DEBT

Bankruptcy, Article 9 and Related Laws

Modern Cases And Materials

By

David G. Epstein
King & Spalding
Atlanta, Georgia

Steve H. Nickles
Roger F. Noreen Chair in Law
University of Minnesota Law School
Minneapolis, Minnesota

AMERICAN CASEBOOK SERIES

WEST PUBLISHING CO.
Eagan, Minnesota 1994

 TEXT IS PRINTED ON 10% POST CONSUMER RECYCLED PAPER

To

Charles and Daniel

and

Ellen and Thomas

Preface

"Debt" is the mildest four-letter work used by lawyers, law students and real people in working with the Bankruptcy Code, Article 9 and related laws. These laws become important when someone is not able or willing to pay what he owes, and his creditors are unhappy.

In a sense, this book starts in the middle of a story. It is a story that had a happy beginning. C thought well enough of D to extend credit to D. Now there are problems with D and C's debtor-creditor relationship: D is not paying C, or C is concerned about whether D will be able to continue paying it. This book is about what lawyers can do to fix the problems.

In the "real world", these problems are typically fixed without lawyers. D pays C, or D and C work out some sort of alternative payment scheme. And, when lawyers do become involved, the problems are typically fixed without litigation or other recourse to the legal process.

Lawyers can be effective in resolving debtor-creditor problems, with or without recourse to bankruptcy and other legal process, only if they know the legal rights and remedies of debtors and creditors. These legal rights and remedies include (i) actions a creditor can take to collect a judgment, (ii) special collection rights created by contract and law, (iii) a debtor's constitutional and statutory protection, (iii) theories for imposing liability on creditors, (iv) debt restructuring possibilities outside of bankruptcy, and (v) various forms of bankruptcy relief.

In practice, a lawyer works with the Bankruptcy Code, Article 9 and other state statutes, documents, pleadings, and reported cases. In this book, you will be working with all of these materials. The cases in the book, with a few "classic" exceptions, are cases decided within the last few years. The cases are, for the most part, heavily edited. Case citations are routinely omitted. We also omitted most footnotes and changed the numbers of the surviving footnotes according to a scheme -- used throughout the book -- that resets the footnote numbering with every page.

Each principal case is typically followed by questions about issues that the case raises and problems that ask you to apply and perhaps doubt the law of the case. Some of the problems have a "right" answer that is sometimes provided after the problems; other problems have several possible answers. All of the problems can be understood and discussed from the materials already considered in the book. We have made a special effort to design problems that could be discussed on the basis of the materials surrounding them.

We want you to learn the basics of debtor-creditor law, to become familiar with the issues of debtor-creditor law that you are likely to encounter in practice, and to think about the policy questions that underlie those issues. While policy questions are consistently and constantly raised, the book does not espouse any particular theory or philosophy of debtor-creditor law. You are left to formulate your own opinions on these policy issues. The only "message" that we are trying to convey is that debtor-creditor law is interesting and intellectually challenging.

We enjoyed working on this book even more than we did the prior edition. Once again, we had great and cheerful secretarial help from **Lynda Walton**; and on this edition **Jonathan Lewis** (*Minnesota 2L*) provided valuable research assistance. **Thanks to both of them.**

DAVID G. EPSTEIN, Atlanta
STEVE H. NICKLES, Minneapolis

Summary of Contents

Table of Contents

TABLE OF CONTENTS

Table of Cases

The principal cases are in bold type. Cases cited or discussed in
the text are roman type. Cases cited in principal cases and within
other quoted materials are not included.

E

F

G

T

U

V

W

Table of Statutes and Regulations

TABLE OF STATUTES AND REGULATIONS

Uniform Arbitration Act

Part 1

NONBANKRUPTCY DEBTOR-CREDITOR LAW

Unit 1

JUDICIAL DEBT COLLECTION

UNIT CONTENTS

———————

A *debtor* is a person who owes money to another person, the *creditor*, because of an obligation such as a bank loan, credit extended for the purchase of property or services, a bill for taxes, a tort claim for damages, or any other money debt. This book is not about how or why the obligation was created, or about the nature or incidents of the obligation. The first part of this book is mostly about the remedies of a creditor under state law when a debtor is unwilling to satisfy the obligation. The second part is largely about the rights of a debtor under federal bankruptcy law to escape or modify the obligation and, in the process, to postpone or avoid the creditor's remedies. The third part is about compromise between debtor and creditor so that each of them avoids the full force of the other's rights. Together, these three parts generally concern the major methods of dealing with debt, whether under state law or in bankruptcy.

When a debtor defaults in paying an obligation, the creditor will first remind the debtor of the obligation and attempt through persuasion to get the debtor to pay it voluntarily. The creditor may even hire a collection agency whose principal job is to convince the debtor to make voluntary payment. The principal limitation on the agency's tactics is the federal Fair Debt Collection Practices Act, 15 U.S.C.A. §1692 et seq., which proscribes overly aggressive, unseemly and oppressive tactics by professional debt collectors and also by lawyers in some of their debt collection activities.

If these collection efforts are unsuccessful, the creditor will resort to the means provided by law or contract whereby property of the debtor is seized and applied in satisfaction of the obligation. The various legal means of so appropriating a debtor's real or personal property constitute the *creditors' remedies* that are the principal subjects of the first part of this book. Some of these remedies are creatures of the common law; others are statutory animals. Most are hybrids. Almost all of them, regardless of their source in law, are parented by the states, not by the federal government.

To a large extent, the states agree on the kinds and general nature of remedies available to creditors; but they disagree widely on the particulars of the remedies. So creditors' remedies, in name and broad substance, are much the same in every state. Yet, the details, especially procedural details, of creditors' remedies vary among the states, except for remedies arising under uniform and model laws. This book focuses not on these differences, but on the general design of the creditors' remedies that are common throughout the country and also on some of the most significant issues associated with these remedies. That each state's set of remedies is peculiar in the fine points is no reason not to study in a debtor-creditor course the broad outline of remedies that all the states share. Just remember to study local law carefully, and pay close attention to all the unique detail when working in the real world on a debtor-creditor case.

□□□□□□

What does the creditor want when a debtor is unwilling or unable to satisfy the obligation. The creditor wants money or property worth money, enough to satisfy the debtor's obligation. The creditor's remedies are ways to get the debtor's property -- ways to take the debtor's property away from her for the purpose of liquidating it and applying the property's value to the debtor's obligation to the creditor.

To maintain order the state alone is authorized to use force in this process. Ordinarily, however, the state will not get involved in grabbing a debtor's property until the creditor gets a judgment against the debtor. It is through the process of the creditor getting a judgment that the state recognizes and measures the debt. (The debt in its original form is entirely replaced by the judgment, which is itself a debt.) Having determined the debt that is reduced to judgment, the state allies itself with the creditor and takes the debtor's property -- forcibly, if necessary -- to satisfy the creditor's judgment. This process of satisfying the judgment is generally known as *enforcement* or *execution of judgment*. Getting a judgment and enforcing it through execution process is the base remedy of all creditors and is the only remedy of general unsecured creditors, meaning creditors without special rights created by contract or law for them.

A. EXECUTION OF JUDGMENTS

1. How The Process Generally Works

a. Levy

A judgment in itself gives a creditor little more than a legal victory and a new form for her claim against the debtor. The greatest value of a judgment as a creditors' remedy lies in what it allows, which is invocation of the state's coercive force in aid of collection. The state aids the creditor through the process of *execution*.

The modern law of execution is mostly statutory and involves a unified, though hardly uniform, process whereby the state seizes and sells as much of the debtor's non-exempt property as is necessary to satisfy the judgment. Executable property typically includes the debtor's non-exempt interests in both realty and personalty, including tangible and intangible personal property. Some states expressly authorize execution on both legal and equitable interests.

A creditor initiates execution usually by applying to the court clerk for a *writ of execution*. The writ of execution is ordinarily issued from the court that rendered the judgment and is directed to a sheriff or other county official. In most states, the court can direct a writ of execution to the sheriff of any county within the state. The writ orders the sheriff to seize property of the debtor, sell it, and apply the proceeds in satisfaction of the judgment. In this process, the act of seizing property is often referred to as *levy* by the sheriff.

> To levy is "[t]o do the acts by which a sheriff sets apart and appropriates, for the purpose of satisfying the command of a writ of execution, a part or the whole of a defendant's property." In levying the execution, the sheriff is "acting as an agent of the law, and not as an agent of the judgment creditor."

Lincoln Lumber Co. v. Elston, 511 N.W.2d 162, 167 (Neb. App. 1993).

Levy is ordinarily effected by the sheriff taking physical possession of the property. When that form of levy is impractical or impossible, constructive possession is taken by somehow giving public notice that the property is *in custodia legis*, as by recording a notice of seizure in the appropriate county records.

The sheriff must levy before the *return date* specified in the writ. This date is determined by reference to enacted law prescribing the number of days within which a sheriff must act in enforcing a writ of execution. Sixty days is not an uncommon period of time for such action. As a general rule, the writ expires on its return date, and the sheriff loses authority to take further steps to enforce it if she has not by that time effected a levy. In such a case, the creditor must initiate the process anew by causing the issuance of another or *alias* writ of execution. If the writ expires after levy but prior to sale, the sheriff in most states is empowered to sell whatever property she has seized so long as she acts within a further period of time established by statute.

In many states, the judgment debtor is given the opportunity to select the property to be levied on by the sheriff. Most states direct that, when the sheriff makes the selection, she must exhaust the debtor's personal property before taking real estate. In practice, the creditor often locates executable property and points the sheriff to it. The sheriff usually is appreciative of the creditor's help, and the two of them work cooperatively as allies in satisfying the judgment. Sometimes, however, the sheriff is unwilling to go as far in her collection efforts as the creditor wishes. If this unwillingness amounts to a serious breach of the sheriff's legal duties, the cost to her can be more than the creditor's vote in the next election. The sheriff can be accountable in damages to the creditor.

Issuance of execution is subject to time limitations in most states. Typically, execution cannot issue during a short grace period following judgment. The debtor is thus given time to pay the judgment or have it set aside. An appeal of the judgment, however, will not of itself stay execution. The judgment debtor must post a bond, commonly referred to as a *supersedeas bond*, if she wishes to hold the sheriff at bay during an appeal of her case. In many states, the outside limit on execution is established either by a specific limitation statute governing execution, or a more general statute of limitation governing actions on judgments. In some of these states, such a statute can be tolled in various ways such as the creditor's issuance of execution during the period of limitation or the debtor's partial payment of the judgment. A statute of limitation on the enforcement of judgments is not tolled, however, by the judgment debtor's appeal of the case, *Farms v. Carlsbad Riverside Terrace Apartments, Inc.*, 102 N.M. 50, 690 P.2d 1044 (1984), unless enforcement of the judgment is stayed as by the judgment debtor posting a supersedeas bond. *North Star*

Development Corp. v. Wolfswinkel, 146 Ariz. 406, 706 P.2d 732 (App.1985).

Problems

1. Debtor owes an obligation to Creditor. The obligation is certain and liquidated. It is also due.

    a. Can Creditor help itself to Debtor's property if Debtor fails to satisfy the obligation?

    b. Can Creditor help itself to Debtor's property if Creditor wins a judgment against Debtor?

    c. Will Sheriff grab Debtor's property on the Creditor's behalf if and when Creditor wins a judgment?

    d. What must happen before Sheriff will grab the Debtor's property in satisfaction of Debtor's obligation to Creditor?

    e. What if the debtor appeals?

2. What property is liable to execution?

    a. Whose property can Sheriff take and apply in satisfaction of Creditor's judgment?

    b. What kinds of property of the Debtor can Sheriff take and sell or otherwise apply in satisfaction of Creditor's judgment?

    c. How much of Debtor's property can Sheriff take and sell or otherwise apply in satisfaction of Creditor's judgment?

3. What kinds of judgments support execution? Does the nature of the underlying liability matter?

4. What if the value of Debtor's property is insufficient to satisfy the judgment?

5. Creditor won judgment in state court in Hennepin County. Debtor owned a vacation home in Itascia County. How can this home be subjected to execution?

b. Execution Liens

A most significant side effect of execution is that the process creates a lien. In the majority of states, this lien attaches to whatever real or personal property the sheriff actually levies on, and the lien dates from the time of the levy. In a large minority of states, the execution lien dates from the delivery of the writ of execution to the sheriff. Everywhere the effect of an execution lien is to give the judgment creditor security against third-party claims during the hiatus between the effective date of the lien and sale of the property on which the sheriff levies. If there is a levy on real estate that is subject to a lien of judgment, the creditor's rights with respect to the property relate back to the time when the judgment lien attached. More is said later about judgment liens.

In states where the lien arises upon delivery of the writ of execution to the sheriff, priority among execution creditors, *inter se*, is usually determined according to the order in which their writs were delivered to the officer; but, when property is levied on pursuant to writs delivered to different officers, priority between the execution creditors is determined in some of these states according to the order in which the levies are made. In states where the lien of execution dates from the time of actual levy by the sheriff, "[t]he execution first levied *** has the first lien on the property, though there may be others in the hands of the sheriff, which were delivered to him before the one levied." *Albrecht v. Long*, 25 Minn. 163, 170 (1878). This rule applies even though the universal rule is that executions should be levied in the order in which the writs are received.

As a general rule, an execution lien attaches only to whatever title or interest the debtor has in the property subject to the lien, which means that the lien does not displace *existing* legal and equitable claims and interests. This deference results from the fundamental principle of derivative title, on which the whole law of private property is based: A transferee of property generally acquires the same rights and priorities as her prior transferors, nothing more and nothing less. The very same principle dictates that an execution lien ordinarily takes priority over *subsequent* claims and interests. This general rule applies not only in states where the lien dates from the time of levy, but also in most jurisdictions where the lien dates from the time the writ is delivered to the sheriff.

Problems

1. Execution Lien Versus Existing Interests

a. A lien of execution attaches to a piece of real estate that is subject to a long existing, though unrecorded, mortgage. State law provides:

"Every conveyance of real estate shall be recorded in the office of the county recorder of the county where such real estate is situated; and every such conveyance not so recorded shall be void as against any subsequent purchaser in good faith and for a valuable consideration of the same real estate, or any part thereof, whose conveyance is first duly recorded, and as against any attachment levied thereon or any judgment lawfully obtained at the suit of any party against the person in whose name the title to such land appears of record prior to the recording of such conveyance."

Is the execution lien or the mortgage entitled to priority?

b. Bank made a loan to Debtor, and to secure the loan Debtor gave Bank a consensual lien on Debtor's widget. This lien was created by contract, is governed by U.C.C. Article 9, and is called an Article 9 security interest. A security interest is akin to a mortgage of personal property. Debtor defaulted in paying another creditor who sued, won judgment, and caused Sheriff to levy execution against the very widget that is Bank's collateral. Is the execution lien or the security interest entitled to priority? See U.C.C. §§9-301(1)(b); 9-301(3); 9-302(1) (general rule is file to perfect). (Unit 2 of this book covers Article 9 in some detail. More problems of priority between lien creditors and secured parties appear in Unit 2, Section D.3., *infra*.)

2. **Execution Lien Versus Subsequent Interests**

   a. C wins a judgment against D and causes a writ of execution to issue against D's property. Before the sheriff levies, D sells equipment which she owns to P. P delays taking delivery of the equipment and the sheriff seizes it. P moves to quash the levy. P's argument is that C's judgment can only be enforced against property of the judgment debtor and that the equipment belonged to her, not D. How should the court rule on P's motion? What result in a state where no execution lien attaches until levy by the sheriff?

   b. Sheriff constructively levies on D's equipment for the purpose of enforcing a judgment against her. D quickly assures the judgment creditor, C, that the judgment will be satisfied without having to sell the equipment. C agrees to wait a spell and asks the sheriff not to dispose of the property. Thereafter, D gets a loan from Bank secured by an Article 9 security interest in the equipment. Instead of applying the loan proceeds in satisfaction of C's judgment, D stuffs the money in her wallet and heads south. C then gives the sheriff the go-ahead to sell the equipment. Bank intervenes and asks for an order directing that the proceeds of the sale be applied first in satisfaction of its secured claim. What is the outcome? See U.C.C. §§9-301(1)(b). Consider whether or not the result is affected by the extra-Code rule of decisional law "that any direction by the execution creditor to the sheriff which suspends the lien or delays the enforcement of the levy renders the execution dormant against subsequent creditors or bona fide purchasers." 2 A. Freeman, A TREATISE ON THE LAW OF EXECUTIONS §206 (3d ed. 1900); see *Illi, Inc. v. Margolis*, 267 Md. 30, 296 A.2d 412 (1972); *Excelsior Needle Co. v. Globe Cycle Works*, 48 A.D. 304, 62 N.Y.S. 538 (1900).

c. Sale

Property on which the sheriff levies execution is usually not turned over to the judgment creditor in satisfaction of her claim. Rather, the sheriff sells the property and, after paying the costs of the sale, gives the net proceeds to the creditor. Any surplus ordinarily goes to the debtor.

Property levied on by the sheriff is the subject of the sale. Yet, the sheriff is permitted to sell only so much of the debtor's property as is necessary to satisfy the execution creditor's judgment and the costs of the sale. In *Griggs v. Miller*, 374 S.W.2d 119 (Mo.1963), the sheriff levied on and sold the debtor's 322 acre farm, valued at $50,000 to $90,000, to satisfy a $2000 judgment. The court canceled the execution sale because, "'[i]f the property can be divided without prejudice, and a part will sell for the debt and costs, a part only shall be sold.'" Id. at 124 (quoting *Gordon v. Hickman*, 96 Mo. 350, 356, 9 S.W. 920, 922 (1888)).

Usually, the execution sale is by public auction. The sheriff's conduct of the sale is thoroughly regulated in most states by detailed statutes prescribing when the sale shall take place, how the sale will be advertised, and how and where it will be conducted. In many states these statutes have remained unchanged for a great many years, and thus they are vulnerable to attack under contemporary notions of procedural fairness.

For example, in the case *Cate v. Archon Oil Co., Inc.*, 695 P.2d 1352 (Okl.1985), an attorney, Cate, got a default judgment for legal fees against Archon Oil. The sheriff levied on an oil and gas lease owned by the judgment debtor. The lease was worth at least $10,000. The sheriff advertised the sale, as the law prescribed, by publishing a notice in a county newspaper and by posting notices in public places, including on the courthouse door. The law did not require any separate effort to notify the judgment debtor personally. At the sale, Cate himself purchased the lease for $500. Archon objected to the sale, but the trial court confirmed it. The Oklahoma Supreme Court reversed, reasoning:

Theoretically, publication may be available for all the world to see, but it is presumptuous to suppose that anyone could read all that is published to see if something may be reported which affects his/her property interest. Exclusive reliance on an inefficacious means of notification cannot be permitted under [the due process clause which requires notice reasonably calculated to reach the interested parties] ***.

Id. at 1356; cf. *Mennonite Bd. of Missions v. Adams*, 462 U.S. 791, 103 S.Ct. 2706, 77 L.Ed.2d 180 (1983) (notice of tax sale was constitutionally inadequate).

Most states have statutory devices to protect judgment debtors from having their property sold at unfairly low prices at execution sales, such as provision for appraisal, redemption, or both.

Appraisal Statutes. These statutes generally provide (1) that an appraisal of the subject property must be made before the sale and (2) either that an execution sale must produce not less than a stated percentage of the appraised value or that a stated percentage of the appraised value must be credited on the debt.

Redemption. Another statutory device providing some protection against inadequate bidding is redemption. Generally, the right of redemption extends only to the execution debtor or her grantee and is limited to the repurchase, within a stated time and at a stated price, of real property. Some states, however, permit redemption of personal property; and some states have extended the right of redemption to junior lienors of the debtor.

d. Setting Sales Aside

While most states do not require judicial confirmation of an execution sale, the court from which the execution issued may, for sufficient cause shown, vacate a sale. As a general rule, however, "mere inadequacy of price, where the parties stand on an equal footing and there are no confidential relations between them, is not, in and of itself, sufficient to authorize vacation of the sale unless the inadequacy is so gross as to be proof of fraud or shocks the conscience of the court." *Wiesel v. Ashcraft*, 26 Ariz.App. 490, 494, 549 P.2d 585, 589 (1976). In the *Wiesel* case, a mortgagor asked the court to set aside the sheriff's sale of his home. The property was purchased by two employees of the original mortgagee who bid one dollar more than the mortgage debt. This amount was less than half of the property's fair market value. Nevertheless, the court upheld the sale.

Although mere inadequacy of price is not sufficient in itself to vacate an execution sale, it may be considered together with other circumstances; and, slight irregularities, when coupled with the low price, may well justify setting aside the sale.

e. Purchaser's Title

In determining whether the price paid at a forced sale is adequate, the court should consider the state of the title acquired by the purchaser at the sale, that is, the extent to which the purchaser takes subject to other claims to the property. As a general rule, a purchaser at any execution sale acquires only such title as the debtor had. Generally, therefore, the purchaser takes the title subject to liens and encumbrances that clung to the property in the hands of the execution debtor.

Significantly, the general rule holds that no implied warranties of title accompany execution sales. The doctrine of caveat emptor applies. Therefore, "where title fails, the purchaser is not entitled to a return from the judgment creditor of the amount paid." *Dixon v. City Nat'l Bank*, 81 Ill.2d 429, 431, 43 Ill.Dec. 710, 711, 410 N.E.2d 843, 844 (1980). "However, *** when the sheriff's deed is a nullity because the judgment debtor held no title or interest whatsoever, the successful bidder has a right to restitution or reimbursement." *Persons v. Bergmann*, 442 A.2d 647, 649 (N.J. Super. 1982).

In exceptional situations, the purchaser at a execution sale is protected against preexisting interests:

1. Where Law Provides For Execution Sales Free And Clear Of Encumbrances. It is possible, but very rare, for applicable law to dictate that the purchaser of property at an execution sale takes title free and clear of *all* liens theretofore existing. Suppose, for example, that Seller of equipment obtained judgment against the Buyer for the price of the goods and caused the equipment to be seized and sold under execution in Delaware. The equipment was subject to a prior, perfected Article 9 security interest in favor of Bank, whose claim to the property was superior to the Seller's claim. The execution sale could nevertheless discharge the Bank's interest. "Chattels sold at an execution sale should be sold free and clear of all encumbrances in order to ensure the highest price and to stimulate bidding. The creditor with the highest priority is not prejudiced in his reliance on the value of the chattel to secure the debt since he is satisfied first from the proceeds." *Maryland Nat'l Bank v. Porter-Way Harvester Mfg. Co.*, 300 A.2d 8, 12 (Del.1972).

2. Where Recording Laws Provide Protection Of The Purchaser. Recording statutes in many jurisdictions protect buyers of real estate at execution sales from secret liens and interests. If the statute does not explicitly include such buyers as a class protected from unrecorded interests, decisional law may categorize execution buyers as bona fide purchasers, which is a class of claimants always protected by recording statutes. The courts disagree whether a judgment creditor herself can ever ascend to the status of bona fide purchaser when she buys real property at her own execution sale by merely crediting the amount of the bid against the judgment.

An execution buyer of goods, as a buyer not in the ordinary course of business, should take free of an unperfected security interest in the property to the extent that she gives value and receives delivery of the goods without knowledge of the security interest. Uniform Commercial Code (U.C.C.) §9-301(1)(c).

3. Where Buyer Is Sheltered By Judgment Creditor's Priority. Even if a purchaser at an execution sale is herself unprotected by real estate recording statutes or Article 9, she should take free of any encumbrances that were subordinate to the execution creditor's lien on the property.

Suppose, for example, that Bank acquired an Article 9 security interest in Debtor's boat but failed to perfect the interest. Creditor got a judgment against Debtor and caused the sheriff to levy execution on the boat. This levy gave Creditor an execution lien on the property. At the execution sale of the boat, a Bank representative appeared and announced the existence of the Bank's security interest. Buyer who purchases the boat should take free of the Bank's interest even though Buyer knew of it when she bought the boat. Although Buyer is not shielded by 9-301(1)(c), which protects innocent, non-ordinary course buyers from unperfected security interests, Buyer should be *sheltered* by the priority of Creditor's execution lien over the Bank's security interest under 9-301(1)(b). Permanent Editorial Board Commentary on the Uniform Commercial Code, PEB Commentary No. 6 Section 9-301(1) (March 10, 1990). Unless the Creditor's priority extends to the purchaser at the execution sale, the Creditor is denied the full protection that Article 9 gives her.

A technical means of achieving this shelter effect is to reason that the buyer at an execution sale acquires the debtor's title to the property as the title existed not when the sale occurred, but at the time when the lien creditor acquired her encumbrance on the property. Alternatively, the shelter effect can be achieved in technical terms by deeming that the title acquired by the buyer at the execution sale relates back to the time when the lien attached, to wit: "'when a levy and sale are made under execution on the judgment, the title under the sheriff's deed relates back to the inception of the lien and so takes precedence over all transfers and incumbrances made subsequently to such inception.'" *Hogan v. Carter,* 431 So.2d 1160, 1165 (Ala.1983)

(quoting *Barber v. Beckett*, 251 Ala. 569, 39 So.2d 17, 19 (1949))
(Beatty, J., dissenting).

Problems

1. Why should the state of the title acquired by a purchaser at an execution sale be considered in determining whether the price paid at the sale was adequate?

2. Suppose Sheriff takes and sells a boat that actually belongs to Debtor's neighbor.

    a. Can the neighbor recover the boat from the buyer?

    b. Does it matter that the neighbor had acquired the boat from Debtor just before Sheriff levied?

    c. What are the buyer's rights if Debtor and the neighbor are co-owners of the boat?

3. Bank has an unperfected, Article 9 security interest in equipment belonging to D. A judgment creditor of D caused execution to issue and the sheriff levied on the equipment. The sheriff later sold the equipment at a forced sale to Buyer. What arguments can you make that Buyer's title is superior to Bank's security interest?

4. Bank has an unrecorded mortgage on business realty belonging to D. Creditor won a judgment against D. In enforcing this judgment, the sheriff levied on D's business real estate, and sold the property to Buyer. What arguments can you make that Buyer's title is superior to Bank's mortgage?

f. Judgment Liens

Priority with respect to real property is greatly affected by judgment liens, which are not created by execution process but are dependent on it. Consider this example: C won a judgment against D in Washington County, where D owns an undeveloped parcel of real estate located on the shore of Scout Lake. The court clerk docketed C's judgment by noting, in a set of records called a "docket", information such as the name of the judgment debtor, the amount of the judgment, and the precise time of making the notation. This process created a lien on all the executable real property that D presently owns or later acquires in Washington County. The lien will spread to D's real property in any other county wherein C registers the judgment. The immediate consequences of the lien attaching to D's lakeside lot in Washington County, or D's real property elsewhere, are practically insignificant. The lien of judgment is general rather than specific and thus gives C no immediately enforceable interest in, or rights with respect to, the property or its products or proceeds.

The judgment lien on D's Scout Lake lot is potentially very valuable, however, as security for C's judgment. If C causes execution to issue against D, the sheriff can levy on the lot for the purpose of satisfying the judgment. In that event, C's rights with respect to the land, i.e., the rights to have the land seized and sold and the proceeds paid to her, relate back to the time the general lien of judgment attached to the property. The result is the subordination of intervening third-party claims.

In all but a handful of states, a judgment creates a lien on real property in which the debtor has an interest at the time of judgment, and extends to realty interests the debtor thereafter acquires. (In a handful of states the judgment lien extends to personal property.) In most states the judgment lien arises when the judgment is formally recorded, as through docketing. In a minority of states the lien arises as soon as the judgment is rendered.

What constitutes real property for judgment lien purposes varies somewhat from state to state. The following are examples of interests that are considered real property for judgment lien purposes in some states, but not in others:

- equitable interests such as the vendee's or vendor's interest under a contract to sell real property;
- leasehold interests;
- reversionary interests and contingent remainders;
- beneficial interests in land trusts;
- shares in a cooperative apartment;
- crops growing on, or harvested from, land that is subject to a judgment lien;
- timber cut from land that is subject to a judgment lien;
- oil and gas leaseholds and other mineral rights.

As a general rule, the only type of judgment that produces a lien is a final, personal judgment of a court of record, for a definite sum of money, that can be enforced through execution against the debtor's real property. Most states have statutes that expressly or implicitly deal with the issue whether a decree for support or alimony creates a judgment lien. A typical statute provides, or is interpreted to provide, that a decree for support or alimony constitutes a lien in the same manner and under the same circumstances as any other money judgment. In construing this sort of statute, the courts disagree whether a lien attaches for future installments of alimony or support, or only for matured installments.

Although a judgment lien is typically enforced through execution process, a judgment creditor in some states may elect to enforce her lien through foreclosure proceedings rather than through execution. In a few states, foreclosure is the exclusive method of enforcement.

Basil v. Vincello
Supreme Court of Ohio, 1990
50 Ohio St.3d 185, 553 N.E.2d 602

Moyer, Chief Justice. The question presented is whether a general judgment creditor may satisfy the unpaid balance of a judgment lien by marshaling a lien against a parcel of property that the debtor conveyed to a third party by means of a defectively executed deed.

The rights and status of the parties must first be defined.

I

Perrico and Slowey paid $50,887 to Vincello and Teague on April 25, 1979. In exchange Vincello and Teague were to execute a quitclaim deed transferring ownership of the property known as Parcel No. 2. Such deeds have the force and effect of a deed in fee simple to the grantee when duly executed in accordance with R.C. Chapter 5301. R.C. 5302.11. Pursuant to R.C. 5301.01, a deed must be signed by the grantor and such signing must be acknowledged in the presence of two witnesses, who shall attest the signing and subscribe their names to the attestation. Furthermore, the acknowledgment must be made before a clerk of a court of the state, a county auditor, county engineer, notary public, mayor, or county court judge, "who shall certify the acknowledgment and subscribe his name to the certificate of such acknowledgment."

In this case, the grantors signed the document outside the presence of both witnesses and did not appear before the notary public who certified the acknowledgment. The acknowledgment required by the statute is for the purpose of affording proof of the due execution of the deed by the grantor, sufficient to authorize the register of deeds to record it. It has been held that "a defectively executed conveyance of an interest in land is valid as between the parties thereto, in the absence of fraud. * * * " Citizens Natl. Bank v. Denison (1956), 165 Ohio St. 89, 95, 59 O.O. 96, 99, 133 N.E.2d 329, 332; Naso v. Daniels (1964), 8 Ohio App.2d 42, 48, 37 O.O.2d 48, 52, 220 N.E.2d 829, 833. In *Citizens*, an improperly acknowledged mortgage was recorded, and the court held that where a deed is executed as the result of fraud, such instrument is ineffective to convey the land. Legal title to the property is not conveyed.

Here, the trial court found from the evidence that no fraud had been perpetrated as between Perrico and Slowey and the Basil Trust. The record supports that finding, although the deed was defectively executed. We find no abuse of discretion and will not disturb this finding of fact. Nevertheless, because the deed was not executed in accordance with R.C. 5301.01 and therefore was defective, legal title did not pass from Vincello and Teague to Perrico and Slowey. The question then is what interest, if any, in Parcel No. 2 did Vincello and Teague pass to Perrico and Slowey?

Vincello and Teague agreed to convey their interest in Parcel No. 2 in exchange for a price. Perrico and Slowey performed their part of the agreement by paying the full consideration required under the contract, $50,887, but received neither title nor possession in exchange. In such instances, courts have created an equitable interest in the purchaser as having a cause of action for breach of an executory contract or as having a "vendee's lien" over the property itself. The "lien" is based on the assumption that the vendor still holds the legal title, either because he has never conveyed it or because some act has been committed which justifies rescission of the contract and return of the purchase price. At most then, it can be said that Perrico and Slowey have an equitable interest in the property still titled in Vincello and Teague that was created upon payment of consideration in April 1979, or they have a cause of action for breach of contract arising when the defective deed was executed in September 1979.

II

The Basil Trust is a general judgment creditor that properly obtained a certificate of judgment from the clerk of courts to satisfy the debt owed by Vincello and Teague for default on the mortgage given it on Parcel No. 12. See R.C. 2329.02. The certificate of judgment was filed on January 23, 1981, and we must assume the truth of plaintiff's assertion in the complaint that the Basil Trust obtained a judgment against any interest Vincello and Teague still had in Parcels 1 through 12. We are required to determine the effect the Basil judgment lien has upon the interest of Perrico and Slowey since the judgment lien against Vincello and Teague is based on an in personam debt.

R.C. 5301.25(A) provides in pertinent part:

"All deeds, * * * and instruments of writing properly executed for conveyance or encumbrance of lands, * * * shall be recorded in the office of the county recorder of the county in which the premises are situated, and until so recorded or filed for record, they are fraudulent, so far as relates to a subsequent bona fide purchaser having, at the time of purchase, no knowledge of the existence of such former deed or land contract or instrument."

This statute is designed to protect subsequent bona fide purchasers of property.

However, the law is clear that judgment lien creditors are not bona fide purchasers for value. The general rule was stated in University Assoc. v. Sterling Finance Co. (1973), 37 Ohio App.2d 17, 19, 66 O.O.2d 32, 33, 305 N.E.2d 924, 925:

"'Accordingly, the interest of a person to whom a judgment debtor has conveyed real estate before the attachment of the judgment or execution lien is preferred to the interest of the judgment creditor, unless such priority is affected by the provisions of recording statutes, or statutes relating to fraudulent conveyances, or the conveyance is void for other reasons, or the grantee is estopped from asserting his claim as against the judgment creditors.' * * *" (Emphasis deleted.)

The trial court found that no fraud was perpetrated upon the Basil Trust by reason of the transaction between Vincello and Teague and Perrico and Slowey. Neither was the transfer of Parcel No. 2 made for the purpose of defrauding the Basil Trust as a judgment creditor since Basil had not achieved that status at the time the transactions were executed. Nor was Parcel No. 2 a part of the security given in exchange for a loan or mortgage between the Basil Trust and Vincello and Teague. Lake County Federal Savings & Loan had the first and paramount mortgage on Parcel No. 2 as well as possession of the property.

Basil contends that Perrico and Slowey may not seek equity from the courts because they do not come to court with "clean hands." The maxim, "He who seeks equity must come with clean hands," requires only that the party must not be guilty of reprehensible conduct with respect to the subject matter of his suit. * * * "[A] court of equity is not an avenger of wrongs committed at large by those who resort to it for relief, however careful it may be to withhold its approval from those which are involved in the subject-matter of the suit and which prejudicially affect the rights of one against whom relief is sought." Kinner v. Lake Shore & Michigan So. Ry. Co. (1904), 69 Ohio St. 339, 344-345, 69 N.E. 614, 615. It does not appear from the record that Perrico and Slowey's conduct, i.e., receiving an improperly executed deed with respect to Parcel No. 2, rises to such a level of reprehensible conduct which would estop their equitable chose in action or interest in the property.

III

Having found Perrico and Slowey's equitable interest to be valid, we consider then the issue of priority. Do the recording statutes protect the Basil Trust as a judgment creditor? The answer must be no.

It is undisputed that by force of R.C. 2329.02, as between two judgment lien creditors, the lien filed prior in time takes priority over the subsequently filed lien. Similarly, pursuant to R.C. 5301.23, " * * * [i]f two or more mortgages are presented for record on the same day, they shall take effect in the order of presentation. The first mortgage presented must be the first recorded, and the first recorded shall have preference." Clearly, the transactions in dispute here do not fall into either category contemplated by these two provisions.

R.C. 5301.03 is a notice statute which permits creation of an equitable interest, and does not protect judgment creditors who have not relied upon the existence and/or ownership of the subject real estate in the extension of credit. Bank One of Milford v. Bardes (1986), 25 Ohio St.3d 296, 297-298, 25 OBR 346, 347, 496 N.E.2d 475, 476. "'* * * [The statute] provides that certain language in a deed or mortgage which purports to create an equitable interest will not be sufficient to notify other parties of limitations on the grantee's or mortgagee's powers. Noncompliance with the statute does not defeat the creation of an equitable interest: it simply prevents enforcement of that interest against the parties named in the statute. Those parties include " * * * bona fide purchasers, mortgagees, lessees, and assignees for value * * *," but not judgment creditors.'" Id.

We conclude that R.C. 2329.01 (former G.C. 11655) determines the issue. It provides:

> "Lands and tenements, including vested legal interests therein, permanent leasehold estates renewable forever, and goods and chattels, not exempt by law, shall be subject to the payment of debts, and liable to be taken on execution and sold as provided in sections 2329.02 to 2329.61, inclusive, of the Revised Code."

The statute, in its predecessor form, G.C. 11655, was construed by this court in Culp v. Jacobs (1930), 123 Ohio St. 109, 174 N.E. 242.

G.C. 11655 was amended (111 Ohio Laws 366) to insert the word "legal," so that the section read:

> "Lands and tenements, including vested legal interests therein, permanent leasehold estates renewable forever, and goods and chattels, not exempt by law, shall be subject to the payment of debts, and liable to be taken on execution and sold * * *."

In *Culp*, the court held that this amendment was enacted to specifically limit the interest in lands and tenements liable to be taken on execution solely to "vested legal interests." To permit equitable interests to be liable on execution would disregard the meaning of the statute and intent of the General Assembly. "[E]quitable interests in real estate cannot be levied upon and sold under execution." Id. at 114, 174 N.E. at 243.

The court of appeals relied on Standard Oil Co. v. Moon (1930), 34 Ohio App. 123, 170 N.E. 368. We find that case distinguishable and not controlling here. In *Standard Oil Co.*, Moon was the owner in fee simple of a certain property. Moon executed a land contract to Smith, who took possession and filed his contract for record. Moon then assigned his remaining interest (the legal title) to West Side Banking Company as security for a loan of $500. This assignment was not recorded. Nearly five months later, Moon executed and delivered a mortgage in favor of Home Building Savings & Loan Company upon this same property. The mortgage was duly recorded. The question in the case was, who had priority over the purchase money owing from Smith to Moon as between West Side Banking Co. and Home Building Savings & Loan? Clearly under the recording statutes, Home Building Savings & Loan could not and did not have notice of the unrecorded assignment. Home Building Savings & Loan's mortgage was recorded first and therefore took priority over the assignment made to West Side Banking Co. This, however, was a priority against any interest remaining in Moon, not Smith, the holder of an equitable chose in action. The court did not hold that the levy of judgment should be against Smith's equitable interest.

Accordingly, we hold that the priorities of interest covered by these statutes have no effect upon the case before us. Perrico and Slowey have an "equitable interest" in either the land still owned by Vincello and Teague, or an equitable chose in action for breach of contract against them individually. We follow this court's ruling in *Culp v. Jacobs*, supra, and hold that equitable interests in real estate cannot be levied upon or sold under execution.

IV

Accordingly, the judgment of the court of appeals is reversed, and the trial court's decision in favor of defendants Perrico and Slowey is reinstated.

Judgment reversed.

Sweeney, Holmes, Wright And Herbert R. Brown, JJ., concur.

Douglas and Resnick, JJ., dissent.

Douglas, Justice, dissenting.

A reading of the facts in the case at bar and the majority's conclusions drawn from those facts should send a chill through real estate lawyers, bankers, investors, title companies and anyone with an interest in searching real estate titles.

Vincello and Teague were the title owners of several parcels of land. In early 1979, Vincello and Marvin Basil negotiated a loan agreement from the Basil Trust ("Basil") to Vincello. As part of the negotiations, on January 10, 1979, Vincello gave Basil a financial statement in which Vincello listed his income and property interests. According to the financial statement, Vincello owned one-half interest in a particular parcel of land known as Parcel No. 2. The interest in Parcel No. 2 was represented to be worth at least $140,000. On March 22, 1979, Vincello, Teague and Basil reached a final agreement concerning the loan.

On April 25, 1979, just over one month after the agreement with Basil had been reached, Vincello and Teague received $50,887 from Perrico and Slowey. In exchange for the $50,887, Vincello and Teague signed a quitclaim deed which purported to transfer Parcel No. 2 to Perrico and Slowey. Hence, Parcel No. 2 which approximately three months earlier had been represented to be worth at least $140,000 was attempted to be transferred for $50,887. Additionally, the quitclaim deed was backdated to show an effective date of November 20, 1978.

However, as the majority correctly notes, the quitclaim deed was ineffective in passing legal title to Perrico and Slowey.

Vincello and Teague defaulted on their loan agreement with the Basil Trust. Consequently, Basil obtained a judgment lien against Vincello and Teague and then filed a certificate of judgment with the clerk of courts on January 23, 1981. In February 1981, Basil filed a complaint alleging that it had obtained a judgment lien against the interests of Vincello and Teague in certain parcels of property, including Parcel No. 2. In December 1981, the faulty quitclaim deed which purported to transfer Parcel No. 2 to Perrico and Slowey was recorded.

Based upon these facts, the majority holds that Perrico and Slowey have an "equitable interest" in Parcel No. 2, or an equitable chose in action for breach of contract against Vincello and Teague and, hence, these equitable interests may neither be levied upon nor sold under execution. In doing so, today's majority misconstrues this case and, as a result, allows Vincello and Teague to thwart the efforts of their judgment creditor when the creditor had no knowledge of an invalid conveyance because the invalid conveyance was neither recorded nor attempted to be enforced.

The majority concludes, and I agree, that R.C. 2329.01 determines the issue in the case at bar. R.C. 2329.01 provides: "Lands and tenements, including vested legal interests therein * * * shall be subject to the payment of debts, and liable to be taken on execution and sold * * *." (Emphasis added.) The majority also concludes, and I agree, that Vincello and Teague still held legal title to Parcel No. 2 after the execution of the faulty quitclaim deed because the deed failed to transfer legal title to the property.

In my judgment, Basil properly executed on Vincello's and Teague's "vested legal interests" in Parcel No. 2. Hence, under R.C. 2329.01, the vested legal interests of Vincello and Teague are proper subjects for the payment of their debts and, accordingly, may be taken on execution and sold. While I agree with today's majority that Perrico and Slowey should have an action (legal or equitable or both) against Vincello and Teague, it does not follow that Perrico's and Slowey's chose in action somehow affects the rights of a judgment creditor that has first executed on the legal interests of its judgment debtors.

Apparently the majority of this court believes that Basil has attempted to levy on Perrico's and Slowey's equitable chose in action or their "equitable interest" in Parcel No. 2. That is incorrect. It is the legal interests of Vincello and Teague that Basil seeks to reach. In ruling otherwise, the majority has misconstrued the entire case before this court. In doing so, the majority's holding establishes a dangerous precedent that will foster and reward secret or illicit real estate transactions, thereby having the potential to bring havoc to the real estate industry.

Seemingly, the court of appeals, while seeing many of these same problems without specifically so articulating them, reached the same conclusion and the judgment of that court should be affirmed. To do otherwise leads me to the conclusion that the basic law we all learned so long ago, to wit: that recording a document with the county recorder is "notice to all the world," has today a new meaning--or no meaning at all. It seems that the answer now is to secretly prepare a quitclaim deed, backdate it even though that is a violation of law, have it signed but not in the presence of witnesses or a notary, have the purported grantee not record it and then later argue that you have no real interest in the property to be levied against. What a sweet deal--but very dangerous, I think--to be sanctioned by this court!

For the foregoing reasons, I must respectfully dissent.

Resnick, J., concurs in the foregoing dissenting opinion.

Problems

1. In *Basil* the majority and the dissent may both be right. Please explain.

2. C won a judgment against D in Washington County, where D owns an undeveloped parcel of real estate located on the shore of Scout Lake. The court clerk docketed C's judgment. What rights does C have with respect to D's Scout Lake lot prior to enforcement of C's judgment lien on the property?

   a. Can C use the lot for week-end picnics?

   b. Can C share in rents, royalties and other revenues from the property?

   c. Can C sell the lot?

3. Suppose D transferred the lot to her neighbor just before Sheriff levied on the property. Describe the rights of a person who buys the home at an execution sale.

4. What are C's rights if D sells the lot? Suppose that C's $10,000 judgment against D was docketed, but before execution was issued to enforce the judgment, D sold the Scout Lake property to B. A proper deed was immediately recorded. B paid $6000, which was close to the property's market value. Shortly thereafter, the land's value increased by fifty percent.

   a. Does C, the judgment creditor, have a claim to the $6000 purchase price which D deposited in her checking account at a local bank?

   b. The sale of the property to B did not disturb the judgment lien. The rule of derivative title applies. If execution issues to enforce C's judgment, the sheriff can levy on and sell the Scout Lake property as if the transaction between D and B had not taken place. Another explanation of the relationship between execution process and the judgment lien in this sort of case is that the lien of execution on the property relates back to the point at which the judgment lien attached and cuts off intervening claims. In any event, the effect in this case is the same. If B wants to settle with C and offers $6000, would you advise C to hold out for more? How much more? See Kinney v. Vallentyne, 15 Cal.3d 475, 124 Cal.Rptr. 897, 541 P.2d 537 (1975) (a judgment lien enlarges commensurate with any increase in the equity in the property occurring after the judgment debtor's disposition of it).

5.   Inasmuch as a subsequent buyer of the property takes subject to the judgment lien, one can safely assume that the same is generally true of a subsequent mortgagee. An exception is made, however, for purchase-money mortgagees. Can you reason why?

6.   Return to Problem 4. Suppose that C and B cannot reach an agreement, and C causes D's Scout Lake property to be seized under process of execution. The sheriff advertises a planned sale of the property. The land and the particulars of the sale are fully described in the ad. A prospective buyer researches record title and discovers D's deed to B and also discovers a mortgage given before, but not recorded until after, C acquired her judgment against D. The prospective buyer is your client. She wants to know if her purchase of the property at the sheriff's sale will cut off B's claim to the property and also the claim of the mortgagee. What is your opinion? The answer with respect to cutting off the mortgagee's claim may well depend on whether the applicable real estate recording statute gives a judgment lien priority over prior, unrecorded conveyances. Some states construe their recording statutes to protect only subsequent encumbrances and transferees, and not general creditors who obtain a lien through judgment or the like. The liens of these creditors are thus subordinate to prior, unrecorded conveyances. Other states protect any creditor, such as C, who obtains a lien before the prior conveyance is recorded. An intermediate position would protect C unless C had notice of the unrecorded conveyance when the judgment lien was obtained.

7.   An unsatisfied judgment against a debtor is often followed by other judgments won by different creditors. When two or more judgment liens attach to property that the debtor presently owns, priority is usually determined according to the order in which the judgments were docketed. There is less agreement on how to determine priority when the land is acquired by the debtor after docketing of the competing judgments. Some courts are consistent and hold that priority as to after-acquired property is determined by order of docketing. A majority of courts take the different view that judgment liens attaching simultaneously to after-acquired property rank equally inter se. Actually, however, even the courts in the majority fail to agree completely. Keeping in mind that the enforcement of a judgment lien depends on the process of execution, can you guess the issue on which these courts divide?

g.   Limitations on Judgments, Enforcement, and Liens

Just as states limit actions on contracts, negotiable instruments, and other types of debts, they similarly limit action on a judgment,

which is a form of debt. Ten years is the typical period during which
an action on a judgment must be commenced. A judgment lien cannot
survive the running of such a statute of limitation.

Yet, before the statute of limitation on the enforcement of her
judgment has run, the judgment creditor can institute a new action
based on the debtor's failure to pay the existing judgment.   The rule
everywhere is that "[w]hen a judgment is obtained, the precedent
cause of action is merged into and extinguished by the judgment.
*The judgment is a debt of record,--a new cause of action,--upon which
a new suit may be maintained.*" *Williams v. Merritt*, 109 Ga. 213, 34
S.E. 312 (emphasis added). Prosecuting this new action, which essentially is an action for debt, is referred to as *renewing* the judgment. If
the creditor prevails -- as she surely will unless the debtor has satisfied the original judgment -- a new judgment will be rendered that
will itself give rise to a new lien and a new limitation period.

A judgment lien may become ineffective well before the running of
the statute of limitation governing actions on judgments. Under the
common law, a judgment lien became *dormant* a year and a day after
the rendition of the judgment because, after that time, execution process, which is the usual vehicle for enforcing judgments and judgment
liens, would not issue in the absence of an earlier effort to enforce the
judgment. In effect, the law presumed that a judgment was satisfied
during the 366-day period.

The states now have statutes that, in one way or another, effectively delay dormancy for a period of time that is longer than a year
and a day. In some states this period of delay is shorter than the
usual statute of limitation governing actions on judgments. If dormancy of the judgment lien results, it may still be possible to issue
execution until expiration of the statute of limitation governing enforcement of the judgment. In this event execution can issue even
though the judgment lien has lapsed. Moreover, the sleeping lien can
usually be *revived*. The traditional means of reviving a dormant judgment lien is a judicial proceeding in *scire facias*. This proceeding essentially involves the judgment creditor causing the issuance of a
judicial writ ordering the judgment debtor to show cause why the
judgment as originally entered should not be enforced against her. In
some states a revivor proceeding can be instituted prior to dormancy
so that the lien never sleeps.

In other states the declared life span of a judgment lien is the
same as both the period of limitation applicable to actions in judgments and the time during which a judgment is enforceable through
execution. There is little doubt in such a state that a judgment lien
cannot be extended through revival. Renewing the judgment is

generally possible, however, so long as the renewal occurs, or is initiated, during the limitation period governing the original judgment.

The most modern statutes provide for perpetuating a judgment lien upon motion or through other simplified process whereby the creditor files a petition or other application with a court functionary that will have the effect of continuing the judgment lien unless the debtor, upon notice, makes a good defense to enforcement of the judgment. Procedurally, this process is akin to *scire facias*; nominally, however, the statutes may refer to the process as renewal. Whether in substance the process creates a new judgment and fresh lien, or merely extends the originals, is unclear.

Problems

J gets a money judgment in a state where the law governing the enforcement of judgments includes these statutes:

Lien of Judgment on Land. A judgment in a District Court of this State, or in a United States District Court within this State, shall be a lien on the real estate owned by the defendant in the county in which the judgment was rendered from the date the judgment is docketed as provided by law. This lien shall continue in force for three years from the date of the judgment and may be revived.

Scire Facias to Revive Judgment. The plaintiff may at any time before or after the expiration of the lien on any judgment, sue out a scire facias to revive the same.

Judgment of Revivor and Continuation of Lien. If, upon service of the scire facias as required by law, the defendant does not appear and show cause why such judgment or decree shall not be revived, the same shall be revived, and the lien continued for another period of three years, and so on from time to time as often as may be necessary.

Time When Lien Begins. If a scire facias be sued out before the termination of the lien of any judgment, the lien of the judgment revived shall have relation to the day on which the scire facias issued; but if the lien of any judgment or decree shall have expired before suing out the scire facias, the judgment of revival shall only be a lien from the time of the rendition of such judgment.

Execution May Issue Until Collection Barred. An execution may be issued upon a judgment at any time until the collection of it is barred by the statute of limitations, although no execution may have been previously issued within a year and a day.

Limitation of Action on Judgment. Actions on all judgments shall be commenced, and execution to enforce same shall be issued, within ten years after the cause of action shall accrue, which is when the judgment is rendered, and not afterward.

1. J got a judgment against D in Hazard County where D, at the time of docketing, owns no real estate. Four years later, D acquires a parcel of non-exempt land in Hazard County.

   a. Does J have a lien on real property purchased by D four years after rendition of J's judgment?

   b. If J has no lien on the property, can she acquire a lien on it? How?

   c. Can J cause execution to issue against D without reviving the judgment? If J has execution issued so that the sheriff levies on the property prior to the sale by D, does the buyer take subject to a lien in favor of J?

2. Suppose that D acquires the real estate in the eleventh year following rendition of the original judgment.

   a. If J had revived the judgment two years earlier, does she acquire a judgment lien on the property?

   b. Is the answer the same if J had renewed the judgment two years earlier?

3. Suppose that J renewed the judgment in the tenth year following rendition of the original judgment. Can she renew it again in the twentieth year and successively at ten-year intervals until the judgment is finally satisfied, and during the entire time keep a judgment lien alive?

4. Will D's death free the land in her estate from a lien of judgment in J's favor?

2. Garnishment

Ordinary execution was originally designed to reach real and personal property of the debtor that she holds or controls in her own name and right. To reach tangible property of a debtor held by third persons, and to collect debts owed the debtor and seize (constructively) other intangible property of the debtor, there is a special proceeding at law in the nature of process and an adversary suit against the person who holds the debtor's property or owes her money: *garnishment* (a/k/a *trustee process*).

Garnishment is available in most states before and after judgment. Although this part of the book focuses on postjudgment garnishment, much of the discussion also applies to prejudgment garnishment, which is highlighted later.   As a postjudgment remedy, garnishment is nothing more than a special form of execution -- a customized form that is designed and used for reaching property of the debtor that is held or controlled by a third party.

Postjudgment garnishment typically begins with the judgment creditor, the garnishor, filing with the court an affidavit describing the judgment, complaining that the judgment is unsatisfied, and alleging that a third person, the garnishee, is indebted to, or holds property of, the judgment debtor. The judge or the court clerk then issues a garnishment summons or writ that is served on the garnishee and the judgment debtor. The most modern procedure allows limited self-help garnishment with the creditor's lawyer serving the process.

Service of the garnishment process on the garnishee creates a lien of garnishment on property of the debtor held by the garnishee and also on debts and other credits the garnishee owes the debtor. Such property and credits are, in effect, impounded by the garnishment for the purpose of applying them to the creditor's judgment. Thus, after proper service of a writ of garnishment, the garnishee acts at her peril if she disposes of the debtor's property held by the garnishee at the time of service, or if she pays an obligation then owed to the debtor.

In some states the impoundment and lien of garnishment reach only the assets that the garnishee holds or owes the debtor at the time the writ is served.   Any property of the debtor thereafter received by the garnishee, or any obligation to the debtor thereafter incurred by the garnishee, is not affected by the garnishment. In other states, the impoundment and lien of garnishment not only reach property held, and credits owed, by the garnishee at the time the summons is served; the garnishment also reaches property of the debtor that comes into the garnishee's possession, and debts of the garnishee that accrue, in the interim between service on the garnishee and answer by her. In order to avoid hassling a debtor's employer, a few states specially provide that a single garnishment of wages automatically continues to impound the debtor's earnings for a specified period after service of the garnishment or until the judgment is satisfied.

The garnishee is required to answer the garnishment summons within a stated time, usually 20 or 30 days. Failure to answer can result in contempt proceedings or a default judgment, which may require the garnishee to pay the value of the debtor's property that the garnishor alleged was held or owed by the garnishee or, in some states, the full amount of the garnishor's judgment against the debtor. In its answer the garnishee must describe what, if any, credits or effects of the debtor it holds. The garnishee can then tender to the court the debtor's property and credits and pray for discharge from any further liability to the garnishor.

If the garnishor controverts the garnishee's answer, the disputed issues are tried as in other civil cases. In this trial the garnishee may assert any defenses available to it, principally including most claims and defenses the garnishee could assert against the debtor should the latter sue the former with respect to the property or credits held or owed by the garnishee. An uncontroverted answer is taken as true. If the garnishee is obligated to the debtor, the court will render judgment against the garnishee for the amount of the obligation. Similarly, any property of the debtor that the garnishee holds will be ordered turned over to the court or the sheriff for sale in satisfaction of the garnishor's judgment.

A frequent target of garnishment actions are debtors' wages. Many states have special procedural rules that govern the garnishment of wages. A common example is the requirement that the debtor receive notice of a garnishment of wages ten days in advance of service on the garnishee. See, e.g., Minn. Stat. §571.41(5); N.D. Cent. Code §2-09.1-04. During this time the debtor may pay the judgment, contest the garnishment, or assert any federal or state restrictions on, and exemptions of, earnings. Most states shield some of a debtor's wages from garnishment through exemption laws, which are discussed later. Federal law, Title III of the Consumer Credit Protection Act, 15 U.S.C.A. §§1671-1676, limits the garnishment of wages, but it is *not* an exemption law inasmuch as the statute affords no protection of wages after they are paid. Title III provides only a temporary shelter over part of a debtor's wages that collapses when the wages leave the employer's control. Thus, the law does little more than its name implies, that is, it restricts garnishment, which explains why the law is presented in this book as part of the section on garnishment.

Bray v. Ed Willey & Son
Supreme Court of Arkansas, 1965
239 Ark. 855, 395 S.W.2d 342

McFaddin, Justice. This is a garnishment case; and the issue is the alleged liability of the garnishee to the judgment plaintiff. Although the amount here involved is very small in monetary value, the legal principles are so important that much time has been spent in research.

On January 10, 1963, appellant Bray recovered a damage judgment against Dave Haneline for $215.97. On January 25, 1963 Bray caused a writ of garnishment after judgment to be served on Ed Willey & Son (hereinafter sometimes referred to as "garnishee" or as "Appellee"). On January 31, 1963 the garnishee filed answer to the interrogatories, stating that the garnishee was not indebted to the defendant on and after the service of the writ of garnishment. Shortly thereafter the garnishee paid the defendant $34.35. On February 8, 1963 Bray controverted and denied the correctness of the answer of the garnishee, claiming that the garnishee had been indebted to Dave Haneline. Trial to the Court on February 10, 1965 resulted in a judgment discharging the garnishee; and from that judgment Bray prosecutes this appeal, relying on one point:

"That the Court erred in discharging the garnishee."

The evidence, viewed in the light most favorable to the judgment, as is our rule in law cases, discloses: that some time prior to the writ of garnishment Haneline had borrowed $75.00 from Willey, and was "working it out"; that on January 25, 1963 when the writ of garnishment was served, Haneline was actually indebted to Willey for $75.00 for a bona fide debt; and that after Willey filed his answer on January 31, 1963 he let Haneline have $34.35 for living expenses. It is this payment of $34.35 that gives rise to this appeal. It is not claimed that there was any collusion or fraud between Haneline and Willey to cover up assets in order to defeat Bray's judgment. It is a simple question of whether Willey had a right to deliver to Haneline $34.35 after the service of the writ of garnishment. Appellant insists that when the writ of garnishment was served on Willey, such service determined the status of the parties; and that Willey could not pay any amount of money to Haneline after that date ****

Our cases hold with practical unanimity that if the garnishee makes any payment to the defendant after the service of the writ of garnishment he does so at his own peril. The authorities generally also recognize the right of offset; that is, if the defendant is indebted to the garnishee for some amount and the garnishee has in his hands any goods, credits, or money belonging to the defendant, then the garnishee can keep enough of same to satisfy his claim against the defendant. In 38 C.J.S. Garnishment §183, p. 409, the holdings are summarized:

"A garnishment lien or right is subject to equities and demands existing in favor of the garnishee at the time the lien or right attached, but is superior to claims which came into existence thereafter."

Likewise, in 6 Am.Jur.2d p. 873, "Attachment and Garnishment" §449, the holdings are summarized:

"As a general rule, a garnishee cannot be placed in any worse condition than he would be if the defendant's claim against him were enforced by the defendant himself, except in cases of fraud and collusion between the defendant and the garnishee. Consequently, the liability, legal and equitable, of the garnishee to the defendant, or the property of the defendant in his possession, is a measure of his liability to the plaintiff, and the plaintiff can have no greater right against the garnishee than the defendant."

We recognize all of these rules; but the question here is whether Willey has become liable to Bray for $34.35, which he could have offset against Haneline's indebtedness to him. Again we emphasize that there is no evidence or indication of fraud or collusion between Willey and Haneline to defeat Bray's judgment. If there had been, what we hereafter hold would not apply.

In view of what we have said, we therefore hold: that when Willey was garnisheed he had a right to offset $34.35 that he owed Haneline on the $75.00 debt that Haneline owed Willey. So when Willey paid Haneline $34.35 then, as far as Bray was concerned, the debt of Haneline to Willey was reduced in that amount. If Willey had ever paid Haneline or credited to his account, more than $75.00, then for such excess over the $75.00 bona fide indebtedness Willey would have been liable to Bray. This is all in the absence of fraud or collusion. * * * We emphasize again that the record here shows a bona fide indebtedness of $75.00 due from Haneline to Willey, and only $34.35 due by Willey to Haneline for services rendered. The payment of $34.35 could not be in addition to some credit on the note, but was the full amount due by Willey to Haneline.

We adhere to our rule that whenever the writ of garnishment is served, any moneys, credits, goods, or effects, in the hands of the garnishee due the defendant must be reported to the Court, and if any such is surrendered by the garnishee to the defendant, such surrender is at the peril of the garnishee. But, here, all such surrender was less than the indebtedness the defendant owed the garnishee; so the judgment rendered by the Court in this case was correct.

Affirmed.

Problems

1. Debtor owned a boat that she had loaned to a neighbor. Is the boat subject to execution? If so, how?

2. Obligor is indebted to Debtor. Creditor is entitled to collect the debt in satisfaction of her judgment against Debtor.

    a. How?

    b. What if Obligor pays the debt to Debtor?

    c. Obligor has a defense to payment that arises from the very same transaction that produced the debt. Is this defense good against Creditor?

    d. Obligor has a counterclaim against Debtor arising from a different transaction. Is this counterclaim good against Creditor?

3. Federal District Court

Judgments in federal district court are also enforced through a writ of execution. Fed.R.Civ.Pro. (F.R.C.P.) 69(a). Generally, the procedure governing execution from federal district courts "shall be in accordance with the practice and procedure of the state in which the district court is held, existing at the time the remedy is sought ***." Id. Of course, federal marshals rather than local officials enforce federal writs of execution. 28 U.S.C.A. §566(b). Also, "a writ of execution [issued from a federal district court] may run and be served anywhere within the territorial limits of the state in which the district court is held that rendered the judgment, although a state writ of execution will not run throughout the state." 7 (pt. 2) J. Moore & J. Lucas, MOORE'S FEDERAL PRACTICE ¶69.04[2] at 69-17 (2d ed. 1983); see also F.R.C.P. 4(e). Moreover, a writ obtained for the use of the United States may be executed in any state or the District of Columbia. 11 Fed.Proc., L.Ed. 31:62 at 247 (1982); see also 28 U.S.C.A. §2413. Liens of execution based on federal judgments are governed, as is the execution process as a whole, by the law of the state in which the district court is held. Thus, state law determines when the lien attaches and its other incidents.

Similarly, judgment liens in federal district court are allowed and controlled by the procedure in the state where the court is located, to wit:

> Every judgment rendered by a district court within a State shall be a lien on the property located in such State in the same manner, to the same extent and under the same conditions as a judgment of a court of general jurisdiction in such State, and shall cease to be a lien in the same manner and time. Whenever the law of any State requires a judgment of a State court to be registered, docketed or indexed, or any other act to be done, in a particular manner, or in a certain office or county or parish before such lien attaches, such requirements shall apply *** only if the law of such State authorizes the judgment of a court of the United States to be registered, recorded, docketed, indexed or otherwise conformed to rules and requirements relating to judgments of the courts of the State.

28 U.S.C.A. §1962. As section 1962 clearly provides, docketing and similar steps that are necessary under state law to create a judgment lien apply to judgments of federal courts only if the state so provides and treats state and federal judgments the same. States cannot

impose conditions on the attachment of federal court judgment liens that are more stringent than those applicable to state court judgment liens. If they do, a judgment of a federal court in the state will in and of itself create a lien on the defendant's property. In such a case no state law requirements, such as docketing and the like, need be satisfied. Also, the lien in such a case will not be limited to the county where the federal court sits; rather, the lien will spread throughout the district court's entire jurisdiction. *Rhea v. Smith*, 274 U.S. 434, 47 S.Ct. 698, 71 L.Ed. 1139 (1927).

B. EXEMPTIONS

As a matter of common law, all of a debtor's property of whatever nature is subject to payment of her debts. By constitution or statute, however, all states give debtors a right to retain some of their property free from the claims of creditors. Such a statutory or constitutional provision is known as an *exemption*.[1] Exemption laws normally protect only debtors who are natural persons and, in some states, only protect property that is used for personal rather than for business purposes. Exempt property cannot be reached by creditors through judicial collection process. In some instances, the property is also secure from any other collection means.

A three-pronged purpose is commonly attributed to exemption laws: protection of the debtor; protection of the debtor's family; and protection of society. By allowing the debtor to retain certain property free from appropriation by creditors, exemption statutes give a debtor a chance to support herself so that she and her dependents will not become a public burden.

---

[1]   Some property is functionally exempt because it is inalienable. As a general rule, only property which can be assigned or alienated is subject to the claims of creditors. Consequently, inalienable property generally is exempt in fact from creditors' claims even though the property is not by law explicitly designated as an exemption. Examples of property of this sort are a debtor's unliquidated claim for damages for personal injury, Plumb, *The Recommendations of the Commission on the Bankruptcy Laws -- Exempt and Immune Property*, 61 VIR.L.REV. 1, 43-47 (1975); a beneficiary's rights in a spendthrift trust, *Helmsley-Spear, Inc. v. Winter*, 74 A.D.2d 195, 426 N.Y.S.2d 778 (1980), aff'd, 52 N.Y.2d 984, 438 N.Y.S.2d 79, 419 N.E.2d 1078 (1981); and a cotenant's interest in property held by the entirety. See cases collected in Annot., 75 A.L.R.2d 1172 (1961). This property is not inalienable in every state, yet it may be immune from creditors' claims for other reasons such as public policy, the nature of the property interest, or because it is covered by an exemption statute.

All states exempt certain personal property, tangible and intangible, from creditor process, but they go about it in several different ways. The various methods of identifying exempt personalty include:

- by *type*, e.g., the family Bible, tools of the debtor's trade, wearing apparel;
- by *value*, e.g., any personal property of a value not to exceed $5000;
- by both *type and value*, e.g., an automobile to the extent of $2000 in value;
- by *type or value*, e.g., the debtor can exempt a long list of specifically identified property or any tangible property not exceeding $6500 in total value.

Moreover, there is very little uniformity among the states with respect to the types and amounts of exempted goods and other personal property. Most states, however, specifically provide for the exemption of wages and other income, and life insurance and various forms of social welfare insurance.

The single most important exemption, however, is the homestead exemption, which protects a debtor's interest in property where she lives. In most jurisdictions, a homestead is fundamentally a privilege or right to exempt certain real property from legal process, not an estate or a vested interest in the property. The original purpose of the homestead exemption was "to protect helpless women and children from the improvident acts of an improvident husband" and is "founded in a wise public policy *** [that it is] better that wives and children should have shelter and a place to live than that a creditor should have his debt ***." *Leonard v. Whitman*, 249 Ala. 205, 209, 30 So.2d 241, 244 (1947). A more modern justification is that the exemption protects "the general economic welfare of all citizens, creditors and debtors alike, by promoting the stability and security of our society." *Wilkinson v. Carpenter*, 277 Or. 557, 565, 561 P.2d 607, 611 (1977).

Creditors often ask debtors to waive the benefit of exemption laws so that none of the debtor's property will be shielded from execution and other process should the creditor be forced to sue on the debt. To this end, consumer credit contracts of various kinds commonly include waiver of exemptions clauses. The exemption laws of a few states authorize the waiver of some or all exemptions. The statutes of other states condemn such a waiver. The enacted laws of most states are silent on the waiver issue; but the well-established general rule is that, except where expressly provided otherwise by enacted law, executory waivers of exemptions are void. They offend public policy.

Federal law also restricts executory waivers of exemptions. A rule of the Federal Trade Commission declares that

> [i]n connection with the extension of credit to consumers in or affecting commerce, *** it is an unfair act or practice within the meaning of [the Federal Trade Commission Act] *** for a lender or retail installment seller directly or indirectly to take or receive from a consumer an obligation that: *** (2) constitutes or contains an executory waiver or a limitation of exemption from attachment, execution or other process on real or personal property held, owned by, or due to the consumer, unless the waiver applies solely to property subject to a security interest executed in connection with the obligation.

FTC Trade Regulation Rule On Credit Practices, 16 C.F.R. §444.2(a)(2).

Executory waivers are condemned in bankruptcy, too. The largest number of American bankruptcies, by far, are liquidation proceedings involving individuals. In this sort of case, all of the debtor's assets that are not subject to valid liens are collected, disposed of, and the proceeds are distributed to creditors. The debtor gets to keep exempt property, however. Moreover, any waiver of exemptions favoring a creditor holding an unsecured claim is voided by federal law, 11 U.S.C.A. §522(e), which means that the waiver will be unenforceable despite state law to the contrary.

The creation of an enforceable security interest in personal property amounts to a waiver of exemption rights with respect to the property. Nevertheless, the vast majority of states, by express statutory provision or through decisional law, permit debtors to encumber exempt property not only to secure payment of the purchase price of the property, but also to secure any non-purchase money loan or other extension of credit. A principal justification for approving voluntary encumbrances is that no law "precludes exempt property from being sold; nor is there any which expressly interdicts the less drastic step of encumbering the property." *State v. AVCO Fin. Service*, 50 N.Y.2d 383, 388, 429 N.Y.S.2d 181, 184, 406 N.E.2d 1075, 1077 (1980). The statutes and cases prohibiting waivers of exemption rights in favor of unsecured creditors are distinguished on various grounds, including the very obvious, though not necessarily convincing, basis that an outright waiver of exemptions in a credit contract is executory only; a security interest amounts to an executed waiver. As explained by the New Mexico Supreme Court:

Assuming, without deciding, that the law of this state does not favor waivers intended to operate at a future time, we are not convinced that a security agreement is such a waiver or that, in practical effect, a security interest differs from a chattel mortgage in any way pertinent to the case at bar.

A security agreement "means an agreement which creates or provides for a security interest." §50A--9--105(h), N.M.S.A.1953. A security interest is an 'interest in personal property.' §50A--1--201(37), N.M.S.A.1953. Therefore it appears to us that the effect of a security agreement is to immediately transfer a property interest in the collateral. The waiver is present, not future, regardless of whether the interest transferred be deemed 'title,' 'lien,' or something else.

We recognize that the exemption statutes are designed to protect debtors from becoming destitute as a consequence of unforeseeable indebtedness. But it has never been suggested that such statutes be construed to deprive an individual of his rights of ownership in the exempt property. Often, such property is the poor man's only source of cash in an emergency and, if the law permits him to sell his exempt property, surely it permits the less drastic step of encumbering it.

Hernandez v. S.I.C. Finance Co., 448 P.2d 474, 476 (1968).

Exemptions are mainly state law, even in federal court. Creditors' process issued from a federal court generally is subject to exemptions provided by the law of the state where the court sits. See F.R.C.P. 64 & 69(a). This is true even when the United States seeks to enforce a judgment in its favor, *Fink v. O'Neil*, 106 U.S. (16 Otto) 272, 1 S.Ct. 325, 27 L.Ed. 196 (1882), so long as the exemption would apply against the state as a judgment creditor. *United States v. Miller*, 229 F.2d 839 (3d Cir.1956).

There are, nevertheless, some federally-created exemptions. Federal non-bankruptcy law creates a wide array of typically narrow exemptions from creditors' process that apply without regard to the source of, or the reason for, the process. Most of the exemptions protect various forms of retirement income and social welfare benefits paid by the United States or somehow regulated by federal law. Examples are: veterans' benefits, 38 U.S.C.A. §5301(a) (1979); social security old age and disability benefits, 42 U.S.C.A. §407(a) (1983); disability and death benefits paid to government employees injured while in the performance of their duties, 5 U.S.C.A. §8130 (1980);

federal civil service retirement, 5 U.S.C.A. §8346(a) (1980); compensation and benefits paid under the Longshoremen's and Harbor Worker's Act, 33 U.S.C.A. §916 (1978); annuities paid pursuant to the Railroad Retirement Act, 45 U.S.C.A. §231m(a) (Supp.1984); and annuities paid to members of the armed forces or their survivors, 10 U.S.C.A. §§1440 & 1450(i) (1983). Federal law also establishes that, as a general rule, a foreign nation's property within the United States is exempt from creditors' process except as otherwise provided by statute or international agreement. 28 U.S.C.A. §1609 (Supp.1984).

More widely important is Title III of the Consumer Credit Protection Act, 15 U.S.C.A. §1671 et seq., which limits the amount of a debtor's wages that a creditor can garnish. Its true purpose, however, is to protect employers from the hassles associated with the garnishment of their employees' wages. Consequently, once an employee receives her wages, Title III no longer protects them to any extent. The law thus is not a true exemption statute. It is rather a temporary shelter over part of a debtor's wages that collapses when the wages leave the employer's control.

A debtor in bankruptcy is allowed to exempt property from the bankrupt estate and thereby keep it for herself free from creditors' claims. The Bankruptcy Code provides as a matter of federal law a generous list of exempt property, including a $7500 interest in a residence and an assortment of personalty, that a debtor can remove from the bankrupt estate unless the state of the debtor's domicile has limited its citizens to local exemptions. See 11 U.S.C.A. §522. Most states have done so, which means that the federal schedule of exemptions is not available to most debtors.

Medaris v. Commercial Bank
Appellate Court of Illinois, Fourth District, 1986
146 Ill.App.3d 1014, 497 N.E.2d 833

Justice Spitz delivered the opinion of the court: On or about September 17, 1984, plaintiffs purchased an automobile from defendant. Defendant financed the purchase and retained a security interest in the automobile, which they subsequently perfected pursuant to article 9 of the Uniform Commercial Code--Secured Transactions (Code) (Ill.Rev.Stat.1985, ch. 26, par. 9-101 et seq.). On January 28, 1985, plaintiffs filed for relief pursuant to chapter 7 of the bankruptcy laws of the United States. (11 U.S.C. §§ 701 et seq. (1982).) Plaintiffs both claimed in their bankruptcy schedules a $1,200 exemption in the automobile pursuant to section 12-1001(c) of the Code of Civil Procedure (Ill.Rev.Stat.1985, ch. 110, par. 12-1001(c)). Subsequently, pursuant to an agreement between the parties to this dispute, defendant repossessed and sold the automobile for an amount substantially less than the amount of the indebtedness owed by plaintiffs to defendant, and plaintiffs filed a complaint for declaratory judgment, seeking to resolve the issue of whether plaintiffs were entitled to claim the motor vehicle as exempt and assert that exemption as priority over the defendant's article 9 security interest and thereby become entitled to the first $2,400 from the sale of the motor vehicle prior to the satisfaction of the defendant's security interest.

The trial court initially held that the plaintiffs' statutory exemption was entitled to priority over the defendant's security interest. After a hearing on defendant's motion for new trial and for reconsideration, the trial court reversed its prior ruling and held that the defendant was entitled to pursue its remedies under section 9-501 et seq. of the Commercial Code (Ill.Rev.Stat.1985, ch. 26, par. 9-501 et seq.) and also held that the exemption statute applies only to "judgment, attachment or distress for rent," and that the self-help remedies of article 9 of the Commercial Code do not fall within any of these categories. The court concluded that the plaintiffs were not entitled to the exemption they claimed under the Illinois exemption statute. On April 21, 1986, judgment was entered on plaintiffs' motion for reconsideration.

The only issue before us on appeal is whether the circuit court erred when it reversed itself and held that defendant's article 9 security interest (Ill.Rev.Stat.1985, ch. 26, par. 9-101 et seq.) in the aforementioned automobile was entitled to priority over plaintiffs' claim of exemption in said automobile pursuant to section 12-1001(c) of the Code of Civil Procedure. Ill.Rev.Stat.1985, ch. 110, par. 12-1001(c).

Section 12-1001(c) of the Code of Civil Procedure provides, in pertinent part, that:

"The following personal property, owned by the debtor, is exempt from judgment, attachment or distress for rent: * * * (c) The debtor's interest, not to exceed $1,200 in value, in any one motor vehicle; * * *."

Ill.Rev.Stat.1985, ch. 110, par. 12-1001(c).

We believe that since defendant's secured interest in the automobile greatly exceeded its fair market value, plaintiffs had no interest in the vehicle within the meaning of the term interest as used in section 12-1001(c) of the Code of Civil Procedure.

The three 19th century Illinois Supreme Court cases relied upon by plaintiffs are all distinguishable on the ground that these cases involved judgment creditors, whereas the instant case involves a creditor who possesses an article 9 security interest.

We interpret section 12-1001(c) of the Code of Civil Procedure to simply mean that a debtor has a right to the first $1,200 of the proceeds of the sale of an automobile when the value of said automobile exceeds the amount of secured debt thereon, but when the amount of the secured debt thereon exceeds the value

of said automobile the debtor has no rights to any of the proceeds of the sale of the automobile. Consequently, we affirm the order of the circuit court.
    Affirmed.

Mirolla v. Mendez
California Court of Appeal, Second District, Division 2, 1980
111 Cal.App.3d 518, 168 Cal.Rptr. 735

Fleming, Associate Justice. Plaintiff Victor Mirolla appeals an order of the superior court declaring defendant Larry Mendez' vehicle exempt from execution. The issue is whether unperfected liens are included in the exemption provided in Code of Civil Procedure section 690.4 for the first $2,500 of value "over and above all liens and encumbrances" on certain items used by the debtor in his trade or profession.
    In October 1978 plaintiff brought an action against defendant in which he alleged that defendant had sold him a stolen vehicle. On October 25 the parties settled the suit for $7,000. The sum was to be paid by defendant in monthly installments of $500, but if defendant defaulted judgment could be entered against him for the unpaid balance plus interest and attorneys' fees. Defendant failed to make the payments, and in August 1979 plaintiff secured a judgment against defendant for $7,000 plus interest and attorneys' fees.
    Defendant was in possession of a truck bearing Oregon license plates. Plaintiff's attorney was informed by Oregon's Department of Motor Vehicles that the truck was registered in Oregon to defendant at his Glendale, California, address, that defendant "had clear legal title to the vehicle, and that there (were) no outstanding liens or encumbrances of record on the vehicle." In September 1979 plaintiff directed the Los Angeles County Marshall to levy on the truck.
    Thereafter, defendant filed a claim of exemption under Code of Civil Procedure section 690.4, which exempts from execution $2,500 of "aggregate actual cash value ... over and above all liens and encumbrances on (various items used by the debtor in his trade or profession) at the time of any levy of attachment or execution thereon," items which include "one commercial motor vehicle reasonably necessary to and actually used (by the debtor) in commercial activity." In the affidavit filed in support of his claim for exemption, defendant, a truck driver, declared that he used the truck levied upon to earn his livelihood, that he had purchased it in May 1978 from Asbury Transportation Company, and that Asbury retained a lien on the truck to secure payments due under the purchase contract. Defendant further declared that since he still owed Asbury $7,900, the vehicle was exempt from execution, because its fair market value (estimated at less than $10,000) did not exceed $2,500 "over and above" the $7,900 lien then held by Asbury. In opposition, plaintiff argued that Asbury's lien was invalid for purposes of defendant's exemption under Code of Civil Procedure section 690.4 because it had never been recorded. In December 1979

the trial court concluded that the vehicle was exempt from execution under Code of Civil Procedure section 690.4, and ordered its release.

(1) On appeal, plaintiff contends the trial court erred in finding Asbury's unrecorded security interest valid for purpose of the exemption and in elevating an unperfected lien above a judgment lien acquired by levy on the vehicle. We agree. An unperfected security interest is subordinate to the rights of a judgment creditor who had levied on the property. (Cal.Com.Code, §§ 9301(1)(b), 9301(3); see also Oregon Com.Code §79.3010(1)(b).) Both California and Oregon require a security interest in a motor vehicle to be recorded as a condition of perfection. (Cal.Veh.Code, §6300; Cal.Com.Code, §9302(1)(d); Oregon Revised Stats. 481.410; 481.413.)

(2) At bench, it is undisputed that plaintiff was a judgment creditor, that defendant was a judgment debtor, and that Asbury had not recorded its security interest in defendant's truck either in Oregon or California at the time plaintiff levied execution on the vehicle. Accordingly, plaintiff's execution lien is superior to Asbury's unperfected lien, and the latter cannot be considered for the purpose of calculating defendant's exemption under Code of Civil Procedure section 690.4.

(3) Defendant and Asbury contend, however, that the release of the vehicle subsequent to the trial court's determination that the vehicle was exempt from execution, returned the parties to the status quo ante, and that plaintiff therefore must once again levy upon the property to satisfy his judgment. Defendant and Asbury argue that on a second levy Asbury's lien, which has now been recorded, would be valid for purposes of calculating the exemption which defendant would again assert. We disagree. Code of Civil Procedure section 690.50(h) states that, when feasible, the levying officer shall retain physical possession of the property levied upon pending final determination of the claim of exemption. Code of Civil Procedure section 690.50(j) provides that a copy of the trial court's order shall be transmitted to the levying officer to permit him either to release the property or, if the property is not found to be exempt, to hold it until the judgment becomes final. At bench, the trial court ordered the sheriff to release the vehicle after it concluded that the vehicle was exempt from execution. The release of physical possession of the vehicle pending the appeal in no way disturbed plaintiff's paramount lien under Commercial Code section 9301, and Asbury's lien, perfected only after the judgment creditor's levy upon the vehicle, remains ineffective for purposes of the execution sale and the amount of exemption thereon. (Code Civ.Proc., §689b(10).)

The order is reversed.

Cargill v. Hedge
Supreme Court of Minnesota, 1985
375 N.W.2d 477

Simonett, Justice. Do the owner-occupants of a farm, by placing their land in a family farm corporation, lose their homestead exemption from judgment creditors? The trial court and the court of appeals said no. We agree and affirm.

On October 24, 1973, defendant-respondent Sam Hedge and his wife Annette entered into a contract for deed for the purchase of a 160-acre farm. On March 1, 1974, the Hedges assigned their vendees' interest to Hedge Farm, Inc., a Minnesota corporation qualified as a family farm corporation under Minn. Stat. §500.24, subd. 1(c) (1973), and took possession. Between 1976 and 1979, Sam Hedge purchased farm supplies and services on account from plaintiff- appellant Cargill, Inc., totaling about $17,000. Apparently not until 1980, however, after Cargill had started suit on the account, did it become aware of the Hedges' corporation. Eventually, pursuant to a confession of judgment, judgment was entered in favor of Cargill and against Sam Hedge and Hedge Farms, Inc., for $12,707.08.

An execution sale was held on July 15, 1982, with Cargill as the successful bidder. Shortly before the 1-year redemption period expired, the district court, on motion of the judgment debtor, enjoined further proceedings on the execution, tolled the redemption period, and allowed Annette to join the proceedings as an intervenor. Subsequently, the trial court ruled that the Hedges had a right to exempt from the execution 80 acres constituting their homestead. The court of appeals affirmed, ruling that Annette Hedge, as sole shareholder of Hedge Farm, Inc., had an "equitable interest" in the corporate property, and that this interest, coupled with the Hedges' occupancy, satisfied the homestead statute. The court implied that it was willing to reach the same result by "piercing the corporate veil." We granted Cargill's petition for further review.

The right to a homestead exemption from execution is a constitutional right. Minn. Const. art 1, §12. This right exempts from seizure or sale "[t]he house owned and occupied by the debtor as his dwelling place, together with the land upon which it is situated," Minn. Stat. §510.01 (1984); in rural areas, 80 acres may be exempted, Minn. Stat. §510.02 (1984). Clearly, a corporation, an artificial entity needing no dwelling, is not entitled to a homestead exemption. If there is to be a homestead exemption here, it must be one personal to the Hedges, notwithstanding the existence of their corporation.

Annette Hedge is the sole stockholder of Hedge Farm, Inc. The court of appeals felt that this gave Annette an "equitable interest" in the property which, together with occupancy, constituted the kind of ownership which would allow the Hedges to assert a homestead exemption in the corporate property. But if Annette is the sole "owner" of the farm, there is no need to assert any homestead exemption because Annette is not a debtor. In any event, the "equitable interest" rationale seems to us conceptually ill-adapted to resolving the issue of creditors' rights we have here, especially since the relationship of a shareholder to a corporation is also implicated. We decline to adopt any equitable interest theory.

We do think, however, that the approach of a reverse pierce of the corporate veil may be used. In Roepke v. Western National Mutual Insurance Co., 302 N.W.2d 350 (Minn.1981), we disregarded the corporate entity to further the purposes of the No-Fault Act. Although title to six motor vehicles was in a corporation, in *Roepke* we nevertheless treated the vehicles as if they had been owned by the deceased, sole shareholder of the corporation, so that the decedent could be deemed an "insured" under the no-fault policy for the purpose of survivors' benefits. It seemed unfair to deprive the business owner of no-fault coverage he would have had if he had operated as a sole proprietorship. We stressed that the decedent had been president and sole stockholder of the corporation, that all six vehicles were used as family vehicles, and that no one in the family owned any other vehicles. Later, in Kuennen v. Citizens Security Mutual Insurance Co., 330 N.W.2d 886 (Minn.1983), we made clear that policy reasons for a pierce do not alone justify disregarding the corporate entity. We refused a reverse pierce in *Kuennen*, where the decedent held only 51% of the stock and used only two of the four corporate vehicles for family use. Thus the degree of identity between the individual and his or her corporation, the extent to which the corporation is an alter ego, is important. Also important is whether others, such as a creditor or other shareholders, would be harmed by a pierce.

Here there is a close identity between the Hedges and their corporation. While the Hedges maintained some of the corporate formalities, such as keeping corporate minutes, filing corporate tax returns, and dealing with the Production Credit Association as a corporation, realistically, as the trial court found, they operated the farm as their own. They had no lease with the corporation and paid no rent. The farmhouse was their family home. Annette Hedge owned all the stock. Mr. and Mrs. Hedge and their daughters were the corporate directors with Sam Hedge as president, Patricia as vice-president, and Annette as secretary-treasurer. None of the officers received any salary. The corporation was as much an alter ego for the Hedges as Mr. Roepke's corporation was for him.

In this case, too, we have strong policy reasons for a reverse pierce, much stronger than in *Roepke*, namely, furtherance of the purpose of the homestead exemption. This state has long recognized the importance, notwithstanding the just demands of creditors, for a debtor's home to be a "sanctuary." Denzer v. Prendergast, 267 Minn. 212, 216, 126 N.W.2d 440, 443 (1964). This "wise and humane policy" is not just for the debtor's benefit, but is also "in the interest of the state, whose welfare and prosperity so largely depend upon the growth and cultivation among its citizens of feelings of personal independence, together with love of country and kindred--sentiments that find their deepest root and best nourishment where the home life is spent and enjoyed." Ferguson v. Kumler, 27 Minn. 156, 159, 6 N.W. 618, 619 (1880). The importance of protecting the homestead is further illustrated by recent laws imposing a moratorium on the foreclosure of certain mortgages and contracts for deed when the property involved qualifies for homestead tax treatment. Minn. Stat. ch. 583 (1984); 1984 Minn.Laws ch. 474. Significant, too, is that the legislature has given homestead classification for real estate tax purposes to homesteads held in family farm corporations where a shareholder occupies and actively farms the land. Minn.Stat. §273.13, subd. 6a (1984).

In *Roepke*, in allowing a reverse pierce, we stated that "no shareholder or creditor would be adversely affected." *Roepke*, 302 N.W.2d at 353. Appellant argues that its creditor rights are adversely affected if the corporate entity is disregarded, but Cargill is no more adversely affected by the reverse pierce than the insurance company in *Roepke*. There is no claim that the rights of other shareholders are harmed; and as for creditors such as Cargill, if the Hedges, who live on the farm, are in reality its owners, any unfairness in allowing them the homestead exemption is merely inherent in the exemption itself. Creditors are deemed to extend credit in awareness that, should an individual debtor default, a homestead is exempt. Here, when Cargill extended credit, it was to Sam Hedge, and only after suit was filed did Cargill discover the existence of Hedge Farm, Inc.

One of the features of a corporation is limiting creditor liability to the corporate assets. We are aware of the danger of a debtor being able to raise or lower his corporate shield, depending on which position best protects his property. Consequently, a reverse pierce should be permitted in only the most carefully limited circumstances. This is such a case, and we so hold. Disregarding the entity Hedge Farm, Inc., we treat the Hedge farm as if owned by Sam and Annette Hedge as vendees under their contract for deed. As a co-vendee, Sam Hedge, the debtor, is entitled to claim a homestead exemption in 80 acres of his farm, and the creditors' execution sale of the exempted 80 acres is void.

Affirmed.

Problems

1. State law allows an individual to exempt one motor vehicle to the extent of a value not exceeding $1500. Debtor Dave owns an old Volkswagen Bug worth $500.00. Is it subject to execution to enforce a $10,000 judgment in favor of Creditor?

    a. Suppose the judgment was based on a promissory note in which Debtor "surrenders now and forever any claim of exemptions of any property as against the Payee or any holder hereof."

    b. Alternatively, suppose the note was signed by a corporation that Debtor Dave had formed for the purpose of getting credit. Debtor transferred the car and other property to the corporation. The corporation and its property are liable for the note. Can the corporation assert the vehicle exemption of state law? See *Cargill*, supra.

   c. Alternatively, suppose the note created a consensual lien -- an Article 9 security interest -- in the car to secure Debtor's obligation to pay the note. When Creditor seeks to enforce the security interest in the car by repossessing it, can Debtor Dave prevent the repo by asserting the vehicle exemption of state law?

2. Start again. Same state law. Same Debtor Dave, an individual. Same Creditor with a $10,000 judgment, with no security interest.

   a. The car was worth $8000. Is it subject to execution to satisfy Creditor's $10,000 judgment? See, e.g., *Gutterman v. First Nat'l Bank*, 597 P.2d 969 (Alaska 1979) (when exempt property is worth more than the statutory exempt maximum, the exempt amount is paid to the debtor from the proceeds of sale prior to any payment to the execution creditor).

   b. Suppose the car was financed by Bank which had a perfected security interest in the car for the $6500 balance Debtor still owed Bank. Is the car subject to Creditor's execution? See *Medaris*, supra.

   c. Go back. The car was worth only $8000, but Bank's interest is unperfected. Is the car subject to Creditor's execution? See *Mirolla*, supra.

3. Debtor Dave's parents created a trust to fund Dave's retirement. Dave cannot receive any of the money for another 30 years, and even then a trustee will pay out the funds according to a rigid schedule geared to fund a reasonable lifestyle for a reasonable time. Are the trust funds subject to execution to satisfy Creditor's judgment against Dave?

   a. Suppose the settlor is Dave's employer who funds the trust as part of Dave's compensation.

   b. Suppose the trust is self settled.

C. FRAUDULENT CONVEYANCES

A not untypical reaction of a debtor confronted with the possibility of seizure of property to satisfy the claims of creditors is to convey away his property to friends or relatives for little or no consideration or with the understanding that the debtor shall continue to enjoy the use and benefit of the property. Since Roman law, such attempts to defraud creditors have been ineffective; creditors have been permitted to recover property so conveyed. The Anglo-American law of fraudulent conveyances is generally considered to have begun with Statute 13 Elizabeth, chapter 5 (1570), which provided:

I. For the avoiding and abolishing of feigned, covinous and fraudulent feoffments, gifts, grants, alienation, conveyances, bonds, suits, judgment and executions *** which *** are devised and contrived of malice, fraud, covin, collusion or guile, to the *end purpose and intent, to delay, hinder or defraud creditors* and others of their just and lawful actions, suits, debts, accounts, damages, penalties, forfeitures, heriots, mortuaries, and reliefs. ***

II. Be it therefore declared, ordained, and enacted *** that all and every feoffment, gift, grant, alienation, bargain, and conveyance of lands, tenements, hereditaments, goods and chattels *** and every bond, suit, judgment, and execution *** made *** to or for *any intent or purpose before declared* and expressed, shall be *** deemed and taken (*only as against that person or persons*, his or their heirs, successors, executors, administrators, and assigns *** whose actions, suits, debts, accounts, damages, penalties, forfeitures, heriots, mortuaries and reliefs *** are, shall or might be in anywise *disturbed, hindered, delayed or defrauded*) to be clearly and utterly void, frustrate, and of none effect; any pretence, color, feigned consideration, expressing of use, or any other matter or thing to the contrary notwithstanding.

III. And be it further enacted *** that all and every the parties to such feigned, covinous or fraudulent *** alienation *** and other things before expressed, and being privy and knowing of the same, *** shall incur the penalty and forfeiture of one year's value of the said lands, tenements, and hereditaments, leases, rents, commons, or other profits of or out of the same; and the whole value of the said goods and chattels; and also so much money as are or shall be contained in any such covinous and feigned bond, the one moiety whereof to be the Queen's Majesty *** and the other moiety to the party or parties grieved ***, and also being thereof lawfully convicted, shall suffer imprisonment for one-half year without bail or mainprise. ***

VI. Provided that this Act *** shall not extend to any estate or interest in lands, tenements, hereditaments, leases, rents, commons, profits, goods, or chattels, had, made, conveyed, or assured *** *upon good consideration and bona fide* lawfully conveyed or assured to any person *** not having at the time of such conveyance or assurance to them made, any manner of notice or knowledge of such covin, fraud, or collusion. *** (Emphasis added.)

The law of fraudulent conveyances soon became something other than the language of the statute. The Statute of Elizabeth says that fraudulent conveyances are "void," but void only as to persons "hindered, delayed or defrauded." In other words, a fraudulent conveyance is valid as between the grantor and the grantee; in other words, a fraudulent conveyance is not void but rather is voidable by certain creditors of the grantor. See 1 G. Glenn, FRAUDULENT CONVEYANCES AND PREFERENCES §111 (1940). Note that the language of the Statute indicates that it is a penal statute with the remedy being the delivery of half of the fraudulently transferred property to the crown and the other half to the defrauded creditor. Courts, however, since *Mannocke's Case*, 3 Dyer 293b (1571), have taken the position that the judgment creditor need not rely on the remedy provided in the statute but can ignore the transfer and proceed directly on the property.

Note also that the Statute of Elizabeth requires "intent to delay, hinder or defraud." Since proof of a particular intent is a difficult task, courts soon developed "badges of fraud", i.e., circumstances indicative of intent to defraud. The first such case was *Twyne's Case*, 3 Coke 80b, 76 Eng.Rep. 809 (1601). There P was indebted to T for 400 pounds and to C for 200 pounds. C sued P and, while the action was pending, P secretly conveyed to T by deed of gift all of his chattels (worth 300 pounds) in satisfaction of T's claim. P, however, remained in possession of some of his property -- some sheep -- and treated them as his own. C obtained a judgment against P, but when the sheriff sought to levy on the sheep, friends of P prevented him from doing so, asserting that the sheep belonged to T. Thereupon C sued T to set aside the conveyance from P to T as a fraudulent conveyance. The court held that the transfer was fraudulent, noting the following "badges of fraud":

> 1st. That this gift had the signs and marks of fraud, because the gift is general, without exception of his apparel, or any thing of necessity; for it is commonly said, *quod dolus versatur in generalibus*.
>
> 2nd. The donor continued in possession and used them as his own; and by reason thereof he traded and trafficked with others, and defrauded and deceived them.

3rd. It was made in secret, *et dona clandestina sunt semper suspiciosa.*

4th. It was made pending the writ.

5th. Here was a trust between the parties, for the donor possessed all, and used them as his proper goods and fraud is always apparelled and clad with a trust, and a trust is the cover of fraud.

6th. The deed contains, that the gift was made honestly, truly, and *bona fide; et clausuloe inconsuet semper inducunt suspicionem.*

76 Eng.Rep. at 812-14.

In virtually every American jurisdiction, the Statute of 13 Elizabeth and its judicial gloss have either been recognized as part of the inherited common law or expressly adopted or enacted in similar terms. The concept of "badges of fraud" has also been generally adopted, and numerous facts are now commonly recognized as indicia or "badges" of fraud. In *Philco Finance Corp. v. Pearson*, 335 F.Supp. 33, 40-41 (N.D.Miss.1971), the court relied on the following badges of fraud to set aside the transfer of 25,000 shares of Classic Cleaners, Inc. by Pearson to Heard:

- Pearson transferred the stock, his principal asset, at a time when he was heavily indebted, had an outstanding judgment against him for sales taxes, and was being sued by Philco upon a large claim; after the transfer he was left without property subject to execution.

- The transfer was not made in the usual course of business and, while not secret, it was done through private negotiation and by signing instruments which were not subjected to public recordation or disclosure to creditors.

- Although the stock had a book value of $17,500 and Classic was obligated to pay Pearson $300 monthly until 1973, Pearson did not offer the stock to Triplett, the other stockholder, who was the person most likely to offer a top price for the stock in a bona fide sale.

- Heard, before purchasing the stock, made no inquiry of Classic or Triplett as to financial condition and after the purchase he was indifferent to the business operations of the corporation.

- Heard was actuated to make the transaction because of his other profitable relationships with Pearson, a person who was in known financial trouble when offering the stock to Heard for $10,000.

- The consideration paid, assuming one was paid, was under conditions designed to conceal the true intention of the parties, namely, to make an arrangement whereby Pearson could continue selling laundry equipment without fear of losing the stock to Philco. The parties cleverly contrived to give the transfer an appearance of fairness.

◆ Although the contract Pearson made with Heard covered both Pearson's stock and 'all interest' in Classic Cleaners, Heard nevertheless allowed Pearson to continue drawing monthly payment from the corporation, thus foregoing claim to more than $12,000 paid to Pearson.

◆ The transfer was made under a provision allowing Pearson's wife to repurchase the stock within one year without profit to Heard.

◆ Heard acquiesced in Pearson's assertion that, notwithstanding the transfer, Pearson still had a voice in Classic's control and operation, 'as manager of the Heard interest.'

◆ Despite the transfer, Heard failed to list the stock bought for $10,000 as an asset on his financial records or financial statements submitted to banks for loan purposes.

The circumstances that constitute a badge of fraud and the weight to be given to a particular "badge" (whether it is conclusive of fraud, prima facie evidence of fraud, or merely admissible evidence of fraud) vary from state to state. One of the few points of uniformity under state law has been that with few exceptions, a preference -- as such -- is generally not a fraudulent conveyance. "True, a creditor who collects from an insolvent debtor fares better than other claimants. Yet if the transfer were set aside in favor of another creditor, there would be but a substitution of one preference for another. For that reason a preference cannot be undone by a competing creditor whether the preference was obtained through judicial process or by a transfer from the debtor. * * *" *Smith v. Whitman*, 39 N.J. 397, 402, 189 A.2d 15, 18 (1963).

In 1918, the National Conference of Commissioners on Uniform State Laws proposed the *Uniform Fraudulent Conveyance Act* (*UFCA*) to promote "uniformity in the law of fraudulent conveyances" and eliminate "the existing confusion in the law." The Commissioners' Prefatory Note of the Act states in part:

The confusions and uncertainties of the existing law which have been referred to are due primarily to three things:

First, the absence of any well recognized, definite conception of insolvency.

Second, failure to make clear the persons legally injured by a given fraudulent conveyance.

Third, the attempt to make the Statute of Elizabeth cover all conveyances which wrong creditors, even though the actual intent to defraud does not exist.

The Statute of Elizabeth condemns conveyances as fraudulent only when made with the 'intent' to 'hinder, delay or defraud.' There are many conveyances which wrong creditors where an intent to defraud on the part of the debtor does not in fact exist. In order to avoid these conveyances, the courts have called to their assistance presumptions of law as to intent, and in equity have pushed presumption of fraud as a fact to an unwarranted extent; with the result that, while in the main the decisions under the facts do justice, the reasoning supporting them leaves much to be desired.

In the Act as drafted all possibility of a presumption of law as to intent is avoided. *Certain conveyances which the courts have in practice condemned, such as a gift by an insolvent, are declared fraudulent irrespective of intent.* On the other hand, while all conveyances with intent to defraud creditors (see Section 7) are declared fraudulent, it is expressly stated that the intent must be actual intent, as distinguished from intent presumed as a matter of law.

The Uniform Fraudulent Conveyance Act was adopted in twenty-three states.

Recently, the Conference of Commissioners on Uniform State Laws promulgated a successor to the UFCA. The new law is entitled, *Uniform Fraudulent Transfer Act (UFTA)*. The UFTA is much like the UFCA in form and substance. Many of the differences between the two laws are minor. In large part, the UFTA simply improves somewhat upon the structure of the UFCA, fine tunes here and there (largely in reaction to changes in bankruptcy law), and codifies choices among certain decisional rules that have developed under the UFCA. There are some significant new wrinkles, however, including:

+ a different, broader definition of insolvency;
+ the elimination of good faith on the part of the transferee or obligee as a factor in determining adequacy of consideration;
+ a new category of fraudulent transfer (preferential transfer to an insider);
+ the elimination of any provision aimed specifically at transfers or obligations of insolvent partnerships;

 ◆ the addition of provisions dealing specifically with the enforcement of encumbrances (so as to immunize lawful enforcement from attack as fraudulent when proceeds from the sale of collateral are small);
 ◆ a few changes in remedies (eliminates the distinction between creditors having mature claims and those having unmatured claims with respect to available remedies, and adds language suggesting the general availability of a personal judgment against a transferee).

Dona Ana Savings and Loan Association v. Dofflemeyer
Supreme Court of New Mexico, 1993
115 N.M. 590, 855 P.2d 1054

Frost, Justice. This matter comes before us on appeal from an order granting summary judgment in favor of the defendants/appellees and against the plaintiff/appellant Dona Ana Savings & Loan Association ("DASL"). DASL held deficiency judgments against James Dofflemeyer, and it attempted to execute on the judgments by garnishing his funds in two annuities. In the district court, Dofflemeyer claimed that the annuity funds were exempt from attachment under NMSA 1978, Sections 42-10-2 and -3 (Cum.Supp.1992). The district court found that the funds were exempt and dismissed DASL's writ of garnishment. DASL appeals, and we reverse and remand with instructions.

FACTS
In the return of DASL's initial writ of execution, Dofflemeyer attached a Claim of Exemptions form listing a certificate of deposit in the amount of $54,000.00. Before DASL could garnish this asset, however, Dofflemeyer liquidated it and used the proceeds to purchase one of his two annuities. In addition, he sold certain real estate to his sister and used the proceeds to purchase the other annuity. The record shows that Dofflemeyer purchased the annuities in contemplation of bankruptcy and in furtherance of his need for an immediate source of monthly income. He listed his sister, who was also his business partner, as beneficiary under both annuities.

ISSUES
While he expressed concern about whether Dofflemeyer's claim of exemption on the annuities was legitimate, the trial judge found that the clear language and plain meaning of the statutes compelled him to allow the exemptions and to dismiss DASL's writ of garnishment with regard to the two annuities. On appeal, DASL claims that the annuities are not exempt from garnishment under Sections 42-10-2 and -3. DASL argues that the district court erred by not going beyond the face of the statutes to construe their purpose. A strict or literal reading of the statute, according to DASL, defeats the intended object of the legislation and operates an injustice. DASL claims that going

beyond a cursory review of the statute, it is apparent that the statutes do not allow a debtor to shield funds from creditors on the eve of execution.

Dofflemeyer, on the other hand, claims that he simply was providing himself with retirement funds as a self-employed person, which is proper under the statutes. According to Dofflemeyer, the statutes clearly provide exemptions for annuities and retirement funds, and thus it is unnecessary to look beyond the plain meaning of the statute.

In addition to the annuities, DASL notes that it filed a writ of garnishment against monies owed to Dofflemeyer by a third party to which he also claimed exemption. While pointing this out, however, DASL does not allege any error in this claimed exemption, nor does it request any relief as to this claim by Dofflemeyer. In addition, the district court did not address this issue in its decision to allow the exemptions. Accordingly, we will consider only the issue of whether the annuity funds are exempt under Sections 42-10-2 and -3.

DISCUSSION

Section 42-10-2 states that: any interest in or proceeds from a pension or retirement fund of every person supporting only himself is exempt from ... attachment, execution or foreclosure by a judgment creditor. NMSA 1978, §42-10-2 (Cum.Supp.1992). Section 42-10-3 states:

> The cash surrender value of any life insurance policy, the withdrawal value of any optional settlement, annuity contract or deposit with any life insurance company, all weekly, monthly, quarterly, semiannual or annual annuities, indemnities or payments of every kind from any life, accident or health insurance policy, annuity contract or deposit heretofore or hereafter issued upon the life of a citizen or resident of the state of New Mexico, or made by any such insurance company with such citizen, upon whatever form and whether the insured or the person protected thereby has the right to change the beneficiary therein or not, shall in no case be liable to attachment, garnishment or legal process in favor of any creditor of the person whose life is so insured or who is protected by said contract, or who receives or is to receive the benefit thereof, nor shall it be subject in any other manner to the debts of the person whose life is so insured, or who is protected by said contract or who receives or is to receive the benefit thereof, unless such policy, contract or deposit be taken out, made or assigned in writing for the benefit of such creditor.

Section 42-10-3. In this case, DASL claims that Dofflemeyer essentially transmuted one form of nonexempt funds into another form of nonexempt funds, or that he fraudulently converted nonexempt funds into exempt funds. Dofflemeyer asserts that the district court found that there was no evidence of abuse or fraud on his part and that the plain meaning of the statutes allows for the exemptions.

* * *

We hold that the object of the exemption statutes quoted above is to allow for exemptions in certain funds, but that it does not allow a debtor to find shelter in these statutes by perpetrating a fraud upon his or her creditors. On their face, the statutes allow for unlimited exemptions for life insurance, annuities, and pension and retirement funds. At least one judge, however, has noted the potential for abuse of the legitimate exemptions under the statutes. The legislature did not intend "that these generous provisions should be prostituted to the encouragement of extravagance, and the evasion of just indebtedness...." New Mexico Nat'l Bank v. Brooks, 9 N.M. 113, 129, 49 P. 947, 952 (1897). We believe, and the record shows, that DASL presented evidence that demonstrates the possibility of abuse and which at least escapes dismissal on summary judgment.

To determine whether a debtor fraudulently converted nonexempt assets into exempt assets, we turn to the Uniform Fraudulent Transfer Act. See NMSA 1978, §§ 56-10-14 to -25 (Cum.Supp.1992). * * * Accordingly, the noninclusive enumeration of factors contained in Sections 56-10-18 and -19 are to be considered when determining whether the funds that ordinarily would be exempt from attachment under Sections 42-10-2 and -3 should be set aside as the result of a voidable transfer.

* * *

Dofflemeyer's purchase of the annuities when his creditors were in "hot pursuit," his apparent admission to his broker that the purchase was a preliminary step into bankruptcy, and his request for an immediate source of income from his threatened nonexempt funds all raise a genuine issue of material fact as to whether his conversion of nonexempt funds, which were in imminent danger of attachment, was done with the intent to defraud DASL. On the other hand, it may very well be true that Dofflemeyer legitimately sought a source for retirement funds or life insurance. In any event, it is our holding today that the conversion of nonexempt funds into funds that are ordinarily exempt under Sections 42-10-2 and -3 are not automatically protected from attachment by creditors without an analysis of whether the transfer served the underlying purpose of the exemption statutes and was not in furtherance of an intent to defraud creditors.

* * *

CONCLUSION

A debtor may buy annuities and claim that they are exempt, but a debtor may not claim an exemption that is a result of fraud and thus avoid creditors' claims by using Sections 42-10-2 and -3 as a guise or ruse. To hold that a debtor automatically may find refuge in these statutes on the eve of execution would render the statutes' application absurd, unreasonable, and unjust. We emphasize, however, that the purposeful conversion of nonexempt funds into exempt funds immediately prior to bankruptcy or threatened execution by a creditor is not fraudulent per se; it is only one indicium of fraud and does not necessarily by itself make out a claim of fraudulent conversion. See Zouhar, 10 B.R. at 156. To defeat the exemptions under the statutes here, there must be a showing of an intent to defraud creditors and that showing must be consistent with the provisions of the Uniform Fraudulent Transfer Act.

We conclude that the district court's interpretation of the exemption statutes is consistent with their plain meaning, but that a genuine issue of material fact exists as to whether Dofflemeyer engaged in acts of fraudulent conversion under the Uniform Fraudulent Transfer Act. Accordingly, we reverse the summary judgment and remand this case to the district court for a determination consistent with this opinion of whether Dofflemeyer fraudulently converted his annuity funds from nonexempt to exempt status.

IT IS SO ORDERED.

Baca, Montgomery and Franchini, JJ., concur.

Ransom, C.J., dissenting.

Ransom, Chief Justice (dissenting).

I respectfully dissent. Upon careful study of Dona Ana's briefs and exhibits supporting the allegation of Dofflemeyer's intent to defraud, I fail to find sufficient evidence to raise a genuine issue of material fact. Clearly, in anticipation of Dona Ana's attempt to attach the nonexempt funds, Dofflemeyer simply transferred assets into exempt annuities for no purpose other than retirement. In re Mueller, 71 B.R. 165 (D.Kan.1987), aff'd, 867 F.2d 568 (10th Cir.1989), is instructive as to whether such a transfer of assets was fraudulent as to Dona Ana. There, the court alluded to the common-law judicial exemption (developed before the bankruptcy act) that was applied whenever a creditor challenged a transfer as a fraudulent conveyance. The exception arose only for a creditor who had a "peculiar equity" in the assets converted to exempt property. "Peculiar equities" exist either when converted funds are fraudulently procured from the creditor or when the creditor has a lien on the assets used to procure the exempt property. Id. at 167. Dona Ana has provided no evidence that the funds were fraudulently procured or that the annuities were procured directly or indirectly by the sale of property on which it held a lien.

It is now true that any creditor may challenge a transfer of assets under the Fraudulent Transfer Act, but in determining intent to defraud, consideration must be given to the status of the creditor seeking to challenge the transfer. If the creditor does not have a peculiar equity or the transferor does not have an ulterior fraudulent purpose, more is required than just the fact that the debtor acquired exempt retirement annuities in anticipation of a lien.

The trial court already has made several uncontroverted findings that support Dofflemeyer's claim that his transfer of non-exempt assets into exempt retirement annuities was legitimate and with the intent to provide for his retirement rather than for some ulterior purpose:

5. Defendant Dofflemeyer is 77 years old and retired.

6. Dofflemeyer was self-employed and put aside for his retirement the funds that Dona Ana seeks to garnish.

7. Dofflemeyer derives his income from Social Security and the annuities that Dona Ana seeks to garnish.

8. Dofflemeyer's Social Security income is $700 per month and is not sufficient to pay his medical expenses, taxes, auto expenses, food, clothing and utility expenses.

9. Dofflemeyer receives $710 per month from the annuities that Dona Ana seeks to garnish.

10. Without the income from the retirement fund/annuities, Dofflemeyer would lack the resources to continue his independent living existence.

11. Without the income from the retirement fund/annuities, Dofflemeyer would either be forced on the public dole or would increase the likelihood of his becoming a public charge.

The Legislature has expressed clearly its intent to protect the retirement income of individuals. This Court has long held that exemption statutes are to be liberally construed in favor of the debtor. Like the homestead exemption statute, the retirement exemption statute "was adopted as a humane policy to prevent families from becoming destitute as the result of misfortune through common debts which generally are unforeseen." See Hewatt v. Clark, 44 N.M. 453, 457, 103 P.2d 646, 649 (1940). "By permitting the debtor to keep those assets necessary for his economic survival, state exemption laws fulfill important social policies which must be balanced against the need for creditor protection." Alan N. Resnick, Prudent Planning or Fraudulent Transfer? The Use of Nonexempt Assets to Purchase or Improve Exempt Property on the Eve of Bankruptcy, 31 Rutgers L.Rev. 615, 615 (1978).

> "[I]t is consistent to permit the debtor to ... purchase new exempt property on the eve of bankruptcy, so long as the items ... purchased will at least partially relieve the debtor of the need for governmental assistance."

Id. at 627.

The trial court had before it evidence that Dofflemeyer's intent in transferring his assets from certificates of deposit to retirement annuities was to provide retirement income in order to pay for necessities. There was no extrinsic evidence that Dofflemeyer's intent was to defraud his creditors. "Fraud can never be predicated on an act which the law permits." In re Tveten, 402 N.W.2d 551, 553 (Minn.1987). Therefore, I would affirm the trial court.

Rubin v. Manufacturers Hanover Trust Co.
United States Court of Appeals, Second Circuit, 1981
661 F.2d 979

[This case was decided under the statutory predecessor to Bankruptcy Code section 548, which was Bankruptcy Act section 67(d). The old and new sections are much the same but the former used the term "fair consideration" instead of the modern "reasonably equivalent value." The definitions are only slightly different. Although decided under the old statute, the Rubin *case is very good law today, both in bankruptcy and under state law. Indeed, it is frequently cited and relied on by lawyers, courts, and commentators and remains a very important case in the law of fraudulent transfers, especially on the issue of indirect transfers as fraudulent..]*

Kearse, Circuit Judge. This appeal arises from the collapse and ultimate bankruptcy of two affiliated firms, U.S.N., Inc. ("USN"), and Universal Money Order Co., Inc. ("UMO"), companies in the business of issuing money orders. Plaintiffs Herbert Rubin and Eliot H. Lumbard, bankruptcy trustees of USN and UMO, respectively, appeal from a judgment of the United States District Court for the Southern District of New York, 4 B.R. 447, Milton Pollack, Judge, dismissing their claims to recover the value of certain funds and securities of the bankrupts from defendant Manufacturers Hanover Trust Co. ("MHT"). The trustees contend that MHT took these assets pursuant to fraudulent conveyances within the meaning of §67(d) of the Bankruptcy Act of 1898, former 11 U.S.C. §107(d) (1976), in satisfaction of debts arising from defaulted loans made, at the behest of the bankrupts, to companies that acted as sales agents for the bankrupts. The district court held, after a bench trial, that the loans against which MHT applied the bankrupts' property were supported by fair consideration and did not render the bankrupts insolvent, so that the transactions could not be set aside pursuant to §67(d). Because we conclude that the district court did not apply the proper legal standards in considering the issues of fair consideration and insolvency, we vacate its judgment and remand the matter for further proceedings.

I. HISTORY OF THE BANKRUPTS' BUSINESS

The bankruptcy of UMO and USN was part of the collapse of a sort of private banking empire controlled by Messrs. John M. Trent and Eugene Skowron. The Trent/Skowron companies were a major factor in what the plaintiffs have termed the "auxiliary banking system," a group of businesses that provide banking-type services primarily to lower-income persons who do not maintain ordinary checking accounts. As part of this system UMO and USN (sometimes referred to as "issuers") engaged in the business of issuing money orders. Defendant MHT was the principal banker for the Trent/Skowron network and, as detailed below, made loans to various members of the network and held as collateral assets owned by UMO and USN. As a result of the collapse of the

Trent/Skowron network, an as yet undetermined, but undoubtedly quite large, number of money orders issued by UMO and USN became unredeemable and worthless. In the present litigation, the trustees of the issuers seek to recover for the benefit of purchasers of unredeemed UMO and USN money orders the value of certain collateral pledged by the issuers and applied by MHT to debts of other companies, most of which were Trent/Skowron affiliates. Resolution of the difficult legal questions raised by the trustees' appeal requires a fairly detailed recounting of the history of the Trent/Skowron enterprises.

A. Basic Organization of the Enterprise

UMO, USN, and their parent corporation, International Express Co. ("International"), were apparently the central elements of the Trent/Skowron network. USN, a New York corporation formed by Trent and Skowron in 1962, sold money orders primarily in New York State. UMO, incorporated by Trent and Skowron in New Jersey in 1970, sold money orders primarily in California, Colorado, Massachusetts, New Jersey, Ohio, and West Virginia. Although the two firms had different sales territories, they were run as a single enterprise. Each was wholly owned by International; 89% of the stock of International was owned by Trent and Skowron. UMO, USN, and International had the same principal officers and directors, including Trent as president and Skowron as secretary-treasurer. The funds of UMO and USN were mingled in a single bank account and were used fungibly to redeem either firm's money orders as they were presented. Although the companies' accounts were so "jumbled together" that their monthly sales rates could not be stated separately, their combined monthly sales volume amounted to about 900,000 money orders, having an average daily face value of about $1,850,000.

UMO and USN did not sell their money orders directly to the public. Instead, each firm enlisted a number of small businesses in its sales territory to act as sales agents. Although a variety of retail stores, particularly drug stores, acted as sales agents in smaller communities, the firms' principal sales agents were check cashing establishments located in large cities. These check cashing "stores" were well situated to sell money orders, for they were equipped for the safe handling of large amounts of money, and their check cashing services provided customers with the cash needed to buy the bankrupts' money orders. By the same token, the sale of money orders aided the check cashers in their principal business by reducing the cash outlays associated with it. This symbiotic relationship with the check casher sales agents was vital to the money order issuers. Robert Sparago, an officer and former general counsel of both UMO and USN, testified that the check cashers did "the major part of the money order business of USN" and that "(w)ithout the check cashers there was no USN." UMO was similarly dependent upon its check casher sales agents.

At some point in the development of their businesses, Trent and Skowron sought to expand into the check cashing business. Toward this end they formed Empire Small Business Investment Corp. ("Empire"), which they used as a holding company to acquire a controlling 50% interest in National Payroll Services Ltd. ("National"), itself a holding company that owned eleven check cashing corporations that operated at 18 locations, and to acquire a controlling 331/3% interest in TWO Check Cashing Corp. ("TWO"), another holding company that owned four check cashing outlets.   All of the check casher subsidiaries of National and TWO were located in New York City, and all were sales agents of USN.

Thus, for the period relevant to this appeal, the relationships between Trent and Showron and the principal businesses they controlled can be summarized schematically as shown below:

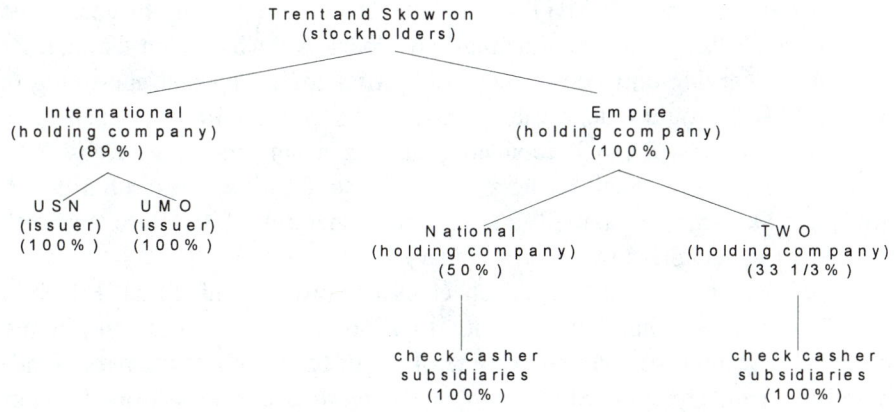

Numbers in parentheses indicate the percentage of the
stock of each corporation owned by the entity immediately
above it in the chain of ownership.

B. The Banking Arrangements and the System of Guarantees

Because their check cashing business required continuous outlays of currency, the check cashers who served as sales agents for UMO and USN experienced a constant need for cash, a need that the inflow of funds from the sale of money orders could never wholly satisfy. The resulting imbalance posed obvious problems for both the check cashers and the money order issuers. If the cashers ran out of currency, they could not conduct their principal business; if the cashers became unable to cash checks, then many prospective customers of UMO and USN would be unable to obtain the cash needed to purchase money orders.

In addition, the currency shortfalls of the check cashers presented a somewhat more fundamental problem for the money order issuers. To the extent that a check casher ran low on cash, he would be tempted to retain the proceeds of his money order sales for use in his own business rather than remit them promptly to the issuer. Such foot-dragging could have disastrous consequences for the issuer, whose profit depends largely on his freedom to exploit the "float" inherent in his business—i. e., on his ability to use and invest the proceeds of money order sales between the time of purchase and the time when the money orders are presented for collection. Any delay in the remittance of sales proceeds to the issuer necessarily diminishes the "float," and therefore the profitability of the issuer's business.

As a means of resolving these problems Trent and Skowron settled on short-term bank financing for the check cashers. In 1964, the two entrepreneurs caused USN to arrange for certain of its check casher sales agents to receive loans from MHT, with which USN maintained an account. Under the initial 1964 arrangement, MHT opened a "loan line" against which USN's check casher sales agents were permitted to borrow for three-day periods. Each month, Trent and Skowron submitted to MHT a schedule of requested loans to each check casher for each day of the month; the daily loans were based on estimates of each casher's varying daily needs for cash. After reviewing and approving the schedules, MHT would extend the specified credit for each day to each of the listed check cashers. This three-sided financing arrangement, whereby MHT loaned money to the check cashers according to the schedules submitted by Trent and Skowron, remained an essential operating procedure until the Trent/Skowron network collapsed in January 1977.

The initial 1964 loan line for the check cashers was provided by MHT on the basis of the check cashers' own credit. In 1966, Trent and Skowron obtained from MHT a second, supplementary line of credit for the check cashers. Under this arrangement, Trent and Skowron pledged certain securities, owned by them, as collateral, and MHT extended credit to the check cashers, in accordance with monthly schedules submitted by Trent and Skowron as described above, in a total amount that was fixed as a varying multiple of the value of the collateral. Thus, under the 1966 arrangement, the check cashers were able to borrow under the 1964 loan lines (which remained in place) to the extent of their own creditworthiness, and were able to draw on the supplementary loan line, on the strength of Trent and Skowron's collateral, as necessary to meet the peak demands of their business. The debts incurred under either line of credit were of course to be repaid by the check cashers themselves.

On November 13, 1970, Trent and Skowron formalized, and altered somewhat, their relationship with MHT and the check cashers by executing the first of a series of agreements whereby they guaranteed the debts of the check cashers to MHT. Under this agreement, Trent and Skowron personally guaranteed "the prompt and unconditional payment of all obligations" of the check cashers to MHT under the loan lines. As security for their obligations under the guarantee, Trent and Skowron gave MHT a lien on their accounts at the bank and pledged other property belonging to them, apparently including the securities that were previously pledged under the 1966 arrangement. Under the 1970 guarantee, the check cashers' loan lines were no longer tied to their own creditworthiness, but were predicated entirely on the financial strength of Trent and Skowron. The permissible borrowings of individual check cashers continued to be determined on the basis of monthly schedules submitted by Trent and Skowron, and the maximum available credit was again set as a varying multiple of the collateral supplied by Trent and Skowron.

Apparently well aware of the size and complexity of the Trent/Skowron business interests, MHT subsequently obtained a series of guarantees and cross-guarantees from various entities in the network in order to ensure that it would be able to look to the assets of any of the Trent/Skowron entities in the event of default by the check cashers. In particular, USN and UMO each guaranteed the joint and individual debts of Trent and Skowron, Trent and Skowron jointly guaranteed the separate debts of USN and UMO, and USN and UMO guaranteed each other's debts. Most of the guarantees were executed in 1972, although some of the Trent/Skowron entities executed additional guarantees in later years as MHT deemed them necessary.

Under each guarantee agreement, the guarantor pledged to MHT, or granted MHT a lien on, certain of its assets as security for its obligations under the guarantee. Of particular importance in this appeal are the security provisions contained in the guarantees given by the money order issuers, several of which were executed on November 28, 1972. On that day, in guarantees of the debts of Trent and Skowron and those of UMO, USN granted MHT a lien on "any and all moneys, securities and any and all other property" of USN then or thereafter in MHT's actual or constructive possession. On the same day, UMO executed a guarantee of Trent and Skowron's debts, granting MHT a similar broad lien. Subsequently, in a guarantee of Trent and Skowron's debts dated July 30, 1975, UMO pledged as collateral some 44,000 shares of stock and other securities. Finally, in a guarantee of Trent and Skowron's debts dated September 21, 1976, UMO repledged these securities holdings, as modified by substitutions of collateral that had taken place since the execution of the July 1975 guarantee, and also pledged as new collateral a $187,000 certificate of deposit held in its name.   For several years after 1964, the Trent/Skowron enterprises functioned fairly smoothly under this system of loan lines and guarantees. After the execution of the initial guarantee in 1970, the number of check cashers financed under the loan lines increased. Although MHT had initially loaned money only to New York City check cashers who were sales agents of USN, check cashers who were sales agents of UMO located in Colorado, Massachusetts, New Jersey, and Ohio soon became regular borrowers under the loan lines. In addition, at various times between 1972 and December 27, 1976, MHT loaned money directly to UMO on the strength of the system of guarantees; on some or all of these occasions, UMO loaned the funds it borrowed from MHT to its check casher sales agents in California. At their peak, the check cashers' combined borrowings from MHT totaled approximately $12 million, and were secured by $3 million worth of collateral under the guarantees.

C. The Food Stamp Episode

In 1972, MHT and the Trent/Skowron enterprise joined forces in selling food stamps to the public. Pursuant to an agreement with the New York City Department of Social Services (the "City Department"), the agency that supervised food stamp operations in metropolitan New York, MHT became a vendor of food stamps, selling them on a wholesale basis to sub-vendors, including check cashers, who retailed them to recipients. Like the sale of money orders, the sale of food stamps benefited the check cashers by reducing somewhat the outflow of cash associated with their principal business. Many of USN's check casher sales agents, including those owned by the Trent/Skowron affiliates National and TWO, acted as sub-vendors of food stamps supplied by MHT.

Applicable federal regulations required sub-vendors of food stamps to pay to the City Department the proceeds of their food stamp sales on a daily or weekly basis, depending on the volume of food stamp sales. Nonetheless, several check cashers, including some sales agents owned by National and TWO, failed to remit these funds in timely fashion, using the resulting "float" to finance their check cashing operations. In 1976, an audit of National conducted by the United States Department of Agriculture ("USDA") revealed that its check cashers had accumulated food stamp arrears totaling $300,000. Apparently TWO's check casher subsidiaries were also substantially in arrears on their food stamp payments.

MHT insisted that Trent and Skowron clear up the food stamp arrears of National and TWO, and apparently went so far as to threaten to cut off credit to the offending check cashers—a move that would have sharply curtailed USN's money order business-if the arrears were not promptly paid. The method adopted for resolving the food stamp problem was an increase in the loan lines available to the affected check cashers. On September 16, 1976, MHT made an additional $500,000 in credit available to the affected firms, increasing National's debt ceiling under the loan line from $1,250,000 to $1,550,000, and increasing TWO's from $290,000 to $490,000. National and TWO used the extra funds provided under the loan lines to settle the food stamp accounts of their check casher subsidiaries. Under the system of guarantees, Trent, Skowron, and their affiliated companies, including USN and UMO, were obligated to repay the increased loan line debts of National and TWO.

D. Investigation, Collapse, and Setoff

A few months before MHT increased its loan lines to National and TWO in order to enable them to settle their food stamp accounts with the City Department, the first warning note of the financial instability of the Trent/Skowron empire was sounded. An informal examination of UMO's financial condition conducted by the California Banking Department expressed the opinion that UMO was insolvent as of March 31, 1976. At that time, UMO's books indicated that the company's net worth was $2,474,000. The California bank examiner who reviewed UMO's finances concluded, however, that some $3,035,000 in assets claimed by UMO on its books should not have been in its capital accounts because they were held not in UMO's name, but in the names of various other companies and persons associated with the Trent/Skowron network. Once these assets were removed from the books, UMO had a negative net worth of roughly $561,000. In addition, the examiner opined that UMO's book value should be further reduced by eliminating from its capital accounts approximately $1.9 million in loans receivable that the examiner considered uncollectable, and by eliminating certain intangible assets valued on the books at about $878,000. Taking into account all the adjustments recommended in his report, the California examiner concluded that UMO had a negative net worth of some $3,645,000. He expressed the opinion that UMO was operating in violation of several California banking laws, particularly those specifying minimum levels of capital and liquidity, and that the company had frequently engaged in "illegitimate float transactions, check swaps, and transactions that appear to be (check) kites." UMO officials were permitted to review the report, and they sharply, but unsuccessfully, disputed many of the adjustments made by the examiner.

A few months after the California authorities conducted their review of UMO, the Trent/Skowron empire began to show outward signs of collapse. The financial problems of National and TWO became particularly acute. Since some time in 1975, National and TWO had not actually repaid the loans extended to them under the loan line, but had simply rolled the loans over every three days as they became due, repaying the old loan with the proceeds of the new one. Between September 1976, when the check casher subsidiaries of National and TWO borrowed the additional $500,000 under the loan lines in order to eliminate their food stamp arrears, and December 1976, National and TWO began to overdraw their accounts at MHT with alarming frequency. At a meeting with MHT personnel held on December 21, 1976, an official of these firms apparently acknowledged that they were in financial difficulty and unveiled a rather desperate plan to raise capital by selling their check casher subsidiaries to the individuals who managed the various check cashing outlets. This plan was never effectuated. On December 27, 1976, National and TWO fell into default on their borrowings from MHT under the December 24, 1976 loan lines, which amounted to $1,550,000 and $390,000, respectively. Despite these defaults, MHT loaned a total of $1 million directly to the firms' check casher subsidiaries on December 31, 1976. In connection with the December 31 loan, USN executed on that day a guarantee of the debts of National and TWO and their subsidiaries.

By December 1976, UMO also had begun to experience financial difficulties. On December 6, for reasons that were not explained at trial, MHT discontinued the extension of credit under the loan lines to UMO check casher sales agents, except for those owned by Propper Demonstration Sales Corp. ("Propper"), a company that operated a number of check cashing outlets and sold

UMO money orders in Massachusetts, Ohio, and New Jersey, but was not otherwise affiliated with Trent/Skowron. Propper received $300,000 under the loan lines at some time after December 6, 1976.

Early in January 1977, the Trent/Skowron empire collapsed completely. Upon learning of the severe financial problems facing the Trent/Skowron firms, several banks with which USN and UMO maintained accounts discontinued their former practice of permitting the issuers to draw against checks deposited to their accounts on the day after deposit, requiring instead that they wait until collection before drawing. With the loss of this "next day availability" of check deposits, USN and UMO lost at least one day's worth of the "float" of funds on which their viability depended, at a total cost that Trent, testifying at trial, put at about $2 million. Almost immediately, USN and UMO became unable to redeem their money orders as they were presented for collection.

On January 10, 1977, the New York State Banking Department ordered USN to discontinue the sale of money orders. On January 12, 1977, UMO petitioned for an arrangement under Chapter XI of the Bankruptcy Act, announcing that it was unable to redeem outstanding money orders having a total face value exceeding $5.3 million. UMO was eventually adjudicated a bankrupt on December 1, 1978. On January 20, 1977, USN filed a petition in bankruptcy, announcing that it was unable to redeem outstanding money orders with a face value of about $5 million. USN was adjudicated a bankrupt the next day.

MHT quickly moved to protect itself from losses on its outstanding loans to the financially troubled check cashers National, TWO, and Propper. Because Trent and Skowron did not honor their obligations, under the guarantees executed by them, to repay these check cashers' debts, MHT looked to the assets of USN and UMO that had been pledged in guarantee of the debts of Trent and Skowron. On January 11, 1977, evidently acting pursuant to the lien provisions of the guarantees executed by USN and UMO, MHT seized the funds remaining in the checking accounts of USN and UMO, about $295,000 and $80,000, respectively, and applied the funds as partial repayment of the loans, totaling $1,550,000 and overdue since December 27, 1976, that it had extended to National's check casher subsidiaries under the loan lines on December 24, 1976. Subsequently, acting in accordance with a stipulation entered into with the bankruptcy trustees, under which the trustees reserved their rights to challenge the transaction, MHT sold for a total of approximately $1,387,000 the various securities pledged by UMO as collateral under its September 21, 1976, guarantee of the debts of Trent and Skowron. MHT applied roughly $78,000 of the sale proceeds as an additional partial repayment of the National loans of December 24, 1976. It also applied roughly $318,000 as partial repayment of the December 24, 1976 loans to the TWO affiliates, whose indebtedness had totaled. $390,000 and had been overdue since December 27, 1976. An additional $531,000 was applied to debts of Propper; these included a balance of $300,000 that had been overdue under the loan lines since sometime after December 6, 1976, a $172,000 overdraft, and interest. On November 27, 1978, MHT delivered to plaintiff Lumbard, UMO's trustee, the balance of the sale proceeds, approximately $459,000.

From these setoffs arose the present litigation.

II. THE PROCEEDINGS BELOW

On January 12, 1979, plaintiffs Rubin and Lumbard, acting in their capacities as bankruptcy trustees of USN and UMO, commenced the present action against Trent, Skowron, and MHT, seeking to recover for the benefit of the bankrupts' creditors-comprised principally of holders of unredeemed money orders-the value of the various assets of USN and UMO that had been applied to the debts of National, TWO, and Propper pursuant to the system of guarantees. In their amended complaint, the trustees asserted ten causes of action of which only two, counts 2 and 10, are at issue in this appeal.

In count 2, plaintiff Lumbard, UMO's trustee, asserted that the guarantees of the debts of Trent and Skowron executed by UMO on November 28, 1972, July 30, 1975, and September 21, 1976, and the granting of liens and pledges of collateral made by UMO in connection with those guarantees, were fraudulent conveyances within the meaning of §67(d)(2)(a), (b) of the Bankruptcy Act, 11 U.S.C. §107(d)(2)(a), (b), and were therefore void against the bankruptcy trustee under §67(d)(6) of the Act, 11 U.S.C. §107(d)(6). Under this theory UMO's trustee sought to recover from MHT approximately $1,008,000; this amount apparently represented the $1,387,000 received by MHT from the sale of securities pledged by UMO under the September 1976 guarantee, plus the $80,000 seized by MHT from UMO's checking account pursuant to the lien contained in its November 1972 guarantee, less the $459,000 in excess proceeds from the sale of UMO's collateral that MHT had returned to the trustee in November 1978.

In count 10, the so-called food stamp count, both trustees asserted, on behalf of their respective bankrupts, that the various guarantees executed by USN and UMO from November 28, 1972 through December 31, 1976, and the various liens and pledges associated with those guarantees, were void as fraudulent conveyances under the Bankruptcy Act insofar as they pertained to the loan line debts of National and TWO incurred on and after September 16, 1976, as a means of settling their food stamp accounts with the City Department. Although the food stamp-related debts of National and TWO apparently never exceeded $500,000, the trustees sought to recover under count 10 approximately $1,489,000. This amount apparently represented the $1,387,000 received from the sale of UMO's securities and the $80,000 seized from its checking account, plus the $295,000 seized from USN's checking account pursuant to the liens created by USN's guarantee of the debts of Trent and Skowron executed in November 1972 and its guarantee of the debts of National and TWO executed on December 31, 1976, plus $186,000 received from the sale of other securities held in the issuers' names that were in MHT's custody and were seized pursuant to the lien provisions of the various guarantees, less the $459,000 that MHT returned to plaintiff Lumbard in November 1978.

After a bench trial, the district court ruled for MHT. Noting that §67(d) of the Bankruptcy Act required the trustees to prove, with respect to each of the fraudulent conveyance counts, both a lack of fair consideration to the bankrupts in the challenged transactions and insolvency or insufficiency of capital of the bankrupts at the time of the transactions, the court held that the trustees had failed to prove lack of fair consideration with respect to each count. In analyzing the fair consideration issues, the district court emphasized the fact that despite apparent barriers of corporate form, the Trent/Skowron enterprises were really "one ball of wax." On count 2, the court held that the November 1972 and September 1976 guarantees, pursuant to which MHT had applied UMO assets to offset the debts of USN's sales agents National and TWO and of UMO's sales agent Propper, were supported by fair consideration because MHT had occasionally loaned money directly to UMO and its sales agent Propper on the strength of those guarantees, and because UMO had received "indirect benefits" from loans to National and TWO by virtue of its "affiliation and identity of interest with" those firms. Similarly, on count 10, the court reasoned that the increased obligations assumed by USN and UMO under the guarantees in connection with the September 1976 expansion of the loan lines for National and TWO were supported by fair consideration because the entire Trent/Skowron enterprise benefited from the settling of the delinquent food stamp accounts made possible by the increased loans.

Alternatively, at least with respect to UMO, the court held that the trustee had failed to carry his burden of showing insolvency or insufficiency of capital. Although the court noted the opinion of the California State Banking Department that UMO was insolvent as of March 31, 1976, it discounted this conclusion because the California examiner had considered UMO separately from its affiliated companies. The court credited testimony of Trent and Sparago that UMO was solvent until at least the last week of 1976, and it observed that UMO's books showed a positive net worth until sometime in 1977. Finally the court noted that although an audit of UMO as of January 31, 1977 had initially shown a $6.1 million deficit, the auditors had ultimately disclaimed any opinion concerning the company's solvency. Viewing the evidence of insolvency as unpersuasive, the court found that the evidence tended to show that UMO was solvent until at least the last week of December 1976, and that therefore insolvency at the pertinent time had not been proven.

Accordingly, the district court dismissed the claims asserted against MHT in counts 2 and 10 and ordered the immediate entry of judgment in MHT's favor, pursuant to Fed.R.Civ.P. 54(b).

On appeal, the trustees renew their contentions that the obligations to repay the debts of National, TWO, and Propper assumed by USN and UMO under the system of guarantees were not supported by fair consideration, that these obligations were incurred at a time when USN and UMO were insolvent, and that MHT must therefore return to the trustees, pursuant to §67(d) of the Bankruptcy Act, the value of the collateral given by the bankrupts that was applied to the debts of National, TWO, and Propper. For the reasons below we conclude that the district court's rulings as to fair consideration and insolvency were based on erroneous legal principles, and that the judgment must be vacated and the matter remanded for further proceedings.

III. DISCUSSION

When an overburdened debtor perceives that he will soon become insolvent, he will often engage in a flurry of transactions in which he transfers his remaining property, either outright or as security, in exchange for consideration that is significantly less valuable than what he has transferred. Although such uneconomical transactions are sometimes merely final acts of recklessness, the calculating debtor may employ them as a means of preferring certain creditors or of placing his assets in friendly hands where he can reach them but his creditors cannot. Whatever the motivation, the fraudulent conveyance provisions of §67(d) of the Bankruptcy Act, 11 U.S.C. §107(d), recognize that such transactions may operate as a constructive fraud upon the debtor's innocent creditors, for they deplete the debtor's estate of valuable assets without bringing in property of similar value from which creditors' claims might be satisfied. In addition, §67(d) recognizes that the incurring of an obligation chargeable against the debtor's property, as distinguished from the actual grant of an interest in that property, may unfairly deplete the debtor's estate if the debtor does not receive in exchange a consideration roughly equal in value to the obligation incurred. Thus, §67(d)(2) provides in relevant part as follows:

> Every transfer made and every obligation incurred by a debtor within one year prior to the filing of a petition initiating a proceeding under this title by or against him is fraudulent (a) as to creditors existing at the time of such transfer or obligation, if made or incurred without fair consideration by a debtor who is or will be thereby rendered insolvent, without regard to his actual intent; or (b) as to then existing creditors and as to other persons who become creditors during the continuance of a business or transaction, if made or incurred without fair consideration by a debtor who is engaged or is about to engage in such business or transaction, for which the property remaining in his hands is an unreasonably small capital, without regard to his actual intent ....

Section 67(d)(6) of the Act, 11 U.S.C. §107(d)(6), empowers the bankruptcy trustee to set aside transfers made or obligations incurred on uneconomical terms, and to recover for the benefit of creditors the value of the property removed from the debtor's estate through such transactions.

In the present case, in order to prove their claims that UMO's and USN's guarantees of the obligations of National, TWO, and Propper were constructively fraudulent, and therefore voidable under criteria set forth in §67(d)(2)(a) and (b), the trustees were required to show: (1) that USN and UMO made transfers or incurred obligations to MHT within one year of the January 1977 filings of their bankruptcy petitions, (2) that these transactions were entered into without "fair" consideration to USN and UMO, and (3) that the bankrupts were, or were rendered, insolvent or insufficiently capitalized as a result. We discuss these issues in turn.

A. The Timing of the Transactions
* * *

With respect to both counts 2 and 10, the trustees contend that USN and UMO incurred obligations as guarantors of the debts of National, TWO, and Propper whenever those firms drew on the loan lines, and that because National, TWO, and Propper drew on the loan lines in September and December 1976, within one year of the January 1977 filings of their bankruptcy petitions, the statutory timing requirement was met. MHT responds that USN and UMO made transfers and incurred obligations only in 1972 and 1975, when they executed their principal guarantees and created the various security interests under them, i. e., more than one year before the January 1977 filing dates. * * *
* * *

[W]e conclude that both USN and UMO "incurred" "obligation(s)" within the meaning of the Act on or about September 16, 1976, when National and TWO drew an additional $500,000 against their increased credit line to cover their food stamp arrearages, and in December 1976, when National, TWO, and Propper last drew on the loan lines. Whenever National, TWO, and Propper borrowed under the loan lines, they of course incurred an obligation of repayment under the terms of their financing agreements with MHT. At the same time, as principal guarantors of the loan line debts under the system of guarantees, Trent and Skowron became contingently liable to discharge the check cashers' obligations if those firms defaulted. Similarly, USN and UMO, as secondary guarantors, became contingently liable if both the principal debtors and the principal guarantors defaulted. Undoubtedly, therefore, USN and UMO "incurred" an "obligation" of repayment, although admittedly a contingent one, whenever National, TWO, and Propper borrowed under the loan line, as they did in September and December 1976.

That the obligations thus incurred by USN and UMO were contingent on others' defaults does not remove them from the scope of §67(d)(2). The statute does not distinguish between fixed and contingent obligations; rather, it applies to "every obligation incurred" within one year of filing, regardless of its nature. 11 U.S.C. §107(d)(2) (emphasis added). While these obligations existed only because of the system of guarantees, it does not follow that the execution of the guarantees, rather than the creation of contingent liabilities under them, constituted the incurring of the obligations for purposes of §67(d)(2). Even after the guarantees were executed, there could be no liability under them until MHT had actually loaned money to National, TWO, and Propper. Until the loans were made, there existed only a framework through which USN and UMO might incur obligations, but they had not done so yet.

Thus we conclude that USN and UMO "incurred" "obligation(s)" within the meaning of the Act when MHT loaned money to National, TWO, and Propper in December 1976. This event of course occurred within the one-year period dealt with by the statute.

B. "Fair" Consideration

Even if the debtor has transferred property or incurred an obligation within one year of filing a bankruptcy petition, the trustee cannot set aside the transaction under §67(d)(2), (a), (b) if the debtor received "fair" consideration for his property or obligation. "Fair" consideration under the Bankruptcy Act, which is defined in §67(d)(1)(e), means more than just the "good and valuable" consideration needed to support a simple contract:

> (C)onsideration given for the property or obligation of a debtor is "fair" (1) when, in good faith, in exchange and as a fair equivalent therefor, property is transferred or an antecedent debt is satisfied, or (2) when such property or obligation is received in good faith to secure a present advance or antecedent debt in an amount not disproportionately small as compared with the value of the property or obligation obtained.

11 U.S.C. §107(d)(1)(e). The reason for this requirement is obvious: if the debtor receives property or discharges or secures an antecedent debt that is substantially equivalent in value to the property given or obligation incurred by him in exchange, then the transaction has not significantly affected his estate and his creditors have no cause to complain. By the same token, however, if the benefit of the transaction to the debtor does not substantially offset its cost to him, then his creditors have suffered, and, in the language of §67(d), the transaction was not supported by "fair" consideration.

Three-sided transactions such as those at issue here present special difficulties under the §67(d)(1)(e) definition of fair consideration. On its face, the statute appears to sanction, as supported by "fair" consideration, a transaction in which the debtor transfers property or incurs an obligation as security for the debt of a third person, provided that the debt is "not disproportionately small" in comparison to that property or obligation. Nonetheless, if the debt secured by the transaction is not the debtor's own, then his giving of security will deplete his estate without bringing in a corresponding value from which his creditors can benefit, and his creditors will suffer just as they would if the debtor had simply made a gift of his property or obligation. Accordingly, courts have long recognized that "(t)ransfers made to benefit third parties are clearly not made for a 'fair' consideration," and, similarly, that "a conveyance by a corporation for the benefit of an affiliate (should not) be regarded as given for fair consideration as to the creditors of the conveying corporations." 4 Collier on Bankruptcy ¶67.33, at 514.1-14.2 (14th ed. 1978) (citing cases). See also In re Christian & Porter Aluminum Co., 584 F.2d 326, 337 (9th Cir. 1978); Bennett v. Rodman & English, Inc., 2 F.Supp. 355 (E.D.N.Y.), aff'd per curiam, 62 F.2d 1064 (2d Cir. 1932).

The cases recognize, however, that a debtor may sometimes receive "fair" consideration even though the consideration given for his property or obligation goes initially to a third person. As we have recently stated, although "transfers solely for the benefit of third parties do not furnish fair consideration" under §67(d)(1)(e), the transaction's benefit to the debtor "need not be direct; it may come indirectly through benefit to a third person." Klein v. Tabatchnick, 610 F.2d 1043, 1047 (2d Cir. 1979) (emphasis added). Accord, Williams v. Twin City Co., 251 F.2d 678, 681 (9th Cir. 1958); McNellis v. Raymond, 287 F.Supp. 232, 238-39 (N.D.N.Y.1968), aff'd in relevant part, 420 F.2d 51 (2d Cir. 1970). If the consideration given to the third person has ultimately landed in the debtor's hands, or if the giving of the consideration to the third person otherwise confers an economic benefit upon the debtor, then the debtor's net worth has been preserved, and §67(d) has been satisfied-provided, of course, that the value of the benefit received by the debtor approximates the value of the property or obligation he has given up. For example, fair consideration has been found for an individual debtor's repayment of loans made to a corporation, where the corporation had served merely as a conduit for transferring the loan proceeds to him. McNellis v. Raymond, supra. Cf. Mayo v. Pioneer Bank & Trust Co., 270 F.2d 823 (5th Cir. 1959), cert. denied, 362 U.S. 962, 80 S.Ct. 878, 4 L.Ed.2d 877 (1960) (fair consideration found for corporate debtor's repayment of loan to its sole stockholder where stockholder had contributed loan proceeds to corporation's capital). Similarly, fair consideration will often exist for a novation, where the debtor's discharge of a third person's debt also discharges his own debt to that third person, see Barr & Creelman Mill & Plumbing Supply Co. v. Zoller, 109 F.2d 924, 926 (2d Cir. 1940), and it may sometimes be found in multi-party transactions of greater intricacy, see, e. g., Klein v. Tabatchnick, supra (fair consideration might exist for corporation's grant of security interest in corporate property in exchange for secured party's pledge of personal property as collateral for bank loan to majority stockholder, who loaned proceeds to corporation). In each of these situations, the net effect of the transaction on the debtor's estate is demonstrably insignificant, for he has received, albeit indirectly, either an asset or the discharge of a debt worth approximately as much as the property he has given up or the obligation he has incurred. Thus, although these "indirect benefit" cases frequently speak as though an "identity of (economic) interest" between the debtor and the third person sufficed to establish fair consideration, see, e. g., McNellis v. Raymond, supra, 287 F.Supp. at 238; In re Winslow Plumbing, Heating & Contracting Co., 424 F.Supp. 910, 914-15 (D.Conn.1976), the decisions in fact turn on the statutory purpose of conserving the debtor's estate for the benefit of creditors.

With these principles in mind, we turn to the parties' contentions concerning the obligations assumed by USN and UMO to repay the debts of National, TWO, and Propper.

The trustees' position is very simple. Pointing out that USN and UMO incurred obligations under their guarantees as security for advances made not to themselves but to National, TWO, and Propper, they argue that the advances did not confer any benefit upon USN and UMO, and that the money order issuers' obligations to repay those advances were therefore unsupported by fair consideration. MHT, seizing on the indirect benefit cases, adopts a subtler position. With respect to count 2, which pertained only to UMO, MHT contends that its loans to National, TWO, and Propper provided fair consideration for UMO's guarantee of their debts because the loans enabled the check cashers to settle their accounts with USN and UMO more quickly, thus increasing both the pool of funds available to redeem UMO money orders and the "float" from which UMO's profits were derived. Similarly, with respect to count 10, which pertained to both issuers, MHT asserts that there was fair consideration to both USN and UMO for the food stamp-related increase in the loans to National and TWO because the increased loans replaced the food stamp "float" as a source of working capital for the check cashers, enabling them to stay in business and securing the stream of money order sales proceeds relied on by both issuers. Finding that there was an "identity of interest" between USN and UMO on the one hand and National and TWO on the other, the district court agreed with MHT. We conclude that the district court should reconsider the matter after additional factfinding on remand.

Initially, we note that the trustees take too narrow a view of the fair consideration requirement of §67(d). As was explained above, the fact that a third party initially receives the consideration given for the debtor's property or obligation does not automatically mean that fair consideration was lacking. Thus the simple fact that National, TWO, and Propper, rather than USN and UMO, received the loan line advances need not compel a ruling in favor of the trustees on this point. The relationships among the Trent/Skowron firms and Propper were such that the advances to National, TWO, and Propper very likely did facilitate transfers of funds from those firms to the bank account shared by USN and UMO, benefiting each of those firms to some degree. Accordingly, the district court did not err in rejecting the trustees' argument that the corporate separateness of the loan recipients from their guarantors necessarily precluded a finding of fair consideration.

On the other hand, the district court did err in accepting MHT's argument that the existence of any indirect benefit whatever to USN and UMO from the advances to National, TWO, and Propper meant that the issuers' obligations as guarantors were necessarily supported by fair consideration. In a transfer for security, §67(d)(1)(e) requires that the present advance or antecedent debt be "not disproportionately small as compared with the value of the property or obligation" given by the bankrupt to secure it. In a three- sided transaction such as that presented here, it is not enough merely to compare the absolute amount of the third person's debt with the amount of security given by the bankrupt. The trustee, who has the burden of proving that the transaction was "without fair consideration," see 4 Collier on Bankruptcy, supra, ¶67.43, at 620-21 (citing cases), could establish lack of fair consideration under §67(d) by proving that the value of what the bankrupt actually received was disproportionately small compared to the value of what it gave. Accordingly, the court must attempt to measure the economic benefit, if any, that accrued to each bankrupt as a result of the third person's indebtedness, and it must then determine whether that benefit was "disproportionately small" when compared to the size of the security that that bankrupt gave and the obligations that it incurred.

The district court did not undertake such an analysis. The court observed that both USN and UMO "had a vital interest in inducing MHT to make ... loans to (National, TWO, and Propper)," and it stated that the issuers' "receipt of indirect benefits because of (their) affiliation and identity of interest with the direct recipients of the loans was receipt of fair consideration"; but it did not attempt to quantify the indirect benefits to either issuer or to compare those benefits with the obligations assumed by the issuers under the guarantees. Without such an analysis, it was impossible for the court to determine whether the estate of either issuer had been conserved in accordance with the principles of §67(d), and it was therefore error for the court to conclude that those purposes had been satisfied.

[Nor should the court have concluded that the money order issuers necessarily received fair consideration by virtue of the benefit to them of the loans made directly to UMO and its check casher sales agents, and of the guarantees of the debts of USN and UMO given by other Trent/Skowron affiliates. The loans to UMO were fully collateralized, and we may assume that UMO's giving of collateral to secure them was supported by fair consideration; but this does not mean that there was fair consideration for UMO's guarantee of the debts of other companies. The loans made to UMO's sales agent Propper may have facilitated remittances from Propper to UMO, but would only constitute fair consideration to UMO if the amount of money passing to it as a result of the loan was "not disproportionately small" in comparison with its obligation of repayment. Finally, while the various cross-guarantees of USN and UMO may have induced MHT to loan money to the check cashers, the crucial issues are whether any of that money found its way to USN and UMO and, if it did, whether its amount was "not disproportionately small" as compared to the issuers' respective obligations.]

Since the court's alternative ground for dismissal was also flawed, see Part C infra, we vacate the judgment of the district court and remand the matter for review of the fair consideration issue under the proper legal standards.

Given the complexity of the transactions and relationships at issue here, we think it advisable to detail the inquiry to be pursued on remand. First, the court must attempt to determine the extent to which the December 1976 loans to

National and TWO increased remittances from those firms to USN, their principal in the money order business. Next, it must attempt to determine the extent to which UMO shared in the increased remittances to USN by virtue of the pooling of the issuers' funds. Similarly, it must attempt to determine the extent to which the December 1976 loans to Propper increased remittances from Propper to UMO, and the extent to which USN shared in any such increases by virtue of the pooling arrangement. The court must then compare its estimate of the value thus received by each issuer with the magnitude of the obligation charged against that issuer under its guarantee. If the value received by either issuer is found to be disproportionately small as compared with its obligation, then, to that extent, the trustee for that issuer will have proved lack of fair consideration, and the court must proceed to consider the insolvency issue, discussed below. However, if either trustee fails to establish that the value is disproportionately small, the court must rule for MHT against that trustee.

In making the determinations and comparisons called for above, the court need not strive for mathematical precision. Section 67(d) requires only "fair" consideration, not a penny-for-penny exchange. At the same time, however, the court must keep the equitable purposes of the statute firmly in mind, recognizing that any significant disparity between the value received and the obligation assumed by either issuer will have significantly harmed the innocent creditors of that firm. Given the financial weakness of National and TWO revealed by the present record, it may well be that the trustees will be able to show that those firms absorbed much of the money provided them under the loan lines, remitting little or nothing to their principal, USN. Or it may be that USN received the lion's share of any remittances, perhaps even an amount properly proportionate to its obligations as guarantor, but that UMO's benefit from the loans was "disproportionately small." Of course, we leave these factual questions to the district court.

C. Insolvency or Insufficiency of Capital

As the third principal element of their causes of action under § 67(d)(2)(a), (b), the trustees were required to show that USN and UMO were, or were rendered, insolvent or insufficiently capitalized when they incurred obligations under their guarantees in September or December 1976. Under §67(d)(1)(d), a person is insolvent "when the present fair salable value of his property is less than the amount required to pay his debts." The statute does not define insufficiency of capital, and the amount of capital deemed sufficient under § 67(d)(2)(b) for the carrying on of a particular business will of course depend on its nature and size. We take up these issues separately with respect to the two debtors.

1. Financial Status of UMO

The evidence concerning UMO's financial health was conflicting. Trustee Lumbard's principal proof of UMO's insolvency was the report of the California

Banking Department, which opined that as of March 31, 1976, UMO had a negative net worth of at least $561,000, and perhaps as much as $3.6 million. In addition, Lumbard adduced testimony of John Waters, an accountant and partner in Arthur Andersen & Co., who supervised an audit of UMO conducted shortly after it petitioned in bankruptcy; Waters testified that UMO had a capital deficit of approximately $6 million as of January 31, 1977, and that the results of his examination of UMO's finances were consistent with the conclusions drawn in the California report. On examination by the court, however, Waters stated that Arthur Andersen had ultimately disclaimed any opinion as to UMO's solvency "(b)ecause of significant uncertainties (concerning efforts "to reach the holders of money orders to firmly establish the liability," and concerning the outcome of the present and other litigation) that could not be resolved at that particular time." In addition, Sparago testified that UMO's books showed a net worth of some $2.4 million throughout 1976, and that the company's net worth was some $900,000 even if one of the most significant adjustments sought by the California authorities were made on its books. Similarly, Trent testified that UMO had "a positive net worth" until January 1977.

Reviewing this evidence, the court stated that the trustee, and the California report, had "artificially segregated (UMO) ... from the overall (Trent/Skowron) enterprise," and that the solvency or insolvency of the enterprise had not been shown. The court chose to credit the testimony of Trent and Sparago over the conclusions of the California report, and observed that UMO's "books * * * showed a positive net worth at all relevant times well into 1977." The court discounted the testimony of Waters as to UMO's negative net worth, on the grounds that Waters had ultimately disclaimed any opinion respecting UMO's solvency and that his initial conclusions concerning UMO's financial position as of January 31, 1977 were "unhelpful in ascertaining the solvency of UMO at the time (months, even years earlier) when the guarantees were made, or even as of December 1976," when the disputed loans were made. Accordingly, the district court concluded that UMO's trustee had failed to meet his burden of proving insolvency "at the time the guarantees were made." We are persuaded that this ruling was made in the context of incorrect legal standards, and that we must vacate the court's judgment and remand for further consideration in light of the principles set forth below.

First, we think the district court placed undue emphasis on the financial health of the Trent/Skowron enterprise as a whole as a determinant of UMO's solvency. Section 67(d)(2) condemns as fraudulent conveyances transactions entered into "by a debtor who is or will be thereby rendered insolvent ... (or) by a debtor who is engaged or is about to engage in (a) business or transaction, for which the property remaining in his hands is an unreasonably small capital." 11 U.S.C. §107(d)(2) (emphasis added). Thus the insolvency issue hinges on the financial position of the debtor, not on that of related entities. Admittedly, the solvency or insolvency of controlling stockholders and related corporations may often shed some light on the fiscal soundness of a corporate debtor, and the district court did not err in considering the finances of Trent, Skowron, USN, and other affiliates in its effort to gauge the status of UMO. Nonetheless, the trustees were not required to prove that all of the Trent/Skowron entities were insolvent or insufficiently capitalized, or that as a whole the enterprise was in that condition. That burden pertained only to the debtor, UMO.

Second, to the extent that the court focused on UMO alone, its emphasis on the testimony concerning book value suggests that the court lost sight of the statutory definition of insolvency, which is cast in terms of "the present fair salable value of (the debtor's) property." The market value of particular property may of course differ substantially from its book value, and the market value of certain of UMO's assets may have been greater or less than their book value. While it was the parties' responsibility to bring any such disparities to the court's attention and to establish market value if the need arose, we think that the court may have overlooked the possibility of such disparities in reviewing the welter of figures with which it was presented.

Finally, we think the court's uncertainty concerning the time when the relevant obligations were incurred may have impeded its examination of the questions of insolvency and insufficiency of capital. The district court stated that UMO's trustee had failed to prove that UMO was insolvent "at the time the guarantees were made." As discussed above, however, UMO's incurring of obligations as guarantor must also be tested as of December 1976, when the loans for which it was charged were made. Accordingly, the question for decision was whether UMO was, or was rendered, insolvent or insufficiently capitalized as of December 1976, not just as of September 1976, when it executed its third guarantee in connection with the food stamp loans, or as of any earlier time.

In view of the court's misapprehensions of the legal framework within which proof as to UMO's insolvency should have been evaluated, the dismissal of Trustee Lumbard's claims for failure of proof of insolvency or insufficiency of capitalization cannot stand. On remand the district court should reconsider the matter, taking additional evidence if necessary, under the proper standards.

2. Financial Status of USN

The question of USN's insolvency presents us with a rather different problem. As nearly as we can tell, trustee Rubin did not offer proof that USN was insolvent or insufficiently capitalized; certainly the district court did not purport to rule on the issue, and the matter has not been mentioned at any time in this appeal. Possibly Rubin sought to establish USN's insolvency simply by showing the proximity in time between, on the one hand, USN's assumption of obligations in connection with loans to National, TWO, and Propper in December 1976 and, on the other hand, its debarment from the money order business by the New York State Banking Department on January 10, 1977, and its adjudication as a bankrupt on January 21, 1977. If this was his intention, however, he apparently has not yet invited any court to consider the theory.

Accordingly, we must consider whether Rubin should be given an opportunity to pursue this issue on remand, or whether we should simply affirm the district court's dismissal of Rubin's claims on the ground of failure to prove this crucial element of his cause of action.

Ordinarily, of course, strong policies favoring finality in litigation and conservation of judicial resources lead an appellate court to disregard contentions that a party has not asserted at trial or has failed to raise on appeal. Were Rubin suing in his own right, we would not hesitate to levy this most appropriate sanction for inattention to vital detail. In the present case, however, Rubin appears not as an entirely self-interested private litigant, but as a trustee, representing the interests of the creditors of USN. Undoubtedly numerous, these creditors-primarily purchasers of USN money orders-possess relatively small individual claims, but are likely to have suffered with disproportionate severity during the long period that those claims have remained unsatisfied. We exercise our discretion in their favor and instruct the district court to consider the issue of USN's insolvency on remand, if trustee Rubin wishes to pursue it. Cf. Cohen v. West Haven Board of Police Commissioners, 638 F.2d 496, 500 n.6 (2d Cir. 1980). Otherwise, we instruct the court to enter judgment in favor of MHT with respect to Rubin's claims.

CONCLUSION

We vacate the judgment of the district court and remand the matter for further consideration of the issues of fair consideration and insolvency in accordance with this opinion. * * *

In re Young
United States District Court, D. Minn. 1993
152 B.R. 939

MacLaughlin, District Judge. This matter is before the Court on defendant Crystal Evangelical Free Church's appeal of the bankruptcy court's order granting summary judgment in favor of plaintiff Julia A. Christians, the trustee. The bankruptcy court's order will be affirmed.
* * *

The parties stipulated to the following facts. Bruce and Nancy Young (debtors) filed a Chapter 7 bankruptcy petition on February 3, 1992. Plaintiff Julia A. Christians is the trustee in their case. In the year immediately preceding the debtors' filing, debtors contributed a total of $13,450 to defendant Crystal Evangelical Free Church. Debtors were insolvent at the time the contributions were made. In addition to their financial contributions, debtors held a variety of volunteer positions in the church. At no time did the church require debtors to pay any membership or attendance fee, but the church does teach that people should make regular financial contributions.

The trustee brought an adversary proceeding seeking to recover the contributions as "fraudulent transfers" within the meaning of the Bankruptcy

Code. The trustee and the church both moved for summary judgment. The bankruptcy court granted the trustee's motion and denied the church's motion. The church appeals.

* * *

III. Fraudulent Transfers Under The Bankruptcy Code

* * *

For the Court to find that a fraudulent transfer occurred, the trustee must prove the following: 1. there was a transfer of an interest of the debtor in property; 2. the transfer was made within one year before the date of the filing of the petition; 3. the debtor was insolvent on the date the transfer was made; and 4. the debtor received less than a reasonable equivalent value in exchange for the transfer. The parties stipulated that the first three elements were satisfied; the only issue is whether the debtors received "reasonably equivalent value in exchange for" the contributions.

* * *

The Court finds that the bankruptcy court adopted the proper analytical framework and interpreted section 548 correctly. There are two issues: (1) did the debtors receive "reasonably equivalent value" for their contributions, and if so (2) were the contributions given "in exchange for" that "value."

1. Did Debtors Receive "Reasonably Equivalent Value"?

The Court concludes that debtors did not receive "reasonably equivalent value," within the meaning of the Bankruptcy Code, for their contributions. "Value" is defined by the Bankruptcy Code. "Value" must be either "property, or satisfaction or securing of a present or antecedent debt." 11 U.S.C. s 548(d)(2)(A). The parties agree that the key issue is whether debtors received some sort of property right. The Court finds that they did not. Debtors stipulated that they could have taken advantage of the services offered by the church regardless of whether they made any financial contributions, but that the church encouraged regular donations. In other words, debtors made the contributions out of a "sense of religious obligation." A debtor cannot receive reasonably equivalent value for payments that are made out of a sense of moral obligation rather than legal obligation. Moreover, emotional support received in exchange for a transfer, without more, cannot satisfy the requirement for reasonably equivalent value. "The object of section 548 is to prevent the debtor from depleting the resources available to creditors through gratuitous transfers of the debtor's property." Charitable contributions are clearly gratuitous transfers, despite the fact that debtors feel morally obligated to tithe. Strictly as a matter of statutory interpretation, there are no justifiable grounds to differentiate between religious donations and other gratuitous transfers, such as gifts to family members, which are clearly avoidable.

The Court concludes that the church's argument that the tax deduction debtors received for the contributions was "reasonably equivalent value" is also unpersuasive. The ability to deduct an amount of money from gross income cannot, in economic terms, be of "reasonably equivalent value" to that same amount in cash that has been removed from the estate. See Durrett v. Washington Nat. Ins. Co., 621 F.2d 201, 203 (5th Cir.1980) (establishing rule that any transfer for less than 70 percent of market value of the property is per se not reasonably equivalent value).

Finally, the bankruptcy court was correct to look to Supreme Court precedent in connection with the Internal Revenue Code for assistance. In Hernandez v. C.I.R., 490 U.S. 680, 109 S.Ct. 2136, 104 L.Ed.2d 766, reh'g denied, 492 U.S. 933, 110 S.Ct. 16, 106 L.Ed.2d 630 (1989), the Supreme Court addressed the issue of whether fixed-level donations to a religious organization can be deducted from taxable income when specific services are provided by the religious organization in return for the fixed donation. The Court found that a quid pro quo analysis was appropriate. The Court held that a charitable contribution is deductible only if it is without adequate consideration. Given this ruling, by definition if a charitable contribution is deductible, i.e. without adequate consideration, it cannot be in exchange for "reasonably equivalent value." See Rubin v. Manufacturers Hanover Trust Co., 661 F.2d 979, 991 (2d Cir.1981) (fair consideration for bankruptcy purposes is more than consideration needed to support a simple contract).

2. If Debtors Received "Reasonably Equivalent Value," Was It "In Exchange For" Contributions?

Even if the debtors received "reasonably equivalent value," the Court finds that the church did not provide that value "in exchange for" the debtors' contributions. The parties stipulated that the church's support and services are available to all, regardless whether contributions are made. This stipulation precludes a finding that the church provided its services "in exchange for" debtors' contributions. The church's argument that debtors received a tax deduction "in exchange for" the contributions is also unpersuasive. A charitable contribution is deductible only if there is no quid pro quo. The Court declines to hold that although a tax deduction is not a quid pro quo for a donation, a tax deduction is given "in exchange for" a donation.

3. Other Case Law

The Court agrees with the bankruptcy court's conclusion that the other cases addressing this issue have glossed-over the statutory requirements in order to reach the "right" result. In Wilson v. Upreach Ministries (In re Missionary Baptist Found. of Am.), 24 B.R. 973 (Bankr.N.D.Tex.1982), the bankruptcy court concluded that "reasonably equivalent value" did not require that a monetary equivalent be received in exchange. The bankruptcy court held that the "good-will" received in return for the contributions satisfied the "reasonably equivalent value" requirement and the contributions could not be recovered as fraudulent transfers. Upreach Ministries is inconsistent with this Court's precedent stating that the benefits received must be "fairly concrete." First Nat'l

Bank in Anoka v. Minnesota Utility Contracting, Inc. (In re Minnesota Utility Contracting, Inc.), 110 B.R. 414, 420 (D.Minn.1990). Moreover, the Upreach Ministries court did not discuss whether the contributions were given "in exchange for" the good-will it received. For these reasons, the Court declines to follow Upreach Ministries.

Turning to Ellenberg v. Chapel Hill Harvester Church, Inc. (In re Moses), 59 B.R. 815 (Bankr.N.D.Ga.1986), while the Court finds that this case's analysis suffers from many of the same flaws of Upreach Ministries, it is also distinguishable from the case at bar. In Ellenberg, the bankruptcy court premised its holding in part on the fact that the church required the contributions as a condition of one of the debtor's employment as a deacon and thus the contributions could be directly tied to the monetary compensation and benefits he received through his employment by the church. Id. In this case, the debtors have stipulated that they were not required to tithe. Accordingly, the Court concludes that debtors did not receive value in exchange for their contributions.

4. Summary

The church states that it is offended at the characterization of the transfers as "fraudulent." Unfortunately, that is the label the Bankruptcy Code places on transactions that harm the interests of creditors in general, and fraudulent intent is not required. Ellenberg, 59 B.R. at 819. While describing the donations as "avoidable transfers" rather than "fraudulent transfers" may be more appropriate because it lessens the inference of culpability, the purpose of section 548 is where attention should be focused. The avoiding powers of the Bankruptcy Code are designed to maximize the size of the estate in order to maximize the distribution to innocent creditors. Minnesota Utility, 110 B.R. at 417. The fact that debtors made gratuitous transfers to their church rather than to, for example, family members or some non-religious charity does not materially alter the analysis. In short, the Court concludes that, as a matter of statutory interpretation, debtors did not receive "reasonably equivalent value" from the church's services and, even if the church's services constituted "reasonably equivalent value," the services were not provided "in exchange for" the debtors' $13,450 in donations.

IV. Constitutional Issues

The church argues that if the Court finds that the debtors' donations were avoidable transfers under section 548, applying section 548 in this case would violate the Free Exercise and Establishment Clauses of the Constitution. * * * In short, the Court holds that an order for the church to turn over debtors' contributions, which were made while the debtors were insolvent, does not violate debtors' free exercise or free speech rights * * * [and] that an order for the church to turn over debtors' contributions does not violate the Establishment Clause.

Accordingly, based on the foregoing, and upon all the files, records and proceedings herein,

IT IS ORDERED that the order of the bankruptcy court is affirmed.
LET JUDGMENT BE ENTERED ACCORDINGLY.

Problems

1. Can a conveyance of property exempt from execution under state law be attacked as a fraudulent conveyance?

2. Can an insolvent debtor's use of nonexempt assets to acquire exempt property be attacked as a fraudulent conveyance? Assume, for example, that Debtor has suffered financial reverses. State law exempts a rural homestead of two hundred acres regardless of worth. Can Debtor sell all of his nonexempt personal property and use the proceeds to purchase and improve a homestead ranch?

3. Decide which of the following transactions might be fraudulent under the Uniform Fraudulent Transfer Act. In each case, assume that the debtor, D, is an individual and was insolvent or became so as a result:

    a. At the time his daughter started law school, D promised her a new car if she graduated first in her class. She graduates first in her class. D buys her a new car even though he is beset by financial difficulties and unable to pay all of his creditors.

    b. D sells his antique bottle collection to his sister Y for $20,000, about its fair market value. D then hides the $20,000 in foreign bank accounts under various aliases.

    c. S lends D $30,000 and obtains a first mortgage on Greenacre, property worth $100,000.

    d. D, heavily in debt to a number of people, uses his last $1,000 to pay debts he owes to his brother, B, and his good friend, F.

    e. With respect to the *Young* case:

        i.   "The doctrine is firmly declared to be that one must be just before generous. * * * A debtor may make a conveyance with the must upright intentions, and yet, if the transfer hinders, delays or defrauds his creditors, it may be set aside as fraudulent." *In re Martin*, 124 B.R. 69, 73 (Bankr. N.D. Ill. 1991); see generally 1 G. Glenn, FRAUDULENT CONVEYANCES AND PREFERENCES, pp.. 264-72 (rev. ed. 1940).

        ii. "The parties agreed that the key issue is whether the debtor received some sort of property right." Do you agree? What if the Youngs send their child to private school and paid $5,000 tuition within a year of their bankruptcy? Is the $5,000 tuition payment a fraudulent conveyance? Is it relevant whether the private school is operated by Crystal Evangelical Free Church?

iii. What result if the Youngs' contributions fulfilled a written pledge of money that they had earlier made to the Church?

iv. Were the district court and the bankruptcy court "correct to look to Supreme Court precedent in connection with the Internal Revenue Code for assistance"?

v. In the problems preceding the *Younq* case, insolvency was assumed. In the Younq case, the parties stipulated that the debtors were insolvent at the time of the transfer. How can a bankruptcy trustee's attorney prove insolvency?

4. Decide which of the following transactions might be fraudulent under the Uniform Fraudulent Transfer Act. In each case, assume that the debtor, Ace Corporation, was insolvent or became so as a result:

a. Ace Corporation gave its president, Dave, a lake-front home, as a gift, in appreciation of Dave's many years of faithful service.

b. Ace repaid Dave a legitimate loan he had made to the company years earlier.

c. Ace sold a patent and trademark license, that was transferable, to Another Co., Inc. The price was substantially less than market value.

d. First Bank foreclosed on a parcel of Ace's real estate that was collateral for a First Bank loan to Ace. The property was sold at a foreclosure sale -- which fully complied with local law -- for a price that, by some expert accounts, is only about 65% of market value. The mortgage was created and recorded many years earlier. Only the foreclosure occurred recently.

e. Ace made a free transfer of certain assets to Child Corp., its corporately separate subsidiary.

f. Ace became a surety for personal loans that Commerce Bank made to Dave, and Ace backed its commitment with liens on its property.

g. Another Corporation and its principals bought Ace. They purchased all of Ace's stock. The deal was complicated, ill-conceived and too costly. Commerce Bank funded the deal. The stockholders netted about one million dollars in cash which the new owners paid with the proceeds of a loan to them by Commerce Bank. This loan, like all of the other financing, was secured by all of Ace 's property.

h. Ace gave First Bank additional collateral for additional loans.

i. Ace gave First Bank additional collateral to secure preexisting, unsecured debt. (Alternatively or additionally, is this transaction a preference?)

j. Ace paid its lawyer, Sarah Johnson, a $100,000 retainer.

5. With respect to each transaction that is fraudulent, who is accountable for what?

6. Who in these problems is protected by the Uniform Fraudulent Transfer Act?

   a. On January 11, D borrows $1,000 from W. On February 22, X obtains a $2,000 judgment against D. On March 13, D tortiously injures Y. On April 4, D makes a fraudulent conveyance of property worth $4,000 to T. On May 5, Z, who does not know of the April 4 transfer, lends D $5,000. Which creditors can attack the April 4 conveyance?

   b. D makes a fraudulent conveyance to T. D's creditors never discover the conveyance. They all settle their claims against D for two cents on the dollar. Can D now compel T to reconvey?

7. What remedies are given creditors by the Uniform Fraudulent Transfer Act?

   a. Are its remedies in rem only, or is personal liability for damages possible?

   b. Are punitive damages ever possible? Although a fraudulent conveyance, in and of itself, does not give rise to punitive damages, the conduct involved may constitute a tort of some kind that can support punitive damages. *Locafrance United States Corp. v. Interstate Distribution Services, Inc.*, 6 Ohio St.3d 198, 451 N.E.2d 1222 (1983) (common-law remedies, including the law of fraud, may be applied when appropriate in fraudulent conveyance cases so that the grantor can be liable for punitive damages for conduct involving malicious and intentional conduct); *Dalton v. Meister*, 71 Wis. 504, 239 N.W.2d 9 (1976) (facts supported cause of action in tort for civil conspiracy to commit fraudulent conveyance which provides damage remedies that are independent of fraudulent conveyance law, including punitive damages for which grantor and grantee may be liable).

D. REACHING PROPERTY BEFORE JUDGMENT (PRE-JUDGMENT REMEDIES)

A creditor trying to collect a claim through the judicial process is not always going to be able to obtain a default judgment. Litigation (even collection litigation) is costly and time-consuming. While the collection lawsuit is pending, the debtor may dispose of his assets, or other creditors may seize the debtor's property to satisfy their claims. *In exceptional circumstances* the law allows a creditor, in one way or another, to impound property of the debtor for safekeeping or protection during the pendency of the creditor's action against the debtor.

1. Attachment

At early common law, attachment was a form of process to compel the defendant to appear and answer if he failed to appear in response to the summons or original writ. The writ commanded the sheriff to attach the property of the defendant to compel his appearance. If he appeared the property was returned to him; if he failed to appear, the property was forfeited. In the 17th century, the nature of attachment changed from a means of compelling the defendant's appearance to a prejudgment (provisional) collection remedy: attached property was no longer released upon the appearance of the defendant but remained attached until after judgment and collection of same. No longer is the main objective of attachment to coerce the defendant debtor to appear by seizure of his property; today the writ of attachment seizes the debtor's property in order to secure the debt or claim of the creditor in the event that a judgment is obtained.

Today attachment is purely statutory. The statutes vary considerably as to when attachment is available. [Federal courts follow the local rules relating to attachment. Fed.R.Civ.Proc. 64.]

In no state is attachment available to every creditor in every collection action. Rather, the use of attachment is generally limited in the following ways:

(1) The statutes providing for attachment commonly spell out specific kinds of actions that may be the basis for the issuance of an attachment. Attachment statutes in many states distinguish between claims *ex contractu* and claims *ex delicto,* sometimes establishing different requirements with respect to attachment for each type of claim, and sometimes providing for attachment only upon claims *ex contractu.*

(2) Attachment is usually possible only on a showing of special statutory grounds. In general the statutory grounds deal with one of three situations: (i) where the plaintiff is unable to obtain personal

service upon a defendant because the defendant is absent from the state, concealing himself, or a nonresident; (ii) where the nature of the plaintiff's underlying claim entitles it to special treatment such as a claim based on fraud or a claim for "the necessaries of life"; (iii) where the defendant has assigned, disposed of, or secreted, or is about to assign, dispose of, or secrete property with the intent to defraud creditors.

(3) A bond is commonly required. The usual condition of the bond is that the plaintiff shall pay all costs that may be awarded to the defendant and all damages that defendant may sustain by reason of the attachment, if the order of attachment is dissolved or if the plaintiff fails to obtain judgment against the defendant.

(4) For reasons of modern due process, an increasing number of states now require that the debtor be provided notice and an opportunity for a hearing before the debtor's property may be attached.

Attachment procedure varies considerably from state to state. In most states, a creditor seeking attachment must first file a complaint. The creditor then files an affidavit stating that a ground for attachment exists and also files a bond. A writ of attachment can then issue.

Originally, the clerk of the court in which the action had been or was being commenced was authorized to issue writs of attachment ex parte. Today, for reasons of modern due process, most states require the opportunity for some form of hearing before a judge. The writ of attachment is directed to the sheriff of a county in which property of the defendant is located. The order instructs the sheriff to levy on and safely keep all non-exempt property of the defendant within the sheriff's county, or so much thereof as is sufficient to satisfy the plaintiff's demand together with costs and expenses. It also directs the sheriff to make a written return to the clerk of the court in which the action is pending showing all property attached and the date of seizure.

Levy on property creates a lien thereon. In most states this lien of attachment dates from the time of the levy although in some states the date of the lien relates back to the date of the issuance of the writ.

A creditor with an attachment lien enjoys a number of advantages:

(1) *Security.* While a collection action is pending, a debtor may try to dispose of his assets. An attachment lien is effective against subsequent purchasers from the debtor. To illustrate, D is in default on its loan obligations to C. C files a lawsuit and obtains an attachment lien on D's collection of Franklin Mint coins by having the sheriff seize the coins pursuant to a writ of attachment. While C's lawsuit against D is pending, D sells the coins to B. C then obtains its

judgment against D. C will be able to sell the Franklin Mint coins to satisfy its judgment. C's attachment lien is effective against B, a subsequent purchaser from the debtor, D.

To obtain its attachment lien, C had to levy on, i.e., actually or constructively seize, the Franklin Mint coins. This seizure put third parties such as B on notice of possible creditor's claims.

(2) *Priority.* Often, a debtor lacks sufficient assets to pay all of his creditors. In such instances, state law does *not* provide for pro rata distributions. Rather, state law provides a series of priority rules. Most of the rules are "first-in-time" rules: the earlier the creditor obtains its lien, the greater its priority. For example, a creditor with an attachment lien takes priority over a creditor who subsequently obtains a judgment lien on the same property. To illustrate, D owes A $10,000 and B $20,000. D is in default on both debts, and D's only significant non-exempt asset is Greenacre. A sues D and obtains an attachment lien on Greenacre. Subsequently, B sues D, obtains a $20,000 judgment against D, and obtains a judgment lien on Greenacre. Then, A obtains a $10,000 judgment against D. If a sale of Greenacre only yields $17,000, A will receive $10,000 of the sale proceeds and B will receive the remaining $7,000.

The rule of first-in-time, first-in-right governs the priority between attachment liens on the same property. This priority is unaffected by the order in which the attaching creditors win judgments and acquire judgment liens against the debtor. Usually, the winner of the first-in-time race is determined either by the order in which attachments were levied or by the order in which the writs were issued. The authorities disagree. Yet, the attachment laws of many states explicitly direct that attachments shall be levied in the order in which the sheriff receives the writs.

Generally, an attachment lien reaches only the debtor's interest in the property and thus does not displace prior claims, rights, and interests. See, e.g., *Travelers Indemnity Co. v. West Georgia Nat'l Bank*, 387 F. Supp. 1090, 1095-96 (N.D.Ga.1974) (transfer of equipment to surety takes priority over later attachment by bank); *Fount-Wip, Inc. v. Golstein*, 29 Cal.App.3d 751, 757, 105 Cal. Rptr. 780, 784 (1972) (apparently unpublicized assignment of interest in estate had priority over attachment of the interest levied against assignor because "a creditor can levy effectively only on the debtor's present interest; if debtor has none because he has assigned that interest to another, there is nothing for the creditor to reach"). If, however, the prior interest is subject to a recording law which has not been satisfied when the attachment lien arises, the attachment will have priority if an attaching creditor is within the class of claimants which the recording law is designed to protect. See, e.g., *Abramson v. Boedeker*, 379 F.2d 741, 748-49 (5th Cir.1967), cert. denied, 389 U.S. 1006, 88 S.Ct. 563, 19 L.Ed.2d 602 (1967) (bank's rights under unrecorded assignment inferior to subsequent attaching or garnishing creditors).

An attachment lien that is perfected by judgment for plaintiff has priority over any conflicting claim, right, or interest (except a federal tax lien) created after the attachment lien arises, which usually is at the time of levy and before the plaintiff's judgment. See, e.g., *In re Gibbons*, 459 A.2d 938 (R.I.1983). The judgment makes the attachment lien final and relates the effectiveness of the lien back to the date of its inchoate origin. Suppose, for example: On February 2, C sues D for $2000, obtains a writ of attachment and causes the sheriff to levy on D's horse. On March 3, B, who is ignorant of C's attachment, buys the horse from D for $3000. On April 4, C obtains judgment against D. Who has priority? C's rights to the horse prevail over B's.

A federal tax lien has priority over an earlier attachment lien that is perfected by judgment for the attaching creditor after the tax lien attaches. The reason is that inchoate interests are ineffective against federal tax liens, and the lien of the attaching creditor is inchoate prior to judgment for her. Moreover, as against a federal tax lien, there can be no relation back of the perfected attachment lien to the time of its inchoate origin. Example: In October, 1946, M sued S on an unsecured note and attached land of the defendant. In December, 1946, the United States filed notices of federal tax liens. In April, 1947, M won judgment, which was recorded in the next month. The tax liens have priority. *United States v. Security Trust & Sav. Bank*, 340 U.S. 47, 71 S.Ct. 111, 95 L.Ed. 53 (1950). Federal tax liens are discussed later.

(3) *Jurisdiction.* The priority and security afforded by the lien are not the only advantages to a creditor of obtaining a writ of attachment. Attachment can also be used as a basis for jurisdiction. State courts can take jurisdiction over nonresidents who have property in the state if that property is brought within the court's jurisdiction by attachment and if substituted service (such as service by publication) is made. Such jurisdiction, called "quasi-in-rem" jurisdiction is generally less valuable to plaintiffs than personal jurisdiction: a judgment quasi-in-rem binds only the parties to the action and not the entire world, and it imposes no personal liability on the defendant, the award being limited to the property seized.

The importance of quasi-in-rem jurisdiction — and hence of attachment as a jurisdictional mechanism — has declined over the years.

Long-arm statutes have increased the availability of in personam jurisdiction. *Shaffer v. Heitner,* 433 U.S. 186, 97 S.Ct. 2569 (1977), has decreased the availability of quasi-in-rem jurisdiction.

Prior to *Shaffer,* presence of property in a state was itself sufficient basis for quasi-in-rem jurisdiction of the courts of that state. In *Shaffer,* however, the Court held that the "minimum contacts" standard of *International Shoe Co. v. Washington,* 326 U.S. 310, 66 S.Ct. 154 (1945), governs not only *in personam* jurisdiction but also *in rem* jurisdiction.

(4) *Leverage.* A more important advantage of attachment is the leverage that it gives the plaintiff. By directing the sheriff to levy on property essential to the defendant/debtor, the creditor greatly strengthens its bargaining position. Deprivation of property used daily or essential to a business may induce the debtor to pay even if the claim is of questionable validity.

Notwithstanding the advantages of attachment discussed above, plaintiff/creditors do not always and should not always obtain a writ of attachment. There are at least three distinct hazards in attachment:

(1) *Fees.* As indicated above, a bond is generally required of the creditor. And, the sheriff will usually require an indemnity bond before levying on property to protect him from liability should he attach the wrong property and incur liability for conversion. The sheriff is also entitled to reimbursement of expenses incurred in levying on the property and in preserving the attached property. Last, but not least, an attaching creditor must pay its attorney for the legal work involved in obtaining an attachment lien.

(2) *Liability for wrongful attachment.* Attachment of personal property deprives the debtor of the use of the property for the duration of the litigation. Attachment of real property makes it difficult if not impossible for the debtor to sell the property for the duration of the litigation. If the debt collection action ends in a judgment for the debtor, the debtor can recover any actual damages she has suffered as a result of the attachment. Additionally, if the creditor attached the debtor's property maliciously and without probable cause, the debtor can recover punitive damages.

Tort liability has even been imposed on a creditor who *prevails* in the debt collection action. If the creditor has directed the sheriff as to which property to seize, the creditor is liable to the debtor if excessive property is seized, and is liable to third parties if their property is wrongfully seized.

(3) *Bankruptcy of the debtor.* Attachment benefits a single creditor at the expense of the debtor and other creditors. A debtor

deprived by attachment of the use of important property may decide to file a bankruptcy petition. Moreover, attachment may motivate the debtor's other creditors to initiate involuntary bankruptcy proceedings. Under section 547 of the Bankruptcy Code, an attachment lien obtained within 90 days of the filing of the bankruptcy petition is invalid if the debtor was insolvent when the lien was obtained.

Failure to obtain a judgment will result in the attachment being dissolved. A debtor may also terminate the attachment and obtain the attached property by posting a "discharging" or "dissolution" bond. These bonds are conditioned that the defendant in the attachment suit will perform whatever judgment will be entered against him and that, in the event of his default thereof, the surety will pay the amount of the judgment. A second class of bond available in most jurisdictions are "forthcoming" or "delivery" bonds. These are conditioned that if judgment in the attachment suit is rendered against the defendant, the property shall be forthcoming to satisfy such judgment, otherwise the surety will be liable to the extent of the value of the property. Such bonds release the property only from the custody of the levying officer; they do not release the attached property from the lien of attachment.

2. Prejudgment Garnishment

Garnishment (in some states a/k/a *trustee process*) is a collection remedy directed not at the defendant but rather at some third person, the garnishee, who owes a debt to the principal debtor, has property of the principal debtor, or has property in which the principal debtor has an interest. Postjudgment garnishment is a form of execution process to collect a judgment. See pages 27-31 *supra*. Prejudgment garnishment is a warning or notice to the garnishee that the plaintiff/creditor claims the right to have such debt or property applied in satisfaction of his claim, and that the garnishee should hold such property until the creditor's suit has been tried and any judgment satisfied. For example, if C brought an action against D to collect a debt that was due and owing and C learned that G held property of D, C might garnish this property. Then, if C was successful in her action against D, C's judgment could be satisfied by the property of D held by G, and, if G no longer had such property, C could recover from G personally. The most common examples of garnishees are the employer of the principal debtor and the bank in which the principal debtor has a savings or checking account.

Prejudgment garnishment is frequently referred to as a form of attachment. The two remedies are similar in many respects. Indeed, in a number of states garnishment is not an independent remedy but rather is a proceeding ancillary to attachment. In other states, however, garnishment is an independent action available for grounds other than those required for the issuance of an attachment and subject to different provisions for bond.

3. Replevin

At early common law, a landlord could enforce its rights to rent by the self-help remedy of distraint, i.e., seizing the personal property of the tenant. If the tenant disputed the landlord's claim of unpaid rent, the landlord could, upon giving the sheriff security, obtain a writ of replevin directing the sheriff to recover possession of the seized personal property, pending litigation of the tenant's rent liability.

In this country, replevin has developed into a more general remedy. Today *replevin* (a/k/a/ *sequestration* or *claim and delivery*) is a proceeding to recover possession of any personal property. At the commencement of the action, the sheriff seizes, i.e., replevies the property, and turns it over to the plaintiff pending outcome of the litigation over possession. If the defendant wishes to regain possession of the goods replevied, he may give a delivery or forthcoming bond.

Replevin cannot be used by all creditors. Replevin can only be maintained by one who has title or the right to possession of the property sought to be recovered. Unpaid unsecured creditors do not have a right to possession of their debtors' property. Unpaid secured creditors do have a right to possession of the property encumbered by their liens.

To illustrate, assume that Pizza Inc. owes U $1,000 and S $2,000. U is an unsecured creditor. S has a security interest in Pizza Inc.'s oven. Pizza Inc. defaults on both debts. The remedy of replevin is not available to U; S can *possibly replevy* the pizza oven. Either U or S *possibly* can *attach* the pizza oven and/or other property of Pizza Inc.

4. Equitable Remedies

McKain v. Rigsby
Supreme Court of Indiana, 1968
250 Ind. 438, 237 N.E.2d 99

Lewis, Chief Justice. This is an appeal prosecuted by the appellant herein seeking reversal of an order entered by the Trial Court, which *** [enjoined]:

*** [T]he defendant, Marshall McKain, from operating the business formerly known as Rigsby's Salvage Yard and now known as Mac's Auto Parts in any manner other than in the usual and customary manner of operating an automobile salvage and used parts business and further

enjoining said defendant from conveying or encumbering any real estate
or interest in real estate owned by him. ***

The appellees were owners and operators of an automobile salvage yard and
used-parts business. The appellant bought this business from the appellees on a
contract by which the purchaser agreed to make installment payments on the
purchase price to the sellers until the entire purchase price was paid. The sellers
made a covenant not to compete against the buyer in a similar business for a
period of fifteen (15) years.

The sellers, after executing the contract, then entered into the automobile
body-repair business near the vicinity of their former enterprise. A dispute arose
between the buyer and sellers as to whether or not the sellers of the automobile
salvage yard were now engaged in a similar business, under the guise of an
automobile body-repairing shop, thereby breaching the covenant not to compete.

Believing the sellers had breached the contract, the buyer refused to make
his final payment when due. Also, there is evidence that he was financially
unable to make this payment. Treating the buyer's refusal to make his last
payment as a failure of performance, the sellers commenced their cause of action
in the Jackson Circuit Court against the buyer for breach of contract, and such
damages as they were entitled. It is important to note at this point that the
sellers-appellees brought a suit for damages as a result of the alleged breach by
the buyer-appellant.

The sellers of the automobile salvage yard did not cause any security interest
to be created in themselves in the salvage yard save for a vendor's
purchase-money lien which arises at law, and the buyer of the property executed
a mortgage on the property to a third party after he acquired it. Also, the buyer,
while operating the business, sold some of his other assets in order to make
improvements on the property and to expand the inventory of the business.
Some of the proceeds from the sale of these other assets were used to pay his
general creditors as well. These transactions, however, do not form the basis of
the sellers' complaints; but, instead, the buyer's manifest intentions to liquidate
the business, as well as his other assets, in order to thwart the sellers in the
collection of their judgment for damages are those which caused concern to the
sellers. The evidence as to the buyer's intent to defraud his creditors is
conflicting.

However, in order to be sure that there would be sufficient assets to pay the
judgment, the sellers, in their initial complaint for breach of contract included a
request for a restraining order and temporary injunction to keep the buyer from
making any sales of his assets thereby preventing him from conveying any assets
in defraud of his creditors. It is from the granting of this temporary injunction,
which was modified by the Court to enable the buyer to make sales in the
ordinary course of his business, that the appellant seeks relief.

Appellant assigns as error, in the granting of the temporary injunction, these
two (2) points:

1. That this case is not a proper situation in whic injunctive relief should be granted.

2. That there was insufficient evidence to support the relief granted.

Appellees rely upon Burns' Indiana Statutes, Anno., §3-2102, [1968 Repl.] to support the granting of the injunction:

"Where it appears by the complaint that the plaintiff is entitled to the relief demanded, and the relief, or any part thereof, consists in restraining the commission or continuance of some act, the commission or continuance of which, during the litigation, would produce great injury to the plaintiff; or, when, during the litigation, it appears that the defendant is doing, or threatens, or is about to do, or is procuring or suffering some act to be done, in violation of the plaintiff's rights, respecting the subject of the action, and tending to render the judgment ineffectual, or when such relief, or any part thereof, consists in restraining proceedings upon any final order or judgment, an injunction may be granted to restrain such act or proceedings, until the further order of the court, which may, afterwards, be modified upon motion. And when it appears in the complaint at the commencement of the action, or during the pendency thereof, by affidavit, that the defendant threatens, or is about to remove or dispose of his property, with intent to defraud his creditors, a temporary injunction may be granted, to restrain the removal or disposition of his property."

Appellees contend that the appellant was about to dispose of his property with the intent to defraud his creditors and that injunctive relief was available under the above-cited statute. Appellees support this contention with Morey et al. v. Ball (1883), 90 Ind. 450, which contains the following statement:

"It is next insisted that the court erred in granting and in refusing to dissolve the injunction, on the ground that a general creditor, before judgment, cannot enjoin his debtor from disposing of his property. This is the rule in the absence of a statute. High Injunctions, secs. 131, 326.

Our statute, however, provides, among other things, that 'where it appears in the complaint, at the commencement of the action, or during the pendency thereof, by affidavit that the defendant threatens, or is about to remove, or dispose of his property, with intent to defraud his creditors, a temporary injunction may be granted to restrain the removal or disposition of his property.' 2 R.S. 1876, p. 93, section 137.

Under this statute, a creditor before judgment may restrain his debtor from disposing of his property. In such case, it must appear that such debtor threatens or is about to dispose of his property with intent to defraud his creditors. ***"

The remedy of injunction is an extraordinary one which should be issued with great caution and only where the reason and necessity are clearly established. The granting of a temporary injunction rests in the sound discretion of the Trial Court and the decision will not be disturbed on appeal unless it is shown that the Trial Court's action was arbitrary or constituted clear abuse of discretion. ***

Also, it must be borne in mind that the equitable relief of injunction does not lie where there is an adequate remedy at law available to the seeker.   ***   However, the rule concerning the existence of other legal remedies is tempered by the following statements:

"It is not enough to defeat injunction that there is a remedy at law. It must be as plain, complete and adequate—or, in other words, as practical and efficient to the ends of justice and its prompt administration—as the remedy in equity. ***

"In determining the adequacy of legal remedies and the consequent superiority of equitable remedies, some force is given to the fact, if it exists, that the former are vexatiously inconvenient, or that a denial of the latter results in irritation, annoyance and embarrassment readily relieved by the application of such remedy. ***

These cases support the principle that a trial court has discretion as to whether or not to grant a temporary injunction even when there is a theoretical remedy at law and it is the duty of the Court to look at the remedy and measure its fullness and its adequacy as it applied in the case at bar. This general principle harmonizes with the other principles concerning the dispensation of equitable relief.

Appellant suggests that since there were other remedies at law available to the appellees, that this extraordinary remedy of injunction did not lie. He points to the alternative remedies of the appointment of a receiver, and a writ of attachment pursuant to Burns' Indiana Statutes, Anno., §3-2601 and §3-501 respectively, as well as a judgment for damages for breach of contract.

The remedy of appointing a receiver would not be one to prevent the issuance of this injunction for these two (2) reasons: First, it is not an alternative remedy at law.

The appointment of a receiver involves the exercise of an extraordinary equitable power which will not be exerted where there is a full and adequate remedy at law. ***

Secondly, the appointment of a receiver is not proper here because the appellee wanted to prevent the conveyance of any of appellant's assets, not just the property over which he had a lien.

"As to the second question, it is enough to say that the courts of this state do not have jurisdiction to appoint a receiver for the property of an individual owner, and seize possession of it, upon mere allegations that he is indebted for borrowed money, and that he is so conducting himself as to be in danger of insolvency, without any showing that the plaintiff has a lien of any kind upon such property, created by contract, attachment, levy or otherwise. No such right existed at common law, and the statutory provision which makes threatened insolvency of a corporation cause for the appointment of a receiver *** does not apply to individuals alleged to be indebted beyond their ability to pay."

Under the authority of the foregoing cases it is apparent that the remedy of temporary injunction is much more benign than the remedy of the appointment of a receiver. The Court would have been without authority to appoint a receiver for the whole of appellant's property and certainly appellant is not damaged by the temporary injunction as he well might have been by the appointment of a receiver.

Moving to the remedy of writ of attachment, we are constrained to agree with the Trial Judge in his decision against denying the injunction because of the existence of this remedy. Attachment requires an actual taking of possession of the goods in question by the party seeking the remedy. This would have disabled appellant from operating his business and prevented him from deriving income, thereby impairing his economic situation. Appellees only brought suit for damages, they didn't want the property in question returned, nor did they wish to impair appellant's financial status. Indeed, appellees wanted to enhance the appellant's ability to withstand the rendering of the judgment. In exercising his discretion, the Trial Judge wisely allowed the injunction to issue because the writ of attachment, under these facts, was not an *adequate* remedy at law.

Appellant next states that since appellees could recover damages as a result of the suit on the contract, an injunction was unnecessary. We only need to refer back to the statute under which the injunction was issued to reconcile this agreement. The injunction issues when the defendant has shown that he was about to dispose of his property to defraud his creditors. After such a conveyance, a judgment for damages would hardly be sufficient compensation. Therefore, the issuance of the injunction was a proper ancillary act to the suit for damages.

As his last argument against an injunction being the proper form of relief in this case, appellant states that since appellees sold the property to the appellant, they have an insufficient interest remaining to seek the protection of the remedy of injunction. The remedy of injunction lies to protect both civil and property rights. State ex rel. Harris et al. v. Superior Court of Marion County et al. (1964), 245 Ind. 339, 197 N.E.2d 634. Where the plaintiff is suing for damages for breach of contract, and the defendant has shown that he intends to make fraudulent conveyances to avoid the judgment, and there are no other adequate remedies at law, the remedy of injunction is proper to protect the plaintiff's judgment from being rendered ineffective. Burns', §3-2102 (supra) is intended to apply to this particular situation.

We now consider appellant's second major objection to the issuance of this injunction; that being, that there was insufficient evidence to support the allegations made by the appellees. The evidence is conflicting. The appellee, Robert Rigsby, testified that appellant told appellees he was going to liquidate the business. Appellant also told them that he couldn't raise the money due under the contract. While not denying that he was financially pressed, appellant maintains that he was not going to liquidate the business and that he was continuing to operate it in a normal manner. There was corroborating testimony to this as well.

In McGoldrick et al. v. Slevin et al. (1873), 43 Ind. 522, the creditors of an individual who was operating a business as a sole proprietorship became concerned that the debtor was going to liquidate the assets and flee with the proceeds. They brought an action for an injunction under a statute very similar to the one relied upon by the appellees. The Court refused to grant the injunction because the creditors couldn't sufficiently prove the debtor's intent to liquidate the assets. However, this Court made the following statement:

" *** But injunctions are granted to restrain the commission of acts threatened or anticipated, injurious to the plaintiff, pending the litigation, and not where the act complained of has been consummated either before or after the action is commenced, and before judgment. *** "

We conclude since the appellant had told the appellees that he was going to liquidate the business, and that since the appellees knew that the appellant was in financial difficulties and was unable to make his last installment payment when due under the contract, that the appellees were justified in seeking, and the Trial Court was justified in issuing, the temporary injunction in question.

This Court held in Indiana Annual Conf. Corp. et al. v. Lemon, etc. (1956), 235 Ind. 163, 131 N.E.2d 780, as follows:

"In our determination of whether or not the trial court committed any error in granting the temporary injunction in this case, the appellee (the plaintiff below) need only show a prima facie case for an injunction and that injury to him would be certain and irreparable if the application be denied and that injury to the defendant below if the temporary injunction be granted, may be adequately indemnified by bond. It is not necessary that a case should be made that would entitle the plaintiff to relief in all events. *** "

The order of the Trial Court granting a temporary injunction in this case is affirmed, and this cause is remanded with directions for further proceedings consistent with this opinion.

Arterburn, Hunter and Jackson, JJ., concur.

Mote, J., not participating.

Notes and Problems

1. Compare the remedies of injunction and attachment in terms of availability, how the remedies protect the creditor, and the effectiveness of the remedies in providing protection.

2. The *McKain* case discusses the appointment of a *receiver pendente lite*, which refers to a receiver appointed during the pendency of an action. Courts exercising equity jurisdiction have the inherent power to appoint such a receiver when "the property in dispute is in danger of loss, destruction, deterioration or other impairment of its value through the neglect, waste, misconduct or other acts or failure to act on the part of the defendant or others who are holding the property." 1 R. Clark, A TREATISE ON THE LAW AND PRACTICE OF RECEIVERS §178 (3d ed. 1959). Most states now have statutes that codify this power, and some of them widen the grounds for appointing a receiver pendente lite.

3. Because the purpose of a receivership is to preserve the substantive rights (legal or equitable) of the plaintiff in the property in dispute, the general rule is that creditors without liens are not entitled to the appointment of receivers. The courts repeatedly state that, generally, a receiver may only be appointed when the person who asks for the remedy has some legally recognized right in the property she wishes seized that amounts to more than a mere claim against the defendant. For the same reason, unsecured creditors generally cannot preliminarily enjoin their debtors from disposing of property, cannot obtain injunctions for other purposes, and cannot get other extraordinary relief in equity. *Mar-Pak Michigan, Inc. v. Pointer*, 225 Ga. 307, 168 S.E.2d 141 (1969); see also *Whisenhunt v. Park Lane Corp.*, 418 F. Supp. 1096 (N.D.Tex.1976) (no basis for injunction or receiver existed on the face of things because the plaintiff-movant was not a secured creditor); *DeAngelis v. Commonwealth Land Title Ins. Co.*, 467 Pa. 410, 358 A.2d 53 (1976) (judgment creditors not entitled to receiver to liquidate personal property of judgment debtor because creditors had not yet caused execution to issue and thus did not have a lien

on the property). Unsecured creditors are limited to relief at law such as attachment and the like.

4.   The converse of the rule is not entirely true. Having a lien is ordinarily a prerequisite to equitable relief, but is not sufficient reason in itself for giving such relief. Legal remedies for enforcing the lien must be inadequate; and there must be a real, demonstrable threat of serious injury to the creditor's interests because receivers and injunctions are extraordinary remedies which are appropriate only in cases of necessity and upon a clear showing that an emergency exists. So, in *Parr v. First State Bank*, 507 S.W.2d 579 (Tex.Civ.App.1974), the court overturned the appointment of a receiver to protect a bank's collateral because the record did "not support the trial court's implied finding that Bank's security was in danger of being lost, removed or materially injured **** " Id. at 583. Compare *Bookout v. Atlas Financial Corp.*, 395 F. Supp. 1338 (N.D.Ga.1974), where, in an action to enforce secured notes, the court appointed a receiver because the debtors were virtually insolvent and there was "a sufficient inference of fraud [by the debtors] to indicate *** that if affirmative protective measures are not implemented immediately, the collateral in question [$12 million worth of notes secured by real estate] may be further transferred or dissipated to the irreparable detriment of plaintiff **** " Id. at 1342. The receiver's duties were these:

(a) The receiver shall institute such legal actions, as shall be necessary, to collect, hold and preserve the collateral and proceeds therefrom;

(b) the receiver shall provide for and direct the continued collections upon the collateral, to convert the proceeds into cash and invest same in interest bearing accounts or certificates of deposit issued by a National Bank;

(c) the receiver shall expend such funds as may be reasonably necessary to effect the collections upon the collateral, including paying reasonable salaries, fees and/or commissions to individuals and entities for the maintenance, preservation and collection of the collateral and the proceeds therefrom;

(d) in order to effectuate maintenance, preservation and collection of the collateral, the receiver is hereby authorized to fully utilize the services of defendants, including their employees, agents or other officers and is authorized to expend reasonable sums in compensation for such services, or alternatively, upon approval of the court, the receiver is authorized to expend such reasonable sums as may be required to employ a competent collection agency or other entity for the purpose of servicing and maintaining the collateral;

(e) the receiver shall hold and conserve the collateral, the attending documents and the proceeds from the collateral, with the exception of the foregoing authorized expenditures, for the parties as their interests may be ultimately determined by the court;

(f) the receiver shall file a timely and periodic report showing the nature of the collateral, its value and the disposition of the proceeds therefrom.

Id. at 1343-44.

Similarly, in the case *B & W Cattle Co. v. First Nat'l Bank*, 692 S.W.2d 946 (Tex.App.1985), a bank sued to enforce a promissory note secured by cattle. Upon filing suit, the bank had caused the cattle to be attached. The debtor moved to vacate the attachment, and in response to this motion the bank asked for a receiver. A receiver was appointed because: (1) the value of the livestock was less than the claims of the bank and other people who had intervened in the action; (2) the debtor could not identify the locations of the livestock securing the bank's notes; (3) some of the livestock had been removed by third parties without the bank's consent; and (4) the livestock could be lost or materially injured absent appointment of a receiver. Id. at 949-50.

Is there an adequate legal remedy in a case such as *Bookout* or *B & W Cattle*? Even when there is (in theory, if not in practice) an adequate legal remedy, a court may be empowered by statute to order a receiver. Some state statutes broaden the right to a receiver and make the remedy available in situations where a court exercising its inherent equitable power is unable to grant the remedy.

5. Notwithstanding *Bookout* and *B & W Cattle*, Article 9 secured parties, having security interests in personal property, seldom seek, and rarely are entitled to, the appointment of a receiver to guard their collateral because they have other adequate legal remedies: self-help repossession or replevin. Using these remedies Article 9 secured parties can quickly dispossess the debtor of the collateral and thereby prevent harm to the property.

In contrast, real estate mortgagees and the like cannot so quickly oust the debtor from possession. Real estate foreclosure proceedings often take considerable time. So receivers are commonly appointed to take over and manage mortgaged realty pending foreclosure or to effect the foreclosure and, even more often, for the specific purpose of collecting rents and profits of real estate to which an encumbrancer is entitled. See, e.g., *Hartford Federal Savings And Loan Ass'n v. Tucker*, 196 Conn. 172, 491 A.2d 1084 (1985) (rent receiver appointed in connection with actions to foreclose mortgages); *First Federal Savings And Loan Ass'n v. Nat'l Boulevard Bank*, 104 Ill.App.3d 1061, 60 Ill.Dec. 798, 433 N.E.2d 1036 (1982) (receiver appointed to secure and manage real property pending foreclosure action); but see *Citicorp Savings v. Occhipinti*, 136 Ill.App.3d 835, 91 Ill.Dec. 360, 483 N.E.2d 706

(1985) (mortgagee suing to foreclose was not entitled to appointment of receiver because the proof of waste was inadequate and less drastic remedy was available); cf. *Brown v. Muetzel*, 358 N.W.2d 725 (Minn.App.1984) (vendor of farm suing to rescind sale contract was not entitled to receiver because the evidence failed to establish that the purchasers were insolvent and that the value of the property was inadequate to protect the debt).

6. Receivers are quite commonly appointed to assist judgment creditors in enforcing their judgments when execution and other ordinary collection remedies have been pursued fruitlessly. The appointment of receivers for this purpose is usually in connection with a creditor's bill or a statutory supplemental proceeding, and in both types of actions the courts have somewhat greater power to issue injunctions aimed at collecting, and preventing the loss of, the debtor's property.

7. Receivers are appointed upon the application of unsecured creditors without judgments in a few, very limited instances. The best known example is a receivership to distribute the assets of a dissolved corporation. Very often, however, such a distribution is part of an insolvency proceeding that occurs under federal bankruptcy law rather than through a receivership pursuant to other law; and, with respect to some aspects of this process, such as the discharge of debts, bankruptcy law displaces and preempts other law so as to limit the attainable ends of local receiverships and other means of dissolution and liquidation outside of bankruptcy.

8. Compare the remedies of attachment, injunction and receivership in terms of availability, how the remedies protect the creditor, and the effectiveness of the remedies in providing protection.

5. Due Process Before Judgment

Connecticut v. Doehr
United States Supreme Court, 1991
___ U.S. ___, 111 S.St. 2105, 115 L.Ed.2d 1

Justice White delivered an opinion, Parts I, II, and III of which are the opinion of the Court. (The Chief Justice, Justice Blackmun, Justice Kennedy, and Justice Souter join Parts I, II, and III of this opinion, and Justice Scalia joins Parts I and III.)

This case requires us to determine whether a state statute that authorizes prejudgment attachment of real estate without prior notice or hearing, without a showing of extraordinary circumstances, and without a requirement that the person seeking the attachment post a bond, satisfies the Due Process Clause of the Fourteenth Amendment. We hold that, as applied to this case, it does not.

I

On March 15, 1988, Petitioner John F. DiGiovanni submitted an application to the Connecticut Superior Court for an attachment in the amount of $75,000 on respondent Brian K. Doehr's home in Meridan, Connecticut. DiGiovanni took this step in conjunction with a civil action for assault and battery that he was seeking to institute against Doehr in the same court. The suit did not involve Doehr's real estate nor did DiGiovanni have any pre-existing interest either in Doehr's home or any of his other property.

Connecticut law authorizes prejudgment attachment of real estate without affording prior notice or the opportunity for a prior hearing to the individual whose property is subject to the attachment. The State's prejudgment remedy statute provides, in relevant part:

"The court or a judge of the court may allow the prejudgment remedy to be issued by an attorney without hearing as provided in sections 52-278c and 52-278d upon verification by oath of the plaintiff or of some competent affiant, that there is probable cause to sustain the validity of the plaintiff's claims and (1) that the prejudgment remedy requested is for an attachment of real property...."

Conn.Gen.Stat. §52-278e (1991).

The statute does not require the plaintiff to post a bond to insure the payment of damages that the defendant may suffer should the attachment prove wrongfully issued or the claim prove unsuccessful.

As required, DiGiovanni submitted an affidavit in support of his application. In five one-sentence paragraphs, DiGiovanni stated that the facts set forth in his previously submitted complaint were true; that "I was willfully, wantonly and maliciously assaulted by the defendant, Brian K. Doehr"; that "[s]aid assault and battery broke my left wrist and further caused an ecchymosis to my right eye, as well as other injuries"; and that "I have further expended sums of money for medical care and treatment." The affidavit concluded with the statement, "In my opinion, the foregoing facts are sufficient to show that there is probable cause that judgment will be rendered for the plaintiff."

On the strength of these submissions the Superior Court judge, by an order dated March 17, found "probable cause to sustain the validity of the plaintiff's claim" and ordered the attachment on Doehr's home "to the value of $75,000." The sheriff attached the property four days later, on March 21. Only after this did Doehr receive notice of the attachment. He also had yet to be served with the complaint, which is ordinarily necessary for an action to commence in Connecticut. As the statute further required, the attachment notice informed Doehr that he had the right to a hearing: (1) to claim that no probable cause existed to sustain the claim; (2) to request that the attachment be vacated, modified, or that a bond be substituted; or (3) to claim that some portion of the property was exempt from execution. Conn.Gen.Stat. §52-278e(b) (1991).

Rather than pursue these options, Doehr filed suit against DiGiovanni in Federal District Court, claiming that §52-278e(a)(1) was unconstitutional under the Due Process Clause of the Fourteenth Amendment. The District Court upheld the statute and granted summary judgment in favor of DiGiovanni. Pinsky v. Duncan, 716 F.Supp. 58 (Conn.1989). On appeal, a divided panel of the United States Court of Appeals for the Second Circuit reversed. Pinsky v. Duncan, 898 F.2d 852 (1990). Judge Pratt, who wrote the opinion for the court, concluded that the Connecticut statute violated due process in permitting ex parte attachment absent a showing of extraordinary circumstances. "The rule to be derived from Sniadach v. Family Finance Corp. of Bay View, 395 U.S. 337, 89 S.Ct. 1820, 23 L.Ed.2d 349 (1969) and its progeny, therefore, is not that postattachment hearings are generally acceptable provided that the plaintiff files a factual affidavit and that a judicial officer supervises the process, but that a prior hearing may be postponed where exceptional circumstances justify such a delay, and where sufficient additional safeguards are present." Id., at 855. This conclusion was deemed to be consistent with our decision in Mitchell v. W.T. Grant Co., 416 U.S. 600, 94 S.Ct. 1895, 40 L.Ed.2d 406 (1974), because the absence of a preattachment hearing was approved in that case based on the presence of extraordinary circumstances.

A further reason to invalidate the statute, the court ruled, was the highly factual nature of the issues in this case. In *Mitchell*, there were "uncomplicated matters that len[t] themselves to documentary proof" and "[t]he nature of the issues at stake minimize[d] the risk that the writ [would] be wrongfully issued by a judge." Id., at 609-610, 94 S.Ct., at 1901. Similarly, in Mathews v. Eldridge, 424 U.S. 319, 343-344, 96 S.Ct. 893, 907, 47 L.Ed.2d 18 (1976), where an evidentiary hearing was not required prior to the termination of disability benefits, the determination of disability was "sharply focused and easily documented." Judge Pratt observed that in contrast the present case involved the fact-specific event of a fist fight and the issue of assault. He doubted that the judge could reliably determine probable cause when presented with only the plaintiff's version of the altercation. "Because the risk of a wrongful attachment is considerable under these circumstances, we conclude that dispensing with notice and opportunity for a hearing until after the attachment, without a showing of extraordinary circumstances, violates the requirements of due process." 898 F.2d, at 856. Judge Pratt went on to conclude that in his view, the statute was also constitutionally infirm for its failure to require the plaintiff to post a bond for the protection of the defendant in the event the attachment was ultimately found to have been improvident.

Judge Mahoney was also of the opinion that the statutory provision for attaching real property in civil actions, without a prior hearing and in the absence of extraordinary circumstances, was unconstitutional. He disagreed with Judge Pratt's opinion that a bond was constitutionally required. Judge Newman dissented from the holding that a hearing prior to attachment was constitutionally required and, like Judge Mahoney, disagreed with Judge Pratt on the necessity for a bond.

The dissent's conclusion accorded with the views of Connecticut Supreme Court, which had previously upheld §52-278e(b) in Fermont Division, Dynamics Corp. of America v. Smith, 178 Conn. 393, 423 A.2d 80 (1979). We granted certiorari to resolve the conflict of authority. 498 U.S. ----, 111 S.Ct. 42, 112 L.Ed.2d 18 (1990).

II

With this case we return to the question of what process must be afforded by a state statute enabling an individual to enlist the aid of the State to deprive another of his or her property by means of the prejudgment attachment or similar procedure. Our cases reflect the numerous variations this type of remedy can entail. In Sniadach v. Family Finance Corp. of Bay View, 395 U.S. 337, 89 S.Ct. 1820, 23 L.Ed.2d 349 (1969), the Court struck down a Wisconsin statute that permitted a creditor to effect prejudgment garnishment of wages without notice and prior hearing to the wage earner. In Fuentes v. Shevin, 407 U.S. 67, 92 S.Ct. 1983, 32 L.Ed.2d 556 (1972), the Court likewise found a Due Process violation in state replevin provisions that permitted vendors to have goods seized through an ex parte application to a court clerk and the posting of a bond. Conversely, the Court upheld a Louisiana ex parte procedure allowing a lienholder to have disputed goods sequestered in Mitchell v. W.T. Grant Co., 416 U.S. 600, 94 S.Ct. 1895, 40 L.Ed.2d 406 (1974). *Mitchell*, however, carefully noted that *Fuentes* was decided against "a factual and legal background sufficiently different ... that it does not require the invalidation of the Louisiana sequestration statute." Id., 416 U.S., at 615, 94 S.Ct., at 1904. Those differences included Louisiana's provision of an immediate postdeprivation hearing along with the option of damages; the requirement that a judge rather than a clerk determine that there is a clear showing of entitlement to the writ; the necessity for a detailed affidavit; and an emphasis on the lien-holder's interest in preventing waste or alienation of the encumbered property. Id., at 615-618, 94 S.Ct., at 1904-1905. In North Georgia Finishing, Inc. v. Di-Chem, Inc., 419 U.S. 601, 95 S.Ct. 719, 42 L.Ed.2d 751 (1975), the Court again invalidated an ex parte garnishment statute that not only failed to provide for notice and prior hearing but that also failed to require a bond, a detailed affidavit setting out the claim, the determination of a neutral magistrate, or a prompt postdeprivation hearing. Id., at 606-608, 95 S.Ct., at 722-723.

These cases "underscore the truism that '[d]ue process unlike some legal rules, is not a technical conception with a fixed content unrelated to time, place and circumstances.' " Mathews v. Eldridge, supra, 424 U.S., at 334, 96 S.Ct., at 902 (quoting Cafeteria Workers v. McElroy, 367 U.S. 886, 895, 81 S.Ct. 1743, 1748, 6 L.Ed.2d 1230 (1961)). In *Mathews*, we drew upon our prejudgment remedy decisions to determine what process is due when the government itself seeks to effect a deprivation on its own initiative. *Mathews*, 424 U.S., at 334, 96 S.Ct., at 902. That analysis resulted in the now familiar threefold inquiry requiring consideration of "the private interest that will be affected by the official action"; "the risk of an erroneous deprivation of such interest through the procedures used, and the probable value, if any, of additional or substitute safeguards"; and lastly "the Government's interest, including the function involved and the fiscal and administrative burdens that the additional or substitute procedural requirement would entail." Id., at 335, 96 S.Ct., at 903.

Here the inquiry is similar but the focus is different. Prejudgment remedy statutes ordinarily apply to disputes between private parties rather than between an individual and the government. Such enactments are designed to enable one of the parties to "make use of state procedures with the overt, significant assistance of state officials," and they undoubtedly involve state action "substantial enough to implicate the Due Process Clause." Tulsa Professional Collection Services, Inc. v. Pope, 485 U.S. 478, 486, 108 S.Ct. 1340, 1345, 99 L.Ed.2d 565 (1988). Nonetheless, any burden that increasing procedural safeguards entails primarily affects not the government, but the party seeking control of the other's property. See *Fuentes v. Shevin*, supra, 407 U.S., at 99-101, 92 S.Ct., at 2003-2005 (WHITE, J., dissenting). For this type of case, therefore, the relevant inquiry requires, as in *Mathews*, first, consideration of the private interest that will be affected by the prejudgment measure; second, an examination of the risk of erroneous deprivation through the procedures under attack and the probable value of additional or alternative safeguards; and third, in contrast to *Mathews*, principal attention to the interest of the party seeking the prejudgment remedy, with, nonetheless, due regard for any ancillary interest the government may have in providing the procedure or forgoing the added burden of providing greater protections.

We now consider the Mathews factors in determining the adequacy of the procedures before us, first with regard to the safeguards of notice and a prior hearing, and then in relation to the protection of a bond.

III

We agree with the Court of Appeals that the property interests that attachment affects are significant. For a property owner like Doehr, attachment ordinarily clouds title; impairs the ability to sell or otherwise alienate the property; taints any credit rating; reduces the chance of obtaining a home equity loan or additional mortgage; and can even place an existing mortgage in technical default where there is an insecurity clause. Nor does Connecticut deny that any of these consequences occurs.

Instead, the State correctly points out that these effects do not amount to a complete, physical, or permanent deprivation of real property; their impact is less than the perhaps temporary total deprivation of household goods or wages. See *Sniadach*, supra, 395 U.S., at 340, 89 S.Ct., at 1822; *Mitchell*, supra, 416 U.S., at 613, 94 S.Ct., at 1903. But the Court has never held that only such extreme deprivations trigger due process concern. See Buchanan v. Warley, 245 U.S. 60, 74, 38 S.Ct. 16, 18, 62 L.Ed. 149 (1917). To the contrary, our cases show that even the temporary or partial impairments to property rights that attachments, liens, and similar encumbrances entail are sufficient to merit due process protection. Without doubt, state procedures for creating and enforcing attachments, as with liens, "are subject to the strictures of due process." Peralta v. Heights Medical Center, Inc., 485 U.S. 80, 85, 108 S.Ct. 896, 899, 99 L.Ed.2d 75 (1988) (citing *Mitchell*, supra, 416 U.S., at 604, 94 S.Ct., at 1898; Hodge v. Muscatine County, 196 U.S. 276, 281, 25 S.Ct. 237, 239, 49 L.Ed. 477 (1905)).

We also agree with the Court of Appeals that the risk of erroneous deprivation that the State permits here is substantial. By definition, attachment statutes premise a deprivation of property on one ultimate factual contingency--the award of damages to the plaintiff which the defendant may not be able to satisfy. See Ownbey v. Morgan, 256 U.S. 94, 104-105, 41 S.Ct. 433, 435-436, 65 L.Ed. 837 (1921); R. Thompson & J. Sebert, Remedies: Damages, Equity and Restitution §5.01 (1983). For attachments before judgment, Connecticut mandates that this determination be made by means of a procedural inquiry that asks whether "there is probable cause to sustain the validity of the plaintiff's claim." Conn.Gen.Stat. §52-278e(a). The statute elsewhere defines the validity of the claim in terms of the likelihood "that judgment will be rendered in the matter in favor of the plaintiff." Conn.Gen.Stat. §52-278c(a)(2) (1991); Ledgebrook Condominium Assn. v. Lusk Corp., 172 Conn. 577, 584, 376 A.2d 60, 63-64 (1977). What probable cause means in this context, however, remains obscure. The State initially took the position, as did the dissent below, that the statute requires a plaintiff to show the objective likelihood of the suit's success. Brief for Petitioner 12; *Pinsky*, 898 F.2d, at 861-862 (Newman, J., dissenting). DiGiovanni, citing ambiguous state cases, reads the provision as requiring no more than that a plaintiff demonstrate a subjective good faith belief that the suit will succeed. Brief for Respondent 25-26. Ledgebrook Condominium Assn., supra, 172 Conn., at 584, 376 A.2d, at 63-64; Anderson v. Nedovich, 19 Conn.App. 85, 88, 561 A.2d 948, 949 (1989). At oral argument, the State shifted its position to argue that the statute requires something akin to the plaintiff stating a claim with sufficient facts to survive a motion to dismiss.

We need not resolve this confusion since the statute presents too great a risk of erroneous deprivation under any of these interpretations. If the statute demands inquiry into the sufficiency of the complaint, or, still less, the plaintiff's good-faith belief that the complaint is sufficient, requirement of a complaint and a factual affidavit would permit a court to make these minimal determinations. But neither inquiry adequately reduces the risk of erroneous deprivation. Permitting a court to authorize attachment merely because the plaintiff believes the defendant is liable, or because the plaintiff can make out a facially valid complaint, would permit the deprivation of the defendant's property when the claim would fail to convince a jury, when it rested on factual allegations that were sufficient to state a cause of action but which the defendant would dispute, or in the case of a mere good-faith standard, even when the complaint failed to state a claim upon which relief could be granted. The potential for unwarranted attachment in these situations is self-evident and too great to satisfy the requirements of due process absent any countervailing consideration.

Even if the provision requires the plaintiff to demonstrate, and the judge to find, probable cause to believe that judgment will be rendered in favor of the plaintiff, the risk of error was substantial in this case. As the record shows, and as the State concedes, only a skeletal affidavit need be and was filed. The State urges that the reviewing judge normally reviews the complaint as well, but concedes that the complaint may also be conclusory. It is self-evident that the judge could make no realistic assessment concerning the likelihood of an action's success based upon these one-sided, self-serving, and conclusory submissions. And as the Court of Appeals said, in a case like this involving an alleged assault, even a detailed affidavit would give only the plaintiff's version of the confrontation. Unlike determining the existence of a debt or delinquent payments, the issue does not concern "ordinarily uncomplicated matters that lend themselves to documentary proof." *Mitchell*, 416 U.S., at 609, 94 S.Ct., at 1901. The likelihood of error that results illustrates that "fairness can rarely be obtained by secret, one-sided determination of facts decisive of rights.... [And n]o better instrument has been devised for arriving at truth than to give a person in jeopardy of serious loss notice of the case against him and an opportunity to meet it." Joint Anti-Fascist Refugee Committee v. McGrath, 341 U.S. 123, 170-172, 71 S.Ct. 624, 647-649, 95 L.Ed. 817 (1951) (Frankfurter, J., concurring).

What safeguards the State does afford do not adequately reduce this risk. Connecticut points out that the statute also provides an "expeditiou[s]" postattachment adversary hearing, §52-278e(c); notice for such a hearing, §52-278e(b); judicial review of an adverse decision, §52-278l (a); and a double damages action if the original suit is commenced without probable cause, §52-568(a)(1). Similar considerations were present in *Mitchell* where we upheld Louisiana's sequestration statute despite the lack of predeprivation notice and hearing. But in *Mitchell*, the plaintiff had a vendor's lien to protect, the risk of error was minimal because the likelihood of recovery involved uncomplicated matters that lent themselves to documentary proof, *Mitchell*, supra, 416 U.S., at 609-610, 94 S.Ct., at 1901, and plaintiff was required to put up a bond. None of these factors diminishing the need for a predeprivation hearing is present in this case. It is true that a later hearing might negate the presence of probable cause, but this would not cure the temporary deprivation that an earlier hearing might have prevented. "The Fourteenth Amendment draws no bright lines around three-day, 10-day or 50- day deprivations of property. Any significant taking of property by the State is within the purview of the Due Process Clause." *Fuentes*, 407 U.S., at 86, 92 S.Ct., at 1997.

Finally, we conclude that the interests in favor of an ex parte attachment, particularly the interests of the plaintiff, are too minimal to supply such a consideration here. Plaintiff had no existing interest in Doehr's real estate when he sought the attachment. His only interest in attaching the property was to ensure the availability of assets to satisfy his judgment if he prevailed on the merits of his action. Yet there was no allegation that Doehr was about to transfer or encumber his real estate or take any other action during the pendency of the action that would render his real estate unavailable to satisfy a judgment. Our cases have recognized such a properly supported claim would be an exigent circumstance permitting postponing any notice or hearing until after the attachment is effected. See *Mitchell*, supra, 416 U.S., at 609, 94 S.Ct., at 1901; *Fuentes*, supra, 407 U.S., at 90-92, 92 S.Ct., at 1999-2000; *Sniadach*, 395 U.S., at 339, 89 S.Ct., at 1821. Absent such allegations, however, the plaintiff's interest in attaching the property does not justify the burdening of Doehr's ownership rights without a hearing to determine the likelihood of recovery.

No interest the government may have affects the analysis. The State's substantive interest in protecting any rights of the plaintiff cannot be any more weighty than those rights themselves. Here the plaintiff's interest is de minimis. Moreover, the State cannot seriously plead additional financial or administrative burdens involving predeprivation hearings when it already claims to provide an immediate post-deprivation hearing. Conn.Gen.Stat. §§ 52-278e(b) and (c) (1991); *Fermont*, 178 Conn., at 397- 398, 423 A.2d at 83.

Historical and contemporary practice support our analysis. Prejudgment attachment is a remedy unknown at common law. Instead, "it traces its origin to the Custom of London, under which a creditor might attach money or goods of the defendant either in the plaintiff's own hands or in the custody of a third person, by proceedings in the mayor's court or in the sheriff's court." *Ownbey*, 256 U.S., at 104, 41 S.Ct., at 435. Generally speaking, attachment measures in both England and this country had several limitations that reduced the risk of erroneous deprivation which Connecticut permits. Although attachments ordinarily did not require prior notice or a hearing, they were usually authorized only where the defendant had taken or threatened to take some action that would place the satisfaction of the plaintiff's potential award in jeopardy. See C. Drake, Law of Suits by Attachments, §§ 40-82 (1866) (hereinafter Drake); 1 R. Shinn, Attachment and Garnishment §86 (1896) (hereinafter Shinn). Attachments, moreover, were generally confined to claims by creditors. Drake §§ 9-10; Shinn §12. As we and the Court of Appeals have noted, disputes between debtors and creditors more readily lend themselves to accurate ex parte assessments of the merits. Tort actions, like the assault and battery claim at issue here, do not. See *Mitchell*, supra, 416 U.S., at 609-610, 94 S.Ct., at 1901. Finally, as we will discuss below, attachment statutes historically required that the plaintiff post a bond. Drake §§ 114-183; Shinn §153.

Connecticut's statute appears even more suspect in light of current practice. A survey of state attachment provisions reveals that nearly every State requires either a preattachment hearing, a showing of some exigent circumstance, or both, before permitting an attachment to take place. Twenty-seven States, as well as the District of Columbia, permit attachments only when some extraordinary circumstance is present. In such cases, preattachment hearings are not required but postattachment hearings are provided. Ten States permit attachment without the presence of such factors but require prewrit hearings unless one of those factors is shown. Six States limit attachments to extraordinary circumstance cases but the writ will not issue prior to a hearing unless there is a showing of some even more compelling condition. Three States always require a preattachment hearing. Only Washington, Connecticut, and Rhode Island authorize attachments without a prior hearing in situations that do not involve any purportedly heightened threat to the plaintiff's interests. Even those States permit ex parte deprivations only in certain types of cases: Rhode Island does so only when the claim is equitable; Connecticut and Washington do so only when real estate is to be attached, and even Washington requires a bond. Conversely, the States for the most part no longer confine attachments to creditor claims. This development, however, only increases the importance of the other limitations.

We do not mean to imply that any given exigency requirement protects an attachment from constitutional attack. Nor do we suggest that the statutory measures we have surveyed are necessarily free of due process problems or other constitutional infirmities in general. We do believe, however, that the procedures of almost all the States confirm our view that the Connecticut provision before us, by failing to provide a preattachment hearing without at least requiring a showing of some exigent circumstance, clearly falls short of the demands of due process.

IV

A

Although a majority of the Court does not reach the issue, Justices MARSHALL, STEVENS, O'CONNOR, and I deem it appropriate to consider whether due process also requires the plaintiff to post a bond or other security in addition to requiring a hearing or showing of some exigency.

As noted, the impairments to property rights that attachments affect merit due process protection. Several consequences can be severe, such as the default of a homeowner's mortgage. In the present context, it need only be added that we have repeatedly recognized the utility of a bond in protecting property rights affected by the mistaken award of prejudgment remedies. *Di-Chem*, 419 U.S., at 610, 611, 95 S.Ct., at 724, 725 (Powell, J., concurring in judgment); id., at 619, 95 S.Ct., at 728 (BLACKMUN, J., dissenting); *Mitchell*, 416 U.S., at 606, n. 8, 94 S.Ct., at 1899, n. 8.

Without a bond, at the time of attachment, the danger that these property rights may be wrongfully deprived remains unacceptably high even with such safeguards as a hearing or exigency requirement. The need for a bond is especially apparent where extraordinary circumstances justify an attachment with no more than than the plaintiff's ex parte assertion of a claim. We have already discussed how due process tolerates, and the States generally permit, the otherwise impermissible chance of erroneously depriving the defendant in such situations in light of the heightened interest of the plaintiff. Until a postattachment hearing, however, a defendant has no protection against damages sustained where no extraordinary circumstance in fact existed or the plaintiff's likelihood of recovery was nil. Such protection is what a bond can supply. Both the Court and its individual members have repeatedly found the requirement of a bond to play an essential role in reducing what would have been too great a degree of risk in precisely this type of circumstance. *Mitchell*, supra, at 610, 619, 94 S.Ct., at 1901, 1906; *Di-Chem*, supra, 419 U.S., at 613, 95 S.Ct., at 725 (Powell, J., concurring in judgment); id., at 619, 95 S.Ct., at 728 (BLACKMUN, J., dissenting); *Fuentes*, 407 U.S., at 101, 92 S.Ct., at 2005 (WHITE, J., dissenting).

But the need for a bond does not end here. A defendant's property rights remain at undue risk even when there has been an adversarial hearing to determine the plaintiff's likelihood of recovery. At best, a court's initial assessment of each party's case cannot produce more than an educated prediction as to who will win. This is especially true when, as here, the nature of the claim makes any accurate prediction elusive. See *Mitchell*, supra, 416 U.S., at 609-610, 94 S.Ct., at 1901. In consequence, even a full hearing under a proper probable-cause standard would not prevent many defendants from having title to their homes impaired during the pendency of suits that never result in the contingency that ultimately justifies such impairment, namely, an award to the plaintiff. Attachment measures currently on the books reflect this concern. All but a handful of States require a plaintiff's bond despite also affording a hearing either before, or (for the vast majority, only under extraordinary circumstances) soon after, an attachment takes place. Bonds have been a similarly common feature of other prejudgment remedy procedures that we have considered, whether or not these procedures also included a hearing. See Ownbey, 256 U.S., at 101-102 n. 1, 41 S.Ct., at 435 n. 1; *Fuentes*, supra, 407 U.S., at 73, n. 6, 75-76, n. 7, 81-82, 92 S.Ct., at 1990, n. 6, 1991-1992, n. 7, 1994-1995; *Mitchell*, supra, 416 U.S., at 606, and n. 6, 94 S.Ct., at 1899; *Di-Chem*, supra, 419 U.S., at 602-603, n. 1, 608, 95 S.Ct., at 721, n. 1, 723.

The State stresses its double damages remedy for suits that are commenced without probable cause. Conn.Gen.Stat. §52-568(a)(1). This remedy, however, fails to make up for the lack of a bond. As an initial matter, the meaning of "probable cause" in this provision is no more clear here than it was in the attachment provision itself. Should the term mean the plaintiff's good faith or the facial adequacy of the complaint, the remedy is clearly insufficient. A defendant who was deprived where there was little or no likelihood that the plaintiff would obtain a judgment could nonetheless recover only by proving some type of fraud or malice or by showing that the plaintiff had failed to state a claim. Problems persist even if the plaintiff's ultimate failure permits recovery. At best a defendant must await a decision on the merits of the plaintiff's complaint, even assuming that a §52-568(a)(1) action may be brought as a counterclaim. Hydro Air of Connecticut, Inc. v. Versa Technologies, Inc., 99

F.R.D. 111, 113 (Conn.1983). Settlement, under Connecticut law, precludes seeking the damages remedy, a fact that encourages the use of attachments as a tactical device to pressure an opponent to capitulate. Blake v. Levy, 191 Conn. 257, 464 A.2d 52 (1983). An attorney's advice that there is probable cause to commence an action constitutes a complete defense, even if the advice was unsound or erroneous. Vandersluis v. Weil, 176 Conn. 353, 361, 407 A.2d 982, 987 (1978). Finally, there is no guarantee that the original plaintiff will have adequate assets to satisfy an award that the defendant may win.

Nor is there any appreciable interest against a bond requirement. Section 52-278e(a)(1) does not require a plaintiff to show exigent circumstances nor any pre-existing interest in the property facing attachment. A party must show more than the mere existence of a claim before subjecting an opponent to prejudgment proceedings that carry a significant risk of erroneous deprivation. See *Mitchell*, 416 U.S., at 604-609, 94 S.Ct., at 1901; *Fuentes*, supra, 407 U.S., at 90-92, 92 S.Ct., at 1999-2000; *Sniadach*, 395 U.S., at 339, 89 S.Ct., at 1821.

B

Our foregoing discussion compels the four of us to consider whether a bond excuses the need for a hearing or other safeguards altogether. If a bond is needed to augment the protections afforded by preattachment and postattachment hearings, it arguably follows that a bond renders these safeguards unnecessary. That conclusion is unconvincing, however, for it ignores certain harms that bonds could not undo but that hearings would prevent. The law concerning attachments has rarely, if ever, required defendants to suffer an encumbered title until the case is concluded without any prior opportunity to show that the attachment was unwarranted. Our cases have repeatedly emphasized the importance of providing a prompt postdeprivation hearing at the very least. *Mitchell*, supra, 416 U.S., at 606, 94 S.Ct., at 1899; *Di-Chem*, 419 U.S., at 606-607, 95 S.Ct., at 722-723. Every State but one, moreover, expressly requires a preattachment or postattachment hearing to determine the propriety of an attachment.

The necessity for at least a prompt postattachment hearing is self- evident because the right to be compensated at the end of the case, if the plaintiff loses, for all provable injuries caused by the attachment is inadequate to redress the harm inflicted, harm that could have been avoided had an early hearing been held. An individual with an immediate need or opportunity to sell a property can neither do so, nor otherwise satisfy that need or recreate the opportunity. The same applies to a parent in need of a home equity loan for a child's education, an entrepreneur seeking to start a business on the strength of an otherwise strong credit rating, or simply a homeowner who might face the disruption of having a mortgage placed in technical default. The extent of these harms, moreover, grows with the length of the suit. Here, oral argument indicated that civil suits in Connecticut commonly take up to four to seven years for completion. (Tr. of Oral Arg. 44.) Many state attachment statutes require that the amount of a bond be anywhere from the equivalent to twice the amount the plaintiff seeks. See, e.g., Utah Rule of Civ.Proc. 64C(b). These amounts bear no relation to the harm the defendant might suffer even assuming that money damages can make up for the foregoing disruptions. It should be clear, however, that such an assumption is fundamentally flawed. Reliance on a bond does not sufficiently account for the harms that flow from an erroneous attachment to excuse a State from reducing that risk by means of a timely hearing.

If a bond cannot serve to dispense with a hearing immediately after attachment, neither is it sufficient basis for not providing a preattachment hearing in the absence of exigent circumstances even if in any event a hearing would be provided a few days later. The reasons are the same: a wrongful attachment can inflict injury that will not fully be redressed by recovery on the bond after a prompt postattachment hearing determines that the attachment was invalid.

Once more, history and contemporary practice support our conclusion. Historically, attachments would not issue without a showing of extraordinary circumstances even though a plaintiff bond was almost invariably required in addition. Drake §§ 4, 114; Shinn §§ 86, 153. Likewise, all but eight States currently require the posting of a bond. Out of this 42 State majority, all but one requires a preattachment hearing, a showing of some exigency, or both, and all but one expressly require a postattachment hearing when an attachment has been issue ex parte. This testimony underscores the point that neither a hearing nor an extraordinary circumstance limitation eliminates the need for a bond, no more than a bond allows waiver of these other protections. To reconcile the interests of the defendant and the plaintiff accurately, due process generally requires all of the above.

V

Because Connecticut's prejudgment remedy provision, Conn.Gen.Stat. §52-278e(a)(1), violates the requirements of due process by authorizing prejudgment attachment without prior notice or a hearing, the judgment of the Court of Appeals is affirmed, and the case is remanded to that court for further proceedings consistent with this opinion.

It is so ordered.

* * *

Chief Justice Rehnquist with whom Justice Blackmun joins, concurring.

I agree with the Court that the Connecticut attachment statute, "as applied in this case," fails to satisfy the Due Process Clause of the Fourteenth Amendment. I therefore join Parts I, II and III of its opinion. Unfortunately, the remainder of the Court's opinion does not confine itself to the facts of this case, but enters upon a lengthy disquisition as to what combination of safeguards are required to satisfy Due Process in hypothetical cases not before the Court. I therefore do not join Part IV.

As the Court's opinion points out, the Connecticut statute allows attachment not merely for a creditor's claim, but for a tort claim of assault and battery; it affords no opportunity for a pre-deprivation hearing; it contains no requirement that there be "exigent circumstances," such as an effort on the part of the defendant to conceal assets; no bond is required from the plaintiff; and the property attached is one in which the plaintiff has no pre- existing interest. The Court's opinion is, in my view, ultimately correct when it bases its holding of unconstitutionality of the Connecticut statute as applied here on our cases of Sniadach v. Family Finance Corp., 395 U.S. 337, 89 S.Ct. 1820, 23 L.Ed.2d 349 (1969); Fuentes v. Shevin, 407 U.S. 67, 92 S.Ct. 1983, 32 L.Ed.2d 556 (1972); Mitchell v. W.T. Grant Co., 416 U.S. 600, 94 S.Ct. 1895, 40 L.Ed.2d 406 (1974), and North Georgia Finishing v. Di-Chem, Inc., 419 U.S. 601, 95 S.Ct. 719, 42 L.Ed.2d 751 (1975). But I do not believe that the result follows so inexorably as the Court's opinion suggests. All of the cited cases dealt with personalty--bank deposits or chattels--and each involved the physical seizure of the property itself, so that the defendant was deprived of its use. These cases, which represented something of a revolution in the jurisprudence of procedural due process, placed substantial limits on the methods by which creditors could obtain a lien on the assets of a debtor prior to judgment. But in all of them the debtor was deprived of the use and possession of the property. In the present case, on the other hand, Connecticut's pre-judgment attachment on real property statute, which secures an incipient lien for the plaintiff, does not deprive the defendant of the use or possession of the property.

The Court's opinion therefore breaks new ground, and I would point out, more emphatically than the Court does, the limits of today's holding. In Spielman-Fond, Inc. v. Hanson's, Inc., 379 F.Supp. 997, 999 (D.Ariz.1973), the District Court held that the filing of a mechanics' lien did not cause the deprivation of a significant property interest of the owner. We summarily affirmed that decision. 417 U.S. 901, 94 S.Ct. 2596, 41 L.Ed.2d 208 (1974). Other courts have read this summary affirmance to mean that the mere imposition of a lien on real property, which does not disturb the owner's use or enjoyment of the property, is not a deprivation of property calling for procedural due process safeguards. I agree with the Court, however, that upon analysis the deprivation here is a significant one, even though the owner remains in undisturbed possession. "For a property owner like Doehr, attachment ordinarily clouds title; impairs the ability to sell or otherwise alienate the property; taints any credit rating; reduces the chance of obtaining a home equity loan or additional mortgage; and can even place an existing mortgage in technical default when there is an insecurity clause." Ante ***. Given the elaborate system of title records relating to real property which prevails in all of our states, a lienor need not obtain possession or use of real property belonging to a debtor in order to significantly impair its value to him.

But in Spielman-Fond, Inc., supra, there was, as the Court points out * * * ante, an alternate basis available to this Court for affirmance of that decision. Arizona recognized a pre-existing lien in favor of unpaid mechanics and materialmen who had contributed labor or supplies which were incorporated in improvements to real property. The existence of such a lien upon the very property ultimately posted or noticed distinguishes those cases from the present one, where the plaintiff had no pre-existing interest in the real property which he sought to attach. Materialman's and mechanic's lien statutes award an interest in real property to workers who have contributed their labor, and to suppliers who have furnished material, for the improvement of the real property. Since neither the labor nor the material can be reclaimed once it has become a part of the realty, this is the only method by which workmen or small businessmen who have contributed to the improvement of the property may be given a remedy against a property owner who has defaulted on his promise to pay for the labor and the materials. To require any sort of a contested court hearing or bond before the notice of lien takes effect would largely defeat the purpose of these statutes.

Petitioner in its brief relies in part on our summary affirmance in Bartlett v. Williams, 464 U.S. 801, 104 S.Ct. 46, 78 L.Ed.2d 67 (1983). That case involved a lis pendens, in which the question presented to this Court was whether such a procedure could be valid when the only protection afforded to the owner of land affected by the lis pendens was a post-sequestration hearing. A notice of lis pendens is a well established traditional remedy whereby a plaintiff (usually a judgment creditor) who brings an action to enforce an interest in property to which the defendant has title gives notice of the pendency of such action to third parties; the notice causes the interest which he establishes, if successful, to relate back to the date of the filing of the lis pendens. The filing of such notice will have an effect upon the defendant's ability to alienate the property, or to obtain additional security on the basis of title to the property, but the effect of the lis pendens is simply to give notice to the world of the remedy being sought in the lawsuit itself. The lis pendens itself creates no additional right in the property on the part of the plaintiff, but simply allows third parties to know that a lawsuit is pending in which the plaintiff is seeking to establish such a right. Here, too, the fact that the plaintiff already claims an interest in the property which he seeks to enforce by a lawsuit distinguishes this class of cases from the Connecticut attachment employed in the present case.

Today's holding is a significant development in the law; the only cases dealing with real property cited in the Court's opinion, Peralta v. Heights Medical Center, Inc., 485 U.S. 80, 85, 108 S.Ct. 896, 899, 99 L.Ed.2d 75 (1988), and Hodge v. Muscatine County, 196 U.S. 276, 281, 25 S.Ct. 237, 239, 49 L.Ed. 477 (1905), arose out of lien foreclosure sales in which the question was whether the owner was entitled to proper notice. The change is dramatically reflected when we compare today's decision with the almost casual statement of Justice Holmes, writing for a unanimous Court in Coffin Brothers v. Bennett, 277 U.S. 29, 31, 48 S.Ct. 422, 423, 72 L.Ed. 768 (1928): "[N]othing is more common than to allow parties alleging themselves to be creditors to establish in advance by attachment a lien dependent for its effect upon the result of the suit." The only protection accorded to the debtor in that case was the right to contest his liability in a post-deprivation proceeding.

It is both unwise and unnecessary, I believe, for the Court to proceed, as it does in Part IV, from its decision of the case before it to discuss abstract and hypothetical situations not before it. This is especially so where we are dealing with the Due Process Clause which, as the Court recognizes, "unlike some legal rules, is not a technical conception with a fixed content unrelated to time, place and circumstances," ante ***. And it is even more true in a case involving constitutional limits on the methods by which the states may transfer or create interests in real property; in other areas of the law, dicta may do little damage, but those who insure titles or write title opinions often do not enjoy the luxury of distinguishing between dicta and holding.

The two elements of due process with which the Court concerns itself in Part IV--the requirement of a bond, and of "exigent circumstances"--prove to be upon analysis so vague that the discussion is not only unnecessary, but not particulary useful. Unless one knows what the terms and conditions of a bond are to be, the requirement of a "bond" in the abstract means little. The amount to be secured by the bond and the conditions of the bond are left unaddressed--is there to be liability on the part of a plaintiff if he is ultimately unsuccessful in the underlying lawsuit, or is it instead to be conditioned on some sort of good faith test? The "exigent circumstances" referred to by the Court are admittedly equally vague; non-residency appears to be enough in some states, an attempt to conceal assets is required in others, an effort to flee the jurisdiction in still others. We should await concrete cases which present questions involving bonds and exigent circumstances before we attempt to decide when and if the Due Process Clause of the Fourteenth Amendment requires them as prerequisites for a lawful attachment.

Justice Scalia, concurring in part and concurring in the judgment.

Since the manner of attachment here was not a recognized procedure at common law, cf. Pacific Mutual Life Ins. Co. v. Haslip, 499 U.S. ----, ----, 111 S.Ct. 1032, ----, 113 L.Ed.2d 1 (1991) (SCALIA, J., concurring in judgment), I agree that its validity under the Due Process Clause should be determined by applying the test we set forth in Mathews v. Eldridge, 424 U.S. 319, 96 S.Ct. 893, 47 L.Ed.2d 18 (1976); and I agree that it fails that test. I join Parts I and III of the Court's opinion, and concur in the judgment of the Court.

Wyatt v. Cole

United States Supreme Court, 1992
___ U.S. ___, 112 S.Ct. 1827, 118 L.Ed.2d 504

Justice O'Connor delivered the opinion of the Court.

In Lugar v. Edmondson Oil Co., 457 U.S. 922, 102 S.Ct. 2744, 73 L.Ed.2d 482 (1982), we left open the question whether private defendants charged with 42 U.S.C. §1983 liability for invoking state replevin, garnishment, and attachment statutes later declared unconstitutional are entitled to qualified immunity from suit. Id., at 942, n. 23, 102 S.Ct., at 2756, n. 23. We now hold that they are not.

* * *

Title 42 U.S.C. §1983 provides a cause of action against "[e]very person who, under color of any statute ... of any State ... subjects, or causes to be subjected, any citizen ... to the deprivation of any rights, privileges, or immunities secured by the Constitution and laws...." The purpose of §1983 is to deter state actors from using the badge of their authority to deprive individuals of their federally guaranteed rights and to provide relief to victims if such deterrence fails.

In *Lugar* * * * the Court considered the scope of §1983 liability in the context of garnishment, prejudgment attachment, and replevin statutes. In that case, the Court held that private parties who attached a debtor's assets pursuant to a state attachment statute were subject to §1983 liability if the statute was constitutionally infirm. Noting that our garnishment, prejudgment attachment, and replevin cases established that private use of state laws to secure property could constitute "state action" for purposes of the Fourteenth Amendment, id., at 932-935, 102 S.Ct., at 2751-2752, the Court held that private defendants invoking a state-created attachment statute act "under color of state law" within the meaning of §1983 if their actions are "fairly attributable to the State." Id., at 937, 102 S.Ct., at 2753. This requirement is satisfied, the Court held, if two conditions are met. First, the "deprivation must be caused by the exercise of some right or privilege created by the State or by a rule of conduct imposed by the State or by a person for whom the State is responsible." Ibid. Second, the private party must have "acted together with or ... obtained significant aid from state officials" or engaged in conduct "otherwise chargeable to the State." Ibid. The Court found potential §1983 liability in Lugar because the attachment scheme was created by the State and because the private defendants, in invoking the aid of state officials to attach the disputed property, were "willful participant[s] in joint activity with the State or its agents." Id., at 941, 102 S.Ct., at 2756 (internal quotation marks omitted).

* * *

Section 1983 "creates a species of tort liability that on its face admits of no immunities." Imbler v. Pachtman, 424 U.S. 409, 417, 96 S.Ct. 984, 988, 47 L.Ed.2d 128 (1976). Nonetheless, we have accorded certain government

officials either absolute or qualified immunity from suit if the "tradition of immunity was so firmly rooted in the common law and was supported by such strong policy reasons that 'Congress would have specifically so provided had it wished to abolish the doctrine.'" Owen v. City of Independence, 445 U.S. 622, 637, 100 S.Ct. 1398, 1408, 63 L.Ed.2d 673 (1980) (quoting Pierson v. Ray, 386 U.S. 547, 555, 87 S.Ct. 1213, 1218, 18 L.Ed.2d 288 (1967)). * * *
* * *

Qualified immunity strikes a balance between compensating those who have been injured by official conduct and protecting government's ability to perform its traditional functions. * * * Accordingly, we have recognized qualified immunity for government officials where it was necessary to preserve their ability to serve the public good or to ensure that talented candidates were not deterred by the threat of damage suits from entering public service. * * *

These rationales are not transferable to private parties. Although principles of equality and fairness may suggest, as respondents argue, that private citizens who rely unsuspectingly on state laws they did not create and may have no reason to believe are invalid should have some protection from liability, as do their government counterparts, such interests are not sufficiently similar to the traditional purposes of qualified immunity to justify such an expansion. Unlike school board members, * * * or police officers * * * or Presidential aides, * * * private parties hold no office requiring them to exercise discretion; nor are they principally concerned with enhancing the public good. Accordingly, extending * * * qualified immunity to private parties would have no bearing on whether public officials are able to act forcefully and decisively in their jobs or on whether qualified applicants enter public service. Moreover, unlike with government officials performing discretionary functions, the public interest will not be unduly impaired if private individuals are required to proceed to trial to resolve their legal disputes. In short, the nexus between private parties and the historic purposes of qualified immunity is simply too attenuated to justify such an extension of our doctrine of immunity.

For these reasons, we can offer no relief today. The question on which we granted certiorari is a very narrow one: "[W]hether private persons, who conspire with state officials to violate constitutional rights, have available the good faith immunity applicable to public officials." Pet. for Cert. i. The precise issue encompassed in this question, and the only issue decided by the lower courts, is whether qualified immunity * * * is available for private defendants faced with §1983 liability for invoking a state replevin, garnishment or attachment statute. That answer is no. In so holding, however, we do not foreclose the possibility that private defendants faced with §1983 liability * ** could be entitled to an affirmative defense based on good faith and/or probable cause or that §1983 suits against private, rather than governmental, parties could require plaintiffs to carry additional burdens. Because those issues are not fairly before us, however, we leave them for another day.

IV

As indicated above, the District Court assumed that * * * Cole was liable under §1983 for invoking the state replevin under bond statute, and intimated that, but did not decide whether, Robbins also was subject to §1983 liability. The Court of Appeals never revisited this question, but instead concluded only that respondents were entitled to qualified immunity at least for conduct prior to the statute's invalidation. Because we overturn this judgment, we must remand since there remains to be determined, at least, whether Cole and Robbins, in invoking the replevin statute, acted under color of state law within the meaning of Lugar, supra. The decision of the Court of Appeals is reversed and the case is remanded for proceedings consistent with this opinion.

It is so ordered.

Problems

1. Debtor Dave defaulted on a Bank loan. Bank sues.

    a. Can Bank attach Dave's car?

    b. Can Bank replevy Dave's car?

    c. Are the answers the same or different if Bank has a consensual lien (an Article 9 security interest) in the car that secures the loan?

2. Brumby filed a general creditor's suit in the Chancery Court of Hamilton County, seeking, among other things, to make available to the general creditors of Ten-Tex Corporation (hereinafter "Ten-Tex"), assets of said corporation, attached in a prior suit and still in the hands of the Clerk and Master. In said prior suit against Ten-Tex Corporation, UCT sued out an original attachment resulting in a levy upon two U.S. patents. In the final decree in that case the attachment was sustained and the assets levied upon were subjected to the satisfaction of the money judgment. * * * In the instant case, on motion for partial summary judgment by UCT, the learned Chancellor held that the lien of the attachment in the earlier suit was effective from the date of levy, November 13, 1968; that UCT's right to the assets attached was therefore prior and superior to the claims of general creditors of Ten-Tex. On Brumby's appeal, the Court of Appeals reversed the Chancellor * * *. *Spunt v. Brumby*, 518 S.W.2d 345 (Tenn. 1974). What should have been the result on further appeal to the Supreme Court of Tennessee?

3. Plaintiff is a Massachusetts bank that allegedly loaned money in excess of $15,500 to defendant Avram. Sometime in late April of 1987, plaintiff sought to secure that debt by attaching Avram's property located at 2711 Ordway Street, N.W., Washington, D.C. At about the same time, Avram was endeavoring to sell that piece of property to defendant Bryant. To this end, a contract of sale had been

entered into on February 13, 1987, and ratified on February 19, 1987. Settlement took place on April 27, 1987, and on that date the deed was delivered to Bryant. On April 28, 1987, plaintiff filed this action, accompanied by a motion for writ of attachment; Judge Sporkin granted the motion the same day, and the Clerk of the Court issued the writ on April 29, 1987. At 11:29 a.m. on the 29th, plaintiff recorded the Court's order with the Recorder of Deeds for the District of Columbia. On the same day, plaintiff delivered the order and writ to the United States Marshal. Bryant recorded the deed of sale for the subject property at 10:38 a.m. on April 30, 1987. At 3:05 p.m. on that date, Deputy U.S. Marshal Walter N. Rich posted the order and attachment on the front door of those premises. *Cape Cod Bank & Tr. Co. v. Avram*, 697 F. Supp. 8 (D. D.C. 1988). Both parties claim priority and have moved for summary judgment. Who should win?

4. Creditor sued on July 1 and caused attachment of Debtor's property on the same day. The property was subject to a consensual lien in favor of Bank. Creditor won judgment and sought to apply the property in satisfaction of its judgment. Bank objected, claiming priority. Who wins?

5. The priority issues are much easier if the attaching creditor fails to win judgment against the debtor. Why?

6. Appellants Watertown Equipment Company and Edward J. Moe bring this 42 U.S.C. §1983 action against appellees Norwest Bank of Watertown, its vice president, Jerry Miller, and its attorney, Thomas Green. The appellants claim that the appellees violated their rights to procedural due process by attaching property of Watertown Equipment Company under a South Dakota attachment statute. The district court granted summary judgment for each appellee, holding that each had qualified immunity from liability.

    Appellant Moe was the majority stockholder of three farm implement dealers, Watertown Equipment Company in Watertown, South Dakota, and two others in Dawson and Appleton, Minnesota. From 1976 to 1982, Norwest Bank of Watertown (then First National Bank of Watertown) extended a general line of credit to Watertown Equipment which was secured by an interest in Watertown Equipment's inventory and receivables. Moe also personally guaranteed most of the loans. Altogether, Watertown owed Norwest about $488,000 on the loans.

    Beginning in 1978, Watertown Equipment had difficulties meeting its loan obligations. Norwest and Moe tried to work out the difficulties. Norwest helped Moe list for sale a plot of about 180 acres which Watertown Equipment owned to finish payment on a mortgage and to help reduce the amount owing on the loans.

    In 1982, Watertown Equipment's financial state worsened. Norwest made frequent demands on Moe for payment, but Moe was only able to make several small payments in 1982. In the spring of 1982, Norwest required monthly and even weekly formal inventories at Watertown Equipment. By summer, Norwest decided to cut Watertown Equipment's line of credit. At this time, Norwest also claims to have discovered equipment missing from the dealership. According to Norwest, the manager of Watertown Equipment, Dan Toben, also warned Norwest that some of the collateral was going to be moved out of the state. In his affidavit, however, Toben stated that he never told this to Norwest, and, in fact, he said that Watertown Equipment had often moved equipment to one of Moe's other dealers and that its behavior in the six months prior to the attachment was no different than it had been in the past. Moe stated that Norwest was aware of such transfers in the past.

Norwest's vice president, Jerry Miller, claims that Norwest began to consider prejudgment attachment upon the suggestion of its attorney, Thomas Green, because of the movement of equipment out of the state and possible concealment of proceeds from sales. In early October of 1982, Miller more fully discussed the use of prejudgment attachment proceedings with Green. In a letter of October 25, 1982, Green cautioned that the South Dakota attachment statute in effect at that time might be unconstitutional, although his research of the case law construing attachment statutes in other states led him to the conclusion that the South Dakota law was "distinguishable." Miller discussed the matter with Norwest's Discount Committee which decided to undertake the attachment. Green prepared the necessary papers, and, on October 25, 1982, Norwest secured an order from the clerk of court of Codington County.

Pursuant to the writ of attachment, the sheriff arrived at Watertown Equipment, told all the employees to leave, and secured the building and all the equipment in it by changing the locks. After several months while the business was still under the attachment, Norwest and Watertown Equipment reached a settlement agreement. Watertown Equipment apparently was closed as a result.

The appellants instituted this action and pendent state claims in federal district court. On November 27, 1985, the district court granted summary judgment for appellee Green. On October 6, 1986, the district court granted partial summary judgment for appellees Norwest Bank and Miller on the section 1983 claim and dismissed the state claims without prejudice. *Watertown Equipment Co. v. Norwest Bank Watertown*, 830 F.2d 1487 (8th Cir. 1987).

Watertown had two major complaints against the South Dakota attachment statute. First, the writ was obtainable from the clerk of court. No judge was to be involved in the matter unless a hearing was requested. Second, the bond required of the creditor, for the purpose of indemnification of the debtor in case of a wrongful attachment, was limited to $10,000. Thus, the defendant is only protected from plaintiff's wrongful attachment for damages up to $10,000.

If you were a judge on the court of appeals, how would you decide these questions:

a. Is the South Dakota attachment statute constitutional?

b. Are the Bank and its lawyer personally liable if the attachment was unconstitutional?

7. On July 8, 1981, plaintiff Jordan, on behalf of Joe J. Jordan, FAIA, Inc., a Pennsylvania corporation, executed a lease to rent the fifth floor of an office building at 1920 Chestnut Street in Philadelphia from defendant Arnold T. Berman, trading as H.P. Realty, for a term commencing September 1, 1981 and ending August 1, 1986. On or about October 1, 1981, plaintiffs Jordan and Mitchell formed Jordan, Mitchell, Inc., an architectural firm that operated out of said premises.

On May 2, 1986, by its terms, this lease automatically renewed for a one-year period commencing August 1, 1986. On May 16, 1986, H.P. delivered a lease termination notice to Jordan, Mitchell, Inc. dated April 30, 1986. When the plaintiffs' attorney advised H.P. that in their view the lease had been renewed automatically, defendant Myron Berman told plaintiff Jordan that he would "retaliate" if plaintiffs continued to occupy the premises pursuant to the purported renewal. Acting on instructions from Myron Berman, unnamed individuals disconnected electrical wiring in plaintiffs' offices on May 22, 1986 and obstructed the entrance thereto on May 23, 1986 by placing trash nearby. As a result, plaintiffs allegedly had to expend sums of money to rectify this situation.

Through counsel, the parties to the lease thereafter negotiated an extension, substituting Jordan, Mitchell, Inc. as lessee and extending the lease for a term of three years, commencing August 1, 1986. The extension agreement was executed by plaintiffs on October 29, 1986 and by H.P. on December 8, 1986, and contained a mutual release of all claims arising under the initial lease.

The lease provided to lessor the option of charging lessee additional rent in an amount equal to their proportionate share of any increases in taxes or operating expenses. Such rent increases would be predicated upon notice by the lessor. H.P. never increased the rent pursuant to this clause during the term of the original lease. The parties never specifically discussed this provision of the lease during the course of their negotiations over the lease extension.

On February 10, 1988, H.P. billed plaintiffs for $1,416.20, a proportional amount of real estate tax increases for the years 1982 to 1988. Plaintiffs paid this amount to the lessor before "realizing" what it was for. Plaintiffs refused to pay the lessor additional rent adjustments that were claimed on October 13, 1988 as a result of increased operating expenses. Defendant Myron Berman then requested Philadelphia Gas Works to terminate gas service to the leased premises. Plaintiffs avoided a termination of service by having PGW bill them directly.

Plaintiffs allege that defendants engaged in similar conduct with respect to other tenants. When Diversified Community Services ("DCS"), another tenant in another building under defendants' control, refused to pay a retroactive rent increase billed on December 7, 1987 and attempted to move, defendants "refused" them permission to utilize the service elevators for this purpose until they had paid the rent demanded. DCS was permitted to move from the building after it settled a suit they filed against defendants as a result of that dispute.

The standard preprinted "Form 60" lease contained a cognovit clause entitling H.P. to confess judgment upon a default in rental payments. The warrant of attorney authorizing the confession of judgment appears on the reverse side of the page with the parties' signatures. This clause also was not specifically discussed during the lease extension negotiation.

Plaintiffs rejected an offer of March 7, 1989 from H.P. to waive its October 13, 1988 claim for additional rent if plaintiff corporation would execute a new three-year lease. On May 16, 1989, counsel filed with the Prothonotary of the Court of Common Pleas of Philadelphia a Complaint in Confession of Judgment against plaintiffs on behalf of Arnold Berman and H.P. Realty, claiming $41,082.62 in overdue rent plus related charges, minus plaintiffs' security deposit. The required verification and affidavit were executed by Myron Berman as "managing agent." Later that day, the Prothonotary issued a Writ of Execution which was served by the Sheriff on Fidelity Bank, effectively freezing plaintiffs' corporate checking account in the amount of the judgment. As a result, the account became overdrawn and six items were returned unpaid.

On May 19, 1989, plaintiffs received from the garnishee notification of the Writ and copies of the documents filed in the Common Pleas Court. On May 24, 1989, plaintiffs filed a petition in the Court of Common Pleas of Philadelphia to open and/or strike the confessed judgment. The state court immediately issued a Rule to Show Cause why the judgment should not be opened or stricken and vacated the garnishment of plaintiffs' account upon the posting of $10,000. On July 21, 1989, the state court ordered that the judgment be opened, and plaintiffs' $10,000 was returned to them.

[Plaintiffs assert six claims in their complaint. In the first count, plaintiffs seek declaratory and injunctive relief against defendant Pettit, the Prothonotary of the Court of Common Pleas of Philadelphia, for alleged due process violations in issuing writs of execution permitting the garnishment of bank accounts pursuant to confessed judgments, under Pa.R.Civ.P. 2950 et seq. The remaining counts, all against defendants Arnold and Myron Berman, assert a violation of the Racketeer Influenced and Corrupt Organizations Act ("RICO"), 18 U.S.C. §1961 et seq., violation of plaintiffs' civil rights under 42 U.S.C. §1983, and state law claims of fraud and malicious use and abuse of process.]

* * *

Plaintiffs seek only injunctive and declaratory relief in their cause of action against Mr. Pettit as Prothonotary of the Court of Common Pleas of Philadelphia. They seek a declaration that the Pennsylvania procedures pertaining to confession of judgment are unconstitutional to the extent that: (a) they permit the entry of judgment without a prior judicial or quasi-judicial review of the supporting documents to determine that it is warranted; and, (b) they permit the issuance of writs of execution for the garnishment of bank accounts prior to notice and an opportunity to move to strike the judgment or a judicial finding of exigent circumstances. They also seek to enjoin the enforcement of those procedures by the Prothonotary. *Jordan v. Berman*, 758 F. Supp. 269 (E.D. Pa. 1991).

What would be your initial reactions to these issues if you were the district court judge?

8. On April 2, 1984, Central Jersey obtained a judgment against Dr. Markouski. On June 15, 1984, Central Jersey delivered a writ of execution on that judgment to the Sheriff of Middlesex County. Pursuant to the writ, the Sheriff levied on the real property owned by Markouski and his wife at 120 Ainsworth Avenue, East Brunswick. To satisfy Central Jersey's judgment, the Sheriff held a sale of Markouski's entirety interest in the property on January 9, 1985. At that sale, Equity purchased Markouski's entirety interest for $7,000.

On August 1, 1984, Heritage Bank obtained a judgment against Markouski in the amount of $45,202. The judgment was docketed on August 6, 1984, but Heritage did not execute on its judgment. Heritage did not receive notice of the January 9, 1985, sheriff's sale. Pursuant to N.J.S.A. 2A:61-1 and Rule 4:65-2, the Sheriff of Middlesex County posted notice of the sale in his office and at 120 Ainsworth Avenue at least three weeks before the sale, and also published notice at least once a week during four consecutive weeks in two Middlesex County newspapers, the Daily Home News and The News Tribune.

On May 29, 1986, New Brunswick Savings Bank commenced an action to foreclose two mortgages it held on the Markouskis' property, totaling $14,945.25. In addition to the Markouskis, New Brunswick named as defendants Equity, as the holder of Markouski's entirety interest in the property, and the parties holding judgment liens against Markouski, including Heritage. After the Chancery Division had granted New Brunswick final judgment, a foreclosure sale of the real property was held on July 1, 1987. At that sale, Audrey Polito and Richard Henderson bought the property for $142,500.

After the mortgage debts were satisfied from the proceeds of the foreclosure sale, there were surplus moneys totaling approximately $127,600, one-half of which was payable to Markouski. Markouski's half of the surplus moneys was not sufficient to satisfy all the claims of his remaining creditors. Thus, in July 1987, Heritage, as one of the parties holding a judgment against Markouski, applied to the Chancery

Division, pursuant to Rule 4:64-3, for an order establishing the priority of claims for the distribution of his share of the surplus. Equity cross-moved, seeking payment of all of the surplus attributable to Markouski's entirety interest. Equity asserted that it owned that interest free and clear of all encumbrances, including Heritage's unexecuted judgment lien, contending that Heritage had not been entitled to actual notice of the January 9, 1985, sheriff's sale.

Heritage conceded that Rule 4:65-2 did not require Central Jersey to notify it, either personally or by mail, of the sheriff's sale. Heritage maintained, however, that lack of actual notice deprived it of its interest in the property without due process of law. It sought, therefore, to have the sheriff's sale set aside as defective, in effect challenging the constitutionality of New Jersey's pre-sale notice procedures as applied to non-levying judgment creditors. *New Brunswick Savings Bank v. Markouski*, 123 N.J. 402, 587 A.2d 1265 (1991).

The trial court held that Equity, as owner of his entirety interest, was entitled to Markouski's one-half interest in the surplus proceeds. The court found that New Jersey's pre-sale notice procedures did not violate the due-process clause, apparently concluding that an unexecuted judgment lien is not a protectible property interest. Heritage appealed, challenging the constitutionality of the notice requirements for judicial sales in execution of judgment liens. The Appellate Division granted the State's motion for leave to intervene and affirmed the trial court's judgment in an unpublished opinion. The New Jersey Supreme Court granted Heritage's petition for certification.

If you were a clerk on New Jersey's highest court, how would you describe the major issues that should be considered?

E. REACHING PROPERTY OUT OF STATE (EXTRA-TERRITORIAL ENFORCEMENT)

Suppose that Creditor gets a judgment against Debtor in State A. Debtor owns little or no property there, but does own substantial property in State B. If Creditor wishes to enforce her judgment through execution process in State B, she must somehow get a judgment there. She is not required, however, to re-litigate in State B her cause of action against Debtor.

When Creditor got the judgment in State A, her cause of action against Debtor was merged in the judgment. The judgment is a fresh, and the only, cause of action Creditor now has against Debtor. As a cause of action, the judgment may be the basis of a later lawsuit against Debtor in State A or in State B. So Creditor can sue Debtor in

State B on the basis of the State A judgment, which is a debt, and get a new, separate judgment in State B.

In this process State B is constitutionally bound to give full faith and credit to the State A judgment. U.S. Const. art. IV, §1, cl. 1. The country's leading conflicts scholar, Robert A. Leflar, has explained what this means:

> Full faith and credit to judgments has been almost altogether a matter of applying part of the relevant common-law rules of res judicata as though they were embodied in the constitutional provision. ***
>
> As it now stands, the clause requires the courts of each state, and the federal courts sitting in the states, to give to the judgments of other states the same conclusive effect between the parties and their privies as is given such judgments in the state in which they were rendered. This does not mean that, in the absence of appropriate federal or state statute providing for it, execution will be levied in one state on account of a judgment rendered in another. It does mean that each state must allow the bringing and maintenance of actions based on extrastate judgments to the extent that it has judicial machinery appropriate for the purpose, and that it must recognize such judgments as constituting a defense to suits on original causes of action already adjudicated by them. The state in which later action is brought is free to apply its own procedural rules, including its nondiscriminatory statute of limitations, to such suits. But it may not retry any matter, any defense, which was properly at issue under the pleadings in the prior proceeding. It makes no difference whether the particular point was argued or was neglected in the earlier action.

Robert A. Leflar, Luther L. McDougal, III & Robert L. Felix, AMERICAN CONFLICTS LAW §73 (4th ed. 1986).

Two points are worth emphasizing: First, the full faith and credit clause only applies to valid judgments conclusively binding on the parties and their privies. Whether a judgment meets this test depends on the law of the state where it was rendered and also, of course, on federal constitutional law. For example, if in rendering judgment against Debtor, State A violated its own procedural law so as to make the judgment void and subject to collateral attack under that law, or exercised jurisdiction over Debtor beyond that allowed by the due process clause without deciding (and without having the opportunity to decide) the jurisdictional question, the judgment is not valid for purposes of full faith and credit. The judgment is thus, on these grounds, subject to collateral attack in State B.

Second, a valid, final judgment is entitled to full faith and credit in another state even though "the original cause of action upon which the first judgment was rendered was one upon which the second state would not in the first place have entertained an action. The local public policy of the second state, however strong it may be, is not a ground for denying full faith and credit to a valid sister state judgment." Id. §75.

Bringing a full-blown, common-law action on an extrastate judgment in State B is inefficient and serves no useful purpose in most cases inasmuch as the defendant had her day in court in State A. Thus, most states have enacted an alternative, stream-lined procedure whereby a sister state's judgment can be established as a local judgment through a comparatively simple registration system.

Uniform Enforcement Of Foreign Judgments Act
1964 Revised Act

§1. Definition
In this Act "foreign judgment" means any judgment, decree, or order of a court of the United States or of any other court which is entitled to full faith and credit in this state.

§2. Filing and Status of Foreign Judgments
A copy of any foreign judgment authenticated in accordance with the act of Congress or the statutes of this state may be filed in the office of the Clerk of any [District Court of any city or county] of this state. The Clerk shall treat the foreign judgment in the same manner as a judgment of the [District Court of any city or county] of this state. A judgment so filed has the same effect and is subject to the same procedures, defenses and proceedings for reopening, vacating, or staying as a judgment of a [District Court of any city or county] of this state and may be enforced or satisfied in like manner.

§3. Notice of Filing
(a) At the time of the filing of the foreign judgment, the judgment creditor or his lawyer shall make and file with the Clerk of Court an affidavit setting forth the name and last known post office address of the judgment debtor, and the judgment creditor.

(b) Promptly upon the filing of the foreign judgment and the affidavit, the Clerk shall mail notice of the filing of the foreign judgment to the judgment debtor at the address given and shall make a note of the mailing in the docket. The notice shall include the name and post office address of the judgment creditor and the judgment creditor's lawyer, if any, in this state. In addition, the judgment creditor may mail a notice of the filing of the judgment to the judgment debtor and may file proof of mailing with the Clerk. Lack of mailing notice of filing by the Clerk shall not affect the enforcement proceedings if proof of mailing by the judgment creditor has been filed.

(c) No execution or other process for enforcement of a foreign judgment filed hereunder shall issue until [ ] days after the date the judgment is filed.

* * *

§4. Stay

(a) If the judgment debtor shows the [District Court of any city or county] that an appeal from the foreign judgment is pending or will be taken, or that a stay of execution has been granted, the court shall stay enforcement of the foreign judgment until the appeal is concluded, the time for appeal expires, or the stay of execution expires or is vacated, upon proof that the judgment debtor has furnished the security for the satisfaction of the judgment required by the state in which it was rendered.

(b) If the judgment debtor shows the [District Court of any city or county] any ground upon which enforcement of a judgment of any [District Court of any city or county] of this state would be stayed, the court shall stay enforcement of the foreign judgment for an appropriate period, upon requiring the same security for satisfaction of the judgment which is required in this state.

§6. Optional Procedure

The right of a judgment creditor to bring an action to enforce his judgment instead of proceeding under this Act remains unimpaired.

§7. Uniformity of Interpretation

This Act shall be so interpreted and construed as to effectuate its general purpose to make uniform the law of those states which enact it.

* * *

Notes And Problems

1. J gets a money judgment against D in Oklahoma, where D owns nothing. D owns a gold mine in Alaska, and for this reason J files her judgment there pursuant to Alaska's law, which includes the Uniform Enforcement of Foreign Judgments Act.

    a. What is the effect of J's Alaska filing in terms of the enforcement remedies available to J in that state?

    b. Can D assert any of the following defenses to enforcement of J's judgment in Alaska? (Keep in mind the constitutional admonition that a final judgment on the merits, which is valid in the state which rendered it, is entitled to full faith and credit throughout the country. U.S. Const. art. IV, §1.)

i.　　The basis of J's Oklahoma judgment is breach of a contract by D, but D did not agree to the contract's terms.

ii.　The judgment is invalid under Alaskan law because service of process on D in the Oklahoma action was achieved in a manner not permitted by Alaskan law.

iii.　Exercise of jurisdiction over D by the Oklahoma court violated federal due process requirements.

iv.　D's only connection with Alaska is ownership of property there; J's claims against D are unrelated to the property; D has not consented to jurisdiction in Alaska; so Alaskan courts cannot exercise jurisdiction over D consistent with federal due process requirements; thus, the judgment against D cannot be enforced in Alaska.

v.　 The judgment is for some reason void and unenforceable under Oklahoma law.

vi.　The Oklahoma judge misconstrued and misapplied the applicable substantive law governing the contractual obligations of D to J.

vii.　The contract that is the basis of J's judgment provided for an interest rate well beyond the maximum rate permitted by Alaskan law, so that enforcing the Oklahoma judgment in Alaska would violate the forum's strong public policy against usury.

viii.　Although the Oklahoma judgment remains enforceable there, enforcement of the judgment in Alaska is barred by the forum's statute of limitation on the enforcement of judgments.

2.　On May 14, 1971, the plaintiff obtained a judgment in Minnesota against the defendant and others in the amount of $39,402.78. This judgment was rendered by the district court of Ramsey County, Minnesota. On December 7, 1971, the plaintiff filed an action in the district court of Shawnee County based upon the Minnesota judgment. The Kansas court entered summary judgment in favor of the plaintiff on February 15, 1972, in the amount of $39,402.78 plus interest. On May 9, 1972, plaintiff attempted to levy execution on the property of the defendant but the execution was returned unsatisfied. Thereafter, no additional action was taken by plaintiff on that Kansas judgment, and it became dormant under the provisions of K.S.A. 60-2403. Plaintiff failed to revive that judgment within two years after the date the judgment became dormant as required by K.S.A. 60-2404.

On September 24, 1973, plaintiff received payment of the sum of $12,902.22 in partial satisfaction of the plaintiff's judgment from a trustee in bankruptcy appointed by a federal court in Minnesota. Thereafter, no further action was taken by the plaintiff upon its 1971 Minnesota judgment until May of 1981 when plaintiff initiated an action in the district court of Ramsey County, Minnesota, based upon the 1971 Minnesota judgment. The record shows that personal service in that action was made on the defendant in Shawnee County on May 12, 1981. On July 16, 1981, the district court of Ramsey County, Minnesota, entered a new judgment in favor of the plaintiff in the amount of $46,418.25 and costs. Thereafter, the plaintiff filed its 1981 Minnesota judgment in the district court of Shawnee County and proceeded to enforce the same in compliance with the Uniform Enforcement of Foreign Judgments Act (K.S.A. 60-3001 et seq.).

On April 27, 1982, the district court of Shawnee County entered judgment in favor of the plaintiff holding the 1981 Minnesota judgment to be properly filed and enforceable under the uniform act. The defendant * * * brought a timely appeal * * *."

The Kansas statute of limitations governing actions brought on foreign judgments is K.S.A. 60-511(5) which sets a period of limitation of five years for an action for relief not provided for otherwise in the article governing the statute of limitations. In passing, it should be noted that K.S.A. 60-16 provides that where the cause of action has arisen in another state and where the cause of action cannot be maintained thereon by reason of lapse of time, no action can be maintained in this state except in favor of one who is a resident of this state and who has held the cause of action from the time it accrued.

K.S.A. 60-2403 provides, in substance, that if execution shall not be sued out within five years from the date of any judgment rendered in any court of record of this state or within five years from the date of any order reviving such judgment or, if five years have intervened between the date of the last execution issued on any judgment and the time of suing out another writ of execution thereon, such judgment shall become dormant and shall cease to operate as a lien on the estate of the judgment debtor. When a judgment shall become dormant and shall so remain for a period of two years, it is the duty of the clerk of the court to release the judgment of record.

K.S.A. 60-2404 provides, in substance, that a dormant judgment may be revived within two years of the date on which such judgment became dormant. The holder is required to file a motion for a revivor and a request for the immediate issuance of an execution thereon if such motion is granted. As noted above, the judgment obtained by plaintiff in Shawnee County district court on February 15, 1972, became dormant and was not revived under the statutory provisions. In Kansas, under these statutes, a party may, by the issuance of an execution every five years, keep a judgment alive indefinitely. The judgment remains in force without execution for five years, and the plaintiff may revive it at any time within two years if it has become dormant thereafter, so that a plaintiff may neglect his judgment for seven years, lacking a day, and then revive it and put it in force for five years more. *Johnson Bros. Wholesale Liquor Co. v. Clemmons*, 233 Kan. 405, 661 P.2d 1242 (1983).

Should the judgment have been affirmed or reversed?

3. Vivian G. Carter (Vivian) and James Newman Carter (Newman) were divorced March 11, 1964, by final decree of the Circuit Court of Palm Beach County, Florida. In the final decree, the court ordered Newman to pay child support and awarded Vivian a judgment against him in the amount of $36,100, plus costs of $27 and counsel fees of $1,500. Although some child support payments were made, no payments were made on Vivian's judgment.

    When this judgment was entered, Florida law provided that a judgment became dormant three years after its rendition, and no execution could be issued thereafter unless and until the judgment was revived by writ of scire facias. In 1967, the Florida statutes were revised to provide that judgments would not become dormant but would continue to furnish the basis for the issuance of execution until barred by the 20-year statute of limitations affecting domestic judgments. The writ of scire facias thus became obsolete. Because the new legislation made no provision for judgments which had become dormant under the former law but which were not yet barred by the statute of limitations, the Supreme Court of Florida adopted Rule of Civil Procedure 1.100(d) providing for revival of a judgment by motion, after notice, in lieu of scire facias.

    Vivian's judgment became dormant under the former law in March 1967. In 1977, she filed a motion to revive judgment in lieu of scire facias in the Circuit Court of Palm Beach County. Both parties appeared by counsel. The court entered an order on August 26, 1977, reviving the 1964 judgment and ordering that execution issue thereon. Newman appealed the revival to the Florida Fourth District Court of Appeal, which affirmed the circuit court by order entered December 27, 1978.

    Vivian instituted this action in the trial court on July 23, 1981, seeking a Virginia judgment based on the Florida judgment. Newman pleaded the statute of limitations. Vivian relied upon documentary evidence in the record and a stipulation that interest on the Florida judgment accrued at an annual rate of 6%. The trial court sustained Newman's motion to strike the evidence, ruling that Vivian's right of action on the judgment was barred by the 10-year period of limitations of Code §8.01-252. * * * Vivian first argues that this statute should be construed to mean that a judgment "rendered" includes a judgment 'revived' so that her action on the 1964 judgment that she revived in 1977 will not be barred. * * * Vivian's alternative argument that Code §8.01-252 is unconstitutional as violative of the Full Faith and Credit and Equal Protection Clauses of the United States Constitution. *Carter v. Carter*, 232 Va. 166, 349 S.E.2d 95 (1986).

    How would you rule on the appeal?

4. A foreign judgment is not properly filed under the Uniform Enforcement of Foreign Judgments Act, and thus is without potency in the forum state, until the judgment is "authenticated" as prescribed by either federal or state law. Federal law provides:

The Acts of the legislature of any State, Territory, or Possession of the United States, or copies thereof, shall be authenticated by affixing the seal of such State, Territory, or Possession thereto.

The records and judicial proceedings of any court of any such State, Territory or Possession, or copies thereof, shall be proved or admitted in other courts within the United States and its Territories and Possessions by the attestation of the clerk and seal of the court annexed, if a seal exists, together with a certificate of the judge of the court that the said attestation is in proper form.

Such Acts, records and judicial proceedings or copies thereof, so authenticated, shall have the same full faith and credit in every court within the United States and its Territories and Possessions as they have by law or usage in the courts of such State, Territory or Possession from which they are taken.

28 U.S.C.A. §1738.

5. Federal law provides for the registration of federal court judgments. The law is as follows:

A judgment in an action for the recovery of money or property now or hereafter entered in any district court which has become final by appeal or expiration of time for appeal may be registered in any other district by filing therein a certified copy of such judgment. A judgment so registered shall have the same effect as a judgment of the district court of the district where registered and may be enforced in like manner.

A certified copy of the satisfaction of any judgment in whole or in part may be registered in like manner in any district in which the judgment is a lien.

28 U.S.C.A. §1963.

6. "Apart from possible treaties or federal common law, there is no compulsion on any American state to recognize or enforce judgments from foreign countries. An American court can deny effect to a foreign judgment because it does not like the kind of service employed even though the service was valid, or because the foreign judgment is on a cause of action that the forum court for any reason dislikes. If a real difference in social policy exists this result is justifiable, since it is possible that alien lands enforcing their own systems of law may render judgments on strange claims unknown to our law and contrary to our motives. This, however, would be unusual.

"Ordinarily American courts should give effect to foreign judgments, and refuse to do so only in extraordinary situations. *** Differences in strong public policy among civilized states today should not readily be found when judgments have been rendered under circumstances which satisfy our own basic concepts of due process of law.

"The Uniform Foreign Money-Judgments Recognition Act is not a reciprocal act, in that what American courts do under it is not made to depend on what foreign courts would do with comparable judgments from this country. Nor does it provide separate enforcement procedures, but prescribes only that foreign judgments shall be enforced in the same manner as judgments of sister states. Several types of judgments are excluded from the finality afforded by the act. These exclusions are judgments for taxes, fines or other penalties and for matrimonial and family support, judgments rendered under a judicial system which does not provide impartial tribunals, and judgments rendered by courts lacking jurisdiction, largely in a due process sense. The act also authorizes exercise of judicial discretion as to enforcement of foreign judgments in cases where notice to the defendant was unduly short, the foreign forum was seriously inconvenient to the defendant, the judgment was obtained by fraud, or the cause of action is repugnant to the public policy of the state in which enforcement is sought.

"General adoption of this act by the states will solve most of the uncertainties which now prevail in the area. If it is not generally adopted, two other avenues remain. One is the adoption of treaties between the United States and the nations of the world with which we engage in commerce. Such treaties would be 'the law of the land' in the United States. The other alternative would involve a holding that the recognition of foreign judgments is so much a federal question that it should become a matter of 'federal common law', as is already true of some other matters of international import." Robert A. Leflar, Luther L. McDougal, III & Robert L. Felix, AMERICAN CONFLICTS LAW §84 at 251-53 (4th ed. 1986).

For a bibliography of primary and secondary sources on the enforcement of foreign country judgments in the United States (inbound judgments), see Robert E. Lutz, *Enforcement of Judgments, Part I: A Selected Bibliography of U.S. Enforcement of Judgments Rendered Abroad*, 27 INT'L LAW. 471 (1993).

7. On the different matters of enforcing American judgments abroad, see Robert E. Lutz, *Enforcement of Judgments, Part II: A Selected Bibliography on Enforcement of U.S. Judgments in Foreign Countries*, 27 INT'L LAW. 1029 (1993).

□□□□□□

Uniform Interstate Family Support Act
National Conference of Commissioners on Uniform State
Laws and the American Law Institute, 1992

PREFATORY NOTE
I. BACKGROUND INFORMATION

Congressional legislation in 1975, 1984, and 1988 has had a major impact on state child support enforcement law, both substantive and procedural. Not only did Congress mandate that states adopt child support guidelines, but it also required the states to establish child support enforcement procedures such as wage withholding, tax intercepts, and credit reporting. In addition, federal law has begun to invade the area of substantive rules for child support; for example, the Bradley Amendment, adopted in 1986, prohibits retroactive reduction of a child support arrearage stemming from a court order.

To respond to these new developments, in 1988 the Conference established a Drafting Committee to review the Uniform Reciprocal Enforcement of Support Act (URESA) and its revised version (RURESA), and to adopt revisions to URESA or propose a free-standing act on the subject of child support enforcement. Some version of URESA or RURESA has been adopted in all states and therefore is familiar to people who work in this field. After reviewing the congressional legislation of the 1980's and the Model Interstate Income Withholding Act drafted in 1984 by the American Bar Association and the National Conference of State Legislatures, the Committee originally decided that the interstate aspects of child support enforcement could be adequately addressed through amendments to RURESA.

At the Conference's Annual Meeting in the summer of 1989, the Drafting Committee presented for first reading some limited initial changes to RURESA. Subsequently, after obtaining the views of numerous persons who are familiar with URESA, the Committee decided to revise the Act much more extensively, and presented those changes for another first reading at the Conference's 1990 Annual Meeting.

Following receipt of extensive comments at the 1990 Annual Meeting and from numerous groups and individuals, the Drafting Committee recommended, and the Executive Committee of the Conference decided, that final approval of the revised URESA should be delayed until the Conference's 1992 Annual Meeting because that timetable would coincide with the work of the U.S. Commission on Interstate Child Support. Throughout 1991 and 1992, the Drafting Committee continued to work on the Act, in conjunction with numerous knowledgeable Advisors and Observers, including five persons who also served as members of the U.S. Commission.

The Drafting Committee and Executive Committee determined that the Act should have a new name--the Uniform Interstate Family Support Act (UIFSA). This new Act is intended to completely revise and replace URESA and RURESA.

A description of the major changes proposed to be made in RURESA presented by UIFSA follows below.

* * *

A. In General

1. TERMINOLOGY. The terminology of URESA and RURESA has been retained as much as possible to ease the transition to the new act, i.e., "responding" and "initiating" state. One notable change is the substitution of the term "tribunal" for "court," in recognition of the fact that many states have created administrative agencies to establish, enforce, and modify child support.

2. REORGANIZATION. The Act has been reorganized into a more logical and understandable order than found in RURESA. The order in which civil and criminal proceedings are dealt with is reversed, which more accurately reflects the frequency and utility of those approaches. Within civil proceedings, separate articles have been created for provisions common to all types of actions (Article 3); for the establishment of support (Article 4); for the enforcement of a support order of another state without registration (Article 5); for the enforcement and modification of support orders after registration (Article 6); and for the determination of parentage (Article 7). In addition, new jurisdictional provisions (Article 2) establish uniform long-arm jurisdiction over nonresidents in order to facilitate one-state proceedings whenever possible.

3. RECIPROCITY NOT REQUIRED. Reciprocity of laws between states is no longer required because at present all states have quite similar laws, and the enacting state should enforce a support obligation irrespective of another state's law. Nonetheless, consistent with past practice URESA, RURESA and all substantially similar state laws are deemed equivalent to UIFSA for purposes of interstate actions (Section 101(7), (16)). This means that any of these acts can be used if different states have different versions in effect, which should help ease the transition to the new Act.

4. LONG-ARM JURISDICTION. The Act contains a broad provision for asserting long-arm jurisdiction to give the tribunals in the home state of the supported family the maximum possible opportunity to secure personal jurisdiction over an absent respondent (Section 201), thereby converting what otherwise would be a two-state proceeding into a one-state lawsuit. Where jurisdiction over a nonresident is obtained, the tribunal may obtain evidence, provide for discovery, and elicit testimony through use of the "information route" sections of the Act (Sections 202, 316 and 318).

B. Establishing a Support Order

1. FAMILY SUPPORT. The revision makes clear that the Act may be used only for proceedings involving the support of a child or spouse of the support obligor, and not to enforce other duties such as support of a parent (Sections 101(2), (18)). Under URESA child support and spousal support are treated identically. However, under UIFSA spousal support is modifiable in the

interstate context only after such a request is forwarded to the original issuing state from another state (Sections 205 and 206).

2. LOCAL LAW. URESA provides a somewhat complex choice of law for establishment of duties of support, i.e., the law of the state where the obligor was present for the period during which support is sought. Otherwise that Act generally refers to the law of the forum. The new Act provides that the procedures and law of the forum apply, with some significant additions or exceptions:

(a) Certain procedures are prescribed for interstate cases even if they are not consistent with local law, e.g., the contents of interstate petitions (Sections 311 and 602); the nondisclosure of certain sensitive information (Section 312); authority to award fees and costs including attorneys fees (Section 313); elimination of certain testimonial immunities (Section 314); and limits on the assertion of nonparentage as a defense to support enforcement (Section 315).

(b) Visitation issues cannot be raised in child support proceedings (Section 305(d)).

(c) Special rules for the interstate transmission of evidence and discovery are added to help place the maximum amount of information before the deciding tribunal. These procedures are available even in one-state cases in which the tribunal asserts long-arm jurisdiction over a nonresident (Sections 202, 316, and 318).

(d) The choice of law for the interpretation of registered orders is that of the state issuing the underlying support order. If there are different statutes of limitation for enforcement, however, the longer one applies (Section 604).

3. ONE-ORDER SYSTEM. Under the present URESA, the majority of support proceedings are de novo. Even when an existing order of one state is "registered" in a second state, the registering state often asserts the right to modify the registered order. This means that more than one valid support order can be in effect in more than one state. Under UIFSA, the principle of continuing, exclusive jurisdiction is introduced into the Act for the first time; this aims, so far as possible, to allow only one support order to be effective at any one time. This principle is carried out in Sections 204 (rules for resolving actions pending in two or more states); 205 and 206 (rules for determining which tribunal has continuing, exclusive jurisdiction over an order); 207 (reconciliation with orders issued before the effective date of the Act); and 208 (multiple orders for two or more families supported by the same obligor).

4. EFFICIENCY. A number of improvements are made to the former Act to streamline interstate proceedings:

(a) Proceedings may be initiated by or referred to administrative agencies rather than to courts in those states that use those agencies to establish support orders (Section 101(22)).

(b) Initiation of an interstate case in the initiating state is expressly made ministerial rather than a matter of court adjudication or review. Further, a party in the initiating state may file an action directly in the responding state (Section 301(c)).

(c) Forms which are federally mandated for use in certain interstate cases must be used in all interstate cases for transmission of information from the initiating to the responding state (Section 311(b)), and the information in those forms is declared to be admissible evidence (Section 316(b)).

(d) Authority is provided for the transmission of information and documents through electronic and other modern means of communication (Section 316(e)).

(e) A tribunal may permit an out-of-state party or witness to be deposed or to testify by telephone conference (Section 316(f)).

(f) Tribunals are required to cooperate in the discovery process for use in a tribunal in another state (Section 318).

(g) A tribunal and a support enforcement agency providing services to a supported family must keep the parties informed about all important developments in a case (Sections 305 and 307).

(h) A registered support order is confirmed and immediately enforceable unless the respondent files a written objection within 20 days after service and sustains that objection (Section 603 and 607).

5. PRIVATE ATTORNEYS. In support actions the Act explicitly authorizes parties to retain private legal counsel (Section 309), as well as to use the services of state support enforcement agency (Section 307(a)). It expressly takes no position on whether the support enforcement agency assisting a supported family establishes an attorney-client relationship with the applicant (Section 307(c)).

6. INTERSTATE PARENTAGE. UIFSA clearly authorizes establishment of parentage in an interstate proceeding, even if not coupled with a proceeding to establish support (Section 701).

C. Enforcing a Support Order

1. DIRECT ENFORCEMENT. The Act provides two direct enforcement procedures that do not require assistance from a tribunal. First, the support order may be mailed directly to an obligor's employer in another state (Section 501), which triggers wage withholding by that employer without the necessity of a hearing unless the employee objects. Second, the Act provides for direct administrative enforcement by the support enforcement agency of the obligor's state (Section 502).

2. REGISTRATION. The registration process of the Act is modeled after that procedure originated in RURESA, but is far more comprehensive. All judicial enforcement activity must begin with the registration of the existing support order in the responding state (Sections 601-604). However, the registered order continues to be the order of the issuing state, and the role of the responding state is limited to enforcing that order except in the very limited circumstances where modification is permitted (Sections 605-608).

D. Modifying a Support Order

1. REGISTRATION. A party (whether obligor or obligee) seeking to modify an existing child support order is directed to follow the identical procedure for registration as when enforcement is sought. Any combination sequence is allowable, e.g., registration for enforcement and later modification, or, contemporaneous modification and enforcement.

2. MODIFICATION LIMITED. Under RURESA most courts have held that a responding state can modify a support order for which enforcement has been sought. Except under narrowly defined fact circumstances, under the new Act the only tribunal that can modify a support order is the one having continuing, exclusive jurisdiction over the order. If the parties no longer reside in the issuing state, a tribunal with personal jurisdiction over both parties or with power given by agreement of the parties, has jurisdiction to modify (Sections 205, 206, 603(c), 609-612).

E. Parentage

It is not entirely clear whether RURESA provides for an interstate determination of parentage without also seeking establishment of support. UIFSA clearly states that interstate determination of parentage is authorized. It may be accomplished without an accompanying establishment of support, or in a contemporaneous manner to both determine parentage and establish support. The Act provides no substantive or procedural alterations to the existing law of the forum with regard to determination of parentage.
* * *

§501. Recognition of Income-Withholding Order of Another State.

(a) An income-withholding order issued in another state may be sent by first class mail to the person or entity defined as the obligor's employer under [the income-withholding law of this State] without first filing a [petition] or comparable pleading or registering the order with a tribunal of this State. Upon receipt of the order, the employer shall:

(1) treat an income-withholding order issued in another state which appears regular on its face as if it had been issued by a tribunal of this State;

(2) immediately provide a copy of the order to the obligor; and

(3) distribute the funds as directed in the withholding order.

(b) An obligor may contest the validity or enforcement of an income-withholding order issued in another state in the same manner as if the order had been issued by a tribunal of this State. Section 604 (Choice of Law) applies to the contest. The obligor shall give notice of the contest to any support enforcement agency providing services to the obligee and to:

(1) the person or agency designated to receive payments in the income-withholding order; or

(2) if no person or agency is designated, the obligee.

§502. Administrative Enforcement of Orders.

(a) A party seeking to enforce a support order or an income-withholding order, or both, issued by a tribunal of another state may send the documents required for registering the order to a support enforcement agency of this State.

(b) Upon receipt of the documents, the support enforcement agency, without initially seeking to register the order, shall consider and, if appropriate, use any administrative procedure authorized by the law of this State to enforce a support order or an income-withholding order, or both. If the obligor does not contest administrative enforcement, the order need not be registered. If the obligor contests the validity or administrative enforcement of the order, the support enforcement agency shall register the order pursuant to this [Act].

§601. Registration of Order for Enforcement.

A support order or an income-withholding order issued by a tribunal of another state may be registered in this State for enforcement.

§602. Procedure to Register Order for Enforcement.

(a) A support order or income-withholding order of another state may be registered in this State by sending the following documents and information to the [appropriate tribunal] in this State:

(1) a letter of transmittal to the tribunal requesting registration and enforcement;

(2) two copies, including one certified copy, of all orders to be registered, including any modification of an order;

(3) a sworn statement by the party seeking registration or a certified statement by the custodian of the records showing the amount of any arrearage;

(4) the name of the obligor and, if known:

(i) the obligor's address and social security number;

(ii) the name and address of the obligor's employer and any other source of income of the obligor; and

(iii) a description and the location of property of the obligor in this State not exempt from execution; and

(5) the name and address of the obligee and, if applicable, the agency or person to whom support payments are to be remitted.

(b) On receipt of a request for registration, the registering tribunal shall cause the order to be filed as a foreign judgment, together with one copy of the documents and information, regardless of their form.

(c) A [petition] or comparable pleading seeking a remedy that must be affirmatively sought under other law of this State may be filed at the same time as the request for registration or later. The pleading must specify the grounds for the remedy sought.

§603. Effect of Registration for Enforcement.

(a) A support order or income-withholding order issued in another state is registered when the order is filed in the registering tribunal of this State.

(b) A registered order issued in another state is enforceable in the same manner and is subject to the same procedures as an order issued by a tribunal of this State.

(c) Except as otherwise provided in this article, a tribunal of this State shall recognize and enforce, but may not modify, a registered order if the issuing tribunal had jurisdiction.

§604. Choice of Law.

(a) The law of the issuing state governs the nature, extent, amount, and duration of current payments and other obligations of support and the payment of arrearages under the order.

(b) In a proceeding for arrearages, the statute of limitation under the laws of this State or of the issuing state, whichever is longer, applies.

§605. Notice of Registration of Order.

(a) When a support order or income-withholding order issued in another state is registered, the registering tribunal shall notify the nonregistering party. Notice must be given by first class, certified, or registered mail or by any means of personal service authorized by the law of this State. The notice must be accompanied by a copy of the registered order and the documents and relevant information accompanying the order.

(b) The notice must inform the nonregistering party:

(1) that a registered order is enforceable as of the date of registration in the same manner as an order issued by a tribunal of this State;

(2) that a hearing to contest the validity or enforcement of the registered order must be requested within [20] days after the date of mailing or personal service of the notice;

(3) that failure to contest the validity or enforcement of the registered order in a timely manner will result in confirmation of the order and enforcement of the order and the alleged arrearages and precludes further contest of that order with respect to any matter that could have been asserted;   and

(4) of the amount of any alleged arrearages.

(c) Upon registration of an income-withholding order for enforcement, the registering tribunal shall notify the obligor's employer pursuant to [the income-withholding law of this State].

§606. Procedure to Contest Validity or Enforcement of Registered Order.

(a) A nonregistering party seeking to contest the validity or enforcement of a registered order in this State shall request a hearing within [20] days after the date of mailing or personal service of notice of the registration.   The nonregistering party may seek to vacate the registration, to assert any defense to an allegation of noncompliance with the registered order, or to contest the remedies being sought or the amount of any alleged arrearages pursuant to Section 607 (Contest of Registration or Enforcement).

(b) If the nonregistering party fails to contest the validity or enforcement of the registered order in a timely manner, the order is confirmed by operation of law.

(c) If a nonregistering party requests a hearing to contest the validity or enforcement of the registered order, the registering tribunal shall schedule the matter for hearing and give notice to the parties by first class mail of the date, time, and place of the hearing.

§607. Contest of Registration or Enforcement.

(a) A party contesting the validity or enforcement of a registered order or seeking to vacate the registration has the burden of proving one or more of the following defenses:

(1) the issuing tribunal lacked personal jurisdiction over the contesting party;

(2) the order was obtained by fraud;

(3) the order has been vacated, suspended, or modified by a later order;

(4) the issuing tribunal has stayed the order pending appeal;

(5) there is a defense under the law of this State to the remedy sought;

(6) full or partial payment has been made; or

(7) the statute of limitation under Section 604 (Choice of Law) precludes enforcement of some or all of the arrearages.

(b) If a party presents evidence establishing a full or partial defense under subsection (a), a tribunal may stay enforcement of the registered order, continue the proceeding to permit production of additional relevant evidence, and issue other appropriate orders. An uncontested portion of the registered order may be enforced by all remedies available under the law of this State.

(c) If the contesting party does not establish a defense under subsection (a) to the validity or enforcement of the order, the registering tribunal shall issue an order confirming the order.

§608. Confirmed Order.

Confirmation of a registered order, whether by operation of law or after notice and hearing, precludes further contest of the order with respect to any matter that could have been asserted at the time of registration.

    * * *

Jo Anne B. Barnhart, *The Federal Office of Child Support Enforcement: Strengthening and Supporting State Programs*
11 Del. Law. 57 (Summer 1993)

During the last decade, federal social policy has placed increasing emphasis on family self sufficiency. The passage of the Family Support Act ("FSA") in

1988 brought new mandates and opportunities for reinforcing the importance of helping families become self sufficient. Among the many provisions included in the FSA were major enhancements of the Child Support Enforcement Program. The new requirements built on the Child Support Enforcement legislation passed in 1984 and 1988, which mandated that all states adopt proven techniques to improve, simplify, and otherwise strengthen methods of securing child support and establishing paternity.

An ever increasing legislative resolve at both federal and state levels to improve the collection of child support payments has led the Federal Office of Child Support Enforcement ("OCSE") to innovative guidelines for setting the amount of support awards, simplified administrative methods of acknowledging paternity, the swifter securing and enforcement of orders, and the use of effective enforcement techniques such as wage withholding and reporting support debts to credit bureaus.

To draft, pass, and enforce better child support statutes and to apply more effective practices takes time, but after eight years of collegial cooperation the national government and the states are beginning to reap the benefits of these stronger laws.

In aiding the states, OCSE delivers a variety of services to strengthen and support state programs. OCSE provides locator services, coordinates tax offset services with the IRS, conducts and contracts out research and demonstration projects, and provides training and technical assistance.

    * * *

There are many other federal services to help states improve their child support programs, including the Federal Parent Locator Service, a computerized national location network operated by OCSE. The locator service has access to addresses and Social Security numbers from the Internal Revenue Service and such other federal agencies as Social Security Administration, National Personnel Records Center, the Department of Defense, the Department of Veterans Affairs, the Selective Service System, and state employment security agencies.

These agencies make the most current information available to the locator service, which then furnishes addresses and information to state and local agencies to locate absent parents and to establish or enforce child support orders.

The locator service has recently developed cross-matches on interstate cases with individual state employment security agency databases. Because accurate Social Security numbers are essential in locating absent parents, OCSE is also instituting a new Social Security Number verification system.

The Federal Office also acts as an intermediary between the Internal Revenue Office and the states in offsetting Federal income tax refunds of absent parents who have accumulated arrearages. States submit cases for offset to the Federal Office, which certifies and formats them and sends them on to the IRS. The money successfully intercepted by the IRS is then distributed to the states. As of July 1992 933,818 cases had been offset for over $619 million, up from

$503 million, or a 23 percent increase for the same period for 1991. The average amounts offset are $645 for AFDC cases and $718 for Non-AFDC cases.

The Federal Office also assists the states in developing statewide automated systems. Currently nine states have fully certified operational systems; twelve are in the final stages preliminary to full operation; eleven are in the transfer/development phase, and the remaining eighteen are in the planning phase.

The Federal Office is developing a national Child Support Enforcement Network ("CSENet") that will improve communications and expedite interstate case processing. CSENet will enable all types of interstate case information, including location data, to flow between the states' automated child support systems.

The Federal Office is conducting a pilot project in the use of Electronic Funds Transfer/Electronic Data Interchange for immediate wage withholding. The four participating states are Delaware, Iowa, Nebraska, and New York. The interchange should make wage withholding convenient and quick for employers. The money would follow an electronic transfer from the bank of the employer to the bank of the state or local child support agency, and from there to the custodial parent's bank.

The Federal Office and the Health Care Financing Administration have reviewed the medical support program in 31 states. The reviews emphasized the discrete functional responsibilities of agencies engaged in the medical support process (Medicaid, Child Support Enforcement, AFDC, and Foster Case), such as cooperation and timely information exchange. Generally, the reviews found gaps and inconsistencies, and showed that a need for improved cooperation and swifter exchange of information.

As a result of these reviews, federal regional offices are providing state child support programs with technical assistance designed to improve program performance. In addition, the Federal Office is in the initial stages of developing written products, which will address such issues as line worker training, best practices, and demonstrating to state executives and legislators the benefits of medical support.

The Federal Office is also helping states improve the application process for non-AFDC parents by questioning whether applications forms as now structured in many states create unnecessary barriers to seeking child support. The Office has developed a best practice guide to help states redesign these forms.

The Federal Office has assisted states in improving allocation of personnel by providing technical assistance derived from an Office manual and videotape entitled "Designing a Model Child Support Enforcement Program: A Resource Allocation Workbook." The Office also assists states in improving enforcement through the use of revised and automated standardized interstate forms.

The Federal Office, recognizing the importance of training, has recently reorganized to place greater emphasis on instruction by creating the National Training Center. The Center develops and conducts workshops for state trainers and serves as a resource for states in obtaining state developed materials and courses.

In September 1991, the Federal Office held the first National Child Support Enforcement Training Workshop for state trainers. Representatives from 29 states attended the three- day session, which was devoted to training trainers, locating non-custodial parents, applying effective enforcement techniques, and engaging medical support. A second workshop for state agency training personnel held in September 1992 concentrated on the collaboration among the Child Support Enforcement, AFDC, and JOBS programs and improving interstate enforcement. State agencies evidenced their commitment by their overwhelming participation and their willingness to attend at their own expense. In April and May of 1992, the Federal Office conducted two sessions of a course entitled "Training of Trainers in Child Support Enforcement."

The Federal Office is now working to identify and promote best practices found in state programs. For example, it is publicizing the efforts of several states to establish paternity in the hospital at the time of birth.

The Child Support Report is a monthly newsletter sent to 15,000 members of the child support enforcement community, promoting efficient operations and management.

The Federal Office has been, above all, committed to changing society's perceptions of child support. The Office has worked to elevate the issues of child support and parental responsibility in the public eye so that non-support of children will be deemed a serious offense -- as well as a burden on taxpayers. To foster this public attitude, the Office recently invited a representative from Mothers Against Drunk Driving ("MADD") to attend a national child support conference. The MADD representative shared strategies that had proven effective in making drinking and driving socially unacceptable.

Recognizing the importance of accurate data in measuring program success, the Federal Office has developed an initiative, Measuring Excellency Through Statistics, which is designed to improve the accuracy of state-submitted data about IV-D programs. This is a continuing initiative, which covers both interstate and intrastate data collection. It includes:

- developing a new design for the annual report to Congress and developing a new periodic report stressing achievements that will help states to promote their programs.
- simplifying and clarifying reporting form instructions to ensure consistency among state reports and dropping unnecessary reporting requirements.
- establishing new reporting requirements to coincide with state systems development.

Another tool for measuring progress and an individual state's compliance with federal law is the Child Support Audit. Through the audit process the

Federal Office has been able to identify problems and deficiencies in state programs. Identification of state failures to achieve substantial compliance with program requirements has been the impetus for them to improve their program performance. Many states have come into compliance with Federal requirements during a corrective action period following an audit. In addition audits help state and local child support agencies focus attention and obtain additional needed resources from state executive and legislative decision-makers.

OCSE audit findings have been upheld at Departmental Appeals Board and Federal District Court levels in all but one challenge, in which the determination was based on a statistical sampling technicality.

While much has been accomplished in child support enforcement and while many families are better off today as a result of these accomplishments, an important question is: What is on the horizon for child support enforcement?

One indication of where the country is headed can be found in the Commission on Interstate Child Support's, "Blueprint for Reform," which was released on August 4, 1992. The Commission's recommendations call for far-reaching improvements affecting both interstate and intrastate child support issues. The Commission recommendations include:

- keeping the state-based programs, but strengthening them by mandating proven techniques for establishing paternity, for enforcement, and for providing adequate resources and training.
- improving state ability to locate noncustodial parents and their assets, to establish paternity through simple acknowledgement procedures at hospitals or in administrative hearings, and to minimize interstate cases by reaching across state lines to establish paternity and secure support.
- a national system for the reporting of new hirings, using a revised W-4 form. New employees would report support obligations on W-4's, which would be matched against a state-based central registry of orders. I believe that targeting employer reporting in some manner (for example by selected industries), rather than requiring all employers to report, would allow for a more efficient use of time and money. This process would eliminate delays in finding those who owe support and would hasten wage withholding. States would also be allowed to initiate withholding with employers in other states directly, thus avoiding delays associated with communications between state agencies.
- enhancing and linking state and federal location sources to allow easy, expeditious access to information across state lines. Such a link would be easily accomplished by expanding (CSENet), described above. CSENet is expected to improve communication and expedite interstate case processing.

- paternity establishment, using state experience in hospital-based paternity acknowledgement and expedited and administrative procedures. At least half the states have these advancements in place or have them under consideration.
- requiring all states to adopt the Uniform Interstate Family Support Act ("UIFSA"). UIFSA is a model act developed by the National Conference of Commissioners of Uniform State Laws that outlines how states should handle child support cases when the parties live in different states. Adoption of UIFSA by all states would standardize interstate case processing and limit the need for interstate activity whenever possible. UIFSA's predecessor, the Uniform Reciprocal Enforcement of Support Act or URESA, was revised numerous times, and different states have adopted different versions, which significantly complicate interstate cases today. UIFSA would be a straightforward and effective remedy for solving interstate problems.

Other interesting approaches to child support enforcement are emerging in a number of states. Since its inception child support has operated through cooperative agreements. The states have agreements with district attorneys, collection agencies, sheriffs' offices, courts, lawyers, etc. to run different parts of the program. Recently, however, faced with budget cuts in many states, more and more legislatures are searching for ways to cut state costs. Many of them are looking to private companies to provide child support services. For example, Tennessee has now privatized two of its judicial districts. In March 1992 they were faced with a District Attorney who refused to renew a contract to continue providing child support services because he did not think he could meet new federal program standards. As a result, the state contracted with a private contractor. Progress to date has been beyond expectations. In the first seven months total collections were up 37 percent (AFDC 41 percent and non-AFDC 36 percent) over the same period in the previous year.

Privatization is clearly on the forefront of emerging enforcement techniques. At the two largest child support conferences in 1992 programs about privatization drew capacity audiences. Increasingly state legislatures allocate funding without staff, thus promoting the move toward privatization of collections.

For the past 17 years we have committed significant federal, state, and local funding and substantially strengthened efforts to address the ever-increasing problem of nonsupport. Fortunately child support continues to be an urgent issue. Creative child support professionals at state and local levels persist in seeking new ways to increase paternity establishment and support collections. The Federal Office of Child Support Enforcement complements state efforts by developing more accurate methods for measuring and documenting program accomplishments, by new techniques for providing technical assistance, and by insuring a strong national commitment to making family self sufficiency a reality.

Problem

Jean and John were happily married in Wisconsin for several many years but they recently divorced. Jean applied to the local family aid office to receive child support from John, and the local county attorney petitioned the court on Jean's behalf. The court authorized the payments but John moved to Minnesota. So, the Wisconsin family aid agency wrote to John's Minnesota employer and demanded that the employer pay the child support out of John's salary. What result in the absence of UIFSA? What result under the UIFSA?

F. EXECUTING PRIVATE JUDGMENTS (ENFORCING ARBITRATION)

Uniform Arbitration Act
Uniform Laws Annotated, 1955 Act

§1. Validity of Arbitration Agreement.

A written agreement to submit any existing controversy to arbitration or a provision in a written contract to submit to arbitration any controversy thereafter arising between the parties is valid, enforceable and irrevocable, save upon such grounds as exist at law or in equity for the revocation of any contract. This act also applies to arbitration agreements between employers and employees or between their respective representatives [unless otherwise provided in the agreement].

§2. Proceedings to Compel or Stay Arbitration.

(a) On application of a party showing an agreement described in Section 1, and the opposing party's refusal to arbitrate, the Court shall order the parties to proceed with arbitration, but if the opposing party denies the existence of the agreement to arbitrate, the Court shall proceed summarily to the determination of the issue so raised and shall order arbitration if found for the moving party, otherwise, the application shall be denied.

(b) On application, the court may stay an arbitration proceeding commenced or threatened on a showing that there is no agreement to arbitrate. Such an issue, when in substantial and bona fide dispute, shall be forthwith and summarily tried and the stay ordered if found for the moving party. If found for the opposing party, the court shall order the parties to proceed to arbitration.

(c) If an issue referable to arbitration under the alleged agreement is involved in an action or proceeding pending in a court having jurisdiction to hear applications under subdivision (a) of this Section, the application shall be made therein. Otherwise and subject to Section 18, the application may be made in any court of competent jurisdiction.

(d) Any action or proceeding involving an issue subject to arbitration shall be stayed if an order for arbitration or an application therefor has been made under this section or, if the issue is severable, the stay may be with respect thereto only. When the application is made in such action or proceeding, the order for arbitration shall include such stay.

(e) An order for arbitration shall not be refused on the ground that the claim in issue lacks merit or bona fides or because any fault or grounds for the claim sought to be arbitrated have not been shown.

§3. Appointment of Arbitrators by Court.

If the arbitration agreement provides a method of appointment of arbitrators, this method shall be followed. In the absence thereof, or if the agreed method fails or for any reason cannot be followed, or when an arbitrator appointed fails or is unable to act and his successor has not been duly appointed, the court on application of a party shall appoint one or more arbitrators. An arbitrator so appointed has all the powers of one specifically named in the agreement.

§4. Majority Action by Arbitrators.

The powers of the arbitrators may be exercised by a majority unless otherwise provided by the agreement or by this act.

§5. Hearing.

Unless otherwise provided by the agreement:

(a) The arbitrators shall appoint a time and place for the hearing and cause notification to the parties to be served personally or by registered mail not less than five days before the hearing. Appearance at the hearing waives such notice. The arbitrators may adjourn the hearing from time to time as necessary and, on request of a party and for good cause, or upon their own motion may postpone the hearing to a time not later than the date fixed by the agreement for making the award unless the parties consent to a later date. The arbitrators may hear and determine the controversy upon the evidence produced notwithstanding the failure of a party duly notified to appear. The court on application may direct the arbitrators to proceed promptly with the hearing and determination of the controversy.

(b) The parties are entitled to be heard, to present evidence material to the controversy and to cross-examine witnesses appearing at the hearing.

(c) The hearing shall be conducted by all the arbitrators but a majority may determine any question and render a final award. If, during the course of the hearing, an arbitrator for any reason ceases to act, the remaining arbitrator or arbitrators appointed to act as neutrals may continue with the hearing and determination of the controversy.

§6. Representation by Attorney.

A party has the right to be represented by an attorney at any proceeding or hearing under this act. A waiver thereof prior to the proceeding or hearing is ineffective.

§7. Witnesses, Subpoenas, Depositions.

(a) The arbitrators may issue (cause to be issued) subpoenas for the attendance of witnesses and for the production of books, records, documents and other evidence, and shall have the power to administer oaths. Subpoenas so issued shall be served, and upon application to the Court by a party or the arbitrators, enforced, in the manner provided by law for the service and enforcement of subpoenas in a civil action.

(b) On application of a party and for use as evidence, the arbitrators may permit a deposition to be taken, in the manner and upon the terms designated by the arbitrators, of a witness who cannot be subpoenaed or is unable to attend the hearing.

(c) All provisions of law compelling a person under subpoena to testify are applicable.

(d) Fees for attendance as a witness shall be the same as for a witness in the .... Court.

§8. Award.

(a) The award shall be in writing and signed by the arbitrators joining in the award. The arbitrators shall deliver a copy to each party personally or by registered mail, or as provided in the agreement.

(b) An award shall be made within the time fixed therefor by the agreement or, if not so fixed, within such time as the court orders on application of a party. The parties may extend the time in writing either before or after the expiration thereof. A party waives the objection that an award was not made within the time required unless he notifies the arbitrators of his objection prior to the delivery of the award to him.

§9. Change of Award by Arbitrators.

On application of a party or, if an application to the court is pending under Sections 11, 12 or 13, on submission to the arbitrators by the court under such conditions as the court may order, the arbitrators may modify or correct the award upon the grounds stated in paragraphs (1) and (3) of subdivision (a) of Section 13, or for the purpose of clarifying the award. The application shall be made within twenty days after delivery of the award to the applicant. Written notice thereof shall be given forthwith to the opposing party, stating he must serve his objections thereto, if any, within ten days from the notice. The award so modified or corrected is subject to the provisions of Sections 11, 12 and 13.

§10. Fees and Expenses of Arbitration.

Unless otherwise provided in the agreement to arbitrate, the arbitrators' expenses and fees, together with other expenses, not including counsel fees, incurred in the conduct of the arbitration, shall be paid as provided in the award.

§11. Confirmation of an Award.

Upon application of a party, the Court shall confirm an award, unless within the time limits hereinafter imposed grounds are urged for vacating or modifying or correcting the award, in which case the court shall proceed as provided in Sections 12 and 13.

§12. Vacating an Award.

(a) Upon application of a party, the court shall vacate an award where:

(1) The award was procured by corruption, fraud or other undue means;

(2) There was evident partiality by an arbitrator appointed as a neutral or corruption in any of the arbitrators or misconduct prejudicing the rights of any party;

(3) The arbitrators exceeded their powers;

(4) The arbitrators refused to postpone the hearing upon sufficient cause being shown therefor or refused to hear evidence material to the controversy or otherwise so conducted the hearing, contrary to the provisions of Section 5, as to prejudice substantially the rights of a party; or

(5) There was no arbitration agreement and the issue was not adversely determined in proceedings under Section 2 and the party did not participate in the arbitration hearing without raising the objection; but the fact that the relief was such that it could not or would not be granted by a court of law or equity is not ground for vacating or refusing to confirm the award.

(b) An application under this Section shall be made within ninety days after delivery of a copy of the award to the applicant, except that, if predicated upon corruption, fraud or other undue means, it shall be made within ninety days after such grounds are known or should have been known.

(c) In vacating the award on grounds other than stated in clause (5) of Subsection (a) the court may order a rehearing before new arbitrators chosen as provided in the agreement, or in the absence thereof, by the court in accordance with Section 3, or if the award is vacated on grounds set forth in clauses (3) and (4) of Subsection (a) the court may order a rehearing before the arbitrators who made the award or their successors appointed in accordance with Section 3. The time within which the agreement requires the award to be made is applicable to the rehearing and commences from the date of the order.

(d) If the application to vacate is denied and no motion to modify or correct the award is pending, the court shall confirm the award. As amended Aug. 1956.

§13. Modification or Correction of Award.

(a) Upon application made within ninety days after delivery of a copy of the award to the applicant, the court shall modify or correct the award where:

(1) There was an evident miscalculation of figures or an evident mistake in the description of any person, thing or property referred to in the award;

(2) The arbitrators have awarded upon a matter not submitted to them and the award may be corrected without affecting the merits of the decision upon the issues submitted; or

(3) The award is imperfect in a matter of form, not affecting the merits of the controversy.

(b) If the application is granted, the court shall modify and correct the award so as to effect its intent and shall confirm the award as so modified and corrected. Otherwise, the court shall confirm the award as made.

(c) An application to modify or correct an award may be joined in the alternative with an application to vacate the award.

§14. Judgment or Decree on Award.

Upon the granting of an order confirming, modifying or correcting an award, judgment or decree shall be entered in conformity therewith and be enforced as any other judgment or decree. Costs of the application and of the proceedings subsequent thereto, and disbursements may be awarded by the court.

§15. Judgment Roll, Docketing.

(a) On entry of judgment or decree, the clerk shall prepare the judgment roll consisting, to the extent filed, of the following:

(1) The agreement and each written extension of the time within which to make the award;

(2) The award;

(3) A copy of the order confirming, modifying or correcting the award; and

(4) A copy of the judgment or decree.

(b) The judgment or decree may be docketed as if rendered in an action.

§16. Applications to Court.

Except as otherwise provided, an application to the court under this act shall be by motion and shall be heard in the manner and upon the notice provided by law or rule of court for the making and hearing of motions. Unless the parties have agreed otherwise, notice of an initial application for an order shall be served in the manner provided by law for the service of a summons in an action.

§17. Court, Jurisdiction.

The term "court" means any court of competent jurisdiction of this State. The making of an agreement described in Section 1 providing for arbitration in this State confers jurisdiction on the court to enforce the agreement under this Act and to enter judgment on an award thereunder.

§18. Venue.

An initial application shall be made to the court of the [county] in which the agreement provides the arbitration hearing shall be held or, if the hearing has been held, in the county in which it was held. Otherwise the application shall be made in the [county] where the adverse party resides or has a place of business or, if he has no residence or place of business in this State, to the court of any [county]. All subsequent applications shall be made to the court hearing the initial application unless the court otherwise directs.

§19. Appeals.

(a) An appeal may be taken from:

(1) An order denying an application to compel arbitration made under Section 2;

(2) An order granting an application to stay arbitration made under Section 2(b);

(3) An order confirming or denying confirmation of an award;

(4) An order modifying or correcting an award;

(5) An order vacating an award without directing a rehearing; or

(6) A judgment or decree entered pursuant to the provisions of this act.

(b) The appeal shall be taken in the manner and to the same extent as from orders or judgments in a civil action.

      * * *

Mewbourne Oil Co. v. Blackburn
Court of Appeals of Texas, Amarillo, 1990
793 S.W.2d 735

[S]ince the contracting parties agreed in writing to arbitrate their contractual disputes, the dispute concerning the performance of the contracts does not affect the validity of the arbitration agreement. Merrill Lynch v. Longoria, 783 S.W.2d 229, 230-31 (Tex.App.--Corpus Christi 1989, orig. proceeding). Then, Mewbourne's claim that Transwestern breached and repudiated the contracts does not preclude the right to arbitration provided by the contracts, USX Corp. v. West, 759 S.W.2d 764, 767 (Tex.App.--Houston [1st Dist.] 1988, orig. proceeding); instead, the claim merely presents issues to be determined by the arbitrators, not by the trial court.

Park Imperial, Inc. v. E. L. Farmer Construction Co., Inc.
Court of Appeals of Arizona, 1969
9 Ariz.App. 511, 513-14, 454 P.2d 181, 183-84

Generally, in the absence of fraud or mistake the action of an arbiter empowered by a contract or statute to construe and determine its conditions is final and conclusive upon the parties. United States v. Ellis, 2 Ariz. 253, 14 P.

300 (1887): 'It is well settled law that the award of an arbitrator in a matter properly submitted to arbitration is final and conclusive, unless it be shown that the arbitrator was guilty of fraud, misconduct, or such gross mistake as would imply bad faith or failure to exercise an honest judgment. (citations omitted) Generally speaking, a valid award of the arbitrator in the matter submitted to him is given the same effect as a valid judgment.' Albert v. Albert, 391 S.W.2d 186, 188, Tex.Civ.App., (1965).

Were the trial court required to try each case de novo the reason for arbitration agreements would be nugatory: 'Were we empowered to view the matter De novo, we would find much to persuade in the arguments advanced by the dissenting arbitrator. But as respondent recognizes, the court's function in confirming or vacating an arbitration award is severely limited. If it were otherwise, the ostensible purpose for resort to arbitration, i.e., avoidance of litigation, would be frustrated.' Amicizia Societa Nav. v. Chilean Nitrate & Iodine S. Corp., 2 Cir., 274 F.2d 805, 808 (1960). In the instant case the person objecting to the award had the burden of making an 'adequate showing' to the trial court wherein the award should be set aside. This Court on appeal is bound to view the action of the trial court in a light most favorable to upholding the trial court's determination, just as the trial court was required to view the arbitration award in a light most favorable to upholding the said award: '* * * A party seeking to set aside an arbitration award on account of error has the burden to affirmatively establish the existence of such error and the fact that it was prejudicial.' Franz v. Inter-Insurance Exchange of Auto. Club of So. Cal., 229 Cal.App.2d 269, 40 Cal.Rptr. 218, 221 (1964).

In the instant case there was a binding arbitration agreement in the contract. A reading of the testimony before the arbitration board and the trial court leads us to the conclusion that there was no abuse of discretion on the part of the trial court in refusing to set aside the award of arbitration.

Questions

1. Is an arbitration agreement enforceable that consists of a clause buried in a standard-form contract nobody actually reads? An example might be a sentence in a deposit agreement with a bank that a customer signs when she opens a checking account. The sentence essentially provides that any complaint by the customer regarding the bank's handling of the account shall be decided by arbitration. Suppose the sentence gives the bank the option of having the complaint decided in court or by arbitration.

2. Suppose the contract between A and B provides that any dispute "arising hereunder" shall be arbitrated. B believes A breached the contract and files suit in state court. How should A respond?

3. What happens if B sues A for tort based on conduct leading to the contract or conduct in performing the contract? For defamation because A got mad and spread tacky rumors about B?

4. What is the source of the procedural rules and other details that govern the conduct of arbitration proceedings?

5. What are the costs of arbitration, how much do they total, and who pays them?

6. Suppose that a dispute between A and B is handled by arbitration. The arbitrator decides for B. Under what circumstances can A appeal? Specifically, can she appeal simply because she is dissatisfied with the decision? Because the arbitrator misapplied the law? Because the arbitration clause provides for appeal?

7. If the arbitrator decides that A owes B money, what are B's remedies to collect the sum?

8. Is an arbitrator limited to awarding damages or can she give other legal or equitable relief?

9. As a general matter, would you advise creditor clients to agree to arbitrate? Same answer for debtor clients?

10. As a general matter, what are the effects of arbitration on lawyering?

American Arbitration Association, A Guide to Arbitration for Business People (1993)

Administrative Fees

The AAA's administrative fees are based on service charges. There is a filing fee based on the amount of the claim or counterclaim, ranging from $500 on claims below $10,000 to a maximum of $5,000 for claims in excess of $1 million. In addition, there are service charges for hearings held and postponements and a processing fee for prolonged cases. This fee information allows the parties to exercise control over their administrative fees. The fees cover AAA administrative services; they do not cover arbitrator compensation or expenses, if any, reporting services, or any postaward charges incurred by the parties in enforcing the award.

The following charges are based on filing and service fees. Arbi trator compensation, if any, is not included in this schedule. Unless the parties agree otherwise, arbitrator compensation and administra tive fees are subject to allocation by the arbitrator in the award.

Filing Fees

A non-refundable filing fee is payable in full by a filing party when a claim, counterclaim or additional claim is filed, as provided below.

Amount of Claim	Filing Fee
Up to $10,000	$500
Above $10,000 to $50,000	$750
Above $50,000 to $250,000	$1,500
Above $250,000 to $500,000	$3,000
Above $500,000 to $1,000,000	$4,000
Above $1 million	$5,000

When no amount can be stated at the time of filing, the minimum filing fee is $1,500, subject to increase when the claim or counterclaim is disclosed.

When a claim or counterclaim is not for a monetary amount, an appropriate filing fee will be determined by the AAA.

The minimum filing fee for any case having three or more arbitrators is $1,500.

Expedited Procedures, outlined in sections 5357 of the rules, are applied in any case where no disclosed claim or counterclaim exceeds $50,000, exclusive of interest and arbitration costs. Under those procedures, arbitrators are directly appointed by the AAA. Where the parties request a list of proposed arbitrators under those procedures, a service charge of $150 will be payable by each party.

Hearing Fees

For each day of hearing held before a single arbitrator, an administrative fee of $150 is payable by each party.

For each day of hearing held before a multiarbitrator panel, an administrative fee of $200 is payable by each party.

There is no hearing fee for the initial hearing in cases administered under the Expedited Procedures.

Postponement/Cancellation Fees

A fee of $150 is payable by a party causing a postponement of any hearing scheduled before a single arbitrator.

A fee of $200 is payable by a party causing a postponement of any hearing scheduled before a multiarbitrator panel.

Processing Fees

On single-arbitrator cases, a processing fee of $150 per party is payable 180 days after the case is initiated, and every 90 days there after, until the case is withdrawn or settled or the hearings are closed by the arbitrator.

On multi-arbitrator cases, a processing fee of $200 per party is payable 180 days after the case is initiated, and every 90 days there after, until the case is withdrawn or settled or the hearings are closed by the arbitrators.

Suspension for Nonpayment

If arbitrator compensation or administrative charges have not been paid in full, the AAA may so inform the parties in order that one of them may advance the required payment. If such payments are not made, the arbitrator may order the suspension or termination of the proceedings. If no arbitrator has yet been appointed, the AAA may suspend the proceedings.

Hearing Room Rental

The Hearing Fees described above do not cover the rental of hearing rooms, which are available on a rental basis. Check with our local office for availability and rates.

The American Arbitration Association

The AAA provides services in administration of arbitration, educational programs, and publications as well as research into the uses of arbitration for settling all types of dispute.

* * *

Unit 2

SPECIAL COLLECTION RIGHTS CREATED BY CONTRACT -- UCC ARTICLE 9 SECURED TRANSACTIONS

UNIT CONTENTS

A. ARTICLE 9 ROAD MAP

Uniform Commercial Code Article 9 governs most consensual liens on personal property or fixtures. "Governs" means that the statute is the primary source of law on the issues addressed by the statute. Article 9 addresses virtually all issues related to consensual liens within its scope, including: how such a lien is created; when and how the creditor can enforce it against the debtor, i.e., seize the property subject to the lien; and the priority of the lien in relation to third parties' claims to the property.

Article 9 invents its own extensive vocabulary of terms that describe secured transactions, and the Code's peculiar definitions of these terms must be read into every provision where the terms appear. So start learning, right now, Article 9's terminology. The most fundamentally important term in Article 9 is *security interest*, U.C.C. §1-201(37), which in essence is the Code's name for a consensual lien on personal property or fixtures. The person in whose favor a security interest exists is a *secured party*. U.C.C. §9-105(1)(m). The property subject to a security interest is the *collateral*. U.C.C. §9-105(1)(c).

The formal definition of "security interest" is "an interest in personal property or fixtures which secures payment or performance of an obligation." U.C.C. §1-201(37) (first sentence). A person is attempting to create a security interest whenever she purports to give someone else *any kind of claim*, however labeled, to personal property or fixtures so that the property can be seized in satisfaction of an *obligation of any kind*. Whether the attempt succeeds or fails is determined by Article 9 because it generally governs security interests, U.C.C. §9-102(1), and addresses through §9-203(1) the issue how a security interest in personal property or fixtures is created.

U.C.C. §9-203(1) lists four prerequisites to the creation of a security interest. First, there must always be a security agreement between the debtor and the creditor, U.C.C. §9-203(1)(a), which is not surprising inasmuch as Article 9 deals with *consensual* liens. A security agreement is the bargain of the debtor and creditor that provides for a security interest. U.C.C. §§9-105(1)(*l*); 1-201(3). The essence of a security agreement is the debtor's consent to the creditor having a security interest in whatever property the parties have agreed will serve as collateral. The second prerequisite to the creation of a security interest is that the security agreement must be in writing, U.C.C. §9-203(1)(a), except when the secured party takes possession of the collateral. The writing must describe the collateral and be signed by the debtor. Third, value must have been given. U.C.C. §9-203(1)(b). Value is broader than, and subsumes, common-law consideration.

U.C.C. §1-201(44). Fourth and finally, the debtor must have rights in the collateral. U.C.C. §9-203(1)(c). Whether and when a debtor acquires rights in collateral is not determined by Article 9. These issues are decided by the law that governs the debtor's connection or claim to the collateral.

These four events can occur in any order, but no security interest is created unless, and until, all four events concur. For example, suppose that Debtor applies to Bank for a loan with which to buy an identified piece of business equipment from Dealer. The parties agree that the equipment will serve as collateral for the loan, thereby satisfying the first prerequisite for the creation of a security interest (AGREEMENT). They reduce this agreement to a writing, which Debtor signs, that describes the equipment and recites that Bank will have a security interest in it. The second prerequisite is thus satisfied (WRITING). Bank then issues a check for the purchase price to Dealer, and in doing so satisfies the third prerequisite (VALUE). At this point Bank has a security interest only if the Debtor has acquired rights in the collateral, which is the final perquisite (RIGHTS). Debtor has such rights only if, and when, a sale contract is made between her and Dealer. If this contract was made before Debtor visited Bank, a security interest existed as soon as the security agreement was signed and Bank issued the purchase-money check. Otherwise, creation of the security interest was delayed until execution of the sale contract because only then did Debtor acquire rights in the collateral.

Once created, a security interest can automatically enlarge to cover further obligations of the debtor to the secured party and additional collateral subsequently acquired by the debtor. Suppose that Debtor expects to buy additional equipment as her business grows. She plans to finance the purchase of the equipment through Bank, and also to borrow money for other purposes from Bank. The parties will not want to execute a separate written security agreement each time more money is loaned to Debtor by Bank. So, in the security agreement they executed in connection with the original loan, Debtor and Bank included a clause providing, "The collateral described and otherwise provided for in this Agreement will secure any and all indebtedness of every kind and class that Debtor at any time, directly or indirectly, owes Bank." This language constitutes a *future-advance* or *future-advance clause*, which Article 9 sanctions. U.C.C. §9-204(3). Through this clause Debtor consents prospectively that the security interest she created should grow in terms of the value it secures.

Of course, as more loans are made to Debtor, Bank will want more collateral so that the value of the security at least equals the amount of the secured debt. This concern can be addressed without the parties executing a new security agreement each time more collateral is needed. In the written security agreement executed in connection with the original loan, Bank and Debtor can include another clause providing, "Any and all indebtedness Debtor owes Bank will be secured by not only by the equipment specifically described herein, but also by any other business equipment in which Debtor now or hereafter has rights." This language constitutes an *after-acquired property clause*, which Article 9 sanctions. U.C.C. §9-204(1). Through this clause, Debtor consents prospectively that the security interest she created should enlarge to cover later acquired property of the kind identified in the security agreement.

So, when Debtor subsequently acquires more equipment for use in her business, Bank's security interest will attach to it immediately, assuming Debtor is then indebted to Bank. As per the terms of the after-acquired property clause, Bank's interest will spread to *any* equipment Debtor acquires, not just equipment Bank finances. Moreover, because of the future-advance clause, any subsequently acquired equipment, along with the equipment that was the original collateral, are security not only for the original loan. All of the equipment is also security for any other indebtedness within the scope of the future-advance clause. Because of the after-acquired property clause, this whole indebtedness is also secured by any other business equipment Debtor acquires. And on and on it goes, each clause feeding on the other so that the security interest grows both in terms of the value it secures and the amount of property that is collateral.

This growth of a security interest through future-advance and after-acquired property clauses is bottomed on the debtor's consent given in advance. A security interest can grow solely by force and operation of law without the debtor's consent. The best example is a security interest in *proceeds*. Suppose Debtor purchases the equipment that is Bank's original collateral. Debtor later sells the equipment and gets $100,000 for it. Bank does not have a security interest in this money on the basis of Debtor's consent because the security agreement, which sets the boundaries of Debtor's consent, describes the collateral only as business equipment. The money is money, not business equipment.

Bank nevertheless has a security interest in the money as proceeds. Proceeds is anything received upon the disposition of collateral. U.C.C. §9-306(1). The equipment was collateral; it was disposed of by the Debtor who got the money in exchange; the money thus is proceeds. A security interest continues in any identifiable proceeds received by a debtor. U.C.C. §9-306(2). This continuing interest in proceeds arises by law and is not dependent on the debtor's consent. As long as the $100,000 remains identifiable, Bank has a security interest in it.

A creditor who by law or agreement has an Article 9 security interest in property of a debtor is a secured party and thus enjoys all the rights that Article 9 accords secured parties with respect to their collateral. These rights attach whether the collateral is property covered specifically in the security agreement; property in which the security interest arose through an after-acquired property clause; or property that is proceeds. A secured party's most important rights are, upon the debtor's default, to repossess, i.e., seize, the collateral, dispose of it, and apply the proceeds in satisfaction of the secured debt. U.C.C. §§9-503 & 9-504.

A secured party can repossess collateral "by action," U.C.C. §9-503, meaning that she can have the state take the property from the debtor through appropriate judicial proceedings such as replevin. Alternatively, a secured party can help herself to collateral: she can act on her own without the state's aid to repossess the property so long as she does not *breach the peace*. Id. The Code does not define "breach of the peace". It is a common-law concept meaning "'a disturbance of public order by an act of violence, or by any act likely to produce violence, or which by causing consternation and alarm, disturbs the peace and quiet of the community.'" *Hilliman v. Cobado*, 131 Misc.2d 206, 499 N.Y.S.2d 610, 614 (1986).

Upon somehow repossessing collateral, a secured party must usually dispose of it. The ordinary means of disposition is public or private sale after notice to the debtor. U.C.C. §9-504(3). The debtor is notified of the disposition so as to enable her to exercise her right of redemption before the sale takes place, U.C.C. §9-506, and also for the purpose of enabling her to police the disposition in the event she does not redeem.

The debtor has a great interest in seeing that the sale is aboveboard and brings the best possible price for the collateral because she gets so much of the proceeds as exceeds the sum of the secured debt and costs of disposition. U.C.C. §9-504(2). This excess is known as a *surplus*. If, on the other hand, the proceeds are too few to satisfy fully the secured debt and costs, the debtor will be personally liable for the outstanding balance. Id. This balance is known as the *deficiency*.

A deficiency is collected by the secured party suing the debtor for the sum in an action for a personal judgment. The judgment is enforced through the standard creditors' remedy: execution. See Unit 1 *supra*. In virtually every deficiency action, the debtor will defend or counterclaim on the basis that the disposition was unlawful for failing to comply with Article 9's requirements for disposing of collateral. These requirements are outlined in Part 5 of Article 9 (principally in U.C.C. §9-504(3)) and basically demand that every aspect of the disposition, and every aspect of the notice to the debtor, be commercially reasonable. In some states, a secured party who fails to satisfy these requirements is barred from recovering a deficiency. At the very least, the secured party is everywhere liable for the loss this failure caused the debtor. U.C.C. §9-507(1).

The rights to repossess and liquidate collateral that Article 9 gives a secured party are not just enforceable against the debtor, they are also enforceable against the debtor's creditors and transferees of the collateral, U.C.C. §9-201, assuming the secured party's interest has priority over the claims of the third parties. Having created a security interest in property does not prevent the debtor from conveying her rights in the collateral. U.C.C. §9-311. She can sell the collateral, or give it away. Moreover, a security interest does not immunize the collateral from consensual or nonconsensual liens of other creditors. Id. Indeed, a piece of property can be subjected to an infinite number of Article 9 security interests and other liens.

Yet, as a general rule, a security interest is unaffected by a debtor's disposition of the collateral, U.C.C. §9-306(2), and is also unaffected by the attachment of another lien of similar or different kind. Notwithstanding disposition or further encumbrance of collateral, the security interest survives and, according to U.C.C. §9-201, is effective against a purchaser of the collateral and against other creditors of the debtor, including creditors acquiring liens on the property.

In effect, §9-201 is Article 9's most general rule of priority which, in part, reflects the common-law principle of derivative title. No one can convey or encumber more than she has. So a debtor who has previously created a security interest in property can only sell, or create or suffer a lien on, the balance of her rights in the collateral. A buyer of the collateral, or a subsequent lienor, thus takes these rights subject to the preexisting security interest.

The rule of U.C.C. §9-201 is not absolute, however. The section begins with the language, "Except as otherwise provided by this Act * * *." This except clause suggests that the U.C.C. (which is "this Act") creates exceptions to the rule of §9-201 and the principle of derivative title so that, in some cases, subsequent purchasers and lienors of collateral will have priority over a preexisting security interest in the property. You better believe it! Indeed, most of Article 9 is concerned with such exceptions.

The major exceptions are rules giving priority under certain circumstances to buyers of collateral, principally U.C.C. §§9-301(1)(c),

9-307(1) and 9-307(2); to judicial lien creditors, U.C.C. §9-301(1)(b); to certain suppliers, U.C.C. §9-310; and to other Article 9 secured parties, U.C.C. §9-312(5).

Some of these rules give priority to subsequent claimants of collateral only when the secured party has not perfected her interest in the property. Perfection ordinarily refers to the steps prescribed by law for giving public notice of a security interest, and can be understood as the critical marking point for applying the first-in-time rule of priority to perfectible interests. The usual means of perfecting an Article 9 security interest is filing an Article 9 filing statement (which is described in U.C.C. §9-402) in the place or places required by U.C.C. §9-401 (which is ordinarily in the office of the secretary of state, or in a local county office, or in both offices). Other means of perfection are possible both under Article 9 and other law. In some cases, these other means are the exclusive steps of perfection so that filing pursuant to Article 9 accomplishes nothing in law.

Other Article 9 priority rules subordinate even perfected security interests to certain subsequent claims. These rules protect subsequent claims that are *enabling interests*, which is a lien or other claim of a person who—by making a loan or otherwise extending value—enables the debtor to buy or otherwise acquire or improve the collateral. Other Article 9 priority rules subordinate perfected security interests to claims of certain buyers who purchase in markets where, for overriding policy reasons, property must pass freely and without concern for encumbrances.

To illustrate a couple of these priority rules, suppose that Debtor buys an additional piece of equipment from Dealer. Dealer itself finances the purchase by extending credit to Debtor. This credit is secured by Dealer retaining an Article 9 security interest in the property. (Title to the equipment passes to Debtor upon delivery of the property to her even though she has not paid for it. U.C.C. §2-401.) Dealer perfects this interest by filing an Article 9 financing statement.

Even though Bank did not finance Debtor's purchase of this equipment, Bank's security interest automatically spreads to the property because of the after-acquired property clause in the security agreement between it and Debtor.

The general rule for deciding whether Bank's or Dealer's interest has priority is U.C.C. §9-312(5)(a), which gives priority to the secured party who first filed or perfected its security interest. If Bank's interest is unperfected, Dealer wins under this rule. Bank probably perfected by filing, however, at the time of Bank's original loan to Debtor. So Bank would win under the rule of §9-312(5)(a).

Yet, Dealer's interest is special because it is an enabling interest. An enabling interest ordinarily has priority notwithstanding the wide-spread principle of first-in-time, first-in-right. In Article 9 terminology, Dealer's interest is a purchase-money security interest. U.C.C. §9-107(a). Notwithstanding §9-312(5)(a), a purchase-money security interest in equipment has priority if it is perfected within ten days after the debtor takes possession of the collateral. U.C.C. §9-312(4). So Dealer's interest outranks the Bank's interest if Dealer's filing was made within the ten-day period.

Suppose, however, that Dealer's inventory, including the piece of equipment sold to Debtor, was collateral for credit extended to Dealer by Manufacturer. Dealer has defaulted under its security agreement with Manufacturer which now seeks to enforce its security interest by repossessing the equipment purchased by Debtor. Manufacturer will argue that its security interest in the equipment survived the sale to Debtor, U.C.C. §9-306(2), and that this security interest is effective against purchasers of the collateral. U.C.C. §9-201.

To escape this argument, and to avoid the repossession rights of Manufacturer, Debtor must find a priority rule that subordinates Manufacturer's security interest in the equipment to her claim as a buyer of the collateral. Debtor's salvation is U.C.C. §9-307(1), which gives priority to a buyer in the ordinary course of business (defined in U.C.C. §1-201(9)) even when the security interest is perfected. Debtor is such a buyer because she made a routine purchase of equipment from a person engaged in the business of selling such goods. Sales of goods in the marketplace would be slowed if the law were otherwise. Moreover, Manufacturer knew and expected that the property serving as its collateral would be offered for sale to the public and cannot rightly complain about such sales occurring. Finally, the Manufacturer is not really harmed by allowing Debtor to take the equipment free of the security interest inasmuch as Manufacturer acquires a security interest in Dealer's right to receive payment for the equipment from Debtor. This right is proceeds, U.C.C. §9-306(1), in which Manufacturer's security interest continues by operation of law. U.C.C. §9-306(2).

In contrast, recall that Debtor sold the different piece of equipment she bought with Bank's loan. The buyer of this property is not a buyer in the ordinary course of business because Debtor is not in the business of selling equipment. Thus, that buyer cannot rely on U.C.C. §9-307(1) to give her priority over Bank's interest in the property. U.C.C. §9-301(1)(c) is no help to the buyer if Bank's interest in the equipment was perfected at the time of the buyer's purchase. U.C.C. §9-307(2) is no help because it only protects buyers of consumer goods who purchase for their own personal, family or household purposes. The collateral was business equipment, not consumer goods. U.C.C. §9-109. Thus, because none of Article 9's priority rules protect the buyer, Bank's rights with respect to the collateral are effective against the buyer, §9-201, which means that upon Debtor's default Bank can repossess the equipment from the buyer. Alternatively, because the Bank had a better right to possession of the property due to its priority, Bank can successfully sue the buyer for conversion of the collateral. In either event, Bank can also claim the $100,000 proceeds. U.C.C. §9-306 comment 3. In any event, Bank's recovery is limited to the amount of the secured debt plus costs of repossession and disposition.

We cannot stress too much that the rights to repossess collateral from a debtor and dispose of the property, to enforce security interests against subordinate third-party claimants of the property, and to pursue all other rights that Article 9 gives creditors, belong only to a secured party, meaning a person in whose favor there is a security interest. Article 9's requirements for creating a security interest must be satisfied in order for a security interest to exist. If these requirements are not met, there is no security interest. If there is no security interest, there is no collateral and no secured party. In this event, a creditor enjoys none of the rights and privileges that Article 9 gives secured parties, which means that the creditor cannot seize property from anyone on the authority of Article 9. Any right to do so must come from other law. If other law does not give the creditor such a right, a seizure of property from the debtor or anyone else is illegal and amounts to conversion. The creditor is therefore liable for compensatory and, in an appropriate case, punitive damages.

Similarly, even when a creditor is a secured party, her Article 9 rights apply only to her collateral, meaning the specific property subject to her security interest. The reach of a security interest is determined by the terms of the security agreement (principally, the description of collateral in the agreement and any after-acquired property clause) and by the few provisions of Article 9 and other law that extend a security interest by force of law. A secured party is accountable if she grabs property that is not somehow covered by the terms of the security agreement and that is not otherwise made subject to her security interest.

So, when analyzing any Article 9 problem, a good way to start is by asking whether the creditor who asserts the rights of a secured party actually has a security interest in the property she claims. In answering this question the first issue is whether the requirements of U.C.C. §9-203(1) were satisfied so that, as to some property, the creditor was a secured party. The next issue is whether the interest so created extended, by agreement or by law, to the specific property the secured party wants. A related issue is the size of the interest, i.e., how much debt does the collateral secure. These three issues are the principal concerns of the next two sections of this unit, which deal with creating and enlarging security interests.

☐☐☐☐☐

In early 1990, the Permanent Editorial Board for the Uniform Commercial Code ("PEB"), with the support of its sponsors, the American Law Institute ("ALI") and the National Conference of Commissioners on Uniform State Laws ("NCCUSL"), established a committee to study Article 9 of the Uniform Commercial Code ("UCC"). This committee, known as the Uniform Commercial Code Article 9 Study Group or Study Committee, was charged with recommending whether Article 9 and related provisions of the UCC need revision. The Committee also was requested, if it concluded that revision was desirable, to recommend the nature and the substance of the revisions. In December, 1992, the Study Committee recommended the appointment of a drafting committee to revise Article 9 and issued a report suggesting many detailed changes. The Study Committee's recommendations of the report (sans commentary) are reprinted throughout this unit under the label, Report of the Article 9 Study Committee.

Barkley Clark, a very prominent and highly respected commercial law teacher, scholar and practitioner, was a member of the Study Committee. He composed the following poem which humorously summarizes, with large accuracy, the Committee's attitude and its work:

A Job Well Done

A Kripe named Homer
and a Gilmore named Grant
Had left us a wonderful monument

We hated to mangle this greatest of works
Or suggest that the previous drafters were jerks

But we sought to update and message it a lot
In order to make sure the statute don't rot

9 is the linchpin of the universe
Could be better, though it could be worse
So we gathered together some 20 great sages
To fine-tune this puppy for all of the ages
We broadened the scope of our article much
To help with securitization and such
We brought in insurance, deposits and tort
In hope that these interests will stand up in court

Though real estate weren't in our province as such
We still thought this subject was worthy of touch
So we tinkered with fixtures and real estate notes
And oil and gas and all that connotes

And at some times we wished for the ultimate sin--
That Article 9 would suck Greenacre in!

On conflicts of law we did mighty reform
By making the debtor's location the norm
But the part of this change that is clearly the best--
Getting rid of that goddamn last-event test!

Should equitable principles continue to be
As strong as they've been under 1-103?
If Steve Nickles has his own way on this deal,
Strict Article 9 we would simply repeal!

The filing system we need to improve
So filers and searchers are more in the groove
But our primary goal here is stopping the spectacles
Of filing clerks acting as more than receptacles!

Filing's okay now with notes and CD's
and L/C's and even with securities

We played with the rules on post-closing events
And even of dual debtors finally made sense

We acted with wisdom and not out of whimsy
When we strengthened the hand of the UCC pimsy
In order to make it a more useful tool
We murdered the transformation rule

Yes, we strengthened those pimsies while avoiding the sin
Of sinking our best friend, the old floating lien
To shore up the floater we did many deeds
The greatest of which was to fatten proceeds
But in all of this tinkering perhaps our best fix
Was to jettison big chunks of 9-306!

Although our committee's a citified gang
We dove into AG lending with a big bang

We shored up consignments and financing buyers
And for dear chattel paper, we put out some fires

Our report makes it clear that you never put fetters
Upon sacred cows that we call account debtors
This theorem applies with particular bounce
When the goodies involved are deposit accounts

Issues of federalism really got tough
When we wrestled with patents and trademarks and stuff
For, though we are all truly states' rights blokes
We know we must work with the Federal folks

Then finally we turned to enforcement, perforce
We deep-sixed the absolute bar rule, of course
Strict foreclosure was strengthened
But on this we still rave--
Oh what, pray, Oh what, can the surety waive?

We heard our Rapson sound his clarion call--
What's good for CIT's good for us all!
We heard Fred Miller mouth his standard refusal
To allow any drafting--except my NCCUSL.
And we heard from mild-mannered Chairman, Bill Burke
Whose Superman status made everything work

History sings of kings of legalese
Of Justinian, Hamarab, and wise Pericles
But none I think produced stuff half as fair as
The work product we got from Mooney and Harris!

Above all, we fervently tried, you and me,
To assure that the lender would [beat] the trustee!
                                        Pindar

B. CREATING SECURITY INTERESTS

1. Security Agreement

Remember that Article 9 governs *consensual* security interests. So, as U.C.C. §9-203(1)(a) demands, an agreement between the debtor and secured party is always necessary to create an Article 9 security interest. This agreement is cleverly referred to as a *security agreement.* U.C.C. §9-105(1)(l).

A security agreement must be in writing unless the secured party takes and keeps possession of the collateral. U.C.C. §9-203(1)(a). The requirement of a writing serves two different, albeit related, purposes: first, the writing is designed to minimize "the possibility of future dispute as to the terms of a security agreement and as to what property stands as collateral." U.C.C. §9-203 comment 3. So the writing must describe the collateral, U.C.C. §9-203(1)(a), by reasonably identifying it. U.C.C. §9-110.

Second, the writing is demonstrable evidence that, as claimed by the creditor, a security agreement was actually made. In addressing this purpose, §9-203(1)(a) is in the nature of a Statute of Frauds. Not surprisingly, therefore, the writing is sufficient only if the debtor signs it.

The requirements that a security agreement describe the collateral and be signed by the debtor are explicitly stated in §9-203(1)(a). Another requirement is hidden there. Not just any writing that a debtor signs describing property is sufficient as a security agreement. U.C.C. §9-203(1)(a) requires a writing that is a *security agreement.* This term means "an agreement which creates or provides for a security interest." U.C.C. §9-105(1)(l). Thus, §9-203(1)(a) requires, in addition to a description of collateral and the debtor's signature, some further evidence that the purpose of the writing was to create or provide for security.

In the absence of a writing that satisfies these three requirements, a creditor cannot have a security interest in any property, except property in her possession. No writing whatsoever is required to create a security interest in property the secured party possesses because her possession completely serves both purposes of a written security agreement. Yet, possession of property alone is not enough to satisfy U.C.C. §9-203(1)(a). The putative secured party must be in possession for the purpose of creating a security interest. Thus, even when a creditor relies on her possession of collateral as a substitute for a written security agreement, she must still prove that such an agreement, albeit oral, was actually made covering the property she holds. REMEMBER: Possession of the collateral does not excuse the requirement of a security agreement, only the requirement that the agreement be in writing.

In most cases, the debtor has possession of the collateral. So a written security agreement that satisfies U.C.C. §9-203(1)(a) is required. If there is none, no security interest exists.

U.C.C. §9-203(1)(a) is not satisfied by the debtor signing just any writing that in some sense describes the collateral. Whatever is signed must evince the purpose of creating or providing for a security interest, and the description of the collateral contained therein must reasonably identify the property. A failure in *either* respect means there is no security agreement within the terms of §9-203(1)(a) and thus there is no security interest.

a. Composing a Written Security Agreement

When lawyers plan secured transactions they almost always use a standard form security agreement that, when properly completed, satisfies all of the requirements of U.C.C. §9-203(1)(a) in a single document and often goes further to provide the secured party with all sorts of "bargained for" protections, including a long and wide list of events and circumstances that constitute default by the debtor.

A written security agreement required by §9-203(1)(a) should not be confused with a financing statement described in §9-402(1). The former is necessary to the creation of a security interest whenever the secured party is not in possession of the collateral. The latter is filed in the local court house or with the secretary of state, or in both places, to perfect a non-possessory security interest. A single writing can serve as both a security agreement and a financing statement if the writing, as completed, satisfies the requirements of both §9-203(1)(a) and §9-402(1). Yet, a standard form financing statement that contains only the information required by §9-402(1), which is commonly known as a *UCC-1*, will not by itself pass as a security agreement sufficient under §9-203(1)(a).

Standard Form Security Agreement

SECURITY AGREEMENT

Made on　　　　　　　　　　, between

(Date)

(Name of all Debtors)　　　　　(Street & No.)　　　　　(City)　　　　　(State)

(herein called "Debtor"), a corporation partnership individual(s), said address being Debtor's mailing address and place of business address at which the property covered hereby is, or promptly after the making of the loan herein referred to will be, located and

(Secured Party)　　　　　(Street & No.)　　　　　(City)　　　　　(State)

(herein called "Secured Party"), said address being Secured Party's address at which information concerning Secured Party's Security Interest hereunder may be obtained.

　　Debtor warrants and agrees that the property covered hereby　is or is to be　is not or is not to be　so affixed or related to realty as to become a part thereof, and that if it is or is to be so affixed, the realty is the same as Debtor's address above given; and that said property is or is to be used by Debtor primarily　[Check (1), (2), or (3)]

- ☐　(1)　in business, and that all the Debtor's places of business are in the same county as Debtor's place of business above set forth except
- ☐　(2)　for personal, family or household purposes.
- ☐　(3)　in farming operations.

Debtor will promptly notify Secured Party, in writing, of any discontinuance of any place of business, the establishment of any new place of business, or any change of location of said property if block (1) is checked, and of any change in Debtor's residence or the location of said property if block (2) or (3) is checked.

　　WHEREAS, Debtor desires to grant Secured Party a Security Interest pursuant to the Uniform Commercial Code in the following described property:

and all replacements thereof and all accessories, parts and equipment now or hereafter affixed thereto or used in connection therewith (hereinafter collectively called the "Goods"); and

WHEREAS, Debtor, upon the execution and delivery of this Agreement and completion of other required details, will borrow $ from Secured Party, which borrowing will be evidenced by the Debtor's promissory note(s) in the total amount of $, representing a loan of $ and interest of $, to maturity, said promissory note (s) being payable and bearing interest as therein set forth and any delinquent payment thereon bearing interest at   % per annum:

NOW, THEREFORE, THIS AGREEMENT WITNESSETH That Debtor, intending to be legally bound. hereby grants to Secured Party, a Security Interest in said Goods, in order to secure the payment of: (1) said note(s); (2) all costs and expenses incurred in the collection of same and enforcement of Secured Party's rights hereunder; (3) any future advances made by Secured Party for taxes, levies, insurance and repair to or maintenance of said Goods; (4) all other money heretofore or hereafter advanced by Secured Party to or for the account of Debtor at the option of Secured Party, and all other present or future, direct or contingent liabilities of Debtor to Secured Party of any nature whatsoever; and (5) interest on (2), (3), and (4).

UNTIL DEFAULT hereunder, Debtor shall be entitled to the possession of the Goods and to use and enjoy the same.

DEBTOR WARRANTS AND AGREES (if applicable) THAT:

☐ (a) Debtor will immediately use the entire proceeds of said borrowing, together with such additional funds of Debtor as may be necessary, to pay the purchase price of the above specifically described property and for no other purpose.

☐ (b) Debtor hereby authorizes Secured Party to disburse the proceeds of said borrowing directly to the seller of the above specifically described property and/or to the insurance agent or broker for insurance thereon.

The additional terms on the reverse side hereof, including the authorization by Debtor to confess judgment, are hereby made a part hereof.

The rights and privileges of Secured Party under this Agreement shall inure to the benefit of its successors and assigns. All representations, warranties and agreements of Debtor contained in this Agreement are joint and several if Debtor is more than one and shall bind Debtor's personal representative, heir, successors and assigns; if any provision of this Agreement shall for any reason be held to be invalid or unenforceable, such invalidity or unenforceability shall not affect any other provision hereof, but this Agreement shall be construed as if such invalid or unenforceable provision had never been contained herein.

_____   _____

(Debtor)   (Secured Party)

_____   _____

BY: (Name & Title)   (Name & Title)

DEBTOR FURTHER REPRESENTS, WARRANTS AND AGREES THAT:

The statements herein as to Debtor's residence or places of business and possession and location of the property specifically described herein are true, and that Debtor has [or if para6raph (a) on reverse side is checked, will acquire] absolute title thereto free and clear of all liens, encumbrances and Security Interests except the Security Interest hereby given to Secured Party and other rights, if any, of Secured Party, and Debtor will defend the Goods against the claims and demands of all persons;

Without the prior written consent of Secured Party, Debtor will not sell, exchange, lease or otherwise dispose of the Goods or any of Debtor's rights therein or under this Agreement, or permit any lien or Security Interest to attach to same except that created by this Agreement and other rights. if any, of Secured Party;

Debtor will maintain the Goods in good condition and repair but without permitting any lien to affix to the Goods as a result thereof, and will pay and discharge all taxes, levies and other impositions levied thereon as well as the cost of repairs to or maintenance of the same and will not permit anything to be done that may impair the value of any of the Goods; if Debtor fails to pay such sums Secured Party may do so for Debtor's account, adding the amount thereof to the other amounts secured hereby;

Debtor will insure the Goods against such casualties and in such amounts as Secured Party shall require; all insurance policies shall be written for the benefit of Debtor and Secured Party as their interests may appear and such policies or certificates evidencing the same shall be furnished to Secured Party. If Debtor fails to pay the premiums on any such insurance Secured Party may do so for Debtor's account, adding the amount thereof to the other amounts secured hereby. Debtor hereby assigns to Secured Party any return or unearned premiums which may be due upon cancellation of any such policies for any reason whatsoever and directs the insurers to pay Secured Party any amounts so due. Secured Party is hereby appointed Debtor's attorney in fact to endorse any draft or check which may be payable to Debtor in order to collect such return or unearned premiums or the proceeds of such insurance; any balance of insurance proceeds remaining after payment in full of all secured hereunder shall be paid to Debtor;

Debtor will not permit any of the Goods to be removed from the location specified herein, except for temporary periods in the normal and customary use thereof, without the prior written consent of Secured Party and will permit Secured Party to inspect the Goods at any time.

Debtor will not permit anything to be done that may impair the value of any of the Goods or the security intended to be afforded by this Agreement;

Debtor will pay all costs of filing any financing, continuation, or termination statements with respect to the Security Interest created by this Agreement; Secured Party is hereby appointed Debtor's attorney in fact to do, at Secured Party's option and at Debtor's expense, all acts and things which Secured Party may deem necessary to perfect and continue perfected the Security Interest created by this Agreement and to protect the Goods;

If the Goods include a motor vehicle or any other type of property for which a Certificate of Title is issuable, Debtor will join with Secured Party in doing whatever may be necessary to have a statement of the Security Interest created by this Agreement noted on said Certificate and will deposit said Certificate with Secured Party.

In case of default in the payment when due of any amount payable on any of the sums secured hereby, or in the due observance or performance of any of the other agreements of Debtor herein contained, or in case any of the representations or warranties of Debtor herein contained shall prove to be false or misleading, or if any proceedings are instituted by or against Debtor under any of the provisions of the Bankruptcy Act or any state insolvency law or for the appointment of a Receiver for Debtor, or if Debtor shall make an assignment for the benefit of creditors, or shall become insolvent, then, in any such event, or whenever Secured Party shall deem itself insecure, Debtor shall be in default hereunder. Therefore, all sums secured hereby shall become immediately due and payable at Secured Party's option without notice to Debtor, and Secured Party may proceed to enforce payment of the same and to exercise any or all of the rights and remedies provided by the Uniform Commercial Code, as well as all other rights and remedies possessed by Secured Party. Whenever Debtor is in default hereunder, Debtor, upon demand by Secured Party, shall assemble the Goods and make them available to Secured Party at a place reasonably convenient to both parties.

Whenever there shall be a default in payment of any sum or sums secured hereby, Debtor hereby authorizes the Clerk or any Attorney of any Court of Record to appear for and confess judgment against Debtor for all sums secured here by together with collection costs. Debtor waives inquisition, stay of execution, errors, appeals and the benefit of all exemption laws, and agrees to condemnation and that any real estate may be sold on a writ of fieri facias.

If Debtor is more than one, the liability hereunder is joint and several.

Standard Form Financing Statement (UCC-1)

This **FINANCING STATEMENT** is presented to a Filing Officer for filing pursuant to the Uniform Commercial Code.	3. Maturity date (if any):

1. Debtor(s) Name (Last Name First)	2. Debtor(s) Address	This space for use of Filing Officer. (Date, time, number and Filing Office.)

4. Secured Party(ies)	5. Secured Party(ies) Address

6. Assigned Party(ies)	7. Assigned Party(ies) Address

8. This financing statement covers the following types (or items) of property:

Description of Real Estate. (Use this only if applicable)

Check (X) if covered: (X) Proceeds of collateral are also covered. ( ) Products of Collateral are also covered. No. of additional sheets presented: ( )

Filed with Circuit Clerk of_____ County. ( ) Secretary of State.

By:_____
       Signature(s) of Debtor(s)

By:_____
       Signature(s) of Secured Party(ies)

FILING OFFICER COPY

This form of financing statement is approved by the Secretary of State and the Arkansas Commission on Uniform State Laws.
STANDARD FORM – UNIFORM COMMERCIAL CODE – FORM UCC-1. Forms may be purchased from Calvert-McBride Printing Company, Fort Smith, Arkansas.

Why does a properly completed UCC-1, that is sufficient under §9-402(1) as a financing statement, not satisfy the requirements of §9-203(1)(a) for a written security agreement? The requirements of the former appear, at first glance, to subsume the requirements of the latter. The functions of the two kinds of writings are different, however, and this functional difference gives rise to an important substantive difference.

Remember that a security agreement is designed to evidence the debtor's consent to creation of a security interest. So a security agreement must create or provide for security. In contrast, a financing statement is intended merely to notify the world that a security interest *might* have been created through conduct beyond the filing of the statement. Indeed, Article 9 expressly provides that a financing statement can be filed before a security interest exists and even before a security agreement is executed. U.C.C. §9-402(1). Thus, a financing statement need not create or provide for security, and the courts believe that a standard form UCC-1 does not have this feature which is required of a security agreement.

Yet, if language creating or providing for security is added to a properly completed UCC-1, the requirements of a security agreement are satisfied, assuming the description of collateral is sufficient for purposes of §9-203(1)(a). That the writing in such a case is labeled "financing statement" rather than "security agreement" is unimportant.

Substantive content controls over form in deciding whether the requirements of §9-203(1)(a) have been satisfied. So, even though lawyers ordinarily use stand-alone, standard-form security agreements, Article 9 does not mandate such a formal, dedicated document. Any writing in any form that satisfies the requirements of §9-203(1)(a) is sufficient as a security agreement. Indeed, a security agreement can be pieced together from several documents that collectively satisfy §9-203(1)(a) when none of them is sufficient in itself.

Tilghman v. Larrimore
Court of Appeals of Maryland, 1993
331 Md. 390, 628 A.2d 215

Rodowsky, Judge. This case involves the credit sale of a Chesapeake Bay skipjack, the Nellie L. Byrd.[2] The sole issue is whether the deferred portion of

---

[2] A skipjack is a working sailboat indigenous to the Chesapeake Bay. The vessel is characterized by a flat-V bottom, sides, a schooner bow, centerboard, and sloop-type rigging on a strongly raked mast with a long boom. It is used in the dredging of oysters. See H. Owens, Baltimore on the Chesapeake 66-67 (1941); M.V. Brewington, Chesapeake Bay, A Pictorial Maritime History 65-66 (1953).

the purchase price was secured by a security interest in the vessel, or whether the transaction was an unsecured sale on credit.

On March 10, 1989, petitioner, Tilghman Hardware, Inc. (Tilghman), agreed to purchase the Nellie L. Byrd from respondent, Darryl Larrimore (Larrimore), "subject to the terms and conditions contained in" a written contract, signed by both parties (the Agreement). * * *

The price was $55,000, payable over time. The Agreement called for a series of deposits: an initial deposit of $500, an additional deposit of $4,500 payable within forty days of execution of the Agreement, $5,389 payable by June 15, 1989, and a debt exchange valued at $2,111. * * * The balance of the purchase price, $42,500, referred to as the "[a]mount to be financed," was to be paid, with interest at nine percent per annum, over five years in accordance with an amortization schedule attached to the Agreement.

Section Six of the Agreement, "Warranties," reads in part:

"Vessel is being sold and purchased free and clear of all debts, claims, liens and encumbrances of any kind whatsoever, except as noted hereinafter and seller warrants and will defend that seller has good and marketable title and *will deliver to the buyer all necessary documents for transfer of the title to buyer on or before the dates set forth for final payment.*"

Section Eight, "Risk of Loss," provides:

"It is agreed by the parties that the risk of loss, injury or destruction of the above described vessel and equipment shall be borne by seller until this transaction is closed and the vessel delivered."

Section Ten, "Binding Effect," provides, in part: "Seller agrees not to sell vessel or to enter into any contract for the sale of vessel while this agreement is in effect." The Agreement did not state what constitutes a buyer's default; nor did it set forth, directly or by reference, any remedies available to Larrimore in the event of Tilghman's default.

Tilghman took delivery, but failed to make the payments as agreed. In August 1990, Larrimore filed with the District Court of Maryland in Talbot County a "Complaint for Replevin" and a "Request for Emergency Ex Parte Order." The complaint alleged that "title [was] to remain in plaintiff until final payment," and that the historic vessel was not being maintained. Larrimore's request for an ex parte injunction, authorizing him to take immediate possession of the vessel, was granted.

At the hearings in the action, and by a memorandum of law, Tilghman argued that the Agreement transferred all ownership rights in the vessel to Tilghman and that Larrimore had not obtained a security interest in the vessel under Article 9, the Secured Transactions Article, of the Uniform Commercial

Code (U.C.C.), Md.Code (1975, 1992 Repl.Vol.), Title 9 of the Commercial Law Article (CL). Thus, Tilghman submitted, Larrimore's remedies were to be found exclusively in Title 2, the Sales Article of the U.C.C. Title 2 remedies do not include replevin by a seller.

The District Court ruled that, under the Agreement, Larrimore held a security interest in the vessel. First it noted that "the contract itself, which was drawn ... by Tilghman ... has to be construed, if there is any doubt with regards to the meaning of any specific term ... in favor of Mr. Larrimore and against Tilghman Hardware." Next the court observed that "the contract itself ... appears to be basically a ... conditional sales contract, whereby title ... to the vessel was held by Mr. Larrimore and never actually delivered to Tilghman Hardware" and that "at the time of the default ... title to the vessel had never been transferred to Tilghman." The District Court found

> "that the intention of the parties ... was that Mr. Larrimore would retain title to the vessel to secure any interest which he might have, pursuant to the conditional sales, and the sales nature of the contract, rather than pursuing the Uniform Commercial Code security interest requirements."

The court said that the U.C.C. was not the exclusive "means" by which a security interest could be created; rather, Larrimore could have the remedy of repossession or replevin by retaining title subject to Tilghman's making the agreed payments. Accordingly, the court concluded that Larrimore's remedy was not limited to a contract action for the unpaid balance of the price. The writ of replevin issued.

Tilghman appealed to the Circuit Court for Talbot County, which affirmed. The circuit court, relying heavily on §9-201, reasoned that the U.C.C. had not abolished the ability of a creditor to create an enforceable security interest by a conditional sales contract. The circuit court additionally held that the record supported the District Court's finding that the intent of the parties was to create what amounted to an enforceable security interest in the Nellie L. Byrd.

We granted Tilghman's petition for certiorari which raises fundamental questions concerning security interests in credit sales.

Tilghman's various arguments can be summarized as follows:

I. Because the Agreement does not undertake to create a security interest specifically under U.C.C. Art. 9, the Agreement cannot create any enforceable security interest; and

II. The Agreement fails to create a security interest because (A) there is no language granting a security interest and (B) repayment of the amount to be financed is not a condition of the transfer of title.

I

In its certiorari petition Tilghman framed the question presented to be: "Does Maryland recognize a common law right to create consensual security interests in personal property which are exempt from the mandates of [Title] 9 of the Commercial Law Article?" That phraseology is a hyperbolic characterization of the District Court's rationale. We understand the District Court to have held that an enforceable Title 9 security interest can be created by manifesting the intent to do so through language referring to a delivery of possession with a reservation of title to be delivered upon satisfaction of a condition. The circuit court affirmed on that same basis. We agree.

A "security interest" is "an interest in personal property ... which secures payment ... of an obligation." §1-201(37). With an exception not relevant here, §9-102 provides, in part, that Title 9 applies

> (1) ... (a) To any transaction (regardless of its form) which is intended to create a security interest in personal property or fixtures including goods....
>
> ....
>
> (2) This title applies to security interests created by contract including pledge, assignment, chattel mortgage, chattel trust, trust deed, factor's lien, equipment trust, conditional sale, trust receipt, other lien or title retention contract and lease or consignment intended as security.

The comments to §9-102 make the rule even more plain, stating, in part:

> Purposes: "The main purpose of this section is to bring all consensual security interests in personal property and fixtures under this Title, except for certain types of transactions excluded by Section 9-104.... 1. Except for sales of accounts and chattel paper, the principal test whether a transaction comes under this Title is: is the transaction intended to have effect as security? ... When it is found that a security interest as defined in Section 1-201(37) was intended, this Title applies regardless of the form of the transaction or the name by which the parties may have christened it. The list of traditional security devices in subsection (2) is illustrative only; other old devices, as well as any new ones which the ingenuity of lawyers may invent, are included, so long as the requisite intent is found. The controlling definition is that contained in subsection 1 [of §9-102].
>
> The Title does not in terms abolish existing security devices. The conditional sale or bailment-lease, for example, is not prohibited; but even though it is used, the rules of this Title govern.

Similarly, the comments to §9-101 state in part:

> Under this Title the traditional distinctions among security devices, based largely on form, are not retained; the Title applies to all

transactions intended to create security interests in personal property and fixtures, and the single term 'security interest' substitutes for the variety of descriptive terms which had grown up at common law and under a hundred-year accretion of statutes. This does not mean that the old forms may not be used, and Section 9-102(2) makes it clear that they may be.

This Court had occasion to comment on the foregoing sections of Title 9 in *Universal C.I.T. Credit Corp. v. Congressional Motors, Inc.*, 246 Md. 380, 228 A.2d 463 (1966), a case involving the priority of creditors' claims to the debtor's inventory. This Court said:

> The official comment states that the purpose of §9-102 is to bring all consensual security interests in personal property, with exceptions specified in §§9-103 and 9- 104, under subtitle 9. "The Subtitle does not in terms abolish existing security devices" but if they are used the rules of subtitle 9 govern.

Id. at 389, 228 A.2d at 469.

    * * *

Thus, the fact that the Agreement employs language invoking concepts that are more appropriate to a pre-U.C.C. conditional contract of sale does not prevent the Agreement from creating a security interest governed by CL Title 9.

II

We now consider those aspects of the Agreement that Tilghman argues prevented the Agreement from effecting a security interest in the vessel. * * *

A

The principal defect asserted is that the Agreement fails to "contain 'language which grants to the creditor a security interest.' " Appellant's Brief at 8 (quoting *L & V Co. v. Asch*, 267 Md. 251, 258, 297 A.2d 285, 288-89 (1972)). Tilghman's position is that words of grant are required.

At issue in *Asch* was whether a financing statement could serve as a security agreement. The debtor, a manufacturing corporation, had received advances under a line of credit from the creditor, The L and V Company (L and V). The parties did not memorialize their bargain with a security agreement, but L and V had recorded a financing statement covering most of the debtor's assets. Later the debtor also had executed three demand promissory notes to L and V, the total of which equalled the outstanding principal balance of the advances.

When the debtor executed a deed of trust for the benefit of its creditors, and L and V petitioned for a preferred claim to the assets, the claim was denied. This Court stated the issue on appeal, and its holding, to be whether the appellant, L and V, had an enforceable security interest on the basis of the notes and financing statement alone which would entitle it to a preferred claim. We hold that L & V cannot have an enforceable security interest because there was no security agreement signed by the debtor ... as required under [§9-203(1)(a)].

267 Md. at 254, 297 A.2d at 286-87. We said that the definition of security agreement ("an agreement which creates or provides for a security interest") and §9-203(1)(a) "have been consistently interpreted by courts as requiring a writing in which the debtor grants a security interest to the secured party." Id., 297 A.2d at 287.

The opinion in *Asch* concluded:

The filing of a financing statement may indicate the existence of a security agreement and, indeed, if it contains language which grants to the creditor a security interest, it may then serve both as a financing statement and a security agreement. There is no language in the UCC to make a financing statement, without words granting a security interest, the equivalent of a security agreement. The granting words are necessary to indicate the intention of the parties to create a security interest; and in the absence of such words, it seems rather clear that the parties did not intend to create a security interest. See, e.g., In re Nottingham [, 6 U.C.C. Rep. Serv. (Callaghan) 1197, 1969 WL 11098 (Bankr.E.D.Tenn.1969)]."

Id. at 258, 297 A.2d at 288-89 (citation omitted).

Here, Tilghman seeks to extend the language employed in the holding in *Asch* to a factual situation that was not presented there. That case held that the "short form" of financing statement permitted under §9-402, standing alone, does not contain words that create or grant a security interest. *Asch* noted, however, that if the financing statement contained "language which grants to the creditor a security interest, it may then serve both as a financing statement and a security agreement." Id. at 258, 297 A.2d at 288-89. *Asch* did not pass upon the sufficiency of any wording in an agreement to constitute a "security agreement."

The cases cited in *Asch*, and the way in which they were cited, further clarify the *Asch* holding. *Asch* relied in part on *American Card Co. v. H.M.H. Co.*, 97 R.I. 59, 196 A.2d 150 (1963), a case in which a claim of priority in receivership was rejected where the creditor relied on a filed financing statement and promissory note, but where there was no security agreement. We quoted with approval from *American Card*, 196 A.2d at 152, the statement that "'it is not possible for a financing statement which does not contain the debtor's grant of a security interest to serve as a security agreement.' (Emphasis supplied.)." *Asch*, 267 Md. at 254, 297 A.2d at 287. Here there is an agreement providing for deferral of the passage of title and, although there is no financing statement, no third party rights are involved.

In re Nottingham, 6 U.C.C. Rep. Serv. (Callaghan) 1197, 1969 WL 11098 (Bankr.E.D.Tenn.1969), cited in *Asch*, also is illustrative. The sole question there was "whether a document signed by the bankrupt when he bought a color television set [met] the requirements of a 'Security Agreement.'" Id. at 1197.

After reviewing the document in question, the court concluded:

> It is neither a title retention contract nor a conditional sales contract. It does not create or provide for any security interest in the property. It is therefore my conclusion that such document does not meet the requirements of a security agreement. "There are no magic words that create a security interest. There must be language, however, in the instrument which when read and construed leads to the logical conclusion that it was the intention of the parties that a security interest be created * * *. The requirements of the Code for creating a security interest are simple--an intention to create a security interest is all that need be shown--a dozen words or less are sufficient, but the security agreement must contain language that meets this simple requirement.

Id. at 1198-99.
  * * *

Even more clearly demonstrating that neither *Asch* nor the U.C.C. requires that an agreement contain words expressly granting a security interest in order to constitute a security agreement is the Code's treatment of reservations of title. Section 1-201(37), which defines "security interest," states that "[t]he retention or reservation of title by a seller of goods notwithstanding shipment or delivery to the buyer (§2-401) is limited in effect to a reservation of a 'security interest.'"

Section 2-401(1), in part, provides: * * * "(1) ... Any retention or reservation by the seller of the title (property) in goods shipped or delivered to the buyer is limited in effect to a reservation of a security interest. Subject to these provisions and to the provisions of the title on secured transactions (Title 9), title to goods passes from the seller to the buyer in any manner and on any conditions explicitly agreed on by the parties." * * * [Here] "[t]he Code cryptically declares * * * [w]here a seller retains title to the goods until paid and delivers possession of the goods to the buyer, the seller's interest is a security interest and is governed by Article 9. When it is the intention of the parties, an instrument which purports to relate to title will be deemed to create merely a security interest. Thus, although the transaction purports to reserve title to the seller, this reservation is limited to a security interest."

In *Sommers v. IBM*, 640 F.2d 686 (5th Cir.1981), the trustee in bankruptcy sought to have a creditor declared unsecured on the grounds, inter alia, that a purchase order "did not qualify as a security agreement under the UCC since it failed to contain language granting the vendor a security interest in the goods." Id. at 688. The court responded:

> "[A] 'security agreement' [is defined] as 'an agreement which creates or provides for a security interest.' A 'security interest' is defined as 'an interest in personal property ... which secures payment or performance of an obligation. The retention or reservation of title by a seller of goods notwithstanding shipment or delivery to the buyer ... is limited in effect to reservation of a "security interest." ' Tex.Bus. & Comm.Code Ann. §1.201(37) (Vernon Supp.1980-1981) (emphasis added). Although 'there must be language in the instrument which "leads to the logical conclusion that it was the intention of the parties that a security interest be created,"' Mitchell v. Shepherd Mall State Bank, 458 F.2d 700, 703 (10th Cir.1972), we conclude the language in the purchase order to the effect that [the creditor] 'retains title to said books until paid ...' was sufficient to reserve a security interest in the books to [the creditor]."

Id. at 689.

In the instant matter the theory followed by the person drafting the Agreement was to separate possession and title. Larrimore agreed to deliver possession of the vessel after the series of deposits was paid, but Larrimore reserved title for later transfer. Where, as here, the intent of the parties was to secure the deferred purchase price, the Code operates to give effect to that intent by treating the outmoded reservation of title as creating a security interest. Language expressly granting a security interest from buyer to seller is not required under these circumstances.

B

The agreement provides that seller "will deliver to the buyer all necessary documents for transfer of the title to buyer on or before the dates set forth for final payment." Tilghman argues that "[h]ad the seller desired to retain an interest in the vessel to secure payment, the contract would have provided that title be transferred following final payment, rather than 'on or before the dates set forth for final payment.'" Appellant's Brief at 9. No cases are cited.

The "on or before" phraseology does not alter our conclusion. The schedule for the monthly payments, incorporated into the Agreement, covered a period of five years. Use of the "on or before" language makes it clear that the debtor may prepay and thereby avoid any question whether the common law rule applicable to real estate mortgages applies to the subject transaction. * * *

JUDGMENT OF THE CIRCUIT COURT FOR TALBOT COUNTY AFFIRMED. COSTS TO BE PAID BY THE PETITIONER, TILGHMAN HARDWARE, INC.

Problems

1. In 1969 plaintiff brought suit against defendant Michael Diodato, and on November 18, 1970 judgment was entered in favor of plaintiff and against Diodato for $2,402.65. Between the time of commencement of said action and the entry of judgment therein defendant Anthony L. Canna claims to have loaned to Diodato (his brother-in-law) the sum of $2,200 to enable the latter to purchase a used Cadillac automobile. The loan was all in cash—defendant Anna B. Canna, the wife of Anthony and the sister of Diodato, testified that she "gave the money to my husband, he gave it to my brother." According to the testimony of Anthony Canna, the entire transaction was consummated on February 28, 1970; the parties had no legal advice and simply "worked (the) . . . papers up" themselves. Diodato executed a handwritten promissory note, dated February 28, 1970, in the following form:

    > I, Michael Diodato, promise to pay $2,200.00 which was loaned to me for the purchase of a 1968 Cadillac, Serial # A--B8135760 Z, to be paid to Anthony L. Canna within 3 years time of above date.

    There was no provision for the payment of interest. The note bore the signature of Diodato, as well as that of a notary public. There was no jurat or other attestation by the notary, although it did bear his seal and the notation "2/28/70" along side his signature. The notary was present and signed the note because Canna "felt this was the best way to do it." Canna testified further that, following the execution of the note, both he and Diodato proceeded to the "division of motor vehicles" where a new title certificate to the Cadillac was issued in the same of Diodato as owner, and designating Anthony L. Canna as "secured party". No instruments or papers other than the note and the title certificate appear to have been drawn or signed by any of the parties with regard to the transaction of February 28, 1970.

    An additional loan of "around $900" was claimed by Canna to have been made by him to Diodato in April, 1970. Another handwritten promissory note signed by Diodato, dated April 15, 1970, and bearing the signature of the same notary public, stated:

    > I, Michael Diodato promise to pay an additional $900.00, for personal expense, which will be added to the $2,200.00 original loan on a 1968 Cadillac, Serial #A--B8135760 Z, making the total amount of $3,100.00 to be paid within 3 years time of the original note to Anthony L. Canna.

    Again the note made no provision for interest.

    Following the entry of its judgment on November 18, 1970 plaintiff levied execution upon Diodato's Cadillac. As a result plaintiff became aware of the fact that Canna was designated as "secured party" on the certificate of ownership of the vehicle, and was asserting a lien against it as security for the two loans, prior to the lien of plaintiff's execution on its judgment. Thereupon plaintiff initiated the present action to set aside as invalid the lien claimed by Canna upon the automobile. After hearing, the trial judge rejected contentions by the plaintiff "that no consideration passed between the parties . . . (and) that no value was given"; in essence found that the transaction between Diodato and Canna created a valid security interest in the automobile in Canna, which was perfected by the designation of Canna as "secured party" on the certificate of ownership, and held that Canna's lien was prior to that of plaintiff. The present appeal has been taken from said determination. The single ground urged for reversal is that the transaction between Canna and Diodato did not create in Canna a security interest in the Cadillac, prior to and enforceable against the plaintiff's lien. *First County Nat'l Bank & Trust Co. v. Canna*, 305 A.2d 442 (N.J. Super. 1973). How should the appeals courts have decided the issue?

2. Dr. William C. Owens loaned $25,000 to Chester Howard. The loan was evidenced by two promissory notes. To secure the notes, Howard endorsed the certificate of title of his 1956 G.M.C. bus and delivered the certificate to Owens.

    [E]ach promissory note contained the words "SECURITY: 1956 GMC Bus." Howard also endorsed his motor vehicle certificate of title to the G.M.C. bus on the line labeled "transfer of title."] On August 26, 1985, Howard sold the same bus to Don J. Simplot for $45,000, to be paid in installments. Simplot paid the last installment on January 22, 1986. He then took possession of the bus and received a bill of sale from Howard. The bill of sale recited that the bus was free from all liens and encumbrances. * * * Meanwhile, in April, 1986, Owens approached Howard and demanded payment of the loan. No payment was made. *Simplot v. Owens*, 805 P.2d 477 (Idaho Ct. App. 1990). The Idaho Department of Transportation decided that Simplot owned the bus but that his title was subject to a security interest in favor of Owens. Simplot sued. The trial court agreed with the Department. Simplot appealed. How would you have decided the appeal?

3. Norman Greer, who was engaged in farming operations in Gibson County, financed his corn and soybean crops through Miles. On May 21, 1991, Greer executed a financing statement[2] identifying himself as the debtor, Miles as a secured party, and "[a]ll corn and soybeans, presently growing, or to be planted on the following farms, and not limited to, including any additional acreage cultivated in 1991 (See exhibit A)" as collateral. Record at 50. The UCC-1 financing statement also included the addresses of both parties. Exhibit A identified by legal description, the Gibson County real estate on which the collateral was growing or was to be planted. Record at 51. Greer signed both the UCC-1 financing statement and Exhibit A. On June 19, 1991, Miles filed the UCC-1 financing statement with Exhibit A attached in the office of the recorder of Gibson County, Indiana. * * * Greer and Miles did not execute a

---

[2]   The financing statement was the standard form prescribed in IND.CODE 26-1-9-402, also known as the UCC-1 financing statement.

document labeled a security agreement. The only document executed was [the] UCC-1 financing statement and its attachment, Exhibit A. Greer signed the UCC-1 financing statement which listed his name and address in the space provided for information on the debtor. Miles' name and address appear in the space provided for information on the secured party. *Gibson County Farm Bureau Cooperative Ass'n, Inc. v. Greer*, 622 N.E.2d 551 (Ind. Ct. App. 1993). Was Miles a secured party?

4. S sold widgets to B on credit. Their written sales contract, which both parties signed, described the widgets and provided that "title to the goods remains in S until B fully pays the price of the goods." The goods were delivered. They conformed to the contract but B never paid for them. S wants to get the widgets back.   Can she repossess the goods under §9-503? See *Tilghman v. Larrimore*, supra.

5. Debtor took her car to Dealer for repairs. The Dealer described the work to be done on a work order which also described Debtor's car. Debtor signed this order. In small print in the corner of the work order this language appeared:

> Customer authorizes the work described below and gives Dealer an express mechanic's lien in the vehicle until the work is paid for.

State law does not provide for an express mechanic's lien, as such. Does Dealer have a mechanic's lien on the car? A security interest in the car? Does it matter?

ロロロロロ

b. Describing the Collateral

World Wide Tracers, Inc. v. Metropolitan Protection, Inc.
Supreme Court of Minnesota, 1986
384 N.W.2d 442

Amdahl, Chief Justice. This case arises from an action brought by appellant, World Wide Tracers, Inc., against respondent, Metropolitan State Bank (bank), Metropolitan Protection, Inc. (debtor), and three guarantors of debtor, to enforce its rights under a security agreement with debtor. The trial court granted bank's motion for summary judgment, declaring that the descriptions of collateral in appellant's security agreement and in the accompanying financing statement were insufficient as a matter of law to perfect appellant's security interest in debtor's accounts receivable. The court of appeals affirmed the trial court. We affirm.

The facts in this case are not in dispute. On July 15, 1980, appellant sold to debtor certain of its assets and properties, including equipment, furniture, uniforms, accounts receivable, and contract rights. To secure payment of the purchase price, debtor executed a security agreement and financing statement in favor of appellant. The financing statement was filed with the Minnesota Secretary of State on July 16, 1980.

Both the security agreement and the financing statement contained the following language describing the collateral:

> All of the property listed on Exhibit "A" attached hereto and made a part hereof, together with any property of the debtor acquired after July 15, 1980.

Both documents had the same Exhibit "A" attached. Exhibit "A" is a list of equipment, furniture, and fixtures owned by appellant and sold to debtor. Exhibit "A" does not include any accounts receivable or contract rights.

In February 1982, bank loaned monies to debtor, for which debtor executed two security agreements containing the following language:

> All accounts of borrower now existing or hereafter at any time acquired, and all contract rights of borrower now existing or hereafter at any time arising.

> All equipment now owned or hereafter acquired, including, but not limited to, office furniture and uniforms.

Debtor also executed a financing statement containing the following language to describe the collateral:

> All accounts receivable and contract rights owned or hereafter acquired.

> All equipment now owned or hereafter acquired, including but not limited to, office furniture and uniforms.

The financing statement was filed with the secretary of state's office on March 3, 1982.

When debtor defaulted on its agreement with appellant in fall 1982, appellant brought suit against debtor, guarantors of debtor's obligations, and bank, asserting the priority of its alleged security interest in the debtor's accounts receivable. Bank answered and counterclaimed, asserting its perfected security interest in debtor's accounts receivable. Debtor filed a petition in bankruptcy, and the bankruptcy trustee disclaimed any interest in and to the accounts receivable.

This appeal presents the following issues:

> 1. How strictly should the Uniform Commercial Code (UCC) requirements regarding the sufficiency of descriptions of collateral in security agreements and financing statements be applied?

2. Is the description of collateral as "all of the property listed on Exhibit 'A' and made a part hereof, together with any property the debtor acquired after July 15, 1980," a sufficient description of the collateral to perfect appellant's security interest in debtor's accounts receivable acquired after July 15, 1980?

1. Under Minnesota's version of the UCC, to perfect a security interest in an item of property, the creditor must have possession of the item, or there must be a signed security agreement between the creditor and the debtor. Minn.Stat. §336.9-203(1)(a) (1984). Additionally, to perfect a security interest in most types of collateral, a financing statement must be filed with the appropriate state or county office. Minn.Stat. §§336.9-302, 336.9-401 (1984).

Article 9 of chapter 336 requires both the financing statement and the security agreement to contain an identification of the property to be secured. *See* Minn.Stat. §§336.9-203(1)(a), 336.9-402(1). Regarding a security agreement, Minn.Stat. §336.9-203 requires the agreement to contain "a description of the collateral." With respect to a financing statement, Minn.Stat. §336.9-402(1) requires "a statement indicating the types or describing the items, of collateral." To perfect a security interest, both the description in the security agreement and the description in the financing statement must be "sufficient." The sufficiency of a description is governed by Minn.Stat. §336.9-110 (1984), which states that "any description of personal property or real estate is sufficient whether or not it is specific if it reasonably identifies what is described."

There is a split of authority regarding the analysis and application of the UCC collateral description requirements. Some courts have read the language of these UCC provisions narrowly and strictly. These courts have been unwilling to accept broad descriptions of collateral in financing statements and security agreements. Under the view adopted by these courts the description "any property" would be clearly insufficient.

Other courts, probably a majority, adopt a more liberal view. *See, e.g., United States v. First National Bank*, 470 F.2d 944 (8th Cir. 1973); * * * *Klingner v. Pocono International Raceway, Inc.*, 289 Pa.Super. 484, 433 A.2d 1357 (1981); *Milwaukee Mack Sales, Inc. v. First Wisconsin National Bank*, 93 Wis.2d 589, 287 N.W.2d 708 (1980). The court in *Klingner* explained this view by stating: "The Code is meant to be comprehensive and flexible, and to free the law from artificial distinctions restricting the rational conduct of commercial financing." 289 Pa.Super. at 489, 433 A.2d at 1360.

Under this view, broad descriptions of collateral in security agreements have been held sufficient so long as it was possible to "reasonably identify" the items subject to the security interests. The court in *First National Bank* stated:

[W]e are not convinced that the requirement in Section 9-203 *** that the collateral be described, is a device for minimizing the amount of collateral a creditor can secure. That may be a laudable goal, but it is not encompassed by §9-110. *** [T]he purpose of a description of collateral in a security agreement is only to evidence the agreement of the parties and therefore it need only "make possible the identification of the thing described."

470 F.2d at 947. In *First National Bank*, the court held that the description in the security agreement as "all farm and other equipment" was adequate to perfect a security interest in the debtor's after-acquired irrigation equipment. *Id.* at 947-48. Similarly, in *Milwaukee Mack Sales*, the Wisconsin Supreme Court held that the description "all debtor's equipment" sufficed to perfect a security interest in the debtor's trucks. 93 Wis.2d at 599, 287 N.W.2d at 714. A Pennsylvania appellate court permitted an even broader description by holding in *Klingner* that the language "all of Borrower's personal property and fixtures" created a security interest in "tickets and their proceeds." 289 Pa.Super. at 492, 433 A.2d at 1361. Finally, in *Leasing Service Corp. v. American National Bank & Trust Co.*, 19 U.C.C. Rep. Serv. (Callaghan) 252, 263 (D.N.J.1976), a federal district court allowed the very broad description in a security agreement of "any and all property wherever located" to create a security interest in all of the debtor's property. *See also In re JCM Cooperative, Inc.*, 8 U.C.C. Rep. Serv. (Callaghan) 247 (Bankr.W.D.Mich.1970) (description of collateral as "the proceeds and products [thereof] of all other equipment -- including but not limited to -- all tangible personal property now owned by the debtor" sufficiently described accounts receivable funds resulting from proceeds or products of the debtor's tangible property).

Courts adopting this broad view of the UCC collateral description requirements have generally demanded even less detail and specificity for descriptions in financing statements. *See, e.g., Thorp Commercial Corp. v. Northgate Industries, Inc.*, 654 F.2d 1245 (8th Cir.1981) ("assignment accounts receivable" perfected a security interest of all the debtor's accounts receivable); *In re F.R. of North Dakota, Inc.*, 41 U.C.C. Rep. Serv. (Callaghan) 265 (Bankr.D.N.D.1985) ("all furniture, fixtures, and small wares" was a sufficient description of the debtor's assets for the financing statement, but not for the security agreement); *In re Mitchell Bros. Construction, Inc.*, 41 U.C.C. Rep. Serv. (Callaghan) 1124 (Bankr.W.D.Wis.1985) ("super-generic" descriptions which do not indicate the types or describe the items of collateral are sufficient in financing statements where the intent is to indicate a blanket lien on all the debtor's assets); *Bankers Trust Co. v. Zecher*, 103 Misc.2d 777, 426 N.Y.S.2d 960 ("all present and hereafter acquired equipment wherever located" was a sufficient description in financing statement to perfect a security interest in the debtor's restaurant equipment). The bankruptcy court in *In re F.R. of North Dakota* explained this difference in treatment of descriptions in security agreements and financing statements:

[A] financing statement has as its purpose only to reasonably [identify] the nature of the secured collateral such that a third party might be placed on notice or such that it would be reasonable for a third party to make further inquiry. Liberality in defining language is permissible in a financing statement if that language does not mislead and at least suggests that further inquiry is appropriate. With regard to the financing statements, the inquiry must be whether the information thereon suggests the existence of additional security leading one to inquire further. The same degree of flexibility as to language is not accorded to the security agreement itself. The security agreement embodies the intention of the parties and is the primary source to which a creditor must direct his inquiry regarding the true nature of the security interest intended. A security interest is defined by the description contained in the security agreement.

41 U.C.C. Rep. Serv. at 271 (citations omitted). The basis for the distinction is found in the language of UCC §9-402(1) that permits a description in a financing statement to be sufficient if it merely indicates the "type" of collateral secured rather than describes each item individually.

In *James Talcott, Inc. v. Franklin National Bank*, 292 Minn. 277, 194 N.W.2d 775 (1972), the sole case in which we have considered this issue, we adopted a broad view of the collateral description requirements of Minn.Stat. §§336.9-203(1)(a) and 336.9-110 and held that the description of collateral in a security agreement as "all goods (as defined in Article 9 of the Uniform Commercial Code) whether now owned or hereafter acquired" was sufficient to perfect a security interest in the debtor's after-acquired motor vehicles and construction equipment. We stated:

The description of the collateral in the extension agreement did what it was meant to do -- namely, it included all of the goods then owned, or to be owned in the future, by the debtor. *** The parties sought to create a security interest in substantially all of the debtor's property. That is what was stated and that is what was meant. The parties did not particularize any further, and the statute does not require it.

Id. at 287, 194 N.W.2d at 782. Although we have adopted the broad view with respect to collateral descriptions in security agreements, we have never had occasion to interpret the requirements for collateral descriptions in financing statements.[2]

---

[2]   In a footnote in *Talcott*, we indicated that although a broad description of collateral sufficed in a security agreement, more restrictive language might be required in a financing statement. *See Talcott*, 292 Minn. at 287, n. 3, 194 N.W.2d at 782 n. 3. This statement, however, was *dicta* because the description in the financing statement in *Talcott* was much more specific than that in the security agreement.

The Eighth Circuit, in construing Minnesota law, adopted the liberal view that collateral descriptions in financing statements are sufficient if they would put a subsequent creditor on inquiry notice regarding the type of property at issue. The court has stated:

> Because the purpose of the financing statement is to warn subsequent creditors rather than to identify the collateral, the UCC makes clear that the collateral need not be specified in the financing statement but may be described by "type." ***
>   * * *
> [T]he UCC requires a description of only the *type* of collateral, not the collateral itself, in the financing statement to perfect a security interest. Under §336.9-110, a description of the collateral in a financing statement "is sufficient whether or not it is specific if it reasonably identifies" the *type* of collateral. The drafters of the UCC contemplated that the financing statement would need to give only enough description of the collateral to induce a subsequent creditor to make further inquiries.

Thorp Commercial Corp., 654 F.2d at 1249 (emphasis supplied).

Commentators on the UCC seem to agree that this is the better view. They are critical of cases requiring precise legal descriptions and argue that a description in a financing statement is sufficient if it would put a third party on notice. According to one commentator:

> [B]ecause the financing statement simply gives notice to the world *** a too-broad notice is, if anything, beneficial to third parties because it gives them warning to stay away. ***
>
> *** [I]f the result of finding a financing statement invalid because of a technical mistake is simply to benefit third parties who have in no way been misled -- and they are not likely to have been misled to their detriment in extending credit by a too-broad description of collateral -- then the result is plainly wrong and clearly unjust.

R. Henson, Secured Transactions §4-7, at 75 (1979). In the view of these commentators, a functional approach to applying the requirements of UCC §9-402(1) is best, with emphasis on the practical effect of the description rather than on whether it literally complies with section 9-402. *See* Comment, *Secured Transactions -- The Use of Generic Classifications as Descriptions of Collateral in Security Agreements and Financing Statements Under Article Nine of the Uniform Commercial Code*, 19 N.Y.L.F. 365, 371 (1973).

The language of the UCC and the official comments support a liberal interpretation of the collateral description requirements for financing statements and indicate that less specificity is required of descriptions in financing statements than in security agreements. While section 336.9-203(1)(a) requires a description of the collateral in the security agreement, section 336.9-402(1) permits either a description of the items of collateral *or* an indication of the "types" of collateral in the financing statement. Also, Minn.Stat. §336.9-402(8) (1984) permits a financing statement to be effective "even though it contains minor errors which are not seriously misleading." Section 336.9-203 contains no such provision for security agreements.

The official comment to UCC §9-402 indicates that the section adopts a system of "notice filing" in which the financing statement serves as "only a simple notice." UCC §9-402, comment 2. "The notice itself indicates merely that the secured party who has filed may have a security interest in the collateral described. Further inquiry from the parties concerned will be necessary to disclose the complete state of affairs." *Id.* The provisions of Article 9 and the official comments thereto support the conclusion that the security agreement embodies the actual agreement between the debtor and the secured party, and the financing statement need only provide inquiry notice to prospective creditors. Accordingly, we conclude that the collateral description requirements for financing statements set forth in Minn.Stat. §336.9-402(1) should be liberally construed and applied. A collateral description in a financing statement should be held adequate to perfect a security interest in an item of property if the description reasonably provides prospective creditors with inquiry notice regarding the type of property at issue.

2. Having concluded that the collateral description requirements of Article 9 should be liberally construed with respect to both security agreements and financing statements, we now consider the adequacy of the collateral description in appellant's documents to perfect a security interest in debtor's accounts receivable. In doing so, we need only consider the sufficiency of the description in the security agreement because the descriptions are identical in both documents. Since less specificity is required of descriptions in financing statements, in cases where the descriptions in the financing statement and the security agreement are identical, the collateral description requirements for security agreements will be dispositive.

As discussed above, under *Talcott*, broad descriptions are allowed in security agreements. Although the collateral description in *Talcott* was not as broad as that in appellant's documents, cases in other jurisdictions have approved such broad language in security agreements. *See Leasing Service Corp.*, 19 U.C.C. Rep. Serv. 252 ("any and all property wherever located"); *In re JCM*, 8 U.C.C. Rep. Serv. 247 ("all tangible personal property"); *Klingner*, 289 Pa.Super. 484, 433 A.2d 1357 ("all of Borrower's personal property and fixtures").

Appellant claims that the language "any property of the debtor acquired after July 15, 1980" accurately conveys the intent of the parties to encumber all of debtor's after-acquired assets. We have specifically acknowledged that such attempts to create blanket liens on a debtor's assets are permissible under Minnesota law. "If the debtor himself is willing to give a creditor a security interest in everything he owns, the code does not prevent it, whether his action is prudent or not." *Talcott*, 292 Minn. at 287, 194 N.W.2d at 782. In *Talcott*, we held:

> [T]he policy of Art. 9 is to uphold security agreements according to their terms. *** A security agreement should not be held unenforceable unless it is so ambiguous that its meaning cannot reasonably be construed from the language of the agreement itself.

Id. at 288, 194 N.W.2d at 782. However, we will not enforce security agreements where such a broad description of the collateral is misleading or ambiguous.

In the security agreement here, the word "property" is used twice to describe collateral -- first in reference to the assets listed on the attached Exhibit "A"; second in reference to after-acquired assets. The word is otherwise undefined. The only guidance one receives in the security agreement as to the meaning of "property" comes from assets listed on Exhibit "A," all of which are tangible personal property. When read in conjunction with Exhibit "A," the word "property" reasonably can be taken to mean only tangible property. At a minimum, the meaning is ambiguous.

Ambiguity and the likelihood of confusion is enhanced by other language in the security agreement. In addition to the language in the collateral description, the agreement contains another after-acquired property clause that grants a security interest in "all increases, parts, fittings, accessories, equipment, renewals and replacements of all or any part thereof, and other goods *of the same class* whether now owned or hereafter acquired by Debtor." (emphasis added). This language raises the question whether only after-acquired property "of the same class" is to be encumbered. If so, no security interest in the accounts receivable is created.

Appellant argues that the intent of the parties as expressed in the security agreement is clear and unambiguous; if it had meant to encumber only tangible property it would not have said "any property." The clear intent of the parties is called into question, however, by the fact that debtor informed bank at the time it acquired the loan that its accounts receivable were unencumbered. Also, if appellant had intended to encumber more than just tangible property, it could have so stated by using the description "any property, tangible or intangible." Where there is an ambiguity in a contract, the contract will be construed against the drafter.

Appellant also argues that the description should not be held inadequate so long as it provides inquiry notice to prospective creditors. Notice, however, is at issue only with respect to financing statements, not security agreements.

Although the description "any property of the debtor" in the security agreement might be sufficient in some circumstances, we conclude that here the description, when read in conjunction with the attached list of tangible assets, is too ambiguous and misleading to create a security interest in debtor's accounts receivable.

Affirmed.

World Wide Tracers, Inc. v. Dudley & Smith
Court of Appeals of Minnesota, 1988
1988 WL 83687 (unpublished opinion)

Schultz, Judge.

FACTS

This is an appeal from a grant of summary judgment. Appellant World Wide Tracers (WWT) had sued its attorneys, Dudley & Smith, for legal malpractice.

In 1980, appellants sold part of their business to Metropolitan Protection, Inc. To secure the sale, a security agreement and financing statement were executed. In an appendix to the financing statement, the property secured was described. Although the list of property was extensive, respondent failed to include accounts receivable or contract rights.

In 1982, Metropolitan Protection took a loan from Metropolitan State Bank. This loan was secured by a promissory note and security agreements in favor of the bank. The security agreement and financing statement for this transaction included accounts receivable and contract rights.

When business turned sour in the fall of 1982, a dispute arose over the priority of appellants' and Metropolitan Bank's respective security interests. The bank brought and succeeded on a motion for summary judgment. On appeal, the trial court was affirmed. See World Wide Tracers, Inc. v. Metropolitan Protection, Inc., 373 N.W.2d 839 (Minn.Ct.App.1985). The Minnesota Supreme Court also affirmed. See World Wide Tracers, Inc. v. Metropolitan Protection, Inc., 384 N.W.2d 442 (Minn.1986).

Appellants then turned to their counsel, suing for legal malpractice. Respondent brought a motion for summary judgment. The trial court granted this motion and WWT appeals.

At hearings on the motion, respondents presented no affidavits. Appellant presented the affidavit of a Minneapolis attorney expert in commercial matters. Appellants' expert testified that respondents' omission of accounts receivable and contract rights from the 1980 financing statement "failed to satisfy the standard of reasonable care applicable to the rendering of legal advice in the area."

The trial court granted summary judgment for respondents, finding as a matter of law that the respondents were neither negligent nor in breach of contract with appellants.

DECISION
Standard of Review

Appellate review of an order for summary judgment is concerned with (1) whether there exist any genuine issues of material fact; and (2) whether the trial court erred in its application of the law.

* * *

2. Under Minnesota law, the elements of legal malpractice are (1) the existence of an attorney/client relationship; (2) acts constituting negligence; (3) the negligent act was the proximate cause of the alleged damage; and (4) but for such negligence the client would have been successful in the prosecution or defense of the action. An attorney is required to act in good faith and with a reasonable degree of care and skill. An honest error of judgment by an attorney does not create liability if it is within the bounds of an honest exercise of professional judgment.

In considering this matter, the trial court also relied on the standard jury instruction relative to duty of an attorney. See 4 Minnesota Practice CIV. JIG 429 (1986). This jury instruction provides:

> In performing professional services for a client, an attorney must use a reasonable degree of skill and learning. In the application of this skill and learning, the attorney must act in good faith and with reasonable care. The attorney is not negligent if he makes an error or mistake in judgment as long as the attorney acts in the reasonable belief that his advice or acts are well founded and in the best interests of the client.

> In performing professional services for a client, an attorney must use that degree of skill and learning which is normally possessed and used by attorneys in good standing under like conditions. In the application of this skill and learning, the attorney must also use reasonable care.

Appellants presented the testimony (through affidavit) of a Minneapolis attorney expert in corporate and commercial law. Appellants' expert testified that reasonable care mandated the inclusion of accounts receivable and contract rights in the property description in the financing statement. The expert noted that at the time respondents drafted the financing statement, there was a split of state authority on the sufficiency of property descriptions in such statements. Reasonable care dictates that a specific reference to accounts receivable be included. The expert concluded by stating that in his opinion, respondents did not meet the "standard of reasonable care applicable to the rendering of legal advice in this area."

In any event, there certainly exist issues of material fact relative to respondents' conduct, which render the trial court's grant of summary judgment to respondents error.

Reversed and remanded.

In re Boogies Enterprises, Inc.
United States Court of Appeals, Ninth Circuit, 1988
866 F.2d 1172

William A. Norris, Circuit Judge: * * * The SBA is a creditor of Boogie under a 1983 loan agreement which gives the SBA a security interest in Boogie's assets. In 1984, Boogie filed a Chapter 11 bankruptcy petition. * * * Shortly afterward, the trustee for Boogie filed suit against one of Boogie's former customers. The suit was settled.

After reaching the settlement, the trustee sought a declaration in the bankruptcy court that the SBA did not have an interest in the proceeds of the settlement that was superior or prior to the rights of the trustee. The SBA contended, as it does on appeal, that a financing statement filed in 1983 pursuant to Cal. Comm.Code §9203 had given the SBA a "perfected" or superior interest in the settlement proceeds.

The bankruptcy court granted summary judgment to the trustee, holding that the financing statement was insufficient to perfect the SBA's security interest in the settlement proceeds. On appeal by the SBA, the district court reversed. The trustee now appeals.
      * * *

At issue in this case is whether the SBA's financing statement was sufficiently descriptive to confer a perfected security interest in the settlement proceeds. The financing statement asserted an interest in the following:

> All furniture, fixtures, equipment, personal property, machinery, inventory, and accounts receivable now owned or hereafter acquired.

The parties agree that the settlement proceeds are a "general intangible" within the meaning of the security agreement and the Code. The SBA argues, and the district court held, that the phrase "personal property" in the financing statement is sufficient to perfect the SBA's encumbrance of the proceeds.

We disagree. The weight of authority indicates that financing statements under the Uniform Commercial Code must describe collateral with greater precision than that furnished by the term "personal property." Professor Gilmore, who helped draft Article 9 of the UCC, wrote of §9402's requirement that financing statements describe collateral by "type" or "item": "The description by 'types' is understood to require a certain degree of specificity: it would not be sufficient for the notice to claim 'all the debtor's property.' " 1 G. Gilmore, Security Interests in Personal Property §15.3, at 477. This view is echoed in decisions of other courts holding that the term "personal property" is insufficiently specific to perfect security interests. * * *

We agree with the analysis of those courts and of Professor Gilmore. Section 9402's requirement of identification by "types" or "items" obliges the drafter of a financing statement to designate the collateral for a loan with greater specificity than the language "personal property" provides.   "Personal property" encompasses all of the items--including general intangibles, among others--covered by the division of the Code regulating secured transactions. See Cal.Comm.Code §9102(1)(a).   The term refers to essentially everything that a creditor can perfect an interest in pursuant to the Code.   "Personal property" cannot satisfy §9402's required identification of "types" or "items" of collateral without effectively nullifying §9402's requirement of identification of assets by "types" or "items," because "personal property" refers to no more and no less than every kind of collateral perfectible under the statute.

If the language "personal property" were sufficient to perfect a security interest, creditors would never need to use any other language to designate collateral. This is plainly at odds with §9402's policy of requiring disclosure to potential creditors of the nature of encumbered collateral. Moreover, it makes no difference that in this case the SBA's financing statement uses the term "personal property" in conjunction with specific types of property such as equipment and accounts receivable: the term is simply redundant with all the other terms in the financing statement, and adds no new "items" or "types." We conclude that the financing statement did not perfect SBA's interest in the general intangibles at issue in this case.

Perhaps it would make more sense, in instances where a creditor had a security interest in all the debtor's assets, for the Code to release the creditor from the identification requirements for financing statements. But we are not free to create such an exception.   Section 9402 requires that collateral be designated either by individual item or by type, which necessarily means in terms more specific than the catch-all term "personal property."

The judgment of the district court is REVERSED.

Questions

1. The Minnesota Supreme Court seems to have concluded in *World Wide v. Metropolitan* that the description of collateral in World Wide's security agreement -- and also in its financing statement -- was okay. World Wide nevertheless lost. Please explain.

2. Compare *Boogies* and *World Wide v. Metropolitan*. How far does the former contradict the latter?

3. How would the Minnesota Supreme Court have decided *Boogies*?

4. On March 28, 1989, David S. Ziluck applied for a Radio Shack credit card by filling out and executing a Radio Shack RSVP Credit Card Application. The front of the application contained blanks for Ziluck to enter various employment, personal, and financial information. The front of the application also provided a space for Ziluck's signature, above which was the following language: I have read the Radio Shack

Credit Account and Security Agreement, including the notice provisions in the last paragraph thereof, and it contains no blanks or blank spaces. I agree to the terms of the Agreement and acknowledge receipt of a copy of the Agreement.

On the back of the application was what was labeled Radio Shack Credit Account and Security Agreement. Significantly, paragraph 12 of the Radio Shack Credit Account and Security Agreement provided:

> 12. SECURITY INTEREST. We retain a security interest under the Uniform Commercial Code in all merchandise charged to your Account. If you do not make payments on your Account as agreed, the security interest allows us to repossess only the merchandise that has not been paid in full. You are responsible for any loss or damage to the merchandise until the price is fully paid. We give up any right to retain or acquire any lien which we might be automatically entitled to by law on your principal dwelling. This does not apply to a lien created by a court judgment or acquired by a filing as provided by statute.

Ziluck filled in the blanks on the front of the application. Ziluck also affixed his signature on the signature line provided on the front of the application. Ziluck did not sign the back of the application, which bore the language of the security agreement, because the back of the application had no space for Ziluck to do so.

Tandy issued Ziluck a credit card, and Ziluck used the card to purchase several items from Radio Shack retail stores. On December 21, 1990, Ziluck and his wife filed for protection from their creditors under Chapter 7 of the United States Bankruptcy Code.

Tandy applied to the bankruptcy court for an order directing the trustee of the bankruptcy estate to deliver possession of the goods Ziluck had purchased with the credit card. Tandy believed it was entitled to take possession of the goods pursuant to what it believed to be its properly perfected security interest in the subject goods. The bankruptcy court denied the motion and Tandy appealed. *In re Ziluck*, 139 B.R. 44 (S.D. Fla. 1992). What should have been the outcome of the appeal?

c. Relying on Extrinsic Evidence

Because the writing requirement of U.C.C. §9-203(1)(a) is in the nature of a Statute of Frauds, a creditor cannot establish an Article 9 security interest in property out of her possession by proof of a verbal understanding to create security. For the same reason, where there is a signed writing but the description of collateral fails the test of U.C.C. §9-110, a creditor should not be allowed to salvage a security interest by using parol evidence to identify further the property. Moreover, a secured party who acquires a security interest in some property of the debtor is nevertheless barred from relying on extrinsic evidence to add collateral that is not described in the security agreement.

Some courts have held, however, that a secured party can introduce parol evidence for the different purpose of determining the meaning of the description of collateral in the parties' security agreement. The purpose here is interpreting the parties security agreement which, after all, is a kind of contract. Neither the parol evidence rule nor any Statute of Frauds prohibits the use of parol evidence for purposes of interpreting contract language. The hard issue with respect to security agreements is deciding whether proffered parol evidence serves the prohibited purpose of adding collateral beyond that described in the writing, or serves the legitimate purpose of interpreting the description. The line between the two purposes can be very thin.

Riviera Equipment, Inc. v. Omega Equipment Corp.
155 Ga.App. 522, 271 S.E.2d 662 (1980)

Shulman, Judge. *** The judgment from which this appeal is taken resulted from a hearing mandated by this court [in an earlier opinion directing] *** that the trial court conduct a hearing to determine whether the security agreement involved in *** [this] case, which agreement referred only to 'concrete pumps,' included the trucks on which the pumps were mounted. The trial court complied with the direction of this court, conducting the trial as a hearing on a motion to set aside a judicial sale. The jury found for the defendant/secured party, Omega. We affirm the judgment entered on that verdict.

* * *

The description in the security agreement of the property involved here was "One Thompsen Model 745 Concrete Pump, Serial 79555. One Thompsen Model 745 Concrete Pump, Serial 74507." Both pumps were mounted on trucks when they were delivered to appellant [the debtor]. When appellant surrendered the pumps to appellee [the secured party] at an earlier stage of these proceedings, they were still mounted on trucks. The controversy which subsequently arose, and the resolution of which is the subject of this appeal, was whether the description in the security agreement was intended to include pumps and trucks, or just the pumps. We agree with appellee that the description is inherently ambiguous and is especially so in the context of the transaction between the parties. That being so, there was no error in admitting evidence to resolve the ambiguity or in giving instructions to the jury to aid them in the process of that resolution.

Problems

1. C loaned D money. They orally agreed that C would have a lien on D's car to secure the loan. This agreement was not in writing but both parties will testify that the agreement was made.

   a. Does C have a security interest in the car?

   b. Suppose they execute a written security agreement now. Will C then acquire a security interest in the car?

2. C loaned D money. They agreed in writing, which both of them signed, that C would have a lien on D's car to secure the loan. Later, they orally agreed that C's collateral would also include D's truck. Does C have a security interest in the truck?

3. C loaned D money. They agreed in writing, which both of them signed, that C would have a lien on D's cars to secure the loan. The question now is whether C's security interest attaches to D's truck. C argues that the term "cars" in the security agreement was intended to mean vehicles and included trucks. Is this evidence of the parties' intention admissible to establish the range of C's collateral?

2. Value

A security interest cannot attach until "value has been given." U.C.C. §9-203(1)(b). The Code provides a clear and detailed definition of "value" in U.C.C. §1-201(44), and the reported cases suggest virtually no troublesome issues in connection with this prerequisite to the existence of a security interest. You too can avoid problems with the value requirement by remembering three main points.

First, the definition of value is very broad. It includes common-law consideration but is not limited to consideration. For example, a promise to perform a pre-existing duty is not consideration under the common law. In contrast, under the Code "a person gives 'value' for rights if he acquires them as security for or in total or partial satisfaction of a pre-existing claim." U.C.C. §1-201(44)(b). So value is given, within the meaning of §9-203(1)(b), when a lender or other creditor acquires a security interest in property to secure an old debt. Giving the debtor something new, such as a further loan or an extension of time to pay, is not necessary. The pre-existing debt will alone support the security interest.

Also, value is not limited to loans made or credit extended to enable the debtor to buy the property that is collateral. Value includes the giving of credit for any purpose, including the acquisition of services, even when there is no connection between the collateral and the purpose for which the value is intended or used. So a bank can acquire a security interest in an automobile to secure a loan the debtor uses to buy tickets for a flight to Hawaii, or to buy a boat. The debtor's boat or automobile can also serve as collateral for a lawyer who has agreed to represent the debtor, on credit, in a divorce proceeding.

Second, who gets the value and who gives it are unimportant under §9-203(1)(c). Ordinarily, the person who owns the collateral gets the value, and the secured party gives the value. Other arrangements can produce security interests, however. For example, a corporation can agree to provide personal property it owns as collateral for Bank's loan to Ellen to enable Ellen to buy the corporation. U.C.C. §9-203(1)(b) is satisfied even though, in strict terms, the value, i.e., the loan proceeds, go to Ellen.

Third, value is not only necessary to the creation of a security interest; value is also necessary to the maintenance of a security interest. This corollary of §9-203(1)(b) is inferred from the scheme and purpose of Article 9. As explained by the United States Court of Appeals for the Fifth Circuit,

> The UCC defines security interest as "an interest in personal property or fixtures which secures payment or performance of an obligation." A security interest thus has no validity absent its underlying obligation; the satisfaction of that obligation extinguishes the security interest.

Bank of Lexington v. Jack Adams Aircraft Sales, Inc., 570 F.2d 1220, 1225 (5th Cir.1978). A security interest can be revived, however, if the debtor again becomes indebted to the secured party and the value given is within the scope of a future-advance clause in the parties' original security agreement, OR is within the scope of a modification of the original agreement or of a fresh agreement.

Questions

1. Usually, value is given by Creditor to Debtor But does the statute REQUIRE that the value be given *by* the creditor who gets the interest and be given *to* the debtor who creates the interest?

2. Because of Debtor's negligence, she is obligated in tort to Creditor. Debtor settles with Creditor and agrees to pay the obligation on an installment basis. The settlement agreement gives Creditor a security interest in certain of Debtor's personal property that is completely described. Creditor thereby acquires a security interest. What value was given?

3. Creditor makes an unsecured loan to Debtor but Creditor later begins to worry about Debtor's financial condition. Debtor agrees at this later point to give Creditor a security interest in Debtor's personal property. Must Creditor give Debtor something new for this interest?

4. Creditor makes a loan to Debtor's Sister. Debtor agrees in writing that Creditor shall have a security interest in certain described property of Debtor to secure the loan. Is there value given for this security interest inasmuch as Debtor herself receives no money?

5. Creditor makes an unsecured loan to Debtor's Sister. Debtor later agrees in writing that Creditor shall have a security interest in certain described property of Debtor to secure the loan. Is there value given for this security interest?

3. Rights In The Collateral

Notwithstanding an effective security agreement and the giving of value, a security interest does not attach to collateral unless the debtor has rights in the property. U.C.C. §9-203(1)(c). The drafters of the U.C.C. did not fully explain the meaning of "rights," declaring only that "'rights' includes remedies." U.C.C. §1-201(36). Nevertheless, the conceptual boundaries of the term "rights" are fairly clear and certain: Some interest short of complete property or full legal title provides sufficient rights to support a security interest, but mere possession in and of itself is probably not enough.

Between these two extremes of mere possession and full legal title is a wide variety of possible interests, claims, powers, and privileges with respect to property. To decide whether any one of these, or a combination of them, is sufficient for the purpose of creating a security interest, the general approach is to consult the appropriate body of law that defines and governs the debtor's connection with or claim to the property in the particular case. This usually requires looking to law that is extraneous to Article 9. If, according to that other law, the debtor has some transferable rights or interest with respect to the property, then to this extent she has "rights in the collateral."

The "rights" requirement is simply an embodiment of the common-law doctrine of derivative title: One cannot convey more than she has. As applied to the creation of security interests, this doctrine breaks down into two basic rules: Rule # 1. A debtor cannot create a security interest in property in which she has no rights. Rule # 2. When a debtor has rights in collateral, the security interest she creates is coextensive with her rights.

The second rule is less obvious but just as real and important under Article 9. A debtor's rights in property may be less than complete and absolute, that is, her rights may be limited or qualified, as is true of a lessee of property. These limitations or qualifications equally limit or qualify a security interest because a security interest attaches to the debtor's rights in property, not to the property itself, and the debtor cannot convey rights greater than her own. For these reasons, a security interest is necessarily coextensive with the debtor's rights in the collateral.

Thus, a debtor who leases goods can create a security interest in her rights as lessee; but she cannot affect the greater residual rights of the lessor. Similarly, a debtor who jointly owns goods can use her interest as collateral; but she cannot encumber the interest of the co-owner.

Both Rules # 1 and # 2 are subject to two principal exceptions:

Exception # 1. A debtor-obligor's rights can exist or grow if another person having an interest in the collateral legally can, and actually does, consent to the use of her interest as collateral for the debtor's obligations. In such a case, however, no security interest is created in the other person's property rights unless the person signs a security agreement. U.C.C. §9-203(1)(a) requires the signature of the "debtor". Look closely at the definition of this term in U.C.C. §9-105(1)(d) ("debtor" means obligor, owner, or both). Even if the debtor-obligor owns no rights in the property, she too must sign the security agreement because the term "debtor" as used in §9-203(1)(a) is a provision dealing with both the collateral and the obligation.

Exception # 2. A debtor-obligor's rights can exist or grow if another person having an interest in the collateral is estopped, or is otherwise precluded, by force of law from objecting to the enforcement of a security interest in her interest. Estoppel can result by operation of common law or statute. In the case *In re Pubs, Inc.*, 618 F.2d 432 (7th Cir.1980), a corporation stood by and watched as two of its officers treated corporate property as their own in securing a bank loan made to them personally. The bank was unaware that the property actually belonged to the corporation. Applying Illinois common law, the court held that the corporation, which was charged with the knowledge of the two officers, was thereafter estopped to deny the validity of the bank's security interest in the property.

Estoppel can also result from statute. Suppose, for example, that Manufacturer of widgets consigns them to Merchant for sale to the public. Merchant is a bailee for a limited purpose. Title and all other rights stay with Manufacturer. Merchant includes the widgets in her inventory in which Bank has a security interest. Bank has no notice, actual or constructive, that Merchant is merely a consignee of the widgets with no rights other than to possess and sell them for Manufacturer.

On these facts there is no common-law estoppel. Yet, because of U.C.C. §2-326, Merchant's creditors can treat the widgets as if title to them were in Merchant. So Bank's security interest attaches to the widgets and enjoys priority over Manufacturer's claim. In effect, Manufacturer is estopped by statute to assert its ownership and to deny the validity of Bank's interest. There are other statutes that in other circumstances similarly estop an owner of property from asserting her interest against third parties.

Whenever an owner of property is estopped by common-law or statute to assert her rights against a secured party, the secured party can enforce her security interest free of the owner's rights even though the owner did not sign a security agreement. In essence, as against the secured party, the estoppel transferred the true owner's rights to the debtor-obligor who did sign such an agreement. This explains why cases such as *Pubs* are often described as creating rights by estoppel.

Questions and Problems

1.   What rights are sufficient to support a security interest?

2.   Creditor makes a loan to Debtor who signs a security agreement perfectly describing property that Debtor stole from another person. Does Creditor have a security interest in this property?

3.   Can Debtor create a security interest in equipment that she has leased?

4.   Can Debtor create a security interest in personal property that she jointly owns with someone else?

5.   Creditor makes a loan to Brother. Brother's Sister agrees to give Creditor a security interest in certain described property of Sister to secure the loan. Is this possible inasmuch as Article 9 requires that the "debtor" must have rights in the collateral?

6.   Creditor makes a loan to Brother. Brother's Sister agrees to give Creditor a security interest in certain described property of Sister to secure the loan. Who must sign the security agreement?

7.   Creditor makes a loan to Brother who signs a security agreement perfectly describing property that entirely belongs to Brother's Sister, who knows nothing of the deal. Does Creditor have a security interest in the property?

8. Creditor makes a loan to Brother who signs a security agreement perfectly describing property that entirely belongs to Brother's Sister, but Brother represents that he is the owner. To make sure, Creditor calls Sister. Sister lies and says the property belongs to Brother. Later, when Brother defaults, Sister fights Creditor's claim to the property, arguing that Brother had no rights and that she signed no security agreement. Who wins?

4. Enlarging Security Interests By Agreement

a. To Cover Later Property — After-Acquired Property Clauses

By including appropriate language in their security agreement, the secured party and debtor can expand the reach of a security interest to include property of the kind described in the agreement that the debtor acquires after the agreement is executed. Article 9 expressly sanctions this sort of clause by declaring, in U.C.C. §9-204(1), "a security agreement may provide that any and all obligations covered by the secured agreement are to be secured by after-acquired collateral."

The courts did not always give effect to after-acquired property clauses in chattel mortgages or other pre-Code security agreements. The early common-law rule was that "nothing can be mortgaged that is not in existence and does not at the time belong to the mortgagor, for a person cannot convey that which he does not own." *Hickson Lumber Co. v. Gay Lumber Co.*, 150 N.C. 282, 63 S.E. 1045, 1047 (1909). A creditor was often forced to rely on equitable principles and remedies to enforce a lien on property that the debtor acquired after the security agreement was made.

Article 9 does not purport to change the principle that a person can convey a present interest in property only if she has rights in it. Indeed, U.C.C. §9-203(1)(c) expressly perpetuates this principle by providing that a security interest attaches only to property in which the debtor has rights. Yet, §9-204(1) expressly validates after-acquired property clauses, which means that

> a security interest arising by virtue of an after-acquired property clause has equal status with a security interest in collateral in which the debtor has rights at the time value is given under the security agreement. That is to say: the security interest in after-acquired property is not merely an "equitable" interest; no further action by the secured party -- such as the taking

of a supplemental agreement covering the new collateral -- is required.

U.C.C. §9-204 comment 1.

U.C.C. §9-204(1) only sanctions an agreement reached by the parties with respect to after-acquired collateral. The section does not give the secured party by operation of law a security interest in any of the debtor's after-acquired property. When a debtor subsequently acquires additional property of a type described in the security agreement, no security interest attaches to the property unless the agreement contains language giving the secured party an interest in the after-acquired property. In the absence of such language, the after-acquired property is not collateral unless the security agreement is amended to cover the property or a wholly new security agreement covering it is executed by the parties.

If the original security agreement contains language giving the secured party an interest in the after-acquired property, the security interest attaches automatically as soon as the debtor has rights in the property. A separate agreement specifically covering the newly-acquired collateral is not needed. Nor is it necessary that additional value be given to support a security interest in the after-acquired collateral. The existence of a pre-existing debt that the property secures is itself "value" within the meaning of U.C.C. §9-203(1)(b). See U.C.C. §1-201(44).

Whether or not a secured party's interest attaches to particular after-acquired property of the debtor usually depends on the parties' security agreement satisfying three requirements:

First, the security agreement must contain a description of some property that "reasonably identifies what is described." U.C.C. §9-110. Otherwise, the secured gets an interest in nothing, except property pledged to her, i.e., collateral in her possession.

Second, the security agreement must indicate that the collateral includes property of the kind described that the debtor thereafter acquires. Otherwise, the collateral is limited to the kind of property described in which the debtor had rights when the agreement was executed. The typical security agreement makes explicit the intention to cover subsequently acquired property by appending to the property description the declaration that the collateral also includes such property "hereafter acquired by the debtor."

Explicit after-acquired property language is not always necessary, however. A number of courts have held, for example, "that when a security interest is taken in *inventory* of a business, after-acquired inventory is automatically covered by the agreement." *In re Nickerson*

& Nickerson, Inc., 329 F.Supp. 93, 96 (D.Neb.1971), *aff'd*, 452 F.2d 56 (8th Cir.1971). The courts reason that

> inventory subject to a security agreement should be looked upon as a single entity and not as a collection of individual items. "In other words, the *res* which is the subject of the lien *** is the merchandise or stock in trade, conceived as a unit presently and continuously in existence -- a 'floating mass', the component elements of which may be constantly changing without affecting the identity of the res." Inventory is like a river, the water in which continually flows, rises and falls, but which always constitutes a river.

329 F.Supp. at 96. This "floating mass", "flowing river" analysis could conceivably be applied to security interests in other kinds of collateral.

Third, the subsequently acquired property that the secured party claims must be of a kind described in the security agreement. For example, if the collateral is described as "*equipment,* presently owned or hereafter acquired", the security interest does not attach to subsequently acquired *inventory.*

A related concern is an after-acquired property clause that is itself restrictive. Suppose, for example, that the security agreement describes the collateral as the debtor's "cattle"; and, instead of providing that the collateral includes such property "hereafter acquired by the debtor," the agreement provides that it covers "replacements of the collateral." The security interest may attach only to after-acquired cattle that are in fact replacements for animals which comprised the original herd and not other cattle subsequently acquired by the debtor to enlarge the herd. An after-acquired property clause may be similarly restrictive if it covers only property that the debtor "hereafter owns" inasmuch as a debtor can have rights in property that she does not "own" in the sense of having title to the property.

Problems

1. Creditor makes a loan to Debtor who signs a written security agreement perfectly describing a piece of equipment that Debtor owns. Later, Debtor acquires additional equipment. Does Creditor's security interest spread to this new equipment?

2. Creditor makes a loan to Debtor who signs a written security agreement perfectly describing a piece of equipment that Debtor owns. Later, Debtor acquires additional

equipment. The parties sign another writing providing that this new equipment secures the loan. Does Creditor's security interest spread to the new equipment?

3. Creditor makes a loan to Debtor who signs a written security agreement perfectly describing a piece of equipment that Debtor owns. Later, Debtor acquires additional equipment. The parties sign no new security agreement, but the original security agreement describes the collateral as all of the Debtor's equipment, including all equipment in which Debtor may thereafter acquire rights.

    a. Does Creditor's security interest spread to the new equipment?

    b. Would Creditor's security interest spreading to the new equipment violate the rule that a security interest can only attach to property in which the debtor has rights?

4. Creditor makes a loan to Debtor who signs a written security agreement perfectly describing a piece of equipment that Debtor owns. Later, Debtor acquires additional equipment. The parties sign no new security agreement, but the original security agreement describes the collateral as all of the Debtor's equipment. Does Creditor acquire a security interest in the new equipment as soon as Debtor acquires rights in the property?

5. Creditor makes a loan to Debtor who signs a written security agreement perfectly describing the collateral as all of the debtor's inventory. Later, Debtor acquires additional inventory. The parties sign no new security agreement. Does Creditor acquire a security interest in the new inventory as soon as Debtor acquires rights in the property?

6. Creditor makes a loan to Debtor who signs a written security agreement perfectly describing the collateral as all of Debtor's consumer goods, present and after-acquired. Two months later, Debtor acquires a new huge-screen television for her home. The parties sign no new security agreement. Does Creditor acquire a security interest in the new TV as soon as Debtor acquires rights in the property? See 9-204(2).

b. To Cover Later Value – Future-Value Clauses

You have learned that, by way of after-acquired property clauses and otherwise, security interests can "float" as to the collateral covered. Security interests can also float as to the amount of debt secured. A secured party and a debtor may include a clause in their security agreement providing that the collateral will secure not only contemporaneous advances of value or other debt, but also value that may be given in the future. U.C.C. §9-204(3) validates such *future-advance* or *future-value clauses*, but the provision accomplishes no more. Neither it nor any other section purports to swell a creditor's security interest in collateral so that solely by operation of law it will secure later value given by her.

The rule under Article 9 is that a future-value interest is enforceable, that is, future value is secured by the collateral, only if "the [subsequently incurred] obligation is *** covered by the security agreement." U.C.C. §9-204 comment 5. This means two things: First, the security agreement must provide that the collateral will secure future value; and second, the subsequent value must be within the scope of the parties' agreement with respect to collateralizing future value.

Security agreements typically include language that is all encompassing with respect to future value. It is not uncommon for the parties to agree that the collateral will secure not only contemporaneous advances but also

> all other money heretofore or hereafter advanced by the Secured Party to or for account of the Debtor at the option of the Secured Party, and all other present or future, direct or contingent liabilities of the Debtor to the Secured Party of any nature whatsoever, and interest on all of the above obligations.

Nothing in Article 9 itself prevents the enforcement of dragnet clauses such as this one, but, as Professor Gilmore reported, the courts often refuse to enforce them "when a lender, relying on a broadly drafted clause, seeks to bring within the shelter of his security arrangement claims against the debtor which are unrelated to the course of financing that was contemplated by the parties." 2 G. Gilmore, SECURITY INTERESTS IN PERSONAL PROPERTY §35.5 at 932 (1965).

The courts long ago created a rule under which collateral -- whether personalty or realty -- is subject to a future-value interest only if the value is "of the same class as the primary obligation *** and so related to it that the consent of the debtor to its inclusion may be inferred." *National Bank of E. Arkansas v. Blankenship*, 177 F.Supp. 667, 673 (E.D.Ark.1959), aff'd sub nom., *National Bank of E. Arkansas v. General Mills, Inc.*, 283 F.2d 574 (8th Cir.1960). The rule is a variant of a more general principle that has traditionally guided courts in the enforcement of future-advance interests. This principle is that a subsequent indebtedness is secured by virtue of a future-advance clause only if the indebtedness was reasonably within the parties' contemplation at the time the security agreement was executed.

The courts have sometimes applied the "same class of indebtedness" rule in Article 9 cases, but the argument for displacement is strong. The drafters of Article 9 absolutely rejected judicial limitations on future-value arrangements that developed under pre-Code law. U.C.C. §9-204 comment 5.

Problems

1. Creditor makes a $50,000 business loan to Debtor, and at this time Debtor signs a security agreement granting Creditor a security interest in Debtor's equipment, inventory, and receivables. Later, Debtor gets a second $50,000 business loan from Creditor. To what extent does Creditor have a security interest in the collateral?

2. Reconsider Problem 1. Suppose the security agreement provides that the collateral secures present and future advances. To what extent does Creditor have a security interest?

3. Continue with Problem 2. Suppose that Creditor subsequently makes a $10,000 personal loan to Debtor. Is this loan secured?

4. Continue with Problem 3. Months later and in self defense, Creditor pays a $5,000 special tax assessment levied against Debtor's business property.

   a. The collateral does not secure this amount. Why not?

   b. How would you have drafted the original security agreement so that the collateral would secure the amount paid for the tax assessment?

5. Creditor makes a $50,000 business loan to Debtor, and at this time Debtor signs a security agreement granting Creditor a security interest in Debtor's equipment, inventory, and receivables that secures all future advances and later value of any kind, whether related or not. Later, Debtor gets a second $50,000 business loan from Creditor. Creditor has a security interest in the collateral for $100,000, both loans. Does the collateral include inventory, equipment, receivables, and proceeds acquired before and after the second loan?

6. Wichita Piano and Organ, Inc. ("Wichita") and Nelson Music Company, Inc. ("Nelson") are Kansas corporations wholly owned by Charles W. Davison. On February 25, 1985, Wichita entered into a loan agreement with First National Bank, Kingman, Kansas ("Kingman Bank"). In return for the loan, Wichita executed a promissory note and security agreement to Kingman Bank. The following day--February 26, 1985--Nelson, through Charles Davison, executed a guaranty agreement whereby it guaranteed Wichita's indebtedness to Kingman Bank. On February 27, 1985--the very next day--Nelson entered into its own loan agreement

with Kingman Bank. The promissory note for that loan specifically referenced a security agreement dated February 27, 1985, which granted Kingman Bank a security interest in Nelson's inventory of Gulbransen organs. That promissory note stated that "[t]his loan is secured by Security Agreement dated 2-27-85, executed by or for the debtor in favor of the holder. This Security Agreement will secure future or other indebtedness and will cover after acquired property." That security agreement contained a "dragnet clause" which stated the following: "The security interest ... shall secure all obligations of the undersigned to the Bank, howsoever created, evidenced or arising, whether direct or indirect, absolute or contingent, or now or hereafter existing, or due or to become due...." (emphasis added). On February 28, 1985, Kingman Bank perfected the security agreement by filing a financing statement with the Kansas Secretary of State.

Almost one year later, on February 13, 1986, Nelson entered into a revolving loan agreement with a second bank, the Bank of Kansas. Under the terms of that agreement, Nelson granted the Bank of Kansas a security interest in "[a]ll inventory and accounts receivable...." The Bank perfected that security interest on February 26, 1986.

In June of 1986, Nelson paid off the February 27, 1985 promissory note. However, some time later, Wichita defaulted on the February 25, 1985 note. Kingman Bank commenced a suit in Kansas court against Wichita (and Davison and Nelson as guarantors) and won a judgment to recover the balance of its loan to Wichita. Bank of Kansas subsequently brought this suit to protect and foreclose its security interest in the Nelson inventory. Kingman Bank was joined as a defendant and it argued that it had a prior claim over Nelson's Gulbransen organ inventory. According to Kingman Bank, Nelson's February 26, 1985 guaranty was an obligation covered by the "dragnet clause" of the February 27, 1985 security agreement. Thus, Kingman Bank asserted that the guaranty obligation was secured by the interest in the Gulbransen organs. Bank of Kansas countered that the February 27, 1985 security agreement between Nelson and Kingman Bank secured only the promissory note entered into on the same date and that Kingman Bank's security interest in Nelson's Gulbransen organ inventory expired when the Nelson promissory note was paid off in June 1986.

The case was removed to federal court, where both sides moved for summary judgment. The district court granted summary judgment for Bank of Kansas, and Kingman Bank now appeals. *Bank of Kansas v. Nelson Music Co., Inc.*, 949 F.2d 321 (10th Cir. 1991). How should the appeals court have decided the case?

C. ENFORCING SECURITY INTERESTS AGAINST THE DEBTOR

1. Determining Default

When a debtor breaches the terms of a security arrangement, she thereby defaults and the secured party is entitled immediately to repossess the collateral, dispose of it, and apply the proceeds in satisfaction of the secured debt. U.C.C. §§9-503 & 9-504. These remedial rights are the reasons for having a security interest; they are the very essence of security. Part 5 of Article 9 establishes and governs these rights, and most of the materials that follow in this section of the book deal with the particulars of repossessing and disposing of collateral upon a debtor's default.

Preliminarily, however, you should consider that default has other, equally devastating consequences for the debtor. The debtor can stave off repossession and sale of her property that is collateral by paying the secured debt. Indeed, Article 9 guarantees the debtor the right of redemption. U.C.C. §9-506. The problem is that the debtor cannot save her property by paying only part of the secured debt, not even when the default occurred because the debtor missed a single installment payment. Security agreements almost always provide that upon default, however defined, the whole balance of the debt becomes due. This provision is called an *acceleration clause* which, when triggered, means that all amounts, heretofore due only in the future, are due now. So, instead of having to come up with a relatively small amount of money to ransom the collateral, such as an installment payment or two, the debtor must pay the balance of everything she owes the secured party.

Default has another consequence for the debtor that is especially devastating for a business debtor. The secured party may very well have been the debtor's principal, perhaps her only, source of credit. Upon default, the creditor will almost certainly refuse to make additional loans, and the debtor thereby is denied operating and capital funds when she most needs them. The debtor is effectively put out of business.

So a secured party's rights upon the debtor's default go beyond grabbing her collateral and include accelerating the secured debt and stopping all other credit. Practically speaking, a secured party's exercise of these additional rights is really what kills a debtor's business. Realizing on the collateral is the anticlimactic removal of the corpse.

A secured party's decision to exercise her default rights is virtually unregulated by law and traditionally has been left, to a large extent, to the almost unlimited discretion of the secured party. Article 9 does not define the term "default" which triggers default rights. The parties define it themselves in the security agreement which, of course, the secured party drafts.

The typical agreement includes a very long list of specific, demonstrable events and circumstances that constitute default. The agreement authorizes a secured party to pursue her default rights if any of these events occurs, even when the default is a technical default, that is, the occurrence of the event does not really jeopardize the collateral or the debtor's ability or willingness to pay the secured debt.

Moreover, there usually is additional language in the security agreement entitling the secured party to accelerate when, for any reason, she feels "insecure". This type of acceleration clause, which is very common, is called a *whim acceleration clause.* The name itself suggests that the secured party needs no compelling justification, or even a good reason, to act. Also, the debt may be evidenced by a promissory note that is payable on demand, i.e., whenever the secured party wants the money.

A secured party's reliance on insecurity or other whim to accelerate a secured debt is explicitly conditioned on the secured party acting in good faith. U.C.C. §1-208. Yet, for these purposes, the Code seems to measure good faith according to a subjective test. A secured party fails this test only when she acts dishonestly in fact, U.C.C. §1-201(19), i.e., with a dark heart. Proving subjective dishonesty is always terribly difficult. So good faith, subjectively defined, is not much of a limit on any kind of conduct.

Debtors often argue, therefore, for an objective or somehow wider meaning of "good faith." In 1990, the meaning was widened for purposes of Article 3, see 3-103(a)(4). Debtors may argue, at least when negotiable instruments are involved in their secured transactions, that the Article 3 definition controls even the Article 9 issues. This argument will be strongest when default under the instrument is the contractual trigger on default for purposes of Article 9. Even a subjective test, however, is not purely subjective.

To avoid this debate entirely, secured parties sometimes structure the transaction so that the debt is a "demand obligation" -- i.e., the debt is payable "on demand," i.e., whenever the secured party wants her money for whatever reason or no reason. Secured parties argue that under this structure, enforcement upon default is not subject to any good faith limitation. The argument is typically based on language in the commentary to 1-208 that "this section has no application to demand instruments or obligations whose very nature permits call at any time with or without reason." U.C.C. §1-208 comment. It's somewhat hard, however, to structure a deal so that -- truly, certainly

-- the debt is due on demand. Moreover, even when a debt is really due "on demand," debtors often argue that a limitation of good faith applies from sources other than §1-208—sources such as §1-203 ("Every contract or duty within this Act imposes an obligation of good faith in performance or enforcement.") and supplemental common law (§1-103). This argument usually fails. (For an especially helpful rendition of this debate, see *Bank One v. Grantham*, 1991 WL 206733 (Court of Appeals of Ohio 1991).) Debtors are better off when default is triggered by some event or the creditor's whim.

J. R. Hale Contracting Co., Inc. v. United New Mexico Bank
Supreme Court of New Mexico, 1990
110 N.M. 712, 799 P.2d 581

Ransom, Justice. This suit involves the claimed wrongful acceleration of a $400,000 promissory note given by J.R. Hale Contracting Company (the company) to the United New Mexico Bank at Albuquerque. At a trial on the merits the district court granted the bank's motion for a directed verdict, finding that the acceleration was justified because an interest payment was twenty-three days past due when the decision to accelerate was made. The company appeals and we reverse, holding that a factual question exists on whether the bank is estopped from using the default clause in the contract in order to justify acceleration without prior notice and an opportunity to cure.

In addition to its defense under the default provision in the contract regarding past due payments, the bank relied upon an insecurity clause and asserted that the company had failed to make a prima facie showing that the bank lacked good faith in accelerating payment under that clause. We agree with the trial court that sufficient facts were introduced on this issue to raise a jury question. Therefore, denial of the bank's motion for a directed verdict on this basis was proper. We remand the cause for a new trial to encompass both the estoppel and lack of good faith issues. The company must prevail on both issues in order to recover on its claim for damages.

The company had been a customer of the bank for about eleven years prior to the circumstances that gave rise to this suit. During this period of time the company entered into numerous revolving credit notes with the bank in gradually increasing amounts. These notes routinely were renewed on or about the due date despite the   fact that the company frequently was late a number of days or even weeks in making its payments. The bank seems not to have been troubled by the payments being past due and took no action in each instance other than possibly contacting the company to request that the payments be brought up to date. The company would send a check or the bank simply would deduct the payment from one of the company's accounts at the bank and send a notice of advice regarding the transaction.

The note at issue in this case was executed in November 1982 in the amount of $400,000. This was double the amount of any previous note. The first and only interest payment on the note was due March 1, 1983, and the note itself was due on July 31, 1983. The note provided that: If ANY installment of principal and/or interest on this note is not paid when due ... or if Bank in good faith deems itself insecure or believes that the prospect of receiving payment required by this note is impaired; thereupon, at the option of Bank, this note and any and all other indebtedness of Maker to Bank shall become and be due and payable forthwith without demand, notice of nonpayment, presentment, protest or notice of dishonor, all of which are hereby expressly waived by Maker * * * *

Toward the end of February 1983, J.R. and Bruce Hale, on behalf of the company, approached the bank to borrow additional funds to cover contracting expenses associated with construction at the Double Eagle II Airport in Albuquerque. The existing $400,000 line of credit was fully drawn. Beginning in the first week in March, the Hales met with the bankers several times a week hoping to arrange for additional financing. The company had not made the March 1 interest payment on the existing loan. J.R. and Bruce Hale stated that no one ever contacted them concerning the delinquent payment and the matter never came up during the March meetings. J.R. Hale carried a blank check to these meetings for the purpose of making the interest payment but stated that he forgot to do so. He stated that on one occasion he called the bank officer assigned to his account and asked the officer to remind him at the next meeting and he would make the payment, but the officer had not done so. Apparently, it was necessary for the bank to calculate the interest payment in order to know the specific amount to be paid.

At the same time that the company was seeking to secure additional financing, the bankers had become concerned about the existing $400,000 loan. The financial statements that the company periodically supplied the bank indicated that the company had lost approximately $800,000 during the last six to seven months. While the Hales were under the impression that additional financing was in the works (a loan application to this effect had been prepared and had been taken to the loan committee for discussion), the bank seriously was considering calling in the company's existing obligations. This possibility never was communicated to the Hales as the bank wished them to remain cooperative. After a meeting on March 22 the bank requested and received from the Hales a list of customers for the undisclosed purpose of using it to collect directly the company's accounts.

The bank called a meeting on March 24 and presented the Hales with a letter stating that all amounts due on the $400,000 revolving line of credit were due and payable immediately. The grounds for the acceleration were stated to be that "The promissory note is in default due to your failure to pay the March 1, 1983 interest payment when due, and also due to the Bank's review of your financial situation which causes the Bank to believe that its prospect for receiving payment of the note is impaired." J.R. Hale produced a blank check and offered to pay the delinquent interest charges but the bank would not reconsider. The bank was able to collect the balance of the note with interest, $418,801.86, in about two weeks after exercising its right to set off the company's accounts at the bank and after receiving payments from the company's customers on their outstanding accounts.

As mentioned, the court directed a verdict for the bank stating that, although a jury issue existed regarding the bank's acceleration under the insecurity clause, none existed regarding the bank's right to accelerate payments under the interest default clause. The company claims on appeal, as it did before the trial court, that a jury issue existed on whether the bank had waived the interest default clause, or whether there was an implied modification of the note to require notice and demand prior to exercising the clause, or whether the bank was estopped to assert the clause. The bank answers that there was no evidence to show waiver, modification, or estoppel and, in any case, the entry of a directed verdict can be upheld under the insecurity clause since there was no genuine issue over the fact that the bank acted in good faith in concluding that its prospect for repayment was impaired.

Waiver, modification, and estoppel distinguished. The company's arguments regarding waiver, modification, and estoppel are intertwined and rely upon the same root proposition: that the conduct of the bank negated the express default provision in the note. The distinctions to be made in the application of these concepts, especially in that of waiver and estoppel, have not always been clear in our cases and some discussion on the point is warranted.

Professor Corbin states that waiver cannot be defined without reference to the particular circumstances to which it is being related, nor can one determine the legal effect of a "waiver" without knowing the facts the term is being used to describe. 3A A.L. Corbin, Corbin on Contracts §752 (1960). To illustrate the concept of waiver of contractual obligations or conditions, he presents the following example within the context of a land conveyance:

> The vendor's "waiver" * * * is his own voluntary action; and in order to be legally effective, it is not necessary that the purchaser shall have given any consideration for it or shall have changed his position in reliance upon it. If the vendor offers to eliminate the condition in exchange for a requested consideration, and the purchaser gives that consideration, the case can still be described as a "waiver"; but it is also a modification by mutual agreement--by a substituted contract--a modification that is not subject to retraction by the vendor. If the vendor requests and receives no consideration for his waiver, but, as he had reason to foresee, it causes the purchaser to change his position materially in reliance upon it, this too deprives the vendor of his power of retraction for, at the least, a reasonable time. The vendor is then said to be estopped; his own action can still be described as a "waiver",

while the resulting action of the purchaser justifies the added description of estoppel.

Id. at §752 p. 481 (footnote omitted).

As Professor Corbin also acknowledges, expressions or conduct that lead a party reasonably to believe that certain conditions or obligations will not be insisted upon may operate as a waiver, and courts will then speak in terms of estoppel as well as waiver. Id. at §754 p. 494-96. In this last situation, where one party has induced material changes of position in the other, a waiver of a contractual obligation or condition actually may not have been intended. There is no requirement that this be the case. While waiver depends upon what one himself intends to do, estoppel depends only upon what one's conduct has caused another party to do. Id. at §752 p. 481, n. 2. Professor Corbin also notes that a party may re- establish a condition or obligation that had been eliminated by waiver in the absence of an exchange of consideration or factors that support estoppel. Id. at §764.

Generally, New Mexico cases have defined waiver as the intentional relinquishment or abandonment of a known right. Our decisions recognize that the intent to waive contractual obligations or conditions may be implied from a party's representations that fall short of an express declaration of waiver, or from his conduct. While not express, these types of "implied in fact" waivers still represent a voluntary act whose effect is intended.

In Ed Black's Chevrolet Center, Inc. v. Melichar, 81 N.M. 602, 471 P.2d 172 (1970), we stated that, based upon the honest belief of the other party that a waiver was intended, a waiver might be presumed or implied contrary to the intention of the party waiving certain rights. Id. at 604, 471 P.2d at 174. Following that decision a number of our opinions discussed a waiver "implied" from a course of conduct in terms of estoppel. These cases represent what we would term here as waiver by estoppel. To prove waiver by estoppel the party need only show that he was misled to his prejudice by the conduct of the other party into the honest and reasonable belief that such waiver was intended.[2] The estoppel is justified because the estopped party reasonably could expect that his actions would induce the reliance of the other party. However, unlike the case of a voluntary waiver, either express or implied in fact, the waiver of the

---

[2]   Although it was not raised and argued to this Court by the parties we wish to reject certain language in Albuquerque Nat'l Bank v. Albuquerque Ranch Estates, Inc., 99 N.M. 95, 101, 654 P.2d 548, 554 (1982), regarding estoppel and the waiver of contractual provisions for timely payments. A party asserting such a claim need not establish that the conduct or silence relied on to create the estoppel was willfully intended to cause the party to act on a false representation or concealment. It is sufficient if any representation by conduct or silence would induce a reasonable and prudent person to believe it was intended to be acted on, or the estopped party should have known that it was both natural and probable that the other party would act upon the conduct or silence under the circumstances.

contractual obligation or condition and the effect of the conduct upon the opposite party may have been unintentional.

The law of waiver as discussed by Professor Corbin and our own cases suggests several possible situations: (1) actual waiver, either express or implied in fact, not supported by consideration, which may be retracted in the absence of detrimental reliance; (2) modification, which is not subject to retraction, based upon mutual agreement to waive certain obligations or conditions and the exchange of consideration; or (3) waiver by estoppel based upon either an actual waiver or certain "expressions or conduct" where the reliance of the opposite party and his change of position justifies the inhibition to assert the obligation or condition. We think these distinctions will clarify what appears to be some confusion of definition and expression in our cases.

Course of conduct in prior commercial dealings. The company's waiver argument relies, in the main, on our decision in Clovis National Bank v. Thomas, 77 N.M. 554, 425 P.2d 726 (1967). The Court in *Thomas* held that a creditor with a perfected security interest in certain cattle had consented to a sale of the cattle, if not expressly, then "certainly impliedly." Id. at 560, 425 P.2d at 730. The Court decided that under the Uniform Commercial Code consent to the sale of the collateral constituted a waiver of the creditor's security interest. Id. at 563, 425 P.2d at 735. The Court treated the consent issue as an election on the part of the creditor and found no evidence to support estoppel.

The evidence cited by the *Thomas* Court to support a finding of consent involved an extended course of commercial conduct between the parties. Specifically, the creditor on a number of occasions previously had allowed the debtor to sell cattle without the written authorization called for in his contracts. This had occurred under numerous earlier financing agreements as well as on a number of occasions under the particular financing agreement creating the security interest at issue in the *Thomas* case. The Court also referred to the similar custom and practice of the creditor generally with regard to all debtors.

Based upon its reading of Thomas, the company would look to the series of financing agreements between it and the bank prior to execution of the $400,000 note, and find, in the bank's willingness to accept late payments without reproach on those earlier obligations, a waiver of the clause giving the bank the right to declare a default due to delinquent payments without prior notice in the current note. We cannot agree that *Thomas* should be read and applied as broadly as the company suggests.

The facts on which the *Thomas* Court relied to find implied consent related to the performance of the particular contract at issue as well as earlier ones. We think that the multiple instances of acquiescence to the sale of cattle under the one financing agreement at issue were sufficient to uphold the judgment without reliance upon the conduct of the parties in performing other agreements. In addition, there was evidence to which the Court referred that the creditor expressly had consented to the sale, indeed that the creditor had "requested" that the sale take place. The decision should not be read to suggest that consent (or waiver) can be implied solely from general custom and usage or the course of conduct between two parties prior to the execution of a particular contractual agreement. We think that any suggestion to the contrary in Thomas was unnecessary to the Court's decision and should not be followed.

In the present case the company was in default on the first and only payment that was due on the obligation. Any previous conduct of the bank in accepting late payments involved other obligations. An actual intent to waive the requirement for timely payment, or to waive the contractual right to declare a default without notice, as provided for in their agreement, must be implied from the parties conduct in the performance of that obligation. Cf. Continental Nat'l Bank of Fort Worth v. Schiller, 89 Ill.App.3d 216, 44 Ill.Dec. 471, 411 N.E.2d 593 (1980) (evidence that bank had accepted late payments on earlier debts insufficient to show a waiver, express or implied, of timely payments on present debt). Otherwise the express terms of the agreement would have no meaning at the time of its execution. While conduct under previous contracts may be relevant to show the intent meant to be expressed by provisions in a current contract, here we must assume that the parties intended the unequivocal import of their agreement. Whether their conduct after the execution of the agreement indicates an intention to waive a particular provision is another question.

We believe our treatment of this issue comports with relevant provisions of the Uniform Commercial Code. NMSA 1978, Section 55-1-205 of the UCC states in pertinent part:

> (1) A course of dealing is a sequence of previous conduct between the parties to a particular transaction which is fairly to be regarded as establishing a common basis of understanding for interpreting their expressions and other conduct.
>
> * * * * * *
>
> (3) A course of dealing between parties and any usage of trade * * * give particular meaning to and supplement or qualify terms of an agreement * * * * (4) The express terms of an agreement and an applicable course of dealing or usage of trade shall be construed wherever reasonable as consistent with each other; but, when such construction is unreasonable, express terms control both course of dealing and usage of trade * * * * Thus, when the previous conduct of the parties is in direct conflict with the unequivocal express terms of an agreement, the latter is determinative as to the nature of their agreement. See NMSA 1978, §55-1-205(4); Celebrity, Inc. v. Kemper, 96 N.M. 508, 632 P.2d 743 (1981).

By contrast, the UCC recognizes that the conduct of the parties in performing an agreement may be relevant to show a modification or waiver of a provision inconsistent with their conduct in the performance of that agreement. See NMSA 1978, §55-2-208. While this particular UCC provision appears in

Article 2 which involves the sale of goods, we find its principles are consistent with our own cases regarding performance.

No actual waiver, express or implied in fact. Here, any inference that the bank actually intended to waive its right under the contract to declare a default without notice must rest on postagreement events. We believe that the postagreement conduct of the bank does not suggest that the bank actually intended to waive its rights under the contract. When a party accepts a late payment on a contract without comment he waives the default that existed. With repetition his actions may suggest an intention to accept late payments generally. In this case, the overdue interest payment was the first payment due under the contract; the bank had not accepted any earlier late payments on that contract. The payment was overdue, the company did not request an extension, and after twenty-three days the bank declared a default. The parties agree that the matter of the overdue interest payment was not discussed during the series of meetings when the company sought to obtain additional financing. For good reasons, the fact that the bank would declare a default based upon the unpaid interest payment may have come as a surprise to the Hales, the bank's silence may have been misleading in the light of the earlier commercial behavior of the parties, but we do not believe that the bank's conduct during the month of March gives rise to a factual question that it was the bank's actual intention to relinquish any contractual rights. At most, the bank's conduct indicated an intention simply to ignore the delinquency for about three weeks.

No modification. Likewise, we agree with the trial court that the facts of this case do not raise an issue of contract modification. We have concluded in our discussion of the waiver issue that no factual question exists on whether the bank for its part actually intended to waive its right to declare a default based upon the past due interest payment. It follows that there can be no issue of whether the parties intended to substitute a new agreement for their earlier one, or whether the parties mutually agreed to amend the contractual provision concerning default and acceleration, and whether this agreement was supported by consideration. An issue of contract modification should be approached in these terms.

"Waiver by estoppel" presented an issue of fact. The company's estoppel argument rests upon an important distinction from actual waiver. Here the previous course of dealings between the parties is relevant to show the meaning that the company reasonably might attribute to the bank's conduct in not mentioning the overdue interest payment. Implicit in Section 55-1-205(1) of the UCC is the recognition that, as a practical matter, one party to a contract will use his past commercial dealings with another party as a basis for the interpretation of the other party's conduct. Thus it is to be expected that the company would interpret the bank's behavior during the month of March in light of their earlier dealings and we believe the bank should have been aware of this consideration.

As we have discussed, to prove waiver by estoppel the company only need show that by the conduct of the bank it was misled to its prejudice into an honest and reasonable belief that the bank would not assert its right under the contract to declare a default without first notifying the company and providing an opportunity to make the payment. The conduct of the bank during the month of March, reasonably interpreted in light of their earlier commercial dealings, is sufficient to create a jury question on this issue.

The company introduced evidence to show that the parties had extensive contact during the month of March in order to discuss the company's financial status. Despite ample opportunity, the bank did nothing to alert the company that it was concerned about the past due payment or that the nature of their financial relationship might take a new course. In the words of one bank officer, the bank wished the company to remain "cooperative." J.R. Hale mentioned the interest payment to a bank officer and it is not recorded that the officer in return indicated that the bank attached any importance whatsoever to the matter. His failure to calculate the exact amount due and then remind Hale of the payment at the next conference would communicate just the opposite impression. Additionally, on March 18 the bank gave a written financial reference to Bruce Hale who apparently intended to use the credit reference in seeking financial assistance from other institutions. The reference stated: "All experience with J.R. Hale Contracting Company has been satisfactory." We believe it would not be unreasonable for the Hales to interpret this conduct as an indication that the bank was unconcerned about the past due payment and intended to conduct its business with the company in the same fashion as it had previously. That is, the bank would approach the Hales about any overdue payment and ask how they would care to arrange for payment.

Some of the facts to which we refer can be regarded as silence on the bank's part in the face of an apparent false sense of security of the company. Silence may form the basis for estoppel if a party stands mute when he has a duty to speak. As we have discussed, the circumstances here suggest that the bank reasonably could expect that the company would rely on the bank's failure to request the interest payment. If so, we believe the bank would have had a duty to inform the company that the bank would enforce performance under the contract according to the letter of their agreement.

On the question of detrimental reliance we note that the company cannot be said to have been lulled by the postagreement conduct into missing the payment when it was first due on March 1. However, we believe the company reasonably might have been induced into not taking the initiative to correct the delinquency and waiting instead for the bank to request the payment or in some fashion draw the matter to the company's attention. Certainly to have the bank declare a default without warning and then accelerate all payments can be considered the detrimental result of the reliance on the impression that the bank's conduct reasonably might have conveyed.

"Lack of good faith" presented an issue of fact under clause providing for acceleration because of insecurity. At trial the bank moved for a directed verdict on a second ground, that the company failed to introduce sufficient evidence showing the bank lacked a good faith belief that its prospect for repayment was impaired. The company had the burden of proof on that issue. NMSA 1978, §55-1-208. The trial judge denied the bank's motion, stating that he believed there were facts in the record from which a jury could conclude that the bank lacked good faith. The bank asserts that the judge applied the wrong standard regarding "good faith" as used in an insecurity clause giving a secured party the power to accelerate payments.

Section 55-1-208 governs the acceleration of notes. It provides that a party may accelerate payment or performance "only if he in good faith believes that the prospect of payment or performance is impaired." Id. "Good faith" is defined by Section 55-1-201(19) as "honesty in fact in the conduct or transaction concerned."

There are two schools of thought and corresponding lines of cases addressing the standard of good faith under Section 1-208 of the UCC. The first requires only that a creditor genuinely believe the prospect for repayment is impaired; he need not be reasonable in that belief. This standard is purely subjective and has been described as "the pure heart and the empty head" standard. Van Horn v. Van De Wol, Inc., 6 Wash.App. 959, 960, 497 P.2d 252, 253 (1972). The second standard includes an objective element of whether the creditor was reasonable under the circumstances in believing that the prospect for repayment was impaired.

The subjective standard is probably the majority view today, but the standard has been criticized strongly as allowing the creditor excessive latitude that imposes a heavy burden of proof on the debtor. See Black v. Peoples Bank & Trust Co., 437 So.2d 26 (Miss.1983); Universal C.I.T. Credit Corp. v. Shepler, 164 Ind.App. 516, 329 N.E.2d 620 (1975) (Garrard, J., concurring). In his concurrence in *Universal C.I.T.*, Judge Garrard stated:

> [A] purely subjective test is subject to arbitrary abuse. It would allow a creditor to be unreasonable and place the debtor in an unjust position since the creditor might at any time call the entire debt and require the debtor to prove the non-existent state of mind of the creditor. Thus, under this interpretation, the code would permit a creditor to destroy a viable contractual relationship without requiring him to justify his actions.

164 Ind.App. at 524-25, 329 N.E.2d at 626 (footnotes omitted). The subjective standard also has been criticized because:

> [a] declaration of insecurity is a unilateral decision made by the creditor which places a severe hardship upon the debtor. This hardship is unjust if the creditor's decision is unreasonable or based upon mistaken facts which the creditor may honestly believe to be true.

Richards Engrs., Inc. v. Spanel, 745 P.2d 1031, 1033 (Colo.Ct.App.1987).

The original definition for "good faith" in the Proposed Final Draft of the Uniform Commercial Code, published in 1950, differed significantly from the present one. In addition to "honesty in fact," the general definition of good faith in Article 1 was to include "observance of reasonable commercial standards of any business or trade in which [a party] is engaged." See The American Law Institute, Uniform Commercial Code §1-201(18) (Proposed Final Draft, 1950). The requirement of reasonable commercial standards was dropped in the Proposed Final Draft No. 2, published in 1951. See The American Law Institute, Uniform Commercial Code §1-201(19) (Proposed Final Draft, 1951). A provision for commercial reasonableness thereafter has been included only in other scattered sections of the Code, notably the definition of good faith applicable to merchants. See §55-2-103(1)(b); see also §§55-2-311(1), 55-3-406, 55-3-419(3), 55-9-318(2). This history suggests an intention to adopt an objective standard of good faith based upon commercial reasonableness only in particular types of transactions and commercial situations.

The only New Mexico case addressing the standard of good faith under an insecurity clause is McKay v. Farmers & Stockmens Bank of Clayton, 92 N.M. 181, 585 P.2d 325 (Ct.App.), writ quashed, 92 N.M. 79, 582 P.2d 1292 (1978). By a vote of two to one the panel reversed the summary judgment entered on behalf of a bank on the issue of whether the bank in good faith deemed itself insecure in the acceleration of a note. Judge Sutin's special concurrence expressed his view that Section 55-1-208 has both subjective and objective elements. See id. at 184, 585 P.2d at 328. The opinion of the court stated little more on the issue of the meaning of "good faith" under Section 55-1-208 than to conclude that the question is usually one of fact rather than a question of law that is amenable to summary judgment. See id. at 182-83, 585 P.2d at 326-27.

After an examination of the decisions to which we have referred, and the various provisions in the UCC concerning good faith, we find that the Code does not impose an objective standard of commercial reasonableness on the decision of the bank to accelerate when the bank was honest in its belief that its prospect for repayment was impaired. The requirement of good faith under Section 55-1-208 is quite specifically a standard of honesty in fact. This standard is, however, a minimum one that the parties are free to supplement by agreement. See §55-1-102(3). The company in this case certainly possessed a level of sophistication to have bargained for an agreement more specifically addressing the circumstances under which an acceleration of payments would be allowed. The company does not suggest that the agreement was a contract of adhesion between parties of unequal bargaining position.

In essence, the requirement of honesty in fact is subjective and is concerned with the actual state of mind of the creditor. Nevertheless, the determination of ultimate fact, whether or not the bank lacked a good faith belief in the impairment of its prospect for repayment, should be based on the facts and circumstances surrounding the acceleration and not solely on the bank's testimony concerning its state of mind. Even under a subjective test of good faith the trier of fact may evaluate the credibility of a creditor's claim and in doing so may take into account the reasonableness of that claim. Thus, the conduct and credibility of the creditor may be tested by objective standards subject to proof and conducive to the application of reasonable expectations in commercial affairs.

We do not mean to suggest that dual elements of reasonableness and good faith are required. Put simply, in the absence of an objective basis upon which a reasonable person would have accelerated the note, the fact finder could infer that the creditor really did not perceive his prospect for repayment to be impaired. This inquiry necessarily will focus on the facts and circumstances that were known to the creditor. As Judge Sutin noted in *McKay*, expert testimony may be necessary to assist the trier of fact. 92 N.M. at 185, 585 P.2d at 329.

Additionally, honesty is inconsistent with willful ignorance of the facts and circumstances available to the creditor, and thus the facts and circumstances that reasonable investigation would have disclosed may be relevant. While "honesty" may require no more than a pure heart, it is questionable that a pure heart can co-exist with closed eyes. It is not honest to close one's eyes so as to maintain an empty head.

We hold that a fact finder can find that a creditor acted without a good faith belief that its prospect for repayment was impaired when (1), under the facts and circumstances that were known to the creditor, there existed a reasonable inference that the creditor in fact did not conclude that its prospect for repayment was impaired and that acceleration was necessary to protect its interests, or (2) there existed a reasonable inference that the creditor chose not to undertake such investigation as (a) was necessary to make an informed decision and (b) would have shown that the foreseeable risk of nonpayment was not materially greater than when the loan was made.

We agree with the trial court that the company introduced sufficient evidence to establish a prima facie case on the lack of good faith on the part of the bank. Notwithstanding the company's profitability problems and declining working capital position, a banking expert testified that the bank's collateral position was more than adequate. Additionally, between March 1 and 23 the company had on deposit with the bank more than enough funds to cover the interest payment. This evidence is sufficient to require that the issue be resolved by the fact finder under the standard of good faith necessary to justify acceleration of payments under an insecurity clause.

Conclusion. For the reasons stated above, we reverse the district court's grant of a directed verdict in favor of the bank based on the interest default clause and hold that an issue of waiver by estoppel exists to be resolved by the jury. In addition, the company also must prove that the bank lacked a good faith belief that its prospect for repayment was impaired.

IT IS SO ORDERED.

2. Repossessing Collateral

Perhaps the single most important provision in Article 9 is §9-503, which provides in part:

> "Unless otherwise agreed a secured party has on default the right to take possession of the collateral. In taking possession a secured party may proceed without judicial process if this can be done without breach of the peace or may proceed by action."

U.C.C. §9-503. The debtor, of course, is contractually bound to observe the secured party's right to possession. *Taylor v. Fedders Corp.*, 635 F.2d 682, 683 (8th Cir.1980). Moreover, the debtor risks tort liability for conversion by refusing to yield possession of the collateral. Restatement (Second) of Torts §237 (1965) (conversion by demand and refusal).

The reality is, however, that some debtors simply will not obey security agreements; and others, who will generally observe their contractual obligations, may nevertheless dispute the contention that a secured party's right to possession has accrued under the terms of the parties' agreement. Thus, §9-503 gives a secured party the right to take collateral from an uncooperative debtor. Having this right to repossess collateral and thereby force a satisfaction of the secured debt is the whole motive for a creditor taking an Article 9 security interest.

A secured party has the option of repossessing "by action," which means seizing collateral with the aid of judicial process such as that available through claim and delivery, replevin or the like. Alternatively, a secured party can elect to help herself to collateral without invoking the state's assistance.

a. Conditions on Self-Help Repossession

Article 9's Conditions. There are three very basic, fundamentally important conditions on a creditor's right to repossess under §9-503: (1) the creditor must be a secured party seizing property subject to her security interest; (2) the debtor must be in default; and (3) the taking must be done without breaching the peace. The first two conditions apply whether the repossession is by action, i.e., replevin, or by self-help. The ban on breaching the peace is there primarily to restrain secured parties who elect to help themselves to their collateral.

The Uniform Conditional Sales Act, the Uniform Trust Receipts Act and all other modern, pre-Code security statutes expressly gave secured creditors the right of self-help repossession. The right has always been conditioned, however, as it is under §9-503, on the creditor proceeding without "breach of the peace." This concept is nowhere defined in the Code. Therefore, in many instances, courts deciding Article 9 cases have looked to pre-Code decisions in searching for the line between acceptable and unacceptable repossession tactics. On this issue, pre-Code law remains valid. Of course, each case turns on its own facts, and the facts of the reported cases vary significantly. Thus, each case tends to make its own law.

It should be said, however, that the true prohibition on breaching the peace is not only that the secured party shall not actually cause a breach of the peace; the prohibition extends to conduct that only threatens to breach the peace. For instance, a secured party may be guilty of wrongful repossession if she reclaims collateral by the use of fraud, artifice, stealth, or trickery. *Ford Motor Credit Co. v. Byrd*, 351 So.2d 557 (Ala.1977) (debtor tricked into driving the collateral, which was a vehicle, to the secured party's office); but see 2 G. Gilmore, SECURITY INTERESTS IN PERSONAL PROPERTY §44.1 at 1212 (1965) (a little trickery is acceptable as by inviting debtor to the office to discuss refinancing and repossessing the collateral, which is a vehicle, as soon as she arrives); cf. *Pierce v. Ford Motor Credit Co.*, 373 So.2d 1113 (Ala.Civ.App.1979) (no breach of the peace when the secured party secretly followed the debtor and repossessed the collateral when it was momentarily left unattended).

Many courts find a breach of the peace when a secured party repossesses collateral over the protest of the debtor who stands between the secured party and the collateral. Clearly in these cases the conduct is culpable not because it actually led to a breach of the peace, but because the conduct easily could have triggered an actual breach.

Extra-Code Conditions. Notice and an opportunity for a hearing upon self-help repossession are not required by any uniform version of Article 9; nor are they required by the United States Constitution because the activity does not involve the state to a degree that triggers fourteenth amendment due process protections. Cf. *Flagg Bros., Inc. v. Brooks*, 436 U.S. 149, 98 S.Ct. 1729, 56 L.Ed.2d 185 (1978) (no state action when warehouseman enforces U.C.C. §7-210 statutory lien for storage charges). It is possible, however, that state constitutional law may require giving the debtor notice and a meaningful opportunity for a hearing.

Also, the security agreement can provide for notice and hearing prior to self-help repossession, although such a contractual provision is a rarity. Much more common are federal and state, non-Code statutes governing specialized transactions, such as credit sales of consumer goods and agricultural equipment, which require a secured party to notify a debtor of an intent to repossess and impose other extraordinary limitations on the rights of secured creditors.

b. Liability for Wrongful Repossession

A creditor violates §9-503 if she (1) repossesses property in which she has no security interest; (2) repossesses collateral when the debtor is not in default; or (3) breaches the peace while effecting self-help repossession of collateral. The courts sometimes refer to this violation as "unwarranted" or "improper" or "unjustified," but the most frequently used descriptive term is *wrongful repossession*. All these terms describe the same misconduct, i.e., action by a secured party in repossessing property without the right to do so or at a time or in a manner not sanctioned by Article 9.

U.C.C. §9-503 does not prescribe the debtor's remedy for wrongful repossession by a creditor. U.C.C. §9-507(1) provides that "the debtor *** has a right to recover from the secured party any loss caused by a failure to comply with the provisions of this Part [5 on default]." A literal reading of this provision and the accompanying commentary suggests, however, that this statutory "any loss" remedy is appropriate only when a secured party wrongly disposes of collateral, not when she wrongfully repossesses it. See U.C.C. §9-507 comments 1 & 2. Arguably, therefore, the remedy provided by §9-507(1) is not the basis of a debtor's cause of action for wrongful repossession.

A secured party's liability for wrongful repossession is usually based on the common-law tort of conversion. Chattel mortgagees and conditional vendors in virtually every state were routinely found liable for conversion under pre-Code law when they wrongfully repossessed collateral from the debtor. This pre-Code law is followed today by courts deciding wrongful repossession cases under Article 9. The courts never fully explain the reason for perpetuating a remedy applied in analogous situations under pre-Code law. They necessarily decide, however, that Article 9 has not displaced the conversion remedy.

The usual measure of damages for conversion based on wrongful repossession is the value of the property at the time of the conversion less the balance of the obligation owed the creditor. In an appropriate case, the debtor can also recover punitive damages. Although the Code provides that penal damages are unrecoverable except as provided in the Code itself or "by other rule of law," U.C.C. §1-106(1), conversion is another rule of law which supports punitive damages. Wrongful repossession is conversion, and debtors suing Article 9 secured parties for having committed this tort are frequently awarded not only actual, compensatory damages, but also punitive damages if the secured party acted maliciously, willfully, or with reckless disregard for the rights of others. This higher degree of culpability is everywhere required for punitive damages, and is the fact that makes a conversion case "appropriate" for such damages.

A secured party cannot escape liability for wrongful repossession through exculpatory language in the security agreement. Although freedom of contract is an important Code principle, no party to a covered transaction can successfully disclaim her obligations of good faith, diligence, reasonableness and care. U.C.C. §1-201(3). Moreover, wrongful repossession sounds in tort, and as a matter of policy the law generally does not look favorably on waivers of tort liability. Similarly, a secured party cannot certainly escape responsibility by hiring an "independent contractor" to repossess. As explained by the Minnesota Court of Appeals:

> The uniform commercial code defines the relationship between secured parties and debtors by establishing specific rights, remedies and duties with respect to repossession and disposition of collateral upon default. See Minn.Stat. §§336.9-501-.9-508 (1988). The code requires a secured party to exercise its self-help remedy rights only when repossession can be accomplished "without breach of the peace." See id. §336.9-503. The conditional nature of the secured party's self-help remedies and the language of section 336.9-503 indicate that a secured party must ensure there is no risk of harm to the debtor and others if the secured party chooses to repossess collateral by self- help methods. The duty to repossess property in a peaceable manner is specifically imposed on a "secured party" by the uniform commercial code and is intended to protect debtors and other persons affected by repossession activities. See id. (a "secured party" may repossess by self-help methods "if this can be done without breach of the peace"). Accordingly, a secured party may not delegate to third persons the secured party's duty to repossess in a peaceable manner. Cf. Restatement (Second) of Torts §424 (1965) (a person under a statutory duty to provide specific safeguards or precautions for the safety of another is liable for injuries to the other person caused by a contractor's failure to provide the necessary safeguards or precautions).

Nichols v. Metropolitan Bank, 435 N.W.2d 637, 640 (Minn.Ct.App. 1989).

3. Disposing Of Collateral

After getting possession of the collateral, the secured party must do something with it, something permitted by Article 9. She cannot safely sit on (or in) the collateral and simply do nothing. "When a secured party takes possession of the collateral and fails to proceed to obtain a valid foreclosure, it acts at its peril." *Jackson v. Star Sprinkler Corp. of Florida*, 575 F.2d 1223, 1234 (8th Cir.1978).

A secured party has a choice between two courses of action. She can strictly foreclose under §9-505, which permits a secured party to retain the collateral in full satisfaction of the secured debt. Alternatively, she can dispose of the collateral under §9-504. The former course is almost never deliberately chosen because the true value of the collateral seldom equals the secured debt. In virtually every case, the secured party elects to dispose of the collateral pursuant to §9-504.

U.C.C. §9-504 begins by explaining that "[a] secured party after default may sell, lease, or otherwise dispose of any or all of the collateral ***." U.C.C. §9-504(1). There are only a couple of reported cases in which a secured party attempted to satisfy the secured debt by leasing the collateral. Every other case involves a sale of the property by the secured party.

Article 9 allows either a public or private sale, U.C.C. §9-504(3), but the statute does not describe in detail how to conduct the foreclosure. There is little more than the general admonition that "every aspect of the disposition including the method, manner, time, place and terms must be commercially reasonable." U.C.C. §9-504(3). Of the few specific directives, clearly the most important is that, ordinarily, the debtor must be notified of the sale. Id. In the usual case no other notification need be sent. Id.

When courts are asked to judge the legality of a secured party's disposition of collateral, the issues that most often arise are

1. Whether or not the secured party properly notified the debtor, and
2. Whether or not the sale was commercially reasonable.

If a court decides either of these issues against a secured party, she is accountable to the debtor, which means that the secured party is liable to the debtor for damages or is barred from suing the debtor for any deficiency or both.

Chemlease Worldwide, Inc. v. Brace, Inc.
Supreme Court of Minnesota, 1983
338 N.W.2d 428

Kelley, Justice. Respondent Chemlease Worldwide, Inc. (Chemlease), the lessor of personal property, sought a deficiency judgment against the lessee (Brace, Inc.) and two personal guarantors of the lessee's lease obligations (Charles and Clayton Brace) for the difference between the unpaid amount due it under the lease and the amount received following a repossession sale. Following trial, the court directed a verdict for the lessor. Subsequently, judgment was entered against the lessee and both personal guarantors. On appeal, appellants claim (1) that the lessor failed to give the lessee and personal guarantors reasonable notice of private sale, as required by the Uniform Commercial Code, and (2) that a directed verdict was inappropriate because there existed factual questions as to whether the private sale was commercially reasonable. We hold that the lessor's notice of private sale was unreasonable and that a jury issue exists as to whether the private sale of the leased equipment was commercially reasonable. Accordingly, we reverse and remand for retrial.

In October of 1975, Brace, Inc. entered into a 62-month lease for computer equipment with Chemlease. Monthly payments were $500.48, for a total of $29,836.26 over the lease term. Brace, Inc. had an option to buy the equipment for $1 at the end of the lease. The price of the equipment was $20,477.83. Contemporaneously with the execution of the lease, Charles and Clayton Brace executed personal guaranties of the lessee's payment obligation. In June of 1977, Brace, Inc. went out of business, but a business called Brace Company continued to do business at the former business address of Brace, Inc. Brace Company assumed and paid the monthly computer lease obligation. Chemlease was not informed of the change in lessee and did not consent to any assignment of the lease. The Brace Company, in turn, went out of business in the fall of 1977. However, the lease payments were made through October of 1978. In November of 1978, Chemlease was informed by Gamet Manufacturing (Gamet), the new tenant of the premises where the computer equipment was located, that the equipment had been left on the premises and requested disposition instructions.

After receiving this information from Gamet and because Brace, Inc. was in default on the lease, Chemlease's collection agent undertook steps to repossess the equipment. The agent testified that he contacted three companies who were potential buyers in the used computer market. Ultimately, sale terms were agreed to with Chicago Cash Register Company, one of those three potential buyers, on or about January 10, 1979. Chemlease's agent instructed Chicago Cash Register Company to pick up the equipment on February 2, 1979. On or about February 1, 1979, Chemlease sent all of the appellants two documents by certified mail: a final demand for payment and a notice of private sale. Notices sent to Brace, Inc. and Clayton Brace were returned without forwarding address.

Charles Brace received and signed a receipt for both documents on February 7 and 8, 1979, respectively. The notice of private sale stated Chemlease would sell the equipment "on or after the 12th day of February, 1979." Meanwhile, the equipment had been picked up from Gamet on behalf of Chicago Cash Register Company by a trucking firm on February 2, 1979. Upon receiving the final demand and notice of private sale, neither Charles Brace nor the other appellants contacted Chemlease nor did they make an effort to find a buyer. On March 13, 1979, upon receipt of $2,500 purchase price, Chemlease gave Chicago Cash Register Company a bill of sale for the computer equipment.

Thereafter, Chemlease commenced the instant action against Brace, Inc. and against Clayton and Charles Brace as guarantors seeking a deficiency judgment. The appellants defended on the grounds Chemlease failed to provide reasonable notice of the private sale and that the sale was commercially unreasonable. At the close of the evidence, the trial court issued an order for directed verdict in favor of Chemlease for $10,406.95, the stipulated amount of the deficiency. Subsequently, the court issued findings of fact, conclusions of law and an order for judgment on which judgment was entered. Appellants appeal from the order granting the directed verdict and from the judgment.

* * *

1. The appellants first contend that they were not provided commercially reasonable notice of the private sale. The lease between Chemlease and Brace, Inc. provided that at the end of the lease period Brace, Inc. had the option to become the owner of the computer equipment for the nominal consideration of $1. Under the Uniform Commercial Code, the interest retained by Chemlease was a security interest. U.C.C. §1-201(37). Therefore, provisions of Article 9 of the Uniform Commercial Code would apply to the transaction.

As the secured party, Chemlease had, on default, a right to take possession of the computer equipment. U.C.C. §9-503. Chemlease also had a right to dispose of the equipment, either by private or public sale, pursuant to section 9-504. Section 9-504(3) provides in part:

> Unless collateral *** is of a type customarily sold on a recognized market, reasonable notification of the time and place of any public sale or reasonable notification of the time after which any private sale or other intended disposition is to be made shall be sent by the secured party to the debtor, if he has not signed after default a statement renouncing or modifying his right to notification of sale.

This provision entitled Brace, Inc., as debtor to the lease agreement, to receive reasonable notice of sale. But are Charles and Clayton Brace, as guarantors on the lease, also entitled to receive such notice? While we have not heretofore considered the question, the New York courts and a majority of jurisdictions addressing the issue hold that a guarantor is a debtor within the meaning of section 9-504. In our view, this construction is consistent with the purpose of the reasonable notification requirement, that is, to enable the debtor to protect his interest in the secured property by paying the debt, finding a buyer, or bidding on the property. A guarantor faces potential liability when the sale price does not cover the deficiency. Additionally, a personal guaranty given by a primary participant in a family-owned corporation often means the guarantor is, in essence, the debtor. The view that a guarantor is a debtor under section 9-504 should be applied to Charles and Clayton Brace. Thus, we conclude they were entitled to receive notice of the proposed sale of the collateral.

Chemlease argues that by the terms of the guaranty the guarantors waived their rights to the collateral and therefore to notice of sale. It appears to us, however, that the fact the guarantors had no rights to the collateral is irrelevant to their interest in insuring Chemlease made the best sale available. The interest Charles and Clayton Brace have in the best sale price is their interest in their potential liability on the guaranty. The waiver in the guaranty does not waive any right to notice they may have under the Uniform Commercial Code. Additionally, by virtue of section 9-501(3)(b), the provisions of section 9-504(3) may not be waived or varied by agreement. *See* Minn.Stat.Ann. §336.9-504(3) Code Comment (West 1966).

Finally, Chemlease argues that Charles and Clayton Brace and Brace, Inc. are barred by estoppel or waiver from claiming the notice and sale were unreasonable because of their activities. Chemlease points out that Brace, Inc. assigned the lease of the equipment to Brace Company in violation of lease provisions and without notice to, or consent of, Chemlease. Additionally, the equipment was abandoned on the property occupied by Gamet when Brace Company went out of business. A violation of lease provisions regarding assignment of the lease would not waive Brace, Inc.'s interest in the property but would entitle Chemlease to any damages incurred by the violation. The abandonment of the computer equipment, like the alleged waiver in the guaranty, could only constitute waiver of rights to the property, not the interest of the guarantors in seeing that the property is sold for the highest price.

2. The trial court found Charles Brace received reasonable notice of the private sale and that the notice provided by Chemlease to the other appellants was also reasonable. As indicated, notices sent to Clayton Brace and Brace, Inc. were returned without forwarding addresses. Appellants here argue notification provided by Chemlease was unreasonable on its face and in effect. They argue that Chemlease's disposition of collateral did not comply with the requirements of U.C.C. §9-504(3) notification.

With regard to the question of whether the notification was commercially unreasonable on its face, an examination of the facts establishes the final demand letters were all apparently postmarked February 1, 1979. The notice of private sale letters were postmarked February 2, 1979. Charles Brace received the final demand letter on February 7, 1979, and the notice of private sale letter on Thursday, February 8, 1979. The notice of private sale stated the sale would be made on or after Monday, February 12, 1979. As received, the notice provided Charles Brace 2 working days to act to protect his interests.

The rule for determining whether notification under U.C.C. §9-504(3) is reasonable is whether the notice was sent in sufficient time to enable those entitled to notice to take appropriate steps to protect their interest in the collateral. A majority of the jurisdictions which have considered the matter hold that return of the letters mailed to Clayton Brace and to Brace, Inc. does not automatically make the notice unreasonable. A reasonable way to fulfill the purpose of the notification requirement, so as to protect debtors without placing an unduly onerous burden on the secured party to hunt down and serve the debtor, is a rule that determines the reasonableness of notice by the secured party upon his proof that notice was dispatched within a commercially reasonable time prior to the date of private sale rather than on actual receipt of notice by the guarantors.

In the instant case, the notifications were mailed on February 1 or 2, 1979, to the former business address of Brace, Inc. and to Clayton Brace and to the home address of Charles Brace. These certified mailings were sent 10 days prior to the date after which, according to the notices, the private sale was proposed to be made. The Uniform Commercial Code provides no statutory period constituting commercially reasonable notification. Moreover, no notice period was provided in the lease for the computer equipment. We note that the case law is not very helpful in this area, especially since the reasonableness of the notification generally depends upon the collateral involved and other circumstances peculiar to each case. However, we conclude, in the absence of contrary evidence, that a mailing 10 days prior to the sale date does not per se appear commercially unreasonable. Accordingly, the burden of producing evidence of specific unreasonableness would shift to the appellants. At trial, they provided no evidence that prior to the proposed sale date they objected to the method or date of sale, attempted to restrain the sale by court order, attempted to find potential purchasers or made any other effort to protect their interests. Had the appellants initiated some protective action which they could not complete prior to the proposed sale date, such would be specific evidence that the notice was not commercially reasonable.

To constitute commercially reasonable notification, the letter containing the notice of sale must be properly addressed. Section 1-201(26) of the Uniform Commercial Code provides the following guidance:

> A person "notifies" or "gives" a notice or notification to another by taking such steps as may be reasonably required to inform the other in ordinary course whether or not such other actually comes to know of it. A person "receives" a notice or notification when

.....

(b) it is duly delivered at the place of business through which the contract was made or at any other place held out by him as the place for receipt of such communications.

Here, the letters of notice of private sale for Brace, Inc. and Clayton Brace were sent to the business address of Brace, Inc. at the time the lease of computer equipment was executed. Chemlease had not received from the Braces notice that they would receive such communications elsewhere. The notice letter to Charles Brace actually notified him. It appears to us the commercial reasonableness of the addresses to which Chemlease sent notification letters is established.

But in determining further whether the notice was commercially reasonable we must decide when the actual sale of the computer equipment to Chicago Cash Register Company occurred. Appellants argue that the sale actually occurred prior to the date of February 12, 1979 -- the proposed date of sale provided in the notice. They claim that the sale agreement with Chicago Cash Register Company was made January 10, 1979, and title to the equipment passed on February 2, 1979, when the computer equipment was picked up by a trucking firm on behalf of Chicago Cash Register Company after authorization of Chemlease. On the other hand, respondent asserts, and the trial court found, that the sale occurred on March 13, 1979, when the bill of sale passed.

Article 9 of the Uniform Commercial Code adopts a definition of "sale" as found in U.C.C. §2-106(1). U.C.C. §9-105(3). Section 2-106(1) provides that a sale "consists in the passing of title from the seller to the buyer for a price." Section 2-401 provides in part:

***

(2) Unless otherwise explicitly agreed title passes to the buyer at the time and place at which the seller completes his performance with reference to the physical delivery of the goods, despite reservation of a security interest and even though a document of title is to be delivered at a different time or place; ***

In the instant case, the computer equipment was moved from Minnesota to Illinois on February 2, 1979. The factual situation here of Gamet delivering the goods to a carrier hired by Chicago Cash Register Company most approximates a shipment contract. Accordingly, we hold that subsection 2 would apply and title would have passed "at the time and place at which the seller completes his performance with reference to the physical delivery of the goods." U.C.C. §2-401(2). The last date at which Chemlease can argue that it completed its performance in this shipment contract is the date the goods were handed over to the carrier on February 2, 1979. Because title passed on February 2, 1979, the "sale" of the equipment, by definition, would have occurred on that date. Because the notices of the sale were not postmarked until February 2, 1979, the date the sale technically occurred, the notification appears to be unreasonable to all appellants because the notices were not sent in sufficient time to enable Brace, Inc. or its guarantors to take protective action.

3. We must next examine the remedy which those entitled to notification have since Chemlease's notification was unreasonable. Section 9-507(1) of the Uniform Commercial Code provides the following remedy:

> If it is established that the secured party is not proceeding in accordance with the provisions of this Part disposition may be ordered or restrained on appropriate terms and conditions. If the disposition has occurred the debtor or any person entitled to notification or whose security interest has been made known to the secured party prior to the disposition has a right to recover from the secured party any loss caused by a failure to comply with the provisions of this Part.

Ordinarily, the damages recoverable for an improper disposition of collateral are the difference between the amount for which the secured party sold the collateral and the collateral's true market value at time of disposition. G. Gilmore, Security Interests in Personal Property, §44.9.2 at 1258 (1965). The question of the market value of the computer equipment is a factual matter for determination by the jury. In the instant case, we note that little evidence was presented by either party on the value of the equipment. Consequently, the determination of which side had the burden of proving the value of the equipment is essential to deciding whether the trial court was correct in directing a verdict.[2] We conclude the same reasons for placing the burden upon the secured party to prove the commercial reasonableness of the notice of sale support placing the burden upon the secured party to prove a fair price was received despite lack of a commercially reasonable notice of sale. Generally in law, the party who stands to benefit from the establishment of the affirmative of a proposition of fact essential to a claim bears the burden of proof as to that proposition. Consequently, once the debtor establishes that the sale was commercially unreasonable because of failure to give commercially reasonable notice of sale

---

[2]   Some jurisdictions have held that U.C.C. 9-507(1) is not a debtor's exclusive remedy against a wrongdoing secured creditor and that failure to comply with commercial reasonableness requirements may constitute an absolute bar to the secured party's recovery of deficiency. In our view, such a harsh remedy does not agree with the underlying assumption of Article 9 that good faith is common and bad faith is rare.

On the other hand, U.C.C. §9-507(1) can be read to require the debtor to show the loss and that the loss would not have occurred but for the failure to comply with statutory commercial reasonableness requirements. The path we choose to follow of the proposed placement of burdens of proof in the text is an intermediary position and an equally acceptable construction of section 9-507(1). Fair price is an element of a commercially reasonable sale. It seems proper to place the burden of proof on the same party on this single factual issue as to both the commercial reasonableness issue and the damages question.

and alleges an amount of loss incurred, it seems to us reasonable to require the secured party to prove that the debtor suffered less or no loss by the disposition. As is the case with the burden of proving the commercial reasonableness, once the secured party makes a prima facie case indicating the debtor did not suffer the damage alleged, the burden of persuasion but not the burden of proof would shift to the debtor.

In this case, the appellants allege the computer equipment was worth $10,000 to $12,000. The equipment sold for $2,500. Respondent presented testimony of its agent that the best offer received by Chemlease was $2,500 and that it was "a fair price under the circumstances." Neither side presented non-party expert testimony on the market value of the equipment at the time of disposition. The burden of proving its entitlement to the deficiency remained on Chemlease. The trial court's placing the burden on appellants to show the sale price was commercially unreasonable was misplaced. The reasonableness of the sale price to Chicago Cash Register Company was a close factual question. Considering the closeness of the factual question and that Chemlease had the burden of proving the commercial reasonableness of the sale, and accepting as true the evidence favorable to appellants, the directed verdict against them was inappropriate.

Accordingly, we reverse and remand to the trial court for a new trial on the question of damages, if any, sustained by appellants under U.C.C. §9-507(1).

Reversed and remanded.

CIT Corp. v. Nielson Logging Co.
Court of Appeals of Oregon, 1985
75 Or.App. 267, 706 P.2d 967

Young, Judge. This action concerns the resale of collateral after defendants' default on a security agreement. ORS 79.5040. Plaintiff sought a deficiency judgment for the difference between the debt, plus personal property taxes and expenses incurred in retaking and reselling the collateral, and the proceeds obtained from the sale of the collateral. Defendants denied the debt and affirmatively alleged that the sale of the collateral was commercially unreasonable. ORS 79.5070.

The jury returned a verdict for plaintiff in the amount of $8,393.03. The trial judge determined that the jury's answers to the interrogatories in the special verdict form were inconsistent with its general verdict and entered judgment for defendants. ORCP 61 C. We conclude that the verdict form is consistent and reinstate the verdict.

Nielson Logging is a partnership consisting of defendants Nielson. In February, 1980, defendants purchased a hydraulic log loader. The purchase was financed. Plaintiff took a security interest in the log loader and in defendants' tractor. The security agreement provided that, in case of default, defendants would be liable to plaintiff for any deficiency remaining on the debt after a disposition sale and for reasonable attorney fees.

Defendants had difficulty making the payments. In April, 1982, they were in default, having failed to pay the monthly installments and personal property taxes assessed against the equipment. In May, plaintiff repossessed the log loader and the tractor. In June, the equipment was sold to plaintiff at a public auction.

After the sale, plaintiff continued to seek buyers for the equipment. It sold the tractor for $28,000 and the log loader for $167,500. Both amounts were credited to defendants' account. Demand was made on defendants to pay the deficiency. They refused, and this action followed. The jury returned a special verdict, which was received by the court without objection, and the jury was discharged. Defendants then filed a "Motion for Judgment N.O.V. and for Judgment in Accordance With Interrogatories Inconsistent With the General Verdict." The trial court granted defendants' motion and, pursuant to ORCP 61C, entered a verdict in defendants' favor.

Plaintiff makes three assignments of error; we need decide only the first, which contends, inter alia, that the jury's verdict complied with the special verdict form and applicable law. The special verdict provided:

"1. After repossession, but before making any adjustment for expenses of resale of the equipment, what amount, if any, do you find was owing from Defendants to Plaintiff? "$224,402.40"

2. Do you find that the Plaintiff incurred any reasonable expenses in retaking, holding, preparing and advertising the equipment for sale? " X YES "   NO

"If your answer is YES, state the amount of such expenses: "$1,587.88 "

3. Do you find that Plaintiff incurred any expenses for personal property taxes in connection with the equipment? " X YES as stipulated "   NO

"If you answer YES, state the amount of such expense: "$6,805.15 as stipulated "

4. Add the amounts in questions 1, 2 and 3 and write the answer here: "$232.795.43

"5. What amount did Plaintiff derive from the sale of the equipment? "$195,500.00

"6. Subtract the amount in question 5 from the amount in question 4 and write the answer here: "37,295.43

"7. Do you find that CIT's sale of the equipment after repossession was commercially reasonable? "   YES " X NO

"If your answer to question 7 is YES, enter your judgment in question 10 for the Plaintiff for the amount in question 6.

"If your answer to question 7 is NO, continue to the next question.

"8. What was the actual fair market value of the equipment on the date it was sold by Plaintiff? "$224,402.40

"9. Subtract the amount in question 8 from the amount in question 4 and write the answer here. "$8,393.03

"If your answer [is] $0 or less, enter your verdict for Defendants in question 10 below.

"If your answer is more than $0, enter that amount as your verdict for Plaintiff in question 10 below.

"10. We, the jury, being first duly sworn and empanelled, render our verdict in favor of the: " X Plaintiff, in the amount of $8,393.03 " Defendants."

The trial court concluded that the jury's answers to questions 1, 7 and 8 of the special verdict form contradicted its verdict for plaintiff (question 10).

The disposition of collateral following default is controlled by ORS 79.5040 and 79.5070. * * *

A creditor's failure to sell the collateral in a commercially reasonable manner pursuant to ORS 79.5040(3) gives rise to a presumption that the collateral was worth the amount of the outstanding debt at the time of the default. All-States Leasing v. Ochs, 42 Or.App. 319, 600 P.2d 899 (1979). In Ferrous Financial Services Co. v. Wagnon, 70 Or.App. 285, 291, 689 P.2d 974 (1984), we held that a creditor is entitled to recover the commercially reasonable costs of resale under ORS 79.5040(1)(a), despite a sale that is determined to have been commercially unreasonable in some other respect. In the present case, the jury was instructed: "If you find that the collateral was not sold in a commercially reasonable manner, a presumption arises which holds that the collateral has a fair market value that was equal to the amount of the unpaid debt owing at the time of default. In such a situation, there can be no deficiency, unless the secured party proves that the fair market value of the equipment * * * was less than the amount of the debt. In that kind of an event, the secured party is entitled to a deficiency in the amount equal to the difference between the fair market value and the amount of the debt."

The jury, by the special verdict form, found that the sale was commercially unreasonable. The jury also found that plaintiff had incurred commercially reasonable expenses of $8,393.03 (sale expenses of $1,587.88 and taxes of $6,805.15). That sum represents the commercially reasonable expenses of resale that plaintiff was entitled to recover under ORS 79.5040(1)(a). The special jury findings are internally consistent and consistent with ORS 79.5040 and 79.5070,[2] as interpreted by *All-States Leasing v. Ochs*, supra, and *Ferrous Financial Services Co. v. Wagnon*, supra.

Reversed; remanded with instructions to reinstate jury verdict and enter judgment thereon.

Notes and Problems

1. Please decide if a default occurs, that entitles a secured party to repossess collateral, under any of these circumstances:

    a. the debtor [inconsequentially] violated an [insignificant] term of the security agreement.

    b. the secured party fears that the value of the collateral is about to slip below the amount of the secured debt.

    c. the secured party has a better use for the money loaned the debtor.

---

[2] The debtor is entitled to any "loss" caused by the creditor's failure to sell the collateral in a commercially reasonable manner. ORS 79.5070(1). The measure of the loss is the difference between the price actually obtained and the price that could have been obtained by proceeding in a commercially reasonable manner. Plaintiff's recovery was computed as follows:

Debt	224,402.40
Sale expenses	8,393.03
	232,795.43
Actual sale price	(195,500.00)
Deficiency	37,295.43 (FMV 224,402.40 - sale
"Loss"	(28,902.40) price 195,500 = 28,902.40)
Verdict for Plaintiff	8,393.03

See *Ferrous Financial Services Co. v. Wagnon*, supra, 70 Or.App. at 289n. 2, 689 P.2d 974.

    d. the debtor failed to pay on time six months ago.

    e. the debtor fails to pay on time this month, just as happened in each of the past six months.

    f. When and how does "good faith" affect the meaning or occurrence of "default" under these circumstances?

2. Please decide which of the following costs are chargeable to the proceeds of the sale of collateral:

    a. interest that accrued between the date of repossession and the date of sale

    b. interest on repossession expenses

    c. attorneys' fees for legal services in connection with respect to repossession and sale

3. What is the consequence of a secured party violating 9-503 in repossessing the collateral?

    a. Debtor recovers compensatory damages

    b. Debtor recovers punitive damages

    c. Secured party cannot recovery any deficiency

    d. Combination of the above or all of them

4. What is the consequence of a secured party violating 9-504 in disposing of the collateral?

    a. Debtor recovers compensatory damages (common law and/or 9-507(1))

    b. Debtor recovers punitive damages (common law and/or 9-507(1) if consumer goods)

    c. Secured party cannot recovery any deficiency (Can you argue that a proper disposition is a condition of the right to recover a deficiency under 9-504(2)?)

    d. Combination of the above or all of them

5. Was a sale unreasonable if the debtor proves that another way of disposing of the collateral would have brought a higher price?

6. Was a sale reasonable if the secured party failed to notify the debtor but the secured party proves that proper notice would not have produced a higher price for the collateral?

7. Suppose the debtor is a corporation that is principally owned by two individuals. These principals guaranteed the debt, i.e., they are sureties. *Chemlease* says they are entitled to notice. Why? What if they aren't notified?

8. Suppose the collateral is co-owned by the debtor's partner?

    a. Is the co-owner liable for any deficiency?

    b. Is the co-owner entitled to notice of the sale of the collateral?

    c. Is the co-owner entitled to any of the proceeds?

9. Suppose the secured party gets the debtor to agree that instead of selling the collateral, the secured party will keep the collateral in satisfaction of the secured debt.

    a. If the secured party then sells the collateral for a sum that is larger than the secured debt, who gets this "surplus"?

    b. Is the debtor liable for any "deficiency" if the sale price is less than the secured debt?

    c. Can the parties "legally" agree that the secured party will keep the collateral in partial satisfaction of the secured debt?

    d. What is the proper procedure for the secured party keeping the collateral in satisfaction of the secured debt when the collateral is software rights?

10. What is the consequence of the secured party waiting an unreasonably long time before selling the collateral? Is the secured party deemed to have kept the collateral in satisfaction of the secured debt, or is the consequence the same as any other violation of 9-504?

11. Nonrecourse agreements change 9-507(2). They eliminate or reduce a debtor's liability for a deficiency . To satisfy the secured debt, the secured party is limited, more or less, to its remedies against the collateral. The debtor is completely or partly freed from personal liability for the secured debt.

a. What's the difference between a nonrecourse agreement and strict foreclosure under 9-505?

b. USX Corporation appeals the district court's grant of summary judgment to Prime Leasing, Inc. on all three counts of USX's complaint. USX's predecessor, USX Credit Corporation [For convenience, we will refer to both USX Corporation and USX Credit Corporation as "USX."], had made a loan to Prime for the purchase of telecommunications equipment that Prime had leased to MBank Alamo of San Antonio, Texas. MBank later was declared insolvent, and the purchaser of its assets, Bank One, Texas, N.A., disaffirmed the equipment leases. USX then repossessed and sold the telecommunications equipment, and subsequently brought this diversity action * * * to recover the difference between the unpaid debt from the original financing transaction and the resale price of the equipment. USX predicated its claims on Prime's failure to notify it of developments concerning the MBank leases. Prime's defense, which the district court found persuasive, was that nonrecourse provisions in certain agreements between USX and Prime precluded USX from seeking any remedies beyond the repossession and resale of the leased equipment.

The facts relating to the formation of the transaction are not in dispute. On February 26 and 27, 1987, USX and Prime entered into the various agreements providing for USX's financing of Prime's purchase of the telecommunications equipment leased to MBank. The agreements between USX and Prime included a Loan Agreement, Installment Note ("Note"), Master Security Agreement and Assignment ("Security Agreement"), and two Collateral Assignments of Lease. The two Collateral Assignments relate to separate but contemporaneous leases of equipment to MBank, a main lease covering an AT & T System 85 and another lease covering several smaller systems. The Collateral Assignment for the AT & T lease was executed by Prime on February 26, 1987; however, the Collateral Assignment for the lease of the smaller systems was not executed until April 21, 1987. There is no explanation in the record for this disparity in execution dates. At any rate, the differing dates of the Collateral Assignments are not relevant to the issues presented on this appeal.

The Note and the Security Agreement both contained nonrecourse provisions. The Note provided:

> This Note is made pursuant to and in connection with the [Loan] Agreement and is to be paid from payments due or to become due and judgments recovered under the Master Lease Agreement between [Prime], as Lessor, and MBank Alamo as Lessee, and in the event of default, from the re-marketing proceeds of the Equipment covered thereby. All the terms, conditions and covenants of the [Loan] Agreement and

Security Agreement, including a full description of the rights of the holder hereof and the definitions set forth therein, are incorporated herein by reference. The Obligations of [Prime] under this Note shall be without recourse or liability against [Prime] for payment of the Note or any related costs or expenses except as to a breach by [Prime] of any assignment, representation, covenant, or warranty described in Sections 4, 5(b) or 6 of the Security Agreement.

Sections 4, 5(b), and 6 of the Security Agreement set forth, inter alia, Prime's obligation to deliver lease payments to USX, Prime's warranties as to the correctness of leases and security agreements, and Prime's obligations to preserve the collateral.

Similarly, the Security Agreement provided:

[USX] shall only have recourse with respect to the Collateral as set forth in Section 1 herein, except that [USX] shall have recourse to the general assets of [Prime] for any representation or warranties of [Prime] which shall have been false when made and for material misrepresentations or omissions made by [Prime] in any document provided by [Prime] to [USX] in connection with this transaction.

Further, and this is the crux of USX's claims in this action, the Collateral Assignments of Lease contained provisions requiring Prime to communicate to USX certain notices pertaining to the leases:

[Prime] hereby agrees ... (iii) to notify promptly [USX] or any subsequent assignee of any default or alleged default (of which [Prime] has knowledge) by any party to the Lease or any termination or alleged termination thereof, (iv) without prior written consent of [USX] or any subsequent assignee, not to extend, amend, supplement or terminate (except as expressly permitted therein), or agree to, or permit, any modifications, waiver or other alteration of the terms thereof, and (v) to deliver to [USX] all notices or other communications received by [Prime] in connection with the Lease or any aspect thereof.

* * *

The leased equipment was installed at MBank. Subsequently, on March 28, 1989, the United States Comptroller of the Currency declared MBank insolvent and appointed the Federal Deposit Insurance Corporation as its receiver. Most of the assets of MBank later were sold by the FDIC to Bank One. In December 1989, Bank One decided to replace the leased equipment and requested Prime to remove it by February 1, 1990. USX, as holder of the security interest in the equipment, foreclosed, took possession, and ultimately resold most of the telecommunications systems, but for substantially less than the payments USX would have collected under its financing agreements with Prime.

In March 1990, USX filed this action, contending that Prime had known throughout 1989 that the FDIC and Bank One wanted to disaffirm the leasing agreement, and that Prime had been negotiating with them, without disclosing such negotiations to USX, about restructuring the leases. USX claims that Prime's failure to disclose negotiations with, and notices from, the FDIC and Bank One constituted a breach of the notification provisions of the Collateral Assignments of Lease. In its complaint, USX alleged a first count based on breach of the specific provisions of the Collateral Assignments; a second count based on breach of the covenant of good faith and fair dealing; and a third count of tortious misrepresentation. Because USX already had taken possession of the equipment, it requested only the remedy of damages.

Following discovery, both parties moved for summary judgment, with USX requesting judgment establishing Prime's liability for breach of the specific notification provisions of the Collateral Assignments; and Prime requesting summary judgment in its favor on all three counts. The motions were referred to a magistrate judge whose report, dated February 4, 1992, recommended that summary judgment should be granted for Prime on Counts I and II of the Amended Complaint. The magistrate judge further noted that although Prime also had requested summary judgment on Count III, it had not made a legal argument on that point; therefore, the magistrate judge did not recommend at that time any particular disposition of that claim. By order dated February 26, 1992, the district court adopted the report and entered summary judgment in favor of Prime on Counts I and II. Prime again moved for summary judgment on Count III; by report dated June 5, 1992, the magistrate judge recommended summary judgment for Prime on that Count, reasoning that USX could not manufacture a tort out of a contract claim. On June 24, 1992, the district court adopted the report and granted summary judgment for Prime on Count III, thus completing disposition of the entire case. USX then appealed. *USX Corp. v. Prime Leasing Inc.*, 988 F.2d 433 (3d Cir. 1993). Should the appeals court have affirmed or reversed?

ᗡᗡᗡᗡᗡ

Report of the Article 9 Study Committee
Permanent Editorial Board for the Uniform Commercial Code
American Law Institute and National Conference of Commissions on Uniform State Law,
1992

Committee Recommendations:

D. Enforcement
28. Consequences of Secured Party's Noncompliance with Article 9, Part 5

A. Article 9 should be revised to set forth clearly the extent to which a secured party's failure to comply with Part 5 of the Article affects the secured party's right to a deficiency. The baseline rule should be the "rebuttable presumption" rule: Once it is established that a secured party has not complied with Part 5, the aggrieved party should be entitled to a rebuttable presumption that compliance with Part 5 would have yielded an amount sufficient to satisfy the secured debt in full. A secured party who seeks to recover a deficiency notwithstanding its failure to comply with Part 5 should have the burden of establishing the amount that would have been recovered had the secured party complied with Part 5, and the secured party's deficiency recovery should be limited to the difference between the amount of the secured debt and that amount.

B. The Drafting Committee should consider defining one or more special classes of transactions to which the "absolute bar" rule would be applied (e.g., those in which the collateral is consumer goods or those in which the secured debt is less than a specified amount). For these transactions, a secured party who failed to comply with Part 5 would be barred from recovering a deficiency. The Committee reached no consensus on the appropriate scope of this special class.

C. The rebuttable presumption rule, when applicable, should be applied to both collections under 9-502 and dispositions under 9-504 and should be applied to both the failure to give notification and the failure to dispose of collateral in a commercially reasonable manner. The rule should not be applied to a junior claimant's remedy against a noncomplying senior secured party; rather, the junior should have the burden of proving the amount of loss it suffered as a consequence of the senior's noncompliance.

D. The absolute bar rule, when applicable, should not prevent a debtor from recovering compensatory damages from a noncomplying secured party to the extent that the exculpation from liability for a deficiency would be inadequate compensation for the loss.

However, the absolute bar rule should not be applied to permit a consumer debtor to block a deficiency and also recover a penalty under 9-507(1). In addition, the rule should not necessarily prohibit a noncomplying secured party from recovering the secured obligation from collateral against which it has not yet enforced its security interest.

E. If a secured party fails to comply with Part 5 of Article 9 with respect to its collection on or disposition of some of the collateral and thereafter the secured party enforces the security interest in remaining collateral, and a court subsequently determines that, by operation of the rebuttable presumption rule or the absolute bar rule, the original collection or disposition satisfied the secured debt in an amount greater than what the secured party actually recovered, then the secured party should be liable to the debtor under 9-507 for any excess recoveries from the remaining collateral. The official comments should be revised to explain this result.

F. Section 9-507(1) should be revised so as to afford a remedy to any aggrieved junior secured party or junior lienholder with an interest in the collateral, rather than providing a remedy only to those aggrieved Article 9 secured parties who were "entitled to notification or whose security interest has been made known to the [enforcing] secured party prior to the disposition."

29. Waiver and Variance of Rights of Debtors and Duties of Secured Parties Under Article 9, Part 5

Part 5 should be revised to clarify which rights of debtors and duties of secured parties can be waived or varied and the circumstances under which such waivers or variances will be effective.

30. Duties Owed to Competing Secured Parties and Lienholders By a Secured Party Who Disposes Of or Makes Collections on Collateral

A. The Drafting Committee should consider whether to expand the class of secured parties that is entitled, under 9-504(3), to notification of a disposition of collateral by an enforcing secured party.

B. Section 9-504(1) should be revised to entitle any holder of a subordinate interest in collateral (a "Junior") to receive a distribution of excess proceeds following a disposition of the collateral by a holder of a senior security interest (a "Senior"), as long as the Junior has given the Senior a timely "written notification of a demand" for the distribution. The right to a distribution should not be confined to junior Article 9 secured parties, as under the current 9-504(1).

C. The official comments should be revised to explain that a Senior who acts in good faith in paying out proceeds of a disposition of collateral is not liable to a person who did not receive a payment to which the person was entitled.

D. The Drafting Committee should consider whether Part 5 should be revised to include a detailed and comprehensive treatment of the enforcement of security interests by junior secured parties.

Comments:

Although they are not entirely problem-free, the rules applicable to multiple security interests in collateral seem to work reasonably well when a Senior conducts a disposition pursuant to 9-504. The only major issue as to dispositions by Seniors concerns the appropriateness of the current notification requirement, addressed by Recommendation A above.

Article 9 explicitly acknowledges junior security interests in collateral. It would be anomalous indeed if the Article did not permit a junior secured party to enforce its security interest by taking possession of and disposing of collateral. Moreover, there is nothing in Article 9 to indicate that a Junior does not have the right to enforce its security interest. Beyond this general conclusion, however, questions abound concerning enforcement by Juniors. In its deliberations, the Committee considered in detail many of these questions, but it did not endeavor to reach a consensus on all of them or to develop a comprehensive new scheme that would address every open issue. Instead, it decided to address some discrete issues of practical importance. The Committee recognizes that a comprehensive statutory treatment of the issues surrounding enforcement by Juniors would require significant changes to Part 5. It encourages the Drafting Committee to consider all of the issues. But, given the relative infrequency of multiple security interests in the same collateral, the Committee believes that many of the problems are not significant enough to warrant comprehensive revision.

E. Section 9-504 should be revised to provide explicitly that a junior secured party who disposes of collateral pursuant to 9-504 is entitled to retain and apply the proceeds to the secured debt and to turn over any surplus proceeds to the debtor. The Junior should not be obliged to turn over the proceeds to a Senior.

F. The statute or official comments should be revised to state explicitly that, unless disclaimed or modified, the warranties provided by 2-312 (warranties of title and against infringement) and 2A-211 (warranties against interference and against infringement) apply to a sale or lease (respectively) of collateral pursuant to 9-504.

Comments:

The purchaser from a foreclosing Junior secured party typically will acquire the collateral subject to the Senior's security interest. If the debtor defaults on its obligations to the Senior, the Senior may prefer to assert a claim against some or all of the proceeds of the Junior's disposition rather than against the collateral. Permitting the Senior to recover proceeds from the Junior to the extent of the Senior's claim against the debtor would put the Junior in the same position it would have been in had the Senior sold the collateral. But, if the purchaser knows about the debt owed to the Senior, then the price that the purchaser pays may reflect the presence of the Senior's security interest, ie., the price would not exceed the value of the collateral less the amount of the senior debt. And if the proceeds were applied to the satisfaction of the Senior's security interest and the disposition operated to discharge the Junior's security interest, then the purchaser would receive a windfall at the expense of one or both of the secured parties. On the other hand, the purchase price may reflect the purchaser's reasonable belief that the Junior holds a first-priority security interest. If so, then permitting the Junior to retain the proceeds at the expense of the Senior may result in the purchaser losing goods for which the purchaser has paid full value and may afford the Junior a windfall as well.

The Committee believes that clarification or adoption of two principles would deal adequately with most cases of enforcement by a Junior secured party. First, a Junior should be entitled to receive and retain the proceeds of a disposition pursuant to 9-504, with no obligation to turn them over to the Senior. Second, a secured party who disposes of collateral should make a warranty under 2-312 or 2A-211 (depending on whether the disposition is by sale or by lease) unless the warranty is effectively modified or disclaimed.

Consider the application of these two rules under alternative assumptions. First, assume that the Junior knows about the Senior's claim. In that case, it is likely that the Senior, the Junior, and the purchaser (say, a buyer) will deal with all of the potential disputes by agreement, in which case the baseline statutory rules would not control. If no such agreement is reached, then it is a safe assumption that the Junior will insist on limiting its warranty of title and the purchase price will, accordingly be adjusted downward. Having taken account of the Senior's claim in the purchase price, the purchaser will be left to deal with the Senior. Second, assume that the Junior does not know about the Senior's claim. In that case, it can be expected that the purchaser would not reduce the purchase price to take account of the Senior's claim and the Junior would not limit its warranty of title. If, subsequently, the Senior successfully asserted its senior claim to the collateral against the purchaser, the purchaser could look to the Junior for damages under 2312. Consequently, although the Junior would not be required to turn over any proceeds to the Senior, the Junior's liability under 2312 would preclude the Junior from receiving a windfall.

G. The official comments should make clear that neither repossession nor disposition of collateral by a Junior *ipso facto* constitutes a conversion of the collateral, but that a Senior is entitled to recover possession of the collateral from a Junior if the Senior has a right to possession as against the debtor.

H. The official comments should be revised to explain that a Junior who makes collections on collateral, pursuant to 9-502 or an agreement with the debtor, and who acts in good faith and without knowledge that the collections violate the rights of a Senior, is entitled to retain the collected proceeds free of the claims of the Senior.

I.   The official comments should be revised to make clear that the equitable doctrine of marshaling should be applied to Article 9 security interests in appropriate cases.

31. Duties Owed to Sureties By a Secured Party Who Disposes Of or Makes Collections on Collateral

A. Part 5 should be revised to make clear that a surety for (including a guarantor of) a secured obligation is a "debtor" for purposes of 9-504 and 9-507.

B. Part 5 should be revised to permit a debtor (including a guarantor or other surety) to waive effectively, either before or after default, its right to notification of a disposition of collateral pursuant to 9-504(3), if the debtor does not have an interest in the collateral.

C. The Drafting Committee should consider whether to revise Part 5 to permit a debtor who is a surety for (including a guarantor of) a secured obligation to waive or vary effectively, before default, any of the debtor's other rights or the secured party's other duties under Part 5 concerning collateral in which the debtor does not then have an interest.

D. The official comments should be revised to make clear that Article 9 generally defers to non-UCC principles of suretyship.

32. Standards for a "Reasonable Notification" of a Disposition of Collateral

A. Section 9-504 should be revised to provide that (i) ten days' advance notice is timely for purposes of the "reasonable notification" requirement in 9-504(3) and (ii) less than ten days' notice can be timely in appropriate circumstances.

B. Section 9-504 should be revised to include a form of notification and to provide that timely use of the statutory form is sufficient to comply with a secured party's duty to send "reasonable notification" of a disposition of collateral.

33. Assignments of Security Interests and Transfers of Collateral to Recourse Parties Under 9-504(5)

A. Section 9-504(5) should be revised to make clear that if a secured party assigns a security interest or transfers collateral to a party against whom the secured party has recourse on account of the debtor's default and who has agreed to accept the rights and assume the duties of the secured party, the assignment or transfer is not a disposition under Article 9, Part 5, and the assignee or transferee thereafter has the rights and duties of the secured party under Article 9.

B. Section 9-504 should be revised to specify the circumstances under which a secured party continues to be responsible to the debtor for compliance with Part 5 notwithstanding the secured party's assignment of a security interest or transfer of collateral to a recourse party pursuant to 9-504(5).

34. Retention of Collateral in Satisfaction of Secured Obligations "Strict Foreclosure" Under 9-505

A. Section 9-505 should be revised to eliminate the requirement that the secured party be in possession of collateral when the collateral is intangible and cannot be possessed. The Drafting Committee should consider whether (i) the possession requirement should be removed for other, tangible collateral, and (ii) if it is eliminated generally, whether it nevertheless should be retained in the case of consumer goods.

B. Section 9-505 should be revised to provide that, in addition to those claimants currently entitled to notice under 9-505, one other group of claimants should be entitled to notice: persons whose written statements claiming an interest in the collateral the secured party receives before sending notice of a proposed strict foreclosure or before the debtor waives its right to notice. The Drafting Committee should consider seriously whether to revise 9-505 to require that notice be given to holders of security interests or liens as to which a financing statement (or other filing) is of record against the debtor a specified number of days before the strict foreclosure is to take effect, in the office where one would file a financing statement as of that date.

C. Part 5 of Article 9 should be revised to validate post-default agreements between a debtor (including a surety) and a secured party to the effect that (i) the secured party may retain collateral in partial satisfaction of the secured obligation or (ii) the secured party may purchase collateral at a private disposition. Such an agreement should not take effect if the secured party fails to comply with the requirement to give notice of the proposed retention or private disposition or if a junior claimant objects to the proposed retention or private disposition.

D. Section 9-505 should be revised to provide that (i) strict foreclosure extinguishes the interest of any junior claimant who failed to object in a timely fashion, whether or not the person was entitled to notice, and (ii) the holder of any junior encumbrance, whether or not the holder is entitled to notice, is entitled to prevent a strict foreclosure by giving a written objection to the secured party before the strict foreclosure becomes effective.

E. Part 5 or the official comments should be revised to make clear that a delay in a secured party's disposition of collateral does not constitute a "constructive" strict foreclosure. Instead, a delay that is unreasonable may be a factor relating to whether the secured party acted in a commercially reasonable manner for purposes of 9-504(3).

35. Debtor's Right to Redeem Collateral

Section 9-506 should be revised to provide that holders of judicial, statutory, and common-law liens may exercise redemption rights on the same terms and conditions as the debtor and other secured parties.

E. Other Topics
36. "Good Faith" and the Relationship Between 1-203 and Article 9

A. The Drafting Committee should give serious consideration to revising the definition of good faith in 1201(19), as it may apply to Article 9, by adding "the observance of reasonable commercial standards of fair dealing" to the current standard of "honesty in fact."

B. Article 9, 1-203, or the official comments should be revised to make clear that an obligation that is secured by a security interest is not necessarily a "contract or duty within [the UCC]," upon which 1-203 imposes an obligation of good faith.

D. RESOLVING PRIORITY DISPUTES

Resolving a priority dispute under Article 9 always involves deciding the order in which multiple claims to collateral rank in relation to each other. The claims that compete with a security interest for priority can be other liens, including other Article 9 security interests, or ownership interests, or both. The purpose of deciding priority may be to determine the order in which the claims will be satisfied from the proceeds of a sale of property, or to determine whether a claimant who has handled the collateral is accountable to a more senior claimant for having done so. In any event, the very existence of a priority dispute assumes that the rights of a debtor in property can be subjected to more than one claim.

This assumption is true in the sense that, so long as the debtor does not transfer all of her rights in property, she can subject the property (more precisely, her rights in the property) to an infinite number of liens. The assumption is also true in the sense that, even when the debtor's rights in property are subject to one or more liens, she can transfer all of her rights to someone else, either through sale or gift, so as to give the transferee a claim to the property. Ordinarily, however, the transfer does not affect preexisting claims. They usually run with the property.

As a general rule of priority, the law—including Article 9—ranks liens and other claims to property in the order in which the claims were created or perfected, i.e., first in time is first in right. The law, especially including Article 9, also recognizes a host of exceptions to the general rule of priority. This section of the book is largely dedicated to exploring the first-in-time rule, as expressed in Article 9, and to investigating the exceptions that Article 9 creates to the rule for certain classes of claimants. We start with buyers of collateral because, apart from bankruptcy, the most common priority disputes involve buyers, and also because the priority rules for buyers of collateral are, *relatively speaking*, the easiest.

Preliminary to exploring Article 9's priority rules for buyers of collateral, we focus on a few very important issues that arise in connection with sales of collateral. These issues do not themselves concern the precise and narrow question of priority between the secured party and the buyer with respect to the property that was sold. Rather, they deal with closely related matters that look very much like priority issues but are really more fundamental concerns that properly should be addressed before reaching the priority issue, including:

- whether the debtor can effectively sell or otherwise alienate her rights in collateral (If not, the buyer acquires nothing and no priority dispute erupts between the putative buyer and the debtor's secured party.);
- if the debtor could and did sell her rights in collateral, whether the secured party's interest in the property survived the sale (If not, there is no priority dispute for the reason that the secured party qua secured party has no claim to the property.); and,
- finally, whether in any event the secured party has a claim to proceeds of the sale of the collateral (If so, the secured party may be satisfied with grabbing the proceeds and not fuss with the buyer over the original collateral.).

1. Alienation Of Collateral

a. Debtor's Right and Power to Alienate Collateral

Production Credit Ass'n Of Madison v. Nowatzski
Supreme Court of Wisconsin, 1979
90 Wis.2d 344, 280 N.W.2d 118

Heffernan, Justice. This is an action for conversion brought by Production Credit Association of Madison (PCA), a corporation engaged in making farm loans, against Walter Nowatzski, the transferee of its debtors, Allan R. and Rosalie Hein (the Heins).

On May 6, 1974, the Heins borrowed from PCA for the purchase of cows. The Heins gave PCA a security interest in various personal property, including "[a]ll farm equipment, now owned or hereafter acquired by Debtor." Listed among the farm equipment was a tractor and a self-propelled swather. The Heins later acquired a windrower, which is one of the items of personal property involved in this litigation, with insurance proceeds after the swather burned.

At a time which the record does not make clear, Walter Nowatzski, an uncle of Allan Hein, lent money to Allan for the purchase of farm equipment. Nowatzski testified that he had an unwritten agreement with Hein that if the loan was not repaid, Hein would turn over the farm equipment to Nowatzski. After the Heins defaulted in their loan payment to PCA, Hein turned over the tractor and windrower to Nowatzski. Nowatzski did not know of PCA's prior security rights, although it is undisputed that the financing statement was on file in the appropriate office.

After the default and after Hein commenced bankruptcy proceedings, PCA learned that the tractor and windrower were in the possession of Nowatzski. It made a demand upon Nowatzski asking that the collateral be returned. That demand was refused by Nowatzski, and PCA brought an action for conversion against him.

The trial court found that PCA's security interest was perfected by the filing of a financing statement on May 6, 1974, and that after the Heins defaulted on the obligation to PCA, PCA made a demand that the collateral be turned over but that Nowatzski refused. The court also found that the tractor at the time of trial had a fair market value of $3,069 and a rental value of $600 per year and the windrower had a fair market value of $4,220 and an annual rental value of $700. The court found that the Heins' indebtedness to PCA exceeded $25,000. The court concluded that, as a matter of law, Nowatzski converted the tractor and windrower and that PCA's damages were $8,589, the sum of the value of the two pieces of equipment at the time of the trial plus one year's rental value for each item.

Two issues are presented by Nowatzski's appeal from the judgment: One, was Nowatzski, a transferee of the debtors, liable for conversion when he refused a demand by the debtor's secured party, PCA, to turn over collateral to which PCA had the right of possession under the Uniform Commercial Code and its security agreement with the debtors; and, two, were damages sufficiently proved and was the proper standard used for the measurement of damages?

The record shows that PCA had a perfected security interest in the Heins' farm equipment. After default in payment of the loan to PCA, the Heins transferred two items of the collateral -- the tractor and windrower -- to Nowatzski, contrary to the contract between PCA and the Heins. Both the failure to make payments when due and the transfer of the collateral without consent of the secured party constituted a breach of the contract. Each breach constituted a default, and upon default the secured party could declare the entire debt due and require the debtors to turn over the collateral.

While it is undisputed that upon default PCA had the right to take immediate possession of the property from the Heins, Nowatzski asserts that he had no obligation to turn over the collateral. Although Nowatzski's brief on appeal asserts that PCA never demanded that Nowatzski turn over the property, this argument is unsupported by the record. Nowatzski's answer to the plaintiff's complaint specifically admitted that a demand was made upon him for the tractor and for the windrower and that he refused to turn them over. The trial court found that a demand was made and refused. That finding is not contrary to the great weight and clear preponderance of the evidence.

As a legal matter, Nowatzski argues that he had the right to possession of the collateral because sec. 409.311, Stats., authorizes a debtor to transfer collateral to third parties. Sec. 409.311 states:

"409.311 Alienability of debtor's rights: judicial process. The debtor's rights in collateral may be voluntarily or involuntarily transferred (by way of sale, creation of a security interest, attachment, levy, garnishment or other judicial process) notwithstanding a provision in the security agreement prohibiting any transfer or making the transfer constitute a default."

On its face Nowatzski's argument, based solely on sec. 409.311, Stats., has some plausibility. That section of the statutes authorizes a physical transfer of the collateral, but it is equally apparent that only the debtor's rights inure to the benefit of the transferee. The rights of a security holder in the collateral are protected by the provisions of sec. 409.306(2) and survive transfer of the collateral made without the secured party's consent.

It is undisputed that the transfer from the Heins to Nowatzski was without PCA's knowledge or approval. Hence, Nowatzski took the property subject to PCA's right of possession because the debtors had defaulted. *See, Production Credit Association of Chippewa Falls v. Equity Coop Livestock Sales Assn.*, 82 Wis.2d 5, 16, 261 N.W.2d 127 (1978). In *Production Credit Association of Chippewa Falls, supra,* we did not reach the question of whether a transfer of collateral which constitutes a default or a transfer which occurs after the debtor's default is a conversion. In that case it was assumed that the transfers occurred before default. In the instant case, however, the transfer occurred after default in payment, and under the agreement an unconsented transfer of the collateral was in itself a default. Sec. 409.503, Stats., provides that, unless otherwise agreed, a secured party upon default by the debtor has the right to take possession of the collateral. Accordingly, it is apparent that sec. 409.311, relied upon by Nowatzski, does not avoid a contract provision making an unconsented transfer of the collateral a default. A reasonable reading of sec. 409.311 is that, although it allows a debtor to transfer collateral, it does not invalidate the security agreement if the agreement makes the unconsented transfer a default.

One writer, in an article giving practical advice on the drafting of security agreements, disputes the interpretation of sec. 409.311, Stats., advanced by Nowatzski. Hogan, *Pitfalls in Default Procedure*, 2 U.C.C.L.J. 244, 246-47 (1970), states:

"One of the troublesome areas in the statute is Section 9-311, which seems to say that the debtor has a right to transfer his interest in the collateral, and it seems to be an unrestricted right to transfer his interest in the collateral. That raises a question. Suppose in the security agreement, as you should, you have said that a default occurs if the debtor sells the collateral. If you have as collateral anything that is not inventory, you want that kind of protection in the definition of default in your security agreement.

"Some people have suggested that Section 9-311 prohibits you from using a transfer of the collateral as the basis of a default. I think that thus far neither the statute nor the cases support that conclusion. Section 9-311 merely preserves the interest of the transferee. If the debtor sells the car, the transferee gets whatever the debtor had. Yet the sale can still be a default, and the buyer of that asset takes subject to the secured claim created by the debtor, and the buyer's ability to keep the assets would be subject to the third party's right to repossess.

"The definition of default is not provided in the Code. Default is a matter to be defined by your agreement. [Footnote omitted.]."

* * *

Under secs. 409.311 and 409.306(2), Stats., the Heins could indeed transfer the collateral to Nowatzski, but Nowatzski took subject to PCA's security interest. By the terms of the agreement between the Heins and PCA, the transfer itself constituted a default which gave PCA the right to require that the collateral be surrendered. PCA also had the right to immediate possession because the debtors had defaulted on their loan payments. On the basis of either default, PCA had the right to the immediate possession of the property, and it could assert that right against Nowatzski. We conclude that PCA's action for conversion was the appropriate remedy when Nowatzski refused to surrender the collateral.

The Official U.C.C. comment 3 to sec. 409.306, Wis.Stats.Ann., states:

"[S]ince the transferee takes subject to the security interest, the secured party may repossess the collateral from him or in an appropriate case maintain an action for conversion."

Following the adoption of the Uniform Commercial Code, courts have generally recognized that conversion actions can be used to secure the rights of secured parties against transferees. ***

Some aspects of the law of conversion and its relevance to ch. 409, Stats., were discussed in the recent case of *Production Credit Association of Chippewa Falls v. Equity Coop. Livestock Sales Assn., supra* 82 Wis.2d at 10, 261 N.W.2d at 129. We said therein, "Conversion is often defined as the wrongful exercise cf dominion or control over a chattel." Conversion may result from a wrongful taking or a wrongful refusal to surrender property originally lawfully obtained. *** Where, however, there is no wrongful taking and the defendant rightfully comes into possession of the chattels, a demand by the rightful owner and a refusal by the alleged tortfeasor are necessary elements of the tort.

Although the trial court found that PCA's financing statement was on file and that Nowatzski failed to check the record to determine whether he was violating the rights of PCA when he took possession of the chattels from the Heins, it is not necessary to determine whether Nowatzski's original taking was wrongful. The record shows that Nowatzski converted the tractor and windrower when he refused to surrender them to PCA upon demand. PCA had the right to possession. There was a demand and a refusal. Facts showing the elements of the tort of conversion were specifically found by the trial court, and those facts are not contrary to the great weight and clear preponderance of the evidence.

The general rule in Wisconsin is that, in an action for conversion, the wronged party may recover as damages the value of the property at the time of the conversion plus interest to the date of trial. *Traeger v. Sperberg,* 256 Wis. 330, 333, 41 N.W.2d 214 (1950).

The trial court's award for the conversion of the tractor and the windrower totaled $8,589. This award was based on the testimony of Thomas J. Zwettler, PCA's Portage branch manager. When Zwettler was called as a witness, defense counsel stipulated to Zwettler's "expertise." Zwettler testified that at the time of trial the book value of a tractor of the type involved was $3,069 and the book value of the windrower was $4,220. He also testified that a year's rental value of the tractor was $600 and the rental value of the windrower was $700. Zwettler acknowledged that he had not examined either piece of machinery, but he based his opinion on his familiarity with the type of equipment, his knowledge of current sales, and the figures which appeared in a guide published by the Wisconsin Retail Equipment Dealers.

The court, relying on the testimony of Zwettler, computed the value of the converted property not at the time of conversion, as is usually done, but at the time of trial. The record does not establish clearly the date of conversion. The records shows, however, that PCA's demand was made after a hearing in Hein's bankruptcy action on March 17, 1975, and prior to the filing of the complaint on February 6, 1976.

Traeger v. Sperberg, supra, recognized the general rule that in conversion the plaintiff may recover the value of the property at the time of the conversion plus interest to the date of trial. It qualified that rule, however, by stating:

> "[I]t is universally recognized that the purpose of this rule is to compensate the plaintiff for the loss sustained because his property was taken." (256 Wis. at 333, 41 N.W.2d at 216)

It is clear that the trial court's computation does not comport with the usual rule concerning the time of valuation. The valuation is not erroneous, however, because, in accordance with the rationale of *Traeger,* it reasonably compensates the wronged party for the loss. The properly admissible expert testimony of Zwettler was sufficient to show value at the time of trial. The book value and testimony of Zwettler constituted a reasonable basis of computation, and the determination of the trial court based on that evidence was adequate proof of value on the date of trial. No attempt was made to dispute the evidence of value as offered by Zwettler. That proof of value, however, was value at the time of the trial rather than at the time of conversion. The conversion, the refusal of Nowatzski to surrender the property, occurred at least nine months prior to trial. In view of the fact that the book value was based upon normal depreciation schedules, it is reasonably certain that the value on the date of conversion was greater than on the date of trial. While PCA may have proved less damages than it was entitled to, it is bound by that proof and Nowatzski, who is not aggrieved, cannot complain. In respect to him, if there was error, the error was harmless.

The rental figures were also supported by expert testimony and were undisputed by proof to the contrary. While interest has usually been accepted as a proper measure of damages to be added to the value of the property from the date of conversion to the date of trial, *Traeger*, as stated above, points out that the purpose of the award is to compensate the plaintiff for the loss sustained because of the taking of property. The rental value of the property is as appropriate a measure of damages as the interest which would be computed on the value of the property taken.

The general rule is that damages must be proved with reasonable certainty. The rental value was established with reasonable certainty by the testimony of Zwettler.

The trial court's computations resulted in a reasonable award based on the relevant evidence adduced at trial and achieved the basic purpose of damages in an action for conversion. The award compensated the plaintiff, PCA, for the loss it sustained when Nowatzski refused to surrender the property to which PCA had the right to immediate possession.

Judgment affirmed.

Notes and Problems

1. SP has a security interest in D's widget. D sells the widget to B.

    a. Is the sale valid?

    b. Does it matter whether or not the security agreement prohibits any disposition of the property?

    c. Does it matter whether or not the secured party approves the sale?

2. A debtor who sells her rights in collateral always remains personally liable for the secured debt unless the secured party releases her from liability. In no event, however, is the buyer of the property personally obligated on the secured debt, unless she assumes it or non-Code statutory law makes her liable even in the absence of an assumption. This is true even when the buyer takes the collateral subject to the security interest, meaning that the interest survives the sale and is superior to the buyer's claim to the property. In this event, the secured party can repossess the property from the buyer upon the debtor-obligor's default. If the

secured party pursues this remedy, she owes the buyer all of the duties that run in favor of a debtor under Part 5 of Article 9 because the buyer, as owner of the collateral, is a "debtor" as that term is defined in Article 9. U.C.C. §9-105(1)(d). So the buyer must be allowed to redeem; the secured party must notify the buyer of the disposition; the buyer is entitled to any surplus, although she is not liable for any deficiency; and the buyer can recover from the secured party for wrongful repossession or wrongful foreclosure. See U.C.C. §9-112.

Instead of repossessing the collateral from the buyer, the secured party can usually recover damages from the buyer for conversion. In practice, a secured party almost always vindicates her priority over a buyer through a conversion action rather than by repossessing the collateral. A buyer of collateral who takes subject to the security interest is personally liable for conversion if she purchased the collateral after the debtor's default, or -- if the purchase preceded default -- the buyer will not surrender the collateral upon demand by the secured party after default occurs, or cannot surrender the property because she has disposed of it. Damages are measured by the value of the property at the time of the tort or the amount of the debt secured by the collateral, whichever is less. See generally Steve H. Nickles, *Enforcing Article 9 Security Interests Against Subordinate Buyers of Collateral*, 50 GEO.WASH.L.REV. 511 (1982).

3. A debtor who wrongfully sells collateral is civilly liable for conversion to the secured party, in addition to remaining personally liable for the secured debt. (Is this extra, conversion liability important inasmuch as the debtor is already liable for the debt?) Moreover, in most states any wrongful sale of collateral by a debtor is a crime. Federal law makes such conduct criminal in some cases, such as wrongfully selling collateral in which the Farmers Home Administration or a production credit association has a security interest.

4. Bank has a security interest in all of the equipment and inventory of ABC Corp., present and after-acquired. ABC Corp. and DEF Corp. merge. DEF is the survivor of the merger. Is DEF liable for the secured debt? To what extent, if at all, is Bank's security interest enforceable against DEF Corp.?

b. Secured Party's Waiver of Security Interest

The *Nowatzski* case and U.C.C. §9-311 teach that, notwithstanding a provision in the security agreement purporting to prohibit the disposition of collateral, the debtor has the power to sell or otherwise alienate her rights in the property. Yet, because of the principle of derivative title as expressed in U.C.C. §9-306(2) (first clause), the security interest attached to these rights survives the sale and continues despite the disposition. The result is that, as a general rule, the buyer takes the property subject to the security interest and is accountable to the secured party for the property or its value.

There are two huge exceptions to the general rule that a buyer of collateral takes the property subject to the security interest. Both exceptions are suggested by §9-306(2) itself. First, the section begins, "Except where this Article otherwise provides ***." This phrase refers to Article 9's priority rules. If these rules give the buyer of collateral priority, she effectively takes free of the security interest. This freedom is either complete or partial, i.e., to the extent the buyer gave value, depending on the terms of the priority rule that protects the buyer.

Second, the first clause of §9-306(2) ends in an "unless" phrase: a security interest survives a sale of the collateral "*unless the disposition was authorized by the secured party in the security agreement or otherwise.*" In other words, a sale of collateral that the secured party authorized terminates the security interest, fully and completely, without regard to the amount of value paid by the buyer. The termination results solely from the authorization and §9-306(2), wholly apart from Article 9's priority rules. The buyer in such a case needs no priority rule to protect her from accountability to the secured party because there is no priority conflict. By authorizing the disposition of collateral, the secured party, in effect, waives her security interest in the property. The secured party thereby completely loses her interest in the property that was sold and thus has no claim against the buyer even though none of Article 9's priority rules would have protected the buyer had there been a priority dispute.

How a secured party authorizes a sale of collateral within the meaning of §9-306(2) is an issue that has bothered and divided the courts. The division concerns both the form and content of authorization. As to form, every court agrees that a secured party can authorize a disposition *expressly* not only through language in the security agreement, but also orally or in a writing that is separate from the security agreement. Virtually every court also agrees, in theory, that authority to dispose of collateral can be *implied* (more precisely, *inferred*) from non-verbal conduct. Implied authorizations, and express authorizations apart from the security agreement, are recognized by the "or otherwise" language of §9-306(2).

Disagreement occurs, however, on the question whether an implicit authorization results from a previous course of dealing between secured party and debtor whereby the former on repeated occasions accepted proceeds of sales of collateral by the latter. There is also disagreement on whether, in any event, the force of such a course of dealing is always completely negated by language in a subsequent security agreement prohibiting sales of collateral or requiring the secured party's prior written consent to them.

The sharpest division among the courts concerns the contents or substance of authorizations. There is general agreement that limits on consent to dispose of collateral must be observed to trigger the death of a security interest on the basis of §9-306(2). By "limits" we mean such things as the class of persons to whom the collateral may be sold, and also the terms and other circumstances of the actual sale itself. So, if a secured party expressly authorizes a debtor to sell collateral to Ms. Jones and no one else, the security interest survives a sale to Ms. Smith. Protection against the interest is afforded Ms. Smith only if she can find a priority rule that covers her. Similarly, if the secured party consents to a sale of collateral to anyone for cash during the month of March, neither a cash sale during April nor a credit sale in March affects the security interest as far as §9-306(2) is concerned.

The courts sharply disagree, however, on whether conditions on consent to sell that are somewhat extraneous to the actual sale must be satisfied in order for a security interest to terminate on the authority of §9-306(2). This disagreement is most evident in cases where: (1) the consent to sell is conditioned on the debtor remitting the proceeds of the sale to the secured party; (2) the debtor sells the collateral to the person, and under the circumstances, agreed to by the secured party; but (3) the debtor misapplies the proceeds. Some courts have held that the security interest dies in such a case despite failure of the condition. Among this group are courts that ordinarily enforce limits on consent to sell, that is, they recognize that such limits must be satisfied before a sale kills a security interest. Their reconciliatory reasoning is that the requirement of surrendering proceeds after a sale occurs is a condition subsequent, while restrictions on the terms and other circumstances of the sale itself are conditions precedent. From a buyer's perspective, the practical significance of this distinction is not immediately clear; nor is it obvious to a buyer why the termination or survival of a security interest under §9-306(2) should depend on whether the boundaries of consent that the sale violated were directly related to the sale or were, in relative terms, extraneous to it.

Problems

1. SP has a security interest in D's widget. The security agreement prohibits any disposition of the collateral without SP's prior, written consent. D sells the widget to B. Decide if SP's security interest continues in the widget under these circumstances:

a. SP gives oral consent before the sale.

b. SP tells D, after the sale, not to worry about having disposed of the collateral without getting the required consent.

c. SP learns of the sale beforehand and fails to object.

d. D pays the proceeds of the sale to SP.

e. SP gives prior written approval of the sale on condition that the sale is subject to SP's security interest.

2. On implied waiver based course of conduct, see the discussion of that issue in the *J.R. Hale Contracting,* which is reprinted at pages 209-19 *supra.*

c.   Continuing Security Interest By Law In Proceeds

The second clause of U.C.C. §9-306(2) provides that, upon the disposition of collateral, the security interest in the property "continues in any identifiable proceeds including collections received by the debtor." This continuing interest in proceeds is not dependent on an agreement between the secured party and debtor. The proceeds interest arises automatically by law, unless the parties agree otherwise, U.C.C. §9-203(2), which they never do.

"Proceeds" is broadly defined in U.C.C. §9-306(1) to mean "whatever is received upon the sale, exchange, collection or other disposition of collateral or proceeds." Thus, whenever there is a disposition of property subject to a security interest, *whatever* is received constitutes proceeds in which a security interest *may* continue under §9-306(2).

We emphasize the word "may" because a security interest does not continue by law in all proceeds as defined in §9-306(1). Except with respect to insurance payments, §9-306(1) is only a definitional provision. The provision that creates or provides for a continuing security interest in proceeds, apart from agreement, is §9-306(2), which states that a security interest continues only in identifiable proceeds including collections received by the debtor. A security interest will not continue in property that admittedly is proceeds as defined in §9-306(1) if the property is not identifiable, or was not received by the debtor, as required in §9-306(2).

So, when a secured party claims an interest in property solely on the basis of the proceeds language in §9-306(2), she must establish that:

√ the property is proceeds as defined in §9-306(1), that is,

-- the property was received upon the disposition of other property, and,

-- this other property -- which was disposed of -- was collateral, i.e., was subject to a security interest in the creditor's favor; and,

√ (2) the proceeds are identifiable; and,

√ the proceeds were "received by the debtor" (Some authorities dispute this requirement.).

Proceeds are *"whatever"* is received upon the disposition of collateral. U.C.C. §9-306(1). If the debtor exchanges collateral for cash, the money is proceeds. If she sells the collateral on credit, the right to receive payment of the purchase price is proceeds whatever form the right takes, i.e., account, chattel paper, instrument, or general intangible. When she enforces such a right that is collateral, the money or whatever else she collects is proceeds. If the debtor swaps collateral for goods, the property she takes in trade is proceeds. In sum, "whatever" means property of any kind, shape or form, whether tangible or intangible, so long as the property is personalty. Article 9 does not apply to real estate as original collateral or as proceeds.

"Whatever" amounts to "proceeds", however, only if it is received upon the "sale, exchange, collection, or other disposition of collateral or proceeds." This requirement is not usually troublesome because, in the ordinary case, the debtor either sells or otherwise voluntarily exchanges collateral in hand for other property, or she collects a debt that is collateral. Hard cases occasionally arise, however, that mark the limits of "proceeds" by limiting the meaning of "disposition" of collateral.

In any event, a security interest continues only in proceeds that are identifiable. U.C.C. §9-306(2). This condition requires a secured party to establish that the property she claims as proceeds is a product -- a direct descendant -- of collateral in which she had a security interest. She must trace the heritage of the property and show a direct ancestral line to collateral. The difficulty in satisfying this condition increases in proportion to the number of transformations the collateral has undergone.

Satisfying the identifiability condition is most difficult when money resulting from the sale of collateral has been mingled with other funds. The commingling itself is not an absolute bar to identifying the proceeds. Yet, the commingling does not result in the security interest spreading to the other funds. So the secured party must somehow segregate the proceeds from the other funds. She cannot actually, physically pinpoint the proceeds, of course, because funds are usually fungible. Rather, identification is accomplished fictionally by using equitable principles of tracing, but only when the facts necessary to the application of these principles are sufficiently proved.

In re Hastie
United States Court of Appeals, Tenth Circuit, 1993
2 F.3d 1042

Brorby, Circuit Judge. The issue in this case is whether a perfected security interest in registered and certificated common stock continues in cash dividends paid on that stock under the Uniform Commercial Code as enacted in the state of Oklahoma.

I

Acquisition Management, Inc., a successor in interest of the Federal Deposit Insurance Corporation, acquired a security interest in shares of stock owned by a debtor, Mr. John Hastie. FDIC/Acquisition Management [hereinafter "FDIC"] and Mr. Hastie also entered into a security agreement in favor of FDIC covering dividends paid on the stock.[1] The security interest in the stock was effectively transferred, and perfected, by FDIC taking possession of the certificated and registered securities. The issuer of the stock, however, was not requested to, and did not, register a change of ownership of the stock and Mr. Hastie was at all relevant times the registered owner of the securities. Mr. Hastie subsequently filed for bankruptcy protection under Chapter 11 of the Bankruptcy Code. After the date of the bankruptcy petition the issuer of the stock paid cash dividends to Mr. Hastie. Mr. Hastie as debtor-in-possession reported the dividend income in his monthly operating report and intended to use the cash dividends to fund the plan of reorganization. FDIC asserted a claim against the cash dividends claiming its security interest in the dividends was perfected. The bankruptcy court granted summary judgment in favor of Mr. Hastie, holding FDIC's security interest in the dividends was not perfected. The district court affirmed. FDIC appeals claiming that the cash dividends are proceeds from the disposition of the stock under Okla.Stat.Ann. tit. 12A, §9-306(1) (West Supp.1993), and its security interest continues in the dividends.

---

[1]   The security agreement provided:
"[T]he Debtor hereby sells, assigns, transfers and conveys unto the Secured Party and grants to the Secured Party a Security interest in and to all of the Debtor's interest and property rights, ... including, without limitation, all moneys and claims for moneys due and to become due to the Debtor under all dividends, distributions, accounts, contract rights, voting rights and general intangibles relating to and/or due from [the issuers].... The Secured Party will have the right to receive from [the issuers] the share of dividends, profits, return of contributions and other distributions to which the Debtor would be entitled."

II

* * *

The threshold issue in this case is whether after-acquired property is subject to a pre-petition security interest under bankruptcy law. Mr. Hastie acquired the cash dividends after the date of the bankruptcy petition. Property acquired after the commencement of a bankruptcy proceeding is not subject to the lien of any security agreement entered prior to the bankruptcy petition, 11 U.S.C.A. §552(a) (West 1993), except that a security agreement covering proceeds of property acquired before commencement covers proceeds acquired after commencement. 11 U.S.C.A. §552(b) (West 1993). Accordingly, FDIC's claim is based upon the determination that cash dividends are proceeds of the stock and that its security interest in the stock continues in the dividends. In making this argument, FDIC asserts that the definition of proceeds under bankruptcy law is broad. We find it unnecessary to decide whether the definition of proceeds under bankruptcy law is broader than the applicable definition under state law, however, as for FDIC to prevail its security interest must be perfected under state law. We turn now to this dispositive issue.

Mr. Hastie was a debtor-in-possession having the powers and duties of a trustee, including the rights and powers of a hypothetical lien creditor with a judicial lien over property in the estate as of the commencement of bankruptcy proceedings. Under Oklahoma law, a lien creditor has priority over an unperfected security interest. Okla.Stat.Ann. tit. 12A, §9- 301(1)(b) (West Supp.1993). Therefore, since Mr. Hastie was in possession of the cash dividends during the pendency of the bankruptcy proceedings, he prevails over FDIC unless FDIC's security interest in the dividends was perfected. FDIC, of course, contends that its interest was perfected. Its position is that the cash dividend was: (1) paid from the earnings and profits of the issuer of the stock; and (2) a disposition of a portion of the stockholder's equity in the underlying corporation. Therefore, according to FDIC, the cash dividends are proceeds of the stock.

Was FDIC's security interest perfected? Whether the cash dividends are proceeds and whether the FDIC has a perfected interest in such proceeds is determined by state law. Under Oklahoma law, "a security interest ... continues in any identifiable proceeds," Okla.Stat.Ann. tit. 12A, §9-306(2) (West Supp.1993), and "proceeds" are defined as "whatever is received upon the sale, exchange, collection or other disposition of the collateral or proceeds." Okla.Stat.Ann. tit. 12A, §9-306(1) (West Supp.1993). With respect to this definition, the term "sale" may be defined generally as "[a] revenue transaction where goods or services are delivered to a customer in return for cash or a contractual obligation to pay. [The] [t]erm comprehends [a] transfer of property from one party to another for valuable recompense." Blacks Law Dictionary, 5th ed. at 1200 (1979). Similarly, the term "exchange" may be defined as "[the] [a]ct of giving or taking one thing for another," id. at 505, and the term "collect" in the context of a debt or claim may be defined as "payment or liquidation of it," id. at 238. Lastly, the phrase "other disposition" may be defined generally as the "[a]ct of disposing; [or] transferring to the care or possession of another; [or] [t]he parting with, alienation of, or giving up [of] property." Id. at 423. Accordingly, each of the foregoing events describes an event whereby one asset is disposed of and another is acquired as its substitute.[1] A survey of Oklahoma law and that of other jurisdictions reveals no case in which the status of ordinary cash dividends as proceeds of the underlying common stock is squarely addressed. Nevertheless, the foregoing definitions are consistent with the conventional usage of such terms.

Based on the recited definitions, FDIC's position is contrary to the language of the statute, and therefore we believe Oklahoma courts would find FDIC's security interest in the cash dividends not perfected. The receipt of cash dividends by a registered owner of certificated securities bears no resemblance to the events specified in the definition of proceeds or to an act of disposition generally. Common stock represents an ownership interest in the issuing corporation. Under Oklahoma law, a cash dividend is a distribution of the issuing corporation's capital surplus or retained earnings. Okla.Stat.Ann. tit. 18, §1049 (West 1986). Thus, although the cash dividend distributes assets of the corporation, it does not alter the ownership interest represented by the stock. The cash dividend, therefore, is not a disposition of the stock. Normally, stock is not disposed of, sold, or exchanged in any way unless a change in the ownership interest in the issuing corporation is thereby effected. We need not decide if a different rule would be appropriate for a liquidating dividend as the issue is not presented. We note only that in such situations an exchange of stock is frequently required. Nor do we view ordinary cash dividends as something akin to a "recovery" for damage to the underlying stock. See generally McGonigle v. Combs, 968 F.2d 810, 828 (9th Cir.) ("[i]f the purpose of [§9-306] is to be served, however, the security-holder must be protected against diminutions in the value of the security that arise not only from sale, but also from other events or transactions that damage the security"), cert. dism'd, --- U.S. ----, 113 S.Ct. 399, 121 L.Ed.2d 325 (1992). The impact of cash dividends on the value of common stock and on the equity of the stockholder therein is a factual matter of a kind and complexity outside the scope of this litigation. We are aware that under certain conditions so-called "ordinary cash dividends" under Oklahoma law might be paid out to a point at or near the point of insolvency for the issuing corporation. * * * In our judgment, the Byzantine factual inquiry that would attend a proceeds rule based upon whether the cash

---

[1] The parties make no argument with respect to Okla.Stat.Ann. tit. 12A, §9-306(4) (West Supp.1993), so we offer no opinion on the effect of this section on this appeal. See generally, In re Bumper Sales, 907 F.2d at 1437-38. Section 9-306(4) provides that: In the event of insolvency proceedings instituted by or against a debtor, a secured party with a perfected security interest in proceeds has a perfected security interest only in the following proceeds: .... (b) identifiable cash proceeds in the form of money which is neither commingled with other money nor deposited in a deposit account prior to the insolvency proceedings.

dividends did or did not diminish the value of the stockholder's equity in the stock would not be justified in expense or helpfulness given that as a matter of practice there exist other conventions for obtaining a perfected security interest in cash dividends. Accordingly, the holding of this case is that ordinary cash dividends out of capital surplus and earned income are not proceeds of the common stock as the distribution of the dividend is not a disposition of the stock.

* * *

The decision of the district court is AFFIRMED.

Chrysler Credit Corp. v. Superior Court
California Court of Appeal, First District, 1993
22 Cal.Rptr.2d 37, 17 Cal.App.4th 1303

Stein, Associate Justice. East County Dodge was in the business, among other things, of selling vehicles supplied to it by Chrysler Credit Corporation (Chrysler) under a security agreement. For reasons which will be discussed, East County Dodge ostensibly deposited the proceeds from the sales of the vehicles in an account at Bank of the West to which both it and Chrysler were signatories. Chrysler ultimately obtained a writ of possession against the funds held in that account. The State Board of Equalization and the Employment Development Department filed third-party claims against the same funds. (Hereafter, except as indicated, these agencies will be referred to as third parties.) Chrysler here appeals the superior court's denial of its motion to dismiss the third-party claims.

* * *

Factual/Procedural Background
The essential facts are not in dispute.
On September 13, 1988, Chrysler entered into a master credit agreement with East County Dodge by which Chrysler agreed to provide financing to East County Dodge for the purpose of purchasing new vehicles from Chrysler and used vehicles from their sellers. The agreement gave Chrysler a "first and prior security interest" in every vehicle financed under the agreement and "all proceeds thereof." Chrysler perfected its security interest by filing its financing statement on October 6, 1988. (See, generally, Com.Code, §§9203, 9302, subd. (1)(a), and 9306.)
East County Dodge began having financial problems, and in April 1990, filed a Chapter 11 petition in the United States Bankruptcy Court. As part of those proceedings, the bankruptcy court authorized East County Dodge to sell vehicles financed by Chrysler under its master credit agreement, and ordered East County Dodge to "deposit into a special trust account ... in the name of East County Dodge and Chrysler the ... wholesale value upon the debtor completing a sale of any ... collateral vehicles (i.e., the vehicles secured under the security agreement.)" In purported compliance with this order, East County Dodge

opened a trust account with the Bank of America for the deposit of funds received from the sales of collateral vehicles. East County Dodge later, with the agreement of Chrysler, moved those funds into an account at Bank of the West--the account at issue here. For purposes of clarity, we will adopt Chrysler's practice and refer to this account as the "cash collateral account."

Thereafter, in connection with any sale of a financed vehicle, East County Dodge provided Chrysler with information referring to that sale, including the purchaser, the price, and a copy of the vehicle's invoice. East County Dodge also forwarded to Chrysler copies of bank deposits reflecting amounts deposited into the cash collateral account. East County Dodge, however, did not directly deposit the funds from the sales of collateral into the cash collateral account. Rather, it deposited these funds into its general operating account and, then, from time to time withdrew funds from the general account and deposited them into the cash collateral account. Thus, Armand Frumenti, the president of East County Dodge, declared, as relevant:

> "The usual practice of East County Dodge, Inc. was to initially deposit all proceeds, including monies received from the sale of automobiles, automotive parts and remuneration for automotive repair services, into the general operating bank account ... Thereafter, monies were periodically transferred from the general operating bank account to the debtor-in-possession bank account by way of a check written against East County Dodge, Inc.'s general operating bank account to the East County Dodge, Inc.'s debtor-in- possession bank account."

Thus, it was East County Dodge's practice to deposit the full purchase price, including sales tax, of vehicles into the general operating account. Chrysler, of course, had no security interest in the sales tax. In addition, Chrysler had no security interest in the funds received by East County Dodge for labor, and these funds, too, were deposited into the general operating account. It follows that the funds in which Chrysler had a security interest--the proceeds of sales of collateral--were commingled with other funds.[1]   The record contains no evidence tracing those funds to any account or entity other than to the cash collateral account. As Chrysler concedes, however, the general operating account regularly reflected a negative balance. Apparently, the Bank of the West would cover the checks drawn on the account and would then use the following day's deposits to recover the overdraft. As Chrysler asserts, "During this time, and without Chrysler's knowledge, Bank of the West allowed a $282,000 overdraft balance to build-up in the Operating Account. [East County Dodge] deposited funds to reduce the overdraft balance and the Bank continued to honor overdrafts, by advancing its own funds."

[1]   Indeed, from July 25, 1990, to December 18, 1990, East County Dodge deposited $1,782,883.85 into its operating account. For the same period Chrysler claimed proceeds from sales of collateral of only $353,131.82.

The bankruptcy proceedings were dismissed on May 1, 1991. On May 8, Chrysler filed a complaint, seeking as relevant here, to recover the funds held in the cash collateral account. In the meantime, third parties levied against East County Dodge's bank accounts, including the cash collateral account, claiming that East County Dodge owed the State Board of Equalization $211,165.07, plus interest, and the Employment Development Department $23,600.54. Chrysler obtained a writ of possession as to the cash collateral account on June 24, 1991. Third parties subsequently filed third-party claims, claiming an interest in the funds held in that account.

DISCUSSION

As all parties agree, the basic issue is whether the court erred in determining that Chrysler had no perfected security interest in the funds in the cash collateral account, a finding which means that the Board of Equalization and the Employment Development Department have the right to levy against those funds, and that their claims have priority over any claim Chrysler has to the funds as an unsecured creditor. There is no question but that Chrysler had a perfected security interest in the collateral--the financed automobiles--itself. The question, rather, is whether the funds deposited into the cash collateral account are the "identifiable proceeds" of the collateral such that Chrysler's security interest attached also to them. (Com.Code, §9306, subd. (2).)

Chrysler's position is that the funds were intended to be, and were, receipts from the sales of the collateral. The third parties' position is that by depositing the amounts received upon sale of the vehicles into the general account and then withdrawing funds from that account and depositing them into the cash collateral account, East County Dodge so commingled the proceeds with other funds that they are not "identifiable" as proceeds from the sales. The superior court adopted this position, finding that "Chrysler has failed to establish that the contents of the so-called Cash Collateral Account constitute 'identifiable cash proceeds' from the sale of its collateral."

* * *

II.

The Evidence Supports the Trial Court's Conclusion that the Funds in the Cash Collateral Account Are Not the Identifiable Proceeds of the Sales of Collateral

The question remains whether Chrysler met its burden of showing that the funds in the cash collateral account were in fact the proceeds of the sales of collateral. The trial court, on such evidence as was submitted by the parties, concluded that the funds in the account were not the identifiable proceeds of those sales. To the extent that the submitted evidence was conflicting, we must, of course, resolve those conflicts in favor of the trial court's conclusion. (Bowers v. Bernards (1984) 150 Cal.App.3d 870, 873-874, 197 Cal.Rptr. 925.)

We do not agree, as third parties have argued, that the ability to trace the proceeds was destroyed the moment that they were commingled with other funds in the general operating account. Again, the issue has not been discussed in any California case, but the applicable principles of law appear to be well established. Addressing the argument that Professor Gilmore (see, generally, II G. Gilmore, Security Interest in Personal Property (1965) §27.4) theorized that commingling should   destroy any identity of proceeds, the court in Harley-Davidson Motor Co. v. Bank of New England (1st Cir.1990) 897 F.2d 611, 619-620, held:

> "The problem with this argument, however, is that the courts have subsequently, with virtual unanimity, rejected Professor Gilmore's early view. They have held that, in certain special circumstances, a secured party may trace 'identifiable proceeds' through a commingled bank account and into the hands of a recipient who lacks the right to keep them. [Citations.] ... Courts, in justifying the use of tracing, have pointed out that the Code itself says that they are to supplement its provisions with general 'principles of law and equity.' [Citations.]"

These principles ordinarily apply to permit tracing where the debtor has acted collusively with a stranger to the secured transaction and permit the secured party to trace funds transferred to the stranger. Such a situation is distinguished from that occurring where the stranger obtains funds from a commingled account in the ordinary course of business. (Id. at p. 620.) We see no reason why the same principles should not apply here, where, although no collusion took place, the funds ostensibly were placed into the cash collateral account so that they would be available to Chrysler.

    * * *

It follows that, as the superior court also concluded, Chrysler was entitled, if it could, to trace the proceeds through the operating account into the cash collateral account. As to each secured vehicle, Chrysler submitted evidence of (1) the date and amount of sale, (2) the amount of proceeds due to Chrysler for such sale, (3) the date the total proceeds from the sale were deposited into East County Dodge's general operating account, and (4) the date funds, earmarked by East County Dodge as the amount due Chrysler, were deposited into the cash collateral account, and (5) the amount of these funds.

The Commercial Code does not provide any aid in determining whether this information sufficiently traced the proceeds of the sales of collateral. We, as have other courts before us, will resort to principles developed in the common law.

The common law rule applicable here is the "lowest intermediate balance rule" used in tracing trust funds. Witkin describes it: "If the trustee withdraws money and dissipates it, the trust funds are only those which remain on deposit. Subsequent deposits ordinarily do not inure to the benefit of the trust. Hence, the beneficiary can have his prior lien only upon the lowest intermediate balance left in the account. And if at any time the trustee withdraws and dissipates the entire fund, the beneficiary loses all prior claim and is merely a general creditor of the trustee." (11 Witkin, Summary of Cal. Law (9th ed. 1990) Trusts, §144(3), p. 1000. The court in Ex Parte Alabama Mobile Homes, Inc. (1985) 468 So.2d 156, 160, elaborates:

> "When proceeds of a sale of collateral are placed in the debtor's bank account the proceeds remain identifiable and a security interest in the funds continues even if the funds are commingled with other funds. [Citation.] The rules employed to distinguish the identifiable proceeds from other funds are liberally construed in the creditor's favor by use of the 'intermediate balance rule.' [Citations.] This rule provides a presumption that proceeds of the sale of collateral remain in the account as long as the account balance equals or exceeds the amount of the proceeds. The funds are 'identified' based on the assumption that the debtor spends his own money out of the account before he spends the funds encumbered by the security interest. If the account balance drops below the amount of the proceeds, the security interest in the funds on deposit abates accordingly. This lower balance is not increased if funds are later deposited into the account. [Citation.] This rule is analogous to the presumption which arises when a trustee commingles trust funds with his own. [Citation.]"

In the present case East County Dodge deposited the proceeds of the sales of collateral into its general operating account. Assuming no further action was taken, Chrysler's security interest attached to those funds notwithstanding that they were commingled with other funds. But further action was taken. It appears that East County Dodge maintained a deficit balance in its general operating account and that the Bank of the West applied any funds deposited into that account to reduce the indebtedness. Under the intermediate balance rule, any nonproceeds would be applied first to reduce East County Dodge's debt to Bank of the West. Once those funds were exhausted, however, and proceeds were attached, Chrysler's security interest in the funds abated. When East County Dodge deposited funds into the cash collateral account, it wrote checks against the general operating account. If at the time such a check was written the general operating account had a positive balance, and if the funds might be deemed proceeds under the intermediate balance rule, the funds taken from the general operating account and deposited into the cash collateral account were in fact the identifiable proceeds of sales of collateral. The evidence, however, is that at the time East County Dodge wrote these checks there were no proceeds in the general operating account. Those funds, together with any other funds deposited, had been used to reduce the deficit in the account. Chrysler's security interest in the funds in the general operating account, accordingly, was reduced to zero. When Bank of the West honored the checks, it essentially advanced its own funds, increasing the deficit in the general operating account. Unless, as does not appear to be the case, Chrysler somehow obtained a security interest in these loan funds, it had no security interest in the funds deposited into the cash collateral account because they were not the proceeds of any sales of collateral; they were funds loaned by Bank of the West.

Chrysler urges us to adopt an exception to the intermediate balance rule. It has been held that where a trustee commingles personal funds with trust funds, and dissipates the commingled funds such that the trust funds are affected, and then deposits additional personal funds into the account, it may be presumed that the trustee was intending to reimburse the trust funds. In such a situation, the trust funds will be replenished. The case law does not recognize this exception in a situation such as exists here; and in our view this exception, if broadly applied, would completely emasculate the rule. Rather, it is properly limited to contests between trustee and beneficiary, where the trustee essentially embezzles trust funds and subsequently intends to, and does, replace them. A different situation exists where, as here, third parties have competing interests in the funds at issue. Here, not only proceeds from the sales of collateral, but funds due other creditors, including third parties, were deposited into the general operating account. It would be inequitable to conclude that after that account was reduced to zero, any money deposited into it belonged only to Chrysler. In addition, were we to adopt the position urged by Chrysler we would, in effect, be giving the debtor, rather than the Commercial Code, the power to determine priorities among creditors. We decline to adopt such a rule. It follows that, as the trial court concluded, the funds in the cash collateral account are not the identifiable proceeds of the sales of collateral.

The superior court correctly denied the motion to dismiss the third party claims. The petition for writ of mandate, as we have so construed Chrysler's appeal, is denied.

Notes and Problems

1. In 1985, Bank makes a loan to Farmer who signs a security agreement describing the collateral as "all the Debtor's crops, present and after-acquired." The agreement also describes the Farmer's land. This land description is required by U.C.C. §9-203(1)(a) whenever "the security interest covers crops growing or to be grown or timber to be cut." In 1986, Farmer participates in a program of the federal government that gives a farmer a right to federally-owned surplus grain in exchange for the farmer not growing fresh crops. Bank argues that Farmer's entitlements are "crops" within the meaning of the security agreement. Is this argument a winner or loser?

    a. Same facts except that the security agreement does not contain a land description.

b. Same facts except that Bank bases its claim to the entitlements on the argument that the entitlements are proceeds of Farmer's crops. Would the answer be different if the Farmer had enrolled in the government program after having planted crops in 1986 and, thereafter, plowed under the crops?

c. Same facts except that the security agreement includes in the description of collateral "all the Debtor's receivables, including all accounts, contract rights, and general intangibles."

2. Bank has a security interest in Dealer Debtor's inventory of automobiles. Some customers buy cars on credit, signing installment sales contracts. Other customers lease cars for typical terms ranging from two to five years.

a. Are the installment sales contracts proceeds of the cars?

b. Are the lease contracts proceeds? The lease payments? See 9-306 comment 6 (based on PEB Commentary No. 9, June 25, 1992).

c. Debtor also rents cars at the airport for very short periods typically ranging from one to three days. Bank's security interest also reaches this fleet of cars. Are the airport rental contracts proceeds?

3. The Debtor is an Arizona limited partnership whose main asset is the Ventana Canyon Golf and Racquet Club (the "Club") in Tucson, Arizona. The Club is a first class golf and tennis club with two 18 hole golf courses, numerous tennis courts, 50 rental suites, a clubhouse and restaurants. Adjacent to the Club is the Loew's Ventana Canyon Resort Hotel (the "Resort") which, by contract with the Debtor, has the right to allow its occupants to have first priority to play one of the golf courses every day. Pursuant to that agreement, the Resort guarantees minimum annual revenue to the Debtor, primarily from green fees. If the minimum revenue is not paid by the Resort occupants, the Resort will pay the difference to the Debtor. To date, the revenue generated from Resort occupants has exceeded the minimum required and, accordingly, the Resort has never become obligated to make a payment to the Debtor pursuant to this commitment.

The Debtor operates, in part, as a private country club with approximately 800 members who have membership agreements with the Debtor. The membership agreements entitle the members to certain exclusive rights at the Club, primarily the right to have the exclusive use of one of the 18 hole golf courses. Further, the members are required to spend minimum annual amounts at the Club. The Debtor is not a totally private club because tee times are available to the public daily on one of the 18 hole golf courses. Although the record is less than clear in this regard, the public's use of one of the golf courses appears to be on an "as available basis," i.e., it appears that as the tee times are available because they are not being used by the members or Resort occupants they can be used by the public. Further, the 50 suites are available to the public and as used the occupants have the use of the Club.

Grefco lent the Debtor $20,000,000.00. The agreement between the Debtor and Grefco authorized negative amortization resulting in Grefco claiming that it was owed a principal debt of approximately $25,600,000.00 on the date the petition was filed. This debt was secured by a first deed of trust on the real property, an assignment of the rents, issues and profits from the real property, a security interest in all personal property used at the Club together with the membership agreements and the above described agreement between the Resort and the Debtor and a reserve account maintained at a designated bank. For purposes of this ruling it is significant to note that the security interest granted covered "all income, rents, royalties, revenues, issues, profits, fees and other proceeds of the Real Property, including, without limitation, all of the right, title and interest of the Debtor, now or hereafter acquired, and as tenant or landlord or seller, in and to all leases, occupancy agreements and use agreements (whether written or oral and whether for a definite term or month to month)".
* * *

Most of the revenues in dispute between these parties involve the post petition revenues of the Debtor. Section 552 of the Code provides the extent to which pre-petition security interests will extend to property acquired post petition. Section 552(a) of the Code states the general rule that 'property acquired by the estate or by the debtor after the commencement of the case is not subject to any lien resulting from any security agreement entered into by the debtor before the commencement of the case,' except as provided in Section 552(b). Section 552(b) of the Code allows a pre-petition security interest in "property of the debtor acquired before the commencement of the case' and 'to proceeds, product, offspring, rents or profits of such property acquired by the estate after the commencement of the case" to remain effective notwithstanding the bankruptcy if all of the requirements of that section are met. Section 552(b) provides a narrow exception to the general rule of Section 552(a) that pre-petition security interests do not extend to property acquired by the estate after the filing of the petition.
* * *

Generally, the revenue earned by the Debtor can be categorized as follows: (1) green fees and golf cart fees paid by members of the Club, occupants of the Resort and the public, (2) charges for the use of the 50 suites, (3) charges at the restaurants by such members, occupants and public, (4) general pro shop charges such as lessons, equipment rental, bag storage, range balls and the like, (5) tennis fees and (6) members fees, dues and minimum spending obligations. *In re Everett Home Town Limited Partnership*, 146 B.R. 453 (Bankr. D. Ariz. 1992). Which of these revenues are "proceeds" of the secured party's collateral so that the security interest will continue in the revenues postpetition?

4.   In March, F sells S inventory on credit. F retains and perfects a security interest in the very inventory sold to S. S later sells some of this inventory, and the cash

received from the sale of the inventory is deposited in a special escrow account. No other funds are deposited into the account. S then uses this escrow account to purchase new inventory. Is this new inventory "proceeds" of the inventory sold by F to S in March? If so, does F's security interest continue in this new inventory? In proceeds of the new inventory? How is this problem different from *Chrysler Credit*?

5. On January 10, S lends D $10,000 and obtains a security interest in all of D's inventory. As of January 10, D's bank account has a $3,000 balance. D then makes the following deposits and withdrawals:

    ♦   On January 13, D deposits $4,000 it received from the sale of inventory.
    ♦   On January 16, D withdraws $6,000 from the account for payroll, rent and other expenses.
    ♦   On January 30, D deposits $9,000 from the sale of a vacant lot it owned.

    What is the extent of D's security interest in D's bank account under U.C.C. §9-306(2)?

6. Same facts as Problem 5, except that the $6,000 withdrawal on January 16 was paid to C. If any of this amount was subject to S's security interest, can S recover the amount from C? See U.C.C. §9-306 comment 2(c). Suppose C was paid the money in exchange for a piece of equipment. If any of the $6,000 paid to C was subject to S's security interest when the amount was withdrawn, does S's security interest continue in the equipment? See U.C.C. §9-306(2) (first clause).

7. A security interest continues in identifiable proceeds received by the debtor *whether or not* the secured party authorized the disposition of the original collateral. So a secured party who consents to a sale of collateral and thereby waives her security interest in the property that is sold nevertheless has the security of the proceeds as collateral, assuming she can identify them. Also, even when a disposition of collateral is unauthorized and the buyer takes subject to the security interest, the secured party can claim the proceeds. In this case, can she claim both the proceeds and the original collateral? Yes. See U.C.C. §9-306 comment 3. The secured party's collateral is effectively doubled; but, as the comment points out, her recovery from the collateral is in every case limited to the amount of the secured debt.

8. SP had a security interest in D's crops. D sold the collateral and bought a Buick and a house. D later traded the Buick for a Jeep. Should SP's security interest have spread to the Buick and the house if proceeds of collateral were traced directly into this property? See U.C.C. §9-104(j); compare, e.g., §§9-104(g) & (l). Would your answer change if the house had been a mobile home?

9. U.C.C. §9-306(2) expressly requires that proceeds be "received by the debtor." An issue here is whether this requirement in subsection (2) on the continuation of a

security interest applies to all proceeds, or only proceeds in the form of "collections". The commentary pretty clearly says that the "received by the debtor" requirement applies generally to all proceeds. In applying this requirement, remember that the term "debtor" is broadly defined to include not only the obligor, but also the owner of the collateral "[w]here the debtor and the owner are not the same person." U.C.C. §9-105(1)(d). So "debtor" includes a person to whom collateral is transferred subject to the security interest. U.C.C. §9-105 comment 2. Have this in mind when you reach the very last part of the next problem.

10. Debtor made an unauthorized sale of collateral to Buyer. None of Article 9's priority rules protected Buyer. Buyer then resold the collateral to Buyer 2.
    a. Can the secured party replevy the collateral from Buyer 2?
    b. Is Buyer 2 liable for the secured debt?
    c. Is Buyer 2 liable for conversion?
    d. Is Buyer liable for the secured debt?
    e. Is Buyer liable for conversion of the collateral?
    f. Is Debtor liable for the secured debt?
    g. Is Debtor liable for conversion?
    h. Is the secured party entitled to whatever property Debtor received from Buyer?
    i. Must Buyer account to the secured party for the property she got from Buyer 2?

2. Secured Party Versus Buyer

a. Usual Operation of Usual Rules

You learned from the preceding materials that a debtor retains the power to sell or otherwise dispose of collateral, thereby transferring her rights in the property, despite provisions in the security agreement that purport to limit her ability to convey the property. You also learned that the debtor's disposition of collateral does not in itself terminate the security interest attached to the property: A security interest generally continues in collateral notwithstanding sale or other disposition. U.C.C. §9-306(2). Although this rule does not prevent the debtor's rights in collateral from passing to her transferee, it does insure (except where Article 9 provides otherwise) that the property remains subject to the security interest despite disposition by the debtor and thus continues to be collateral for the debt owed the secured party. You learned, too, of a major exception to §9-306(2): a security interest does not survive a disposition of collateral if the secured party somehow authorized the disposition. In this event, the secured party loses her interest in the property and has no further claim to it, although she still has a claim to proceeds.

If the disposition was not authorized by the secured party so that her interest survives and continues in the property in the hands of the transferee, the secured party has the prima facie right, upon the debtor's default, to take possession of the collateral. The right to repossess is enforceable against a buyer or other transferee of the property either by peaceable self-help or by judicial action, including replevin. Alternatively, the secured party can usually recover damages from the transferee for conversion. The secured party will rely on U.C.C. §9-201 which provides that a security agreement, and thus the interest on which it is based, are enforceable not only against the debtor, but also against purchasers of the collateral.

The buyer cannot successfully defend against the secured party's repossession efforts or conversion action simply by showing that she acquired the debtor's rights in good faith, for value, and without knowledge of the security interest. The buyer's principal defense, if the disposition was unauthorized, is that her claim to the collateral has priority over the security party's interest. The various rules of Article 9 that give priority to a buyer of collateral are exceptions to both §9-306(2) and §9-201. If any of these priority rules protect the buyer, she effectively takes free of the security interest either completely or partially, that is, to the extent the buyer gave value for the property. Whether this freedom is complete or partial depends on the terms of the protective priority rule.

A buyer enjoys the freedom given by a priority rule even when the disposition through which she claims the collateral was not authorized by the secured party. Indeed, only when the disposition was unauthorized will a buyer need the protection of a priority rule because, if the disposition was authorized, the secured party has no interest in the property and there is no priority contest between her and the buyer.

The principal priority rules protecting buyers of goods are U.C.C. §§9-307(1), 9-307(2), and 9-301(1)(c).

Problems

1. Xerxes Electronics, Inc. is a company in the business of retailing computer hardware to the general public. Xerxes is financed by First Bank St. Paul, which has an Article 9 security interest in all of Xerxes' inventory. The parties' security agreement defines inventory in the same way U.C.C. §9-109 defines the term. Xerxes sold a computer to Cynthia Lundquist, a retail customer, who purchased the computer with cash for her own personal, family and household purposes. Is Ms. Lundquist protected by U.C.C. §9-307(1) from First Bank's security interest? (The answer depends in large part on whether Ms. Lundquist is a "buyer in ordinary course of business." See U.C.C. §1-201(9).)

2. Does the answer to Problem 1 depend on whether First Bank's security interest is perfected?

3. Same facts as Problem 1 except that Ms. Lundquist knows of First Bank's security interest when she buys the computer. Is Ms. Lundquist protected by U.C.C. §9-307(1) from First Bank's security interest?

4. Same facts as Problem 1 except that Ms. Lundquist knows of First Bank's security interest when she buys the computer and also knows that Xerxes is prohibited by its security agreement with First Bank from selling inventory without first getting First Bank's permission. Is Ms. Lundquist protected by U.C.C. §9-307(1) from First Bank's security interest?

5. Same facts as Problem 1 except that Ms. Lundquist buys the computer on credit and secures her obligation to pay the price by giving Xerxes a security interest in the machine. Is Ms. Lundquist protected by U.C.C. §9-307(1) from First Bank's security interest?

6. After buying the computer on credit and using it for several months, Ms. Lundquist decides she wants a better model. So she sells it to her next-door neighbor who intends to use the machine primarily for her own personal, family, and household purposes. Instead of using the proceeds to satisfy Xerxes' security interest in the computer, Ms. Lundquist uses the proceeds as a down-payment on another machine purchased from Zeos. Is the neighbor protected by §9-307(1) from Xerxes' security interest? By §9-307(2)? (CAUTION: Xerxes did not file a financing statement, but its interest is automatically perfected because of U.C.C. §9-302(1)(d).)

7. What could Xerxes have done to protect itself against buyers of its collateral such as Ms. Lundquist's neighbor?

8. Same facts as Problem 6 except that the neighbor bought the machine to use in her law practice. Does U.C.C. §9-307(2) protect the neighbor? Does U.C.C. §9-307(1)? How about U.C.C. §9-301(1)(c)?

9. Continue with Problem 8. Suppose the neighbor resold the computer to a law clerk who used the machine primarily for her own personal, family and household purposes. Is the clerk protected by U.C.C. §9-307(2) from Xerxes' security interest?

10. Suppose Ms. Lundquist purchased the computer on credit from Xerxes primarily to use in her business office. Xerxes retained a security interest but neglected to file a financing statement. Ms. Lundquist sold the machine to a neighbor who bought it for use in her law practice. Is the neighbor protected by §9-301(1)(c) from Xerxes' security interest?

11. Same facts as Problem 10, except that neighbor gave the machine away after using it for several months. Is the donee protected from Xerxes' security interest? See 9-301 comment 9 (reference to "shelter principle").

12. Same facts as Problem 10 except Xerxes properly filed a financing statement before the sale by Lundquist to her neighbor. Does U.C.C. §9-301(1)(c) protect the neighbor? U.C.C. §9-307(2)? U.C.C. §9-307(1)? Would the neighbor be protected if Xerxes had authorized the sale?

13. Two other priority rules protect buyers of goods, but only in limited circumstances. See U.C.C. §§9-103(2)(d) & 9-504(4) (which protects any purchaser of any kind of collateral, not just a buyer of goods). Under what circumstances do these rules apply?

b. Special Problems Involving §9-307(1)

Problems

1. Several farmers ordered fertilizer from Farm Co-Op, a dealer in agricultural supplies. The farmers paid in advance. The Co-Op did not carry a large inventory of fertilizer. Rather, the Co-Op ordered directly from the manufacturer based on customers' own orders. In this case the Co-Op ordered the necessary goods, and the fertilizer was shipped by rail. A whole boxcar of the stuff was delivered to the Co-Op but, just after the boxcar's doors were opened, Local Bank seized the whole load. It turns out that Local Bank had a perfected security interest in all of the Co-Op's inventory, present and after-acquired; and Co-Op had defaulted on the secured debt owed Local Bank. The farmers sued Local Bank for conversion. Who wins?

2. On February 10, 1989, DePerry, a housing contractor, executed a security agreement with plaintiff describing a Volvo dump truck and a Hitachi excavator, as collateral given by DePerry to secure his debt to plaintiff. On February 11, 1989, plaintiff filed a financing statement which perfected plaintiff's security interest. On February 2, 1991, DePerry sold the Hitachi excavator to Wholesalers (a dealer in such goods) and on June 24, 1991, Wholesalers sold the Hitachi excavator in due course to an innocent third party. Wholesalers has not turned over possession of the Hitachi excavator to plaintiff since the commencement of litigation against Wholesalers. *Associates Commercial Corp. v. DePerry*, 1993 WL 307704 (Conn. Super. Ct. Aug. 3, 1993). On these facts plaintiff has the better claim to the excavator. Why? The result would be different if DePerry were himself a dealer in heavy equipment. Why?

3. What result if DePerry had defaulted; plaintiff repossessed the excavator and stored it for safekeeping with Wholesalers; and Wholesalers without authority sold the excavator to the innocent third person? See 2-403(2)&(3).

4. Transportation Specialists, Inc., d/b/a Cavalier Vans ("Cavalier"), a licensed manufacturer of shuttle buses, used a Ford Econoline chassis which it obtained from Mid-Tenn. in Nashville. Cavalier made the required modifications and sold the finished product to its customers. The transactions between Mid-Tenn. and Cavalier, followed for several years almost without exception, involved a delivery of the chassis to Cavalier on credit with the purchase price to be paid when Cavalier completed the unit and sold it. Mid-Tenn. held the manufacturer's certificate of origin until Cavalier paid the purchase price. In the summer and fall of 1990, the defendants/appellees, Lease Plan USA, Inc. and Master Lease, Inc., ordered five vehicles from Cavalier. It appears from the record that the vehicles ultimately delivered to the buyers were not in Cavalier's inventory at the time the order was placed. Cavalier followed its usual course of dealing with Mid-Tenn. in filling the orders. This time, however, Cavalier gave the buyers it's own certificates of origin showing that Cavalier was the owner of the vehicles, that each vehicle was a "new vehicle" as described in the certificate, and that the transfer was "the first transfer of such new motor vehicle in ordinary trade and commerce." It is asserted that Cavalier used this scheme to hide from Mid-Tenn. the fact that the units had been sold. With the certificates furnished by Cavalier, the buyers were able to obtain certificates of title in Louisiana and Massachusetts where the vehicles were leased to third parties. Neither buyer had actual knowledge that Mid-Tenn. had originally sold these vehicles or asserted any ownership or security interest in them. When Mid-Tenn. did not receive payment from Cavalier, it sued the buyers seeking immediate possession or in the alternative the value of the vehicles. The Chancery Court of Davidson County granted summary judgment to the buyers. *Mid-Tenn. Ford Truck Sales, Inc. v. Lease Plan USA, Inc.*, 1993 WL 266865 (Tenn.Ct. App. July 16, 1993). What should the appellate court have done?

   (a) Affirmed because the buyers had priority
   (b) Affirmed because Mid-Tenn. has no interest
   (c) Reversed because Mid-Tenn. had priority
   (d) Reversed because buyers had no interest
   (e) Remanded (indeterminate)

5. In January, 1988, the secured creditors transferred to the debtor, Richard Skolnick, molds, equipment, inventory and other assets necessary to manufacture and sell replica car kits of a 1953 Corvette. In consideration, the debtor executed a promissory note for $185,000.00, with the debt secured by all assets related to the replica car kits, including inventory and all after-acquired property. The promissory note and security agreement provided that the debtor would pay $500 upon the note each time he collected full payment for a kit, and the debtor was obligated to sell a minimum of 50 car kits the first fifteen months and every twelve months thereafter, or be deemed in default. The debtor also promised to provide monthly financial reports. In April, 1989, the debtor defaulted upon the note and security agreement by failing to make payments when due and not providing the required monthly financial

reports. As a result of the default, the secured creditors accelerated the balance due under the note and filed suit against the debtor seeking damages for the unpaid balance and seeking possession of the property covered by the security agreement. On November 2, 1989, the secured creditors served upon the debtor a pre-judgment writ of replevin directing seizure of the assets under the security agreement. Among the items seized were steel frames, fiberglass bodies, molds, and other component parts and inventory used in the assemblage of replica car kits. After the execution of the writ of replevin, the debtor ceased to conduct business. Seven customers of the debtor were allowed by the trial court to file complaints in intervention alleging that they each had made a contract with the debtor to buy a replica car kit which had been wrongfully converted by the secured creditors. The customers had each paid full price for a car kit, but the debtor's assets were seized before he could assemble and deliver them.

After a non-jury trial, the trial court entered final judgment in favor of the seven customers for money damages, finding that the secured creditors converted a car kit belonging to each customer and that the secured creditors did not have an interest in the car kits under the after-acquired property clause of the security agreement since they were "consumer goods." The judgment awarded the customers damages individually in the amount each paid for a replica car kit, plus interest. *Kit Car World, Inc. v. Skolnick*, 616 So.2d 1051 (Fla. Dist. Ct. App. 1993). How should the case have been decided on appeal?

(a) Affirmed based on the trial court's reasoning
(b) Affirmed for different reasoning
(c) Reversed because of reasoning opposite the trial court's
(d) Reversed for different reasons
(e) Remanded (indeterminate)

6. Augustine and Barbara Caron purchased a new motor home from Bradford Trailer Sales, Inc. under a retail installment contract and security agreement. Bradford's security interest was perfected. On or about April 6, 1990, the Carons, without Bradford's knowledge, traded the motor home to Wildcat Van Center, Inc., a merchant dealing in motor homes and recreational vehicles. Thereafter, the Carons made no further installment payments to Bradford. On April 9, 1990, the Zimermans purchased the motor home from Wildcat. Wildcat did not advise the Zimermans that there was a lien on the motor home, and the record is devoid of any showing that Wildcat or the Zimermans inquired of the Department of Highway Safety and Motor Vehicles as to the condition of the motor home's title. When the Caron's account with Bradford became delinquent on May 5, 1990, Bradford contacted them and learned that the motor home had been sold. Bradford wrote to Wildcat, requesting payoff on the Carons' account. The lien was never satisfied. The Zimermans filed their action for declaratory judgment. Bradford filed a complaint alleging an action for replevin against the Zimermans, an action for conversion against Wildcat, and an action for damages against the Carons. The actions were consolidated. *Green Tree*

Acceptance, Inc. v. Zimerman, 611 So.2d 608 (Fla. Dist. Ct. App. 1993). What's the correct outcome?

(a) Bradford wins against everyone.
(b) Bradford wins only against Carsons
(c) Bradwin loses against Wildcat.
(d) Bradford loses against Zimermans.
(e) Bradford loses against everyone.

c. Buyers of Farm Products

Protection For Purchasers Of Farm Products
7 U.S.C.A. §1631

(c) Definitions

For the purposes of this section--

(1) The term "buyer in the ordinary course of business" means a person who, in the ordinary course of business, buys farm products from a person engaged in farming operations who is in the business of selling farm products.

(2) The term "central filing system" means a system for filing effective financing statements or notice of such financing statements on a statewide basis and which has been certified by the Secretary of the United States Department of Agriculture; the Secretary shall certify such system if the system complies with the requirements of this section; specifically under such system--

(A) effective financing statements or notice of such financing statements are filed with the office of the Secretary of State of a State;

(B) the Secretary of State records the date and hour of the filing of such statements;

(C) the Secretary of State compiles all such statements into a master list--

(i) organized according to farm products;

(ii) arranged within each such product--

(I) in alphabetical order according to the last name of the individual debtors, or, in the case of debtors doing business other than as individuals, the first word in the name of such debtors; and

(II) in numerical order according to the social security number of the individual debtors or, in the case of debtors doing business other than as individuals, the Internal Revenue Service taxpayer identification number of such debtors; and

(III) geographically by county or parish; and

(IV) by crop year;

(iii) containing the information referred to in paragraph (4)(D);

(D) the Secretary of State maintains a list of all buyers of farm products, commission merchants, and selling agents who register with the Secretary of State, on a form indicating--

(i) the name and address of each buyer, commission merchant and selling agent;

(ii) the interest of each buyer, commission merchant, and selling agent in receiving the lists described in subparagraph (E); and

(iii) the farm products in which each buyer, commission merchant, and selling agent has an interest;

(E) the Secretary of State distributes regularly as prescribed by the State to each buyer, commission merchant, and selling agent on the list described in subparagraph (D) a copy in written or printed form of those portions of the master list described in paragraph (C) that cover the farm products in which such buyer, commission merchant, or selling agent has registered an interest;

(F) the Secretary of State furnishes to those who are not registered pursuant to (2)(D) of this section oral confirmation within 24 hours of any effective financing statement on request followed by written confirmation to any buyer of farm products buying from a debtor, or commission merchant or selling agent selling for a seller covered by such statement.

(d) Purchases free of security interest

Except as provided in subsection (e) of this section and notwithstanding any other provision of Federal, State, or local law, a buyer who in the ordinary course of business buys a farm product from a seller engaged in farming operations shall take free of a security interest created by the seller, even though the security interest is perfected; and the buyer knows of the existence of such interest.

(e) Purchases subject to security interest

A buyer of farm products takes subject to a security interest created by the seller if--

(1)(A) within 1 year before the sale of the farm products, the buyer has received from the secured party or the seller written notice of the security interest organized according to farm products that--

(i) is an original or reproduced copy thereof;

(ii) contains,

(I) the name and address of the secured party;

(II) the name and address of the person indebted to the secured party;

(III) the social security number of the debtor or, in the case of a debtor doing business other than as an individual, the Internal Revenue Service taxpayer identification number of such debtor;

(IV) a description of the farm products subject to the security interest created by the debtor, including the amount of such products where applicable, crop year, county or parish, and a reasonable description of the property; and

(iii) must be amended in writing, within 3 months, similarly signed and transmitted, to reflect material changes;

(iv) will lapse on either the expiration period of the statement or the transmission of a notice signed by the secured party that the statement has lapsed, whichever occurs first; and

(v) any payment obligations imposed on the buyer by the secured party as conditions for waiver or release of the security interest; and

(B) the buyer has failed to perform the payment obligations, or

(2) in the case of a farm product produced in a State that has established a central filing system--

(A) the buyer has failed to register with the Secretary of State of such State prior to the purchase of farm products; and

(B) the secured party has filed an effective financing statement or notice that covers the farm products being sold; or

(3) in the case of a farm product produced in a State that has established a central filing system, the buyer--

(A) receives from the Secretary of State of such State written notice as provided in subparagraph (c)(2)(E) or (c)(2)(F) that specifies both the seller and the farm product being sold by such seller as being subject to an effective financing statement or notice; and

(B) does not secure a waiver or release of the security interest specified in such effective financing statement or notice from the secured party by performing any payment obligation or otherwise; and

Problems

1. First Bank has a security interest in all of Farmer's crop. First Bank has complied with Article 9's rules with respect to filing a financing statement covering its collateral. Farmer makes an unauthorized sale of this year's corn crop to Cargill, Inc., which is a buyer in the ordinary course of business. State law does not include a central filing system for farm products as described by 7 U.S.C.A. §1631(a). Does Cargill take free of, or subject to, First Bank's security interest?

2. Same as Problem 1, except that Cargill learned before the sale, in a conversation with the debtor, that the sale would violate the security agreement between First Bank and Farmer.

3. Same as Problem 1, except the state does have such a central filing system. Bank had compiled with the system by filing an effective financing statement, but Cargill had not registered as the system requires.

4. Continue with Problem 3. Suppose that neither First Bank nor Cargill had complied with the central filing system.

5. Same as Problem 1 with these additional facts: Cargill's mountains of corn purchased from farmers throughout the Midwest are subject to a security interest in favor of Second Bank. Cargill makes an unauthorized sale of part of this collateral to General Mills. Does General Mills take free of, or subject to, Second Bank's security interest? First Bank's interest?

6. The Bank loaned large sums of money (in excess of $3,000,000) to Freddie and Marlys Mutschler, who were prominent farmers in Jamestown, North Dakota. The Mutschlers gave the Bank a lien on their crops, as partial security for the loans. The loan agreement provided that when the Mutschlers sold the grain they were obligated to turn over the proceeds to cover their indebtedness. Freddie Mutschler was also the owner, but not the manager, of the Jamestown Farmers Elevator, which bought and sold various farmers' grain. The Mutschlers themselves sold grain to the elevator. *** Sometime in the fall of 1982, the Mutschlers sold their crop to the Jamestown Farmers Elevator, but did not apply the proceeds to their debt at the Bank. The elevator in turn sold some of the grain *** to the Pillsbury Company. The Bank did not discover these events until the Mutschlers and Jamestown Farmers Elevator filed bankruptcy in early 1983. The Bank then sued Pillsbury for conversion of its collateral. *First Bank v. Pillsbury Co., 801 F.2d 1036, 1037-38* (8th Cir.1986). What result? Would the result be different or more certain if Freddie were not the owner of the elevator?

d. Buyer's Vulnerability to Future Value, §9–307(3)

The typical security agreement contains a future-advance clause whereby the collateral secures loans and other credit the secured party extends beyond the value given when the agreement was executed. See U.C.C. 9-204(3). A secured party who is unaware that her collateral has been sold by the debtor may well make future advances after the sale. Does a buyer who takes subject to the security interest also take subject to future advances made after she purchased the collateral? U.C.C. 9-307(3) addresses this question.

The answer turns in part on whether or not the future advances are made "pursuant to a commitment." Advances not made pursuant to a commitment are known as optional advances. An *advance pursuant to commitment* is an advance (i.e., a loan or some other extension of credit) that is made because of a contract, entered into before the advance, that legally bound the secured party to make the advance at a time specified in the contract providing for the advance. See U.C.C. 9-105(1)(k). An *optional future advance* is any other future advance: an advance made whenever the secured party decides, in her discretion, to extend more credit to the debtor under an existing security arrangement without being bound by contract or otherwise to make the advance.

Problems

1. Bank has a perfected security interest in all of D's industrial equipment. The security agreement provides that the collateral secures all future advances. At a time when the secured debt equals $25,000, D makes an unauthorized sale of a piece of its equipment to B. The price approximates the equipment's market value of $45,000. B is not a buyer in the ordinary course of business because D is not in the business of selling the kind of goods involved. Bank later makes a future advance of $20,000. D now owes Bank $45,000. In any event, B takes subject to First Bank's security interest to the extent of $25,000, the initial advance. Consider whether B also take subject to the $20,000 future advance in these circumstances:

   a. The Bank made the advance, which was optional, 30 days after the sale without knowledge of the sale.

   b. The Bank made the advance, which was optional, 30 days after the sale with knowledge of the sale.

   c. The Bank made the advance, which was optional, 50 days after the sale without knowledge of the sale.

   d. The Bank made the advance 50 days after the sale with knowledge of the sale, but the advance was pursuant to a commitment that was made in ignorance of the sale 30 days after the sale occurred.

2. First Bank partly finances Frontier Home Sales, which retails mobile homes. The agreement between them gives First Bank a security interest in all of Frontier's inventory, which is collateral for all future advances. At a time when the secured debt is $25,000, Frontier sells a mobile home from its inventory to Cynthia Lundquist for $50,000. Ms. Lundquist is a buyer in the ordinary course of business. Thirty days later, First Bank loans Frontier an additional $100,000 without knowledge of the sale to Ms. Lundquist. Is Ms. Lundquist protected partly or fully against First Bank's security interest? (Hint: "[A] buyer in the ordinary course of business who takes free of the security interest under subsection (1) is not subject to any future advances." U.C.C. 9-307 comment 4.)

3. U.C.C. 9-307(1) does not protect a buyer in the ordinary course of business from a security interest created by someone other than her seller. Does such a buyer who takes subject to such an interest, that is, an interest created by a person not her seller, nevertheless take free of all future advances under 9-307(3)?

3. Secured Party Versus Lien Creditor

The term *judicial lien* commonly refers to a creditor's claim to property of the debtor that is acquired through judicial process.

Judgment liens and liens of execution or attachment are judicial liens. When a judicial lien reaches personal property that is also subject to an Article 9 security interest, the holder of the judicial lien is known, in Article 9's terminology, as a *lien creditor*, which "means a creditor who has acquired a lien on the property involved by attachment, levy or the like *** " U.C.C. §9-301(3). The basic priority rule for any conflict between an Article 9 secured party and a lien creditor is that a security interest is subordinate to the rights of a person who becomes a lien creditor before the security interest is perfected. U.C.C. §9-301(1)(b). In other words, an unperfected security interest is "subordinate" to a judicial lien on the same property. This general rule contemplates a situation where a judicial lien arises in the gap between the creation and perfection of a security interest: if D gave S a security interest in her truck on October 7, and S perfected this security interest on October 21, any creditor who obtained an attachment or execution lien on the truck between October 7 and October 21 would have priority over S.

Section 9-301 is also important for what it does not say. It does not govern priority as between a secured creditor and a creditor with a statutory lien (see section 9-310) or between two secured creditors (see section 9-312). It does not expressly state that a creditor with an unperfected security interest has priority over general creditors although that is certainly implied. Moreover, section 9-301 is silent as to the relative priority when the judicial lien arises before the security interest attaches. In such cases, it would seem that the first in time rule should apply regardless of whether the security interest is perfected immediately.

A lien creditor whose lien attached after a security interest was perfected in the collateral loses priority to the secured party, 9-201, except that section 9-301(2) creates an exception favoring purchase money security interests:

> If the secured party files with respect to a purchase money security interest before or within ten days after the debtor receives possession of the collateral, he takes priority over the rights of a transferee in bulk or of a lien creditor which arise between the time the security interest attaches and the time of filing.

U.C.C. §9-301(2). The term "purchase money security interest" is defined as a security interest

(a) taken or retained by the seller of the collateral to secure all or part of its price; or

(b) taken by a person who by making advances or incurring an obligation gives value to enable the debtor to acquire rights in or the use of collateral if such value is in fact so used.

U.C.C. §9-107.

The 9-301(2) exception effectively gives a grace period for filing purchase money interests. It is limited, however, for reasons that are not entirely clear. For example, a purchase money secured party can take advantage of §9-301(2) only by filing. Perfection otherwise than by filing won't trigger the exception. Also, the exception apparently does not apply when the claim of a lien creditor attaches to collateral before the purchase money security interest attaches. In this event, even though the secured party later perfects by filing within ten days of the debtor getting possession of the collateral, §9-301(2) is inapplicable because the lien creditor's claim did not arise between the times of attachment and perfection of the security interest. Nevertheless, the purchase money security interest qua enabling interest may be given priority by the extra-Code law governing the judicial lien.

A lien creditor who loses priority to a secured party is vulnerable, to some extent, to future advances made by a secured party. Suppose, for example, that S had a perfected security interest in D's equipment worth $50,000. A judgment creditor of D caused an execution lien to attach to the equipment. Before the lien attached, the secured loan owed S was $25,000. The day after the lien attached, S made another loan to D of $25,000 that was also secured by the equipment. S enjoys priority to the full extent of $50,000. There is nothing left for the lien creditor.

Section 9-301(4) limits this future-advance priority, but this section is itself limited because "future advance" within the meaning of the section does not include every kind of secured obligation. With respect to secured obligations that are not future advances, a secured party's priority over a lien creditor can continue to grow after the lien attached without, say some authorities, any apparent limits.

UNI Imports, Inc. v. Aparacor, Inc.
United States Court of Appeals, Seventh Circuit, 1992
978 F.2d 984

Crabb, Chief District Judge. This appeal raises an issue best described as one of those "delicious academic morsels so dear to the hearts and minds of commercial law teachers," 2 James J. White & Robert S. Summers, Uniform

Commercial Code, §26-1, 491 (Practitioner's ed. 1988). The actual circumstances in which it arises occur very seldom; similar cases are "as scarce as hen's teeth." Id. at 493. The case arises out of supplementary proceedings held in the district court on a petition by UNI, Inc., for a turnover of assets in the possession of Exchange National Bank of Chicago. It involves the relative priorities between a judgment creditor and a secured lender of lines of credit, the applicability of Ill.Rev.Stat. ch. 26, ¶9-301(4), and the treatment of non-advance expenditures by a secured creditor.

On UNI's motion for summary judgment, the district court held that Exchange was required to turn over assets sufficient to satisfy UNI's lien. That holding may be correct, but the present record does not allow an affirmance. Under §9-301(4), Exchange's perfected security interest has priority over UNI's judgment lien to the extent that the interest secures advances made within 45 days after the lien attached; the $274,000 payment that Exchange made after the expiration of the 45-day grace period following attachment of UNI's lien and before the assignment for the benefit of creditors is not protected from subordination to that lien. Whether Exchange has claims to reimbursement that take priority over UNI's security interest in the $274,000 advance is a question we cannot answer on the present record. The district court did not analyze the various expenditures and payments made by Exchange after the 45-day period to determine whether Exchange has a right to reimbursement superior to that of UNI. We will remand the matter to allow the district court to make that analysis.

The parties do not dispute any of the following material facts.

FACTS

On August 12, 1987, Exchange National Bank and Aparacor, Inc. executed a document entitled "Security Agreement," which granted Exchange a security interest in Aparacor's assets at Exchange. On October 9, 1987, the two executed a note due April 30, 1988, which incorporated the security agreement and established a revolving line of credit of up to $7.2 million for Aparacor and related entities. After the note expired, Exchange continued to make advances of funds without an additional written agreement.

On November 18, 1988, UNI obtained a $66,000 judgment against Aparacor in the United States District Court for the Central District of California. UNI registered the judgment in the United States District Court for the Northern District of Illinois. On January 12, 1989, UNI tried to enforce the judgment against Aparacor's assets at Exchange by delivering a writ of execution to the United States Marshals Service. The marshals service served the writ on Exchange the following day, but Exchange refused to turn over any of Aparacor's assets, contending that it had priority status.

Exchange continued to advance money to Aparacor. On February 3, 1989, Exchange and Aparacor executed a document titled "Modification Note" that purported to modify the October 1987 note and to reduce Aparacor's revolving credit to $5.4 million. By February 26, 1989 (45 days after Exchange had been served with the writ), the principal balance of Aparacor's loan had grown to approximately $2.8 million from a balance of approximately $780,000 as of January 12, 1989. Between February 26, 1989 and March 2, 1989, Exchange advanced an additional $274,000 to Aparacor. On March 2, 1989, Aparacor executed an assignment for the benefit of creditors. Between March 2 and May 31, 1989, Exchange made additional payments of over $2 million as follows:

Advances to Assignee--	$ 636,595
Payment of Sales Commissions--	419,080
Payment of Real Estate Taxes--	728,753
Payment of Interest under Modification Note to Mar. 2--	27,056
Payment of Mechanics' Lien--	2,200
Payment of Legal Fees--	30,708
Letter of Credit Draws--	277,716
Miscellaneous--	19,326

TOTAL	$2,141,438

After the assignment on March 2, 1989, Exchange credited to Aparacor's outstanding balance the following: credit collections from accounts receivable, $2,584,638.21; proceeds from the sale of real estate and equipment, $1,414,287.30; and proceeds from the application of a certificate of deposit, $51,203.00, for a total of $4,050,128.51.

On September 27, 1990, UNI petitioned the district court for turnover of Aparacor's assets in the possession of Exchange. The court granted the petition and this appeal followed. UNI's $66,000 judgment has not been satisfied. Aparacor still owes $938,553.78 to Exchange.

* * *

OPINION

When a person in need of money borrows a lump sum secured by specific collateral, such as real estate, the question of priorities between the lender and any subsequent person who obtains a judgment against the borrower is relatively straightforward: the judgment creditor's interest is subordinate to the lender's, so long as the lender has obtained and perfected a security interest in the borrower's realty before the lien attaches. This straightforward situation becomes complicated when the borrower wants a line of credit rather than a lump sum loan and when the collateral is a constantly changing one in the form of inventory or accounts receivable. Scholars and practitioners have debated whether the lender's security interest in the collateral attaches from the outset, that is, from the first advance under the line of credit (the "unitary" theory), or whether each advance gives rise to a new security interest, each of which arises no earlier than the time the creditor extends value (the "multiple" theory). See discussion in Dick Warner Cargo Handling Corp. v. Aetna Business Credit, 746 F.2d 126, 130-33 (2d Cir.1984); Jeanne L. Schroeder & David Gray Carlson,

Future Nonadvance Obligations Under Article 9 of the UCC: Legitimate Priority or Unwarranted Squeeze-Out? 102 Banking L.J. 412 (1985); William T. Plumb, Federal Tax Liens and Priorities--Agenda for the Next Decade II, 77 Yale L.J. 605, 659-61 (1968).

The passage of the Federal Tax Lien Act of 1966 focused attention on the scope of the "floating lien" that attached to inventory or other changing collateral. Supreme Court rulings prior to 1966 had subordinated security interests based on after-acquired property or future advances to federal tax liens on the ground that such interests were "inchoate," that is, not certain in amount, identity of collateral or identity of creditor. See generally, Peter F. Coogan, The Effect of the Federal Tax Lien Act of 1966 Upon Security Interests Created under the Uniform Commercial Code, 81 Harv.L.Rev. 1369, 1375-80 (1968). The Tax Lien Act addressed the perceived need to save such security interests from subordination to subsequent tax liens. See David Gray Carlson and Paul M. Shupack, Judicial Lien Priorities Under Article 9 of the Uniform Commercial Code: Part I, 5 Cardozo L.Rev. 287, 349 (1984). The drafters of the Tax Lien Act defined a security interest as "any interest in property acquired by contract for the purpose of securing payment or performance of an obligation or indemnifying against loss or liability," 26 U.S.C. §6323(h)(1), adding that such an interest exists at any time "if, at such time, the property is in existence and the interest has become protected under local law against a subsequent judgment lien arising out of an unsecured obligation...." Id. This definition of a "choate" security interest made it a matter of practical importance to determine whether a particular interest would or would not be subordinated to a judgment lien because the drafters of the Tax Lien Act did not want tax liens subordinated to floating liens that would be subordinate in turn to judicial liens. Schroeder & Carlson, supra, 5 Banking L.J. at 421. To protect revolving credit security interests from subordination to tax liens under the hypothetical lien creditor test in the Tax Lien Act, the drafters of the 1972 amendments to the Uniform Commercial Code added subsection (4) to §9-301 to provide that [a] person who becomes a lien creditor while a security interest is perfected takes subject to the security interest only to the extent that it secures advances made before he becomes a lien creditor or within 45 days thereafter or made without knowledge of the lien or pursuant to a commitment entered into without knowledge of the lien.

The section rests on the assumption that the multiple theory is operative for future advances, that is, each advance gives rise to a new security interest, which arises when the creditor extends value. See Dick Warner Cargo Handling Corp. v. Aetna Business Credit, 746 F.2d at 133:

> Sections 9-301(4) and -307(3) generally accepted Coogan's conclusion that security interests relating to advances created subsequent to the intervention of a third party as lien creditor or purchaser should be subordinated to the interest of the third party. [Citing Coogan &

Gordon, The Effect of the Uniform Commercial Code upon Receivables Financing, 76 Harv.L.Rev. 1529, 1549-51 (1963).]

Section 9-301(4) applies to situations in which there is a "perfected" security interest in existence when the judgment lien attaches. (Perfection occurs when a debtor signs a security agreement containing a description of the collateral, value has been given and the debtor has rights in the collateral. Ill.Rev.Stat. ch. 26, ¶9-203(2).) Under P 9-301(4), future advances are protected (1) in all cases for 45 days following attachment of the lien; (2) beyond 45 days if the secured party makes the advance without knowledge of the lien; and (3) beyond 45 days if the secured party is committed to make advances, provided the commitment was entered into without knowledge of the lien. As Carlson and Shupack point out, the first two situations provide important protections: "A lender with knowledge will certainly cease advancing funds, if he can, and a lender without knowledge will be protected if he manages to maintain his ignorance." Carlson & Shupack, supra, 5 Cardozo L.Rev. at 349 (footnotes omitted). In the third situation, the special provision for commitments made before the lien attached reflects pre-UCC law that "the security interest for advances made pursuant to a binding commitment came into existence when that commitment was made and therefore comes ahead" of a lien creditor even if the lien attaches between the time the commitment is made and the first actual advance of funds. Id. Such binding commitments are differentiated from agreements providing for advances but not committing the lender to make them.

Left unanswered by the drafters of §9-301(4) was the question of the treatment of the other parts of a secured obligation such as interest and collection expenses. Were these different parts of the obligation subsumed by the term "advances" (and treated identically) or did they give rise to their own security interests and, if so, did those security interests arise when value was given or at the outset when the obligation was entered into? In the only case to address this issue, Dick Warner Cargo Handling Corp. v. Aetna Business Credit, 746 F.2d 126, the Court of Appeals for the Second Circuit concluded that the separate parts of the obligation were not intended to be treated as advances. Although the court did not say so explicitly, in effect it treated such obligations as giving rise to their own security interests, at least some of which arose with the execution of the financing agreement.

Exchange relies on §9-301(4) and the Second Circuit's opinion in *Dick Warner* for its contention that it is entitled to be reimbursed ahead of UNI for all of the funds it provided Aparacor after January 12, 1989, the date on which the lien attached.[1] Exchange's position is that the funds provided to Aparacor before March 2, 1989 (the day of the assignment for the benefit of creditors)

---

[1]   Under Illinois law, the lien attached when UNI delivered the writ of execution to the marshal. Asher v. United States, 570 F.2d 682, 683 (7th Cir.1978). Neither UNI nor Exchange denies that when UNI delivered the writ to the marshal it obtained a lien on the money in Aparacor's accounts at Exchange.

were advances made pursuant to binding commitments agreed to in the original loan agreement with Aparacor, modified and revived by the modification agreement of February 3, 1989. Therefore, argues Exchange, those advances have priority over UNI's judgment lien under the exception in §9-301(4) for advances made "pursuant to a commitment entered into without knowledge of the lien." Alternatively, Exchange maintains, the payments it made after March 2, 1989 were not advances, but were payments related to other aspects of the secured obligation: the kinds of expenses that Judge Friendly chose to refer to as "non-advances" in the *Dick Warner* case. Exchange contends that it has a priority interest in those expenditures that overrides that of UNI. Exchange concedes that if the modification note is considered a new agreement, UNI might have a priority interest in the $274,000 advanced to Aparacor between February 26 and March 2, but contends that because it has not yet been reimbursed in full for its protected (pre-February 26) advances and for its protected "non-advances," the question of the relative priorities to the $274,000 never arises.

The district court addressed only the first of these arguments. It concluded that the February 3, 1989 agreement was not a mere modification of the 1987 revolving line of credit, but a new commitment entered into after Exchange had knowledge of UNI's lien, and therefore one that offered Exchange no protection for any advances made after the expiration of the 45-day period on February 26, 1989.[1] UN Imports, d/b/a UNI, INC. v. Aparacor, slip op. at 5-6, 1991 WL 49563 (N.D.Ill. Apr. 3, 1991). The court noted that although the 1987 note expired on April 30, 1988, nine months before the execution of the modification agreement, the modification note was not executed until almost one month after Exchange received formal notice of UNI's lien. The court was not impressed by the language in the note stating the parties' intent to "further modify and restate the obligations set forth in the Note...." Modification Note at 1. The "crucial fact beyond dispute is that any prior commitment requiring [Exchange] to make continued advances to Aparacor ended in April, 1988." UN Imports, slip op. at 5.

Exchange makes little effort to explain how it could have retained a binding commitment from a matured note. The cases it cites do not support its assertion. The district court was well justified in finding that the modification note was a new commitment entered into by Exchange with full knowledge of UNI's intervening lien, and that the parties had not succeeded in reviving the original, expired note by their execution of the modification note.[2] Given this finding, the

---

[1] Technically, the period expired on February 25, 1989, 45 days after the lien attached upon delivery to the marshal for service. The district court counted from the date of service (January 13). UNI has advised this court that it has no objection to the use of the later date.

[2] This does not mean that Exchange was not secured or that it lost its priority as a secured creditor during the period between written agreements. Its interest in the property and the priority of that interest vis-a-vis other secured creditors were protected from the time it filed its financing statement. See U.C.C. §9-312, Official Comment n. 5,

district court did not need to analyze the nature of the original security agreement between the parties to determine whether the agreement constituted a binding commitment as Exchange contended.

Having reached the conclusion that the modification note represented a new commitment made with knowledge of UNI's lien, the district court ordered the bank to turn over to UNI assets sufficient to satisfy its lien. * * * The district court did not address the second argument advanced by the bank: that it had a priority interest in all of the assets it withdrew for crediting to Aparacor's outstanding loan balance because the money from those assets was applied to reimburse the bank for payments it had made "to preserve and protect collateral," and that under the Second Circuit's holding in *Dick Warner*, 746 F.2d 126, such payments are "non-advances" for which the lender is entitled to priority reimbursement.

Neither this court nor the state courts of Illinois have had occasion to address §9-301(4)'s treatment of "non-advances." Exchange argues that in such a situation the Illinois courts would defer to the decision of the Court of Appeals for the Second Circuit in *Dick Warner*, in order to promote the Uniform Commercial Code's policy of uniformity.

In *Dick Warner*, 746 F.2d 126, Aetna and Best Banana had entered into a financing arrangement under which Aetna had agreed to lend money to Best Banana in its discretion and to obtain letters of credit to enable Best Banana to make purchases from overseas suppliers. The security agreement obligated Best Banana to indemnify Aetna for any liability incurred in connection with any letter of credit or with Aetna's application for such a letter, and to reimburse Aetna for its expenses in enforcing or protecting its security interest or its rights under any of the Agreements or in respect of any of the transactions under the agreement, and to pay Aetna a minimum monthly payment of $7,500. After Aetna had advanced funds and applied for the issuance of an irrevocable letter of credit for the benefit of the banana shipper, Dick Warner Cargo Handling unloaded two shipments of bananas, both of which Best Banana rejected as defective. Aetna asked the issuer of the letter of credit not to honor the letter. Dick Warner sued Best Banana for its services and obtained a judgment in Virginia that it sought to enforce in Connecticut through garnishment of Best Banana's credit balance with Aetna. Aetna had in its possession a "lockbox" bank account consisting of collections of Best Banana's encumbered accounts. After Aetna deducted $353,577 to discharge Best Banana's current indebtedness for advances, interest and other charges, the bank account had a net credit

---

example 5 (1990); Thomas H. Jackson & Anthony T. Kronman, Secured Financing and Priorities Among Creditors, 88 Yale L.J. 1143, 1178 (1979) ("[I]f C 1 files a financing statement on May 30, and C 2 files a financing statement covering the same collateral on June 30, C 1's interest in the property will have priority over C 2's, regardless of the order in which they actually make their loans or satisfy the requirements for perfection.") Whether Exchange had priority over a judgment lien creditor at that time is a separate issue.

balance of about $46,000, which Aetna was keeping as additional security for obligations of Best Banana that might accrue later, including liability for the dishonored letter of credit, attorneys' fees and the "minimum monthly charge."

The Second Circuit held that Aetna's interest in the credit balance had priority over Dick Warner's lien, based on Best Banana's undertaking in the original financing agreement to reimburse Aetna for attorneys' fees and other expenses it might incur in defending against suits such as Dick Warner's. According to the court, the drafters of §9-301(4) did not intend to include such expenditures by the lender in the term "advances" because the lender's obligation to advance funds to the borrower differs from the lender's obligation for expenses in connection with the loan, such as attorneys' fees. Expenditures in the latter category

> do not constitute "advances" as that term is commonly used; in the ordinary meaning of language, "advances" are sums put at the disposal of the borrower-- not expenditures made by the lender for his own benefit. See, e.g., Black's Law Dictionary, 48 (5th ed. 1979).

Id. at 130. The Second Circuit suggested use of the term "non-advances" for the debtor's obligation to pay interest and indemnify the lender for various expenses it has incurred. The court held that a lender that perfects its security interest with respect to such obligations is entitled to protection against a subsequent lien creditor. In other words, the lender is entitled to priority reimbursement insofar as a prior-perfected security interest

> secures a non-advance obligation relating to a transaction prior to the levy, like that of the debtor to pay interest or even to reimburse the creditor for attorneys' fees incurred reasonably and in good faith with respect to loans made prior to the imposition of the lien or otherwise protected by it.

Id. at 134. The court took the view that the drafters of §9-301(4) never intended to include non-advance obligations under this section. Thus, although for the purpose of the section, advances were treated as multiple (giving rise to a new security interest with each new advance), the treatment of future "non-advance" obligations was not affected by the new §9-301(4). Such obligations retained their unitary character, relating back to the original agreement. They continued to have priority over a later judicial lien if they had been undertaken before the lien attached, even if they did not mature until after attachment. The court acknowledged that a straightforward reading of §9-301(4) would not support such an interpretation, but concluded that it was what the drafters must have meant and that any other result "would be so plainly unreasonable and inconsistent with commercial practice that such an interpretation must be avoided." *Dick Warner*, 746 F.2d at 134.

The result reached in *Dick Warner* is not wholly convincing. As a general rule, security interests under Article 9 do not arise until value is extended. The court does not explain satisfactorily why it should be different for "non-advances." Although protecting non-advances benefits revolving credit lenders and thus, presumably improves debtors' chances of obtaining such loans, it does so at the cost of squeezing out lien creditors. One can reasonably ask whether it is fair or commercially useful to strike the balance in favor of the financier. After all, the lender in these situations has a close and continuing relationship with the debtor, enabling him to supervise and control all of the debtor's transactions, whereas the judgment lien creditor may well be an involuntary creditor of the debtor. * * * The drafters of the 1972 amendment noted this unfairness with respect to future advances:

> It seems unfair to make it possible for a debtor and secured party with knowledge of the judgment lien to squeeze out a judgment creditor who has successfully levied on a valuable equity subject to a security interest, by permitting later enlargement of the security interest, by an additional advance, unless that advance was committed in advance without such knowledge. [Footnote omitted.]

U.C.C. §9-312 (1972) Reasons for 1972 Change. Ironically, the possibility of squeeze-out posed by future advances is less than for non-advance value. Future advances have the positive value of enlarging the estate; reimbursing the secured creditor for non-advance value only depletes the estate. In *Dick Warner*, for example, Best Banana was obligated to pay Aetna a $7500 minimum monthly charge. Aetna had no incentive and no apparent obligation to stop the running of the charge, other than the declining balance of Best Banana's lockbox account.

Nonetheless, the *Dick Warner* result is endorsed by the Permanent Editorial Board for the Uniform Commercial Code. In Commentary No. 2, March 10, 1990, the board added the following paragraph to the commentary to §9- 301(4):

> The word "only" in subsection (4) is limited in its effect to the lien creditor's subjection to the specified advances. It does not limit the lien creditor's subjection to whatever other rights the secured party may have by contract or law, e.g., the right to interest before or after the attachment of the judgment lien to the collateral or the right to foreclosure expenses or other collection expenses.

In light of this commentary and the holding of the Second Circuit, we conclude that the Illinois courts would hold that §9-301(4) does not apply to non-advances. This conclusion is not the end of the inquiry in this case, however. It remains to be determined just which non-advance payments and expenditures have priority under UNI's lien. Neither *Dick Warner* nor the

Permanent Editorial Board's commentary can be read as giving priority to every expense claimed by a secured creditor, whenever incurred and for whatever purpose.

In *Dick Warner*, Judge Friendly gave priority to non-advance obligations that "related to transactions before the date of the levy," even if the obligation did not become due until after the levy. 746 F.2d at 134. Included in this category were attorneys' fees and other litigation expenses, id., and interest on protected advances accruing after the creation of the lien, as well as interest obligations accruing before the levy, id. at 130-31. With respect to letters of credit, Judge Friendly found it unnecessary to decide whether a creditor's placing itself at risk in connection with letters of credit would constitute an advance or a non-advance whose priority would be protected under the court's interpretation of §9-301(4), although he leaned toward treating the commitment to back a letter of credit as an advance. Finally, he refrained expressly from deciding whether Best Banana's obligation to pay minimum monthly charges for interest and commissions should receive priority as a non-advance.

In this case, the next inquiry will be to determine the rights Exchange had under its original agreement with Aparacor and to decide which of Exchange's post-February 26 payments are reimbursable under the terms of that agreement, or under any applicable law. Since those questions have not been briefed and the factual record has not been developed, we cannot resolve it. However, we can decide whether Exchange has any contractual right to priority arising from non-advance obligations incurred in connection with the protected advances it made within the 45-day period after the levy. We conclude that it has no such right. At the time of the levy, the agreement between Exchange and Aparacor had expired. In these unusual circumstances, Exchange can rely only on the original, expired agreement as the source of any preexisting contractual right to reimbursement for interest, collection expenses, or other costs paid for after the levy on January 12, 1989. When UNI levied on the funds in the possession of Exchange, UNI's lien was subordinate to (1) all of the advances Exchange made prior to the levy; (2) the advances Exchange made between the date of the levy and February 26, 1989; and (3) whatever other rights Exchange had under the law and its original agreement with Aparacor, including the right to pre-lien and post-lien interest on advances made under that agreement. The lien was not subject to any rights Exchange may have acquired under the modification agreement, since those rights did not exist until after the levy.[1] In other words, Exchange has no priority over UNI with respect to interest on advances made after the levy, expenses of collection of the collateral securing the post-lien advances, or attorneys' fees not incurred under the terms of the original agreement.

---

[1]   We leave for another day the question whether a secured creditor is entitled to priority for obligations incurred in connection with post-lien advances paid out within 45 days of the levying of a judgment lien that are made pursuant to an unexpired agreement.

On remand, the district court may find it more helpful to use the Permanent Editorial Board's terminology: "rights under contract or law" rather than *Dick Warner*'s definition: "relating to transactions before the date of the levy." It will be Exchange's burden to show what pre-lien contract rights give it priority to reimbursement out of the funds collected during the assignment for benefit of creditors, as well as to show that its non-advance expenses were "incurred reasonably and in good faith." *Dick Warner*, 746 F.2d at 134. (Because the record contains no facts about the assignment for benefit of creditors, we leave that subject unaddressed. It may well be, however, that the district court will have to examine the assignment to determine whether it has any bearing on Exchange's priority rights under Illinois law.)

     * * *

This matter will be remanded to the district court for further proceedings in accordance with this opinion. Circuit Rule 36 shall not apply.

Problems

1. Sheriff levies execution on a widget that is subject to an Article 9 security interest in favor of Beneficial Finance which had loaned the debtor money for a vacation trip to Greece. Is the execution lien or the security interest entitled to priority? See U.C.C. §§9-301(1)(b); 9-301(3); 9-302(1) (general rule is file to perfect).

    a. Would the result change if the secured party were a bank that had financed the debtor's purchase of the widget? See U.C.C. §§9-301(1)(b); 9-301(2); 9-107; 9-109; 9-302(1)(d) (purchase money security interest in consumer goods automatically perfected by operation of law).

    b. Bank has an unperfected security interest in equipment belonging to D. Business Finance makes an unsecured loan to D, which D fails to repay. Business Finance wins a judgment on the debt and causes execution to issue against D's property. The sheriff levies on the equipment that is subject to the Bank's security interest. The day before this levy the Bank perfected its security interest. Does Bank or Business Finance have priority?

2. Bank has a perfected security interest in all of D's industrial equipment. The security agreement provides that the collateral secures all debts and liabilities of every kind and class, whether related or unrelated, that D at any time owes Bank. At a time when the secured debt equals $25,000, D suffers a $45,000 judgment in a suit by a general, unsecured creditor, LC, who causes execution to issue against D. The sheriff levies on D's equipment. (Local law dates a lien of execution from the time of levy.) Bank later makes a further loan, i.e., a future advance, of $20,000. D now owes Bank $45,000. In any event, LC takes subject to First Bank's security interest

to the extent of $25,000, the initial advance. Consider whether LC also take subject to the $20,000 future advance in these circumstances:

    a. The Bank made the advance, which was optional, 30 days after the levy without knowledge of the lien.

    b. The Bank made the advance, which was optional, 30 days after the levy with knowledge of the lien.

    c. The Bank made the advance, which was optional, 50 days after the levy without knowledge of the lien.

    d. The Bank made the advance 50 days after the levy with knowledge of the lien.

    e. The Bank made the advance 50 days after the levy with knowledge of the lien, but the advance was pursuant to a commitment that was made in ignorance of the levy 30 days after the lien occurred.

    f. The Bank made the advance 50 days after the levy with knowledge of the lien, but the advance was pursuant to a commitment that was made with knowledge of the levy 30 days after the lien occurred.

3. Frontier Home Sales, a retailer of mobile homes, applies to First Bank for a loan. The parties meet and discuss the matter, and it appears likely that First Bank will make the loan and take a security interest in Frontier's inventory as collateral. Although no security agreement is executed at this meeting, Frontier signs a standard form financing statement which fully describes Frontier's inventory. First Bank files the financing statement the very next day. A week later, a judgment creditor of Frontier levies execution on Frontier's inventory. Shortly thereafter, First Bank and Frontier reach a final understanding with respect to financing; they execute a security agreement covering Frontier's inventory; and the Bank advances loan proceeds to Frontier. Who has the superior claim to the inventory, First Bank or the creditor with the execution lien? See U.C.C. 9-301(1)(b) & (4); 9-303(1).

4. Reconsider Problem 2a, but don't change the facts. Change the analysis. Suppose LC argues there is not one security interest, but two interests: the initial loan created a security interest, and the second loan created a second security interest. The second security interest was not perfected until the loan was made, which was after LC became a lien creditor. Thus, under both 9-301(1)(b) and 9-301(4), LC has priority as to this second interest.

5. Reconsider Problem 2a with this change in facts: Suppose the initial loan of $25,000 was fully satisfied before LC's lien attached to the equipment.

6. Once again reconsider Problem 2a, and again change the facts. No second loan
    was made. Instead, 30 days after LC's lien attached to the equipment, First Bank
    satisfied a $25,000 tax debt D owed the government. First Bank took this action
    pursuant to a clause in the security agreement signed by D which authorized the
    Bank in its discretion "to satisfy Debtor's obligations to creditors and other third
    parties who have, or might assert, claims against the collateral or other assets of
    Debtor." So, in paying D's tax debt, First Bank did not act as a volunteer or otherwise
    officiously. Is the answer different or more certain if the initial $25,000 loan had been
    fully satisfied before the levy?   In addition to *UNI Imports*, see Permanent Editorial
    Board of the Uniform Commercial Code, PEB Commentary No. 2, Section 9-301(4)
    (March 10, 1990).

4. Secured Party Versus "Supplier" With Common-Law Or Statutory Lien

The law of every state gives certain suppliers of property and services a lien on the property they supply or on the object of their work.
The lien is not dependent on the debtor's consent, and it usually
arises independently of judicial proceedings. Ordinarily, the lien attaches automatically as soon as the property or services are supplied,
or when the debtor refuses to pay for them.

The class of people entitled to suppliers' liens is not the same in
every state. Differences are largely attributable to economic, political,
and social peculiarities among the states. Everywhere, however, suppliers' liens are given to persons who repair or otherwise improve
goods (artisans) and persons who supply labor or materials for improving real estate (construction lienors). See Unit 3.A., *infra*. In
every state sellers of goods also enjoy a limited sort of suppliers' lien,
or collection of liens, in the form of rights of stoppage in transit and
rights of reclamation.

When suppliers' liens on personal property or fixtures conflict with
Article 9 security interests in the property, the proper priority rule is
not U.C.C. §9-301(1)(b) if, as is usually the case, the lien arises entirely apart from judicial proceedings. Remember that §9-301(1)(b)
applies in a contest between a secured party and a "lien creditor." A
person whose lien arises automatically, apart from judicial proceedings, is not a lien creditor. See U.C.C. §9-301(3).

Article 9 contains no general priority rule dedicated to all conflicts
between security interests and suppliers' liens. Indeed, in express
terms, Article 9 addresses only one such conflict: a conflict between
an artisan and a secured party who both claim goods in the artisan's
possession. See U.C.C. §9-310. (In more general terms, Article 9
seems also to deal with priority disputes over fixtures when the competing parties are a secured party and a construction lienor. See
U.C.C. §§9-313 & 9-105(1)(g) (definition of encumbrancer seems to

embrace construction lienor). Priority problems involving fixtures are considered later in this unit.)

How are we to decide priority between some other kind of suppliers' lien and a security interest in the absence of a specific rule in Article 9? If the lien is statutory, as is often true, the statute providing for the lien might also contain a provision governing its priority. If the lien statute, too, lacks a specific priority rule, there is authority for falling back on U.C.C. §9-201 as a residual principle of priority favoring a security interest, except when Article 9 or some other part of the Code provides otherwise. See, e.g., *Farmers & Merchants Nat'l Bank v. Schlossberg*, 306 Md. 48, 507 A.2d 172 (1986) (awarding priority to perfected security interest over subsequent state tax lien). Supporting priority for a security interest in such a case is the negative implication of §9-310: A perfected security interest prevails over any suppliers' lien on the collateral, for goods and services furnished with respect to the property, in all circumstances not covered by the terms of §9-310. See, e.g., *Blazer Mach. Co. v. Klineline Sand & Gravel Co.*, 271 Or. 596, 533 P.2d 321 (1975) (secured party prevails over nonpossessory artisan's lienor on the basis of the negative implication of §9-310); *Forest Gate Ford, Inc. v. Fryar*, 62 Tenn.App. 572, 465 S.W.2d 882 (1970) (same).

Some courts believe, however, that Article 9 is altogether inapplicable in resolving priority disputes that Article 9 does not specifically cover. In effect, these courts refuse to recognize §9-201 as a general rule of priority, and decline to infer anything from the inapplicability of §9-310. See, e.g., *McGahey v. Fuller*, 131 Ill.App.3d 663, 86 Ill.Dec. 937, 476 N.E.2d 438 (1985) (rejecting secured party's reliance on §9-201 as a general rule of priority in deciding conflict between security interest in crops and statutory claim to crops by vendor of land upon vendee-debtor's forfeiture under contract for deed).

If the lien statute says nothing about priority, and if Article 9 is found inapplicable in the absence of a specific priority provision, the court will decide the conflict on the basis of a decisional rule that is purely judge-made, or that is based ostensibly on an inference of legislative intent drawn from the lien statute.

5. Secured Party Versus Secured Party

a. Ordinary Cases Under U.C.C. §9-312(5)

The general rules of priority that rank conflicting Article 9 security interests are U.C.C. §§9-312(5)(a) and (b). If neither interest is perfected, the applicable priority rule is §9-312(5)(b), which awards priority to the secured party whose interest first attached pursuant to

§9-203(1)(a). If either or both interests are perfected, §9-312(5)(a) applies and gives priority to the secured party who first filed or perfected.

In applying 9-312(5)(a), remember these two big points:

* THE EFFECT OF ACTUAL KNOWLEDGE. The first secured party to file or perfect wins under section 9-312(5)(a) even though this person actually knows of the other security interest.

* FIRST TO FILE *OR* PERFECT -- NOT FIRST TO PERFECT. The rule of section 9-312(5)(a) is not the first to perfect; the rule is first to *file or perfect*. The difference is significant. Remember that perfection occurs only if a security interest has been created, §9-303(1), and remember too that a financing statement can be filed before the creation of a security interest. §9-402(1).

But be careful! Even though you should avoid thinking of §9-312(5)(a) as establishing a rule of first-to-perfect, don't go overboard and think of the section as giving priority whenever, and only if, a secured party is the first to file. In cases where a secured party relies for priority on having been the first to have filed, or the first to have perfected by filing, the secured party will succeed only if the collateral is a kind of property in which a security interest can be perfected by filing. Filing is an appropriate step for perfection whenever the collateral is goods, and an interest in certain intangibles can be perfected by filing, including chattel paper, general intangibles, and documents. Security interests in instruments and money, however, can only be perfected by the secured party taking possession of the collateral. U.C.C. §9-304(1). Filing as to instruments and money has no legal consequence whatsoever.

On the other hand, a secured party can win under §9-312(5)(a) even though she has neither filed nor taken possession of the collateral. There are a few instances where a security interest is perfected without the secured party taking any action whatsoever beyond creating the interest. The interest, once created, is deemed perfected without filing or possession. A good example is a purchase money security interest in consumer goods. U.C.C. §9-302(1)(d). Suppose that S sells B a television on credit and retains a security interest in the set. B takes the set home with her where she plans to use it for personal entertainment. S does not file. B later gives Finance Company a security interest in the television. Finance Company files. S's interest is entitled to priority under §9-312(5)(a). Although Finance Company was the first to file, S's interest was the first perfected through

§9-302(1)(d). The rule of §9-312(5)(a) is the first to file *or* perfect, and how the perfection is accomplished is unimportant.

Citizens State Bank v. Peoples Bank
Court of Appeals of Indiana, First District, 1985
475 N.E.2d 324

Neal, Judge. * * * Defendant-appellant, The Citizens State Bank (Citizens), appeals from a judgment of the Bartholomew Circuit Court determining plaintiff-appellee, The Peoples Bank (Peoples), possessed a lien superior to that of Citizens on personal property of Kenneth Bode (Bode) in Peoples' action to foreclose on a promissory note and security interest in Bode's farm equipment.

STATEMENT OF THE FACTS

The facts are undisputed. In November 1979, Bode, a resident of Bartholomew County, executed an installment note and security agreement with Peoples. A financing statement was prepared and improperly filed with the Recorder of Jackson County by Peoples on November 9, 1979, in spite of the fact that the instrument had Bartholomew County written on it and Bode lived in Columbus. A list of farm equipment owned by Bode and located in Bartholomew County was attached to the security agreement.

At some time Bode also executed a promissory note with Citizens concerning his consignment hog operation. Citizens refused to renew this obligation in 1982 unless Bode could provide it with some security on the loan, as the hog business had ceased operation. Citizens was aware of Peoples' security interest in Bode's equipment.

In February of 1982 Peoples' loan officer and vice-president, Ralph Spurgeon (Spurgeon), spoke with Citizens' president, Curtis Benter (Benter) via telephone to discuss the possibility of Peoples' releasing its security interest in Bode's equipment so that Citizens could use it as security. Spurgeon advised Benter that Peoples would release the equipment if it obtained a third mortgage on Bode's real estate. There was no further communications between the banks on this matter. Citizens had no knowledge of any negotiations between Bode and Peoples concerning either the release of the equipment or a third mortgage.

On March 4, 1982, Spurgeon prepared and signed a document which stated Bode's name, address, and equipment covered by its security agreement. At the bottom of the list is typed "The above list of equipment is to be used as security by the Citizens State Bank." Above Spurgeon's signature, also in his handwriting, is the sentence "We will release these items." Spurgeon delivered this document to Bode, who also signed it and delivered it to Benter that same day. Bode relayed to Benter that Spurgeon had told him the equipment had been released and he was "free to take it to Citizens". Benter telephoned the Recorder of Bartholomew County to inquire as to any financing statement on file between Bode and Peoples, and was assured there was none. Benter further requested and received a written search from the Bartholomew Recorder verifying the absence of such a financing statement. Citizens then prepared a promissory note, a security agreement with an attached list of Bode's equipment and a financing statement, all of which were executed by Bode on March 4. Citizens filed its financing statement with the Recorder of Bartholomew County on March 8, 1982.

In January of 1983 Peoples discovered it had erroneously filed its financing statement on the Bode loan in Jackson County. A second financing statement was prepared and filed in Bartholomew County by Peoples on January 17.

On February 3, 1983 Peoples filed a complaint to foreclose on its lien on Bode's equipment. Instead of giving Peoples a third mortgage on his real estate, Bode filed Chapter 7 bankruptcy on May 2 and was thereafter relieved of any debt owed Peoples or Citizens. Citizens filed a counterclaim and cross- claim alleging an interest superior to Peoples in Bode's equipment on September 2, 1983. Following a bench trial on December 27, judgment was entered in favor of Peoples on December 28, 1983.

ISSUES

Citizens raises two issues for our review; however, we find reversal is warranted upon examination of but one: whether the trial court erred in ruling the lien of Peoples was superior to that of Citizens regarding Bode's equipment.

DISCUSSION AND DECISION

The judgment of the trial court reads, in pertinent part:

"The evidence leaves no doubt that Peoples received a security interest in the personalty of Bode in November of 1979, and that Citizens had actual knowledge of that interest on March 4, 1982. Given this, Citizens has three possible theories of recovery: one--a direct contract of release between it and Peoples; two--as a third party beneficiary of a contract of release between Bode and Peoples; and third--promissory estoppel of Peoples' alleged promise of release. As to the direct contract theory, there is no consideration by Citizens to support the promise of Peoples to release the security. Similarly, Citizens cannot prevail as a third party beneficiary of a contract of release between Bode and Peoples. Bode never completed his part of the bargain, ie., a promised third mortgage on realty of Bode was never executed to secure the November, 1979 loan by Peoples to Bode. Finally, Citizens cannot claim that it substantially changed its position to its prejudice by its reliance on the alleged promise to release by Peoples. The evidence reveals that Citizens had previously executed an unsecured loan with Bode, the antecedent debt which was to be secured by the personalty in question."

* * *

Contrary to the ruling of the trial court, this case fits squarely into the frame of promissory estoppel. This court has ruled the doctrine is applicable to commercial transactions. See IND.CODE 26-1-1-103. The use of promissory estoppel is also consistent with the Uniform Commercial Code's (UCC) obligation of good faith, found in Title 26 of the IND.CODE. See IND.CODE 26-1-1-203.

Indiana follows the format of promissory estoppel embodied in Section 90 of the Restatement of Contracts * * *:

"A promise which the promisor should reasonably expect to induce action or forbearance of a definite and substantial character on the part of the promisee and which does induce such action or forebearance is binding if injustice can be avoided only by the enforcement of the promise."

Promissory estoppel is most often applied where one party signifies his intention to abandon an existing right, leading another to act to his detriment in the event such right is subsequently asserted. Here, Peoples signified its intention to release Bode's equipment leading Citizens to use it as collateral for the renewal of its loan to Bode.

The promisor need not receive any benefit or consideration from the transaction. Actual fraud on the part of the promisor is not a requisite but there must be some false representation or concealment of facts. Whether Spurgeon's handwritten statement "We will release these items" constitutes a misrepresentation of current fact or an unfulfilled promise as to future action is irrelevant to the application of promissory estoppel. However, it is necessary that Citizens reliance on the representation was reasonable. The list of equipment prepared by Peoples and furnished to Citizens stated both that equipment was to be used as security by Citizens and that Peoples would release it. Benter, acting for Citizens, was justified in relying on this document which was consistent with Bode's relayed message from Spurgeon, especially in light of his own prior conversation with Spurgeon and his independent investigation of the county records. We have no insight into Peoples reasons for preparing and delivering to Citizens the ostensible release of Bode's equipment. We can only infer from the face of it that Peoples intended Citizens to rely upon the information and statements contained therein. In any case, Peoples should reasonably have expected such reliance following Spurgeon's discussion with Benter, knowing Citizens was not involved in and unaware of the status of Peoples negotiations with Bode regarding a third mortgage.

The trial court found Citizens had not substantially changed its position because it had previously executed an unsecured loan with Bode on his hog operation. However, Citizens initially refused to renew that loan, and intended to try to collect on it because the hog business had ceased operation. Only if Bode could provide collateral to secure the obligation would Citizens agree to renew it. Upon receipt of the list of Bode's equipment prepared by Peoples, Citizens positively acted to renew its loan to Bode and perfect its security interest by properly filing a financing statement covering the equipment. Citizens also forbore suing to recover the amount outstanding on Bode's loan. This conduct is "of a definite and substantial character" and meets the strictures of Sec. 90.

Finally, Citizens reliance on Peoples' representations of release would produce "substantial economic loss" to Citizens if Peoples is permitted to reassert its prior right to the equipment. Assuming Peoples' lien on Bode's equipment had been effective as against Citizens before the release, Citizens' lien would then be subordinate to that of Peoples. The failure of Peoples to follow through on its statements to release Bode's equipment was due to its unsuccessful attempt to secure a third mortgage on his real estate. Citizens should not be the scapegoat for the shortcomings of Peoples' business dealings to which Citizens was not a party.

Having met the rigors of this equitable doctrine, Citizens should be permitted to benefit from the enforcement of Peoples representation to release Bode's equipment. As Citizens properly filed a financing statement on March 8, 1982 its lien on Bode's equipment was perfected before Peoples properly filed on January of 1983. Therefore, Citizens' lien has priority over that of Peoples.

The same result is appropriate under the UCC * * *. Peoples did receive a security interest in Bode's farm equipment in 1979; however, the question remains whether such interest was perfected as against Citizens when it filed its financing statement on March 8, 1982.

Under 9-401(2) Peoples' filing in Jackson County was wholly ineffective because it was not proper as to any of the collateral. An exception does exist where a party has "knowledge of the contents of such financing statement". 9-401(2). Knowledge means actual knowledge. 1-201(25). It has been suggested in light of the language of the current statute, which replaced a prior version stating knowledge of the filing was sufficient, that an "eyeing the document" test is required. Whether the party must have actually observed the financing statement to be bound by it is not clear; however, most jurisdictions agree mere knowledge of a security agreement is inadequate. But see In re Davidoff, (S.D.N.Y.1972) 351 F.Supp. 440. As stated in Goldberg Co. v. County Green Limited Partnership, (W.D.Va.1977), 438 F.Supp. 693: "The Uniform Commercial Code is a carefully planned and systematic compilation of logic and experience. Words are painstakingly defined and used in accordance with their intended impact on the everyday commercial transaction. A security agreement is not the same thing as a financing statement. Had the legislature intended for knowledge of a security agreement to be the same as knowledge of the contents of a financing statement it could have said so." 438 F.Supp. at 697-8.
* * *

Indiana courts have not previously had an opportunity to decide what level of knowledge is sufficient to bring a party under the exception of IND.CODE

26-1- 9-401(2); however, some basic requirements are obvious from an analysis of the UCC itself. As stated above, a security agreement and a financing statement are two different instruments with distinct purposes. The former is a document setting out an arrangement between a creditor and a debtor, while the latter is a paper which must be filed in a designated public office to perfect a security interest and notify any interested party that such exists. 9-105(h); 9-302; 9-401; 9-402. Priority between conflicting security interests in the same collateral is determined strictly by the order of filing. 9-312(5) and comments thereto. This pure race section operates without regard to the parties state of knowledge and nowhere requires the holder of a security interest second in time to be without knowledge of the prior interest in order to prevail when he has filed his financing statement first. Thus, the threshold amount of knowledge by a subsequent creditor under 9-401(2) must necessarily be greater than this.

Section 9-401(2) contemplates (1) filing of a financing statement somewhere; and (2) knowledge by a subsequent secured party of the contents of such financing statement, referring to the one filed. It follows that knowledge the financing statement was filed somewhere is included in the requirement of "knowledge of the contents". As previously mentioned, before the 1956 changes in 9-401(2), knowledge of the filing sufficed. This minimal knowledge is still required but now, additional fact-specific proof that a creditor was aware of an earlier filed interest is necessary to defeat the second, perfected interest.

At this point, reference to apposite decisions of our sister states would be helpful. In Goldberg, supra, a bank which financed a construction project properly filed a financing statement covering appliances to be installed in the completed building. The vendor of these appliances, which would ordinarily have a superior purchase money security interest under 9-312, filed its financing statement in the improper county. The court held that 9-401(2) would not protect the vendor where the bank had notice of the vendor's security interest and had even received a photostatic copy of its security agreement but was unaware of the financing statement. The bank had searched the records of the proper county for the vendor's financing statement but had not located one. Upon the bankruptcy of the debtor/purchaser, the bank's lien took priority over the vendor's.

United States v. Waterford No. 2 Office Center, (1980) 246 Ga. 475, 271 S.E.2d 790 involves a pledge of equipment located in the debtor's office in the Waterford building to secure a bank loan guaranteed by, and later assigned to, the Small Business Association (SBA). The bank filed a financing statement in the improper county. After the debtor defaulted on the loan, the SBA orally informed Waterford of its security interest in the equipment located there. Waterford became a judgment lien creditor of the debtor. Following the sale of the equipment a priority dispute arose between the SBA and Waterford. The Supreme Court of Georgia held that under that state's version of 9- 301(1)(b), which states an unperfected security interest is subordinate to the rights of one who becomes a lien creditor before the security interest is perfected,[1] Waterford had priority. The SBA's argument under 9-401(2) failed because it had not proven Waterford had knowledge of the contents of its financing statement; only its security interest.

The court in In re Davidoff, supra, rejected the notion that knowledge of a security interest is necessarily not the same as knowledge of the contents of the financing statement. In Davidoff, the court ruled an equipment supplier, through conversations with the debtor, had all knowledge of a bank's prior chattel mortgage covering the equipment as if he had read the financing statement. It applied New York's law of notice to the UCC's obligation of good faith in 1-203 to find the supplier had been put on inquiry and possessed the means of acquiring knowledge of the contents of the financing statement, and therefore should be charged with that actual knowledge which was available through "ordinary diligence".

We decline to accept New York's broad view of what constitutes knowledge under 9-401(2). Section 1-102 states the UCC provisions shall be liberally construed and applied. However, if mere knowledge of a security interest or agreement is deemed equivalent to knowledge of the contents of the financing statement, the pure race aspect of 9-312(5) would be undermined. Nor do we hold actual examination of the financing statement is always necessary. In keeping with the UCC's policy of flexibility, we believe the intermediate level of knowledge required under 9-401(2) should not be rigidly fixed. Rather, each case must be evaluated on its particular facts keeping in mind the UCC's catch phrases of good faith, diligence, reasonableness and due care. See 1-102 and comments thereto.

In the case at bar Citizens admits to having knowledge of Peoples security interest in Bode's equipment prior to March 4, 1982. Peoples had the further burden of proving Citizens somehow had knowledge of the contents of its financing statement, including the fact that a filing occurred, when Citizens became a lien holder and perfected its security interest in the equipment. 9-401(2). Peoples has not proven, and did not even allege, Citizens had any knowledge of the existence, filing or contents of its financing statement when it completed the paperwork necessary to use Bode's equipment as collateral for the renewal of his loan. In fact, all of the evidence supports the opposite conclusion. Benter testified:

"I assumed by the statement made by Ralph Spurgeon on [the document he sent to me] and by the statement made by Kenneth Bode to me that this equipment had been released and by the fact that no Financing Statement was found in Bartholomew County, Indiana that the equipment had been released by the Peoples Bank and was free of any

---

[1]   Georgia has adopted the 1972 amendment to 9-301(1)(b). Cf. IND.CODE 26-1-9-301(1)(b) which contains the original text of 9-301(1)(b).

security interest in the farm machinery and equipment as listed on [the document]."

We need not decide whether the document delivered to Citizens purporting to release Bode's equipment was adequate under 9-406, as that section deals with a statement presented to the filing officer and notes that such is merely a "permissive devise". Comment to 9-406. Rather, the document serves to buttress Citizens position that it had no reason to know of Peoples improperly filed financing statement or its continued interest in Bodes equipment when citizens perfected its security interest. Moreover, Citizens employed due diligence, as required in Davidoff, supra, in searching the records before perfecting its security interest and discovered no financing statement. "Given this fact, it is difficult to perceive of how a party can know the contents of something which [it] does not know exists." Goldberg, supra at 697.

We find Peoples has not carried its burden of proving Citizens had any knowledge whatsoever of the contents of its financing statement when it took a security interest in Bode's equipment. Therefore, Peoples' argument under 9-401(2) must fail. Even if created with knowledge of Peoples' security interest, absent knowledge that a financing statement had been filed, Citizens properly perfected security interest takes priority. 9-312(5).

For all the above stated reasons, the judgment of the trial court that Peoples' lien is superior to that of Citizens as to Bode's equipment is reversed. The proceeds of the sale of such equipment shall first be applied to pay for the cost of this action and the sale, then applied to the debt due Citizens and finally to the debt due Peoples.

Judgment reversed.

First Wyoming Bank v. Mudge
Supreme Court of Wyoming, 1988
748 P.2d 713

Urbigkit, Justice. This is an appeal from an action instituted by Robert M. Mudge, Sybil A. Mudge, Edward W. Mudge, and Edna F. Mudge (Mudges), appellees, by a third-party complaint in response to a foreclosure action instituted by First Wyoming Bank, Casper (Bank), appellant, to foreclose a security interest in a corporate enterprise inventory. This third-party complaint was severed from the original foreclosure action when the earlier decision was appealed and the foreclosure decision affirmed in M & M Welding v. Pavlicek, Wyo., 713 P.2d 236 (1986). The third-party complaint alleging intentional interference with a contract by the Bank resulted in a jury verdict for the Mudges of $123,997.33.

We affirm this decision also * * *.

Appellant Bank presents the issues for review as trial-court error: 1. Improper instructions to the jury. 2. Failure to grant defendant's motions for a directed verdict. 3. Exclusion of certain evidence.

I. FACTS

The parties and the facts involved in this appeal are essentially identical to those in M & M Welding v. Pavlicek, supra, where the facts are set out in more detail, and only the facts pertinent to this appeal will be highlighted here. On July 31, 1981, the Mudges made an agreement to sell the family corporate welding business to Redding. This written agreement included transfer of the Mudges' stock in M & M Welding, Inc., with inventory, equipment, and the business site real property. Additionally, the document contained a nonencumbrance covenant clause, Section 3(f), which later led to this litigation, and which provided: "3(f). It is agreed that the assets of M & M Welding, Inc., a Wyoming corporation, or its successor corporation shall not be mortgaged for more than the presently existing indebtedness without Sellers['] consent until the total purchase price herein agreed to be paid shall have been paid in full. Such consent shall not be unreasonably withheld." To facilitate the security status of the transaction, the corporate stock was placed in escrow until the buyer completed payments under the contract while operating the business during the purchase payment period.

The sales transaction closed in September, 1981, and the buyer took over the operation of M & M Welding. Almost immediately, he applied to appellant for a loan of $100,000 to cover obligations from other investments. At some time, as evidenced by its inclusion in the Redding loan file, the Bank's lending officers had been given an unsigned copy of the purchase agreement that contained the nonencumbrance covenant. The date when the Bank actually received the agreement is disputed, as well as by whom it was seen. In any event, no encumbrance consent was ever obtained from the Mudges, and the Bank took a security interest in the inventory and equipment for the purpose of securing a first priority upon loan default.

Subsequently, Redding did go into default on his purchase payments, causing the Mudges to cancel the sales agreement and in August, 1982 reclaim the M & M stock from escrow. The Mudges first became aware of the security agreement given by Redding to the Bank when the Bank made foreclosure claim to the inventory and equipment as a result of the disputed security agreement, which action effectively shut down M & M Welding. To free up their collateral and be able to continue the business, the Mudges individually put up a letter of credit for $100,000, which was substituted for the property which was the subject of the pending bank foreclosure action. The Bank subsequently drew down the letter of credit. The Bank won the first go-around in M & M Welding v. Pavlicek, supra, but in the second round, now here on appeal, lost the jury verdict on a theory of intentional interference with a contractual relationship for the amount of the letter of credit, purchase cost, and interest.

II. INTENTIONAL INTERFERENCE RULE IN WYOMING LAW

This court has adopted the Restatement (Second) of Torts, §766, p. 7 (1979) definition of the tort of intentional interference with a contract: """One who intentionally and improperly interferes with the performance of a contract (except a contract to marry) between another and a third person by inducing or otherwise causing the third person not to perform the contract, is subject to liability to the other for the pecuniary loss resulting to the other from the failure of the third person to perform the contract.""" Davenport v. Epperly, Wyo., 744 P.2d 1110, 1111 (1987), quoting Toltec Watershed Improvement District v. Johnston, Wyo., 717 P.2d 808, 813-814 (1986).

It is well established in Wyoming that the elements of a claim of tortious interference with a contract that the plaintiff must prove are: (1) the existence of the contract; (2) the defendant's knowledge; (3) intentional and improper interference inducing or causing a breach; and (4) resulting damages.

III. JURY INSTRUCTION

Appellant argues that it was error to give to the jury Instruction No. 3: "In this case, the Plaintiffs have the burden of proving by a preponderance of the evidence the following: "(1) The existence of a valid contractual relationship; "(2) knowledge of the contractual relationship on the part of the Defendant; and "(3) intentional and improper interference by the inducing or otherwise causing a breach of the relationship; "(4) which resulted in damage to the Plaintiffs." We would disagree, since this instruction correctly recites the Restatement of Torts (Second) §766 (1979) elements of proof of the tort of intentional interference with contractual relations which this court has previously adopted. The instruction succinctly followed prior Wyoming case law which will not here be rewritten.

IV. DIRECTED VERDICT

Appellant next argues that it was erroneous not to grant appellant's motions for a directed verdict because appellees failed to prove damages, lacked standing to sue, and failed to present evidence to satisfy the elements of tortious interference with a contractual relationship. We disagree. * * *

The appellant argues that there was insufficient evidence presented specifically on the second, third, and fourth elements of the tort, and that therefore his motion for directed verdict should have been granted. However, the contention is unsustained when the evidence is viewed most favorably to the Mudges as appellees. Directed to the second element, knowledge of the contract, the Mudges presented testimony through Redding that he gave a copy of the purchase agreement to the Bank's lending officers before the $100,000 note transaction occurred. Also, more critically, Bordewick, president of the Bank during that time frame, testified as a subpoenaed witness that in his opinion the Bank file reflected knowledge, and:

"Q. Now, would you expect, as a question of lending policy or banking policy, that if a lender was after a hundred thousand dollar loan and that he had been involved in purchasing a million dollar business, that the bank would in fact want to have access to and examine the agreement that was involved?

"A. I would think so."

Thus, considering the evidence most favorable to the Mudges, there was sufficient evidence in the record to conclude that the Bank had knowledge of the terms of the purchase agreement from a document to be found in its files which had been provided before it took a security interest in the contractually constrained chattels.

The third element, intentional interference with a contract without justification, is also alleged not to be present because the interference was not improper. This court recently clarified the definition for improper interference in Wyoming in Toltec Watershed Improvement District v. Johnston, supra, 717 P.2d at 814:

> "Factors to be considered for the action are listed as follows:
>
> "'In determining whether an actor's conduct in intentionally interfering with a contract or a prospective contractual relation of another is improper or not, consideration is given to the following factors:
> "'(a) the nature of the actor's conduct,
> "'(b) the actor's motive,
> "'(c) the interests of the other with which the actor's conduct interferes, "
> '(d) the interests sought to be advanced by the actor,
> "'(e) the social interests in protecting the freedom of action of the actor and the contractual interests of the other,
> "'(f) the proximity or remoteness of the actor's conduct to the interference and
> "'(g) the relations between the parties.' Restatement (Second) of Torts, §766, pp. 26-27 (1979)."

Further, this court recognizes Restatement (Second) of Torts, §773 (1979), that one who interferes with a contract by asserting a bona fide claim in good faith is not liable for tortious interference with contractual relations. Evidentiary analysis establishes a justified basis for the jury to have found as a predicate for liability that the Bank did not act in good faith in inducing the borrower to violate his purchase agreement so that the lender would obtain priority chattel security for its $100,000 loan. While the Bank's motive to have a first priority in the collateral for loan is not in itself improper, the fact, as the jury concluded, that the Bank knew about the restrictive covenant and then preempted the collateral in requiring the Mudges to post a letter of credit to pay to get their property back, displayed a classic case of the tort of intentional interference with a contractual relation. In simplistic terms, it consisted of inducing the buyer to break his purchase contract terms in order to offer a new loan security priority to the Bank.

Next, the argument is made that the real parties in interest were not the Mudges as third-party complainants. The facts do not sustain their argument. The Mudges originally sold and sought protection in sale-price payment by the nonencumbrance clause. Upon repossession, they individually were faced with protection of the reclaimed business, and purchased the letter of credit with attendant cost.

Appellant additionally contends that the fourth element, resulting damages, was not proven. Again, we disagree. This argument has the same character and contention found in the real-party-in-interest denial. A party is entitled to all damages which will compensate for all the detriment proximately caused by the breach of the duty. The letter of credit was in the amount of $100,000; the initial cost of the letter was $2,000; and the interest was $21,997.38. Thus, the jury's decision that the Mudges were entitled to recover their incurred costs in the total amount of the verdict is justified, considering that but for the Bank's improper interference the Mudges would not have obtained the letter of credit or incurred the consequent cost of $123,997.38. The letter of credit was acquired to provide validity to the corporate stock repossession and proximately measured the sustained damage. There was no error in denying the directed verdict motion.

We answer the first two issues affirmatively, and there is no need to proceed to appellant's third issue because we find there was sufficient evidence to uphold the jury's verdict. The case was submitted to and decided by the jury on a theory of contractual interference for monetary benefit with a known nonencumbrance covenant between the prospective borrower and a third party. This case, in classical terms, fits the historical perspective of this tort theory. The practical litigative issue was knowledge and consequent disregard, which was adversely determined by jury verdict.

Affirmed.

Problems

1. SP-1 acquires a security interest in D's farm machinery on January 1. On February 1, D gives SP-2 a security interest in the same property. Neither interest is perfected. See U.C.C. §9-312(5)(b).

2. Same facts as Problem 1, except that SP-2 perfects its security interest before SP-1's security interest is perfected. See U.C.C. §9-312(5)(a).

3. Same facts as Problem 2, except that, before SP-2 perfects, she learns of SP-1's unperfected interest. See U.C.C. §9-312 comment 5 (Example 2).

4. Same facts as Problem 3 except that SP-2 learns of the other interest before her security interest attaches.

5. SP-1 and D discuss the possibility of a loan to D secured by a security interest in farm machinery. Although no agreement is reached and no loan is made, D signs a financing statement covering the property and SP-1 properly files the statement. (Article 9 permits filing a financing statement before a security interest attaches. U.C.C. §9-402(1).) SP-2 thereafter makes a loan to D and takes as collateral a perfected security interest in the property described in SP-1's financing statement. Eventually, D borrows money from SP-1, and these parties execute a security agreement covering the farm machinery.

6. SP-1 makes a loan to D that is secured by a negotiable promissory note on which D is the payee. SP-1 files a financing statement covering the Article 3 instrument. D later borrows money from SP-2 and again uses the note as collateral. This time, however, D delivers possession of the note to SP-2. SP-1 claims priority with respect to the note on the basis of U.C.C. §9-312(5)(a).

7. SP-1 finances D's farm machinery dealership. The parties have executed a security agreement which covers D's inventory, present and after-acquired. SP-1's interest is perfected by filing. D experiences a temporary cash flow problem and asks SP-1 for a short-term loan of $25,000 to pay employees and satisfy other expenses. SP-1 refuses to lend any more money to D. D thus asks SP-2 for the money, agreeing to give SP-2 a security interest in two farm tractors on their way to D from the manufacturer. SP-2 makes the loan and acquires a perfected security interest in the tractors, which are inventory.

8. Same facts as Problem 7, except that, before D acquired the two new tractors, the secured debt owed to SP-1 was $75,000. Some time after D acquired the tractors, SP-1 made an additional loan of $25,000 pursuant to a future-advance clause in its security agreement with D. The value of the tractors at a forced sale is about $100,000. See U.C.C. §9-312(7).

9. Same facts as Problem 8, except that the initial $75,000 loan by SP-1 had been repaid in full when the $25,000 future advance was made.

b. Enabling Security Interests: Purchase- and Production-Money Security Interests

The most important exceptions to the first-to-file-or-perfect rule of U.C.C. §9-312(5) are §§9-312(3) or 9-312(4). Both of exceptional provisions are designed to protect secured parties having *purchase money security interests* in collateral. A "purchase money security interest", which is defined in U.C.C. §9-107, is a special type of enabling lien. An enabling lien is a term we use to describe the lien of a person who, by making a loan or extending credit, enabled the debtor to acquire, or improve, the very property that is collateral. The law of creditors' remedies generally favors enabling liens of all kinds over conflicting liens for unrelated debt. In line with this widespread policy of the law, Article 9, through §§9-312(3) and (4), gives priority to a purchase money security interest over a nonpurchase money security interest in the collateral even if the nonpurchase money interest was first filed or perfected. Both sections condition the super-priority of a purchase money security interest on the satisfaction of certain procedural requirements, but the sections differ as to the number and content of these requirements.

U.C.C. §9-312(2) is another enabling lien exception to §9-312(5)(a). In theory, §9-312(2) gives "priority to a new value security interest in crops based on a current crop production loan." U.C.C. §9-312 comment 2. In other words, a creditor with a security interest in crops she helped to produce, which we call a kind of *production-money security interest*, is entitled to priority over an earlier security interest, even though perfected, that is unrelated to production of the collateral. In practice, however, §9-312(2) is meaningless because the circumstances under which it applies are so extraordinarily narrow and largely fortuitous.

More than one purchase money or crop production money security interest can attach to the same collateral. In this event, how is priority to be determined between the conflicting enabling liens? Professor Grant Gilmore, the principal architect of Article 9, analyzed the issue in this fashion:

> There can be more than one purchase-money interest in the same property. Assume, for example, that a lender makes an advance for 50 per cent of the purchase price, the seller retaining a security interest in the goods for the unpaid balance. The seller would have a purchase-money interest under paragraph (a) [of §9-107], the lender would have one under (b). Or two lenders could contribute toward the purchase money, each taking a paragraph (b) interest to the extent that his money was "so used." *** In cases of the type just supposed, there is nothing in §9-107 to give priority to one of the purchase-money interests over the other. If both of them attached and became perfected at the same time, they would presumably rank equally. If they attached or became

perfected at different times, priority between them would be regulated by §9-312(5) [which is the first-in-time first in right principle].

2 G. Gilmore, SECURITY INTERESTS IN PERSONAL PROPERTY §29.3 at 784 (1965).

MBank Alamo National Association v. Raytheon Co.
United States Court of Appeals, Fifth Circuit, 1989
886 F.2d 1449

Reavley, Circuit Judge: MBank Alamo National Association ("MBank") and E.I. DuPont de Nemours Company, Inc. ("DuPont") pressed this conversion action against Raytheon Company ("Raytheon"), claiming that Raytheon collected certain accounts receivable, in which MBank and DuPont had security interests superior to those of Raytheon.   Raytheon's defense was that it had a purchase money security interest in the accounts receivable.   Concluding that Raytheon had no purchase money security interest in the accounts, the district court held that Raytheon's security interests were subordinate to those of MBank and DuPont, and granted MBank's and DuPont's motions for summary judgment. We affirm.

I. Background
MBank and DuPont entered various security agreements with Howe X-ray ("Howe").   By January 10, 1983, in accordance with these agreements, both DuPont and MBank held perfected liens in Howe's present and future accounts receivable.   MBank also held a perfected security interest in Howe's present and after acquired inventory.

Beginning in January 1983, Raytheon, an x-ray equipment manufacturer, entered a series of transactions with Howe who was one of its distributors. Raytheon agreed to ship x-ray equipment to Howe after Howe contracted with one of its customers for the sale, delivery, and installation of certain Raytheon equipment.   In exchange, Howe agreed to assign the specific accounts receivable to Raytheon.   Subsequent to the assignments, Raytheon filed financing statements in specific accounts receivable of Howe. Between July 1983 and December 1984, Raytheon collected over $850,000.00.

By November 1984, Howe had defaulted on its obligations to MBank and DuPont. MBank and DuPont, pursuant to their security interests, demanded payment from Raytheon from the accounts receivable that it had collected. Raytheon refused, claiming that it had a purchase money security interest ("PMSI") in the accounts receivable and that its interests were therefore superior to those of MBank and DuPont.

In addition to its contention that it had a PMSI in the accounts receivable, Raytheon claimed that even if it did not have a PMSI in those accounts, MBank waived its security interest in the accounts. The district court granted MBank's and DuPont's motions for summary judgment, deciding that Raytheon had no PMSI in the accounts receivable and that Raytheon had not raised an issue of MBank's alleged waiver.

Raytheon appeals the district court's determination that it did not have a PMSI in the accounts receivable. In the alternative, Raytheon contends that if our construction of the PMSI statutory provisions excludes the Raytheon-Howe transaction, the ruling should not apply to this case under the doctrine of nonretroactivity. Raytheon also appeals the district court's finding that Raytheon failed to produce sufficient evidence of waiver to overcome MBank's motion for summary judgment.

II. Analysis

A. Purchase Money Security Interests

The rules governing the rights of creditors are set out in Chapter 9 of the Texas Business and Commerce Code ("Code"), which essentially adopted the provisions of the Uniform Commercial Code--Secured Transactions. See Tex.Bus. & Com.Code Ann. §9.101 et seq. (Vernon 1989). These provisions were enacted "to provide a simple and unified structure within which the immense variety of present-day secured financing transactions can go forward with less cost and with greater certainty." §9.101, 1972 Official U.C.C. Comment. In keeping with these goals, rules were enacted prioritizing conflicting security interests in the same property.

The general rule provides that the first perfected security interest to be filed has priority and other perfected interests stand in line in the order in which they were filed. See §9.312(e). PMSIs are excepted from the first- to-file rule and take priority over other perfected security interests regardless of the filing sequence. §9.312(c), (d). The district court found that Raytheon did not fall within the PMSI exception, that MBank had priority as the first to file, under §9.312(e)(1), and that DuPont takes second priority since it filed next.

Raytheon claims the district court erred by not recognizing its priority in the accounts receivable as a PMSI under §9.312(d).[1] Section 9.312(d) provides that "[a] purchase money security interest in collateral other than inventory has priority over a conflicting security interest in the same collateral or its proceeds if the purchase money security interest is perfected at the time the debtor receives possession of the collateral or within 20 days thereafter."

As a threshold matter, Raytheon must establish that it meets the statutory definition of a PMSI. Raytheon contends that it fits the statutory requirements of a PMSI under §9.107(2), which provides: A security interest is a "purchase money security interest" to the extent that it is

---

[1] Raytheon claims a PMSI in the accounts receivable and not in the inventory. Raytheon cannot claim a PMSI in this inventory because it did not comply with §9.312(c)(2), which requires a PMSI holder to notify in writing the holder of a conflicting security interest in the same inventory.

.... (2) taken by a person who by making advances or incurring an obligation gives value to enable the debtor to acquire rights in or the use of collateral if such value is in fact so used.

To meet these requirements Raytheon must show: (1) that it gave value; (2) that the value given enabled Howe to acquire rights in the accounts receivable; and (3) that the accounts receivable qualify as collateral within the meaning of the statute.

The value requirement is satisfied by any consideration sufficient to support a simple contract. See Thet Mah and Assoc. v. First Bank of North Dakota, 336 N.W.2d 134, 138 (N.D.1983); §1.201(44)(D) (Vernon 1968). Assuming arguendo that Raytheon gave value by extending credit to Howe in exchange for Howe's promise to assign the accounts receivable to Raytheon, see Thet Mah, 336 N.W.2d at 138, Raytheon has failed to satisfy the other two requirements.

To create a PMSI, the value must be given in a manner that enables the debtor to acquire interest in the collateral. This is accomplished when a debtor uses an extension of credit or loan money to purchase a specific item. See Ingram v. Ozark Prod. Credit Assoc., 468 F.2d 564, 565 (5th Cir.1972); In re Dillon, 18 B.R. 252, 254 (Bkrtcy.E.D.Cal.1982) (PMSI lien attaches to item actually purchased); Jackson & Kronman, Secured Financing and Priorities Among Creditors, 88 Yale L.J. 1143, 1165 (1979) (PMSI priority limited "to loans that can be traced to identifiable, discrete items of property.").

The collateral at issue here is the accounts receivable. In an attempt to force its interest into the PMSI mold, Raytheon has characterized the transaction as follows:

> "Raytheon, by agreeing to extend credit on its equipment, enabled Howe
> X-Ray to enter into subsequent contracts of sale with its customers,
> thereby acquiring rights in the contract accounts which, upon the
> specific advance and delivery of equipment, blossomed into a right to
> the collateral accounts receivable."

Raytheon, however, cannot force this transaction to fit. To accept this characterization, we would have to close our eyes to the true nature of the transaction.

Raytheon, in essence, is claiming that it advanced x-ray machines to Howe on credit, which then enabled Howe to purchase accounts receivable from its customers. This, however, does not comport with our view of commercial reality. While, as Raytheon suggests, it may be theoretically possible to create a PMSI in accounts receivable by advancing funds for their purchase, the same cannot be done by advancing x-ray machines. We view this as a two-step transaction in which Raytheon first advanced machines to Howe for retail sale and, once these machines were sold, Howe then assigned the accounts receivable to Raytheon. Through the credit advance, Howe acquired an interest in the machines, not the accounts receivable. Raytheon's credit advance, therefore, did not enable Howe to acquire an interest in the accounts receivable, as collateral within the meaning of the statute.

Additionally, in its characterization of the transaction, Raytheon is attempting to benefit from the PMSI's preferred status in a manner that was not contemplated by the U.C.C. drafters. PMSIs provide an avenue for heavily burdened debtors to obtain credit for specific goods when creditors who have previously loaned money to the debtor may be unwilling to advance additional funds. By giving a PMSI holder a priority interest in the specific goods purchased, there is some incentive for a lender to advance funds or credit for the specific transaction. The scope of a PMSI holder's preferred interest, however, is specifically limited by the Code.

Under §9.312(c), a PMSI in inventory is limited to that inventory or to "identifiable cash proceeds received on or before the delivery of the inventory to a buyer...." The drafters noted that general financing of an inventory business is based primarily on accounts resulting from inventory, chattel paper and other proceeds. §9.312, Official U.C.C. Reasons for 1972 Change comment (4). Reasoning that "[a]ccounts financing is more important in the economy than the financing of the kinds of inventory that produce accounts, and [that] the desirable rule is one which makes accounts financing certain as to its legal position," id., they specifically excluded accounts resulting from the sale of inventory from the protections of a PMSI. Thus, financing statements that are filed on a debtor's accounts take precedence over any subsequent claim to accounts as proceeds of a PMSI in inventory. Additionally, to protect lenders who make periodic advances against incoming inventory, the PMSI holder is required to notify other secured parties before it can take priority. §9.312(c)(2); see id., 1972 Official U.C.C. Comment comment 3.

The priority scheme, however, differs in the context of collateral other than inventory. Under §9.312(d), a PMSI in collateral other than inventory entitles the holder to a superior interest in both the collateral and its proceeds regardless of any intervening accounts. The differing entitlement to proceeds is due to differences in the expectations of the parties with respect to the collateral involved.

Collateral other than inventory generally refers to equipment used in the course of business. Since, unlike inventory, "it is not ordinarily expected that the collateral will be sold and that proceeds will result, [the drafters found it] appropriate to give the party having a purchase money security interest in the original collateral an equivalent priority in its proceeds." §9.312, Official U.C.C. Reasons for 1972 Change comment (3).

Howe's business primarily involved the sale of inventory, which included the Raytheon x-ray machines. See §9.109(4). The accounts receivable are proceeds resulting from the sale of the machines. MBank and DuPont took security interests in the accounts receivable, in accordance with their expectation that sale of the inventory would generate the accounts. If we were to accept Raytheon's argument that it holds a PMSI in Howe's accounts receivable, we would be giving Raytheon a priority interest in the proceeds of inventory, in direct contravention to the express intent of the drafters. Additionally, Raytheon would have successfully avoided the notice requirements of §9.312(c)(2).

Raytheon argues, however, that the policies underlying PMSIs actually favor recognizing Raytheon's priority interest in Howe's accounts. It points out that Howe could find no other source of financing besides Raytheon and that "MBank and DuPont benefited by the financing arrangements because the extension of [credit] by Raytheon helped Howe X-ray stay in business thereby servicing its debts." Raytheon also contends that if the Code is interpreted to limit the security interests of creditors, such as Raytheon, to a mere promise of repayment and the grant of a PMSI in inventory, a "valuable source of credit" to similarly encumbered debtors would "dry up." This is because the risk of default is too great in the face of prior liens on the debtor's accounts.

The Code itself, however, answers this argument. The drafters were apparently well aware that the failure to extend a PMSI holder's priority status to the resulting accounts would provide less incentive for inventory financiers to provide credit. See §9.312, 1972 Official U.C.C. Comment comment 8. Yet, they did not extend the protections of a PMSI and merely noted that "[m]any parties financing inventory are quite content to protect their first security interest in the inventory itself, realizing that when inventory is sold, someone else will be financing the accounts and the priority for inventory will not run forward to the accounts." Id. The drafter's recognition of the problem and the statutory favoring of accounts financing demonstrate that the drafters were not overly concerned that this source of financing would "dry up."

Additionally, Raytheon had alternative means of securing its right to receive payment. Besides obtaining a PMSI in the inventory by complying with the §9.312(c)(2) notice requirements, it could have entered subordination agreements with MBank and DuPont on the specific accounts resulting from the sale of Raytheon's x-ray machines. It also could have sold the machines to Howe's customers who would have paid Raytheon directly, with Howe receiving a commission on the sale. If Raytheon had followed either of these courses, it would not have subverted the notice and filing requirements of the Code. As this transaction goes beyond that contemplated by the PMSI provisions, we decline "to expand the scope of special protection afforded a purchase money security interest, lest in so doing we defeat the underlying purposes of the Code: to bring predictability to commercial transactions." Mark Prod. U.S., Inc. v. Interfirst Bank Houston, N.A., 737 S.W.2d 389, 393 (Tex.App.-- Houston [14th Dist.] 1987).

Since Raytheon did not have a PMSI in Howe's accounts receivable, the first-to-file priority rules govern. As the last to file, Raytheon's interest is subordinate to those of MBank and DuPont.

      * * *

C. Waiver

Lastly, Raytheon contends that the district court erred in holding that Raytheon failed to produce sufficient evidence that MBank waived its security interest in the accounts to overcome MBank's motion for summary judgment. To support its claim, Raytheon presented evidence that MBank was informed that Howe and Raytheon were engaged in ongoing credit negotiations and that Howe was assigning the accounts receivable to Raytheon. Additionally, while MBank was aware that it was not receiving full payment of Howe's accounts receivable, MBank never requested that the accounts proceeds be segregated or held in trust for the bank.

Waiver is a valid defense to an action to enforce a security interest. Weisbart & Co. v. First Nat'l Bank of Dalhart, Texas, 568 F.2d 391, 396 (5th Cir.1978); Montgomery v. Fuquay-Mouser, Inc., 567 S.W.2d 268, 270 (Tex.Civ.App.1978). Under Texas law, "[w]aiver is the intentional relinquishment of a known right or intentional conduct inconsistent with claiming it, with full knowledge of the material facts." Montgomery, 567 S.W.2d at 270.

Although Raytheon's evidence suggests that MBank knew about the assignment of the accounts receivable, the assignment alone did not interfere with MBank's rights, because any assignment would be subordinate to MBank's security interest. MBank's rights were not infringed until Raytheon collected the accounts receivable. To raise the issue of whether MBank intended to relinquish its security interest in the accounts receivable, Raytheon would at least have to present evidence that MBank knew Raytheon was collecting the accounts. Raytheon did not do so. The district court properly granted the motions for summary judgment. The judgments for MBank and DuPont are AFFIRMED.

Goldberg, Circuit Judge, dissenting:

What we confront today is another nettle in the thicket of the Texas Uniform Commercial Code. A thorny question of statutory interpretation that could cause scratch and abrasion if not reconnoitered under the illumination provided by the Texas Supreme Court. After examining the relevant statutes and commentaries, however, I believe that the majority has not construed the code as would the Texas Supreme Court in the face of the same problem. So because the scratch of a thorn may cause infection if not properly treated, I must respectfully DISSENT.

The nettle of this case is whether an account receivable should be considered "collateral" in the words of the purchase money security interest statute so that the purchase money interest has priority over a security interest previously perfected in an identical account. My belief is that accounts receivable are an appropriate form of collateral because they can be used to invigorate marginal businesses. I would thus hold that Raytheon established a purchase money security interest in the specified accounts of Howe x-ray.

I. THE FACTS

Both MBank and DuPont had loaned money to Howe, a dealer in medical equipment including expensive x-ray machines. To guard against the possibility that Howe would default on these loans, MBank, whose loan was made before DuPonts, perfected a security interest in Howe's accounts receivable then existing and subsequently arising and also perfected a similar security interest in Howe's inventory. DuPont's security interest was also perfected in Howe's accounts receivable then existing and subsequently arising but was filed after MBank's interest.

While the MBank/DuPont loans were outstanding, Raytheon entered into a series of transactions with Howe. Each transaction was executed according to a preexisting distribution agreement which allowed Howe to contract with customers for the sale of Raytheon x-ray machines. Under this agreement, Raytheon promised to supply an x-ray machine to Howe in exchange for Howe's promise to assign the account receivable that arose from the sale of the machine to Raytheon. Raytheon gave notice of its security interest in each account by filing a financing statement within the applicable 20 day period after the creation of the account. The structure of this agreement between Howe and Raytheon arose because Howe had begun to experience difficulty in obtaining additional financing and was spiraling down toward bankruptcy, its final fate.

II. DISCUSSION

Before I get involved in the details of Raytheon's purchase money security interest, however, a momentary step back is in order to scan the general landscape of security interests. As a general observation, the usual method for growth in the area of commercial law has been the daring creativity of a company pushing out beyond the boundaries of "normal practice" in response to business exigencies. The history of trust receipts, the factor's liens, and the eventual adoption of Article 9 of the Uniform Commercial Code illustrates this general observation in the area of security interests. See G. Gilmore, Security Interests in Personal Property, Ch. 1-8 (1965).

> "The idea which the draftsmen [of Article 9] started with was that the system of independent security devices [developed in different area of commerce] had served its time; that the formal differences which separated one device from another should be scrapped and replaced with the simple concept of a security interest in personal property; that all types of personal property, whether held for use or for sale, should be recognized as available for security."

Id. at 290. Article nine was thus intended to be a flexible statute that could respond to divergent commercial needs.

The facts of this case present exactly the type of problematic situation which demands a creative solution. Raytheon, as a manufacturer of expensive x-ray equipment, often does not seek out customers itself but instead uses local distributors such as Howe to make sales. But Howe had to borrow money for it to function as a merchant of medical equipment. MBank and DuPont provided this money protecting themselves by with security interests in the collateral Howe had available, Howe's present and future accounts receivable and inventory. This type of security interest in a borrower's intangibles such as accounts receivable is extremely common. The key to who has priority is to determine who filed the security interest in the collateral first. First in time, first in line goes the rhyme.

The problem with this situation is that a manufacturer will not loan or give a heavily indebted merchant any goods to sell on credit because once the merchant sells the goods, the banker, not the manufacturer, will have priority in the resulting accounts under the first in time first in line principle. Raytheon would thus not advance any x-ray machines to Howe because MBank and DuPont would have priority in any accounts that arose from the sale of the machines. Yet it is these very sales which would enable Howe to make profits to pay off its loans to MBank and DuPont. So how does an indebted merchant, who is unable to pay a manufacturer for goods that the merchant must sell to service the banker's loan, stay in business? Often what occurs is a scenario where the banker's loan is not paid, the merchant goes out of business, and the manufacturer loses an opportunity to distribute its goods on the market.

Article 9 provides a solution: the purchase money security interest. This device, with its root in the Railroad Car Trusts of the Nineteenth Century, has priority over security interests filed earlier because of its specific transaction oriented function. Id. at 743-53 (citing U.S. v. New Orleans R.R., 79 U.S. (12 Wall.) 362, 364-65, 20 L.Ed. 434 (1871) (pre Erie commercial case giving priority to the later in time party)). The purchase money security interest operates outside the notice principle which favors early interest holders over later ones. Notice is not the driving force behind the purchase money security interest.

It was this purchase money device that allowed Howe an opportunity to continue doing business to the benefit of MBank, DuPont and Raytheon. Howe did not have enough money to purchase a $140,000 x-ray machine for inventory but Raytheon would not advance a machine on credit to Howe. A creative alternative was necessary. Raytheon agreed to advance a machine to Howe in exchange for Howe's enforceable purchase order or account receivable. Raytheon thus used the account as a vehicle to ensure Howe's payment for the machine. It was a creative solution to the meeting of two creditors, a manufacturer of expensive equipment, and a heavily indebted retailer, that allowed commerce to continue to flow.

But for the law to recognize this creativity, it must be determined whether Raytheon has complied with the elements of the Texas purchase money security interest statute. Admittedly this arrangement does not present a paradigmatic purchase money security interest, but I believe that creativity, when in harmony with the statutory requirements, should be encouraged.

A. THE VALUE REQUIREMENT

Purchase money security interests are defined in section 9.107 of the Texas Uniform Commercial Code. Section 9.107, states, in pertinent part:

> A security interest is a "purchase money security interest" to the extent that it is ... (2) taken by a person who by making advances or incurring an obligation gives value to enable the debtor to acquire rights in or the use of collateral if such value is in fact so used.

Under the statute, Raytheon must satisfy three requirements. Raytheon must demonstrate that: (1) it gave value to Howe by making advances or incurring an obligation; (2) its extension of value enabled Howe to acquire rights in the collateral--the account receivable in each particular transaction; and, (3) the Texas U.C.C. recognizes an account receivable as collateral for the purposes of a purchase money security interest.

There is no question that Raytheon extended value. Raytheon gave value when it shipped, according to the purchase order, an x-ray machine that a particular customer had ordered. This interpretation of the value requirement is consistent with the definition of value as set out in section 1.201(44) of the Texas Uniform Commercial Code. Section 1.201(44) is applicable through the direction of the definitional cross reference of section 9.107. It states in pertinent part, that: "[a] person gives 'value' for rights if he acquires them ... (D) generally, in return for any consideration sufficient to support a simple contract." Raytheon satisfied section 1.201(44) because the advance of the x-ray machine in exchange for a promise from Howe to assign an accounts receivable arising from the sale of that x-ray machine is consideration sufficient to support a contract. Moreover, under section 9.107(2) itself, "'A secured party may give value by committing ... to supply goods or [by] actually supply[ing] the goods.'" Thet Mah and Associates Inc. v. First Bank of North Dakota, 336 N.W.2d 134, 138 (N.D.1983) (citing 1 Bender U.C.C. Service, Secured Transactions, section 4.05(4) p. 304 (1983).

This advance also satisfied the limitation on the type of value that may be given as defined in comment 2 of section 9.107. Comment 2 states, in pertinent part:

> "[t]his section ... provides that the purchase money party must be one who gives value 'by making advances or incurring an obligation': the quoted language excludes from the purchase money category any security interest taken as security for or in satisfaction of a preexisting claim or antecedent debt."

This antecedent debt limitation is satisfied here because Howe's debt to Raytheon was not preexisting but was instead created by the advance of the machine. Only then was Howe indebted to Raytheon for the machine's value. In turn, the debt was secured by the accounts receivable that Howe assigned to Raytheon pursuant to their agreement.

B. THE ENABLING REQUIREMENT

The second element of a purchase money security interest is the requirement that Raytheon give value "to enable" Howe to acquire rights in the particular account receivable. This requirement means that the advance made by Raytheon must have made it possible for Howe X-ray to obtain the collateral.

In the present case, the enabling requirement is satisfied because Raytheon's agreement with Howe, which preceded all of the particular transactions, was that Raytheon would advance an x-ray machine to Howe in exchange for an accounts receivable generated by Howe's sale of the machine to a customer. This preexisting agreement, together with the advance of the machine by Raytheon, enabled Howe to make the sale. At the same moment in time, in the twinkling of an eye, the sale created the particular account receivable payable to Howe which Howe then assigned to Raytheon pursuant to their preexisting agreement. "If the loan transaction appears closely allied to the purchase transaction, that should suffice. The evident intent of paragraph (b) [U.C.C. 9-107(b)] is to free the purchase-money concept from artificial limitations; rigid adherence to particular formalities and sequences should not be required." G. Gilmore, I Security Interests in Personal Property, 782 (1965).

C. THE COLLATERAL REQUIREMENT

The thorny question in this case centers on whether accounts receivable should be considered collateral for the purpose of a purchase money security interest under Section 9-107(b). To my mind, Raytheon has jumped this hurdle.[1]

---

[1]   MBank and DuPont argue that Raytheon does not have purchase money security interest in the accounts receivable of Howe. They contend that the proper way to characterize the transaction between Raytheon and Howe is to view Raytheon as having advanced credit to Howe. This credit, the argument continues, allowed Howe to purchase inventory from Raytheon in the form of the x-ray machine. Thus, according to MBank and DuPont, the x-ray machine served as collateral to secure the advance of the credit from Raytheon. Howe then sold the x-ray machines to its customers. The sales created accounts receivable which Howe assigned to Raytheon. The implication of MBank and DuPont's characterization of the transaction between Raytheon and Howe is that MBank and DuPont have priority in the accounts receivable over Raytheon because Raytheon would not be able to claim a valid purchase money security interest. Raytheon would not be able to claim a purchase money security interest under section 9.312(d) because this section requires that the interest be taken in collateral other than inventory. Section 9.312(d) states that "A purchase money security interest in collateral other than inventory has priority over a conflicting security interest in the same collateral or its proceeds if the purchase money security interest is perfected at the time the debtor receives possession of

Under section 9.105(a)(3), which is listed in the definitional cross references of section 9.107, collateral is defined as "the property subject to a security interest and includes accounts and chattel paper which have been sold...." Moreover, under section 9.106, which is also listed in the definitional cross references of section 9.107, "[a]ccount means any right to payment for goods sold or leased or for services rendered which is not evidenced by an instrument or chattel paper, whether or not it has been earned by performance." The comment to 9.106 states that the section is referring to "ordinary commercial accounts receivable." By reading these two definitional sections in tandem, it is clear that an account receivable can be collateral for the purposes of a purchase money security interest under section 9.107.

There is, however, no other authority to our knowledge that expressly states that accounts receivable should be considered collateral for the purpose of a purchase money security interest. The Supreme Court of Minnesota has suggested that a purchase money security interest in accounts could validly arise. See Northwestern National Bank Southwest v. Lectro Systems, 262 N.W.2d 678, 680 (Minn.1977) ("This is not a case in which funds were advanced and used for purchase of a receivable."). And, Professor Grant Gilmore, one of the original drafters of article 9, has stated in his treatise on security interests, that the purchase money concept might apply to intangible property in occasional cases.

---

the collateral or within 20 days thereafter." Raytheon would thus have to claim a purchase money security interest under another section because according to MBank and DuPont, the collateral in the transaction was inventory. The purchase money security interest would have to be justified under section 9.312(c) which applies to purchase money security interests in inventory. Section 9.312(c)(2) requires "the purchase money secured party [to give] notification in writing to the holder of conflicting security interests if the holder has filed a financing statement covering the same type of inventory." Raytheon, however, failed to give any notice to MBank or DuPont and could not, therefore, establish a valid purchase money security interest under this section. Because Raytheon would be precluded from claiming a purchase money security interest under section 9.312(c) or section 9.312(d), MBank and DuPont would have priority over Raytheon in the accounts receivable of Howe under section 9.312(e). Section 9.312(e) states that "conflicting security interests rank according to priority in time of filing or perfection." Therefore, because both MBank and DuPont filed notice of their claims prior to Raytheon, they would have superior interests under section 9.312(e). This analysis, however, suggested by MBank and DuPont begs the question. The question is whether Raytheon established a purchase money security interest in the accounts receivable of Howe not whether Raytheon properly perfected a purchase money security interest in the inventory of Howe. The analysis of whether Raytheon properly perfected a security interest in the inventory of Howe assumes that MBank and DuPont's characterization of the transaction is correct. But the very question to be decided is how to characterize the transaction for the purposes of defining a purchase money security interest. Nothing in the code mandates that Raytheon to claim a purchase money security interest in Howe's inventory. Raytheon claimed a purchase money security interest in the accounts receivable of Howe. The question is thus whether accounts receivable may be considered collateral for the purposes of a purchase money security interest.

G. Gilmore, I Security Interests in Personal Property, 781 (1965) ("There seems to be no reason, however, why the term 'collateral' should have other than its normal meaning: the purchase-money concept may thus, in an occasional case, apply to intangible property....").

MBank and DuPont have asserted that accounts receivable should not be considered collateral for the purpose of defining a purchase money security interest under Section 9.107(2). Their argument, adopted by the majority, is that because accounts receivable financing has been accorded a special importance by the Texas Uniform Commercial Code, its legal position should not be made less certain by the operation of Sections 9.107(2) and 9.312(d). Once a security interest has been created under section 9.107(2), section 9.312(d) grants it special status. Section 9.312(d) states that "a purchase money security interest in collateral other than inventory has priority over a conflicting security interest in the same collateral or its proceeds if the purchase money security interest is perfected at the time the debtor receives possession of the collateral or within 20 days thereafter."

The significance of this special priority granted to purchase money security interests in subsection (2) becomes apparent when compared to the general priority rule in section 9.312(e). Under section 9.312(e)(1), conflicting security interests in the same collateral rank according to the time of filing. The first party to file notice of its interest in an account has priority over any subsequently filed interests in the identical account.

Because of the operation of section 9.312(d), however, the first party to file notice of a security interest in an account would not necessarily have priority under section 9.312(e)(1). Section 9.312(d) would grant priority over any interest filed previously in the same account if purchase money status in the account was first established under section 9.107. The legal position of accounts receivable financing might thus be made less certain if a purchase money security interest could be claimed in accounts receivable under section 9.107(2). Diminished certainty could result in the sense that the first party to file notice of its interest in an account under section 9.312(e) would be uncertain as to whether it had priority in the account or whether another party has priority because the latter established purchase money status in the same account under 9.107(2).

MBank and DuPont argue that this uncertainty in the legal position of accounts receivable financing should be prohibited because of the special importance accorded to accounts receivable financing under the code. They find this importance in the history of section 9.312(c) which prohibits the establishment of purchase money security interests in accounts receivable, derivatively, as proceeds of inventory. The argument points out that this prohibition was created due to the importance of accounts receivable financing in the economy. Based on these premises, the argument concludes that the possibility of a purchase money security interest in accounts receivable under section 9.107(2) should also be prohibited. The fallacy of this logic, however, is that it equates the value of accounts receivable as applied to a problem that arose in the area of inventory financing with the values behind the section 9.107 purchase money security interest.

The argument thus rests upon MBank and DuPont's interpretation of section 9.312(c). Section 9.312(c) provides that "a perfected purchase money security interest in inventory has priority over a conflicting security interest in the same inventory and also has priority in any identifiable cash proceeds received on or before the delivery of inventory to a buyer." This section of the code was changed in 1972 to address the problem of priority conflicts between a claim to accounts receivable derivatively as proceeds of inventory and a claim to the accounts established by the filing of a direct security interest. The conflict arose between inventory financiers who claimed priority in the accounts as proceeds of the inventory that they helped the debtor to acquire and lenders who had taken a direct security interest in the accounts as collateral for money loaned to the debtor.

Section 9.312(c) offered a solution to this conflict. It states that a prior right to the inventory of a debtor does not confer a prior right to any proceeds that arise from the sale of the inventory except for identifiable cash proceeds. There is no prior right to accounts receivable as proceeds from the sale of the inventory. Under this section, it would not be possible to establish a purchase money security interest in inventory and then claim a purchase money security interest in any of the accounts that arose from the sale of that inventory. This exclusion of accounts receivable as proceeds of inventory under section 9.312(c) rests upon the assumption that accounts receivable financing is more important in the economy than the financing of the types of inventory that produce accounts when sold.

MBank and DuPont thus argue that a purchase money security interest in accounts receivable should not be permitted under section 9.107(2) because a purchase money security interest in accounts receivable may not be claimed derivatively as proceeds of the sale of inventory under section 9.312(c). However, when this argument is examined in light of the policy interests underpinning section 9.107(2), the argument's core assumption, the importance of accounts receivable financing in the economy, dictates precisely the opposite result.

The most important policy justification for a purchase money security interest under section 9.107(2) is the protection that it gives to a debtor who is unable to raise additional funds to remain in business. Creditors who have previously loaned money to the debtor and taken a security interest in the debtor's goods may be unwilling to advance additional value or funds. These additional funds, however, could enable a debtor to purchase goods, make sales, and in turn, generate profits. Profits which could not only be used to create more business, but also, to allow the debtor to pay off the creditor's loans. The purchase money security provisions thus enable a leveraged debtor who is able to find a new lender to give that new lender a first claim on the new collateral purchased notwithstanding a prior filing by another creditor.

The arrangement between Raytheon and Howe exemplifies the use of accounts receivable to advance the policy rationale behind the purchase money security interest. It was the use of the accounts receivable by Raytheon as collateral for the x-ray machines that allowed Howe to continue to do business. The additional business that Howe was able to generate with the advance of the x-ray machines, at minimum, gave Howe an additional opportunity to stay in business. This opportunity was a benefit to creditors such as MBank and DuPont whose loans would not be repaid unless Howe had the ability to generate profits. It also demonstrated the importance of accounts receivable financing in another forum, the creation of purchase money security interests.

The use of accounts receivable as collateral in this case benefited MBank and DuPont as creditors because the consequences of an unpaid account were relatively greater to Raytheon. Raytheon, MBank and DuPont would each have been harmed if Howe's customers failed to pay their accounts. If an account receivable were to remain unpaid, Raytheon would lose the entire value of the x-ray machine advanced to Howe. In contrast, it is unlikely that the failure of one account would drive Howe into bankruptcy so that Howe would be unable to repay MBank and DuPont. Yet it is this additional risk taken by Raytheon which allowed Howe a profit that could be used to fund its business to the advantage of MBank and DuPont.

Finally, any obligation imposed on MBank and DuPont to determine whether Howe was using its accounts receivable to collateralize purchase money security transactions is diminished in two respects. First, as stated, it is these very purchase money transactions that allowed Howe an additional opportunity to service its debts to these creditors. Second, MBank and DuPont as creditors had already established relationships with Howe. In future transactions, it would not have been difficult for them to ascertain whether Howe was using any accounts to collateralize purchase money transactions with other creditors and draft the loan contracts accordingly.

D. THE LIMIT OF RAYTHEON'S PURCHASE MONEY SECURITY INTEREST

I would, however, posit a serious limit on the extent of Raytheon's purchase money security interest. Under section 9.107, a security interest has purchase money character only to the extent of the value given to acquire the collateral. In the present case, the value given by Raytheon was the price of the x-ray machine as measured by the difference in the price Howe charged customers and the price Raytheon charged Howe. This price measures the extent of Raytheon's purchase money security interest in the specific accounts receivable of Howe. I do not mean to imply that the value given to a distributor such as Howe will always be measured by the wholesale price. In some situations, it could be the retail price depending upon what the debtor was meant to gain by the transaction. I would leave these transactional details for the district court.

The difference between the price Raytheon charged Howe and the price Howe charged its customers would thus not be a part of Raytheon's purchase money security interest. There is evidence to the effect that Howe used a portion of this difference, Howe's profit margin, to pay a preexisting debt owing from Howe to Raytheon. This money could not be a part of Raytheon's purchase money security interest because a purchase money security interest may not be used to secure a preexisting debt.

There is also evidence which suggests that Raytheon may have loaned money to Howe to cover Howe's costs of installing the x-ray machine. Any such money would not be a part of Raytheon's purchase money security interest. There should not be any additional opportunities created under the code to give simple loans purchase money character.

To my mind, Raytheon has established a valid purchase money security interest under section 9.107(2) of the Texas Uniform Commercial Code. The x-ray machine advanced by Raytheon constituted the value that enabled Howe to acquire accounts receivable, the collateral, for the purposes of section 9.107(2). As such, this case should be reversed and remanded, where the issue of waiver could be examined with a headlight's incandescence and the retroactivity issue appropriately explored. I therefore respectfully DISSENT.

First National Bank v. Associated Stockdale Companies
Appellate Court of Illinois, Third District, 1991
160 Ill.Dec. 394, 217 Ill.App.3d 384, 577 N.E.2d 524

Justice Gorman delivered the opinion of the court: The plaintiff, First National Bank of Joliet, brought an action for declaratory judgment against the defendant, Associated Stockdale Companies, Inc. (Stockdale), seeking a declaration of whose perfected security interest in certain crops was entitled to priority. The circuit court entered a declaratory judgment in favor of the bank. Stockdale now appeals. We affirm.

Lyle Hecht, Kimberly Hecht, Edward Hecht, and Alice Hecht signed a security agreement dated June 1, 1983, giving the bank a security interest in crops growing or to be grown on specified parcels of land in Grundy County. The security interest was given to secure the payment of any and all indebtedness of Edward and Lyle Hecht to the bank, whether then existing or thereafter arising. On June 29, 1983, the bank filed with the recorder of deeds of Grundy County a financing statement noting the debtors, the secured party, and the collateral that had been the subject of the security agreement. (A continuation of this financing statement was filed on March 4, 1988.)

The Hechts signed two promissory notes dated August 22, 1985, with the bank as payee. Both notes were renewals of previously existing indebtedness, and both were due and payable on February 22, 1986. The principal amounts of the notes were $159,000 and $416,684.83. (The record indicates that the indebtedness represented by these notes has never been satisfied.)

Stockdale sold to the Hechts fertilizer and other supplies needed for production of the 1986 crops. It sold these supplies on open account between November 18, 1985, and June 23, 1986. On October 3, 1986, Stockdale obtained a security agreement from Lyle Hecht granting it a security interest in the 1986 crops to secure payment of the indebtedness for the supplies. A financing statement was duly filed with the recorder of deeds of Grundy County by Stockdale on October 6, 1986.

The Hechts planted their cash crops between April 25, 1986, and May 19, 1986.

On March 18, 1987, the bank brought this declaratory judgment action to determine whose security interest in the Hechts' 1986 crops was superior, its or Stockdale's. The bank and Stockdale had previously agreed to hold in escrow some of the proceeds from the sale of the Hechts' 1986 crops, with disposition of that sum to depend on the outcome of the declaratory judgment action. The bank and Stockdale entered into a stipulation of facts. Based on that stipulation and after considering the written briefs and arguments of the parties, the circuit court decided that the bank's security interest was superior, and entered judgment accordingly.

The sole issue presented is whether section 9-312(2) of the Uniform Commercial Code gives Stockdale's perfected security interest in the Hechts' 1986 crops priority over the bank's perfected security interest in those crops.

Section 9-312(2) of the Uniform Commercial Code states as follows:

"A perfected security interest in crops for new value given to enable the debtor to produce the crops during the production season and given not more than three months before the crops become growing crops by planting or otherwise takes priority over an earlier perfected security interest to the extent that such earlier interest secures obligations due more than six months before the crops become growing crops by planting or otherwise, even though the person giving new value had knowledge of the earlier security interest."

Stockdale argues that in order to give this provision any practical effect, the time when an "obligation" is deemed "due" ought to be the time when value is originally given to the debtor whereby the debtor incurs the obligation. Stockdale argues that the term "obligations" in this provision should not be interpreted to include promissory notes merely embodying antecedent debts. Stockdale reasons that since the original indebtedness to the bank (that eventually became embodied in the promissory notes) had been incurred long before six months prior to the planting of the 1986 crops, Stockdale's security interest for supplies provided in the three- month period prior to planting has priority over the bank's security interest for indebtedness represented by the promissory notes.

Stockdale argues alternatively that "due" should simply be interpreted as "due and owing" rather than "due and payable." Stockdale reasons that since the bank's promissory notes were "due and owing" on August 22, 1985, more than six months before the 1986 crops were planted, Stockdale's security interest for supplies provided in the three-month period prior to planting has priority over the bank's security interest for indebtedness represented by the promissory notes.

A number of Federal and sister state cases have applied section 9-312(2) of the Uniform Commercial Code, and have consistently interpreted the term "due" therein as meaning "overdue." In Decatur Production Credit Association v. Murphy (1983), 119 Ill.App.3d 277, 74 Ill.Dec. 765, 456 N.E.2d 267, the appellate court implicitly adopted the position that the term "due" in section 9-312(2) means "overdue." None of these opinions discusses the purposes the drafters of section 9-312(2) sought to achieve by this section, and the present parties do not present any authority to shed light on why the drafters chose the words they chose.

We recognize that if "due" in section 9-312(2) means "overdue," that section gives less benefit to farmers seeking crop production financing (and those wishing to provide such financing) than if "due" means "due and owing." While previously secured lenders are placed at great advantage in this situation, farmers are not without business options to counter an unscrupulous lender in most instances. On the other hand, a contrary interpretation would probably make it harder to get credit in the first instance, and would probably require lenders to be more aggressive in enforcing their rights in collateral and in doing so at an earlier time. In short, we see no happy medium interpretation here, and no particular policy reason to interpret the term one way or the other.

Given that courts have consistently interpreted "due" in section 9-312(2) as meaning "overdue," that the legislature has not seen fit to amend this provision at any time since it was first adopted in 1962, that there has been no showing that the drafters of this provision had a purpose for it inconsistent with this interpretation, and that the drafters could have easily chosen another word (such as "created") to make clear a contrary interpretation, the trial court correctly interpreted "due" as meaning "overdue" in this provision.

Since the due dates of the bank's promissory notes at issue fell within the six month period prior to the planting of the Hechts' 1986 crops, Stockdale cannot claim that its security interest has priority over that of the bank by virtue of section 9-312(2). As no other basis for priority has been argued by Stockdale, the general priority rule of section 9-312(5)(a) (Ill.Rev.Stat.1985, ch. 26, par. 9-312(5)(a)) applies. This rule, as applied to the facts of the present case, gives priority to the security interest of the first of two secured creditors to file a financing statement covering the collateral. Since the bank filed its financing statement earlier than did Stockdale, the trial court did not err in entering its declaratory judgment in favor of the bank.

Affirmed.

First National Bank v. Bostron

Colorado Court of Appeals, 1977
39 Colo.App. 107, 564 P.2d 964

Sternberg, Judge. The issues presented by this appeal are whether, under the Uniform Commercial Code, a perfected security interest in feed survives after consumption of the feed by cattle in which the secured party has no interest, and if so, whether the secured party is entitled to any of the proceeds from the sale of these cattle. We answer these questions in the negative and therefore affirm the judgment of the trial court.

One Eldon Weiss owned a ranch on which he raised cattle and feed crops. As a separate and distinct part of this operation Weiss entered into a joint venture with the defendant, Reinhold Bostron, under which Bostron was to supply the money and Weiss the labor necessary to raise Holstein heifers. The heifers were purchased by Bostron and Weiss with money borrowed from the plaintiff, First National Bank of Brush, which retained a perfected purchase money security interest in the animals. The Bostron-Weiss joint venture cattle were segregated from other cattle on the Weiss ranch. Feed for all the cattle, however, was commingled and fed to the animals Weiss owned individually and to those owned by the Bostron-Weiss joint venture. Intervenor, Colorado High Plains Agricultural Credit Corporation, held a perfected security interest given by Weiss, individually, in, among other things, "all feed now owned or hereafter acquired, all crops now growing or to be grown, proceeds and products of collateral."

The cattle raised by the joint venture were eventually sold at a loss, and consequently, even after paying most of the proceeds from the sale to First National Bank of Brush, there was a deficiency owing that bank. None of the proceeds from the sale of the Bostron-Weiss cattle were paid to the intervenor.

Plaintiff bank sued Weiss and Bostron to recover the remaining balance of the loan, and Colorado High Plains intervened claiming an interest in any recovery which the bank might obtain against Bostron. Weiss was adjudicated a bankrupt and proceedings against him in this action were stayed. Since the intervenor's security interest attached only to the feed owned by Weiss, its right of recovery, if any, from Bostron must be premised on the benefit which Bostron individually received from the joint venture as a result of the Weiss feed being fed to the joint venture cattle.

The provisions of the Uniform Commercial Code--Secured Transactions, §4--9--101, et seq., C.R.S.1973, govern this case. Section 4--9--315, C.R.S.1973, provides:

"(1) If a security interest in goods was perfected and subsequently the goods or a part thereof have become part of a product or mass, the security interest continues in the product or mass if: (a) The goods are so manufactured, processed, assembled, or commingled that their identity is lost in the product or mass; or (b) A financing statement covering the original goods also covers the product into which the goods have been manufactured, processed or assembled.

In light of the wording of this section, we conclude that cattle are neither a "product" nor a "mass" as these terms are used in the statute. The reference in subsection (a) to "manufactured, processed, assembled, or commingled" precludes any other interpretation. The feed which the cattle ate did not undergo any of these transformations, that is, it was not manufactured, processed, assembled or commingled with the cattle. Cattle consume food as motor vehicles do gasoline. Once eaten the feed not only loses its identity, but in essence it ceases to exist and thus does not become part of the mass in the sense that the code uses the phrase. Section 4--9--315, C.R.S.1973 (Comment 3), makes this evident: "This section applies not only to cases where flour, sugar and eggs are commingled into cake mix or cake, but also to cases where components are assembled into a machine." Feed as consumed by cattle is distinguishable from this notion of accession which the code's drafters visualized.

Moreover, since the financing statement did not specifically cover the product "into which the goods have been manufactured, processed or assembled" the language of §4--9--315(1)(b), C.R.S.1973, does not support intervenor's claim.

Relying on §4--9--306, C.R.S.1973, intervenor next contends that the cattle are proceeds of the feed as that term is defined in that portion of the code. * * * This contention also is unavailing for several reasons. First, the trial court found that the intervenor lost its interest in the proceeds because it authorized the disposition of its collateral, I.e., the feed, by Weiss to the Bostron-Weiss joint venture. See Farmers National Bank v. Ceres Land Co., 32 Colo.App. 290, 512 P.2d 1174 (1973). This finding is supported by evidence in the record and therefore is dispositive. However, we also conclude that even if the intervenor had not authorized the use of the feed subject to its security interest by the joint venture, nevertheless intervenor's interest still would not have survived its consumption by the cattle.

Weiss Received nothing when he disposed of the collateral by feeding it to the joint venture cattle. As noted in our discussion of §4--9--315, C.R.S.1973, the collateral was consumed, and there are no traceable proceeds to which the security interest may be said to have attached. To interpret §4--9--306, C.R.S.1973, as intervenor urges would extend the security interest of one in the position of the intervenor to the parts of the butchered animal, into the supermarket, and ultimately into the hands of the consumers. We cannot attribute such legislative intent to the General Assembly when it adopted this section of the UCC.

Intervenor's final contention is that by §4--9--307(1), C.R.S.1973, it had an interest in the cattle which ate the feed. * * *

Assuming, without deciding, that the joint venture was a buyer in the ordinary course of business from Weiss, a cursory reading of this portion of the code would suggest, as intervenor asserts, that its security interest continues into the cattle. However, the joint venture did not sell the feed; rather, it sold the cattle to which it was fed. As previously noted, in our analysis of §4--9--315, C.R.S.1973, the collateral in which the security interest was initially taken is, after having been fed to the cattle, non-existent, and thus buyers of the cattle cannot reasonably be equated with buyers of the feed in which there exists a security interest.

In summary then, we hold that a security interest in feed does not in and of itself extend to the cattle which eat that feed by application of §4--9--315, C.R.S.1973, nor do cattle which eat the feed constitute proceeds of the collateral by application of §4--9--306, C.R.S.1973. We hold further that under the facts here, §4--9--307(1), C.R.S.1973 does not extend the security interest in the feed after its ingestion by the cattle.

Judgment affirmed.

Problems

1. SP-1 finances D's farming operation. Loans to D are covered by a security agreement giving SP-1 a security interest in all of D's farm machinery and other equipment, including after-acquired such property. SP-1 has properly filed a financing statement. D buys a new farm tractor on credit from SP-2 who retains a security interest in the goods.

   a. Who wins priority if SP-2 perfects by filing before delivering the tractor to D?

   b. Ah-Ne-Pee Dimensional Hardwood, Inc. (Hardwood) manufactures wood products. In the late 1970s, Hardwood began operating from a facility in Ogema, Wisconsin. In the late 1980s, Hardwood decided to expand its operations and open a second facility in Michigan. The new facility was financed by a $200,000 loan from Miners State Bank, a $625,000 loan from the Township, and $125,000 of owner equity.

   On January 20, 1989, Miners State Bank loaned Hardwood $200,000 in exchange for a Promissory Note. The Promissory Note was secured by a mortgage on real property located in the Township of Stambaugh, Michigan. On January 26, 1989, the mortgage was recorded. Additionally, the Promissory Note was secured by a Security Interest in equipment and personal property located at the Michigan facility. The Security Interest included an after-acquired property clause and a future advances clause. That Security Interest was perfected by filing Financing Statements with the Michigan Secretary of State on February 6, 1989, March 7, 1989, and

September 25, 1989. The Township contends that Hardwood used the loan proceeds for building renovations and as a down payment on equipment.

On September 22, 1989, the Township loaned defendant Hardwood $625,000 in exchange for a Promissory Note. This loan was made pursuant to the United States Department of Urban Development's Economic Development Implementation Grant. The Promissory Note was secured by a Mortgage on the same real property as the Promissory Note given to Miners State Bank. Miners State Bank agreed to subordinate its interest in the real property to the Township's interest. In addition, this Promissory Note was secured by an interest in all tangible and intangible personal property and fixtures located at the Michigan facility. However, unlike the real property mortgage, the Township did not obtain a subordination of Miners State Bank's Security Interest in the personal property. Like the Miners State Bank's Security Interest, the Township's Security Interest also contained an after-acquired property and future advances clauses. The Township's Security Interest was perfected by filing a Financing Statement with the Michigan Secretary of State on October 12, 1989--after Miners State Bank filed its Financing Statements.

The Township contends that Hardwood purchased a majority of its equipment shortly after Hardwood received the $625,000 loan from the Township.

In the summer of 1991, Hardwood was acquired by ANP Acquisition Corporation, a corporation wholly owned by Andrew Hunter and Robert Keith.

On July 8, 1991, Miners State Bank assigned its interest in its Promissory Note, Mortgage, and Security Agreement to defendant ANP Dimensional Lumber Michigan, Inc. (Lumber), a subsidiary of Dimensional Lumber Holdings--another corporation wholly owned by Andrew Hunter and Robert Keith. Miners State Bank received $159,933.78 as compensation for the assignment. On July 10, 1991, this assignment was recorded. Dimensional Lumber Holdings earlier had purchased a note secured by equipment and personal property located at the Wisconsin facility.

The Township contends that Hardwood stopped making payments on the $625,000 Promissory Note after June 1991. The Township claims that defendant Hardwood is in default on the $625,000 Promissory Note because no one has made payments pursuant to the terms of the Note. As of March 23, 1992, $579,114.84 of principal and $41,840.40 of interest was owed on the Note.

In June 1991, Lumber executed a $500,000 note with Hardwood secured by Hardwood assets and real property. In July 1991, Lumber executed an additional $300,000 note secured by the January 20, 1989, security agreement between Hardwood and Miners State Bank. The July 1991 note was later increased to $800,000. Robert Keith claims that the money was loaned to pay Hardwood's vendors. The then president of Hardwood, Geron Verville, does not remember any consideration being exchanged for the note, and he stated that Lumber was funneling money through Hardwood to increase the amount of its security interest.

On March 26, 1992, the Township filed this lawsuit against defendant Hardwood seeking this Court to adjudge a foreclosure and sale of the mortgaged property to satisfy the Hardwood obligations to the Township. The Township also seeks a judicial determination against Hardwood as to who has priority in the personal property. The Township argues that it has a purchase money security interest in the equipment purchased shortly after extending the loan to Hardwood. The Township also seeks an order from this Court restraining both defendants from removing property from the premises located in Stambaugh, Michigan.

On September 30, 1992, the Township filed a Motion for Summary Judgment. On October 1, 1992, defendant Lumber filed a Motion for Partial Summary Judgment. *Township of Stambaugh v. AN-NE-PEE Dimensional Hardwood, Inc.*, 841 F. Supp. 803 (W.D. Mich. 1993). How would you rule?

c. Darrell D. Moyer and Community National executed a promissory note, security agreement, and financing statement. The loan proceeds of the promissory note were used to purchase a 1982 International Harvester planter described in the security agreement and financing statement. Community National held a purchase money security interest in the planter and attempted to perfect its interest by filing the financing statement with the Neosho County Register of Deeds on May 12, 1989, rather than with the Kansas Secretary of State. This filing was made in good faith.

Home State Bank held a prior perfected blanket security interest in Moyer's equipment by virtue of two promissory notes, a security agreement dated April 20, 1987, and a financing statement dated September 9, 1986, filed with the Secretary of State. Home State Bank was granted judgment on December 17, 1990, against Moyer for a total sum of $117,105.86. Home State was also granted a judgment foreclosing its security interest in the planter purchased with the loan from Community National. Pursuant to its judgment, Home State Bank sold the collateral securing its indebtedness.

Community National filed a financing statement covering its interest in the planter with the Secretary of State on January 8, 1991. The district court granted judgment in favor of Community National against Moyer for $5,776.82 and also issued an order allowing Community National to foreclose its security interest in the planter or the proceeds from its sale.

The district court found that although Community National's first filing of the financing statement with the Neosho County Register of Deeds was improper because it was in the wrong place, it was effective pursuant to K.S.A.1991 Supp. 84-9-401(2) against the competing prior perfected blanket security interest held by Home State Bank. The court's rationale in awarding Community National priority was that Ray Withers, an officer of Home State Bank, had knowledge of the contents of Community National's financing statement from a Credit Bulletin dated May 15, 1989, and a telephone discussion with Ron Sheddrick, a Community National officer, occurring the week of May 22, 1989. Because Home State Bank sold the planter on January 26, 1991, received proceeds of $4,450, and paid none to Community National, the district court granted Community National a judgment of $4,450 plus costs.

On appeal, Home State contends the trial court incorrectly interpreted K.S.A.1991 Supp. 84-9-401(2). * * * There appear to be no Kansas cases on the relation of 84-9-401(2) to purchase money security interests (PMSI). *Community Nat'l Bank v. Moyer*, 17 Kan.App.2d 218, 836 P.2d 1198 (1992). How should the appeal be decided?

2. SP-1 finances D's farm machinery dealership. The parties have executed a security agreement covering D's inventory, present and after-acquired. SP-1's interest is perfected by filing. D orders two new high-performance tractors from the manufacturer, SP-2. D and SP-2 agree to defer payment of the purchase price, but D's obligation to pay is secured by SP-2 retaining a security interest in the tractors. SP-2 clearly has a purchase money security interest. Before delivering the tractors to D, SP-2 files a proper financing statement in the proper place. What else, if anything, is required for SP-2 to win priority?

3. D borrowed money from two banks to finance the purchase of very expensive equipment. Both banks filed financing statements: National Bank filed before D took delivery of the equipment. State Bank filed on the day the seller delivered the equipment to D. Which bank has priority?

4. D is a widget manufacturer. Bank is D's principal financer and enjoys an earlier perfected security interest in all of D's property, present and after-acquired. S supplies services or components, on credit, that are essential to the production of the widgets that D manufacturers. S is secured by a later perfected security interest in all of the widgets that D produces. Can S rely on 9-312(3) for priority? On 9-314 or 9-315?

5. [I]n 1984, farmer owes lender $250,000, to be satisfied by installment payments spread over the next ten years. Also in 1984, as partial security for the debt, farmer gives lender an Article 9 security interest in the farmer's present and after-acquired crops. Lender properly files a financing statement covering all the farmer's crops. In 1986, the farmer plants a corn crop using $80,000 worth of seed and other goods and services acquired on credit from supplier, to whom the farmer gives a security interest in the corn. Supplier properly files. Within three months after the supplier first extends credit, the crops begin to grow, and several months later the farmer reaps a bountiful harvest worth $125,000. At about this point the lender accelerates the balance of the farmer's $250,000 debt and claims the crops as after-acquired collateral.

The lender wins the priority dispute with the supplier under the first-to- file-or-perfect rule of section 9-312(5)(a). Under this rule the nature of the debt to the lender is irrelevant, and the extent of the lender's priority is measured by the total amount of the unpaid obligation secured by the crops. Section 9-312(2) does not aid the supplier because, as conventionally interpreted, it is completely useless against an earlier perfected interest securing a debt of any kind to the extent the debt is freshly due within or after the six-month period before the crops started to grow. If none of the debt underlying the earlier interest was overdue when the six-month period commenced, section 9-312(2), as currently construed, is altogether inapplicable. The supplier's enabling security interest is thus wholly subordinate, notwithstanding that the earlier secured party contributed nothing to the production of the current crop. If part of the debt securing the earlier interest was overdue at the beginning of the six-month period, the crop production secured party gets a limited priority. That is, the supplier receives priority with respect to the then overdue portion of the debt securing the earlier interest. The crop production secured party wins total priority only if all of the debt securing the earlier interest was overdue at the beginning of the six-month period before the crops started to grow, and only if no new debt was created during the period." Steve H. Nickles, *Setting Farmers Free: Righting the Unintended Anomaly of U.C.C. §9-312(2)*, 71 MINN. L. REV. 1135, 1186-88 (1987).

6. D is a rancher. Bank has a perfected security interest in all of D's cattle. S supplies feed on credit and retains a security interest in the goods. As additional security S also has a later perfected security interest in D's cattle. The cattle eat the feed and grow. Nevertheless, S's security interest in the cattle is entirely subordinate to Bank's interest.   Please explain.

c. Proceeds

"The [secured] party who may have had a prior security interest in inventory [or other collateral] or may have had the only such security interest does not automatically for that reason have priority as to the accounts [or other proceeds resulting from the original collateral]. His claim to accounts [or other proceeds] may or may not have priority over competing filed claims to accounts [or other proceeds]. The priority is based on precedence as to the accounts [or other proceeds] under the rules stated in *** [U.C.C. §§9-306 and 9-312]." U.C.C. §9-312 comment 4.

In other words, when the property in dispute is proceeds, priority as to the original collateral does not always automatically carry over to proceeds of the property. A fresh analysis is ordinarily required applying Article 9's priority and perfection rules directly to the proceeds themselves because the conflict involves the proceeds as collateral, not the property that produced the proceeds.

Problems

7. SP-1 and SP-2 have nonpurchase-money security interests in D's inventory. The two interests are perfected by filing. SP-1 filed first. The security agreements and financing statements of both secured parties are limited to inventory. D disposes of the collateral through sales to customers. The proceeds consist primarily of cash, accounts, and chattel paper. SP-1 and SP-2 both claim the proceeds and disagree on whose claim is entitled to priority. Who wins the dispute? See U.C.C. §§9-306(1)-(3); 9-312(5)(a) & (6).

8. Same facts as Problem 7, except that the security agreements and financing statements of both secured parties covered all of the debtor's personal property.

9. Same facts as Problem 7, except that the original collateral is equipment rather than inventory.

10. SP-1 makes a loan to D who signs a security agreement covering all her equipment, present and after-acquired. SP-1 immediately files a financing statement containing an identical description of collateral. Thereafter, D buys equipment on credit from SP-2 who retains a security interest in the property and perfects by filing on the same day the equipment is delivered to D. D eventually sells this piece of equipment on credit to B who signs a simple contract evidencing her agreement to pay the balance of the price within a year. Both SP-1 and SP-2 claim the account as proceeds of the equipment. See U.C.C. §9-312(4).

11. Same facts as Problem 10, except that the original collateral is inventory rather than equipment. See U.C.C. §9-312(3).

12. Same as Problem 11, except that D buys more inventory with the money that SP-2 paid D for the receivables SP-2 bought from D.

6. Negotiable Paper Collateral

Exceptional priority rules apply to certain intangible personalty that by other law is negotiable, meaning that a transferee, under certain circumstances and upon certain conditions, acquires rights greater than her transferor and cuts off all prior claims to the property. We refer here to negotiable paper of various kinds: money; Article 3 instruments, Article 7 negotiable documents of title, and Article 8 securities.

The common law has long recognized the negotiability of money and its equivalent. More than 200 hundred years ago, in *Miller v. Race*, 97 Eng. Rep. 398 (K.B. 1758), Lord Mansfield declared the negotiability of an English bank note that served as paper currency:

> Now they are not goods, not securities, nor documents for debts, nor are so esteemed: but are treated as money, as cash, in the ordinary course and transaction of business, by the general consent of mankind; which gives them the credit and currency of money, to all intents and purposes. They are as much money, as guineas themselves are; or any other current coin, that is used in common payments, as money or cash.

> * * * It has been quaintly said, "that the reason why money can not be followed is, because it has no ear-mark:" but this is not true. The true reason is, upon account of the currency of it: it can not be recovered after it has passed in currency. So, in case of money stolen, the true owner can not recover it, after it has been paid away fairly and honestly upon a valuable and bona fide consideration * * *.

> * * * Apply this to the case of a bank-note. An action may lie against the finder, it is true; (and it is not at all denied:) but not after it has been paid away in currency. * * * Here, an inn-keeper took it, bona fide, in his business from a person who made an appearance of a gentleman. Here is no pretence or suspicion of collusion with the robber: * * * "he took it for a full and valuable consideration, in the usual course of business." Indeed if there had been any collusion, or any circumstances of unfair dealing; the case had been much otherwise. * * * [A bank-note] never shall be followed into the hands of a person who bona fide took it in the course of currency, and in the way of his business. * * * No dispute ought to be made with the bearer of a cash-note; in regard to

commerce, and for the sake of the credit of these notes; though it may be both reasonable and customary, to stay the payment, till inquiry can be made, whether the bearer of the note came by it fairly, or not.

With respect to instruments and such other negotiable paper, statutes that are beyond Article 9 provide, in various terms, that a good faith purchaser or holder of any of these kinds of property sometimes takes free of all adverse claims, including Article 9 security interests. U.C.C. §3-305(1); 7-502(1); 8-302(3). In every instance the term purchaser or holder can include a person acquiring a security interest in the property. U.C.C. §§1-201(32) & (33).

Article 9 defers to this other law. With respect to money the common law of *Miller* supplements Article 9 or, as federal common law, preempts Article 9. With respect to other kinds of negotiable paper, §9-309 provides that "[n]othing in this Article limits the rights of a holder in due course of a[n Article 3] negotiable instrument, or a holder to whom a negotiable document of title has been duly negotiated or a bona fide purchaser of a security ***." This deference means that such "holders or purchasers *take priority* over an earlier security interest even though perfected." U.C.C. §9-309 (emphasis added). Therefore, when an Article 9 secured party qualifies under Article 3, 7 or 8 for bona fide purchaser status as to an Article 3 instrument, an Article 7 negotiable document, or an Article 8 security so as to entitle her under that law to freedom from adverse claims to the property, her interest is entitled to priority over an earlier perfected security interest notwithstanding U.C.C. §9-312(5). To the extent that these other articles provide for cutting off preexisting security interests that otherwise would have enjoyed priority, they effectively create exceptions to §9-312(5) and other inconsistent priority rules, and Article 9 incorporates these exceptions by reference through §9-309.

Article 9 also creates its own exception that applies to a kind of quasi-negotiable paper collateral not necessarily governed by Article 3, 7 or 8: *chattel paper.* "'Chattel paper' means a writing or writings which evidence both a monetary obligation and a security interest in or lease of specific goods...." U.C.C. §9-105(1)(b). The best example of chattel paper is an installment sales contract for goods through which the seller retains a security interest in the property to secure payment of the price. This kind of chattel paper is not an Article 3 negotiable instrument, an Article 7 document, or an Article 8 security. So, if two secured parties both claim the paper, §9-309 is inapplicable. The usual rules of §9-312(5) would thus apply in determining the priority of their interests, unless the exceptional §9-308 governs the dispute.

U.C.C. §9-308 is a priority rule favoring purchasers of chattel paper who give new value for the property and take possession of it in the ordinary course of business. Because the term "purchasers" (defined by U.C.C. §§1-201(32) & (33)) includes Article 9 secured parties, §9-308 can function as an exception §9-312(5). The explanation for §9-308 is that, under the circumstances the section describes, heavier policies and accepted commercial practice favor the free flow of chattel paper.

P.E.B. Commentary No. 7 -- The Relative Priorities of Security Interests in the Cash Proceeds of Accounts, Chattel Paper, and General Intangibles

American Law Institute and National Conference of Commissioners
on Uniform State Laws
Permanent Editorial Board Commentary, March 10, 1990

Issue

Secured party A and secured party B each has a perfected security interest in the same account, chattel paper, or general intangible, with A having priority over B. If the account debtor makes payment to secured party B, directly or through the debtor, may A recover the payment from B?

Discussion

The issue under discussion arises when two secured parties have a perfected security interest in an account, chattel paper, or general intangible and the secured party that does not have priority (B) receives a payment from the account debtor. The debtor, having received the payment from the account debtor, may remit it to B, or B may receive payment directly from the account debtor. See §9-502(2) (secured parties' right to notify account debtor to make payment to the secured party); §9-318(3) (account debtor may discharge obligation by paying assignee after receiving notification that right to receive payment has been assigned and that payment is to be made to assignee). Under these circumstances, may A, the secured party having priority in the account, chattel paper, or general intangible, recover the payment from B?

A. Payment by Check

Article 9 determines the relative priorities of security interests in accounts, chattel paper, and general intangibles. See §9-312(5) (general rule); §9-308 (special rule with respect to chattel paper). The Article also determines the relative priorities of security interests in payments made by the account debtor, which payments are the proceeds of the original collateral. See §9-312(6); §9-306(1).

When the account debtor pays B by check, or when the debtor indorses and delivers to B a check drawn by the account debtor to the order of the debtor, B will be a holder of the check. If B takes the check under the circumstances described in §3-302(1), B will be a holder in due course. See §3-302(1) and (2). A's filed financing statement does not constitute notice to B of A's claim to the check and does not preclude B from being a holder in due course. See §3-305(1). Specifically, B takes priority over A's earlier, perfected security interest in the check and is entitled to keep the funds received when the check is paid. See §9-309 * * *.

Even if B is not a holder in due course, §9-308 may give priority to B's security interest in the check. But if B takes the check under circumstances that preclude B from being a holder in due course (e.g., if a notation on the check gives B reason to know that the check constitutes A's proceeds) and from taking priority under §9-308, then B would take the check subject to A's security interest. See §3-306(a).

B. Payment in Cash

The Code does not specifically address the right of B to retain a cash payment from the account debtor. Accordingly, resort must be had to the principles of law and equity. See §1-103. Under those principles, when a person assigns the same claim to two persons and the assignee without priority (B) receives payment from the obligor, the assignee receiving payment owes a duty of restitution to the assignee having priority (A). But if B gave value for the assignment (as B must have, see §9-203(1)(b)) and obtained the payment in good faith and without knowledge or reason to know of the prior assignment, then B may retain the payment. See Restatement, Second, Contracts §342(b), Comment e & Illustration 3; see also Restatement of Restitution §126, Comment f & Illustration 8. Cf. §9-306 Comment 2(c) (recipients of cash proceeds paid from the debtor's checking account in the operation of the debtor's business take free of a security interest in the proceeds). In determining whether B had reason to know of A's security interest, courts should apply §9-309 by analogy. Otherwise, cash would be rendered less negotiable than a check.

Conclusion

Whether B will be entitled to keep a cash payment from an account debtor or will be under a duty of restitution to A depends on whether B received the payment in good faith and without knowledge or reason to know of A's security interest. Whether B will be entitled to keep a payment made by a check drawn by the account debtor depends on whether B is a holder in due course of the check or is entitled to priority under §9-308. A's filed financing statement should not constitute notice to B of A's security interest in either case.

The Official Comment to §9-309 is amended by adding the following:

3. The operation of this section can be seen when two secured parties have a perfected security interest in an account, chattel paper, or general intangible and the secured party that does not have priority receives a payment by check directly or indirectly from the account debtor. If the recipient takes the check under circumstances that give the recipient the rights of a holder in due course (Section 3-302), then the recipient's security interest in the check will take priority over the competing security interest and the recipient will be entitled to keep the payment. See Commentary No. 7, dated March 10, 1990.

The Official Comment to §9-312 is amended by adding the following:

9. Under some circumstances, a secured party, who does not have priority in an account, chattel paper, or general intangible may be entitled to keep a cash payment received directly or indirectly from the account debtor. See PEB Commentary No. 7, dated March 10, 1990.

ㅁㅁㅁㅁㅁ

Orix Credit Alliance, Inc. v. Sovran Bank
United States Court of Appeals, Fourth Circuit, 1993
4 F.3d 1262

Hamilton, Circuit Judge: Orix Credit Alliance, Inc. (Orix) appeals the district court's grant of summary judgment in favor of Sovran Bank (Sovran) awarding Sovran a priority claim to the proceeds arising from the sale of a Crane on which Orix maintained a security interest lien. Finding no error, we affirm.

I

This controversy involves a dispute over the right to proceeds from the sale of a debtor's collateral. In September 1988, Orix and its debtor, A.E. Finley and Associates (Finley), entered into an agreement under which Orix agreed to finance, from time to time, Finley's acquisition of large industrial equipment and machinery which Finley would then either rent or resell. On September 30, 1988, Finley executed Orix's standard security agreement which granted Orix a security interest in all equipment financed by Orix.

On July 16, 1990, pursuant to their arrangement, Orix financed Finley's purchase of an American Crawler Crane (the Crane). Finley executed and delivered to Orix a promissory note in the amount of $305,000 and Orix filed a financing statement for the Crane with the appropriate Virginia officials. At the same time, Orix wrote a letter to Finley's lender, Sovran, which stated: We (Orix) have acquired one or more security interests (sic) in the goods described below: [the Crane]. We would appreciate it greatly if you would acknowledge that our interest in the goods described above is, and will be, prior to any interest of your company in such goods. Please confirm by signing in the place provided below and returning the original of this letter to us. Joint Appendix (J.A.) at 786. On July 16, 1990, a loan officer at Sovran, Elspeth McClelland, executed this subordination agreement, expressly acknowledging that Orix had a superior security interest in the Crane.

Finley maintained both a lending and depository relationship with Sovran. Specifically, Sovran provided Finley with a revolving line of credit and three bank accounts. The first account was a "cash collateral account," which was maintained by Sovran to receive all incoming payments from Finley's customers. Finley did not have direct access to or use of the funds in the cash collateral account. Each banking day, on a regular and routine basis, the deposits to the cash collateral account from the previous day were removed and applied to the outstanding balance of Finley's line of credit with Sovran. The second account was the "controlled disbursement account" on which Finley wrote checks. Under normal operating procedures, when the checks written on this account were presented to Sovran for payment, Sovran would notify Finley and, after Finley requested an advance under its line of credit, Sovran would then deposit sufficient funds from the line of credit into this account to pay the checks. Sovran and Finley implemented this arrangement at the inception of their relationship in December 1988, and the established procedures remained unchanged.

In 1991, Finley's financial situation worsened. Thus, when Finley's line of credit formally expired in July 1991, Finley was unable to pay the outstanding balance due Sovran. Consequently, on September 4, 1991, Sovran formally declared default on Finley's line of credit. In an attempt to cure its financial situation, Finley decided to sell some of the equipment which it currently leased. Pursuant to this decision, Finley arranged to sell the Crane to Signet Leasing and Finance Corporation (Signet). Orix authorized this sale on the condition that Finley would first use the proceeds to pay the remaining debt owed to Orix on this Crane. Orix took no other precautionary measures to ensure payment by Finley even though, as the secured party, it was in a position to do so.

On September 20, 1991, Finley informed Sovran that Signet would be wiring $565,000 into Finley's cash collateral account and requested Sovran to notify Finley when the wire transfer arrived. After receiving the wire transfer on that day, Sovran provided Finley with the requisite notice and, on the next banking day, routinely transferred the funds to reduce Finley's line of credit balance.[1]   On September 23, 1991--the first banking day after the wire transfer--Finley wrote a check on its controlled disbursement account to Orix for $257,648, the balance of the debt owed Orix on the Crane.

On September 30, 1991, this check was presented to Sovran for payment. On that day, Sovran advised Finley that a total of $288,388 had been presented

---

[1]   This wire transfer included proceeds arising from Signet's purchase of the Crane and other equipment from Finley.

for payment on the controlled disbursement account. As was customary, Finley then requested Sovran to advance that amount under the line of credit in order to cover these checks. In response, Sovran refused to advance the requested amount because it exceeded the remaining availability under Finley's line of credit. Sovran further advised Finley that the applicable banking laws only required payment of approximately $6,000 in checks presented that day. Finley thus reduced its requested advance to $6,000. On the next day, October 1, 1991, Finley's check to Orix was again presented to Sovran for payment. Because the amount of the Orix check again exceeded Finley's availability under its line of credit, Sovran dishonored the check.

On October 2, 1991, Finley's loan officer at Sovran, McClelland, sent a memorandum to her superiors discussing the Finley line of credit. The memo indicated that, after the $2,000,000 line of credit expired in July 1991, Sovran's credit committee had approved an extension of this line of credit until October 31, 1991. Despite this authorization, the memo indicated that McClelland had verbally informed Finley that Sovran would reduce the line to $1,600,000 through October 1, 1991, and, on that date, reduce the line an additional $200,000 to $1,400,000 until October 31, 1991. The memo also suggested that, in order to avoid "arbitrarily cutting the line" and to protect the bank, Sovran should send written notice to Finley advising of these reductions. J.A. at 404. Finally, the memo indicated that, on October 1, 1991, Sovran "returned ... a large check to [Orix] that was being used to pay off some equipment that was sold." Id. The memo identified two reasons for returning this check: (1) The line [of credit] balance would have been $1,595,000 and this would have been $195,000 over the agreed amount; and (2) The collateral sheet showed that there was not the collateral availability. The availability was $1,574,000. Id. The same day, Sovran had Finley sign a letter formally acknowledging Sovran's reduction in the line of credit to $1,400,000, effective as of October 1, 1991. J.A. at 409-10.

After Sovran dishonored the check to Orix, Orix filed suit against Sovran in the United States District Court for the District of Maryland. After the completion of discovery, the parties filed cross motions for summary judgment. Orix essentially argued that, because the funds in Finley's cash collateral account on September 20, 1991 constituted identifiable proceeds from the sale of Orix's collateral, under Virginia's Uniform Commercial Code (Va.U.C.C.) §8.9-306(2) Orix had a continuing security interest in those funds. Thus, Orix claimed Sovran had no right to use the Signet-remitted funds to reduce Finley's line of credit balance with Sovran.

The district court rejected Orix's argument and granted Sovran's motion for summary judgment. The district court reasoned that the transfer of the funds in question occurred in Finley's ordinary course of business and, therefore, Va.U.C.C. §8.9-306 as qualified by Comment 2(c) to that section, extinguished Orix's security interest in those proceeds.

Orix now appeals to this court.

II

In its appeal, Orix first contends that the use of funds from Finley's cash collateral account to reduce Finley's line of credit with Sovran cannot be considered a transaction in the ordinary course of Finley's business if Sovran knew another creditor had a security interest in those proceeds.[1] Orix reasons that Comment 2(c) to Va.U.C.C. §8.9-306 only protects a transferee who has no knowledge of a prior security interest in the proceeds received. We disagree.

Section 8.9-306(2) of the Va.U.C.C. gives a secured creditor a continuing security interest in "any identifiable proceeds [from the sale of collateral] including collections received by the debtor." However, this security interest in proceeds is not absolute. Comment 2(c) to this provision states, in relevant part:

> Where cash proceeds are covered into the debtor's checking account and paid out in the operation of the debtor's business, recipients of the funds of course take free of any claim which the secured party may have in them as proceeds. What has been said relates to payments and transfers in ordinary course.

Although we found no Virginia authority directly on point, courts have uniformly recognized that a transferee's knowledge of a prior security interest in proceeds does not, by itself, suggest that the transfer of those proceeds occurred outside the ordinary course of the debtor's business. The case relied on by the district court, In re Halmar Distributor's, Inc., 116 B.R. 328 (Bankr.D.Mass.1990), rev'd on other grounds 968 F.2d 121 (1st Cir.1992), provides a good example.

In *Halmar*, a supplier sold inventory to a debtor on credit and took a purchase money security interest in that inventory and any resulting proceeds. The debtor also maintained a banking relationship similar to the arrangement Finley had with Sovran. Specifically, the debtor had a revolving line of credit and a lockbox account with its bank. Under the lockbox arrangement, the debtor's customers mailed all payments to that account and the bank automatically applied those receipts to reduce the debtor's line of credit. As a consequence of this arrangement, the bank often used proceeds from the supplier's collateral to reduce the line of credit even though the bank knew the supplier had a security interest in those proceeds.

When the debtor encountered financial difficulties and did not repay the supplier, the supplier filed suit against the bank. The supplier claimed that, because the supplier had a continuing security interest in the proceeds, the bank had no right to use those proceeds to reduce the outstanding balance on the

---

[1]   The parties dispute whether Sovran actually knew that the September 20, 1991, wire transfer contained proceeds from the sale of collateral in which Orix had a security interest. For purposes of reviewing the district court's summary judgment, however, we must view the facts in the light most favorable to Orix. Thus, we will assume Sovran had such knowledge.

debtor's line of credit with the bank. The bankruptcy court rejected this claim, reasoning in part that "the transfer of proceeds in the ordinary course of business ... [should have] the same consequences as ordinary course transfers of [the] original collateral." Id. at 333. Under §9-307(1) of the Uniform Commercial Code (U.C.C.), a purchaser of goods in the ordinary course of business takes those goods free of any security interest created by his seller, "even though the buyer knows of [the security interest]." Id. Thus, the bankruptcy court concluded that "a transfer [of proceeds] in the ordinary course of a debtor's business terminates a security interest [in those proceeds]" regardless of the transferee's knowledge. Id.

We believe Virginia law would apply the rationale of the *Halmar* court to the present case. As the First Circuit has noted:

> [W]e can imagine good commercial reasons for not imposing, even upon sophisticated suppliers or secondary lenders, who are aware that inventory financers often take senior secured interests in "all inventory plus proceeds," the complicated burden of contacting these financers to secure permission to take payment from a [debtor's] ordinary commingled bank account.

Harley-Davidson Motor Co. v. Bank of New England, 897 F.2d 611, 622 (1st Cir.1990) (emphasis in original). Thus, we hold that a transferee's knowledge of a prior security interest in proceeds does not, by itself, indicate that the transfer of these proceeds occurred outside the ordinary course of the debtor's business. Consequently, Sovran's knowledge of Orix's prior security interest in the proceeds in question does not require a conclusion that Sovran's use of those proceeds to reduce Finley's line of credit occurred outside the ordinary course of Finley's business.

III

Orix next contends that Sovran's use of the proceeds in question does not qualify as a transaction in the ordinary course of Finley's business because those proceeds were not "paid out in the operation of the debtor's business." Va.U.C.C. §8.9-306, Comment 2(c) (emphasis added). We disagree.

To support its argument, Orix relies on Barber-Greene Co. v. National Bank of Minneapolis, 816 F.2d 1267 (8th Cir.1987). In *Barber-Greene,* a supplier sold machinery on credit to a debtor, taking a security interest in that machinery. The debtor also maintained a banking relationship which included a revolving credit facility, a "collateral account" and a "general operating account." Pursuant to their agreement, the proceeds from the sale of the debtor's inventory were deposited in the collateral account. "The bank [then] periodically, and at its discretion, transferred funds from the collateral account" to reduce the debtor's loan balance. Id. at 1269 (emphasis added). Upon the debtor's request for credit, the bank would advance funds from the revolving loan and credit the debtor's general operating account.

When the debtor's financial situation deteriorated, the bank applied funds from all of the debtor's accounts to reduce the loan balance. Because the debtor did not pay the supplier, the supplier filed suit against the bank. The supplier claimed that it had a security interest in the proceeds superior to the bank's. In response, the bank argued that the transfers occurred in the ordinary course of the debtor's business and, therefore, Comment 2(c) to Va.U.C.C. §8.9-306 extinguished the supplier's security interest in those proceeds.

The Eighth Circuit rejected the bank's argument, concluding that "[t]he proceeds were not paid out by [the debtor] in the ordinary course of its business." Id. at 1273. The court reasoned:

> Comment [2(c)] presupposes an account over which the debtor voluntarily makes deposits, and from which the debtor voluntarily makes payments to third parties who take in good faith. [The debtor in the present case] had no control over the collateral account. The bank had sole control. [The debtor] had no choice but to deposit the proceeds from the sale of all inventory into the collateral account. [The debtor] was never faced with decisions as to when and to whom payments from the account should be made, because [the debtor] had no control over the proceeds once they were deposited in the collateral account.

Id. at 1272. In addition, the Barber-Greene court noted that Comment 2(c) to U.C.C. §9-306 was not intended to protect banks which knowingly attempt to place themselves in a stronger position than that of creditors holding a superior claim as to those proceeds. Id.

We think the rationale employed by the *Barber-Greene* court does not apply to the present case. In *Halmar*, a case which closely resembles the instant matter, the court concluded that the proceeds were "paid out" in the ordinary course of the debtor's business. In reaching this conclusion, the court distinguished *Barber-Greene* on the basis that:

> [T]he cash transfers to the bank in [Barber-Greene], far from being in the ordinary course, were precipitated by the debtor's deteriorating financial condition. The bank set off all of the debtor's deposit accounts, not just the collateral account, in payment of its indebtedness. It did so because of the debtor's defaults. Nor was there any of the consent and acquiescence which is present here.... The [*Barber-Greene*] court was presented with conduct amounting to foreclosure, and the decision should be read in that light.

Halmar, 116 B.R. at 334.

We think this distinction applies with equal force to the present case. Unlike the bank's discretionary transfer of funds in *Barber-Greene*, Sovran routinely withdrew the previous day's deposits to Finley's cash collateral account on the next banking day and applied this amount against the outstanding balance due on Finley's line of credit with Sovran. Moreover, the system facilitating the transfer of these funds to Sovran remained unchanged from the inception of Sovran and Finley's relationship in 1988. In contrast, the bank in *Barber-Greene* began offsetting all of the debtor's accounts at the onset of its debtor's financial troubles. Because Sovran merely followed preexisting and long-established procedures, the concerns expressed by the *Barber-Greene* court relating to a bank's knowing attempt to gain a stronger position as to proceeds do not exist in the present case. Instead, under such circumstances we think the proceeds in question were "paid out in the operation of the debtor's business" as contemplated by Comment 2(c) to Va.U.C.C. §8.9-306.

IV

As a final argument, Orix contends that the district court erred in awarding summary judgment in favor of Sovran because the evidence before the district court created a genuine issue of material fact as to whether Sovran's use of the proceeds in question occurred in the ordinary course of Finley's business. Orix relies on two evidentiary facts to support this argument. We think neither evidentiary fact created a triable issue and discuss our reasons with respect to each fact separately.

A

Orix first contends Finley's deteriorating financial condition and Sovran's subsequent declaration of default on Finley's line of credit on September 4, 1991, suggests that, at the time Sovran used the proceeds in question, there was no business as usual between Sovran and Finley. Thus, Orix concludes that the district court should conduct a full trial before determining whether the transaction in question occurred in the ordinary course of Finley's business. We disagree.

Comment 2(c) to Va.U.C.C. §8.9-306 states that, in order for a transferee of proceeds to take free of any security interest in those proceeds, the proceeds must be "paid out in the operation of the debtor's business." Thus, determining whether the transfer of proceeds occurred in the ordinary course of business requires us to focus on Finley's rather than Sovran's business. Despite Finley's financial troubles, we think the payments to Sovran clearly occurred within the ordinary course of Finley's business.

As previously discussed, Sovran and Finley, at the inception of their relationship in 1988, voluntarily established the procedures through which Sovran applied the proceeds in question. In addition, Sovran routinely and daily withdrew these funds automatically, without the exercise of any discretion by either party. Because this system existed before the onslaught of Finley's financial woes, and neither Finley's subsequent financial troubles nor Sovran's declaration of default altered this procedure, we think neither of these facts suggest that the transaction in question occurred outside the ordinary course of Finley's business. Thus, we believe the facts relied on by Orix did not create a triable issue.

B

Orix also argues that Sovran's "retroactive" reduction of Finley's line of credit on October 2, 1991, from $1,600,000 to $1,400,000, and the subsequent dishonoring of Finley's check to Orix also suggest Sovran did not take the proceeds in the ordinary course of Finley's business. Orix reasons that this "retroactive" reduction in Finley's line of credit reflects a deliberate attempt to avoid paying Orix. Orix adds "[i]f Sovran truly would have been operating in the ordinary course of business, it would have honored Finley's check to Orix based on the sufficient [collateral] availability that existed on the [two] days the check was presented for payment." Brief of Appellant at 21. Thus, Orix concludes that a trial is necessary to determine whether the transaction in question occurred in the ordinary course of Finley's business. We disagree.

The "ordinary course" transfers described in Comment 2(c) to Va.U.C.C. §8.9- 306 "ha[ve] a fairly broad meaning" and exclude only that conduct which "in the commercial context, is rather clearly improper." *Harley-Davidson,* 897 F.2d at 622. In the present case, the uncontradicted evidence in the record indicates that Sovran and Finley verbally agreed to the reductions in the line of credit on September 11, 1991. J.A. at 439. Because the parties agreed to these reductions before Sovran knew of Finley's check to Orix--Finley did not even write this check until September 20, 1991--we think the evidence in the record does not support a conclusion that Sovran deliberately implemented a "retroactive" reduction in Finley's line of credit merely to avoid paying Orix. Thus, Sovran's reduction in the line of credit was not "clearly improper" and did not occur outside the ordinary course of Finley's business.

V

For the reasons stated herein, the judgment of the district court is affirmed. AFFIRMED.

Ervin, Chief Judge, dissent[ed] [and filed a dissenting opinion].

Problems

1. SP-1 makes a loan to D, and the parties execute a security agreement describing the collateral as all of D's inventory and receivables, including accounts and chattel paper, present and after-acquired. SP-1 files a financing statement covering the same collateral. Subsequently, D sells inventory on credit to twenty customers. Each of them signs an installment sales contract evidencing her obligation to pay the price and granting to D a security interest in the property she purchased from D. For Article 9 purposes each contract, and the entire collection of contracts, are "chattel

paper." U.C.C. §9-105(1)(b). In reliance on this new paper SP-1 makes additional loans to D. Also, D uses the same accounts and chattel paper as collateral for a loan from SP-2. SP-2 perfects its security interest by filing as to the accounts and chattel paper and also by taking possession of the chattel paper. See U.C.C. §9-305. Everything happens in the ordinary course. D takes the loan proceeds and flees the country. Who has priority with respect to the chattel paper, SP-1 or SP-2?

a. Same facts, except that SP-2, upon acquiring her interest, has knowledge of SP-1's interest.

b. Same facts, except that SP-1 claims the paper merely as proceeds of its inventory. That is, SP-1 does not make new advances in reliance on the paper. See U.C.C. §§9-306(1) & (2). (Assume that SP-1's perfected interest in the inventory carries over as a perfected security interest in the chattel paper, with perfection as to the chattel paper dating from the filing as to the inventory. See U.C.C. §§9-306(3) & 9-312(6).) Also, as in Problem 2, SP-2 knows of SP-1's interest.

c. Same facts, except that D sells the accounts and chattel paper to SP-2 instead of using the paper to secure a debt. Any equity, as well as the risk of non-collection, pass to SP-2.

2. "I am in the banking group here at Faegre & Benson [Minneapolis, Minnesota] and have advised lenders and leasing companies over the years in how to obtain a first security interest in leases or installment sale contracts (both chattel paper) when they either make a loan and take a security interest in the chattel paper or when they buy (discount) the chattel paper. * * * [There are three] kinds of true lease financings that I commonly see and that I believe any revision of UCC 9-308 should contemplate.

[a.] "In the first category, a lender will be asked to make a loan against a specific lease or group of leases. A promissory note will be signed and a security interest taken in the lease. For the reasons mentioned above, the lender will also take a security interest in the equipment to secure the loan. Scheduled payments under the note will generally match payments under the lease. In any event, payments made by the lessees are used to pay back the loan. Sometimes the lender will collect the payments directly and sometimes the borrower will be allowed to collect them but in either case the source of repayment is primarily the leases. This is not strictly speaking inventory financing (type A in [the Article 9 Study Committee Report]) since there is no requirement that the loan be repaid when the inventory is sold (or leased). Rather, it is chattel paper financing. Nor is this a general floating loan or revolving credit (type B [in the Report]) since there is typically no borrowing base to determine availability. Rather, it is financing of specific leases over a fixed term corresponding to the maturity of the paper, the amount of which is based on the creditworthiness of the lessees, the collateral value of the underlying equipment, and the credit strength of the leasing company (sometimes this latter consideration is not a factor since frequently loans against specific leases are nonrecourse loans to the leasing company).

[b.] "The second category is substantively the same as the first but the structure is slightly different. The financing institution will purchase (discount) the lease by paying a lump sum to the leasing company in exchange for an assignment of the lease. The financing institution will take a security interest from the leasing company in the underlying equipment, only this time the security interest will secure the rent because there is technically no "loan" involved as there is in the first category. The amount paid for the leases is based on the present value of the stream of payments payable under the leases determined by using an interest rate that the lender would use if it were making a loan. The purchase is either with or without recourse. The source of payment is obviously the same, namely the leases. The difference in structure is that no promissory note is involved. Thus, the only credit instrument is the paper itself. Some financing institutions like this structure since there is no need to be alert to amending a promissory note if there are changes in the payment schedule for the leases on account of an extension granted to the lessee or a casualty to one of several items covered by the lease or for some other reason.

[c.] "In the third category, the financing institution purchases not only the leases (the stream of payments) but also title to the underlying equipment. In other words, the financing institution steps into the shoes of the leasing company completely and becomes the lessor. It differs from the second category in that in the second category the financing institution takes only a security interest in the underlying equipment, thereby allowing the leasing company to retain the residual value of the equipment once the lessee makes all the rental payments and the lease expires. Article 9 applies to a transaction in this third category since it is the sale of chattel paper. This transaction is not limited to the sale by a leasing company of its entire business. It also occurs when one leasing company originates a lease or leases in its name and thereafter sells its entire interest in those leases to another leasing company. The first leasing company may want to do this either because it wishes to downsize its portfolio or because it is not in the business of operating an ongoing leasing company but really operates as a broker or intermediary, originating leases in its own name and promptly reselling them (at a markup) to other leasing companies that have the staff to administer the leases over their terms (the administration of a portfolio of leases requires a lot of paper work and people to collect and pay sales taxes and personal property taxes, as well as to handle collections).

"The structures in the first two categories are, of course, equally applicable to installment sale contracts and other chattel paper not constituting a true lease. An example is the typical automobile conditional sale contract. Another example is a "lease" that is not really a true lease even though it may be written on a document entitled "Equipment Lease" or the like. Some leases give the lessee the option to buy the equipment at the end of the lease for a $1 or for a stated percentage of original equipment cost. These and other factors may convert what would otherwise be a true lease into an installment sale contract (or a transaction that "creates a security interest" to use the language of UCC 1-201(37)). Sometimes a lender financing leases cannot be sure whether a lease offered as collateral is a true lease or not. For example, if the lessee has a fixed price option to purchase, the price may be on the borderline between "nominal" and "the reasonably predictable fair market value" on the exercise date. The Lender will therefore want to perfect his security interest as if both possibilities were true.

[A] problem I have faced in these three areas * * * is whether L-2's knowledge of the earlier filed financing statement is sufficient knowledge to disqualify him from priority as to the chattel paper. If it is, then there certainly is a suggestion that L-2 would be better off not even making a UCC search. I have considered that alternative but can not bring myself to it on the theory that no court would reward the lender who failed to make a search and punish the lender that did make a search." Letter from David M. Beadie, Esq. to Steve H. Nickles 1, 3-5 (August 6, 1993).

3.   Same as Problem 1, except that the account debtors make payments by checks that are delivered to D and indorsed by D to SP-2 or the account debtors pay SP-2 directly.

4.   Same as Problem 3, except that account debtors make payments by checks and in cash that are funneled to certain of D's unsecured creditors.

5.   Same as Problem 3, except that D deposits some of the checks in a bank account, and D uses the money to satisfy a preexisting, unsecured debt owed the bank or the bank sets off the account to satisfy the debt.

7. Vindicating Priority

Stotts v. Johnson
Supreme Court of Arkansas, 1990
302 Ark. 439, 791 S.W.2d 351

Hays, Justice.   This case involves a priority dispute under the Uniform Commercial Code between two creditors, F.L. and Shirley Stotts, appellants, and Malvern National Bank, appellee. The Stotts and the Bank claimed an interest in property being purchased by the debtor, Jimmy Johnson. The trial court found in favor of the Bank and the Stotts appeal from that decision.

On August 4, 1986, Jimmy Johnson made an agreement with F.L. Stotts to purchase a concession trailer from Stotts. Stotts gave Johnson a bill of sale which described the homemade concession trailer and included a statement that the trailer was free from all liens and encumbrances. Johnson took the bill of sale on the same day to the Malvern National Bank where he obtained a loan of $14,347.60. The Bank took a security interest in the trailer and filed its financing statement, perfecting its interest.

A month later Johnson gave Stotts a $10,000 down payment and signed a contract of sale, a promissory note, financing statement and security agreement. The financing statement was never perfected. By the terms of the contract, Johnson was to pay the down payment and $500 per month to Stotts.

In January of 1988, Johnson defaulted and Stotts repossessed the trailer pursuant to a provision in the contract of sale. Stotts then sold the trailer without giving notice to either Johnson or the Bank.

When Johnson learned of the sale he filed a replevin suit naming Stotts and the Bank as defendants and claiming Stotts had wrongfully repossessed the trailer. The Bank filed a counter claim against Johnson and a cross-claim against the Stotts alleging its lien was superior to that of Stotts. The case was heard by the trial court and it found for the Bank, holding that the Bank's interest was paramount. The Bank was awarded judgment for the past due principal and interest, $8,920.07, against Stotts and Johnson.[1] Other cross-claims and counterclaims by Stotts and Johnson were dismissed because of insufficient evidence.

The only issue on appeal is the Stotts's contention that the trial court erred in awarding judgment in favor of the Bank. We affirm the trial court.

Appellants' argument rests on two provisions of the Arkansas Uniform Commercial Code. The first, Ark.Code Ann. §4-9-504 (1987), provides for the disposition of collateral by a secured party after a debtor's default. The pertinent provision provides for notification of a sale of the collateral: §4-9-504(3). ... "[R]easonable notification of the time and place of any ... sale ... shall be sent by the secured party to the debtor.... In other cases, notification shall be sent to any other secured party from whom the secured party has received ... written notice of a claim of an interest in the collateral." The second provision relied on is Ark.Code Ann. §4-9-507 (1987), which deals with a secured party's liability for failure to comply with Part Five of Chapter 9. It provides in part:

> §4-9-507(1). If it is established that the secured party is not proceeding in accordance with the provisions of this Part disposition may be ordered or restrained on appropriate terms and conditions. If the disposition has occurred the debtor or any person entitled to notification or whose security interest has been made known to the secured party prior to the disposition has a right to recover from the secured party any loss caused by a failure to comply with the provisions of this Part.

---

[1] This may not be the appropriate measure of damages, see R. Hillman, J. McDonnell, S. Nickles, Common Law and Equity Under the Uniform Commercial Code, (1985), ¶25.01[3][a] and ¶25.02[5][a], n.312, however this issue was not raised below nor has it been argued on appeal.

Appellants argue that under these two provisions of the Code there is no requirement that notice be sent to someone in the Bank's position, i.e., the Bank was not the debtor, nor had it notified appellants of its interest, §4-9-504(3). Nor was the Bank within one of the classifications of §4-9-507(1) of parties entitled to recover because of failure to comply with the provisions of Part Five of Chapter 9. Therefore, appellants argue, the Bank was not entitled to any proceeds out of the disposition of the collateral upon default.

While there is authority supporting appellants' position that they were not required to send notice to a senior creditor under §4-9-504(3), see e.g., B. Clark, The Law of Secured Transactions, §4.8[7][d] (1980), that does not answer the question before us. Nor do we find it dispositive whether the Bank was within one of the classifications entitled to recover under §4-9-507(1) from a loss caused by a secured party's failure to comply with the provisions of Part Five of Chapter 9, as also argued by appellants.

While the provisions in Part Five of Chapter 9 arguably do not include a senior creditor in the Bank's position, they are not dispositive in any case, because they are not relevant to a senior creditor's claim of priority in the collateral or its proceeds. Rather, we interpret the provisions in Part Five as directed to those individuals who would have an interest in seeing that the collateral is disposed of in the most productive manner possible, so that a surplus might be realized, which is all a debtor and junior creditor would be entitled to. See §§4-9-504(1)(c), and 4-9-504(2); 9 W. Hawkland, Uniform Commercial Code Series, §9-504:09 (1986); Ark.Code Ann. §4-9-504 Comment 6 (1982); see also, R. Hillman, J. McDonnell, S. Nickles, Common Law and Equity Under the Uniform Commercial Code §25.02[4][a] (1985).

In contrast, a senior creditor is interested, not in any surplus from a junior creditor's sale, after deduction of the junior's interest, but in realizing its priority entitlement as predetermined by the Code. Support for the Bank's position is found in §§4-9-301 and 4-9-312, which provide that a perfected interest, as held by the Bank, takes priority over an unperfected security interest, held by Stotts. See §4-9-301, Comment 2. Were it otherwise, what would be the point of granting priority to the party who has followed the structure outlined in the Code to determine priority disputes? See B. Clark, §3.9[d], The World's Worst UCC Decision (where the author criticizes a Florida case in which the court ignored the clear priority provisions of the Code, and fashioned an award to a junior creditor based on certain equity maxims).

While it has been acknowledged that Article 9 would grant priority to a senior creditor over a junior creditor, it is further acknowledged that, "[N]othing in Article 9 clearly and explicitly gives a senior secured party a prior right to the proceeds of a foreclosure sale conducted by a junior secured party...." R. Hillman, supra, at note 265. However, that same commentator further notes that the priority interests are clearly recognized by the Code, id. at note 265, 293, and that while this issue of a senior creditor's priority to the proceeds has not been squarely addressed in most cases, a number of courts have nevertheless held that a junior secured party who disposes of collateral is accountable to a senior secured party for the sale proceeds. Id. at note 280, and id., 1989 Cum.Supp., note 280, (and cases cited therein); see also B. Clark, supra, §4.6[4], 1987 Cum.Supp. No. 3 (and cases cited therein). These courts have found support for their decisions through various theories including a conversion action by the senior creditor, based on priority sections of the code, or simply on the basis of the senior creditor's request for accounting pursuant to the priorities of the Code.

Our research has produced little discussion of this question, but the one extensive commentary we have found gives support for granting priority in this situation to the senior creditor, based on the priority provisions of the Code, R. Hillman, supra, at note 293, with support from various policy reasons within the code's framework. Id. at §28.02[4][d]. We find that persuasive. That discussion concludes with the following:

> These concerns may suggest that an unexpressed principle or policy underlies Article 9 which supports giving a senior secured party a prior right to the proceeds of a junior creditor's disposition of collateral. If so, the courts are licensed to go beyond the statute's literal dictates and construe its provisions liberally. Specifically, the courts may implement 'a statutory policy with liberal and useful remedies not provided in the statutory test.' Thus the plain meaning and logical implications of Sections such as 9-306 and 9-504 may be preempted by a pervasive spirit of priority that supports giving a senior secured party a claim to the proceeds of a junior creditor's sale of collateral.

* * * We agree with that analysis and hold that the trial court properly found that the Bank had priority over the Stotts.
    * * *

The judgment is affirmed.

□□□□□

Report of the Article 9 Study Committee

Permanent Editorial Board for the Uniform Commercial Code
American Law Institute and National Conference of Commissions on Uniform State Law,
1992

Committee Recommendations:

C. Perfection and Priority
11. Filing

A. The sponsors of the UCC should encourage and support the ongoing efforts to improve and make more uniform the various state systems for filing financing statements and conducting searches for them. These efforts should reach beyond the text of Article 9 to address broadly a wide range of existing deficiencies in filing systems, including those relating to delay, inaccuracy, and inadequate technical support (hardware, software, and staff).

B. The Drafting Committee should revise the text of Part 4 of Article 9 as may be appropriate to improve the operation of the filing systems. The Drafting Committee should give attention to existing problems in the following areas, among others: (i) purging of filed financing statements from the records; (ii) the volume and detail of information provided in response to a search request; (iii) the discretion that filing officers exercise, particularly in determining whether financing statements are "presently effective" (9-407(2)) and in determining whether to refuse to accept a financing statement for filing; (iv) obtaining termination statements when the secured party no longer exists or cannot be found; (v) the duration of the effectiveness of financing statements; (vi) "paper neutral" filing standards that would accommodate existing and future innovations in information technology; (vii) provision for administrative regulations to regulate some aspects of the filing system; (viii) clarification that changes in a secured party's name never renders a financing statement seriously misleading; (ix) clarification of how the filing system deals with successors to a secured party *(e.g,* the Resolution Trust Corporation); (x) indexing financing statements according to numbers *(ie.,* social security or tax I.D. numbers), either in addition to or instead of names; (xi) circumstances when signatures are required and, in a variety of contexts, the appropriate party to sign; (xii) external, remote access to filing systems for the purpose of searching and filing; (xiii) filing against partnerships that do not have names; (xiv) filing against trusts; (xv) improved provisions for the payment of fees; (xvi) consequences of assignments and partial assignments, particularly with respect to termination statements; (xvii) the impact of bankruptcy on filed financing statements; (xviii) subsequent filings that affect an original filing but contain identifying information that differs from the original *(e.g.,* termination statement filed after the secured party has changed its name); (xix) expansion or removal of the 6-month pre-lapse period for filing continuation statements; (xx) the effect, if any, of a change in the address of a secured party; (xxi) the need for a means of effecting "global" amendments to financing statements *(e.g.,* amending all financing statements filed against a particular debtor by filing a single document); and (xxii) extension, as appropriate, to other Part 4 provisions of the principle, contained in 9-402(8), of effectiveness notwithstanding "minor errors which are not seriously misleading."

12. Non-UCC Principles of Law and Equity

Article 9 should not be revised to address explicitly the circumstances under which non-UCC principles of law and equity should override otherwise applicable Article 9 priority rules. The Drafting Committee or the PEB should give serious consideration to revising the official comments or issuing PEB Commentary to point out the risks of using equitable principles to reorder Article 9 priorities and to identify examples of judicial decisions that reflect both inappropriate and appropriate readjustments.

13. Rights in Collateral

Article 9 should not be revised to explain when a debtor has "rights in the collateral" for purposes of attachment of a security interest under 9-203(1). The Drafting Committee or the PEB should give serious consideration to revising the official comments or issuing PEB Commentary to make clear that one with a limited interest in collateral, such as a bailee, has "rights in the collateral" and that a security interest can attach to those limited rights.

14. Purchase Money Security Interests and Purchase Money Priority

A. The definition of "purchase money security interest" (PMSI) in 9-107 should be revised to make clear that:

1. A security interest may be a PMSI notwithstanding (i) the fact that the collateral also secures other, nonpurchase money debt and (ii) the fact that the purchase money debt is secured by additional collateral.

2. A renewal, refinancing, or other restructuring of the debt secured does not destroy the purchase money character of a security interest.

3. In the case of a cross-collateralization or a restructuring, the burden is on the secured party to prove the extent to which a PMSI survives, including the allocation of payments between purchase money and nonpurchase money debt.

B. The Drafting Committee should consider whether to add an allocation formula to 9-107 that, in the absence of a contrary agreement by the parties, would specify how payments are to be allocated to the purchase money and nonpurchase money components of secured obligations.

C. Section 9-107 should be revised to make clear that cross-collateralization in the case of PMSI's in inventory is effective; *ie.,* to the extent any purchase money inventory secures any purchase money debt, the security interest receives PMSI status.

D. The official comment to 9-107 should be revised to make clear that purchase money debt includes related obligations such as interest, collection expenses, and the like.

E. The official comment to 9-107 should be revised to make clear that a security interest does not qualify as a PMSI if: (i) a debtor buys property on unsecured credit and subsequently creates the security interest to secure the purchase price or (ii) a debtor buys property for cash and subsequently creates the security interest in the property to secure a borrowing of an amount equivalent to the purchase price.

F. The period of 10 days specified in 9-301(2) and 9-312(4) should be extended to 20 days.

G. The official comments to 9-301 and 9-312 should be revised to clarify and provide guidance concerning the time at which a debtor "receives possession" of collateral for purposes of the priority rules contained in 9-301(2), 9-312(3), and 9-312(4).

H. Section 9-312 should be revised to provide that competing PMSI's that qualify for PMSI priority in the same collateral pursuant to 9-312(3) or 9-312(4) should receive coequal, pro rata treatment.

15. Proceeds

A. The definition of "proceeds" in 9-306(1) should be revised as follows:

1. The definition should make clear that when collateral consisting of goods is leased the debtor's (lessor's) leasehold interest, including the lease rentals, constitutes proceeds of that collateral. The Drafting Committee should consider whether to revise the definition to provide that royalties arising out of a debtor's licensing of intellectual property constitute proceeds of the intellectual property.

2. The definition should specify that proceeds includes (i) property acquired by a debtor as distributions on account of the interest of a debtor in collateral *(e.g.,* stock splits) and (ii) claims arising out of the loss of, nonconformity of, defects in, or damage to collateral *(e.g.,* warranty and tort claims); the concepts of "sale, exchange, collection or other disposition" found in the current definition may not be broad enough to embrace property of this kind.

3. The definition should make clear that proceeds is not limited to property "received by the debtor" *(ie.,* in the possession of or controlled by the debtor) but

rather that the concept extends to any proceeds to the extent that the debtor acquires rights in the property.

Comments:

1. Effects of classifying property as "proceeds."

Any consideration of what constitutes or should constitute proceeds under 9-306(1) should identify the effects of classifying or not classifying property as proceeds.

a. Continuation of security interest. If property constitutes "identifiable proceeds" of collateral, then a security interest "continues" in the proceeds pursuant to 9-306(2). Because proceeds are a species of after-acquired property, in many cases the same result as that arising under 9-306(2) could be achieved, whether or not the property constitutes proceeds, by describing the after-acquired property in the security agreement. But when property is classified as proceeds, the security agreement need not describe it. Eliminating the need for more expansive drafting under current law also may have other, less obvious, advantages. It may save costs of extended negotiations, inhibit abuse and overreaching by some secured parties, and rescue other secured parties from careless omissions.

b. Continuation of perfection of security interest. Section 9-306(3) provides that if property constitutes proceeds of collateral in which a security interest is perfected, the security interest in proceeds is "continuously perfected." But the security interest in proceeds ceases to be so perfected "ten days after receipt . . . by the debtor," subject to three exceptions.

Under the exception in 9-306(3)(a), a financing statement need not explicitly cover the type or items of collateral that constitute proceeds (except in the case of proceeds acquired with cash proceeds). When proceeds are of a type in which a security interest can be perfected by filing, however, a secured party could achieve the same result as that provided by 9-306(3) continuous perfection merely by filing a financing statement covering that type of collateral, in advance, in the proper office.

Section 9-306(3)(b) creates another exception to the 10-day limitation for "identifiable cash proceeds" when "a filed financing statement covers the original collateral." A security interest in "cash proceeds" (9-306(1) (2d sentence)) as original collateral ordinarily cannot be perfected by filing because deposit accounts currently are excluded from Article 9 and other cash proceeds usually consist of money or instruments. It follows that the continuous perfection conferred by 9-306(3)(b) provides greater protection for proceeds, as such, than would be available under the after-acquired property approach. To the extent that permissive perfection by filing werc to become available for such cash proceeds, however, this advantage would disappear.

Finally, the exception in 9-306(3)(c) allows for continuous perfection beyond the 10-day period if the security interest in proceeds is perfected before the period expires. A security interest in after-acquired property that does not consist of proceeds also can be perfected following the debtor's acquisition of the property, but the continuous perfection provided by 9-306(3)(c) can be important for purposes of priority. Again, to the extent proceeds consist of property not excluded from Article 9's scope, and in which a security interest could be perfected by filing, the same advantage could be had by an initial filing covering the after-acquired property. Moreover, except where the debtor cooperates or the secured party monitors the debtor's activities closely, it may be that secured parties infrequently discover the need to perfect in proceeds prior to the expiration of the 10-day period.

c. *Treatment of proceeds in debtor's bankruptcy proceeding*

(1) Preferences: Bankruptcy Code 547. Whether or not collateral acquired by a debtor within the 90-day period prior to the debtor's bankruptcy filing is classified as proceeds under 9-306(1) generally does not affect the avoidability of a security interest under Bankruptcy Code 547. Even if the security interest in original collateral had been perfected earlier than the 90th day prior to the bankruptcy petition, under Bankruptcy Code 547(e)(3) the *transfer* of the security interest in proceeds would not occur until the debtor acquired rights in the proceeds. For example, assume that a debtor transfers equipment to a non-ordinary course buyer, without the authorization of the secured party, so that the buyer acquires the equipment *subject to* the security interest. Assume further that the debtor receives, in exchange for the transferred equipment, another item of equipment. Applying 9-306(2), the secured party would have a security interest in the transferred item as well as in the newly-acquired item, which would be proceeds. The security interest in the newly-acquired item would not be insulated from attack under Bankruptcy Code 547 merely because it constitutes proceeds.

In the more typical case, a debtor's acquisition of proceeds within the 90-day window prior to a bankruptcy petition ordinarily *does not* give rise to an avoidable transfer under Bankruptcy Code 547. For example, when proceeds are received in exchange for original collateral and the security interest *does not continue in the original collateral,* typically either Bankruptcy Code 547(b)(5) will not be satisfied or the transaction will be sheltered by the "contemporaneous exchange" exception in Bankruptcy Code 547(c)(1). Also, where proceeds of inventory or receivables are concerned, the exception in Bankruptcy Code 547(c)(5) (the "two-point test") will apply.

(2)   Post-Petition   Proceeds: Bankruptcy   Code   552. Bankruptcy Code 552(b) provides that, after the filing of a petition under the Bankruptcy Code, an after-acquired property clause in a debtor's prepetition security agreement ceases to be effective as to postpetition after-acquired property *(ie.,* the "floating lien" stops floating). Bankruptcy Code 552(b) provides an exception, however, for otherwise unavoidable security interests in "proceeds, product, offspring, rents, or profits" of prepetition collateral. "[P]roceeds," as used in Bankruptcy Code 552(b), is not defined. Some courts have looked to the definition in 9-306 for guidance. Indeed, Bankruptcy Code 552(b) validates security interests in postpetition proceeds etc. "to the extent provided by [the] . . . security agreement and by applicable nonbankruptcy law." However, were the definition of proceeds in 9-306(1) materially expanded, bankruptcy courts might be less likely to follow it for purposes of Bankruptcy Code 552(b).

d. Summary. When compared with the use of expansive coverage of after-acquired collateral in security agreements and financing statements, the benefits to secured parties of classifying collateral as proceeds are relatively small. The principal benefits are automatic, continuous perfection in cash proceeds under 9-306(3)(b) and the favorable treatment afforded postpetition proceeds under Bankruptcy Code 552. If the Committee's recommendations concerning permissive filing for instruments and security interests in deposit accounts as original collateral were to be adopted, the same benefits of 9-306(3)(b) for after-acquired cash proceeds would be available without respect to their classification as such. As to the meaning of "proceeds" in Bankruptcy Code 552, that is ultimately a question of federal, not state, law.

2. *Standards for what constitutes or should constitute proceeds.*

a. Exchange and replacement. The current definition of proceeds is transactional. Each of the triggering events specified in 9-306(1) —"sale, exchange, collection or other disposition of collateral or proceeds"—appears to contemplate that proceeds will be received in place of and in substitution for the original collateral, which has been disposed of or reduced in value (such as by collections).

Applying this "replacement" standard, a lease of goods would seem to be an "other disposition" giving rise to proceeds consisting of the debtor's rights under the lease, including its right to receive rentals. Inasmuch as the reported cases are not uniform on this point, the Committee recommends that 9-306(1) be clarified to reflect this result. Although perhaps less clear, royalties arising out of a debtor's licensing of intellectual property likewise would seem to be proceeds of the intellectual property. The Drafting Committee should consider whether to revise the definition to provide accordingly.

Other examples of property received by a debtor in replacement of collateral, otherwise on account of a diminution in value of collateral, or to supplement collateral, do not seem to fit the "other disposition" criterion of   9-306(1). For example, a breach of warranty claim against a seller of goods or a tort claim against a third party for damage to or conversion of goods each involves a chose in action that replaces the value of collateral that would have (or should have) been available to a secured party. Although these intangibles are similar to insurance proceeds that are explicitly included in the definition of proceeds, they are not covered by that inclusion. The (Committee recommends that 9-306(1) be revised so as to include such "replacement" or "compensatory" intangibles as proceeds.[1]

b. Close association. Another way of characterizing what proceeds are or should be does not depend on the exchange concept. Instead, this approach would include as proceeds those things that are so necessarily and obviously associated with an interest in the original collateral that a security agreement and financing statement ought not to be required to mention them explicitly. If the debtor, as owner of the collateral, is necessarily entitled to such property, then a secured party likewise should be entitled to the property as collateral.

This "close association" conceptualization of proceeds would embrace all forms of distributions on account of securities, partnership interests, and other intangibles (which may or may not already be covered as "collections" proceeds), government subsidies, and other payments that do not involve an "exchange." (Claims for damage or loss of collateral and claims for infringement of rights to intellectual property collateral seem to fit this "close

---

[1]   At some point, the acquisition of assets by a debtor, in part as a result of a diminution in value of collateral, will be too attenuated for those assets to be considered proceeds. For example, accounts generated by a construction contractor should not be considered proceeds of the contractor's construction equipment, even though the equipment depreciates as a result of its use in generating the accounts. Nor should inventory fabricated by a debtor's factory equipment be considered proceeds of that equipment. Cash earned from music or video machines presents a case closer to the margin. Has the equipment merely provided a service, or is the better analogy that of a short-term rental? The committee is inclined to leave such marginal cases to the courts.

association" model as well as the "replacement" or "exchange" paradigm discussed above.) The Committee recommends that 9-306(1) be revised so as to embrace this "close association" concept.

3. *Proceeds not received by the debtor.*

"Proceeds" are defined in 9-306(1) as "whatever is received . . ." Moreover, the operative rule of 9-306(2) provides that "a security interest . . . continues in any identifiable proceeds including collections received by the debtor." The statute does not make clear whether "received by the debtor" modifies "proceeds" generally or modifies only "collections," although the drafting history strongly suggests that the limiting language modifies "proceeds" generally, and some courts have so held. The Committee questions the wisdom of limiting proceeds to what is "received by the debtor." It is difficult to rationalize why, for example, a security interest in identifiable collections on accounts collateral should not exist merely because the collections are received by an escrow agent or paid into court.

It might be argued that eliminating the "received by the debtor" limitation would give proceeds too broad a reach by including, for example, what is received by a debtor's transferee upon retransfer of the original collateral. But this result may obtain even if the phrase is not eliminated and is construed to mean that only proceeds that are physically received by a debtor qualify as proceeds subject to a continuous security interest under 9-306(2); a court might reason that a security interest continues in proceeds received by the original debtor's transferee because the transferee, having acquired the collateral, *is a debtor.* Moreover, if the concern is for the creditors of or purchasers from the transferee, that concern would be addressed better by a *priority* rule, not by a rule affecting the continuation of a perfected security interest. (The Committee does not propose to alter the common-law conversion liability of one who wrongfully deals with collateral, such as a buyer or auctioneer in an unauthorized sale.)

Limiting the continuation of a security interest to what is "received" may be too restrictive for yet another reason. It seems to connote something that can be physically possessed, although no one doubts that intangibles such as accounts can be proceeds of inventory.

Removing the "received" requirement from 9-306 and the "received by the debtor" requirement from 9-306(2) would make it necessary to find a replacement for the concept of receipt. The

Committee recommends that the concept of the debtor's acquisition of rights in the property be substituted for the receipt concept.

* * *

B. Section 9-318 and the official comment to 9-318 should be revised as follows:

1. They should make clear that the rights and duties specified in subsections (1) and (3) apply to all account debtors, including account debtors on general intangibles that are proceeds.

2. They should make clear that the term "assignee" (i) embraces any secured party, including a secured party claiming proceeds of original collateral (such as inventory) other than a receivable, and (ii) is not limited to an outright buyer of an account.

C. Section 9-306 or the official comment should be revised either to set forth the applicable tracing rule for purposes of determining whether cash proceeds are "identifiable" (9-306(2) and (3)) or to acknowledge explicitly the appropriateness of applying non-UCC tracing principles, such as the "lower intermediate balance rule."

D. The provision for automatic and continuous perfection of security interests in cash proceeds in 9-306(3)(b) should be extended to proceeds of original collateral in which a security interest is perfected by a method other than filing.

E. Subsection (3) of 9-306 and the official comment should be revised as follows:

1. The period of 10 days for temporary automatic perfection of security interests in proceeds should be extended to 20 days.

2. In conformity with proposed changes to subsections (1) and (2), the 20-day period should begin when the debtor acquires rights to the proceeds instead of the time of the debtor's "receipt of the proceeds."

3. The statute should specify more clearly that, in the absence of a special rule extending perfection beyond the 20-day period (ie., subsection (3)(a), (b), or (c)), the security interest in proceeds becomes unperfected on the 21st day after the debtor's acquisition of rights to the proceeds.

4. The official comment to 9-306 should be revised to explain that if a security interest in proceeds becomes unperfected at the end of the 20-day period

provided by subsection (3), then the unperfected status does not "relate back" to the time that the proceeds were acquired by the debtor, ie., the security interest is to receive perfected status for all purposes during the 20-day period.

5. The statute should make clear that when perfection of a security interest in proceeds is extended under subsection (3)(a) or (b), the perfection lapses when the effectiveness of the filed financing statement lapses or, if the security interest in the original collateral is perfected other than by filing, when the security interest in the original collateral becomes unperfected.

F. The official comments to 9-306 should be revised to reflect that Article 9 does not displace non-UCC rules of negotiability and finality of payment that otherwise would apply to cash proceeds and funds paid from a deposit account constituting proceeds. The revised comments should indicate that a good faith purchaser of cash proceeds or of funds transferred or paid from a deposit account constituting cash proceeds takes free of security interests to the same extent that the purchaser would take free of other competing claims.

G. Subsection (4) of 9-306 should be deleted.

H. Subsection (5) of 9-306 should be deleted.

I. Section 9-308 should be revised to provide that the priority afforded thereunder to purchasers of chattel paper also extends to the goods covered by the chattel paper if the transferor reacquires an interest (other than a bare possessory interest) in the goods.

J. The official comments to appropriate sections of Article 9 should be revised to explain and clarify the application of priority rules to returned and repossessed goods in the absence of 9-306(5).

16. Temporal Limits of Perfection

A. Assuming that the Drafting Committee retains the six-month period in 9-403(2), the statute or the official comment should be revised to make clear that a continuation statement filed more than six months before the lapse date is ineffective.

B. Section 9-403(2) or the official comment should be revised to make clear when insolvency proceedings terminate for purposes of the section. The Drafting Committee should consider whether to expand the application of the tolling provisions of 9-403(2) to security interests that are not perfected by filing and should seek ways in which to prevent the destruction by filing officers of financing statements that remain effective solely by virtue of the debtor's having entered insolvency proceedings.

C. The periods of temporary perfection provided by 8-321(4), 9-304(4), and 9-304(5) should be changed from 21 days to 20 days.

D. Sections 8-321(4), 9-304(4), and 9-304(5) or the official comments should be revised to make clear that if a security interest becomes unperfected at the end of the period of temporary perfection, the unperfected status does not "relate back", ie., for all purposes the security interest is to be considered as having been a perfected security interest during the period of temporary perfection.

17. Post-Closing Events: Attachment, Perfection, and Priority Issues

A. The first sentence of 9-402(7) should be revised to make clear that a financing statement using a debtor's trade name as the debtor's name is ineffective except when the trade name, as compared to the debtor's real name, is not seriously misleading.

B. Section 9-402(7) should be revised to distinguish between a change of a debtor's name, on the one hand, and other changes (including changes of identity and corporate structure) that result in a new legal entity becoming a debtor, on the other.

C. With respect to the change of a debtor's name:

1. Section 9-402 should make explicit that a filed financing statement remains effective with respect to collateral acquired by the debtor within four months after the change, even if the change has rendered the financing statement seriously misleading.

2. Section 9-402 should provide that the effectiveness of a filed financing statement that has become seriously misleading as a consequence of the change can be extended to include collateral acquired more than four months after the change by filing an amendment to the financing statement but not by filing a new financing statement. Conforming revisions to other subsections of 9-402 should permit the secured party to file such an amendment without the debtor's signature and should delete the current authorization to file a new financing statement without the debtor's signature.

D. Section 9-203, 9-204, or the official comments should be revised to indicate that Article 9 does not determine the circumstances under which an after-acquired property clause in a security agreement covers property acquired by a person other than the person who signed the agreement.

E. Section 9-402(7) should be revised to make clear whether, when a person becomes bound by a security agreement signed by another person *(ie.,* when a security agreement signed by one person becomes effective against property acquired by another person), a financing statement filed against the person who signed the security agreement is effective to perfect a security interest in collateral that the person who becomes bound acquires or has acquired from an entity other than the signer.

F. If the Drafting Committee decides to revise 9-402(7) to provide that a financing statement filed against the person who signed a security agreement is effective to perfect a security interest in collateral that a person who becomes bound by the agreement acquires or has acquired from an entity other than the signer, then it should also revise 9-402(7) as follows:

1. A financing statement that is seriously misleading as to the person who becomes bound should be effective only with respect to collateral acquired by the person within four months after the person becomes bound unless a new appropriate financing statement is filed before the expiration of the four months. The Drafting Committee should consider whether the new debtor's signature should be required for the new appropriate financing statement.

2. A new rule would be necessary to resolve the priority of competing security interests that may arise when a person becomes bound by a security agreement signed by another person, the financing statement filed against the signer remains effective to perfect a security interest in collateral that the person acquires or has acquired from an entity other than the signer, and the person creates a security interest in the same collateral in favor of another secured party. Under this new rule, the first secured party to file or perfect should enjoy priority; however, for purposes of this rule, the filing that names the signer should date from the later of the time of fling or the time the person became bound.

G. The third sentence of 9-402(7) should be revised to make clear that it applies only when a security interest continues in the transferred collateral.

H. New provisions should be added to Article 9 to address the priority of a security interest in collateral that the debtor acquires subject to a security interest created by a different debtor. The substance of these provisions should be as follows:

1.   When a person acquires collateral subject to a perfected security interest created by another person, any security interest created by the acquirer in the collateral is subordinate to the security interest created by the other person.

2.   When a person acquires collateral subject to an unperfected security interest created by another person, the priority rules of 9-312 govern as if the acquirer created the security interest.

18. Instruments

A.   Article 9 should be revised to permit perfection of a security interest in an instrument by filing a financing statement.

B.   The priority of a security interest in an instrument that is perfected by filing should be governed by the priority rules otherwise applicable to security interests in instruments, *ie.,* 9-301, 9-306, 9-308, 9-309, and 9-312.

19. Letters of Credit

A.   The UCC should be revised to make clear that a security interest in a letter of credit can attach before demand for payment is made under the credit, and that payment under the credit constitutes the proceeds of the letter of credit.

B.   Article 5 and Article 9 should be revised to permit a security interest in a letter of credit to attach in accordance with 9-203(1); that is, the secured party should acquire a security interest without the need to take possession of the credit.

C.   Article 9 should be revised to permit a security interest in a letter of credit to be perfected either (i) by filing or (ii) in the case of a person who takes a security interest in the ordinary course of its business and for new value, by notifying the issuer of its security interest and taking such steps as are necessary to cause the issuer to acknowledge the security interest.

D.   Article 9 or the official comments should make clear that a security interest in an obligation supported by a letter of credit includes a security interest in the letter of credit.

E.   The ordinary priority rules of 9-312(5) should apply to security interests in letters of credit; however, a person who has perfected a security interest in accordance with Recommendation C (ii) should be entitled to priority over a security interest perfected by filing.

F. Article 5 should be revised to clarify the obligations owed by the issuer to an assignee of a letter of credit, including a secured party who has taken a security interest the credit

20. Articles 8 and 9 should be revised to deal with security interests in investment securities generally along the lines reflected by the Article 8 Drafting Committee's May 1, 1992 draft, which (i) moves the principal provisions relating to security interests in investment securities from Article 8 to Article 9; (ii) defines the rights and benefits enjoyed by a customer of a financial intermediary as a new type of collateral, "securities account entitlement," and defines securities and securities account entitlements together as "investment property"; (iii) provides for automatic perfection of, and affords priority to, a security interest in a securities account entitlement when the secured party is the financial intermediary that maintains the securities account entitlement for its customer; (iv) provides that a financial intermediary that maintains a securities account entitlement for its debtor-customer has no duties or obligations to the customer's secured party except to the extent that the financial intermediary so agrees; (v) provides for the perfection of a security interest in investment property (A) by filing, (B) by possession (in the case of certificated securities), or (C) in the case of a securities account entitlement, by the agreement of the financial intermediary that maintains the securities account entitlement for its customer that the financial intermediary will comply with instructions from the customer's secured party; and (vi) provides for automatic perfection of a security interest when the debtor is a broker.

21. Chattel Paper

A. Section 9-308 should be revised either to (i) eliminate the distinction between subsections (a) and (b) by creating a single set of circumstances under which a purchaser of chattel paper achieves priority over an earlier-perfected security interest or to (ii) clarify the bifurcated standards established by clauses (a) and (b).

B. If 9-304(1) is revised to permit perfection of security interests in instruments by filing (see Recommendation 18.A), then 9-308 should apply to such security interests.

C. The definition of security interest in 1-201(37) or the scope of Article 9 specified in 9-102(1) should be revised to provide that loan participations and other loan sales by financial institutions (and, possibly, sales by other classes of professional lenders) do not constitute the sale of chattel paper that is within the scope of Article 9.

D. Section 9-103(4) should be revised to clarify which state's priority rules apply when a security interest in chattel paper is perfected by both filing and possession.

E. The Drafting Committee should consider seriously whether 9-104(f) should be revised to clarify the exclusion of certain assignments of accounts, chattel paper, and other rights to payment from the scope of Article 9.

22. Goods Subject to a Certificate of Title Statute

A. Article 9 should be revised to provide that perfection of a security interest in goods subject to a certificate of title statute occurs upon receipt by appropriate state officials of a properly tendered application for a certificate of title on which the security interest is to be indicated; an application as to which there has been substantial compliance with the requirements of the statute should be considered properly tendered for these purposes.

B. The Drafting Committee should give serious consideration to revising Article 9 or the official comments to clarify the extent to which the principles of notice filing are applicable to security interests in goods subject to a certificate of title statute.

C. The Drafting Committee should consider whether a security interest in goods subject to a certificate of title statute can be perfected by taking possession of the goods and should revise 9-302(4) or 9-103, comment 4(e), accordingly.

D. The Drafting Committee should consider whether to revise 9-302(3)(b) to enable a secured party to file a financing statement to perfect a security interest in goods that a dealer holds in its possession for the purpose of leasing to others and for which no certificate of title is outstanding.

E. The Drafting Committee should review the way in which Article 9, including 9-314, applies to goods that are installed in or affixed to goods covered by a certificate of title. In particular, the Drafting Committee may wish to devote attention to the following: (i) the circumstances, if any, under which compliance with a certificate of title statute with respect to goods subject thereto *(e.g.,* a truck) should be sufficient to perfect a security interest in goods that previously were or subsequently are affixed to or installed in the goods *(eg.,* a refrigeration unit); (ii) whether and, if so, for how long a security interest perfected by filing in the goods affixed to or installed in goods subject to a certificate of title statute should remain perfected after the goods are affixed or installed; (iii) whether Article 9 should afford priority to a secured party who finances replacement parts or components that are affixed to or installed in goods already subject to a security interest perfected under the certificate of title statute; and (iv) whether a security interest in goods should continue in parts and components removed from the goods (temporarily or permanently) and, if the security interest does continue in the components and parts and the security interest in the goods was perfected under the certificate of title statute, whether the security interest in the parts and components should continue to be perfected.

23. Non-Assignable Contracts, Permits, and Licenses

The Drafting Committee should give serious consideration to whether Article 9 should be revised to provide that a prohibition on the assignment of a private or governmental contract, license, or permit is ineffective to prevent the attachment or perfection of a security interest and that the creation of a security interest in the debtor's rights under the contract, license, or permit does not give rise to a default under the contract, license, or permit notwithstanding any agreement or other law to the contrary.

24. Issues in Agricultural Financing

A. Article 9 should be revised to address at least those important issues dealt with by the proposals in the Final Report on Agricultural Financing Under Article 9 of the Uniform Commercial Code concerning:

(1) extension of the perfection, priority, and enforcement provisions of Article 9 to agricultural statutory liens; and

(2) replacement of 9-312(2) with a special priority rule governing a "production money security interest" ("PrMSI"), *ie.,* a security interest arising in favor of a person who gave new value that is used in the production of crops.

B. The Drafting Committee should give serious consideration to the Final Report's other proposals, as to most of which the Committee generally agrees.

C. The Drafting Committee should give serious consideration to extending the perfection, priority, and enforcement provisions of Article 9 to statutory and common-law liens generally.

D. The Drafting Committee should work with the appropriate ABA task forces in forging a consensus in the agricultural community on the appropriate scope and priority of the PrMSI and on the other issues raised in the Final Report.

25. Consignments

A. Section 2-326 should be revised to make clear that it applies to both "true consignments" and "sale or return" transactions in which goods are delivered to a merchant who deals in goods of that kind.

B. Section 2-326 should be revised to provide that, except as qualified by Recommendation C, goods delivered to a merchant who deals in goods of that kind under a name other than that of the person making delivery, for the purpose of sale by the merchant, whether or not the merchant is to process the goods before sale, are subject to the claims of the merchant's creditors unless the person who delivers the goods files a financing statement against the merchant in compliance with the provisions of Article 9.

C. Section 2-326 should be revised to exclude from its operation transactions for which requiring the filing of a financing statement (on pain of subordination) would be inappropriate *(e.g.,* the delivery for sale of consumer goods by a natural person or of art by artists).

D. The official comments to 1-201(37) or 2-326 should be revised to explain how to distinguish a transaction governed by 2-326 from a consignment "intended as security," which creates a security interest governed by Article 9.

E. Article 9 should be revised to provide that first-in-time principles analogous to 9-312(5) as against a competing secured party and 9-301(b) as against a competing lien creditor govern the priority of a person who delivers goods to a merchant under the circumstances described in Recommendation B and makes an appropriate filing against the merchant, but does not meet the additional requirements specified in 9-114(1).

F. Article 9 should be revised to provide that the interest of a person who delivers goods to a merchant under the circumstances described in Recommendation B attaches to the proceeds of a disposition of the goods and to clarify the priority rules applicable to the proceeds.

26. Buyers in Ordinary Course of Business

A. The definition of "buyer in ordinary course of business" in 1-201(9) should be revised to provide that the earliest time that a buyer can achieve the status of a buyer of goods is the time that the buyer obtains the right to possession of the goods under Article 2.

B. Section 9-307(1) should be revised to provide that a buyer in ordinary course of business does not take goods free of a security interest if the secured party is in possession of the goods, rejecting the holding of *Tanbro Fabrics Corp. v. Deering Milliken, Inc,* 350 N.E.2d 590 (N.Y. 1976).

C. Section 2-403, 2-402, 9-307, or the official comments should be revised to make clear that, notwithstanding the "his seller" limitation in 9-307(1), pursuant to 2-403(2) a buyer in ordinary course of business can take goods free of a security interest created by one other than the buyer's seller if the holder of the security interest itself entrusts the goods to the buyer's seller.

27. Financing Buyers and Non-Lease Bailments

A. Article 2, Article 9, or both should be revised to afford a purchase money-like priority for financing buyers, similar to that provided to purchase money inventory financers, if a priority rule for financing buyers can be fashioned that is practical, not unacceptably complex, and adequately protective of the rights of earlier-in-time inventory financers.

B. The scope of Article 9 should not be expanded to include non-lease bailments. The UCC should not be revised to address the question whether a putative non-lease bailment is a true bailment transaction that is outside the scope of Article 9 or is a security interest subject to the Article.

D. Enforcement
* * *

30. Duties Owed to Competing Secured Parties and Lienholders By a Secured Party Who Disposes Of or Makes Collections on Collateral

[Reprinted at pages 241-44 supra.]

E. PERFECTING SECURITY INTERESTS

Here are the fundamentals of perfection:

First, perfection of a security interest is unimportant between the immediate parties, that is, perfection, or the lack of perfection, in no way affects the secured party's rights against the debtor. Thus, an unperfected security interest is as fully enforceable against the debtor as a perfected security interest.

Second, perfection is important only in priority disputes with third parties. The purpose of perfection is to give a secured party's interest in collateral the most protection possible, i.e., the most protection the law affords, against third parties' claims to the property. The range of claimants over which a secured party enjoys priority is much wider when her security interest is perfected. On the other hand, perfection does not insure that a secured party will prevail over all transferees of the collateral from the debtor, or over all of the debtor's other creditors who claim the property. Some of them will prevail over the holder of even a perfected security interest. Yet, "*in general* after perfection the secured party is perfected against creditors and transferees of the debtor and in particular against any representative of creditors in insolvency proceedings instituted by or against the debtor." U.C.C. §9-303 comment 1 (emphasis added).

Third, perfection occurs when a security interest "has attached and when all the applicable steps for perfection have been taken." U.C.C. §9-303(1). A nonexistent security interest obviously cannot be perfected, and this truism explains the condition to perfection that an interest has attached to the collateral. The requirements for the attachment or creation of a security interest, and the circumstances under which the interest will enlarge, are discussed in Section B, *supra*, of this unit. Here we focus on the "applicable steps" for perfection beyond having an attached interest. You must always remember, however, that although these steps can be taken before a security interest exists, taking the steps accomplishes nothing if a security interest is never created or is not sustained.

Fourth, the usual "applicable step" in perfecting a security interest is filing an Article 9 financing statement. U.C.C. §9-302(1) & comment 1. Filing, however, is not the exclusive means of perfection under Article 9. In some cases, for example, possession of the collateral by the secured party is an acceptable alternative to filing, but not when the collateral is accounts or general intangibles. If the collateral is instruments or money, possession is generally the only way to perfect. In a few cases, security interests are automatically perfected without filing or perfection.

Determining the appropriate applicable steps for perfection under Article 9 thus always requires classifying the collateral according to Article 9's five definitional categories of goods (consumer goods, equipment, farm products, inventory, and fixtures), and the six categories of intangible property (accounts, chattel paper, instruments, general intangibles, documents, and money). Misclassification of the collateral can lead to taking an inappropriate step to perfection; and such a misstep results in failure to perfect.

Fifth, Article 9 does not always govern the question of perfection. The applicable law on perfecting security interests in some kinds of collateral are prescribed by state law outside of Article 9 (e.g., motor vehicles subject to certificate of title laws) or by federal law (e.g., aircraft). Sometimes, especially when the collateral is intellectual property, the relationship between Article 9 and federal law is not entirely clear.

Robert Laurence, The Shortest Article Ever on Secured Transactions
1989 Ark. L. Notes 77

Once and for all, let's get this straight: *unperfected* does not mean *unsecured.*[1] O. K. ?

☐☐☐☐☐☐

1. Filing

Section 9-302(1) "states the general rule that to perfect a security interest under this Article a financing statement must be filed." U.C.C. §9-302 comment 1. Part 4 of Article 9 is dedicated to the details of filing. In general, however, a financing statement is filed only upon the secured party filing what Article 9 requires to be filed (see U.C.C. §9-402) in the place where Article 9 requires it to be filed (see U.C.C. §9-401). Moreover, a proper financing statement filed in the right place is effective only to the extent, and for the time, that Article 9 allows.

The idea of perfection by filing probably brings to mind your first year property study of protection from third party claims by recording. Although the ideas are similar and the objectives the same, there is a fundamental difference between most real estate recording statutes and Part 4 of Article 9. Recording traditionally means placing on record the original instrument—the deed or mortgage. Although an Article 9 security interest can be perfected by filing the written security agreement, U.C.C. §9-402(1), Article 9 does not require it.

---

[1]   The Supreme Court of Arkansas first made this mistake in McIlroy Bank v. First National Bank, 252 Ark. 558, 480 S.W.2d 127 (1972), and was criticized for it in Nickles, A *Localized Treatise on Secured Transactions--Part 11,* 34 ARK. L. REV. 559, 568 (1981).

   They recently made the mistake again in Ward v. First National Bank, 292 Ark. 21, 728 S.W.2d 149 (1987). Having held (properly, I think) that First National's security interest was *unperfected,* the unanimous Court wrote: " . . . because we have decided [First National] has no perfected security in the combine, we need not decide an issue of priority, and thus, we do not address whether *[Ward's] security interest can be considered to be perfected under the Uniform Commercial Code." Wrong, wrong, wrong.*

   If Ward was unsecured, First National wins: secured beats unsecured, perfected or not, 9-201. If Ward was perfected, then Ward beats First National: perfected beats unperfected, 9-312(5). If Ward was unperfected, then the issue is the priority between two unperfected security interests, which attached simultaneously when the debtor acquired "rights" in the combine, 9-203(1)(c). The resolution of that issue is not an easy one and is beyond the limited scope of this article.

Indeed, the statute creates a system of "notice filing" under which a secured party is encouraged to file only

> a simple notice *** before the security interest attaches or thereafter *** [that] indicates merely that the secured party who has filed may have a security interest in the collateral described. Further inquiry from the parties concerned will be necessary to disclose the complete state of affairs. Section 9-208 provides a statutory procedure under which the secured party, at the debtor's request, may be required to make disclosure.

U.C.C. §9-402 comment 2.

This "simple notice" is called a "financing statement". A standard form financing statement appears earlier in this unit, *supra*, at page 170. Every financing statement—standard form or otherwise—must meet the requirements of U.C.C. §9-402(1):

- Give the names of the debtor and the secured party;
- Give an address of the secured party from which information concerning the security interest may be obtained;
- Give a mailing address of the debtor;
- Contain a statement indicating the types, or describing the items, of collateral;
- Contain a description of the real estate concerned if the financing statement covers crops growing or to be grown;
- Be signed by the debtor.
- [Some states add additional, non-uniform requirements, such as a tax identification number.]

Perfection by filing cannot be accomplished unless the financing statement satisfies these requirements.

The most troublesome requirement is the "statement indicating the types, or describing the items, of collateral." This requirement is similar to the demand of U.C.C. §9-203(1)(a) that a written security agreement contain "a description of the collateral." In each instance the statute is satisfied only if the "statement" or "description" is sufficient. You have already considered the issue of sufficiency of descriptions in security agreements. See *World Wide Tracers, Inc. v. Metropolitan Protection, Inc.*, 384 N.W.2d 442 (Minn. 1986), reprinted at pages 181-89, *supra*. The issue is handled no differently when the debate centers on a financing statement, except—as *World Wide* suggests—the courts are usually more lenient in judging the sufficiency of descriptions in financing statements. The reasons are two: First, the purpose of a financing statement is "simple notice" to third parties who are responsible for getting complete information from the immediate parties. Second, the black letter of §9-402(1) permits financing statements to *state* the *types* of collateral in place of describing *the* collateral.

A financing statement and a security agreement are alike in other ways beyond requiring a description of collateral. Each of them is effective only with respect to property that is within the scope of the description of collateral contained therein. The two kinds of writings are also alike in requiring the debtor's signature.

A financing statement is different, however, in that the requirements of §9-402(1) cannot be satisfied by a composite of documents. So a financing statement that is unsigned by a debtor cannot be made effective by linking it to the security agreement the debtor did sign; and such a linkage cannot stretch the scope of a description of collateral in a financing statement to match a wider description in a security agreement. Moreover, the scope of a description in a financing statement can almost never be widened through extrinsic evidence.

A financing statement peculiarly must contain the names and addresses of the secured party and debtor. Do not dismiss the significance of these requirements as a source of grief for secured parties. Especially troublesome is the requirement of giving the debtor's name. Trade names and the like won't do.

A financing statement that fully satisfies the requirements as to content imposed by §9-402 is ordinarily effective to perfect a security interest only if the statement is filed in the place designated by §9-401(1). The uniform text of §9-401(1) is odd because there are three alternatives of it. The first alternative leans very much toward central filing. The third alternative leans toward local filing. The second alternative is a compromise of the other two choices. Local considerations of policy have governed each state's selection among these three alternatives. Most states have enacted the second alternative.

Problems and Notes

What Is Filed

1. Will a security interest in a farmer's tractor and harvester be perfected by a properly filed financing statement that describes the collateral as "farm equipment"?

2. Will a security interest in an individual's tape deck and portable television be perfected by a properly filed financing statement that describes the collateral as "consumer goods"? As "goods"? As "all property of the debtor"?

3. Because a financing statement is designed only to alert the world that the secured party *may* have an interest in the *types* of property stated or otherwise identified therein, there is no requirement that the financing statement announce the coverage of after-acquired property or future advances. See 9-204 comment 5.

   a. SP loans D $50,000, and D signs a security agreement covering "manufacturing equipment, present and after-acquired." A financing statement is filed stating that the collateral is "equipment." D thereafter acquires a new piece of manufacturing equipment. If the word "equipment" is a sufficient statement or description of collateral for purposes of §9-402(1), is the financing statement effective as to the new property even though the statement does not mention after-acquired equipment?

   b. Same facts, except the security agreement also provides that the collateral will secure "all future loans made by SP to D." The financing statement is silent as to future loans. Indeed, the statement provides nothing whatsoever as to value, present or future. Several months after the agreement is executed and the financing statement is filed, SP makes an additional $50,000 loan to D, which is of the same kind and class as the original loan. Is the filing effective as to both loans?

4. Bank makes a loan to D who agrees to give Bank a security interest in all her business property. The security agreement describes the collateral as: "all D's equipment, inventory, and receivables of every kind, including accounts, instruments, chattel paper, and general intangibles." To what extent is Bank's security interest perfected if the financing statement describes the collateral as "all business property"? As "all inventory and equipment."

5. A and B own a farm jointly. Their joint ownership extends to everything. They borrow money from Bank and both of them sign a security agreement that describes the collateral as "all farm equipment, including, but not limited to: automobiles, trucks, tractors, combines, harvesters, and all other implements of husbandry." Only A signs the financing statement which Bank properly files. A year later, A and B suffer a judgment that is enforced by the sheriff seizing all their non-exempt farm equipment. Does Bank or the lien creditor have priority as to equipment the sheriff seized?

6. Your client makes a secured loan to Sanford & Son, Inc. The financing statement, signed by Fred G. Sanford as President of Sanford & Son, Inc., gives the debtor's name as "Sanford & Sons." Does the financing statement meet the requirements of

§9-402(1)? What if the financing statement gives the debtor's name as "Snaford & Son, Inc."?

7. Who searches public records for filed financing statements? What are the mechanics of such a search? Should the answers to these questions affect the answer to the question "are errors in a financing statement 'minor errors that are not seriously misleading'"?

8. "[M]ost of the courts have been willing to tolerate incorrect names and incorrect indexing as effective under 9-402(8) when in their judgment the inaccuracies were not 'seriously misleading.' We believe this to be the proper approach and encourage the courts to focus here on whether a reasonably diligent searcher would be likely to discover a financing statement indexed under the incorrect name. Of course a variety of empirical facts would affect the probability that such a search would find the name." James J. White & Robert S. Summers, UNIFORM COMMERCIAL CODE §22-18 at 1036 (3d ed. 1988).

9. On April 4, P, Inc., extended credit to D and obtained a security interest in D's accounts. The security agreement provided in part that D's accounts secured not only the April 4th loan but also all future obligations of D to P, Inc., or to any subsidiaries of P, Inc. A financing statement was properly filed showing only P, Inc. as the secured party. On May 5, S Co., a subsidiary of P, Inc., makes a loan to D and obtains a security interest in D's accounts. Will it be necessary for S Co. to file a financing statement?

10. S filed a financing statement naming D as the debtor and S as the secured party. Earnie Litella, the filing officer, reversed the names in the filing office records so that the index showed D as the secured party and S as the debtor. Does Mr. Litella's error affect the perfection of S's security interest? *Should* filing officer error affect the perfection of a security interest?

Where It Is Filed

11. In each of the following situations determine where S would file. (Assume in each instance that local law is 9-401(1) (Second Alternative).)

a. S obtains a security interest in the inventory of Disco-O-Mat Record Store.

b. S has a security interest in the accounts of New Ulm Furniture Store.

c. S has a security interest in the inventory and equipment of all the retail stores operated in five counties by Dayton's Department Stores, Inc., which has its main headquarters in Bell County.

d. S takes a security interest in D's bedroom furniture.

e. S's security interest is in crops and farm equipment of farmer D who lives in
Bell County but farms in both Bell and Milam Counties.

12. S has a security interest in the crops and farm equipment of farmer D who lives in
Bell County but farms in both Bell and Milam Counties. S files a financing statement
in Bell County. Is S's security interest perfected? See 9-401(2).

13. S extends credit to Macon Farm Machinery Sales and Service, Inc., M, and obtains a
security interest in M's inventory of Kubota tractors and Owatonna hay equipment. S
files its financing statement in the UCC records in Bibb County. T is considering
extending credit to M. M tells T about S's lien. T nevertheless extends credit to M
and takes a security interest in M's inventory. T files a proper financing statement
with the Secretary of State. Who has priority, S or T? See U.C.C. §§9-312(5)(a) &
comment 5; 9-401(2).

14. Assume you are a member of a bar committee studying possible changes in your
state's version of 9-401(1). Another committee member argues for a completely
centralized, computerized filing system operated exclusively by the Secretary of
State's office. Filings could be made electronically by creditors using their own
computers to communicate directly with the Secretary's computer system. Searches
could be conducted in the same fashion. Any electronic filing would have to be
confirmed by the secured party recording with the Secretary's office a hard copy of a
UCC-1 within ten days. If such a confirmation is not received, the electronic filing
would be deleted. The computerized system would be open for business 24 hours a
day, seven days a week. Identify and balance the advantages and disadvantages of
such a system.

How Durable It Is (Continued Effectiveness)
15. *Change In Debtor's Name, §9-402(7).* Bank had a security interest in the present
and after-acquired equipment, inventory and receivables of Allied Telephone, Ltd., a
partnership. The security interest was perfected by a filed financing statement. On
March 1, Allied changed its name. The debtor acquired new inventory on April 2,
and new equipment on September 28. Consider whether Bank has a perfected
security interest in the new inventory and equipment under these circumstances:

a. Allied changed its name to Allied Telecommunications Company.

b. Allied changed its name to Berger Bros. Sporting Goods.

c. Allied incorporated under the name Allied Telecommunications, Inc.

d. Allied was purchased by, or merged into, Sperry, Inc., and was thereafter
operated as Allied Telephone, A Division of Sperry, Inc. (Be careful with
this one! A very fundamental issue is involved: Is the after-acquired

property clause in the security agreement enforceable so as to give the Bank a security interest in any property acquired after the take-over by Sperry?)

e. Do any of these circumstances affect the perfected status of Bank's security interest in equipment and inventory the debtor owned when the name changed or other event occurred?

16. *Change in Secured Party.* Suppose that a group of lenders act collectively with respect to the debtor, and they appoint an independent third party to be their agent for purposes of the collateral -- to monitor, police, and otherwise tend to the collateral for them.

a. Is their security interest perfected if the financing statement names only the collateral agent and not each of them?

b. If so, does the financing statement continue to be effective if the membership of the lenders group changes?

17. *Change In Facts That Controlled Place Of Filing, §9-401(3).* Bank had a security interest in the equipment of D, a farmer, who lived and farmed on leased land in Bell County, where Bank had filed its financing statement. D decided to quit farming herself and to start a business in Milam County where she would provide her labor and equipment to farmers who needed extra help on a temporary basis. Does Bank's financing statement remain effective with respect to D's equipment? Does the answer depend on whether D moves to Milam County?

18. *Adding New Kinds of Collateral, §9-402(4).* Bank has a security interest in D's inventory and receivables. Bank's filed financing statement covered the same collateral. When the parties agreed to increase D's loan limit, they executed a new security agreement that described the collateral as inventory, receivables and equipment. Must a wholly new financing statement be filed in order for Bank to perfect its security interest in D's equipment?

19. *Termination Of Financing Arrangement, §§9-404 & 9-406.* SP-1 was D's principal financer under a security agreement that covered all of D's inventory, equipment and receivables, present and after-acquired. SP-1's filed financing statement covered the same collateral. The parties' security agreement also included a broadly worded future-advances clause. Two years after it began, however, the relationship between SP-1 and D soured. SP-2 assumed the role of D's financer under a security agreement and filed financing statement covering all of D's business property. The first loan from SP-2 to D was used to satisfy everything D owed SP-1. Shortly thereafter D made a written demand to SP-1 that SP-1 remove from record its financing statement. Consider these subsequent events:

  a. SP-1 did not comply with D's demand that SP-1 terminate its filing. Within a year, D became dissatisfied with SP-2 and started doing business again with SP-1 which made a substantial operating loan to D. D had not repaid its obligations to SP-2. Who has priority with respect to collateral shared by SP-1 and SP-2?

  b. Same facts, except that SP-1 did file a termination statement. Who has priority? Does SP-1 even have a security interest in the property?

  c. Same facts, except that SP-1 gave D a signed statement releasing all collateral described in SP-1's financing statement. See 9-406. Who has priority? Does SP-1 even have a security interest in the property?

20. *Disposition Of The Collateral.* Bank had a security interest in D's farming equipment that was perfected by a filed financing statement. Without authority from Bank, D sold the equipment to B, who is not a buyer in the ordinary course of business. Consider the affect on the Bank's interest if:

  a. B gives a security interest in the equipment to Financer whose loan to B enabled her to purchase the property from D. Financer immediately perfects. See U.C.C. §§9-312; 9-402(7).

  b. B paid in cash using loan proceeds from Financer. D deposits the money in a bank account which is shortly thereafter garnished by a judgment creditor of D. See U.C.C. §§9-301(1)(b); 9-306(1), (2) & (3).

  c. B bought the equipment on credit, signing a simple contract evidencing her obligation to pay the price to D. A judgment creditor of D thereafter garnishes B in an attempt to reach the payments B is obligated to make to D.

  d. Are the answers different if Bank was aware of the sale to B? If Bank consented to the sale to B?

  e. What's the connection between 9-306(2) (which terminates a security interest upon any authorized disposition of collateral) and the last sentence of 9-402(7) (which continues perfection with respect to transferred collateral even though the secured party knows of and consents to the transfer)? See Permanent Editorial Board of the Uniform Commercial Code, PEB Commentary No. 3, Sections 9-3061(2) and 9-402(7) (March 10, 1990).

21. *Assignment Of Security Interest, §§9-302(2); 9-405.* Dealer sold a Ford tractor to Farmer and retained a security interest in the goods. Dealer perfected by filing a financing statement giving its own name as secured party. The installment sales

contract that Farmer signed, which was also a security agreement, was sold by Dealer to Ford Motor Credit Co., Inc. (FMCC). Through this sale FMCC acquired Dealer's right to receive the price of the tractor from B and also acquired the security interest in the tractor. The sale of the contract was without recourse, and nothing about it was filed in the public records. Consider the effects of these subsequent events:

   a. Soon after Farmer purchased the tractor, a judgment creditor of Farmer caused the sheriff to levy on it. FMCC intervenes in the execution proceedings to claim a superior interest in the tractor. Who has the better claim to the tractor, FMCC or the lien creditor? See U.C.C. §§9-301(1)(b); 9-302(2); 9-405.

   b. Suppose that the levy did not occur until six years after Farmer had purchased the tractor. Because a filing is effective for only five years, 9-403(1), FMCC had filed a continuation statement within six months before the filing made by Dealer lapsed. See 9-403(3). FMCC filed the continuation in its own name, making no reference whatsoever to the assignment of the security interest from the Dealer to FMCC.

22. *Lapse/Continuation.* SP-1 was D's principal financer with a security interest in all of D's inventory, equipment and receivables. SP-1 had properly filed a financing statement on January 2, 1989. In July, 1993, D borrowed operating funds from SP-2 and gave SP-2 a security interest in the same collateral. SP-2 immediately made a proper filing. In June, 1994, D collapsed financially. SP-1 and SP-2 claimed the collateral, which was not sufficient to satisfy full both their claims. Who has priority? See U.C.C. §§9-312(5)(a); 9-403(2).

   a. Same facts, except that in September, 1993, SP-1 filed a continuation statement pursuant to §9-403(3).

   b. Same facts, except that in March, 1993, SP-1 filed a fresh financing statement signed by D the same month. This new financing statement was exactly like the original statement. What if this statement was filed in September?

   c. Same facts, except that D's collapse occurred in September, 1993, when a receiver was appointed to dispose of D's property and collect D's receivables. SP-1 and SP-2 both demanded the proceeds, and the receiver interpleaded the funds sometime in October, 1993. The interpleader action was dormant until June, 1994, at which time the court set about determining the issue of priority between SP-1 and SP-2. Who is entitled to priority? (By the way, SP-1 did not file a continuation statement.)

Bank of the West v. Commercial Credit Financial Services, Inc.
United States Court of Appeals, Ninth Circuit, 1988
852 F.2d 1162

David R. Thompson, Circuit Judge: In these cross-appeals, Bank of the West, a California banking corporation ("Bank of the West" or "Bank"), and Commercial Credit Financial Services, Inc., a Delaware corporation ("CCFS"), appeal the district court's judgment for Bank of the West on its suit for conversion of collateral. Bank of the West argues that (1) the district court's findings of fact are erroneous, (2) the court improperly excluded certain evidence, (3) the damages awarded are inadequate as a matter of law, and (4) the court erred in not considering the Bank's fraudulent conveyance claim. On its cross-appeal, CCFS argues the court incorrectly resolved the priority dispute between it and Bank of the West. CCFS contends that had the court applied the correct rule to the priority dispute, the court would have concluded CCFS did not convert the collateral.

We have jurisdiction under 28 U.S.C. §1291. Although the district court's findings of fact are not clearly erroneous, we conclude that the court erred in resolving the conflicting claims to the collateral. Consequently, we hold that CCFS prevails on its cross-appeal, and we do not reach Bank of the West's damages and fraudulent conveyance arguments. We reverse the decision of the district court and remand the case for entry of judgment in favor of CCFS.

* * *

II
FACTS

* * *

On April 5, 1982, Bank of the West entered into a loan and security agreement with Allied Canners & Packers, Inc. ("Allied"), a wholly-owned subsidiary of Boles World Trade Corporation ("BWTC"). Bank of the West lent Allied $4,000,000 in exchange for a security interest in Allied's present and future-acquired inventory, accounts, and proceeds. The Bank perfected its security interest by filing a financing statement with the California Secretary of State on April 7, 1982.

In 1983, Allied's financial condition deteriorated and the Bank demanded repayment of the outstanding loan balance of $1,800,000. Allied persuaded the Bank to renegotiate the loan. This resulted in a restructuring agreement signed on January 13, 1984. Contemporaneously with the restructuring agreement, Allied signed a new security agreement granting Bank of the West a security interest in Allied's "present and hereafter acquired" accounts, inventory, and proceeds. As part of the loan renegotiations, there is evidence that BWTC suggested to Bank of the West that it would transfer a beverage wholesaling and importing business to Allied.

In January 1984, another wholly-owned BWTC subsidiary, Boles & Co., Inc. ("BCI"), entered into a factoring agreement with CCFS. The factoring agreement provided that BCI would assign its accounts to CCFS. CCFS would then collect amounts due from account debtors; three days after collection, CCFS would remit to BCI the amounts collected, less a 1% commission, and less any prior advances, plus interest. Advances were to be made on accounts which remained uncollected 33 days following assignment. In the factoring agreement, BCI granted CCFS a security interest in its present and after-acquired accounts. In a separate security agreement to secure advances made to BCI pending collection of accounts, BCI also granted CCFS a security interest in BCI's present and after-acquired inventory and proceeds. CCFS properly perfected its security interests by filing a financing statement with the California Secretary of State on January 5, 1984.

To understand the issues on appeal, it is necessary to consider the complicated corporate structure of the affiliated companies owned by BWTC. BWTC, formerly called Boles & Co., Inc., owned several subsidiary corporations, which engaged in several different businesses. Before August 1983, the former Boles & Co. (now called BWTC) conducted a beverage importing and wholesaling business. On August 15, 1983, the board of directors of the original Boles & Co. voted to change its name to BWTC and to contribute the beverage business to one of its wholly-owned subsidiaries, Minerals Trading Corporation. On the same day, the directors of Minerals voted to change its name to Boles & Co., Inc. (referred to as BCI), and to accept the contribution of the beverage business assets from BWTC. Between August 1983 and June 30, 1984, BWTC again reorganized its subsidiaries and transferred the beverage business from BCI to Allied. Allied changed its name to Boles International Beverage Co. ("Allied/BIBCO") by vote of its board of directors on December 6, 1983, but did not file a certificate of amendment with the California Secretary of State to reflect this name change until June 11, 1984.

Much of the dispute in this case is over who owned the beverage business accounts factored by CCFS after January 13, 1984, the date on which Bank of the West signed the loan restructuring agreement with Allied/BIBCO. Bank of the West argues that at least by February 1, 1984, Allied/BIBCO was conducting the beverage business and that CCFS consequently was factoring accounts in which Bank of the West held a prior perfected security interest. The district court found that the beverage business was not finally transferred to Allied/BIBCO until July 1, 1984. The court reviewed the extensive evidence presented by both sides and found that while BWTC may have intended to transfer the beverage business to Allied as early as October 1983, id. at 814, BWTC did not complete moving the beverage business to Allied/BIBCO until the end of June 1984. Having examined the record, which is replete with conflicting testimony, vague assertions, and confused recollections, we cannot say that the district court's findings of fact are clearly erroneous. Accordingly, we accept the court's finding that between January 13 and June 30, 1984, BCI owned and operated the beverage business.

In operating that business, BCI generated the accounts factored by CCFS.[1] On July 1, 1984, the beverage business was transferred to Allied/BIBCO. Consequently, from and after that date, any accounts factored by CCFS were generated by sales of the beverage business inventory by Allied/BIBCO, or were accounts in existence at the time of the transfer.

III
ANALYSIS

The principal issue on appeal is the application of the California Commercial Code to determine which of two conflicting security interests in the beverage business's accounts has priority. [R]esolving conflicting claims to the same collateral requires a three-step inquiry. The first step is to determine whether each security interest has "attached," and therefore become enforceable. See Cal.Com.Code §9203(1). Attachment occurs when each of three events has taken place: (1) the secured party has possession of the collateral pursuant to an agreement, or the debtor has signed a security agreement describing the collateral, (2) the secured party has given value, and (3) the debtor has rights in the collateral. Id.

The second step in the analysis is to classify each of the competing security interests as "perfected," id. §9303(1), or as "unperfected." Perfection requires "attachment" of the security interest plus some additional step specified in the code. Id. In general, a security interest which has "attached" is "perfected" by filing a financing statement, id. §9302(1), which complies with certain formal requisites, see id. §9402(1), and is filed in the proper place. Id. §9401(1). Once the competing security interests have been classified, the final step is to apply the priority rules set out in chapter 3 of Division 9 of the California Commercial Code. See id. §§9301-9318.

The collateral claimed by both CCFS and Bank of the West consists of accounts generated from the sale of the beverage business's inventory after the transfer of the beverage business from BCI to Allied/BIBCO. The district court found that the "transfer" of the beverage business to Allied/BIBCO was effected by a process that ended by July 1, 1984. * * * Consequently, the dispute is over those accounts factored between July 1, 1984 and October 15, 1984, the date on which the factoring agreement terminated. To understand the resolution of the priority dispute that we adopt in this opinion, it is necessary to consider the status of the parties' security interests before the transfer of the beverage business.

---

[1]   Bank of the West renews its argument that even if BCI "operated" the beverage business before July 1984, Allied "owned" the inventory used in that business, and hence Allied "owned" any accounts generated by the sale of that inventory. We reject this argument. The district court specifically found that BCI owned the collateral used in the beverage business, which necessarily included inventory. This finding is not clearly erroneous.

A. The Pre-Transfer Security Interests in the Beverage Business

1. The Bank's Security Interest

Until completion of the transfer on July 1, 1984, Bank of the West had no enforceable security interest in the beverage business's inventory or accounts. Bank of the West's debtor is Allied/BIBCO. A security interest cannot attach unless "the debtor has rights in the collateral." Cal.Com.Code §9203(1)(c). The district court specifically found that Allied/BIBCO did not acquire rights in the collateral until the transfer of the beverage business. Consequently, Bank of the West had no security interest in the accounts factored by CCFS under its agreement with BCI until the July 1, 1984 transfer.

2. CCFS' Security Interest

From January 10, 1984 to July 1, 1984, CCFS had a perfected security interest in BCI's inventory, accounts, and proceeds. On January 10, 1984, BCI signed two agreements (the factoring agreement and the separate security agreement) granting CCFS security interests in BCI's present and future-acquired inventory, accounts, and proceeds. CCFS gave "value" to BCI by promising to advance it money on the strength of the accounts assigned under the factoring agreement. See Cal.Com.Code §1201(44). The district court specifically found that BCI had "rights in the collateral." Thus, CCFS's security interest attached to the pre- transfer collateral on January 10, 1984. Cal.Com.Code §9203(1). CCFS filed a financing statement naming BCI as its debtor with the California Secretary of State on January 5, 1984. As a result, CCFS's security interest became perfected on January 10, 1984, the date on which its security interest in the collateral attached. See Cal.Com.Code §9303(1) ("If such [applicable] steps [required for perfection] are taken before a security interest attaches, it is perfected at the time when it attaches.").

B. The Post-Transfer Security Interests

1. The Bank's Security Interest

Bank of the West's security agreement with Allied granted the Bank a security interest in Allied's future-acquired inventory, accounts, and proceeds. As we have stated, Bank of the West's security interest attached to the transferred assets on July 1, 1984, when its debtor, Allied, acquired rights in the collateral. See Cal.Com.Code §9203(1). Bank of the West's security interest became perfected at the moment of attachment as a result of the Bank's financing statement naming Allied as its debtor, which was filed with the California Secretary of State on April 7, 1982. See id. §9303(1). In addition to its perfected security interest in assets actually transferred from BCI to Allied, because of the after-acquired property clause in its security agreement, Bank of the West had a perfected security interest in all inventory, accounts, and proceeds thereafter acquired by Allied.[1]

---

[1]   We note that there is evidence in the record that at the time of the July 1, 1984

2. CCFS's Security Interest

In its opinion, the district court concluded that it was unnecessary for it to determine whether CCFS's security interest remained perfected after the transfer. In light of our resolution of the priority dispute, we must address this question.

Two provisions of the commercial code are relevant to deciding whether CCFS's security interest continued after the transfer of the beverage business to Allied. We begin with section 9306(2), which provides in pertinent part:

> Except where this division ... otherwise provides, a security interest continues in collateral notwithstanding sale, exchange or other disposition thereof unless the disposition was authorized by the secured party in the security agreement or otherwise, and also continues in any identifiable proceeds including collections received by the debtor.

Cal.Com.Code §9306(2). Neither the factoring agreement nor the related security agreement expressly authorized BCI to transfer its assets to another corporation. There is no evidence to show that CCFS otherwise authorized this disposition of its collateral. California courts have made clear that implied authorizations of sales of the debtor's collateral will not be found absent clear evidence based on the prior conduct of the parties. Because there is no evidence that CCFS authorized BCI's disposition of the collateral, CCFS's security interest in the collateral actually transferred (inventory and accounts) and its proceeds continued after the transfer.

While section 9306(2) indicates that a security interest survives an unauthorized disposition of the collateral, we must look to section 9402(7) of the commercial code to determine whether CCFS's security interest in the collateral remained perfected after the transfer.

> A financing statement sufficiently shows the name of the debtor if it gives the individual partnership or corporate name of the debtor, whether or not it adds other trade names or names of partners. Where the debtor so changes his name or in the case of an organization its name, identity or corporate structure that a filed financing statement becomes seriously misleading, the filing is not effective to perfect a security interest in collateral acquired by the debtor more than four months after the change, unless a new appropriate financing statement or an appropriate amendment to the filed financing statement is filed before the acquisition of collateral by the debtor. A filed financing statement remains effective with

---

transfer, Allied was a moribund entity that carried on no business of its own. Consequently, the only post-transfer property acquired by Allied related to the beverage business.

respect to collateral transferred by the debtor even though the secured party knows of or consents to the transfer.

Cal.Com.Code §9402(7).

On its face, section 9402(7) seems to answer the issue posed by the transfer from BCI to Allied simply enough. Under the third sentence of section 9402(7), CCFS's security interest in the collateral actually transferred by BCI to Allied remains perfected. This is the collateral "transferred by the debtor" to which the third sentence of 9402(7) speaks. Section 9306(2) says CCFS's security interest follows its collateral. The last sentence of section 9402(7) says CCFS's filed financing statement remains effective. By necessary implication, CCFS's security interest therefore remains perfected. The more difficult question to answer, however, is whether CCFS has any interest in collateral acquired by Allied after the transfer. At first blush, the answer is no. After the transfer, any collateral acquired by Allied is not collateral acquired by CCFS's "debtor." See, e.g., Cal.Com.Code §9105(1)(d) (" 'Debtor' means the person who owes payment or other performance of the obligation secured, whether or not he or she owns or has rights in the collateral, and includes the seller of accounts or chattel paper."). If the accounts generated after the transfer are not collateral acquired by CCFS's debtor, it would appear that CCFS cannot claim any security interest in the post-transfer accounts, except to the extent that these accounts are traceable as proceeds of the transferred inventory, in which CCFS had a perfected security interest that followed the transfer under sections 9306(2) and 9402(7).

If we were to read section 9402(7) this rigidly we would overlook a difficult problem that commentators have observed. There are a number of transactions that involve both a transfer of collateral and a change in the corporate identity or structure of the debtor. See, e.g., Knippenberg, Debtor Name Changes and Collateral Transfers Under 9-402(7): Drafting from the Outside-In, 52 Mo.L.Rev. 58, 108 (1987) ("It is not always an easy matter, however, to decide whether the activity of an entity debtor should be regarded as a change of identity or corporate structure on the one hand, or a transfer of collateral on the other." (footnote omitted)); Note, Debtors' Name or Identity Changes: Distributing Benefits and Burdens Under Article 9, 31 Hastings L.J. 959, 979 (1980) ("[G]iven the various potential forms of transfers, it may be difficult to distinguish between dispositions of collateral to independent third parties and to successor enterprises of the debtor."). In the present case, assets have been transferred from one wholly- owned subsidiary of a common parent corporation to another wholly-owned subsidiary. There is no evidence that the transferor, BCI, received any consideration for the transfer of the beverage business. The evidence suggests that the transaction represented a simple bookkeeping entry from the perspective of the parent corporation. There is no evidence that the beverage business was conducted differently after the transfer. Indeed, until mid-August 1984, Allied continued to use invoices and transfer lists bearing the BCI name. There also is testimony in the record indicating that "there was confusion among BWTC personnel as to which company operated the beverage business [before the transfer]." In sum, the "transfer" of collateral in this case involves a change in the corporate structure of the debtor.

Comments 7 and 8 to section 9-402(7) of the Uniform Commercial Code, which California has adopted almost unchanged, read as follows:

> 7. * * * Subsection (7) also deals with the case of a change of name of a debtor and provides some guidelines when mergers or other changes of corporate structure of the debtor occur with the result that a filed financing statement might become seriously misleading. Not all cases can be imagined and covered by statutes in advance; however, the general principle sought to be achieved by the subsection is that after a change which would be seriously misleading, the old financing statement is not effective as to new collateral acquired more than four months after the change, unless a new appropriate financing statement is filed before the expiration of the four months. The old financing statement, if legally still valid under the circumstances, would continue to protect collateral acquired before the change and, if still operative under the particular circumstances, would also protect collateral acquired within the four months. Obviously, the subsection does not undertake to state whether the security agreement continues to operate between the secured party and the party surviving the corporate change of the debtor.

> 8. Subsection (7) also deals with a different problem, namely whether a new filing is necessary where the collateral has been transferred from one debtor to another. This question has been much debated both in pre-Code law and under the Code. This Article now answers the question in the negative. Thus, any person searching the condition of the ownership of a debtor must make inquiry as to the debtor's source of title, and must search in the name of a former owner if circumstances seem to require it.

Cal.Com.Code §9402(7) Uniform Commercial Code Comments 7 & 8 (emphasis added).

These comments make clear that the second and third sentences of 9402(7) are meant to apply in different circumstances.[1] The drafters, however, do not

---

[1] Notwithstanding arguments to the contrary, we do not read the third sentence of section 9402(7) as simply stating a necessary conclusion from the second sentence. See, e.g., Note, supra, 31 Hastings L.J. at 984 ("[T]he last sentence appears to state merely what is evident from the second, i.e., that no new financing statement need be filed with

explain how courts are to decide whether an intercorporate transfer unaccompanied by a formal structural change such as a merger of the related entities is a "change of identity or structure" or a "transfer of collateral." This clearly is not a simple matter to resolve. But in this case, we conclude that there has been a change of structure in the debtor entity.

To reach this conclusion, we return to the Code's definition of "debtor," which provides that "[w]here the debtor and the owner of the collateral are not the same person, 'debtor' means the owner of the collateral in any provision of the division dealing with the collateral, ... and may include both where the context so requires." Cal.Com.Code §9105(1)(d). Comment 2 to this section explains that "[o]ccasionally, one person furnishes security for another's debt, and sometimes property is transferred subject to a secured debt of the transferor which the transferee does not assume; in such cases, the term 'debtor' may, depending upon the context, include either or both such persons." Id. Uniform Commercial Code Comment 2 (emphasis added). We already have seen that under section 9306(2), a security interest follows collateral into the hands of the transferee when the transferor's disposition of the collateral was not authorized. It seems reasonable to read the term "debtor" in the second sentence of section 9402(7) to mean not only the transferee, but also to include the transferor, especially when the transferor and transferee are wholly-owned subsidiaries of a common parent and the transfer occurs under the circumstances existing in the present case.

Our conclusion to treat the intercorporate transfer between BCI and Allied/BIBCO as a change in BCI's corporate structure also finds support in our decision in Towers v. B.J. Holmes Sales Co. (In re West Coast Food Sales, Inc.), 637 F.2d 707 (9th Cir.1981). In that case, the creditor, B.J. Holmes Sales Co., lent money to John Granaham d/b/a West Coast Sales Co. in exchange for a security interest in the debtor's accounts. B.J. Holmes filed a financing statement naming "West Coast Sales Company" as its debtor. Later, a newly formed entity, West Coast Food Sales, Inc., succeeded to the assets and liabilities of West Coast Sales Company. B.J. Holmes continued to lend money to West Coast Food Sales, Inc. until June 1, 1977, when that corporation filed a

---

respect to the security interest in the specific property transferred by the debtor to the successor enterprise." (emphasis in original)). We think that the drafters intended the third sentence to apply to bona fide transfers of collateral to third parties unrelated to the transferor. We note, of course, that section 9307(1), which provides that a transfer to a buyer in the ordinary course will cut off the transferor's creditor's security interest, does not apply in this case. This is so because Allied cannot qualify as a "buyer in the ordinary course." The transfer of all of BCI's assets to Allied as a matter of law is not in the ordinary course of business. See Cal.Com.Code §1201(9). The transfer of all of BCI's inventory to Allied is a bulk sale. See id. §6102. "Buying" does not include a bulk transfer. Id. §1201(9). Therefore, Allied, as a transferee in bulk, cannot defeat CCFS's security interest. See Bank of the West, 655 F.Supp. at 816. As we explain later in this opinion, if Allied cannot defeat CCFS's security interest, neither can Bank of the West.

bankruptcy petition. The trustee in bankruptcy challenged B.J. Holmes' security interest in the accounts generated after the incorporation of West Coast Food Sales, Inc. and the transfer of the assets and liabilities of West Coast Sales Co. to it in 1973. The trustee argued that the newly formed entity was not B.J. Holmes' debtor and the security agreement with West Coast Sales Co. did not bind West Coast Food Sales, Inc. We rejected the trustee's argument because we found it repugnant to allow "a debtor ... to evade the obligations of a validly executed security agreement by the simple expedient of an alteration in its business structure." Id. at 709. We noted that the business was operated similarly before and after the change in corporate structure and that ownership of the two entities remained in the same hands before and after the transfer. Id.

The rationale of the *West Coast Food Sales* case applies to the intercorporate transfer between BCI and Allied. We will not validate an attempt by BWTC to switch assets among its affiliated, wholly-owned subsidiaries so that the debt to Bank of the West is satisfied at the cost of CCFS's perfected secured claim against the beverage business's assets. "A debtor cannot destroy the perfected security interest of a secured party by merely changing its name or corporate structure...." Id. (quoting Inter Mountain Ass'n of Credit Men v. Villager, Inc., 527 P.2d 664, 671 (Utah 1974)); see also AC-Delco Div. of Gen. Motors Corp. v. Serrins Automotive Warehouse, Inc. (In re Serrins Automotive Warehouse, Inc.), 18 B.R. 718, 719 (Bankr.W.D.Pa.1980) (citing cases stating that debtor cannot destroy perfected security interest by transferring title to collateral or changing its name or corporate structure, "and the validity of the lien against subsequently acquired assets as well as those presently owned is effective thereagainst"); American Heritage Bank & Trust Co. v. O. & E., Inc., 40 Colo.App. 306, 308, 576 P.2d 566, 568 (1978) (same).

In summary, we hold that when BCI transferred its assets to Allied, this was not a bona fide third party transfer of collateral within the scope of the third sentence of section 9402(7). Rather, BCI simply changed its corporate structure. When the transferor shifts assets to an affiliated company at the behest of their common parent company, and when the transaction has the same effect as a merger of the transferor into the transferee with the transferee as the surviving corporation, we cannot say that this is a simple transfer of collateral. To hold otherwise would permit debtors to decide which sentence of section 9402(7) applies merely by choosing an advantageous formal arrangement for the desired transaction. Thus, applying the second sentence of section 9402(7), we hold that CCFS's security interest continued perfected in those assets actually transferred to Allied as well as in those assets acquired by Allied during the four months following the July 1, 1984 transfer. Because the only collateral at issue in this case consists of those accounts factored in the 3 1/2 -month period between July 1, 1984, and October 15, 1984, we need not consider whether the BCI-Allied transaction rendered CCFS's filed financing statement seriously misleading.

C. Resolving the Priority Dispute

Having concluded that both Bank of the West and CCFS had perfected security interests in the inventory and accounts actually transferred from BCI to Allied/BIBCO, as well as the inventory and accounts acquired by Allied/BIBCO after the July 1, 1984 transfer, we must decide which of these security interests is entitled to priority. The district court resolved this question by looking to section 9312(5), which provides:

> In all cases not governed by other rules stated in this section ... priority between conflicting security interests in the same collateral shall be determined according to the following rules: (a) Conflicting security interests rank according to priority in time of filing or perfection. Priority dates from the time a filing is first made covering the collateral or the time the security interest is first perfected, whichever is earlier, provided that there is no period thereafter when there is neither filing nor perfection. (b) So long as conflicting security interests are unperfected, the first to attach has priority.

Cal.Com.Code §9312(5).

By applying section 9312(5)(a) according to its literal language, the district court concluded that Bank of the West's security interest prevailed over that of CCFS. When BCI transferred the beverage business to Allied/BIBCO, Bank of the West's security interest attached under the after-acquired property clause in its security agreement. See Cal.Com.Code §§9203(1), 9204(1). When Bank of the West's security interest attached, it automatically became perfected pursuant to the earlier filed financing statement naming Allied as its debtor. See Cal.Com.Code §9303(1). Bank of the West's financing statement was filed on April 7, 1982. CCFS's financing statement was filed January 5, 1984, and its security interest became perfected on January 10, 1984 when BCI executed the factoring and related security agreements. Section 9312(5) sets forth a "first to file or first to perfect" rule of priority. Because Bank of the West's financing statement was filed first, the district court concluded that the Bank's security interest prevailed over that of CCFS. Bank of the West, 655 F.Supp. at 817.

The situation we have described above has until this case been regarded by the commentators as only a hypothetical scenario. It is a scenario offered by the commentators, however, to illustrate a failure of the commercial code to resolve a priority dispute properly. The difficulty noted by these commentators is this: Before the transfer from BCI to Allied, CCFS (the transferor's creditor) had a perfected security interest in the collateral. After the transfer, CCFS's perfected security interest suddenly is subordinated to the perfected security interest of Bank of the West (the transferee's creditor). CCFS, which had taken all steps required of it by the commercial code to announce its interest in the collateral to potential creditors of the transferor (BCI), now finds its security interest subordinated to that of the transferee's (Allied's) creditor, (Bank of the West), whose security interest came into play only because BCI made an unauthorized disposition of the collateral to which the Bank's security interest attached solely by operation of an after-acquired collateral clause.

We agree with the commentators that applying section 9312(5) to resolve this priority dispute produces an unsatisfactory result. The principal reason that section 9312(5) fails to produce a proper result is that it does not appear the drafters contemplated * * * the "dual debtor dilemma." * * * Because section 9312(5) does not contemplate the dual debtor scenario, we must resolve this priority dispute by returning to first principles.

As a general rule of construction, the commercial code "shall be liberally construed and applied to promote its underlying purposes and policies." Cal.Com.Code §1102(1). The commercial code is intended to be flexible. "It is intended to make it possible for the law embodied in this Act to be developed by the courts in the light of unforeseen and new circumstances and practices. However, the proper construction of the Act requires that its interpretation and application be limited to its reason." Id. Uniform Commercial Code Comment 1. There are two reasons behind the rule of section 9312(5)(a). First, the "first to file or first to perfect" rule serves to modify the common law notion of "first in time, first in right." Section 9312(5) places a premium on prompt filing of financing statements as a means of protecting future creditors of the debtor. The financing statement alerts potential creditors that collateral against which they are contemplating making a loan already is encumbered. Thus, section 9312(5)(a) penalizes a creditor who has a security interest but who does not promptly file a financing statement by awarding priority to a later creditor who acquires a security interest in the same collateral and who more promptly files a financing statement. The "first to file or first to perfect" rule of 9312(5)(a) thus addresses the problem of secret security interests that so concerned pre-Code courts. But in the present case, the notice giving function of 9312(5)(a) does not apply. Bank of the West is a creditor of another debtor entity, and the Bank's interest in the collateral arises solely out of an after-acquired property clause. Bank of the West cannot claim that it has relied to its detriment on the absence of a filed financing statement by CCFS.[1]

A second purpose behind section 9312(5)(a) is an implied commitment to a secured creditor who has filed a financing statement that, absent special considerations such as a purchase money security interest, see, e.g., Cal.Com.Code §9312(3), (4), no subsequent creditor will be able to defeat the complying creditor's security interest. This notion finds support in comment 5 to section 9402(7), which reads in pertinent part: "The justification for this rule

---

[1]   Indeed, there is evidence that as part of the restructuring agreement, the Bank agreed to subordinate its security interest to any institutional lender who financed the beverage business's accounts. CCFS gave BCI a subordination agreement to send the Bank when CCFS learned of the transfer. For reasons not clear in the record, the Bank did not execute the subordination agreement. The fact remains, however, that the Bank cannot argue that it was misled by the absence of a financing statement filed by CCFS.

lies in the necessity of protecting the filing system--that is, of allowing the secured party who has first filed to make subsequent advances without each time having, as a precondition of protection, to check for filings later than his." Cal.Com.Code §9312 Uniform Commercial Code Comment 5. This has been described as the "claim staking" function of the financing statement. What this means is that by filing a proper financing statement in the proper place, a secured creditor has staked a claim to its collateral and knows that, absent special considerations, its claim will prevail against subsequently arising interests in the same property. By complying with the Code, the creditor is relieved of much of the responsibility of monitoring its debtor's collateral--the Code has allocated the burden of discovering prior filed financing statements to later lenders. Cf. Cal.Com.Code §9402 Uniform Commercial Code Comment 8 ("[A]ny person searching the condition of ownership of a debtor must make inquiry as to the debtor's source of title, and must search in the name of a former owner if the circumstances seem to require it.").

Applying section 9312(5)(a) to the present case serves neither of the rationales behind the "first to file or first to perfect" rule. The notice giving function is irrelevant because the creditor of a different debtor whose sole interest in disputed collateral arises from an after-acquired property clause has no incentive to check for financing statements against the property of another debtor. Certainly the burden is on a transferee's creditor to search the title to property, but this duty arises only when the transferee's creditor first appears on the scene after the transfer. Likewise, it makes no sense to use section 9312(5)(a) to defeat CCFS's perfected security interest when CCFS has taken all steps required of it by the Code to proclaim its interest in the collateral. CCFS is entitled to rely on the Code's promise that a creditor who fully complies usually may expect its security interest to be given priority in a dispute with another secured creditor. To apply section 9312(5)(a) to this case would produce an undesirable result that does not follow from the principles that the section is meant to promote.[1]

---

[1]   It is possible to argue, of course, that our analysis does violence to the interest of the transferee's creditor, whose security interest has been perfected by filing just the same as the transferor's creditor. But it is important to remember that the situation we consider is one in which the transferee's creditor's security interest attaches to the transferred collateral solely by operation of an after-acquired property clause. Although the Uniform Commercial Code expressly validates after-acquired property clauses, see Cal.Com.Code §9204(1), these "floating liens" still have not been whole-heartedly accepted by the drafters.

> Subsection 1 makes clear that a security interest arising by virtue of an after-acquired property clause has equal status with a security interest in collateral in which the debtor has rights at the time value is given under the security agreement. That is to say: security interest in after- acquired property is not merely an "equitable" interest; no further action by the secured party ... is required. This does not mean however that the interest is proof against subordination or defeat....

We think the correct result is reached in this case by applying the common sense notion that a creditor cannot convey to another more than it owns. Put another way, the transferee, Allied, cannot acquire any greater rights in the beverage business's assets than its transferor, BCI, had in them. Our analysis also finds direct support in the California Commercial Code. Section 9312(1) provides, "The rules of priority stated in other sections of this chapter ... shall govern where applicable." And section 9306(2) provides that a security interest follows collateral into the hands of a transferee when there is an unauthorized disposition by the transferor. The drafters tell us that

> "[i]n most cases when a debtor makes an unauthorized disposition of the collateral, the security interest, under ... this Article, continues in the original collateral in the hands of the purchaser or other transferee. That is to say, ... the transferee takes subject to the security interest.... Subsection [9306(2)] codifies this rule."

Cal.Com.Code §9306(2) Uniform Commercial Code Comment 3. If the transferee (Allied) takes the transferred collateral subject to the transferor's creditor's (CCFS's) security interest, certainly the transferee's creditor (Bank of the West) can have no greater rights in the collateral than does its debtor (Allied). Because section 9402(7) preserves CCFS's perfected security interest in the collateral actually transferred as well as in the property acquired in the four months after the transfer, CCFS's security interest continues to be superior to Bank of the West's interest during this period, even though Bank of the West's interest also is perfected. This result is consistent with the principles of the filing system that we have previously discussed. If the notice giving function does not apply because Bank of the West has no reason to check for filings against BCI, the claim-staking function that protects CCFS should be enforced. CCFS has done all that the Code asks of it to protect its interest. Absent some countervailing consideration, CCFS should be entitled to rely on its perfected security interest.

IV
CONCLUSION

BCI's transfer of the assets subject to CCFS's security interest was an unauthorized disposition of the collateral. Consequently, applying section 9306(2), CCFS's security interest followed the transferred assets into the hands of Allied. Because the transfer was in reality a change in corporate structure, CCFS's security interest remained perfected in all assets actually transferred as well as in those acquired by Allied in the four months after the transfer. See

---

Cal.Com.Code §9204(1) Uniform Commercial Code Comment 1 (emphasis added). To the extent our opinion results in holders of after-acquired property clauses not being able to prevail against the perfected security interest of a transferor's secured creditor, this is consistent with the drafters intention in validating after-acquired property clauses but not granting them an assurance of absolute priority in all cases.

Cal.Com.Code §9402(7) (second sentence). Because Allied/BIBCO's interest in the assets transferred and those acquired in the four months thereafter is subject to CCFS's security interest, see Cal.Com.Code §9306(2) Uniform Commercial Code Comment 3, Bank of the West can have no greater rights in the collateral than its debtor. Cf. Cal.Com.Code §2403(1). Therefore, CCFS's perfected security interest is superior to that of Bank of the West. Because Bank of the West's security interest is subordinate to that of CCFS, CCFS could not have converted Bank of the West's property when it factored the post-transfer account. As a result, we reverse the decision of the district court and remand the case for entry of judgment in favor of CCFS.

REVERSED AND REMANDED.

2. Other Steps For Perfection (Exceptions To Filing)

a. Possession

A filing system has not always existed as a means of giving public notice of security interests in personal property. Recording acts providing for the filing of chattel mortgages and other personal property security devices were uncommon in the United States until the second half of the nineteenth century. In the absence of a recording act and compliance with it, a debtor's creditors and purchasers of the collateral could easily be misled by a security arrangement that permitted a debtor freely to hold and use property that she did not fully own. Because there was no system for recording encumbrances on chattels, creditors or purchasers had no reliable means for discovering a secured creditor's interest which, therefore, was a secret lien. For this reason, security arrangements that left a debtor in possession of the collateral generally were unenforceable against innocent third parties.

Thus, in the earliest days of American secured transactions law, taking possession of the collateral was often the only means by which a secured creditor could insure her collateral against the claims of the debtor's other creditors and transferees of the property. This sort of security arrangement, known as the *pledge*, is simply a bailment for the purpose of securing an obligation, which requires a debtor-pledgor to surrender physical control of the collateral to a secured creditor-pledgee. Someone thereafter acquiring an interest in the property cannot justly complain of the pledgee's interest. Inasmuch as the debtor lacked possession and control of the collateral, no reasonably alert and inquisitive person could have been misled about the true state of the debtor's title to the property. On this basis, the courts for centuries have generally enforced pledge arrangements against third parties.

Article 9 sanctions pledges of collateral and facilitates the use of this ancient security device in two ways. First, Article 9 dispenses with the requirement of a written security agreement when a secured party possesses pledgeable collateral. U.C.C. §9-203(1). Second, a security interest in pledgeable collateral is perfected by the secured party's possession of the property. U.C.C. §9-305. In deciding for either or both of these purposes if a pledge has been accomplished under Article 9, you must necessarily consider whether the collateral is *pledgeable* and, if so, whether the secured party is in *possession* of the property as the law of pledges defines the term.

Accounts and general intangibles are not pledgeable. So possession is an *impossible* and *impermissible* means of perfecting security interests in these types of collateral. Filing is always required. Moreover, when the collateral is accounts or general intangibles, a written security agreement is always necessary.

Letters and advices of credit, money, negotiable documents, chattel paper, and instruments, like all kinds of goods, are pledgeable under Article 9. U.C.C. §§9-304(1) & 9-305. Article 9 recognizes possession and filing as *alternative* means of perfecting security interests in goods, negotiable documents, and chattel paper. Possession is the *exclusive* means of perfection when the collateral is money or instruments (other than certificated securities).

Although Article 9 expressly provides for "possession" as a means of perfection, the statute does not define the term. The courts therefore consult the common law of pledges. Under this law, possession generally implies that a person has physical control of property with the intent to exercise such control in her own behalf. Restatement of Security §1 comment a (1941).

Yet, to perfect an Article 9 security interest by possession, a secured party need not control the collateral with the specific intention of thereby perfecting her interest. A security interest in pledgeable property is perfected, for example, when a secured party repossesses collateral for the purpose of disposing of it under Part 5 of Article 9.

On the other hand, a bare intention or naked right to control collateral for whatever purpose, even for the specific purpose of perfecting the security interest, will not result of itself in perfection by possession. Ordinarily, the property must be actually, physically, manually delivered to the secured party, or she must otherwise establish real control over the collateral. Moreover, "'the pledgee's possession *** [must] be complete, unequivocal and exclusive of the pledgor's possession in his own right.'" *Cissell v. First Nat'l Bank,* 476 F.Supp. 474, 491 (S.D.Ohio 1979). In other words, if the secured party shares with the debtor access to and control over the collateral, the secured party is not, in legal terms, in possession of the collateral and thus her security interest is not perfected by possession. U.C.C. §9-205 comment 6. Control of the collateral must rest exclusively with the secured party.

The law of pledges has always recognized that the secured party herself need not personally possess the collateral in order to establish a pledge. Article 9 agrees. So, for example, "possession may be by the secured party himself *or by an agent on his behalf*." U.C.C. §9-305 comment 2 (emphasis added). Yet, because a secured party must exclusively control the collateral, "the debtor or a person controlled by him cannot qualify as such an agent for the secured party." Id.

When collateral is in the possession of a third-party bailee who is not at the time the secured party's agent, the secured party can nevertheless perfect by possession by notifying the bailee of the secured party's interest. U.C.C. §9-305. This means of perfection by possession essentially mirrors the common law under which a pledge can be created, when the collateral is held by a third person, by the pledgor or pledgee notifying the third person that the property has been pledged to the pledgee. Restatement of Security §8 (1941).

Possession by an agent and possession by notice to a bailee are separate constructs. They are different methods by which a secured party can perfect by possession when someone else physically controls and thus actually possesses the collateral. Possession by an agent refers to possession accomplished through the manual or constructive delivery of the collateral to a person who stands legally in the secured party's stead. Possession by notice to a bailee refers to possession achieved through constructive delivery of the collateral to the secured party. The law deems that upon the bailee receiving notification of the security interest, control of the collateral, and thus possession of the property, are transferred to the secured party.

These two methods of perfection operate independently. No notice is necessary to perfect a security interest in collateral held by an agent of the secured party. The agent's possession is legally equivalent to possession by the secured party herself; thus, the agent's possession of itself perfects the security interest.

Where the person who holds the collateral is not the secured party's agent, perfection by possession is nevertheless possible under the notice to bailee rubric of §9-305. The bailee's receipt of notification of the security interest is essential in this case because it operates to make the bailee accountable for the collateral to the secured party. The debtor's control of the property is accordingly limited, and, thus, third parties are alerted to the secured party's claim of an interest. This notification is unnecessary when the person in possession of the collateral is the secured party's agent because, as such, the person already is accountable for the property to the secured party. Perfection by notice to a bailee implicitly assumes that the bailee is not the secured party's agent because, if the situation were otherwise, there would be no need to notify the bailee of the security interest. The bailee's possession as agent would of itself accomplish perfection.

Notice to a bailee is therefore used as a means of perfection in cases where the collateral is in the possession of a third person who holds the property through someone other than the secured party. When this third person, i.e., the bailee, is notified of the secured party's interest, the bailee in effect becomes the secured party's agent and through this agent the secured party possesses the collateral.

This someone through whom the bailee holds is usually the debtor, however, and Article 9 declares that a person controlled by the debtor cannot be the secured party's agent for possession. There is no paradox. Although the bailee was initially the debtor's agent, and in this role originally acquired possession of the collateral, the bailee's allegiance changes upon being notified of the secured party's interest. The bailee thereafter is accountable for the collateral to the secured party and thus is no longer the debtor's agent. The bailee has no choice in this regard: Perfection is accomplished simply by the bailee receiving notification of the secured party's interest. There is no further requirement that "the bailee * * * attorn to the secured party or acknowledge that he now holds on * * * [the secured party's] behalf." U.C.C. §9-305 comment 2.

Perfection by possession begins "from the time possession is taken without a relation back and continues only so long as possession is retained." U.C.C. §9-305. This is true however the secured party takes possession, whether personally, through her agent, or by notifying a third party bailee. In the last instance, the secured party is deemed to have possession from the time the bailee receives notification of the secured party's interest. Determining when a bailee *receives notification* can be a difficult problem. U.C.C. §1-201(26).

A secured party in possession of collateral for the purpose of perfecting her security interest, or for any other purpose, cannot do as she pleases with the property. A pledgee is essentially a bailee whose custody of the property is for the special and limited purpose of securing a duty or debt. Thus, before default, a pledgee is powerless to dispose of the pledgor's interest in the property. Therefore, the pledgee cannot unilaterally effect a lawful sale of the property outright. Moreover, a secured party in possession of collateral is seldom authorized even to use the property except "for the purpose of preserving the collateral." U.C.C. 9-207(4).

Preserving the collateral is a basic duty imposed on a pledgee by the common law and Article 9. U.C.C. §9-207(1) provides that "[a] secured party must use reasonable care in the custody and preservation of collateral in his possession." To determine the range of responsibilities this provision imposes on Article 9 pledgees, the courts often rely on common law because, according to the drafters of Article 9, §9-207(1) merely restates the "duty to preserve collateral imposed on a pledgee at common law." U.C.C. §9-207 comment 1. Generally, the common-law rule of reasonable care "is confined to the physical care of the chattel," Restatement of Security §17 comment a (1941); and, in a typical case involving a pledge of ordinary goods, "only passive custody is usually demanded of the pledgee, who ultimately returns the pledged article in the same form in which it is received." A Dobie, Handbook on the Law of Bailments and Carriers §83 at 220 (1914).

Notes and Problems

1. O is indebted to D, and this debt is evidenced by a negotiable promissory note which O issued to D. D borrowed money from Bank and used the note as collateral. Bank neglected to have D sign a security agreement covering the note, but Bank took possession of the unindorsed note. Does the Bank have a perfected security interest in the note?

2. D purchased a non-negotiable certificate of deposit (CD) from First Bank. D used the CD as collateral for loans from Second Bank and Third Bank. Second Bank was the first to acquire a security interest in the CD, which was delivered by D to Second Bank. Third Bank's interest in the CD was created later, and at the same time Third Bank filed a financing statement covering the property. Who is entitled to priority, Second Bank or Third Bank?

3. Bank had a security interest in D's equipment and inventory. Upon D's default, Bank employees entered D's place of business and made an announcement that all the personal property there should be considered impounded by the Bank. Is the Bank's interest thereby perfected by possession? What if D surrendered the keys to the premises to Bank officials and lost all right and power of entry except by permission of the Bank?

4. Is the bank where debtor maintains her checking accounts in possession of the debtor's money?

5. Under the common law, a pledge of bulky goods can be accomplished without the pledgee obtaining actual, exclusive control of the collateral. Here is an illustration:

A offers to pledge to B a pile of steel scrap lying in an enclosure near A's factory. B accepts the offer and posts a placard to a stake firmly affixed in the ground near the pile on which it is stated that the scrap has been pledged to B. The marking is a sufficient evidence of assumption of control to create a pledge.

Restatement of Security §6 comment a & illustration 2 (1941). This is an example of the common law recognizing constructive delivery as a sufficient substitute for actual possession. Prior to the days of recording acts when the pledge was the only effective security device, the usually rigid rules of possession had to give way, as in this case, in the face of commercial necessity to use as collateral property that practically could not be delivered to the pledgee. To meet these needs the courts very liberally defined the concept of possession. Should modern courts refuse to define so broadly the term "possession" for purposes of §9-305?

6. First State Bank was approached by a grain farmer who needed a loan to finance her farming operations during the next planting season. Last season's grain has been processed and is stored in a warehouse of the Mississippi Storage Co., Inc. (MSC). MSC issued to the farmer a non-negotiable warehouse receipt which describes the kind and quantity of grain that the farmer stored.

First State and the farmer reached an understanding; the loan was made; and a valid security agreement covering the grain stored with MSC was executed on Monday, April 3.

On Tuesday, April 4, First State mailed to MSC's address, which is a post office box, a notification of the Bank's security interest in the farmer's grain stored with MSC. The notice was delivered by regular United States mail and placed in MSC's post office box on Wednesday, April 5. A secretary for MSC ordinarily checks the company's post office box every day; but the secretary was ill on Wednesday and Thursday and did not check the box on those days. When the secretary picked up the mail on Friday, April 7, he discovered the letter from First State and immediately referred it to MSC's manager.

On Wednesday afternoon, April 5, Second National Bank filed a financing statement covering the farmer's grain stored with MSC. A week later a security interest in favor of Second National was created in the grain. Who is entitled to priority, First State or Second National?

a. Same facts, except that First State filed a financing statement on Tuesday, April 4.

b. Same facts, except that farmer indorsed and delivered the warehouse receipt to First State Bank on Monday, April 3.

c. Same facts, except that MSC issued farmer a negotiable warehouse receipt covering the goods and farmer indorsed and delivered it to First State Bank on Thursday, April 6.

7. Prior to the enactment of Article 9, the field warehouse was a common tool of inventory financing. The tool is rarely used today, but it remains a most reliable means of insuring control over collateral and proceeds. A "field warehouse" is to be contrasted with a "terminal warehouse", a separate and independent storage facility operated by a public warehouse company. A "field warehouse" is established on or near the premises of the depositor/debtor by a public warehouseman. The word "field" does not imply open air storage; rather, from the warehouseman's standpoint, the operation is in the field rather than at the warehouseman's permanent facilities.

Generally, the debtor makes arrangements with the bank or other lending agency for the loan against its inventory prior to the establishment of the field warehouse. The loan agreement will require the establishment of a field warehouse and the deposit of inventory in the warehouse. The loan agreement will usually also provide when the debtor will be able to withdraw items from the warehouse—e.g., a specified amount each week provided that the debtor has repaid the portion of the loan represented by the previous week's withdrawal.

A contract is then entered into between the debtor and the warehouseman, which sets the rates and terms under which the field warehouse will be operated. The debtor then leases part of its premises to the warehouse company for use as the field warehouse. The area so leased can be a room, a building, a part of a building, a tank, or an open yard area. The warehouse company cordons off the leased area to indicate clearly its dominion over it. Signs are posted on the enclosed area stating that the goods therein are stored with the warehouse company. Obviously, many field warehouses hardly look like warehouses at all.

After the "warehouse" has been constructed in this manner, the warehouse company hires and bonds a warehouse manager—generally an employee of the debtor. (If the new custodial duties do not require her full time, she can still be employed by the debtor for other work.) In her new job, she receives instructions exclusively from the warehouse company which also pays her wages.

The debtor then stores part of its inventory in the field warehouse. A receiving record is kept, and warehouse receipts are issued to the creditor. Warehousemen issue either negotiable or non-negotiable receipts.

As the goods are placed in the field warehouse and the warehouse receipts are issued to the creditor, the creditor extends credit to the debtor as provided in the loan agreement. The creditor now has control over the inventory in the warehouse—over the collateral. If the collateral is covered by a negotiable receipt, the receipt must be released by the creditor and presented to the warehouseman before the debtor can reacquire the pledged inventory. If the collateral is covered by a non-negotiable receipt, the goods are released only upon the creditor's written instructions.

8. Although perfection by possession continues only so long as possession is retained, U.C.C. §9-305, a security interest in the collateral does not necessarily become unperfected when possession ends. If the secured party otherwise perfects in a manner allowed by Article 9 before yielding possession, the security interest remains perfected after the period of perfection. Id. In effect, the two means of perfection are tacked together so that there is no intervening period of "unperfection." There are situations, however, when the end of perfection by possession causes problems.

    a. SP-1 makes a loan to D, and D pledges her widget as collateral. SP-1 and D execute a valid written security agreement, but no financing statement is filed. SP-1 later releases possession of the widget to D, and D gives a security interest in the widget to SP-2 who perfects by properly filing a financing statement. Which secured party has priority in the widget, SP-1 or SP-2?

    b. Same facts, except SP-1 eventually reacquires possession of the widget. (U.C.C. §9-305 rejects the equitable doctrine of relation back under which a pledgee's taking possession of collateral "was deemed to relate back to the date of the original security agreement." U.C.C. §9-305 comment 3.)

    c. Same facts, except SP-2 acquires and perfects its security interest by filing before SP-1 releases possession of the widget to D.

    d. Same facts, except SP-1 properly files a financing statement before releasing possession of the widget to D.

    e. Same facts as Problem 8.d., except that SP-1 and D had not executed a written security agreement.

9. D borrowed $10,000 from Bank and secured the loan with a pledge of corporate stock valued at $15,000 when the loan was made. While Bank was holding the stock, the market value of the property declined sharply over a period of several months so that, when the loan was due, the stock was worth only $9000. D argues that Bank violated its duty of reasonable care as pledgee in not selling the stock, 9-207, and that the resulting loss should be offset against D's debt to Bank. Should this argument succeed?

10. In each of the following cases, the debtor gives bank a security interest in corporate stock. How does the bank perfect its interest?

   a. The corporation that issued the stock, Little Corp., is a small, inactively traded company. The stock is certificated and is held by the debtor who is the registered owner.

   b. The corporation is a giant company, Big Corp., whose stock is very actively traded on the Big Board. The debtor bought the stock through an account with the local office of a large, national broker. The debtor herself actually holds no stock certificates. Most of the corporation's stock exists in jumbo certificates held by the record owner, Cede & Co., which is the nominee name used by DTC, the Depository Trust Company. DTC is a New York trust company which holds securities for the benefit of its participants—hundreds of broker-dealers and banks. DTC's records show that debtor's broker owns several millions shares of Big Corp. The broker's own records show that the debtor owns 2000 shares.

11. Suppose that bank wishes to effect a pledge of certain of the debtor's pledgeable property. Consider if the bank is in possession of the property in these circumstances:

   a. Someone who is not part of the bank, but who works on the bank's behalf as agent, takes possession of the property.

   b. The debtor keeps possession of the property as bank's agent?

   c. The bank notifies another lender who is already holding the property to secure a another obligation of the debtor.

□□□□□□

<h2 style="text-align:center">Matter of Van Kylen</h2>
United States Bankruptcy Court, W.D. Wisconsin, 1989
98 B.R. 455

    Robert D. Martin, Chief Judge. This is an interpleader action to determine the rights of the Citizens State Bank (the "Bank"), the bankruptcy trustee, and the debtor's spouse in $50,000.00 currently held by Merrill Lynch, Pierce, Fenner & Smith, Inc. ("Merrill Lynch, Inc."). The Bank claims ownership of the entire $50,000.00 by virtue of the prepetition enforcement of a security interest. The trustee asserts that the Bank's security interest was not perfected, and seeks to bring the entire $50,000.00 into the bankruptcy estate by avoiding the enforcement of the security interest. The debtor's spouse, who has not filed bankruptcy, claims a one-half interest in the funds as a joint tenant, and alleges that the encumbrance of her interest was invalid for want of consideration. Merrill Lynch, Inc. has been dismissed pursuant to a stipulation of the parties. After a hearing on cross motions for summary judgment filed by the Bank, the trustee, and the debtor's spouse, the matter was taken under advisement. The parties then completed briefing the issues.

The facts are fairly complex. On April 24, 1981, the Bank advanced $213,000.00 to Mitchell Color Graphics, Inc., n/k/a RVK, Inc. (the "Corporation"), pursuant to a promissory note executed by the Corporation. Mr. Van Kylen, an officer, employee, and stockholder of the Corporation, personally guarantied payment of the note. The guaranty was also signed by Mrs. Van Kylen and was secured by a mortgage on the Van Kylen's homestead, which was owned in joint tenancy.

On May 17, 1982, the Bank advanced $120,000.00 to the Corporation pursuant to a second corporate note. Mr. Van Kylen again guarantied payment of the note, and secured the guaranty by a second mortgage on the homestead which was executed by both Van Kylens.

In August of 1984, Mr. Van Kylen advised the Bank of his desire to sell the homestead. The Bank agreed to release its mortgages in exchange for a security interest in $50,000.00 of the sale proceeds, and a promise that the proceeds subject to the Bank's security interest would be deposited in an account with Merrill Lynch, Inc. in which a balance of at least a $50,000.00 would be maintained at all times.

On August 31, 1984, the Bank executed a release and satisfaction of their two mortgages in return for the Van Kylens granting it a security interest in $50,000.00 of the proceeds from the sale of their home. On or about that same date, the Van Kylens sold their home. Fifty thousand dollars from the sale proceeds were deposited with the Bank in the form of a certificate of deposit, payable to either of the Van Kylens.

On September 27, 1984, the Van Kylens opened a "Cash Management Account" (the "CMA") with Merrill Lynch, Inc. as joint tenants with right of survivorship. Under the terms of the CMA agreement the Van Kylens had the power to direct Merrill Lynch, Inc. to allocate any monies deposited into their CMA among three types of accounts: a conventional securities account; a money account, consisting of either a money market deposit account or money market fund shares; and a card/check account. By the last of these alternatives the Van Kylens could have had direct access to the monies on deposit at any time.

Initially, the Van Kylens directed Merrill Lynch, Inc. to invest the funds in their CMA in $25,000.00 of government securities and $25,000.00 of certificates of deposit. Apparently, certificates evidencing these investments were not issued to the Van Kylens. The Van Kylens never requested the issuance of either a bank credit card or checking privileges for use in relation to their CMA.

Also on September 27, 1984, the Van Kylens and the Bank entered into a written agreement (the "Assignment Agreement") by which the Van Kylens granted the Bank a security interest in their CMA to the extent of $50,000.00 and agreed to maintain a minimum balance of at least that amount.[1] The Assignment Agreement permitted the Van Kylens to direct the use of the

$50,000.00 in the CMA on the condition that "[a]ll amounts in the [CMA] up to $50,000 shall be in instruments, documents, securities or other similar items which are either insured by FDIC/FSLIC or are issued by the United States Government." The Agreement also provided that the Bank could enforce its security interest in the CMA by written notice to Merrill Lynch, Inc. that was either signed by the Bank and the Van Kylens, or signed by the Bank alone, certifying that an " 'event of default' exists as of the date thereof" under the notes or Mr. Van Kylen's personal guaranties.

On October 1, 1984, the Bank cashed the Van Kylens' $50,000.00 certificate of deposit and forwarded a check for $50,000.00 to Merrill Lynch, Inc. to be deposited in the CMA. No financing statement relating to the Bank's security interest in the CMA was ever filed with the Secretary of State.

On February 3, 1987, the Bank sent written notice to the Van Kylens that the Corporation was in default, and demanded payment under Mr. Van Kylen's personal guaranties. On February 12, 1987, the Bank made a written demand upon Merrill Lynch, Inc. that title to the CMA be transferred from the Van Kylens to the Bank, but failed to certify that an event of default had occurred as required by the Assignment Agreement. On February 19, 1987, the Bank provided Merrill Lynch, Inc. with a corrected written notice of the default.

On March 3, 1987, Mr. Van Kylen filed a chapter 7 bankruptcy petition. Merrill Lynch, Inc. has since liquidated the funds in the CMA and currently holds them in escrow pending the outcome of this litigation. At all times relevant, the outstanding balance of the debts secured by Mr. Van Kylens' personal guaranties exceeded $50,000.00.

The trustee has moved for summary judgment on the grounds that the Bank never perfected its security interest under Wisconsin's version of the Uniform Commercial Code (the "U.C.C."), and that the prepetition enforcement of the unperfected security interest constituted a preferential transfer transfer of funds in the CMA to the Bank. The Bank disputes the applicability of the U.C.C. to the transaction and argues that its lien was perfected under the common law of pledges or assignments. Other than arguing that its lien was perfected, the Bank has raised no argument against a finding that the transfer of Mr. Van Kylen's interest was a preference avoidable under Bankruptcy Code section 547. The Bank, however, contests any nullification of the enforcement of its lien on Mrs. Van Kylens' interest.

The threshold issue in this case is the applicability of Wisconsin's version of Article Nine of the U.C.C. If Article Nine does not apply, the transaction is subject to the common law governing pledges or assignments.

The Bank claims its security interest in the CMA by virtue of an instrument denominated an "Assignment." Paragraph 1 of the Assignment Agreement provides:

---

[1]   Contemporaneously, the Van Kylens executed a "Collateral Pledge Agreement," by which they "grant[ed] to [the] Bank a security interest in all property of the Debtor of any kind now in the possession or control of [the] Bank for collateral purposes."

> In consideration for the [Bank] releasing [the Van Kylens'] residence from collateral for the above-mentioned loans, and other good and valuable consideration, [the Van Kylens] do[ ] hereby assign to Assignee, solely as collateral for the above-mentioned notes, all of their rights, title and interest in the cash account up to $50,000.

Presumably, Article Nine applies to the creation of this security interest. As section 409.102(1)(a) provides:

> (1) Except as otherwise provided in s. 409.104 on excluded transactions, this chapter applies: (a) To any transaction (regardless of its form) which is intended to create a security interest in personal property or fixtures including goods, documents, instruments, general intangibles, chattel paper or accounts.

WIS.STAT. §409.102(1)(a) (1987-88). There is no dispute that the CMA is an item of personal property, or that the transaction involving the Van Kylens' respective interests in the CMA was intended to create a security interest in the CMA.

As section 409.102(2) makes clear, the use of the non-U.C.C. nomenclature in the Assignment Agreement does not take the transaction outside Article Nine:

> This chapter applies to security interests created by contract including pledge, assignment, chattel mortgage, chattel trust, trust deed, factor's lien, equipment trust, conditional sale, trust receipt, other lien or title retention contract and lease or consignment intended as security....

WIS.STAT. §409.102(2) (1987-88). Thus, Article Nine applies to this transaction unless it is specifically excluded by the U.C.C. itself.

The parties point to section 409.104(13) as the only basis upon which the transaction may be excluded from Article Nine's coverage. That section provides:

> This chapter does not apply: .... (13) To a transfer of an interest in any deposit account as defined in s. 409.105(1), except as provided with respect to proceeds under s. 409.306 and priorities in proceeds under s. 409.312.

WIS.STAT. §409.104(13) (1987-88). Because the CMA constituted original collateral, rather than proceeds from other items of collateral, neither of the two exceptions to the so-called deposit account exception is applicable. The point of contention is whether the CMA is a "deposit account" within the meaning of section 409.105(1)(e), which states:

(1) In this chapter unless the context otherwise requires: .... (e) "Deposit account" means a demand, time, savings, passbook or like account maintained with a bank, savings and loan association, credit union or like organization, other than an account evidenced by a certificate of deposit.

WIS.STAT. §409.105(1)(e) (1987-88).

Cash Management Accounts have been offered by Merrill Lynch, Inc. since 1977[1] as:

> an integrated program which links together three components: (1) a conventional securities account, (2) a choice of Money Accounts, including several no-load money market funds, and (3) an account which provides card and checking services maintained by the Bank. Cash Management Account Agreement P 1. The unique feature of the CMA is the ability of account holders to utilize both conventional banking services and brokerage services. Account holders can designate how they wish deposited funds invested, having as their choices any mix of the following: (i) conventional securities; (ii) a FSLIC or FDIC insured savings account paying interest at money market rates; (iii) shares in any of three money market funds--a "CMA Money Fund," a tax-exempt fund, or a government securities fund; and (iv) a checking account established with a participating banking institution, which provides access to the funds in the CMA by the use of checks drawn on, or a credit card issued by, that banking institution.

The definition of deposit account found in section 409.105(1)(e) directs attention to three factors: the type of account; the existence of an instrument evidencing the account; and the type of institution with which the account is maintained. The Official Comment to section 9-104 of the Official Text of the U.C.C. indicates that two concerns gave rise to the exception for deposit

---

[1] Cash Management Accounts have been noted as an instance of "competition from non-bank financial institutions" with conventional banking entities. Other non-bank financial institutions also compete with commercial banks and savings institutions to some extent. In the recent period of high interest rates, competition from money-market funds for the savings of depositors who otherwise would use the services of commercial banks and savings institutions has been intense. Moreover, there appears to be a growing tendency for these non-bank institutions to offer services similar to those offered by banks and savings institutions. Major brokerage houses offer their customers diverse financial services. For example, Merrill Lynch, Pierce, Fenner and Smith has a Cash Management Account in which the customer receives interest on balances maintained, checking facilities, a charge card, and lending privileges. F. Beutel & M. Schroeder, Bank Officers' Handbook of Commercial Law 5-45 (5th ed. 1982).

accounts: that security transactions involving deposit accounts were often unique, and thus not susceptible to treatment under a general commercial statute, and that existing law adequately dealt with transactions of this type. U.C.C. §9-104 comment 7 (1977).

The statute speaks of "a demand, time, savings, passbook or like account ... other than an account evidenced by a certificate of deposit." WIS.STAT. §409.105(1)(e) (1987-88). Distinguishing a "like account" from an "un-like account" should be done along functional lines. See U.C.C. §9-101 comment (1977) ("The scheme of the Article is to make distinctions, where distinctions are necessary, along functional rather than formal lines."). The first distinction to be made is between those accounts that are the functional equivalent of money and those that are not.

The examples of accounts set forth in section 409.105(1)(e) share the common trait of being viewed as cash equivalents. Black's Law Dictionary defines "cash" as "[m]oney or the equivalent.... negotiable checks, and balances in bank accounts...." Id. at 196 (5th ed. 1979). Likewise, in the Article Nine provision dealing with deposit accounts as proceeds of other collateral, "money, checks, deposit accounts, and the like" are characterized as "cash proceeds." WIS.STAT. §409.306 (1987-88).

On this point, the Bank's argument that the funds in the CMA were only accessible via checks drawn on an account maintained with a participating bank is relevant. However, the Van Kylens did not utilize the CMA as a checking account. If they had established a Card/Check Account in order to use either the checking or credit card options, the Van Kylens could have had access to their invested money (in excess of $50,000.00) simply by making check or credit card withdrawals. To the extent the funds in the Card/Check Account were insufficient to cover the withdrawals, Merrill Lynch, Inc. would have liquidated the Van Kylens' investments. Were a card or checking account access used, the CMA might more closely approach being a "like" account. Since this was not the case, the Van Kylens' CMA lacks the features of accessibility and liquidity characterizing "deposit accounts."

There is a second distinction between "like" and "unlike" accounts. In bank accounts, the depositor possesses nothing more than a chose in action, i.e., the deposit holder's obligation to repay the money deposited. In a certificate of deposit the indebtedness of the bank is reified in the form of an instrument. By excluding accounts evidenced by certificates of deposit from the definition of "deposit account," the drafters of Article Nine appear to have drawn a distinction between those accounts which remain a mere chose in action and those which have been reified. See WIS.STAT. §403.104(2)(a) (1987- 88) ("A writing ... is ... [a] 'certificate of deposit' if it is an acknowledgment by a bank of receipt of money with an engagement to repay it."). In the latter case, the rationale underlying the deposit account exception--the uniqueness of the account and the inadequacy of Article Nine vis-a-vis common law rules--is no longer applicable. Under the U.C.C., the certificate of deposit is treated as an "instrument," see

WIS.STAT. §403.104(3) (1987-88); id. §409.105(1)(i), and a perfected security interest in it can be acquired under Article Nine, see id. §409.304(1). Thus, the functional importance of this second distinction lies in the fact that as to the accounts evidenced by an instrument, the reified intangible evidencing the account is an item of collateral commonly used in commercial transactions and to which the U.C.C.'s rules are easily and specifically applied.

The form of the funds in the CMA is relevant. The Van Kylens' deposit was placed into government securities and, for some period of time, certificates of deposit. However, there is no evidence that securities certificates or certificates of deposit were issued to the Van Kylens. Therefore, it cannot be fairly said that the CMA was ever "evidenced" by a reified intangible. Nevertheless, the fact that the funds in the CMA were held as types of assets in which security interests are commonly taken cuts against a finding that this was a "like account." See *Nix*, 864 F.2d at 1212 (where funds deposited in Keogh plan were invested in shares of stock, court states that "[w]hereas bank accounts are funded solely with cash, a Keogh plan may be, as [the debtor's] was, funded in whole or in part with stock.").

Finally, it is important that section 409.105(1)(e) speaks of an account "maintained with a bank, savings and loan association, credit union or like organization." The Van Kylens opened their CMA with Merrill Lynch, Inc., which held and invested the Van Kylens' deposit. Merrill Lynch, Inc. issued statements to the Van Kylens. While the Van Kylens could have used a Check/Card Account with a participating bank, they did not do so. Rather than the bank member of the Merrill Lynch family, the Van Kylens maintained their account with the investment brokerage member.

The enumerated types of "like organization[s]" indicate that the deposit account exception is limited to accounts maintained with traditional depository institutions. Merrill Lynch, Inc.--an investment firm--hardly qualifies as such an institution. Cf. Gary Plastic Packaging Corp. v. Merrill Lynch, 756 F.2d 230, 237 (2d Cir.1985) (discussing distinction under federal law between investment banking and deposit banking). As the Fifth Circuit has stated in regard to a Keogh plan maintained with Merrill Lynch:

> Moreover, Merrill Lynch is not 'a bank' or 'like organization,' but a stock broker. It therefore could not accept deposits under Texas law. It held [the debtor's] Keogh plan assets as a fiduciary for him, not simply as a bank receiving a deposit. A Keogh plan therefore is not a 'deposit account' within the meaning of §9.105(a)(5) ...

Nix, 864 F.2d at 1212 (footnotes omitted). For this reason, if for no other, the CMA does not come within the deposit account exception.

The deposit account exception is based on the notion that security interests in savings accounts, etc. are not the stuff of commercial secured financing. Whether the reality of today's commercial practice comports with the drafters' perceptions of commercial financing at the time the exception was drafted is an open question. It is unlikely that the drafters of Article Nine envisioned the existence of hybrid accounts of this type, much less their serving as collateral for commercial loans. However, I do not believe that the stated rationale for the deposit account exception permits an expansive reading of the exception. Rather, the drafters' introductory comment that "[t]he aim of this Article is to provide a simple and unified structure within which the immense variety of present-day secured financing transactions can go forward with less cost and with greater certainty," U.C.C. §9-101 comment (1977), discourages expanding the exception beyond conventional bank accounts maintained with traditional depository institutions. As the CMA brochure itself emphasizes to accountholders, "your CMA account should not be considered a bank account." CMA Brochure at 7.

It is clear from the foregoing that the Article Nine governs the parties' rights in the CMA. Thus, the inquiry shifts to whether the Bank has complied with Article Nine's requirements for the attachment and perfection of its claimed security interest.

A security interest is perfected "when it has attached and when all of the applicable steps required for perfection have been taken." WIS.STAT. §409.303(1) (1987-88). A security interest "attaches" when the following events have occurred:

> (a) The collateral is in the possession of the secured party pursuant to agreement, or the debtor has signed a security agreement which contains a description of the collateral ...;
> (b) Value has been given; and
> (c) The debtor has rights in the collateral.

WIS.STAT. §409.203(1)(a)-(c) (1987-88). Upon attachment, the security interest is valid and enforceable between the debtor and the secured party. WIS.STAT. §409.203(1) (1987-88).

The only condition for attachment which is seriously at issue[1] is whether the Bank "gave value." Section 401.201(44)(d) tells us that: [A] person gives

---

[1] Mrs. Van Kylen also argues, although it must be assumed she is not serious about it, that the Collateral Pledge Agreement was insufficient to create a security interest in the CMA, since its scope is limited to collateral in the possession or control of the Bank. Assuming the collateral was not in the possession of the Bank, Mrs. Van Kylen overlooks the fact that the Assignment Agreement satisfies the requirement of section 409.203(1)(a) that "the debtor has signed a security agreement containing a description of the collateral." The Assignment Agreement was signed by both the Van Kylens. In paragraphs 1 and 2 of the Assignment Agreement, a description of the Bank's collateral is found:

1. ... [the Van Kylens] do[ ] hereby assign to [the Bank], solely as collateral ...,

value for rights if he acquires them: .... (d) Generally, in return for any consideration sufficient to support a simple contract. WIS.STAT. §401.201(44)(d) (1987-88). Mrs. Van Kylen has moved for summary judgment on the grounds that the Bank's security interest did not attach to her interest in the CMA because she did not receive consideration. Because the U.C.C. nowhere defines "consideration," we are left to the common law of contracts to determine whether the Bank's security interest is enforceable against Mrs. Van Kylen's interest in the CMA.[1]

Under Wisconsin law, consideration "may consist of a detriment to the promisee or a benefit to the promisor." First Wisconsin National Bank v. Oby, 52 Wis.2d 1, 6, 188 N.W.2d 454 (1971). With respect to the "benefit to the promisor" prong of this definition, the Wisconsin Supreme Court has quoted the following:

> [A]ny benefit, profit or advantage flowing to the promisor which he would not have received but for the contract constitutes a sufficient consideration therefor. It is not necessary, however, that a benefit should accrue to the person making the promise; it is sufficient that something valuable flows from the person to whom it is made, ... and that the promise is the inducement to the transaction.

Id. at 6 n. 1, 188 N.W.2d 454 (quoting 17 C.J.S. Contracts §74 at 757- 61). As to the "detriment to the promisee" prong, the Court quoted the following from Professor Williston's treatise: 'It would be a detriment to the promisee, in a legal sense, if he, at the request of the promisor and upon the strength of that promise, had performed any act which occasioned him the slightest trouble or inconvenience, and which he was not obligated to perform.' Oby, 52 Wis.2d at 5-6, 188 N.W.2d 454 (quoting W. Jaeger, 1 Williston on Contracts §102A at 380 (3d ed. 1957)). The treatise elsewhere states that the proposition that "a detriment suffered by the promisee at the promisor's request and as the price for the promise is sufficient, though the promisor is not benefited, is well settled." W. Jaeger, 1 Williston on Contracts §102 at 377 (3d ed. 1957).

Mrs. Van Kylen argues that she received no benefit from the loan to the Corporation and thus her granting two mortgages on her home was not supported by consideration. She then argues that since the underlying mortgages were not enforceable their release by the Bank did not constitute consideration for the replacement security interest in the CMA.

---

all of their rights, title and interest in the cash account up to $50,000. 2. All amounts in the Cash Account up to $50,000 shall be in instruments, documents, securities or other similar items which are either insured by FDIC/FSLIC or are issued by the United States Government.

[1]   WIS.STAT. §401.103 (1987-88) ("Unless displaced by the particular provisions of chs. 401 to 409 the principles of law and equity ... shall supplement its provisions.").

Mrs. Van Kylen's granting of the underlying mortgages was indeed supported by sufficient consideration. The first mortgage instrument states that the mortgage was "given to secure the payment of SBA Guaranty dated April 24, 1981 in the principal sum of $213,200.00, signed by Raymond R. Van Kylen." The second mortgage instrument states that the mortgage was "given to secure payment of a promissory note dated May 17, 1982 in the principal sum of $120,000.00 signed by MITCHELL COLOR GRAPHICS, INC."

There is no doubt that the Bank gave something of value in return for the mortgages, i.e., the loan proceeds. That this benefit flowed to the Corporation and to Mr. Van Kylen does not defeat the mortgage contract if that benefit was the inducement to Mrs. Van Kylen's promise. See Oby, 52 Wis.2d at 5-6, 188 N.W.2d 454; see also In re Ousley, 92 B.R. 278, 284 (Bankr.S.D.Ohio 1988) (husband's obligations under security agreements are enforceable where consideration flowed directly to wife rather than to him).

The Restatement (Second) of Contracts sets forth a number of illustrations demonstrating that consideration supported the granting of the mortgages by Mrs. Van Kylen even if the benefit given by the Bank ran solely to Mr. Van Kylen and the Corporation. Comment e to section 71 reads as follows:

> e.   Consideration moving from or to a third person.
>
> It matters not from whom the consideration moves or to whom it goes. If it is bargained for and given in exchange for the promise, the promise is not gratuitous. Illustrations: 14. A promises B to guarantee payment of a bill of goods if B sells the goods to C. Selling the goods to C is consideration for A's promise. 15. A makes a promissory note payable to B in return for a payment by B to C. The payment is consideration for the note.

Restatement (Second) of Contracts §71, comment e at 176 (1981).

Additionally, there is some evidence to indicate that Mrs. Van Kylen herself received a benefit from the transaction. Her husband was a minority shareholder in the Corporation, as well as one of its employees. * * * [B]ecause the loans to the Corporation in some measure permitted it to continue operations and thus to provide income to Mr. Van Kylen, Mrs. Van Kylen benefitted from the transaction. Moreover, for some period of time, Mrs. Van Kylen was herself employed by the Corporation.

Since the mortgages appear to have been enforceable, their release by the Bank conferred a benefit on Mrs. Van Kylen and a detriment on the Bank. The Bank gave up the right to look to the homestead for the satisfaction of any default on the part of the Corporation or Mr. Van Kylen. There is no merit to Mrs. Van Kylen's claim that she did not receive consideration for the mortgages and the security interest granted to the Bank. Therefore, the Bank's security interest attached to the CMA and its contents.

The inquiry now turns to whether the Bank's security interest was perfected. If unperfected, the security interest is junior in priority to a "person who becomes a lien creditor before the security interest is perfected." WIS.STAT. §409.301(1)(b) (1987-88). The bankruptcy trustee holds the rights of a hypothetical lien creditor, and can void the junior lien. 11 U.S.C. §544(a)(1). Thus, if the Bank's security interest was unperfected, it would lose its lien and become an unsecured creditor in Mr. Van Kylen's bankruptcy.

The "essence of the perfection process is furnishing public notice of the secured party's interest in the collateral, thereby protecting third persons against the secret or undisclosed lien." J. Worley, Possessory Security Interests, P 14.01[2][b] at 14-7 in Coogan, Hogan, Vagts & McDonnell, 1B Secured Transactions Under the Uniform Commercial Code (rev. ed. 1988). Excluding those instances where a security interest is deemed to be perfected upon attachment and without any further action by the secured party, see, e.g., WIS.STAT. §409.302(1)(d) (1987-88) (automatic perfection of security interest in consumer goods having a purchase price not in excess of $500.00), the "steps required for perfection" under Article Nine are either the filing of a financing statement in the appropriate public office, see WIS.STAT. §409.302(1) (1987-88), or the secured party taking possession of the collateral, see id. §409.305. Additionally, since April 26, 1986, a revised Article Eight of the U.C.C. has provided the means for perfecting security interests in investment securities. See id. §§408.321, 408.313(1).

The parties address perfection of the Bank's security interest as if it covered only the contents of the CMA (the government securities and certificates of deposit), without any discussion of whether the Bank's security interest in the CMA itself is perfected. However, the Bank's failure to file a financing statement with respect to its security interest in the CMA itself is clearly fatal. The Van Kylens' rights in the CMA are a "general intangible" under section 409.106: 'General Intangibles' means any personal property property (including things in action) other than goods, accounts, chattel paper, documents, instruments and money. WIS.STAT. §409.106 (1987-88). Therefore, the filing of a financing statement was required in order to perfect the Bank's security interest. See WIS.STAT. §409.302(1) (1987-88); U.C.C. §9-305, comment 1 (1977) ("A security interest in accounts and general intangibles--property not ordinarily represented by any writing whose delivery operates to transfer the claim--may under this whose delivery operates to transfer the claim--may under this Article be perfected only by filing....").

Even if we were to focus on the contents of the CMA, which we need not, the Bank's security interest was unperfected. The parties seem to agree that the funds in the CMA were invested in government securities and, at one time, certificates of deposit, and that these investments were not reduced to certificate form.[1] Because it is undisputed that the Bank did not file a financing statement

---

[1]   The parties' agreed proposed findings of fact do not address this point. In their

with respect to any type of collateral, unless the Bank can fit itself within one of various exceptions to the filing requirements of section 409.302(1), its security interest in the Van Kylens' rights in the investments was unperfected.

The Bank claims that either of two exceptions applies: the exception for possessory security interests or the exception for security interests in securities. As to the first of these arguments, the Bank relies on section 409.302(1)(a), which provides:

> (1) A financing statement must be filed to perfect all security interests except the following: (a) A security interest in collateral in possession of the secured party under s. 409.305.

WIS.STAT. §409.302(1)(a) (1987-88). Section 409.305 provides in relevant part:

> A security interest in letters of credit and advices of credit (s. 405.116(2)(a)), goods, instruments (other than certificated securities), money, negotiable documents or chattel paper may be perfected by the secured party's taking possession of the collateral. If such collateral other than goods covered by a negotiable document is held by a bailee, the secured party is deemed to have possession from the time the bailee receives notification of the secured party's interest.

WIS.STAT. §409.305 (1987-88). Thus to merit the exception under section 409.305 the collateral must exist in a tangible form and the secured party must be in "possession" of that collateral.

The Bank's argument fails at the threshold. Because no certificates representing the Van Kylens' rights in the investments were issued, the Bank's collateral must be classified as a "general intangible." As such, the possessory security interest exception is inapplicable. See U.C.C. §9-305 comment 1

---

briefing, however, the parties concur that the funds in the CMA were invested in certificates of deposit and government securities and that neither stock certificates nor certificates of deposit were actually issued. Trustee's Brief at 6, 11; Bank's Brief at 28; Bank's Reply Brief at 11. Actual evidence of the contents of the CMA is found in the document evidencing the opening of the CMA. This document contains a box entitled "Initial Transaction," wherein the information "Buy 25M MLFSX" is recorded. From reference to other portions of this document and the CMA brochure, this data means that $25,000 was to be invested in a government securities fund. As to the remaining $25,000, the document is silent. Mr. Van Kylen testified at a deposition that it was his understanding that the funds in the CMA were held in the form of government bonds. Adversary Deposition of Raymond R. Van Kylen at 34-35. Mr. Van Kylen also testified that he believed Merrill Lynch, Inc. had possession of the bonds. Id. at 36-37. Because the certificated character of the investments in the CMA is a material fact, the perfection of the Bank's security interest is addressed as if certificates were not issued, see infra 465, and as if they were, see infra 465-69.

(1977) ("This section permits a security interest to be perfected by transfer of possession only when the collateral is goods, instruments ...; that is to say, accounts and general intangibles are excluded.").

Even if we assume that certificates representing the investments were issued to the Van Kylens, there is nothing to suggest that the Bank was "in possession" of those instruments. Assuming the government securities were certificated and the certificates of deposit were issued, the collateral existed in the form of instruments. See WIS.STAT. §409.105(1)(i) (1987-88) ("'Instrument' means a negotiable instrument as defined in s. 403.104 or a certificated security as defined in s. 408.102"); id. §403.104(2)(a) (certificate of deposit qualifies as a negotiable instrument "if it is an acknowledgment by a bank of receipt of money with an engagement to repay it"); 1987 Official Text of the Uniform Commercial Code: Reporter's Introductory Comment to 1977 Amendments, app. I at 813 (West 1987) ("The essential difference between a certificated and an uncertificated security ... is that the former is represented by an instrument, which may be treated as the property it represents, and the latter is not."). A security interest in instruments must be perfected by possession under section 409.305[1] . See WIS.STAT. §409.304(1) (1987-88).

Under section 409.305, possession is accomplished when the collateral is physically transferred to the secured party or its agent, or to a bailee who has been notified of the secured party's interest. Section 9-305 requires the secured party, his agent, or the bailee to have actual possession of the collateral in order to perfect his security interest. The debtor's lack of possession coupled with actual possession by the creditor, the creditor's agent or the bailee serves 'to provide notice to prospective third party creditors that the debtor no longer has unfettered use of [his] collateral.' The Bank does not contend that the contents of the CMA were ever actually transferred to it. Rather, the Bank appears to argue that Merrill Lynch, Inc. possessed the collateral either as an agent of the Bank or its bailee. However, "[a]s the functional equivalent of filing, the secured party's taking possession of the collateral is adequate only if it puts third persons on notice that someone may claim an interest in the debtor's property." J. Worley, Possessory Security Interests §14.03[1] at 14--13-14. Therefore, the putative agent for the secured party may not be too closely aligned to the debtor. As the Official Comment to section 9-305 states: Possession may be by the secured party himself or by an agent on his behalf: it is of course clear, however,

---

[1]   Because section 409.305 excludes instruments existing in the form of certificated investment securities from its scope, this provision is only applicable to the extent the funds were invested in certificates of deposit which were in the possession of the Bank at the time the Bank enforced its security interest. See WIS.STAT. §409.305 (1987-88) ("A security interest is perfected by possession from the time possession is taken without relation back and continues only so long as possession is retained....") (emphasis supplied). As to any certificated securities, the Bank must rely on Article Eight's provisions relating to the perfection of security interests in investment securities. See infra 468-69.

that the debtor or a person controlled by him cannot qualify as such an agent for the secured party. U.C.C. §9-305 comment 2 (1977).

The secured party's control of the agent vis-a-vis the collateral must be exclusive of the debtor. See U.C.C. §9-205 comment 6 (1977) ("Th [is] section does not mean that the holder of an unfiled security interest, whose perfection depends on possession of the collateral by the secured party or by a bailee ... can allow the debtor access to and control over the goods without thereby losing his perfected interest."). Any control exercisable by the debtor over the putative agent for the secured party defeats the secured party's claims to possession. The party in possession may not serve as the agent for both the debtor and the secured party.

Under the agreed facts Merrill Lynch, Inc. does not qualify as an agent of the Bank for purposes of perfecting the Bank's security interest. Under Paragraph 2 of the Assignment Agreement, the Van Kylens were permitted to change the mix of investments in the CMA subject only to the requirements that: one, the investments be insured by the FDIC/FSLIC or be issued by the United States Government; and two, at least $50,000.00 worth of investments remain in the CMA at all times. The Van Kylens could effect a change in the investment mix by communicating their wishes to Merrill Lynch, Inc., who quite clearly was acting as their agent with respect to the CMA. See Merrill Lynch, Pierce, Fenner & Smith, Inc. v. Boeck, 127 Wis.2d 127, 145, 377 N.W.2d 605 (1985) (Abrahamson, J., dissenting) ("the nature of the relation between a customer who has a nondiscretionary account and the broker ... is one of principal and agent"). The degree of control the Van Kylens possessed over both the collateral and the putative agent renders the possession of the collateral by Merrill Lynch, Inc. inadequate to impart notice to third parties that the contents of the CMA were encumbered by the Bank's security interest. The Bank's argument that the title of the account would serve this notice function is simply unavailing. See Greiner v. Wilke (In re Staff Mort. & Inv. Corp), 625 F.2d 281, 283-84 (9th Cir.1980) (stapling security agreement to pledged notes did not serve notice function when neither secured party nor agent were in actual possession of the collateral).

The Bank also asserts that Merrill Lynch was a bailee, and that Merrill Lynch had notice of the Bank's security interest. The Bank provides little argument and no citation to authority in support of its assertion. There is no doubt that Merrill Lynch received notification of the Bank's security interest. The question is whether it held the contents of the CMA as a bailee within the meaning of section 409.305. This inquiry is slightly different than that undertaken in regard to Merrill Lynch's status as the agent of the Bank. One commentator distinguishes possession by agency from possession by a bailee with notice under section 9-305 in the following manner:

The possession-by-agency technique contemplates the collateral being held or controlled by a party who is aligned with the secured party. The debtor delivers physical control of the collateral to the agent, and the agent's possession operates as the secured party's possession with the agent acting on behalf of th secured party.   The bailee-with-notice technique, by contrast, contemplates the collateral being held or controlled by someone aligned (at least initially) with the debtor.   The bailee presumably already has possession of the collateral by virtue of some pre-existing relationship with the debtor, and his receiving notification of the secured party's interest merely operates to transfer possession--albeit constructively--to the secured party.

J. Worley, Possessory Security Interests §14.04[2][a][ii] at 14-48.[1]

In In re Copeland, 531 F.2d 1195 (3d Cir.1976) the court stated:

> Where the Code requires perfection by possession of the secured party or his bailee, it is clear that possession by the debtor or an individual closely associated with the debtor is not sufficient to alert prospective creditors of the possibility that the debtor's property is encumbered....   It does not follow ..., however, that possession of the collateral must be under the sole dominion and control of the secured party....   Rather, we believe that possession by a third party bailee, who is not controlled by the debtor, which adequately informs potential lenders of the existence of a perfected security interest satisfies the notice function underlying the 'bailee with notice' provision of §9-305.

Id. at 1204.   Thus, while the collateral need not be "under the sole dominion of the secured party," if the debtor can exercise control over the collateral while it is in the possession of the bailee, perfection is defeated.   Cf. U.C.C. §9-205 comment 6 (1977).

As discussed above, the Assignment Agreement permitted the Van Kylens freely to change the mix of investments in the CMA.   The Van Kylens could accomplish this by the simple expedient of directing Merrill Lynch, Inc. to

---

[1]   At least one case appears to take a somewhat contrary position, holding that the a party standing in a bailment relation with the debtor may not qualify as a bailee under U.C.C. §9-305.   In In re Milam, 4 B.R. 621 (Bankr.M.D.Ga.1980), the debtor granted a security interest in a certain quantity of stock to a bank.   The bank itself never took possession of the stock certificates; rather, the certificates remained in the possession of the issuer.   The bank, relying on U.C.C. §9-305 (1972 version), argued that the since it had orally notified the issuer of the bank's security interest, the issuer was a "bailee with notice."   The court disagreed stating: [U.C.C. §9-305] is of no help to [the secured party] unless [the issuer] was the bailee of the [secured party], and the facts disclose that [the issuer] was the bailee of the debtor and not of the [secured party].   [The issuer] could not serve as bailee of both the debtor and the [secured party]. Milam, 4 B.R. at 622.

convert any particular investment into another form. Both Merrill Lynch, Inc. and the collateral were "under the control" of the Van Kylens.

Because of its general importance in bankruptcy law some comment is appropriate on Hassett v. Blue Cross & Blue Shield of Greater N.Y. (In re O.P.M. Leasing Services, Inc.), 46 B.R. 661 (Bankr.S.D.N.Y.1985). There the debtor granted a security interest in $100,000.00 under an escrow agreement. The escrow agent was obligated to place the funds in an interest bearing account with a federally insured banking institution and to deliver to the debtor all interest earned on the funds. The escrow agent was also required to release the funds to the secured party upon the receipt of written notice that the debtor had defaulted. When the debtor filed bankruptcy, the trustee argued that the security interest was unperfected as the secured party was not in possession of the funds. The court held that the escrow agent was a "bailee with notice" under U.C.C. §9-305, stating:

> As the Escrow Agent was fully informed of [the secured party's] interest in the escrow account, and because the escrow agreement provided adequate notice to any subsequent creditors of [the debtor] that [the debtor] no longer had unfettered use of the funds in the escrow account, the Court is satisfied that delivery of possession to the Escrow Agent as custodian fully satisfied the perfection requirements of the U.C.C.

O.P.M. Leasing, 46 B.R. at 670.

O.P.M. Leasing is analogous to this case in that the debtors were restricted in their use of the collateral. There, the funds deposited were in the exclusive control of the escrow agent; here, the Van Kylens had to maintain $50,000.00 of value in the CMA. Additionally, in each case the security agreement seems sufficient to apprise subsequent creditors of the encumbrance of the collateral. There is, however, a distinguishing feature. In O.P.M. Leasing the collateral, a cash deposit, was static, i.e., the debtor had no power to convert it into other forms of property. See id. at 668 ("The funds were not in control of [the debtor]."). In the present case, the Van Kylens could freely convert the government securities into shares in a money market fund, or various other investments. Further, there is nothing in the Assignment Agreement which prevents the Van Kylens from taking possession themselves of the instruments representing the investments made with the CMA funds. If that were done, a creditor dealing with the Van Kylens would not have the level of notice afforded one seeking to assert an interest in the OPM escrow.

The Bank's last stand on the issue of perfection is made under Article Eight. The Bank states in its brief: Section 408.321(1) stats., provides that a security interest in a security is enforceable and can attach only if transferred to the secured party or person designated by him or [her] under 408.313(1), Stats. In this case, to the extent there were any securities making up the fund, Merrill Lynch, as agent for the Bank, had possession of the security, and therefore the security interest became perfected at that time. Bank's Brief at 30. The Bank's rather truncated statutory argument is apparently as follows. Section 408.321(1) provides that a security interest in a security attaches when it is "transferred to the secured party or a person designated by him or her under s. 408.313(1)." WIS.STAT. §408.321(1) (1987- 88). Under section 408.313(1)(a), the "transfer" of a security interest occurs when the secured party "or a person designated by him or her acquires possession of a certificated security." WIS.STAT. §408.313(1)(a) (1987-88). Merrill Lynch, Inc. was so designated and had possession. Finally, section 408.321(2) provides that when a security interest "is so transferred pursuant to an agreement by a transferor who has rights in the security to a transferee who has given value [it] is a perfected security interest." WIS.STAT. §408.321(2)(1987-88). The Van Kylens had rights in the investments and Merrill Lynch gave value. Therefore, to the extent the contents of the CMA contained certificated securities, the Bank held a perfected security interest.

Because the provision the Bank relies upon is the result of an amendment to Wisconsin's version of the U.C.C. occurring after the security interest was created, see 1985 Wisconsin Act 237 (adopting the "1977 Official Amendments" to the U.C.C.), the trustee argues that "retroactive" application of the provision is improper. I cannot adopt the trustee's argument. Application of the 1977 amendments to this transaction really does not have "retroactive" effect. No legal entitlements were changed. Prior to the amendments the security interest of a pledgee of a certificated security could have been perfected by possession. See WIS.STAT. §409.302(1)(a) (1981-82); id. §409.304(1); id. §409.305. After the 1977 amendments, sections 408.313(1)(a) and 408.321(2) allow creation and perfection of security interests in the same manner. The requirements for prefection of the Bank's security interest are essentially identical under either statutory scheme:

> The typical pledge of a certificated security is unaffected by the [exclusion of certificated securities from section 9-305] since Section 8-313(1)(a) provides for transfer by delivery and Section 8-321(2) provides that a security interest thus transferred is perfected.

1987 Official Text of the Uniform Commercial Code: Reasons for 1977 Change §9-305, app. I at 883 (West 1987). The 1977 Amendments do not change the result in this case.

Again assuming for purposes of disposing of the parties' cross motions for summary judgment that certificated securities were issued and were held by Merrill Lynch, Inc., the issue is whether Merrill Lynch, Inc. was acting as the Bank's "designee." I have found no cases which attempt to define "designee," but the commentary regarding the 1977 Amendments seems to argue in favor of construing it to mean "agent for purposes of possession;" i.e., in the same manner as "agent" was construed under the old section 9-305. This seems faithful to the drafters' intent not to change the law with respect to security interests in certificated securities. If Merrill Lynch was not the Bank's agent before it is not now. The Bank, therefore, has failed to bring itself within either of the two exceptions to filing upon which it relies, and its security interest was unperfected.

* * *

Therefore, the transfer of Mr. Van Kylen's interest in the CMA to the Bank is avoided and pursuant to section 551 is preserved for the benefit of the estate.

ORDER

The court having this day entered its memorandum decision in the above-entitled matter,

IT IS HEREBY ORDERED that Lillian S. Van Kylen's motion for summary judgment is denied;

IT IS FURTHER ORDERED that the trustee's motion for summary judgment is granted in part and the trustee is entitled to one-half of the funds currently held in escrow by Merrill Lynch, Inc. for the benefit of the parties;

IT IS FURTHER ORDERED that Citizen State Bank's motion for summary judgment is granted in part and the Bank is entitled to the remaining one-half of the funds currently held in escrow by Merrill Lynch, Inc.

b. Automatic Perfection

In a few instances, Article 9 provides that a security interest is perfected even though the secured party neither files a financing statement nor keeps possession of the collateral. The interest is perfected automatically without the secured party doing anything. In these few, very limited instances, the strong policy of the law favoring perfection, which ordinarily conditions enforceability of a security interest against third parties on public notice, yields to an even stronger reason for allowing the secured party, in effect, to enforce a secret lien against the world.

In some instances of automatic perfection, the security interest is deemed perfected as soon as the interest attaches to the collateral, and the period of automatic perfection is unlimited. The interest is perfected as long as the interest continues. This is true, for example, with respect to:

* a purchase money security interest in consumer goods; and,
* an assignment of accounts which does not alone or in conjunction with other assignments to the same assignee transfer a significant part of the outstanding accounts of the assignor.

U.C.C. §9-302(1)(d) & (e).

These two instances of automatic perfection are theoretically the most significant because consumer goods purchased on credit and accounts are such common forms of collateral. Practically speaking, however, neither of them is very important. With respect to the first, that is, purchase money security interests in consumer goods, used consumer goods are relatively invaluable and thus are unlikely to be transferred by the debtor, claimed by her other creditors, or (if the truth be known) pursued by the secured party in the event of default.

Of course, there is a direct relationship between the durability of consumer goods that are collateral and (1) the property's worth as used goods, (2) the attractiveness of the property to third parties; and (3) the secured party's willingness to pursue the property upon the debtor's default. Yet, the greatest threat to the property as collateral is probably a sale by the debtor to a buyer who, like the debtor, is a consumer. Such a buyer, however, takes free of a security interest that is perfected only automatically through U.C.C. §9-302(1)(d). See U.C.C. §9-307(2). Also, U.C.C. §9-302(1)(d) does not apply to motor vehicles required to be registered, which includes virtually all cars and trucks purchased by consumers.

U.C.C. §9-302(1)(e) is also practically unimportant. Accounts are commonly used as collateral for business loans, but in virtually every case the security agreement covers all the debtor's accounts, not just an insignificant part of them which is all that U.C.C. §9-302(1)(e) covers. Moreover, the secured party commonly is a professional lender, and the courts have interpreted §9-302(1)(e) as in any event unavailable to a secured party who is experienced in accounts financing, *In re B. Hollis Knight Co.*, 605 F.2d 397 (8th Cir.1979), or experienced in secured lending generally, *H. & Val J. Rothschild, Inc. v. Northwestern Nat'l Bank*, 309 Minn. 35, 242 N.W.2d 844 (1976), even though the percentage of the debtor's total accounts that are collateral is mathematically insignificant in absolute terms.

In some instances of automatic perfection, the period of perfection is not unlimited; rather, the perfection continues for only a short time. This is true of U.C.C. §§9-304(4) & (5) which, in general terms, give "perfected status to security interests in instruments (other than certificated securities) and documents for a short period although there has been no filing and the collateral is in the debtor's possession." U.C.C. §9-304 comment 4. The explanation for this temporary automatic perfection, which last for only 21 days, is very pragmatic: "There are a variety of legitimate reasons *** why such collateral has to be temporarily released to a debtor and no useful purpose would be serves by cluttering the files with records of such exceedingly short term transactions." Id. The importance of these instances of automatic perfection is suggested by the paucity of reported cases in which a secured party has been forced to rely on §9-304(4) or §9-304(5) to establish priority.

Probably the truly most important instance of automatic perfection is U.C.C. §9-306(3), which provides for continuing in proceeds the perfected status of the security interest in the original collateral. This rule applies not only when dealing with priority of security interests *inter se;* it also applies and is equally important in determining the priority of a proceeds security interest relative to any other kind of claim or interest whenever priority turns on perfection.

c. Other Law (Exceptions to Perfection Under Article 9)

Article 9 is not the exclusive source of law on the perfection of security interests, not even when the security interest is created and ranked against other claims under the rules of Article 9. Federal and even state law sometimes provide for perfecting an Article 9 security interest by taking steps under law other than Article 9, even though Article 9 continues to govern issues of creation or priority. The most familiar example is state law requiring certificates of title for motor vehicles.

Problems

1. Myford Car Sales, Inc. is a car dealer selling Ford cars and trucks mainly to individual consumers and occasionally to businesses. Buyer offers to buy a car on credit from Myford, proposing that her obligation to pay the price be secured by the vehicle itself.

    a. What law governs CREATION of a security interest in the vehicle in favor of Myford? See U.C.C. §9-102(1).

    b. How is the interest created? See U.C.C. §9-203(1).

2. Same facts as Problem 1, but the questions are different.

    a. What law governs PERFECTION of the security interest? See U.C.C. §§9-302(1)(d); 9-302(3)(b); Uniform Motor Vehicle Certificate Of Title And Anti-Theft Act (U.M.V.C.T.) §20(a) & (b) (1955 Official Text).

    b. How is the interest perfected? See U.M.V.C.T. §§6, 9, 20(b) & 21. Does this law condition perfection on Myford retaining possession of the certificate the state issues? Should Myford nevertheless retain the title? Can Myford perfect by holding the certificate of title even if its interest is not noted thereon? Can Myford perfect by taking possession of the vehicle rather than by having its interest noted on the certificate?

   c. When is Myford's security interest perfected if Myford perfects by having its interest noted on the certificate of title? See U.M.V.C.T. §20(b).

3. Myford is financed by State Bank, which wants a security interest in the dealer's inventory.

   a. What law governs CREATION of a security interest in Myford's inventory in favor of the Bank? See U.C.C. §9-102(1). How is the interest created? See U.C.C. §9-203(1).

   b. What law governs PERFECTION of the security interest? See U.M.V.C.T. §§2(a)(2) & 3(c); U.C.C. §9-302(3)(b). How is the interest perfected? When is the interest perfected?

4. Suppose Myford also sells Myford tractors, and sold one of them to a customer for use in the customer's farming operations. The sale was on credit with the retention of a security interest in Myford's favor. What law governs creation of the security interest in the tractor? See U.C.C. §9-102(1). What law governs perfection of the interest? See U.M.V.C.T. §§1(d) & 2(a)(6).

5. Continue with Problem 1. Myford sells Buyer a car on credit and retains a security interest in the vehicle. Upon proper application, a certificate of title is issued giving Buyer's name as owner and showing Myford as the holder of a "first security interest or lien." No financing statement is filed.

Buyer purchased the car for her own personal, family, and household purposes, but soon discovered the vehicle was a lemon. She unloaded the car by selling it to Transferee, who intended the same uses for the vehicles. Buyer represented to him that she held "clear title". Transferee did not ask to see the car's certificate of title, and Buyer did not volunteer to show the certificate to him. (On what should have happened with respect to the certificate of title, see U.M.V.C.T. §14.) Shortly thereafter Buyer stopped making car payments to Myford, and Myford traced the vehicle to Transferee who refused Myford's demand that he surrender possession. Myford sues Transferee to replevy the vehicle. Transferee argues that he took free of Myford's security interest under U.C.C. §9-307(2) because Myford had not filed a financing statement covering the vehicle. Is there a flaw in this argument? See U.C.C. §§9-302(3)(b) & (4).

3. Classification Of Collateral

In re Bedford Computer Corp.

United States Bankruptcy Court, D. New Hampshire, 1986
62 B.R. 555

[Bedford Computer Corporation engaged in the development, manufacture, and marketing of "real time" computer text and graphic composition systems. These systems were used primarily by financial and legal printers, and businesses with in-house typesetting requirements. Bedford had manufacturered and sold electronic pre-press composition and editing hardware and software for many years. The principal technology that Bedford developed consisted of source and object codes embodied in magnetic media.[1] In this case the court was asked to decide whether this property was tangible or intangible.] James E. Yacos, Bankruptcy Judge: * * *

Courts and attorneys are used to drawing distinctions between "tangible" and "intangible" property for purposes of various legal rules and principles. They find themselves confronted with a quite perplexing task, however, when called upon to characterize the "software" used in the computer industry. Since the industry itself is relatively new, the case decisions are sparse. Such decisions as there are, and the legal perplexities involved, are discussed in a number of recent articles.

The confusing characteristics of software for legal analysis is well-summarized in the Horovitz article cited above as follows:

> Software has several traits that make its classification within the UCC a complicated question. Software exhibits characteristics of a good, a service, and an intangible. Typical software transactions take place in widely varying forms. When analyzing the applicability of the UCC to software, it is useful to consider the character of the property (whether it is tangible or intangible), the character of the transaction (whether it is a good or a service), the form of the transaction (whether it is a sale, a lease, or a license), and the compatability of software transactions with the goals and effects of the UCC. [65 B.U. Law Rev. at 149]

If the court in the present case were compelled to make a definitive characterization, I believe I would conclude that the software here involved

---

[1]   The "object code" is the engineer's instructions translated into a language that only the computer hardware can "read" to become a functioning machine. It is an essential part of the machine in that sense. The "source code" is the same original set of instructions, expressed in a language that the engineers can read and deal with. Customers are almost never given the source code when they purchase a computer product. As one Bedford engineer testified, the source code is the "lifeblood" of any computer company and is rarely disclosed.

should be characterized as tangible rather than intangible property. The evidence establishes in excruciating detail that the source code and object code embodiment of that "technology" cannot exist independent from the actual hardware components to which it gives operational life. The source code does not demonstrate some broad generalized technology of technical principles and ideas, existing apart from a particular tangible machine already in existence, but instead presupposes the prior existence of particular hardware to give the source code itself any meaning.[1] Moreover, the source code is embodied in tangible magnetic media of various types, and when translated into equally- tangible object code media, becomes just as much a part of the "computer machine" being developed as any of its other tangible facets. In a sense, it could be said that the engineers at Bedford could not work on "technology" in any abstract way at all, but necessarily had to effectuate tangible changes in tangible machines by their very activity.[2]

* * *

---

[1]   It is important to understand that both codes, even when printed out in "hard-copy" form from the magnetic media, are not recognizable as "language" in the ordinary sense. As the testimony in the record indicates, and inspection of Plaintiff's Exhibits 87 and 88 will confirm, the printout just produces "gibberish" of two types. The source code "gibberish" is understandable to engineers if sufficient commentary is provided. The object code "gibberish" is understandable to no one but the computer. Courts have trouble enough reading contractual and statutory language and the undersigned judge has had to take on faith the foregoing gibberish-analysis presented by the expert witnesses. As far as this court is concerned, one of the piles of gibberish looks pretty much like the other pile. Cf. Bank of Marin v. England, Trustee in Bankruptcy, 385 U.S. 99, 103, 87 S.Ct. 274, 277, 17 L.Ed.2d 197 (1966) ("[W]e do not read these ... words with the ease of a computer.").

[2]   The court is aware of the decision in this district in United States v. Antenna Systems, Inc., 251 F.Supp. 1013 (D.N.H.1966), dealing with a question under UCC Article 9 of whether a security agreement that described the security collateral to include inventory, work in process, contract rights, furniture, fixtures, and equipment (but not "general intangibles") covered "blueprint and technical data produced when the company's engineering staff designed a product." The court noted that it was being compelled to classify between mutually exclusive categories "property which arguably fits into both categories but which fits neatly into neither category." The court then ruled that "for purposes of this case these blueprints, drawings, etc. in reality the visual reproductions on paper of engineering concepts, ideas and principles, are general intangibles within the meaning of that term as used in the Uniform Commercial Code." This decision does not appear to be a very strong precedent for a similar ruling involving property having the unique characteristics of computer software. See also, Bonebrake v. Cox, 499 F.2d 951 (8th Cir.1974); Standard Structural Steel Co., v. Debron Corporation, 515 F.Supp. 803 (D.Conn.1980).

Matter of Newman

United States Court of Appeals, Fifth Circuit, 1993
993 F.2d 90

Reynolds G. Garza, Circuit Judge: West Loop Savings Association ("West Loop") appeals from an adverse summary judgment entered by the district court, which held that West Loop held an unperfected security interest in an annuity contract assigned by the debtor Bobby Lynn Newman ("Newman"). The court held that the annuity contract was a general intangible and, as a result, a financing statement was required to be filed with the secretary of state in order to complete perfection. West Loop contends that the annuity contract is not a general intangible, but an instrument and, therefore, its security interest was perfected upon delivery. We agree with the district court that the annuity contract is a general intangible and, therefore, the case is in all respects AFFIRMED.

* * *

The UCC defines a general intangible merely by stating what is not a general intangible.[1] A general intangible is essentially a bundle of rights such as those inherent in a franchise, a chose in action, a copyright, or an annuity. See Flanigan's Enterps., Inc. v. Barnett Bank of Naples, 614 So.2d 1198, 1201 (Fla.Ct.App. 5th Dist.1993) (dicta) (citing 73 C.J.S. Property §15 (1983)); see also In re Holiday Intervals, Inc., 931 F.2d 500, 503 (8th Cir.1991) (land sale installment contract general intangible); In re Nix, 864 F.2d 1209, 1211 (5th Cir.1989) (Keogh plan general intangible); In re Hartman, 102 B.R. 90, 93 (Bankr.N.D.Tex.1989) (one-half partnership interest general intangible); In re Bell Fuel Corp., 99 B.R. 602, 604 (Bankr.E.D.Pa.) (contractual right to receive insurance constitutes chose in action and thus general intangible), aff'd, 891 F.2d 281 (3d Cir.1989); Gold Medal Prods., Inc. v. Love Enterps., Inc., 766 S.W.2d 759, 761 (Mo.Ct.App.1989) (assignment of right to proceeds from pending lawsuit general intangible); cf Smith v. Mark Twain Nat'l Bank, 805 F.2d 278, 285 (8th Cir.1986) (repurchase agreement and certificate of deposit instruments); In re Staff Mortgage & Inv. Corp., 625 F.2d 281, 284 (9th Cir.1980) (promissory note secured by deeds of trust instrument).

---

[1]   Section 9.106 "defines" a general intangible as follows: "any personal property other than goods, accounts, chattel paper, documents, instruments and money." Tex.Bus. & Com.Code §9.106. The term "general intangibles" brings under this Article miscellaneous types of contractual rights and other personal property which are used or may become customarily used as commercial security. Note that this catch-all definition does not apply to money or other types of intangibles that are specifically excluded from the coverage of the Article under Section 9.104. Section 9.104, Uniform Commercial Code provision 9-104, excludes twelve types of transactions from the scope of Article 9. Section 9.104's exclusions fall generally under three main categories: (i) transactions that are subject to overriding governmental interests; (ii) transactions that are nonconsensual; and (iii) transactions that are out of the mainstream of commercial financing. See W. Hawkland, R. Lord, and C. Lewis, Uniform Commercial Code Series §9-104:01 (1988).

There is a dearth of case law on the classification of general intangibles. In fact, most of the cases focus on the difference between an account and a general intangible. In two of the cases that were faced with the issue of general intangible versus instrument, the courts in each instance tersely concluded that the bundle of rights in question were general intangibles. See In re ESM Government Secs., Inc., 812 F.2d 1374, 1377 (11th Cir.1987) (right to payment of funds from repurchase of GNMAs was not an account or instrument and thus general intangible); Union Inv., Inc. v. Midland-Guardian Co., 30 Oh.App.3d 59, 506 N.E.2d 271, 273 n. 2 (1986) ("Without a detailed explanation of our reasons, we find that the [promissory] note ... is a general intangible").

Perhaps the only substantive confrontation with the instrument versus general intangible classification occurred in *Coral Petroleum*. See *Coral Petroleum*, 50 B.R. at 837-39. In *Coral Petroleum*, Bankruptcy Judge Manuel Leal concluded that a promissory note was an instrument. See id. at 838. Interestingly, the creditor in *Coral Petroleum* sought to have the note classified as a general intangible in order to have a perfected security interest because it did not possess the note, but had filed a financing statement. See id. at 835. Conversely, herein West Loop seeks to have the annuity classified as an instrument because it has possession, but did not file a financing statement.[1]

Coral Petroleum approached the problem in a pragmatic manner. The court concluded that the test for determining whether a writing is transferable in the ordinary course of business hinges on what professionals would ordinarily do to transfer such an interest. Id. at 838 (citing Harris, Non-negotiable Certificates of Deposit: An Article 9 Problem, 29 U.C.L.A.L.Rev. 330, 372 (1981)). The court reasoned that if professionals would attach significance to possession of the writing and treat certain collateral as an instrument, then the law should likewise treat the collateral similarly. See id.[2]

After carefully reviewing the record, we find no indication that this or any other annuity is transferred in the regular course of business by endorsement. In

---

[1]   If collateral is classified as an instrument, then the only way to perfect is to take possession via a pledge. Tex.Bus. & Com.Code §9.304(e)(1). On the other hand, if collateral is classified as a general intangible, then the only way to perfect is to file a financing statement. See Barkley Clark The Law of Secured Transactions Under the Uniform Commercial Code, P 7.03 (2d Ed.1988) (hereinafter "Clark Secured Transactions "). This case painfully illustrates the problems that creditors encounter when they fail to account for Article 9 problems. The best practice in cases where a precise categorization is elusive, would be to comply with both requirements. Creditors who foresee Article 9 problems when acquiring collateral are "handsomely rewarded for their knowledge of the breadth of Article 9." Id. at P 1.03.

[2]   In Clark, Secured Transactions, at ¶7.03, p. 7-8, the author discusses *Coral Petroleum*, and states: In short, the definition of 'instrument' in the UCC is broad and intentionally incorporates standard banking practice. The fact that the note was nonnegotiable and of limited transferability did not prevent it from being an instrument that could be pledged as collateral and for which possession was the only proper method of perfection. Id.

an instance such as this, where precise categorization is unclear, it seems to this court that a finding of general intangible is warranted. The cases indicate that collateral such as certificates of deposit and promissory notes are instruments because professionals attach significance to their possession. However, interests such as Keogh Plans and the contractual right to receive insurance are treated as general intangibles because they are not customarily transferred by delivery with endorsement. These annuities are general intangibles because based upon the "reasonable professional standard" outlined in Coral Petroleum there is no indication that they are regularly traded by delivery or that possession of the annuity certificate confers the right to payment.

In a vacuum, if left to formulate our own test for distinguishing between a general intangible and an instrument, our benchmark would begin with the definition of an instrument.[1]   Section 9.105(a)(9) defines an "instrument" as "any other writing which evidences a right to the payment of money and is not itself a security agreement or lease and is of a type of which is in the ordinary course of business transferred by delivery with any necessary indorsement or assignment." Tex.Bus. & Com.Code §9.105(a)(9). Because the annuity contract in question: (i) does not evidence a right to payment on its face; and (ii) is not ordinarily transferred by delivery, it is not an instrument.

> * * *

[W]e AFFIRM the district court's summary judgment in favor of the trustee.

Stephen L. Sepinuck, *Classifying Credit Card Receivables Under The U.C.C.: Playing With Instruments?*
32 Ariz. L. Rev. 789 (1990)

> * * *

Credit card transactions have, in the past several years, become one of the predominant payment methods for American consumers, generating billions of dollars in outstanding receivables. Some of these receivables are used as collateral for loans to those merchants who accept payment by credit card, while others back certain securities issued by credit card banks.

In spite of their prevalence, neither the cards themselves nor the receivables they help create are expressly mentioned in the Uniform Commercial Code. Although federal law does govern some aspects of credit card transactions, most notably the rights of cardholders, much of the remaining operation of credit cards is left to the auspices of state commercial law, which is generally silent. This silence is particularly troubling in Article Nine, which provides different perfection methods for different types of collateral. Although no court has yet determined the proper Article Nine classification of and perfection method for credit card receivables, the issue is one upon which attorneys and other commercial law experts do differ. Because the issue is also one upon which

---

[1]   We note that the annuity contract is not a "good, account[ ], chattel paper, document ... or money." Tex.Bus. & Com.Code §9.106.

billions of dollars may be won or lost, the present level of uncertainty is simply too great.

* * *

To illustrate * * * [a] likely scenario, assume that a hypothetical Beacon Airlines ("Beacon") operates a fleet of twenty commuter aircraft with which it transports cargo and passengers between several medium- sized midwestern cities. Like many small businesses, Beacon has numerous creditors. Many of these creditors are suppliers to whom Beacon owes an unsecured debt for fuel, spare parts, and other materials provided on a regular basis. One creditor is a bank (the "Bank") which financed Beacon's initial start-up and subsequent expansion and which, in connection with this financing, took a security interest in Beacon's aircraft, equipment, and accounts. The Bank perfected its security interest in Beacon's airplanes by filing the appropriate documents with the FAA Aircraft Registry in Oklahoma City, and perfected its interest in the remaining collateral by filing a properly executed financing statement in the appropriate state office.

Shortly after its initial start-up, Beacon contracted with another bank (the "Credit Card Bank") to participate in the MasterCard and Visa systems and contracted with American Express to honor that organization's series of cards. Since that time, Beacon has accepted payment from its customers via cash, check, and each of these major credit cards. At a time when some money remains due to Beacon on credit card receivables in its possession and others undergoing processing by American Express and the Credit Card Bank, Beacon's financial situation worsens. In response, Beacon seeks protection from its creditors by filing a petition for relief under Chapter 11 of the United States Bankruptcy Code.

If we assume, as often occurs, that the resale value of the Bank's tangible collateral -- Beacon's aircraft and equipment -- fails to equal the total outstanding indebtedness Beacon owes to the Bank, the Bank will look to its remaining collateral: Beacon's accounts. * * * [O]n any given day, hundreds of millions of dollars in freshly generated credit card receivables are in the hands of merchants, such as Beacon, and these credit card receivables are likely to make up a sizable percentage of these merchants' total receivables. Accordingly, the Bank will likely be very interested in obtaining Beacon's credit card receivables and the Bankruptcy Court may be asked to determine whether the Bank has a perfected security interest in the money owed by Credit Card Bank and American Express to Beacon.

* * *

Under Article Nine of the Uniform Commercial Code, a creditor must perfect a security interest in order to render that interest generally effective against both other creditors of the debtor and subsequent purchasers of the collateral. For most types of collateral, the creditor may perfect by either properly filing a financing statement which adequately describes both the debtor and the collateral or by taking physical possession of the collateral. For certain types of collateral, however, Article Nine restricts perfection to only one of these alternative methods. For example, a creditor may perfect a security interest in accounts or general intangibles only by filing a financing statement. Conversely, a creditor may generally perfect a security interest in instruments only by taking possession. Accordingly, it is essential for a creditor wishing to perfect a security interest in a merchant's credit card receivables to ascertain whether the receivables constitute accounts, general intangibles, or instruments.

* * *

From the outset it is clear that credit card receivables do not qualify as instruments under either of the first two clauses of the instrument definition. They are not negotiable instruments because they lack the "magic words" of negotiability: they fail to state that they are payable to the order of the merchant or to the bearer. They are not certificated securities for similarly obvious reasons. Accordingly, the relevant question becomes whether such a receivable is "any other writing which evidences a right to the payment of money * * * and is of a type which is in ordinary course of business transferred by delivery with any necessary indorsement or assignment."

* * *

It seems apparent that such receivables do evidence a right to the payment of money and therefore satisfy the first half of this definition. Indeed, they appear to evidence no rights other than the right to receive payment in money. The mere fact that payment of such a receivable is likely to be discounted from the face amount would not seem to alter this conclusion.

The difficult question centers on the latter half of the definition: whether such receivables are of a type which is in ordinary course of business transferred by delivery. It remains somewhat unclear whether this phrase requires merely that transfers of writings, however infrequent, customarily be effected through delivery, or whether it alternatively or additionally requires that the writings be of a type which is transferred frequently.

The weight of authority seems to be that transfer by delivery -- not frequency of transfers -- is the main focus of this statutory language. In other words, delivery of the writing must generally be necessary to transfer the right to payment which the writing represents. As one commentator put it, the Article Nine classification should depend on how professionals who deal with such writings handle them. If such professionals attach importance to possession of the writing, then the law should do the same. This is merely a way of restating the traditional maxim that the right to collect must be bound to the writing. If the right to payment exists independent of the writing, it cannot be an instrument, but if possession of the writing alone entitles the holder to receive payment, the writing is an instrument.

When, interpreted in this manner, the rationale for having different perfection mechanisms for accounts and instruments becomes evident. If the transfer of a particular right to money is generally effected through delivery of a writing, a secured creditor must obtain possession of that writing to prevent future -- and possibly fraudulent -- deliveries and transfers of the right. Although filing a financing statement with respect to such collateral might provide notice to the world, it would undermine the ease and operation of the normal transfer-by-delivery process. Moreover, if collection of a right to money requires delivery of a writing to the obligor, possession of the writing by a secured creditor is often essential to prevent the obligor from discharging its obligation by paying the debtor upon presentment.

On the other hand, for rights which are transferred other than by delivery, such as accounts and general intangibles, neither of these concerns applies. While such rights may be referenced in one or more writings, such as a sales or service contract, an order confirmation, a simple bill, or the seller's books and records, they exist independent of such writing and may readily be sued upon separately. Indeed, because such rights may be evidenced in multiple writings, possession of any one writing is not only unnecessary to prevent future, and perhaps fraudulent, transfers, it is insufficient.

Hence, the thrust of section 9-105(1)(i) appears to be that transfer by delivery and collection by presentment is what makes an instrument out of a writing which evidences the right to the payment of money. Even though a specific writing expressly restricts or prohibits transfers to third parties, if it is of a type for which delivery to the obligor is customarily required for collection, possession of the paper is necessary for the secured creditor to be truly secure.

The difficulty with classifying credit card receivables is that they seem to possess some, but not all, of the attributes of instruments. Specifically, while the right to payment on a credit card receivable often requires presentment of a writing -- at least when a writing exists -- presentation of the writing will not alone be sufficient to entitle the holder to payment. To obtain payment, the holder must also have some contractual relationship with one or more members of the credit card system: a member bank for Visa or MasterCard; American Express itself for Optima or the American Express card. Without such a relationship, no one will honor a credit card slip presented for payment. Even when a writing does exist, bank card slips are not always transferred to the issuing bank; the merchant or the merchant bank may retain them and electronically transmit the information necessary to obtain payment and bill the cardholder. This truncation of the collection procedure suggests that the right to collect is not intrinsically bound to the writing. In short, presentment of the writings representing credit card receivables is sometimes required, but is insufficient to obtain payment, and transfer of such writings -- by delivery or otherwise -- is usually not permitted.

Given these facts, the two reasons for classifying a writing as an instrument, and thus requiring possession to perfect a security interest in it, appear not to apply to credit card receivables. First, while possession of an instrument is often necessary to prevent additional and perhaps fraudulent transfers of the writing (and the right to payment which it represents), the receivables are not transferable. Indeed, no one without a contractual relationship with someone in the clearinghouse procedure can hope to collect by mere presentment of the written slip. Second, while the obligor on a receivable may be able to discharge its obligation despite knowing that someone other than the presenter has a claim to it, the mechanism by which payment is made -- at least on bank cards -- undermines the ability of the debtor to use this fact to defraud secured creditors.

Even when merchants do present written bank card slips for payment, the merchant bank makes only a provisional settlement to the merchant's deposit account. Most credit card processing contracts between merchants and merchant banks restrict the merchant's right to withdraw the provisional settlement for quite some time, usually at least 120 days. If a creditor had a security interest in the credit slips redeemed for payment, that interest would extend to the deposit account as proceeds of the credit card slip. The merchant would then have little ability to use the funds for some other purpose. Thus, even assuming that concerns over the obligor's ability to discharge its obligation in circumstances detrimental to the secured creditor is what prompts courts to treat nontransferable writings as instruments, such concerns do not apply to the classification of credit card receivables.

* * *

CONCLUSION

Billions of dollars will be at stake when courts finally determine how credit card receivables and the little slips of paper which evidence them should be classified under Article Nine of the Uniform Commercial Code. Although such writings appear to meet the literal wording of the Code's definition of "instruments," and at least some commentators have suggested that they are instruments, no persuasive reason exists to classify them as such. They are not transferable, they are generally not presented back to the issuer in the collection process, and creditors usually have no access to the clearinghouse procedure through which they are paid. Classifying them as instruments, and thereby requiring secured creditors to take possession of them in order to perfect their interest, would serve no useful purpose.

Moreover, requiring possession to perfect an interest in credit card receivables would undermine the ability of creditors to perfect their security interests and would effectively prevent them from using credit card receivables as collateral. It would also require creditors and debtors to continuously distinguish between credit card receivables created in point-of-sale transactions and those arising from telephone and mail orders, for which no writing exists. The Uniform Commercial Code was not intended to so frustrate commercial transactions.

* * *

4. Multistate Transactions

The Uniform Commercial Code, as enacted by the states, is not really uniform in the sense of being the same throughout the country. Four major reasons explain this lack of uniformity:

First, there are competing official versions of the U.C.C.

Second, even among states sharing the same official version of the U.C.C., there are differences based on non-uniform, local legislative amendments.

Third, the exact same enacted law can be, and often is, interpreted differently by courts throughout the country. The U.C.C. has not been spared from disagreements among judges as to the meaning of its provisions. Indeed, the major reason the U.C.C. fails as a nationally uniform law is that the judicial gloss varies so widely from state to state.

Finally, provisions of each state's Code that refer to a municipal or state officer, such as the Secretary of State, have reference—quite obviously—to the officer within that state. Thus, although Georgia and Minnesota may agree that a financing statement should be filed centrally in a certain case, the Georgia §9-401 contemplates the Georgia Secretary of State and the same provision in Minnesota means the Minnesota Secretary of State.

Thus, conflicts questions, including choice-of-law questions, are often decisive in a multistate, secured transactions case even though the case is governed by Article 9 in each of the several states whose law could be applied. In such a case, two Code provisions guide the court in deciding which state's Article 9 to apply: U.C.C. §1-105(1), which is the general choice-of-law rule for the whole Code; and §9-103, which directs choice of law only on matters of perfecting security interests and related issues.

We should warn you that conflicts questions are often difficult, and choice-of-law questions are especially tough in Article 9 cases. The difficulty is compounded in such cases not only because two choice-of-law statutes are applicable, but also because of the concept known as *depecage*, which means that different issues in a single case arising out of the same facts may be decided according to the laws of different states. The possibility of this happening in Article 9 cases is increased for the very reason that two choice-of-law statutes (§§1-105 and 9-103) apply in any such case that involves an issue of perfection, which is often.

Some advice: In a secured transactions case the safer approach is to consider conflicts questions, especially the matter of choice of law, for each issue (or collection of similar issues) instead of asking which state's Article 9 governs the whole case. The first step is to decide which states' laws constitutionally can be applied on the issue. The next step is to determine whether §1-105 or §9-103 governs the judge's decision on choosing among the several states whose law could be applied. When §9-103 governs, the final step, which is the hardest, is to apply the applicable subsection in making the choice.

Problems

1. Hormel is a meatpacking company whose main plant and corporate headquarters are in Austin, Minnesota, which is the site of the Miss Minnesota pageant. Hormel also has plants in Iowa. Hormel borrows money from Citicorp Bank of New York City. The loan is secured by Hormel's inventory and manufacturing equipment in Austin. Decide which state's law governs creation of the security interest in the collateral under these circumstances:

    a. The security agreement provides that "this contract is governed by the law of New York." See U.C.C. §1-105(1).

    b. The security agreement provides that "this contract is governed by the law of South Dakota," where a large division of Citicorp is located.

    c. The security agreement provides that "this contract is governed by the law of Iowa," where Hormel operates several manufacturing plants.

    d. The security agreement is silent with respect to governing law.

2. In answering Problem 1, which state's §1-105 were you applying?

3. Suppose Hormel and Citicorp agree in their security agreement that the law of New York shall govern their rights and duties. What steps should Citicorp take to perfect its security interest? Be careful! See U.C.C. §§1-105(2); 9-103.

4. Suppose Hormel borrows money from Citicorp to buy a new piece of manufacturing equipment to be located in Hormel's plant in Austin, Minnesota. The new equipment is the collateral for the loan under a security agreement the parties executed. The equipment is manufactured by a company in New Jersey which has already been paid for the equipment. What steps does Citicorp take to perfect its security interest in the new equipment? Assume that filing is an appropriate "applicable step for perfection" in each of the three states. See U.C.C. §9-103(1)(c).

5. Same as Problem 1 with a few additional facts: Citicorp acquires a security interest in the Austin inventory and equipment, and properly files in Minnesota a financing statement covering the collateral. A year later, unbeknownst to Citicorp, Hormel moves part of the equipment in its Austin plant to a plant in Des Moines, Iowa. Two months after this move, Hormel gets a loan from First State Bank of Des Moines, Iowa, which is secured, in part, by a security interest in all of Hormel's equipment located in Iowa. First State promptly files in Iowa. A year after the Austin equipment was moved to Iowa, Citicorp and First State litigate in Iowa which of them has priority with respect to the equipment that was moved from Minnesota to Iowa and remains

in Iowa. Citicorp files in Iowa shortly before the litigation begins. Which bank is entitled to priority? See U.C.C. §§9-103(1)(b) & (1)(d).

6. Now, using variations of the Hormel/Citicorp/First State case, study the language of, U.C.C. §9-103(1)(d)(i). Supplement the facts of Problem 1. Citicorp acquires a security interest in the Austin inventory and equipment and properly files in Minnesota a financing statement covering the collateral. A year later, unbeknownst to Citicorp, Hormel moves part of the equipment in its Austin plant to a plant in Des Moines, Iowa. Consider these variations in later events:

   a. Six months later, Hormel sells to Buyer the equipment moved to Iowa from Minnesota. Citicorp finally learns of the removal and the sale and, upon Hormel's default, demands the equipment from Buyer, who refuses the demand. Citicorp sues Buyer for conversion. Who wins?

   b. Suppose the sale to Buyer takes place two months after the equipment is removed to Iowa.

   c. Suppose the event in Iowa is not a sale of the equipment to Buyer. Rather, a judgment creditor levies execution on the equipment within two months after the property is removed to Iowa. Who is entitled to priority, Citicorp or the execution lien creditor?

   d. Suppose the judgment creditor does not levy execution on the equipment until six months after the property is removed to Iowa. Be careful! Take a long look at U.C.C. §9-103 comment 7 (second paragraph).

7. As a final examination on U.C.C. §9-103(1), return to the Hormel/Citicorp/First State case and consider these variations:

   a. Same facts as Problem 5 with two changes: First, Citicorp properly files in Iowa within four months after the equipment is removed to Iowa.

      Second, First State acquires its interest in the equipment through an after-acquired property clause in a security agreement between First State and Hormel made three years before the equipment was moved to Iowa. This agreement, and a proper Iowa filing that accompanied it, antedate both the agreement between Hormel and Citicorp and also the Minnesota filing by Hormel.

   b. Same facts as Problem 5 with only these changes: The equipment is returned to Minnesota one year after it was taken to Iowa, and one month later First State files suit in Minnesota to replevy the property. Citicorp intervenes and opposes the replevin, claiming that its security interest in the equipment is entitled to priority.

8. Now we move to U.C.C. §9-103(2). Bank financed Debtor's purchase of a car in Minnesota. Debtor granted Bank a security interest in the vehicle, and Minnesota issued a certificate of title showing Debtor as "owner" and Bank as holder of a "first security interest." Bank kept possession of the certificate. Debtor moved to Iowa and took the car with her. Iowa law requires that any person moving to the state must—within a period of two months—get Iowa license plates through a process of registering her vehicles with Iowa officials and must also, in a related process, have Iowa certificates of title issued for the vehicles. Anyone failing to comply with these requirements risks criminal sanctions. (Iowa law is actually somewhat different. The law reported here is "made up" for purposes of these problems.)

   Debtor never registered or titled her car in Iowa. Three months after moving there, she sold the vehicle to Buyer, an individual consumer. Shortly thereafter Bank sought to repossess the car from Buyer because Debtor had defaulted under the terms of the security agreement with Bank. Buyer argues priority under Iowa's U.C.C. §9-301(1)(c). Who wins?

9. Same as Problem 8, except that the sale to Buyer occurred five months after Debtor moved to Iowa.

10. Bank financed Debtor's purchase of a car in Minnesota. Debtor granted Bank a security interest in the vehicle, and Minnesota issued a certificate of title showing Debtor as "owner" and Bank as holder of a "first security interest." Bank kept possession of the certificate. Debtor moved to Iowa and took the car with her. A month after moving to Iowa, Debtor undertook to register and title her car there. The Iowa authorities asked Debtor for the Minnesota title. Debtor reported that Bank had possession of it because Bank had a security interest in the vehicle. The authorities explained they could not register or title Debtor's car in Iowa without surrender of the Minnesota title. The authorities further explained they would write the Bank and ask Bank to surrender the Minnesota title. After getting the Minnesota title, the authorities would send Debtor proof of Iowa registration and Iowa license plates; and they would issue an Iowa title, showing Bank's security interest, which would be sent to Bank.

   Because of a bureaucratic foul-up, the Iowa authorities never contacted the Bank in Minnesota. Moreover, a month later, the Iowa authorities issued directly to Debtor an Iowa certificate of title that was "clean," that is, the title did not show Bank's security interest. They also sent Debtor proof of Iowa registration and Iowa license plates. Debtor thereafter sold the car to Buyer in Des Moines. Consider whether the Buyer or the Bank has priority under these circumstances:

a. The sale occurred five months after Debtor moved to Iowa, and the Buyer was a used car dealer. See U.C.C. §9-103(2)(b).

b. The sale occurred three months after Debtor moved to Iowa, and the Buyer was a used car dealer. Bank did not seek to repossess the car, however, until six months later.

c. The sale occurred three months after Debtor moved to Iowa, and the Buyer was a used car dealer. Immediately after the sale, Bank sought to repossess the car from Buyer.

d. The sale occurred three months after Debtor moved to Iowa, and the Buyer was an accountant who purchased the car for her own personal and family purposes. See U.C.C. §9-103(2)(d).

11. Same facts as Problem 10, except that the Iowa authorities did contact the Bank, and the Bank sent the Minnesota title to them. Still, however, Iowa plates and a clean certificate of title were issued to Debtor. Thereafter, within three months of moving to Iowa, Debtor sold the car to a used car dealer. Bank immediately sought to repossess the car from the dealer. See U.C.C. §9-103(2)(b).

12. Would any of the answers to the questions in Problems 8 through 11 change if Iowa law included U.M.V.C.T. §20(2)?

13. The final examination on U.C.C. §9-103(2) is as follows: "On April 28, 1979, the Wattendorfs, under the assumed names of Marion and Margaret Jones, purchased a motorhome from the defendant Bob Moore, Inc., a dealer in motorhomes. The Wattendorfs financed this purchase through an installment sales contract, which the dealer assigned to Rockland. On May 23, 1979, Rockland secured from the Massachusetts Registry of Motor Vehicles a certificate of title which contained a notation of Rockland's lien.

"In the fall of 1979, the Wattendorfs drove the motorhome to Florida, where they usually spent the winter months. While in Florida, the Wattendorfs registered the motorhome and obtained Florida license plates. They subsequently returned to *** Massachusetts, in the spring of 1980, more than four months later.

"In September, 1980, George Wattendorf owed the city [of Boston] more than $100,000 in real estate taxes. On September 4, 1980, upon learning of the Wattendorfs' ownership of the motorhome, the city seized and distrained the vehicle [pursuant to state law that gave the city the status of a lien creditor within the meaning of U.C.C. §9-301]. *** The trial judge *** held the city liable in conversion." *City of Boston v. Rockland Trust Co.*, 391 Mass. 48, 460 N.E.2d 1269, 1270-71 (1984). Assume U.C.C. §9-103(2) governs choice of law. Should the appellate court have affirmed or reversed?

14. Debtor is in the business of providing harvesting services to farmers. Her home and office is in Lincoln, Nebraska. In the fall of each year, however, Debtor and her employees travel around the Mid-West with Debtor's combines and other equipment to help farmers harvest corn and other grains. A Chicago bank is Debtor's principal financer.

   a. What law governs the bank's perfection of security interests in Debtor's harvesting equipment such as combines? See U.C.C. §9-103(3).

   b. Which part of §9-103 supplies the choice-of-law rule with respect to the perfection of security interests in the Debtor's trucks that transport the combines around the Mid-West, and the vans that transport employees?

   c. What law governs perfection of the bank's security interest in Debtor's receivables in the form of rights to payment for services rendered? Does it matter whether these rights are secured by the grain Debtor harvests?

15. A California syndicate of investors owns a race horse named "U.C.C." that is stabled in Kentucky when the animal is not racing elsewhere. U.C.C. spends much of each year, however, at race tracks in other states such as Florida, Arkansas, New York, Georgia and Minnesota. A Los Angeles bank has a security interest in U.C.C. Where and how should the bank perfect its interest?

⬚⬚⬚⬚⬚⬚

Report of the Article 9 Study Committee

Permanent Editorial Board for the Uniform Commercial Code
American Law Institute and National Conference of Commissions on Uniform State Law,
1992

Committee Recommendations:

B. Applicable Law
8. In General (1-105)

Given the apparent infrequency with which choice-of-law questions under 1-105 have arisen in Article 9 transactions, the Committee sees no need for changes to the section.

9. Law Applicable to Perfection and the Effect of Perfection or Non Perfection

A. Section 9-103 should be revised to provide that, except where perfection is accomplished by taking possession of the collateral,   the law of the jurisdiction in which the debtor is located should determine perfection and the effect of perfection or nonperfection of a security interest.

B. Section 9-103(1)(b) should be revised to eliminate the "last event" test and to provide that the law of a particular jurisdiction governs perfection and the effect of perfection or nonperfection of a security interest during the time that the collateral is located in that jurisdiction. Analogous language should be added to 9-103(3)(b).

C. If the "location of the collateral" rule is retained for nonpossessory security interests, the "thirty-day" rule in 9-103(1)(c) should not be expanded to cover nonpurchase money security interests.

D. Section 9-103(1)(d) or the official comments thereto should be revised to make clear that the "four-month" rule applies regardless of whether the goods are relocated to the forum state or to another jurisdiction and regardless of the circumstances surrounding the removal of collateral and its presence in another jurisdiction.

E. Section 9-103(3)(e) should be revised to provide that a security interest that becomes unperfected under the section is deemed to have been unperfected as against all persons who acquire an interest in the collateral after the debtor's location changes and to clarify that the debtor's entry into bankruptcy before the expiration of the four-month period tolls the expiration of the period.

F. The Drafting Committee should consider whether, under 9-103(3)(b), the conflict-of-law rules of the jurisdiction of the debtor's location should continue to be relevant to a determination of the law governing perfection and the effect of perfection or non perfection of a security interest.

10. Certificates of Title

A. Section 9-103(2) or the official comments should be revised to clarify that the section applies to a certificate of title issued jurisdiction having no other contacts with the goods covered by the certificate or with the debtor.

B. At least insofar as it relates to automobiles and other motor vehicles, 9-103(2) should be revised to provide that perfection continues beyond the four-month period until another jurisdiction issues a certificate of title covering the goods; registration of the goods in another jurisdiction should not of itself result in loss of perfection.

C. Section 9-103(2) should be revised to clarify that it applies to goods covered by a certificate of title and as to which a security interest may be perfected under applicable non-UCC law by delivering designated documents to a state official for the purpose of causing an indication of the security interest to be placed on the certificate.

F. SCOPE OF ARTICLE 9

Unless the transaction between a creditor and debtor is within Article 9's scope, the creditor has none of the rights regarding the debtor's property or protections against third-party claimants that Article 9 provides a secured party; and the debtor cannot hold the creditor accountable under the provisions of Article 9 that regulate, for the benefit of the debtor, a secured party's handling of collateral. Deciding if a transaction falls within the scope of Article 9 is a two-step process.

The first step is to apply the true-false test of applicability imposed by U.C.C. §9-102(1), which is the general scope provision of Article 9. The test is pretty easy: Notwithstanding the form of the transaction, is it "intended to create a security interest in personal property or fixtures," (U.C.C. §9-102(1)(a)) or to effect a "sale of accounts or chattel paper" (U.C.C. §9-102(1)(b))? If the answer is false, the exercise is completed. Article 9 does not apply.

If the answer to the test of §9-102(1) is true, the exercise continues to the second step which is a multiple-choice test. Is the transaction described in any of the subdivisions (a)-(l) of §9-104? This section lists transactions expressly excluded from Article 9. If the transaction matches any of the §9-104 exclusions, Article 9 is altogether inapplicable, or applies only to the limited extent explained in the pertinent §9-104 subdivision, even though the transaction satisfies the test of §9-102(1).

1. Transactions Intended As Security, U.C.C. §9-102(1)(a)

U.C.C. §9-102(1) is Article 9's general scope provision which makes the statute applicable "to any transaction (regardless of its form) which is intended to create a security interest in personal property or fixtures", U.C.C. §9-102(1)(a), and also "to any sale of accounts or chattel paper." U.C.C. §9-102(1)(b). The reach of this language is somewhat restricted by §9-104, which expressly excludes from Article 9 some transactions that are within the ambit of §9-102(1). The §9-104 exclusions are discussed later, as is Article 9's coverage of sales of accounts and chattel paper. The focus here is on the meaning of §9-102(1)(a), extending Article 9's reach to transactions in which the parties intend to create a security interest. This language is responsible for bringing within Article 9's scope the great majority of transactions covered by the statute.

Because of §9-102(1)(a), Article 9 opens wide like a huge umbrella to cover "*all* consensual security interests in personal property and fixtures," U.C.C. §9-102 comment (emphasis added), except those excluded by §9-104. With a few minor exceptions, Article 9 does not apply when security is created by law without the debtor's consent[1] as is true of an artisan's lien or a bank's equitable right of setoff. Article 9 never applies to real estate except when the collateral is fixtures. The topic of fixtures as collateral is discussed later. On the other hand, virtually nothing (save §9-104) precludes application of Article 9 whenever a creditor claims security based on an agreement with the debtor and the collateral is personal property or fixtures. In such a case, Article 9 comprehensively governs the validity and enforceability of the secured transaction between the immediate parties, and also against third parties, whether the transaction is between family members or between a merchant or bank and its customer;[2] whether the transaction secures an obligation to pay the price of property or services, repay a loan, or perform some other kind of contractual duty;[3] and without regard to the way in which the parties structure or characterize their arrangement with respect to security. This last point is terribly important.

Pre-Code law recognized a host of different devices for creating security in personal property by way of agreement between creditor and debtor. The best-known examples are the pledge, conditional sale

---

[1]   The exceptions include the security interests arising without a debtor's consent under various provisions of U.C.C. Article 2 such as §§2-505 (seller's procurement of a negotiable bill of lading reserves in her a security interest in the goods) and 2-711(3) (buyer who rejects goods or revokes her acceptance of them given a security interest in the goods to secure her right to recover price she has paid). An Article 2 security interest is made subject to Article 9 through §§9-203(1) and 9-113. The exceptions also include the Article 4 security interest that a collecting bank is given in items for which it extends credit. See U.C.C. §4-208(1). This security interest is brought within Article 9's scope through §§9-203(1) and 4-208(3)

[2]   Some parts of Article 2 apply only in transactions involving merchants. See, e.g., U.C.C. §§2-201 (written confirmation satisfies statute of frauds with respect to contract between merchants); 2-314 (warranty of merchantability is implied only in sale by merchant). Nothing in Article 9 is so limited. Article 9 applies to secured transactions without regard to the business, occupation, or hobbies of the creditor or debtor and regardless of the levels of their sophistication in the ways and means of security arrangements.

[3]   The Code defines security interest as an interest securing an *obligation*, U.C.C. §1-201(37) (emphasis added), but "obligation" is undefined. The term may well include commitments arising apart from contract, but the real world of secured financing provides no examples.

contract, chattel mortgage, trust receipt, and factor's lien.[1] These devices differed in form but not in essential purpose or design. Each of them enabled the creditor to claim as against the world certain goods or intangibles of the debtor as a means of satisfying the latter's obligation to the former. Each device made possible this claim by reserving or creating in the creditor some kind of interest in the property that the parties had agreed would serve as collateral security. The name and precise nature of the interest depended on which security device was used.

The test of Article 9's applicability is stated in terms of the purpose and design shared by these pre-Code security devices. U.C.C. §9-102(1)(a) extends the statute to any kind of transaction "(regardless of its form)" intended by the parties to create a security interest in personal property or fixtures; and the Code defines "security interest" to mean any kind of interest in such property "which secures payment or performance of an obligation." U.C.C. §1-201(37). The form of the transaction is completely immaterial, including the name that the parties give the interest retained by the creditor. U.C.C. §9-102 comment 1 ("this article applies regardless of the form of the transaction or the name by which the parties may have christened it"). Consequently, the pledge, the chattel mortgage, the conditional sale contract and the other members of this heretofore divided family of pre-Code security devices are all brought together under the same statutory roof and subjected to a single, well-integrated scheme of secured transactions law.[2]

The traditional forms and names can still be used. Article 9 does not abolish in terms any of the pre-Code security devices. U.C.C. §9-102 comment 1. Yet, irrespective of the form used, Article 9 governs the transaction through rules that eliminate distinctions among traditional devices based on form and that apply the generic label "security interest" to any secured party's encumbrance on collateral no matter what form was used to create it.

New-fangled security arrangements involving personal property or fixtures also are brought within the scope of Article 9 by the broad language of §9-102(1)(a). Because the section makes the applicability

---

[1]   For complete descriptions of these devices, with emphasis on historical development, see 1 G. Gilmore, Security Interests in Personal Property 5-145 (1965).

[2]   This reunion is confirmed by U.C.C. §9-102(2), which provides that Article 9 "applies to security interests created by contract including pledge, assignment, chattel mortgage, chattel trust, trust deed, factor's lien, equipment trust, conditional sale, trust receipt, other lien or title retention contract and lease or consignment intended as security." The commentary adds that this "list of traditional devices *** is illustrative only: other old devices *** are included, so long as the requisite intent [to create a security interest] is found." U.C.C. §9-102 comment 1.

of Article 9 depend solely on a finding that the parties intended to create a security interest, innovations in the form and terminology of security devices offer no escape from rules of the statute. "[O]ld devices, as well as any new ones which the ingenuity of lawyers may invent, are included [within Article 9's scope], so long as the requisite intent is found." U.C.C. §9-102 comment 1. Indeed, an important aim of the drafters of Article 9 was to keep the statute flexible and formalities simple so as to "make it possible for new forms of secured financing, as they develop, to fit comfortably under its provisions ***." U.C.C. §9-101 comment.

The applicability of Article 9 does not depend on the parties having intended to create a "security interest" in so many words. Moreover, the parties' subjective intentions are wholly irrelevant. The controlling issue is whether the arrangement agreed to by the parties, if enforced, would have the effect of giving the creditor a right to look to specific property of the debtor should the debtor default in paying or otherwise performing an obligation owed the creditor.[2] The pertinent intent concerns the goal of the parties' transaction determined objectively, not the methods they consciously adopted in trying to achieve the goal.

In sum: U.C.C. §9-102(1)(a) causes Article 9 to apply whenever a creditor and debtor (regardless of the means they use) intend the creditor (whatever she is called) to have an interest (however the parties label it) in personal property or fixtures of the debtor (whatever she is called) for the purpose of securing payment or performance of an obligation (no matter what it may be).

a. True Lease Versus Lease Intended as Security

Edwin E. Huddleson, *Old Wine in New Bottles:*
UCC Article 2A--Leases
39 Ala. L. Rev. 615, 623-25 (1988)

A. True Leases of Goods Distinguished from
"Sales" and "Security Interests"

A threshold task in drafting Article 2A was to define a lease of goods and to distinguish it from a conditional sale or disguised security interest. True leases long have been distinguished from sales for many purposes in commercial law,

---

[2]   The drafters put it similarly in commenting that "[t]ransactions in the form of consignments or leases are subject to this Article if the understanding of the parties or the effect of the arrangement shows that a security interest [as defined by §1-201(37)] was intended." U.C.C. §9-102 comment 1.

including determining remedies on default, a lessor's rights under section 365 of the Bankruptcy Code, and whether a transaction is covered by state usury laws.

The UCC definition of a true lease determines not only the rights and remedies of the parties to the lease but those of third parties. If a transaction creates a lease and not a security interest, the lessee's interest in the goods is limited to its leasehold estate; the residual interest in the goods belongs to the lessor. This has significant implications to the lessee's creditors.

Moreover, a secured sale, unlike a lease, is subject to Article 9, which contains rules of priority and generally requires the filing of a financing statement for secured interests.   True leases henceforth generally will be governed by the provisions of Article 2A, while sales and "security interests" will continue to be covered by UCC Articles 2 and 9 respectively.

The original language of section 1-201(37) partially defined the distinction between a true lease and a "lease intended for security." But drawing this distinction in specific cases has proved to be a difficult and frequently litigated problem. After considering a variety of suggestions, the Commissioners on Uniform State Laws decided to clarify the definition of a true lease by amending section 1-201(37) to preserve common law principles and reaffirm the importance of the residual as a source of potential gain or loss in the business of equipment leasing.

At common law, the central feature of a true lease is the reservation of an economically meaningful interest to the lessor at the end of the lease term. Ordinarily this means two things: (1) at the outset of the lease the parties expect the goods to retain some significant residual value at the end of the lease term; and (2) the lessor retains some entrepreneurial stake (either the possibility of gain or the risk of loss) in the value of the goods at the end of the lease term. Over the years, the equipment leasing industry has developed a wide variety of practices that affect the lessor's residual. These include options for the lessee to renew the lease or buy the goods, "open-end" leases with terminal rental adjustment clauses (TRAC), "puts" that provide the lessor with an option to require the lessee to purchase the goods, and lease remedy provisions that allocate the economic risks of ultimate disposal of the residual. Article 2A provides a reasonable set of rules for assessing the impact of these practices on the true lease status of a transaction.

1. The statutory framework.--Given the difficulties of crafting a comprehensive definition of a true lease, as well as the importance of maintaining flexibility in structuring lease transactions, the draftsmen of Article 2A decided that the definition should generally leave the issue to be "determined by the facts of each case," rather than an overly rigid definition woodenly resolving every imaginable case. The outcome is a loosely defined statutory trichotomy: transactions are either leases, sales, or security interests.

The old common law touchstone of a true lease--the lessor's meaningful residual interest--is reflected in Article 2A. Section 2A-103(1)(j) of the statute defines a "lease" as "a transfer of the right to possession and use of goods for a term in return for consideration, but a sale, including a sale on approval or a sale or return, or retention or creation of a security interest is not a lease." Thus, the term "lease" is defined by comparison to a sale (section 2-106(1)) and a "security interest" (section 1-201(37)). Yet by elaborating upon common-law principles in the amendment to section 1-201(37), sharpening the distinction between a lease and a sale, the new statute provides significantly more guidance than current law as to the essence of a true lease.

The Comment to section 2A-103(1)(j) contains a set of "hypotheticals [to] indicate the perimeters of the issue" and states that "[t]his section as well as Section 1-201(37) must be examined to determine whether the transaction in question creates a lease or a security interest." The structure of the amended statutory definition in section 1-201(37) is first to state the general rule: "Whether a transaction creates a lease or security interest is determined by the facts of each case." Next, several specific factors are identified that will destroy true lease status and create a "security interest." Finally, other factors are listed that are consistent with true lease status.

Two basic factors, either of which will destroy true lease status and create a "security interest," where the lessee is obligated to pay rents for the lease term, are in essence: (1) where the lease is for the full economic life of the goods; or (2) where the lessee has an option to become the owner for "nominal" additional consideration. Where either factor exists, the transaction is not a true lease because the lessor has no reasonable expectation of a meaningful residual. The Comment to section 1-201(37) emphasizes that "these tests focus on economics, not the intent of the parties."

Other factors are identified in amended section 1-201(37) as being consistent with true lease status. These include: (1) a "full payout" lease (where the present value of the lessee's payments are substantially equal to the fair market value of the goods at the outset of the lease); (2) typical "net lease" provisions where the lessee assumes the risk of loss, or agrees to pay taxes, insurance, filing, recording, or registration fees, or service or maintenance costs; (3) the mere existence of a option to renew the lease or buy the goods; and (4) options to renew or buy at a fixed price equal to or greater than reasonably predictable fair market value (as predicted at the time the transaction is entered into).

Moreover, the amended statutory definition deletes all reference to "the parties' intent." The Comment to the section explains that most of the criteria that courts have relied upon to show intent, including "typical net lease provisions, a purported lessor's lack of storage facilities or its character as a financing party rather than a dealer in goods," are "as relevant to true leases as to security interests." Objective criteria, not a search for subjective intention, is the order of the day.

These are significant clarifications of the law. Yet no attempt was made to answer all questions, since the variety of transactions that parties to a "lease" can produce is almost unlimited. Rather, the general standard is that whether a particular transaction creates a lease or a "security interest" will be determined on the basic of all the facts and circumstances.

2. Options to renew or buy.--One linchpin in the definition of a true lease that goes to the heart of the lease-sale distinction is the subject of options. This is a sensitive area for both lessors and lessees, since the price of an option to renew or buy directly affects the lessor's monetary return. In general, amended section 1-201(37) contains a sensible treatment of options in a true lease. The statute retains some ambiguity in treating the subject of "bargain options," which may be inevitable or even desirable.

(a) Development.--Originally, the Drafting Committee considered tying the definition of a true lease to artificial percentages and formulas for determining what constitutes "nominal consideration" for options to renew or buy. These formulas were of two types. One required the option price to have some minimum absolute value, measured as a percentage of the original value of the goods. The other type of formula required the option price to be some substantial fixed percentage of the "reasonably predictable fair market value" of the goods at the time the option was to be exercised, with the "reasonable prediction" determined at the time the transaction was entered into.

Ten percent of the original value of the goods was considered and rejected as a possible benchmark for defining "nominal consideration." One such proposal, for example, would have accorded true lease status to "leases" with fixed price purchase options whenever the option was "equal to or greater than ten percent of the fair market value of the goods at the time the lease was entered into." This sweeping proposal was quickly rejected, as being at odds with settled law, since it would have accorded true lease status to transactions with ten percent fixed-price options where the reasonably predictable fair market value of the goods was eighty percent, not ten percent, at the time the option was to be exercised.

The Committee draftsmen also considered and rejected a similar "ten percent" rule that would have stamped some transactions as "security interests" by amending section 1-201(37) to provide with respect to options that "[a]dditional consideration is nominal if it is less than . . . 10 percent of the fair market value of the goods at the time the lease agreement was entered into."

This proposal overlooked the fact that a nine percent fixed- price purchase option would not be nominal where nine percent was a reasonable estimate of the fair market value of the goods at the time the option was to be exercised. True lease status may be present in such cases.

Equally without merit was an early proposal that would have accorded true lease status to "leases" having fixed-price purchase options whenever the option was "equal to or greater than 75% of the reasonably predictable fair market value of the goods or renewal option at the time the option is to be performed if exercised, as predicted or predictable at the time the lease was entered into." This proposal would have accorded true lease status to leases containing "bargain" options to renew or buy. When the lessor and the lessee agree at the outset to give the lessee a twenty-five percent discount on the anticipated fair market option price, they have written a "bargain" option agreement that "tilts the scales" to encourage exercise of the option. Well-settled principles of law indicate that this sort of bargain option agreement may not constitute a true lease.

The Drafting Committee also rejected a proposed amendment to section 1-201(37) that would have provided, with respect to options, that "[a]dditional consideration is nominal if it is less than . . . ___ percent of the reasonably predictable fair market value of the goods or renewal option at the time the option is to be performed if exercised." The proposal overlooked the fact that any percentage number less than 100 percent, might be interpreted implicitly to sanction "bargain" options as clearly consistent with "true lease" status.

After considering these and other proposed formulas, the Commissioners abandoned the notion of using artificial formulas and percentages to define an option in a true lease. Instead, they adopted the functional approach that had developed at common law.

(b) Guiding principles.--The important principle recognized in amended section 1-201(37) is that lessors under a true lease are economic investors possessing a real economic stake in the residual value of the leased goods. Well-settled legal principles, reflected in the amendment to section 1-201(37), confirm that the option price in a true lease must be related to "reasonably predictable fair market value" and not simply to a bargain or "nominal" option that is so low that, as a matter of economics and so far as the parties can foresee, it effectively "cashes in" the lessor's residual interest. The original agreement in a true lease cannot contain an economically irresistible option, which the parties expect from the outset will be exercised by the lessee to purchase the goods or renew the lease for the remaining economic life of the goods. To have a true lease, the original agreement must leave the lessor with some meaningful economic interest in the residual.

The statute rejects the view, expressed during the Drafting Committee sessions, that "[i]t doesn't make any difference whether you have a lease or a sale, as long as you know which is which." Traditional common-law principles recognize that it makes a difference whether the lessor has a meaningful residual interest in the goods. A meaningful residual interest has a significant effect on lease pricing as well as on practical assessments of the risks, rewards, and expertise involved in being a successful lessor. A lease is not simply an installment sale with a balloon payment at the end. And the lessee's acquisition of the goods for their full economic life is not a foregone conclusion. In a true lease, the lessor has a real entrepreneurial stake in the residual.

The implications of this principle are far-reaching: As a matter of economic self-interest, a true lessor cares about the quality, energy efficiency, durability, and long-term value of the leased goods, since there is some legitimate possibility that he may get back the goods or otherwise have to dispose of them. The residual is not just a "throw-in" in a true lease. It is a significant source of potential gain or loss for the lessor. Ordinarily, all other things being equal, one might expect rental payments under a true lease to be lower than periodic payments under a disguised sale where the seller, at the outset of the transaction, plans never to deal with the residual. Viewed from the perspective of the economy as a whole, lessees will have more marketplace choices and will receive more meaningful information about the goods they wish to use when the law recognizes the substantive economic differences between a true lease and a sale. One essential difference between the two is that the lessor in a true lease retains a real, economically meaningful interest in the residual.

(c) Treatment of options by the new statute.--The amendments to section 1-201(37) reflect the central importance of the lessor's meaningful residual. True lease status is not destroyed by the mere existence of an option to renew the lease or buy the goods. Where the option price in a lease is "stated to be the fair market value of the goods," amended section 1- 201(37) creates a safe harbor validating such options as consistent with true lease status. This safe harbor defines the classic case where the lessor retains a real, economically meaningful interest in the residual.

Another part of amended section 1-201(37) validates certain fixed-price options as clearly consistent with true lease status by stating:

A transaction does not create a security interest merely because it provides that

. . .. (e) the lessee has an option to become the owner of the goods for a fixed price that is equal to or greater than the reasonably predictable fair market value of the goods at the time the option is to be performed.

This safe harbor for true leases with fixed-price purchase options at "reasonably predictable fair market value" also requires the lessor to retain a meaningful residual. Given the widespread use of fixed-price purchase options, this part of amended section 1-201(37) should be helpful to equipment lessors, particularly in bankruptcy and usury cases.

Options can transform a lease agreement into one for security if the lessee cannot terminate its obligations under the lease (simply "walk away" from it) and "the lessee has an option to become the owner of the goods for no additional consideration or nominal additional consideration upon compliance with the lease agreement." This portion of amended section 1-201(37) shows how the concept of a "nominal" purchase option is related to the concept of the lessor's meaningful residual. Transactions are not true leases where the parties anticipate, at the outset of the transaction, that the option will be irresistible in the sense that the option price is extremely low in comparison to the fair market value of the property.

One criticism leveled at amended section 1-201(37) is that it fails to validate, as clearly consistent with true lease status, agreements with a fixed-price option that "approximates reasonably predictable fair market value." This criticism is unsound. The only purpose of substituting "approximates" for "equal to or greater than" would be to validate, as clearly consistent with true lease status, agreements with fixed-price options at less than predictable fair market value. This seems unwarranted. When the lessor and lessee agree at the outset to give the lessee a discount on the option price so that the option is less than the reasonably predictable fair market value, the parties have entered a "bargain" option agreement that "tilts the scales" to encourage exercise of the option. That sort of agreement, which may or may not constitute a true lease, undercuts the importance of a lessor's entrepreneurial stake in the residual. Neither reason nor authority supports a sweepingly overbroad provision granting safe harbor true lease status to such agreements.

Moreover, as a matter of drafting statutes, it does not make sense to use a vague word like "approximates" in what is supposed to be a safe harbor test for valid fixed-price options in a true lease. It would be difficult for a lessor to determine whether the lease agreement falls within a safe harbor that is defined by the word "approximates." Extensive litigation would arise over the meaning of this one vague word. Courts might well search for a percentage formula to give meaning to the word. Viewed in this light, the word "approximates" appears to be a stalking horse for a mathematical or percentage formula of the kind that was considered and rejected. The Commissioners properly rejected the proposal to insert the vague word "approximates" in the safe harbor for fixed-price options.

True leases are defined sensibly in Article 2A. Amended section 1-201(37) provides that some transactions are clearly true leases, that other transactions are clearly secured transactions, and that everything else is to be determined by reference to "the facts of each case." This clarifies current law to some extent, while accommodating the whole spectrum of existing leasing practices. The safe harbor for true leases with fixed-price purchase options "equal to or greater than" reasonably predictable fair market value parallels the wording of IRS Revenue Procedure 75-21, a basic set of tax law guidelines that has been familiar to the leasing industry for over a decade. No business justification exists for switching to "approximates": The safe harbor phrased in terms of "equal to or greater than" covers a wide range of predicted option values. The overall standard for judging true lease status, under amended section 1-201(37), is by reference to "the facts of each case." These standards should give businessmen all the flexibility that they need. As equipment lessors requested, moreover, the statute preserves, rather than undercuts, the importance of the residual as a source of potential gain or loss in the business of equipment leasing. In commenting on the new leasing statute, Ned Mundell, President and Chief Executive Officer of California-based U.S. Leasing International, stated: "The long-term interests of the equipment leasing industry, and the public interest, are best served by recognizing the importance of a lessor's entrepreneurial stake in the residual. We are satisfied that the new UCC provisions on leasing do that."

(d) Bargain options.--Transactions with fixed-price "bargain options" that are exerciseable for less than "reasonably predictable fair market value" will be assessed on the basis of "the facts of each case" under amended section 1-201(37), as under current law. The Comments to new section 1-201(37) are ambiguous on the proper treatment of such bargain options. We are told that:

> A fixed price purchase option in a lease does not of itself create a security interest. This is particularly true if the fixed price is equal to or greater than the reasonably predictable fair market value of the goods at the time the option is to be performed. A security interest is created only if option price is nominal and the conditions stated in the introduction to the second paragraph of this subsection are met [i.e., if the lessee cannot simply "walk away" from the lease by terminating its obligations]. There is a set of purchase options whose fixed price is less than fair market value but greater than nominal that must be determined on the facts of each case to ascertain whether the transaction in which the option is included creates a lease or a security interest. The courts are left to interpret, as best they can, this Delphic pronouncement on fixed-price purchase options for "less than fair market value."

Two possible interpretations are immediately apparent. One is that some bargain options--at less than reasonably predictable fair market value--are consistent with true lease status, as long as the option price is not so low as to become "nominal." This interpretation, of course, invites courts to search for some percentage formula (fifty-one percent? seventy-five percent? or ninety percent?) to try to pin down the metaphysical difference between a permissible "bargain" option and an impermissible "nominal" option in a lease. Such a view of the Comment lends a schizophrenic quality to amended section 1- 201(37), in light of the statutory text's rejection of formulas and percentages as an approach to defining a true lease. This sort of schizophrenia has ample precedent in the law. But the search for a mathematically precise definition of a lease seems a vain quest for illusory benefits. Economic uncertainties of life (such as technological obsolescence and changes in the rate of inflation) are such that a wide range of values should quality as "reasonably predictable fair market value" option prices in any given transaction. Given this reality, it seems unrealistic and artificial to seek mathematically precise percentages or formulas to define an impermissibly low option price that will destroy true lease status. It should take an extreme case to show a "bargain" fixed-price option totally outside the ballpark of "reasonably predictable fair market value" option prices.

The other interpretation of the Comment would be that its reference to "a set of purchase options whose fixed price is less than fair market value" means "less than [what] fair market value" turns out to be at the time the option is exercised. This view of the Comment would fit well within the decided cases: True leases may include fixed-price options that are not nominal in light of the "reasonably predictable fair market value" of the goods, as predicted at the outset of the transaction, even if later unexpected events make the option price a bargain (or even "nominal") at the time the option is actually exercised. When a fixed-price purchase otpion turns out to be "less than fair market value," a question may arise as to whether the transaction is a true lease. But the statutory text and Comment on amended section 1-201(37) make it clear that it is "the facts and circumstances at the time the transaction is entered into" that are controlling. Where a fixed-price purchase option is not "nominal," when viewed in light of the circumstances known at the outset of a transaction, the option is consistent with true lease status. Overall the test remains whether, as a practical matter, at the outset of a transaction, the lessor had an economically meaningful interest in the residual.

    * * *

3.   TRAC leases.--"Open-end" leases, with terminal rental adjustment clauses (TRAC), have been widely used in the motor vehicle leasing industry for over thirty years. Essentially, this type of lease sets out a schedule of rental payments, together with a corresponding estimate for the value of the residual at the end of the lease term. TRAC provisions in the agreement then provide that the actual value of the residual will be determined at the end of the lease term by appraisal, sale to a third party, or otherwise, and that a payment then will be made by the lessee or a credit given by the lessor to reflect the difference between the actual and estimated residual values. Widely different variations on this basic format may appear in specific "open- end" leases.

Theoretically, "open-end" TRAC leases reward lessees who take good care of the leased goods, while compensating the lessor for any unusual wear and tear. TRAC lessees pay fair value for their use of the goods, according to supporters of the "open-end" lease, while the TRAC lessor retains the residual value. One view of TRAC clauses is that they simply allow the parties to determine the amount of actual depreciation on the leased goods. Others point out, however, that typical TRAC provisions give the lessee (not the lessor) the potential gain or loss from disposition of the residual. This point arguably undercuts any meaningful residual interest of the lessor and suggests that TRAC transactions are not true leases.

TRAC motor vehicle leases to commercial lessees are specifically recognized as true leases by the federal tax laws. But the case law is divided on whether TRAC leases are true leases under state law.   The Commissioners decided that amended section 1-201(37) would be silent on the thorny question of whether TRAC leases are true leases.

"Open-end" leases also raise the issue of whether TRAC provisions or some variations of them are validated by the liberal provisions of new section 2A- 504 on "liquidation of damages." TRAC provisions that essentially deprive the lessor of any meaningful interest in the goods at the end of the lease term may or may not pass muster as true leases. Viewed as liquidated damage formulas, however, some more narrowly drawn TRAC provisions seem "reasonable." One common lease provision, according to the Comment in section 2A-504, leaves the lessor with potential profits from a sale of the residual, while essentially making the lessee a guarantor of the estimated residual value set out in the lease. This "one-sided" TRAC provision leaves the lessor with a meaningful interest in the residual. Where reasonable, the courts should find that it qualifies as an enforceable provision in a true lease. Other kinds of narrowly drafted TRAC-like provisions, which charge the lessee for excessive use or poor maintenance as opposed to changes in value due to market trends, also seem consistent with true lease status.

Whether true lease status should be accorded to more broadly drafted TRAC vehicle leases currently in widespread use is less clear. Three additional major arguments might be advanced for recognizing these transactions as true leases under state law. First, TRAC vehicle leases, in order to qualify as "operating leases" under accounting rules, often leave the lessor with some minimum "at risk" investment in the vehicle (e.g., twenty percent of original cost) that cannot be recouped from the lessee under the TRAC clause. The vehicle lessor's minimum "at risk" investment arguably leaves the TRAC vehicle lessor with a meaningful economic stake in the residual and thereby establishes true lease status. Second, TRAC vehicle leases commonly provide the lessee with an option to return the vehicle at any time. This sort of TRAC transaction is not a sale, since it involves no "passing of title," and the lessor remains liable as title holder of the vehicle. Moroever, the transaction would not appear to be a security interest, since if the lessee can return the goods at any time, there may not be a sufficient "obligation" to secure. Viewed in light of the UCC trichotomy under which transactions are either leases, sales, or security interests, this sort of TRAC transaction in the end may be characterized as a lease. Third, vehicles are a unique kind of asset, in that the marketplace for used vehicles in America establishes the reasonably predictable market value of used vehicles to a very high degree of certainty. As a practical matter, it is the market for used vehicles and not the lessor or lessee that guarantees the residual value of used vehicles. Even broadly phrased TRAC vehicle leases operate, under this view, to charge the lessee only for excessive use or poor maintenance, as opposed to changes in value due to market trends. Under this "legal realist" argument, TRAC vehicle leases are true leases because in the special case of vehicles they are functionally the same as true leases with more narrowly drawn provisions that simply charge the vehicle lessee for excessive use. Courts have not yet had occasion to come to grips with these and other considerations about TRAC leases. Thus, the question of whether TRAC vehicle leases are true leases under state law remains unsettled.

Outspoken critics of Article 2A include some motor vehicle lessors who fault the new statute for failing specifically to validate "open-end" TRAC leases as true leases. The statute mirrors the common law, however. To this date, the weight of the case law has not recognized broadly phrased "open-end" TRAC leases as true leases under state law. Moreover, equipment lessors in the past have opposed according true lease status to "open-end" TRAC leases outside the specific context of motor vehicle leasing. The Commissioners acted reasonably in leaving the status of "open-end" TRAC leases to be determined by the courts under the general "facts of each case" test of amended section 1- 201(37) and the evolving common law. This approach simply preserves the status quo under state law regarding "open-end" TRAC leases.

Amelia H. Boss, *The New (1990) Article 2A Leases*
ALI-ABA Course of Study, 1991
C664 ALI-ABA 125

* * *

VI. FINANCE LESSORS

One of the most innovative concepts incorporated by Article 2A is the notion of a "finance lease," and the corresponding notion of a "finance lessor." This concept recognizes the commercial reality that many leasing situations are not two-party, but rather three-party transactions consisting of a supplier (who is the manufacturer, distributor or seller of the goods), the lessee (who chooses the goods, often contacting the supplier directly) and the "lessor" (who in most instances simply furnishes the money to purchase the goods, and then leases them to the ultimate user, the lessee). Recognizing that these three-party transactions should be subject to slightly different rules than the traditional two-party transaction, Article 2A first defines a finance lease, and then provides a subset of rules to govern them.

The primary area where finance leases are subject to a different set of rules is in the warranty area. In a finance lease, it is the supplier (not the lessor) who is supplying the goods, while the lessor is merely the provider of financing. Article 2A recognizes that reality. Thus, in a finance lease, the main effect of the rules is to insulate the lessor from responsibility for matters not related to the lessor's function as a financing source. The finance lessor will not be deemed to have made any implied warranties with respect to the goods, notwithstanding the absence of an otherwise effective disclaimer. On the other hand, the lessee is expected to look directly to the supplier [or, in some cases, to a third party other than the supplier who has made warranties] for any recourse with respect to the leased property; §2A-209 automatically extends all warranties made by the supplier [and other third parties] in the supply contract to the lessee, even though the lessee was not a party to that supply contract. In addition to this "pass through," Article 2A restricts the ability of the supplier and lessor to modify those warranties without the consent of the lessee.

In addition to the separate set of warranty provisions, there are other provisions giving additional protection to the lessor. For example, the lessee's obligations to the lessor under a finance lease are deemed to be "irrevocable and independent" upon the lessee's acceptance of the goods. Thus, even though the lease does not specifically include one, there is implied in every finance lease the equivalent of a "hell or high water" clause.

* * *

IX. FILING REQUIREMENTS

One of the major debates surrounding the drafting of Article 2A was whether to establish a system of public notice or filing for true leases, as currently exists for leases "intended as security" under Article 9. Traditionally, true lessors of personal property have not been required to file or give any other public notice to protect their interests in goods under a true lease from third parties including the trustee in bankruptcy. For a variety of reasons, the drafters eschewed the requirement of any filing for personal property leases, with the limited exception of fixtures (§2A-209).

Despite the absence of a requirement of filing for true leases, Article 9 in §9-408 allows lessors to file a protective financing statement (thereby guarding against the possibility that the transaction will be found to create a security interest under §1-201(37). Prudent lessors should continue to file such protective filing statements.

* * *

XI. THIRD PARTY ISSUES

A. Transfers in General.

Generally, a lessee's or lessor's rights under a lease contract or the residual rights of a lessor are freely transferable, unless (i) the transfer is voluntary and the contract prohibits the transfer or (ii) the transfer materially increases the burden or risk on the other party and the transferee does not give the necessary assurances of performance to that party. §2A-303.

It should be noted that Article 2A, while emphasizing free alienability, recognizes the enforceability of contractual restrictions or anti-assignment clauses. Moreover, it incorporates the limitations on assignments found in the Bankruptcy Code, 11 U.S.C. §365.

An assignment, so-called, of lease rights is treated as any other transfer is, and is presumed to transfer both rights and obligations, unless otherwise specified in the lease agreement.

B. Rights of Non-Creditor Transferees.

If a subsequent lease in entered when there is an existing lease, the subsequent lease is subject to the prior lease. See §2A-304 (subsequent lease of goods by lessor); §2A-305 (sale or sublease of goods by lessee). However, where the transferee, be it a lessee or a buyer, takes in the ordinary course of business from one in the business of leasing or selling goods of the kind, the transferee may take free of the lease interest. Thus, a subsequent "lessee in the ordinary course of business," who deals with a lessor who is a merchant dealing in goods of the kind leased and to whom the goods are entrusted under the prior lease, will take the goods free of the prior existing lease contract. §2A-304(2). Similarly, if the lessee is a merchant dealing in goods of the kind, it can pass good title to a buyer in the ordinary course of business or a sublessee in the ordinary course of business. §2A-305(2). A lessee in the ordinary course also takes the leasehold free of any security interest created by the lessor.

§2A-307(3). These rules are consistent with other rules which have been developed to protect the marketplace and transferees in the ordinary course.

C. Lien priorities.

Lien priorities are dealt with in §§2A-306 and 2A-307. These sections are based on many of the priority provisions of Article 9. A materialperson's possessory lien (whether arising under statute or by rule of law) has priority over any interest of the lessor or lessee under a lease contract, unless other law sets a different priority. Otherwise, lessee's creditors take subject to the lease contract. §2A-307. Lessors's creditors with liens arising prior to, or security interests perfected before, the lease contract became enforceable generally take priority over interests arising under the contract. §2A-307(2)a and (b).

D. Lessee in the ordinary course of business.

As noted above in (B), Article 2A introduces the notion of a "lessee in the ordinary course of business," and grants such a lessee special protection. A "lessee in the ordinary course of business" is defined in §2A-103(1)(o) as

a person who in good faith and without knowledge that the lease to him is in violation of the ownership rights or security interest or leasehold interest of a third party in the goods leases in ordinary course from a person in the business of selling or leasing goods of that kind but does not include a pawnbroker. . .

E. Fixtures and Accessions.

When goods become fixtures or accessions, the third party rights and claims of those holding an interest in the real estate or in the whole are implicated. * * *

b. Repo Agreements

Resolution Trust Corp. v. Aetna Casualty
& Surety Co. Of Illinois
United States District Court, N.D. Illinois, 1993
831 F.Supp. 610

Marovich, District Judge.   [This case involves transactions commonly referred to as] repurchase ("repo") and reverse repurchase ("reverse repo") agreements * * *. The typical repo is a two-part transaction.[1]   The first part

---

[1]   Although the parties, for purposes of the stipulated facts, have agreed to describe repo and reverse repo transactions and the parties engaged therein using words such as "purchase," "sale," "buyer," and "seller," the parties do not thereby agree on whether repo and reverse repo transactions are or should be characterized substantively as purchases and sales, loans, or any other types of transactions. In their respective memoranda of law, RTC argues that repos and reverse repos are purchases and sales of securities and Aetna argues that repos and reverse repos are transactions in the nature of a loan.

consists of the agreement to transfer a specified security by one party to another party in exchange for a fixed price. The second part consists of the contemporaneous agreement by the seller to return or "repurchase" the security on a specified future date at the original price plus an agreed upon rate of return.

The typical reverse repo consists of the same two-part transaction viewed from the perspective of the other side of the transaction. (For purposes of this opinion, the terms "repo" and "reverse repo" will be used to describe transactions from the perspective of the dealers, AMC or BBS. Thus, in a repo transaction, AMC or BBS "repoed out" or transferred a security to a repo participant, the buyer, and simultaneously agreed to repurchase the security on a future date. Conversely, in a reverse repo transaction, AMC or BBS, as buyer, "reversed in" or purchased a security from a reverse repo participant, who agreed to repurchase the security on a future date.)

Once a repo or reverse repo transaction is entered into, the parties generally have three choices regarding custody of the underlying security: a repo transaction may be (a) a possessory, delivery repo transaction; (b) a non-possessory repo transaction; or (c) a tripartite repo. In a delivery repo transaction, the dealer actually transfers the security to the repo participant at the outset of the transaction. Certificated securities are physically delivered in exchange for cash. In a non-possessory repo transaction, the dealer retains possession of the securities in an account with its clearing agent. In a tripartite repo, the securities are delivered to a third party, usually a custodial bank that contracts to hold the securities for the benefit of both parties.

Dealers frequently do not themselves physically retain the securities that they are holding. Many dealers instead utilize the services of clearing agents. A clearing agent may perform a number of different services for its customers, including the receipt and delivery of securities, payment for securities, and collection or transfer of funds for securities sold. A clearing agent also often provides financing to a customer in the form of a line of credit (a "clearing loan") generally collateralized by those securities owned by the customer which are deposited at the clearing agent.

The dealer's transactions with its clearing agent are accomplished through two general types of accounts maintained by the clearing agent for its customer: (a) the clearing account; and (b) the safekeeping account. A clearing account is a general account used for deposits of cash and of securities owned by or otherwise available to the dealer for resale or for securing a loan from the clearing agent. A safekeeping account, on the other hand, is usually used to segregate those securities which are owned or fully paid for by the dealer's own customers and not generally available for serving as collateral to secure the loans from the clearing agent.

* * *

[In this case] RTC argues that the repo and reverse repo transactions in question were purchases and sales of securities * * *. Aetna, on the other hand, argues that these transactions, although not outright loans, were either "de facto" loans or "transactions in the nature of the loan or extension of credit." * * * [The repo transactions were between GreatAmerican Federal Savings & Loan Association and Bevill, Bresler & Schulman (BBS), a securities broker-dealer. RTC was the conservator for GreatAmerican which suffered losses in the transactions. RTC claimed that these losses were covered by insurance agreements between GreatAmeircan and Aetna. This insurance expressly excluded losses from loans. This exclusion explains Aetna's argument that the repo deals were loans.]

Given the hybrid nature of repo transactions, it is not surprising that RTC and Aetna have such differing opinions as to the proper characterization of a repo and reverse repo.[1] There is simply no question that repo and reverse repo transactions have functional attributes which resemble short-term collateralized loans. As one court stated:

> From a purely economic perspective, ... a repo is essentially a short-term collateralized loan, and the parties to these transactions tend to perceive them as such. The element of the transaction over which the most bargaining usually occurs is in the interest rate. The parties customarily refer to the underlying securities as "collateral," and the risk of a change in the value of the collateral remains with the borrower, even though the lender "owns" it for the term of the agreement. S.E.C. v. Miller, 495 F.Supp. 465, 467 (S.D.N.Y.1980). However, repos also possess many of the benefits of an outright sale and purchase of a security. See In the Matter of Bevill, Bresler and Schulman Asset Management Corporation v. Army Moral Support Fund, 67 B.R. 557 (D.N.J.1986).

When determining whether a particular repo transaction should be treated as a loan or a sale and purchase of security must be made on a case by case basis. First Federal Savings & Loan Assoc. of Toledo v. Fidelity & Deposit Co. of Maryland, 895 F.2d 254, 260 (6th Cir.1990). In *First Toledo*, the court laid out the factors that should be considered in determining whether a particular repo transaction should be considered a loan. These factors include: (1) whether the seller could require the purchaser to resell; (2) whether the purchaser could require the seller to repurchase; (3) whether a definite remedy was provided in the event of either party's default; (4) whether the seller agreed to pay interest at a stipulated rate; (5) whether the value of the securities equalled the amount advances; (6) whether there was evidence of a debt; and (7) whether any collateral was pledged. Id. at 260 (citing Citizens National Bank v. United

---

[1] Most courts and commentators would agree that a repo is not a collateralized loan or a security but, instead, a hybrid of the two. In After the Trade, Dr. Stigum, Aetna's expert, wrote: repos have certain of the characteristics of a collateralized loan and certain of the characteristics of a securities transaction. They are in truth a sort of legal jackass: part horse (securities transaction) and part donkey (collateralized loan). Dr. Marcia L. Stigum After The Trade (1988), at 215.

States, 551 F.2d 832, 838, 841, 213 Ct.Cl. 236 (1977)). After weighing these factors and carefully examining the transactions in question, the history and development of the repo market, the nature of the savings and loan industry and the intent of the parties who entered into these two transactions, we conclude that the repos and reverse repos at issue in this case are best characterized as "transactions in the nature of a loan" for purposes of the Bond. * * *

First, the agreements entered into between [the parties involved] set forth specific maturity dates, settlement dates for repayment of funds and specific rates of interest to be paid at the time of settlement. Second, the interest rates were negotiated at a rate which had no relationship to the interest rate of the underlying securities. Third, on the front end, the securities were not sold for full market value as in standard purchases or sales. Instead, the funds disbursed were less than the market value of the collateral securities. Fourth, like a loan, principal and interest payments on securities underlying these transactions were to be paid to the original owner of the security during the term of the transactions. Moreover, GreatAmerican could enforce the agreement and require BBS to either repay the funds that were lent or to deliver the underlying securities at the end of the term of the agreement. Finally, the written agreement between the parties provided that in the event of a default, GreatAmerican was able to sell the underlying securities without notice and for the best price available, charging the loss, if any, to the account of BBS. Clearly, under the factors set forth in *First Toledo*, the repos and reverse repos appear to be, at the very least, "transactions in the nature of a loan."

More telling is the fact that the officers of GreatAmerican who were involved in the repo transactions in question considered the repos and reverse repos involved in this case to be lending and borrowing transactions even though the language of the agreements speaks in terms of the sale and purchase of securities. Ralph Bellon, Chief Financial Officer and Vice President of GreatAmerican, described repo transactions as the "lending of money on short term basis for which in turn the customer is given government securities, agencies or mortgage-backed securities as collateral." Bellon further described reverse repos as transactions "whereby their institution initiating that (sic) would be borrowing funds from the other institution." On its books and records, Bellon confirmed that GreatAmerican considered repo and reverse repo transactions to be the lending and borrowing of funds respectively and accounted for them differently than the purchase and sale of securities.
    * * *

Aetna's motion for summary judgment is granted. * * *

2. Accounts And Chattel Paper

a. Article 9's Coverage of Security Transfers and Outright Sales of Accounts and Chattel Paper

Shmatte Dress Co. sells dresses on credit to clothing stores that agree to pay in 30, 60, or 90 days. Shmatte's right to receive payment for dresses sold to a clothing store is called an *account* if the right arises from a simple sales contract, written or oral. U.C.C. §9-106. Shmatte's right is called *chattel paper* if the contract is in writing and not only evidences the store's obligation to pay the price of the dresses, but also retains a security interest in the goods to secure that obligation. U.C.C. §9-105(1)(b). In either event, the store is called an *account debtor*. U.C.C. §9-105(1)(a). Thus, when Shmatte sells dresses on credit to several stores, it has accounts, chattel paper, or both. Shmatte, however, needs cash so that it can pay its employees and buy more material. Shmatte can use the accounts or chattel paper to obtain cash.

Shmatte can use the accounts or chattel paper for a loan or line of credit from Chemical Bank. Obviously, such a security transfer of accounts or chattel paper is within the scope of Article 9. U.C.C. §9-102(1)(a). This means, among other things, that:

- The Shmatte/Chemical Bank loan agreement must satisfy the requirements of §9-203(1) for the Bank to acquire any interest in the accounts or chattel paper.
- In determining whether Chemical Bank's claim to the accounts or chattel paper has priority over the claims of other creditors of Shmatte or purchasers of the accounts or chattel paper from Shmatte, courts will look to the priority rules of Article 9.
- Thus, the Shmatte/Chemical Bank transaction is subject to the perfection rules of Article 9 to the extent Article 9 makes perfection a decisive issue in determining Chemical Bank's priority.

Alternatively, Shmatte can use its accounts and chattel paper to obtain cash by selling the rights to payment to Midtown Factors. Such an absolute transfer of accounts or chattel paper is also governed by Article 9. U.C.C. §9-102(1)(b). This means that:

- The Shmatte/Midtown factoring agreement must satisfy the requirements of §9-203(1) for Midtown to acquire any interest in the accounts or chattel paper.
- In determining whether Midtown's claim to the accounts and chattel paper has priority over the claims of other creditors of Shmatte or

purchasers of the accounts or chattel paper from Shmatte, courts will look to the priority rules of Article 9.

♦ Thus, the Shmatte/Midtown transaction is subject to the perfection rules of Article 9 to the extent Article 9 makes perfection a decisive issue in determining Midtown's priority.

Even though Article 9 would apply to both Shmatte's security transfer of accounts and chattel paper to Chemical Bank and Shmatte's sale of such property to Midtown Factors, there are differences in the two transactions. In the Shmatte/Chemical loan transaction, unless the loan agreement provides otherwise:

♦ Shmatte is obligated to repay the cash it receives from Chemical;
♦ Chemical looks first to Shmatte for repayment;
♦ Shmatte continues to collect from the account debtors;
♦ Chemical can collect from account debtors only in the event that Shmatte defaults, U.C.C. §9-502(1); and
♦ If Chemical is unable to collect from the account debtors a sum sufficient to satisfy full Shmatte's debt to the Bank, Shmatte is liable for the deficiency. U.C.C. §§9-502(2) & 9-504(2).

In the Shmatte/Midtown Factors factoring agreement, unless the agreement provides otherwise:

♦ Shmatte is not obligated to repay the cash it receives from Midtown;
♦ Midtown relies exclusively on payments by account debtors for reimbursement of the cash paid to Shmatte;
♦ Midtown takes over collecting from the account debtors as soon as it buys the accounts or chattel paper;[1] and
♦ Shmatte is not liable for any deficiency. U.C.C. §9-504(2).

---

[1]   Midtown has this right notwithstanding U.C.C. §9-502(1).   This subsection conditions a secured party's direct collection rights on the debtor's default, unless there is an agreement otherwise; and Midtown is a secured party even though it purchased the accounts and chattel paper. U.C.C. §9-105(1)(m). Yet, in selling the property to Midtown, Shmatte lost all its rights against the account debtors, including the right to collect from them; these rights, including the right presently to collect directly from the account debtors, passed to Midtown. Moreover, as a practical matter, implicit in every sale of accounts or chattel paper is an agreement that, unless the parties explicitly provide otherwise, the assignee secured party can collect directly from the account debtors whenever she wishes. On either of these bases a factor must necessarily have the right to notify account debtors to pay her directly as soon as she buys the rights against them. Otherwise, she would never have the right, by law, to effect direct collection because the assignor-debtor never defaults under a sale of accounts or chattel paper inasmuch as she owes no obligation to the assignee-secured party.

As the use of the qualifying phrase "unless the agreement other-wise provides" suggests, either the loan arrangement or the factoring agreement can be structured by the parties to look and operate, wholly or in part, like the other kind of deal. Indeed, in practice, "[c]ommercial financing on the basis of accounts and chattel paper is often so conducted that the distinction between a security transfer and a sale is blurred * * *." U.C.C. §9-102 comment 2. For this rea-son, "a sale of such property (accounts and chattel paper) is therefore covered by [Article 9] *** whether intended for security or not, unless excluded by Section 9-104." Id.

Octagon Gas Systems, Inc. v. Rimmer
United States Court of Appeals, Tenth Circuit, 1993
995 F.2d 948

Baldock, Circuit Judge. Octagon Gas Systems, Inc. ("Octagon") appeals from the decision of the United States District Court for the Western District of Oklahoma affirming the bankruptcy court's order granting Appellee Roy T. Rimmer's motion for summary judgment.

Poll Gas, Inc. ("Poll") was in the business of gathering and selling natural gas in Oklahoma. As part of its business, Poll owned and operated a gas gathering system ("the System"). Prior to 1976, Amcole Energy Corporation ("Amcole") owned ten percent of the Poll stock and four other shareholders owned the remainder of the stock. In May 1976, Amcole entered into an agreement with Poll's remaining four shareholders to purchase all of their shares. Pursuant to the terms of the purchase agreement ("the 1976 Agreement") between Amcole and the other shareholders, the selling shareholders agreed to sell Amcole their 90% of the Poll stock and certain other assets. In exchange, Amcole transferred to each shareholder a proportionate "overriding royalty interest" in the gross proceeds received by Amcole from gas sold through the Poll System. As a result of the 1976 Agreement, Amcole became Poll's sole remaining shareholder. Approximately one-half of Rimmer's "overriding royalty interest" originates from the 1976 Agreement.

On May 31, 1982, Poll, assigned to SINA 79/80 Limited ("SINA") an "overriding royalty interest" in the gross proceeds derived from the Poll System. The remaining half of Rimmer's "overriding royalty interest" arises from the 1982 Assignment.

In 1983 and 1984, Rimmer purchased, from the original assignees, a portion of the "overriding royalty interests" created by the 1976 Agreement and the 1982 Assignment. Subsequently, on January 28, 1987, Amcole, Poll, and Rimmer executed an agreement entitled Assignment of Overriding Royalty Interest ("1987 Assignment"). See infra note 3. Pursuant to the parties' various cross-transfers, the 1987 Assignment provided that "... Rimmer will own from this date forward a full Five Percent (5%) perpetual overriding royalty interest on all proceeds payable to [Poll] under the [System]...." Appellant's App. at 83- 86.

In 1988, Poll commenced this Chapter 11 bankruptcy case. Prior to filing the petition in bankruptcy, Poll, pursuant to the 1987 Assignment, paid Rimmer five percent of its proceeds from the sale of gas through the System. During the pendency of the bankruptcy estate, the bankruptcy trustee continued to pay this five percent interest to Rimmer.

In January 1990, the bankruptcy court confirmed the trustee's reorganization plan. Under the plan, the Poll System[1] was conveyed to Norwest Bank Minnesota ("Norwest") or its designee, in satisfaction of Norwest's secured claim. The Plan provided that the Poll System would be transferred to Norwest "free and clear of liens, claims, interests, and encumbrances." Appellant's App. at 130. Thereafter, Norwest conveyed the System to Octagon. After assuming control of the System, Octagon refused to recognize any interest held by Rimmer in the System gas sale proceeds and failed to make any payments to Rimmer. Consequently, this action was commenced by a creditor of Rimmer, Bonnet Resources Corporation, alleging it is secured by Rimmer's interest in the System's gas sale proceeds. Rimmer subsequently brought a motion for intervention. The bankruptcy court granted Rimmer's motion and exercised jurisdiction to determine whether the Plan effectuated a transfer of Rimmer's five percent interest to Octagon, or whether Rimmer's interest survives as personal property owned by Rimmer.

On cross motions for summary judgement, the bankruptcy court held that Rimmer owned a five percent interest in the proceeds of gas sold through the Poll System which was not affected by the Plan or the transfer of the Poll System to Octagon. The court, rejecting Octagon's argument that Article 9 of the Uniform Commercial Code ("U.C.C.") applied, reasoned that Rimmer's partial interest in the proceeds from the sale of gas was a "good" and amounted to a proportionate ownership right. The court found that Rimmer's interest was not property of Poll's bankruptcy estate and therefore could not be transferred by the estate to Octagon. The bankruptcy court granted summary judgment in favor of Rimmer, and the district court summarily affirmed.

On appeal Octagon raises numerous issues, among them: (1) whether the bankruptcy court erred in finding that Rimmer had an interest in the Poll System gas sale proceeds, and (2) whether the bankruptcy court erred in determining that Article 9 of the U.C.C. was inapplicable to Rimmer's interest. Because we remand in order for the court to apply Article 9, we do not address Octagon's remaining issues.

* * *

---

[1]   The Poll System included all gas purchase and sales contracts pursuant to which the System buys and sells gas and all accounts receivable from the sale of gas or gas liquids by the System.

I.

Octagon argues that Rimmer had no enforceable interest in the Poll System gas sales proceeds. Octagon's only argument concerning this issue that merits extensive discussion pertains to the 1976 Agreement. Octagon contends that because Poll was not a party to the 1976 Agreement, the portion of Rimmer's interest that derives from the 1976 Agreement is not an enforceable interest in the Poll System gas sale proceeds; rather it is only an enforceable interest against Amcole in the amount Amcole received from Poll.[1]

* * *

All of Poll's shareholders and directors were parties to the 1976 Agreement. This being the case, the shareholders had the capacity to dispose of Poll's assets and bind Poll to the Agreement. Because this was the intent of the parties, the effect of the 1976 Agreement was to create enforceable interests in Poll's proceeds. Alternatively, Poll's continuous payment of the interests over nearly fourteen years evidences its ratification of the 1976 Agreement. See Blunt v. Blunt, 198 Okl. 138, 176 P.2d 471, 472 (1947). Because we hold that the 1976 Agreement, in addition to the 1982 Assignment and the 1987 Assignment, created an enforceable interest in the Poll System gas sale proceeds, we uphold the bankruptcy court's determination that Rimmer had an interest in the Poll System's gas sale proceeds.

II.

Throughout this litigation, Octagon has maintained that Rimmer's interest is an "account" governed by Article 9 of the U.C.C. as adopted by Oklahoma. Rimmer has conceded that his interest is an "account," but argues that regardless of Article 9, he "owns" the interest, not Poll, and therefore his interest has never been property of Poll's bankruptcy estate. The bankruptcy court held that Article 9 was inapplicable because Article 9 provides a classification of interests for the purpose of determining competing secured interests, "not a classification for the creation of an ownership right in personal property." Order of July 26, 1991 at 6-7, In Re Meridian Reserve, Inc., No. BK-88-06519-BH, (Bankr.W.D.Okla. July 29, 1990).

* * * Although Article 9 applies mainly to transactions intended to create security interests, it also applies to sales of accounts, Okla.Stat.Ann. tit. 12A, §9-102(1)(b) (West Supp.1993), because sales of wholly intangible interests in accounts create the same risks of secret liens inherent in secured transactions.

As a starting point in our analysis, we must determine whether Rimmer's interest in the Poll System's gas sale proceeds is an "account" as defined by Article 9 of the U.C.C. as adopted by Oklahoma. See Okla.Stat.Ann. tit. 12A, §§9-101 to 9-507 (West 1963 & Supp.1993). Article 9 applies to transactions

---

[1]   As a threshold matter, we agree with the bankruptcy court that the use of the term "overriding royalty interest" in the underlying transactions is technically incorrect for lack of an oil and gas leasehold estate. See Appellant's App. at 63. Nevertheless, the transactions created an enforceable interest in the Poll System's gas sale proceeds. See infra.

involving personal property. Okla.Stat.Ann. tit. 12A, §9- 102(1) (West 1963). One form of personal property to which Article 9 applies is an "account" which is defined as "any right to payment for goods sold ... which is not evidenced by an instrument or chattel paper." Okla.Stat.Ann. tit. 12A, §9-106 (West Supp.1993). Section 9-105(1)(h) states that "goods" includes "all things which are movable at the time the security interest attaches ... but does not include ... minerals or the like, including oil and gas, before extraction." Id. §9-105(1)(h) (emphasis added).

Natural gas, once extracted, becomes personal property in Oklahoma, and as such, is subject to Article 9. Also, by negative implication, section 9-105(1)(h) indicates that minerals, including gas, following extraction, come within Article 9's definition of a "good." Here, the gas sold is extracted. Because extracted gas is a "good," Poll's right to payment for gas sold, as well as Rimmer's five percent interest in Poll's right to payment, is an account.

Having determined that the interest acquired by Rimmer is an account under Article 9, it follows that Article 9 applies to Rimmer's five percent interest in the Poll System's gas sale proceeds (hereinafter referred to as "Rimmer's account"), even though the transactions giving rise to Rimmer's account were not intended to secure a debt. The U.C.C. Official Comment 2 to Okla.Stat.Ann. tit. 12A, §9-102 (West Supp.1993), explains that in the case of commercial financing on the basis of accounts,

> "the distinction between a security transfer and a sale is blurred, and a sale of such property is therefore covered by [9-102(1)(b)] whether intended for security or not. The buyer is then treated as a secured party and his interest as a security interest."

Section 9-102(1)(b) states that Article 9 applies "to any outright sale of accounts." Further, the term "security interest" as defined by Article 9, expressly includes "any interest of a buyer of accounts," Okla.Stat.Ann. tit. 12A, §1-201(37) (West Supp.1993), and "secured party" includes "a person to whom accounts ... have been sold." Id. §9-105(1)(m). Additionally, section 9-105(1)(d) defines "debtor" as including "the seller of accounts," and, under section 9-105(1)(c), "collateral" includes "accounts ... which have been sold." These provisions clearly indicate that the buyer of an account is treated as a secured party, his interest in the account is treated as a security interest, the seller of the account is a debtor, and the account sold is treated as collateral.

We must now determine whether the fact of Poll's bankruptcy alters the application of Article 9 to Rimmer's account. Under §541 of the Bankruptcy Code, the property of the bankrupt's estate includes, "all legal or equitable interests of the debtor in property as of the commencement of the case." In United States v. Whiting Pools, Inc., 462 U.S. 198, 103 S.Ct. 2309, 76 L.Ed.2d 515 (1983), the Supreme Court, noting that §541 has an expansive scope, determined that §541 merely defines what is included in the bankrupt's estate rather than placing a limit on the scope of the estate. Id. at 203, 103 S.Ct. at 2312. The Court also pointed out that, under §541, property of the bankrupt's estate includes any property subject to a security interest. Id. at 203-04, 103 S.Ct. at 2312-13. The impact of applying Article 9 to Rimmer's account is that Article 9's treatment of accounts sold as collateral would place Rimmer's account within the property of Poll's bankruptcy estate. Further, if it is determined that Rimmer's account was not properly perfected, then, upon Poll's filing of bankruptcy, the bankruptcy trustee as a lien creditor would have a security interest superior to that of Rimmer.[1]

Rimmer contends, and the bankruptcy court held, that because Rimmer "bought" the account, he had title to the account and "owned" the account, and Poll no longer had any ownership interest in the account. Therefore, Rimmer argues, when Poll filed for bankruptcy, Poll's bankruptcy estate did not include Rimmer's account. Although acknowledging that Article 9 applies to sales of accounts, Rimmer argues that when deciding whether the account is property of the bankrupt's estate, the sale of an account must be distinguished from the transfer of an account for security. Simply put, Rimmer's argument rests on the principle that he, not Poll, owned the account as of the date of the sale.

We do not agree that the assignment of the account to Rimmer effectuated a transfer to Rimmer of all property interests in the account, leaving Poll with no property interest in Rimmer's account which the bankruptcy trustee could reach under 11 U.S.C. §541. Rimmer has advanced no sound argument, based either on post-U.C.C. case law or policy, as to why Article 9 should not be applied here. In fact, our review of the structure of Article 9, the available case law, and the policies underlying Article 9 and the Bankruptcy Code convinces us that a debtor's sale of an account, prior to filing for bankruptcy, does not necessarily place that account beyond the reach of the bankruptcy trustee.

* * * Article 9 does not attempt to classify a debtor's interest in the collateral as a property right or a specific legal interest. Article 9 also does not speak in terms of who has title to collateral among competing parties. Okla.Stat.Ann. tit. 12A, §9-101 (West 1963) (Official Comment). Rather, Article 9 "focuses on the rights and duties of the secured party, the debtor, and third parties." Okla.Stat.Ann. tit. 12A, §9-101 (West 1963) (Official Comment). Article 9 grants rights in the collateral to creditors in the event a secured party fails to perfect his interest, Okla.Stat.Ann. tit. 12A, §9-301 (West Supp.1993), regardless of the location of title and regardless of the debtor's or secured party's legal interest in the collateral. Id.. This Article 9 scheme applies with equal force to the sale of accounts. Article 9 treats the interest acquired by a buyer of accounts as a security interest and treats the buyer as a secured party.

---

[1] Under the Bankruptcy Code, the bankruptcy trustee has the rights of a hypothetical lien creditor. 11 U.S.C. §544; see also 4 Collier on Bankruptcy, ¶544.02 (Lawrence P. King ed., 15th ed. 1993). Accordingly, the trustee prevails over an Article 9 claimant whose interest is unperfected as of the date of filing of bankruptcy. Okla.Stat.Ann. tit. 12A, §9-301(1)(b) (West Supp.1993).

Accordingly, the seller or assignor of the account "does not part with all transferable rights in [the] account[ ] even following an absolute assignment."

[A]cceptance of Rimmer's transfer of ownership or title argument would allow an account buyer to benefit unfairly, at the expense of the bankrupt debtor's other creditors, from the debtor's filing for bankruptcy. For example, it is beyond dispute that, outside the realm of bankruptcy, a lien creditor would have rights in the accounts superior to the rights of the unperfected buyer of the accounts. See Okla.Stat.Ann. tit. 12A, §9-301 & §9-312 (West Supp.1993). However, under Rimmer's theory, once the debtor declares bankruptcy, the fact of bankruptcy alone places the accounts sold to the unperfected account buyer beyond the reach of the bankruptcy trustee and all of the bankrupt's creditors. This result is contrary to the similar aims of Article 9 and the Bankruptcy Code. The current Bankruptcy Code was designed, in part, to make bankruptcy law more congruent with the U.C.C. The policy behind Article 9 is to ensure certainty for creditors and provide notice of security interests to third parties. See Okla.Stat.Ann. tit. 12A, §9-101 (West 1963) (Official Comment). Likewise, certain provisions of the Bankruptcy Code "are designed to protect creditors by eliminating secret liens." In keeping with these policies, we hold that because, under Article 9, a sale of accounts is treated as if it creates a security interest in the accounts, accounts sold by a debtor prior to filing for bankruptcy remain property of the debtor's bankruptcy estate.[1]

Accordingly, we hold that the bankruptcy court erred in concluding that Article 9 was inapplicable to Rimmer's interest. The bankruptcy court must therefore readdress, in light of Article 9, the central issue of whether the reorganization plan effectuated a transfer of Rimmer's interest to Octagon, or whether Rimmer's interest survives the Plan. The court must make findings regarding whether Rimmer's account was a perfected security interest-- i.e., whether U.C.C. filings were required or made.[2] The court must also determine the effect, if any, of the trustee's actions concerning Rimmer's account, and the effect, if any, of Rimmer's actions. For these reasons, we REVERSE the entry of summary judgment in favor of Rimmer and REMAND to the district court with

---

[1]   Of course, this is not to say that an account buyer with a perfected security interest in an account forfeits his interest upon the debtor's filing for bankruptcy. Although property subject to a security interest is property of the debtor's bankruptcy estate, secured creditors of the debtor are provided "adequate protection" for their interest. See 11 U.S.C. §363(e) (providing that upon a secured creditor's request, bankruptcy court must place limits, as necessary to protect creditor, on trustee's power to sell, use, or lease property of the estate).

[2]   The dissent implies that the application of Article 9 to the facts of this case automatically divests Rimmer of his interest. We do not agree that such a result is mandated. For example, upon remand, the court may determine that Rimmer retains his interest because no U.C.C. filing was required under Okla.Stat.Ann. tit. 12A, §9-302(e) (West Supp.1993) (no filing required if account assignment does not transfer a significant part of outstanding accounts of assignor).

instructions to vacate its judgment and remand the case to the bankruptcy court for further proceedings consistent with this opinion.

Seth, Circuit Judge, dissenting:

I must respectfully dissent from the majority opinion as I agree with the determinations made by the United States District Court for the Western District of Oklahoma and by the United States Bankruptcy Judge. Briefly, these were that the "interest" in issue was never part of the Poll, Inc. bankruptcy estate. The "interest" owned by Mr. Rimmer was in the proceeds of the sale of natural gas collected from producing wells and sold to distributors, especially to Oklahoma Natural Gas Company. It apparently was secured from Amcole.

The Bankruptcy Court, in substance, held that Appellee Rimmer owns a separate and distinct interest in 5% of the proceeds of gas and liquids sold through the Poll Gas System, and that this interest was not in Poll's bankruptcy estate nor impacted by the Trustee's conveyance of the system.

The "interest" of Rimmer which I consider is only that portion derived from what is referred to as the 1976 Agreement or the Agreement, which is herein described. By the Agreement undivided interests were sold by Amcole outright to "Sellers" who were Rimmer's predecessors.

The Agreement was an outright sales agreement signed by all the stockholders and directors who thereby sold all their stock in Poll, Inc. (and two gas wells) to Amcole as Buyer. Amcole was also a stockholder in Poll. As consideration for the purchase of the stock in Poll, Inc., Amcole agreed to pay the purchase price in full, and did so. This purchase price, as stated in the Agreement (including some cash also from Poll, Inc.), was: "an Override of the gross proceeds received by BUYER through Poll Gas Inc. from Oklahoma Natural Gas Company under their existing contract and any and all amendments thereto, and all other gas, and liquids purchased and sold, and all additional connections, gas processing and gathering facilities and systems, through the Poll Gas System ... [in three named counties in Oklahoma]." The "override" was to total 9% of the proceeds of gas sales and 5% of proceeds from sales of liquids. The Agreement said these were "to be owned" as therein divided among the three named individuals and two corporations. These were the former Poll, Inc. stockholders except for Amcole.

The Agreement was to apply to any purchases of gas or liquids as well by the Oklahoma Natural Gas Company. The Agreement was filed in the county records. Appellee Rimmer was not one of these original sellers of stock, as mentioned, but bought interests from them.

The rest of Rimmer's interest originated in later agreements with other parties. The interests there concerned were also called overriding royalties.

We are concerned with Poll, Inc. as the Debtor, and its bankruptcy estate, not with Amcole. There remained nothing relating to the interests to go into the Poll bankruptcy estate. The ownership had passed by the 1976 Agreement to Amcole, and it as consideration agreed to and did create the "interests," as above described, out of what it bought--Poll Gas, Inc. I agree with the majority that enforceable interests were created by the 1976 Agreement including that owned by Rimmer, but I must disagree that they were part of the Poll bankruptcy estate.

I.

There is a significant aspect of the appeal which relates to the decision of the District Court, and of the Bankruptcy Court, that the "interests" of Rimmer were not part of the Debtor Poll, Inc. bankruptcy estate.

The relationship of the parties and the early transactions, particularly the changes brought about by the 1976 Agreement, must be examined. The Agreement is the source of the particular interests here considered. Before the 1976 Agreement the Poll corporation gathered gas in the field, transported it, and sold much of it to Oklahoma Natural Gas Company under contracts. Amcole decided to acquire Poll, Inc. by the 1976 Agreement. Under the Agreement all stock of Poll which Amcole did not already own vested in Amcole as "Buyer." All stockholders and directors of Poll signed the 1976 Agreement. The majority holds that Poll, Inc. was bound by the Agreement, and I agree.

The unusual part of the Agreement was that Amcole, as Buyer (of the stock), was obligated to use assets of Poll, that is, the gas sales contracts with Oklahoma Gas Company or the proceeds therefrom to pay the former Poll stockholders--the Sellers. To do this, and it was done, Amcole necessarily had to exercise ownership of these interests formerly of Poll, Inc. The actions of Amcole, and its performance as Buyer for its own benefit, demonstrated this ownership. It was the only way it could perform its obligation. "Control" of Poll could not do this. There would be no ownership of the interests in question after the 1976 Agreement remaining in Poll. Poll obtained no benefits under the Agreement and it lost assets. It undertook the duty to remit sales proceeds formerly its own. This was done in the capacity of a cestui que trust as would arise under an oil payment or similar interest. It had a duty to remit and nothing more. See Corbin on Contracts, §873 at 823 and §902 at 853.

Thus the "interests," which the majority defines as "accounts" under the 1976 Agreement, passed to Amcole as part of the sale of Poll, Inc. U.C.C. §9-104(e) Supp. They could not then be part of the Poll, Inc. estate. Whether they were part of the Amcole estate the record does not reveal. This is one of the elements supporting the District Court's holding that the interests were not part of the Poll estate.

II.

There is another reason why the Rimmer interest did not become part of the Poll estate.

The use by the original parties to the 1976 Agreement, and the continued use of the term "override" in later agreements between successors to the interests as a description of the interests created, is significant and cannot be ignored. It was obvious that the parties adopted the accepted characteristics and consequences of "overrides" as applicable and descriptive of the interests created. This was a clear and obvious description for them to apply to the "interests." It was in commonly used terms in the business. They adopted and applied the consequences and characteristics of such an interest in their agreements. This was clearly expressed, the intent was clear, and it can make no difference that the term is not applied to an interest of the type here concerned if its meaning they adopted and applied. We are not concerned with how the term may have been used by others. Certainly the 17+ years of "continued course of dealing" shows what the parties meant. See U.C.C. (with comments) §1-102 and §1-105.

It is apparent that the consequences, nature and scope of an "override" were adopted as descriptive as there were no time limits or period to restrict the perpetual term of such an interest and there was also no dollar limit. With such a permanent interest and without limits of time and money, the use or misuse of the term "override" was a clear expression or description. The nature and scope were well known and accepted.

The years of "continued course of dealing" by the parties and successors adopted its meaning and this should be sufficient under the U.C.C. An "agreement" under the U.C.C. as to consequences which would otherwise flow from the provisions of the U.C.C. includes the effect of a course of dealing (§1-102, §1-105).

The intent of the parties must be applied. There is no indication whatever that the Agreement or the interests were in any way intended to be a security agreement. The course of dealing was the equivalent to an "agreement" of the parties as described in the U.C.C., which modifies the U.C.C. terms, and determines the real nature of the interests.

III.

The position taken by the majority is that the interest of Mr. Rimmer was put in the Poll bankruptcy estate by Article 9 of the U.C.C. This position is based only on the theory that the interest fell within the Article 9 definition of an "account," and if it was an "account" it automatically was included in the Debtor's estate. This was, according to the majority, to follow regardless of the intention of the parties to the Agreement and the years of "course of dealing." When the definition was applied it was automatically something none of the parties intended, nor what it actually was as demonstrated over the 17 years. The record shows there was no debt, the interest was paid for in full, the intent was perpetual, and the interest had no dollar limit. There was no hint of commercial financing.

To apply the "account" definition is to reverse the completed 1976 sale and revest the interest in Poll. Rimmer apparently paid several hundred thousand dollars to buy the interest and the application of Article 9 would divest him of the interest. By all indications in the majority opinion he would become at most an unsecured creditor in the estate of the corporation which probably was never the source of interest to permit the application of Article 9.

The consequences of the application of Article 9 demonstrates that it is not applicable. The U.C.C. by fiat cannot change the consequences and legal nature of a transaction contrary to the intent of the parties.

The most that the statute could do, in Article 9, and this may be what it does, is to require the consequences therein provided, that is, to require this to be a security transaction, unless a contrary intention and purpose of the parties can be shown.

I would affirm the trial court.

b. Risks in Financing Accounts and Chattel Paper

Professor Grant Gilmore once described intangibles such as accounts and chattel paper as *precarious* collateral, which is an apt description whether the property is assigned as security or sold to the transferee. Here we consider the risks a secured party faces, and ways to reduce them, whenever the collateral consists of rights to payment of money. Such rights take four basic forms: accounts; chattel paper; instruments (principally promissory notes, which are less intangible than other intangibles); and general intangibles (such as a right to repayment of a loan when the right is not embodied in a note or other instrument or in chattel paper). The two forms most often used as collateral are accounts and chattel paper, and thus we focus almost exclusively on them. We sporadically discuss negotiable instruments only to illustrate how this form avoids certain risks common to accounts and chattel paper. General intangibles are not separately mentioned; but virtually everything said about accounts applies equally well to rights to the payment of money in the form of general intangibles, except that Article 9 only applies to security transfers of general intangibles and not to outright sales of such property. The same is true with respect to instruments, that is, sales of negotiable instruments are not within the scope of Article 9. The statute applies to instruments, if at all, only when they are used as collateral for a loan.

Before reading further, review the vocabulary. Whether a transferee of accounts or chattel paper purports to take the property as collateral for a loan, or through an absolute sale transaction, the only interest she can acquire, if Article 9 applies, is an Article 9 *security interest*; and she acquires such an interest only if U.C.C. §9-203(1) is satisfied. Upon satisfying §9-203(1), the transferee is an Article 9 *secured party* and the accounts or chattel paper is *collateral*, even though the transferee purports to have purchased the property. The transferor, that is, the person who used the property as collateral or sold it to the secured party, is the *debtor*, even though the rights to payment were owed originally to this person and she purported to effect an absolute transfer of them to the secured party. Each person obligated on an account or piece of chattel paper, that is, the person who owes the right to payment, is the *account debtor* without regard to whether the obligation she owes is sold or transferred as security.

For Article 9 to work for you in this context, you must use its terms and avoid thinking in terms of buyer and seller with respect to sales of accounts and chattel paper. We understand, however, that thinking of buyers and sellers is natural when there is a sale. To make things a little easier for you right now, the following discussion uses the more neutral term assignor to refer to any transferor of accounts or chattel paper, and the term assignee to refer to any transferee, whether the transaction is a sale or for security. As your courage builds, try to substitute the correct terms "debtor" and "secured party."

The value in accounts or chattel paper, whether the property is sold or used as collateral, are the payments of money that account debtors owe presently and in the future. Circumstances that might inhibit the assignee of accounts or chattel paper in getting these payments are risks to the assignee's security or the return on her investment. There are two general classes of such risks: risks as to priority and risks as to collection.

i. Priority Risks

You already know about this risk, which takes two forms: successive and earlier assignments. The risk of successive assignments is the possibility that the assignor will reassign the collateral, voluntarily or involuntarily, to a third party who will have first right to the payments made and owed by account debtors. The third party might be a lien creditor who garnishes the account debtors, or -- much more likely -- another assignee/secured party who acquires a security interest in the collateral. To protect against this risk the assignee must perfect its security interest.

If the assignor/debtor of accounts or chattel paper reassigns the property to a second assignee/secured party, the conflict of interests between the two assignees will be decided under the priority rules of Article 9, usually U.C.C. §9-312(5)(a). To protect its interest to the fullest extent possible, the first assignee must perfect its interest in accounts by filing, and in chattel paper by either filing or taking possession of the chattel paper. U.C.C. §§9-304(1) & 9-305. Taking possession of chattel paper is better insurance than filing because, if the assignee is holding the paper, no subsequent assignee could possibly qualify for the super-priority of U.C.C. §9-308.

The greater risk is that another secured party will claim the accounts or chattel paper through an earlier, perfected assignment. Such a claim might very well be made by the assignor's inventory financer who can assert a security interest in accounts and chattel paper as proceeds of inventory. In this event, the second assignee will surely lose the priority dispute under the general rule of U.C.C. §9-312(5)(a). With respect to accounts, and chattel paper that does not qualify for protection under §9-308, the second assignee has no escape, except through U.C.C. §9-312(4) which arguably is applicable -- but not clearly so -- to protect the second assignee to the extent that the value she gives the debtor is used to buy more inventory.

ii. Collection Risks

These risks, which take several forms outlined below, concern the problems of collecting from the account debtor the money she pays or is obligated to pay.

Account Debtor Paid The Assignor. An "account debtor is authorized to pay the assignor until the account debtor receives notification that the amount due or to become due has been assigned and that payment is to be made to the assignee." U.C.C. §9-318(3). As long as an account debtor is so authorized, she is not responsible to the assignee for payments made to the assignor that are not remitted to the assignee. Thus, to insure that she actually collects payments the account debtor is obligated to make, the assignee must give the notice described in §9-318(3). In giving this notice, there are substantive and procedural problems.

The substantive problem is that the assignee is not entitled to give the §9-318(3) notice to account debtors whenever she wishes simply because she has a security interest in the accounts or chattel paper on which the account debtors are obligated. U.C.C. §9-502(1) provides that a secured party can notify an account debtor to pay her directly only "in the event of default" and no sooner, unless the assignee/secured party and assignor/debtor have "so agreed." If such an agreement is made so that the assignee/secured party can notify account debtors to pay her directly sooner than the assignor's default, the arrangement between the assignee/secured party and the assignor/debtor is referred to as "notification" or "direct collection" financing. If such an agreement is not made, their arrangement is called "non-notification" or "indirect collection" financing. Both methods of financing are in "wide-spread use." U.C.C. §9-308 comment 1. For example,

> In the automobile field, *** when a car is sold to a consumer buyer under an installment purchase agreement and the resulting chattel paper is assigned, the assignee usually takes possession, the obligor is notified of the assignment and is directed to make payments to the assignee. In the furniture field, for an example on the other hand, the chattel paper may be left in the dealer's hands or delivered to the assignee; in either case the obligor may not be notified, and payments are made to the dealer assignor who receives them under a duty to remit to the assignee.

Id.

When, by agreement or otherwise, an assignee is entitled to notify account debtors and direct them to pay her directly, the assignee faces the problem of satisfying the procedural requirements of §9-318(3) so that the notice is effective to thereafter bind the account debtors to her. The notification must reasonably identify the rights assigned. Also, the assignee must make clear that payments on the account should be made to the assignee rather than to the assignor. U.C.C. §9-318(3). Unless all of these steps are taken, the account debtor is free to pay the assignor without any liability to the assignee, id., even though the account debtor actually knows of the assignment. U.C.C. §9-318 comment 3. Apparently, however, the notice need not always be in writing. Oral notice will sometimes suffice, *State Bank of Young America v. Vidmar Iron Works, Inc.,* 292 N.W.2d 244, 252 (1980), assuming the assignee can prove having given the notice.

The risk of the account debtor paying the assignor, with no accountability to the assignee for the payments, is theoretically nonexistent when a right to payment of money is embodied in a negotiable instrument, such as a promissory note, that the assignee holds as a holder in due course. Payment of an instrument to anyone other than the holder in due course is not a valid defense against the holder's enforcement of the instrument, whether the payment was made before or after the instrument was negotiated to the holder. It makes no difference that the obligor was not notified of the transfer of the instrument. U.C.C. §9-318(3) protects only account debtors, and an obligor on a negotiable instrument is not an account debtor. U.C.C. §9-105(1)(a). Of course, payment to someone else will be effective, even as against a holder in due course, if the holder's agent took the payment, the holder authorized payment to the other person, or she ratified the payment. Thus, if a creditor takes instruments as collateral but allows the debtor to collect from the obligors, the creditor cannot complain against the obligors if she never actually gets the payments, not even if she is a holder in due course of the instruments.

A holder of instruments might in any event prefer to protect herself fully by notifying the obligors to pay her directly as soon as the instruments are negotiated to her. In this regard, however, the holder is in no better position that an assignee of accounts or chattel paper: She can give such notice only upon the debtor's default, unless the agreement between her and the debtor provides otherwise. U.C.C. §9-502(1).

Account Debtor Defaults. The most common event that devalues accounts or chattel paper as collateral is the account debtor's unwillingness to pay the obligation she owes, that is, the account debtor defaults. In this event, the assignee can sue for a personal judgment against the account debtor and enforce the judgment through execution process. Whether the assignee has other, more effective remedies depends on the nature and terms of the arrangement between her and the assignor, and also on whether the collateral is accounts or chattel paper.

The agreement between the assignee and assignor may expressly provide that uncollected accounts may be charged back against the assignor, so that the assignor effectively becomes a surety for the account debtor. This kind of agreement is called a "recourse agreement." If the assignee acquired the collateral through a security transfer rather than by way of an outright sale, the assignee can in any event hold the assignor personally liable for the difference between the secured debt and the amount collected from account debtors, that is, the deficiency. U.C.C. §9-502(2).

The assignee of chattel paper enjoys a remedial option not available when the collateral is accounts. The obligation of an account debtor on chattel paper is secured by an Article 9 security interest in goods. This security interest was transferred to the assignee along with the account debtor's obligation. Because the security interest now runs in favor of the assignee, the assignee can repossess and dispose of the goods upon the account debtor's default. If the secured debt is not fully satisfied by the proceeds of this disposition, the assignee can sue the account debtor for the deficiency.

If a recourse agreement exists when the collateral is chattel paper, the assignee might simply force the assignor to repurchase paper in default instead of pursuing the underlying collateral and, thereafter, the account debtor personally. If such a charge back occurs, the assignor once again is the owner of the chattel paper, i.e., the secured debt, and thus can repossess and sell the goods and hold the account debtor liable for any deficiency.

Account Debtor On Chattel Paper Transfers Her Rights In The Underlying Collateral. Chattel paper is more valuable as collateral than accounts in the sense that the obligations represented by chattel paper are themselves secured by goods. To maximize this value the assignee must minimize the risk of third parties acquiring superior claims to the underlying collateral, meaning creditors of the account debtor, a purchaser from her, or her trustee in bankruptcy. In other words, the assignee must insure perfection of the security interest the account debtor granted the assignor. The assignee having perfected her security interest in the chattel paper does not perfect the security interest in the goods that are the collateral underlying the chattel paper. The interest in the underlying goods must be separately perfected. Usually, however, the assignor has perfected the interest; and, if so, the interest in the goods remains perfected despite the assignment of the security interest to the assignee as part and parcel of the chattel paper assignment. U.C.C. §9-302(2) and comment 7.

If the underlying collateral is for some reason returned to the assignor, an especially complicated priority dispute is likely to erupt between the assignee and the assignor's inventory financer. Article 9 devotes special attention to this dispute in §9-306(5). Here's a hypothetical situation that this section covers: Island Equipment Company is a farm equipment dealer which sells goods manufactured by J.I. Case Company. Case sells equipment on credit to Island, and secures the credit with a security interest in Island's inventory that is perfected by filing. Included among equipment Case sold to Island was a tractor which Island resold to Buyer. Buyer's purchase was on credit, and she signed an installment sale contract through which Island retained a security interest in the tractor. Island then sold this contract to Borg-Warner Acceptance Corporation, which purchased all of Island's chattel paper and took possession of it in the ordinary course of Borg-Warner's business.

Stop! Look at what has happened to this point. Case lost its security interest in the tractor because of U.C.C. §9-307(1), and probably because Case also authorized the disposition in the security agreement. U.C.C. §9-306(2). Case's interest continued in the chattel paper Buyer signed, U.C.C. §§9-306(1) & (2); but this proceeds interest in the chattel paper was lost when Island assigned the paper to Borg-Warner. U.C.C. §9-308. Case is really not harmed, however, because its interest continues in the money that Borg-Warner paid for the chattel paper. This money is proceeds of the chattel paper. See U.C.C. §§9-306(1) & (2).

Borg-Warner, as assignee of the chattel paper, not only has a security interest in the paper, but also in the tractor which is security for Buyer's obligation on the paper.

A short time later, Buyer rejects the tractor or revokes her acceptance, or Buyer defaults and the tractor is repossessed. In either event, the tractor ends up back in Island's inventory. Case once again acquires a security interest in the tractor either because its security agreement with Island covers after-acquired inventory, or by operation of law, that is, §9-306(5)(a). Take a look at that subsection.

Case's security interest will conflict with Borg-Warner's security interest in the tractor, which survives the tractor's return to Island. U.C.C. §9-306(2). Because Case's filing as to inventory predates Borg-Warner's filing or perfection as to the tractor, Case will claim priority under U.C.C. §9-312(5)(a).

Borg-Warner can nevertheless win on the basis of §9-306(5)(b), which is an exception to §9-312(5)(a), depending on how paragraph (d) is interpreted and applied.

Account Debtor Has A Defense To Payment. When an assignee of accounts or chattel paper looks directly to the account debtor for payment, the account debtor very often asserts some defense or claim arising out of the transaction between her and the assignor. Such a claim or defense can ordinarily be asserted against the assignee, U.C.C. §9-318(1), except where (1) the account debtor has made an enforceable agreement not to assert this sort of claim or defense against an assignee, id. & U.C.C. §9-206, or (2) the account debtor's obligation takes the form of a negotiable instrument of which the assignee is a holder in due course. U.C.C. §§3-305 & 9-309. Neither of these exceptions is likely to apply when the underlying transaction between the assignor and account debtor is a consumer credit transaction, i.e., involves the sale and financing of goods for personal, family or household purposes.

Many states have laws banning the use of negotiable instruments in consumer credit sales, except for checks for the purchase price of the goods or services. Similar laws prohibit including in consumer credit contracts an agreement by the debtor not to assert against an assignee any claim or defense arising out of the consumer credit sale. Moreover, even if such an agreement is part of such a contract, or a negotiable instrument is used notwithstanding a prohibition against the use in a consumer deal, these consumer protection laws may dictate that an assignee of the contract or the instrument nevertheless takes subject to the claims and defenses of the consumer against the assignor.

Also, federal law mandates that consumer credit contracts, including negotiable instruments used in consumer deals, must contain a provision that any assignee is subject to such claims and defenses. Any taker of a contract that includes this provision is bound by it just as she is bound by all the other terms of the contract. See Federal Trade Commission Preservation of Consumer Claims And Defenses Trade Regulation Rule, 16 C.F.R. pt. 433, which is reprinted in West's Commercial Statutes (latest ed.) or comparable work.

Whenever U.C.C. §9-318(1) allows an account debtor to assert against an assignee the claims and defenses she has against the assignor, the account debtor can also offset against her liability to the assignee any unrelated claims the account debtor has against the assignor that accrued before the account debtor received notice of the assignment. Some states allow this sort of offset in an action to enforce a negotiable instrument if the plaintiff lacks the rights of a holder in due course.

Assignee Is Affirmatively Liable To Account Debtor. Taking subject to the account debtor's claims and defenses against the assignor is not a new wrinkle in the law. The rule has always been that an assignee steps into the shoes of the assignor. Until recently, everyone agreed on the meaning of this rule: When sued by the assignee, the account debtor can defensively raise claims she has against the assignor. The account debtor cannot, however, assert those claims affirmatively against the assignee and recover damages from the assignee. Thus, the account debtor can reduce or totally eliminate her liability to the assignee, but she cannot look to the assignee to pay damages for which the assignor is liable. In other words, in her relationship to the assignee, the account debtor can wield her claims and defenses against the assignor only as a shield, not as a sword.

The doctrinal basis for this rule is the principle that a bank or other person who takes an assignment of accounts or chattel paper as collateral acquires only the assignor's rights against the account debtor or other obligor. The assignee is not a delegate who takes over the assignor's duties of performance to the account debtor. See U.C.C. §§2-210(4) & 9-317; but see Federal Trade Commission Preservation of Consumer Claims And Defenses Trade Regulation Rule, 16 C.F.R. pt. 433 (consumer can recover amounts paid to assignee). In a few modern cases the courts appear to have relaxed the traditional rule that immunizes an assignee from affirmative liability to an account debtor or other obligor. Actually, however, these cases are best explained as limited exceptions to, and not wholesale repudiations of, the traditional rule.

3. Explicit Exclusions

Characterizing a transaction under U.C.C. §9-102(1) as one intended to create a security interest in property or fixtures, or as a sale of accounts or chattel paper, is only the first step in deciding if Article 9 applies. The obligatory second step is to determine if §9-104 nevertheless expressly excludes the transaction from Article 9's scope. A transaction may satisfy one of the tests of the general scope provision, §9-102(1), but not be governed by Article 9 because the transaction falls within an explicit exclusion of §9-104. This is well demonstrated by comparing the language of §§9-102(1)(b) and 9-104(f) regarding the applicability of Article 9 to sales of accounts and chattel paper. The former section pulls within Article 9 "*any* sale of accounts or chattel paper," U.C.C. §9-102(1)(b) (emphasis added), but the latter section kicks out some such sales "which, by their nature, have nothing to do with commercial financing transactions." U.C.C. §9-104 comment 6.

R. Braucher & R. Riegert, INTRODUCTION TO
COMMERCIAL TRANSACTIONS
447-48 (1977)

Certain transactions have been excluded from the coverage of Article 9 for various reasons. [Section 9-104 contains twelve] *** [p]aragraphs listing excluded transactions * * *. We attempt to arrange these exceptions in accordance with the probable reason for their exclusion.

Security Interests Subject to Federal Statutes. Paragraph (a) excludes any security interest subject to federal statute "to the extent that such statute governs the rights of parties to and third parties affected by transactions in particular types of property" covered by the statute. ***

A federal law would, of course, take precedence over a State law in any event; the significance of Paragraph (a) is its intent to make the UCC applicable in the areas of the relevant federal laws to questions not dealt with by those laws. The federal laws dealing with secured transactions are usually not very comprehensive; Paragraph (a) makes it clear that the draftsmen intended that the Code be used to fill in the gaps.

Transactions Not Within the Stated Scope of Article 9. Three exclusions involve transactions not within the stated scope of Article 9. These are the landlord's lien of Paragraph (b), the liens for services or materials of Paragraph (c), and the interest in real estate of Paragraph (j).

* * *

[In addition t]he right of set-off excluded by Paragraph (i) does not involve a security interest, but rather involves the right of a debtor to set off against his creditor any claims he has against the creditor. When the debtor is a bank, the right of set-off is sometimes inaccurately referred to as a banker's lien. To avoid any possibility that Article 9 might be applied to the right of set-off, Paragraph (i) was included.

Transactions Thought Not to Be of Commercial Importance. Several Paragraphs list transactions which are excluded from the coverage of Article 9 because they are not of commercial importance. These include: *** claims for compensation of an employee (Paragraph (d)), *** the right represented by a judgment (Paragraph (h)), *** and a claim arising out of a tort and any deposit account maintained with a bank, savings institute or the like (Paragraph[s] (k) [and (l)]).

Exclusions of Specialized Types of Financing. Some exclusions reflect the views of people engaged in specialized types of financing. *** [Governmental transfers, Paragraph (e), fall into this group.] The exclusion of Paragraph (g) relating "to a transfer of an interest or claim in or under any policy of insurance" reflects an insurance company point of view that pre-Code practices worked satisfactorily.

Notes and Problems

1. The §9-104(a) exclusion recognizes federal preemption to the extent that a federal statute governs a secured transaction. The language "to the extent" implies that federal law and Article 9 can both apply to the same transaction, albeit different aspects of the transaction.

    This exclusion does not recognize federal preemption otherwise than by statute of the United States; but, of course, federal administrative regulations can also override Article 9 and so can federal common law. Preemption by federal common law is a possibility when the United States, or an instrumentality of the United States, claims a consensual lien on personal property. The United States Supreme Court has declared that "the priority of liens stemming from federal lending programs [such as those of the SBA and FHA] must be determined with reference to federal law," and, the interstices of the statutes authorizing these programs are to be filled by the federal courts "'according to their own standards'" in the absence of statutory provisions specifying the appropriate rules of decision. United States v. Kimbell Foods, Inc., 440 U.S. 715, 727, 99 S.Ct. 1448, 1457, 59 L.Ed.2d 711 (1979). In the very same case, however, the court adopted nondiscriminatory state law, including Article 9, as the federal rule of decision in determining priority between the consensual security interest of the Small Business Administration and a private creditor, and between the security interest of the Farmers Home Administration and an artisan claiming a supplier's lien for repairs to the collateral.

2. L leased office space to T. T failed to pay her rent, and shortly thereafter a judgment creditor of T levied execution on T's office equipment. L argues that she has a first claim to the equipment to secure the rent due her from T. The lien creditor argues she has priority because L did not file an Article 9 financing statement. See U.C.C.

§9-301(1)(b). Consider whether the lien creditor's argument is sound under these circumstances:

   a. L's claim to the equipment is based on a non-Code statute giving every landlord a right to distrain a tenant's personal property in satisfaction of unpaid rent.

   b. L's claim is based on a provision in the lease agreement with T providing that "the Landlord shall have a lien on all of Tenant's equipment and other personal property located in leased premises to secure payment of rent."

3. Bank makes a loan to D, a construction company, to help D begin performance of a contract that obligates D to build a structure for O. The loan is secured by an assignment to Bank of D's rights to payment under D's contract with O. Is the arrangement between Bank and D within Article 9's scope? If so, must Bank file a financing statement covering the collateral to protect its interest against third parties' claims?

4. Z wronged D, and D thus sued Z for damages. While the case was pending, D assigned her claim against Z to Bank as security for a preexisting debt D owed Bank. Thereafter, in the action by D against Z, judgment was rendered against Z in the amount of $150,000. Z paid this amount to D, and D deposited the amount in a passbook savings account at Minnesota Federal Savings & Loan, which account she thereafter assigned to her Mother as collateral for a loan. Does Bank have an Article 9 security interest in the bank account? Does D's Mother?

5. Same facts as Problem 4, except that D bought a $150,000 certificate of deposit from Minnesota Federal instead of putting the money in a passbook savings account.

6. Bank makes a loan to Skyway Hotel. The collateral includes "room charges paid by Hotel guests and residents." Is this aspect of the security arrangement between the parties within the scope of Article 9?

Report of the Article 9 Study Committee
Permanent Editorial Board for the Uniform Commercial Code
American Law Institute and National Conference of Commissions on Uniform State Law,
1992

COMMITTEE RECOMMENDATIONS:

A. Scope of Article 9

1. Sales of General Intangibles; Credit Card Receivables

A. Article 9 should be revised to include within its scope sales of general intangibles for the payment of money. However, the Drafting Committee should ensure that the expanded scope does not embrace sales of receivables as to which regulation by Article 9 would be impractical or unnecessary (e.g., loan participations and other loan sales by financial institutions and, possibly, sales by other classes of professional lenders).

B. Article 9 should be revised to define "credit card receivables" as a new type of collateral, to provide that Article 9 covers sales of credit card receivables (as well as security interests therein that secure obligations), and to provide that filing a financing statement is the only means of perfecting a security interest in credit card receivables.

2. Intellectual Property

A. Both Article 9 and federal law should be revised to make clear the extent to which each governs the creation, perfection, priority, and enforcement of security interests in federally regulated intellectual property rights. At a minimum, the Drafting Committee should revise 9-104(a) or the official comments to state that Article 9 applies to such security interests to the extent permitted by the Constitution and should revise 9-302(3) and the official comment to clarify the applicability of the subsection.

B. The federal recording systems for interests in intellectual property should be reformed to establish one or more notice-filing systems for security interests. These systems, which should be similar to the Article 9 system, would supplement the current recording systems, which are indexed according to particular property ("tract indexes").

C. Article 9 and federal law should be revised to provide that a security interest can be perfected *(ie.,* can achieve priority over the rights of a judicial lien creditor) either in accordance with Article 9 or by recordation in the appropriate federal tract index. Recordation in the federal notice-filing system would not be necessary or sufficient to perfect a security interest.

D. Article 9 and federal law should be revised to provide that, in general, priorities of claimants (including secured parties who have perfected their security interests) who record in the federal system should be determined on the basis of priority in time of recordation; *ie.,* a purchaser would take subject to an interest (including a perfected security interest) recorded earlier in either the federal tract index or the federal notice-filing system. A purchaser (including a secured party) who records in the federal tract index would take free of (or take priority over) a security interest that was perfected in accordance with Article 9 and not recorded in either federal system.

E. Article 9 and federal law should be revised to provide that Article 9 governs a secured party's rights upon the debtor's default but that federal law determines the requirements for making an effective transfer of the collateral in connection with the enforcement of a security interest.

F. The Drafting Committee should work with the Task Force on Security Interests in Intellectual Property of the Business Law Section of the American Bar Association to develop additional priority rules necessitated by the unique nature of the collateral and the coexistence of federal and state systems, including rules with respect to licensees of intellectual property. The PEB should support the effort to amend the applicable federal laws in ways that will facilitate secured transactions.

3. Insurance Policies as Collateral

The Drafting Committee should give serious consideration to revising 9-104(g) to expand the scope of Article 9 to include security interests in most forms of business insurance policies and at least some forms of "personal" *(e.g,* life, health, and disability) insurance. In its consideration of personal insurance, the Drafting Committee should consider the potential for abuse that might arise by virtue of the applicability of Article 9.

4. Tort Claims as Collateral

A. Section 9-104(k) should be revised to expand the scope of Article 9 to include security interests in claims (other than claims for personal injury) arising out of tort, to the extent that such claims are assignable under applicable non-UCC law.

B. The Drafting Committee should consider seriously whether to expand the scope of Article 9 to include security interests in claims for personal injury arising out of tort.

C. Article 9 or the official comments should be revised to make clear that Article 9 applies to security interests in rights to payment that derive from claims arising out of tort *(e.g.,* rights to payment under a settlement agreement or a promissory note given to evidence liability in tort).

5. Fixtures and Real Estate-Related Collateral

A. Section 9-313(4)(c) should be extended to "readily removable equipment that is not primarily used or leased for use in the operation of the real estate."

B. Article 9 should be revised to provide that perfection in an obligation *(e.g.,* a note) secured by real estate should be accomplished by perfection as to the obligation under Article 9 in the same manner as if the obligation were not secured by the real estate and to make clear that no additional perfection is required with respect to the real estate.

C. The Drafting Committee should give serious consideration to the reports of the advisory group on real estate-related collateral.

6. Oil, Gas, and Minerals-Related Collateral

The Drafting Committee should give serious consideration to revising the UCC to comport with the recommendations made by the American Bar Association UCC Committee Task Force on Oil and Gas Finance, including:

(1) clarification of the boundary between real and personal property law, by providing that (a) real property law governs oil, gas, and other minerals in the ground, together with related contractual arrangements *(e.g,* oil and gas leases and production payment contracts); (b) other contractual interests *(e.g.,* farmout, operating, production, and processing agreements) are general intangibles covered by Article 9; (c) extracted minerals are personal property governed by the UCC (including 9-307(1)); and (d) vehicles and other non fixture equipment are governed by the UCC; and

(2) revision of 9-401 to make clear that all financing statements relating to security interests that attach to oil and gas immediately upon extraction are to be filed in the office where a real estate mortgage is to be filed, and that the filing rules for other security interests *(ie.,* those that attach after extraction) should be the same as those for other goods.

7. Deposit Accounts

A. Article 9 should be revised to include deposit accounts within its scope as original collateral.

B. Article 9 should be revised to provide that a depositary institution owes no duties to a secured party claiming a security interest in a deposit account maintained with that institution unless, and then only to the extent that, the institution agrees to assume such duties or is served with legal process concerning the deposit account.

C. The Drafting Committee should give serious consideration to the recommendations contained in the Report of the Subcommittee on the Use of Deposit Accounts as Original Collateral.

ᑎᑎᑎᑎᑎᑎ

4. Secured Transactions Involving Real Estate

Problems

Real Estate As Collateral
1. Sun Town, Inc. sells a parcel of real estate to B. B's obligation to pay the price of the lot is evidenced by a promissory note, and this note is secured by a mortgage on the lot.   Does Article 9 govern this security arrangement? See U.C.C. §9-102(1) & 9-104(j).

2. Bank had a security interest in D's corps. They were sold to buyer in the ordinary course who paid cash. D used the money to buy a house. Does Bank's security interest continue in the house?

Real Estate Paper
3. Continue with Problem 1. Sun Town, Inc. borrows money from Bank. The loan is secured by an assignment of B's secured note to Sun Town. Is this security arrangement within Article 9's scope? See U.C.C. §9-102(3).

4. Sun Town subsequently makes a further assignment of the secured note to General Finance, Inc. Who has priority with respect to the secured note, Bank or General Finance?

5. Return to Problem 3. Sun Town defaults. Bank looks to B to pay the note assigned to Bank as collateral. B is bankrupt; so Bank decides to foreclose on the real estate mortgage that secures the note. There is a problem, however. B sold the lot to C, and C paid the purchase price to Sun Town which was the mortgagee of record. The

assignment from Sun Town to Bank, which occurred before C purchased the lot, was never recorded. C argues that her claim to the real estate outranks the Bank's claim. How is this priority dispute resolved? Does Article 9 supply the rule of decision? See U.C.C. §9-102 comment 4.

Fixtures

6.   D gives S & L a mortgage on real estate where D operates her butcher shop. Later, Bank takes a security interest in all D's business equipment and files pursuant to Article 9. D defaults under her security agreement with Bank. Bank wants to repossess D's equipment, including a large, walk-in freezer. S & L objects to Bank's repossession of the freezer, claiming it has a superior claim to the property as real estate mortgagee. Who has the better claim to the freezer? See U.C.C. §9-313.

> [*Authors' Note*: We will walk you through this problem. The first issue is whether both parties have a claim to the freezer. Bank has an Article 9 security interest in the freezer even if the freezer is a fixture. Article 9 governs the creation of security interests in fixtures. U.C.C. §§9-102(1) & 9-313(2). Moreover, a security interest in goods that become fixtures continues in the property notwithstanding the transformation, unless the goods are ordinary building materials incorporated into an improvement on land. U.C.C. §9-313(2).
>
> If the freezer is not a fixture, S & L has a claim to the property only if it and D complied with §9-203(1) to create a security interest in the goods. They probably did not comply with that section. If the freezer is a fixture, S & L could have acquired an interest either by complying with Article 9, or "pursuant to real estate law." U.C.C. §9-313(3). Under the real estate law of most states, the interest of a real estate encumbrancer usually extends automatically to fixtures added to the real property.
>
> Thus, S & L has no interest in the freezer if the property did not become a fixture. There is no priority conflict, and Bank wins. If the freezer is a fixture, both Bank and S & L have interests. There is a priority conflict, and the rule of decision is somewhere in U.C.C. §9-313.
>
> Bank will argue that its Article 9 security interest in the freezer is good against the world, U.C.C. §9-201, and that, upon the debtor's default, it can repossess its collateral, U.C.C. §9-503, even if the collateral is a fixture. U.C.C. §9-313(8).
>
> S & L will counter that the right to repossess a fixture is conditioned on the secured party having priority over all encumbrancers of the real estate. U.C.C. §9-313(8). S & L is an encumbrancer, U.C.C. §9-105(1)(g), and the general rule of priority between a real estate

encumbrancer and an Article 9 secured party is that the encumbrancer wins. U.C.C. §9-313(7).

Bank's response is that the general priority rule of §9-313(7) is riddled with exceptions, which are embodied in subsections (4) and (5). The general rule among the exceptions is §9-313(4)(b), which essentially states the first-in-time, first-in-right principle. This exceptional rule will aid Bank only if (1) S & L failed to record in the appropriate real estate records before (2) Bank perfected by a fixture filing. A fixture filing implies satisfaction of special rules regarding the contents of the financing statement and also the place where it is filed. U.C.C. §§9-313(1)(b); 9-401(1); 9-402(5).

If S & L recorded before Bank perfected, Bank can nevertheless win under §9-313(4)(a) if (1) the Bank's interest is a purchase money security interest and (2) the Bank perfected by a fixture filing before the freezer became a fixture or within ten days thereafter. A regular Article 9 filing that, for purposes of what and where to file, treats the freezer as plain equipment, that is, as pure personal property rather than as a fixture, will not suffice.

If neither subsection (4)(b) or (4)(a) works in favor of Bank, S & L is entitled to priority (and so Bank cannot repossess the freezer) unless S & L, in effect, waives its claim to the property, U.C.C. §9-313(5)(a), or D is entitled as against S & L to remove the freezer, U.C.C. §9-313(5)(a), which right will inure to the benefit of Bank and effectively shelter Bank's repossession from the complaints of S & L.

Now, you work the rest of the problems on your own, using the general analytical framework we used for this first problem.]

7. D mortgaged her business realty to Bank, which recorded the mortgage in accordance with state and local real estate law. D purchased a large, walk-in freezer and installed it in her place of business. The freezer became a fixture. C.I.T. made a business loan to D, and took a security interest in all of D's equipment, including the freezer. C.I.T. made a proper fixture filing. Bank thereafter assigned D's mortgage to SBA, which immediately recorded the assignment in local real estate records. D defaulted under her security agreement with C.I.T., and C.I.T. now wants to repossess D's equipment, including the freezer. Does SBA or C.I.T. have priority as to the freezer?

8. D asks Bank for a loan. The parties discuss the request and agree that, if the Bank makes the loan, the collateral will include all of D's equipment, including fixtures. No final agreement is reached at this first meeting, but Bank has D sign financing statements, including a fixture filing, which Bank properly files. Thereafter, D gives S

& L a real estate mortgage on her place of business. S & L properly records. A week later, Bank and D reach a final agreement, a security agreement is executed covering equipment and fixtures at D's place of business, and the loan proceeds are disbursed. Whose claim to fixtures is entitled to priority, the Bank's or S & L's?

9. D gives Bank a mortgage on her place of business. Bank records. SP sells D equipment for use in D's business. The equipment is installed so that it becomes a fixture that would require very much work to remove; and, five days later, SP files a financing statement with the Secretary of State as per the second alternative of U.C.C. §9-401(1), which is local law. D defaults under her security agreement with SP who now wants to repossess the equipment. Bank objects. Who has priority?

10. Same as Problem 9, except that SP makes a proper fixture filing.

11. Same as Problem 9, with these changes in facts: The equipment is a large Xerox machine. The machine is properly classified as a fixture under local law because a special room was constructed to house it. The machine, however, can easily be removed inasmuch as nothing other than the electrical cord plugged into the wall connects it to the room where it sits, and the room has wide doors designed for readily moving the machine when major repairs are necessary.

12. D buys a 25-year old house where she and her family now reside. The purchase is financed by S & L which has a recorded mortgage on the place. D decides to replace a built-in kitchen oven with a new model. SP sells D a new oven on credit and installs the oven for D. The installment is easily accomplished by removing six screws that held the old oven in place, pulling out the old oven, snipping the electrical wires and connecting them to the new oven, wiring and sliding in the new oven, and replacing the screws. SP retained a security interest in the new oven to secure D's obligation to pay the price. Does S & L have a claim to the new oven? If so, does SP's security interest enjoy priority over S & L's claim?

13. D purchased a large, walk-in freezer and installed it in her place of business. The freezer became a fixture that is not easily removed. C.I.T. made a business loan to D, and took a security interest in all of D's equipment, including the freezer. C.I.T. filed pursuant to Article 9. G, a general, unsecured creditor of D, thereafter won a judgment against D in the county where D's place of business is located. When D defaulted under her security agreement with C.I.T., C.I.T. decided to repossess the freezer. G objected. Does G's judgment give her a claim to the freezer, or must G levy execution against the freezer in order to establish a claim to the property? Assuming G has a claim to the freezer, is this claim or C.I.T.'s security interest entitled to priority?

14. Uno Pizzeria contracts with General Martar Construction, GM, for the construction of a new building. The contract calls for progress payments at defined stages of construction. Construction Mortgage Co. agrees to lend the sums needed for the

progress payments and obtains a mortgage on the land and the building. Construction promptly records its mortgage. GM buys the light fixtures for the new building on credit from your client, Seetha Light, Inc. If GM fails to pay Seetha, does U.C.C. §9-313 protect Seetha? Is there any non-Code protection for Seetha?

Unit 3

SPECIAL COLLECTION RIGHTS
CREATED BY LAW

UNIT CONTENTS

A. NONCONSENSUAL LIENS

1. Sellers' Rights Of Reclamation And Stoppage

Suppose that Seller sells goods to Buyer on credit. Buyer accepts the goods and later defaults, i.e., fails to pay the price when due under the terms of the credit arrangement. The Seller can sue the Buyer for damages under Article 2. See U.C.C. §2-709. As a general rule, Seller cannot recover the goods themselves unless she has an Article 9 security interest in the property. The fudge word "ordinarily" is used because Article 2 provides an explicit, though narrowly circumscribed, exception in U.C.C. §2-702(2), which gives unpaid credit sellers a right to *reclaim* goods supplied to insolvent buyers.

A seller in a cash transaction who exchanges the goods for a check that bounces, i.e., that is dishonored upon presentment to the drawee-bank, also has a right to reclaim the goods. This right of unpaid cash sellers to reclaim is inferentially recognized by U.C.C. §§2-507 and 2-511.

Wholly separate from both of these rights of reclamation is the different right of a seller to stop delivery of goods that have been shipped to a buyer. This right of *stoppage of delivery in transit* is defined in U.C.C. §2-705, which allows stopping delivery of any quantity of goods when the reason is the buyer's insolvency but limits the right to large shipments when the reason for stoppage is the buyer's repudiation or default.

Third parties often resist a seller's efforts to reclaim or stop delivery of goods under Article 2. A common opponent of these efforts is a person to whom the buyer has resold the goods, or a person to whom the buyer has given a security interest in the goods. How should these priority battles be resolved?

Graniteville Co. v. Bleckley Lumber Co., Inc.
United States Court of Appeals, Eleventh Circuit, 1991
944 F.2d 819

PER CURIAM:

The appellant, Dixie Bonded Warehouse & Grain Company, Inc. ("Dixie"), appeals the district court's grant of summary judgment in favor of the appellee. For the reasons which follow, we affirm the judgment of the district court but for a different reason than that stated by the district court.

This case began as an interpleader action filed by Graniteville Company ("Graniteville") to determine whether Dixie or Allstate was entitled to the proceeds of accounts receivable Graniteville owed to Bleckley Cotton Company ("Bleckley") for cotton purchased. All of Dixie's claims involve the question of who is entitled to the proceeds of Bleckley's accounts receivable, not claims involving Dixie's cotton. While the district court ultimately reached the correct conclusion, its finding that Dixie had standing to challenge Allstate's right to Bleckley's accounts receivable was based on its misinterpretation of §2-401 and §9-113 of the Uniform Commercial Code ("U.C.C.").

The record demonstrates that Allstate had a perfected security interest in Bleckley's accounts receivable and the contractual right to collect the proceeds of the receivables directly from Bleckley's account debtors. In fact, this court determined in a related appeal that Allstate's perfected security interest in Bleckley's accounts receivable was valid and enforceable and that Allstate had the right to collect the accounts directly from Bleckley's account debtors. Unless Dixie can demonstrate that it has some legal claim to Bleckley's accounts receivable, it has no standing to attack or challenge Allstate's ownership of the proceeds.

Relying on the district court's reasoning, Dixie contends in this appeal that it has some amorphous, unperfected security interest in Bleckley's accounts receivable that arises by operation of law under U.C.C. §2-401. A close review of the U.C.C., however, demonstrates that Dixie has no such security interest and is no more than an unsecured creditor of Bleckley. Allstate, on the other hand, bought, paid for, and rightfully owns the accounts receivable.

Under the U.C.C., unpaid sellers retain rights in their goods even after they are identified to the contract: (1) the right to reclaim the delivered goods upon demand made within ten days after delivery (U.C.C. §2-702); (2) the right to withhold delivery of the goods and resell them to another buyer (U.C.C. §2-703, §2-706); and (3) the right to ship under reservation of a security interest (U.C.C. §2-505). If properly exercised, these provisions create rights in the sold goods that, although subordinate to the rights of Article IX secured creditors like Allstate, may nevertheless give the sellers standing to challenge the validity of the secured creditors' interest. In the present case, the record demonstrates that Dixie failed to reserve title and did not obtain an Article IX security interest in its cotton or Bleckley's accounts receivable before releasing possession and control of its goods. Thereafter, Dixie failed to reclaim its cotton under U.C.C. §2-702 and never sued its buyer, Bleckley, on the bad checks used to purchase the cotton or for breach of contract. Since the cotton is now gone, Dixie is thus "relegated to the position of unsecured creditor[ ]." Teton Int'l v. First Nat'l Bank, 718 S.W.2d 838, 840 (Tex.Ct.App.1986). Without some security interest in Bleckley's accounts receivable, Dixie simply has no standing to challenge Allstate's ownership rights. Without standing, the issue of Allstate's good faith becomes irrelevant as a matter of law.

Accordingly, we affirm the district court's grant of summary judgment in favor of Allstate.

AFFIRMED.

Burk v. Emmick

United States Court of Appeals, Eighth Circuit, 1980.
637 F.2d 1172.

Heaney, Circuit Judge.

I

This appeal arises out of a transaction in which plaintiff Willard Burk contracted to sell approximately 950 head of yearling steers to defendant Bob Emmick, d/b/a Emmick Cattle Company. The terms of the sales contract provided that the buyer would make a $15,000 down payment and tender the balance upon delivery.

The contract was amended, postponing the delivery date and modifying the manner in which payment would be made. The amended agreement called for payment of a major portion of the purchase price at delivery by sight draft drawn upon the codefendant, Northwestern National Bank of Sioux City. The balance of the purchase price was to be covered by the buyer's personal note. Just prior to delivery, the defendant Bank orally guaranteed to the seller that funds were available to cover the sight draft so that delivery could be made. The seller made delivery, but the sight draft was not accepted by the Bank and the buyer's personal note was never honored.

Subsequent to these transactions, the seller reclaimed the cattle and resold them for less than the original contract price. Thereafter, the seller sued the buyer in the United States District Court for the Northern District of Iowa, alleging breach of contract and fraud. The seller also sued the Bank on a promissory estoppel theory, reasoning that he detrimentally relied upon the Bank's oral assurance that funds were available to cover the sight draft, thus inducing the seller to make delivery and suffer pecuniary injury. The case was tried to a jury and a verdict was returned on the seller's breach of contract claim against the buyer in the amount of $19,300. The jury also returned a verdict in the seller's favor against the Bank on the promissory estoppel claim in the amount of $24,700.

All parties filed post trial motions. The seller moved to amend the judgment by increasing the amount of the award. The buyer and the Bank moved for judgment notwithstanding the verdict, for a new trial, and to amend the judgment. All motions were denied, and all parties appealed. We affirm.

II

The buyer and the Bank argue that Iowa Code §554.2702 controls this case. The buyer contends this section bars a seller who successfully reclaims goods from further recovering a deficiency judgment. The Bank agrees that section 2-702 applies, but asserts that because the seller failed to demand return of the goods within ten days of delivery, the reclamation was improper. The Bank asserts that it has an interest in the cattle superior to the unpaid seller based upon a preexisting security interest covering after-acquired property of the defendant buyer.

In resolving the questions posed by this appeal, we first determine the relative rights of the parties involved in this sales transaction.

A. The Rights of the Secured Party Under Section 2-403.

Section 2-403 gives a transferor power to pass good title to certain transferees even though the transferor does not possess good title. This section contemplates the situation in which a cash seller delivers goods to a buyer who pays by a draft that is subsequently dishonored, and then transfers title to a good faith purchaser. U.C.C. §§2-403(1)(b) & (c). In such a situation, as between the good faith purchaser and the unpaid seller, the former's claim is clearly superior.

Furthermore, section 2-403 does not limit the power of a transferor to pass good title only through sales transactions. The language of the Code specifically provides that "purchasers" may take good title from transferors. The term purchaser is broadly defined in the Code to include an Article IX secured party. *See* U.C.C. §§1-201(32) & (33). Here, if the Bank had acted in good faith, its interest in the cattle would be superior to the aggrieved seller. However, as the district court noted, the issue was properly submitted to the jury and the jury determined that the Bank did not exercise good faith. Accordingly, the Bank does not qualify as a good faith purchaser under section 2-403. As between the seller and the Bank, the seller's interest in the cattle is superior.

B. The Rights of the Cash Seller Under the U.C.C.

Section 2-703 indexes the remedies available to a seller upon the buyer's breach. The right of reclamation is not specifically mentioned there. The cash seller's right to reclaim has been drawn from the language of sections 2-507 and 2-511.

Section 2-507(2) gave the seller in this case the right to reclaim the cattle which were sold and not paid for. The buyer's main contention is that once the seller had successfully reclaimed the goods, he could not also seek a deficiency judgment. The buyer asserts the election of remedies provision in section 2-702(3) is applicable to a cash seller's section 2-507 right of reclamation. We do not agree. There is nothing in the language of the Code or the Comments to suggest that the election of remedies provision applies to a cash seller's reclamation under section 2-507. In fact, the concept of election of remedies is foreign to the liberal remedial provisions intended by the drafters of the U.C.C. *See* §2-703 Comment 1.

The buyer also asserts that the seller failed to demand reclamation within ten days of delivery of the cattle. Some courts have decided that a cash seller's reclamation right is subject to the ten-day limitation provision covering credit sale transactions involving insolvent buyers under section 2-702, but those decisions are factually dissimilar. The courts that have imposed the ten-day limitation have concerned the respective rights of a good faith purchaser or trustee in bankruptcy and an unpaid seller. But here, a good faith purchaser is not involved. Nor are we faced with the conflicting interests of an unpaid seller and a trustee in bankruptcy representing the interests of a bankrupt's creditors. Rather, the conflict is between the unpaid cash seller and the breaching buyer, and the question is whether the seller may reclaim and recover a deficiency judgment from that buyer.

It is instructive to note that the buyer in the case at bar has never forcefully opposed the seller's right to reclaim; rather, it has focused its primary attention upon the seller's right to a deficiency. This is understandable in light of the fact that the buyer was not prejudiced by the seller's reclamation, improper or not. Had the seller not reclaimed the goods, he could have sued for the full contract price. See U.C.C. §§2-703, 2-709.

Our holding is quite limited. We determine that as between the seller and the buyer, where a cash seller reclaims goods sold to a breaching buyer, the only limitation imposed upon the seller's right is a reasonableness requirement. Since we determine that the buyer was not prejudiced by the seller's delay in reclaiming the cattle, we find the seller's reclamation was not unreasonable.

Furthermore, the district court was correct in determining that section 2-702 did not properly apply to the instant case. By its very terms, that section applies when the seller discovers the buyer to be insolvent *and* when the underlying transaction is a credit sale. The transaction that gave rise to this lawsuit was a cash sale. As the district court reasoned, the fact that payment was made by a draft that was subsequently dishonored does not alter the nature of the underlying transaction.

The district court properly determined that section 2-703 controls this case. This section declares the right of the aggrieved seller to: (1) withhold delivery; (2) stop delivery by any bailee; (3) proceed under section 2-704; (4) *resell and recover damages as provided in section 2-706;* (5) recover damages for nonacceptance or the price; or (6) cancel. In this case, the seller properly chose the fourth alternative. This section's applicability to this case is highlighted by Official Comment 3, which provides: "In addition to the typical case of refusal to pay or default in payment, the language in the preamble, 'fails to make a payment due,' is intended to cover the dishonor of a check on due presentment, or the non-acceptance of a draft ***." U.C.C. §2-703 Official Comment 3.

In this case, when the draft was not accepted by the Bank, the seller chose to reclaim the cattle pursuant to section 2-507 and resell them. Section 2-703(d) allows the seller to recover a deficiency judgment upon a reasonable resale.

III

Finally, section 2-706 provides that the recoverable deficiency is the difference between the original contract price and the amount realized upon a commercially reasonable resale. The jury was properly instructed on the section 2-706 damage formula. The district court further instructed the jury that

> in the event you find for the plaintiff Burk and against the defendant Emmick in Count I of the Complaint but find that the plaintiff Burk's resale of the cattle was not effected in good faith and in a commercially reasonable manner, the actual and compensatory damages to which the plaintiff Burk is entitled is the difference between the market price at the time and place for delivery and the unpaid contract price agreed upon by Burk and Emmick, together with any incidental damages, but less expenses saved in consequence of buyer's breach.

> If the measure of damages provided in the above paragraph is inadequate to put the seller in as good a position as full performance of the contract by the defendant Emmick would have done, then the measure of damages is the profit (including reasonable overhead) which the plaintiff Burk would have made from full performance by the defendant Emmick, together with any incidental damages and giving due allowance for costs reasonably incurred and due credit for payments or proceeds of resale.

This was a proper instruction and the jury could rationally have used this damage formula in arriving at its damage award. The award is supported in the record as a whole. A jury award may not be set aside unless it is flagrantly inadequate or not supported by the record. Since we determine that such is not the case here, the jury's verdict stands as rendered.

2. Other Suppliers' Liens

Larry Moffett, Priority Of Artisan's Lien Under
U.C.C. Section 9-310
48 Miss.L.J. 1113, 1113-19 (1977)

At common law an artisan who repaired [personal] property or otherwise enhanced its value or life was given the right to retain possession of the property until he had been paid for his services. This right, known as an artisan's lien, depended on the artisan's exclusive and continuous possession of the item. Consequently, once possession was voluntarily surrendered, [the lien was lost and] a subsequent retaking would not revive the lien **** The artisan generally encountered no substantial problems unless his lien came into conflict with an earlier interest. Although questions of priority were often decided in favor of an owner or prior lienor if he did not give his consent to or had no knowledge of the repairs, many courts found an owner's implied consent to necessary repairs.

Despite such liberal interpretations establishing the liens, artisans encountered problems because the lien was merely possessory; the artisan's sole relief was to hold the property until payment was made. To alleviate this situation, states enacted statutory liens, which for the first time provided means of enforcement for the artisan [such as giving the artisan a right to enforce the lien through judicial foreclosure or through a private sale of the property]. **** Most courts agree that the statutory possessory lien, like its common law ancestor, is based on possession and is waived when the lienholder voluntarily and unconditionally parts with possession; a subsequent reacquisition of the property will not revive the lien. Consequently, besides codifying the strictly possessory artisan's lien, several states also enacted a statutory lien for artisans not in possession of repaired property. ***

Against this background of common law and statutory, possessory and nonpossessory artisan's liens, the Uniform Commercial Code speaks directly to the issue of priority between an artisan's lien and a prior security interest. U.C.C. section 9-310 provides that a lien created "by statute or rule of law" will be given priority in all cases where services and materials are furnished in the ordinary course of business and where the goods are in the lienor's possession. The sole exception occurs when the statute creating the lien expressly subordinates it to other interests.

Because of the requirement of possession, it is not entirely clear how section 9-310 affects nonpossessory liens. One interpretation provides that such liens are totally outside the scope of the section and that priority is governed by previous statute and case law. According to this interpretation, section 9-310 does not affect pre-Code nonpossessory lien priority. A different interpretation *** holds nonpossessory liens inferior to prior secured interests in all instances despite contrary pre-Code statutory and case law. [According to this interpretation, section 9-310 impliedly denies priority to a nonpossessory lien.]

Michael G. Walsh, A Mechanics' Lien Primer
for the General Practitioner
37 No. 5 Prac. Law. 77 (July 1991)

Mechanics' liens are the bane of mortgage and construction lenders as well as property owners. For contractors, subcontractors, and real estate developers, on the other hand, a properly perfected mechanics' lien is often the only means they have for obtaining payment for a project. To competently represent any of these parties, you must therefore know the law of mechanics' liens. This knowledge is usually self-taught, since law school courses more often than not omit or gloss over this important subject.

This article will introduce you to the subject of mechanics' liens. Although the mechanics' lien act of each state is unique, mechanics' lien statutes share many similarities and reflect certain basic principles. The examples in this article are drawn from the mechanics' lien statutes of some of the more populous states: these will guide you in analyzing the mechanics' lien laws in your own state.

THE NATURE OF THE MECHANICS' LIEN

Unknown to common law, mechanics' liens are entirely statutory in origin and nature. Although mechanics' liens are creatures of state law, certain principles are common to most mechanics' lien statutes. Perhaps the most important principle to remember is that you must follow the letter of a mechanics' lien statute, no matter how overly technical or unreasonable those requirements may appear. Courts generally interpret these statutes strictly, and the slightest variance from what the statute requires may result in the court's striking the lien.

* * *

A mechanics' lien does not stem from the contract governing the erection or the repair of the structure, but rather from the use of the materials furnished and the labor expended by the contractor, subcontractor, or other professional. The lien is considered security for the underlying debt. A claim for a mechanics' lien is generally an action in rem in the nature of collateral security for the payment of the debt due for work done or materials furnished. Usually, enforcing the mechanics' lien is only one remedy available to the claimant. The claimant may also maintain a personal action to recover the underlying debt from the responsible party.   * * *

As a general rule, a mechanics' lien is created only when an owner of property * * * contracts for an improvement to the property that requires the furnishing of labor or materials. ***

Mechanics' lien statutes primarily protect certain named classes of professionals or tradesmen who furnish labor, materials, or both in connection with new construction or an improvement to existing property. * * * At a minimum, the protected groups include contractors, subcontractors, and materialmen.

PROPERTY ENCUMBERED BY THE LIEN

A properly perfected mechanics' lien usually encumbers property in addition to the structure on which the work was performed. Typically, the lien also encumbers the land on which the structure stands. * * * Note, however, that work performed on a structure sitting on a vast tract of land may not necessarily give rise to a lien encumbering the entire tract.

LABOR AND MATERIALS SUPPORTING A LIEN

Mechanics' lien laws typically protect claimants for the payment of debts owed them for the furnishing of labor or materials in connection with some sort of property improvement. Once again, closely review your state's lien law to determine what qualifies as lienable "labor" and "materials."

* * *

THE PRIORITY OF A MECHANICS' LIEN

A mechanics' lien is a mighty weapon in the claimant's battle to be paid for his work on a project, because it generally gets priority over conflicting encumbrances, such as judgment liens or mortgage liens. Some states grant the lien priority over conflicting liens notwithstanding that the lienable labor was performed or materials supplied after the competing liens were recorded.

For example, California law provides that mechanics' liens generally are preferred to any other lien, mortgage, deed of trust, or other encumbrance on the improvement and the site of the improvement that attach after the beginning of the work on the improvement. Moreover, the mechanics' lien takes priority over any other liens, regardless of when they attached, if the claimant had no notice of them, and if they were not recorded when the claimant began work on the improvement.

* * *

WAIVER OF THE LIEN

The potentially devastating consequences of a properly perfected mechanics' lien have led many property owners, mortgage lenders, and others to insist on lien waivers from the contractor and all subcontractors on a project before agreeing to finance, authorize, or participate in the project. The proliferation of lien waivers has prompted some states to refuse to enforce them.

* * *

RELEASING OR DISCHARGING THE LIEN

The attorney of an owner or other interested party who wishes to discharge a mechanics' lien should, of course, consult and follow the letter of the law in his jurisdiction when attempting to discharge a mechanics' lien.

Mechanics' lien statutes usually list a number of ways that a party--the claimant, the property owner, or one acting on the behalf of either--may discharge the lien. To illustrate, a state may permit the discharge of a mechanics' lien by:

--The entry by the claimant of satisfaction of the lien on the margin of the record of the lien or in a separate writing.

--The failure of the claimant to begin an action to enforce the lien within the time specified by the statute.

--The dismissal, with prejudice, of an action to enforce or foreclose the lien, or the entry of judgment that no lien exists.

--The claimant's willful inclusion in his claim of any labor, materials, or equipment that were not actually furnished for the property described in the claim.

--Depositing with the court a sum of money or posting a bond or other security.

Unless the statute provides that a particular action results in a discharge of the lien, the lien will be unaffected by that action. For example, the sale of the property on which the mechanics' lien attached normally has no effect on the lien.

ENFORCING THE LIEN

The usual way to enforce a mechanics' lien is to institute an action to enforce the claim, or, as it is stated in some states, to foreclose on the lien. Generally, the action is considered an in rem proceeding, not a personal action on the contract for the repair or improvement.   * * *

All states require mechanics' lien claimants to follow certain steps before bringing an action on the claim of lien. Typically, the claimant has to provide some type of preliminary notice to the property owner, to the contractor (if the claimant is not the contractor), and, in some states, to the construction lender as well.

After providing a preliminary notice to the parties as required by the statute, the claimant ordinarily:

--Has to record or file his claim of lien with a court official, such as the clerk of court, within a prescribed period of time following the completion of the work;

--Serve the owner with a written notice of the filing, or, if the owner's address is unknown, post a notice on the structure on which the work was performed; and

--File an affidavit or other proof of service of notice, or an acceptance of service.

In some states, a subcontractor may have to send an additional, preliminary notice to the property owner in some cases.

STATUTORY REQUIREMENTS STRICTLY ENFORCED

Courts will hold a lien claimant (and her attorney) strictly to the time limits found in the statute. They will also strictly enforce statutory requirements regarding the contents of the claim of lien. As always, there is no substitute for careful reading of, and compliance with, all statutory requirements.
   * * *

CONCLUSION

A mechanics' lien is a powerful weapon in the hands of a contractor, subcontractor, materialman, or other professional or tradesman whose claim for payment is denied. Since the lien is a purely statutory remedy, it goes without saying that you must become thoroughly familiar with the mechanics' lien statute in your state and consult that statute whenever you are confronted with an actual or potential mechanics' lien problem.

In gaining a good working knowledge of your lien law, be certain that you understand:

--Who can claim the lien;

--What types of services and materials are considered lienable;

--How to determine the amount of the lien;

--How to perfect the lien so that it will have priority over conflicting claims and liens;

--Whether and how a lien may be waived;

--How a lien may be discharged; and

--How the lien may be enforced.

Georgia's Liens For Mechanics And Materialmen
Ga. Code 44-14-360 et seq. (1993)

44-14-360 Definitions.

As used in this part, the term:

(1) "Contractor" means a contractor having privity of contract with the owner of the real estate.

(2) "Land surveyor" means the same as the definition thereof in Code Section 43-15-2.

(3) "Materials," in addition to including those items for which liens are already permitted under this part, means tools, appliances, machinery, or equipment used in making improvements to the real estate, to the extent of the reasonable value or the contracted rental price, whichever is greater, of such tools, appliances, machinery, or equipment.

(4) "Materialmen" means all persons furnishing the materials, tools, appliances, machinery, or equipment included in the definition of materials in paragraph (3) of this Code section.

(5) "Professional engineer" means the same as the definition thereof in Code Section 43-15-2.

(6) "Registered forester" means the same as the definition of such term in Code Section 12-6-41.

(7) "Registered land surveyors" and "registered professional engineers" means land surveyors or professional engineers who are registered as land surveyors or professional engineers under Chapter 15 of Title 43 at the time of performing, rendering, or furnishing services protected under this part.

(8) "Residential property" means single-family and two-family, three-family, and four-family residential real estate.

(9) "Subcontractor" means, but is not limited to, subcontractors having privity of contract with the contractor.

44-14-361 Creation of liens; property to which lien attaches.

(a) The following persons shall each have a special lien on the real estate, factories, railroads, or other property for which they furnish labor, services, or materials:

(1) All mechanics of every sort who have taken no personal security for work done and material furnished in building, repairing, or improving any real estate of their employers;

(2) All contractors, all subcontractors and all materialmen furnishing material to subcontractors, and all laborers furnishing labor to subcontractors, materialmen, and persons furnishing material for the improvement of real estate;

(3) All registered architects furnishing plans, drawings, designs, or other architectural services on or with respect to any real estate;

(4) All registered foresters performing or furnishing services on or with respect to any real estate;

(5) All registered land surveyors and registered professional engineers performing or furnishing services on or with respect to any real estate;

(6) All contractors, all subcontractors and materialmen furnishing material to subcontractors, and all laborers furnishing labor for subcontractors for building factories, furnishing material for factories, or furnishing machinery for factories;

(7) All machinists and manufacturers of machinery, including corporations engaged in such business, who may furnish or put up any mill or other machinery in any county or who may repair the same;

(8) All contractors to build railroads; and

(9) All suppliers furnishing rental tools, appliances, machinery, or equipment for the improvement of real estate.

(b) Each special lien specified in subsection (a) of this Code section may attach to the real estate for which the labor, services, or materials were furnished if they are furnished at instance of the owner, contractor, or some person acting for the owner or contractor.

44-14-361.1 How liens declared and created; record; commencement of action; notice; priorities; parties; limitation on aggregate amount of liens.

(a) To make good the liens specified in paragraphs (1) through (8) of subsection (a) of Code Section 44-14-361, they must be created and declared in accordance with the following provisions, and on failure of any of them the lien shall not be effective or enforceable:

(1) A substantial compliance by the party claiming the lien with his contract for building, repairing, or improving; for architectural services furnished; for registered forester services furnished or performed; for registered land surveying or registered professional engineering services furnished or performed; or for materials or machinery furnished or set up;

(2) The filing for record of his claim of lien within three months after the completion of the work, the furnishing of the architectural services, or the furnishing or performing of such surveying or engineering services or within three months after the material or machinery is furnished in the office of the clerk of the superior court of the county where the property is located, which claim shall be in substance as follows:

"A.B., a mechanic, contractor, subcontractor, materialman, machinist, manufacturer, registered architect, registered forester, registered land surveyor, registered professional engineer, or other person (as the case may be) claims a lien in the amount of (specify the amount claimed) on the house, factory, mill, machinery, or railroad (as the case may be) and the premises or real estate on which it is erected or built, of C.D. (describing the houses, premises, real estate, or railroad), for satisfaction of a claim which became due on (specify the date the claim was due) for building, repairing, improving, or furnishing material (or whatever the claim may be)."

At the time of filing for record of his claim of lien, the lien claimant shall send a copy of the claim of lien by registered or certified mail to the owner of the property or the contractor, as the agent of the owner;

(3) The commencement of an action for the recovery of the amount of his claim within 12 months from the time the same shall become due. In addition, within 14 days after filing such action, the party claiming the lien shall file a notice with the clerk of the superior court of the county wherein the subject lien was filed. The notice shall contain a caption referring to the then owner of the property against which the lien was filed and referring to a deed or other recorded instrument in the chain of title of the affected property. The notice shall be executed, under oath, by the party claiming the lien or by his attorney of record. The notice shall identify the court wherein the action is brought; the style and number of the action, including the names of all parties thereto; the date of the filing of the action; and the book and page number of the records of the county wherein the subject lien is recorded in the same manner in which liens specified in Code Section 44-14-361 are filed. The clerk of the superior court shall enter on the subject lien so referred to the book and page on which the notice is recorded and shall index such notice in the name of the then purported owner as shown by the caption contained in such notice. A separate lis pendens notice need not be filed with the commencement of this action; and

(4) In the event any contractor or subcontractor procuring material, architect's services, registered forester's services, registered land surveyor's services, or registered professional engineer's services, labor, or supplies for the building, repairing, or improving of any real estate, building, or other structure shall abscond or die or leave the state within 12 months from the date such services, labor, supplies, or material are furnished to him, so that personal jurisdiction cannot be obtained on the contractor or subcontractor in an action for the services, material, labor, or supplies, or if the contractor or subcontractor shall be adjudicated a bankrupt, or if, after the filing of an action, no final judgment can be obtained against him for the value of such material, services, labor, or supplies because of his death or adjudication in bankruptcy, then and in any of these events, the person or persons furnishing material, services, labor, and supplies shall be relieved of the necessity of filing an action or obtaining judgment against the contractor or subcontractor as a prerequisite to enforcing a lien against the property improved by the contractor or subcontractor. Subject to Code Section 44-14-361, the person or persons furnishing material, services, labor, and supplies may enforce the lien directly against the property so improved in an action against the owner thereof, if filed within 12 months from the time the lien becomes due,

with the judgment rendered in any such proceeding to be limited to a judgment in rem against the property improved and to impose no personal liability upon the owner of the property; provided, however, that in such action for recovery, the owner of the real estate improved, who has paid the agreed price or any part of same, may set up the payment in any action brought and prove by competent and relevant evidence that the payments were applied as provided by law, and no judgment shall be rendered against the property improved. Within 14 days after filing such action, the party claiming the lien shall file a notice with the clerk of the superior court of the county wherein the subject lien was filed. The notice shall contain a caption referring to the then owner of the property against which the lien was filed and referring to a deed or other recorded instrument in the chain of title of the affected property. The notice shall be executed, under oath, by the party claiming the lien or by his attorney of record. The notice shall identify the court wherein the action is brought; the style and number of the action, including the names of all parties thereto; the date of the filing of the action; and the book and page number of the records of the county wherein the subject lien is recorded in the same manner in which liens specified in Code Section 44-14-361 are filed. The clerk of the superior court shall enter on the subject lien so referred to the book and page on which the notice is recorded and shall index such notice in the name of the then purported owner as shown by the caption contained in such notice. A separate lis pendens notice need not be filed with the commencement of this action.

(b) As between themselves, the liens provided for in Code Section 44-14-361 shall rank according to the date filed; but all of the liens mentioned in this Code section for repairs, building, or furnishing materials or services, upon the same property, shall, as to each other, be of the same date when declared and filed for record within three months after the work is done or before that time.

(c) The liens specified in Code Section 44-14-361 shall be inferior to liens for taxes, to the general and special liens of laborers, to the general lien of landlords of rent when a distress warrant is issued out and levied, to claims for purchase money due persons who have only given bonds for titles, and to other general liens when actual notice of the general lien of landlords and others has been communicated before the work was done or materials or services furnished; but the liens provided for in Code Section 44-14-361 shall be superior to all other liens not excepted by this subsection.

(d) In any proceeding brought by any materialman, by any mechanic, by any laborer, by any subcontractor, or by any mechanic of any sort employed by any subcontractor or by any materialmen furnishing material to any subcontractor, or by any laborer furnishing labor to any subcontractor, to enforce such a lien, the contractor having a direct contractual relationship with the subcontractor shall not be a necessary party; but he may be made a party. In any proceedings brought by any mechanic employed by any subcontractor, by any materialmen furnishing material to any subcontractor, or by any laborer furnishing labor to any subcontractor, the subcontractor shall not be a necessary party; but he may be made a party. The contractor or subcontractor or both may intervene in the proceedings at any time before judgment for the purpose of resisting the establishment of the lien or of asserting against the lienor any claim of the contractor or subcontractor growing out of or related to the transaction upon which the asserted lien is based.

(e) In no event shall the aggregate amount of liens set up by Code Section 44-14-361 exceed the contract price of the improvements made or services performed.

44-14-361.2 *Dissolution of lien.*

(a) The special lien specified in subsection (a) of Code Section 44-14-361 shall be dissolved if the owner, purchaser from owner, or lender providing construction or purchase money or any other loan secured by real estate shows that:

(1) The lien has been waived in writing by lien claimant; or

(2) (A) They or any of them have obtained the sworn written statement of the contractor or person other than the owner at whose instance the labor, services, or materials were furnished, or the owner when conveying title in a bona fide sale or loan transaction, that the agreed price or reasonable value of the labor, services, or materials have been paid or waived in writing by the lien claimant; and

(B) When the sworn written statement was obtained or given as a part of a transaction:

(i) Involving a conveyance of title in a bona fide sale;

(ii) Involving a loan in which the real estate is to secure repayment of the loan; or

(iii) Where final disbursement of the contract price is made by the owner to the contractor

there was not of record, at the time of the settlement of the transaction a valid preliminary notice or claim of lien which had not been previously canceled, dissolved, or expired.

(b) As used in paragraph (2) of subsection (a) of this Code section, the term:

(1) "Person other than the owner" shall not include a subcontractor.

(2) "Final disbursement" of the contract price means payment of the agreed price between the owner and contractor for the improvements made upon the real estate or the reasonable value of the labor, services, and materials incorporated in the improvements upon the real estate and shall include payment of the balance of the contract price to an escrow agent.

44-14-361.3 *Preliminary notice of lien; form; notice to contractor; filing; necessity of preliminary notice.*

(a) Prior to filing a claim of lien, a person having a lien under paragraphs (1) through (8) of subsection (a) of Code Section 44-14-361 may at such person's option file a preliminary notice of lien rights. The preliminary notice of lien rights in order to be effective shall:

(1) Be filed with the clerk of superior court of the county in which the real estate is located within 30 days after the date a party delivered any materials or provided any labor or services for which a lien may be claimed;

(2) State the name, address, and telephone number of the potential lien claimant;

(3) State the name and address of the contractor or other person at whose instance the labor, services, or materials were furnished;

(4) State the name of the owner of the real estate and include a description sufficient to identify the real estate against which the lien is or may be claimed; and

(5) Include a general description of the labor, services, or materials furnished or to be furnished.

(b) A party filing a preliminary notice of lien rights except a contractor shall, within seven days of filing the notice, send by registered or certified mail a copy of the notice to the contractor on the property named in the notice or to the owner of the property. The lien claimant may rely on the building permit issued on the property for the name of the contractor.

(c) The clerk of each superior court shall maintain within the records of that office a record separate from all other real estate records in which preliminary notices specified in subsection (a) of this Code section and affidavits specified in subsection (c) of Code Section 44-14-361.4 shall be filed. Each such notice and affidavit shall be indexed under the name of the owner as contained in the preliminary notice. The clerk shall collect a filing fee of $5.00 for the filing of each preliminary notice.

(d) A person having a lien under paragraphs (1) through (8) of subsection (a) of Code Section 44-14-361 may enforce the lien without filing a preliminary notice of lien.

44-14-361.4 Cancellation or expiration of preliminary notice; demand for filing of claim of lien.

     * * *

44-14-361.5 Liens of persons without privity of contract.

(a) To make good the liens specified in paragraphs (1), (2), and (6) through (9) of subsection (a) of Code Section 44-14-361, any person having a right to a lien who does not have privity of contract with the contractor and is providing labor, services, or materials for the improvement of property shall, within 30 days from the filing of the Notice of Commencement or 30 days following the first delivery of labor, services, or materials to the property, whichever is later, give a written Notice to Contractor as set out in subsection (c) of this Code section to the owner or the agent of the owner and to the contractor for a project on which there has been filed with the clerk of the superior court a Notice of Commencement setting forth therein the information required in subsection (b) of this Code section.

(b) Not later than 15 days after the contractor physically commences work on the property, a Notice of Commencement shall be filed by the owner, the agent of the owner, or by the contractor with the clerk of the superior court in the county in which the project is located. A copy of the Notice of Commencement shall be posted on the project site. The Notice of Commencement shall include:

(1) The name, address, and telephone number of the contractor;

(2) The name and location of the project being constructed and the legal description of the property upon which the improvements are being made;

(3) The name and address of the true owner of the property;

(4) The name and address of the person other than the owner at whose instance the improvements are being made, if not the true owner of the property;

(5) The name and the address of the surety for the performance and payment bonds, if any; and

(6) The name and address of the construction lender, if any.

The owner, the agent of the owner, or the contractor shall be required to give a copy of the Notice of Commencement to any subcontractor, materialman, or person who makes a written request of the owner, the agent of the owner, or the contractor. Failure to give a copy of the Notice of Commencement within ten calendar days of receipt of the written request from the subcontractor, materialman, or person shall render the provision of this Code section inapplicable to the subcontractor, materialman, or person making the request.

(c) A Notice to Contractor shall be given to the owner or the agent of the owner and to the contractor at the addresses set forth in the Notice of Commencement setting forth:

(1) The name, address, and telephone number of the person providing labor, services, or materials;

(2) The name and address of each person at whose instance the labor, services, or materials are being furnished;

(3) The name of the project and location of the project set forth in the Notice of Commencement; and

(4) A description of the labor, services, or materials being provided and, if known, the contract price or anticipated value of the labor, services, or materials to be provided or the amount claimed to be due, if any.

(d) The failure to file a Notice of Commencement shall render the provisions of this Code section inapplicable. The filing of a Notice of Commencement shall not constitute a cloud, lien, or encumbrance upon or defect to the title of the real property described in the Notice of Commencement, nor shall it alter the aggregate amounts of liens allowable, nor shall it affect the priority of any loan in which the property is to secure payment of the loan filed before or after the Notice of Commencement, nor shall it affect the future advances under any such loan. Nothing contained in this Code section shall affect the provisions of Code Section 44-14-361.2.

(e) The clerk of each superior court shall file the Notice of Commencement within the records of that office and maintain an index separate from other real estate records or an index with the preliminary notices specified in subsection (a) of Code Section 44-14-361.3. Each such Notice of Commencement shall be indexed under the name of the true owner and the contractor as contained in the Notice of Commencement.

44-14-362   Cancellation of preliminary notice upon final payment; form of cancellation.

* * *

44-14-363   Special liens on personalty; notice; enforcement; priorities; maximum claims for storage; recordation.

(a) All mechanics of every sort shall have a special lien on personal property for work done and material furnished in manufacturing or repairing the personal property and for storage of the personal property after its manufacture or repair, which storage begins accruing after 30 days' written notice to the owner of the fact that storage is accruing and of the daily dollar amount thereof; and said notice shall be mailed to the owner by certified mail addressed to the owner at his last known address. Such special liens may be asserted by the retention of the personal property or the mechanic may surrender the personal property and give credit when the lien is enforced in accordance with Code Section 44-14-550; and if such special liens are asserted by retention of the personal property, the mechanic shall not be required to surrender the property to the holder of a subordinate security interest or lien. Such liens shall be superior to all liens except liens for taxes and, except as provided in subsection (2) of Code Section 11-9-310, such other liens as the mechanic may have had actual notice of before the work was done or material furnished.

(b) The maximum amount of storage that may be charged shall be $1.00 per day. Nothing contained in this Code section shall allow a fee for storage to be charged on any item with a fair market value in excess of $200.00. Storage charges pursuant to this Code section shall not apply to motor vehicles now or hereafter covered by Chapter 3 of Title 40 nor shall the storage fee be charged if there is a bona fide dispute between the customer and the mechanic as to the manner of repair or the charges for repair.

(c) (1) When possession of the property is surrendered to the debtor, the mechanic shall record his claim of lien within 90 days after the work is done and the material is furnished or, in the case of repairs made on or to aircraft or farm machinery, within 180 days after the work is done and the material is furnished. The claim of lien shall be recorded in the office of the clerk of the superior court of the county where the owner of the property resides. The claim shall be in substance as follows:

> "A.B., mechanic, claims a lien on _____ (here describe the property) of C.B., for work done, material furnished, and storage accruing (as the case may be) in manufacturing, repairing, and storing (as the case may be) the same."

(2) If possession of the personal property subject to a special lien as provided in this Code section is surrendered to the debtor and if such special lien is not preserved by recording the claim of lien as provided in paragraph (1) of this

subsection, the mechanic acquires a special lien on other personal property belonging to the debtor which comes into the possession of the mechanic, except that this sentence shall not apply to consumer goods which are being used by a consumer for personal, family, or household purposes or which have been bought by a consumer for use for personal, family, or household purposes. The special lien created by this paragraph shall be subject to the provisions of this Code section as to foreclosure and recording.

44-14-364 Release of lien on filing of bond; amount; real property bonds; schedule, affidavit, and recordation.
        * * *

44-14-365 Rights as to liens of partnerships, corporations, and associations made up of or employing registered architects, foresters, land surveyors, or professional engineers.
        * * *

44-14-366 Waiver of lien or claim upon bond in advance of furnishing labor, services, or materials void; interim waiver and release upon payment; unconditional waiver and release upon final payment; affidavit of nonpayment.
        * * *

44-14-513 Liens in favor of planing mills, etc.
        Proprietors of planing mills and other similar establishments shall have the same lien as provided in Code Section 44-14-363 for work done on material furnished by others; and, when they furnish material, they shall have the same liens provided for in Code Section 44-14-361 for materialmen. Proprietors of sawmills, when furnishing material for the improvement of real estate to purchasers from them for that purpose, shall be entitled to the lien provided for in Code Section 44-14-361, said lien to be governed by the rules laid down in Code Section 44-14-361 when the same are applicable.

Minnesota Veterinarians Lien
Minn. Stat. §514.92 (1993)

514.92. Veterinarian's lien
        Subdivision 1. Attachment. A licensed veterinarian who performs emergency veterinary services that cost more than $25 for animals at the request of the owner or a person in possession of the animals has a lien on the animals for the value of the services.   Veterinary services include emergency surgical procedures, administering vaccines, antisera, and antibiotics, and other veterinary medicines and treatments. Veterinary services also include services performed primarily to protect human health, prevent the spread of animal diseases, or to preserve the immediate health of an animal.
        Subd. 1a. Filing and perfecting lien. The veterinarian must file a lien statement in the appropriate filing office for a financing statement covering the animals to be

filed under section 336.9-401 by 180 days after the veterinary services are performed. The lien is perfected by properly filing the lien statement.

Subd. 2. Lien statement. (a) A lien statement must be verified and state:

(1) the name of the owner, or reputed owner, of the animals;

(2) the name of the person for whom the veterinary services were performed;

(3) the kind, number, and reasonable identification of animals treated;

(4) the dates when the veterinary services were begun and finished;

(5) the fraction of veterinary services performed which were primarily for the purpose of protecting human health, preventing the spread of animal diseases, or preserving the health of the animal or animals treated;

(6) the reasonable value of the veterinary services rendered, or the price contracted between the parties; and

(7) the name and address of the veterinarian claiming the lien.

(b) The provisions of section 514.74 relating to inaccuracies in lien statements apply to lien statements under this subdivision.

Subd. 3. Enforcement of lien. An action to enforce a perfected lien under this section must be started by one year after the date the last veterinary service was performed. A perfected lien may be enforced in the manner prescribed for security interests under sections 336.9-501 to 336.9-508.

Subd. 4. Priority of lien. (a) A perfected veterinarian's lien under this section has priority over other liens and security interests on the same animals to the extent the veterinary services were performed primarily for the purpose of protecting human health, preventing the spread of animal diseases, or preserving the health of the animal or animals treated.

(b) A veterinarian's lien has priority over a security interest perfected before the veterinarian's lien only if the security interest is perfected after March 22, 1986.

(c) The priority among veterinarian's liens filed under this section is according to the first lien filed.

Subd. 5. Termination. (a) A veterinarian's lien under this section terminates:

(1) 180 days after the last veterinarian's services was performed if a proper lien statement is not filed; or

(2) one year after the lien is filed if an action to enforce the lien has not been started.

(b) A filing officer may remove and destroy terminated lien statements in the same manner as provided for a financing statement under section 336.9-410.

Minnesota Agricultural Production Input Lien
Minn. Stat. §514.950 et seq. (1993)

514.950. Definitions

Subdivision 1. Applicability. The definitions in this section apply to sections 514.950, 514.952, 514.954, 514.956, 514.958, and 514.959.

Subd. 2. Agricultural chemical. "Agricultural chemical" means fertilizers or agricultural chemicals that are applied to crops or to land that is used for raising crops, including fertilizer material, plant amendment, plant food, and soil amendment as defined in section 18C.005, and pesticide and plant regulator as defined in section 18B.01.

Subd. 3. Agricultural production input. "Agricultural production input" means crop production inputs and livestock production inputs.

Subd. 4. Crop production input. "Crop production input" means agricultural chemicals, seeds, petroleum products, the custom application of agricultural chemicals and seeds, and labor used in preparing the land for planting, cultivating, growing, producing, harvesting, drying, and storing crops or crop products.

Subd. 5. Feed. "Feed" means commercial feeds, feed ingredients, mineral feeds, drugs, animal health products, or customer-formula feeds that are used for feeding livestock, including commercial feed as defined in section 25.33.

Subd. 6. Lender. "Lender" means a person in the business of lending money identified in a lien-notification statement.

Subd. 7. Letter of commitment. "Letter of commitment" means a binding, irrevocable and unconditional agreement by a lender to honor drafts or other demands for payment upon the supplier presenting invoices signed by the purchaser or other proof of delivery.

Subd. 8. Livestock production input. "Livestock production input" means feed and labor used in raising livestock.

Subd. 9. Person. "Person" means an individual or an organization as defined in section 336.1-201, paragraph (30).

Subd. 10. Petroleum product. "Petroleum product" means motor fuels and special fuels that are used in the production of crops and livestock, including petroleum products as defined in section 296.01, alcohol fuels, propane, lubes, and oils.

Subd. 11. Proceeds. "Proceeds" means proceeds as defined in section 336.9-306 except that if rights or duties are contingent upon express language in a financing statement, the requisite language may exist in a lien-notification statement under section 514.952, and includes farm products, inventory, warehouse receipts, and documents of title.

Subd. 12. Seed. "Seed" means agricultural seeds that are used to produce crops, including agricultural seed as defined in section 21.72.

Subd. 13. Supplier. "Supplier" means a person who furnishes agricultural production inputs.

514.952. Notification; lien-notification statement; effect of notification

Subdivision 1. Notification to lender. A supplier may notify a lender of an agricultural production input lien by providing a lien-notification statement to the lender in an envelope marked "IMPORTANT-LEGAL NOTICE". Delivery of the notice must be made by certified mail or another verifiable method.

Subd. 2. Lien-notification statement. The lien-notification statement must be in a form approved by the secretary of state and disclose the following:

(1) the name and business address of the lender that is to receive notification;

(2) the name and address of the supplier claiming the lien;

(3) a description and the date or anticipated date or dates of the transaction and the retail cost or anticipated costs of the agricultural production input;

(4) the name, residential address, and signature of the person to whom the agricultural production input was furnished;

(5) the name and residential address of the owner and a description of the real estate where the crops to which the lien attaches are growing or are to be grown; or for a lien attaching to livestock, the name and residential address of the owner of the livestock, the location where the livestock will be raised, and a description of the livestock; and

(6) a statement that products and proceeds of the crops or livestock are covered by the agricultural input lien.

Subd. 3. Response of lender to notification. (a) Within ten calendar days after receiving a lien-notification statement, the lender must respond to the supplier with either:

(1) a letter of commitment for part of all of the amount in the lien- notification statement; or

(2) a written refusal to issue a letter of commitment.

(b) A copy of the response must be mailed to the person for whom the financing was requested.

Subd. 4. Effect of response. (a) If a lender responds with a letter of commitment for part or all of the amount in the lien-notification statement, the supplier may not obtain a lien for the amount stated in the letter of commitment.

(b) If a lender responds with a refusal to provide a letter of commitment the rights of the lender and the supplier are not affected.

Subd. 5. Effect of no response. If a lender does not respond under subdivision 3 to the supplier within ten calendar days after receiving the lien-notification statement, a perfected agricultural production input lien corresponding to the lien-notification statement has priority over any security interest of the lender in the same crops or livestock or their proceeds for the lesser of:

(1) the amount stated in the lien-notification statement;

(2) the unpaid retail cost of the agricultural production input identified in the lien-notification statement; or

(3) for livestock any limitation in section 514.954, subdivision 2.

Subd. 6. Lien priority. An agricultural production input lien does not have priority over liens that arise under chapter 395 or 514, or over perfected security interests for unpaid rent for the land where the crops were grown. Agricultural production input liens are a security interest and have priority according to chapter 336, the uniform commercial code, except as provided in subdivision 5.

514.954. Lien attachment

Subdivision 1. Lien on crops. A supplier who furnishes crop production inputs has an agricultural input lien for the unpaid retail cost of the crop production inputs. The lien attaches to: (1) the existing crops upon the land where a furnished agricultural chemical was applied, or if crops are not planted, to the next production crop within 16 months following the last date on which the agricultural chemical was applied; (2) the crops produced from furnished seed; or (3) the crops produced, harvested, or processed using a furnished petroleum product. If the crops are grown on leased land and the lease provides for payment in crops, the lien does not attach to the lessor's portion of the crops. The lien continues in crop products and proceeds.

Subd. 2. Lien on livestock. A supplier who furnishes livestock production inputs has an agricultural production input lien for the unpaid retail cost of the livestock production input. The lien attaches to all livestock consuming the feed and continues in livestock products and proceeds. A perfected agricultural production input lien that attaches to livestock may not exceed the amount, if any, that the sales price of the livestock exceeds the greater of the fair market value of the livestock at the time the lien attaches or the acquisition price of the livestock.

Subd. 3. Time of attachment. An agricultural input lien attaches when the agricultural production inputs are furnished by the supplier to the purchaser.

514.956. Perfection of lien; filing

Subdivision 1. Perfection. To perfect an agricultural production input lien, the lien must attach and the supplier entitled to the lien must file a lien-notification statement with the appropriate filing office under section 336.9- 401 by six months after the last date that the agricultural production input was furnished.

Subd. 2. Failure to perfect. An agricultural production input lien that is not perfected has the priority of an unperfected security interest under section 336.9-312.

Subd. 3. Duties of filing officer. The filing officer shall enter on the lien-notification statement the time of day and date of filing. The filing officer shall file, amend, terminate, note the filing of a lien-notification statement, and charge the fee for filing under this section in the manner provided by section 336.9-403 for a financing statement, except that the social security number of an individual debtor or the Internal Revenue Service taxpayer identification number for a debtor other than an individual is not required. A lien-notification statement is void and may be removed from the filing system 18 months after the date of filing. The lien-notification statement may be physically destroyed after 30 months from the date of filing.

Subd. 4. Rules. The secretary of state shall adopt rules for the filing, amending, termination, and removal of lien-notification statements.

514.958. Enforcement of lien

The holder of an agricultural production input lien may enforce the lien in the manner provided in sections 336.9-501 to 336.9-508 subject to section 550.17. For enforcement of the lien, the lienholder is the secured party and the person for whom the agricultural production input was furnished is the debtor, and each has the respective rights and duties of a secured party and a debtor under sections 336.9-501 to 336.9-508. If a right or duty under sections 336.9-501 to 336.9-508 is contingent upon the existence of express language in a security agreement or may be waived by express language in a security agreement, the requisite language does not exist.

514.959. Enforcement actions; lien extinguished

An action to enforce an agricultural production input lien may be brought in district court in a county where some part of the crop or livestock is located after the lien is perfected. A lien-notification statement may be amended, except the amount demanded, by leave of the court in the furtherance of justice. An agricultural production input lien is extinguished if an action to enforce the lien is not brought within 18 months after the date the lien- notification statement is filed.

Notes And Problems

1. The Georgia statutes distinguish between materialmen (44-14-360(4)) and mechanics (44-14-363). What's the difference? Do the State of Georgia and Attorney Michael Walsh disagree about the meaning of "mechanic"?

2. Suppose a local garage works on your car.

    a. Could the garage take an Article 9 security interest in the car or other property to secure the value of its parts and work?

    b. Suppose there's no security interest.
        i.   Can the garage keep the car if you don't pay?
        ii.   Can they let you take it on condition you pay later and come and get it if you don't pay?
        iii. What happens if GMAC's got a security interest in the car to secure the purchase price?
        iv.   What happens if a local bank has a security interest in the car that secures an unrelated debt?.

    c. Suppose the car is leased.
        i.   Can the local garage or anyone else acquire a security interest?
        ii. Can the garage acquire a lien under a law such as Georgia's 44-14-363?

3. A veterinarian who works on a farmer's cattle in Minnesota is certainly entitled to a lien under the Veterinarians Lien law, but she might also fit within the terms of the Ag Input Lien.

    a. Under which law would she be better off?

    b. Would it be possible (legally? politically?) to widen the Vet Lien law to cover not only veterinarians but also anybody who supplies ag inputs of any kind? (The effect would be to make the Ag Input Lien unnecessary.)

    c. Would it be possible (legally? politically?) to widen the priority of a vet lien by giving it priority over every perfected security interest without regard to when the security interest was created or perfected?

    d. Both Minnesota lien statutes incorporate pieces of U.C.C. Article 9. The Minnesota liens, however, are not Article 9 security interests. What's the connection between the lien laws and Article 9?

    e. A vet or ag input supplier could easily acquire an Article 9 security interest in the debtor's property to secure the price of the vet's or supplier's goods and services. Why are these Minnesota statutory liens even necessary?

4. Your client is acquiring a building in Atlanta. Does she need to know whether there are any construction liens on the building? Why? How can you determine whether there are any such liens?

5. First Bank loaned $10 million for construction of the new East Lake Shopping Center in Athens, Georgia. The Bank filed a construction mortgage on April 2. The day before, on April 1, FlatTop Co. had begun bulldozing the building site pursuant to a contract with the general contractor that required FlatTop to clear and level the site. If FlatTop is not paid for its services:

    a. Can FlatTop assert a construction lien?

    b. If FlatTop can assert a construction lien, can the owner of the shopping center property successfully defend on the basis that it paid the general contractor everything due under the construction contract?

    c. How will a construction lien in FlatTop's favor rank in relation to First Bank's mortgage?

6. Suppose First Bank recorded its mortgage before any work commenced on the shopping center; so the construction liens of FlatTop and other unpaid suppliers are subordinate to the mortgage, at least to the extent of advances previously made by First Bank. Are the lienors also subordinate to advances the Bank thereafter makes? In many states the answer depends on whether the later advances are optional or pursuant to a commitment. An optional advance under a construction loan, if made by a lender having actual notice of intervening liens, will generally be subordinate to them. G. Nelson & D. Whitman, REAL ESTATE FINANCE LAW §12.6 & §12.7 (3dd ed. 1994).

7. "The mechanics' lien, the traditional refuge of unpaid subcontractors and suppliers, is often useless to them in construction projects. Increasingly construction lenders have learned to record their mortgages before any work is done, and to avoid optional advances; under these circumstances the mechanics' lien claimants are almost certain to be subordinate to the construction loan, and its foreclosure will seldom produce any surplus for them. An alternative source of payment to the subcontractors and suppliers is the payment bond, but its use is generally confined to large commercial projects and those being built with public funds. In residential subdivisions and small apartment projects, neither the lien nor the bind is likely to be available. * * * At least ten states have attempted to provide another route to the unpaid subcontractors and suppliers: the stop notice. In essence, it is a right to make and enforce a claim against the construction lender (or in some states, the owner) for a portion of the undisbursed construction lien proceeds, if any. It is somewhat like a garnishment of the loan funds, although the analogy is not entirely accurate; a stop notice may be effectively filed, for example, even if the borrower-developer has defaulted and is therefore not entitled to any further construction draws. Obviously the stop notice is effective only if some funds remain in the lender's or owner's own hands. The remedy is statutory, and specific time requirements must be met; often the claimant must file a bond to indemnify the lender against damages which might result from a wrongful claim. The lender may simply pay the claim and discharge the stop notice, but if the claim is disputed or there are insufficient funds to pay all stop notice claims, litigation may be necessary." G. Nelson & D. Whitman, REAL ESTATE FINANCE LAW §12.6 at 910-12 (3d ed. 1994).

ooooo

Citizens Fidelity Bank & Trust Co. v. Fenton Rigging Co.
Court of Appeals of Kentucky, 1975
522 S.W.2d 862

Catinna, Commissioner. The Jefferson Circuit Court, Chancery Branch, First Division, adjudged that a mechanic's lien filed by Fenton Rigging Company was a superior lien to one asserted by Citizens Fidelity Bank and Trust Company under a security agreement executed to it by Hughes Erecting and Rigging Company, Inc. The bank appeals.

Hughes Company contracted with International Harvester Company to perform certain work on its property located in Louisville, consisting primarily of the removal of heavy equipment and the relocating and installing of steel floors. The contract price was $18,737.50. Hughes Company contracted a major portion of the projected work to Fenton, thereby becoming indebted to it in the sum of $10,399.50.

In April 1970 Hughes Company established a line of credit with Citizens and executed a financing statement covering its accounts receivable, primarily those to become due from Harvester pursuant to the terms of the contract between Hughes Company and Harvester. On May 27, 1970, a security agreement was executed to Citizens by which it acquired a security interest in the accounts receivable. After execution of the financing statement and security agreement, Citizens advanced Hughes Company certain sums of money including the sum of $7,000 represented by a note which was not paid.

Fenton completed its work for Hughes on May 18, 1970, and on July 28, 1970, filed a mechanic's lien pursuant to KRS 376.010 on Harvester's property on Crittenden Drive in Louisville to secure the amount due it as a subcontractor for Hughes Company, Fenton filed this action against Hughes and Harvester, demanding judgment against Harvester for $10,399.50, and directing Harvester to pay Fenton from the proceeds of monies becoming due to Hughes Company under the contract, or for a judgment enforcing its mechanic's lien against the Harvester property. Citizens intervened, asserting a prior lien on any sums which might be due Hughes as a result of its contract with Harvester to secure the payment of the $7,000 note. Harvester admitted that it was indebted under the Hughes Company contract in the sum of $10,399.50 (later determined to be $11,720).

The trial court found that Fenton had a mechanic's lien on the property of Harvester to secure it in the payment of sums due from Hughes Company, which lien was prior to the lien asserted by Citizens under its security agreement upon any accounts due from Harvester pursuant to the terms of its contract with Hughes. The court also adjudged that there be paid to Harvester's attorneys, Ogden, Robertson, and Marshall, fees in the amount of $200 for services rendered in the proceeding.

Upon this appeal, Citizens claims that the lien acquired by it upon the accounts receivable of Hughes by reason of the recorded financing statement and security agreement was prior to that asserted by Fenton.

KRS 355.9-101 through 355.9-507, Secured Transactions, detail the procedure parties must follow in order to obtain a lien upon accounts receivable. The problem area we here encounter concerns a determination of what constitutes the accounts receivable upon which Citizens had a lien by reason of its security agreement. KRS 355.9-106 defines "account" as meaning any right to payment for goods sold or leased or services rendered which is not evidenced by any instrument or chattel paper. "Contract right" is defined as meaning any right to payment under a contract not yet earned by performance and not evidenced by any instrument or chattel paper. The line of credit established by Hughes Company with Citizens was therefore secured by its "contract right" arising out of the Harvester agreement. The security agreement executed to Citizens granted a lien on all sums accruing and payable to Hughes Company in the future; however, it was essential that such future accruals be payable to Hughes Company and not to someone else.

When Hughes Company failed to pay Fenton as required by their agreement and Fenton filed its mechanic's lien upon Harvester's property to secure it in the payment of that amount, Harvester became directly obligated to pay Fenton sums claimed by it for the purpose of discharging the debt of Hughes and obtaining a release of the lien asserted by Fenton on its real property and equipment. Fenton's services were performed as a part of the Hughes' contract with Harvester, and, consequently, when Harvester became obligated to pay Fenton sums which otherwise would have been due Hughes Company under the contract, they ceased to be a part of Hughes' "contract right" and therefore did not become accounts receivable covered by the security agreement executed by Hughes to Citizens.

As a consequence of Harvester's becoming primarily liable to Fenton for services performed, the amounts due did not become subject to the lien of Citizens. Harvester was, therefore, obligated to Fenton first for the amount due it and, second, to Hughes Company for the balance that might be due under the contract, and upon that balance Citizens had a lien to secure it in the payment of the note executed by Hughes Company to the bank.

We have held in the past that the statutory lien of KRS 376.010 is restricted to land, buildings, and improvements, and will not encumber personal property or funds belonging to the party against whom the lien is asserted. There are other jurisdictions which have construed the Commercial Code and particularly Section 9-310 (KRS 355.9-310) so that a validly filed mechanic's lien becomes prior to any lien created by the Code regardless of the fact that it is confined to personal property and accounts receivable or contract rights. Cf. National Bank of Detroit v. Eames and Brown, 50 Mich.App. 447, 213 N.W.2d 573 (1973); Corbin Deposit Bank v. King, Ky., 384 S.W.2d 302 (1964).

Citizens also asserts that it was error to allow an attorney's fee to the lawyers representing Harvester. However, the attorneys were not made parties to this appeal; therefore, the court cannot consider this claimed error.

The judgment is affirmed.

All concur.

3. Federal Tax Lien

Sections 6321 through 6323 of the Internal Revenue Code are commonly referred to as the Federal Tax Lien Act. A lawyer or law student should look to these provisions for answers to the following questions:

- When does a federal tax lien arise
- What property is covered by a federal tax lien
- What are the rights of a third party who buys property from the taxpayer after a federal tax lien arises
- What are the rights of the taxpayer's other creditors.

a. When Does the Federal Tax Lien Arise

Section 6321 sets out three requirements for the creation of a federal tax lien:

✓ IRS' assessment of the tax liability; and
✓ IRS' demand for payment of this tax liability;
✓ The taxpayer's failure to pay.

The next section, section 6322, provides that a tax lien dates from the time of assessment. It is thus necessary to know when assessment occurs. Although assessment is only the first of three requirements for creating a tax lien, section 6322 makes the date of assessment important to the taxpayer, buyers from the taxpayer, and creditors of the taxpayer.

The date of assessment depends on whether the taxpayer acknowledged the liability in his return. When a person files a return acknowledging unpaid taxes, assessment simply involves noting the liability on a list in the office of the district director of the IRS, section 6203. If, for example, D sends the IRS a check for $3,000 along with her return that shows her tax liability is $7,000, assessment of the $4,000 liability would occur almost immediately after the return is received.

If the tax liability is not acknowledged on the return, considerably more time will elapse between the filing the return and assessment. If the tax liability is understated on the return, the deficiency must be discovered through an audit of the return. The taxpayer then must be notified and given the opportunity to respond to the finding of a deficiency. The actual assessment of the tax deficiency cannot be made until the taxpayer either acquiesces in the adjustment of his tax liability or exhausts his opportunities for administrative review.

Section 6303 requires that, after assessment, "as soon as practicable," the taxpayer be given notice, stating the amount of the tax liability and demanding payment. The notice form that the IRS uses gives the taxpayer ten days to make payment.

Remember that while creation of the lien requires (1) assessment, (2) demand, and (3) failure to pay, the lien relates back to the time of the assessment. Remember also that the creation of the lien does not require recordation or other public notice of the lien.

A valid tax lien arises without the federal government filing notice thereof in a public recordation system. It is quite possible that a taxpayer will not know that a tax lien has been imposed upon its property, that buyers from the taxpayer will not know, that other creditors of the taxpayer will not know. An unfiled federal tax lien is valid against the taxpayer and *most* third parties. Later we explain which third parties are protected from unfiled federal tax liens.

b. What Property is Covered By a Federal Tax Lien

Section 6321 describes the property covered by a federal tax lien: "All property and rights to property, whether real or personal, belonging to such person." "All" in this context truly means all. The federal tax lien reaches not only all the property that the debtor has an interest in as of the time of assessment but also all property interests later acquired. If the taxes are assessed in June of 1984 and the taxpayer acquires Greenacre in August of 1984, the tax lien would encumber Greenacre. Greenacre would be subject to the tax lien even if Greenacre was the debtor's homestead and exempt under state exemption laws. The tax lien reaches that part of the taxpayer's property that would otherwise be protected by state law from the reach of creditors. The Internal Revenue Code contains its own, nominal exemption provisions in section 6334.

c. What Are the Rights of a Third Party Who Buys
Property From the Taxpayer After the Tax Lien Arises

What is the impact of a federal tax lien on a buyer from the taxpayer? For example, X claims that she is entitled to Greenacre because she bought it from D for $10,000. The IRS claims that it is entitled to Greenacre because D owes $10,000 in back taxes and the IRS has a tax lien.

The facts creating such a buyer/IRS priority contest will fit into one of the three patterns:

1. The sale by the taxpayer occurred before creation of the tax lien, i.e. before tax assessment;
2. The sale by the taxpayer occurred after creation of the tax lien but before filing of the federal tax lien;
3. The sale by the taxpayer occurred after creation and filing of the federal tax lien.

Clearly, the purchaser prevails in the first situation. Sections 6321 provides for a tax lien on property of the taxpayer. If X buys Greenacre from the taxpayer before tax assessment, then Greenacre is not "property *** belonging to such person" at the time the lien arises.

It is equally clear that buyers prevail in the second situation. Section 6323 is in part a recording statute; subsection (f) of section 6323 provides for recording the federal tax lien in the state record systems. Section 6323(a) protects "purchasers" from unrecorded tax liens; an unfiled federal tax lien is not valid as against a "purchaser." If X paid "adequate and full consideration," he is a purchaser, as defined in section 6323(f)(6). If X paid or became legally obligated to pay adequate and full consideration before the federal tax lien was filed, he takes Greenacre free from the federal tax lien. X would be protected by section 6323(a) even if he knew of the unfiled federal tax lien.

Some buyers prevail even over filed federal tax liens. Under section 6323(b) certain third parties take free from a federal tax lien that was filed prior to the sale. For example, section 6323(b)(3) protects purchasers of personal property at retail. If B buys living room furniture from D Furniture Store Inc. the government can not look to this furniture to satisfy its tax claim against D Furniture Store Inc. even though the government filed its federal tax lien.

A filed federal tax lien is, however, effective against most subsequent buyers from the taxpayer. If X buys Greenacre from D after the IRS files its federal tax lien, the IRS will have priority over X.

d. What Are the Rights of the Taxpayer's Other Creditors

A person who is not paying his federal taxes is probably not paying his non-governmental creditors and probably lacks sufficient assets to pay all claims against him. Which claims have priority? Remember, under section 6322, the tax lien dates from the time that the taxes were assessed. What if private creditors obtained liens on the debtor's property before the time that the taxes were assessed? Will all such earlier in time liens have priority or will earlier in time liens take priority over the IRS' tax lien only if they are "choate"?

United States v. Security Trust & Sav. Bank, 340 U.S. 47, 71 S.Ct. 111 (1950), was the first case to apply the "choate lien doctrine" to a priority problem under the Federal Tax Lien Act. *Security Trust* involved the relative priority of a federal tax lien and an attachment lien. Since an attachment lien is subject to contingencies that might terminate its enforceability, the lien was deemed inchoate and therefore ineffective against the subsequently arising federal tax lien.

Security Trust relied on choateness cases decided under Revised Statutes (R.S.) 3466. This federal law gives priority to federal claims in certain situations, such as when an insolvent debtor makes an assignment of property or her estate is insolvent. Subsequent federal tax lien cases have followed this practice. The Supreme Court, however, has yet to find a competing lien choate in a case arising under section

3466. On the other hand, there are several Supreme Court federal tax lien cases in which the competing lien was held to be choate.

In *Crest Finance Co. v. United States*, 368 U.S. 347, 82 S.Ct. 382 (1961), the Supreme Court accepted the government's concession that the competing lien was choate. The lien there involved was an assignment of accounts; the accounts were earned and due prior to the time that the federal tax lien attached.

In both *United States v. City of New Britain*, 347 U.S. 81, 74 S.Ct. 367 (1954) and *United States v. Vermont*, 377 U.S. 351, 84 S.Ct. 1267 (1964), prior statutory liens on personal property were held choate. The liens involved in these tax lien cases are difficult to distinguish from the liens held *inchoate* in federal priority cases such as *United States v. Gilbert Associates, Inc.*, supra. In neither *New Britain* nor *Vermont* was the taxpayer divested of title or possession. The Court in *Vermont* distinguished *Gilbert* saying "different standards apply where the United States' claim is based on a tax lien arising under §§6321 and 6322."

To summarize, case law indicates that (1) a private creditor will have priority over the IRS if its lien was choate before the federal taxes were assessed, and (2) the choateness standard in federal tax lien act cases is different from the choateness standard in federal priority cases.

Since 1966, section 6323(a) of the Federal Tax Lien Act indicates that a private creditor will have priority over the IRS if it obtains a security interest, a mechanics lien, or a judgment lien before the federal tax lien is filed.

Like a lot of statutes, the Federal Tax Lien Act uses words differently than you or we ordinarily use them. For example, section 6323(a) gives a "holder of a security interest" priority over an unfiled federal tax lien. Section 6323(h) defines "security interest" so as to limit the protection of section 6323(a) to creditors with *perfected* security interests.[56]

---

[56] Under section 6323(h), "security interest" includes consensual liens on both personal property or real property. The security interest is deemed to exist only after it is valid under local law against a "judgment lien." This was obviously intended to limit section 6323(a)'s protection to perfected security interests and recorded mortgages.

The use of the term "judgment lien" was unfortunate. Under the laws of most states, a judgment lien does not reach personal property, and therefore even an unperfected UCC security interest would be superior to a judgment lien and thus superior to an unfiled federal tax lien. Such a result would be inconsistent with prior law. There is no indication that Congress intended to change the law and accord priority to unperfected security interests. Instead, it is more likely that Congress did not understand the difference between "judgment lien" and "judicial lien." Most courts read the term "judgment lien" in section 6323(h) as including other types of judicial liens so

Section 6323(a) also provides that a "judgment lien creditor" takes priority over an unfiled federal tax lien. There is no statutory definition of a "judgment lien creditor." The term is, however, defined in Treasury Regulation section 301.6323(h)-1(g) in a way that includes all post-judgment *judicial* liens and execution liens as well as judgment liens.[1]

Section 6323(a)'s protection of a judgment lien creditor from an unfiled federal tax lien raises the question of the relationship between section 6323(a) and the *choateness doctrine*. It should still be clear that a judgment lien is not choate. [A judgment lien reaches all of the debtor's real property in the county, now owned or later acquired; a judgment lien is thus not sufficiently specific as to property to meet the requirements of the common law choateness doctrine.] What is not at all clear is the relationship between section 6323(a) and the choateness doctrine.

The Federal Tax Lien Act nowhere mentions the choateness doctrine. To what extent does section 6323(a) displace the choateness doctrine?

Most authorities suggest that if a creditor comes under section 6323(a), it does not also have to satisfy the choateness requirement. For example, in *Aetna Ins. Co. v. Texas Thermal Ind.*, 591 F.2d 1035, 1038 (5th Cir. 1979), a security interest v. tax lien case, the court stated, "[W]hatever role the "choateness' rule of federal common law may play in other contexts, it has been supplanted by the provisions of section 6323 with respect to tax lien priority questions as to which the statute provides an unambiguous federal law answer." There are, however, cases to the contrary.

The following hypotheticals illustrate the application of section 6323(a):

> On January 10, a federal tax lien arises. February 2, E obtains a judgment against the taxpayer, obtains a writ of execution, and causes the sheriff to levy on personal property of the taxpayer. March 3, IRS files its federal tax lien in accordance with section 6323(f).

---

that only perfected security interests qualify for the protection of section 6323(a).

[1]   Remember that a "judgment lien" is a particular kind of judicial lien. Under the laws of most states, a judgment lien is obtaining by docketing a judgment in the real property record system and only reaches real property. Thus if the term "judgment lien creditor" in section 6323(a) were given its usual meaning, a judgment creditor who obtained a judgment lien on real property by docketing its judgment would take priority over an unfiled federal tax lien while a judgment creditor who obtained an execution lien on personal property by causing the issuance of a writ of execution and the levy on the debtor's property would not take priority over an unfiled federal tax lien.

E's execution lien would have priority (assuming that the term "judg-ment lien creditor" in section 6323(a) is given the meaning suggested in the Treasury Regulation.)

> On March 3, a federal tax lien arises. April 4, J obtains a judgment against the taxpayer and dockets its judgment in a county in which the taxpayer owns real property. May 5, IRS files its federal tax lien in accordance with section 6323(f).

J's judgment lien would have priority (assuming that a creditor who satisfies the requirements of section 6323(a) does not also have to sat-isfy a choateness test.)

> January 10, a federal tax lien arises. February 2, S makes a secured loan to the taxpayer and perfects its security interest. March 3, IRS files its federal tax lien in accordance with section 6323(f).

S's security interest would have priority.

> April 4, a federal tax lien arises. May 5, X makes a secured loan to the taxpayer but neglects to file a financing statement or otherwise perfect its lien. June 6, IRS files its federal tax lien in accordance with section 6323(f).

IRS would have priority. X did not obtain a security interest *as de-fined in the federal tax lien act* prior to federal tax lien filing.

e. Priority of floating liens

Article 9 security interests are often "floating liens." Security agreements commonly contain after-acquired property clauses such as "This debt is secured by all of the debtor's inventory, now owned or hereafter acquired," or future advances clauses such as "This collat-eral secures all of the debtor's debts to the secured party, whenever incurred."

Section 6323(c) governs the extent to which the priority enjoyed by a secured party extends to property acquired by the taxpayer after the federal tax lien filing. Section 6323(c) imposes the following limitations:

1. The secured party must have obtained and perfected its security interest prior to the filing of the federal tax lien.
2. The collateral must be commercial financing security, i.e., accounts, chattel paper, or inventory not equipment.
3. The property must have been acquired within 45 days of the federal tax lien filing.

Assume for example that:

* January 10, S lends D $100,000 and obtains and perfects a security interest in all of D's present or future inventory.
* February 2, federal tax lien arises.
* March 3, federal tax lien is filed.
* April 4, D acquires additional inventory.

S's priority extends to the April 4 inventory. S's $100,000 claim must be satisfied in full before IRS has any rights in any of D's inventory. Sections 6323(c) and (d) both extend the secured party's priority to future advances in certain situations. Under both,

✓ The secured party must have obtained and perfected its security interest prior to the filing of the federal tax lien.
✓ The extension of credit must have occurred within 45 days of the federal tax lien filing *or* before the creditor obtained knowledge of the federal tax lien filing, whichever first occurs.[56]

Note, however, that section 6323(c) is limited to "commercial financing security" *but* section 6323(d) is *not*. Assume for example that:

* January 10, S lends D $100,000 and obtains and perfects a security interest in D's *equipment*.
* February 2, federal tax lien arises.
* March 3, federal tax lien is filed.
* April 4, S lends D an additional $40,000.

S's priority would extend to the April 4 loan unless S on April 4 knew of the federal tax lien filing. In other words, S must be paid $140,000 before IRS has rights to D's equipment.

---

[56] There is no time limitation on future advances made pursuant to an "obligatory disbursement agreement" as defined in section 6323(c)(4).

United States v. McDermott
United States Supreme Court, 1993
___ U.S. ___, 113 S.Ct. 1526, 123 L.Ed.2d 128

Justice Scalia delivered the opinion of the Court.

We granted certiorari to resolve the competing priorities of a federal tax lien and a private creditor's judgment lien as to a delinquent taxpayer's after-acquired real property.

I

On December 9, 1986 the United States assessed Mr. and Mrs. McDermott for unpaid federal taxes due for the tax years 1977 through 1981. Upon that assessment, the law created a lien in favor of the United States on all real and personal property belonging to the McDermotts, 26 U.S.C. §§6321 and 6322, including after-acquired property, Glass City Bank v. United States, 326 U.S. 265, 66 S.Ct. 108, 90 L.Ed. 56 (1945). Pursuant to 26 U.S.C. §6323(a), however, that lien could "not be valid as against any purchaser, holder of a security interest, mechanic's lienor, or *judgment lien creditor* until notice thereof ... has been filed." (Emphasis added.) The United States did not file this lien in the Salt Lake County Recorder's Office until September 9, 1987. Before that occurred, however--specifically, on July 6, 1987--Zions First National Bank, N.A., docketed with the Salt Lake County Clerk a state-court judgment it had won against the McDermotts. Under Utah law, that created a judgment lien on all of the McDermotts' real property in Salt Lake County, "owned ... at the time or ... thereafter acquired during the existence of said lien." Utah Code Ann. §78-22-1 (1953).

On September 23, 1987 the McDermotts acquired title to certain real property in Salt Lake County. To facilitate later sale of that property, the parties entered into an escrow agreement whereby the United States and the Bank released their claims to the real property itself but reserved their rights to the cash proceeds of the sale, based on their priorities in the property as of September 23, 1987. Pursuant to the escrow agreement, the McDermotts brought this interpleader action in state court to establish which lien was entitled to priority; the United States removed to the United States District Court for the District of Utah.

On cross-motions for partial summary judgment, the District Court awarded priority to the Bank's judgment lien. The United States Court of Appeals for the Tenth Circuit affirmed. McDermott v. Zions First Nat'l Bank, N.A., 945 F.2d 1475 (1991). We granted certiorari.

II

Federal tax liens do not automatically have priority over all other liens. Absent provision to the contrary, priority for purposes of federal law is governed by the common-law principle that "'the first in time is the first in right.'" United States v. New Britain, 347 U.S. 81, 85, 74 S.Ct. 367, 370, 98 L.Ed. 520 (1954); cf. Rankin & Schatzell v. Scott, 12 Wheat. 177, 179, 6 L.Ed. 592 (1827)

(Marshall, C.J.). For purposes of applying that doctrine in the present case--in which the competing state lien (that of a judgment creditor) benefits from the provision of §6323(a) that the federal lien shall "not be valid ... until notice thereof ... has been filed"--we must deem the United States' lien to have commenced no sooner than the filing of notice. As for the Bank's lien: our cases deem a competing state lien to be in existence for "first in time" purposes only when it has been "perfected" in the sense that "the identity of the lienor, *the property subject to the lien*, and the amount of the lien are established." United States v. New Britain, 347 U.S., at 84, 74 S.Ct., at 369 (emphasis added); see also id., at 86, 74 S.Ct., at 370; United States v. Pioneer American Ins. Co., 374 U.S. 84, 83 S.Ct. 1651, 10 L.Ed.2d 770 (1963).

The first question we must answer, then, is whether the Bank's judgment lien was perfected in this sense before the United States filed its tax lien on September 9, 1987. If so, that is the end of the matter; the Bank's lien prevails. The Court of Appeals was of the view that this question was answered (or rendered irrelevant) by our decision in United States v. Vermont, 377 U.S. 351, 84 S.Ct. 1267, 12 L.Ed.2d 370 (1964), which it took to "stan[d] for the proposition that a non-contingent ... lien on all of a person's real property, perfected prior to the federal tax lien, will take priority over the federal lien, regardless of whether after-acquired property is involved."[1] 945 F.2d, at 1480. That is too expansive a reading. Our opinion in *Vermont* gives no indication that the property at issue had become subject to the state lien only by application of an after-acquired-property clause to property that the debtor acquired after the federal lien arose. To the contrary, the opinion says that the state lien met (presumably at the critical time when the federal lien arose) "the test laid down in New Britain that ... 'the property subject to the lien ... [be] established.' " 377 U.S., at 358, 84 S.Ct., at 1271 (citation omitted).[2] The argument of the United States that we rejected in *Vermont* was the contention that a state lien is not perfected within the meaning of New Britain if it "attach[es] to *all* of the taxpayer's property," rather than "to

---

[1]   As our later discussion will show, we think it contradictory to say that the state lien was "perfected" before the federal lien was filed, insofar as it applies to after-acquired property not acquired by the debtor until after the federal lien was filed. The Court of Appeals was evidently using the term "perfected" (as the Bank would) in a sense not requiring attachment of the lien to the property in question; our discussion of the Court of Appeals' opinion assumes that usage.

[2]   The dissent cannot both grant the assumption "that the debtor in Vermont acquired its interest in the bank account before the federal lien arose," post, * * *, and contend that "the debtor's interest in the bank account ... could have been uncertain or indefinite from the creditors' perspective." In the same footnote, the dissent misdescribes the "critical argument that we rejected" in Vermont. It was not that "the State's claim could not be superior unless the account had been 'specifically identified' as property subject to the State's lien," but rather that the State's claim could not be superior unless it had "*attach[ed]* to specifically identified portions of that property," United States v. Vermont, 377 U.S. 351, 355, 84 S.Ct. 1267, 1269, 12 L.Ed.2d 370 (1964) (emphasis added).

specifically identified portions of that property." 377 U.S., at 355, 84 S.Ct., at 1269 (emphasis added).[1] We did not consider, and the facts as recited did not implicate, the quite different argument made by the United States in the present case: that a lien in after-acquired property is not "perfected" as to property yet to be acquired.

The Bank argues that, as of July 6, 1987, the date it docketed its judgment lien, the lien was "perfected as to all real property then and thereafter owned by" the McDermotts, since "[n]othing further was required of [the Bank] to attach the non-contingent lien on after-acquired property." Brief for Respondents 21. That reflects an unusual notion of what it takes to "perfect" a lien.[2] Under the Uniform Commercial Code, for example, a security interest in after-acquired property is generally not considered perfected when the financing statement is filed, but only when the security interest has attached to particular property upon the debtor's acquisition of that property. §§9-203(1) and (2), 3 U.L.A. 363 (1992); §9-303(1), 3A U.L.A. 117 (1992). And attachment to particular property was also an element of what we meant by "perfection" in *New Britain.* See 347 U.S., at 84, 74 S.Ct., at 369 ("when ... the property subject to the lien ... [is] established"); id., at 86, 74 S.Ct., at 370 ("the priority of each statutory lien contested here must depend on the time it attached to the property in question and became [no longer inchoate]").[3] The Bank concedes that its lien did not actually

[1]   The dissent claims that "the Government's 'specificity' claim rejected in Vermont is analytically indistinguishable from the 'attachment' argument the Court accepts today," since "[i]f specific attachment is not required for the state lien to be 'sufficiently choate,' then neither is specific acquisition." Post, * * *. But the two are not comparable. Until the debtor has acquired the subject property, it is impossible to say that "the property subject to the lien [has been] ... established," United States v. New Britain, 347 U.S. 81, 84, 74 S.Ct. 367, 369, 98 L.Ed. 520 (1954). Judicial attachment, on the other hand (and it is important to note that judicial attachment of the property, rather than attachment of the lien to the property, was what the Government's argument in Vermont involved), merely brings into the custody of a court property that is already--prior to judicial attachment--known to be subject to the lien.

[2]   The dissent accepts the Bank's central argument that perfection occurred when "there was 'nothing more to be done' by the Bank 'to have a choate lien' on any real property the McDermotts might acquire." Post * * * (quoting United States v. New Britain, supra, at 84, 74 S.Ct., at 369); see also post, at 1533-1534. This unusual definition of perfection has been achieved by making a small but substantively important addition to the language of New Britain. "[N]othing more to be done to have a choate lien" (the language of New Britain) becomes "nothing more to be done by the Bank to have a choate lien." Once one recognizes that the dissent's concept of a lien's "becom[ing] certain as to the property subject thereto," see post, ***, is meaningless, it becomes apparent that the dissent, like the Bank, would simply have us substitute the concept of "best efforts" for the concept of perfection.

[3]   The dissent refuses to acknowledge the unavoidable realities that the property subject to a lien is not "established" until one knows what specific property that is, and that a lien cannot be anything other than "inchoate" with respect to property that is not yet subject to the lien. Hence the dissent says that, upon its filing, the lien at issue here

attach to the property at issue here until the McDermotts acquired rights in that property. Brief for Respondents 16, 21. Since that occurred after filing of the federal tax lien, the state lien was not first in time.[1]

But that does not complete our inquiry: Though the state lien was not first in time, the federal tax lien was not necessarily first in time either. Like the state lien, it applied to the property at issue here by virtue of a (judicially inferred) after-acquired-property provision, which means that it did not attach until the same instant the state lien attached, viz., when the McDermotts acquired the property; and, like the state lien, it did not become "perfected" until that time. We think, however, that under the language of §6323(a) ("shall not be valid as against any ... judgment lien creditor until notice ... has been filed"), the filing of notice renders the federal tax lien extant for "first in time" priority purposes regardless of whether it has yet attached to identifiable property. That result is also indicated by the provision, two subsections later, which accords priority, even against filed federal tax liens, to security interests arising out of certain agreements, including "commercial transactions financing agreement[s]," entered into before filing of the tax lien. 26 U.S.C. §6323(c)(1). That provision protects certain security interests that, like the after-acquired-property judgment lien here, will have been recorded before the filing of the tax lien, and will attach to the encumbered property after the filing of the tax lien, and simultaneously with the attachment of the tax lien (i.e., upon the debtor's acquisition of the subject property). According special priority to certain state security interests in these circumstances obviously presumes that otherwise the federal tax lien would prevail--i.e., that the federal lien is ordinarily dated, for purposes of "first in time" priority against §6323(a) competing interests, from the time of its filing, regardless of when it attaches to the subject property.[2]

"was perfected, even as to the real property later acquired by the McDermotts, in the sense that it was definite as to the property in question, noncontingent, and summarily enforceable." Post, * * *. But how could it have been, at that time, "definite" as to this property, when the identity of this property (established by the McDermotts' later acquisition) was yet unknown? Or "noncontingent" as to this property, when the property would have remained entirely free of the judgment lien had the McDermotts not later decided to buy it? Or "summarily enforceable" against this property when the McDermotts did not own, and had never owned, it? The dissent also says that "[t]he lien was immediately enforceable through levy and execution against all the debtors' property, whenever acquired." Post, at 1532 (emphases added). But of course it was not "immediately enforceable" (as of its filing date, which is the relevant time) against property that the McDermotts had not yet acquired.

[1]   The dissent suggests, post, at 1532, n. 1, that the Treasury Department regulation defining "judgment lien creditor," 26 CFR s 301.6323(h)-1(g) (1992), contradicts our analysis. It would, if it contained only the three requirements that the dissent describes. In fact, however, it says that to prevail the judgment lien must be perfected, and that "[a] judgment lien is not perfected until the identity of the lienor, *the property subject to the lien*, and the amount of the lien are established." Ibid. (emphasis added).

[2]   The dissent contends that "there is no persuasive reason for not adopting as a

The Bank argues that "[b]y common law, the first lien of record against a debtor's property has priority over those subsequently filed unless a lien- creating statute clearly shows or declares an intention to cause the statutory lien to override." Brief for Respondents 11.[1] Such a strong "first-to-record" presumption may be appropriate for simultaneously-perfected liens under ordinary statutes creating private liens, which ordinarily arise out of voluntary transactions. When two private lenders both exact from the same debtor security agreements with after-acquired-property clauses, the second lender knows, by reason of the earlier recording, that that category of property will be subject to another claim, and if the remaining security is inadequate he may avoid the difficulty by declining to extend credit. The Government, by contrast, cannot indulge the luxury of declining to hold the taxpayer liable for his taxes; notice of a previously filed security agreement covering after-acquired property does not enable the Government to protect itself. A strong "first-to-record" presumption is particularly out of place under the present tax-lien statute, whose general rule is that the tax collector prevails even if he has not recorded at all. 26 U.S.C. §§6321 and 6322; United States v. Snyder, 149 U.S. 210, 13 S.Ct. 846, 37 L.Ed. 705 (1893). Thus, while we would hardly proclaim the statutory meaning we have discerned in this opinion to be "clear," it is evident enough for the purpose at hand. The federal tax lien must be given priority.

The judgment of the Court of Appeals is reversed, and the case is remanded for further proceedings consistent with this opinion.

So ordered.

Justice Thomas, with whom Justice Stevens and Justice O'connor join, dissenting.

---

matter of federal law the well-recognized common-law rule of parity and giving the Bank an equal interest in the property." Post * * *. As we have explained, the persuasive reason is the existence of §6323(c), which displays the assumption that all perfected security interests are defeated by the federal tax lien. There is no reason why this assumption should not extend to judgment liens as well. A "security interest," as defined in §6323, is not an insignificant creditor's preference. The term includes only interests protected against subsequent judgment liens. See 26 U.S.C. §§6323(h)(1) and 6323(c)(1)(B). Moreover, the text of §6323(a) ("The lien ... shall not be valid as against any purchaser, holder of a security interest, mechanic's lienor, or judgment lien creditor") treats security interests and judgment liens alike. Parity may be, as the dissent says, a "well-recognized common-law rule," post, * * *, but we have not hitherto adopted it as the federal law of tax liens in 127 years of tax lien enforcement.

[1]   The dissent notes that "[n]othing in the law of judgment liens suggests that the possibility, which existed at the time the Bank docketed its judgment, that the McDermotts would not acquire the specific property here at issue was a 'contingency' that rendered the Bank's otherwise perfected general judgment lien subordinate to intervening liens." Post, * * *. Perhaps. But priorities here are determined, not by "the law of judgment liens" but by §6323(a), as our case-law has interpreted it. The requirement that competing state liens be perfected is part of that jurisprudence.

I agree with the Court that under 26 U.S.C. §6323(a) we generally look to the filing of notice of the federal tax lien to determine the federal lien's priority as against a competing state-law judgment lien. I cannot agree, however, that a federal tax lien trumps a judgment creditor's claim to after-acquired property whenever notice of the federal lien is filed before the judgment lien has "attached" to the property. Ante * * *. In my view, the Bank's antecedent judgment lien "ha[d] [already] acquired sufficient substance and ha[d] become so perfected," with respect to the McDermotts' after-acquired real property, "as to defeat [the] later-filed federal tax lien." United States v. Pioneer American Ins. Co., 374 U.S. 84, 88, 83 S.Ct. 1651, 1655, 10 L.Ed.2d 770 (1963).

Applying the governing "first in time" rule, the Court recognizes--as it must--that if the Bank's interest in the property was "perfected in the sense that there [was] nothing more to be done to have a choate lien" before September 9, 1987 (the date the federal notice was filed), United States v. New Britain, 347 U.S. 81, 84, 74 S.Ct. 367, 369, 98 L.Ed. 520 (1954), "that is the end of the matter; the Bank's lien prevails," ante, * * *. Because the Bank's identity as lienor and the amount of its judgment lien are undisputed, the choateness question here reduces to whether "the property subject to the lien" was sufficiently "established" as of that date. *New Britain*, supra, at 84, 74 S.Ct., at 369. Accord, Pioneer American, supra, 374 U.S., at 89, 83 S.Ct., at 1655. See 26 CFR §301.6323(h)-1(g) (1992). The majority is quick to conclude that "establish[ment]" cannot precede attachment, and that a lien in after-acquired property therefore cannot be sufficiently perfected until the debtor has acquired rights in the property. See ante, * * *. That holding does not follow from, and I believe it is inconsistent with, our precedents.

We have not (before today) prescribed any rigid criteria for "establish[ing]" the property subject to a competing lien; we have required only that the lien "*become certain* as to ... the property subject thereto." *New Britain*, supra, 347 U.S., at 86, 74 S.Ct., at 370 (emphasis added). Our cases indicate that "certain" means nothing more than "[d]etermined and [d]efinite," *Pioneer American,* supra, 374 U.S., at 90, 83 S.Ct., at 1656, and that the proper focus is on whether the lien is free from "contingencies" that stand in the way of its execution, United States v. Security Trust & Savings Bank, 340 U.S. 47, 50, 71 S.Ct. 111, 113, 95 L.Ed. 53 (1950). In *Security Trust,* for example, we refused to accord priority to a mere attachment lien that "had not ripened into a judgment," *New Britain*, supra, 347 U.S., at 86, 74 S.Ct., at 370, and was therefore "contingent upon taking subsequent steps for enforcing it," 340 U.S., at 51, 71 S.Ct., at 114. And in United States v. Vermont, 377 U.S. 351, 84 S.Ct. 1267, 12 L.Ed.2d 370 (1964), we recognized the complete superiority of a general tax lien held by the State of Vermont upon all property rights belonging to the debtor, even though the lien had not "attach[ed] to [the] specifically identified portions of that property" in which the Federal Government claimed a competing tax lien. Id., at 355, 84 S.Ct., at 1269. With or without specific attachment, Vermont's general lien was "sufficiently choate to obtain priority over the later federal lien," because it was "summarily enforceable" upon assessment and demand. Id., at 359, and n. 12, 84 S.Ct., at 1272, and n. 12.

Although the choateness of a state-law lien under §6323(a) is a federal question, that question is answered in part by reference to state law, and we therefore give due weight to the State's "'classification of [its] lien as specific and perfected.'" *Pioneer American*, supra, 374 U.S., at 88, n. 7, 83 S.Ct., at 1655, n. 7 (quoting Security Trust, supra, 340 U.S., at 49, 71 S.Ct., at 113). Here, state law establishes that upon filing, the Bank's judgment lien was perfected, even as to the real property later acquired by the McDermotts, in the sense that it was definite as to the property in question, noncontingent, and summarily enforceable. Pursuant to Utah statute, from the moment the Bank had docketed and filed its judgment with the clerk of the state court on July 6, 1987, it held an enforceable lien upon all nonexempt real property owned by the McDermotts or thereafter acquired by them during the existence of the lien. See Utah Code Ann. §78-22-1 (1953). The lien was immediately enforceable through levy and execution against all the debtors' property, whenever acquired. See Belnap v. Blain, 575 P.2d 696, 700 (Utah 1978). See also Utah Rule Civ.Proc. 69. And it was "unconditional and not subject to alteration by a court on equitable grounds." Taylor National, Inc. v. Jensen Brothers Constr. Co., 641 P.2d 150, 155 (Utah 1982). Thus, the Bank's lien had become certain as to the property subject thereto, whether then existing or thereafter acquired, and all competing creditors were on notice that there was "nothing more to be done" by the Bank "to have a choate lien" on any real property the McDermotts might acquire. *New Britain*, 347 U.S., at 84, 74 S.Ct., at 369. See *Vermont*, supra, 377 U.S., at 355, 84 S.Ct., at 1269.[1]

The Court brushes aside the relevance of our Vermont opinion with the simple observation that that case did not involve a lien in after-acquired property. Ante, * * *. This is a wooden distinction. In truth, the Government's "specificity" claim rejected in *Vermont* is analytically indistinguishable from the "attachment" argument the Court accepts today. Vermont's general lien applied to all of the debtor's rights in property, with no limitation on when those rights were acquired, and remained valid until the debt was satisfied or became unenforceable. See 377

---

[1]   The Department of Treasury regulations defining "judgment lien creditor" for purposes of §6323(a) set forth only three specific requirements for a choate lien (corresponding to the three "establish [ment]" criteria of New Britain). The judgment creditor must "obtai[n] a valid judgment" (thus establishing the lienor) for the recovery of "specifically designated property or for a certain sum of money" (thus establishing the amount of the lien), and if recording or docketing is "necessary under local law" for the lien to be effective against third parties, the judgment lien "is not perfected with respect to real property until the time of such recordation or docketing." 26 CFR §301.6323(h)-1(g) (1992). The last requirement--recording or docketing--is the only specific requirement recognized in the regulations for establishing the real property subject to the judgment lien. The regulations in no way suggest that §6323(a) imposes any "attachment" condition for after- acquired property. Such a condition would be, in effect, an additional recordation requirement that is not otherwise imposed by local law.

U.S., at 352, 84 S.Ct., at 1268. The United States claimed that its later-filed tax lien took priority over Vermont's as to the debtor's interest in a particular bank account, because the State had not taken "steps to perfect its lien by attaching the bank account in question" until after the federal lien had been recorded. Brief for United States in United States v. Vermont, O.T.1963, No. 509, p. 12. "Thus," the Government asserted, "when the federal lien arose, the State lien did not meet one of the three essential elements of a choate lien: that it attach to specific property." Ibid. In rejecting the federal claim of priority, we found no need even to mention whether the debtor had acquired its property interest in the deposited funds before or after notice of the federal lien. If specific attachment is not required for the state lien to be "sufficiently choate," 377 U.S., at 359, 84 S.Ct., at 1272, then neither is specific acquisition.[1]

Like the majority's reasoning today, see ante, * * *, the Government's argument in *Vermont* rested in part on dicta from *New Britain* suggesting that "attachment to specific property [is] a condition for choateness of a State-created lien." Brief for United States in United States v. Vermont, supra, at 19. See *New Britain*, 347 U.S., at 86, 74 S.Ct., at 370 ("[T]he priority of each statutory lien contested here must depend on the time it *attached* to the property in question and became choate") (emphasis added). *New Britain*, however, involved competing statutory liens that had concededly "attached to the same real estate." Id., at 87, 74 S.Ct., at 371. The only issue was whether the liens were otherwise sufficiently choate. Thus, like *Security Trust* (and, in fact, like all of our cases before *Vermont*), *New Britain* provided no occasion to consider the necessity of attachment to property that was not specifically identified at the time the state lien arose.

Nothing in the law of judgment liens suggests that the possibility, which existed at the time the Bank docketed its judgment, that the McDermotts would not acquire the specific property here at issue was a "contingency" that rendered the Bank's otherwise perfected general judgment lien subordinate to intervening liens. Under the relevant background rules of state law, the Bank's interest in after-acquired real property generally could not be defeated by an intervening statutory lien. In some States, the priority of judgment liens in after-acquired property is determined by the order of their docketing. 3 R. Powell, Law of Real Property ¶ 481[1], p. 38-36 (P. Rohan rev. 1991) (hereinafter Powell). See, e.g.,

---

[1]   Even assuming, as the majority does, that the debtor in Vermont acquired its interest in the bank account before the federal lien arose, the critical argument that we rejected in that case was the contention that the State's claim could not be superior unless the account had been "specifically identified" as property subject to the State's lien. 377 U.S., at 355, 84 S.Ct., at 1269. At the time of the federal filing, the debtor's interest in the bank account, like the McDermotts' interest in the property at issue here, could have been uncertain or indefinite from the creditors' perspective. Nevertheless, in both cases, the particular property was "known to be subject to the [state] lien," ante, * * *, simply because that lien, by its terms, applied without limitation to all property acquired at any time by the debtor.

Lowe v. Reierson, 201 Minn. 280, 287, 276 N.W. 224, 227 (1937). In others, the rule is that "[w]hen two (or more) judgments are successively perfected against a debtor and thereafter the debtor acquires a land interest[,] these liens, attaching simultaneously at the time of the land's acquisition by the debtor, are regarded as on a parity and no priority exists." 3 Powell ¶481[1], pp. 38-35 to 38-36. See, e.g., Bank of Boston v. Haufler, 20 Mass.App. 668, 674, 482 N.E.2d 542, 547 (1985); McAllen State Bank v. Saenz, 561 F.Supp. 636, 639 (SD Tex.1982). Thus, under state common law, the Bank would either retain its full priority in the property by virtue of its earlier filing or, at a minimum, share an equal interest with the competing lienor.[1] The fact that the prior judgment lien remains effective against third parties without further efforts by the judgment creditor is enough for purposes of §6323(a), since the point of our choateness doctrine is to respect the validity of a competing lien where the lien has become certain as to the property subject thereto and the lienor need take no further action to secure his claim. Under this federal-law principle, the Bank's lien was sufficiently choate to be first in time.[2]

I acknowledge that our precedents do not provide the clearest answer to the question of after-acquired property. See ante * * *. But the Court's parsimonious reading of Vermont undercuts the congressional purpose--expressed through repeated amendments to the tax lien provisions in the century since United States v. Snyder, 149 U.S. 210, 13 S.Ct. 846, 37 L.Ed. 705 (1893)--of "protect[ing] third persons against harsh application of the federal tax lien," Kennedy, *The*

---

[1]   Article 9 of the Uniform Commercial Code is inapposite, and the Court's reliance on it misplaced. See ante, * * *. The technical rules governing the perfection and priority of the special security interests in personal property created by Article 9 have no application to traditional judgment liens in real property, see §9-102, 3 U.L.A. 73 (1992), and should have no bearing on the federal doctrine of "choateness." In the context of determining the relative priority of a competing statutory judgment lien, it is Article 9's notion of perfection that is the more "unusual." Ante, * * *.

[2]   Even if the Court were correct that attachment is the determinative criterion of choateness, we would have a tie, since the federal lien "did not attach [to the after-acquired property] until the same instant the state lien attached." Ante, * * *. That being so, there is no persuasive reason for not adopting as a matter of federal law the well- recognized common-law rule of parity and giving the Bank an equal interest in the property. See 3 Powell ¶481[1]. Section 6323(a)'s requirement that the federal lien be "filed" to be effective may determine when the lien arises for general priority purposes, but the word "filed" provides no textual basis for concluding that a tie goes to the Government, and simply declaring that it does, see ante, * * *, does not make it so. The special exception in §6323(c), which protects later-arising security interests that are based on certain preferred financing agreements, see ante, at 1530, does not imply that judgment creditors lose out. Indeed, §6323(c) demonstrates that Congress has considered the question of later-arising property, and the absence of an analogous provision in §6323(a) suggests that Congress was content to let the courts apply one of the existing background rules to determine the relative priority (or parity) of the federal lien as against competing judgment liens in after- acquired property.

Relative Priority of the Federal Government: The Pernicious Career of the Inchoate and General Lien, 63 Yale L.J. 905, 922 (1954). The attachment requirement erodes the "preferred status" granted to judgment creditors by §6323(a), and renders a choate judgment lien in after- acquired property subordinate to a "secret lien for assessed taxes." *Pioneer American*, 374 U.S., at 89, 83 S.Ct., at 1655. I would adhere to a more flexible choateness principle, which would protect the priority of validly docketed judgment liens.

Accordingly, I respectfully dissent.

B. SETOFF

Stephen L. Sepinuck, *The Problems With Setoff: A Proposed Legislative Solution*
30 Wm. & Mary L. Rev. 51, 51-53 (1988)

The Origins of Setoff

In its most basic form, setoff is the cancellation of cross demands, that is, the satisfaction of all or part of a debt owed by X to Y through the simultaneous discharge or forgiveness of a debt due to X from Y. Setoff began in ancient Rome with the doctrine of compensatio. During the time of Gaius, setoff was limited to certain claims arising out of the same contract and its use remained a matter of judicial discretion. Under Marcus Aurelius and Justinian, the doctrine was expanded to include claims arising from different transactions and was extended to reach both real and personal actions.

Eventually, the doctrine made its way to France, where it can be traced to the fourteenth century. In England, however, the doctrine generated less enthusiasm. Under the English legal system, the forms of action and the system of pleadings were designed to bring opposing parties to a single issue, affirmed on one side and denied on the other. Interjection of a collateral issue or claim ran counter to this basic philosophy and must have seemed intolerable. Nevertheless, some early courts of chancery, exercising equitable jurisdiction and conscious of the unfairness of denying setoff against parties with few or dwindling financial resources, found a basis for setoff outside the formalities of law. They also recognized its concomitant benefit of avoiding circuity and multiplicity of suits.

In 1705, the doctrine finally received legislative support through a temporary bankruptcy statute. It reemerged in 1729, as part of an act reforming debtors' prisons and insolvency proceedings. This time the doctrine had a much broader application, extending beyond insolvency proceedings and applying generally:

[w]here there are mutual Debts between the Plaintiff and Defendant, . . . one Debt may be set against the other, and such Matter may be given in Evidence upon the General Issue, or pleaded in Bar, as the Nature of the Case shall require, so as at the Time of his pleading the General Issue,

> where any such Debt of the Plaintiff . . . is intended to be insisted on in
> Evidence, Notice shall be given of the particular Sum or Debt so intended
> to be insisted on, and upon what Account it became due.

Throughout the eighteenth and nineteenth centuries, however, setoff was available only in judicial proceedings and remained subject to all the formalities of English law.

Surprisingly, setoff on this side of the Atlantic predates the English statutes. As early as 1645, the colony of Virginia permitted civil defendants to set off debts due to and debts owing from a plaintiff. By 1654, Maryland had followed with a similar measure for discounting debts. In 1682, Pennsylvania added its own version, one somewhat more comprehensive than the subsequent English legislation. Moreover, as reenacted shortly after the turn of the eighteenth century, the Pennsylvania statute permitted a defendant to obtain affirmative relief if, after setoff, he remained a creditor of the plaintiff.

New York adopted its own statute in 1714, largely identical to the Pennsylvania act, but requiring that written notice of the offsetting debt be given with the responsive plea. In 1722, New Jersey enacted its version, closely tracking the New York statute, but also requiring that the defendant plead his setoff 'or else forever after be barred of bringing any action for that which he might or ought to have pleaded by virtue of this act.' Although certain formalities remained for some time, these acts evidently evolved into the permissive and compulsory counterclaims present in modern American pleading systems.

Setoff thus began as an innovative pleading tool. Yet, with the advent of the liberal pleading rules embodied in the Federal Rules of Civil Procedure, much of the original purpose and early complexities of setoff have vanished. Still, the spirit and substance or setoff lives on, now outside the courtroom and the narrow confines of pleading formalities. Setoff has become a widely recognized area of substantive law.

The Current Uses of Setoff

Although the precise actions necessary to effect setoff are unclear, setoff can now certainly be effected without judicial involvement. The circumstances under which privately effected setoff may arise are quite varied. For example, merchants occasionally set off the account debts generated when they buy from and sell to each other. More frequently, banks will use account deposits to set off overdue loans made to their depositors. In fact, in reliance upon their ability to effect setoff swiftly, banks occasionally require borrowers of large sums to maintain their deposit accounts with the lending institution.

Even when setoff arises during litigation, courts not longer treat it as a procedural device but instead recognize it as a substantive right. The exact nature and scope of this right is varied and unclear. Yet, setoff undeniably affects the priority of creditors and, therefore, remains a significant concern in structuring commercial transactions.

The Importance of Setoff

The importance of setoff perhaps is best demonstrated when one party to a pair of mutual debts becomes bankrupt or insolvent. In such a case, when a debtor lacks the ability to fully satisfy his debt, setoff becomes more than a mere alternative to bringing suit to enforce an obligation. It frequently becomes the only means by which a creditor can fully collect.

The general scheme of modern bankruptcy law requires that the bankruptcy trustee or debtor-in-possession marshall all of the bankrupt's unencumbered assets before distributing assets to creditors with unsecured claims. This action includes collecting debts owed to the bankrupt. In a reorganization proceeding, these assets then are used by the debtor-in- possession to generate additional assets for later distribution to creditors. In a liquidation, the trustee sells the assets and distributes the proceeds to creditors in what is supposed to be a more expedited fashion. In both cases, creditors are divided into classes and arranged in a hierarchy specified by statute. The equitable distribution that the Bankruptcy Code then seeks to effect requires that no creditor in a class receive a greater percentage of his claim than any other creditor in the same or higher class.

In theory, therefore, one who is both a creditor and a debtor of the bankrupt will be compelled to pay his debt in full, and then receive payment with his class on what is likely to be only a small percentage of his claim. Setoff permits a creditor to avoid this basic scheme of the Bankruptcy Code by netting out his claim and his debt.

Not surprisingly, several courts have noted that the availability of setoff seems to run counter to the fundamental policy underlying bankruptcy law: a fair and proportionate distribution to creditors. For this reason, some courts have prohibited its exercise against a debtor undergoing a bankruptcy reorganization. Nevertheless, because setoff is firmly grounded in fundamental notions of fairness, it has been incorporated in every United States bankruptcy statute. Most courts now permit setoff absent 'compelling circumstances,' and treat it essentially as a security interest, rather than as the equitable remedy of its origin. Accordingly, a creditor owing a mutual debt available for setoff is entitled to adequate protection of his claim or relief from the automatic stay. Moreover, setoff apparently remains available to satisfy creditors' claims that would otherwise be subordinated, and as a procedural matter, the right to setoff does not depend on the timely filing of a proof of claim.

Even outside the bankruptcy context, setoff remains an extraordinarily fast and inexpensive means of debt collection. In addition, its availability can provide a unique alternative to traditional forms of security, as well as a means of reducing the judiciary's ever-increasing backlog. Setoff is thus a valuable commercial tool--a tool which should be standardized to avoid frustrating the reasonable expectations of those who deal in the fast-paced, modern world of interstate commerce.

Thomas G. Dobyns, *Banking Setoff: A Study In Commercial Obsolescence*
23 Hastings L.J. 1585, 1587-88 (1972).

When a depositor opens a general account *** with a bank, a debtor-creditor relationship is created. The bank has legal title to any money deposited and becomes indebted to the depositor in the amount of the deposit; the latter has a chose in action ***. [W]hile the bank is the debtor of the customer, should the customer become similarly indebted to the bank, the latter has the right *** to debit the customer's account in satisfaction of his indcbtcdncss to thc bank. This procedure is accomplished without resort to formal judicial proceedings, legal or equitable. Moreover, the right exists apart from any setoff statute and operates automatically in those cases where it is applicable. Finally, by the majority view, the right is exercisable unless the depositor objects prior to exercise. The depositor's prior consent is unnecessary.

Thus, banking setoff allows a bank in the position of creditor to rely on a security interest of which the customer is unaware. The practice of preemptorily debiting the customer's account before proof of his indebtedness to the bank is only one example how banking setoff has diverged from the equitable principles on which it was ostensibly founded.

Randall Lawson Dunn, *Banker's Lien And Equitable Setoff: Constitutional And Policy Considerations For Protecting Bank Customers*
27 Stan.L.Rev. 1149, 1152-53 (1975)

Two distinct types of setoff are recognized ***. Ultimately derived from the Roman law of *compensatio*, the statutory setoff procedure provides for recognition at trial of automatic offsets of cross-demands. Equitable setoff is a nonstatutory remedy that the creditor bank can apply on its own authority. The timing of the operation of equitable setoff distinguishes it from the statutory procedure. When a creditor, whether a bank or any other, invokes *compensatio* before a court, he declares that the mutual obligations of the parties extinguished one another the first moment they coexisted. Equitable setoff operates as a mutual cancellation of indebtedness at whatever point in time the bank chooses to declare obligations offset. The effects of the two procedures are otherwise substantially alike.

The practice of setoff was recognized early in English courts of equity. It originated from a perception that 'natural justice' requires mutually existing obligations to be set off and only the balance of the debts recovered. Through natural law doctrine is no longer recognized as the compelling justification that it once was, the concept that mutual debtors should cancel corresponding debts and determine liability on the basis of the remaining balances retains the appeal of intrinsic rationality. In general, it appears only fair and just that debtors offset their mutually coexisting demands and deal further in terms of the net difference of their obligations. However, vital questions must be answered regarding who is to make the critical determinations as to the validity of asserted claims and the appropriate timing for setoff. The existence of unrestricted power in the hands of creditor banks to make setoff decisions poses a grave threat to debtor-depositors.

Equitable setoff may currently be used whenever a bank and its depositor are mutually indebted. To employ the setoff procedure, the bank requires neither the aid of a court nor the sanction of statute but can proceed on its own initiative. Equitable setoff may be applied, however, only against certain limited classes of property, namely the undifferentiated funds in a depositor's checking or savings accounts. Deposits earmarked for special purposes *** may not be offset. In spite of these limitations, equitable setoff provides banks with a potent means to collect delinquent debts.

1. Setoff Versus Checks Drawn Against Debtor's Account

Four Circle Co-Op v. Kansas State Bank & Trust Co.
United States District Court, D. Kansas, 1991
771 F. Supp. 1144

Crow, District Judge. These cases arise out of the bankruptcy of Fleming Grain Company, Inc. (Fleming). In 1984, Fleming, a company which profited from the resale of grain, became financially insolvent due to the principals' losses in the commodities market. On the day Kansas State Bank and Trust Company (KSBT) learned of these losses, it set off the amounts owed by Fleming. This setoff caused numerous checks issued by Fleming to bounce. The plaintiffs in these cases are persons who were issued checks by Fleming but were unable to collect from the account upon which they were issued due to KSBT's setoff. The plaintiffs have received partial payments on the checks through distributions in bankruptcy.

The plaintiffs in this case are suing KSBT for conversion, alleging that KSBT wrongfully setoff against the funds in Fleming's account. The plaintiffs allege that KSBT knew that the funds in Fleming's account were their property. KSBT denies any wrongful action and challenges the plaintiffs ownership interest in the funds. KSBT named the trustee in bankruptcy as a third-party defendant, claiming that the bankruptcy estate should compensate KSBT for any amounts it may owe to the plaintiffs. The trustee challenges whether it should be liable to KSBT if the plaintiffs are successful in their conversion claim.

This case comes before the court upon KSBT's motions for summary judgment in all three cases, upon the plaintiffs' cross-motion for summary judgment in Case Number 89-1316-C, and upon the trustee's motion for summary judgment against KSBT in all three cases.

Facts

Fleming Grain was founded in December 1978 by John Fleming, Tom Forenshell and K. Zack Zigler, three individuals who each had experience in the grain industry. Fleming's business consisted of purchasing grain from grain producers/sellers, and acting as middle-man, would sell the grain to buyers for a profit of approximately three to five cents a bushel (net after expenses, including the cost of transportation). Fleming's profits on its grain transactions amounted to 1.5% to 2.5% of the total resale price of the grain Fleming sold. Fleming did not raise any grain itself, nor did Fleming have grain storage capabilities.

In 1979 Fleming began banking at KSBT. From 1979 until 1984, Fleming maintained a business demand deposit checking account at KSBT. The documents governing that account did not indicate that the account was "special," "trust" or "custodial". From this account, Fleming paid essentially all of its bills, including payments to grain sellers. Throughout this same time, Fleming also maintained a line of credit with KSBT. As a condition of the line of credit, KSBT required Fleming to maintain an exclusive banking relationship. As security for the line of credit, Fleming granted KSBT a security interest in its accounts receivable and proceeds therefrom and contract rights. The line of credit enabled Fleming to pay sellers of grain, notwithstanding the untimely receipt of sale proceeds. Prior to July 1984, KSBT had written several letters addressed "To Whom It May Concern" with an understanding that these letters would be forwarded to potential customers of Fleming and that the desired effect of the letters was to induce reliance by potential customers in extending credit to Fleming.

KSBT, as part of its analysis of Fleming for loan purposes, acquired a fairly detailed understanding of Fleming's operations. Fleming sold plaintiffs' grain under separate contracts; plaintiffs were not parties to Fleming's contracts with third parties (the ultimate buyers of the grain). Apparently, the vast majority of all of Fleming's transactions were made on what is called a "back-to-back" agreement, whereby a purchase is not made without a confirmed buyer.

Until the beginning of 1984, Fleming was apparently a profitable enterprise. However, in the first few months of 1984, KSBT officials began to notice that Fleming was encountering financial difficulties. On July 3, 1984, Fleming was in default on two notes issued in favor of KSBT. The total principal amount of those notes was $1,200,000. On July 24, 1984, Fleming was in default on a third promissory note in the principal amount of $300,000, bringing the total principal amount on which Fleming had defaulted as of July 24, 1984, to $1,500,000.

On July 25, Fleming, Forenshell and Zigler, advised KSBT that they had lost over $1,000,000 of Fleming's assets by speculating in the commodity futures market in the principals' individual names. Later that day, KSBT seized all of the funds in the Fleming account. On July 26, 1984, KSBT applied $1,235,707.93 from Fleming's business checking account at KSBT to Fleming's indebtedness to the bank. On July 26, 1984, after KSBT had seized the funds in the Fleming account, KSBT demanded immediate payment from Fleming on the defaulted notes.

As a result of the setoff, the checks which Fleming had written to the plaintiffs and deposited by the plaintiffs into regular banking channels on and after July 25, 1984, were returned to the plaintiffs unpaid.

The plaintiffs in case number 89-1314-C and case number 89-1315-C are farmers or other grain suppliers who sold grain to Fleming prior to July 25, 1984. Fleming sold that grain to its customers prior to July 25, 1984. Prior to July 25, 1984, Fleming issued checks drawn on its business checking account at KSBT in payment to the plaintiffs for their grain. The total of checks is $417,658.32. The plaintiffs in case number 89-1316-C are grain suppliers and/or transportation providers who sold grain and/or transportation services to Fleming prior to July 25, 1984. The total value of the checks issued to the plaintiffs in this case is $318,895.75. Each check at issue was transmitted to the payee on the check by Fleming through the mail or by hand and was deposited for collection in the ordinary course of the payee's operations as a grain seller. Each draft at issue was transmitted by the drafting party identified on the draft to KSBT for payment by Fleming in the ordinary course of banking operations and the drafting party's operations as a grain seller.

The amount of compensatory damages claimed by each plaintiff is equal to the amount of the returned checks or drafts each plaintiff holds, plus interest, and less any reduction made by the court for partial payment received from the Fleming Trustee applicable to the checks or drafts at issue.

As of the dates the grain payment checks held by plaintiffs were issued, Fleming's business checking account balance at KSBT was sufficient to cover all the checks issued to the plaintiffs. From July 1 through July 25, 1984, when all the checks held by the plaintiffs were presented for payment, approximately 84% of all deposits to Fleming's account at KSBT were proceeds of grain sales. Fleming's account balance on July 1, 1984 was $162,112.14.

* * *

The Right of Setoff

Bank setoff is the legal right of a financial institution to appropriate the deposit of its customer upon the customer's default and apply those funds against the customer's debts to the institution. See Tulkova Affiliates, Inc. v. Security State Bank, 229 Kan. 544, 627 P.2d 816 (1981). The right of setoff is an ancient doctrine tracing its origin back to the Roman doctrine of "compensatio," which is the extinction of cross-demands. In Kansas, the right of setoff is established by statute. K.S.A. 9-1206 provides: "Any bank shall have the right to set off any obligation or claim which it has, when the same is matured against any depositor." The right of setoff has long been recognized by Kansas courts.

Before exercising the right of setoff, certain conditions must be satisfied. First, a valid debtor-creditor relationship must exist between the bank and the depositor. Second, the depositor's debt must be due and owing or "mature." Third, the funds must be the depositor's property and deposited without restrictions. Fourth, there must be mutuality of obligation between the debtor and creditor, as well as between debt and funds on deposit.

A bank's right to setoff may be denied under certain situations where the bank has knowledge of a third party's interest in the deposited funds. Two rules have evolved: the "legal" rule and the "equitable" rule.

All courts, including Kansas, prohibit setoff when a bank has actual knowledge that the deposits in the debtor's account belong to a third person. See Iola State Bank v. Bolan, 235 Kan. 175, 188, 679 P.2d 720 (1984). "A bank is also denied the right of setoff where it has knowledge of circumstances sufficient to necessitate inquiry concerning the sums." *Bolan*, 235 Kan. at 188, 679 P.2d 720 (quoting Commercial Disc. Corp. v. Milw. Western Bank, 61 Wis.2d 671, 680-81, 214 N.W.2d 33 (1974). This is known as the "legal" rule.

Under the equitable rule, under certain circumstances a bank may not setoff even though it has no knowledge of the interests of third parties in the funds. In order to recover under the equitable theory, the third party must demonstrate that (1) the bank's lack of knowledge has not resulted in any change in the bank's position, and (2) no superior equities have been raised in its favor. See Commercial Disc., 214 N.W.2d at 37-39. Kansas has discussed, but has not expressly adopted, the equitable rule.

The plaintiffs contend that *Bolan* precludes summary judgment. The plaintiffs contend that the facts of *Bolan* are virtually indistinguishable from the facts of this case and that any facts that are different only indicate that KSBT's behavior in this case is more reprehensible. The plaintiffs extol the virtues of the *Bolan* case and note that the case has been frequently cited by the Kansas appellant courts.

KSBT contends that *Bolan* is an aberration of Kansas law which has been the subject of criticism by legal scholars and should be limited to its specific facts. KSBT acknowledges that *Bolan* has been cited on many occasions by Kansas appellate courts, but contends that the central holding of that case has not been followed in subsequent cases. KSBT contends that even under *Bolan* it is entitled to summary judgment.

The *Bolan* Case

In *Bolan*, decided March 24, 1984, Biggs Feed and Grain, Inc. (Biggs) operated a feed and grain elevator at Waverly, Kansas, and conducted its banking business with the Iola State Bank (Bank). Biggs purchased and sold grain. The Bank financed the grain operation since its inception in 1974. Biggs executed a promissory note on February 13, 1981, in the sum of $294,000 with interest at a rate of 17%. Security agreements were executed granting the Bank a security interest in all inventory of seed and grain and a purchase money security interest in all wheat, soybeans and feed grains owned or acquired by Biggs.

Biggs did not make any principal or interest payments on the note, which became due on July 1981. Examiners of the Bank criticized the Biggs' indebtedness and the Bank assured the examiners that the Biggs matter would be taken care of within 90 days. After the discussion with the bank examiners, the Bank met with Biggs to inform him that the note was past due and that he had 90 days from the bank examination, to the middle of October, to find other financing or a buyer of the business. The Bank discovered that its deadline fell during the middle of soybean harvest. At Biggs' request, the deadline was extended to November 15, 1981.

The November 15, 1981, deadline passed; Biggs failed to respond to the Bank's demand for payment. On December 7, 1981, checks issued by Biggs to farmers/sellers for past grain sales began to arrive at the Bank. At the time those checks were issued there were sufficient funds in the Biggs' account to cover all outstanding checks. The Bank setoff Biggs' general checking account and applied the funds against the balance due on Biggs' note. At the time of the setoff, proceeds from Biggs' resale of grain constituted 95% of all deposits in the account. On the same day as the setoff, the Bank filed suit against Biggs, its principal and the guarantors of the note. The farmers/sellers intervened in the suit alleging that the Bank had converted their money.

The case was tried to a jury. At the close of the evidence, the district court directed a verdict in favor of the farmers/sellers for $26,663.14. The district court held that Biggs had only a voidable title in the grain, and that when the Bank dishonored Biggs' checks given for payment of the grain, the Bank voided Biggs' title and returned title to the farmers/sellers. The district court also concluded that the Bank knew the nature of the funds in Biggs' bank account and that the setoff was a willful act of conversion of the farmers/sellers' property. On the issue of punitive damages, the jury awarded the farmers/sellers $150,000.

On appeal, the Supreme Court affirmed the award of both compensatory and punitive damages, concluding that the district court had reached the correct result, but for the wrong reason. The court concluded that the adoption of the U.C.C. abolished the cash sale doctrine. The court then proceeded to analyze whether the Bank had acted in good faith: (1) The farmer's tender of delivery of the grain was conditional upon payment, and Biggs, a merchant, acquired voidable title to the grain under K.S.A. 84-2-403; (2) The Bank's security interest attached to the grain; (3) The Bank was a purchaser as defined by K.S.A. 84-1-201(33); (4) Biggs' sale of the grain to good faith purchasers in the normal course of business defeated the Bank's title to the grain, but the proceeds of the grain sales were identifiable cash proceeds; (5) as a secured creditor, the bank had a right to the proceeds of the grain sales and had a right to the money deposited in Biggs' checking account.

The farmers/sellers argued, and the Supreme Court agreed, however, that the Bank had failed to act in good faith as required by the U.C.C., and was therefore not a "good faith purchaser." K.S.A. 84-1-201(19) defines "good faith" as meaning honesty in fact in the conduct or transaction concerned. Since the Bank failed to act in good faith, it was not a good faith purchaser, and its security interest did not attach against the farmers/sellers. In determining that the Bank had not acted in good faith, the Supreme Court relied on several facts including: (1) the size of Biggs' debt and the fact that he had never made a payment; (2) The Bank knew that Biggs would not be able to pay the note; (3) The Bank extended the 90-day limitation to pay the loan to coincide with the harvest season; (4) The Bank knew that the funds setoff in the Biggs' account were funds from sales of grain harvested by the farmers; (5) The Bank knew how Biggs conducted the operations of purchasing and selling grain.

The Supreme Court then commented:

> Since the Bank's security interest did not attach against the farmers/sellers, what is their relationship? Under the UCC a drawee is not liable to the holder of a check until it is accepted by the drawee. The UCC does not affect the Bank's liability to the farmers/sellers in contract, tort or otherwise by its failure to accept the check when presented for payment. K.S.A. 84-3-409. Under normal circumstances, when the farmers/sellers sold the grain to Biggs and Biggs' bank dishonors Biggs' checks payable to the farmers/sellers, in spite of sufficient funds and in absence of a stop order, the farmers/sellers had no direct recourse against Biggs' bank until the Bank accepted the check for payment. The UCC continues the prior law that there is no privity between the holder of a check and the drawee bank, assuming no certification or retention of the check beyond the midnight deadline. 235 Kan. at 187, 679 P.2d 720.

The Bank argued in the alternative that if it was not entitled to the funds under the U.C.C., it was entitled to the funds under the common law and K.S.A. 9-1206. After reviewing the law in regard to setoff, the court concluded:

> A holder cannot sue the drawee bank for wrongful dishonor of an insolvent depositor's check just because the bank dishonors the check in order to protect its own interest. Where a bank knows sums deposited in the account of one of its depositors belongs to a third party, it does not act in good faith when it applies such funds of the third party against the depositor's debts to the bank. Under such circumstances the third party has an action directly against the bank for conversion of the third party's funds from the debtor's accounts. 235 Kan. at 189, 679 P.2d 720.

In concluding that the bank had actual knowledge that the funds in Biggs' account belonged to third parties, the court relied on the statements made by a bank employee during trial which conceded that the money in the account belonged to the plaintiffs. 235 Kan. at 191, 679 P.2d 720. The court concluded that this admission, coupled with the Bank's knowledge of how Biggs operated, indicated actual knowledge. "Where a Bank actually knows the sums deposited in the account of one of its debtors belong to a third person, it cannot apply such funds against the debtor's obligation to the bank. The setoff was improper under K.S.A. 9-1206." Id.

The Supreme Court also concluded that the award of punitive damages was appropriate.

Discussion and Disposition

For whatever reason, the plaintiffs in this case are unable to trace the proceeds of the sale of their grain to funds in Fleming's account at KSBT. The court concludes that the failure to demonstrate a sufficient property interest in those funds compels summary judgment in favor of KSBT, as the plaintiffs have failed to demonstrate a necessary element of their case.

The plaintiffs repeatedly assert that the money in Fleming's account on July 25, 1984 is "their" money. Unfortunately for the plaintiffs, they are unable to demonstrate that the money in the account is the proceeds of the sale of their grain. As KSBT suggests, there is no evidence in the record indicating the source of the money in the account. The plaintiffs have not traced the funds in the account to Fleming's purchase of their grain.

Proof of ownership in the funds in the Fleming account is essential to the plaintiffs' claims. "[T]he plaintiff in a conversion action assumes the burden of proving a sufficient interest in the property allegedly converted." Security Nat. Bank v. Belleville Livestock, 619 F.2d 840, 849 (10th Cir.1980) (applying Kansas law). As noted above, the account was not designated for a specific purpose.

The plaintiffs essentially argue that *Bolan* alleviates grain sellers holding checks dishonored by the bank (after a purportedly wrongful setoff) of the burden of proving ownership in the allegedly converted funds. It is the plaintiffs' position that a bank's knowledge of the source of funds in an account (i.e., grain sales) simply allows the plaintiffs to side-step the issue of ownership by merely presenting the dishonored check to the court, and upon proving bad faith, automatically collect compensatory and punitive damages from the bank. Simply put, *Bolan* does not stand for that proposition. In *Bolan*, the bank did not dispute the plaintiffs' ownership interest in the account funds. Therefore, the proof of ownership element of the plaintiffs' case was satisfied and uncontested. The court in *Bolan* appears to acknowledge that the plaintiffs must prove ownership interest in the funds. 235 Kan. at 189, 679 P.2d 720.

In the case at bar, KSBT has put the plaintiffs to the task of proving ownership in the funds, a burden they are unable to shoulder. Because the court concludes that the plaintiffs have failed to establish an element of their cause of action, the court need not reach the issue of whether KSBT acted in bad faith in exercising its right of setoff.

The plaintiffs urge the court to accept its argument that once the checks were issued to the plaintiffs, the funds in Fleming's account were converted from proceeds of accounts receivable (from grain buyers) into funds committed for accounts payable (to plaintiffs) in which KSBT had no interest, and that KSBT agreed to this transition in form, particularly when Fleming was "holding the money close." This argument simply ignores K.S.A. 84-3-409, which provides in pertinent part:

(1) A check or other draft does not of itself operate as an assignment of any funds in the hands of the drawee available for its payment, and the

drawee is not liable on the instrument until he accepts it. (2) Nothing in this section shall affect any liability in contract, tort or otherwise arising from any letter of credit or other obligation or representation which is not an acceptance.

OFFICIAL UCC COMMENT

. . . . .

1. As under the original sections, a check or other draft does not of itself operate as an assignment in law or equity. The assignment may, however, appear from other facts, and particularly from other agreements, express or implied; and when the intent to assign is clear the check may be the means by which the assignment is effected.

. . . . .

KANSAS COMMENT 1983

. . . . .

(2) Makes clear that this section does not affect liability which may arise apart from the instrument. Examples of such liability are: Ballard v. Bank, 91 K. 91, 136 P. 935 (1913) (foundation for long line of Kansas decisions) ... This section makes it clear that the drawing of a check or other draft does not operate "of itself" to transfer to the payee pro tanto the funds in the account.·

. . . . .

Most important, if a seller sells goods to a buyer and the buyer's bank dishonors the buyer's check payable to the seller in spite of sufficient funds and the absence of a stop order, the seller has no direct recourse against the buyer's bank. The best that the seller can do is to move against the buyer on the check or on the underlying obligation; the buyer can then move against his bank for wrongfully dishonoring an item that was "properly payable." See 84-4-402. In short, this section continues prior law in recognizing not one ounce of privity between the holder of a check and the drawee bank, assuming no certification and no retention beyond the midnight deadline. Nor can the holder sue the drawee bank for wrongful dishonor of an insolvent depositor's check just because the bank dishonored the item in order to protect its own interests. In such a case, the holder's recourse is against the drawer and any indorsers ...

The position urged by the plaintiffs is simply irreconcilable with the law of Kansas.

Nor have the plaintiffs attempted to demonstrate in a meaningful fashion the timing of the transactions surrounding their grain sales. Of course, the fact that Fleming was incurring losses in the commodities market and paying those losses, contributes to the fact that it is impossible to determine the source of the money in the account.

KSBT is entitled to summary judgment on the issue of conversion.

Pro Tanto

The Ad-Rem plaintiffs also contend that they are, irrespective of *Bolan*, entitled to a pro tanto assignment under Ballard v. Home Nat. Bank, 91 Kan. 91, 136 P. 935 (1913). They contend that the uncontroverted facts indicate that KSBT agreed or impliedly agreed not to setoff funds that were committed to accounts payable. The plaintiffs contend that the KSBT's tacit agreement coupled with its knowledge of Fleming's operation entitle them to a pro tanto assignment of funds. KSBT rather casually dismisses this argument in a footnote. The court is, however, compelled to agree with KSBT's analysis.

In *Ballard*, the Supreme Court of Kansas held:

"All the authorities are agreed upon the rule of law declared in the above case, that a bank which accepts a deposit of money made by a depositor for a special purpose, under an agreement that it will pay the amount when needed for that purpose, can not rightfully appropriate such deposit to discharge the depositor's indebtedness to it." (Note, 30 L.R.A., n.s., 517; see, also, Notes, 111 Am.St.Rep. 415; 2 Ann.Ca. 206; 19 Ann.Cas. 488.) It is not necessary, in order for this rule to apply, that there shall be what is strictly and technically known as a "special deposit." It is enough that there is an agreement for a particular application of the fund. The bank's right to a lien upon deposits is not of such character that it may not be waived....

"Of the general rule that a bank to whom a depositor is owing a matured indebtedness may appropriate the general deposit of its debtor to the discharge of the obligation, there can be no doubt.... But it is no less certain that a deposit made for a special purpose, or under a special agreement, can not rightfully be so appropriated.... Indeed, the proposition that a bank enjoys no exemption from the general rule by which every party to a business transaction or agreement is legally bound to respect the obligation of his contract is one which ought to require neither argument nor citation of authority."

91 Kan. at 94, 136 P. 935.

In short, there is no evidence indicating that such an agreement existed. The written agreements between KSBT and Fleming did not create such an agreement. On the contrary, those agreements gave KSBT the right to setoff or otherwise collect funds in Fleming's account. The court rejects the plaintiffs' contention that KSBT's failure to exercise the right of setoff (at Fleming's request) prior to July 25, 1984, waived that right and gave rise to an implicit or tacit agreement as to the ownership of funds in the Fleming account.

The court recognizes that the plaintiffs in this case are the unfortunate victims of the financial ruin of Fleming. While the court is not unsympathetic to this series of events which leaves the plaintiffs only partially compensated, the court is compelled to conclude that the plaintiffs have not demonstrated a sufficient property interest to survive summary judgment.

IT IS THEREFORE ORDERED that KSBT's motions for summary judgment in * * * are granted, * * * that the plaintiffs' motion for cross-summary judgment in Case Number 89-1316 (Dk. 46) is denied; [and] * * * that the trustee's motions for summary judgment * * * are dismissed as moot.

Uniform Commercial Code §4-303 (1990 Official Text)

§4-303. When Items Subject to Notice, Stop-Payment Order, Legal Process, or Setoff; Order in Which Items May be Charged or Certified

(a) Any knowledge, notice, or stop-payment order received by, legal process served upon, or setoff exercised by a payor bank comes too late to terminate, suspend, or modify the bank's right or duty to pay an item or to charge its customer's account for the item if the knowledge, notice, stop-payment order, or legal process is received or served and a reasonable time for the bank to act thereon expires or the setoff is exercised after the earliest of the following:

(1) The bank accepts or certifies the item;

(2) The bank pays the item in cash;

(3) The bank settles for the item without having a right to revoke the settlement under statute, clearing-house rule, or agreement;

(4) The bank becomes accountable for the amount of the item under Section 4-302 of this title dealing with the payor bank's responsibility for late return of items; or

(5) With respect to checks, a cutoff hour no earlier than one (1) hour after the opening of the next banking day after the banking day on which the bank received the check and no later than the close of that next banking day or, if no cutoff hour is fixed, the close of the next banking day after the banking day on which the bank received the check.

(b) Subject to subsection (a) of this section, items may be accepted, paid, certified, or charged to the indicated account of its customer in any order.

Official Comment

1. While a payor bank is processing an item presented for payment, it may receive knowledge or a legal notice affecting the item, such as knowledge or a notice that the drawer has filed a petition in bankruptcy or made an assignment for the benefit of creditors; may receive an order of the drawer stopping payment on the item; may have served on it an attachment of the account of the drawer; or the bank itself may exercise a right of setoff against the drawer's account. Each of these events affects the account of the drawer and may eliminate or freeze all or part of whatever balance is available to pay the item. Subsection (a) states the

rule for determining the relative priorities between these various legal events and the item.

2. The rule is that if any one of several things has been done to the item or if it has reached any one of several stages in its processing at the time the knowledge, notice, stop-payment order or legal process is received or served and a reasonable time for the bank to act thereon expires or the setoff is exercised, the knowledge, notice, stop-payment order, legal process or setoff comes too late, the item has priority and a charge to the customer's account may be made and is effective. With respect to the effect of the customer's bankruptcy, the bank's rights are governed by Bankruptcy Code Section 542(c) which codifies the result of Bank of Marin v. England, 385 U.S. 99 (1966). Section 4-405 applies to the death or incompetence of the customer.

* * *

2. Setoff Versus Garnishment

Wenneker v. Physicians MultiSpecialty Group, Inc.
Supreme Court of Missouri, 1991
814 S.W.2d 294

Blackmar, Judge. Here we treat of the right of a garnishee to set off claims it has against the judgment debtor. The essential facts are stipulated and both sides agree that there are no factual disputes. Most of the somewhat complicated facts are not necessary to the resolution of the legal issues.

The garnishor, Wenneker Delmar Partnership, recovered a judgment against Physicians Multispecialty Group, Inc. (PMG.) in the amount of $122,934.46, including attorney's fees of $2,000.00. It caused South Side National Bank in St. Louis to be summoned as garnishee. At the time the garnishment summons was served, July 12, 1989, PMG had a total of $176,166.71 on deposit in two accounts.

The bank sought to set off the amount of $151,384.08, representing installments of rent, at the time of the service of the garnishment, against its deposit liability to PMG in responding to the garnishment. It conceded that PMG had an outstanding balance over and above the asserted indebtedness in the amount of $24,330.97, and that amount was paid into court.

The indebtedness the bank asserts arose out of a lease transaction between Netherton Building Partnership as lessor and PMG as lessee. The leased premises (the Project) were the subject of a bond issue. Netherton executed a note which was secured by a deed of trust and security agreement on the leased premises, and the bank acquired the note. The note states that the principal and interest were payable out of rent and revenue from the building project. Netherton explicitly assigned the rents coming due from PMG as further security for this note. PMG agreed that its lease would be subordinate to any deeds of trust placed on the premises and also agreed that Netherton had the right to assign its interest in the lease as security for financing the project. In October of 1988 PMG abandoned the premises and ceased paying rent. The bank took possession under the terms of the assignment without terminating the lease. Netherton defaulted on the note held by the bank. On March 16, 1989 the bank foreclosed its deed of trust and purchased the leased premises at the foreclosure sale for $400,000. Thus the bank was entitled to all unpaid rents, whether accruing before or after the foreclosure, and these, together with charges such as taxes and insurance which PMG was obliged to pay by contract, amounted to $106,262.97 at the time the garnishment was served. The bank also claims that it was entitled to set off the rents accruing after the service of the garnishment, which amounted to $45,121.11 at the time the bank sold the property on September 13, 1989.

Wenneker argues that debts owed to the bank as lessor and as assignee of rents may not be set off against deposits. It also claims that the bank waived any right of setoff by paying two checks after the service of the garnishment.

The trial court entered summary judgment for the bank. The Court of Appeals, Eastern District, reversed, essentially accepting Wenneker's arguments. We granted transfer because of the importance of the question of a garnishee's right of setoff and the paucity of authority. We now sustain the bank's right to set off only the indebtedness due it at the time of the garnishment, and reverse and remand for the entry of a modified judgment. We also reject Wenneker's claim of waiver.

1. Set-Off of Rental Payments

Wenneker argues that a garnishee's right of set-off exists only as to claims which satisfy a requirement of "mutuality." Thus, it argues, claims arising out of an assignment and claims for rent may not be set off against bank deposits. It does not adduce persuasive authority for its contention.

* * *

Missouri law rather holds that garnishees may set off any matured and liquidated claims they hold against judgment debtors. Garnishment is a legal process through which a holder of a judgment may apply sums which others owe the judgment debtors to the satisfaction of the judgment. See generally Ch. 525, RSMo 1986. It is said that the garnishor stands in the shoes of the judgment debtor. It follows that the garnishor may reach the indebtedness which the garnishee has a present obligation to pay to the judgment debtor at the time of service, and nothing beyond this. In Firebaugh v. Stone, 36 Mo. 111, 115 (1865) this Court quoted from Drake on Attachments, § 672, as follows:

> an attaching creditor can hold the garnishee only to the extent of the defendant's claim against the garnishee, and he can acquire no rights against the latter, except such as the defendant had; and as he is not permitted to place the garnishee in any worse condition than he would occupy if sued by defendant, it follows necessarily, that whatever defence the garnishee could urge against an action by the defendant, for the debt in respect of which he is garnished, he may set up in bar of a judgment

against him as garnishee. The garnishment freezes the mutual debts and credits of the garnishee and the judgment debtor at a point in time.

Wenneker argues that, if the setoff is allowed, it will be possible for banks to purchase obligations of their customers, perhaps at a discount, in order to set them off against deposits. We do not find this professed fear sufficiently disturbing to justify an alteration of the law as we understand it. Here there is no suggestion that the bank did not acquire its claims against PMG in the normal course of business, as additional security for the Netherton note.

Wenneker also argues that the liquidation of garnishments may be indefinitely delayed if trial is required as to issues between the garnishee and the judgment debtor. It would not be appropriate to deny a right of setoff simply because that right might be contested. The garnishor has no equity in recovering more than the garnishee owes the judgment debtor. Catching something by garnishment process is a fortuitous event.

It follows that the bank is entitled to set off its matured claims against the deposits reached by the garnishment.

2. Future Installments of Rent

The bank also claims a right to set off rent accruing after the service of the garnishment, relying on language of the "written depositor's contract" (commonly called "signature card") signed by PMG, as follows: Bank has a security interest in any monies in this account or any other now or hereafter in possession of Bank for the payment of any indebtedness or liability now or hereafter owing the Bank by both or either.

We do not believe that this language is sufficient to allow a setoff of installments of rent not yet due when the garnishment is served. As has been said earlier, the garnishment causes the striking of a balance. The language "now or hereafter" speaks as of the time the depositor's contract was signed, and allows the bank a lien on installments of rent as they come due, but is not sufficient to defeat the right of the garnishor to reach the net amount due the judgment debtor at the time of service. Future installments of rent were neither "indebtedness" nor "liability" at the time the garnishment was served. Numerous cases hold that there may be setoff only of matured demands. Under these authorities future installments of rent may not be set off. Our holding of course does not relieve PMG of such liability as it may have to the bank for these installments. We deal here only with the question of setoff.

We express no opinion as to the right of setoff of a note due on demand, or as to the effect of an acceleration clause. We simply hold that the contractual language in this case is not sufficient to justify the setoff of future installments of rent.

3. The Effect of Payment of Checks

The stipulation shows that the bank paid two small checks of PMG which were presented after the service of the garnishment, one in the amount of $331.66

on July 13, 1989 and one in the amount of $120.00 on July 17, 1989. Two checks presented later were not honored. Wenneker argues that the bank, by paying the two checks, waived its right of setoff, citing numerous authorities.

The stipulated facts do not establish the affirmative claim of waiver, which is consistently defined in our cases as the "intentional relinquishment of a known right." In the authorities relied on the courts appear to have sensed a deliberate purpose on the part of the garnishee of aiding the judgment debtor by ignoring the garnishment. Where the bank appears simply to have been careless in paying checks drawn on a garnished account, other courts have not found waiver. The turndown of two later checks, after having paid the first two presented after the service of the garnishment, is more probative of carelessness than of waiver. The bank, however, must account to the garnishor for the proceeds of the improperly paid checks.

The judgment is reversed and the case is remanded with directions to enter a new judgment allowing the bank to set off the indebtedness due it from PMG for rent and related expenses as of July 12, 1989, less $451.66 on account of the two checks improvidently paid.

Bray v. Ed Willey & Son
Supreme Court of Arkansas, 1965
239 Ark. 855, 395 S.W.2d 342

[Reprinted at pages 29-31 supra.]

3. Setoff Versus Security Interest

Citizens National Bank v. Mid-States Development Co.
Court of Appeals of Indiana, Third District, 1978
177 Ind. App. 548, 380 N.E.2d 1243

Garrard, Presiding Judge. This appeal requires us to resolve the conflict that arises when a bank exercises a right of set-off against funds in a depositor's account that represent proceeds of accounts receivable and inventory in which a secured party has a perfected interest under the Uniform Commercial Code. The trial court, sitting without a jury, determined that the secured party was entitled to these funds so that the bank's set-off amounted to a wrongful conversion of the property. We affirm the trial court's decision and hold that, on these facts, the Uniform Commercial Code requires that the bank, as an unsecured creditor, be subordinated to the perfected security interest in proceeds.

* * *

The Bank argues that rights of set-off are excluded from the Code's treatment of secured transactions. It therefore contends that we are enjoined to resolve this dispute without reference to the UCC and Code's adoption.

* * *

In determining whether the Code's chapter on secured transactions is applicable to the assertion of a bank's right of set-off we are confronted with statutory language that "This article (chapter) does not apply . . . to any right of set-off . . . ." IC 26-1-9-104(i). While the language is plain enough, the conclusion that this section removes from operation of the Code any controversy between a setting-off bank and a secured party is not warranted by the narrow purpose this provision was intended to serve. Professor Gilmore, a principal reporter for Article 9 of the Code, gives this explanation for the set-off exclusion:

> "This exclusion is an apt example of the absurdities which result when draftsmen attempt to appease critics by putting into a statute something that is not in any sense wicked but is hopelessly irrelevant. Of course a right of set-off is not a security interest and has never been confused with one: the statute might as appropriately exclude fan dancing. A bank's right of set-off against a depositor's account is often loosely referred to as a 'banker's lien,' but the 'lien' usage has never led anyone to think that the bank held a security interest in the bank account. Banking groups were, however, concerned lest someone, someday, might think that a bank's right of set-off, because it was called a lien, was a security interest. Hence the exclusion, which does no harm except to the dignity and self-respect of the draftsmen."

Plainly banks need not comply with the requirements of Chapter 9 in order to assert set-offs against their depositors. But given the narrow purpose of the set-off exclusion we are unwilling to read it as removing commercial transactions or conflicts from the operation of the UCC whenever a bank's set-off is involved.

Acceptance of the narrow view of the set-off exclusion does not, however, resolve the priority dispute between the Bank and Soya. It is a predicate of the consideration of statutory and case authority relevant to the secured party versus setting-off bank conflict. We believe that the Code's priority rules require the proceeds security interest to prevail over a bank's right of set-off against funds placed in a general deposit.

    * * *

[U]nderlying the complex of Code priority provisions is the keystone rule of IC 26-1-9-201 which states: "General validity of security agreement. Except as otherwise provided by this act (26-1-1-101 26-1-10-106) a security agreement is effective according to its terms between the parties, against purchasers of the collateral and against creditors. Nothing in this article (chapter) validates any charge or practice illegal under any statute or regulation thereunder governing usury, small loans, retail instalment sales, or the like, or extends the application of any such statute or regulation to any transaction not otherwise subject thereto." The effect of this section is to give the Chapter 9 secured party, upon a debtor's default, priority over "anyone, anywhere, anyhow" except as otherwise provided by the remaining Code priority rules. The Bank as a creditor of Huntington falls within the ambit of this section. There being nothing else in the Code to resolve the priority conflict between Soya and the Bank, section 9- 201 is controlling. As an unsecured general creditor[1] the Bank's claim of set-off should be subordinated to the proceeds security interest asserted by Soya.

* * *

[W]e believe the secured party should be able to rely on his compliance with the Code's requirements for perfection and his search of the public recording system as against the unrecorded interest of the setting-off bank. Were this otherwise a secured party with an interest in proceeds could not rely on recording but would be required to take additional steps to insure that he was accorded full protection. For example, the secured party might have proceeds deposited in a special account thus precluding a bank's set-off rights. Under such a rule the secured party would have to require special accounts or inquire into loan transactions which are not a matter of public record. Putting such a duty on a secured party, as well as permitting a bank to prevail if that duty is not met, undercuts significant values of certainty, efficiency and reliance which are at the heart of the Code's emphasis on public filing. On the other hand a secured party might require that proceeds be payable to it before future advances would be made to the debtor. While this may be safe practice for a creditor, it is purposefully not required by the Code for the maintenance of a proceeds security interest since it tends to curtail commercial practice and business operation. IC 26-1-9-205; IC 26-1-9-306(2) and (3). In short, if Chapter 9 is to be a comprehensive system for the perfection of security interests in personal property we see no reason for requiring special standards, with their increased costs, that must be met if a secured party is to prevail over a bank's right of set-off. The Code's priority rules are sufficient.

* * *

The judgment is affirmed.

---

[1] In characterizing the Bank as a general unsecured creditor of Soya we do not diminish longstanding Indiana law which recognizes the special character of a bank's right of set-off. Money deposited in a general account becomes the property of the bank; the depositor becomes the bank's creditor to the extent of the deposit. When the depositor becomes indebted to the bank, a mutual debtor-creditor relationship arises that justifies a bank's right of set-off, I. e., a self-help device for extinguishing mutual debts. The right arises by operation of law and is founded both on fairness and on the nature of the bank deposit which permits the depositor to erase any mutual indebtedness by his withdrawal. However, where this right is exercised unilaterally, no Code provision extends special protection to the bank vis-a-vis the proceeds security interest. Of course, if the depositor made a voluntary transfer to the bank in the ordinary course of his business, the bank cold seek the protection of IC 26-1-9-206.

Bank of Kansas v. Hutchinson Health Services, Inc.
Court of Appeals of Kansas, 1989
13 Kan. App. 2d 421, 773 P.2d 660

Davis, Judge: This appeal involves conflicting claims by the Bank of Kansas (Bank) and the State of Kansas to Medicaid reimbursement funds owed by the Kansas Department of Social and Rehabilitation Services (SRS) to Hutchinson Health Services, Inc., (HHS) a nursing home operator. The Bank holds a perfected security interest in HHS' accounts receivable, which include the Medicaid reimbursement funds, based on three loans it made to HHS, which loans are in default. The State of Kansas through the Department of Human Resources (DHR) claims the right of setoff for delinquent unemployment contributions owed by HHS. The trial court held that the Bank's perfected security interest prevailed over the State's right of setoff. We affirm in part, reverse in part, and remand for further proceedings.

The resolution of this case requires us to answer two questions: (1) Whether the priority rules of Article 9 of the Uniform Commercial Code (UCC) apply to a priority battle between a creditor's right of setoff and another creditor's perfected security interest in the debtor's accounts receivable; and (2) if so, what specific rules apply and with what result?

The facts are not in dispute. The Bank made three separate loans to HHS totaling $281,384.58. These loans were secured by a perfected security interest in HHS' accounts receivable, which include Medicaid reimbursement funds.

HHS defaulted. The Bank filed suit on November 16, 1984, and on November 19, 1984, filed an amended petition against HHS and SRS, seeking judgment against HHS on the promissory notes for $186,141.51 plus interest and seeking orders requiring the SRS to pay all of HHS' Medicaid reimbursement accounts to the Bank. DHR intervened in the suit, alleging that HHS owed $14,916.42 in delinquent unemployment contributions and that the State of Kansas was entitled to offset this amount against the Medicaid reimbursement funds owed by SRS to HHS.

On March 15, 1985, the Bank and the DHR entered into an agreed order recognizing that the State of Kansas had acquired by setoff $14,916.42 from the Medicaid reimbursement funds owed to HHS. Both parties agreed that the question of priority to these funds would be reserved for a later determination. The Bank was granted judgment against HHS for $197,812.42 plus interest. The Medicaid reimbursement funds were then paid into court by SRS and distributed to the Bank in partial satisfaction of its judgment. The trial court held that the Bank's perfected security interest in the Medicaid reimbursement funds had priority over DHR's right of setoff and granted judgment for the Bank for the $14,916.42 plus interest.

Before addressing the questions raised by this appeal, we note that this court has resolved a priority battle between Bank of Kansas and Central State Bank in this same case involving different funds. Bank of Kansas v. Hutchinson Health

Services, Inc., 12 Kan.App.2d 87, 735 P.2d 256, rev. denied 241 Kan. 838 (1987). Central State Bank offset the funds in HHS' checking account against debts HHS owed to it, but the Bank of Kansas claimed that it was entitled to the funds because they were identifiable proceeds of HHS' accounts receivable, in which the Bank of Kansas held a perfected security interest. We held that while a bank or other creditor seeking to exercise a right of setoff need not comply with the requirements of Article 9, "the priority as between a right of setoff and a perfected security interest is governed by Article 9." 12 Kan.App.2d at 93, 735 P.2d 256. (1) Do the priority rules of Article 9 of the Uniform Commercial Code apply to a priority battle between a creditor's right of setoff and another creditor's perfected security interest in the debtor's accounts receivable?

While our previous decision provides a direct answer to our first question, DHR argues that we should limit this holding to priority battles between banks and other financial institutions. Although the previous appeal involved a priority battle between two banks, our holding applies to any priority battle involving a right of setoff and a perfected security interest. We again hold that "the priority as between a right of setoff and a perfected security interest is governed by Article 9." 12 Kan.App.2d at 93, 735 P.2d 256.

* * *

The determination of priorities under Article 9 requires that we identify the respective parties within the context of Article 9. The Bank is a perfected secured party. K.S.A.1988 Supp. 84-9-105(1)(m); K.S.A. 84-9-303. HHS is a "debtor" since it owes payment of the obligation secured. K.S.A.1988 Supp. 84-9-105(1)(d). The collateral, HHS' accounts receivable, including the Medicaid reimbursement funds, is an "account" since it represents HHS' right to payment for services rendered. K.S.A. 84-9-106. Since the State is obligated through SRS to pay on the account, that is, to make Medicaid reimbursement payments to HHS, the State is an "account debtor." K.S.A.1988 Supp. 84-9-105(1)(a).

This appeal involves accounts receivable financing. Accounts receivable financing involves an assignment of the debtor's accounts receivables to the secured party as security for the debtor's obligation. When the account debtor is not informed of the arrangement, as is the case here, the financing is on a "non-notification" basis. The Kansas Comment explains:

> "[I]f the assignment is on a 'non-notification' basis, as with the typical security interest in accounts, the secured party does not notify account debtors to make payment direct to it until default of the assignor. Once direct collection is triggered, the secured party can 'take control' of the proceeds, as by crediting checks to the unpaid balance of the assignor's debt."

Kansas Comment 1983 to K.S.A. 84-9-502. In such a case, the assignment can be thought of as taking effect only after the debtor defaults and notice of the assignment is given to the account debtor.

The general priority rule in Article 9 is stated in K.S.A. 84-9-201: "Except as otherwise provided by this act a security agreement is effective according to its terms between the parties, against purchasers of the collateral and against creditors." We applied this rule to resolve the priority battle in Bank of Kansas v. Hutchinson Health Services, Inc., 12 Kan.App.2d 87, 735 P.2d 256. The parties and the trial court applied the same rule to resolve the present dispute. However, when the setoff is asserted by the account debtor, the priority rule is "otherwise provided" by Article 9.

When an account receivable has been assigned as security, "[t]he account debtor is authorized to pay the assignor until the account debtor receives notification that the amount due or to become due has been assigned and that payment is to be made to the assignee." K.S.A. 84-9-318(3). Notification may be made "when so agreed" or "in any event on default." K.S.A. 84-9-502(1).

The date of notification is critical when the claims arise independently of the contract creating the account because it determines what claims the assignee is subject to. K.S.A. 84-9-318(1)(b) provides:

> "[T]he rights of an assignee are subject to ... any other defense or claim of the account debtor against the assignor which accrues before the account debtor receives notification of the assignment." The Official UCC Comment explains that, when an account debtor has claims against the assignor which arise independently of the contract creating the account, "an assignee is subject to all such claims which accrue before, and free of all those which accrue after, the account debtor is notified."

Official UCC Comment No. 1 to K.S.A. 84-9-318. The Kansas Comment explains:

> "A financing assignee also takes subject to the account debtor's right of setoff from defenses or claims arising out of other contracts, under subsection (1)(b), so long as the right of setoff accrues before the account debtor receives notification of the assignment." Kansas Comment 1983 to K.S.A. 84-9-318.

* * *

RESULT

Applying K.S.A. 84-9-318(1)(b) to this case, we conclude that whether the State of Kansas through DHR may offset its claim for HHS' delinquent unemployment contributions against the funds SRS owes HHS depends on when the State's claim accrued. If the State's claim accrued before the Bank notified SRS of the assignment, the Bank's assignment is subject to the claim. If the State's claim accrued after the Bank notified SRS, the Bank takes free of the claim.

A secured party "notifies" an account debtor "by taking such steps as may be reasonably required to inform the [account debtor] in ordinary course whether or not [the account debtor] actually comes to know of it." K.S.A.1988 Supp. 84-1-201(26). The record shows that the Bank first notified SRS that it was entitled to payment when it filed its amended petition naming SRS as a defendant on November 19, 1984. Arguably, notice was not "in ordinary course"; however, it is sufficient to satisfy the requirements of the UCC because SRS received actual notice of the Bank's claim. See K.S.A. 84-1-102. We conclude that notice was given on November 19, 1984.

The UCC leaves the definition of when a claim "accrues" to the law under which the claim arose. The Employment Security Law, however, does not expressly state when contributions accruc. In the absence of an express definition, two possibilities suggest themselves. A claim could "accrue": (1) when the obligation to pay is incurred; or (2) when the obligation is actually due and payable. The first definition reflects a fiscal view, appropriate to accounting or tax law. The second definition reflects the more usual sense of accrue, that is, that "a claim or setoff accrues when a cause of action exists." Seattle-First Nat'l Bk. v. Ore. Pac. Inc., 262 Or. 578, 583, 500 P.2d 1033 (1972).

On balance, we believe that the policies of simplicity and commercial certainty underlying the UCC favor the second definition. See K.S.A. 84-1-102. Under the first definition, the value of accounts assigned as security could never be accurately determined because the accounts would always be subject to an independent claim arising against the assignor after the assignment is made, but accruing beforehand. Under the second definition, the value of accounts can be determined with reasonable certainty at the time of the assignment. As the Oregon court noted, an assignment must have "value and stability" to "be used as an effective security device." 262 Or. at 582, 500 P.2d 1033.

When an unemployment contribution payment is due and payable is specified in the administrative regulations adopted pursuant to law: "[C]ontributions ... shall become due on, and shall be paid on or before, the 25th day following the close of the calendar quarter in which the wages are paid." K.A.R. 50-2-3(b). Thus, HHS' contributions for the third quarter of 1984 were due on October 25, 1984, before the Bank gave notice, and its fourth quarter contributions were due on January 25, 1985, after the Bank gave notice.

We conclude that State of Kansas through DHR is entitled to offset the amount owed for the third quarter of 1984--approximately $10,122.36--together with any interest or penalties thereon against the money SRS owes to the Bank as HHS' assignee. We further conclude that the security interest of the Bank is superior to the State of Kansas' right of setoff for the amount owed for the fourth quarter of 1984--approximately $4,678.72. On remand, the trial court is directed to compute the exact amounts to which each party is entitled and to enter judgment in favor of the Bank for the amount it is still owed.

Affirmed in part, reversed in part, and remanded with directions.

4. Setoff Versus Federal Tax Lien

Jersey State Bank v. United States
United States Court of Appeals, Seventh Circuit, 1991
926 F.2d 621

Posner, Circuit Judge. The Internal Revenue Service, having assessed (demanded) taxes due from Marion Price, served a notice of levy on the Jersey State Bank, in which Price had a demand deposit account--a notice, in other words, that the Service intended to seize the account in order to collect the assessment. 26 U.S.C. §6331. Price had borrowed money from the bank for his business in exchange for a note that not only promised to repay the loan but also purported to give the bank a security interest in the deposit account and a right to set off money in that account against Price's debt to the bank. The loan was in default, so after receiving the Internal Revenue Service's notice of levy the bank exercised its right of set off by seizing the balance in the deposit account, some $5,000. Later the Service filed a notice of tax lien, which it claims established its priority over the bank's right of set off. The district court disagreed and gave judgment for the bank in this suit for wrongful levy, and the Service has appealed. The bank has cross-appealed, arguing that it is entitled to reasonable attorney's fees under 26 U.S.C. §7430, which entitles the prevailing party in a suit for wrongful levy to attorney's fees unless the government's position was substantially justified. The cross-appeal must fail. The statute defines prevailing party to exclude not only the United States but also the taxpayer's creditor, §7430(c)(4)(A), which is what the bank is.

The making of the tax assessment against Price created a lien upon his property, and the lien arose on the date of the assessment. 26 U.S.C. §§6321, 6322. If, however, the competing creditor, that is, the bank, obtained a "security interest" in the property (the money on deposit) before the Internal Revenue Service filed its notice of tax lien, the creditor prevails. §6323(a). (The notice of levy was not the assessment, was not a notice of tax lien, was not filed, and, in short, has no significance with respect to the question which lien had priority.) We must go therefore to section 6323(h)(1)(A), which defines "security interest," so far as pertinent here, as any interest in property "protected under local law against a subsequent judgment lien arising out of an unsecured obligation." This shunts us to Illinois law, where the controlling case is Pines Trailer Corp. v. Roaring Express Co., 127 Ill.App.2d 46, 261 N.E.2d 709 (1970). A bank was owed money by one of its depositors, who just as in this case had defaulted on an obligation to the bank. Another creditor of the depositor obtained a judgment entitling it to garnish the depositor's account. Before he could do so the bank exercised its right to set off the money in the account against the depositor's debt to it. The court held that this was a proper set off, and by so holding put the bank ahead of a subsequent judgment lienor, the garnishing creditor. This shows that the interest which a bank acquires in its depositor's account as a result of his defaulting is a security interest as defined by the federal statute. So even if the set off had been made after the Internal Revenue Service filed its notice of tax lien, the bank would have won, because the security interest that the set off enforced had been obtained before that filing. Indeed, it may have been obtained even before the promissory note came due by virtue of the default--may have been obtained when the loan was made in the first place. Bee Jay's Truck Stop v. Dept. of Revenue, 86 Ill.App.3d 7, 13, 41 Ill.Dec. 257, 262, 407 N.E.2d 755, 760 (1980).

It is arguable (though Jefferson Bank & Trust v. United States, 894 F.2d 1241, 1244 (10th Cir.1990), is to the contrary) that the bank's security interest was "inchoate" until the bank exercised its right of set off or took other steps to prevent the depositor from withdrawing the money in the account. But that is of no consequence. The set off was made before the notice of tax lien was filed, and a security interest that predates such notice takes priority over the federal tax lien. All this assumes, moreover--what is by no means clear--that the doctrine of inchoate liens survived the enactment of the Tax Lien Act of 1966, which added to the Code the provisions cited earlier relating to the priority of state-created security interests (§§6323(a), (h)(1)(A)). That was a judge-made doctrine designed to determine whether a prior state law lien had acquired "sufficient substance" that it ought to be permitted to defeat a federal tax lien. United States v. Pioneer American Ins. Co., 374 U.S. 84, 88, 83 S.Ct. 1651, 1655, 10 L.Ed.2d 770 (1963). The test of "sufficient substance" required that the identity of the state law lienor, the amount of his lien, and the property subject to the lien all have been ascertained, made determinate, before the filing of the federal tax lien. Id. at 89, 83 S.Ct. at 1655; United States v. City of New Britain, 347 U.S. 81, 84, 74 S.Ct. 367, 369, 98 L.Ed. 520 (1954). The 1966 Act, passed as it was in part to alleviate the perceived harshness of the doctrine of inchoate liens, Aetna Ins. Co. v. Texas Thermal Industries, Inc., 591 F.2d 1035, 1038 (5th Cir.1979) (per curiam), is markedly, perhaps pregnantly, silent in regard to any requirement that the state tax lien be "choate"; all that is required is that the state security interest have been obtained prior to the filing of the federal tax lien. And the Committee reports state that security interests as defined in the Act "are to have a priority over a nonfiled Federal tax lien ... whether or not in all other regards they are definite and complete at the time notice of the tax lien is filed." H.R.Rep. No. 1884, 89th Cong., 2d Sess. 4 (1966); S.Rep. No. 1708, 89th Cong., 2d Sess. 4 (1966), U.S.Code Cong. & Admin.News 1966, pp. 3722, 3724, 3725. Aetna concluded that the Tax Lien Act had wiped out the doctrine of inchoate liens. A number of other decisions, however, including our own J.D. Court, Inc. v. United States, 712 F.2d 258, 262 (7th Cir.1983), and decisions in the Fifth Circuit itself, cited in Texas Commerce Bank-Fort Worth, N.A. v. United States, 896 F.2d 152, 161 n. 8 (5th Cir.1990), disagree; and United States v. Bell Credit Union, 860 F.2d 365, 371 (10th Cir.1988), tries to split the difference. The present case is hardly the one in which to try to resolve the question what if anything of the doctrine of inchoate liens survived the passage of the Tax Lien Act. Certainly with the actual making of the set off all the requirements of "choateness" had been satisfied, and the set off preceded the notice of tax lien. The testing case would be one in which the bank had made the set off after the notice of tax lien was filed.

It is true, as the government argues, that the Internal Revenue Service is not a garnishment creditor, that the bank's interest was not "perfected" by any act of sequestration or announcement prior to the exercise of the right of set off, and that it was not a common law pledge. But so what? Illinois law would protect the bank's interest in the taxpayer's deposit against a judgment lien creditor of the depositor by allowing the bank to set off the depositor's debt to it with its debt to the depositor (that is, with the deposit) when the other creditor appeared on the scene. This shows that the bank had a security interest within the meaning of the Tax Lien Act when the notice of the federal tax lien was filed. We repeat that, if it is necessary, as it may not be, the security interest was not inchoate at the time the notice of federal tax lien was filed, since the identity of the state law lienor, the amount of his lien, and the property subject to the lien had all been unequivocally fixed earlier, when the bank exercised its right of set off (even earlier, if one agrees with Jefferson Bank & Trust).

Neither the appeal nor the cross-appeal has merit, and the judgment of the district court is therefore

AFFIRMED.

C. EQUITABLE LIENS AND THE LIKE

Darr v. Muratore
United States District Court, D. Rhode Island, 1992
143 B.R. 973

Lagueux, District Judge. This matter is presently before the Court on defendants' motion to quash and remove the notices of lis pendens filed by a creditors' committee and adopted by plaintiff on thirty-nine parcels of real estate. For the reasons that follow, the Court denies defendants' motion.

I. BACKGROUND

Columbus Mortgage & Loan Corporation of Rhode Island, Inc. ("Columbus Mortgage") is an insolvent corporation licensed by the State to act as a primary and secondary mortgage lender. Columbus Mortgage filed for bankruptcy on February 15, 1991. Plaintiff Stephen Darr was appointed the Trustee in bankruptcy ("Trustee") of Columbus Mortgage on December 23, 1991.

Defendant Joseph R. Muratore, Sr. ("Muratore") is a shareholder, director, president, treasurer, and executive officer of Columbus Mortgage. Muratore is also a shareholder, director, and officer of Muratore Agency, Inc. ("Muratore Agency") and Muratore Realty Corp. ("Muratore Realty"), and a general partner of Shawomet Holding Association ("Shawomet Holding"). Rose E. Muratore, Muratore's wife, is a shareholder in Columbus Mortgage, Muratore Agency, and

Muratore Realty. She is also a director and secretary-treasurer of Columbus Mortgage, an officer and director of Muratore Agency and Muratore Realty, and a partner in Shawomet Holding.

The Trustee asserts that Muratore Agency, Muratore Realty, and Shawomet Holding ("the affiliated entities"), and Columbus Mortgage were the alter egos of Muratore, with virtually all of their business affairs controlled by him. They shared common ownership, employees, premises, phone lines, fax numbers, and equipment. Their assets were commingled, and few corporate formalities existed to establish them as independent entities.

The Trustee further asserts that Muratore, having had nearly absolute control over Columbus Mortgage, transferred at least two million dollars from Columbus Mortgage to himself, his wife, the affiliated entities, and their creditors. These were essentially unsecured loans, not evidenced by promissory notes or any other documentation. Muratore used the funds to acquire and maintain real estate and other assets held by defendants. Accordingly, the Trustee brought suit to impose a constructive trust on the property standing in the name of various defendants, and ratified the notices of lis pendens filed by the creditors' committee to preserve the interests of Columbus Mortgage pending the outcome of the litigation.

Defendants present two separate grounds in support of quashing and removing the notices of lis pendens. First, defendants claim that the Rhode Island lis pendens statute, R.I.Gen.Laws §9-4-9 (West Supp.1991), has been misused and that this action is an attempt to obtain the equivalent of an ex parte prejudgment attachment on real property. Second, defendants argue that the Rhode Island lis pendens statute is invalid because it lacks constitutional safeguards mandated by the due process clauses of the United States and Rhode Island Constitutions.

After having heard arguments on the motion, the Court took the matter under advisement. The motion is now in order for decision.

II. APPLICATION OF LIS PENDENS STATUTE

At early common law a judgment in a lawsuit could bind only the actual parties to the suit and those in privity with them, but in cases concerning title to real property, it was necessary to notify potential real estate buyers of the pending litigation. Chrysler Corp. v. Fedders Corp., 670 F.2d 1316, 1319 (3d Cir.1982). The common law doctrine of lis pendens stipulated that the filing of the lawsuit itself served as constructive notice that the property was the subject of litigation, and any buyer of the property would take title subject to the outcome of the litigation, even if he or she had no actual notice. Id.; Picerne v. Redd, 72 R.I. 4, 11, 47 A.2d 906, 910 (1946). State legislatures subsequently enacted lis pendens statutes to require parties claiming an interest in real property to file a notice of the pending litigation in the land records for that property. This provided buyers with the means of obtaining actual notice of the pending lawsuit, thereby alleviating the harsh rule of the common law doctrine. Campbell v. Metcalf, 20 R.I. 352, 353, 39 A. 190 (1898). A bona fide purchaser of real property, with or without actual notice, would be bound by the outcome of the litigation only if the plaintiff had filed a notice of lis pendens. Chrysler Corp., 670 F.2d at 1320; Debral Realty, Inc. v. DiChiara, 383 Mass. 559, 560-61, 420 N.E.2d 343, 345 (1981).

Section 9-4-9, the Rhode Island lis pendens statute, provides in pertinent part that a notice of lis pendens may be filed in an action "concerning the title to any real estate, in this state, or to any interest or easement therein." A plaintiff may not file a notice of lis pendens in a suit for monetary relief in order to obtain the benefit of an equitable attachment. Picerne, 72 R.I. at 15, 47 A.2d at 912.

Defendants argue that the notices of lis pendens have been improperly filed in this case because the Trustee has presented no claim concerning an interest in real estate. They assert that the Trustee has obtained the equivalent of an ex parte prejudgment attachment as security for Columbus Mortgage's claims against defendants. The Trustee counters that defendants' use of the unsecured funds from Columbus Mortgage entitles the Trustee to enforce an equitable lien on the land, sufficient to support the filing of a notice of lis pendens.

A.

The first question for the Court is whether an equitable lien falls within the scope of the lis pendens statute.

An equitable lien is a special form of constructive trust. Coventry Homes, Inc. v. Scottscom Partnership, 155 Ariz. 215, 218, 745 P.2d 962, 965 (Ct.App.1987). It is based upon the great maxim, "equity regards as done that which ought to have been done." Finkelstein v. Finkelstein, 502 A.2d 350, 354 (R.I.1985). In a constructive trust situation, a court imposes an in personam obligation on one party to convey real estate to the other party in order to prevent unjust enrichment. Matarese v. Calise, 111 R.I. 551, 562, 305 A.2d 112, 119 (1973). An equitable lien, however, is a proceeding against the property itself to enforce an equitable interest in the property. Coventry Homes, 155 Ariz. at 218, 745 P.2d at 965. Where a defendant has used the funds of a plaintiff to purchase new property, the plaintiff may have the option of enforcing either a constructive trust of the property or an equitable lien against the property. Restatement of Restitution §161 cmt. a (1936); accord In re Lela & Co., 551 F.2d 399, 406-07 (D.C.Cir.1977); Middlebrooks v. Lonas, 246 Ga. 720, 272 S.E.2d 687, 689 (1980). Where the funds have been used to improve property already owned by the defendant, the plaintiff would be entitled to enforce only an equitable lien. Restatement of Restitution §206.

Other jurisdictions have determined that a cause of action to impose an equitable lien is an action concerning title to or an interest in real property, sufficient to support the filing of a notice of lis pendens. In Coventry Homes, supra, the plaintiff had brought suit for anticipatory breach of a personal services contract and filed a notice of lis pendens against the defendant's property as security for his claim. 155 Ariz. at 216, 745 P.2d at 963. The Court stated that a valid cause of action to impose an equitable lien was an action affecting title to property that would support the filing of a notice of lis pendens. Id. at 218, 745

P.2d at 965. The Court found, however, that the plaintiff had no right to impose an equitable lien because the contract was unrelated to an interest in the property. Id. at 218-19, 745 P.2d at 965-66.

In Busch v. Doyle, 141 B.R. 432 (D.Utah 1992), the plaintiff sought damages and a constructive trust for breach of an oral employment contract, and filed a notice of lis pendens on defendant's property. Id. at 436. The Court found that the lis pendens was unjustified because the cause of action was a suit for money damages and did not affect title to land. Id. at 436. The Court noted that the plaintiff, while seeking to impose a constructive trust, had failed to allege an equitable lien in the complaint, thereby suggesting that if plaintiff had made a valid claim for an equitable lien, the lis pendens might have been upheld. Id.

In Burger v. Superior Court, 151 Cal.App.3d 1013, 199 Cal.Rptr. 227 (1984), plaintiff filed a notice of lis pendens on defendant's property, asserting imposition of a constructive trust because plaintiff's funds had been used to improve the property. Id. at 1016, 199 Cal.Rptr. at 229. The Court found that the value of the improvements was far less than the value of the land, and that plaintiff was actually seeking money damages, which would not justify a notice of lis pendens. Id. at 1018-19, 199 Cal.Rptr. at 230-31. The Court added that enforcement of an equitable lien might be an alternative ground on which to base the notice of lis pendens. Id.

At least two courts have found that an action to impose a constructive trust is an action affecting title to or right of possession of real property, sufficient to support a notice of lis pendens. Coppinger v. Superior Court, 134 Cal.App.3d 883, 891, 185 Cal.Rptr. 24, 29 (1982); Polk v. Schwartz, 166 N.J.Super. 292, 298, 399 A.2d 1001, 1004 (App.Div.1979). The Rhode Island Supreme Court, however, has never decided that precise point.

In Matarese, supra, the Rhode Island Supreme Court stated that a constructive trust did not create an equitable interest in land. 111 R.I. at 562, 305 A.2d at 118-19. This case is distinguishable because the plaintiff in Matarese sought merely to remedy breach of a fiduciary duty, not to assert an interest in the defendant's land. Id. Furthermore, the land in question was located in Italy, outside the jurisdiction of the Rhode Island lis pendens statute. The plaintiff's only remedy, therefore, was to impose a constructive trust on the land, requiring the defendant to convey it in accordance with his agency agreement. Id.

This Court concludes that when the Rhode Island Supreme Court faces the issue, it will decide that a cause of action to enforce an equitable lien is an action affecting title to or an interest in real property, sufficient to support the filing of a notice of lis pendens.

B.

The next issue is whether the facts in this case adequately support a request for an equitable lien.

The Court must determine from the allegations in the complaint, taken as true, whether the Trustee has asserted a claim concerning title to or an interest in real property. American Motor Club, Inc. v. Neu (In re American Motor Club, Inc.),

109 B.R. 595, 598 (Bankr.E.D.N.Y.1990); Sutherland v. Aolean Dev. Corp., 399 Mass. 36, 40, 502 N.E.2d 528, 531 (1987). The Trustee need not establish that Columbus Mortgage will ultimately succeed on the merits. American Motor Club, 109 B.R. at 598; Coppinger, 134 Cal.App.3d at 888, 185 Cal.Rptr. at 27. Furthermore, Muratore's absolute control over the businesses and his commingling of their assets complicates the tracing of the funds at this stage of the proceedings. Accordingly, the parties may address the actual tracing of the funds at a later time. See American Motor Club, 109 B.R. at 599.

The Trustee asserts that Columbus Mortgage is entitled to an equitable lien on defendants' real property because the funds transferred from Columbus Mortgage were used to purchase and maintain the property in question. In his complaint the Trustee alleges that over two million dollars of Columbus Mortgage's funds were used to acquire, maintain, and improve defendants' property. Some of the property was sold, but the proceeds were not used to repay the funds taken from Columbus Mortgage.

This is a classic case for the imposition of an equitable lien on the real estate owned by Muratore and his entities. The maxim that equity regards as done that which should have been done is applicable here. When Muratore "borrowed" money from Columbus Mortgage to purchase or improve defendants' properties, he should have executed a mortgage in favor of Columbus Mortgage. Therefore, Columbus Mortgage now has an equitable lien on those premises.

The decisions from other jurisdictions support this proposition. In a factually similar case, In re Lela, supra, the petitioners' investments in several partnerships were fraudulently diverted to pay the mortgages on two pieces of real estate owned by a separate corporation. 551 F.2d at 402. The corporation subsequently became insolvent, and the petitioners sought to file a petition for involuntary reorganization of the corporation. Id. The District Court determined that the petitioners were ineligible to file such a petition on the ground that they were not secured creditors. Id. Reversing the lower court, the Circuit Court concluded that the wrongful diversion of the funds had created a constructive trust of corporate property on behalf of the petitioners. Id. at 406. Furthermore, the petitioners held an equitable interest against the property that permitted them the option of "trac[ing] the path of their money to the property acquired and impos[ing] a lien upon it as a security for their claims" against the corporation. Id. at 407; accord Sherman v. Rhode Island Hosp. Trust Co., 68 R.I. 525, 533, 30 A.2d 498, 502 (1943) (equitable lien imposed where husband misappropriated funds from mother to pay mortgage on property).

The Trustee also asserts an equitable interest in the real estate on the basis of two counts of the complaint that allege breaches of contracts to transfer land. Count IV alleges a breach of Muratore's agreement to transfer all the assets of the affiliated entities to Columbus Mortgage in repayment for the unsecured loans. The Trustee claims that no such assets were transferred. Count VI alleges a breach of Muratore's agreement to convey additional real estate if the transferred property amounted to less than two million dollars. The fair market value of the property was assessed at less than two million dollars, but the Trustee claims that no additional assets were transferred.

A cause of action to enforce an executory contract for a conveyance of real estate asserts an interest in land sufficient to support a notice of lis pendens. George v. Oakhurst Realty, Inc., 414 A.2d 471, 473 (R.I.1980). Whereas the contracts allegedly breached in this case are less formal than a purchase-and-sale agreement, the Court opines that the Trustee has alleged facts that, if proven to be true, would entitle Columbus Mortgage to assert an equitable interest in the real estate.

The Trustee has also alleged breaches of fiduciary duty by Muratore in his dealings with Columbus Mortgage. There is evidence that Muratore routinely applied loan repayments first to principal, rather than to interest. The Trustee requests, therefore, that a constructive trust be imposed on the assets transferred from Columbus Mortgage to defendants and on any assets obtained with the transferred funds. As discussed above, a party seeking to impose a constructive trust on a wrongdoer may have the option of asserting a claim for an equitable lien against the property itself. Accordingly, this Court determines that the Trustee has alleged sufficient facts to claim an equitable lien on the thirty-nine parcels of land.

III. CONSTITUTIONALITY OF LIS PENDENS STATUTE

Defendants also assert that the Rhode Island lis pendens statute is unconstitutional because it violates the due process clauses of the United States and Rhode Island Constitutions. Procedural due process is necessitated only where there is a taking of a protected interest and sufficient state involvement to invoke due process guarantees. Board of Regents v. Roth, 408 U.S. 564, 569, 92 S.Ct. 2701, 2704, 33 L.Ed.2d 548 (1972); Chrysler Corp., 670 F.2d at 1321. The Rhode Island lis pendens procedure meets neither prerequisite.

First, there has been no significant taking of property. Whereas the filing of a notice of lis pendens may cloud title and complicate alienation of the property, it does not amount to a taking nor to an interference with alienation. In George, supra, the Rhode Island Supreme Court stated: We have long rejected the proposition that a notice of lis pendens is the equivalent of an attachment. Lis pendens is fundamentally different from prejudgment garnishment, attachment, or replevin. Those actions are confiscatory and therefore improper without prior notice and opportunity to be heard. Lis pendens instead is not a lien but merely puts all prospective purchasers on notice that there is a suit pending involving an issue of title to the real property. We therefore find that due process of law does not mandate notice and opportunity to be heard before the filing of a notice of lis pendens under G.L.1956 (1969 Reenactment) §9-4-9. 414 A.2d at 474 (citations omitted); accord American Motor Club, 109 B.R. at 597 (notice of pendency does not prevent sale nor create lien on property).

The primary purpose of the notice of lis pendens is, as its name suggests, to give notice to potential buyers of a pending lawsuit concerning real property. The party in possession is free to use and enjoy the property on which the notice of lis pendens is filed. Furthermore, he or she may alienate the property if a willing buyer can be found. Accord Batey v. Digirolamo, 418 F.Supp. 695, 697 (D.Haw.1976); Empfield v. Superior Court, 33 Cal.App.3d 105, 108, 108 Cal.Rptr. 375, 377 (1973); Debral Realty, 383 Mass. at 565, 420 N.E.2d at 347-48; cf. Spielman-Fond, Inc. v. Hanson's, Inc., 379 F.Supp. 997, 999 (D.Ariz.1973) (filing of mechanics' or materialmen's lien does not amount to taking), aff'd, 417 U.S. 901, 94 S.Ct. 2596, 41 L.Ed.2d 208 (1974).

Second, the extent of the State's involvement in the filing of a notice of lis pendens is minimal. Unlike an attachment or seizure procedure, where a state agent takes actual possession of the property, the filing of a notice of lis pendens requires only a superficial, ministerial involvement by the state. Chrysler Corp., 670 F.2d at 1327; Debral Realty, 383 Mass. at 565-66, 420 N.E.2d at 348. The true purpose of the statute is to provide notice to potential buyers of a disputed interest in the land, not to dispossess a defendant of land. Although the filing of a notice of lis pendens may impair the marketability of real property to some degree, "the countervailing interest of the state in an orderly recording and notice system for transactions in real property makes imperative notice to buyers of property of the pending cause of action concerning that property." Empfield, 33 Cal.App.3d at 108, 108 Cal.Rptr. at 377.

The defendants contend that the Rhode Island Supreme Court is poised to declare the Rhode Island lis pendens statute unconstitutional. They point to the case of DeLeo v. Anthony A. Nunes, Inc., 546 A.2d 1344 (R.I.1988), cert. denied and appeal dismissed, 489 U.S. 1074, 109 S.Ct. 1522, 103 L.Ed.2d 828 (1989), in support of this claim. In DeLeo the plaintiff had filed a notice of lis pendens in order to impede development of the land, not to give notice of a legitimate interest in the property. Id. at 1347. The Court stated: the filing of a lis pendens can become a pernicious practice that has the same effect as attaching one's property without the benefit of a court hearing.... [A]ny property "encumbered" by a lis pendens is "unmarketable" because the property would never be sold so long as the lis pendens remained in effect. Filing such a document without a colorable claim is done at the filer's peril. Id. at 1347-48. The Court in DeLeo was concerned with the malicious filing of a notice of lis pendens "without a colorable claim." Id. This is clearly inapposite to the present situation, where there has been no abuse of the lis pendens procedure. Furthermore, the holding of DeLeo signifies that an abuse of the lis pendens procedure may make a plaintiff liable for slander of title, abuse of process, and malicious use of process. Id. at 1346. This holding does not portend that the Rhode Island Supreme Court is poised to invalidate the lis pendens statute itself as unconstitutional.

Defendants also rely upon the case of Kukanskis v. Griffith, 180 Conn. 501, 430 A.2d 21 (1980), in which the Supreme Court of Connecticut declared the Connecticut lis pendens statute unconstitutional because it did not comport with the due process requirements of the United States and Connecticut Constitutions. 430 A.2d at 25. Although similar to §9-4-9 in some respects, the Connecticut statute "fail[ed] to provide even the barest minimum of due process protection" because it contained no provision for a timely hearing, either before or after the filing of a notice of lis pendens, and no notice requirement. Id. The Connecticut Legislature subsequently amended the statute to provide for a post-filing hearing, and the amended statute's constitutionality was upheld in Williams v. Bartlett, 189 Conn. 471, 457 A.2d 290, appeal dismissed, 464 U.S. 801, 104 S.Ct. 46, 78 L.Ed.2d 67 (1983).

The Kukanskis Court found that the effect of filing a notice of lis pendens interfered sufficiently with the alienability of real estate to require at least minimum due process safeguards. 430 A.2d at 25. Even if this Court were to agree that the filing of a notice of lis pendens constituted a taking with sufficient state involvement, the Rhode Island lis pendens procedure provides adequate constitutional safeguards. Section 9-4-9 specifies that a plaintiff shall give notice to all named parties within seven days after recording a notice of lis pendens, and a defendant may subsequently file a motion to quash an improperly filed lis pendens. That accords a defendant all the process that is due. There is no constitutional requirement that the landowner be given a hearing before the notice of lis pendens is filed. George, 414 A.2d at 474.

IV. CONCLUSION AND ORDER

Accordingly, defendants' motion to quash and remove the notice of lis pendens is hereby denied.

It is so ordered.

Unit 4

COLLECTING FROM OTHER DEBTORS

UNIT CONTENTS

A. SURETIES

Restatement (Third) of Suretyship
Tentative Draft No. 1 -- March 23, 1992

§ 1. Transactions Giving Rise to Suretyship Status
(1) A "secondary obligor" has suretyship status whenever:

(a) one person (the "principal obligor") owes performance of a duty (the "underlying obligation") to another person (the "obligee"); and

(b) pursuant to contract, a third person (the "secondary obligor") is subject to a "secondary obligation," whereby either:

(1) the secondary obligor also owes performance, in whole or in part, of the duty of the principal obligor to the obligee; or

(2) the obligee has recourse against the secondary obligor or its property:

(i) in the event of the failure of principal obligor to perform the underlying obligation; or

(ii) to protect the obligee against loss

arising from potential nonperformance by

the principal obligor; and

(c) to the extent that the underlying obligation or the secondary obligation is performed the obligee is not entitled to performance of the other; and

(d) as between the principal obligor and the secondary obligor, the principal obligor has a duty to perform the underlying obligation or bear the cost of performance.

(2) If the criteria of subsection (1) are fulfilled, the secondary obligor has suretyship status:

(a) regardless of the form of the transaction fulfilling the criteria;

(b) regardless of any term used by the parties to describe the secondary obligor or the sec ondary obligation;

(c) whether the secondary obligation is conditional or unconditional;

(d) whether or not the secondary obligation is known to the principal obligor; and

(e) whether or not the obligee has notice that the secondary obligor has suretyship status.

§4. Formation of the Contract Creating the Secondary Obligation -- Generally

The requisites of contract formation apply generally to formation of a contract creating a secondary obligation.

§9. When Secondary Obligation Is Voidable Due to Misrepresentation

(1) If the secondary obligor's assent to the secondary obligation is induced by a fraudulent or material misrepresentation by the obligee upon which the secondary obligor is justified in relying, the secondary obligation is voidable by the secondary obligor.

(2) If the secondary obligor's assent to the secondary obligation is induced by a fraudulent or material misrepresentation by either the principal obligor or a third person upon which the secondary obligor is justified in relying, the secondary obligation is voidable by the secondary obligor unless the obligee, in good faith

and without reason to know of the misrepresentation, gives value or relies materially on the secondary obligation.

(3) If, before the secondary obligation becomes binding, the obligee or principal obligor:

    (a) knows facts unknown to the secondary obligor that materially increase the risk beyond that which such person has reason to believe the secondary obligor intends to assume; and

    (b) has reason to believe that these facts are unknown to the secondary obligor; and

    (c) has a reasonable opportunity to communicate them to the secondary obligor; the nondisclosure of these facts to the secondary obligor by such person constitutes a material misrepresentation.

Comment on Subsection (3):

f. Nondisclosures. Under the rule stated in subsection (3), some nondisclosures by the obligee or principal obligor are deemed to be material misrepresentations, thereby subjecting them to the rules in subsections (1) and (2). Three criteria must be fulfilled for a nondisclosure to constitute a material misrepresentation. First, the obligee or principal obligor must know facts materially increasing the secondary obligor's risk beyond that which it is reasonable to believe the secondary obligor intends to assume. Second, the obligee or principal obligor must believe the facts are unknown to the secondary obligor. Third, the obligee or principal obligor must have an opportunity to communicate the facts to the secondary obligor, but fail to do so before the secondary obligation becomes binding. It should be noted that this subsection places no burden on the obligee to investigate for the benefit of the secondary obligor. Nor does it require the obligee to take any particular steps to ascertain whether the secondary obligor is acquainted with facts that the obligee may reasonably believe are known to both of them.

Illustration:

    5. Developer A will enter into a construction contract with contractor C only if C procures payment and performance bonds satisfactory to A. C asks B, who has issued bonds for C in the past, to issue the bonds. Unknown to B, C has just suffered a series of business reverses leaving C equitably insolvent. C does not disclose this to B. C's nondisclosure is a material misrepresentation.

g. Continuing guaranties. In the case of a continuing guaranty (see §12(e)), the secondary obligor's offer typically can be revoked before each extension of credit. Thus, nondisclosure of facts occurring after the execution of a continuing guaranty may constitute material misrepresentation with respect to such subsequent extensions of credit.

Illustrations:

> 6. S has given C a continuing guaranty of all indebtedness of D to C. After C has made several extensions of credit to D, C learns that D has become insolvent. S does not know this fact and C is aware of S's ignorance. C, without disclosing D's insolvency to S, makes further advances to D. Since S could have revoked the continuing guaranty before the subsequent advances, C's nondisclosure is a material misrepresentation.

> 7. S has given C a continuing guaranty of all indebtedness of D to C. Previous extensions of credit by C to D have been in the form of unsecured loans. C then makes a nonrecourse loan to D, secured by an item of real estate; i.e., if D defaults on the loan, C has recourse only against the real estate and not against D personally. S did not anticipate that C would make a nonrecourse loan to D and C was aware of S's ignorance. If the nonrecourse feature of the loan to D increases S's risk beyond that which C would have reason to believe S intended to assume, and S could have revoked the guaranty before the nonrecourse loan was made, C's nondisclosure is material.

h. Nondisclosure after formation of contract establishing secondary obligation. This section applies to misrepresentations that induce the secondary obligor's assent to the secondary obligation. Misrepresentation or nondisclosure by the obligee as to certain facts during the suretyship relationship may provide the secondary obligor with a defense to the secondary obligation.

i. Other grounds for avoidance. The secondary obligation, as a contract, may also be voidable in other situations that result in the voidability of a contract. Such other situations resulting in voidable contracts include those in which one party was an infant and those in which the contract was induced by mistake or duress.

§13.   Effect of Suretyship Status on Rights and Duties of the Secondary Obligor--Generally

(1) The rights of the secondary obligor against the principal obligor are (i) those existing as a result of any contract between them, and (ii) those that arise out of suretyship status.

(2) The duties of the secondary obligor to the obligee, and of the obligee to the secondary obligor, are those existing pursuant to the contract creating the secondary obligation, subject to defenses arising out of suretyship status.

§14.   Suretyship Status -- Recourse of Secondary Obligor Against Principal Obligor

(1) Suretyship status gives the secondary obligor the right to require the principal obligor to perform the underlying obligation or bear the cost of performance.

(2) The right to require the principal obligor to perform the underlying obligation or bear the cost of performance may be effectuated by:

(a) enforcement of the principal obligor's duty of performance * * *; or

(b) enforcement of the principal obligor's duty to reimburse the secondary obligor * * *; or

(c) subrogation of the secondary obligor to the rights of the obligee ***.

(3) The secondary obligor's recourse against the principal obligor pursuant to this section may be augmented, modified or limited by contract between the secondary obligor and the principal obligor.

§15.   Suretyship Status -- Defenses of Secondary Obligor Against Obligee

Suretyship status gives the secondary obligor a defense to its duty pursuant to the secondary obligation to the extent that:

(a) the underlying obligation has been discharged by performance or other satisfaction by the principal obligor; or

(b) there is a defense of the principal obligor to the underlying obligation that is available to the secondary obligor * * *; or

(c) the principal obligor has tendered performance of the underlying obligation and (i) if the underlying obligation is the payment of money, the obligee has refused such tender, or (ii) otherwise, if the obligee has unreasonably refused such tender; or

(d) the secondary obligor has a "suretyship defense" * * *.

Comment:

a. Performance or satisfaction by principal obligor. To the extent that the underlying obligation is discharged by performance or other satisfaction by the principal obligor, the secondary obligation is also discharged. The obligee is entitled to only one performance.

b. Defense to underlying obligation. Some defenses of the principal obligor on the underlying obligation are available to the secondary obligor. The secondary obligor has a defense to the secondary obligation to the extent of such a defense.

c. Tender of performance. Performance by the principal obligor of the underlying obligation discharges the secondary obligor on the secondary obligation; thus, if the obligee refuses tender of due performance of the underlying obligation, then the obligee by its action denies the secondary obligor a discharge. This places the secondary obligor at risk of being liable for performance and, perhaps, being unable effectively to shift the cost of performance to the principal obligor pursuant to its rights against the principal obligor. It is inequitable for the obligee to spurn performance that would both (i) fulfill the duty owed to the obligee and (ii) place the cost of that performance on the person who ought to bear that cost, only later to seek performance from the person who ought not bear that cost.

d. Suretyship defenses. [Later sections] provide the secondary obligor with its most important defenses -- the so called "suretyship defenses." These defenses provide discharge arising from impairment by the obligee of the secondary obligor's right of recourse against the principal obligor, from modification of the underlying obligation, and from conduct of the obligee.

e. Other defenses to secondary obligation. Of course, the secondary obligor may also have a defense to its duty pursuant to the contract establishing the secondary obligation. The secondary obligor is excused from fulfillment of the secondary obligation to the extent of such a defense.

Restatement (Third) of Suretyship
Tentative Draft No. 2, April 2, 1993

TITLE B. SURETYSHIP DEFENSES

Introductory Note:

There is probably no area of suretyship law in which there is less consensus than the law of suretyship defenses. Rules vary from jurisdiction to jurisdiction, from context to context, and from common law to the Uniform Commercial Code. Title B seeks to rationalize this complex area and to set forth a series of rules that flow from a common concept.

Suretyship is, essentially, a nexus of three relationships: the relationship between the principal obligor and the obligee (embodied in the underlying obligation), the relationship between the secondary obligor and the obligee (embodied in the secondary obligation), and the relationship between the principal obligor and the secondary obligor (embodied in the du ties of performance and reimbursement and the doctrines of restitution and subrogation). The first two relationships are created by the actions of the parties; the third, however, is created by law. The duties of performance and reimbursement and the doctrines of restitution and subrogation are imposed by suretyship law to complete the bargain of the secondary obligor. As between the principal obligor and the secondary obligor, it is the principal obligor who ought to perform or bear the cost of performance. Thus, when a secondary obligor enters into the secondary obligation, it undertakes an obligation to the obligee but becomes the beneficiary of a corresponding obligation of the principal obligor. Accordingly, a secondary obligor who is called on to perform will, in most cases, have a cause of action against the principal obligor which, if the principal obligor is solvent, will enable the secondary obligor to be saved harmless from the cost of its performance of the secondary obligation.

As a result of the duties flowing from the principal obligor to the secondary obligor, the secondary obligor's decision as to whether to enter into the secondary obligation typically depends on a risk assessment. The secondary obligor must assess the risks that the principal obligor will not perform the underlying obligation and that, if so, the secondary obligor will not be able successfully to pass the cost of its performance to the principal obligor despite the existence of the principal obligor's duties.

If, after the secondary obligor enters into the secondary obligation, the obligee does an act that changes the risks that were the subject of the secondary obligor's assessment, there is the potential for a loss to the secondary obligor. The subject of this Title is the effect on the secondary obligor's relationship with the obligee of acts that change that risk. Generally speaking, this Title discharges a secondary obligor to the extent that such acts would otherwise cause the secondary obligor to suffer a loss.

§33. Impairment of Secondary Obligor's Recourse

(1) The duty of the secondary obligor to perform the secondary obligation is subject to the condition that the obligee refrain from impairing the recourse of the secondary obligor against the principal obligor.

(2) Acts that impair the recourse of the secondary obligor against the principal obligor include:

        a) release of the principal obligor with respect to the underlying obligation * * *;

        (b) extension of time granted to the principal obligor to perform the underlying obligation * * *;

        (c) other modification of the underlying obligation * * *;

        (d) impairment of collateral * * *; and

(e) any other act that impairs the principal obligor's duty of performance * * *, the principal obligor's duty to reimburse * * *, or the secondary obligor's right of restitution * * * or subrogation * * *.

(3) If the obligee impairs the recourse of the secondary obligor against the principal obligor, the secondary obligor is discharged from any unperformed portion of the secondary obligation to the [appropriate] extent * * *.

(4) If the obligee impairs the recourse of the secondary obligor against the principal obligor

(a) after the secondary obligor performs any portion of the secondary obligation; or

(b) before the secondary obligor performs a portion of the secondary obligation, if the secondary obligor performs:

(i) without knowledge of such act;

(ii) for the benefit of an intended beneficiary who can enforce the secondary obligation notwithstanding the impairment of recourse; or

(iii) under business compulsion; then, the secondary obligor has a claim against the obligee with respect to any portion of the secondary obligation that has been performed to the extent that such impairment would have discharged the secondary obligor with respect to that performance.

§42.   Waiver of Suretyship Defenses; Consent

(1) The secondary obligation is not discharged * * * if:

(a) the secondary obligor consents to an act that would be the basis of the discharge; or

(b) in the contract creating the secondary obligation or otherwise, the secondary obligor waives discharges based on those sections either specifically or by general language indicating that the secondary obligor waives defenses based on suretyship.

(2) Consent, for purposes of subsection (1)(a), may be express or implied from the circumstances. Unless the circumstances indicate otherwise, when the secondary obligor either controls the principal obligor or deals with the obligee on behalf of the principal obligor, agreement by the principal obligor to an act that would lead to discharge * * * constitutes consent to that act by the secondary obligor.

SMALL BUSINESS ADMINISTRATION (SBA)
GUARANTY
(SBA Form 148 (4-91) REF. SOP 70-50 USE 5-87 EDITION)
U.S. Government Printing Office: 1991 -- 524-616/40181

_____, 19__

    In order to induce [   ]
[SBA or other Lending Institution], (hereinafter called "Lender") to make a loan or loans, or renewal or extension thereof, to [   ]
(hereinafter called "Debtor"), the Undersigned hereby unconditionally guarantees to Lender, its successors and assigns, the due and punctual payment when due, whether by acceleration or otherwise, in accordance with the terms thereof, of the principal of and interest on and all other sums payable, or stated to be payable, with respect to the note of the Debtor, made by the Debtor to Lender, dated _____ in the principal amount of $ _____, with interest at the rate of _____ per cent per annum. Such note, and the interest thereon and all other sums payable with respect thereto are hereinafter collectively called "Liabilities." As security for the performance of this guaranty the Undersigned hereby mortgages, pledges, assigns, transfers and delivers to Lender certain collateral (if any), listed in the schedule on the reverse side hereof. The term "collateral" as used herein shall mean any funds, guaranties, agreements or other property or rights or interests of any nature whatsoever, or the proceeds thereof, which may have been, are, or hereafter may be, mortgaged, pledged, assigned, transferred or delivered directly or indirectly by or on behalf of the Debtor or the Undersigned or any other party to Lender or to the holder of the aforesaid note of the Debtor, or which may have been, are, or hereafter may be held by any party as trustee or otherwise, as security, whether immediate or underlying, for the performance of this guaranty or the payment of the Liabilities or any of them or any security therefor.

    The Undersigned waives any notice of the incurring by the Debtor at any time of any of the Liabilities, and waives any and all presentment, demand, protest or notice of dishonor, nonpayment, or other default with respect to any of the Liabilities and any obligation of any party at any time comprised in the collateral. The Undersigned hereby grants to Lender full power, in its uncontrolled discretion and without notice to the undersigned, but subject to the provisions of any agreement between the Debtor or any other party and Lender at the time in force, to deal in any manner with the Liabilities and the collateral, including, but without limiting the generality of the foregoing, the following powers:

    (a) To modify or otherwise change any terms of all or any part of the Liabilities or the rate of interest thereon (but not to increase the principal amount of the note of the Debtor to Lender), to grant any extension or renewal thereof and any other indulgence with respect thereto, and to effect any release, compromise or settlement with respect thereto;
    (b) To enter into any agreement of forbearance with respect to all or any part of the Liabilities, or with respect to all or any part of the collateral, and to change the terms of any such agreement;

(c) To forbear from calling for additional collateral to secure any of the Liabilities or to secure any obligation comprised in the collateral;

(d) To consent to the substitution, exchange, or release of all or any part of the collateral, whether or not the collateral, if any, received by Lender upon any such substitution, exchange, or release shall be of the same or of a different character or value than the collateral surrendered by Lender;

(e) In the event of the nonpayment when due, whether by acceleration or otherwise, of any of the Liabilities, or in the event of default in the performance of any obligation comprised in the collateral, to realize on the collateral or any part thereof, as a whole or in such parcels or subdivided interests as Lender may elect, at any public or private sale or sales, for cash or on credit or for future delivery, without demand, advertisement or notice of the time or place of sale or any adjournment thereof (the Undersigned hereby waiving any such demand, advertisement and notice to the extent permitted by law), or by foreclosure or otherwise, or to forbear from realizing thereon, all as Lender in its uncontrolled discretion may deem proper, and to purchase all or any part of the collateral for its own account at any such sale or foreclosure, such powers to be exercised only to the extent permitted by law.

The obligations of the Undersigned hereunder shall not be released, discharged or in any way affected, nor shall the Undersigned have any rights or recourse against Lender, by reason of any action Lender may take or omit to take under the foregoing powers.

In case the Debtor shall fail to pay all or any part of the Liabilities when due, whether by acceleration or otherwise, according to the terms of said note, the Undersigned, immediately upon the written demand of Lender, will pay to Lender the amount due and unpaid by the Debtor as aforesaid, in like manner as if such amount constituted the direct and primary obligation of the Undersigned. Lender shall not be required, prior to any such demand on, or payment by, the Undersigned, to make any demand upon or pursue or exhaust any of its rights or remedies against the Debtor or others with respect to the payment of any of the Liabilities, or to pursue or exhaust any of its rights or remedies with respect to any part of the collateral. The Undersigned shall have no right of subrogation whatsoever with respect to the Liabilities or the collateral unless and until Lender shall have received full payment of all the Liabilities.

The obligations of the Undersigned hereunder, and the rights of Lender in the collateral, shall not be released, discharged or in any way affected, nor shall the Undersigned have any rights against Lender: by reason of the fact that any of the collateral may be in default at the time of acceptance thereof by Lender or later; nor by reason of the fact that a valid lien in any of the collateral may not be conveyed to, or created in favor of, Lender; nor by reason of the fact that any of the collateral may be subject to equities or defenses or claims in favor of others or may be invalid or defective in any way; nor by reason of the fact that any of the Liabilities may be invalid for any reason whatsoever; nor by reason of the fact that the value of any of the collateral, or the financial condition of the Debtor or of any obligor under or guarantor of any of the collateral, may not have been correctly estimated or may have changed or may hereafter change; nor by reason of any deterioration, waste, or loss by fire, theft, or otherwise of any of the collateral, unless such deterioration, waste, or loss be caused by the willful act or willful failure to act of Lender.

The Undersigned agrees to furnish Lender, or the holder of the aforesaid note of the Debtor, upon demand, but not more often than semiannually, so long as any part of the indebtedness under such note remains unpaid, a financial statement setting forth, in reasonable detail, the assets, liabilities, and net worth of the Undersigned.

The Undersigned acknowledges and understands that if the Small Business Administration (SBA) enters into, has entered into, or will enter into, a Guaranty Agreement, with Lender or any other lending institution, guaranteeing a portion of Debtor's Liabilities, the Undersigned agrees that it is not a co-guarantor with SBA and shall have no right of contribution against SBA. The Undersigned further agrees that all liability hereunder shall continue notwithstanding payment by SBA under its Guaranty Agreement to the other lending institution.

The term "Undersigned" as used in this agreement shall mean the signer or signers of this agreement, and such signers, if more than one, shall be jointly and severally liable hereunder. The Undersigned further agrees that all liability hereunder shall continue notwithstanding the incapacity, lack of authority, death, or disability of any one or more of the Undersigned, and that any failure by Lender or its assigns to file or enforce a claim against the estate of any of the Undersigned shall not operate to release any other of the Undersigned from liability hereunder. The failure of any other person to sign this guaranty shall not release or affect the liability of any signer hereof.

                 _____

                 _____

                 _____

NOTE.--Corporate guarantors must execute guaranty in corporate name, by duly authorized officer, and seal must be affixed and duly attested; partnership guarantors must execute guaranty in firm name, together with signature of a general partner. Formally executed guaranty is to be delivered at the time of disbursement of loan.

(LIST COLLATERAL SECURING THE GUARANTY)

⬚⬚⬚⬚⬚⬚

Gant v. NCNB National Bank
Court of Appeals of North Carolina, 1989
94 N.C.App. 198, 379 S.E.2d 865
review denied by Supreme Court of North Carolina, 1989
325 N.C. 706, 388 S.E.2d 453

EAGLES, Judge. Plaintiff argues on appeal that the trial court erred in dismissing her complaint. After careful consideration of the record on appeal and the applicable law, we agree in part.

* * *

The crux of plaintiff's complaint is that defendant failed to fulfill its obligation to inform her of the financial condition of the company whose loans she guaranteed. Although there is no fiduciary relationship between creditor and guarantor, in some instances a creditor owes a duty to the guarantor to disclose information about the principal debtor. If the creditor knows, or has good grounds for believing that the surety [or guarantor] is being deceived or misled, or that he is induced to enter into the contract in ignorance of facts materially increasing the risks, of which he has knowledge, and he has an opportunity, before accepting his undertaking, to inform him of such facts, good and fair dealing demand that he should make such disclosure to him; and if he accepts the contract without doing so, the surety [or guarantor] may afterwards avoid it.

Plaintiff has alleged the defendant knew that she was unaware of the financial condition of the principal debtor and knew that she was relying on defendant's "good faith and financial expertise" in making the loans. Further, plaintiff alleged the defendant at all times knew or had sufficient information to know the principal debtor was insolvent. Plaintiff has alleged sufficient facts to state a claim against defendant, whether the cause of action is ultimately determined to be one for negligence or "breach of duty of good faith," as plaintiff has labeled her claims. Allegations of sufficient facts to state any legal claim are all that is generally required to withstand a Rule 12(b)(6) motion [to dismiss].

* * *

Plaintiff has also alleged a cause of action based on fraud. The essential elements of actionable fraud are well established. There must be a misrepresentation of material fact, made with knowledge of its falsity and with intent to deceive, which the other party reasonably relies on to his deception and detriment. Equally well-established is the requirement that the plaintiff allege all material facts and circumstances constituting the fraud with particularity in the complaint. Mere generalities and conclusory allegations of fraud will not suffice. The pleader must state with particularity the time, place and content of the false representation.

Here because plaintiff has failed to allege the circumstances constituting fraud with sufficient particularity, the trial court was correct in granting defendant's Rule 12(b)(6) motion [to dismiss] on the fraud claim. The fatal deficiency in plaintiff's allegations is that the complaint contains no facts whatsoever setting forth the time, place or specific individuals who purportedly made the fraudulent misrepresentations to plaintiff. It is not sufficient to allege conclusorily that a corporation made fraudulent misrepresentations.

   * * *

For the reasons stated, the trial court's order of dismissal is affirmed in part and reversed in part, and the case remanded for proceedings on the breach of duty of good faith claim and the negligence claim.

Affirmed in part, reversed in part and remanded.

Manufacturers Hanover Trust Company v. Yanakas

United States Court of Appeals, Second Circuit, 1993
7 F.3d 310
motion for vacatur denied
1993 WL 513370 (1993)

Kearse, Circuit Judge: Defendant Nicholas Yanakas appeals from a final judgment of the United States District Court for the Southern District of New York, John F. Keenan, Judge, ordering him to pay plaintiff Manufacturers Hanover Trust Company ("MHT" or the "Bank") $1,036,381.42 on its claim for enforcement of Yanakas's personal guarantee of certain loans. The district court (a) dismissed three of Yanakas's affirmative defenses and counterclaims, which asserted that Yanakas had been fraudulently induced to sign the guarantee, on the ground that the guarantee stated that it was "absolute and unconditional," (b) dismissed Yanakas's remaining affirmative defenses and counterclaims, which asserted that the Bank had breached its fiduciary duty, on the ground that the answer failed to show the existence of such a duty, and (c) granted summary judgment in favor of the Bank. On appeal, Yanakas contends that the district court erred in dismissing his affirmative defenses and counterclaims and in granting summary judgment against him. For the reasons below, we affirm in part, vacate in part, and remand for further proceedings with respect to the defenses of and counterclaims for fraudulent inducement.

I. BACKGROUND

The present lawsuit arises out of loans from MHT to Advance Ring Manufacturers, Inc. ("ARM"), which, prior to December 1986, was owned in part by defendant Charles Buonincontri ("Buonincontri") and in part by one Arthur Abraham. Since this appeal centers on the sufficiency of Yanakas's affirmative defenses and counterclaims, we take the allegations of the defenses and counterclaims as true. The following description of the events is taken largely from those allegations.

A. *The Events*

In December 1986, Buonincontri and Abraham entered into an auction to determine which of them would purchase the other's interest in ARM.

Buonincontri won the auction and became president of ARM. Prior to the auction, Yanakas had made a loan of $250,000 to ARM to help Buonincontri finance his proposed purchase of Abraham's shares. In June 1987, Yanakas converted his initial loan to capital and paid ARM an additional $250,000, thereby acquiring a 25% interest in the company. In 1988, he made further loans and capital contributions totaling $500,000 and acquired an additional 25%; in October of that year, he became the owner of all issued and outstanding shares of ARM.

MHT had entered into a lending relationship with ARM in 1985. At the time of the December 1986 auction, ARM was indebted to MHT in an amount that the Bank places at $700,000. In April 1987, the Bank loaned ARM an additional $350,000 (the "1987 loan"), in connection with which it obtained financial information and personal guarantees from Buonincontri and his wife, defendant Camille Buonincontri.

In 1987 and part of 1988, ARM obtained financing from both MHT and National Westminster Bank ("NatWest"). Initially, both banks were unsecured creditors. Yanakas asserts that in early 1988, however, NatWest surreptitiously obtained the signature of Buonincontri to a document that, unbeknownst to Yanakas, Buonincontri, and ARM, converted NatWest's unsecured position into one secured by the assets of ARM.

On March 31, 1988, MHT told Yanakas that the Bank would call its loans to ARM and would cease to finance ARM's operations unless Yanakas signed a personal guarantee of the loans and paid down part of ARM's outstanding balance. In reliance on these representations and on the Bank's promise to continue financing ARM if he complied with its demands, Yanakas (a) paid $100,000 of ARM's 1987 loan, (b) invested an additional $200,000 in ARM, and (c) executed a personal guarantee of all of ARM's obligations to MHT, agreeing, in part, as follows:

> [Yanakas] hereby *absolutely and unconditionally guarantees to Bank the prompt payment of claims of every nature and description of Bank against Borrower ... and any and every obligation and liability of Borrower* to Bank or another or others of whatsoever nature and howsoever evidenced, whether now existing or hereafter incurred, originally contracted with Bank and/or with another or others and now or hereafter owing to or acquired in any manner, in whole or in part, by Bank, or in which Bank may acquire a participation, whether contracted by Borrower alone or jointly and/or severally with another or others, whether direct or indirect, absolute or contingent, secured or not secured, matured or not matured. (All of foregoing are hereinafter referred to as "Obligations").
>
>   * * *
>
> Guarantor waives any and all notice of acceptance of this guarantee or the creation or accrual of any of said Obligations.... *This guarantee shall be a continuing, absolute and unconditional guarantee of payment*

regardless of the validity, regularity or enforceability of any of said Obligations or purported Obligations....

(Guarantee of All Liability and Security Agreement, dated March 31, 1988 ("Guarantee"), at 1 (emphasis added).) Unbeknownst to Yanakas, on the day that he executed the Guarantee, MHT also got Buonincontri, as ARM's president, to execute a new demand promissory note to MHT in the amount of $550,000 (the "1988 note").

In April 1988, after learning of NatWest's security interest in ARM's assets, Yanakas urged MHT to purchase that interest, for which Yanakas would put up $700,000, roughly the amount of the debt to NatWest, as security. Yanakas stressed the need for a prompt response in order to allow ARM to process orders for the 1988 Christmas season. The Bank promised to consider the proposition but delayed acting on it, and eventually rejected it. Shortly after acquiring Yanakas's Guarantee, the Bank ceased funding ARM's operations and demanded repayment of all ARM loans.

ARM was ultimately unable to obtain adequate financing for the 1988 Christmas season, and it filed for bankruptcy.

B. *The Present Lawsuit and the Opinion Below*

In 1990, MHT commenced the present action against Yanakas and the Buonincontris as guarantors of its loans to ARM. MHT sought $210,000, the outstanding balance on the 1987 loan, plus interest, and $550,000 plus interest on the 1988 note. Yanakas, while denying knowledge of the precise details of ARM's indebtedness to the Bank, asserted five affirmative defenses and counterclaims against the Bank. His first three affirmative defenses and counterclaims alleged that MHT had induced him to sign the Guarantee (1) by affirmatively representing that if Yanakas complied with its demands, the Bank would not call its loans to ARM and would continue to finance ARM's operations, and (2) by concealing from him material information, including (a) the fact that on the day it extracted the Guarantee from Yanakas, the Bank had Buonincontri sign the 1988 note for $550,000, (b) the fact that the Bank had discovered that, beginning in late 1986, the Buonincontris had misrepresented their financial circumstances, and (c) the fact that the Bank had no intention of continuing to provide financing to ARM:

> 31. Upon information and belief, at the time Yanakas' guarantee was requested; (a) the Bank had discovered that NatWest had been given a secured position in the assets of ARM; (b) the Bank had also discovered that Charles and Camille had given the Bank a false financial statement in late 1986, which did not reflect [a $1,000,000] mortgage on their home; (c) the Bank had decided to terminate the loans to ARM and not to continue financing ARM but to seek Yanakas' guarantee before it made its position public; (d) the Bank had assigned ARM's loans to its "workout" department which, upon information and belief, was for problem loans

which the Bank wanted to liquidate rather than continue; and (e) the Bank had previously released Abraham's guarantee.

32. None of the foregoing significant and material facts were made known by the Bank to Yanakas prior to the time that Yanakas signed the guarantee. Had Yanakas been advised of any of said facts, he would not have signed the guarantee.

(Answer ¶¶31, 32.)

Yanakas's fourth and fifth affirmative defenses and counterclaims alleged that the Bank controlled the finances of ARM, that Yanakas had no other financial options, and that a relationship of trust and confidence therefore existed between MHT and ARM. Yanakas alleged that the Bank had breached its fiduciary duty to ARM and Yanakas by not responding promptly to, and by then rejecting, Yanakas's proposal that MHT purchase NatWest's position. He alleged that while delaying its response, the Bank never had any intention of forbearing from calling ARM's loans or of continuing to finance its operations; that the Bank had already taken an internal step toward liquidation of those loans; and that

[t]he Bank acted in a heavy-handed, commercially unreasonable and grossly negligent manner without regard to the rights of Yanakas or ARM, in bad faith, and willfully and maliciously by not accepting the aforesaid proposal, in delaying in acting on the proposal, and in demanding payment of the loans to ARM. The Bank's acts caused ARM to file for bankruptcy resulting in a total loss of Yanakas' investment and loans to ARM.

(Answer ¶48.)

Yanakas requested rescission of the Guarantee, $300,000 in compensatory damages on account of his payment of $100,000 on ARM's loans and his last capital contribution of $200,000, and $7.5 million in compensatory damages because the Bank's actions caused ARM to terminate its business, depriving Yanakas of his investment and his expected profits. He also requested $7.5 million in exemplary damages.

MHT moved pursuant to Fed.R.Civ.P. 12(b)(6) to dismiss Yanakas's counterclaims for failure to state a claim on which relief can be granted. It moved pursuant to Fed.R.Civ.P. 12(f) to strike his affirmative defenses as immaterial. In an Opinion and Order dated February 20, 1992 ("Dismissal Order"), the district court granted MHT's motions. Citing Citibank, N.A. v. Plapinger, 66 N.Y.2d 90, 495 N.Y.S.2d 309, 485 N.E.2d 974 (1985), the court dismissed Yanakas's first three affirmative defenses and counterclaims, ruling that "under New York law fraudulent inducement is not a valid defense to enforcement of a [ ] guarantee which, by its terms, is 'absolute and unconditional.' " Dismissal Order at 6. "Because the guarantee that Yanakas signed states that it [is] 'absolute and unconditional,' the defense of fraudulent inducement is unavailable to Yanakas."

Id. at 6-7. The court also dismissed Yanakas's fourth and fifth affirmative defenses and counterclaims, rejecting his contention that the debtor-creditor relationship between ARM and the Bank was fiduciary in nature, and concluding that Yanakas had failed to allege any facts that would have created a duty on the part of MHT to respond to or accept Yanakas's April 1988 proposal within a particular period of time. Id. at 9.

MHT promptly moved for summary judgment on its claim against Yanakas. In an Opinion and Order dated July 31, 1992 ("Summary Judgment Decision"), the district court granted the motion, stating that despite his affirmative defenses Yanakas had "admit[ted] all relevant allegations upon which [his alleged] liability is premised," and had "fully acknowledged his guarantee of ARM's outstanding debt to MHT." Summary Judgment Decision at 3. Since the affirmative defenses had been stricken, the court concluded that Yanakas's "[a]dmission of this debt and the execution of a guarantee for the full extent of that debt le[ft] no unresolved genuine issue of material fact to be addressed." Id. at 3-4. Further finding no genuine issue to be tried as to the amount of the debt, the court ruled that MHT was entitled to judgment against Yanakas for $1,036,381.42, representing a total of $760,000 outstanding on the two ARM debts, plus accrued interest.

Noting that the Buonincontris had filed for bankruptcy, thereby delaying the resolution of any claims against them, the court ordered that a final judgment be entered in favor of MHT against Yanakas pursuant to Fed.R.Civ.P. 54(b). This appeal followed.

II. DISCUSSION

On appeal, Yanakas contends principally that the district court erred in ruling (1) that the fact that his Guarantee stated that it was "absolute and unconditional" precluded his claims of fraudulent inducement, and (2) that the Bank had no fiduciary duty to accept or respond promptly to his proposal to restructure ARM's debts. For the reasons below, we agree in part with the first contention but reject the second.

A. *The Claims of Fraudulent Inducement*

Under New York law, which by the terms of the Guarantee governs this diversity action, if a contract recites that all of the parties' agreements are merged in the written document, parol evidence is not admissible to vary, or permit escape from, the terms of the integrated contract. Such a general merger clause is ineffective, however, to preclude parol evidence that a party was induced to enter the contract by means of fraud. Thus, even when the contract contains "an omnibus statement that the written instrument embodies the whole agreement, or that no representations have been made," a party may escape liability under the contract by establishing that he was induced to enter the contract by fraud. Danann Realty Corp. v. Harris, 5 N.Y.2d 317, 320, 184 N.Y.S.2d 599, 601-02, 157 N.E.2d 597, 598-99 (1959) (*"Danann"*).

When, however, the contract states that a contracting party disclaims the existence of or reliance upon specified representations, that party will not be allowed to claim that he was defrauded into entering the contract in reliance on those representations. See Citibank, N.A. v. Plapinger, 66 N.Y.2d 90, 94-95, 495 N.Y.S.2d 309, 311, 485 N.E.2d 974, 976 ("*Plapinger* "); *Danann*, 5 N.Y.2d 317, 320-21, 184 N.Y.S.2d 599, 602, 157 N.E.2d 597, 599. In *Danann*, the purchaser of a lease on a building sought damages for fraud, claiming that it had entered into the contract of sale as a result of the selling defendants' false representations "as to the operating expenses of the building and as to the profits to be derived from the investment." Id. at 319, 184 N.Y.S.2d at 600, 157 N.E.2d at 598. The contract itself, however, stated that " '[t]he Seller has not made ... any representations as to the ... *expenses* [or] *operation* ... [of] the aforesaid premises ... and the Purchaser hereby *expressly acknowledges that no such representations have been made ....*'" Id. at 320, 184 N.Y.S.2d at 601, 157 N.E.2d at 598 (emphasis in *Danann*). The contract also stated that all of the parties' understandings and agreements were merged in the contract, " '*neither party relying upon any statement or representation*, not embodied in this contract, made by the other.' " Id. (emphasis in *Danann*). The *Danann* court, after noting that a general and vague merger clause would not bar parol evidence to support a fraud claim, ruled that the fraud claim in the case before it was barred by the purchaser's express disclaimer in the contract of any reliance on that specific representation. "[P]laintiff has in the plainest language announced and stipulated that it is not relying on any representations as to the very matter as to which it now claims it was defrauded. Such a specific disclaimer destroys the allegations in plaintiff's complaint that the agreement was executed in reliance upon these contrary oral representations...." Id. at 320-21, 184 N.Y.S.2d at 602, 157 N.E.2d at 599.

In *Plapinger*, the court applied the *Danann* principle to an "absolute and unconditional" guarantee of a company's debts given by corporate officers in connection with an agreement by the plaintiff banks to restructure the company's indebtedness. The guarantee stated that its " 'absolute and unconditional' " nature was " 'irrespective of (i) any lack of validity ... of the ... Restated Loan Agreement ... or any other agreement or instrument relating thereto', or '(vii) any other circumstance which might otherwise constitute a defense' to the guarantee." *Plapinger*, 66 N.Y.2d at 95, 495 N.Y.S.2d at 312, 485 N.E.2d at 977. Following a default by the corporation, the banks brought suit to enforce the guarantee against the officers. The officers sought to defend by alleging that they had been induced to enter into the guarantee agreement by the plaintiff banks' fraudulent representation that the banks had committed themselves to providing the corporation an additional line of credit.

The *Plapinger* court, while confirming the traditional principle that a general merger clause is insufficient to bar a defense of fraud in the inducement, see id. at 94-95, 495 N.Y.S.2d at 311, 485 N.E.2d at 976, affirmed the dismissal of the guaranteeing officers' fraud defense on the ground that it was inconsistent with their specific recitals in the contract. First, though noting that the guarantee before it was "not the explicit disclaimer present in *Danann*, " the *Plapinger* court observed that the guarantee was by no means a generalized boilerplate clause but rather was a "multimillion dollar personal guarantee" that was signed "following extended negotiations between sophisticated business people." 66 N.Y.2d at 95, 495 N.Y.S.2d at 312, 485 N.E.2d at 977.

Second, the court found that the "substance" of the guarantee encompassed not only the financing agreements for the debtor corporation, but also " 'any other agreement or instrument relating thereto,' " which included the guarantee itself. Id. Thus, the officers had agreed that their guarantee was "absolute and unconditional irrespective of any lack of validity or enforceability of the guarantee," id. at 92, 495 N.Y.S.2d at 309, 485 N.E.2d at 974 (emphasis added), and "irrespective of ... any other circumstance which might otherwise constitute a defense" with respect to the guarantee, id. The court concluded that if it were to allow the officers to plead fraudulent inducement of the guarantee, it would in effect condone a fraudulent representation by the officers themselves of their own intentions vis-a-vis the guarantee. See id. at 95, 495 N.Y.S.2d at 312, 485 N.E.2d at 977; see also *Danann*, 5 N.Y.2d at 323, 184 N.Y.S.2d at 604, 157 N.E.2d at 600 (same).

Following *Danann* and prior to *Plapinger*, this Court noted that in order to be considered sufficiently specific to bar a defense of fraudulent inducement under *Danann*, a guarantee must contain explicit disclaimers of the particular representations that form the basis of the fraud-in-the- inducement claim. See Grumman Allied Industries, Inc. v. Rohr Industries, Inc., 748 F.2d 729 (2d Cir.1984). We stated that "[t]he *Danann* rule operates where the substance of the disclaimer provisions tracks the substance of the alleged misrepresentations." 748 F.2d at 735. Given the *Plapinger* court's emphasis on the fact that the defendants there had negotiated an agreement in which they expressly waived any challenge to the validity of the guarantee itself, we are of the view that the ruling in *Plapinger* does not materially alter the principle established by *Danann*.

This view is supported by many state court decisions since *Plapinger* that have ruled that the mere general recitation that a guarantee is "absolute and unconditional" is insufficient under *Plapinger* to bar a defense of fraudulent inducement, and that the touchstone is specificity. Thus, where specificity has been lacking, dismissal of the fraud claim has been ruled inappropriate. See, e.g., Zaro Bake Shop, Inc. v. David, 176 A.D.2d 721, 721, 574 N.Y.S.2d 803, 804 (2d Dep't 1991) (mem.) (" 'absolutely and unconditionally' liable ... language, in and of itself, was ... insufficient to preclude ... proof of fraud in the inducement"); DiFilippo v. Hidden Ponds Associates, 146 A.D.2d 737, 737-38, 537 N.Y.S.2d 222, 223-24 (2d Dep't 1989) (mem.) (contract provision not a bar to fraud-in-inducement claim where contract provision "d[id] not specifically disclaim reliance on any oral representation concerning the particular matter as to which plaintiff now claims he was defrauded"); GTE Automatic Electric Inc. v. Martin's Inc., 127 A.D.2d 545, 546-47, 512 N.Y.S.2d 107, 108 (1st Dep't 1987) (mem.) (recitation that underlying notes are absolute and unconditional does not bar proof of fraud in inducement of guarantee since there was "not ... a specific disclaimer, as in both *Plapinger* and *Danann* Realty and, therefore, the principle of those cases does not apply"); Goodridge v. Fernandez, 121 A.D.2d 942, 945, 505 N.Y.S.2d 144, 147 (1st Dep't 1986) (mem.) (defendant Fernandez, sued on his guarantee, not barred from asserting fraud- in-inducement defense because, "in sharp contrast to the guarantee in [*Plapinger*], [Fernandez's guarantee] contains no specific disclaimer of defenses available to the guarantor with respect to the guarantee").

Where the fraud claim has been dismissed, the disclaimer has been sufficiently specific to match the alleged fraud. See, e.g., Manufacturers Hanover Trust Co. v. Restivo, 169 A.D.2d 413, 414, 564 N.Y.S.2d 141, 141 (1st Dep't) (mem.) (claims that "MHT representative fraudulently represented that [defendants'] guarantees were temporary and conditional upon MHT's advancing sufficient funds to consummate a business merger are barred by the language of the guarantees stating that they were continuing and unconditional " (emphasis added)), appeal dismissed, 77 N.Y.2d 989, 571 N.Y.S.2d 914, 575 N.E.2d 400 (1991); First City National Bank & Trust Co. v. Heaton, 165 A.D.2d 710, 711-12, 563 N.Y.S.2d 783, 783-84 (1st Dep't 1990) (mem.) (guarantee barred fraud-in-inducement defense that was "in direct contradiction to the[ ] specific acknowledgement" made in the guarantee); Marine Midland Bank, N.A. v. CES/Compu-Tech, Inc., 147 A.D.2d 396, 397, 537 N.Y.S.2d 818, 819-20 (1st Dep't 1989) (mem.) (contractual disclaimer in which defendant expressly "waive[d] ... the right to assert defenses, setoffs and counterclaims ... in any action or proceeding in any court arising on, out of, under, by virtue of, or in any way relating to this Note or the transactions contemplated hereby " (emphasis added) was "sufficiently specific to foreclose the defense of fraudulent inducement"). But see Bank Leumi Trust Co. v. Block 3102 Corp., 180 A.D.2d 588, 589, 580 N.Y.S.2d 299, 300 (1st Dep't) (mem.) ("The language of the guarantees specifies that they are absolute and unconditional, negating the claim of fraudulent inducement....") (precise language of guarantees not disclosed in opinion), appeal denied, 80 N.Y.2d 754, 587 N.Y.S.2d 906, 600 N.E.2d 633 (1992).

In the present case, Yanakas's Guarantee is, for the most part, significantly different from the guarantee at issue in *Plapinger*. First, there is no indication that the Yanakas Guarantee, which is in a preprinted form, is anything but a generalized boilerplate exclusion. The form was one that MHT apparently used routinely; an affidavit submitted by MHT's counsel in support of the Bank's motion to dismiss the affirmative defenses and counterclaims attached copies of an identical MHT guarantee form executed by others in connection with financing unrelated to ARM. There was no evidence that the scope or character of the Guarantee was the product of any negotiations between the parties.

More importantly, the Yanakas Guarantee does not purport to waive any defenses to its own validity. Rather, the Guarantee states that Yanakas "absolutely and unconditionally guarantees" all "obligation[s] and liabilit[ies] of Borrower to Bank or another or others," and states that the "guarantee shall be a continuing, absolute and unconditional guarantee of payment regardless of the validity, regularity or enforceability of any of said Obligations". The term

"Obligations" is explicitly defined in the Guarantee with reference only to obligations of ARM. Thus, the Yanakas Guarantee contains no disclaimer as to the validity, regularity, or enforceability of the Guarantee itself. It also contains no disclaimer of the existence of or reliance upon representations by MHT, no express reference to any promise of continued financing, and no blanket disclaimer of the type found in *Plapinger* as to "any other circumstance which might otherwise constitute a defense" to the Guarantee.

One of Yanakas's bases for claiming fraud in the inducement, however, is barred by the Guarantee. Yanakas alleged that the Bank had failed to disclose to him its same-day procurement of the $550,000 note signed by Buonincontri. The Guarantee, however, expressly covers ARM debts "whether now existing or hereafter incurred," and expressly "waives any and all notice of ... the creation ... of any of said Obligations." These terms are sufficiently specific to preclude any claim that the Bank defrauded Yanakas by failing to disclose the existence or imminence of the 1988 note.

In other respects, the Guarantee given by Yanakas does not, in words or substance, contain disclaimers of the representations that formed the basis of his claim of fraudulent inducement. Accordingly, the decision of the district court to dismiss the first three affirmative defenses and counterclaims must be vacated. The court's ruling that MHT was entitled to summary judgment against Yanakas, premised as it was on the dismissal of those defenses, must likewise be set aside.

B. *The Remaining Counterclaims*

Yanakas's fourth and fifth affirmative defenses and counterclaims, which center on his April 1988 proposal to restructure ARM's debt by having MHT purchase NatWest's security interest, asserted that MHT's rejection of, and failure to respond promptly to, his proposal constituted a breach of MHT's fiduciary duty. His challenge to the district court's dismissal of these claims is without merit.

Under New York law, the "usual relationship of bank and customer is that of debtor and creditor," Aaron Ferer & Sons Ltd. v. Chase Manhattan Bank, N.A., 731 F.2d 112, 122 (2d Cir.1984), "and does not create a fiduciary relationship between the bank and its borrower or its guarantors," id. Though in unusual circumstances, a fiduciary relationship may arise even between a bank and a customer if there is either "a confidence reposed which invests the person trusted with an advantage in treating with the person so confiding," Fisher v. Bishop, 108 N.Y. 25, 28, 15 N.E. 331, 332 (1888), or an assumption of control and responsibility, the mere fact that a corporation has borrowed money from the same bank for several years is insufficient to transform the relationship into one in which the bank is a fiduciary.

Seeking to avoid the application of this well-established principle, Yanakas relies on K.M.C. Co. v. Irving Trust Co., 757 F.2d 752 (6th Cir.1985) ("K.M.C."). His reliance is misplaced. K.M.C. involved an agreement by Irving Trust Co. ("Irving") to extend the debtor a $3.5 million line of credit, in consideration of which the debtor assigned all of its business receipts to an account to which only Irving had access. Thus, the debtor had an express agreement for a certain sum of credit, and Irving had control over assets of the debtor, impeding the debtor from seeking new financing. The Sixth Circuit held that, in these circumstances, Irving's termination of the line of credit without advance notice breached an implied covenant of good faith. This Court has held that the fiduciary obligation found in K.M.C. is not present where a bank has "never represented that credit of a certain amount would be provided, and [the borrower] had no reasonable expectation of continued, much less expanded, credit." Fasolino Foods Co. v. Banca Nazionale del Lavoro, 961 F.2d 1052, 1058 (2d Cir.1992).

Yanakas's answer did not allege any facts sufficient either to convert MHT's position from that of creditor into that of fiduciary or to liken his circumstances to those in K.M.C. The answer did not allege that MHT controlled the assets or operations of ARM or that MHT otherwise exercised powers beyond those of a typical lender-creditor. Yanakas did not allege that MHT had agreed to provide ARM with any certain amount of financing. He did not allege any agreement by MHT to Yanakas's proposed restructuring of ARM's debt, nor any representations by MHT suggesting that it would agree to that proposal. Though Yanakas alleged that ARM was unable to find financing elsewhere, there was no allegation that ARM's agreements with MHT precluded ARM from making a search for such financing or that the Bank failed to give proper notice of its decision to cease providing financing. We agree with the district court that Yanakas failed to allege any facts showing a fiduciary duty on the part of the Bank.

CONCLUSION

We have considered all of the contentions of the parties in support of their respective positions on this appeal and, except as indicated above, have found them to be without merit. We vacate so much of the judgment of the district court as dismissed Yanakas's first three affirmative defenses and counterclaims and granted judgment in favor of MHT; we affirm so much of the judgment as dismissed the fourth and fifth affirmative defenses and counterclaims; and we remand to the district court for further proceedings not inconsistent with the foregoing.

No costs are awarded at this time. In the event that Yanakas ultimately prevails on any of his affirmative defenses or counterclaims, the district court may award him the costs of the present appeal.

B. LETTERS OF CREDIT

Amelia H. Boss, Suretyship and Letters of Credit: Subrogation Revisited
34 Wm. & Mary L. Rev. 1087, 1091-93 (1993)

Relationships giving rise to suretyship status * * * involve three parties: the principal obligor, who owes a duty of performance (the underlying obligation) to an other person (the obligee), and a secondary obligor (the surety), who, pursuant to contract, promises to perform -- in whole or in part -- the duty of the principal obligor to the obligee. The two most common contractual mechanisms resulting in suretyship status are "suretyship" [in which the promise of the surety is unconditional yet is a secondary, collateral obligation] and "guaranty" [in which the guarantor's obligation is conditional yet is deemed to be independent and primary].

At the outset, a letter of credit may appear to fit within the framework of [suretyship] * * *. The letter of credit transaction generally involves three parties. The applicant or customer is the person who requests the issuer, generally a bank, to issue the letter of credit. The credit will allow a third person, the beneficiary, to draw upon the credit by presentation of the required documents. In a conventional commercial letter of credit transaction, the applicant will have a contract with the beneficiary (the underlying obligation) requiring it to pay a sum for the delivery of certain goods; the letter of credit functions as a payment mechanism, and by drawing on the letter of credit, the beneficiary receives the amounts on the underlying contract. In a standby letter of credit situation, the beneficiary is entitled to draw upon default of the applicant in the underlying contract; payment of the letter of credit functions in satisfaction of the applicant's per formance.

The difficulty in bringing letters of credit [within the suretyship framework] * * * emerges with the requirement * * * that * * * a transaction gives rise to suretyship status only if "to the extent that the underlying obligation or the secondary obligation is performed the obligee is not entitled to performance of the other." Thus, in the traditional guaranty situation, full payment by the debtor or principal obligor would dis charge the guarantor's obligation to the creditor. Similarly, pay ment by the guarantor would discharge the debtor's obligation to the creditor as well. Presumably, in a letter of credit context, payment of a letter of credit (the secondary obligation) would discharge the principal obligor or applicant of its obligation on the underlying obligation for which the letter of credit was issued. The difficulty is that payment or performance by the applicant or prin cipal obligor is not a defense to a draw under a letter of credit.21 Thus, the requirement of [suretyship] * * * technically is not met.

Gerald T. McLaughlin, Standby Letters of Credit and Guaranties: An Exercise in Cartography
34 Wm. & Mary L. Rev. 1139, 1140-45 (1993)

The standby letter of credit and the contract of guaranty are both credit enhancement devices. By nature, however, the standby letter of credit is "beneficiary oriented," meaning that the standby credit favors the interests of the beneficiary of the credit who in most financial transactions will be the obligee/creditor. A contract of guaranty, on the other hand, is more "applicant oriented." "Applicant oriented" means that, when compared to a standby letter of credit, the contract of guaranty tends to favor the interests of the party applying for the guaranty (who in most fi nancial transactions will be the obligor/debtor), rather than the party who is the beneficiary of the guaranty.

A. Standby Letters of Credit

To help understand the beneficiary-oriented nature of a standby letter of credit, let me describe a classic standby letter-of-credit transaction. Typically, a standby letter-of-credit transaction is composed of three separate and independent contracts. For example, assume that X and Y enter into a contract whereby X promises to build Y a house by June 1. X promises to pay Y $50,000 in liquidated damages if X fails to build the house by that date. To guarantee payment of that sum, Y requires that X have Solid Gold Bank issue a $50,000 standby letter of credit in favor of Y. The terms of the credit entitle Y to demand payment from Solid Gold Bank by presenting the bank with a $50,000 sight draft and a written certificate attesting to X's failure to complete the necessary construction of the house by June 1 and failure to pay the $50,000 in liquidated damages.

This contract between X and Y, whereby X must complete construction of the house by June 1, is the underlying contract, Con tract I, that necessitates the issuance of the standby credit. The contract between X and Solid Gold Bank whereby X applies to the bank for the issuance of the standby credit and promises to reimburse Solid Gold Bank in the event that the bank must honor its letter-of-credit payment obligation is Contract II. Finally, Contract III is the actual standby letter of credit that is issued by Solid Gold Bank and established in favor of Y whereby Solid Gold Bank irrevocably obligates itself to pay Y $50,000 if Y presents the required sight draft and written certificate attesting to X's failure to complete the timely construction of the house and pay the liquidated damages amount.

There are two cardinal principles of letter of credit law. First, Solid Gold Bank's (issuing bank's) payment obligation to beneficiary Y under the letter of credit (Contract III) is documentary in nature; that is, Solid Gold Bank is obligated to pay beneficiary Y only if Y presents the necessary draft and written certificate at testing to X's default in advance of the expiry date of the credit. Second, absent fraud, Solid Gold Bank's payment obligation under Contract III is separate from, and independent of, the other contracts that generated it--Contract I (the construction contract be tween X and Y) and Contract II (the reimbursement agreement between Solid Gold Bank as the issuer of the credit and X as the applicant for the credit).

It is these two principles that mainly account for the beneficiary oriented nature of a standby letter of credit. In deciding whether to honor its credit, the issuing bank is obligated to review only the facial compliance of the documents presented. The bank need not, and in fact may not, embroil itself in the timeconsuming pro cess of evaluating the facts that underlie those documents. Be cause the issuing bank undertakes an obligation to pay only against documents and not against the truth or falsity of the facts stated in those documents, the beneficiary of the credit is thereby assured of swift payment. Similarly, because the issuing bank undertakes a payment obligation that is independent of Contracts I and II, the beneficiary will be assured of payment despite the existence of disputes (other than those based on fraud) that arise with respect to the underlying contract (Contract I) or the reimburse ment agreement (Contract II).

Of course, once the beneficiary of the credit has been paid and the issuing bank's Contract III payment obligation has been fully satisfied, nothing in letter-of-credit law prevents the rights of the beneficiary with respect to Contract I from being subsequently readjusted--either through negotiation or litigation. One thing is certain, however: during any subsequent negotiation or litigation, the beneficiary-oriented nature of a letter of credit means that the beneficiary will be the stakeholder of the proceeds of the letter-of-credit payment.

B. Contracts of Guaranty

A contract of guaranty is more applicant oriented in nature than a standby letter of credit. In its classic form at least, a contract of guaranty is nondocumentary, requiring the guarantor to honor its guaranty after evaluating not the facial conformity of documents, but rather the truth or falsity of facts. Similarly and almost as a corollary of what has just been said, a contract of guaranty is, therefore, dependent on the contracts that give rise to its issuance.

Assume again that X and Y enter into the aforementioned construction contract, the terms of which obligate X to complete Y's house by June 1 or pay $50,000 in liquidated damages if X fails to complete construction by that date. To secure payment of this sum, Y requires that X have a third party, Q, issue a $50,000 guaranty in favor of Y. Q's guaranty entitles Y to claim $50,000 from Q if X defaults on its obligation to complete construction of the house by June 1 and fails to pay Y the necessary $50,000 in liquidated damages. According to classic principles of guaranty law, Q's contract of guaranty (Contract III) is dependent upon the underlying construction contract (Contract I). Put another way, Q will be obligated to pay on its guaranty only if X in fact defaults on its obligations to complete construction of the house by June 1 and to pay the $50,000 in liquidated damages. If, for example, X were coerced by Y into accepting the June 1 completion date, then Q would not be required to honor its guaranty because X would not in fact have defaulted on its Contract I performance obligation and been required to pay Y $50,000 in liquidated damages. Because a contract of guaranty does not necessarily assure beneficiary Y of payment if disputes arise with respect to the underlying con struction contract, it is to that extent less beneficiary oriented than a standby letter of credit. Looked at from the other side, because the contract of guaranty allows guarantor Q to utilize the defenses of X, the principal obligor, as defenses to its own payment obliga tion, the guaranty is more applicant oriented in nature than the standby letter of credit.

Rose Developments, Inc. v. Pearson Properties, Inc.
Court of Appeals of Arkansas, 1992
38 Ark.App. 215, 832 S.W.2d 286

Mayfield, Judge. Rose Developments appeals from the order of the circuit court which permanently enjoined the drawing on, or honor of, a letter of credit, pursuant to Ark.Code Ann. §4-5-114(2)(b) (Repl.1991), on the finding that appellant had committed fraud.

On December 6, 1988, appellee Pearson contracted with the appellant Rose to provide material and labor in connection with the construction of building "K" in a condominium project known as Solomons Landing Project. The amount of the contract was $458,200.00. In lieu of a performance bond, Pearson delivered an irrevocable letter of credit in the amount of $25,000.00 to secure its performance under the contract. The letter of credit authorized Rose to draw up to $25,000.00 available by "your drafts at sight" accompanied by an authorized statement that Pearson (d/b/a Homes, Inc.) had failed to perform its obligations as required under the terms and conditions of its construction contract and the original of the letter of credit. Under the terms of the letter of credit, drafts had to be drawn and negotiated no later than July 15, 1989. Subsequently, buildings "E" and "L" were made addendum to the original contract. The only change was an increase in the price.

On July 5, 1989, S. Brooks Grady, Sr., Vice-President of Rose, stated in a letter to First National Bank (Bank) that "Homes, Inc. has been working on our job at Solomons Landing in Maryland since November 1988. We have been very satisfied with their work, and they are presently working on our third building." On July 15, 1989, the letter of credit was extended until January 12, 1990, for the purpose of working on buildings "E" and "L".

On December 4, 1989, the Bank was notified that Homes, Inc., had failed to perform its obligations as required under the terms and conditions of its construction contract and immediate payment of $25,000.00 was requested under the letter of credit.

On December 12, 1989, Pearson filed a petition for a temporary restraining order against Rose and the Bank alleging among other things that the draft was fraudulently presented upon misrepresentations by Rose, and alternatively that "Ark.Code Ann.Section 4-5-114 specifically grants the Court authority to enjoin the honor of a draft or demand based on 'fraud, forgery, or other defect not apparent on the face of the documents.'"

On December 13, 1989, the court granted the petition. Subsequently, the Bank filed an answer admitting its obligation to honor the draft drawn against the letter of credit unless enjoined by the court and tendered a cashier's check for $25,000.00 to the clerk of the court for safekeeping until further orders.

After a hearing, held May 31, 1990, the trial court found Rose had committed fraud which should prevent it from drawing on the letter of credit and permanently enjoined the Bank from honoring the draft and Rose from drawing on the letter of credit.

A letter of credit is a three-party arrangement involving two contracts and the letter of credit:

> 1) the underlying contract between the customer and the beneficiary, in this case between Pearson and Rose; 2) the reimbursement agreement between the issuer and the customer, in this case between First National Bank and Pearson; and 3) the letter of credit between the issuer and the beneficiary, in this case between First National Bank and Rose. The significant part of this arrangement is the "independence principle" which states that the bank's obligation to the beneficiary is independent of the beneficiary's performance on the underlying contract.

2 J. White & R. Summers, *Uniform Commercial Code* §19-2 (3d ed.1988). "Put another way, the issuer must pay on a proper demand from the beneficiary even though the beneficiary may have breached the underlying contract with the customer." Id. at 8. "It is not a contract of guarantee ... even though the letter fulfills the function of a guarantee." Id. at 9.

The letter of credit involved in this case is a standby letter of credit which has been characterized as a "back-up" against customer default on obligations of all kinds. Id. §19-1, at 4. Such letters function somewhat like guarantees because it is the customer's default on the underlying obligation that prompts the beneficiary's draw on the letter. Id. at 4. The risk to the issuer is somewhat greater than in a commercial letter of credit in that the commercial letter gives the issuer security in goods whereas the standby letter gives no ready security, and the banker behaves as a surety. Id. at 6. The standby letter of credit is somewhat akin to a performance bond in that:

> In place of a performance bond from a true surety, builder (customer) gets his bank (issuer) to write owner (beneficiary) a standby letter of credit. In this letter, issuer engages to pay beneficiary-owner against presentment of two documents: 1) a written demand (typically a sight draft) which calls for payment of the letter's stipulated amount, plus 2) a written statement certifying that customer-builder has failed to perform the agreed construction work.

Id. at 4.   One difference between the standby letter of credit and the surety contract is that the standby credit beneficiary has different expectations.

> In the surety contract situation, there is no duty to indemnify the beneficiary until the beneficiary establishes the fact of the obligor's nonperformance. The beneficiary may have to establish that fact in litigation. During the litigation, the surety holds the money and the beneficiary bears most of the cost of delay in performance. In the standby credit case, however, the beneficiary avoids that litigation burden and receives his money promptly upon presentation of the required documents. It may be that the account party has in fact performed and that the beneficiary's presentation of those documents is not rightful. In that case, the account party may sue the beneficiary in tort, in contract, or in breach of warranty; but during the litigation to determine whether the account party has in fact breached his obligation to perform, the beneficiary, not the account party, holds the money.

J. Dolan, *The Law of Letters of Credit*, at 1-18, 1-19 (2d ed.1991).

Letters of credit are governed by the "Uniform Commercial Code--Letters of Credit," Ark.Code Ann. §4-5-101 through 117 (Repl.1991). Section 4-5-114(1) provides that an issuer must honor a draft which complies with the terms of the relevant credit regardless of whether the goods or documents conform to the underlying contract between the customer and the beneficiary. However, the issuer does not have an absolute duty to honor a draft authorized by the letter of credit. An exception is provided by §4-5-114(2) which provides that an issuer need not honor the draft if "a required document does not in fact conform to the warranties made on negotiation or transfer of a document of title (§4-8-306) or of a certificated security (§4-8-306) or is forged or fraudulent or there is fraud in the transaction." Section 4-5-114(2)(b) provides that in all other cases as against its customer an issuer may honor the draft despite notification from the customer of fraud, forgery, or other defect not apparent on the face of the documents but a court of appropriate jurisdiction may enjoin such honor.

On appeal, it is argued that the trial court erred in finding the appellant committed fraud which would prevent it from drawing on the letter of credit. Appellant admits that courts have allowed injunctions for "fraud in the transaction" but argues an injunction is proper only if there is no bona fide claim to payment, and the wrongdoing of the beneficiary has so vitiated the entire transaction that the legitimate purposes of the independence principle would no longer be served. See *Intraworld Industries, Inc. v. Girard Trust Bank*, 461 Pa. 343, 336 A.2d 316 (1975); *Sztejn v. Henry Schroder Banking Corp.*, 177 Misc. 719, 31 N.Y.S.2d 631 (1941). Appellant contends that Pearson has established only that there may be a dispute as to some of the "back charges". (Back charges have to do with material and labor that needs or needed to be performed, that Pearson was supposed to be responsible for, but appellant had to take over.)

Appellees agree the only issue on appeal is whether appellant committed fraud which would justify the issuance of the injunction and argue the injunction was proper. Appellee Pearson contends that in December 1989 or January 1990 it received a number of back charges dating as far back as December 1988; that it had never previously received these charges; that appellant, while in possession of documents it claimed were back charges, wrote a letter to obtain an extension of the letter of credit stating it was "very satisfied with the work of Homes, Inc."; and that appellant knowingly misrepresented the facts in order to obtain an extension of the letter of credit.

In support of its argument, appellee Pearson cites *W.O.A. Inc. v. City National Bank of Fort Smith, Ark.*, 640 F.Supp. 1157 (W.D.Ark.1986), and *Shaffer v. Brooklyn Park Garden Apartments*, 311 Minn. 452, 250 N.W.2d 172 (1977). Those cases, however, involved false certification accompanying drafts for payment and have no application here. In *City National Bank* the appellant intentionally misrepresented the state of affairs when, though it had been paid, it presented drafts for payment under a letter of credit. That case relied on *Roman Ceramics Corp. v. Peoples National Bank*, 714 F.2d 1207 (3d Cir.1983), which held that a beneficiary who tenders a draft knowing that its certification of nonpayment by the buyers is false, is guilty of fraud in the transaction. Similarly, *Shaffer* involved a situation where letters of credit guaranteed payment of certain promissory notes. The issuer received documents which appeared to comply with the presentation requirements under the letters of credit; however, the certifications which stated the customers had defaulted on their loans were false.

In the instant case, the certification stated that "Homes, Inc., has failed to perform its obligations as required under the terms and conditions of their construction contract." At trial, Robert Pearson III, Vice-President of Homes, Inc., testified they did not allege that there were forgeries "or anything like that" involved in the demand for payment on the letter of credit. Pearson admitted the letter of credit was to protect appellant in the event Pearson did not pay for labor, materials and other supplies that might be incorporated into the structure; that there were outstanding materialmen's and laborers' liens against the project; and that some of those liens were for materials, labor, and supplies that were the responsibility of Pearson. Pearson testified his allegation of fraud was based on the contention that he had been billed for work outside his contract and that Rose had called upon the letter of credit based upon certain back charges. Pearson said the majority of the back charges were unacceptable, but acknowledged that 10% of the charges were legitimate.

Appellee Bank admits this case does not involve forgery or "other defect not apparent on the face of the documents". John Thornton, Executive Vice-President of the Bank, testified he would not have extended the original letter of credit without Rose's statement that the jobs were being done in a satisfactory manner. Appellee Bank argues that none of the back charges, that predated the extension of the letter of credit, were mentioned in appellant's letter which induced the Bank to extend the letter of credit. And the Bank contends that Rose's fraud can be categorized as both egregious and intentional and that the injunction was a proper statutory remedy.

The narrow question to be decided by this court is whether the evidence will support a finding that there was "fraud in the transaction." Our research has revealed no Arkansas cases containing a definition of "fraud in the transaction" as used in the section of the Uniform Commercial Code that is involved in this case. Some courts have held that fraud in the transaction must be of such an egregious nature as to vitiate the entire underlying transaction so that the legitimate purposes of the independence of the bank's obligation would no longer be served. See *Roman Ceramics Corp. v. Peoples National Bank*, 517 F.Supp. 526 (M.D.Pa.1981), aff'd, 714 F.2d 1207 (3d Cir.1983); *Intraworld*, supra; *Sztejn*, supra. Other cases and writers have suggested intentional fraud should be sufficient to obtain injunctive relief in letter of credit cases. See *NMC Enterprises, Inc. v. Columbia Broadcasting System, Inc.*, 14 U.C.C.Rep.Serv. 1427 (N.Y.Sup.Ct.1974); 6 W. Hawkland, *Uniform Commercial Code Series*, §5-114:09 (1984); Edward L. Symons, Jr., *Letters of Credit: Fraud, Good Faith and the Basis for Injunctive Relief*, 54 Tul.L.Rev. 338 (1980). Professor Symons concludes "a proper definition of fraud will necessarily encompass and be limited by the requirement of scienter: that there be an affirmative, knowing misrepresentation of fact or that the beneficiary state a fact not having any idea about its truth or falsity, and in reckless disregard of the truth." Symons, supra at 379. It has also been suggested that the lesson to be learned from this section of the Uniform Commercial Code (Ark.Code Ann. §4-5-114(2) (Repl.1990)), is that a court should seldom enjoin payment under a letter of credit on the theory that there is fraud in the documents or fraud in the underlying transaction. See 2 J. White & R. Summers, *Uniform Commercial Code* §19-7 (Supp.1991).

From our consideration of the law and the evidence in this case, we think the trial court erred in enjoining payment under the letter of credit. In the first place, we do not believe appellant's general statement "we have been very satisfied with their work" is sufficient for a finding of fraud. At the time this statement was made, appellant had extended Pearson's contract for building "K" to include buildings "E" and "L", and it seems obvious that appellant's statement was truthful or appellant would not have extended the contract. Also, the testimony shows that the total amount of the contract for building "K" was $458,200.00 and that the back charges which pre-date the statement complained of totalled only approximately $1,944.81. We do not believe the existence of back charges in that small amount supports a finding that appellant committed fraud when it said "we have been very satisfied with their work."

As to the argument that appellant's fraud consisted of billing for work that was outside its contract and other disputed back charges, Robert Pearson III testified his allegation of fraud was that the letter of credit was being called upon because appellant said that based upon "these back charges" they were still owed money, but Pearson testified that as far as "these back charges" are concerned "the majority of them are unacceptable." Pearson testified appellant was claiming a total of $50,000.00 to $60,000.00 in back charges on a project which totaled over $1.2 million. This is simply a contract dispute relating to back charges which may have to be resolved in litigation. However, as explained in Dolan, supra, in the standby letter of credit case "the beneficiary avoids that litigation burden and receives his money promptly" and during the litigation "the beneficiary, not the account party, holds the money."

When we apply the law to the evidence in this case, we think it was clearly erroneous to find that appellant committed fraud that should prevent it from drawing on the letter of credit; therefore, it was error to grant permanent injunctive relief to appellee Pearson and prevent the Bank from honoring the draft drawn on the letter of credit.

Reversed and remanded for any necessary proceedings consistent with this opinion.

Bank of Newport v. First National Bank & Trust Co.
United States Court of Appeals, Eighth Circuit, 1982
687 F.2d 1257

Gibson, Senior Circuit Judge. Bank of Newport appeals from the dismissal by the district court after a bench trial of Bank of Newport's diversity action against First National Bank and Trust Company of Bismarck (First National) for alleged wrongful dishonor of a draft drawn under a letter of credit issued by First National. We affirm the district court.

I

The events leading to this action began when First National at the request of Drs. Robert Honkola, Ralph Honkola, and Richard Fettig (the doctors) issued an irrevocable letter of credit, dated June 30, 1976, in the amount of $125,775.00 to Fiscal Concepts, Inc., a California corporation (Fiscal). The doctors sought issuance of the letter of credit pursuant to an investment program under which they were to provide Fiscal with $60,000.00 in cash and a letter of credit in the amount of $125,775.00 in exchange for the ownership interest in distributorships of coin-operated blood pressure machines. Specifically, the doctors were to receive forty-five blood pressure machines for sale or lease in Minnesota, North Dakota, South Dakota, and Wisconsin.

Fiscal and the doctors agreed that the First National letter of credit was to guarantee the manufacture and delivery of the blood pressure machines and, therefore, should serve as collateral for a second letter of credit issued at Fiscal's request for the benefit of Filac Corporation (Filac), the manufacturer of the machines. However, Fiscal made a commitment to the doctors that the First National letter of credit would never be drawn upon. The First National letter of credit,[72] issued June 30, 1976, provides that the letter was issued " *** [f]or guaranty that Drs. Honkola, Fettig, and Honkola will sell 25 BPM-1200 systems in Minnesota, North Dakota, and South Dakota, and 20 like machines in Wisconsin ***." The letter further provides that drafts drawn under the credit must be endorsed and state the reason for the draw.

On June 14, 1976, Fiscal entered into a general loan and blanket collateral agreement with the Bank of Newport, giving the bank a security interest in Fiscal property. At this time, Fiscal also assigned the proceeds of the First National letter of credit to the bank. The doctors were not told of the assignment until the summer of 1977 and of the security agreement until after this action was commenced.

In December of 1976, Bank of Newport issued, at Fiscal's request, a letter of credit in the amount of $125,760.00 to Filac to guarantee the shipment of ninety-six blood pressure machines to Fiscal. The First National letter of credit was designated as collateral for this letter of credit. In March 1977, Fiscal executed a promissory note in favor of the Bank of Newport in the amount of $125,750.00. This note was secured by the proceeds of the First National letter of credit pursuant to the general loan and collateral agreement of June 14, 1976. Bank of Newport made periodic disbursements under this note to cover draws made by Filac on the Bank of Newport letter of credit.

First National first became aware that the letter of credit had been assigned to Bank of Newport as collateral for Bank of Newport loans to Fiscal in July 1977. Consequently, First National's attorney Jerome Zamos wrote Bank of Newport a letter, stating that the First National letter of credit was not to be used as security for any loans by Bank of Newport to Fiscal, that such use would violate the terms of the letter of credit, and that First National would not honor calls upon its letter of credit. In this letter, Zamos referred to the Fiscal's earlier written commitment to the doctors that the First National letter of credit would never be drawn upon and would only be used "to guarantee manufacturing [of the blood pressure machines] in the first instance."

---

[72]   The letter of credit provides as follows:

"Gentlemen:

"Our Irrevocable Letter of Credit No. 30 Amount -- $125,775.00 -- U.S. Funds for account of Drs. Honkola, Fettig, and Honkola

"For guaranty that Drs. Honkola, Fettig, and Honkola will sell 25 BPM-1200 Systems in Minnesota, North Dakota, and South Dakota, and 20 like machines in Wisconsin.

"The drafts drawn under this Credit are to be endorsed thereon and must bear the clause, drawn under the First National Bank and Trust Company of Bismarck Letter of Credit No. 30 dated June 30, 1976. [sic]

"The drafts drawn under this Credit should state the reason for the draft.

"We hereby agree with drawers, endorsers, and bona fide holders of drafts drawn under and in compliance with the terms of this credit that the same shall be duly honored upon presentation at the First National Bank and Trust Company of Bismarck, Bismarck, North Dakota if drawn and negotiated on or *before December 30, 1977*."

Despite receiving this notice from First National, on September 13, 1977, Bank of Newport prepared a sight draft, executed by Fiscal's president, authorizing First National to pay Bank of Newport $125,775.00 under the letter of credit. The front side of the draft provided that it was "[d]rawn under the First National Bank and Trust Company of Bismarck Letter of Credit # 30 dated 6/30/76 and subsequent amendments thereof." On November 30, 1977, Bank of Newport endorsed the reverse side of the draft, stating that it was "[d]rawn for Letter of Credit face value for application to beneficiary's obligation incurred for the purchase of merchandise in accordance with the letter of credit purpose." When Bank of Newport made this endorsement, it had no knowledge that any blood pressure machines had been purchased by Fiscal for eventual delivery to the doctors and made no effort to determine whether such purchases had been made. Further, at this time, the Bank of Newport retained possession of some 200 blood pressure machines warehoused pursuant to its blanket security agreement with Fiscal and knew that the doctors had not received their forty-five blood pressure machines as required by the agreement between Fiscal and the doctors, the agreement which was the underlying purpose for the letter of credit.

Bank of Newport subsequently presented the draft to First National along with Fiscal's assignment statement and the letter of credit. First National refused to honor the draft because: (1) the condition of the letter of credit had not been met -- i.e., the blood pressure machines had not been delivered to the doctors; and (2) Bank of Newport had received notice that the letter of credit was being improperly used to repay loans from Bank of Newport to Fiscal rather than to guarantee delivery of the machines to the doctors.

The District Court dismissed both of Bank of Newport's claims, holding that First National's dishonor was justified on two independent grounds: First, Bank of Newport failed to provide documentation evidencing delivery of the machines to the doctors as was required under the court's interpretation of the letter of credit. Second, prior to drawing the draft, Bank of Newport had actual knowledge of nondelivery of the machines to the doctors, had possession and control of 200 such machines warehoused pursuant to its security agreement with Fiscal, and had notice that the letter of credit was being improperly used by Fiscal as security for loans from Bank of Newport to Fiscal.[72] As to the second grounds for dishonor, the court concluded that Bank of Newport was "attempting to manipulate the

---

[72]   The court further found that:

   "[P]laintiff had knowledge that delivery of the machines may have been required under the [First National] letter of credit and a number of other letters of credit for the benefit of Fiscal issued for other investors not party to this action. In situations when plaintiff found such letters of credit to be ambiguous in regard to conditions precedent, plaintiff informed Fiscal of the fact and requested Fiscal to seek revision of the letters of credit to provide simply that funds be used 'for general corporate purposes.'"

requirements of [the] letter of credit *** to recover its loan to Fiscal without giving up any of the machines it held as collateral."

Bank of Newport now appeals from the district court's dismissal of its claim for wrongful dishonor; it does not appeal the district court's dismissal of its claim for declaratory relief as to its status as a holder in due course.

II
(A)

This appeal focuses on the question of whether Bank of Newport's draft on the First National letter of credit was tainted by "fraud in the transaction," giving First National the right to dishonor that draft under Uniform Commercial Code §5-114(2). Bank of Newport makes two arguments in support of its position that there was no "fraud in the transaction." First, Bank of Newport argues that it complied fully and truthfully with the terms of the letter of credit by providing the following statement of reason for the draw:

> "Drawn for letter of credit face value for application to beneficiaries' obligation incurred for purchase of merchandise in accordance with the letter of credit purpose."

Bank of Newport urges that the veracity of this statement was not impaired by the fact that the purpose for which the draft was drawn -- to repay loans Bank of Newport made to Fiscal -- was wholly inconsistent with the purpose for which the letter of credit was issued -- to assure delivery of blood pressure machines to the doctors. Bank of Newport further argues that its actual knowledge of nondelivery of the blood pressure machines, its retained possession and control of such machines, and its knowledge of the improper use of the letter of credit did not impair its right to receive payment on the draft presented to First National. Both of these arguments are hinged upon the long-standing principle that a letter of credit is completely divorced from the underlying transaction between the issuing bank's customer (the doctors) and the beneficiary under the letter of credit (Fiscal).

We do not accept Bank of Newport's arguments and conclude that where, as here, no innocent third parties are involved and where the draft itself and the underlying transaction are tainted with fraud or actual knowledge that the underlying transaction is being wholly thwarted by the beneficiary or its assignee, the draft need not be honored. Under the circumstances here presented, the salutory commercial doctrine of the independence of the letter of credit from the underlying transaction has no application. Bank of Newport, as assignee, stands in the shoes of Fiscal, and obviously Fiscal had no right to draw on the letter of credit without making provision for the delivery of the machines. Bank of Newport, as assignee, only had the right to receive payment on drafts properly drawn by the beneficiary, Fiscal.

(B)

A letter of credit is a commitment on the part of the issuing bank that it will pay a draft or demand for payment presented to it under the terms of the credit. Typically, three separate and distinct contracts are involved:

(1) The contract of the bank (First National) with its customer (the doctors) by which the bank agrees to issue the letter of credit to the beneficiary (Fiscal).

(2) The underlying contract between the customer and the beneficiary which results in the letter of credit issuance.

(3) The letter of credit itself, which is a contract between the issuing bank and the beneficiary by which the bank agrees to pay the drafts drawn under the letter of credit and presented to it by the beneficiary if they are accompanied by the requisite documents.

Long-standing case law, codified in the Uniform Commercial Code, establishes that the letter of credit is separate and distinct from the underlying contractual transaction between the issuing bank's customer and the beneficiary. Accordingly, the issuing bank's duty to honor drafts presented for payment is dependent only on the terms and conditions of the letter of credit and not the underlying contract between the bank's customer and the beneficiary. The rule of the independence of the letter of credit from the underlying transaction is based on two policy considerations. First, the issuing bank can assume no liability for the performance of the underlying contract because it has no control over making the underlying contract or over selection of the beneficiary. Second, the letter of credit would lose its commercial vitality if, before honoring drafts, the issuing bank were obliged to look beyond the terms of the letter of credit to the underlying contractual controversy between its customer and the beneficiary.

In the instant case, First National's duty to honor Bank of Newport's draft is governed by §5-114(1) of the Uniform Commercial Code, which provides that:

"An issuer must honor a draft or demand for payment which complies with the terms of the relevant credit regardless of whether the goods or documents conform to the underlying contract for sale or other contract between the customer and the beneficiary."

However, §5-114(2) of the Uniform Commercial Code permits an issuer to dishonor where "fraud in the transaction" has been shown and the holder has not taken the draft in circumstances that would make it a holder in due course. Here, because Bank of Newport does not (and cannot in this factual context) claim holder in due course status, we only address whether or not the defense of "fraud in the transaction" has been shown.

The "fraud in the transaction" defense is a statutory codification of the landmark case of *Sztejn v. J. Henry Schroder Banking Corp.*, 177 Misc. 719, 31

N.Y.S.2d 631 (N.Y.Sup.Ct.1941). In *Sztejn*, a letter of credit was issued to a seller to insure payment for a quantity of bristles. The letter of credit provided that drafts would be paid upon presentation of invoices and a bill of lading showing that shipment of the bristles had been made. The buyer who had procured the letter of credit sued to enjoin payment of the drafts drawn under the letter of credit. The buyer's complaint alleged that while the documents complied on their face with the terms of the letter of credit, the seller shipped worthless cowhairs instead of bristles. Thus, the buyer claimed the seller had engaged in "active fraud" in presenting the documents. The seller's correspondent bank who presented the draft moved to dismiss the buyer's injunction claiming that in a letter of credit transaction, the issuing bank was required to honor drafts where the accompanying documents on their face conformed to the requirements of the letter of credit, notwithstanding fraud in the underlying transaction.

The *Sztejn* court denied the correspondent bank's motion. The court stated that although a letter of credit is independent of the primary contract of sale between the buyer and the seller, and a bank is not required to go behind documents presented for payment before honoring drafts, "[t]he application of this doctrine presupposes that the documents accompanying the drafts are genuine."

The court went on to conclude that where no innocent parties are involved and where the documents and underlying transaction are tainted with intentional fraud, the draft need not be honored, even though the documents conform on their face. The court remarked that "the principle of the independence of the bank's obligation under the letter of credit should not be extended to protect the unscrupulous [beneficiary]." The court accordingly held that a bank presenting a draft on the beneficiary's behalf rather than as a holder in due course stood in no better position than the beneficiary charged with fraud. In the instant case no goods had been shipped at all.

Courts applying *Sztejn's* "fraud in the transaction" defense, as codified in UCC §5-114(2), have given varying interpretations to the term "fraud in the transaction." Some courts interpret the "fraud in the transaction" defense to permit an issuer to dishonor where fraud in the *underlying transaction* has been shown *and no innocent parties are involved*.

Other courts have interpreted the "fraud in the transaction" defense to apply only where fraud has been found in respect to the documents presented to the issuer and not as to the underlying transaction.

Bank of Newport urges that the "fraud in the transaction" defense is available only where the required documents presented along with the draft for payment are intentionally misleading or false, and, fraud in the underlying transaction cannot give rise to a defense to payment. Thus, Bank of Newport suggests that the only issue raised in this case is whether the required document, the draft setting forth the reason for the draw, was itself false; and contends that the statement was true, even though the purpose for the draw -- to repay Bank of Newport loans to Fiscal -- may have been inconsistent with the purpose underlying the letter of credit issuance -- delivery of the machines to the doctors.

(C)

Even accepting Bank of Newport's framing of the issue, we cannot agree that the statement of reason for the draw was itself truthful and that the purpose underlying the letter of credit was of no importance. The statement for the draw may have been artfully worded, but it was in total variance from the purpose of the transaction and not at all in keeping with the obligations of the beneficiary to manufacture and deliver the machines. We analyze this issue in three steps.

First, the purpose underlying the letter of credit is important in determining the truthfulness of the statement of reason because in that statement Bank of Newport explicitly warrants that its draft is "drawn *** in accordance with the letter of credit purpose." Clearly, the ultimate purpose behind the letter of credit issuance here was to assure delivery of the machines to the doctors. Bank of Newport's suggestion that the district court found that the letter of credit was intended merely to serve as collateral to secure manufacture of the machines is based on an incomplete reading of the district court's decision. Furthermore, the district court expressly found that Fiscal and the doctors agreed that the letter of credit was issued "to guarantee the manufacture and delivery of the BPM machines." That court also concluded that "it would be incongruous for the doctors to guarantee to sell machines without being able to acquire the machines to complete their sale."

Second, Bank of Newport knew or at least had reason to know that the purpose behind the letter of credit issuance was delivery of the machines to the doctors. The letter of credit itself indicates that its purpose was to "guaranty that the doctors will sell [blood pressure machines]." Even though the language may have been insufficient to impose a documentary evidence of delivery requirement, it clearly put Bank of Newport on notice that the *purpose* underlying the letter of credit issuance was to assure delivery of the machines. Furthermore, as the district court found, "Bank of Newport was intrinsically involved in the financing and supervising of Fiscal Concepts, Inc. *** and was aware that a number of letters of credit *** may have required delivery of machines as a condition precedent." In view of Bank of Newport's close supervision over Fiscal's financing, it is reasonable to assume that Bank of Newport was aware of the purpose behind a sizable letter of credit made in Fiscal's favor, particularly where Bank of Newport was an assignee of proceeds under that credit. Finally, the letter sent by First National's attorney, Jerome Zamos prior to presentation of the draft put Bank of Newport on notice of the purpose behind the letter of credit. In that letter Zamos indicated that the letter of credit was not to be used to secure loans by Bank of Newport to Fiscal. The Zamos letter also referred to the letter of agreement between Fiscal and the doctors in which Fiscal promised never to draw against the letter of credit.

Third, as the district court found and Bank of Newport concedes, Bank of Newport had knowledge of nondelivery of the machines when it submitted its draft including the statement of reason for the draw. Furthermore, Bank of Newport made no effort to determine whether any machines were *ever* going to be delivered to the doctors.

Therefore, synthesizing steps one through three, the following conclusion emerges: when Bank of Newport submitted its statement of reason that the draft was drawn "in accordance with the letter of credit purpose," it knew that the purpose for which the draft was drawn -- repayment of loans Bank of Newport made to Fiscal -- could not possibly be "in accordance with" the purpose for which the letter of credit was issued -- delivery of the machines to the doctors. Hence, the statement was itself intentionally inaccurate. However, the real fraudulent effect of this statement is amplified when it is considered in conjunction with Bank of Newport's participation in frustrating the letter of credit purpose by retaining possession and control over the machines rather than shipping them to the doctors. Thus, while expressly warranting on its draft that the draft was made in accordance with the letter of credit purpose, Bank of Newport knew that such purpose would be frustrated by its own refusal to ship the machines.[72] We therefore conclude that Bank of Newport's draft was tainted by "fraud in the transaction"[73] and affirm the district court, with costs assessed against appellant.

Affirmed.

Problems

1. Woodmoor planned to develop a mountain recreation community in Routt County, Colorado (the County), to be known as Stagecoach. Early in 1973, Woodmoor obtained plat approval from the Routt County Board of County Commissioners (the Commissioners) for several Stagecoach subdivisions. Pursuant to section 30-28-137, C.R.S.1973 (1977 Repl. Vol. 12), and county subdivision regulations, approval of three of these subdivision plats was conditioned upon Woodmoor's agreement to provide a bond or other undertaking to ensure the completion of roads in accordance with the subdivision design specifications. Accordingly, subdivision improvements agreements were executed between Woodmoor and the County.

---

[72]   This case is therefore distinguishable from cases Bank of Newport relies upon which hold that the purposes for the draw on a letter of credit need not be consistent with the purpose of the underlying transaction. Indeed, this case falls squarely within the exception enunciated in *Sztejn* that "the principle of the independence of the bank's obligation under a letter of credit should not be extended to protect the unscrupulous [beneficiary]." *Sztejn*, 31 N.Y.S.2d at 634. Bank of Newport, as an assignee, had a direct interest in payment under a letter of credit, the purpose of which the Bank knew was being frustrated by its own actions. Bank of Newport stands in no better position than Fiscal, which clearly had no right to draw the draft under these circumstances.

[73]   While not expressly characterizing the Bank of Newport's actions as constituting "fraud in the transaction," the district court did conclude:

"It is clear that [Bank of Newport] had control of the machines and was attempting to manipulate the requirements of [the] letter of credit in regard to the machines. [Bank of Newport's] intent was obviously to recover its loan to Fiscal without giving up any of the machines it held as collateral."

At Woodmoor's request, the Bank issued three letters of credit to secure Woodmoor's obligations under the agreements. The first two letters of credit, No. 1156 and No. 1157, were issued January 23, 1973 in the respective amounts of $158,773 and $77,330 bearing expiry dates of December 31, 1975. The third letter of credit No. 1168 was issued March 7, 1973 in the amount of $113,732 bearing an expiry date of December 31, 1976. The face amounts of the letters of credit were identical to the estimated costs of the road and related improvements in the respective subdivision improvements agreements. The County was authorized by each letter of credit to draw directly on the Bank, for the account of Woodmoor, up to the face amount of each letter of credit. Each letter of credit required the County, in order to draw on the letters of credit, to submit fifteen-day sight drafts accompanied by: "A duly-signed statement by the Routt County Board of Commissioners that improvements have not been made in compliance with a Subdivision Improvements Agreement between Routt County and the Woodmoor Corporation dated (either January 9, 1973 or March 7, 1973) and covering the (respective subdivisions) at Stagecoach and that payment is therefore demanded hereunder."

Woodmoor never commenced construction of the roads and related improvements. On December 31, 1975, the expiry date of letters of credit No. 1156 and No. 1157, the County presented two demand drafts to the Bank for the face amounts of $158,773 and $77,330. The demand drafts were accompanied by a resolution of the Commissioners stating that Woodmoor had failed to comply with the terms of the subdivision improvements agreements and demanded payment of the face amounts of the letters of credit. On January 5, 1976, within three banking days of the demand, the Bank dishonored the drafts. The Bank did not specifically object to the County's presentation of demand drafts rather than fifteen-day sight drafts as required by the letters of credit.

On December 22, 1976, the County presented the Bank with a demand draft on letter of credit No. 1168 which was accompanied by the required resolution of the Commissioners. The Bank dishonored this draft because of the County's nonconforming demand, viz., that a demand draft was submitted rather than a fifteen-day sight draft. On December 29, 1976, the County presented a fifteen- day sight draft to the Bank. This draft was not accompanied by the resolution of the Commissioners. On December 31, 1976, the Bank dishonored this draft.

The County sued to recover the face amounts of the three letters of credit plus interest from the dates of the demands. The Bank answered the County's complaints alleging several affirmative defenses. The fundamental premise of the Bank's defenses was the assertion that the County would receive a windfall since it had not expended or committed to spend any funds to complete the road improvements specified in the subdivision improvements agreements. *Colorado Nat'l Bank v. Bd. of*

County Comm'rs, 634 P.2d 32 (Colo. 1981). Who should prevail, the County or the Bank?

2.   Bank A issued a letter of credit to D, the beneficiary, but Bank A kept possession of the credit. D agreed in writing that Bank B had a security interest in the credit to secure a loan from Bank B to D. Bank B thereafter notified Bank A that Bank B claimed a security interest in the credit. Does Bank B have a perfected security interest?

3.   "Certain European banks currently have agreements with large customers that permit those customers to place electronic 'orders' for the issuance of commercial credits. If the order 'tests' against the authorization procedure, the bank's computer automatically issues a commercial documentary credit to the advising bank * * *. The advising bank will then either print out, or in some cases electronically transmit, the credit to the beneficiary. The ICC [International Chamber of Commerce] takes the position that these arrangements should be left to the private contracting arrangements of the parties * * *. The ICC does not currently, and does not apparently intend, to try to establish standards for such arrangements." R. David Whitaker, *Electronic Documentary Credits*, 46 Bus. Law. 1781, 1782 (August 1991). Can such an electronic letter of credit be used, reliably, as collateral? How?

C. INSIDER LIABILITY

Morgan v. United States

United States District Court, N.D.Tex., Jan. 25, 1990
90-1 U.S.Tax Cas. (CCH) P 50,106, Unempl.Ins.Rep. (CCH) P 15407A, 1990 WL 39106),
aff'd, 937 F.2d 281 (5th Cir. 1991)

Fitzwater, District Judge: This motion for summary judgment presents the question whether plaintiff-counterdefendant Tommy D. Morgan ("Morgan") was a "responsible person" who "willfully" failed to account for and pay withholding taxes within the meaning of 26 U.S.C. §6672(a). Concluding as a matter of law that the summary judgment evidence establishes Morgan's liability, the court grants summary judgment and enters judgment in favor of the government.

I

The summary judgment evidence establishes the following uncontested facts. Morgan is an accountant who resides in Denton, Texas. He has been employed by Two Jacks Wireline Service Corporation since 1970.

In 1980 or 1981 he became an officer of the corporation. He never attended any meetings of the officers or the board of the corporation because none were held. He was never a director of the corporation. Plaintiff's responsibilities included typing invoices, keeping monthly records, preparing tax returns,

included typing invoices, keeping monthly records, preparing tax returns, preparing Form 941's (the Employer's Quarterly Federal Tax Return), preparing state unemployment forms, and preparing state withholding reports. He did not prepare payroll checks.

The corporation maintained three bank accounts--one in Denton, Texas and two in Louisiana. Morgan had signature authority over the Denton account. No payroll checks were issued from that account. The account was used to issue checks to the IRS, to the State of Louisiana for state taxes, to Morgan, and to Two Jacks Wireline Services. The funds in the account were proceeds from factoring receivables. If the proceeds from such receivables exceeded the monthly expenses, the excess was transferred to Louisiana. Additionally, Morgan transferred money to Louisiana whenever the president of the corporation requested money, whether or not there was an excess in the Denton bank account for the month. If the Denton account had insufficient funds to pay withholding taxes when due, Morgan sent the withholding tax return to the president of the company and instructed him to pay the taxes. Morgan was aware that the withholding taxes were not being paid, yet he made transfers from the Denton account to the president of the corporation, to himself, and to the State of Louisiana for payroll taxes.

II

Funds required to be withheld from employees' payroll checks are held in trust by the employer for the United States. If the trust funds are not paid over, the government may impose a 100 percent penalty for the withheld taxes pursuant to 26 U.S.C. §6672(a).[72] Liability under §6672(a) is imposed only on a responsible person who has willfully failed to perform a duty to collect, account, and pay over the taxes.[73]

A

Whether a taxpayer is a responsible person within the meaning of §6672(a) is a matter of status, duty, and authority. There can be more than one responsible person, and the Fifth Circuit generally takes a broad view of who qualifies as such.

The central question is whether an individual had the effective power to pay taxes. The threat of adverse action by a superior or direct instructions not to pay taxes owed does not relieve one from his status as a responsible person. Mere access to corporate funds, however, does not make one a responsible person. A

---

[72]   26 U.S.C. §6672(a): "Any person required to collect, truthfully account for, and pay over any tax imposed by this title who willfully fails to collect such tax, or truthfully account for and pay over such tax, or willfully attempts in any manner to evade or defeat any such tax or the payment thereof, shall, in addition to other penalties provided by law, be liable to a penalty equal to the total amount of the tax evaded, or not collected, or not accounted for and paid over. No penalty shall be imposed under section 6653 for any offense to which this section is applicable."

[73]   A responsible person's willful failure to perform any of the three enumerated functions results in §6672(a) liability.

corporation may deny an employee the actual authority to pay taxes. In that circumstance, requiring the employee to pay taxes would amount to requiring him to steal company funds. Morgan's deposition testimony demonstrates that he had actual authority to pay withholding taxes, at least to the extent funds were available in the Denton account.

Morgan argues, however, that there is no evidence to show he had control over sufficient funds in the Denton account to pay all the withholding taxes due. A person cannot be a responsible person unless he has the effective ability to pay the taxes. A person who controls insufficient corporate funds to pay the taxes in full does not have the effective ability to pay the taxes beyond the funds in the account he controls. Thus, he is a responsible person only to the extent of the funds entering his accounts after the tax liability arises.

The burden of proving that Morgan did not control sufficient funds to pay the tax liability is upon Morgan. A plaintiff seeking refund of a partial payment of a §6672 penalty has the burden of proving that he was not a responsible person even if the government has counterclaimed for the remaining unpaid tax. Morgan merely points out that the government "has offered no summary judgment evidence to show [Morgan] had control over sufficient funds in the one account he could sign on to cause payment of the tax liability." Because Morgan will bear the burden at trial of proving he is not a responsible person, on motion for summary judgment he bears the burden of adducing sufficient evidence which, if believed by a jury, would entitle him to relief. Morgan offers no evidence of the insufficiency of the funds over which he had control. He has thus failed to satisfy his burden of proof.

Morgan testified he had the authority to draw checks on the Denton account to pay taxes. He was an officer of the corporation and was fully aware of the corporation's tax obligations. Morgan did not adduce evidence from which a reasonable jury could find he had control only over funds that were insufficient to pay the taxes. The court thus concludes Morgan has not adduced evidence sufficient to create a genuine issue regarding whether he was a responsible person. [Other courts have found the following persons to be responsible for purposes of §6672 liability: president of corporation held responsible person despite limited check writing authority; president and vice-president with signing authority over bank accounts held responsible persons; chairman of board with check signing authority held responsible person; minority shareholder acting as treasurer and executive and executive vice-president held responsible person; general manager with check signing authority held responsible person; president of corporation with check signing authority held responsible person; officer with check signing authority held responsible person.]

B

Morgan also contends he did not willfully fail to pay the taxes. Willfulness under §6672(a) requires a voluntary, conscious, and intentional act, but not a bad motive or evil intent. Willfulness is normally proved by evidence that the responsible person paid other creditors with knowledge that withholding taxes were due at the time to the government. Willfulness is also established if the responsible person acted with reckless disregard of a known or obvious risk that tax withholdings would not be paid over to the government. Reckless disregard includes failure to investigate or correct mismanagement after being notified that withholding taxes have not been paid.   Mere negligence does not establish willfulness.   A responsible person's decision not to pay over withholding taxes does not cease to be willful because the person is ordered by another not to pay. The responsible person bears the burden of proving his actions were not willful.

It is undisputed that Morgan wrote checks to himself and the State of Louisiana subsequent to discovering that Two Jacks Wireline Services owed withholding taxes to the government. No later than April 1984 Morgan was aware that withholding taxes were not being paid. Morgan argues that the corporation's president was responsible for the decision not to pay. Morgan's willful failure to remit taxes is not affected by the fact that he may have delegated to the president the duty to pay. Moreover, Morgan's actions in not ensuring that the president in fact was paying the taxes constitute at least a reckless disregard of a known risk that tax withholdings would not be paid over to the government.

Morgan was aware of the tax deficiencies and made payments to himself and others during 1984 despite this knowledge. Morgan had a duty to ensure the taxes were paid. The court concludes he willfully failed to pay the taxes owed for each quarter. [Other courts have found willfulness in these cases: reckless disregard for risk IRS would not apply deposits to withholding taxes sufficient to establish willfulness; taxpayer acted willfully in allowing company to continue in business and use trust funds to pay other creditors; taxpayers acted willfully despite their reliance on controller's assertions that taxes had been paid; taxpayer acted willfully despite delegation of duty to pay taxes to subordinates.]

On the basis of the evidence that Morgan has adduced in response to the government's summary judgment motion, a reasonable jury would be unable to conclude Morgan was not a responsible person and did not act willfully in failing to pay the withholding taxes in question. Accordingly, the government's motion for summary judgment is granted.

So Ordered.

Nachazel v. Mira Co., Mfg.
Supreme Court of Iowa, 1991
466 N.W.2d 248

Schultz, Justice.   The issues on this appeal arise out of the plaintiffs', Laddie and Linda Nachazel (Nachazels), attempt to collect a judgment of $48,462 plus interest awarded against Mira Co., Manufacturing (Mira). See Nachazel v. Miraco Mfg., 432 N.W.2d 158 (Iowa 1988). After plaintiffs' execution against Mira was returned unsatisfied, plaintiffs commenced this action against several defendants in an attempt to satisfy their judgment.

Plaintiffs sued two corporations, Miracle Recreation Equipment Co. (Miracle) and Ahrens Agricultural Industries Co. (Ahrens Co.). Miracle owns all of Mira's stock. Ahrens Co. manufactures and sells products formerly sold by Mira. Plaintiffs also sued three individuals, C.W. Ahrens, Paul W. Ahrens, and Randy Juhl, who were officers and directors of both Mira and Miracle. Paul W. Ahrens is now deceased and his estate is substituted as a party to this appeal. Mira was also a defendant to the present action, however, no judgment was entered against it.

The trial court entered judgment against the three individuals and Miracle. It dismissed the action against Ahrens Co. We affirm the judgment against Miracle as modified. We reverse the judgment against the individuals and the dismissal of the action against Ahrens Co.

Miracle manufactures and sells recreational equipment. In December 1977 it entered the agricultural market and incorporated Mira. Miracle referred to its agricultural division in its minutes from a meeting of Miracle's Board of Directors; however, Mira was only a part of Miracle's agricultural division. Mira sold and warranted the agricultural products but Miracle manufactured them.

Mira's operation as a separate entity was quite limited. Mira's office was located in Miracle's headquarters but did not maintain a separate telephone, checking account, or accounting department. Mira did not file separate tax returns; its taxable income was included in Miracle's consolidated tax return. Mira did have two employees but they were on Miracle's payroll. Miracle received all cash receipts, paid all bills, and provided all of the accounting services for Mira. Miracle did maintain a ledger showing the relationship of Mira's and Miracle's financial status.

Late in 1983, changes occurred within Miracle's agricultural division. Problems had developed in the manufacture, sale, delivery, and use of Mirahuts which resulted in claims being filed against Mira and Miracle. Defendant C.W. Ahrens planned to retire as Miracle's Director and Chairman of the Board in late 1983. The man chosen to succeed Ahrens did not have faith in the profitability of the agricultural line of products and Miracle decided to remove itself from the agricultural market. However, Ahrens believed that the agricultural lines had merit. On November 10, 1983, Miracle's Board of Directors decided to sell the assets of Mira to C.W. Ahrens and empowered Miracle's executive committee to enter a contract of sale with Ahrens.

In December 1983, Ahrens retired from Miracle and incorporated Ahrens Co., which was formed to continue the business of Miracle's former agricultural division. Mira and Ahrens Co. entered a contract for the sale of Mira's assets, which included some vehicles (ten trucks), accounts receivable, and leases. Later, the vehicles were valued at $82,339 and the receivables and leases at $166,745. Also, Miracle transferred its tooling equipment and inventory by the peculiar action of a bill of sale from Mira to Ahrens Co. Miracle received the entire proceeds from the sale of these assets, but Mira's ledger account reflected a credit for the sale.

Mira ceased to do business in 1983. In 1985, the Secretary of State issued a certificate of cancellation to Mira for failure to file a 1985 annual corporation report. Meanwhile, Miracle settled other claims against Mira and provided for Mira's defense in plaintiffs' earlier suit, which was tried and appealed in 1987 and 1988.

Plaintiffs' petition contained eight counts alleging several theories of recovery against the various defendants. The event common to all theories advanced by plaintiffs was the transfer of assets in 1983 and early 1984 between Mira, Miracle, and Ahrens Co. Following trial, the court awarded plaintiffs a judgment against the three individual defendants for $48,462 with interest, and a judgment against Miracle to the extent of the value of the assets transferred from Mira to Miracle. It found against plaintiffs on their claims against Ahrens Co.

On appeal, the individual defendants and Miracle challenge the trial court's separate determination of liability against them. They also claim that the trial court erred when it denied a motion to compel the withdrawal of plaintiffs' attorneys. Plaintiffs cross-appeal, challenging the amount of the award against Miracle and the court's dismissal of its claims against Ahrens Co. We discuss the various issues separately.

* * *

III. Equitable lien and continuing corporation theory of liability. Plaintiffs sought recovery against Miracle and Ahrens Co. under an equitable lien or continuing corporation theory. The trial court ruled that Miracle was responsible under this theory to the extent of the assets transferred, which amounted to ten trucks or the proceeds therefrom. The court rejected plaintiffs' similar claim against Ahrens Co.

On appeal, Miracle challenges the court's factual determination and its application of a lien in plaintiffs' favor. On cross-appeal, plaintiffs urge that the award of damages against Miracle was inadequate and that they were also entitled to recover against Ahrens Co.

We have recognized principles that allow the attachment of an equitable lien to properly transferred property or its traceable proceeds. Tubbs v. United Central Bank, N.A., 451 N.W.2d 177, 185 (Iowa 1990); Cox v. Waudby, 433 N.W.2d 716, 719-20 (Iowa 1988); In re Receivership of Hollingsworth, 386 N.W.2d 93, 96-97 (Iowa 1986). An equitable lien is a remedial alternative to a constructive trust. Hollingsworth, 386 N.W.2d at 96. An equitable lien is a restitution concept applied by courts of equity to avoid injustice. Tubbs, 451 N.W.2d at 185 (citing Restatement of Restitution §161, at 650-52 (1937)). It may be "implied and declared by a court of equity out of general considerations of a right and justice as applied to the relations of the parties and the circumstances of their dealings." Tubbs, 451 N.W.2d at 185 (quoting Farmers & Merchants Bank v. Commissioner of Internal Revenue, 175 F.2d 846, 849 (8th Cir.1949)). The right to acquire an equitable lien may be cut off by the superior rights of innocent third parties, such as a good faith purchaser for value who takes the property without notice of the lien. Cox, 433 N.W.2d at 720; Luedecke v. Des Moines Cabinet Co., 140 Iowa 223, 228, 118 N.W. 456, 457 (1908).

Transfers by corporations may be subject to the application of this equitable rule. In a proper case, creditors of a corporation possess an equitable lien upon the assets of a corporation and may pursue this right against the property in the hands of one who is not a good faith purchaser. Nelson v. Pampered Beef-Midwest, Inc., 298 N.W.2d 281, 285 (Iowa 1980). In Nelson we further elaborated:

> The rule is recognized that, where one corporation transfers all its assets to another, not in the ordinary course of business, the very circumstances of the case imply full knowledge on the part of the transferee of all the facts necessary to charge the property in the hands of the purchaser with the debts of the seller; and this is especially true where the purchasing corporation is a product of the ingenuity of the stockholders of the old corporation, who took the property with full knowledge of the right of the plaintiff and transferred it to the new body of their own creation.

Id. (quoting Farnsworth v. Muscatine Produce & Pure Ice Co., 177 Iowa 21, 36, 158 N.W. 741, 747 (1916)). We now examine these equitable lien principles in light of the respective claims of the parties in this case.

A. Miracle. Under this record, we conclude that plaintiffs have established an equitable lien against Miracle for the proceeds of the assets transferred from Mira to Miracle and sold to Ahrens Co. At a November 10, 1987, meeting, Miracle's Board of Directors took action to sell Mira's assets to C.W. Ahrens, who was Chairman of the Boards of Miracle and Mira. Miracle's Board authorized its executive committee to carry out this sale. There is no record that Mira took any independent action on this sale. All of the proceedings originated with Miracle's Board except that the transfer of the agricultural division's assets was made by Mira.

We agree with the trial court's finding that "Mira was absorbed by Miracle and was then phased out ... notwithstanding no formal articles of merger were filed." This de facto merger of the assets of Mira into Miracle was neither a sale nor a transfer in the ordinary course of business.

We agree with the trial court's holding that plaintiffs, as creditors of Mira, are entitled to pursue their claim against Miracle. Under the authority of Tubbs and Nelson, we hold that the circumstances of this case entitle plaintiffs to an equitable lien against either the assets transferred to Miracle or to the traceable proceeds of these transferred assets.

The trial court limited plaintiffs' recovery against Miracle to the extent of ten trucks. We disagree with the court's limitation. In addition to the ten trucks, Miracle took control of Mira's accounts receivable and leases and then caused their sale to Ahrens Co.

We are aware the ledger shows that Mira owed Miracle money and that Miracle claims an entitlement to the accounts receivable, leases, and vehicles. We find little merit in this contention. Miracle had complete control of the figures that appeared on Mira's ledger accounts. Miracle set its own prices on the products it manufactured and supplied to Mira. Miracle maintained Mira's books. Miracle's Board proceedings of January 31, 1983, reveals a statement by its financial officer that Miracle's books "did not truly reflect the proper allocation of costs of goods produced between the companies. That these figures were based purely upon imagination rather than basic costs." Mira's employees simply sold the products and drew their salaries; Miracle completely controlled all decisions that affected Mira's profitability and net worth.

Under these circumstances, it would be inequitable to give Miracle, as a creditor of Mira, priority over plaintiffs' claim against Mira. Miracle received $200,000 in cash and a note for the sale balance. We hold that plaintiffs may have a personal judgment against Miracle.

We affirm the trial court's judgment against Miracle based on an equitable lien theory of recovery. We modify the amount of the judgment. Plaintiffs shall have judgment against Miracle for the sum of $48,462 with interest at the rate of ten percent per annum from November 28, 1983.

B. Ahrens Co. The trial court denied application of an equitable lien theory of recovery against Ahrens Co. It reasoned that: (1) Ahrens Co. did not agree to assume Mira's debts; (2) there was no merger between Mira and Ahrens Co.; (3) Ahrens Co. was not a mere continuation of Mira; and (4) the transaction was not entered into for the purpose of avoiding creditors. However, these are not the appropriate findings for the creation of an equitable lien. Rather, these findings are independent requirements for establishing personal liability against a purchasing company for the debts of a selling corporation. See Nelson, 298 N.W.2d at 287 (quoting Luedecke, 140 Iowa at 226, 118 N.W. at 457). We agree with the trial court's conclusion that these independent requirements are not met in this case and that personal liability should not be imposed on Ahrens Co. However, whether or not plaintiffs may impose an equitable lien on purchased assets or proceeds presents a separate issue.

The record in this case presents the issue of whether Miracle's transfer of Mira's assets to Ahrens Co. without making adequate provision for the payment of Mira's unsecured debts provides plaintiffs an equitable lien remedy against these assets or the proceeds therefrom. We conclude that plaintiffs are entitled to an equitable lien remedy against Ahrens Co. The assets of Mira came under the ownership of Ahrens Co. by a series of decisions made by Miracle's Board and C.W. Ahrens, who also founded Ahrens Co. When the transfer of Mira's assets was initiated, C.W. Ahrens was the director and chief officer of both Mira and Miracle. This was not an arm's-length transaction in the ordinary course of business; rather, the transaction was an in-house deal. Defendant Juhl, who was the financial officer and director of both Mira and Miracle, determined the value of Mira's assets in December 1983 and subsequently made major adjustments before setting the final price in 1984. Later, Juhl also worked as a certified public accountant for Ahrens Co.

More important, Juhl, who engineered Mira's accounting and sale price, did not protect plaintiffs as creditors of Mira. Miracle set up a reserve for the payment of Mira's debts; however, this reserve was another venture guided by imagination and proved to be inadequate. C.W. Ahrens was in a position to control Juhl and the three corporations that were involved in the sale of Mira's assets.

We conclude that the transfer of Mira's entire assets was not an ordinary business transaction. Nor can Ahrens Co. claim to be a good faith purchaser. Therefore, we hold that plaintiffs are entitled to an equitable lien against the ten vehicles, accounts receivable, leases, or the proceeds therefrom, to the extent of their judgment against Mira. We reverse that portion of the trial court's ruling denying application of the equitable lien theory of recovery against Ahrens Co. and direct it to enter judgment in accordance with this section.

IV. Statutory liability. Defendants contend that the trial court erred by holding C.W. Ahrens, Paul Ahrens, and Randy Juhl jointly and severally liable for breaching the statutory duty imposed by Iowa Code section 496A.44(3) (1983) to make adequate provision for Mira's debts, obligations, and liabilities in the distribution of Mira's assets. The trial court found that these individual defendants breached this statutory duty by failing to "provide for the contingent liability which could arise ... in the event of recovery by [the Nachazels]." We reverse the trial court's ruling holding the individual defendants liable under section 496A.44(3).

[Section 496A.44(3) provides in relevant part:

In addition to any other liabilities imposed by law upon directors and officers of a corporation, a director shall be liable in the following circumstances, unless the director complies with the standard provided in this chapter for performance of the duties of directors: ....

3. A director who votes for or assents to any distribution of assets of a corporation to its shareholders during the liquidation of the corporation without the payment and discharge of, or making adequate provision for, all known debts, obligations, and liabilities of the corporation shall be liable to the corporation jointly and severally with all other directors so voting or assenting for the value of such assets which are distributed, to the extent that such debts, obligations and liabilities of the corporation are not thereafter paid and discharged.]

The plain language of section 496A.44(3) allows only a corporation, not a third-party creditor, to bring an action. In allowing plaintiffs to recover under section 496A.44(3), the trial court relied on the reasoning of the Colorado supreme court in Ficor, Inc. v. McHugh, 639 P.2d 385 (Colo.1982), which allowed a creditor to bring suit under a Colorado statute containing language identical to section 496A.44(3). However, Ficor appears to be a minority view and we decline to adopt its reasoning. See Lowell Staats Mining Co. v. Philadelphia Elec. Co., 878 F.2d 1271, 1277 (10th Cir.1989) (stating that Ficor created a narrow exception for when a creditor can sue on its own behalf).

In the absence of statutory language giving creditors a direct cause of action against corporate officers and directors, the rule generally followed is that a creditor of a corporation may not maintain a personal action at law against officers or directors who have committed a wrong against the corporation, such as mismanagement, waste, or diversion of assets. See 18B Am.Jur.2d Corporations §1842, at 693 (1985). The reason is that officers and directors owe a duty to the corporation and not to third parties who might be injured incidentally by the wrong committed against the corporation. Id. at 693-94. Additionally, privity is lacking due to the absence of a contractual relationship between corporate officers and creditors. Id. at 693.

The common reason advanced by other courts in interpreting the same or similar corporate statutes is that a creditor does not have the right to bring an action directly against corporate officers and directors when the governing statute does not contain the word "creditor." See, e.g., Lowell Staats, 878 F.2d at 1277 (refusing to apply Ficor 's reasoning to same Colorado statute and holding that judgment creditor in individual capacity could not sue director); Louisiana World Exposition v. Federal Ins. Co., 858 F.2d 233, 239-40 (5th Cir.1988) (cause of action runs solely in favor of corporation when plain language of Louisiana statute does not give creditor direct cause of action against director of insolvent corporation); Delgado Oil Co., Inc. v. Torres, 785 F.2d 857, 860-61 (10th Cir.1986) (rejecting application of Ficor reasoning to bankruptcy statute and holding that creditor's cause of action can be enforced only by bankruptcy trustee for debtor corporation); Planned Consumer Mktg., Inc. v. Coats & Clark, 127 A.D.2d 355, 369, 513 N.Y.S.2d 417, 426 (1987) (holding that judgment creditor is not proper party to bring an action against director for unlawful distribution of corporate assets under New York statute giving corporation the exclusive right to enforce liability against directors), aff'd on other grounds, 71 N.Y.2d 442, 522 N.E.2d 30, 527 N.Y.S.2d 185 (1988); Schaeffer v. DeChant, 11 Ohio App.3d 281, 282, 464 N.E.2d 583, 585 (1983) (same as Planned Consumer). Even when the relevant statutory language provided that directors "shall be jointly and severally liable to the corporation for the benefit of its creditors" the court held that creditors did not have standing to sue. See Aries Ventures Ltd. v. Axa Finance, 729 F.Supp. 289, 297-98 (S.D.N.Y.1990). The rule announced in Ficor has appeal, but we believe that the statute's plain language must be followed. Any change must be left to future legislation.

Thus, upon consideration of the foregoing cases and the plain language of Iowa Code section 496A.44(3), we hold that the right to bring an action under this section runs only to the corporation, and not to creditors.

The trial court also awarded a judgment against Miracle under count IV of plaintiffs' petition which we perceive to be an offshoot from the statutory claim against the individual directors. Defendants do not include this as an issue on appeal. Therefore, we must affirm the trial court's judgment against Miracle.

V. Other theories of liability. On cross-appeal, plaintiffs urge that the trial court erred in failing to hold Miracle liable on a fraudulent conveyance theory and in failing to pierce the corporate veil of Mira and find its sole shareholder, Miracle, liable for Mira's debts. In section III, we held Miracle liable for the same relief requested under these theories of liability. Thus, we decline to discuss these theories.

Plaintiff also requests an award of punitive damages. The trial court determined that defendants' conduct falls short of the type necessary to impose punitive damages. We agree. To justify such an award, the wrongful conduct must be committed with willful or reckless disregard for the rights of another. Moreover, punitive damages are always discretionary. We have not considered the issue of liability under every count of plaintiffs' petition; however, our review of the entire record causes us to conclude that defendants' conduct did not rise to a level which justifies an award of punitive damages.

VI. Summary. Our holding can be summarized as follows: (1) We affirm the trial court's refusal to disqualify plaintiffs' counsel; (2) we reverse the judgment and decree against C.W. Ahrens, Randy Juhl, and the Estate of Paul Ahrens; (3) we affirm the judgment against Miracle but modify it to allow a judgment and decree against Miracle for $48,462 plus interest at ten per cent per annum from November 28, 1983; (4) we reverse the dismissal of plaintiffs' claim against Ahrens Co. and direct that a judgment and decree be entered against Ahrens Co. for the imposition of an equitable lien, not to exceed the amount of the judgment against Miracle, against the vehicles, accounts receivable, and leases or the proceeds therefrom; and (5) we affirm the trial court in all other respects. Finally, we assess the costs incurred in both the trial court and on appeal against Miracle, Ahrens Co., and plaintiffs equally.

Affirmed In Part As Modified And Reversed In Part.

ADT Security Systems Mid-South, Inc. v. Central Distribution, Inc.

Court of Appeals of Minnesota, 1994
1994 WL 43872 (unpublished opinion)

Huspeni, Judge. Appellant Gerald Trooien challenges the district court's grant of summary judgment holding him personally liable to respondent ADT Security Systems for debts owed by corporate parties to a contract. Because appellant's misuse of the corporate form and unfairness to respondent justifies piercing the corporate veil, we affirm.

FACTS

Appellant Gerald L. Trooien is the sole shareholder of JLT Group, Inc., a Minnesota corporation that manages real estate. Appellant also is the sole shareholder of JLT Real Estate Company, which is the general partner in a limited partnership called JLT Warehouse Limited Partnership. Appellant was the sole limited partner in JLT warehouse until March 1989.

Central Distribution, Inc. (Central) and Central Distribution Carriers (Carriers), Central's wholly-owned subsidiary, originally were owned by the Bratnober family. In March 1989, Central transferred all equipment and assets associated with operating its trucking and warehousing business to Carriers. Central's principal asset after the transfer consisted of real estate occupied by a warehouse complex housing a number of tenants, including Carriers.

At the same time that Central transferred equipment and assets to Carriers, appellant purchased all of Carriers' stock from the Bratnobers. On April 12, 1989, appellant also purchased all of Central's stock. On the same day, Central contributed its only asset, the warehouse complex real estate, to JLT Warehouse in exchange for a 35% limited partnership in JLT Warehouse. After appellant purchased the companies, JLT Group assumed management of the warehouse complex real estate.

Respondent ADT Security Systems provided security systems and services to the warehouse complex before appellant bought the companies, billing its services to Central. After appellant acquired Central and Carriers in 1989, respondent approached JLT Group to discuss upgrading the security systems in the complex. JLT Group directed respondent to bill existing alarm services directly to third-party tenants instead of to Central and to bill "CDI, Inc." for portions of the warehouse occupied by Central Distribution. Respondent understood "CDI, Inc." to mean Central.

When respondent contracted for the upgraded security services, it dealt with Barry Weber, whom appellant identified as Carriers' CEO. Weber consulted with appellant and Williamson, a JLT Group employee, and received Williamson's approval to enter into the contracts. The three contracts identify CDI, Inc. as customer and Weber as CEO. Appellant claims that Weber signed the contracts on behalf of Carriers only.

In early 1990, Carriers experienced financial difficulties. In particular, the company fell behind in rent payments owed to JLT Warehouse, the owner of the real estate. On September 26, 1990, in exchange for forgiveness of some of the accrued rent, Carriers agreed to sell equipment and assets (Carriers' equipment) to JLT Warehouse. Four days later, on September 30, JLT Warehouse distributed Carriers' equipment to appellant, adjusting appellant's capital account in the limited partnership. On the same day, Williamson purchased Carriers' equipment from appellant, giving appellant a nonrecourse promissory note secured by the stock in Midway Cold and Storage (Midway), a company appellant incorporated on September 21, 1990, to lease the warehouse complex space occupied by Carriers. Williamson purchased the stock from appellant on October 1, 1990, with Carriers' equipment as consideration.

Since Carriers' space in the warehouse complex was now occupied by Midway, Carriers began the process of winding down. The company attempted to work out debt repayment plans with its creditors and managed to settle its accounts with all but respondent and three other creditors. In the meantime, respondent terminated its services in the warehouse complex.

Respondent commenced an action to recover amounts due under its service contract with CDI, Inc., naming Central and Carriers as primarily liable on the debt and appellant and Midway liable as alter egos, instrumentalities, or successors in interest to Central Distribution Companies. The district court granted respondent partial summary judgment on the issue of whether the Central Distribution Companies were merely appellant's alter ego, thus rendering appellant individually liable on the debt the companies owed respondent. Later, the district court issued an order setting the amount of damages at $46,898.

DECISION

On appeal from a summary judgment, this court must determine (1) whether there are any genuine issues of material fact, and (2) whether the trial court erred in its application of the law.

1. Appellant argues that he cannot be individually liable for Carriers' debt to respondent because he did not disregard the corporate entity. We disagree.

We begin by noting that it is appropriate to pierce the corporate veil in the context of a summary judgment motion. Disregard of the corporate entity will allow a corporation's creditor to hold shareholders liable for a corporate obligation. Creditors may "pierce the corporate veil" to impose liability on an individual shareholder when the reality of the shareholder's relationship with the corporation's operation meets a two-prong test. Victoria Elevator Co. v. Meriden Grain Co., 283 N.W.2d 509, 512 (Minn.1979).

Under the first prong of the *Victoria Elevator* test, the court looks at the relationship between the shareholder and the corporation, considering the following factors:

(1) insufficient capitalization for purposes of corporate undertaking,
(2) failure to observe corporate formalities,
(3) nonpayment of dividends,
(4) insolvency of debtor corporation at time of transaction in question,
(5) siphoning of funds by dominant shareholder,
(6) nonfunctioning of other officers and directors,
(7) absence of corporate records, and
(8) existence of the corporation merely as a facade for individual dealings.

Id.

Some of these factors are present in appellant's relationship with Central and Carriers. While appellant generally observed corporate formalities, there is evidence that he did not always clarify that Central and Carriers were separate entities. Weber, whom appellant claimed was Carriers' CEO, stated that Central and Carriers "weren't separate corporations, they were just run together." Furthermore, respondent dealt with Central before appellant purchased the companies and reasonably believed that "CDI, Inc." was simply another name for Central when appellant directed him to bill CDI directly. Respondent's contracts with CDI for upgraded security services were signed by Weber, Carriers' CEO, but there is no indication on the contract that Weber was acting on behalf of Carriers rather than Central. Those contracts were approved by Williamson, a JLT Group employee, not a Central or Carriers employee.

We also find evidence of siphoning assets, particularly with regard to Carriers' equipment. Carriers acquired the equipment from Central in March 1989, and then sold it to JLT Warehouse on September 26, 1990, in return for forgiveness of unpaid rent. JLT Warehouse distributed the equipment to appellant four days later and adjusted the amount of appellant's capital contribution to the limited partnership. Appellant then sold the equipment to Williamson, who gave appellant a nonrecourse note in the amount of $273,410 secured by Midway stock, which Williamson purchased by selling the equipment to Midway. As a result, Carriers was left with virtually no assets except, as conceded by appellant, "a couple little, small pieces of equipment * * *, but nothing of any significance." Carriers' equipment essentially belongs to appellant because Williamson paid for it with a nonrecourse note secured by a company that was not intended to survive and in fact did not survive. There is no evidence that Williamson paid the note, thus leaving appellant the sole shareholder of all of Midway's assets, including the equipment.

We also find proof that appellant operated Central and Carriers merely as a facade for his own dealings. Appellant admitted that he was most interested in Central's real estate holdings when he purchased the company. As soon as he bought the company he transferred the real estate, which was Central's primary asset, to JLT Warehouse. Rather than operate Central and Carriers as trucking and warehouse companies, he sold off essentially all of their assets to other companies he controlled. His goal was to attract long-term tenants so that he could mortgage the property, and he finally accomplished that goal when he leased to a third-party tenant the space originally leased by Carriers and the short-lived Midway. Accordingly, we find that appellant satisfies the first prong of the Victoria Elevator test, that he operated the corporations for his own benefit.

Under the second prong of the *Victoria Elevator* test, the court must find an element of injustice or fundamental unfairness in the relationship between respondent and the corporation. This does not require a finding of strict common law fraud, but the proponent of disregarding the corporate entity must produce "evidence that the corporate entity has been operated as a constructive fraud or in an unjust manner."

We note unfairness in the way in which the companies dealt with respondent, and thus find the second prong satisfied as well. First, although respondent's long-term relationship with Central changed when appellant purchased the company, there is no indication that respondent understood the change. Respondent was directed to bill "CDI, Inc.," which respondent believed was

Central, and when respondent entered new contracts with CDI, Inc., Weber signed them as CEO, not CEO of Carriers.

Second, the transfer of Carriers' equipment amounts to intentional or constructive fraud.

> A transfer made or obligation incurred by a debtor is fraudulent as to a creditor, whether the creditor's claim arose before or after the transfer was made or the obligation was incurred, if the debtor made the transfer or incurred the obligation with actual intent to hinder, delay, or defraud any creditor of the debtor.

Minn.Stat. §513.44(a)(1) (1990). Appellant's conduct indicates actual intent to hinder, delay, or defraud creditors. See Minn.Stat. §513.44(b) (identifying factors to consider in determining whether actual intent exists). First, the transfers of Central's real estate and Carriers' equipment involved substantially all of the companies' assets. Appellant testified at his deposition that neither company had many physical assets remaining. Second, the debtor (Carriers) was insolvent at the time of the transfer of its equipment or became insolvent shortly after the transfer was made. It sold the equipment because it could not pay its rent. Furthermore, at the time of the sale, Midway already occupied Carriers' space in the warehouse complex, making it impossible for Carriers to continue as a business able to repay its debts. Third, the transfers were not disclosed to respondent. Under these facts we find that there exists unfairness sufficient to justify disregarding the corporate entity.

2. Appellant claims that because the district court's grant of partial summary judgment determined only that appellant was liable, there remains an issue of fact regarding the amount of liability or whether the corporations have any obligation at all to respondent. We disagree.

Although appellant argues that Carriers did not pay respondent because respondent did not provide the services it promised under the contract, the evidence does not support such a claim. Weber, who supposedly was in charge during all relevant times in question, was not aware of any unusual problems with the alarms. The only other evidence of respondent's allegedly defective services are three 1991 memoranda. One refers to an incident that occurred after Carriers' demise, and the other two were written by Weber's replacement after Carriers was already in arrears with several vendors. There is no evidence linking any of the incidents in the memoranda to respondent's conduct in installing or servicing the systems. Furthermore, there appears to be no other documentation of appellant's or Carriers' complaints to respondent regarding its services, despite appellant's claim that Carriers reported its problems to respondent. Accordingly, the evidence presented is not sufficient to raise an issue of material fact regarding the amount of damages.

3. Respondent requests attorney fees on appeal. Attorney fees generally are not recoverable in the absence of a contract or statute. The agreement between

respondent and Central/Carriers provided for the customer "to pay all costs, expenses and fees of ADT's enforcement of their Agreement, including collection expenses, court costs, and attorneys' fees." Respondent thus is entitled to fees and costs of $7,433.69, which we find to have been reasonably incurred on appeal.

Affirmed.

Unit 5

COLLECTING FROM CREDITORS

UNIT CONTENTS

A. LIABILITY OF CREDITORS TO THE DEBTOR (a/k/a "LENDER LIABILITY")

A debtor who has borrowed money usually has no direct defense to her obligation to repay the loan. After all, she asked for the money and got it.

The debtor often argues, however, that her obligation is reduced or eliminated by offsetting culpable conduct of the lender. This allegation is sometimes based on breach of enacted (statutory or regulatory) law that governs the loan itself or, more often, such law that governs the collateralization of the the loan. Equally or more often, the debtor's complaint against the lender is based on the common law of contracts or tort. The debtor argues that the lender is guilty of breach of contract in deciding default, in dealing with collateral, or by not providing more funds just when the debtor most needed more money. Very often this argument is based on breach of an implied obligation—such as "good faith"—rather than on breach of an express contract term. Or, the debtor contends that the lender caused harm by some misrepresentation, and that this conduct allows the debtor to avoid liability herself in contract or to impose tort liability on the lender. Other torts may also be alleged—torts as old as interference with contract and torts that, as yet, don't widely exist such as breach of good faith.

Part of the debtor's strategy is to establish that in dealing with the debtor, the lender was a fiduciary and owed commensurate responsibilities. Breach of fiduciary duty is itself a tort; but the debtor's principal reason for alleging a fiduciary relationship is something else. If such a relationship existed between the bank and the debtor, the former's duties to the latter were higher under contract law and tort law. Therefore, the threshold of bank liability to the debtor is lower.

Irrespective of the basis or theory behind the debtor's claims, this offsetting accountability of banks and other creditors is commonly known as *lender liability*."[1] It dilutes the force and harshness of creditors' rights that are largely founded on and protected by traditional contract doctrine. It therefore limits—even undermines—creditors' rights even though other law provides for and sanctions them. It is on the battlefield of lender liability that we can see, more clearly than anywhere else, the constant war between contract and tort.

The debtor usually (almost always) loses arguments of lender liability. A creditor is almost always an *adversary* in its relationship with the debtor, not a fiduciary. For this reason, creditor's duties are typically less than normal rather than more. Also, contracts are usually enforced to the letter and not beyond—very little is implied; terms are interpreted generously in favor of the banks because the banks themselves drafted the terms generously in their favor; and breach of contract itself, even of a duty of good faith, has never been-- and still is not-- a tort. The courts refuse to stretch and apply the the contrary,

---

[1]   For a complete and very useful analysis of the whole area, see Professor Mark Budnitz's revision of Helen Chaitman, THE LAW OF LENDER LIABILITY (forthcoming 1994) (Warren, Gorham & Lamont).

narrow cases involving breach of insurance contracts. Moreover, doing so ordinarily won't help the debtor because the test of a lender's good faith is generally and mostly a subjective test, which means that the test is very easy for the lender to satisfy and thus breach of the duty is actually extremely rare.

Still, debtors' lawyers are encouraged by the rare case of lender liability, even when the case is very narrow and fact specific. They keep trying to widen lenders' duties under contract and tort law. A debtors' lawyer's rare win in an isolated case is enough to make lenders and bank lawyers worry in almost every case.

Security Pacific National Bank v. Williams
California Court of Appeals, Fourth District, 1989
262 Cal. Rptr. 260 (ordered not published)

Work, Associate Justice. Security Pacific National Bank (Bank) appeals a judgment awarding James J. Williams more than $2 million in compensatory damages, $2.5 million in punitive damages and $200,000 in attorney's fees for fraudulently inducing Williams to purchase an additional automobile dealership, Viking Dodge, which ultimately resulted in his bankruptcy and the closure of his original, and previously successful, automobile dealership, Baron Buick. The trial court alternatively found the Bank's conduct constituted a tortious breach of the covenant of good faith and fair dealing implied in his personal guarantees on the loans for the dealerships.

* * *

For the reasons which follow, * * * we affirm the judgment.

FACTUAL AND PROCEDURAL BACKGROUND

We state the facts in the light most favorable to the judgment. In 1975, Williams purchased Baron Buick with three partners, Mick Chesrown, Theo Lamb and Emanuel Bugelli, each of whom invested $50,000. With almost a decade of automobile dealership experience,[1] Williams managed the dealership with Bugelli visiting periodically to discuss the financial aspects of the enterprise. Under Williams's guiding hand, Baron Buick evolved from a losing dealership into a very profitable one. In 1976, he bought out his partners for $72,000 each and at the age of 25 became the youngest holder of a General Motors franchise.

Although Williams was a skillful car salesman, he had little training, experience or knowledge in automobile financing and banking, relying instead on

---

[1]   Williams's automobile dealership experience started at age 16 as a lot boy. He quickly advanced to a lube man, parts department employee and service manager. He obtained his salesman license at 18 and began selling cars. He gained sales and service experience in higher volume dealerships in Riverside County, where he met Chesrown and Bugelli. In 1973, he became used car manager at Lamb Chevrolet in National City.

the guidance of others. He was particularly unsophisticated in interpreting and understanding dealer financial statements.[1]

After acquiring Baron Buick, Williams developed a close personal and business relationship with Charles Walker, who was the Bank's vice-president responsible for dealership credit in San Diego County and who maintained a hands-on relationship with the Baron Buick account. Williams and Walker had daily contact, discussing problems involving the finances of the dealership. They lunched several times a week; Walker's oldest son was a close acquaintance of Williams; and Williams considered Walker like a father. Walker considered Williams like a son. Williams not only trusted Walker, but loved him.

Williams also developed and maintained a close personal relationship with Howard Butler, who ran the Bank's El Cajon service center and took over the Baron Buick account. Their relationship was both business and social. They met frequently, permitting Butler to tutor Williams on the Bank's financial expectations for Baron Buick. Socially, they went fishing and bought a boat together. They became not only "very close friends," but also "business partners, so to speak."

Williams also developed a personal and trusting relationship with John Robert Ross, who was the Bank's credit coordinator responsible for handling problem dealerships. He was the Bank's aggressive crisis manager, responsible for determining whether a dealership could be saved and if not, what the Bank could salvage. Williams was encouraged by Butler to get to know and rely on Ross's superior knowledge of dealership financing. They too developed a social relationship, exemplified by a three or four-day trip to the 1979 Superbowl. Their close personal relationship resulted in foregoing customary business formality; for, when Ross dealt with Williams, his word and representations were considered binding upon both him and the Bank. Williams trusted Ross who admitted he knew Williams was "deficient" in the critical area of interpretating financial statements.

Unlike ordinary bank lender/borrower commercial relationships, extensive evidence, including testimony of banking experts, revealed that automobile dealership bank financing customarily engenders close relationships between staffs at automobile dealerships and financial institutions with the dealers viewing the bankers as their partners. Williams entertained this view which prevailed in the industry, and the Bank's representatives continually advised him their treatment as partners would guarantee their relationship would go a long way. The mutual trust relationship entertained by similar Bank-financed dealers was reflected by their complete reliance on the Bank's financial expertise. This reliance was consistent with Williams providing complete access to all financial information from Baron Buick. The Bank assumed an active role in managing Baron Buick. For example, if Walker advised Williams he had a problem regarding his financial

---

[1]   Within his statement of decision, the trial court characterized "Williams' basic understanding of the car business was that he had to sell cars to make money. ..."

statements, the latter would do whatever the former suggested, including laying off employees or lowering or raising inventory. He trusted and depended upon their superior knowledge of financial matters.[1]

The Bank regarded Williams as a favored car dealer by mid-1978. So much so that in late 1977 Walker prevailed upon Williams to temporarily manage Lamb Chevrolet to protect the Bank's interest which was jeopardized because of financial difficulties. For this it paid him $1,000 a day. Williams resolved the problems at Lamb Chevrolet to the Bank's delight. Butler declared he had done "a very good job."

The Bank gave Williams special financing privileges, including (1) instant credit on used car drafts, (2) instant credit on conditional sales contracts, (3) a contingent reserve less than 3 percent required in the master flooring agreement,[2] (4) a liberal credit policy with regard to the granting of overdraft privileges, and (5) a liberal policy of extending capitalization loans. Although offering a distorted picture of a dealership's true financial condition, these privileges were designed to provide the dealerships with more working capital than they actually possessed and were extended by the Bank to solicit conditional sales contracts from high volume dealerships. These contracts were more profitable and less risky than other financial arrangements, such as flooring financing or capitalization loans.

While Williams was general manager at Lamb Chevrolet during 1978, Baron Buick experienced some overdrafts, causing Ross to come down from Los Angeles to discuss the matter with Williams. Concluding Baron Buick was not being properly managed because Williams was dividing his time between the two dealerships, the matter was resolved within 60 days of Ross's visit. By January 1, 1979, Williams left Lamb Chevrolet and returned full time to Baron Buick, which quickly returned to profitability. With earnings high, Williams was confident and eager to acquire other dealerships.

At about this time, Bugelli's dealerships in Los Angeles, Universal Ford, Westchester Ford and Viking Dodge, were for sale. The management of these dealerships was the antithesis of the Williams approach and the Bank faced the prospect of a substantial financial loss. Universal Ford and Westchester Ford, in particular, employed classic, high-pressure sales techniques, including the "TO" (turn over) sales method where customers would be turned from one salesman to

---

[1] In its statement of decision the trial court found: "Williams understood his relationship with the bank to be a partnership relationship based on mutual trust and complete disclosure. Charlie Walker, Howard Butler, and Gerry Bruno had a similar understanding. Each understood Mr. Williams' lack of expertise when it came to understanding the financial affairs of a car dealership, and sought to assist him with this end of the business and they were aware that Williams relied on them for their financial expertise."

[2] Before Williams acquired an interest in Baron Buick, the flooring financial arrangement was provided by GMAC and the conditional sales contracts were being purchased by both GMAC and the Bank. However, after Williams and his partners acquired the dealership, the Bank assumed all financing.

another, almost literally kept prisoners as they were passed on from one salesman to the next until a deal was finally consummated. In working class areas, these tactics produced a high volume of sales and a correspondingly large number of "risky" conditional sales contracts, which generated a high percentage of repossessions and a great deal of friction between Bugelli and the Bank. Nevertheless, the Bank had loosened credit standards for Bugelli because of the large volume of conditional sales contracts being generated, and their relationship, though sometimes tense, proved mutually very profitable until February 1979, when a four-day Los Angeles television news expose blew the whistle on Bugelli's Universal Ford "bait and switch" tactics. With its revelation of other questionable high pressure techniques, the expose created a sensation in the relevant market area and the Department of Motor Vehicles began to investigate the Bugelli dealerships. Concerned, Robert Montieth, president of the Bank's credit division, without notice and contrary to the Bank's agreement with Bugelli halted purchase of conditional sales contracts from the Bugelli dealerships. The television expose coupled with the Bank's restriction on the purchase of conditional sales contracts rendered Universal Ford and Westchester Ford worthless.

The Bank successfully insisted the flooring at Universal Ford and Westchester Ford be transferred to Ford Motor Credit during January and February 1979. However, the Bank remained at risk for at least $1.5 million on a flooring line at Viking Dodge and an approximately $220,000 capitalization loan to Bugelli for the purchase of the dealership.

Ross orchestrated the process of transferring the flooring and insuring the Bank's flooring lien was paid by placing his examiners in the Ford dealerships on a daily basis. In fact, Ross had approved Bugelli's purchase of Viking Dodge at the same time the Bank had decided to get out of the flooring of Universal Ford and Westchester Ford. At a time when the Bank had a verbal policy not to establish any new credit relationships with Chrysler dealerships, Ross helped Bugelli acquire Viking Dodge to use as a "dump" for his repossessions when he sold Universal Ford and Westchester Ford, although Bugelli told him the dealership would not be profitable for a year.

After the television news expose, Williams met with Ross to discuss the possibility of his acquiring Universal Ford. Ross counseled against the purchase because of the adverse publicity and his belief it was too large a dealership for Williams to manage simultaneously with Baron Buick. Threatening to "pull the chain" (the Bank's flooring credit) at Baron Buick if Williams persisted, Ross refused to permit him to make the acquisition. Williams then inquired about Westchester Ford, but Ross again counseled against it. However, when Williams then asked about Viking Dodge, the Bugelli dealership from which the Bank needed a financial bail-out, Ross responded: "Now, that's a good one; I'll help you buy that one." He advised Williams to negotiate with Bugelli, but not to sign anything unless he first approved it. He extolled Viking Dodge as financially sound, a profitable dealership in which, in light of its size and manageability, Williams could prosper.

When Bugelli asked $50,000 for "blue sky" (goodwill), Ross told Williams there would be no payment for blue sky. Ross then stated he would dictate the deal on Williams's behalf and get him "a good deal." First, he told Williams he wanted Chrysler Credit to take over the flooring from the Bank, explaining this would provide Viking Dodge with greater working capital, because the dealership could benefit from a "legitimate float." Secondly, he wanted Williams to assume the contingent liability on 73 conditional sales contracts the Bank had purchased from Viking Dodge, which Ross had reviewed and characterized as all good. Ross promised that if Williams assumed this contingent liability, the Bank would permit him to assume Bugelli's capitalization loan for Viking Dodge and purchase the conditional sales contracts from Viking Dodge after Williams acquired the dealership. Dealing personally with Williams, the Bank required he sign personal guarantees on the Viking Dodge liability. Ross told Williams an examination of the financial statements of Viking Dodge showed that it was making $20,000 per month. He declared, "he was monitoring the situation" of Viking Dodge, which with his representation he was acting in Williams's interest in the purchase implied his people were watching over the books to make sure Williams would not be cheated.

On March 28, 1979, the parties agreed on terms dictated by Ross for Williams's purchase of Viking Dodge. Bugelli characterized Ross as "King Kong" and Williams as Ross's "fair-haired boy" in describing their respective roles in the transaction. After this meeting, the Bank facilitated Chrysler's approval of the transaction by sending a letter misleadingly stating the Bank was making a capitalization loan for $225,000 (Exh. 28), falsely implying the Bank was capitalizing the dealership with an additional $225,000 of working capital when in reality Williams was simply assuming Bugelli's existing obligation. Because Viking Dodge's actual capitalization was far below Chrysler's stated guidelines for adequate capital, Chrysler would not have approved the change of ownership had the Bank truthfully stated the facts. Williams commenced managing Viking Dodge on March 31, before the proposed sale was approved by Chrysler. Actual ownership was transferred on May 1.

Viking Dodge was doomed to fail from the day Williams purchased it. The true financial condition of the dealership at that time known to the Bank, but not Williams, was: (1) contracts in transit (conditional sales contracts purchased by banks other than the bank providing the flooring credit) were up dramatically; (2) working capital was critically low; (3) February 1979 showed a loss of $1,700; (4) March 1979 showed a loss of $133,000; (5) April 1979 showed a loss of $96,000; (6) new car inventory had increased from $1.5 million to in excess of $1.7 million; and (7) sales were down. Further, on March 15, 1979, the dealership had wholesaled used cars to avoid being sold- out-of-trust. Viking Dodge was in serious trouble and the Bank knew it. Not only were monthly financial statements sent to the Bank by Bugelli, but in March and April, Bank representatives directly supervised by Ross monitored the dealership operations daily.

A substantial part of the business of Viking Dodge was from the sale of vans. In fact, before Williams acquired the dealership, approximately $900,000 of its total $1.3 million to $1.5 million inventory was in vans, the source of approximately 50 percent of the dealership's profits. Nearly 90 percent of the vans sold were custom or conversions. Unlike Williams's experience at Baron Buick where the Bank purchased conditional sale contracts on custom vans, the Bank refused to finance such conversions when Williams took over Viking Dodge. Ross never forewarned Williams the Bank would pursue any different conversion financing policy at Viking Dodge. Consequently, the Bank's new policy as to Viking Dodge eliminated a major source of profit. The Bank's newly implemented restrictive policies concerning the purchase of conditional sales contracts, Viking Dodge's inadequate capitalization, the 1979 gas crisis, Chrysler's financial problems, and a sluggish domestic market, cumulatively drove the dealership into bankruptcy during the following months.

As the overall situation became more bleak, the Bank's policies concerning the purchase of conditional sales contracts became increasingly restrictive. Loose credit and special privileges were withdrawn from Williams when they were really needed. Instant credit on contracts or used car drafts was no longer available and Viking Dodge suffered substantial losses on repossessions it had to sell as used cars. Williams put an additional $15,000 of his money into Viking Dodge in January 1980, as well as another $35,000 borrowed from the Bank which was secured by UCC-1 on all his used cars at Baron Buick. By investing the additional $50,000, Chrysler agreed to permit Williams to keep the dealership open until another buyer could be found. However, since there were few buyers of Chrysler dealerships at that time, Williams reluctantly released Viking Dodge to Chrysler Credit on March 12, 1980. Chrysler obtained a $274,000 deficiency judgment based upon Williams's personal guarantee of the flooring credit. Additionally, Williams had lost his $50,000 personal investment and the value of his time allocated to Viking Dodge.

Williams then returned full time to Baron Buick, the financial condition of which had been substantially weakened during Williams's ownership of Viking Dodge. Williams had used a "special" reserve released in April 1979, of $50,000 from Baron Buick to purchase Viking Dodge. Additionally, during mid-1979, Baron Buick transferred from $30,000 to $50,000 to Viking Dodge for general operating funds, as well as 20 to 30 used cars.

In March 1980, Baron Buick's commercial checking account was overdrawn. Concerned with the dealership's financial problems, the Bank and Ross specifically wanted $100,000 to $125,000 additional capital invested in it. He authorized further overdrafts on the Baron Buick account to meet payroll. To satisfy the Bank's request, Williams solicited Robert Alcorn for additional capital, who invested $19,000 into Baron Buick as earnest money. Williams agreed to sell him 50 to 51 percent of Baron Buick for $100,000, and an additional $50,000 if needed. On March 31, 1980, Ross, Bruno, Williams, Alcorn and Chesrown met at Baron Buick.[1] Alcorn agreed to immediately put $100,000 of additional capital in Baron Buick, as soon as the Bank provided a letter of understanding that for six months it would not remove the flooring and would do business as usual on conditional sales contracts. When Ross agreed to submit this letter, Alcorn left for the state of Washington to raise the funds. Alcorn promptly forwarded a check for $100,000, payable to Chesrown and Baron Buick, to be deposited when the Bank exchanged the promised letter of understanding. Williams was given the check by Chesrown on April 10th or 11th and Williams attached it to a deposit slip dated April 11, 1980, for the Bank's Baron Buick commercial account and showed the check to Butler that day.

During the April 12-13 weekend, Baron Buick held a liquidation sale, which drew a good public response resulting in the sale of 30 to 40 cars. Bruno worked the entire weekend at Baron Buick preapproving credit on the conditional sales contracts. However, on Monday, Butler rejected all conditional sales contracts Bruno preapproved. Apparently, a confrontation occurred and Williams withheld the $45,000 generated from the sale, depositing it instead in the Bank of America. He then showed the Alcorn check to Butler and requested the letter of understanding, but Butler replied "that's between you and Ross." Williams explained he could not deliver the check without receipt of the letter and suggested Ross come down.

Ross arrived at Baron Buick April 15, at approximately 6 p.m., but Williams was not there. The next morning Ross and Butler prepared a demand letter for payment of all flooring liability. Williams, Ross, Butler and Gary Ellingson (Williams's personal friend and an attorney) met in Williams's office. Ross was upset and told Williams that he was going to close the place down. Williams again explained he had the $100,000 check as agreed and offered to deposit it when he was shown the promised letter of understanding. Ross responded there would be no letter of understanding; he was closing the place down; and there was not a "fucking thing" Williams could do about it. He pulled the keys, ordered guard service, had the dealership locked and chained, and left for Los Angeles.

After the closure, Williams still controlled the showroom and office. Consequently, the next day he wholesaled used cars to raise cash to pay his bills and his employees' salaries, as well as the earnest money loans made by Alcorn and Chesrown. Although he tried to keep the business open, it was impossible without new and used cars.[2]

On April 25, the Bank filed involuntary bankruptcy proceedings against Baron Buick. With substantial television and other media coverage, the trustee took physical control of the dealership.[3]

---

[1]   When Williams was temporarily out of the office, Ross advised Alcorn that Baron Buick was a gold mine and that Williams was not properly managing it.

[2]   With the closure of the dealership, salespersons abandoned the premises and some absconded with their demonstrator vehicles as security for payment of their salaries. Williams helped Bank employees locate missing new cars, with the result that only 4 vehicles out of 137 could not be located.

[3]   One of the experts testified that with the influx of the promised $150,000 capital

Bank employees and agents told others that Williams was a thief, was involved in illegal practices, could not be trusted, had stolen 40 cars and his family members were all driving 1980 Buicks. These allegations were false, however, the word spread rapidly throughout the automobile finance industry making it impossible for Williams to find work locally. He was essentially blackballed from the car industry in California as the allegations continued to be relayed for several years. Williams was eventually reduced to tending bar in Sacramento.

* * *

WILLIAMS ESTABLISHED ACTUAL FRAUD BASED UPON AFFIRMATIVE MISREPRESENTATIONS

Asserting no fiduciary duty can ever exist between a commercial borrower and lender, the Bank contends the judgment should be reversed because the trial court erred in finding a fiduciary duty here and applying the breach of that duty as the foundation for the fraud judgment permitting circumvention of the essential elements of justifiable reliance and proximate cause. Moreover, it argues without a fiduciary relationship Williams failed to prove his fraud claim because the statements found to be actionable were either statements of opinion or nondisclosures rather than affirmative misrepresentations.

However, perhaps the most fundamental principle of appellate review is that where the trial court's decision is itself correct in law, it will not be disturbed on appeal simply because the trial court relied on erroneous grounds in reaching its conclusion. In other words, "[i]f right upon any theory of the law applicable to the case, [the decision] must be sustained regardless of the considerations which may have moved the trial court to its conclusion." Because the trial court based its decision alternatively on the causes of actions pleading fraud, negligent misrepresentation and breach of the implied covenant of good faith and fair dealing, the judgment must be affirmed if either fraud or negligent misrepresentation has been proved. Here, the Bank was not surprised by either theory at trial and these counts were based on affirmative misrepresentations by the Bank to Williams on which he reasonably relied, and not solely predicated upon a fiduciary relationship giving rise to a duty to disclose material information which the Bank had concealed from Williams.

Generally, the "concept of fraud embraces anything which is intended to deceive, including all statements, acts, concealments and omissions involving a breach of legal or equitable duty, trust or confidence which results in injury to one who justifiably relies thereon." Consequently, the elements of actionable fraud giving rise to the tort action for deceit include: (1) a misrepresentation (false representation, concealment or nondisclosure); (2) knowledge of falsity (scienter); (3) intent to defraud or induce reliance; (4) justifiable reliance; and (5) resulting

---

investment by Alcorn, Baron Buick would have made it. The Bank had Williams sign Exhibit 51 purportedly constituting a waiver of any defenses on April 25, 1980. Although the Bank contended this constituted a complete defense to the lawsuit, the trial court found Williams's consent under the circumstances was coerced and involuntary, rendering the waiver ineffective.

damages. All of the cited elements must be established in order to find actionable fraud, as the absence of any one element is fatal to recovery. Within the context of this case, a party to a contract commits actual fraud when doing any of the following acts with the intent to deceive another or simply to induce that individual to enter into a contract: suggesting as a fact that which is not true by one who does not believe it to be true, or positively asserting, in a manner not warranted by the information known to that person, of that which is not true, though the actor believes it to be true. (Civ.Code, §1572, subds. 1, 2.)[1] Williams correctly asserts he alleged and obtained judgment based upon an actual fraud theory within the context of sections 1572 and 1710. In his fifth cause of action, he only alleged actual fraud based upon affirmative misrepresentations made by Ross on behalf of the Bank. He did not allege fraudulent concealment by the Bank premised upon any alleged duty of disclosure.[2] Although the trial court found fraud based upon not only affirmative misrepresentations, but also for failure to disclose material facts arising from the parties' fiduciary relationship, the court's statements of decision shows it treated the affirmative misrepresentations and the failures to disclose as independent and distinct bases supporting its fraud determination.[3] Consequently, the trial court's judgment rests independently upon affirmative misrepresentations unrelated to any duty to disclose arising from a fiduciary relationship and the failure in that context to disclose certain material facts.

The record is replete with affirmative false representations by Ross on behalf of the Bank, including Viking Dodge was a good dealership; Viking Dodge was financially sound and a profitable dealership which was making approximately

---

[1]   All statutory references are to the Civil Code unless otherwise specified. Deceit is further statutorily defined within sections 1709 and 1710. The former expressly provides: "One who willfully deceives another with intent to induce him to alter his position to his injury or risk, is liable for any damage which he thereby suffers." The latter defines deceit as either: "1. The suggestion, as a fact, of that which is not true, by one who does not believe it to be true; 2. The assertion, as a fact, of that which is not true, by one who has no reasonable ground for believing it to be true; 3. The suppression of a fact, by one who is bound to disclose it, or who gives information of other facts which are likely to mislead for want of communication of that fact; or, 4. A promise, made without any intention of performing it."

[2]   The allegation of fraud did not incorporate by reference any of the fiduciary duty allegations contained within the ninth cause of action involving breach of the implied covenant of good faith and fair dealing within the fourth amended complaint.

[3]   The trial court stated in pertinent part: "This court's statement of facts and conclusions drawn therefrom establish the elements of this tort [fraud]. Security Pacific National Bank, through its officers, employees, and agents made affirmative misrepresentations and additionally concealed, suppressed and failed to disclose material facts. The bank was under a duty to disclose these material facts and this is especially so in light of the existing fiduciary relationship. The bank officer, agents and employees acted with the intent to defraud Williams. Williams justifiably relied on the statements, actions and non-actions of the bank officers, employees and agents to his detriment (resultant damages)." (Italics added.)

$20,000 per month, when in fact Ross was aware Bugelli had purchased it as a "dump" for repossessions from other dealerships, Bugelli was having financial problems, and Bugelli would not obtain a profit for at least a year at Viking Dodge; the 73 conditional sales contracts purchased by the Bank from Viking Dodge had been inspected by Ross and were good, when in fact Ross was aware of Bugelli's "ramrodding" sales techniques and 23 actual "unwinds" of conditional sales contracts; that he was representing Williams's best interests in the acquisition of Viking Dodge when in fact he was representing the adverse interests of the Bank; the Bank wanted Chrysler to take over the flooring credit of Viking Dodge in order to provide the dealership with additional credit through a "legitimate float," when in fact the Bank wanted Chrysler to take over the flooring so that its own risk and liability could be substantially reduced; he was monitoring the situation at Viking Dodge, when construed in the light of the representation Ross was representing Williams in the purchase at minimum implied the Bank would protect Williams's interests through the surveillance; and the Bank would back Williams like they had "always done business" and continue to purchase additional sales contracts from Viking Dodge. However, consistent with the allegations of the complaint, the essence of the actual misrepresentations related to Ross's representations Viking Dodge was a good and financially sound dealership, he was representing Williams in the deal, he was monitoring the situation at Viking Dodge and he had inspected the conditional sales contracts of the dealership and found them all to be good.[1]

---

[1]   Mindful Williams seeks affirmance of the judgment based upon actual affirmative misrepresentations and without relying upon any fiduciary relationship between the parties, the Bank contends Ross's evaluation of Viking Dodge as a dealership and its conditional sales contracts as being "good" constituted unactionable statements of opinion. "Generally, actionable misrepresentation must be one of existing fact; 'predictions as to future events, or statements as to future action by some third party, are deemed opinions, and not actionable fraud....' (4 Witkin, Summary of Cal.Law (8th ed. 1974) Torts, §447, p. 2712.) But there are exceptions to this rule: '(1) where a party holds himself out to be specially qualified and the other party is so situated that he may reasonably rely upon the former's superior knowledge; (2) where the opinion is by a fiduciary or other trusted person; [and] (3) where a party states his opinion as an existing fact or as implying facts which justify a belief in the truth of the opinion.' (Borba v. Thomas (1977) 70 Cal.App.3d 144, 152 [138 Cal.Rptr. 565]....) Examples of actionable statements under these exceptions include a sales agent's representation that a condominium with structural defects was nevertheless luxurious and an outstanding investment (Cooper v. Jevne (1976) 56 Cal.App.3d 860, 866 [128 Cal.Rptr. 724] ...) and a realtor's opinion that the purchaser of a particular lot would have an enforceable access easement. (Southern Cal. etc. Assemblies of God v. Shepherd of Hills etc. Church (1978) 77 Cal.App.3d 951, 959 [144 Cal.Rptr. 46]....)" (Cohen v. S & S Construction Co. (1983) 151 Cal.App.3d 941, 946, 201 Cal.Rptr. 173.) Here, the record clearly supports applying either of the two remaining exceptions to this general rule without requiring reliance upon a fiduciary relationship. In any event, as we shall explain, a fiduciary relationship may exist between a lender and borrower and substantial evidence

The crucial issue here is whether substantial evidence supports the trial court's determination Williams proved his fraud claim by showing he reasonably relied upon Ross's and the Bank's false affirmative representations regarding the financial health of Viking Dodge.

The determination of whether reliance is justified under the circumstances of a particular case must be made by evaluating whether reliance was justified in light of a party's own knowledge and experience and without an independent inquiry and investigation. Consequently, where a trial court's finding of fact is challenged on appeal for lack of substantial evidence, our inquiry is limited to determining whether there is substantial evidence, contradicted or uncontradicted, supporting the challenged finding.

"Testimony concerning one's own reliance is legally insufficient evidence if such reliance is without justification [citation]; a party plaintiff's misguided belief or guileless action in relying on a statement on which no reasonable person would rely is not justifiable reliance. [Citation.] 'If the conduct of the plaintiff in light of his own intelligence and information was manifestly unreasonable, ... he will be denied a recovery.'" However, "[i]t is only where a party to whom a representation is made has the means at hand for determining its truth or falsehood and resorts to such means, without interference by the other party, and after investigation learns that the statement was false, that he is precluded from asserting that he relied upon the representation." In other words, if one is justified in relying and in fact does rely upon false representations, recovery will not be precluded simply because means of knowledge were available. "In such a case, no duty in law is devolved upon him to employ such means of knowledge."[1] Moreover, "[n]egligence on the part of the plaintiff in failing to discover the falsity of a statement is no defense when the misrepresentation was intentional rather than negligent. [Citations.] As a general rule negligence of the plaintiff is no defense to an intentional tort. [Citation.] The fact that an investigation would have revealed the falsity of the misrepresentation will not alone bar ... recovery...."[2]

Guided by the foregoing, we conclude ample evidence supports the trial court's determination Williams justifiably and reasonably relied upon the misrepresentations of Ross and the Bank. The record establishes that in general bank-financed automobile dealership business relationships are more like joint

---

supports the trial court's finding here such a relationship existed as a matter of fact between these parties.

[1]   "The rule of unjustifiable reliance ... is seldom applied in practice, for the old notion of 'caveat emptor' is thoroughly discredited. There is ordinarily no duty to investigate, and the former defense of contributory negligence of the plaintiff was held not to be a defense to the intentional tort of fraud." (5 Witkin, Summary of Cal.Law (9th ed. 1988) Torts, §715, p. 814; Arthur L. Sachs, Inc. v. City of Oceanside (1984) 151 Cal.App.3d 315, 323, 198 Cal.Rptr. 483.)

[2]   "'No rogue should enjoy his ill-gotten plunder for the simple reason that his victim is by chance a fool.'" (Seeger v. Odell, supra, 18 Cal.2d at p. 415, 115 P.2d 977, quoting Chamberlin v. Fuller (1887) 59 Vt. 247, 9 A. 832, 835.)

ventures than ordinary commercial arms-length lender-borrower activities. As Williams explained in his testimony, he was always advised by the Bank his accepting it as a partner would guarantee a successful financial relationship. Our detailed factual summary highlights the underpinning of this relationship was Williams's complete reliance on the financial expertise of the Bank which was provided complete access to all financial information within the dealerships. All parties, including the Bank officials, conceded Williams was unsophisticated when it came to reading and evaluating dealer financial statements. All Bank officials were aware Williams totally relied upon and trusted the Bank and its representatives (Walker, Butler and Ross) in all matters pertaining to finance because of his deficiencies in matters of financing.

Granted, Williams had access to the financial statements of Viking Dodge before acquiring it; however, he accepted Ross's characterization of their "bottom line" after being advised Ross had examined them and was monitoring the dealership on a daily basis. This is consistent with the conceded history of the Bank's relationship and Ross's superior knowledge and expertise in financial matters. In fact, during his Viking Dodge tenure, Williams never knew how to interpret a Dodge statement. Similarly, Williams did not review the dealership's conditional sales contracts, because Ross had done so and assured him they were all good.

Ross's representation he was representing Williams's interests in the negotiations for Viking Dodge and would get him a good deal, was not only false, but specifically intended to obtain Williams's reliance on his advice. That this ploy was successful is corroborated by evidence Ross dictated the terms of the sale and Williams agreed with whatever Ross stated. Williams's passive conduct throughout the negotiating is consistent with not only the "partner-type" relationship the Bank had nurtured with him, but also his reliance on Ross's affirmative representations he was advancing Williams's interests.

The Bank, however, characterizes Williams's claim of justifiable reliance as only related to Ross's opinion Viking Dodge was a "good deal." The Bank emphasizes the evidence shows Williams ignored the advice and information he received from Bugelli, Butler and his partner Mayfield regarding the problems at Viking Dodge. Emphasizing Williams's claim of reliance is solely limited to his own testimony, the Bank argues it is not credible evidence and not substantial enough to support the trial court's finding. This view ignores the totality of Ross's representations and the context in which they were made. Even assuming Williams were aware of the financial problems shackling Viking Dodge before the close of escrow, it does not negate the court's finding his reliance upon Ross's misrepresentations to be reasonable. Rather, the record viewed as a whole supports the conclusion Williams recognized, trusted and relied upon Ross's superior financial expertise in dealing with "problem" and struggling dealerships. Granted, Butler off-handedly declared to Williams before the close of escrow that his purchase of Viking Dodge would result in bailing out of the Bank and the bankruptcy of Baron Buick. However, the record is replete with corroboration that all the many automobile and bank financing personnel who testified considered Ross to be the financial wizard in this area of expertise. No one so described Butler, who acknowledged Ross's superior financial expertise. In any event, under the above authorities, neither Williams's knowledge nor the nature of his conduct preclude his asserting justifiable reliance upon Ross's misrepresentations.

The record firmly establishes Ross was considered by all as the automobile dealership financial expert; as Williams's perceived personal friend he purported to represent the latter's interests; and Williams could justifiably rely on Ross's representations in light of Ross's expertise and experience. However, the Bank further challenges the reasonableness of Williams's reliance in light of Ross's and the Bank's patently adverse interests in the Viking Dodge deal. Granted, Ross had a general reputation in the industry of protecting the Bank's interests. Nevertheless, an adversarial relationship does not necessarily preclude reasonable reliance especially here where Ross specifically assured Williams he was acting in Williams's best interests in saddling him with Viking Dodge's problems. The Restatement Second of Torts section 543 provides: "The recipient of a fraudulent misrepresentation of opinion is justified in relying upon it if the opinion is that of a person whom the recipient reasonably believes to be disinterested and if the fact that such person holds the opinion is material." Applying this rule is appropriate "when the person who misrepresents his opinion has an interest in the transaction adverse to that of the recipient but purports to be disinterested." (Rest.2d, Torts, §543, com. a.) Ross's and the Bank's undisclosed interest in Williams's acquiring Viking Dodge was to release the Bank from its flooring financing and have it replaced by Chrysler. In light of his expertise, his opinion was not only material but highly persuasive to Williams.[1]

The Bank also argues the trial court's fraud theory is deficient because it rests upon findings of fact which show Viking Dodge's failure was caused by being too highly leveraged for the economic crisis facing all dealerships and Chrysler in particular. However, the trial court precisely found the restrictive policies of the Bank concerning the purchasing of conditional sales contracts combined with other factors to cause Viking Dodge to fail. The Bank's argument also misses the mark, because Williams's theory of recovery is not that the Bank's fraud caused Viking Dodge to fail, but rather induced him into purchasing a dealership which according to its own experts was doomed to fail from the time of purchase.

---

[1] Moreover, because we conclude there existed a fiduciary relationship between the parties (infra.), we note that where a duty to disclose material information arises between a lender and borrower because of the existence of such a confidential relationship, any adversity in interest regarding the underlying debt between the parties becomes secondary. (First American Nat. Bank of Iuka v. Mitchell (Miss.1978) 359 So.2d 1376, 1380.)

WILLIAMS ESTABLISHED HIS CAUSE OF ACTION
FOR NEGLIGENT MISREPRESENTATION

The necessary elements for a cause of action sounding in negligent misrepresentation include: (1) the representation as to a past or existing material fact; (2) the representation must have been untrue; (3) regardless of the defendant's actual belief, the representation must have been made without any reasonable ground for believing its truth; (4) defendant must have made the representation with the intent to induce plaintiff's reliance; (5) plaintiff must have been unaware of the false character of the representation, acted in reliance upon its truth and been justified in relying upon it; and (6) plaintiff sustained damages as a result of relying upon the truth of the representation. "As is true of negligence, responsibility for negligent misrepresentation rests upon the existence of a legal duty, imposed by contract, statute or otherwise, owed by a defendant to the injured person. [Citations.].... 'One party to a business transaction is under a duty to exercise reasonable care to disclose to the other before the transaction is consummated, ... facts basic to the transaction, if he knows that the other is about to enter into it under a mistake as to them, and that the other, because of the relationship between them, the customs of the trade or other objective circumstances, would reasonably expect a disclosure of those facts.' [Citations.]"

Here, the record amply supports the trial court's determination Ross had no reasonable ground for believing Viking Dodge constituted a good, financially sound and profitable venture with good conditional sales contracts; Williams could succeed in operating the dealership; or that he was representing Williams's interests in the acquisition of Viking Dodge. Ross always knew the Bank had engineered Bugelli's purchase of Viking Dodge so as to provide him a "dump" for repossessions from his other failed dealerships and that Viking Dodge could not be a profitable venture for at least a year, even if Chrysler's lurking financial difficulties were overcome. Moreover, during March-April 1979, Ross had his bank examiners monitoring Viking Dodge's operations on a daily basis. Ross not only personally reviewed the financial statements which revealed substantial losses during the first quarter of 1979, but he was also aware of the 23 "unwinds" of conditional sales contracts. Finally, as icing on the cake, Ross served on the Bank's consumer loan committee, which was carefully monitoring Chrysler's financial condition and the Bank's outstanding credit to Chrysler dealerships which was precariously at risk. Accordingly, substantial evidence supports the trial court's judgment on the deceit theory of negligent misrepresentation.

THE TRIAL COURT FINDING FIDUCIARY RELATIONSHIP EXISTED
BETWEEN THE BANK AND
WILLIAMS IS SUPPORTED BY THE LAW AND SUBSTANTIAL
EVIDENCE

Emphasizing the Bank's relationship with Williams was not extraordinary within the automobile industry, the Bank contends the trial court erred in "creating" a fiduciary duty running from a lender to its borrower and, in any event, the record is devoid of any evidence supporting any implied findings the Bank accepted fiduciary responsibility toward Williams.

The trial court found "[a] true fiduciary relationship, in fact, existed between bank officials and James Williams." It did not hold the relationship between a borrower and a lender constituted a fiduciary relationship as a matter of law. Consequently, the issues before us are whether a fiduciary relationship can ever arise between a commercial borrower (or guarantor) and a lender and, if so, whether substantial evidence supports the trial court's determination here.

As a general rule, the relationship between a bank and a depositor, borrower or customer is that of a creditor/debtor, dealing at arms-length, and not of a fiduciary giving rise to a duty of disclosure upon the bank. However, while there exists no per se fiduciary relationship between a bank and its customers, a fiduciary duty may nevertheless arise from their business relationship when the customer reposes trust in a bank and relies on the bank for financial advice or under other special circumstances.

The recognition of a fiduciary relationship between a lending institution and a borrower and the accompanying duty of disclosure is the result of contemporary banking business practices and procedures.[1] Indeed,

> "[p]resent-day commercial transactions are not, as in past generations, primarily for cash; rather, modern banking practices involve a highly complicated structure of credit and other complexities which often thrust a bank into the role of an advisor, thereby creating a relationship of trust and confidence which may result in a fiduciary duty upon the bank to disclose facts when dealing with the customer." (Tokarz v. Frontier Federal Sav. & Loan Ass'n, supra, 656 P.2d at p. 1092; Stewart v. Phoenix Nat. Bank, supra, 64 P.2d at p. 106; 70 A.L.R.3d 1344, 1347.)

Although the "special circumstances" relied on by the courts to serve as a predicate for finding a fiduciary relationship and accompanying duty upon the bank to disclose certain information to borrowers or customers vary, the relationship and obligation to disclose generally arises where the bank undertakes to advise a customer as a part of the services it provides; where there is a repose of trust by the customer along with an acceptance or invitation of such trust on the part of the lending institution; where the bank had been the financial advisor for the customer for many years and the bank's advice had been relied upon; where the bank dealt directly with the customer regarding a matter involved in the litigation, had knowledge of the reliance and confidence of the customer, and

---

[1]   In fact, regarding the duty to disclose, Ross testified that a bank considering a loan to a dealer has the obligation to disclose information regarding the transaction adverse to the dealer's interests even though disclosure would hurt the bank's interests. Moreover, similar descriptions of the obligation of a banker to disclose known business risks to potential dealership clients were given by the Bank's expert witnesses Ehrenfeldt, Koenig, Butler and Guptill.

especially where the bank stood to profit from the nondisclosure; where the bank loaned money to a customer to purchase a business, failed to disclose its superior information that business was experiencing financial difficulties, represented to the contrary it was a "going" business and the buyer should be able to "do all right," and stood to benefit from the transaction by reducing its loan on the business and obtaining a consignor of substantial means; where the bank made a loan for a particular purpose knowing that purpose could not be fulfilled and that it involved fraudulent activities of one of its depositors; where the bank loans a customer money for investment with and deposit in the account of another customer whom the bank knows is involved in fraudulent activity and stands to benefit by applying the loan proceeds to offset the latter's overdrawn account; where the bank knows or has reason to know a customer is placing his/her trust and confidence in the bank and relying on the bank for counsel and information; where the bank retained borrower's funds, disbursed them without authorization and demanded repayment of loan; where a mortgagee bank advised and induced mortgagers to sell land under threat of foreclosure knowing the mortgaged property could have been sold for approximately $35,000 more; and, where the bank officer failed to disclose a known material fact to the borrower, there had existed a long-standing relationship between that officer and the borrower and the former had recommended the loan and negotiated its terms for the latter.

California courts have likewise recognized that a fiduciary relationship may exist between a borrower and lender. Such a relationship of trust and confidence arises between a bank and its loan customers where the borrower perceives his relationship with the bank officer as very close, relies on the bank officer's financial advice, discloses confidential financial information to the bank officer, specifically relies on the bank's representation the guarantees would be released upon consummation of a merger when in fact the bank had represented to others the guarantees would not be released, and the bank's position of benefiting from the merger. Consequently, in California and those other jurisdictions which harbor the majority view recognizing the possibility of a confidential relationship arising between a bank and its customers, the existence of such a relationship is generally determined as a matter of fact, predicated upon the facts of the specific case before the court. Needless to say, the extent of the factual showing required has varied from jurisdiction to jurisdiction. "'It is settled by an overwhelming weight of authority that the principle [as to confidential relationship] extends to every possible case in which a fiduciary relation exists as a fact, in which there is confidence reposed on one side and the resulting superiority and influence on the other. The relation and the duties involved in it need not be legal. It may be moral, social, domestic, or merely personal. Hence, the rule embraces both technical fiduciary relations and those informal relations which exist wherever one man trusts in and relies upon another.'"

Relying upon the standard set forth in BAJI No. 12.36,[1] the trial court correctly concluded a fiduciary relationship may well exist between a lending institution and a borrower, as substantial evidence supports its determination a true fiduciary relationship existed in fact between the Bank officials and Williams. Here, the record is replete with evidence Williams developed very close and trusting relationships with Walker, Butler and Ross, both business and social in character. Bank officials actively fostered Williams's perception the Bank and its representatives were his partners, actively engaged in the financing and management of Baron Buick. In financial matters, Williams completely relied on the superior knowledge of Walker, Butler and Ross.[2] As the trial court found based upon substantial evidence, the "Williams-Security Pacific National Bank [relationship] went far beyond a lender-borrower relationship. It was an all-encompassing, mutually beneficial, day-to-day relationship in which both sides reposed trust and confidence in one another.... The relationship here, had much the makings of a mutually beneficial partnership. Williams did in fact repose trust and confidence in the integrity and fidelity and financial judgments of these bank officers and the bank officials knew it."

Consistent with the cited case law emanating from the 1937 *Stewart* decision and continuing through its contemporary progeny, the trial court's factual finding that a fiduciary relationship existed between Williams and the Bank is fully supported by the special circumstances present here. Given the nature of the parties' relationship, the Bank knowingly undertook to act on behalf and for the benefit of Williams in the purchase of Viking Dodge. Regardless how Ross's role is characterized, he, in fact, orchestrated the deal between Bugelli and Williams, as both were "under his charge." Similar to the factual scenario within First National Bank in Lenox v. Brown, supra, 181 N.W.2d 178, the Bank here secretly intended to improve its unfavorable financial position in Viking Dodge by misrepresenting it as a good prosperous venture, persuading Williams to purchase the failing dealership and securing his personal guarantee for that worthless dealership's indebtedness while removing its flooring liability and replacing it with Chrysler's, without revealing the serious financial problems Viking Dodge was experiencing as well as its underlying purpose of freeing it from its flooring liability. In essence, the Bank stood in a fiduciary relationship to Williams because it had superior knowledge regarding the financial condition of Viking Dodge because of its prior and current relationship with that dealership and knew Williams trusted and relied upon its expertise in financial matters including the acquisition of Viking Dodge.

Relying on language in Committee on Children's Television, Inc. v. General Foods Corp. (1983) 35 Cal.3d 197, 197 Cal.Rptr. 783, 673 P.2d 660, the Bank

---

[1]   BAJI No. 12.36 provides in pertinent part: "A fiduciary or a confidential relationship exists whenever under the circumstances trust and confidence reasonably may be and is reposed by one person in the integrity and fidelity of another."

[2]   In fact, Williams testified it was unnecessary for him to read the financial statements of the dealerships because "[t]he Bank--Howard [Butler] or Charlie [Walker], would always tell me what to look for and they had Mr. Ross looking at them. Mr. Ross could look at your financial statements and tell you if you were using too many grease rags."

contends that before a fiduciary relationship can be recognized its affirmative consent to act as a fiduciary is required and the record is devoid of either a finding or any evidence it ever consented to act on behalf of Williams in a fiduciary capacity. Granted, before a party can be charged with a fiduciary obligation, that party "must either knowingly undertake to act on behalf and for the benefit of another, or must enter into a relationship which imposes that undertaking as a matter of law." (Id. at p. 221, 197 Cal.Rptr. 783, 673 P.2d 660.) However, necessarily implied within the trial court's ultimate finding of a fiduciary relationship here was the Bank's knowing and purposeful conduct of acting on Williams's behalf in the acquisition of Viking Dodge. Such an implication arises from the very nature of Ross's conduct, encouraging Williams's acquisition of Viking Dodge and dictating not only the negotiation, but the ultimate "deal." Moreover, the parties' relationship as evinced from the entire record establishes a close and trusting relationship between the parties, akin to a partnership, where both parties recognized Williams's reliance.

Contrary to the Bank's assertion, imposing fiduciary duties is consistent with public policy where the Bank assumes not only an active advisory role, but also that of a dominant participant. The underlying impetus for recognizing de facto fiduciary relationships is the public policy consideration of protecting those who are victimized by fiduciary relations for simply trusting and relying upon another and thus preventing unjust enrichment. Such recognition is compelled where under the circumstances here the Bank, as the principal lender, assumed the role of a "control creditor" by becoming so involved in Williams's daily operations at his dealerships and orchestrated his expansion into Viking Dodge, so as to erode away his separate identity. (See Schechter, The Principal Principle: Controlling Creditors Should Be Held Liable For Their Debtors' Obligations (1986) 19 U.C. Davis L.Rev. 875, 878-880; Comment, The Fiduciary Controversy: Injection of Fiduciary Principles Into The Bank-Depositor and Bank-Borrower Relationships (1987) 20 Loyola L.A.L.Rev. 795, 800-801; Union State Bank v. Woell (N.D.1989) 434 N.W.2d 712, 721, recognizing concept that "actual day-to-day involvement in management and operations of the borrower or the ability to compel the borrower to engage in unusual transactions" shows the requisite "control" by a lending institution over a borrower.) Simply stated, public policy shall never conflict with imposing fiduciary responsibilities where a commercial lender assumes such a dominant role as the Bank did here in Williams's business ventures, so as to render Williams the marionette and the Bank the puppeteer.[1] In

---

[1]   The Bank's reliance on this court's opinion in Wagner v. Benson (1980) 101 Cal.App.3d 27, 161 Cal.Rptr. 516, is misplaced. In *Wagner*, the plaintiffs borrowed money from a bank to invest in a cattle raising venture. When the investment proved unwise, they sued the bank for (among other causes of action) tortious breach of the implied covenant of good faith and fair dealing, theorizing the bank had a duty to disclose certain information about the business entity in which they had invested. Affirming a judgment on the pleadings, this court reasoned the duty of good faith and fair dealing did not include the bank's duty to disclose information to them regarding the

other words, case law recognizes a fiduciary relationship arises between commercial lenders and clients where the bank invites, and the customer reposes, trust and confidence under circumstances transcending an ordinary commercial transaction.

THE TRIAL COURT DID NOT ABUSE ITS DISCRETION IN PERMITTING WILLIAMS TO FILE
HIS FOURTH AMENDED CROSS-COMPLAINT AT TRIAL

Contending it was subject to a "trial by ambush" partially because the trial court permitted Williams to add tort claims to his cross-complaint at trial, the Bank argues the delay was unexcused and the late amendment was extremely prejudicial, injecting new triable issues of fiduciary duty and bad faith within the context of a tortious breach of the implied covenant of good faith and fair dealing. The Bank argues it had taken no pre-trial discovery regarding these issues since they were raised well after the discovery cut-off date. It asserts the amendment so expanded the scope of the evidence from limited specific alleged misrepresentations to encompass a complete analysis of its financing practices, an "open sesame" scenario for which it could not adequately prepare because of the lack of discovery and time to prepare.

A trial court has broad discretion to allow an amendment to any pleading in the furtherance of justice at any time before or after the commencement of trial. "Where no prejudice is shown to the adverse party, the liberal rule of allowance prevails." Indeed, as a matter of policy, a trial court's decision permitting amendment will be upheld unless a manifest or gross abuse of discretion is clearly established.

Here, early in the trial, the court permitted Williams to amend his cross-complaint to allege a tortious breach of the covenant of good faith and fair dealing and a fiduciary relationship. Williams's motion to file such an amendment approximately two months earlier had been denied without prejudice to renew at the time of trial. On the day of trial, he renewed his motion. Within its statement of decision, the trial court addressed the concerns the Bank emphasizes on this appeal, and explained: "Up until trial Williams had been deposed ten times, in addition he testified two times in the bankruptcy proceeding. The facts giving rise to the alleged breach were discovered by the bank in painful detail. In addition the

---

investment because the success of the plaintiffs' investment was not a benefit of the loan agreement the bank had a duty to protect. Within the context of a fiduciary relationship, *Wagner* is consistent with the general rule a debtor/creditor relationship does not constitute a fiduciary relationship as a matter of law. However, *Wagner* does not stand for the proposition a debtor/creditor relationship may never constitute a fiduciary relationship, because there was no claim in Wagner that a fiduciary relationship existed in fact between the parties. Moreover, *Wagner* is distinguishable from the factual context of this case where the Bank not only advised and encouraged Williams to acquire Viking Dodge, but also played a dominant role in negotiating and culminating the ultimate transaction.

trial lasted from August 19 to October 31, 1985, with final argument not until December 3. No surprise can be claimed. The court allowed broad inquiry into every facet of the bank-Williams relationship. The breach of the covenant of good faith and fair dealing is based on the same acts alleged to be fraudulent by Williams and on [the] same contracts which the bank relied in its case in chief. In such a case the amendment relates back to the filing of the cross complaint. [Citations.] The statute of limitations has not run and the act of allowing amendments such as this is discretionary with the court. [Citation.]"

The Bank has failed to meet its burden of establishing a clear abuse of discretion. Preliminarily, the bad faith tort cause of action is predicated upon covenants arising from the same contracts the Bank relies upon in its case in chief and the same conduct which Williams claimed amounted to fraud. Moreover, Williams's request was not designed to surprise or prejudice the Bank, as his counsel attempted the same amendment in June 1985, two months before trial when it was denied without prejudice. At the time of the June motion, plaintiff's counsel had had the case for approximately eight months and the primary case precedent upon which Williams relies for his ninth cause of action for breach of the implied covenant of good faith and fair dealing of Seaman's Direct Buying Service, Inc. v. Standard Oil Co. (1984) 36 Cal.3d 752, 206 Cal.Rptr. 354, 686 P.2d 1158, did not become final until November 15, 1984. Accordingly, any delay in bringing the amendment was neither unreasonable nor unexcusable as a matter of law. Even more significantly, the Bank was aware Williams's affirmative defense to its action to recover under the guarantee was expressly based on its contractual breach of the covenant of good faith and fair dealing. This contractual breach theory was directed at precisely the same conduct as the tortious breach of covenant theory, and had put the Bank on notice of the need to defend against evidence of its specific acts of misconduct to which it now claims surprise. In fact, the Bank had been given permission to further depose Williams and to serve further interrogatories directly on this issue some two months earlier. Only the potential damages differ. Accordingly, absent a long unexcused delay and any resulting prejudice to plaintiff, we conclude the trial court did not abuse its discretion in permitting Williams to amend his cross-complaint to add only a new legal theory for recovery based upon the same contracts and allegations of fraud which had been pled several years earlier. Indeed, "[c]ounsel on the firing line in an actual trial must be prepared for surprises, including requests for amendments of pleading. They cannot ask that a judgment afterwards obtained be set aside merely because their equilibrium was slightly disturbed by an unexpected motion. In order to reverse a case on any such ground there must be a showing that actual unfairness or obvious prejudice has resulted from the allowance of such an amendment, and there has been no such showing in this case. The court acted within proper limits of discretion in allowing the amendment."

        * * *

THE TRIAL COURT DID NOT ERR IN AWARDING WILLIAMS COMPENSATORY DAMAGES WITHOUT REQUIRING AN OFFSET FOR LOSSES SUSTAINED WHICH HE HAD PERSONALLY GUARANTEED

The Bank unmeritoriously contends the trial court erred in awarding Williams compensatory damages without requiring him to perform his obligations under his guarantees. Noting the court found the Bank lost $883,782.25 as a result of the closures of Viking Dodge and Baron Buick and Williams's default on his guarantees and $35,000 note, the Bank argues it is entitled to have this amount deducted from Williams's compensatory damages award which it alleges was generated by the trial court partially rescinding his personal guarantees. This claim rests on a mischaracterization of the nature of the litigation by declaring Williams affirmed his obligations under the guarantees by suing to recover for damages thereunder. From this faulty premise, the Bank reasons the trial court only partially rescinded the guarantees and the note, contrary to the provisions of section 1691, by awarding Williams damages while not requiring him to perform his obligations under the guarantees. However, Williams did not sue to recover damages under the guarantees, the Bank did. Williams affirmatively defended on the grounds that the Bank's conduct made his performance under the agreements impossible, fraudulently induced him into signing them and frustrated their underlying purposes. The trial court expressly found Williams proved his fraud defense and concluded the Bank's fraud rendered it impossible for him to perform his obligations under the contracts, precluding the Bank's recovery for Williams's contractual obligations on its complaint. Williams's cross-complaint recovery was for compensatory damages suffered as a result of the Bank's fraud and negligent misrepresentations in inducing him to purchase Viking Dodge. Consequently, these tort causes of action did not rest upon the guarantees.

Granted, $1,669,554 for lost earnings was included within the compensatory damages award. However, these damages did not flow from breach of contract, but rather from the Bank's unrelated fraudulent conduct and were properly awarded under sections 1709 and 3333. Inferentially, the Bank is arguing Williams would not have been able to earn the lost income awarded but for these guarantees, and thus, receiving the challenged damages constitutes his affirmance of the guarantees and promissory note. However, at most, these guarantees amounted to no more than a "foundational backdrop giving rise to the action." Absent the Bank's fraudulent conduct, the necessary condition precedent to Williams's personal liability under the guarantees would not have occurred. A creditor who is a party to fraud cannot recover either directly or indirectly from a victimized surety.

The compensatory damages award here is not flawed for providing an award more akin to "benefit of the bargain" damages awardable under contract rather than permissible "out of pocket" damages for fraud and deceit, in light of our determination there existed a de facto fiduciary relationship between the parties. For, where the defrauding party stands in a fiduciary relationship to the victim, damages must be measured pursuant to the broad provisions of sections 1709 and 3333, regulating compensation for torts in general, in substantially the same manner as a breach of contract so as to provide the injured party with "the benefit of his bargain" and attempt to place him insofar as possible in the same position he would have been in the absence of the fraud. Consequently, applying "the benefit of the bargain" rule here and presuming Williams's award for lost income represented "net" income after payment of any obligations on the $35,000 promissory note, Williams is entitled to the compensatory damages awarded for lost income as supported by substantial evidence.

    * * *

DISPOSITION

Judgment affirmed.

Kremer, P.J., concurs.

Todd, Associate Justice, dissenting.

I respectfully dissent. In my view the statement of decision by the trial court erroneously failed to address and resolve the issue of justifiable reliance as specifically requested by Bank. * * *

Justifiable reliance must be established as an essential element in Williams's case. The standard to be applied is well stated in Kahn v. Lischner (1954) 128 Cal.App.2d 480, 489, 275 P.2d 539: "Thus if the conduct of the complaining party in the light of his own intelligence and information, or ready availability of information, was manifestly unreasonable, he will be denied a recovery. The test is not only whether the party acted in reliance upon a misrepresentation, but whether he was justified in his reliance."

The trial court, in its statement of decision, concluded "Williams justifiably relied on the statements, actions and non-actions of the bank officers, employees and agents...." This ultimate fact or conclusion of law is contained in that portion of the statement of decision entitled "FRAUD" and included under the general heading "LEGAL ISSUES." Earlier, in detailing "Some of the court's salient factual conclusions," the trial court found: "(7) Williams was justified in relying on Ross and the Security Pacific National Bank because the bank had always stood by him.... Williams did not know (and this lack of knowledge was reasonable) that Viking Dodge had no real chance at succeeding and relied on Ross' representations to the contrary."

The statement of decision containing these quoted portions was adopted and filed by the trial court after specific objections were filed by the Bank. I quote the pertinent objection on the issue of justifiable reliance from Bank's objections to statement of intended decision, filed January 17, 1986: "3. In regard to the Viking Dodge fraud causes of action, the court failed to make specific findings in its Decision on the elements of: "...................... "c. Williams' reasonable reliance on the alleged misrepresentations in light of his knowledge of Bugelli's losses at Viking Dodge (part II, I infra), the extensive publicity regarding Chrysler's problems (part II, K infra), his management of the dealership for one month before the escrow closed, his knowledge of the consequences of the Bank's decision not to finance van conversions (part II, R infra), and the evidence presented by Williams that Security Pacific officers Howard Butler and Charlie Walker warned him not to purchase Viking Dodge before the close of escrow. (Chesrown testimony; Walker testimony.)"

The trial court, in its statement of decision, made clear factual findings concerning the special relationship between Williams and Ross. However, significant findings were also made determining the close personal and fiduciary relationships between Williams and Bank officer Howard Butler. In the statement of decision, the trial court described Williams's relationship with Butler as follows: "After Walker was transferred to northern California, Williams began almost daily contact with Howard Butler, who ran Security Pacific National Bank's service center in El Cajon and who succeeded Walker with respect to the Baron Buick account, both on a business and a social basis." The majority opinion correctly points out, "In financial matters, Williams completely relied on the superior knowledge of Walker, Butler and Ross." Further, "Williams also developed and maintained a close personal relationship with Howard Butler, who ran the Bank's El Cajon service center and took over the Baron Buick account. Their relationship was both business and social. They met frequently, permitting Butler to tutor Williams on the Bank's financial expectations for Baron Buick. Socially, they went fishing and bought a boat together. They became not only 'very close friends,' but also 'business partners, so to speak.'" While Williams knew Ross and appreciated Ross's expertise in dealership finance, the statement of decision made it clear--as does the majority opinion--that Williams was working on a daily basis with Butler, and that his personal relationship with Butler was much closer than it was with Ross. Butler handled Williams's financial transactions with the Bank every day. Ross was only involved when problems reached the crisis level. Regardless of Williams's view of Ross's expertise, the record clearly reflected, and the trial court properly found, that Butler was Williams's confidante, mentor, and most trusted Bank representative long before Viking Dodge was in the picture.

The importance of the Butler-Williams relationship is that at a time when Williams was in the process of investigating Viking Dodge and negotiating to purchase it, but before Williams was bound to go through with that transaction, Williams admitted Butler told him, "Congratulations, you just bailed out the bank and went broke at Baron." This statement was made by Butler in a breakfast meeting with Williams shortly after his "first series of meetings with Mr. Ross and Mr. Bugelli" concerning the Viking Dodge deal. At that time Butler was Williams's "best friend."

This direct warning from Williams's closest Bank associate was made before any of the final negotiations with Ross and Bugelli. More importantly, this warning was made before Williams undertook management of Viking. Williams was in sole control of the Viking Dodge dealership for an entire month before he was bound by the close of the sale escrow. Williams testified Ross insisted he, Williams, take over management of Viking Dodge during the sale escrow period so he could "take a look at how the store had been run for that four or five month period [of Butler's stewardship]...." Thereafter, Williams was personally present as manager of Viking Dodge at least four to five days per week during at least the first two weeks of April 1979. It was during this one-month period that Williams had access to the financial statements of Viking Dodge on a daily basis. (See maj. opn., ante.)

Again, Butler made his explicit warning contemporaneously with Williams's actual knowledge Bank was not going to finance van conversion sales at Viking after Williams acquired it. Williams himself testified he obtained Chrysler flooring for van packages because Bank was no longer in that market. Long before escrow closed on Viking, Williams knew he would no longer have flooring support from Bank. Ross insisted on this as a part of the deal.

Nevertheless, the trial court, in its statement of decision, made no reference whatsoever to Williams's admission of the Butler warning. Thus, the statement of decision reads as though the warning was never made. Yet at one point in the statement of decision, the trial court noted, "Any responsible banker should have warned Williams that the Viking Dodge purchase was not financially viable, or at least that the critical records, on which to make this judgment were missing."

At eight different places in its statement of decision, the trial court based its finding of the "fiduciary relationship" between Williams and Bank on his interaction with Bank officials other than Ross. Besides Howard Butler, the trial court mentioned Charles Walker and Gerald Bruno, among others, as officers of Bank who were in a fiduciary relationship with Williams.

By contrast, the trial court found Williams's first close contact with Ross was in November 1978, only four months before the Viking deal began and only six months before it was completed. The very existence of this fiduciary relationship is based primarily on the interaction of Williams with Walker, then Butler and Bruno between 1976 and late 1978--the period Williams was successfully operating Baron Buick in San Diego. Williams's strongest business contact with Ross during this period resulted from overdrafts at Baron Buick stemming from Williams's dividing his managerial expertise between Lamb Chevrolet and Baron Buick. This problem was quickly resolved when Williams terminated his contract at Lamb Chevrolet and returned full time to Baron Buick.

Only after Bugelli's improper sales practices brought failure to University Ford and Westchester Ford did Williams have any further direct contact with Ross.

The point of this review of the trial court's factual findings is to illustrate the ambiguity inherent in the statement of decision. While relying on the Butler-Williams "partnership" to establish the fiduciary relationship upon which it predicated liability for concealment of material facts, the trial court completely ignored Butler's warning to Williams in finding Williams justifiably relied on Ross's statements and misconduct.

I note the record contained contradictory evidence as to Butler's warning to Williams. At trial, after Williams admitted receiving Butler's warning concerning the likelihood of failure at Viking, Butler denied making the statement at all. Mr.

Chesrown, another Bank official, corroborated Williams's admission the warning had been given to Williams by Butler. In light of the other salient circumstances at the time, resolution of that contradictory evidence was of ultimate importance on the issue of justifiable reliance. The only reason given for the trial court's conclusion that justifiable reliance had been established was "the bank had always stood by him [Williams]." This reason was without any substantial evidentiary support in the record. As already mentioned, Bank insisted Chrysler assume all flooring liability for Viking Dodge when Williams took over. Bank refused to finance any more van conversions, which meant 90 percent of Viking's profit-making business had to be financed by other financial institutions. Essentially, Bank was deserting Williams in his new enterprise at Viking. Regardless of opinions or misrepresentations spoken by Ross as to the potential for success at Viking, Williams had actual knowledge Bank was not going to support his new venture financially. Thus, the statement of decision did not address Bank's request for a specific explanation of the factual and legal basis for its decision on this critical issue, as is required by section 632.

I have searched the California authority and have found nothing to support the proposition implicit in the judgment of the trial court and the opinion of my colleagues: When a trusted fiduciary bank officer [Butler] advises Williams his proposed Viking Dodge acquisition will "[bail] out the bank and [destroy] Baron," Williams is legally justified in relying, instead, on the misrepresentations of another fiduciary bank officer who previously has been only minimally involved as his advisor. If the concept of fiduciary obligation is to be extended to the bank-borrower relationship, and if it is to be based upon the conduct of Butler and other Bank officials in no way involved with the fraudulent conduct, how can that close relationship be ignored when determining the justifiable reliance issue?

As mentioned, although Bank objected to the trial court's failure to address these matters in its statement of decision, the trial court did not mention or discuss Butler's warning in the statement of decision filed in this case. Nowhere in that document did the trial court directly address and reconcile (1) Butler's warning, (2) Williams's knowledge of conditions at Viking, and (3) Williams's opportunity to verify Butler's warning while managing Viking in April 1979. Rather, the trial court apparently concluded Williams could ignore these matters and blithely rush to bankruptcy.

When a material issue is not explained by the trial court after a specific request, it may not be inferred on appeal that the trial court decided in favor of the prevailing party as to those facts or on that issue. In *Miramar Hotel*, supra, the trial court issued an intended statement of decision by way of minute order. Although receiving objections and specific requests for a formal statement of decision from the losing party at trial, the court did not respond but entered judgment with only the intended statement of decision on file. This was held reversible error per se since the result was the issuance of no formal statement of decision. The court held appellant did not need to show prejudice as a prerequisite to reversal. Here, the circumstances were analogous. Bank strongly asserted the failure of Williams to prove justifiable reliance in its defense. The truth or falsity of alleged misrepresentations rested largely on the credibility of Williams and Ross, but the circumstances showing Williams's true knowledge of the risks of the Viking venture were established without controversy except for Butler's warning. Hence, the trial court's total failure to address, resolve or explain its determination on that essential issue made the statement of decision fatally defective and reversible per se. If one presumes the trial court believed Williams's admission as to Butler's warning, as one is authorized to do under section 634, then in relating Butler's warning to the facts clearly within Williams's knowledge, there was no basis for finding Williams justifiably relied on Ross's misconduct.

It is impossible for me to accept the proposition any experienced automobile agency operator with Williams's intelligence would ignore the impact of Butler's comment and sink his financial future in Viking Dodge, in light of the other circumstances well known to him.

Therefore, * * * I dissent. I would reverse and remand for a new trial on all issues.

B. LIABILITY OF CREDITORS TO OTHER CREDITORS

1. By Law

R. Hillman, J. McDonnell & S. Nickles, COMMON LAW AND EQUITY UNDER THE UNIFORM COMMERCIAL CODE
¶24.04[1] (1985)

Occasionally, a claimant of collateral who is just about to lose a priority dispute will make a last ditch effort to win by arguing broadly that notwithstanding Article 9's priority rules that are against him, "the equities" are in his favor; and he thus should prevail on the basis of unspecified "equitable principles" or "equity" in general. This sort of argument, which challenges the intrinsic fairness of Article 9's priority rules, almost never succeeds. It fails primarily for the reason explained by the court in *Security National Bank v. Dentsply Professional Plan* [617 P.2d 1340, 1343 (Okl.1980)]:

> Although strict adherence to the Code requirements may at times lead to harsh results, efforts by some courts to fashion equitable solutions for mitigation of hardships experienced by creditors in the literal application of *** [Article 9] may have the undesirable effect of reducing the degree of reliance the marketplace should be able to place on the Code provisions. The inevitable harm doubtless would be more serious to commerce than the occasional harshness from strict obedience.

A more basic reason is that in drafting and enacting Article 9's priority rules, the usual equities involved in typical cases were considered along with various policy concerns. These rules represent legislative decisions by people who very deliberately balanced competing equities and weighed what is fair between classes of claimants against what is useful and necessary to the overall ends of commerce. By entertaining arguments that attack head on the fairness of Article 9's priority rules, the courts would be forced to judge the wisdom of these decisions and assume for themselves a legislative role. Few courts will openly make claim to the legislator's job.

A very different argument for disregarding Article 9's priority rules is that the person who benefits from them acted unfairly. This argument, which sometimes prevails, seeks to subordinate a person's claim to collateral not because the rules that give the person priority are themselves inequitable; the thrust of the argument is rather that the person entitled to priority engaged in inequitable or otherwise culpable conduct that is properly punishable by denying him the right to enforce his claim. The conduct may consist of fraud or simpler forms of bad faith that may be a sufficient basis in and of itself for subordinating the culprit's claim.

Ostlund Chemical Co. v. Norwest Bank
Supreme Court of North Dakota, 1988
417 N.W.2d 833

Vande Walle, Justice. Ostlund Chemical Company [Ostlund] appealed from a summary judgment dismissing its action against Norwest Bank of Jamestown, formerly known as First National Bank of Jamestown [Bank]. Because genuine issues of material fact have been raised in this case, we reverse and remand for trial.

The evidence, viewed in the light most favorable to the party against whom summary judgment was rendered, reflects that during March 1982, Bruce Glinz, a farmer, was indebted to the Bank for more than $440,000. Glinz sought $600,000 in operating funds for the 1982 farm year, but because of his deteriorating financial condition, the Bank was unwilling to advance such funds to Glinz on its own. The Bank, however, agreed to accept a Farmers Home Administration [FmHA] subordination of security to use as collateral for providing operating funds to Glinz. Under this arrangement the Bank provided Glinz a line of credit for $600,000, placed under the control of an FmHA officer and to be disbursed in accordance with a specifically defined budget. The itemized budget provided for a total of $150,000 to be used for pesticides and fertilizers.

During April 1982, Glinz contacted Ostlund in an effort to purchase on credit between $330,000 and $350,000 of farm chemicals and fertilizers for the crop season. In order to verify that Glinz had adequate credit for the proposed purchase, Howard Fairburn, Ostlund's credit manager, contacted the Bank by telephone. Fairburn spoke with Dennis Renner, a vice-president and manager of the Bank's agriculture department, told him about Glinz's request, and asked him if Glinz would have credit available to pay Ostlund's invoices when they became due. Renner responded that Glinz's line of credit was sufficient to cover his purchase of chemicals and fertilizers.

Ostlund then sold fertilizer and chemicals to Glinz on credit. In June 1982, after Glinz had purchased more than $225,000 in products from Ostlund, Glinz told the company that he was unable to make any payments and that the Bank had terminated his line of credit. Ostlund contacted the Bank, which confirmed this information. According to Ostlund, it nevertheless continued to supply Glinz with its products so he could successfully complete the harvest and use the resulting profits to retire his debt to Ostlund.

Glinz did not pay Ostlund, and he subsequently filed for bankruptcy. Although Ostlund recovered more than $87,000 from the bankruptcy trustee, Ostlund contends it is currently owed, exclusive of interest, approximately $214,000.

In December 1983, Ostlund commenced this action against the Bank seeking damages in excess of $300,000. The count of Ostlund's complaint which is involved in this appeal alleges that

> "[t]he statements and representations made by the Bank to Ostlund ... were statements of material facts made intentionally by the Bank and such statements were false, and such statements were recklessly made by the Bank, and such statements constituted promises made by the Bank without the Bank's intention of performing the same, and such statements were made by the Bank in order to induce [Ostlund] to sell and deliver to Glinz approximately $350,000 worth of chemicals and fertilizers."

The Bank counterclaimed and moved for summary judgment. Based upon the depositions of Renner and Fairburn, the district court determined that

> "[n]o genuine issue of material fact is shown that the conversation between Renner and Fairburn placed Renner in a situation of intending to deceive [Ostlund] or to induce [Ostlund] to enter into a contract with Glinz."

The court concluded that Ostlund had failed to show any basis for actual fraud under §9-03-08, N.D.C.C., or deceit under §§9-10-02 and 9-10-03, N.D.C.C., and granted the Bank's motion for summary judgment. The court declined to rule on the issues raised in the Bank's counterclaim, but issued a Rule 54(b), N.D.R.Civ.P., certification, and this appeal followed.

* * *

Because Ostlund conceded at the motion for summary judgment that it was no longer pursuing a case based upon any contract between the parties, we construe Ostlund's remaining count as a tort action for deceit under §§9-10-02 and 9-10-03, N.D.C.C., rather than for actual fraud or constructive fraud under §§9-03-08 and 9-03-09, N.D.C.C.[1] See Hellman v. Thiele, 413 N.W.2d 321, 325-326 (N.D.1987). Section 9-10-03, N.D.C.C., provides that "[o]ne who willfully deceives another with intent to induce him to alter his position to his injury or risk is liable for any damage which he thereby suffers." Section 9-10-02, N.D.C.C., defines deceit as follows:

> "9-10-02. Deceit--Definition. A deceit within the meaning of section 9-10-03 is: "1. The suggestion as a fact of that which is not true by one who does not believe it to be true; "2. The assertion as a fact of that which is not true by one who has no reasonable ground for believing it to be true; "3. The suppression of a fact by one who is bound to disclose it, or who gives information of other facts which are likely to mislead for want of communication of that fact; or "4. A promise made without any intention of performing."

In *Hellman*, supra, 413 N.W.2d at 326, we noted that a party may be held liable for nondisclosure under §9-10-02(3), N.D.C.C., only if that party is under a duty to disclose the "true facts."[2]

The plaintiffs in *Hellman*, creditors of an insolvent bank customer, sued the bank alleging that it engaged in a pattern of paying the customer's overdrafts, knowing the customer was insolvent, in an effort to keep the customer's business afloat long enough for the bank to become fully secured on its various loans to the customer. We upheld the district court's grant of summary judgment against one group of plaintiffs "who had had no contacts with the Bank regarding [the customer's] financial status." *Hellman*, supra, 413 N.W.2d at 323. We reviewed decisions from other jurisdictions holding that, in general, a bank is under no affirmative duty to disclose to the world a customer's financial condition. We held that the group of plaintiffs who had not communicated with the bank failed to

---

[1]   Because Ostlund has relied principally upon the statutory provisions on fraud and deceit as the basis for its action, we do not consider whether Ostlund's complaint can be construed as alleging a cause of action based upon negligent misrepresentation.

[2]   In Hellman v. Thiele, 413 N.W.2d 321, 326 (N.D.1987), we further noted that this rule is the same under §551(1) of the Restatement (Second) of Torts (1977), which provides: "s 551. Liability for Nondisclosure "(1) One who fails to disclose to another a fact that he knows may justifiably induce the other to act or refrain from acting in a business transaction is subject to the same liability to the other as though he had represented the nonexistence of the matter that he has failed to disclose, if, but only if, he is under a duty to the other to exercise reasonable care to disclose the matter in question."

establish through statute, rule, or other authority that the bank had a duty to disclose to them the customer's true financial condition.

This case differs from *Hellman*. Ostlund alleges that it made a specific inquiry concerning the availability of credit for Glinz's proposed chemical purchases and received a misleading response from the Bank, which stood in a position to benefit from Glinz's production of a good crop.

While the Bank was originally under no duty to divulge any information about Glinz's credit status, we believe that once the Bank chose to reply to Ostlund's inquiry it had a duty to impart full, accurate, and truthful information. See Berkline Corp. v. Bank of Mississippi, 453 So.2d 699, 702 (Miss.1984); Nevada National Bank v. Gold Star Meat Company, 89 Nev. 427, 514 P.2d 651, 653 (1973); Annot., "Liability of bank, to other than party whose financial condition is misrepresented, for erroneous credit information furnished by bank or its directors, officers, or employees," 77 A.L.R.3d 6 (1977); cf. Holcomb v. Zinke, 365 N.W.2d 507, 511-512 (N.D.1985). The Sixth Circuit Court of Appeals responded to criticism of this rule in Central States Stamping v. Terminal Equip. Co., 727 F.2d 1405, 1409 (6th Cir.1984):

> "The Bank argues that this rule is unworkable and would 'dry up' normal communications from banks which are essential to the functioning of the economy. Such a result is not inevitable. In an English case which was similar to ours, Hedley Byrne & Co., Ltd. v. Heller & Partners, Ltd., [1964] A.C. 465, 486, Lord Reid pointed out that a banker who receives an inquiry about the credit-worthiness of a customer has three courses open. The banker can decline to give the information; he can give an answer with a clear qualification that it is given and accepted without any responsibility or is given without reflection or research; or, the banker can give an answer without qualification. Lord Reid concluded that if a banker adopts the third alternative he can be held to have accepted some responsibility for answering carefully or to have accepted a relationship with the inquirer which requires him to exercise such care as circumstances require.

> "Hedley Byrne was not a fraud case but involved a negligent answer by a banker. However, it dealt instructively with the duty to speak once a relationship is established in which the person questioned knows that the inquirer is relying on the fact that he, the person questioned, has superior information. The duty is particularly clear when the party answering the inquiry benefits directly from the actions of the inquiring party...."

In this case, Glinz was indebted to the Bank on other loans for more than $440,000. Regarding the $600,000 line of credit for the 1982 farm season, Renner testified in his deposition as follows:

"Q Why don't you explain to me then this subordination agreement between the Jamestown bank and FHA [sic]?

"A Okay. His credit had deteriorated to the point were [sic] we could not advance operating funds on our own in 1982.

"Q Why was that?

"A Because of the financial health of Mr. Glinz, it had deteriorated, the collateral was insufficient, it just didn't--the credit didn't support the bank going in with that type of an operating request that he had needed. He was looking for about $600,000.

"So, we recognized that, you know, if Mr. Glinz was going to attempt to perform on his debts he would need to grow a crop to generate some income over and above the operating expenses so that he could perform on his other term debts, so to speak. So, we agreed to accept an FHA [sic] subordination."

The evidence also permits a reasonable inference that Renner had knowledge of the itemized budget categories for the $600,000 line of credit at the time Fairburn telephoned him to verify that Glinz had a sufficient line of credit to pay for the proposed chemical and fertilizer purchases. Furthermore, regarding the telephone conversation, Fairburn testified in his deposition as follows:

"Q Now, what specifically--and I want you to be as precise as you can-- did Mr. Renner tell you during the course of this telephone conversation?

"A We discussed the fact that the bank was looking at $600,000 worth of credit for Bruce Glinz for the 1982 crop year. I indicated what our amount or the amount that Bruce had indicated to us would be his chemical needs and I also indicated the date that the payment would be coming due or be expected. And I asked if the credit would be available for him to be able to take his accounts and pay his invoices at that point in time. And our conversation was that there would be credit available.

"Q All right. Are you trying to tell me that Mr. Renner told you that out of a $600,000 line of credit that there would be $350,000 available for chemicals ?

"A He indicated that to me, that they would have credit available to pay the bill when it came due, yes."

Viewed in the light most favorable to Ostlund, the evidence in the record is sufficient to raise genuine issues of material fact on whether the Bank has committed an actionable deceit within the meaning of §§9-10-02 and 9-10-03, N.D.C.C.

Accordingly, the summary judgment is reversed and the case is remanded for trial.

Ninth District Production Credit Association
v. Ed Duggan, Inc.
Supreme Court of Colorado, En Banc, 1991
821 P.2d 788

Justice Lohr delivered the opinion of the Court. We granted certiorari in this case to review the decision of the Colorado Court of Appeals in Ed Duggan, Inc. v. Ninth Dist. Prod. Credit Ass'n, 795 P.2d 1347 (Colo.App.1990). At trial the jury returned a special verdict finding that the defendant, Ninth District Production Credit Association, had been unjustly enriched and awarding the plaintiff, Ed Duggan, Inc., damages in the amount of $101,586.38. The trial court entered judgment on the verdict and the court of appeals affirmed. We conclude that the trial court erred in instructing the jury and therefore reverse the judgment of the court of appeals and direct that the case be remanded for a new trial.

I.

A.

This case involves claims of Ed Duggan, Inc. (Duggan Corporation) for compensation for corn delivered to a failing cattle feedlot business. The issues on certiorari review are limited to the relative rights of Duggan Corporation, an unsecured creditor of the feedlot business, and Ninth District Production Credit Association (PCA), a creditor with a security interest in the proceeds of the feedlot's accounts receivable. A summary of the facts surrounding the dispute provides the necessary context for understanding the legal issues presented. Testimony at trial was conflicting in a number of respects. In summarizing the relevant facts as presented by the evidence, we attempt to identify the areas of material conflict.

Norman Land & Livestock Company (Norman Company) owned and operated a cattle feedlot and also was engaged in the general farming business. Howard Norman was a corporate officer of Norman Company and also managed its operations. The feedlot business supplied Norman Company with its primary source of income. Operating the feedlot involved caring for cattle to maturity and fattening them for slaughter. Norman Company was compensated based on the amount of weight gained by the cattle while at the feedlot. Corn was the primary growth component in the diet of the cattle, and Duggan Corporation was a principal supplier of corn to the feedlot.

Norman Company's operations were financed by PCA. PCA had made annual operating loans to Norman Company beginning in 1978 and held a perfected security interest in the company's accounts receivable and other personal property to secure the annual advances and prior indebtedness. PCA would commit to loan moneys up to a specified amount during a particular year and Norman Company would request and obtain advances under the commitment from time to time as necessary to pay bills incurred in its operations. PCA did not supply advances directly to Norman Company. Instead, Norman Company would issue sight drafts against PCA to pay specific bills. PCA would then review the bills and honor the drafts by making additional funds available under its loan commitment. In return, PCA would collect all the proceeds of Norman Company's accounts receivable to apply against the indebtedness. This arrangement was standard for all ranching and farming loans made by PCA and enabled PCA to assure that the proceeds of a debtor's collateral would be applied to reduce the debtor's obligations to PCA.

In August of 1982, PCA reviewed Norman Company's financial condition and concluded that it was deteriorating rapidly. At that time Howard Norman was exploring various possibilities for refinancing or sale of the feedlot business. PCA decided to allow Norman Company to continue to operate into December 1982. However, if the debt owed to PCA should still be outstanding at that time, PCA planned to foreclose; such action would result in closure of the feedlot business. In connection with this decision, PCA prepared a memorandum, executed by Howard Norman on behalf of Norman Company, outlining certain restrictions on Norman Company's operations from September into December 1982. The memorandum, dated September 17, 1982, stated in pertinent part:

1. No "new" cattle to be put on feed unless approved by [PCA] .... 6. No other feed purchases except dry corn and protein--use own corn as soon as possible   7. Prior approval from [PCA] on all disbursements over $500.00 and such disbursements supported by invoice or statement as of September 20, 1982 .... 11. It is understood and agreed by the undersigned the funds being advanced are to preserve and protect collateral pledged to [PCA] and is in no way a guarantee for future or further extension of credit: PCA intended this memorandum to be confidential, but it contained nothing to indicate this intent.

In the latter part of 1982, C.J. Streit (Streit) became interested in purchasing certain assets of Norman Company, including the feedlot. Although Norman Company was the owner, negotiations for the sale were conducted between Streit and PCA. Streit testified that PCA controlled the moneys involved in the purchase because of its position as a secured creditor of Norman Company and a potential financing source for Streit. Roland Johnson (Johnson), who had been president of PCA during the times relevant to this dispute, testified however that PCA's primary involvement in the sale transaction was as a potential lender to Streit.

Johnson stated that PCA would not have benefitted from Streit's purchase of the operation because PCA would have suffered approximately the same loss on its loan to Norman Company whether or not the sale between Streit and Norman Company was concluded.

Shortly after negotiations for the sale began, Streit moved approximately 750 head of his own cattle onto the Norman Company feedlot. PCA never expressly approved the addition of these cattle to the feedlot, but Johnson and Randall Ford (Ford), who had been the PCA loan officer and office manager at the relevant times, were aware that the cattle had been moved in and did not object to the additional cattle.

Streit testified that he wanted to keep the feedlot operation running throughout the negotiations because he preferred to purchase an ongoing business. Ford testified that the feedlot was kept open at the request of Howard Norman. Streit, Norman, and Ford met early in December to discuss the sale. Norman testified that during the meeting Ford and Streit requested he leave the room, and that at some point after the meeting they told him that the feedlot was to remain open. The lot continued in operation until total liquidation in March of 1983. The evidence suggests that all parties wished the feedlot to continue in operation, principally to facilitate a sale to Streit.

After negotiations with Streit began in December, PCA did not commence foreclosure proceedings as it had planned earlier. Instead, it allowed Norman Company to continue to operate despite the fact that the PCA loan commitment expired on December 15, 1982. PCA also continued to disburse funds after December 15, even though the disbursements exceeded its loan commitment limits. PCA representatives testified that, with one minor exception, these disbursements were made only for the purpose of preparing equipment and property for sale and for paying the salaries of Norman Company employees, and that therefore the disbursements were consistent with the decision to wind down Norman Company's operations. There was conflicting testimony that during this period PCA advanced funds to pay almost all of the feedlot's obligations except Duggan Corporation's bills for supplying corn.

Sometime after Streit began negotiating for the purchase, Norman Company began to place proceeds from collection of its accounts receivable in an escrow account, pursuant to an agreement with Streit. The escrow account was maintained until Streit decided not to purchase the Norman Company assets in late February 1983. At that time the escrow account balance of approximately $250,000 was turned over to PCA. In addition, PCA received payment from Streit of approximately $120,000 for feedlot services provided by Norman Company in connection with the 750 cattle Streit moved onto the lot in December.

Edmond Duggan (Duggan) operated Duggan Corporation, a trucking business that supplied corn to Norman Company for its feedlot operation. Duggan Corporation had been a regular supplier of corn to Norman Company for many years. Norman Company representatives testified that beginning in late November or early December of 1982, in accordance with the requirements of the September

17 memorandum between PCA and Norman Company, PCA was informed each time that Norman Company ordered corn from Duggan Corporation. Norman Company maintained that initially it called PCA before ordering corn to inform it that corn was needed and to obtain approval for the purchase. After Streit became involved in the purchase negotiations, he began approving the corn purchases. Nevertheless, testimony indicated that after Streit's involvement a Norman Company representative continued to call PCA to inform it that corn was being ordered. Duggan testified that he was aware that PCA was being informed in advance of these purchases.

PCA loan officer Ford was present at the Norman Company feedlot during the period when Duggan Corporation was delivering corn, and PCA was aware that cattle in the feedlot were eating corn that had been delivered by Duggan Corporation to Norman Company after the loan commitment had run out. During Ford's visits to the feedlot, he also reviewed records indicating that Duggan Corporation was delivering corn to Norman Company during the period involved in this dispute. PCA president Johnson testified, however, that no PCA representative was making operating decisions for Norman Company; rather, Howard Norman made all business decisions for the company through February 1983.

Duggan Corporation was never paid for corn it supplied to Norman Company during the period from late November 1982 through early February 1983. Howard Norman showed Edmond Duggan a copy of the September 17 memorandum in early December when Duggan first inquired about the nonpayment. Duggan testified that he believed he was protected because the memorandum contemplated continued purchases of dry corn, and in the past PCA had always provided the funds for corn purchases based on sight drafts written by Norman Company. Norman also informed Duggan of the escrow account arrangement sometime in December, and Duggan expected to be paid from the escrowed funds once they were released upon completion of the sale to Streit. However, Duggan Corporation continued to supply the corn as an unsecured creditor. After Streit elected not to purchase the feedlot, Norman Company was financially unable to pay for the corn and Streit declined to pay. Duggan Corporation then sought payment from PCA in the latter part of March or early April of 1983, but this request was denied. PCA maintains that as a secured creditor it is entitled to the proceeds of accounts receivable and should not be required to pay Duggan Corporation, an unsecured creditor, out of those funds.

B.

Duggan Corporation brought suit in Larimer County District Court seeking recovery of $101,586.41 for the purchase price of the corn delivered to Norman Company less a deduction for corn repossessed by Duggan Corporation and resold after the dispute arose. Named as defendants were Norman Company, Streit and PCA. The claims of Duggan Corporation against Norman Company and Streit as well as counterclaims and cross-claims asserted by those parties have been resolved or dismissed and are not relevant to this certiorari review.

Duggan Corporation sought recovery against PCA based on theories of express contract and unjust enrichment. After trial to a jury, the jury returned a special verdict finding that there was no express contract by which PCA agreed to pay for the corn delivered by Duggan Corporation to Norman Company but that there was an "implied contract," based on a theory of unjust enrichment, and that Duggan Corporation had suffered damages in the amount of $101,586.38 by reason of PCA's failure to pay for the corn. On appeal, the Colorado Court of Appeals affirmed. We granted certiorari to consider the following issues: Whether the court of appeals correctly ruled that as a matter of law [PCA] was unjustly enriched and, if so, that [PCA] is liable to Duggan [Corporation] even though [PCA] held a perfected security interest in Norman [Company's] assets. Whether the trial court erred in not submitting to the jury [PCA's] theory of the case, which was that [PCA] had a perfected security interest in Norman [Company's] assets.

II.

The central issue in this case is whether a creditor that holds a perfected security interest in collateral can be held liable to an unsecured creditor based on a theory of unjust enrichment for benefits that enhance the value of the collateral. We conclude that this question cannot be answered categorically. Such a dispute involves tension between the priority system established in Article 9 of the Uniform Commercial Code (UCC or the Code) and equitable principles of unjust enrichment. Although the policies underlying the UCC support a uniform, reliable system of priorities among creditors, we are unwilling to hold that alteration of that hierarchy of priorities is never necessary to implement the equitable principles on which the doctrine of unjust enrichment is based. A sketch of the UCC system of priorities and of the elements of a claim for unjust enrichment will serve as a background for consideration of cases that have grappled with the relationship between these two sets of principles.

Under Article 9 of the UCC, a creditor may obtain security for payment of an obligation by acquiring a security interest in a debtor's collateral. The basis of an enforceable security interest is a security agreement between the debtor and the creditor. Normally, this agreement will be in writing signed by the debtor, and will contain a description of the collateral covered by the agreement. See §§4-9-201, -203(1)(a), 2 C.R.S. (1973 & 1991 Supp.). A security interest does not come into being until the creditor has given value and the debtor has acquired rights in the collateral. §4-9- 203(1)(b) and (c). A creditor with a security interest has superior rights in the collateral as against the debtor and unsecured creditors. See §§4-9- 201, -203(1), -301; 2 J. White & R. Summers Uniform Commercial Code §24-6 (3d pract. ed. 1988). In order to protect its interest to the fullest, a creditor must "perfect" its security interest. See §4-9-312. This normally entails filing a financing statement in the appropriate governmental office. §§44-9- 302, -401. A creditor with a perfected security interest has priority over most other subsequent competing claims to the collateral. See §4-9-312; 2 J. White & R. Summers, Uniform Commercial Code §24-7. It is undisputed in this case that PCA held a perfected security interest in Norman Company's accounts receivable, and that Duggan Corporation was an unsecured creditor.

The UCC also provides for the application of equitable principles in cases governed by Article 9. According to section 4-1-103, "[u]nless displaced by the particular provisions of this title, the principles of law and equity ... shall supplement its provisions." This section has been characterized as the "most important single provision in the Code." 1 J. White & R. Summers, Uniform Commercial Code §5. The UCC was enacted to displace prior legal principles, not prior equitable principles.

> Code sections do not "occupy the equity field." Rather, general equitable principles remain largely intact, for they are only rarely "particularly displaced." In a sense, then, they are the main occupants of the relevant field. This follows from their basic character. Unlike general legal principles, they do not merely supplement Code sections; their function is also to carve exceptions from or otherwise modify Code sections, and the courts have recognized as much. These functions are not peculiar to the bearing of 1-103 equitable principles on Code rules; they are characteristic of the bearing of equitable principles upon legal rules throughout the law. .... With 1-103 and related law on the books, judges can escape the ancient dilemma of either adhering to the legal rule and doing an inequity, or of doing equity but in an unlaw-like fashion. Indeed, 1-103 imposes a duty on the judge to reach the equitable result unless the relevant general equitable principle has been particularly displaced. While equitable doctrines may have the effect of making Article 9 priority law less certain, "they offer flexibility in cases where applying the Code rigorously may result in an unfair outcome."

Id. §26-20.

Unjust enrichment, sometimes referred to as quasi-contract or contract implied in law, is an equitable doctrine that permits recovery when a plaintiff shows

> "(1) that a benefit was conferred on the defendant by the plaintiff, (2) that the benefit was appreciated by the defendant, and (3) that the benefit was accepted by the defendant under such circumstances that it would be inequitable for it to be retained without payment...."

Cablevision of Breckenridge v. Tannhauser Condominium Ass'n, 649 P.2d 1093, 1096-97 (Colo.1982); accord Dass v. Epplen, 162 Colo. 60, 424 P.2d 779 (1967). Since the doctrine of unjust enrichment has not been displaced by the particular provisions of Article 9, the doctrine may supplement its provisions. See

Producers Cotton Oil Co. v. Amstar Corp., 197 Cal.App.3d 638, 242 Cal.Rptr. 914, 927 (1988).

There is obvious tension between the doctrine of unjust enrichment and the priority system established by Article 9. When an unsecured creditor confers a benefit upon a secured creditor by adding to or enhancing the creditor's collateral and a claim for unjust enrichment against the secured creditor is recognized, the secured creditor in effect loses its priority status despite its compliance with the procedures set forth in Article 9. We have recognized in other settings, however, that the scope of the remedy under the doctrine of unjust enrichment "is broad, cutting across both contract and tort law, with its application guided by the underlying principle of avoiding the unjust enrichment of one party at the expense of another." Cablevision, 649 P.2d at 1097. The concept of unjust enrichment centers attention "on the prevention of injustice.... This wide and imprecise idea has played a creative role in the development of an important branch of modern law." Palmer, Law of Restitution §1.1 (1978). We must determine whether the enrichment of a secured creditor as a result of benefits conferred by an unsecured creditor can ever be considered "unjust" and, if so, the standards that will govern that determination.

The court of appeals noted an apparent split of authority on the issue of the availability of an unjust enrichment claim in circumstances where it will upset the order of priorities established under Article 9 of the UCC. The court cited Peerless Packing Co., Inc. v. Malone & Hyde, Inc., 376 S.E.2d 161 (W.Va.1988), and Evans Products Co. v. Jorgensen, 245 Or. 362, 421 P.2d 978 (1966), as cases supporting the view that a secured creditor's claim to collateral cannot be defeated by application of the doctrine of unjust enrichment. On the other side of the controversy it referred to Producers Cotton Oil Co. v. Amstar Corp., 242 Cal.Rptr. 914, and Borg-Warner Acceptance Corp. v. Valentine Associates Ltd. Corp., 192 Ga.App. 123, 384 S.E.2d 223 (1989). These latter cases both allowed a claim of unjust enrichment to prevail over the claim of a secured creditor. We believe that the results reached in these two lines of authority can be reconciled, although the courts' analyses are concededly in tension. The cases are factually distinguishable and consistent with a view that in appropriate circumstances a claim of unjust enrichment can be asserted successfully by an unsecured creditor against a secured creditor.

The facts in the cases denying an unsecured creditor's unjust enrichment claim against a secured creditor are complex. A common thread, however, runs through them. In each, the secured creditor had no more than general knowledge that an unsecured creditor was supplying goods to the debtor. There were no facts to indicate that the secured creditor initiated or encouraged the transaction by which the unsecured creditor enhanced the value of the secured collateral when the unsecured creditor supplied goods or services to the debtor. Thus, in *Peerless Packing* the secured creditor of a grocery store prevailed over unsecured creditors who asserted an unjust enrichment claim for groceries delivered during the week before the secured creditor foreclosed, took over operation of the store, and gave notice that it would not be responsible for debts incurred prior to foreclosure. The claim was based on the contention that the secured creditor allowed groceries to be delivered after it had formed the intent to foreclose one week earlier. There is no suggestion in the case report that the secured creditor participated in ordering the groceries or otherwise initiated or encouraged the purchase of the groceries. *Peerless Packing*, 376 S.E.2d 161. Similarly, in *Evans Products* a secured creditor of a plywood manufacturer, with a lien on finished plywood, prevailed over an unsecured creditor who furnished raw material to the manufacturer and accepted finished plywood in payment. In holding for the secured creditor in a suit to foreclose against the supplier's plywood, the court rejected the defense that to permit the recovery without requiring payment for the raw material would unjustly enrich the secured creditor. The case report contains no indication that the secured creditor was even aware of the transaction between the unsecured supplier of raw material and the manufacturer. *Evans Products*, 421 P.2d 978.

In rejecting the unjust enrichment claims of the unsecured creditors in *Peerless Packing* and *Evans Products*, the appellate courts reasoned that "[t]he purpose and effectiveness of the UCC [Uniform Commercial Code] would be substantially impaired if interests created in compliance with UCC procedure could be defeated by application of the equitable doctrine of unjust enrichment." *Evans Products*, 421 P.2d at 983; *Peerless Packing*, 376 S.E.2d at 164 (quoting *Evans Products*, 421 P.2d at 983).[1]

The leading case allowing an unsecured creditor asserting an unjust enrichment claim to prevail against a secured creditor is *Producers Cotton Oil*, 242 Cal.Rptr. 914. In that case, the foreclosure claim of a creditor holding a security interest in growing crops and proceeds was held subject to reduction by a claim of the purchaser of those crops on a theory of unjust enrichment for money spent by the purchaser in harvesting those crops without first obtaining the secured creditor's consent and subordination. The court stated:

> We agree with the position of [the purchaser] and hold that when a party possessing a security interest in a crop and its proceeds has knowledge of and acquiesces in expenditures made which are necessary to the development of the crop, and ultimately benefits from the expenditures, a party who, through mistake, pays such costs without first obtaining subordination, is entitled to recover.

Producers Cotton Oil, 242 Cal.Rptr. at 927 (emphasis in original).

---

[1] In *Peerless Packing* the Supreme Court of Appeals of West Virginia stated, however, that "[w]e do not hold that an equitable claim for relief never lies in a case controlled by the UCC." It emphasized, nevertheless, that only "virtually fraudulent conduct" would justify such a claim in view of the strong policy for adherence to the priority system of the Uniform Commercial Code. *Peerless Packing*, 376 S.E.2d at 164-65 n. 4.

The secured creditor in *Producers Cotton Oil* was held to have acquiesced in the expenditures necessary to harvest the crop that was subject to its security interest. Under these circumstances the court concluded that the creditor would be unjustly enriched if not required to pay the costs associated with the benefit produced by harvesting the crop. Cf. *Borg-Warner*, 384 S.E.2d 223.[1]

Viewing the evidence in the present case in the light most favorable to Duggan Corporation, the situation in Duggan is more closely analogous to *Producers Cotton Oil* than to the *Peerless Packing* line of cases. Indeed, the evidence of PCA involvement in Duggan is stronger than that present in *Producers Cotton Oil*, where an agent of the secured creditor was simply in the field at harvest time and was aware that a third party was harvesting the crops.

The central point of distinction between Duggan and *Producers Cotton Oil*, on the one hand, and the *Peerless Packing* line of cases on the other, is the extent to which the secured creditor was involved in the transaction by which the unsecured creditor supplied goods or services that enhanced the value of the secured collateral. Where a secured creditor does not itself initiate or encourage[2] the transaction that creates the unsecured obligation giving rise to the unjust enrichment claim, retention of any benefit realized by the secured creditor without compensating the supplier is not unjust and thus an unjust enrichment claim cannot be supported. Certainly a secured creditor is benefitted whenever the collateral that secures its loan is augmented or increased in value without expense to the secured creditor. Such a situation may arise when an unsecured creditor supplies goods to a debtor that automatically become part of the secured creditor's collateral; and in a sense it may seem unfair to allow the secured creditor to accept this benefit without having to pay its full cost. However, the priority system established by Article 9 of the Code contemplates that secured creditors can foreclose on their security interests in collateral free of debts owed by the

---

[1]   In *Borg-Warner*, the plaintiff-creditor provided floor-plan financing to a mobile home dealer and held a security interest in the dealer's inventory. The dealer contracted to sell a home under an installment sales contract, but the purchaser of the home rescinded before the sale became final. Before learning of the rescission, the defendant, who had purchased the installment sales contract from the dealer, had remitted to the plaintiff-creditor the sum required to release the home from the lien. The plaintiff-creditor later foreclosed its lien on the inventory including the home that was the subject of the transaction. The court held that the plaintiff would be unjustly enriched if allowed to retain the repossessed home as well as the sum paid to release it from the lien.

[2]   In *Producers Cotton Oil* the court held that the secured creditor's act of acquiescing in the harvesting of the secured collateral (crops) was a sufficient basis for holding the secured creditor liable on the theory of unjust enrichment. However, in that case, the harvesting was necessary to the actual preservation of the secured collateral. *Producers Cotton Oil*, 242 Cal.Rptr. 914. Here, the delivery of corn was not essential to preserve the secured collateral, but instead served to augment or enhance its value. In such a case, more than mere acquiescence is required to hold a secured creditor liable on the basis of unjust enrichment.

debtor to junior unsecured creditors. See §§4-9-201, -310, -312, -317, 2 C.R.S. (1973 & 1991 Supp.). The UCC makes the unsecured creditor aware of the risks, and supplies a means by which such a creditor can learn in advance of the secured creditor's prior position by referring to the records in the appropriate governmental office. See §4-9-401, and official comment.

The UCC priority system thus reflects the legislative judgment that the value of a predictable system of priorities ordinarily outweighs the disadvantage of the system's occasional inequities. At the same time, however, the Code recognizes that equitable principles may require alteration of the priority system in particular circumstances. See §4-1-103. Although caselaw concerning the application of the equitable doctrine of unjust enrichment in the Article 9 context is scarce, courts have frequently employed other equitable principles to create exceptions to the established priority system. Thompson v. United States, 408 F.2d 1075, 1081-85 (8th Cir.1969) (lack of good faith on part of secured creditor towards the United States government, a junior creditor, held proper basis for altering Article 9 priorities); Limor Diamonds, Inc. v. D'Oro by Christopher Michael, Inc., 558 F.Supp. 709, 711 (S.D.N.Y.1983) (secured party's rights in collateral may be subordinated to rights of holder of junior security interest based on lack of good faith); Citizens State Bank v. Peoples Bank, 475 N.E.2d 324, 326-28 (Ind.App.1985) (promissory estoppel principles can be used to subordinate the lien of a senior creditor); Affiliated Foods, Inc. v. McGinley, 426 N.W.2d 646 (Iowa App.1988) (senior creditor equitably estopped from asserting priority of its secured interest with respect to a junior secured creditor); French Lumber Co., Inc. v. Commercial Realty & Finance Co., Inc., 346 Mass. 716, 195 N.E.2d 507 (1964) (doctrine of subrogation utilized to alter secured creditor priorities under Article 9). Courts have also been willing to alter established priorities on the basis of fraudulent transfer principles. See King v. Ionization Int'l, Inc., 825 F.2d 1180 (7th Cir.1987); Kulik v. Albers, Inc., 91 Nev. 134, 532 P.2d 603 (1975).

Here, there was evidence that would have supported jury findings presenting the following picture: PCA permitted the continued operation of the feedlot in anticipation of closing a sale with Streit rather than liquidating the business as it had previously planned. PCA was the source of all operational funds for Norman Company's feedlot operations, controlled payment of all of its obligations, and received the proceeds of all of its accounts receivable. PCA was informed each time that corn was ordered and never objected to any purchase. Moreover, prior to entry of Streit upon the scene it specifically approved each order. A PCA representative actively reviewed records that evidenced the amount of corn being delivered to Norman Company, and its representative was present at Norman Company on some occasions when Duggan Corporation delivered corn. In addition, Howard Norman showed Edmond Duggan the September 17 memorandum that indicated PCA's intent to permit Norman Company to purchase dry corn. Duggan knew that moneys to pay for corn deliveries were historically obtained by Norman Company from advances made by PCA under the loan to Norman Company. Given these circumstances, Duggan Corporation continued to deliver corn to the Norman Company feedlot. The corn was used to feed the cattle. The owners of the cattle were billed based on weight gain. The proceeds of the accounts receivable so generated were ultimately transferred to PCA and applied toward Norman Company's obligations to PCA.

In a situation where a secured creditor initiates or encourages transactions between the debtor and suppliers of goods or services, and benefits from the goods or services supplied to produce such debts, equitable principles require that the secured creditor compensate even an unsecured creditor to avoid being unjustly enriched. The equitable claim is at its strongest when the goods or services are necessary to preserve the security, as in *Producers Cotton Oil*. A secured creditor can protect itself from unjust enrichment claims by remaining uninvolved or by informing the proper parties of its intent not to pay for debts incurred in maintaining, enhancing, or making additions to secured collateral. Given the evidence concerning PCA's active role in creating a perception that the corn would be paid for, its failure to inform the parties otherwise, and the need for the corn to feed the cattle in order to produce accounts receivable subject to the PCA security interest, under appropriate instructions the jury could have found that the doctrine of unjust enrichment required that PCA compensate Duggan Corporation for the corn it delivered to the Norman Company feedlot.

III.

We next must address PCA's argument that the trial judge erred by not properly instructing the jury on its theory of the case. The court of appeals determined that the trial court did not err in this respect. We conclude that the jury instructions were inadequate and that the judgment entered on the jury verdict must be reversed.

A.

* * *

The following instruction on the theory of unjust enrichment was given to the jury:

> In order for the Plaintiff, Ed Duggan, Inc., to recover from the Defendant, Ninth District Production Credit Association, upon an implied contract to pay for goods, you must find all of the following have been proved: 1. The Plaintiff delivered corn to Norman Land and Livestock Company; 2. The Plaintiff did so without a specific agreement as to compensation, but with the reasonable expectation that it would be paid the reasonable value of the corn by the Defendant, Ninth District Production Credit Association; 3. The delivery of corn by Plaintiff: a. conferred a benefit on the Defendant, Ninth District Production Credit Association; and b. the Defendant, Ninth District Production Credit Association, appreciated or realized the benefit; and c. the Defendant, Ninth District Production Credit Association, accepted the benefit under such circumstances that it would be inequitable for the Defendant, Ninth District Production Credit

Association, to retain the benefit without payment of the reasonable value of the corn. 4. The reasonable value of the corn delivered by Plaintiff and used by Norman Land and Livestock Company resulting in benefit to Defendant, Ninth District Production Credit Association. If you find that any one or more of these propositions has not been proved by a preponderance of the evidence, then an implied contract has not been proven and you should answer question 4 on the Special Verdict "No". On the other hand, if you find that all of these propositions have been proved by a preponderance of the evidence, then an implied contract has been proven and you should answer question 4 on the Special Verdict "Yes".[1]

Jury Instruction No. 23. This instruction sets forth the elements of unjust enrichment as enunciated in *Cablevision* and *Dass v. Epplen*. However, it does not set forth standards by which the jury could determine whether it was inequitable for PCA to retain the benefit of Duggan Corporation's delivery of corn without paying for its reasonable value. Because of the special considerations involved when an unjust enrichment claim is asserted by an unsecured creditor against a creditor secured by a lien created under the UCC, we do not believe that the jury could fairly resolve this issue consistent with the law without further instructions from the court.

Nevertheless, the instructions tendered by PCA were properly rejected. PCA's tendered instructions suggest that a secured creditor's right to obtain the full benefit of its collateral is absolute.[2] In proper circumstances, however, an

---

[1]   The instruction was derived from the model jury instruction for a contract implied in fact, CJI-Civ.3d 30:31, and counsel for Duggan Corporation termed the claim one for an "implied contract," without specifying whether the contract was implied in fact or in law.   Paragraph 3 of the instruction requires that all the elements of an unjust enrichment claim be proven and therefore properly sets forth the elements of a claim for unjust enrichment, sometimes referred to as a contract implied in law. Paragraph 2 of the instruction, however, is appropriate only for a claim based on contract implied in fact and should not have been included. See Section III B, below.

[2]   PCA's tendered instructions stated in part:

      Under laws of the State of Colorado, it is not unjust enrichment for a secured creditor to receive the collateral or security described or covered by a financing statement and a security agreement. PCA's tendered Instruction No. 5. You are instructed that the Statutes of the State of Colorado in full force and effect at all times pertinent here provide that "the mere existence of a security interest or authority given to the debtor to dispose of or use collateral does not impose contract or tort liability upon the secured party for the debtor's acts or omissions." PCA's tendered Instruction No. 6. A creditor who delivers corn without a financing statement and security agreement is an unsecured creditor. A filed financing statement and security agreement gives a secured creditor prior rights to any corn delivered by an unsecured creditor. PCA's tendered Instruction No. 7. The Production Credit Association was a secured creditor

unsecured creditor may obtain compensation from a secured creditor under a claim for unjust enrichment. The distinction that must be drawn in these situations is that between permissible enrichment under Article 9 and unjust enrichment. Under Article 9 a secured creditor is ordinarily authorized to maintain its security interest in collateral and its position of priority without assuming responsibility for unsecured obligations of the debtor even if those obligations were incurred for goods or services that enhanced the value of the collateral--this is not unjust enrichment. On the other hand, if the secured creditor initiates or encourages transactions by which such obligations are incurred and derives a benefit from such transactions, the secured creditor may be held liable on an unjust enrichment claim. A jury cannot be presumed to understand the interrelation of the doctrine of unjust enrichment and the law of secured transactions and therefore must be apprised of how a seeming conflict between the two is to be resolved.

In keeping with the previously stated principles, we suggest that the following instruction on an inequitable retention of benefit by a secured creditor would have been appropriate under the evidence presented at the trial in this case: PCA is a secured creditor with rights in the accounts receivable and other personal property of Norman Company that ordinarily are superior to any rights of an unsecured creditor such as Duggan Corporation. It is not inequitable for a secured creditor to retain a benefit conferred by an unsecured creditor without compensating the unsecured creditor if the secured creditor does not initiate or encourage the transaction between the unsecured creditor and the debtor by which that benefit is conferred. However, when the benefit is provided under circumstances where the secured creditor initiates or encourages such transaction, it is inequitable for the secured creditor to retain the benefit without compensating the unsecured creditor. If you determine that Duggan Corporation conferred a benefit on PCA, you must apply this instruction in determining whether it was inequitable that PCA retain the benefit without compensating Duggan Corporation. Cf. *Producers Cotton Oil*, 242 Cal.Rptr. at 927 (discussed above).

B.

[P]aragraph 2 of Jury Instruction No. 23 erroneously included reliance as an element of a claim for unjust enrichment. The theory underlying the instruction as given was referred to generically as "implied contract" and contained elements of both a contract implied in fact and a contract implied in law. The instruction specifically required, as an element of a contract implied in law, that Duggan Corporation delivered corn to Norman Company "without a specific agreement as to compensation, but with the reasonable expectation that it would be paid the

under the laws of the State of Colorado and was legally entitled to the accounts receivable of [Norman Company]. [Duggan Corporation] is charged with such knowledge and in furnishing feed to [Norman Company], acted as an unsecured creditor.

PCA's tendered Instruction No. 9.

reasonable value of the corn by [PCA]." Jury Instruction No. 23. The elements of a claim for unjust enrichment are correctly set forth in paragraph 3 of that instruction. On retrial, the court should not include paragraph 2 of Jury Instruction No. 23 in instructing the jury on the elements of Duggan Corporation's claim for unjust enrichment.

C.

PCA also argues that the trial court erred in its instruction to the jury on the element of benefit. We address this argument because the issue may arise again on retrial.

The trial court instructed that [a] person confers a benefit upon another if he gives to the other possession of, or an interest in, personal property. He confers a benefit not only where he adds to the property of another, but also where he saves the other from expense or loss. The word "benefit", therefore, denotes any form of advantage. Jury Instruction No. 25. PCA argues that this instruction was given in error because it required the jury to find in favor of Duggan Corporation if it found that PCA received any sort of benefit. This argument mischaracterizes the instructions. "All of the court's instructions ... are to be read and considered as a whole in determining whether all the necessary law has been correctly stated to the jury." Montgomery Ward & Co. v. Kerns, 172 Colo. 59, 63, 470 P.2d 34, 36-37 (1970). Instruction 25 defines the term "benefit" as it is used in Instruction 23, and paragraph 3 of Instruction 23 clearly states that PCA must have "accepted the benefit under such circumstances that it would be inequitable for [PCA] to retain the benefit without payment of the reasonable value of the corn." The benefit in question, when the instructions are read together, was the benefit derived by PCA when corn was delivered. The corn permitted the feedlot to continue in operation and generated accounts receivable that were then automatically subject to the security interest of PCA. We find no error in Instruction 25 in the context of the evidence as presented and the instructions as given.

IV.

We are persuaded that in certain circumstances a secured creditor can be held liable to an unsecured creditor on the basis of unjust enrichment notwithstanding its secured status. Where a secured creditor is benefitted by a transaction between its debtor and an unsecured creditor that enhances the value of the secured collateral, and the secured creditor initiates or encourages the transaction, the secured creditor can be held liable to the unsecured creditor on the theory of unjust enrichment. The jury instructions given here, however, were not adequate to enable the jury to resolve the unjust enrichment issue in accordance with the applicable law. We therefore reverse the judgment of the court of appeals and return the case to that court with directions to reverse the judgment of the trial court and remand the case for a new trial.

Vollack, J., dissents, and Rovira, C.J., and Erickson, J., join in the dissent.

Justice Vollack dissenting:

The majority states that the central issue in this case is "[w]hether a creditor that holds a perfected security interest in collateral can be held liable to an unsecured creditor based on a theory of unjust enrichment for benefits that enhance the value of the collateral," and then observes that "[s]uch a dispute involves tension between the priority system established in Article 9 of the Uniform Commercial Code (U.C.C.) and equitable principles of unjust enrichment." Maj. op. I disagree because neither this issue, nor such a tension, is raised by the facts in this case. PCA's status as a secured creditor is not relevant to whether an express or implied contract exists between Duggan and PCA. Duggan is not claiming a priority or interest in collateral or proceeds held by PCA under its perfected security agreement with Norman. Instead, Duggan is claiming that, by its conduct, PCA has an obligation under an implied contract theory to pay Duggan the reasonable value of the corn that Duggan delivered to Norman.

I.

The cases cited by the majority, which have addressed the relationship between Article 9 of the U.C.C. and unjust enrichment, do not in my opinion apply to the facts in this case because those cases involved disputes over specific collateral or identified proceeds in which one of the parties had a security interest. See Producers Cotton Oil Co. v. Amstar Corp., 197 Cal.App.3d 638, 242 Cal.Rptr. 914 (1988); Borg-Warner Acceptance Corp. v. Valentine Assoc. Ltd., 192 Ga.App. 123, 384 S.E.2d 223 (1989). The present case does not involve a dispute over collateral or proceeds but, as stated above, is a dispute over whether PCA has an obligation to pay Duggan under an implied contract theory.

In *Producers Cotton Oil*, which the majority finds analogous to the facts in this case, Producers had a perfected security interest in the crops and proceeds of Borboa's farm operation. Borboa contracted to sell his crop to Amstar. When Producers was informed of the crop sale, they sent Amstar an assignment of crop proceeds. Amstar agreed to assign the proceeds to Producers, subject to deduction for the indebtedness of Borboa. *Producers Cotton Oil*, 242 Cal.Rptr. at 916.

In 1981, Amstar mistakenly paid the harvesting expenses for Borboa's crop. The 1981 crop yielded proceeds of $231,108.76. Amstar assigned $166,019.38 to Producers after deducting harvesting and other expenses. Producers demanded payment for these deductions. After Amstar refused to pay Producers, Producers brought an action against Amstar, claiming the deductions violated its security interest and constituted conversion of the proceeds. Id. at 917.

The dispute in *Producers Cotton Oil* concerned which party had the better right to the "proceeds" that were deducted by Amstar. Id. The court concluded that Producers had a valid security interest in the proceeds and that Amstar had a valid claim to the proceeds based on unjust enrichment. The court then had to determine which claim prevailed over the other. The court held that the unjust enrichment claim prevailed, but limited its decision to the particular facts of the case. Id. at 927.

The distinction between *Producers Cotton Oil* and the present case is apparent. In *Producers Cotton Oil*, the parties were disputing their rights to proceeds in which Producers had a secured interest, specifically, the amount that Amstar deducted from the crop proceeds. In the present case, no such dispute exists because Duggan's implied contract claim does not assert a right to any secured interest held by PCA under the security agreement with Norman.

In his complaint, Duggan did not assert any claim for relief based on a priority or interest in collateral or proceeds held by PCA. Moreover, Duggan did not contest PCA's position as a secured creditor in Norman's assets. Instead, Duggan based his claim for relief on PCA's conduct. Specifically, Duggan asserts that the PCA/Norman relationship was not an ordinary lender/debtor relationship because PCA had control of the feedlot's activities, including the ordering and delivery of corn.

In this case, without some dispute over a secured item, the fact that PCA was a secured creditor is not relevant to a determination of whether PCA is obligated to pay Duggan for the corn based on a theory of implied contract to avoid unjust enrichment. A secured creditor, like anyone else, can enter into an implied (or express) contract that creates an obligation to pay. As PCA stated in its closing argument, the issue in this case is "whether the Production Credit Association [PCA] somehow stepped in and made an agreement, took on an obligation that it never intended to take on."

II.

Duggan's claim for relief is one of contract. Thus, as the trial court instructed, contract law controls the disposition of the issues in this case, and the Uniform Commercial Code is not applicable. The trial court gave instruction No. 23, which in my opinion correctly stated the law applicable to the evidence and Duggan's asserted claim of implied contract. The case was submitted to the jury on special interrogatories as to express and implied contract.

In order to recover on a theory of implied contract to avoid unjust enrichment, Duggan had to prove, as provided in instruction No. 23, (1) that a benefit was conferred on the defendant by the plaintiff, (2) that the benefit was appreciated by the defendant, and (3) that the benefit was accepted by the defendant under such circumstances that it would be inequitable for it to be retained without payment of its value. Cablevision of Breckenridge, Inc. v. Tannhauser Condominium Assoc., 649 P.2d 1093, 1096-97 (Colo.1982). In the present case, the evidence clearly satisfies all three of these elements.

The jury could reasonably conclude that Duggan conferred a benefit on PCA and that PCA appreciated the benefit. PCA was informed each time that corn was ordered and never objected, and for a period of time specifically approved each order. A PCA representative was present at the feedlot on several occasions when corn was delivered. A PCA representative actively reviewed records that evidenced the amount of corn being delivered to Norman. PCA directed that the feedlot remain open in anticipation of a proposed sale.

The jury's verdict that it would be inequitable to retain the benefit without payment is supported by Norman's showing Duggan the September 17 memorandum that indicated PCA's intent to permit Norman to purchase dry corn. Also, PCA was the source of all operational funds for Norman's feedlot operations, controlled payments of all its obligations, and received the proceeds of all its accounts receivable. Norman was not permitted by PCA to retain or expend funds collected by the feedlot. Duggan knew that payment for corn deliveries to Norman historically came from advances made by PCA to Norman.

III.

The majority's new standard and requirement that an additional instruction be given to inform the jury of the interrelation of the doctrine of unjust enrichment and Article 9 of the U.C.C. is misplaced. The instructions given by the trial court were proper and do not need to be supplemented by additional instructions to provide the jury with an understanding of the law of implied contract. The jury, in applying the evidence to the instructions of law, concluded that Duggan was entitled to damages.

The fact that PCA is a secured creditor would only be relevant if Duggan were claiming that PCA's priority was junior to his claim of an implied contract to avoid unjust enrichment. In such a case, the court would have to decide whether PCA's security interest or Duggan's contract claim controls. The majority does not identify the security, if any, in which Duggan is claiming an interest. Without such a dispute, Article 9 of the U.C.C. is not applicable. I agree with the trial court and the court of appeals that the instructions should not include any reference to PCA's U.C.C. interest. I would affirm the jury verdict.

I am authorized to say that Chief Justice ROVIRA and Justice ERICKSON join in this dissent.

2. By Agreement

a.　　Participations

BANK PARTICIPATION AGREEMENT

_____19____

_____
(Name of Bank)

_____
(Address)

Gentlemen:

We have entered or propose to enter into an agreement with _____ (the "Company") substantially in the form annexed hereto as Exhibit A (the "Agreement") setting forth the terms and conditions governing loans by us to the Company measured by the collateral therein described. The loans will be charged to an open account on our books (the "loan account") in the name of the Company and we will not take notes to evidence the loans. We are pleased to confirm our willingness to sell to you, on a continuing basis, an undivided fractional participation interest in all such loans. The amount of your participation in all such loans (your "Participation") at any time and from time to time shall be an amount equal to ____% of the aggregate principal balance of all such loans outstanding as of the date of determination of the amount of your Participation, and such applicable percentage is hereinafter referred to as the "Participation Percentage". Our sale to you of a participation in such loans is subject to the following terms and conditions:

1. Your initial Participation shall be payable by you to us simultaneously with our making of the initial loan to the Company pursuant to the Agreement or upon your acceptance hereof, whichever is later. Upon our receipt of payment from you of the amount of your Participation we shall issue to you a Participation Certificate in the form annexed hereto as evidence of your Participation.

2. Our loans to the Company outstanding may increase or decrease from time to time through our disbursement of additional loans, collection of proceeds of collateral and through repayments on the loans, and the amount of your Participation may fluctuate, provided that the amount of your Participation will not exceed the Participation Percentage. In order to minimize the transfer of funds between us, however, your Participation shall be computed weekly rather than each time the loan balances fluctuate and shall be adjusted upward or downward on the basis of the balances owing in the loan

account as of the close of business of the preceding week. Each week we will mail to you a participation report showing the amount of all loans to the Company outstanding as of the date of such report and the amount of your Participation therein. With each such report we shall, in the event the amount of your Participation shown in such report differs from the amount shown in the Participation Certificate then held by you, issue to you a new Participation Certificate in an amount equal to your Participation as shown in such participation report. Each Participation Certificate, as issued, shall replace and supersede in all respects all Participation Certificates previously issued to you. If the amount of your Participation shown in any such new Participation Certificate is more than that shown in the Participation Certificate being replaced thereby, you will forthwith remit to us an amount equal to the increase, and conversely, if the amount of your Participation shown in such new Participation Certificate is less than the amount shown in the Participation Certificate being replaced, we will forthwith remit to you an amount equal to such decrease. We shall mark our books and records to show at all times the amount of your Participation. You shall not have the right to transfer all or any part of your Participation to others without our prior written approval.

3. The delivery to you of any Participation Certificate shall constitute a sale and assignment to you of a Participation in the loans to the Company to the extent of the amount stated in such Certificate. No payment by you to us on account of any such Participation shall evidence a loan by you to us. Such Participation shall entitle you only to participate in the loans made by us to the Company to the extent of the Participation Percentage, in all principal payments received by us in reduction of the amounts owing on such loans, all recoveries received by us pursuant to the Agreement, all proceeds of collection on collateral for the loans and in all payments of interest to the extent hereinafter set forth.

4. If we have received all interest, computed at the rate specified and in accordance with the Agreement, on our loans for the previous month, we shall also pay to you, promptly after the same has been col lected by us, an amount computed at the rate of ___% per annum, based on a year of twelve months of 30 days each, on the amount of the average daily balance of your Participation during the previous month, provided, however, that if the amount of the interest charges collected by us from the Company should in crease or decrease as a result of any provision in the Agreement relating to the "prime rate" of banks, the aforesaid percentage to be used in computing your share of such interest shall be increased or decreased by the percentage per annum corresponding to the percentage per annum of such increase or decrease. If the interest collected by us on the loans for any month is less than the amount that should have been collected in accordance with the terms of the Agreement, we will share with you the interest, computed as aforesaid, then and thereafter collected for such month in the same ratio as would have applied if there had been no deficiency in the amount of interest so collected for such period. If because of any minimum income provision of the Agreement we should collect an amount in excess of the amount of interest that would be payable if

based solely on the amount of loans outstanding, we shall retain such excess as ad ditional compensation for servicing the loans.

5. We shall have the exclusive right to carry out the provisions of the Agreement, to enter into amendments thereto, to enforce and collect the loans made thereunder, to grant or withhold waivers, consents and approvals, to release collateral, and to exercise and enforce all rights and privileges accruing to us by reason of the Agreement and any other agreements, security, guaranties or claims given to us in connection with the loans, all in our name alone and in accordance with our sole discretion and the exercise of our business judgment. We shall handle all transactions relating to the loans and any collateral in accordance with our usual practices with respect to loans of this type and shall adhere to the same standards of conduct as would be the case if there were no participation in such loans. We have made no warranties or representations, express or implied, nor do we assume any liability to you with respect to the solvency or financial worth of the Company or of the obligors on any indebtedness constituting collateral or under any instrument of guaranty, or with respect to the validity, enforceability, value or collectibility of any of the loans or any collateral, any guaranties or other security for the loans or of the title of the Company to or authority to transfer collateral. We shall not be liable to you for any action of, or failure to act or mistake on the part of any of our agents, officers, employees or attorneys with respect to any transactions relating to the loans, provided we have acted in good faith and have not been guilty of any willful misconduct. With out limiting any of the foregoing, you hereby expressly confirm your understanding that we need not require the Company to remit to us all proceeds of collateral for the loans.

6. All ordinary overhead costs and expenses incurred by us in administering the loans shall be borne exclusively by us, but any costs, expenses, fees or disbursements incurred by outside agencies or attorneys retained by us to enforce payment or to realize on collateral shall be borne by you and by us pro rata in accordance with the ratio that the Participation Percentage in effect at the date the same are incurred bears to the total loans then outstanding. In the event that either of us should be sued or threatened with suit by any receiver, trustee in bankruptcy or similar official on account of any alleged preference or voidable transfer alleged tohave been received by either of us as the result of any transaction in respect of which you shall have participated with us hereunder, or in the event that any action, claim or demand of any kind shall be asserted against either of us, directly or indirectly, relating to such transactions, then, in any such event, any moneys paid in satisfaction or compromise of such suit, claim, action or demand and any expenses, costs and attorneys' fees paid or incurred in connection therewith, as well as any costs or expenses which you or we may incur in enforcing, maintaining or preserving our rights under the Agreement or which may be incurred in enforcing, protecting or realizing on collateral (but not any expense of ordinary overhead of either party) shall be borne pro rata by each of us in accordance with the ratio that the Participation Percentage

in effect at the date such costs or expenses are incurred bears to the total loans then outstanding.

7. This participation agreement shall continue in full force and effect until the anniversary date of the Agreement and shall automatically be extended from anniversary date to anniversary date in each succeeding year unless sooner terminated as hereinafter provided. As used herein the term "anniversary date" shall have the same meaning as defined in the Agreement. You shall have the right to terminate this participation agreement as of any anniversary date by giving us at least 90 days prior written notice of your intention to so terminate. In such event, this participation agreement shall terminate on such anniversary date but termination shall not affect our respective rights or obligations hereunder incurred prior to the effective date of termination, provided, however, that if we so elect, we may as of such date pay you the full amount of your Participation, together with interest computed thereon as provided above. If we elect not to pay you your Participation as aforesaid, we shall proceed to enforce repayment of the loans outstanding in accordance with our sole discretion and exercise of our business judgment, it being understood and agreed that we may continue to remit to the Company portions of collections of proceeds of collateral from time to time if we deem it advisable to do so to effect an orderly liquidation of the loans.

If the foregoing is in accordance with your understanding, would you kindly sign and return to us one of the enclosed copies of this letter.

Very truly yours,

C.I.T. CORPORATION

By _____

(Title)

READ AND AGREED:

_____

(Name of Bank)

By _____

(Title)

NONNEGOTIABLE
LOAN PARTICIPATION CERTIFICATE

No. _____

C.l.T. Corporation hereby certifies that

(the Bank) has acquired and is the owner of an undivided participating share, to the extent of $, in all loans made and to be made by C.l.T. Corporation to

(the Company) pursuant to an agreement between C.l.T. Corporation and the Company mentioned in the Participation Agreement referred to below.

This Certificate is issued pursuant to and subject to the terms, conditions and provisions of a certain Participation Agreement between the Bank and C.l.T. Corporation dated   , 19   , and any amendments thereof. This Participation Certificate supersedes and replaces all Participation Certificates heretofore issued by C.l.T. Corporation to the Bank pursuant to the Participatlon Agreement.

This Certificate is not an acknowledgement of indebtedness and may not be transferred or assigned either in whole or in part without the prior written consent of C.l.T. Corporation.

C.l.T. CORPORATION

Dated   By

b.   **Subordination**

Williams v. First National Bank & Trust Co.
Supreme Court of Oklahoma, 1971
482 P.2d 595

McInerney, Justice.   Plaintiff in Error, J. D. Williams, as vendor, and Defendant in Error, First National Bank and Trust Company of Vinita, as lender, each extended credit to one Goad (not a party to this appeal), and each took a security interest in certain (identical) property owned by Goad.   Williams then perfected his security interest ahead of the Bank by filing his financing statement, as required by the Uniform Commercial Code, 12A O.S.1961, §§9--302, 9--401(1)(c), before the Bank did.   Goad thereafter went bankrupt with the bulk of the two loans still outstanding, and both the Bank and Williams brought suits against Goad for personal judgments against him and for foreclosure on the two mortgages, both creditors further asserting the superiority of their own mortgages over that of the other's.   The trial court, sitting without a jury, allowed the prayed-for judgments and foreclosures against Goad.   However, notwithstanding Williams' earlier filing, the trial court held the Bank's mortgage senior to Williams' on the basis of a verbal agreement between the Bank and Williams, previous to their actually making the loans herein, to the effect that the Bank's mortgage was to be prior to Williams'.   Since the value of Goad's pledged chattels was insufficient to satisfy both mortgages, Williams thereupon brought this appeal.
        * * *

There appears to be no real doubt but that in the absence of the verbal agreement, Williams' mortgage, having been filed (and thereby perfected) first, would be entitled to priority over the Bank's. 12A O.S.1961, §9--312(5)(a).

The question dispositive of this appeal, as we understand the parties' briefs, is the effect of the prior verbal agreement between the Bank and Williams in view of 12A O.S.1961, §9--316, which provides: "9--316.   Priority Subject to Subordination.   Nothing in this Article prevents subordination by agreement by any person entitled to priority."   "Agreement" is defined in 12A O.S.1961, §1--201(3), as:

> the bargain of the parties in fact as found in their language or by implication from other circumstances including course of dealing or usage of trade or course of performance as provided in this Act (Sections 1--205 and 2-- 208).   Whether an agreement has legal consequences is determined by the provisions of this Act, if applicable; otherwise by the law of contracts (Section 1--103).   (Compare "Contract".)

The Oklahoma Comment to this Section notes that this State had no previous statutory equivalent, and declares that "The term as defined includes all agreements, whether legally enforceable or not."   An "agreement" therefore appears to be distinct from a "contract."

As quoted above, this §1--201(3) itself refers to §§1--205 and 2--208. We find the general Comment to §1--205(1) to be of particular help here:

> 1. This Act rejects both the "lay-dictionary" and the "conveyancer's" reading of a commercial agreement. Instead the meaning of the agreement of the parties is to be determined by the language used by them and by their action, read and interpreted in the light of commercial practices and other surrounding circumstances * * *

It would therefore appear that a subordination 'agreement' as envisioned by §9--316 may be informal, and need not rise to the full dignity of a contract; and being satisfied that the trial court's implied finding of the existence of such an agreement herein is supported by competent evidence, we concur in the trial court's judgment on the legal effect and consequences thereof.
        * * *

We therefore hold that subordination agreements under 12A O.S.1961, §9--316, may be parol; and deciding that, we find no further basis for reversing the trial court's judgment.

Affirmed.

ITT Diversified Credit Corp. v. First City Capital Corp.
Supreme Court of Texas, 1987
737 S.W.2d 803

Gonzalez, Justice. This is a case of first impression concerning the effect of a subordination agreement made between the first and third lienholders on the priority status of a second lienholder. The trial court gave the second lienholder priority over the first and third lienholders. The court of appeals affirmed the judgment of the trial court. We reverse and remand.

First City National Bank (the Bank) acquired a first lien security interest on personal property owned by Sisco Enterprises. First City Capital Corporation (FCCC) obtained a second lien and ITT Diversified Corporation (ITT) obtained a third lien on the same assets.

In order for ITT to lend money to Sisco Enterprises, the Bank executed a subordination agreement to ITT, in which the Bank subordinated its interest in certain assets of the debtor to the interest of ITT. Thereafter, ITT foreclosed on these same assets. FCCC claimed the proceeds of the sale and when it was not paid, filed suit alleging that its security interest was superior to ITT's interest. The trial court held that the subordination agreement between the Bank and ITT did not give ITT priority over the interest possessed by FCCC. The trial court rendered judgment that FCCC recover from ITT the proceeds from the sale of the assets in question, plus interest and costs, and the court of appeals affirmed. ITT asserts that the trial court and the court of appeals erred in holding that the subordination agreement did not allow ITT to succeed to the interest of the Bank.

The Texas Business & Commerce Code provides that nothing in article 9 prevents subordination by agreement by any person entitled to priority. Tex.Bus. & Com.Code Ann. §9.316 (Vernon Supp. 1987). Section 1.102 of the Code specifically allows provisions of the Code to be varied by agreement. Tex.Bus. & Com.Code Ann. §1.102(c) (Vernon 1968). Moreover, a subordination agreement is nothing more than a contractual modification of lien priorities and must be construed according to the expressed intention of the parties and its terms.

The court of appeals relied on McConnell v. Mortgage Inv. Co. of El Paso, 292 S.W.2d 636, 638 (Tex.Civ.App.--El Paso 1955), aff'd, 157 Tex. 572, 305 S.W.2d 280 (1957). *McConnell* is inapplicable because it dealt exclusively with the priorities between a deed of trust, a vendor's lien, and a mechanic's and a materialman's lien. In *McConnell*, we specifically noted that the litigation involved the priority of liens arising from a real estate transaction. In a non-real property situation, the third lienholder should be able to succeed to that part of the interest that was subordinated by the first lienholder, so long as the second lienholder is neither burdened nor benefitted by the subordination agreement. For example, A, B and C have claims against the debtor which are entitled to priority in alphabetical order. "A" subordinates his claim to "C." After foreclosure of the secured interest, the resulting fund is insufficient to satisfy all three claims. The proper distribution of the fund is as follows.

1. Set aside from the fund the amount of "A" 's claim.
2. Out of the money set aside, pay "C" the amount of its claim, pay "A" to the extent of any balance remaining after "C" 's claim is satisfied.
3. Pay "B" the amount of the fund remaining after "A" 's claim has been set aside.
4. If any balance remains in the fund after "A" 's claim has been set aside and "B" 's claim has been satisfied, distribute the balance to "C" and "A".

See Gilmore, Security Interests in Personal Property §39.1 at 1021 (1965).

Thus, "C", by virtue of the subordination agreement, is paid first, but only to the amount of "A" 's claim, to which "B" was in any event junior. "B" receives what it had expected to receive, the fund less "A" 's prior claim. If "A" 's claim is smaller than "C" 's, "C" will collect the balance of its claim, in its own right, only after "B" has been paid in full. "A", the subordinator, receives nothing until "B" and "C" have been paid except to the extent that its claim, entitled to first priority, exceeds the amount of "C" 's claim, which, under its agreement, is to be first paid.

The trial court should set aside from the fund the amount of the Bank's claim and out of this amount, pay ITT the amount of its claim. Then, the trial court should allocate to the Bank any balance remaining after ITT's claim is satisfied, and then allocate to FCCC the amount of the fund remaining after the Bank's claim has been set aside. If any balance remains in the fund after the Bank's claim has been set aside and FCCC's claim has been satisfied, the court should distribute the balance to ITT and then to the Bank.   Thus, ITT, by virtue of the subordination agreement, is paid first but only to the amount of the Bank's claim, to which FCCC was in any event junior. FCCC will receive what it expected to receive, the fund less the Bank's prior claim.

The judgment of the court of appeals is reversed and this cause is remanded to the trial court for rendition of judgment consistent with this opinion.

Problems

1. What exactly is the meaning of the court's conclusion in *Williams* that a subordination agreement "need not rise to the full dignity of a contract"?   Please square this conclusion with the opinion of the court in *Equitable Bank v. Ford Motor Co.*, 138 F.R.D. 455 (D. Md. 1990), that "it takes more than wishful thinking to make [a subordination] agreement. What there must be is a bargain, that is, some conduct on the part of the party sought to be charged from which a reasonable trier of fact could conclude that it in fact agreed to subordinate." Id. at 457.

    a. In the case *In re Bishop*, 52 B.R. 470 (Bankr. N.D. Ala. 1985), the court pointed out that although the courts are reluctant to do so, they can invoke estoppel to reverse prioirities even in the absence of a subordination agreement between the creditors. Id. at 474. Please square this opinion with that of the court in *Equitable Bank* that a subordination agreement requires a bargain.

    b. In *Folkers v. Britt*, 457 N.W.2d 578 (Iowa 1990), a junior secured party tried to reverse priorities by agruing, alternatively, subordination by agreement, estoppel, *and* waiver. Waiver and estoppel are alike in not requiring a bargain. Are waiver and estoppel any different with respect to reversing priorities?

2. Suppose that Ariticle 9 gives A's security interest priority over the security interest that B would acquire in lending to the debtor, D. To encourage B to lend, A decides to subordinate.

    a. Who must make the agreement?

    b. Can A give up some priority but not all?

    c. What must be said?

    d. Must the subordination agreement satisfy the 9-203(1) requirements of form or substance?

    e. Is a financing statement necessary for an effective subordination agreement?

    f. Assuming that an effective subordination agreement is created between A and B, is the effect that A's interest becomes unperfected?

3.   Suppose that Bank1 and Bank2 have security interests in the same collateral. Both of the secured parties mistakenly assume that Bank2 has priority. Article 9 actually gives priority fully to Bank1. Bank2 agrees to *limited* subordination of its mistaken priority. Is Bank2 entitled to priority as to the balance?

4.   A and B have interests in the same collateral. A, who is entitled to priority, subordinates her claim completely to that of B. Z also has an interest in the same collateral. Z's interest is junior ro A's but is senior to B's. The claims of A, B, and Z are $10,000 each. The collateral produces $22,000 (net after expenses of disposition). How should the proceeds be distributed?

5.   Suppose that A fully subordinates to both B and Z and the collateral produces only $17,000. How is priority decided between B and Z?

6.   What is the effect of a secured party subordinating to an unsecured creditor?

□□□□□□

SUBORDINATION AGREEMENT

THIS SUBORDINATION AGREEMENT ("Agreement") is made and entered into by and between the undersigned, _____ _____, having an address at _____ _____ and Financial Corporation ("Financial"), having its principal offices in Chicago, Illinois. Capitalized terms used herein which are not defined herein are used herein as such terms are defined in the Accounts Financing Agreement [Security Agreement] dated as of _____ ____, 19__, by and between Financial [and] _____ ("Debtor "), and Rider No. 1, dated as of _____, 1989 by and between Financial and the Borrower [and that certain letter re: Inventory dated as of   , 19] (collectively, the "Loan Agreement").

<u>WITNESSETH</u>:

WHEREAS, the undersigned is financially interested in the Borrower, in that Debtor is now indebted to the undersigned, pursuant to those certain promissory notes dated _____ __, 19__ in the total amount of _____ Dollars ($_____) (which promissory notes, together with any instrument(s) which may hereafter be substituted therefor under the terms of any agreement between Debtor and the undersigned, are hereinafter referred to as the "Notes").

WHEREAS, Debtor will be indebted to Financial as a result of loans by Financial to Debtor pursuant to the Loan Agreement; and

WHEREAS, the undersigned acknowledges that the loans or other extensions of any financial accommodation or credit to Debtor by Financial is of value to the undersigned;

<u>AGREEMENT</u>

NOW, THEREFORE, for good and valuable consideration, receipt of which is hereby acknowledged by the undersigned, and in order to induce Financial, at its option, now or from time to time hereafter, to make loans or extend credit or any other financial accommodation to or for the benefit of Debtor; or to grant such renewals or extensions thereof as Financial may deem advisable; and to better secure Financial in respect of the foregoing, the undersigned hereby agrees with Financial as hereinafter set forth.

As used herein the following terms shall have the meanings set forth below:

"Bankruptcy Code" shall mean Title 11 of the United States Code (11 U.S.C. §101 et. seq.) or any replacement or supplemental federal statute dealing with the bankruptcy of debtors.

"Borrower" shall mean Debtor and any successor or assign of Debtor, including, without limitation, a receiver, trustee or debtor-in-possession of or for Debtor.

"Permitted Payments" shall mean   .[1]

"Senior Obligations" shall mean the Obligations (as defined in the Loan Agreement) and all interest and costs of enforcement or preservation and protection of collateral which may at any time accrue with respect to the Obligations or which would accrue but for the operation of any provision or doctrine with respect to the Bankruptcy Code and any obligations of, advances made to or claims against Borrower pursuant to or with respect to any financing or extension of credit provided to Borrower by Financial pursuant to Section 363 or 364 of the Bankruptcy Code.

"Subordinated Debt" shall mean any principal, interest, fees or other monies which may now or hereafter be owing by Borrower to the undersigned or be owing by any other person, firm, partnership or corporation to the undersigned for the benefit of Borrower (whether such amounts represent principal or interest, or obligations which are

---

[1]   This term is highly negotiated.

due or not due, direct or indirect, absolute or contingent) including, without limitation, the Notes and any negotiable instruments evidencing such amounts.

1.   Standby; Subordination; Subrogation.   The payment and performance of the Subordinated Debt is hereby subordinated to the Senior Obligations and [except for Permitted Payments,] the undersigned will not ask, demand, sue for, take or receive from Borrower by setoff or in any other manner, the whole or any part of the Subordinated Debt which may now or hereafter be owing by Borrower and will not take any negotiable instruments evidencing such amounts, nor any security (including guaranties and third party credit support) for any of the foregoing, unless and until all such Senior Obligations of Borrower whether now existing or hereafter arising directly between Borrower and Financial, and whether such Senior Obligations arise after the Borrower or the Borrower's estate becomes the subject of proceedings under the Bankruptcy Code or whether such Senior Obligations are acquired outright, conditionally or as collateral security from another by Financial, shall have been fully paid and satisfied with interest, including interest on any loans or advances made to the Borrower after the Borrower or the Borrower's estate becomes the subject of proceedings under the Bankruptcy Code and all commitments under the Loan Agreement have expired or been terminated. All liens and security interests of the undersigned, whether now or hereafter arising and howsoever existing, in any assets of Borrower or any assets securing any of the Senior Obligations shall be and hereby are subordinated to the rights and interests of Financial in those assets; the undersigned shall have no right to possession of any such assets or to foreclose upon any such assets, whether by judicial action or otherwise, unless and until all of the Senior Obligations shall have been fully paid and satisfied and all commitments under the Loan Agreement have expired or been terminated. The undersigned also hereby agrees that, regardless of whether any of the Senior Obligations are secured or unsecured, Financial shall be subrogated for the undersigned with respect to the undersigned's claims against Borrower and the undersigned's rights, liens and security interests, if any, in any of Borrower's assets and the proceeds thereof until all of the Senior Obligations have been fully paid and satisfied and all commitments under the Loan Agreement have expired or been terminated. In the event, at the request of Borrower, Financial releases any of its security for any of the Senior Obligations which constitutes part or all of the security for the Subordinated Debt, the undersigned shall thereupon execute and deliver to Borrower such termination statements and releases as the Borrower shall reasonably request to release the undersigned's security interest in or lien against such property of Borrower. The undersigned acknowledges and agrees that, to the extent the terms and provisions of either this Agreement or the Loan Agreement are inconsistent with the Notes, the Notes shall be deemed to be subject to the Loan Agreement and this Agreement. [Borrower may pay to the undersigned, and the undersigned may accept from Borrower, Permitted Payments.]

2. Enforcement Rights. The undersigned, prior to the payment in full of the Senior Obligations and the termination of all financing arrangements between Borrower and Financial, shall have no right to enforce any claim with respect to the

Subordinated Debt, or otherwise to take any action against Borrower or Borrower's property without the prior written consent of Financial.

3. <u>Subordinated Debt Owed Only to the Undersigned</u>. The undersigned warrants and represents that the undersigned has not previously assigned any interest in the Subordinated Debt or any security interest in connection therewith, that no other person, firm or corporation owns an interest in the Subordinated Debt or security therefor other than the undersigned (whether as joint holders of the Subordinated Debt, participants or otherwise) and that the entire Subordinated Debt is owing only to the undersigned and covenants that the entire Subordinated Debt shall continue to be owing only to the undersigned and all security therefor shall continue to be held solely for the benefit of the undersigned unless assigned in accordance with the terms of this Agreement.

4. <u>Lender Priority</u>. In the event of any distribution, division, or application, partial or complete, voluntary or involuntary, by operation of law or otherwise, of all or any part of the assets of Borrower or the proceeds thereof to the creditors of Borrower or readjustment of the Senior Obligations and Subordinated Debt of Borrower, whether by reason of liquidation, bankruptcy, arrangement, receivership, assignment for the benefit of creditors or any other action or proceeding involving the readjustment of all or any part of the Senior Obligations or the Subordinated Debt, or the application of the assets of Borrower to the payment or liquidation thereof, or upon the dissolution or other winding up of Borrower's business, or upon the sale of all or substantially all of Borrower's assets, then, and in any such event, (i) Financial shall be entitled to receive payment in full of any and all of the Senior Obligations then owing prior to the payment of all or any part of the Subordinated Debt, and (ii) any payment or distribution of any kind or character, whether in cash, securities or other property, which shall be payable or deliverable upon or with respect to any or all of the Subordinated Debt shall be paid or delivered directly to Financial for application on any of the Senior Obligations, due or not due, until such Senior Obligations shall have first been fully paid and satisfied.

5. <u>Payments Received by the Undersigned</u>. Should any payment or distribution or security or instrument or proceeds thereof be received by the undersigned upon or with respect to the Subordinated Debt or any other obligations of Borrower to the undersigned prior to the satisfaction of all of the Senior Obligations and termination of all financing arrangements between Borrower and Financial, the undersigned shall receive and hold the same in trust, as trustee, for the benefit of Financial, and shall forthwith deliver the same to Financial, in precisely the form received (except for the endorsement or assignment of the undersigned where necessary), for application on any of the Senior Obligations, due or not due, and, until so delivered, the same shall be held in trust by the undersigned as the property of Financial. In the event of the failure of the undersigned to make any such endorsement or assignment to Financial, Financial, or any of its officers or employees, is hereby irrevocably authorized to make the same.

6. <u>Instrument Legend</u>. Any instrument evidencing any of the Subordinated Debt (including, without limitation, the Notes), or any portion thereof, will, on the date hereof or promptly hereafter, be inscribed with a legend conspicuously indicating

that payment thereof is subordinated to the claims of Financial pursuant to the terms of this Agreement, and (i) a copy thereof will be delivered to Financial on the date hereof, and (ii) the original of any such instrument will be immediately delivered to Financial upon request therefor by Financial after the occurrence of an Event of Default (as defined in the Loan Agreement) or if Financial at any time determines, in its sole discretion, that the financial condition of the undersigned is or becomes such that Financial wishes to have such possession to protect Financial' interest hereunder. Any instrument evidencing any of the Subordinated Debt, or any portion thereof, which is hereafter executed by Borrower, will, on the date thereof, be inscribed with the aforesaid legend and a copy thereof will be delivered to Financial on the date of its execution or within five (5) business days thereafter and the original thereof will be delivered as and when described hereinabove.[1]

7. <u>Reimbursements for Expenses and Borrowings from Borrower; Assignment of Claims</u>. The undersigned agrees that until the Senior Obligations have been paid in full and satisfied and all financing arrangements between Borrower and Financial have been terminated, the undersigned will not, directly or indirectly, accept or receive the benefit of any remuneration or reimbursement for expenses from or on behalf of Borrower and will not assign or transfer to others any claim the undersigned has or may have against Borrower, unless such assignment or transfer is made expressly subject to this Agreement.

8. <u>Continuing Nature of Subordination</u>. This Agreement shall be effective and may not be terminated or otherwise revoked by the undersigned until the Senior Obligations shall have been fully discharged and all commitments under the Loan Agreement have been terminated. In the event the undersigned shall have any right under applicable law otherwise to terminate or revoke this Agreement which right cannot be waived, such termination or revocation shall not be effective until written notice of such termination or revocation, signed by the undersigned, is actually received by Financial's officer responsible for such matters. In the absence of the circumstances described in the immediately preceding sentence, this is a continuing agreement of subordination and Financial may continue, at any time and without notice to the undersigned, to extend credit or other financial accommodations and loan monies to or for the benefit of Borrower on the faith hereof. Any termination or revocation described hereinabove shall not affect this Agreement in relation to (a) any of the Senior Obligations which arose prior to receipt thereof, (b) any of the Senior Obligations which represent interest on Senior Obligations, or (c) any of the Senior Obligations created after receipt thereof, if such Obligations were incurred either through extensions of credit by Financial pursuant to Financial' financing arrangements with Borrower in an aggregate outstanding amount not to exceed the Maximum Credit, and/or for the purpose of preserving or protecting any collateral (including, but not limited to, all protective advances, costs, expenses) and/or for attorneys' and paralegals' fees, whensoever made, advanced or incurred by Financial in connection with the Senior Obligations. If, in reliance on this Agreement, Financial makes loans or other advances to or for the benefit of Borrower or takes other action under the Loan Agreement after such aforesaid termination or revocation by the undersigned but

---

[1]   The subordinated debt should have a proper legend.

prior to the receipt by Financial of said written notice as set forth above, the rights of Financial shall be the same as if such termination or revocation had not occurred; and, in any event, no obligation of the undersigned hereunder shall be affected pursuant to this Section 8 by the death, incapacity or written revocation of the undersigned or any other subordinated party, pledgor, endorser, or guarantor, if any.

9. Additional Agreements Between Financial and Borrower. Financial, at any time and from time to time, either before or after any such aforesaid notice of termination or revocation, may enter into such agreement or agreements with Borrower as Financial may deem proper, extending the time of payment of or renewing or otherwise altering the terms of all or any of the Senior Obligations or affecting the security underlying any or all of the Senior Obligations, and may exchange, sell, release, surrender or otherwise deal with any such security, without in any way thereby impairing or affecting this Agreement.

10. Undersigned's Waivers. All of the Senior Obligations shall be deemed to have been made or incurred in reliance upon this Agreement. The undersigned expressly waives all notice of the acceptance by Financial of the subordination and other provisions of this Agreement and all other notices not specifically required pursuant to the terms of this Agreement whatsoever, and the undersigned expressly waives reliance by Financial upon the subordination and other agreements as herein provided. The undersigned agrees that Financial has made no warranties or representations with respect to the due execution, legality, validity, completeness or enforceability of the Loan Agreement, or the collectibility of the Senior Obligations, that Financial shall be entitled to manage and supervise its loans, extensions of credit or other financial accommodations to Borrower in accordance with applicable law and Financial's usual practices, modified from time to time as Financial deems appropriate under the circumstances, without regard to the existence of any rights that the undersigned may now or hereafter have in or to any of the assets of Borrower, and that Financial shall have no liability to the undersigned for, and waives any claim which the undersigned may now or hereafter have against, Financial arising out of any and all actions which Financial, in good faith, takes or omits to take (including, without limitation, actions with respect to the creation, perfection or continuation of liens or security interests in the Collateral (as defined in the Loan Agreement) and other security for the Senior Obligations, actions with respect to the occurrence of an Event of Default, actions with respect to the foreclosure upon, sale, release, or depreciation of, or failure to realize upon, any of the Collateral and actions with respect to the collection of any claim for all or any part of the Senior Obligations from any account debtor, guarantor or any other party) with respect to the Loan Agreement or any other agreement related thereto or to the collection of the Senior Obligations or the valuation, use, protection or release of the Collateral and/or other security for the Senior Obligations.

11. Bankruptcy Issues. If Borrower or Borrower's estate becomes the subject of proceedings under the Bankruptcy Code and if Financial desires to permit the use of cash collateral or to provide financing to Borrower under either Section 363 or Section 364 of the Bankruptcy Code, the undersigned agrees that adequate notice of such

financing to the undersigned shall have been provided if the undersigned received notice two (2) business days prior to the entry of any order approving such cash collateral usage or financing. Notice of a proposed financing or use of cash collateral shall be deemed given upon the sending of such notice by telegraph, telecopy or hand delivery to the undersigned at the address indicated above. All allocations of payments between Financial and the undersigned shall, subject to any court order, continue to be made after the filing of a petition under the Bankruptcy Code on the same basis that the payments were to be allocated prior to the date of such filing. In the event that the undersigned has or at any time acquires any security for the Subordinated Debt, the undersigned agrees not to assert any right it may have to "adequate protection" of its interest in such security in any bankruptcy proceeding and agrees that it will not seek to have the automatic stay lifted with respect to such security, without the prior written consent of Financial. The undersigned waives any claim or defense the undersigned may now or hereafter have arising out of the election by Financial, in any proceeding instituted under Chapter 11 of the Bankruptcy Code, of the application of Section 1111(b)(2) of the Bankruptcy Code, and/or any borrowing or grant of a security interest under Section 364 of the Bankruptcy Code by Borrower, as debtor-in-possession. To the extent that Financial receives payments on, or proceeds of collateral for, the Senior Obligations which are subsequently invalidated, declared to be fraudulent or preferential, set aside and/or required to be repaid to a trustee, receiver or any other party under any bankruptcy law, state or federal law, common law, or equitable cause, then, to the extent of such payment or proceeds received, the Senior Obligations, or part thereof, intended to be satisfied shall be revived and continue in full force and effect as if such payments or proceeds had not been received by Financial.

12. Financial's Waivers. No waiver shall be deemed to be made by Financial of its rights hereunder, unless the same shall be in writing signed on behalf of Financial and each waiver, if any, shall be a waiver only with respect to the specific instance involved and shall in no way impair the rights of Financial or the obligations of the undersigned to Financial in any other respect at any other time.

13. Information Concerning Financial Condition of Borrower. The undersigned hereby assumes responsibility for keeping itself informed of the financial condition of Borrower, any and all endorsers and any and all guarantors of the Senior Obligations and of all other circumstances bearing upon the risk of nonpayment of the Senior Obligations and/or Subordinated Debt that diligent inquiry would reveal, and the undersigned hereby agrees that Financial shall have no duty to advise the undersigned of information known to Financial regarding such condition or any such circumstances. In the event Financial, in Financial's sole discretion, undertakes, at any time or from time to time, to provide any such information to the undersigned, Financial shall be under no obligation (i) to provide any such information to the undersigned on any subsequent occasion, or (ii) to undertake any investigation not a part of Financial's regular business routine and shall be under no obligation to disclose any information which, pursuant to accepted or reasonable commercial lending practices, Financial wishes to maintain confidential. The undersigned hereby agrees that all payments received by Financial may

be applied, reversed, and reapplied, in whole or in part, to any of the Senior Obligations, as Financial, in Financial's sole discretion, deems appropriate and assents to any extension or postponement of the time of payment of the Senior Obligations or to any other indulgence with respect thereto, to any substitution, exchange or release of collateral which may at any time secure the Senior Obligations and to the addition or release of any other party or person primarily or secondarily liable therefor.

14. No Offset. In the event the undersigned at any time purchases goods or services from Borrower, the undersigned hereby irrevocably agrees that it shall pay for such goods or services in cash or cash equivalents in accordance with the terms of such purchases and shall not deduct from or setoff against any amounts billed to the undersigned by Borrower in connection with such purchases any amounts the undersigned claims are due to it with respect to the Subordinated Debt and that the non-monetary terms and conditions of any such purchases shall be not more favorable to the undersigned than arms'-length terms and conditions made available by Borrower to third parties.

15. Notices. Unless otherwise provided herein, all notices required or desired to be given hereunder shall be deemed validly given or delivered upon the earlier of (i) actual receipt thereof by the undersigned or Financial or (ii) three (3) days following deposit in the U.S. mails, postage prepaid addressed to the undersigned or Financial at the addresses set forth in the introductory paragraph of this Agreement.

16. Severability. Wherever possible, each provision of this Agreement shall be interpreted in such manner as to be effective and valid under applicable law, but if any provision of this Agreement shall be prohibited by or invalid under applicable law, such provision shall be ineffective to the extent of such prohibition or invalidity, without invalidating the remainder of such provision or the remaining provisions of this Agreement.

17. Headings. The headings contained in this Agreement are and shall be without substantive meaning or content of any kind whatsoever and are not a part of the agreement between the parties hereto.

18. Authority. The undersigned hereby certifies that it has all necessary authority to grant the subordination evidenced hereby and to execute this Agreement on behalf of the undersigned.

19. Binding Effect. This Agreement shall be immediately binding upon the undersigned and its successors and assigns, and shall inure to the benefit of the successors and assigns of Financial.

20. GOVERNING LAW; SUBMISSION TO JURISDICTION; WAIVER OF JURY TRIAL; WAIVER OF DAMAGES. (a) THIS AGREEMENT SHALL BE GOVERNED BY AND INTERPRETED IN ACCORDANCE WITH THE LAWS OF THE STATE OF ILLINOIS AND ANY DISPUTE ARISING OUT OF, CONNECTED WITH, RELATED TO, OR INCIDENTAL TO THE RELATIONSHIP ESTABLISHED BETWEEN THE UNDERSIGNED AND FINANCIAL IN CONNECTION WITH THIS AGREEMENT, AND WHETHER ARISING IN CONTRACT, TORT, EQUITY OR OTHERWISE, SHALL BE RESOLVED IN ACCORDANCE WITH THE INTERNAL LAWS (AS OPPOSED TO THE CONFLICTS OF LAWS PROVISIONS) AND DECISIONS OF THE STATE OF ILLINOIS.

(b)   EXCEPT AS PROVIDED IN THE NEXT PARAGRAPH, THE UNDERSIGNED AND FINANCIAL AGREE THAT ALL DISPUTES BETWEEN THEM ARISING OUT OF, CONNECTED WITH, RELATED TO, OR INCIDENTAL TO THE RELATIONSHIP ESTABLISHED BETWEEN THEM IN CONNECTION WITH THIS AGREEMENT, AND WHETHER ARISING IN CONTRACT, TORT, EQUITY, OR OTHERWISE, SHALL BE RESOLVED ONLY BY STATE OR FEDERAL COURTS LOCATED IN CHICAGO, ILLINOIS, BUT THE UNDERSIGNED AND FINANCIAL ACKNOWLEDGE THAT ANY APPEALS FROM THOSE COURTS MAY HAVE TO BE HEARD BY A COURT LOCATED OUTSIDE OF CHICAGO, ILLINOIS.   THE UNDERSIGNED WAIVES IN ALL DISPUTES ANY OBJECTION THAT IT MAY HAVE TO THE LOCATION OF THE COURT CONSIDERING THE DISPUTE INCLUDING, WITHOUT LIMITATION, ANY OBJECTION TO THE LAYING OF VENUE OR BASED ON THE GROUNDS OF FORUM NON CONVENIENS.

(c)   THE UNDERSIGNED AGREES THAT FINANCIAL SHALL HAVE THE RIGHT, TO THE EXTENT PERMITTED BY APPLICABLE LAW, TO PROCEED AGAINST THE UNDERSIGNED OR ITS PROPERTY IN A COURT IN ANY LOCATION REASONABLY SELECTED IN GOOD FAITH TO ENABLE FINANCIAL TO REALIZE ON SUCH PROPERTY, OR TO ENFORCE A JUDGMENT OR OTHER COURT ORDER ENTERED IN FAVOR OF FINANCIAL. THE UNDERSIGNED AGREES THAT IT WILL NOT ASSERT ANY PERMISSIVE COUNTERCLAIMS IN ANY PROCEEDING BROUGHT BY FINANCIAL TO REALIZE ON SUCH PROPERTY, OR TO ENFORCE A JUDGMENT OR OTHER COURT ORDER IN FAVOR OF FINANCIAL.   THE UNDERSIGNED WAIVES ANY OBJECTION THAT IT MAY HAVE TO THE LOCATION OF THE COURT IN WHICH FINANCIAL HAS COMMENCED A PROCEEDING DESCRIBED IN THIS PARAGRAPH INCLUDING, WITHOUT LIMITATION, ANY OBJECTION TO THE LAYING OF VENUE OR BASED ON THE GROUNDS OF FORUM NON CONVENIENS.

(d)   THE UNDERSIGNED AND FINANCIAL EACH WAIVE ANY RIGHT TO HAVE A JURY PARTICIPATE IN RESOLVING ANY DISPUTE, WHETHER SOUNDING IN CONTRACT, TORT, OR OTHERWISE ARISING OUT OF, CONNECTED WITH, RELATED TO OR INCIDENTAL TO THE RELATIONSHIP ESTABLISHED BETWEEN THEM IN CONNECTION WITH THIS AGREEMENT.   INSTEAD, ANY DISPUTES RESOLVED IN COURT WILL BE RESOLVED IN A BENCH TRIAL WITHOUT A JURY.

(e)   THE UNDERSIGNED (i) AGREES THAT FINANCIAL SHALL HAVE NO LIABILITY TO THE UNDERSIGNED (WHETHER SOUNDING IN TORT, CONTRACT OR OTHERWISE) FOR LOSSES SUFFERED BY THE UNDERSIGNED IN CONNECTION WITH, ARISING OUT OF, OR IN ANY WAY RELATED TO, THE TRANSACTIONS CONTEMPLATED AND THE RELATIONSHIP ESTABLISHED BY THIS AGREEMENT, OR ANY ACT, OMISSION OR EVENT OCCURRING IN CONNECTION THEREWITH, UNLESS IT IS DETERMINED BY A JUDGMENT OF A COURT THAT IS BINDING ON FINANCIAL, (WHICH JUDGMENT SHALL BE FINAL AND NOT SUBJECT TO REVIEW ON APPEAL), THAT SUCH LOSSES WERE THE RESULT OF ACTS OR

OMISSIONS ON THE PART OF FINANCIAL, CONSTITUTING WILLFUL MISCONDUCT OR KNOWING VIOLATIONS OF LAW AND (ii) WAIVES, RELEASES AND AGREES NOT TO SUE UPON ANY CLAIM AGAINST FINANCIAL (WHETHER SOUNDING IN TORT, CONTRACT OR OTHERWISE), EXCEPT A CLAIM BASED UPON WILLFUL MISCONDUCT OR KNOWING VIOLATIONS OF LAW. WHETHER OR NOT SUCH DAMAGES ARE RELATED TO A CLAIM THAT IS SUBJECT TO THE WAIVER EFFECTED ABOVE AND WHETHER OR NOT SUCH WAIVER IS EFFECTIVE, FINANCIAL SHALL NOT HAVE ANY LIABILITY WITH RESPECT TO, AND THE UNDERSIGNED HEREBY WAIVES, RELEASES AND AGREES NOT TO SUE UPON ANY CLAIM FOR, ANY SPECIAL, INDIRECT, CONSEQUENTIAL OR PUNITIVE DAMAGES SUFFERED BY THE UNDERSIGNED IN CONNECTION WITH, ARISING OUT OF, OR IN ANY WAY RELATED TO THE TRANSACTIONS CONTEMPLATED OR THE RELATIONSHIP ESTABLISHED BY THIS AGREEMENT, OR ANY ACT, OMISSION OR EVENT OCCURRING IN CONNECTION THEREWITH, UNLESS IT IS DETERMINED BY A JUDGMENT OF A COURT THAT IS BINDING ON FINANCIAL (WHICH JUDGMENT SHALL BE FINAL AND NOT SUBJECT TO REVIEW ON APPEAL), THAT SUCH DAMAGES WERE THE RESULT OF ACTS OR OMISSIONS ON THE PART OF FINANCIAL, CONSTITUTING WILLFUL MISCONDUCT OR KNOWING VIOLATIONS OF LAW.

IN WITNESS WHEREOF, this instrument has been signed and sealed this _____ day of _____, 19 _.

_____

Acknowledged and accepted in
Chicago, Illinois this __ day
of _____, 19__.

FINANCIAL CORPORATION

By _____
Title:

_____ hereby accepts, and acknowledges receipt of a copy of, the foregoing Subordination Agreement (the "Agreement") this __ day of _____, 19__, and agrees that it will not pay any of the Subordinated Debt (as such term is defined in the Agreement) or grant any security therefor, except as the Agreement provides. In the event of a breach by the undersigned of any of the provisions herein, or by the holder of any Subordinated Debt of any of the provisions of the Agreement, all of the Senior Obligations (as such term is defined in the Agreement) shall, without presentment, demand, protest or notice of any kind, become immediately due and payable, unless Financial shall otherwise elect in writing.

_____

By: _____
Its: _____

Attest:

By: _____
Its: _____

(AFFIX CORPORATE SEAL)

C. LIABILITY OF CREDITORS TO THE GOVERNMENT

Liability for withholding taxes
Minn. Stat. §290.92

Subd. 2a. Collection at source. (1) Deductions. Every employer making payment of wages shall deduct and withhold upon such wages a tax as provided in this section.

* * *

Subd. 22. Liability of third parties paying or providing for wages. (a) For purposes of this section, if a lender, surety, or other person, who is not an employer with respect to an employee or group of employees, pays wages directly to such an employee or group of employees, employed by one or more employers, or to an agent on behalf of such employee or employees, such lender, surety, or other person shall be liable to the commissioner in a sum equal to the taxes required to be deducted and withheld from such wages by such employer.

(b) If a lender, surety, or other person supplies funds to or for the account of an employer for the specific purpose of paying wages of the employees of such employer, with actual notice or knowledge that such employer does not intend to or will not be able to make timely payment or deposit of the amounts of tax required by this section to be deducted and withheld by such employer from such wages, such lender, surety, or other person shall be liable personally to the commissioner in a sum equal to the taxes which are not paid over to the commissioner by such employer with respect to such wages.

(c) For purposes of this subdivision, a person shall be deemed for purposes of a particular transaction to have actual notice or knowledge of any fact from the time such fact is brought to the attention of the individual conducting such transaction, and in any event from the time such fact would have been brought to such individual's attention if the person had exercised due diligence. A person exercises due diligence by maintaining reasonable routines for communicating significant information to the person conducting the transaction and there is reasonable compliance with the routines. Due diligence does not require an individual acting for the person to communicate information unless such communication is part of the individual's regular duties or unless the individual has reason to know of the transaction and that the transaction would be materially affected by the information.

(d) Any amounts paid to the commissioner pursuant to this subdivision shall be credited to the liability of the employer.

Citicorp Industrial Credit, Inc. v. Brock

Supreme Court of the United States, 1987
483 U.S. 27, 107 S.Ct. 2694, 97 L.Ed.2d 23

Justice MARSHALL delivered the opinion of the Court. Section 15(a)(1) of the Fair Labor Standards Act of 1938, 52 Stat. 1068, prohibits "any person" from introducing into interstate commerce goods produced in violation of the minimum wage or overtime provisions of the Act. The question in this case is whether §15(a)(1) applies to holders of collateral obtained pursuant to a security agreement.

I

In 1983, petitioner entered into a financing agreement with Qualitex Corporation, a clothing manufacturer and the corporate predecessor to Ely Group, Inc., and its subsidiaries Rockford Textile Mills, Inc., and Ely & Walker, Inc. (collectively Ely). Under the terms of the financing arrangement, petitioner agreed to loan up to $11 million to provide working capital for Ely. In return, Ely granted petitioner a security interest in inventory, accounts receivable, and other assets. Petitioner perfected its security interest under applicable state law.

The financing agreement imposed various reporting requirements on Ely, including the submission to petitioner of a weekly schedule of inventory, a monthly balance sheet and income statement, and reports of accounts receivable. Petitioner also monitored the collateral upon which it made cash advances through a system of audits and on-site inspections. In the fall of 1984, Ely's sales began to fall below projections, and the balance on the loan began to increase, reaching over $9.5 million by February 1985. Ely stopped reporting to petitioner in January 1985. On February 8, petitioner stopped advancing funds and demanded payment in full. At the request of Ely's management, however, petitioner did not immediately foreclose. It gave Ely an opportunity to devise a plan for continuing its operations, but Ely was unable to do so. Petitioner waited until February 19, at which time it took possession of the collateral, including Ely's inventory of finished goods.

Ely's employees continued to work until February 19, when Ely ceased all operations and closed its manufacturing facilities. Because Ely defaulted on its payroll, the employees did not receive any wages for pay periods between January 27 and February 19. The Department of Labor concluded that the items manufactured during these times were produced in violation of §§6 and 7 of the Fair Labor Standards Act of 1938 (FLSA), 29 U.S.C. §§206 and 207, and that under §15(a)(1), they were "hot goods" that could not be introduced into interstate commerce.[1] Acting on information that petitioner intended to transport these goods in interstate commerce, the Secretary of Labor sought to enjoin shipment.

---

[1]   Section 15(a)(1) of the FLSA, codified at 29 U.S.C. §215(a), provides in relevant part:

"(a) [I]t shall be unlawful for any person-- "(1) to transport, offer for

In an action filed in the United States District Court for the Eastern District of Tennessee, the Secretary moved for a preliminary injunction and sought a temporary restraining order to prohibit Ely and petitioner from placing the goods in interstate commerce. The District Court denied the application for a temporary restraining order but, after a hearing, granted the Secretary's motion for a preliminary injunction. Donovan v. Rockford Textile Mills, Inc., 608 F.Supp. 215 (1985). The Under Secretary of Labor then filed another complaint against Ely and petitioner, this time in the United States District Court for the Western District of Tennessee. This complaint was also accompanied by a motion for a preliminary injunction and application for a temporary restraining order. The District Court granted the temporary restraining order and later granted the Under Secretary's motion for a preliminary injunction. Ford v. Ely Group, Inc., 621 F.Supp. 22 (1985).

Both District Courts held that §15(a)(1), which makes it unlawful for any person to ship "hot goods" in interstate commerce, prohibited not only Ely but also petitioner from transporting or selling items produced by employees who had not been paid in conformity with §§6 and 7 of the FLSA. They found this reading of §15(a)(1) consistent with congressional intent to exclude from interstate commerce goods produced under substandard labor conditions. The courts concluded that " 'in light of the purposes of the Act, it would be an unjust and harsh result for the creditor to get the benefit of the labor of the employees during the period of time they produced goods and were not paid as provided by the Act; a benefit which the creditor would not have without the employees['] labor.'" .

The two cases were consolidated on appeal. The United States Court of Appeals for the Sixth Circuit affirmed, one judge dissenting. Brock v. Ely Group, Inc., 788 F.2d 1200 (1986). Following the plain language of §15(a)(1), the majority concluded that "any person" as used in that section applies to secured creditors. Like the District Courts, it found this result consistent with the purpose of the FLSA: to exclude tainted goods from interstate commerce. The Court of Appeals rejected the reasoning of the Second Circuit in Wirtz v. Powell Knitting

---

transportation, ship, deliver, or sell in commerce, or to ship, deliver, or sell with knowledge that shipment or delivery or sale thereof in commerce is intended, any goods in the production of which any employee was employed in violation of section 206 or section 207 of this title, or in violation of any regulation or order of the Secretary issued under section 214 of this title; except that no provision of this chapter shall impose any liability upon any common carrier for the transportation in commerce in the regular course of its business of any goods not produced by such common carrier, and no provision of this chapter shall excuse any common carrier from its obligation to accept any goods for transportation; and except that any such transportation, offer, shipment, delivery, or sale of such goods by a purchaser who acquired them in good faith in reliance on written assurance from the producer that the goods were produced in compliance with the requirements of this chapter, and who acquired such goods for value without notice of any such violation, shall not be deemed unlawful."

Mills Co., 360 F.2d 730 (1966), which had held §15(a)(1) inapplicable to secured creditors who take possession of goods produced in violation of the FLSA. 788 F.2d, at 1204-1205. The Sixth Circuit noted that Congress created only two exceptions to the broad scope of §15(a)(1), one for common carriers and one for good faith purchasers, and concluded that "*Powell Knitting Mills* created an exception for secured creditors that Congress did not and has not deemed appropriate." The dissenting judge would have followed *Powell Knitting Mills*. He maintained that in enacting the "hot goods" provision, Congress was concerned with violations of the Act occurring in the course of the ongoing production of goods by a solvent manufacturer, not, as here, by an insolvent corporation that has ceased operations.

We granted certiorari to resolve this conflict among the Circuits. We now affirm.

II

A

The FLSA mandates the payment of minimum wage and overtime compensation to covered employees. Section 6(a) provides that every employer, as defined in the Act, "shall pay to each of his employees" wages not less than the specified minimum rate; §7(a)(1) prohibits employment of any employee in excess of 40 hours per week "unless such employee receives compensation" at a rate of not less than one and one-half times the employee's regular rate. Petitioner does not contest the lower courts' findings that Ely failed to pay its employees at all for several weeks immediately preceding the plant closings. Consequently, we conclude, as did the Court of Appeals, that the goods produced during this period were manufactured in violation of §6 and/or §7 of the FLSA and are "hot goods" for the purposes of §15(a)(1).

Section 15(a)(1) prohibits "any person" from introducing goods produced in violation of §6 or §7 of the FLSA into interstate commerce. Section 3(a) defines "person" as "an individual, partnership, association, corporation, business trust, legal representative, or any organized group of persons." 29 U.S.C. §203(a). As a corporate entity, petitioner clearly falls within the plain language of the statute. Section 15(a)(1) contains two exemptions to the general prohibition on interstate shipment of "hot goods." The first, enacted as part of the original FLSA, exempts common carriers from the prohibition on transportation of such goods. The second, added in 1949, exempts a purchaser who acquired the goods for value, without notice of any violation, and "in good faith in reliance on written assurance from the producer that the goods were produced in compliance with the requirements" of the Act.

Petitioner does not claim to come within either statutory exemption. Rather, it argues that the exemptions reflect congressional intent to limit application of the "hot goods" provision to culpable parties, and therefore, "innocent" secured creditors should not be subject to the Act. We disagree. Although §§6 and 7 only require "employers" to pay minimum wage and overtime, §15(a)(1) refers to "any person," not "any employer." Congress limited other provisions of the FLSA as petitioner suggests, which indicates that its failure to do so in §15(a)(1) was not inadvertent. That Congress identified only two narrow categories of "innocent" persons who were not subject to the "hot goods" provision suggests that all other persons, innocent or not, are subject to §15(a)(1). We find no indication that Congress actually considered application of the "hot goods" provision to secured creditors when it enacted the FLSA. By claiming a general exemption for creditors, without any duty to ascertain compliance with the FLSA, petitioner is asking us to put creditors in a better position than good-faith purchasers, for whom Congress specifically added an exemption.

In the past, the Court has refused "[t]o extend an exemption to other than those plainly and unmistakably within [the FLSA's] terms and spirit." A.H. Phillips, Inc. v. Walling, 324 U.S. 490, 493, 65 S.Ct. 807, 808, 89 L.Ed. 1095 (1945). Similarly, where the FLSA provides exemptions "in detail and with particularity," we have found this to preclude "enlargement by implication." We see no reason to deviate from our traditional approach in this case.

B

Petitioner urges us to look beyond the plain language of the statute, citing the often-quoted passage from Holy Trinity Church v. United States, 143 U.S. 457, 459, 12 S.Ct. 511, 512, 36 L.Ed. 226 (1892): "[A] thing may be within the letter of the statute and yet not within the statute, because not within its spirit, nor within the intention of its makers." According to petitioner, the sole aim of the FLSA was to establish decent wages and hours for American workers. This goal, petitioner claims, is not furthered by application of §15(a)(1) to creditors who acquire "hot goods" by foreclosure and are not themselves responsible for the minimum wage and overtime violations. However, we conclude that the legislative intent fully supports the result achieved by application of the plain language.

While improving working conditions was undoubtedly one of Congress' concerns, it was certainly not the only aim of the FLSA. In addition to the goal identified by petitioner, the Act's declaration of policy, contained in §2(a), reflects Congress' desire to eliminate the competitive advantage enjoyed by goods produced under substandard conditions.[1] 29 U.S.C. §202(a). This Court has

---

[1]   Section 2(a), codified at 29 U.S.C. §202(a), provides:

"The Congress finds that the existence, in industries engaged in commerce..., of labor conditions detrimental to the maintenance of the minimum standard of living necessary for health, efficiency, and general well-being of workers (1) causes commerce and the channels and instrumentalities of commerce to be used to spread and perpetuate such labor conditions among the workers of the several States; (2) burdens commerce and the free flow of goods in commerce; (3) constitutes an unfair method of competition in commerce; (4) leads to labor disputes burdening and obstructing commerce and the free flow of goods in commerce; and (5)

consistently recognized this broad regulatory purpose. "The motive and purpose of the present regulation are plainly ... that interstate commerce should not be made the instrument of competition in the distribution of goods produced under substandard labor conditions, which competition is injurious to the commerce." United States v. Darby, 312 U.S. 100, 115, 61 S.Ct. 451, 457, 85 L.Ed. 609 (1941).

Application of §15(a)(1) to secured creditors furthers this goal by excluding tainted goods from interstate commerce. Had the Department of Labor not obtained an injunction in this case, petitioner, as a secured creditor, would have converted several weeks of labor by the debtor's employees into goods covered by its security interest; the "hot goods" produced by these uncompensated employees would have competed with goods produced in conformity with the FLSA's minimum wage and overtime requirements. Moreover, prohibiting foreclosing creditors from selling "hot goods" also advances the goal identified by petitioner. Secured creditors often monitor closely the operations of employer-borrowers, as petitioner did in this case. They may be in a position to insist on compliance with the FLSA's minimum wage and overtime requirements. As the District Court for the Western District observed:

> "[I]f foreclosing creditors are free to ship and sell tainted goods across state lines, the temptation to overextend credit to marginal producers is strong, as is the likelihood that such producers will become unable to meet their payrolls. The reason for this is that finance companies and institutions stand to reap financial gain by keeping such producers in business. A holding by this Court that creditors may not ship and sell in interstate commerce goods produced in violation of the Act will not only protect complying manufacturers from the unfair competition of such

---

> interferes with the orderly and fair marketing of goods in commerce" President Roosevelt's message to Congress, which served as the inspiration for passage of the Act, makes a similar point: "Goods produced under conditions which do not meet rudimentary standards of decency should be regarded as contraband and ought not to be allowed to pollute the channels of interstate trade."

H.R.Doc. No. 255, 75th Cong., 1st Sess., 3 (1937). See Powell v. United States Cartridge Co., 339 U.S. 497, 516, 70 S.Ct. 755, 765, 94 L.Ed. 1017 (1950). The President's message was cited approvingly throughout the legislative history of the 1938 Act. See, e.g., S.Rep. No. 884, 75th Cong., 1st Sess., 1-3 (1937); H.R.Rep. No. 1452, 75th Cong., 1st Sess., 5-7 (1937); H.R.Rep. No. 2182, supra, at 5. Despite these expansive indications of legislative purpose, petitioner insists that Congress was concerned about competition only to the extent that competition from " 'chiselers' " had the effect of driving down wages and working conditions. Brief for Petitioner 24-25. However, based on the statute, its legislative history, and our prior decisions, we conclude that exclusion from interstate commerce of goods produced under substandard conditions is not simply a means to enforce other statutory goals; it is itself a central purpose of the FLSA.

tainted goods, but, we submit, it will also discourage the type of commercial financing which leads to minimum wage and overtime violations."

621 F.Supp., at 26.

C

A literal application of §15(a)(1) does not grant employees a priority in "hot goods" superior to that which a secured creditor has under state law. Petitioner's rights in the collateral as against Ely are unchanged by our holding. Petitioner still owns the goods, subject only to the "hot goods" provision, which prevents it from placing them in interstate commerce. The employees have not acquired a possessory interest in the goods.[1] Indeed, as the District Court for the Western District of Tennessee recognized, the Secretary brought this action "not to compel the foreclosing creditor to pay the statutory wages or to put pressure on the defaulting producer to pay such wages, but to keep tainted goods from entering the channels of interstate commerce." Id., at 25-26. That petitioner can cure the employer's violation of the FLSA by paying the employees the statutorily required wages does not give the employees a "lien" on the assets superior to that of a secured creditor.

In numerous other statutes, Congress has exercised its authority under the Commerce Clause to exclude from interstate commerce goods which, for a variety of reasons, it considers harmful. Like the FLSA, these regulatory measures bar goods not produced in conformity with specified standards from the channels of commerce. As the District Courts in this case recognized, secured creditors take their security interests subject to the laws of the land. See 621 F.Supp., at 26; 608 F.Supp., at 217. If, for example, the goods at issue in this case were fabrics that failed to meet federal flammability standards and were therefore banned from interstate commerce under the Flammable Fabrics Act, 67 Stat. 111, as amended, 15 U.S.C. §1191 et seq., surely petitioner could not argue that it had a right to sell the inventory merely by virtue of its status as a secured creditor. "Hot goods" are not inherently hazardous, but Congress has determined that they are contraband nonetheless. We see no reason for a different result merely because a different form of contraband is involved.

III

We hold that §15(a)(1)'s broad prohibition on interstate shipment of "hot goods" applies to secured creditors who acquire the goods pursuant to a security agreement. This result is mandated by the plain language of the statute, and it furthers the goal of eliminating the competitive advantage enjoyed by goods

---

[1]   Of course, under state law, the employees may have a lien on the employer's property superior to petitioner's lien. See Tenn.Code Ann. §66-13-101 (1982) (creating statutory wage lien on "corporate or firm property of every character and description"). However, any such lien would exist independent of the application of the FLSA to petitioner.

produced under substandard labor conditions. Accordingly, the judgment of the Court of Appeals is

Affirmed.

Justice Scalia, concurring.

While I would affirm the Court of Appeals even if I agreed with petitioner that "the sole aim of the FLSA was to establish decent wages and hours for American workers," ante, at 2700, and that this goal "is not furthered by application of §15(a)(1)" to secured creditors, ibid., I do not disagree with the Court's conclusions in Part II-B, and therefore join its opinion in full.

Justice Stevens, with whom Justice White joins, dissenting.

The statute that the Court construes today was enacted during the Great Depression. Although business failures were an everyday occurrence in 1938, nothing in the language or history of the Fair Labor Standards Act (FLSA or Act) suggests that Congress intended that Act to address the unfortunate situation that arises when an employer is unable to pay his employees for the final days of work that produced the inventory at hand when the plant was forced to close.

Indeed, if there is one conclusion that both parties before us, and every court that has ever considered this matter, agree upon, it is that Congress did not "actually conside[r] application of the 'hot goods' provision to secured creditors when it enacted the FLSA." Ante. This historical fact carries much weight in this case. The subjects of bankruptcy and secured transactions constitute discrete bodies of law, which are generally governed by the Federal Bankruptcy Code and by state law, respectively.[1] Instead of interpreting Congress' silence as evincing intent to invade these areas with an Act whose purposes do not fit nicely into these contexts,[2] I would interpret Congress' utter silence as showing that Congress

---

[1] The FLSA was enacted to prevent employers from paying substandard wages. Section 15(a)(1) is designed to prevent employers from producing goods at such low cost that they could undersell competitors who paid what Congress deemed to be a decent wage. The concern of the statute was the ongoing business with its continuing impact on both the labor market and the commercial market. It was not remotely concerned with the perennial problem of distress sales that follow in the wake of a business failure. Under the Court's novel reading of the Act, any such sale--whether by a secured creditor, a trustee in bankruptcy, or even by a creditor's committee trying to raise funds to meet a shortage in the final payroll-- would be a sale of "hot goods" and therefore illegal.

[2] As Judge Engel explained in dissent from the Court of Appeals' decision:

"The practical effect of the majority's decision is not to remove any tainted goods from competition for, as happened here, almost always the result will be that the goods are sold, if not in foreclosure, then in bankruptcy, or by other attaching creditors. As here, the goods will go out in the market, but whether they are sold for competitively destructive prices will not depend on the cost of their production but upon the manner of their sale in any event. The real effect of the majority's interpretation is simply to create a judicial lien superior to the

never intended to apply the FLSA to these unique areas of the law.[1]   See Kelly v. Robinson, 479 U.S. 36, 47, 107 S.Ct. 353, 359-360, 93 L.Ed.2d 216 (1986).

Even were I not confident in that conclusion, however, I certainly believe that the arguments in favor of petitioner's construction are substantial enough to warrant our adherence to settled precedent.   During the 28 years from the enactment of the FLSA through 1966 it appears that no Secretary of Labor ever sought an injunction against the sale of "hot goods" in circumstances such as these.   See Wirtz v. Powell Knitting Mills Co., 360 F.2d 730, 733 (CA2 1966). When a Secretary did attempt to use the statute in this novel way, the Court of Appeals for the Second Circuit summarily rejected his interpretation, explaining:

> "We believe that there was no Congressional intent that concerns in [the creditor's] position be within §15. The purpose of forcing payment of wages should not apply to the creditor who advanced funds long before the default in wages, and who merely forecloses his lien, at least where the value of the goods acquired does not exceed the debt left unpaid. Since [the creditor] is not giving present consideration, it can neither force [the employer] to make payment nor withhold wages from its payment and pay the wage earners itself. It already provided [the employer] with cash, part of which no doubt went for wages that were paid. Since the only reason to give effect to §15 would be to force [the creditor] to pay the wages, §15

---

otherwise lawful lien which Citicorp possessed in the goods. In my view, this kind of pressure is the only motivation in the government in its present construction of the Act. Had it intended to create a federal lien law, Congress no doubt could have done so, but it did not. State laws governing creditors' rights, state laws protecting employees from non- payment of wages and bankruptcy laws generally, provide a great deal of relief for the protection of employees of defunct and insolvent corporations. It seems to me that in this special area of concern, the operation of these more traditional sources of law was intended by Congress to be sufficient. It is my opinion, therefore, that under a common sense application of section 15(a)(1), Congress was looking instead at application of the Act in the course of the ongoing production of goods and not at the situation obtaining here and in the like cases in the Second and Fourth Circuits."

Brock v. Ely Group, Inc., 788 F.2d 1200, 1207 (1986).

[1]   Aside from my conclusion that secured creditors such as Citicorp are not barred from selling "hot goods," I also have doubts about whether the employees who participated in the production of the goods at issue in this case were "employed in violation of [the FLSA]" within the meaning of §15(a)(1) of the Act at the time the goods were produced. See ante. The terms of their employment complied with the statute and when they performed their services everyone expected and intended that they would be paid in full. It may well be true that the employer committed a violation of the Act when it was subsequently unable to meet its payroll, but I am not sure the inventory can be branded "hot goods" because of that subsequent event.

ought not apply to it, in a backhanded way of attacking its secured position. "The Secretary stresses the point that when the Congress desired to protect bona fide purchasers from the strict wording of the Act it found it easy to do so by amending the Act with appropriate safeguards. This would indeed be persuasive if there were indications that the present problem of the foreclosing secured creditor had been brought to the attention of the Congress. The argument loses force because this was apparently never done, and the Secretary's present contention is much weakened by the fact that since the enactment of the Act in 1938 neither he nor his predecessors appear to have so read the Act, in spite of the myriad of instances in which similar security titles must have been enforced."

Id., at 733.

I would have subscribed to this reasoning in 1966, and certainly do now. In the more than 20 years since the Second Circuit's decision, its construction of the statute has not been called into question by the courts that have addressed the issue, except in the decisions now on review. Given the Secretary's practice prior to the Powell Knitting decision, the judicial acceptance of that decision, and the fact that Congress has not seen fit to amend the statute in light of these decisions, I believe that the Powell Knitting construction should be retained until Congress rejects it.

I respectfully dissent.

United States v. Fleet Factors Corp.
United States Court of Appeals, Eleventh Circuit, 1990
901 F.2d 1550

Kravitch, Circuit Judge: Fleet Factors Corporation ("Fleet") brought an interlocutory appeal from the district court's denial of its motion for summary judgment in this suit by the United States to recover the cost of removing hazardous waste from a bankrupt textile facility. The district court denied summary judgment because it concluded that Fleet's activities at the facility might rise to the level of participation in management sufficient to impose liability under the Comprehensive Environmental Response Compensation and Liability Act ("CERCLA"), 42 U.S.C. §§9601-57 (1982 & West Supp.1988), despite the statutory exemption from liability for holders of a security interest. We agree with the district court that material questions of fact remain as to the extent of Fleet's participation in the management of the facility; therefore, we affirm the denial of Fleet's summary judgment motion.

FACTS
In 1976, Swainsboro Print Works ("SPW"), a cloth printing facility, entered into a "factoring" agreement with Fleet in which Fleet agreed to advance funds

against the assignment of SPW's accounts receivable. As collateral for these advances, Fleet also obtained a security interest in SPW's textile facility and all of its equipment, inventory, and fixtures. In August, 1979, SPW filed for bankruptcy under Chapter 11. The factoring agreement between SPW and Fleet continued with court approval. In early 1981, Fleet ceased advancing funds to SPW because SPW's debt to Fleet exceeded Fleet's estimate of the value of SPW's accounts receivable. On February 27, 1981, SPW ceased operations and began to liquidate its inventory. Fleet continued to collect on the accounts receivable assigned to it under the Chapter 11 factoring agreement. In December 1981, SPW was adjudicated a bankrupt under Chapter 7 and a trustee assumed title and control of the facility.

In May 1982, Fleet foreclosed on its security interest in some of SPW's inventory and equipment, and contracted with Baldwin Industrial Liquidators ("Baldwin") to conduct an auction of the collateral. Baldwin sold the material "as is" and "in place" on June 22, 1982; the removal of the items was the responsibility of the purchasers. On August 31, 1982, Fleet allegedly contracted with Nix Riggers ("Nix") to remove the unsold equipment in consideration for leaving the premises "broom clean." Nix testified in deposition that he understood that he had been given a "free hand" by Fleet or Baldwin to do whatever was necessary at the facility to remove the machinery and equipment. Nix left the facility by the end of December, 1983.

On January 20, 1984, the Environmental Protection Agency ("EPA") inspected the facility and found 700 fifty-five gallon drums containing toxic chemicals and forty-four truckloads of material containing asbestos. The EPA incurred costs of nearly $400,000 in responding to the environmental threat at SPW. On July 7, 1987, the facility was conveyed to Emanuel County, Georgia, at a foreclosure sale resulting from SPW's failure to pay state and county taxes.

The government sued Horowitz and Newton, the two principal officers and stockholders of SPW, and Fleet to recover the cost of cleaning up the hazardous waste. The district court granted the government's summary judgment motion with respect to the liability of Horowitz and Newton for the cost of removing the hazardous waste in the drums. The government's motion with respect to Fleet's liability, and the liability of Horowitz and Newton for the asbestos removal costs was denied. Fleet's motion for summary judgment was also denied. The district court, sua sponte, certified the summary judgment issues for interlocutory appeal and stayed the remaining proceedings in the case. Fleet subsequently brought this appeal challenging the court's denial of its motion for summary judgment.

* * *

DISCUSSION

The Comprehensive Environmental Response Compensation and Liability Act was enacted by Congress in response to the environmental and public health hazards caused by the improper disposal of hazardous wastes. United States v. Maryland Bank & Trust Co., 632 F. Supp. 573, 576 (D. Md. 1986). The essential policy underlying CERCLA is to place the ultimate responsibility for cleaning up hazardous waste on "those responsible for problems caused by the disposal of chemical poison." Accordingly, CERCLA authorizes the federal government to clean up hazardous waste dump sites and recover the cost of the effort from certain categories of responsible parties. Maryland Bank & Trust Co., 632 F.Supp. at 576.

The parties liable for costs incurred by the government in responding to an environmental hazard are: 1) the present owners and operators of a facility where hazardous wastes were released or are in danger of being released; 2) the owners or operators of a facility at the time the hazardous wastes were disposed; 3) the person or entity that arranged for the treatment or disposal of substances at the facility; and 4) the person or entity that transported the substances to the facility. 42 U.S.C. §9607(a) (1982 & West Supp.1988). The government contends that Fleet is liable for the response costs associated with the waste at the SPW facility as either a present owner and operator of the facility, see 42 U.S.C. §9607(a)(1), or the owner or operator of the facility at the time the wastes were disposed, see 42 U.S.C. §9607(a)(2).

The district court, as a matter of law, rejected the government's claim that Fleet was a present owner of the facility. The court, however, found a sufficient issue of fact as to whether Fleet was an owner or operator of the SPW facility at the time the wastes were disposed to warrant the denial of Fleet's motion for summary judgment. On appeal each party contests that portion of the district court's order adverse to their respective interests.

A. Fleet's Liability Under Section 9607(a)(1)

CERCLA holds the owner or operator of a facility containing hazardous waste strictly liable to the United States for expenses incurred in responding to the environmental and health hazards posed by the waste in that facility. See 42 U.S.C. §9607(a)(1); S.Rep. No. 848, 96th Cong., 2d Sess. 34 (1980). This provision of the statute targets those individuals presently "owning or operating such facilit[ies]." See 42 U.S.C. §9601(20)(A)(ii). In order to effectuate the goals of the statute, we will construe the present owner and operator of a facility as that individual or entity owning or operating the facility at the time the plaintiff initiated the lawsuit by filing a complaint.[1]

---

[1]   Although the "owner and operator" language of §9607(a)(1) is in the conjunctive, we construe this language in the disjunctive in accordance with the legislative history of CERCLA and the persuasive interpretations of other federal courts. See Maryland Bank & Trust Co., 632 F.Supp. at 577-78; see also Guidice v. BFG Electroplating and Manufacturing Co., 732 F.Supp. 556, 561 (W.D.Pa.1989) (interpreting statute in disjunctive); Artesian Water Co. v. Government of New Castle County, 659 F.Supp. 1269, 1280 (D.Del.1987) (same), affirmed, 851 F.2d 643 (3d Cir.1988). Additionally, we note that §9607(a)(2) is phrased in the disjunctive. We can perceive no rational explanation, other than careless statutory drafting, for imposing liability upon "owners or operators" under one section but only holding "owners and operators" liable under another section. Cf. Coastal Casting Service v. Aron, No. H-86-4463 slip op. at 3, 1988

On July 9, 1987, the date this litigation commenced, the owner of the SPW facility was Emanuel County, Georgia. Under CERCLA, however, a state or local government that has involuntarily acquired title to a facility is generally not held liable as the owner or operator of the facility. Rather, the statute provides that

> in the case of any facility, title or control of which was conveyed due to bankruptcy, foreclosure, tax delinquency, abandonment, or similar means to a unit of State or local government, [its owner or operator is] any person who owned, operated or otherwise controlled activities at such facility immediately beforehand.

42 U.S.C. §9601(20)(A)(iii).

Essentially, the parties disagree as to the interpretation of the phrase "immediately beforehand." The district court reasoned that Fleet could not be liable under section 9607(a)(1) because it had never foreclosed on its security interest in the facility and its agents had not been on the premises since December 1983. The government contends that the statute should be interpreted to refer liability "back to the last time that someone controlled the facility, however long ago." Appellee's Brief at 23. Thus, according to the government, the period of effective abandonment of the site by the trustee in bankruptcy (from December 1983 to the July 1987 foreclosure sale) should be ignored and liability would remain with Fleet since it was the last entity to "control" the facility.

We agree with Fleet that the plain meaning of the phrase "immediately beforehand" means without intervening ownership, operation, and control. Fleet, therefore, cannot be held liable under section 9607(a)(1) because it neither owned, operated, or controlled SPW immediately prior to Emanuel County's acquisition of the facility. It is undisputed that from December 1981, when SPW was adjudicated a bankrupt, until the July 1987 foreclosure sale, the bankrupt estate and trustee were the owners of the facility. Similarly, the evidence is clear that neither Fleet nor any of its putative agents had anything to do with the facility after December 1983. Although Fleet may have operated or controlled SPW prior to December 1983, its involvement with SPW terminated more than three years before the county assumed ownership of the facility. The fact that the bankrupt estate or trustee may not have effectively exercised their control of the facility between December 1983 and July 1987 is of no moment. It is undisputed that Fleet was not in control of the facility during this period. Although a trustee can

---

WL 35012 (S.D.Tex. April 8, 1988) ("It is well known that CERCLA was hastily drafted and adopted, with resulting ambiguities. ...") (available on WESTLAW as 1988 WL 35012); Maryland Bank & Trust Co., 632 F.Supp. at 578 ("The structure of section 107(a) [9607(a)], like so much of this hastily patched together compromise Act, is not a model of statutory clarity."). Our construction of both statutory provisions in the disjunctive is further supported by the fact that the definitional section of the statute only refers to the phrase "owner or operator." See 42 U.S.C. §9601(20)(A).

obviously abdicate its control over a bankrupt estate, it cannot in such a manner unilaterally delegate its responsibility to a previous controlling entity. To reach back to Fleet's involvement with the facility prior to December 1983 in order to impose liability would torture the plain statutory meaning of "immediately beforehand."[1]

B. Fleet's Liability Under Section 9607(a)(2)

CERCLA also imposes liability on "any person who at the time of disposal of any hazardous substance owned or operated any ... facility at which such hazardous substances were disposed of...." 42 U.S.C. §9607(a)(2). CERCLA excludes from the definition of "owner or operator" any "person, who, without participating in the management of a ... facility, holds indicia of ownership primarily to protect his security interest in the ... facility." 42 U.S.C. §9601(20)(A). Fleet has the burden of establishing its entitlement to this exemption. Maryland Bank & Trust, 632 F.Supp. at 578; see United States v. First City National Bank of Houston, 386 U.S. 361, 366, 87 S.Ct. 1088, 1092, 18 L.Ed.2d 151 (1967). There is no dispute that Fleet held an "indicia of ownership" in the facility through its deed of trust to SPW, and that this interest was held primarily to protect its security interest in the facility. The critical issue is whether Fleet participated in management sufficiently to incur liability under the statute.[2]

The construction of the secured creditor exemption is an issue of first impression in the federal appellate courts. The government urges us to adopt a narrow and strictly literal interpretation of the exemption that excludes from its protection any secured creditor that participates in any manner in the management of a facility. We decline the government's suggestion because it would largely eviscerate the exemption Congress intended to afford to secured creditors. Secured lenders frequently have some involvement in the financial affairs of their debtors in order to insure that their interests are being adequately protected. To

---

[1] This interpretation of §9607(a)(1) is particularly appropriate in the context of the entire statutory scheme. While §9607(a)(1) targets present owners and operators of toxic waste facilities, §9607(a)(2) focuses on the entities that owned or operated the facility at the time the wastes were disposed. A narrow reading of this section would not, therefore, create an unintended loophole for individuals or entities to escape liability for improperly disposing hazardous waste.

[2] The government correctly formulates this issue as being comprised of two distinct, but related, means of finding Fleet liable under §9607(a)(2). First, Fleet is liable under the statute if it operated the facility within the meaning of the statute. Alternatively, Fleet can be held liable if it had an indicia of ownership in SPW and managed the facility to the extent necessary to remove it from the secured creditor liability exemption. See United States v. Kayser-Roth Corp., 724 F.Supp. 15, 20-21 (D.R.I.1989). Although we can conceive of some instances where the facts showing participation in management are different from those indicating operation, this is not such a case. The sum of the facts alleged by the government is sufficient to hold Fleet liable under either analysis. In order to avoid repetition, and because this case fits more snugly under a secured creditor analysis, we will forgo an analysis of Fleet's liability as an operator.

adopt the government's interpretation of the secured creditor exemption could expose all such lenders to CERCLA liability for engaging in their normal course of business.

Fleet, in turn, suggests that we adopt the distinction delineated by some district courts between permissible participation in the financial management of the facility and impermissible participation in the day-to-day or operational management of a facility. In United States v. Mirabile, the first case to suggest this interpretation, the district court granted summary judgment to the defendant creditors because their participation in the affairs of the facility was "limited to participation in financial decisions." No. 84-2280, slip op. at 3 (E.D.Pa. Sept. 6, 1985) (available on WESTLAW as 1985 WL 97). The court explained "that the participation which is critical is participation in operational, production, or waste disposal activities. Mere financial ability to control waste disposal practices ... is not ... sufficient for the imposition of liability." Mirabile, No. 84-2280, slip op. at 4; accord United States v. New Castle County, 727 F.Supp. 854, 866 (D.Del.1989); Rockwell International v. IU International Corp., 702 F.Supp. 1384, 1390 (N.D.Ill.1988); see also Coastal Casting Service, No. H-86-4463, slip op. at 4(complaint alleging that secured creditor's entanglement with facility's management surpassed mere financial control held sufficient). The court concluded that "before a secured creditor ... may be held liable, it must, at a minimum, participate in the day-to-day operational aspects of the site. [Here, the creditor] ... merely foreclosed on the property after all operations had ceased and thereafter took prudent and routine steps to secure the property against further depreciation." Id. at 12.

The court below, relying on *Mirabile*, similarly interpreted the statutory language to permit secured creditors to provide financial assistance and general, and even isolated instances of specific, management advice to its debtors without risking CERCLA liability if the secured creditor does not participate in the day-to-day management of the business or facility either before or after the business ceases operation. Applying this standard, the trial judge concluded that from the inception of Fleet's relationship with SPW in 1976 to June 22, 1982, when Baldwin entered the facility, Fleet's activity did not rise to the level of participation in management sufficient to impose CERCLA liability. The court, however, determined that the facts alleged by the government with respect to Fleet's involvement after Baldwin entered the facility were sufficient to preclude the granting of summary judgment in favor of Fleet on this issue.

Although we agree with the district court's resolution of the summary judgment motion, we find its construction of the statutory exemption too permissive towards secured creditors who are involved with toxic waste facilities. In order to achieve the "overwhelmingly remedial" goal of the CERCLA statutory scheme, ambiguous statutory terms should be construed to favor liability for the costs incurred by the government in responding to the hazards at such facilities. Allis Chalmers, 893 F.2d at 1317; see Maryland Bank & Trust Co., 632 F.Supp. at 579 (secured creditor exemption should be construed narrowly); Note, When a

Security Becomes a Liability: Claims Against Lenders in Hazardous Waste Cleanup, 38 Hastings L.J. 1261, 1285-86, 1291 (1987) (same) [hereinafter Claims Against Lenders]. The district court's broad interpretation of the exemption would essentially require a secured creditor to be involved in the operations of a facility in order to incur liability. This construction ignores the plain language of the exemption and essentially renders it meaningless. Individuals and entities involved in the operations of a facility are already liable as operators under the express language of section 9607(a)(2). Had Congress intended to absolve secured creditors from ownership liability, it would have done so. Instead, the statutory language chosen by Congress explicitly holds secured creditors liable if they participate in the management of a facility.

Although similar, the phrase "participating in the management" and the term "operator" are not congruent. Under the standard we adopt today, a secured creditor may incur section 9607(a)(2) liability, without being an operator, by participating in the financial management of a facility to a degree indicating a capacity to influence the corporation's treatment of hazardous wastes. It is not necessary for the secured creditor actually to involve itself in the day-to-day operations of the facility in order to be liable--although such conduct will certainly lead to the loss of the protection of the statutory exemption. Nor is it necessary for the secured creditor to participate in management decisions relating to hazardous waste. Rather, a secured creditor will be liable if its involvement with the management of the facility is sufficiently broad to support the inference that it could affect hazardous waste disposal decisions if it so chose.[1] We, therefore,

---

[1]   This narrow construction of the secured creditor exemption is supported by the sparse legislative history on the subject. The Senate version of CERCLA initially lacked an exemption for secured creditors in its definition of "owner or operator." See S. 1480, 97th Cong., 2d Sess., reprinted in 2 Senate Comm. on Environmental and Public Works, 97th Cong., 2 Sess., 1 A Legislative History of the CERCLA 470 (Comm. Print 1983). Representative Harsha introduced the exemption to the bill that was finally passed stating:

> This change is necessary because the original definition inadvertently subjected those who hold title to a ... facility, but do not participate in the management or operation and are not otherwise affiliated with the person leasing or operating the ... facility, to the liability provisions of the bill.

Remarks of Rep. Harsha, reprinted in 2 Senate Comm. on Environmental and Public Works, 97th Cong., 2d Sess., 2 A Legislative History of the CERCLA 945 (Comm. Print 1983) (emphasis added). The use of the word "affiliated" to describe the threshold at which a secured creditor becomes liable clearly indicates a more peripheral degree of involvement with the affairs of a facility than that necessary to be held liable as an operator. It also suggests that the interpretation of the exemption intended by Congress is more consistent with the level of secured creditor involvement described in our opinion than with the management of day-to-day operations standard set forth in Mirabile.

specifically reject the formulation of the secured creditor exemption suggested by the district court in *Mirabile*.

This construction of the secured creditor exemption, while less permissive than that of the trial court, is broader than that urged by the government and, therefore, should give lenders some latitude in their dealings with debtors without exposing themselves to potential liability.   Nothing in our discussion should preclude a secured creditor from monitoring any aspect of a debtor's business. Likewise, a secured creditor can become involved in occasional and discrete financial decisions relating to the protection of its security interest without incurring liability.

Our interpretation of the exemption may be challenged as creating disincentives for lenders to extend financial assistance to businesses with potential hazardous waste problems and encouraging secured creditors to distance themselves from the management actions, particularly those related to hazardous wastes, of their debtors.   As a result the improper treatment of hazardous wastes could be perpetuated rather than resolved.   These concerns are unfounded.

Our ruling today should encourage potential creditors to investigate thoroughly the waste treatment systems and policies of potential debtors.   If the treatment systems seem inadequate, the risk of CERCLA liability will be weighed into the terms of the loan agreement.   Creditors, therefore, will incur no greater risk than they bargained for and debtors, aware that inadequate hazardous waste treatment will have a significant adverse impact on their loan terms, will have powerful incentives to improve their handling of hazardous wastes.

Similarly, creditors' awareness that they are potentially liable under CERCLA will encourage them to monitor the hazardous waste treatment systems and policies of their debtors and insist upon compliance with acceptable treatment standards as a prerequisite to continued and future financial support.   Once a secured creditor's involvement with a facility becomes sufficiently broad that it can anticipate losing its exemption from CERCLA liability, it will have a strong incentive to address hazardous waste problems at the facility rather than studiously avoiding the investigation and amelioration of the hazard.

In Maryland Bank & Trust Co., the court aptly described and weighed the competing policy interests of creditors and the government in interpreting the secured creditor exemption:

> In essence, the defendant's position would convert CERCLA into an insurance scheme for financial institutions, protecting them against possible losses due to the security of loans with polluted properties. Mortgagees, however, already have the means to protect themselves, by making prudent loans. Financial institutions are in a position to investigate and discover potential problems in their secured properties.   For many lending institutions, such research is routine.   CERCLA will not absolve them from responsibility for their mistakes of judgment.

632 F.Supp. at 580 (citations omitted).

We agree with the court below that the government has alleged sufficient facts to hold Fleet liable under section 9607(a)(2). From 1976 until SPW ceased printing operations on February 27, 1981, Fleet's involvement with the facility was within the parameters of the secured creditor exemption to liability. During this period, Fleet regularly advanced funds to SPW against the assignment of SPW's accounts receivable, paid and arranged for security deposits for SPW's Georgia utility services, and informed SPW that it would not advance any more money when it determined that its advanced sums exceeded the value of SPW's accounts receivable.

Fleet's involvement with SPW, according to the government, increased substantially after SPW ceased printing operations at the Georgia plant on February 27, 1981, and began to wind down its affairs. Fleet required SPW to seek its approval before shipping its goods to customers, established the price for excess inventory, dictated when and to whom the finished goods should be shipped, determined when employees should be laid off, supervised the activity of the office administrator at the site, received and processed SPW's employment and tax forms, controlled access to the facility, and contracted with Baldwin to dispose of the fixtures and equipment at SPW. These facts, if proved, are sufficient to remove Fleet from the protection of the secured creditor exemption. Fleet's involvement in the financial management of the facility was pervasive, if not complete.[1] Furthermore, the government's allegations indicate that Fleet was also involved in the operational management of the facility. Either of these allegations is sufficient as a matter of law to impose CERCLA liability on a secured creditor. The district court's finding to the contrary is erroneous.

With respect to Fleet's involvement at the facility from the time it contracted with Baldwin in May 1982 until Nix left the facility in December 1983, we share the district court's conclusion that Fleet's alleged conduct brought it outside the statutory exemption for secured creditors.[2] Indeed, Fleet's involvement would

---

[1]   Generally, the lender's capacity to influence a debtor facility's treatment of hazardous waste will be inferred from the extent of its involvement in the facility's financial management. Here, that inference is not even necessary because there was evidence before the district court that Fleet actively asserted its control over the disposal of hazardous wastes at the site by prohibiting SPW from selling several barrels of chemicals to potential buyers. As a result, the barrels remained at the facility unattended until the EPA acted to remove the contaminants.

[2]   The district court summarized the government's allegations of Fleet's conduct at the facility during this period as follows:

Plaintiff alleges that Baldwin moved the barrels that allegedly contained hazardous substances before Baldwin conducted the public auction. Plaintiff contends that after the auction, Baldwin auctioned some, but not all, of the machinery and equipment as is, and in place, and permitted the purchasers to remove the equipment and machinery that they had purchased. Plaintiff asserts that after the auction Fleet signed a document that permitted Nix to have access

pass the threshold for operator liability under section 9607(a)(2).[1]   Fleet weakly contends that its activity at the facility from the time of the auction was within the secured creditor exemption because it was merely protecting its security interest in the facility and foreclosing its security interest in its equipment, inventory, and fixtures. This assertion, even if true, is immaterial to our analysis. The scope of the secured creditor exemption is not determined by whether the creditor's activity was taken to protect its security interest. What is relevant is the nature and extent of the creditor's involvement with the facility, not its motive. To hold otherwise would enable secured creditors to take indifferent and irresponsible actions toward their debtors' hazardous wastes with impunity by incanting that they were protecting their security interests. Congress did not intend CERCLA to sanction such abdication of responsibility.

CONCLUSION

We agree with the district court that Fleet is not within the class of liable persons described in section 9607(a)(1). We also conclude that the court properly denied Fleet's motion for summary judgment. Although the court erred in construing the secured creditor exemption to insulate Fleet from CERCLA liability for its conduct prior to June 22, 1982, it correctly ruled that Fleet was liable under section 9607(a)(2) for its subsequent activities if the government could establish its allegations. Because there remain disputed issues of material fact, the case is remanded for further proceedings consistent with this opinion.

AFFIRMED and REMANDED.

Problem

"Wachovia Bank made a loan to Otto Skipper in 1979 that was secured by 217 acres of land.   The 217 acres securing Wachovia's loan was generally

> to the facility for 180 days and to remove any remaining machinery and equipment.... Plaintiff maintains that friable asbestos was knocked loose from the pipes connected to the machinery and equipment by either the purchasers of the equipment at the auction or Nix. Plaintiff alleges that the condition of the chemicals and the asbestos in the facility after Baldwin, Nix, and the purchasers concluded their business constituted an immediate risk to public health and the environment....

Fleet Factors, 724 F.Supp. at 960-61. Fleet disputes these material facts. Id. at 961.
[1]   During oral argument, counsel for Fleet virtually conceded operator liability for its conduct with respect to the facility when he discussed Fleet's potential for liability were it to have fixed a hole in the roof of an SPW building: JUDGE KRAVITCH: If [Fleet] finds in fixing the roof that there is some asbestos that is being dislodged can it just ignore that? .... MR. GOOD: Once it fixes the roof, once it takes over control of fixing the roof, it has opened a potential pandora's box both as to that asbestos and anything else at that facility underneath it known and unknown. JUDGE KRAVITCH: Why isn't that analogous to what happened here?

undeveloped, rural land. During the 1970s, Skipper allegedly disposed of various hazardous waste materials at the undeveloped Potter's Pits site. In August 1976, the United States Coast Guard responded to complaints of an oil spill at Potter's Pits, and a clean-up operation commenced. Any sludge remaining in the area following the clean-up allegedly was mixed with sand and buried.

"Skipper defaulted on his loan in February 1980, and Wachovia exercised its rights as beneficiary under a deed of trust and foreclosed on the property. As was standard practice at the time, Wachovia referred the foreclosure to outside legal counsel. The counsel and the local court clerk handled the foreclosure process, and the sale was conducted according to state law. Wachovia, however, was the only bidder at the sale. As a result, it purchased the property and took title to the 217 acres on March 25, 1980. It did so, Wachovia has contended, solely to protect its security interest.

"Several days later, Wachovia signed a standard listing contract with local realtors to sell the entire property. No attempt was made by Wachovia following the foreclosure and the listing to develop or manage the 217 acres. Shortly after the placing of the property on the market, Jimmy Cain emerged as a potential purchaser. Both Cain and appellant McLamb visited the property, and on October 8, 1980, the men purchased the 217 acres. There was no discussion at the time of the sale of any prior oil spills at the Potter's Pits area. The district court concluded that the there was no indication that Wachovia had knowledge of the old oil spill prior to taking a security interest. It further found that the record reflected that Wachovia learned of the previous oil spill at Potter's Pits after the foreclosure but prior to selling the property. The district court made no findings in its opinion as to the appellants' knowledge of the past oil spill or as to whether the spill and subsequent clean-up were easily discoverable through reasonable investigations into the property.

"Cain and McLamb began developing the 217 acres into a residential subdivision called Sandy Creek Acres. Lots were sold. Earl Gurkin and his wife purchased Lot 85 in July 1982, and Lot 86 in early 1983. In July 1983, however, Wilbur McLamb received a letter from the Brunswick County Health Department indicating that Lots 85 and 86 were located near or on the site where the contamination had occurred in 1976. The letter also explained that the hazardous waste had not been entirely cleaned up. The Environmental Protection Agency ('EPA') began investigating the Gurkin's property in late 1983, and, shortly thereafter, it conducted a removal action at the site.

["In 1989, the United States filed a civil action pursuant to Section 107(a) of the Comprehensive Environmental Response, Compensation, and Liability Act ('CERCLA'), 42 U.S.C. §9601 et seq., to recover costs incurred for actions taken in response to the release of hazardous substances on several acres of land known as 'Potter's Pits.' Potter's Pits is located in Sandy Creek Acres, North Carolina. Named as defendants in the action were former landowners: Wilbur McLamb and Barbara McLamb, Jimmy F. Cain and Peggy Cain, Hubert J. Anderson and Ada Anderson, Investors Management Corporation ('IMC'), and Otto Skipper.

"In August 1990, the appellants-the McLambs and IMC-joined several of their co-defendants in filing a third-party complaint against appellee Wachovia Bank & Trust Co., N.A. ('Wachovia'). The complaint alleged fraud, negligent misrepresentation, breach of implied warranty, and contribution claims under CERCLA and North Carolina law.

"The district court granted summary judgment in favor of Wachovia on the appellants' CERCLA claim on the grounds that the bank was exempt from liability pursuant to the security interest exemption found in 42 U.S.C. §9601(20)(A) and 40 C.F.R. §300.1100(d) (1992).

"The appellants now appeal the grant of summary judgment in favor of Wachovia. They maintain that Wachovia is liable for contribution under CERCLA because it became an outright 'owner' of the contaminated site when it purchased the property at the foreclosure sale. Therefore, the argument continues, the bank does not qualify under the statutory exemption as a secured holder who had 'indicia of ownership primarily to protect [its] security interest.' They further contend that Wachovia should not fall within the security interest exemption because it did not act in a commercially reasonable manner after it took title to the property."] *United States v. McLamb*, 5 F.2d 69 (4th Cir. 1993).

Part 2

BANKRUPTCY LAW

Unit 6

OVERVIEW OF BANKRUPTCY

UNIT CONTENTS

A. WHAT IS BANKRUPTCY LAW?

The law of bankruptcy is federal law. It is primarily statutory law. For most of the twentieth century, bankruptcy was governed by the Bankruptcy Act of 1898 (commonly referred to as the "Act"). Bankruptcy cases filed since October 1, 1979, are governed by the Bankruptcy Reform Act of 1978 (commonly referred to as the "Bankruptcy Code"). This book will, of course, focus on the Bankruptcy Code, as amended.

The Bankruptcy Code divides the substantive law of bankruptcy into the following chapters:

Chapter 1, General Provisions, Definitions and Rules of
    Construction
Chapter 3, Case Administration
Chapter 5, Creditors, the Debtor, and the Estate
Chapter 7, Liquidation
Chapter 9, Adjustment of the Debts of a Municipality
Chapter 11, Reorganization
Chapter 12, Adjustment of Debts of a Family Farmer with
    Regular Annual Income
Chapter 13, Adjustment of the Debts of an Individual With
    Regular Income
Chapter 15, United States Trustees

The provisions in Chapters 1, 3, and 5 apply in every bankruptcy case, unless otherwise specified.

It is also necessary to deal with the Federal Rules of Bankruptcy Procedure ("Bankruptcy Rules"). They were promulgated by the United States Supreme Court pursuant to the authority of 28 U.S.C.A. section 2075. These Bankruptcy Rules, not the Federal Rules of Civil Procedure, "govern procedure in United States Bankruptcy Courts," Rule 1001. The Bankruptcy Rules are divided into ten parts. Each part governs a different stage of the bankruptcy process.

Bankruptcy law also includes state law. While principles of federal supremacy and the inability of states to impair the obligations of contracts preclude state legislatures from enacting bankruptcy laws, the Bankruptcy Code often expressly incorporates state law. See, e.g. sections 522(b), 544(b). Additionally, in applying the Bankruptcy Code, reference is commonly made to state common law concepts.

There are a few basic differences between bankruptcy law and state debtor-creditor law. State law puts a premium on prompt action by creditors: the first creditor to attach the debtor's property, the first creditor to execute on the property, etc. is the one most likely to be paid. Bankruptcy law, on the other hand, emphasizes equality of treatment, rather than a race of diligence. After the commencement of a bankruptcy case, a creditor generally cannot improve its position vis-a-vis other creditors by obtaining a lien on the assets of the debtor, see section 362. Similarly, a creditor's ability to improve its position before bankruptcy is limited considerably by bankruptcy law, section 547.

Second, the prospects for debtor relief are much greater in bankruptcy. The concept of "discharge" is unique for bankruptcy. A discharge relieves the debtor from any further liability on her debts.

While no debtor is guaranteed a bankruptcy discharge, most debtors who file for bankruptcy do receive a discharge. "One of the primary purposes of the bankruptcy act is to 'relieve the honest debtor from the weight of oppressive indebtedness and permit him to start afresh *** '" *Local Loan Co. v. Hunt*, 292 U.S. 234, 244, 54 S.Ct. 695, 699, 78 L.Ed. 1230, 1235 (1934).

Third, the vocabulary of bankruptcy law is different from the vocabulary in state law. Both ordinary terms such as "debtor" and "insolvent" and more technical terms such as "inventory" and "notice and hearing" are given special and unique meanings by the Bankruptcy Code. As you work with the provisions of the Bankruptcy Code, it is very important that you always check for definitions of the statutory terms. Section 101 of the Code is the primary, but not exclusive, source of such definitions.

A vocabulary list of the people involved in a bankruptcy case is set out below.

B. WHO IS INVOLVED IN A BANKRUPTCY CASE: A VOCABULARY LIST

1. *bankrupt*—no such person under the Bankruptcy Code.
2. *debtor*—person who files a voluntary petition or person against whom an involuntary petition is filed; in other words, the "bankrupt".
3. *holder of claim*—creditor. If D owes C $300,000 and D files a bankruptcy petition, D will be a debtor and C will be the holder of a claim.
4. *holder of a secured claim*—creditor with a lien on property of the debtor or a right of setoff against property of the debtor. The amount of a secured claim is limited by both the debt and the value of the collateral. If D owes C $300,000 and the debt is secured by Greenacre, the amount of C's secured claim will depend on the value of Greenacre. If Greenacre is valued at $200,000, then C's secured claim will only be $200,000. Under these facts, C will also have an unsecured claim for $100,000. A single credit transaction can be the basis for two claims: a secured claim and an unsecured claim.
5. *holder of unsecured claim*—a creditor that does not have a lien or right of setoff against the debtor's property or a creditor that has a lien on or right of setoff against property of the debtor that has a value less than the amount of the debt.
6. *bankruptcy judge*—a judicial officer of the district court.
7. *trustee*—representative of the creditors, generally a private citizen, not an employee of the federal government. There will be a

trustee in every Chapter 7, 12, and 13 case and some Chapter 11 cases. Her powers and duties vary from chapter to chapter. The trustee is generally appointed by the United States trustee. Creditors can elect a trustee to replace an appointed trustee.

8. *creditors' committee*—representatives of creditors in Chapter 11 cases.

9. *United States trustee*—federal government official who performs administrative tasks such as appointing trustees or members of a creditors' committee that a bankruptcy judge would otherwise have to perform.

10. *debtor in possession*—debtor in a Chapter 11 or Chapter 12 case. To illustrate, in a Chapter 11 case either the debtor will remain in control of its business or assets as debtor in possession or a trustee will be appointed to take control of the business or assets.

C. WHAT IS BANKRUPTCY?

There are two general forms of bankruptcy: (1) liquidation and (2) rehabilitation.

Chapter 7 of the Code is entitled "Liquidation." The terms "straight bankruptcy" or "bankruptcy" often are used to describe liquidation cases under the bankruptcy laws because the vast majority of bankruptcy cases are liquidation cases. In a typical Chapter 7 liquidation case, the trustee collects the nonexempt property of the debtor, converts that property to cash, and distributes the cash to the creditors. The debtor gives up all of the nonexempt property she owns at the time of the filing of the bankruptcy petition and hopes to obtain a discharge.

Chapters 11, 12, and 13 of the Bankruptcy Code contemplate debtor rehabilitation. In a rehabilitation case, creditors look to future earnings of the debtor, not to the property of the debtor at the time of the initiation of the bankruptcy proceeding, to satisfy their claims. The debtor generally retains its assets and makes payments to creditors, usually from post-petition earnings, pursuant to a court-approved plan.

Chapter 9 (Adjustment of Debts of a Municipality), Subchapters III and IV of Chapter 7 (Stockbroker and Commodity Broker Liquidation), and Subchapter 14 of Chapter 11 (Railroad Reorganization) are beyond the scope of this book.

D. WHAT HAPPENS IN A BANKRUPTCY CASE?

Is the debtor a business or a consumer? To state the obvious, what happens in a bankruptcy involving a large business such as Johns-Manville is going to be different from what happens in a bankruptcy involving a consumer such as Jane Jones. More than 90% of the bankruptcy cases involve nonbusiness debtors.

What happens in a bankruptcy case also depends on the form of bankruptcy - Chapter 7, Chapter 11, Chapter 12 or Chapter 13. Typically, 80% or more of the bankruptcy filings are under Chapter 7. Typically, a Chapter 11 case or a Chapter 12 case generates more legal issues and involves more lawyers than a Chapter 7 case or a Chapter 13 case.

1. Chapter 7

A Chapter 7 case has five stages:

1. getting the debtor into bankruptcy court;
2. collecting the debtor's property;
3. selling this property;
4. distributing the proceeds of the sale to creditors, and
5. determining whether the debtor is discharged from further liability to these creditors.

a. Commencement

A Chapter 7 case is commenced with the filing of a petition with the Bankruptcy Court, sections 301-303. The petition shall "conform substantially" to the petition set out in the Official Forms.[1]

Generally, the debtor files the bankruptcy petition. While creditors have a limited statutory right to initiate bankruptcy under Chapter 7 against a debtor, less than 1 of the Chapter 7 petitions are filed by creditors.[2] Debtor-initiated proceedings are often referred to as "voluntary;" creditor-initiated proceedings are often labeled "involuntary."

---

[1]   When it adopted Bankruptcy Rules, the Supreme Court also adopted Official Bankruptcy Forms.

[2]   The statistic that less than 1 of the Chapter 7 filings are by creditors probably does not accurately represent the practical significance of the involuntary bankruptcy provisions. It does not reflect the number of debtors who enter into workout agreements or file voluntary petitions because of the possibility of creditors filing an involuntary petition.

b. Collection

Section 704 charges the bankruptcy trustee with the duty of collecting the property of the estate in a Chapter 7 bankruptcy case. Who is the bankruptcy trustee and what is property of the estate?

Recall that the bankruptcy trustee is different from the United States trustee. The bankruptcy trustee is not a government employee; rather she is a private citizen who will be paid for her work in the Chapter 7 case in accordance with a statutory formula that looks to the moneys disbursed to creditors in the case, see section 326. A trustee is typically appointed by the United States trustee. Under section 702, creditors can replace this appointed trustee with a trustee of their choice.

Whether appointed by the United States trustee or elected by the creditors, the bankruptcy trustee is not a neutral observer. She is not neutral in that she is trying to recover from the debtor for creditors as much as possible. She is not an observer in that a Chapter 7 trustee is an active trustee.

One of the most important activities of the Chapter 7 trustee is the collection of the property of the estate from the debtor. The filing of a bankruptcy petition creates "property of the estate." Property of the estate includes all of the debtor's interests in property as of the time of the filing of the petition. (Section 541, which provides a more complete description of property of the estate, is considered later.) The Chapter 7 trustee must collect the property of the estate from the debtor. Additionally, the trustee is statutorily empowered to recover some property that the debtor transferred prior to bankruptcy.

How does the bankruptcy trustee learn what section 541 property the debtor owns and what property the debtor transferred prior to the petition? The schedules that the debtor is required to file by section 521 are one important source of such information; the meeting of creditors is another. Section 343 requires that the debtor appear at a meeting of creditors and submit to questioning under oath. Through such questioning the trustee and creditors try to locate and evaluate assets of the debtor and determine if any previous transfer of property by the debtor can be avoided.

Section 522 allows a debtor to claim as "exempt" from property of the estate "certain assets." In the typical Chapter 7 case of a consumer debtor, all or almost all property is exempt. In such a "no asset" case, there are no assets for the trustee to collect and liquidate.

c. Liquidation

In a Chapter 7 case, any distribution to creditors is typically in cash, not in kind. Accordingly, it is necessary for the trustee to sell the property that he collects. Some of the "property of the estate" will have little if any resale value. Most of the personal property owned by a consumer debtor has little resale value. Property owned by a business debtor may require extensive repairs to be made salable. The trustee has the power to "abandon" such "burdensome" property back to the debtor under section 554.

d. Distribution

A creditor with a valid lien on property will receive either its collateral or the proceeds from its sale.

Section 726 governs the proceeds from the sale of unencumbered property of the estate. Section 726 reflects the bankruptcy policy of treating similar creditors similarly. It provides for a pro rata distribution to the holders of allowed unsecured claims. If, for example, the sale of the *unencumbered* property of the estate nets $3,000 and there is $30,000 of *allowed* unsecured, *non-priority* claims, each general creditor will receive 10 of its claim.

The preceding sentence suggests the three principal exceptions to the general Chapter 7 policy of pro rata distribution. First, creditors whose claims are secured are treated more favorably. Second, certain unsecured claims enjoy a priority in distribution and are paid before other unsecured claims. Section 507 lists the claims with a priority status in bankruptcy. Third, section 726 does not call for dividends to be paid on all claims—only on allowed claims. Section 502 answers the question which claims are allowed.

e. Discharge

A discharge is a release of the debtor from any further personal liability for his or her pre-bankruptcy debts. *If* the debtor receives a discharge, all a creditor will receive will be its pro rata distribution even though the amount of the debt far exceeds the amount of this bankruptcy dividend.

To illustrate, assume that Sluggo files a Chapter 7 petition. At the time of the petition, he owes Mr. Bill $1,000. The amount of Sluggo's debts far exceeds the value of his non-exempt property. The liquidation of Sluggo's non-exempt property only yields $800 for $16,000 of unsecured debts. Remember Chapter 7 provides for a pro rata distribution. Accordingly, on these facts, Mr. Bill and Sluggo's other creditors with unsecured claims would receive only "five cents on the dollar." And, *if* Sluggo receives a discharge, Mr. Bill would be barred from attempting to collect the remaining $950 of his debt from Sluggo.

As the preceding paragraph implies, a discharge is not granted to each and every debtor. Section 727(a) lists ten grounds for barring the debtor from receiving a discharge. Even if he is able to receive a discharge, a debtor will not necessarily be freed from all creditors' claims. Section 523 excepts a number of debts from the operation of any discharge.

2. What Is Chapter 13 And How Does It Differ From Chapter 7?

The typical Chapter 13 cases is not a liquidation case. Generally, in Chapter 13, the debtor retains his or her property and prepares a plan proposing payments to creditors.

A Chapter 13 case has five stages. First, an individual debtor files a petition. Only the debtor can file a Chapter 13 petition. Only certain *individuals* are eligible for Chapter 13 relief. Second, the debtor files a plan providing for payments to creditors. The Code specifies what the plan must provide and what the plan may provide. The Code does not require that the plan provide for full payment of creditors; the plan may alter the rights of creditors. Third, the court reviews and determines whether the plan meets the requirements for confirmation of the plan. Fourth, after confirmation, the debtor makes the payments called for by the plan. Fifth, the debtor receives a discharge.

In Chapter 13 cases, as in Chapter 7 cases, the provisions in Chapters 1, 3, and 5 are applicable.

There are important differences between Chapter 7 cases and Chapter 13 cases. *Some* of these differences are:

- Only debtors can file a Chapter 13 case; debtors *and* creditors can file Chapter 7 cases.
- Chapter 7 relief is more generally available. Use of Chapter 13 is restricted to individual debtors "with a regular income" who meet the debt limits of section 109(e). Chapter 7 can be used by corporations, partnerships and individuals, with no debt limits.
- In a Chapter 7 case, the bankruptcy trustee takes possession of the property of the estate. In a Chapter 13 case, the debtor retains the property of the estate.
- In a Chapter 7 case, creditors are paid from the liquidation of the property of the estate, and the amount a particular creditor receives is governed by statute. The Chapter 7 distribution to creditors generally occurs within months of the bankruptcy filing. In a Chapter 13 case, creditors are generally paid from the debtor's post-petition earnings, and the amount a particular creditor receives

is governed by a court-approved plan. A Chapter 13 plan usually provides for payments over a three to five year period.

- In a Chapter 7 case, the availability of a discharge depends on whether a creditor can establish one of the statutory grounds for withholding a discharge. In a Chapter 13 case, the availability of a discharge depends primarily on whether the debtor makes his payments called for by the plan.
- A Chapter 13 discharge typically covers more kinds of debts than a Chapter 7 discharge.

Please look for other differences between Chapters 7 and 13 as you work through these materials.

3. What Is Chapter 11 And How Is It Different From Chapters 7 And 13?

Chapter 11, like Chapter 13, typically involves rehabilitation rather than liquidation. Although the Bankruptcy Code does not expressly restrict the use of Chapter 11 to business cases, the typical Chapter 11 case is a business case. A Chapter 11 case involving a business will typically have the following stages: (1) getting the debtor into bankruptcy, (2) operating the business, (3) formulating a plan of rehabilitation, (4) creditor acceptance of the plan, (5) court confirmation of the plan, (6) discharge and (7) payments under the plan.

There are important differences between Chapter 11 and Chapter 7. Some of the differences are:

- There is a trustee in every Chapter 7 case. In most Chapter 11 cases, there is not a trustee.
- In a Chapter 7 case, the trustee takes possession of the property of the estate and liquidates it. Creditors are paid from the liquidation of the property, and the amount a particular creditor receives is governed by statute. In a Chapter 11 case, the debtor as "debtor in possession" retains the property of the estate. Creditors are generally paid from the post-petition earnings of the debtor, and the amount a particular creditor receives is governed by a plan approved by both creditors and the court.
- In a Chapter 7 case, the availability of a discharge depends on whether a creditor can establish one of the statutory grounds for withholding a discharge. Typically in Chapter 11, the debtor receives a discharge when its plan is confirmed.

There are also important differences between Chapter 11 cases and Chapter 13 cases. Some of these differences are:

- Debtors and creditors can file a Chapter 11 petition; only certain debtors can file Chapter 13 petitions.
- Chapter 11 is more generally available. Chapter 11 can be used by corporations, partnerships and individuals with no debt limits. Chapter 13 is restricted to individuals with a regular income who meet the debt limits of section 109(e).
- Chapter 11 contemplates creditors' plans as well as debtor plans, and plans are generally filed months, if not years, after the petition. In Chapter 13, the plan can only be filed by the debtor and generally is filed at the same time as the bankruptcy petition.
- In Chapter 11, creditors vote on the plan. Creditors do not vote on a Chapter 13 plan.
- In Chapter 13 cases, discharge is delayed until the debtor performs under the plan. In Chapter 11, the discharge occurs at the confirmation of the plan.

4. What Is Chapter 12 And How Is It Different From The Other Chapters?

Chapter 12 was added to the Bankruptcy Code. It became effective on November 9, 1986. It provides an additional bankruptcy alternative for the "family farmer with a regular income" as defined in section 101.

Chapter 12 is modeled on Chapter 13. In Chapter 12, as in Chapter 13,

- Only the debtor can file the petition.
- The debtor retains the property of the estate.
- Payments to creditors are determined by the plan, and only the debtor can file the plan.
- Creditors do not vote on the plan; only the bankruptcy judge approves the plan.
- Chapter 12 debtors do not receive a discharge until they perform under the plan.

While Chapter 12 was based on chapter 13, it differs from Chapter 13 in a number of important respects. Eligibility is only the most obvious difference. Chapter 13 can be used by individuals with a regular income, regardless of the source of that income. Chapter 12 can only be used by debtors with a regular income from farming operation, regardless of whether the debtor is an individual or a corporation or partnership. Moreover, the debt limits for Chapter 12 are significantly higher than the debt limits for Chapter 13.

Please look for other differences between Chapters 7, 11, 12 and 13 as you work through these materials. And think about the differences in the roles of lawyers in the various chapters. For example, in a Chapter 7 case, the Bankruptcy Code controls (i) what amounts are to be distributed to creditors generally, (ii) how that distribution is to be allocated among the various creditors, and (iii) when the distribution is to occur. In a Chapter 7 case, the attorney for the trustee and the bankruptcy judge simply apply a series of statutory mandates. The lawyers' role is largely limited to litigating the application of these statutory mandates.

While Chapter 11 has its own statutory mandates, the process is basically a consensual one. Chapter 11 contemplates that the debtor and its creditors will themselves agree on (i) what amounts are to be distributed to creditors generally, (ii how that distribution is to be allocated among various creditors, and (iii) when the distribution is to occur. The lawyers' roles include negotiating a deal, drafting a plan and disclosure statement as well as litigating the applications of Chapter 1, 3, 5, and 11's various statutory mandates.

Chapter 13, like Chapter 11, requires a court-approved plan of debt restructuring. Nonetheless, the role of lawyers in Chapter 13 cases is probably more similar to the role of lawyers in Chapter 7 cases, than in Chapter 11 cases. In Chapter 13, like Chapter 7, the Bankruptcy Code mandates what amounts are to be distributed among creditors generally. While the Chapter 13 plan controls how that distribution is to be allocated among the various creditors and when the distribution is to occur, creditors do not have the opportunity to vote on the plan. In the typical Chapter 13 case, like the typical Chapter 7 case, the attorney for the debtor and the bankruptcy judge simply apply a series of statutory mandates, and the role of other attorneys is limited to litigating the application of these statutory mandates.

Unit 7

COMMENCEMENT, DISMISSAL AND CONVERSION OF BANKRUPTCY CASES

UNIT CONTENTS

A. COMMENCEMENT OF VOLUNTARY CASES

Section 301 deals with the commencement of voluntary cases. Please read section 301. Note both what section 301 requires and what it does not require.

It does *not* require "insolvency", as defined in section 101, or the inability to pay debts. It does require that the debtor be "an entity that may be a debtor under such chapter." What does the quoted phrase mean? Section 109 sets out who is eligible to be a debtor under each chapter. [What tells a law student or lawyer who is reading section 301 to look to section 109?]

Section 301 also requires that the debtor file a petition. The Judicial Conference of the United States has developed a form voluntary petition and other official forms. See Bankruptcy Rule 9009. Please review Form No. 1, Voluntary Petition.

A voluntary petition filed by an eligible debtor cannot be contested. The filing results in an automatic entry of an "order for relief."[1]

Notes and Problems

1. See generally Glen Ayers, *Commencing a Case Under the Bankruptcy Act of 1978: A Primer*, 51 Miss.L.J. 639 (1981).

2. Which of the following can file a Chapter 7 petition?

   a. H. Ross Perot

   b. Chaste Manhattan Bank

   c. King & Spalding, a partnership

   d. Toew Maine Lobster to Go, a sole proprietorship one of several businesses owned by Tom Toew

   e. Ward and June Cleaver (cf. section 302)

3. Which of the above can file a Chapter 11 petition?

4. Which of the above can file a Chapter 13 petition?

5. Cases and commentary sometimes refer to Chapter 20's (a debtor who receives a Chapter 7 discharge and later files a Chapter 13 petition) and Chapter 22's (a debtor who obtains confirmation of a Chapter 11 plan and later files another Chapter 11 petition). *See generally* Jeffrey Morris, *Serial Bankruptcy in Good Faith in Chapter 20*, 1 Faulkner & Gray's Bankruptcy Law Review 48 (Winter 1990); Barry Zaretsky, *Chapter 22 Cases* N.Y.L.J., November 21, 1991. The Bankruptcy Code deals with "serial" filing in sections 109(g) and 727(a)(8) and (9). The Supreme Court dealt with serial filing in *Johnson v. Home State Bank, infra*.

B. COMMENCEMENT OF INVOLUNTARY CASES

Most bankruptcy cases are "voluntary" cases; 99% of the Bankruptcy petitions are filed by debtors on Form 1. The other 1% of the bankruptcy petitions are filed on Form 10 by creditors—oops, by holders of claims.

---

[1] The phrase "order for relief" in the last sentence of section 301 replaces the term "adjudication" in the old Bankruptcy Act.

Section 303 deals with bankruptcy petitions filed by creditors. Please read section 303. Creditors may file bankruptcy petitions under Chapter 7 and Chapter 11, but not under Chapter 12 or Chapter 13. Certain debtors are protected from involuntary petitions. Debtors excluded from voluntary bankruptcy—railroads, insurance companies, banking institutions—are also excluded from involuntary bankruptcy. Additionally, farmers and charitable corporations may not be subjected to involuntary petitions. (Legislative history shows that farmers are excluded because of the cyclical nature of agriculture.)

The petition must be filed by the requisite number of creditors. Generally, three creditors with unsecured claims totaling at least $5,000 must join in the petition. If, however, the debtor has less than twelve unsecured creditors, a single creditor with an unsecured claim of $5,000 is sufficient.

An involuntary petition does not operate as an adjudication, or, in the language of the Bankruptcy Code, as an "order for relief." The debtor has the right to file an answer. If the debtor does not timely answer, "the court shall order relief," section 303(h). If the debtor does timely answer the petition, the court "shall order relief against the debtor" only if the petitioning creditor can establish one of the two grounds for involuntary relief in section 303(h).

The first basis for involuntary relief is that the debtor is generally not paying debts as they come due. This is sometimes referred to as "equitable insolvency."[1]

The alternative basis for involuntary relief is that within 120 days before the petition was filed, a general receiver, assignee or custodian took possession of substantially all of the debtor's property or was appointed to take charge of substantially all of the debtor's property. The appointment of a receiver in a mortgage foreclosure action to take possession of Greenacre, less than substantially all of the debtor's property, would not be a basis for involuntary relief.

Usually there will be an interval of at least several weeks between the filing of an involuntary petition and the order of relief against the debtor. During this period, the debtor may continue to buy, use, or sell property and to operate its business, section 303(f). The bankruptcy court may appoint an interim trustee to take possession of the debtor's property or operate the debtor's business "if necessary to preserve the property of the estate or to prevent loss to the estate,"

---

[1]   Insolvency in the equity sense, i.e., failure generally to pay debts as they become due, is the test in section 303. It is not, however, the bankruptcy test for insolvency. The definition of insolvency in section 101(26) is based on the traditional balance sheet test of excess of liabilities over assets at fair valuation. Accordingly, in sections of the Bankruptcy Code that use the term "insolvent", the balance sheet test is to be applied.

section 303(g). If an interim trustee is appointed, the debtor may regain possession by posting a bond.

Notwithstanding the protection of section 303(f), the filing of an involuntary petition adversely affects the debtor's financial reputation and business operations. Section 303(i) attempts to protect debtors from ill-founded petitions by setting out the following remedies in cases in which an involuntary petition is dismissed:

✓ The court *may* grant judgment for the debtor against the petitioning creditors for costs and a reasonable attorney's fee.

✓ If an interim trustee took possession of the debtor's property, the court *may* grant judgment for "any damages proximately caused by the taking."

✓ If the petition was filed in "bad faith," the court *may* award "any damages proximately caused by such filing," such as loss of business, and also punitive damages.

Problems

1. *See generally* Susan Block-Lieb, *Why Creditors File So Few Involuntary Petitions and Why the Number is Not Too Small,* 57 BROOKLYN L. REV. 803 (1991).

2. X, Y, and Z are trade creditors of D Co. D Co. is delinquent in its payments to X, Y, Z, and its other trade creditors. D Co., however, is current on its payment obligations to its bank creditors. X, Y, and Z believe that a prompt liquidation of D Co.'s assets will minimize their losses.

   a. Can X, Y, and Z file an involuntary petition?

   b. If so, should they file an involuntary Chapter 7 petition or an involuntary Chapter 11 petition?

3. C holds the first mortgage on D Shopping Center Ltd. D Shopping Center Ltd. is in default on this mortgage and on its obligations to its ten other creditors. Can C file an involuntary petition? What are the advantages to C, if any, of filing an involuntary bankruptcy petition instead of initiating a state mortgage foreclosure proceeding?

C. DISMISSAL

The Bankruptcy Code deals with dismissal of a bankruptcy case not only in section 303(i), discussed above, but also in sections 305, 707, 1112, 1208 and 1307.

The bankruptcy court may dismiss or suspend a voluntary bankruptcy proceeding even though it was filed by an eligible debtor. And, the bankruptcy court may dismiss or suspend an involuntary bankruptcy case even though all of the requirements are satisfied, section 305. This section empowers the bankruptcy court to dismiss or suspend a case if there is a foreign bankruptcy proceeding pending concerning the debtor or if "the interests of creditors and the debtor would be better served by such dismissal or suspension."

To illustrate, D, Inc. is generally not paying its debts as they come due. D, Inc. is trying to negotiate a workout with its creditors. Three of D, Inc.'s creditors are dissatisfied with the terms proposed in the workout and file an involuntary Chapter 11 petition against D, Inc. The bankruptcy court may decide to dismiss this petition if D, Inc. is making progress in negotiating a workout with its creditors.

A section 305 dismissal must be preceded by "notice and a hearing."[1] The decision to dismiss (or not to dismiss) is not appealable. If an involuntary petition is dismissed under section 305, the petitioning creditors are *not* liable for costs, attorneys fees or damages under section 303(i).

Note that section 305 applies to all forms of bankruptcy cases - Chapter 7 cases, Chapter 11 cases, Chapter 12 cases, and Chapter 13 cases. Additionally, each of these chapters has its own dismissal provision that applies only in cases under that chapter.

The ability of a debtor to effect the dismissal of a bankruptcy petition that she voluntarily filed varies from chapter to chapter. As the case below illustrates, debtors who filed for relief under Chapter 7 must establish "cause" in order to obtain a dismissal of their Chapter 7 petition.

In re Underwood
United States Bankruptcy Court, West Virginia, 1981
7 B.R. 936

Memorandum of Opinion
Edwin F. Flowers, Bankruptcy Judge.
The Debtors seek dismissal of their joint voluntary petition filed March 7,

---

[1]   Notice the definition of notice and hearing in section 102. You are now on notice of this provision.

1980, under chapter 7 of the Bankruptcy Code, in order to file a new petition including a new debt. Following the Debtors' meeting of creditors on April 14, the Trustee filed a report declaring that no assets were available for distribution to creditors, and a discharge hearing was then scheduled for September 16. However, on August 29, 1980, the Debtors filed a motion to dismiss their case. A supporting affidavit to the motion discloses that the Debtor, Mr. Underwood, was involved in an automobile accident on June 16, 1980, which resulted in a claim against him of $2,412.73. The Debtors contend that without a dismissal of the case, and subsequent filing to include this claim, they will be deprived of the fresh start Congress intended a bankruptcy discharge to provide. They argue that:

> [A] cause for dismissal is "adequate" when the Reform Act's purposes are promoted by such dismissal. Applying this test to the instant case, it can be seen that no creditors will be prejudiced by a dismissal. The estate has no assets by which dividends may be paid to creditors. Secondly, dismissal here would comport with the Reform Act's intended purpose of providing a fresh start to the debtor. [Memorandum of Points and Authorities at 2.]

The Debtors further argue that where notice of the motion to dismiss is given and no party objects, the voluntary dismissal must be granted without any showing of cause, citing In re Wirick, 3 B.R. 539, 6 B.C.D. 354 (Bkrtcy.E.D.Va.1980), to support their position. *Wirick* is premised, however, on the fact that "[a]ll creditors were properly noticed and none objected." In the present case, the tort creditor is not identified and there is no indication that notice of the dismissal motion was given to it or any other postpetition creditors. As sought here, the dismissal request does not afford procedural due process to adversely affected parties. Neither the tort creditor nor any other postpetition creditor was given notice of the debtors' motion to dismiss. The only parties who received notice were those who might conceivably be benefited by a dismissal while the parties adversely affected had no notice. Lack of objection to the dismissal request can thus scarcely be held to adequately support the motion.

Provisions of the Code and general equitable principles govern the granting of a dismissal in bankruptcy. Section 707 of the new Bankruptcy Code provides that:

> The court may dismiss a case under this chapter only after notice and a hearing and only for cause, including—
>
> (1) unreasonable delay by the debtor that is prejudicial to creditors; and
>
> (2) nonpayment of any fees and charges required under chapter 123 of title 28.

* * *

The Code perpetuates the American contribution to bankruptcy law of a fresh start through the discharge of past indebtedness. Similarly, the limitation on the frequency of this fresh start is continued from the old Act. Section 14(c)(5) of the Act excepted from discharge those cases filed within six years of a prior bankruptcy discharge. The new Bankruptcy Code provides that:

> The court shall grant a discharge, unless—
>
> ***
>
> (8) the debtor has been granted a discharge under this section *** in a case commenced within six years before the date of the filing of the petition; *** [§727(a)(8).]

Notably, the Code does not restrict the frequency of bankruptcy filings, only the frequency of bankruptcy discharges. Thus, a dismissal for the purpose of a new filing does no offense to any provision of the Code, but the expectation of a discharge of debts more than once every six years is beyond the relief provided under chapter 7.

Case processing burdens had prevented the discharge of the instant Debtors. Had a discharge been entered when the Debtors first became eligible, the tort debt would not have been included. A new bankruptcy petition and schedule of debts would include the liabilities which had accrued in the gap period between the first and second petitions and, in effect, would result in a second discharge within a six-year period. This raises the prospect of carefully timed dismissal requests which delay the entry of the discharge while new debts are being added. Such a course inequitably prejudices the rights of those creditors who extended credit after the initial petition. It is not known who they are or whether they extended credit to the Debtors in confidence that the Debtors were soon to be unburdened of other debts. These post-filing creditors could attempt to have their debts excepted from the discharge, but this substitutes a significant legal burden in place of a routine credit decision. The filing—dismissal—filing sequence leaves creditors uncertain whether a stay remains in effect and whether pursuit of nonbankruptcy relief will be rendered futile by a new petition. This converts the extraordinary relief of the automatic stay into an injunction at the whim of the debtor. Rather than a protective device for the debtor, the enjoinder of creditor action which flows automatically from the filing of a petition could become an unintended bargaining weapon for debtors.

The filing of a bankruptcy petition substantially affects the legal rights of the parties and effects significant results which should not be undermined by an on again—off again option for the debtor. The debtor and his counsel must decide whether it is advantageous to seek bankruptcy relief. They must decide what form of relief should be sought and, equally important, when to file for relief. At the time and in the fashion the debtor chooses, one of the most pervasive injunctions known to the law is entered; an estate is created consisting of the debtor's assets; debts and creditors whose claims will be discharged are identified; the accrual of interest on claims is cut off. These are but several of the legal consequences of the debtor's petition. Their impact on creditors is significant and should not be expended through prerogatives which the law does not clearly give a debtor.

Since a dismissal for the purpose of filing a new petition would result in an enlarged discharge, thus violating the limitations which Congress placed on chapter 7 relief, the Debtors' application should be denied.

Finally, a debtor facing circumstances similar to those in the instant case is not without recourse under the Code. Relief under the provisions of chapter 13 results in a discharge notwithstanding the entry of a discharge under chapter 7 within the previous six years. Considering the administrative burden that would be generated through multiple filings and dismissals, the available alternate statutory remedies should be utilized rather than the avenue sought here.

It is recognized that a debtor's improper action, such as failing to pay filing fees, might result in a dismissal which, by a forthright request, is here being denied. To preclude such an anomalous result, unless the provisions of the Bankruptcy Code are not being subverted, a dismissal ordinarily will be entered with prejudice.

Notes and Problems

1. In seeking dismissal of their voluntary Chapter 7 petition, why did the debtors rely on section 707, instead of section 305?

2. Why did the bankruptcy court deny the Underwoods' motion to dismiss? Would the bankruptcy court have granted the motion to dismiss if all post-petition creditors were given notice of the motion to dismiss and no creditor objected? But cf. section 707.

3. After the conclusion of this bankruptcy case, could the Underwoods file another Chapter 7 bankruptcy case?

4. Section 1307 governs dismissal of Chapter 13 petitions. If the Underwoods had filed a Chapter 13 petition instead of a Chapter 7 petition, would the bankruptcy court have granted their motion to dismiss? Is there any language in section 707 that corresponds to section 1307(b)?

5. Could the Underwoods have converted their Chapter 7 case to a Chapter 13 case and dismissed? See sections 706, 1307(b).

6. Please read section 707(b) which provides the bankruptcy court with discretion to dismiss a Chapter 7 case involving primarily consumer debts if the court "finds that granting relief would be a substantial abuse of the provisions of this Chapter (7)." What is "substantial abuse" for purposes of section 707(b)? Assume, for example, that D earns $150,000 a year. D spends all of this on drink, drugs, and dates, owns

no property and has unsecured debts of $101,000. D files a Chapter 7 petition. Should the court dismiss under section 707(b)? *See generally* Lawrence Young, *The Increasing Impact of Bankruptcy Code Section 707(b)*, 49 Bus. Law. 2043 (1990)

□□□□□□

Underwood involved an effort by debtors to obtain dismissal of a bankruptcy petition that the debtors filed. Most motions to dismiss bankruptcy petitions are filed by creditors in an effort to obtain dismissal of a bankruptcy petition that the debtor filed.

Under sections 707, 1112, 1208, and 1307, dismissal on a creditor's motion requires a showing of "cause." Each of these sections list circumstances constituting cause for dismissal; each of the lists is nonexclusive.

In re Johns-Manville Corp.

United States Bankruptcy Court, Southern District of New York, 1984
36 B.R. 727

Burton R. Lifland, Bankruptcy Judge.

Decision and Order on Motions to Dismiss
Manville's Chapter 11 Petition
Decision No. 1 on Correlated Manville Matters

I

Background and Issues Presented

Whether an industrial enterprise in the United States is highly successful is often gauged by its "membership" in what has come to be known as the "Fortune 500". Having attained this measure of financial achievement, Johns-Manville Corp. and its affiliated companies (collectively referred to as "Manville") were deemed a paradigm of success in corporate America by the financial community. Thus, Manville's filing for protection under Chapter 11 of Title 11 of the United States Code ("the Code or the Bankruptcy Code") on August 26, 1982 ("the filing date") was greeted with great surprise and consternation on the part of some of its creditors and other corporations that were being sued along with Manville for injuries caused by asbestos exposure. As discussed at length herein, Manville submits that the sole factor necessitating its filing is the mammoth problem of uncontrolled proliferation of asbestos health suits brought against it because of its substantial use for many years of products containing asbestos which injured those who came into contact with the dust of this lethal substance. According to Manville, this current problem of approximately 16,000 lawsuits pending as of the filing date is compounded by the crushing economic burden to be suffered by Manville over the next 20-30 years by the filing of an even more staggering number of suits by those who had been exposed but who will not manifest the asbestos-related diseases until some time during this future period ("the future asbestos claimants"). Indeed, approximately 6,000 asbestos health claims are estimated to have arisen in only the first 16 months since the filing date. This burden is further compounded by the insurance industry's general disavowal of liability to Manville on policies written for this very purpose. Indeed, the issue of coverage has been pending for years before a state court in California ("the California Coordinated Litigation").

It is the propriety of the filing by Manville which is the subject of the instant decision. Four separate motions to dismiss the petition pursuant to Section 1112(b) of the Code have been lodged before this Court by: (1) The Committee of Asbestos-Related Litigants and/or Creditors ("the Asbestos Committee"); (2) M.J. Whitman & Co. ("Whitman"); (3) GAF Corporation; and (4) Armstrong World Industries, Inc., Acands, Inc., Brinco Mining, Ltd., Cummings Insulation Co., Inc., Delaware Insulation Co., Eagle-Picher Industries, Inc., Fibreboard Corp., Keene Corp., The McCormick Asbestos Co., Metalclad Insulation Corp., North Bros. Co., Owens-Illinois, Inc., Pacor, Inc., Pittsburgh Corning Corp., Rock Wool Manufacturing Co., Shook & Fletcher Insulation Co., and W.R. Grace & Co. ("the Co-defendants").

Manville has opposed all four dismissal motions and has been joined in opposition to them by the Unofficial Committee of School Creditors and the Equity Holders Committee. The Unsecured Creditors' Committee has filed a brief "in response" to the motions which advocates denial of the motions.

The Asbestos Committee, which is comprised with one exception of attorneys for asbestos victims, initially moved to dismiss this case on November 8, 1982 citing Manville's alleged lack of good faith in filing this petition. However, the Asbestos Committee did not press its motion before the Court until now, more than one year later. In the interim, while engaging in plan formulation negotiations, it has vigorously pursued discovery in order to bolster its factual contention that Manville knowingly perpetrated a fraud on this Court and on all its creditors and equity holders in exaggerating the profundity of its economic distress in 1981 so as to enable it to file for reorganization in 1982. Thus, the Asbestos Committee submitted in November 1983 a multitude of volumes of materials consisting of 55 days of depositions of Manville officers in alleged support of the inference that in 1981 a small Manville group "concocted" evidence to meet the requirements for filing a Chapter 11 petition. The Asbestos Committee alleges that this group manufactured evidence of crushing economic distress so as to demonstrate falsely that pursuant to required principles of accounting (Financial Accounting Standards Board No. 5 ("FASB-5")), Manville had to book a reserve of at least $1.9 billion for asbestos health liability, and thus had no alternative but to seek Chapter 11 protection. The booking of such a reserve would, in turn, have triggered the acceleration of approximately $450 million of outstanding debt, possibly resulting in a forced liquidation of key business segments. Thus, the multitudinous submissions by the Asbestos

Committee are aimed at showing their challenge to the motive, methods and data used by Manville's accounting consultants, its management and its Litigation Advisory Group ("LAG") in determining whether relief under Chapter 11 should be sought.

Mindful that there is no insolvency requirement for Chapter 11 debtor status, the issue presented for determination by this Court is whether these allegations of error by the Asbestos Committee, even egregious error, in over-calculation of Manville's financial problems are relevant to establish the kind of bad faith in the sense of an abuse of this Court's jurisdiction which will vitiate the filing of a Chapter 11 petition. This opinion will thus elucidate whether the tomes of material submitted by the Asbestos Committee defeat the essential fact that as of August 26, 1982 Manville is a real company with real debt, real creditors and a compelling need to reorganize in order to meet these obligations.

The Whitman motion dated November 1, 1982, the GAF motion dated September 29, 1983 and the most recently filed Co-defendants' motion dated December 14, 1983 all advance purely legal arguments and require no factual determination by this Court. They are based on the theory that because the claims of future asbestos victims are not cognizable or dischargeable in bankruptcy, the *raison d'etre* for the filing is vitiated and thus the petition should be dismissed. However, this Court must bear in mind in determining the issues raised by these movants that even if the claims of future claimants are ultimately found not dischargeable, that finding does not necessarily preclude this Court from dealing with the interests of these "parties in interest" under Code Section 1109(b), especially since blinding the reorganization process to their residual interests would doom this reorganization case to ineffectiveness. If future claimants are properly represented as parties in interest, the means for the emergence of a proper plan which fairly provides for the survival and just treatment of their interests post-petition will be better assured.

As background information, it should be noted that throughout the course of the past 16 months, all parties, including the movants herein, have participated to a substantial extent in negotiations aimed at formulating a consensual plan treating all interests justly and fairly. Indeed, it is interesting to note that some of the very co-defendants which now seek to dismiss the petition, notably Owens-Illinois and Keene Corp., have previously expressed on the record before this Court their fervent desire to engraft themselves onto any plan providing for a claims-handling facility with which to deal with asbestos claimants. They have related to the Court their arduous efforts at formulating a sharing arrangement whereby all co-defendants, including Manville, may apportion their relative liabilities to the victims as a first step toward full participation in and contribution to any claims-handling Manville reorganization plan to be funded by an industry "super fund".

The shifting posture of many of the co-defendants is in no small measure impelled by their continued involvement in the nonbankruptcy asbestos litigation and the filing by Manville of a plan that as yet does not provide a sharing and contribution arrangement. In any event, whether or not the co-defendants may for the purpose of the dismissal motions deem it prudent to participate in the reorganization effort and effect a global solution to the asbestos problem, Manville should have the opportunity to attempt to successfully reorganize with or without them so long as it conforms to all Code requirements.

Throughout this 16-month period, the Asbestos Committee, at considerate expense to the debtor, has engaged its own counsel and epidemiologists and, jointly with the Unsecured Creditors' Committee, engaged an investment banking firm to prepare projections of future income in aid of plan formation. It is only now that negotiations have become seemingly deadlocked that the Asbestos Committee has reverted to its original position of attacking the filing. If there was merit in the motion to dismiss on grounds of lack of good faith, it could have been fervently pressed a year ago instead of tolerating this alleged misuse of the courts. This same assertion of untimeliness can be made regarding the other co-defendant proponents of dismissal of the petition because they too may be pressing these motions as a last resort as a result of frustrations at the bargaining table. This Court must therefore bear in mind the strategical motivations underlying the pursuit of these motions at this time as well as recognize the progress toward a successful, perhaps consensual, reorganization that has already taken place. It is against this backdrop of progress and achievement accomplished by the key constituencies toward a resolution on perhaps a sweeping basis of the asbestos problem that the instant motions are now placed before me for determination.

II
Discussion of Law

A. *General Eligibility Requirements For Chapter 11 Status*

The motions to dismiss Manville's petition filed by the Asbestos Committee, GAF, Whitman, and the Codefendants must be denied. Preliminarily, it must be stated that there is no question that Manville is eligible to be a debtor under the Code's statutory requirements. Section 109 of the Code contains its eligibility requirements and provides in pertinent part:

> (a) Notwithstanding any other provision of this section, only a person that resides in the United States, or has a domicile, a place of business, or property in the United States, or a municipality, may be a debtor under this title
>
> (b) A person may be a debtor under Chapter 7 of this title only if such person is not—
>
> (1) a railroad;

(2) a domestic insurance company, bank, savings bank, cooperative bank, savings and loan association, building and loan association, homestead association, or credit union; or

(3) a foreign insurance company, bank, savings bank, cooperative bank, savings and loan association, building and loan association, homestead association, or credit union, engaged in such business in the United States
***

(d) Only a person that may be a debtor under Chapter 7 of this title, except a stockbroker or commodity broker, and a railroad may be a debtor under Chapter 11 of this title.

Clearly, Manville meets the requirements contained in subsection (a) for debtors under all chapters of the Code in that it is domiciled and has its place of business in the United States. Also, the word "person" used in subsection (a), as defined in Code section 101(30), includes an individual, a partnership, and a corporation, but not a governmental unit.

In addition, Manville meets the eligibility requirements contained in subsection (b) and made applicable to Chapter 11 debtors by subsection (d). Manville is obviously not any of the prohibited entities described in subsection (b).

Moreover, it should also be noted that neither Section 109 nor any other provision relating to voluntary petitions by companies contains any insolvency requirement. The Collier treatise so declares with regard to Chapter 7 debtors, stating: "Under this subdivision any person not within the excluded class who owes debts in any amount, no matter how small, may file a petition for liquidation." And, with specific regard to Chapter 11, the Code eliminates the requirement contained in former Sections 77(a), 130(1), 323 and 423 of the Act that the debtor be insolvent or unable to pay his debts as they mature. This is in striking contrast to the requirement of insolvency contained in Code Section 303 with regard to the commencement of involuntary cases. Code Section 303(h) provides in pertinent part:

If the Petition is not timely controverted, the court shall order relief against the debtor in an involuntary case under the chapter under which the petition was filed. Otherwise, after trial, the court shall order relief against the debtor in an involuntary case *** only if—

(1) the debtor *is generally not paying such debtor's debts as they become due.* ***

In contrast, Code Section 301 provides:

A voluntary case under a chapter of this title is commenced by the filing with the bankruptcy court of a petition under such chapter by an entity that may be a debtor under such chapter. The commencement of a voluntary case under a chapter of this title constitutes an order for relief under such chapter.

It is only with regard to Chapter 9 (Adjustment of Debts of a Municipality) that the Code mentions insolvency or inability to meet one's debts. *See* Code Section 109(c)(3).

Accordingly it is abundantly clear that Manville has met all of the threshold eligibility requirements for filing a voluntary petition under the Code. This Court will now turn to the issue of whether any of the movants have demonstrated sufficient "cause" pursuant to Code Section 1112(b) to warrant the dismissal of Manville's petition.

B. The Standard of "Cause" For Dismissal Of A Chapter 11 Petition

Section 1112(b) of the Code provides for conversion or dismissal of a case for "cause". It lists nine examples of cause, but the list is not exhaustive. One court has described the pertinent legislative history, declaring: "The court will be able to consider other factors as they arise, and use its equitable powers to reach an appropriate result in individual cases. What constitutes cause under section 1112(b) is subject to judicial discretion under the circumstances of each case."

Much of the argument in support of all of the motions to dismiss is pitched to the confirmability of Manville's proposed plan. This argument is misplaced. Under the statutory reorganization scheme, there can be many plans advanced by many interests. The essential determination here is the propriety of the filing, and whether "cause" exists to vitiate it, not the confirmability of a particular plan. If Manville is unable to effectuate a particular plan, that is not tantamount to finding that no plan can be effectuated.

C. The Motion To Dismiss Filed By The Asbestos Committee

The motion to dismiss the petition filed by the Asbestos Committee must also be denied. The Asbestos Committee premises its motion to dismiss the petition on what it contends is Manville's "bad faith" in filing for protection under Chapter 11. As the Asbestos Committee states in its brief submitted to the district court in support of its unsuccessful motion to withdraw the reference on the instant motion: "The Asbestos Committee is prepared to prove that Manville's Chapter 11 petition is purely a bad faith maneuver by Manville to curtail its liabilities. ***" And, in its papers in support of that motion to dismiss, the Asbestos Committee states: "These Chapter 11 cases were filed in bad faith, are an abuse of the provisions of Chapter 11 and an imposition on this Court's jurisdiction and should therefore be dismissed without further delay".

Because the allegations of the Asbestos Committee are not supported by concrete facts and thus do not rebut the essential fact that Manville is a real company with a substantial amount of real debt and real creditors clamoring to enforce this real debt, the Asbestos Committee has not sustained its burden of demonstrating sufficient fraud to vitiate the filing *ab initio*.

1. The Code's Policies Of Open Access And Liquidation Avoidance

In determining whether to dismiss under Code Section 1112(b), a court is not necessarily required to consider whether the debtor has filed in "good faith" because that is not a specified predicate under the Code for filing. Rather, according to Code Section 1129(a)(3), good faith emerges as a requirement for the confirmation of a plan. The filing of a Chapter 11 case creates an estate for the benefit of all creditors and equity holders of the debtor wherein all constituencies may voice their interests and bargain for their best possible treatment. It is thus logical that the good faith of the debtor be deemed a predicate primarily for emergence out of a Chapter 11 case. It is after the confirmation of a concrete and immutable reorganization plan that creditors are foreclosed from advancing their distinct and parochial interests in the debtor's estate.

A "principal goal" of the Bankruptcy Code is to provide "open access" to the "bankruptcy process". The rationale behind this "open access" policy is to provide access to bankruptcy relief which is as "open" as "access to the credit economy." Thus, Congress intended that "there should be no legal barrier to voluntary petitions." Another major goal of the Code, that of "rehabilitation of debtors", requires that relief for debtors must be "timely". Congress declared that it is essential to both the "open access" and "rehabilitation" goals that

> [i]nitiating relief should not be a death knell. The process should encourage resort to it, by debtors and creditors, that cuts short the dissipation of assets and the accumulation of debts. Belated commencement of a case may kill an opportunity for reorganization or arrangement.

Accordingly, the drafters of the Code envisioned that a financially beleaguered debtor with real debt and real creditors should not be required to wait until the economic situation is beyond repair in order to file a reorganization petition. The "Congressional purpose" in enacting the Code was to encourage resort to the bankruptcy process. This philosophy not only comports with the elimination of an insolvency requirement, but also is a corollary of the key aim of Chapter 11 of the Code, that of avoidance of liquidation. The drafters of the Code announced this goal, declaring that reorganization is more efficient than liquidation because "assets that are used for production in the industry for which they were designed are more valuable than those same assets sold for scrap." Moreover, reorganization also fosters the goals of preservation of jobs in the threatened entity.

In the instant case, not only would liquidation be wasteful and inefficient in destroying the utility of valuable assets of the companies as well as jobs, but, more importantly, liquidation would preclude just compensation of some present asbestos victims and all future asbestos claimants. This unassailable reality represents all the more reason for this Court to adhere to this basic potential liquidation avoidance aim of Chapter 11 and deny the motions to dismiss. Manville must not be required to wait until its economic picture has deteriorated beyond salvation to file for reorganization. Manville's purported motivation in filing to obtain a breathing spell from asbestos litigation should not conclusively establish its lack of intent to rehabilitate and justify the dismissal of its petition. On the contrary, there has been submitted no evidence that Manville has not bargained to obtain a reorganization plan in good faith.

2. Manville's "Good Faith" Filing Is Measured By The Existence Of Massive Unmanageable Real Debt Owed To Real Claimants

It is this Court's belief that there is no strict and absolute "good faith" predicate to filing a Chapter 11 petition. Earlier bankruptcy laws, for example, former Chapter X relating to corporate debtors specifically required that the court find that the petition "had been filed in good faith". *See* §§141, 146. However, the present Bankruptcy Code contains no such express requirement.

This Court, along with others, has opined that the concept of good faith is an elastic one which can be read into the statute on a limited *ad hoc* basis. Slavish adherence to a good faith concept may redound to the detriment of those non-debtor claimants who are or may putatively be beneficiaries of the reorganization process. Chapter 11 filing creates a bankruptcy estate which exists for the debtor's creditors and equity holders. The filing triggers the springing into existence of important constituencies which, along with the debtor, must be protected by a reorganization court. Accordingly, the intense focus on the debtor's motives in filing is misplaced. In *Manville*, it is undeniable that there has been no sham or hoax perpetrated on the Court in that Manville is a real business with real creditors in pressing need of economic reorganization. Indeed, the Asbestos Committee has belied its own contention that Manville has no debt and no real creditors by quantifying a benchmark settlement demand approaching one billion dollars for compensation of approximately 15,500 prepetition asbestos claimants, during the course of negotiations pitched toward achieving a consensual plan. This huge asserted liability does not even take into account the estimated 6,000 new asbestos health claims which have arisen in only the first 16 months since the filing date. The number of post-filing claims increases each day as "future claims back into the present."

Moreover, asbestos related property damage claims present another substantial contingent and unliquidated liability. Prior to the filing date, various schools initiated litigation seeking compensatory and punitive damages from, *inter alia*, Manville for their unknowing use of asbestos-containing products in ceilings, walls, structural members, piping, ductwork and boilers in school buildings.

In short, there was justification for Manville to elect a course contemplating a viable court-supervised rehabilitation of the real debt owed by Manville to its real creditors. Thus, its petition must be sustained.

D. The GAF, Whitman And Co-defendants' Motions To Dismiss The Petition Must Be Denied

The motion filed by GAF to dismiss this petition raises only legal issues and turns on no factual determinations. It is based on the theory that because the claims of future asbestos claimants are not cognizable and dischargeable in bankruptcy, the *raison d'etre* for the filing is vitiated and thus the petition should be dismissed.

Like the GAF motion, the Whitman motion is premised on a mechanistic interpretation of the provisions of and commentary to the Code to the effect that the future claims are too contingent to be cognizable "claims" under the Code.

The Co-defendants' motion to dismiss the petition similarly must be dismissed as it too is predicated on the theory that future claims are not dischargeable in a Chapter 11 proceeding.

As stated earlier, the type of plan which emerges, *i.e.*, whether or not it treats with future claimants fairly, if at all, is irrelevant to the threshold determination made by this Court today as to the propriety or "good faith" of Manville's filing. These pejorative considerations are more appropriately left to the decision on confirmability of a concrete plan, as applied to a plan proponent, under Section 1129 of the Code.

IV
Conclusion

All four of the motions to dismiss the Manville petition are denied in their entirety.

It is SO ORDERED.

Notes and Problems

1. This case involves a motion to dismiss filed by creditors. Why do creditors file a motion to dismiss? One of the groups filing a motion to dismiss in the *Johns-Manville* case was the Committee of the Asbestos Related Litigants and/or Creditors. Why did it want the bankruptcy case dismissed?

2. D files a Chapter 11 petition, its creditors file a motion to dismiss, and the court dismisses the case. How long does D have to wait before it can file another bankruptcy petition? Cf. section 109(f).

3. As the *Manville* opinion indicates, insolvency is no longer a requirement for filing a voluntary petition. Why? Is the debtor's solvency "cause" for purposes of section 1112? Was Manville "insolvent"?

4. As the *Manville* opinion also notes, the Bankruptcy Code drops the good faith filing requirement of the 1898 Act. Is the debtor's lack of good faith in filing its bankruptcy petition "cause" for dismissal under section 1112? If so, how can creditors establish this lack of good faith?

5. *See generally* Carlos Cuevas, *Good Faith and Chapter 11: Standards that Should Be Employed to Dismiss Bad Faith Chapter 11 Cases*, 60 Tenn. L. Rev. 525 (1993); Janet Flaccus, *Have Eight Circuits Shorted? Good Faith and Chapter 11 Bankruptcy Petitions*, 67 Am. Bankr. L.J. 401 (1993); Lawrence Ponoroff & F. Stephen Knippenberg, *The Implied Good Faith Filing Requirement: Sentinel of an Evolving Bankruptcy Policy*, 85 Nw U.L. Rev. 919 (1991).

6. Most of the reported cases on motions to dismiss for lack of good faith in filing involve debtors with a single real estate asset that file for Chapter 11 relief on the eve of foreclosure of that asset. Single asset real estate cases have been singled out for special treatment and are separately treated in Unit 17.

D. CONVERSION

If a debtor is dissatisfied with his initial choice of form for bankruptcy, he can change his mind and choose another chapter by filing a motion to convert his case to another chapter. Similarly, creditors can request the court to convert a pending case to another chapter.

Section 706 governs conversion from Chapter 7; section 1112 deals with conversion from Chapter 11; section 1208 applies to conversion from Chapter 12; section 1307 controls conversion from Chapter 13. Generally, motions to convert are filed by debtors who try to effect a rehabilitation under Chapter 11 or Chapter 13 and now want to liquidate under Chapter 7.

Section 348 and Rule 1019 deal with the legal consequences of a conversion from one chapter to another. See generally David G. Epstein, *Consequences of Converting a Bankruptcy Case*, 60 Am.Bankr.L.J. 339 (1986).

Unit 8

LEGAL CONSEQUENCES OF THE COMMENCEMENT OF A BANKRUPTCY CASE

UNIT CONTENTS

The mere filing of a bankruptcy petition, voluntary or involuntary, has immediate legal consequences on both the debtor and creditors.

A bankruptcy filing affects the debtor's use and/or possession of her property by creating "property of the estate." Similarly a bankruptcy filing affects the creditors' ability to collect their pre-bankruptcy claims by imposing an "automatic stay" that bars or "stays" any creditor from taking action against the debtor or her property to collect pre-bankruptcy debts.

The bankruptcy filing also serves a date of cleavage. For example, property of the estate is generally limited to the debtor's interests in property as of the filing of the petition. Similarly, the automatic stay and other Bankruptcy Code provisions distinguish between claims that arose before the commencement of the bankruptcy case and postpetition claims.

The basic bankruptcy concepts of "property of the estate" and "automatic stay" are considered below.

A. PROPERTY OF THE ESTATE

1. Why Is Property Of The Estate An Important Concept?

The filing of a bankruptcy petition automatically creates an estate, section 541(a).

In a Chapter 7 case, "property of the estate" is collected by the bankruptcy trustee and sold; the proceeds from the sale of the property of the estate are then distributed to creditors, sections 704, 726. In other words, the loss of property of the estate is the primary cost of Chapter 7 bankruptcy to the debtor; the receipt of the proceeds from the sale of property of the estate is the primary benefit creditors derive from a Chapter 7 bankruptcy.

In most Chapter 11 and 12 cases, the debtor will remain in possession of "property of the estate" as "debtor-in-possession". However, the Chapter 11 or Chapter 12 debtor-in-possession's use of the property of the estate will be subject to bankruptcy court supervision. Consider the example of Chapter 11 cases involving business debtors. Successful rehabilitation of a business generally requires continued operation of the business. Continued operation of the business generally requires continued possession of the business property. A debtor will continue to operate its business in Chapter 11 as debtor-in-possession unless a request is made by a "party in interest" for the appointment of a trustee, and the bankruptcy court, after notice and hearing, grants the request. (When a trustee is appointed in a Chapter 11 case, she takes possession of property of the estate. Even if a trustee is not appointed in a Chapter 11 case, the debtor-in-possession's use and sale of the property of the estate is subject to the supervision of the bankruptcy judge as provided in section 363. Section 363 is considered later.

Similarly, in Chapter 12 cases, the debtor will generally retain possession of the property and continue to operate the farm. As in Chapter 11, a "party in interest" can request that the debtor-in-possession be dispossessed and a trustee takeover. And, again as in Chapter 11, if a trustee is not so installed, the Chapter 12 debtor in possession's use and sale of the property of the estate is subject to the supervision of the bankruptcy court as provided in sections 363 and 1206.

While Chapter 13 contemplates that there will be a trustee in every case, a Chapter 13 trustee does not take possession of property of the estate. A debtor who files for Chapter 13 relief retains possession of his property. Again, however, the use and sale of "property of the estate" is subject to the supervision of the bankruptcy court as provided in section 363.

In both Chapter 12 and Chapter 13 cases, the value of the property of the estate determines the minimum amount that must be offered to holders of unsecured claims in the debtor's plan of repayment, sections 1225(a)(4), 1325(a)(4). Chapter 11 imposes a similar requirement as to nonassenting holders of unsecured claims, section 1129(a)(7)(A)(ii).

Finally, a number of general provisions in Chapters 3 and 5 that are applicable in all bankruptcy cases use the phrase "property of the estate." For example, the automatic stay bars a creditor from collecting a claim from property of the estate, section 362(a)(3), (4).

In short, in all bankruptcy cases and in all bankruptcy classes, it is necessary to be able to answer the question what does property of the estate include.

2. What Does Property Of The Estate Include?

With only minor exceptions, property of the estate includes all property of the debtor as of the time of the filing of the bankruptcy petition.

The seven numbered subparagraphs of section 541 specify what property becomes property of the estate. Paragraph one is by far the most comprehensive and significant. Section 541(a)(1) provides that property of the estate includes "all legal or equitable interests of the debtor in property as of the commencement of the case." This is a very broad statement. Property of the estate thus includes both real property and personal property, both tangible and intangible property, both property in the debtor's possession and property that is held by others in which the debtor has an interest.

The application of section 541(a)(1) requires answering three questions:

1. Is the item in question "property" for purposes of section 541(a)(1)?
2. If so, what is the debtor's interest in that property? [Note that section 541(a)(1) reaches merely the debtor's interest in property rather than simply the debtor's property.]
3. If so, did the debtor have this interest in the property as of the time of the commencement of the bankruptcy case?

The *FitzSimmons* case illustrates the third question. The first two questions will then be discussed in connection with *Chicago Board of Trade v. Johnson*, infra.

In re Fitzsimmons
United States Court of Appeals, Ninth Circuit, 1984
725 F.2d 1208

Goodwin, Circuit Judge: Edward M. Walsh, trustee in bankruptcy of the estate of Edward R. FitzSimmons, appeals from a decision of the Bankruptcy Appellate Panels of the Ninth Circuit.

Edward FitzSimmons is an attorney who operates as a sole proprietorship a law practice known as "Law Offices of Edward R. FitzSimmons." The practice employs other attorneys, along with various other staff members. In July of 1980, FitzSimmons filed a voluntary petition in the United States Bankruptcy Court for the Northern District of California seeking relief under Chapter 11 of the Bankruptcy Code.

At first, FitzSimmons was debtor-in-possession of his entire estate, including his law practice. The Bankruptcy Court subsequently appointed Walsh trustee of FitzSimmons' estate, with the exception of his law practice, and entered an order regulating FitzSimmons' operation of the law practice. This order allowed FitzSimmons to continue to operate the law practice as debtor-in-possession on behalf of the estate, subject to various restrictions. It permitted FitzSimmons to pay himself a salary of $3,500 per month out of the funds of the law practice and required him to remit to the Trustee at the end of each month all funds of the law practice in excess of $15,000.

After unsuccessfully moving for modification of the Bankruptcy Court's order, FitzSimmons appealed to the Bankruptcy Appellate Panels of the Ninth Circuit. A panel reversed the Bankruptcy Court's order, one judge dissenting, "insofar as it holds that post-bankruptcy earnings from services performed by an individual debtor are property of the estate in a Chapter 11 case."

When FitzSimmons filed his petition for bankruptcy relief, an estate was created. §541(a). This estate comprises the property that will ultimately be available to satisfy the costs of bankruptcy administration and pay off the claims of creditors, subject to the right of the debtor to declare some of the estate exempt under §522(b). The scope of the estate is broad: it includes, with two minor exceptions, "all legal or equitable interests of the debtor in property as of the commencement of the case." §541(a)(1). Section 541 goes on to include in the estate "[p]roceeds, product, offspring, rents, and profits of or from property of the estate," subject to one important limitation: "except such as are earnings from services performed by an individual debtor after the commencement of the case." §541(a)(6). This case requires us to determine the scope of the earnings exception contained in §541(a)(6).

FitzSimmons contends that since he operates his law practice as a sole proprietorship, all of the earnings generated by the practice are "earnings from services performed by an individual debtor" and fall within the earnings exception. The trustee contends that all the earnings of the practice belong to the estate, and that FitzSimmons is entitled to only the salary that the bankruptcy court allowed him.

To arrive at a proper construction of §541(a)(6), we consider its interrelationship with the other provisions of the Bankruptcy Code. Chapter 11 seeks to preserve a foundering business as a going concern, because the assets of a business are often more valuable when so maintained than they would be when liquidated. The purpose of Chapter 11, therefore, is to restructure a business' debts so that the business may continue to operate. To this end, §1108 authorizes the trustee (or the debtor in possession, *see* §1107) to operate the debtor's business during the course of the bankruptcy proceedings. Operation of the business is the rule, not the exception, in a Chapter 11 case.

The trustee essentially argues that the authority to operate the debtor's business contained in §§1107 and 1108 overrides the §541(a)(6) earnings exception in Chapter 11 cases. In his view, §§1107 and 1108 entitle the estate, and not the debtor, to all proceeds from the operation of the debtor's business, even if those proceeds were generated by the services of an individual debtor. The trustee maintains that an individual debtor-in-possession such as FitzSimmons, who operates his business on behalf of the estate, is entitled only to whatever salary the estate or the bankruptcy court allocates to him.

We cannot accept the trustee's position because the Bankruptcy Code applies §541(a)(6) in Chapter 11 cases. Section 103 of the Bankruptcy Code states that the provisions of Chapter 5 of the Code, which includes §541, apply to cases brought under Chapters 7, 11 and 13. As the opinion for the Bankruptcy Appellate Panels points out, Congress knew how to override this general applicability of §541(a)(6) when it wanted to do so. For example, Code §1306 removes the earnings exception from Chapter 13 cases by providing that:

(a) Property of the estate includes, in addition to the property specified in section 541 of this title—

.....

(2) earnings from services performed by the debtor after the commencement of the case but before the case is closed, dismissed, or converted to a case under chapter 7 or 11 of this title, whichever occurs first.

If Congress had intended to make the earnings exception inapplicable to Chapter 11 cases, we believe that it would have done so explicitly, as it did in §1306.

Although we hold that the earnings exception of §541(a)(6) does apply to Chapter 11 cases, FitzSimmons overstates the effect of that exception. Once again, consideration of the provisions of Chapter 11 of the Bankruptcy Code aids us in arriving at our construction of §541(a)(6). We hold that the earnings exception applies only to services performed *personally* by an individual debtor, because giving the exception the broader scope that FitzSimmons urges would seriously interfere with the continued operation of a sole proprietorship during the course of a Chapter 11 case.

Businesses operated as sole proprietorships are eligible for Chapter 11 relief. *See* §§109(d), 101(30). FitzSimmons' reading of the earnings exception would effectively preclude operation of sole proprietorships under Chapter 11. His contention that all the earnings of a sole proprietorship constitute "earnings from services performed by an individual debtor" and are excluded from the estate means that the estate—and the creditors who look to the estate for satisfaction of their claims—would not enjoy the benefit of any profits earned by a sole proprietorship operated under Chapter 11. This contrasts with the situation that prevails when the debtor business is a partnership or a corporation. In those cases, there is no "individual debtor" so the earnings exception is not applicable and the earnings of the business all accrue to the estate under §541(a)(6). At the same time, although FitzSimmons maintains that the estate should not enjoy the profits earned by a sole proprietorship operated under §1108, any losses suffered by such a sole proprietorship would be borne by the estate, since such losses would reduce the value of the estate's assets.

We do not believe that Congress intended such an anomalous result. To avoid it, we hold that §541(a)(6) excepts from the proceeds of the estate only those earnings generated by services personally performed by the individual debtor. FitzSimmons is thus entitled to monies generated by his law practice only to the extent that they are attributable to personal services that he himself performs. To the extent that the law practice's earnings are attributable not to FitzSimmons' personal services but to the business' invested capital, accounts receivable, good will, employment contracts with the firm's staff, client relationships, fee agreements, or the like, the earnings of the law practice accrue to the estate.

Our interpretation accords with the plain meaning of the language of §541(a)(6). The section speaks only of "services performed by an *individual* debtor," (emphasis added), reinforcing our conclusion that it excepts only earnings from services personally performed by an individual debtor, since the services of a debtor's employee or return on capital are not services of the individual debtor himself.

In this case, the Bankruptcy Court's order permitted FitzSimmons to retain a salary of $3,500 per month. We affirm the Bankruptcy Appellate Panels' reversal of that order because it is not evident that $3,500 per month constitutes those proceeds of FitzSimmons' law practice that were attributable to the services personally rendered by FitzSimmons himself. The value of FitzSimmons' services may have been higher—or lower—than $3,500 per month. On remand, the Bankruptcy Court should ascertain the portion of the law practice's earnings that were attributable to FitzSimmons' personal efforts and exclude that amount from the bankruptcy estate. The practice's earnings from all other sources belong to the estate.

Notes and Problems

1. Dave files a Chapter 7 petition on January 15th. On April 5th, he receives a $10,000 royalty check from West Publishing Co. for royalties on his excellent student aid, DEBTOR-CREDITOR LAW IN A NUTSHELL. Is the $5,000 property of the estate?

2. Dave's Car Rental Co., D, files a Chapter 11 petition on January 15th and continues to rent cars and otherwise operate its business. Are rentals received after January 15th property of the estate?

3. Dave's Court Reporting Service, Inc., files a Chapter 11 petition on January 15th and continues to prepare transcripts and otherwise operates its business. Are fees received after January 15th property of the estate? Would the answer be different if Dave has not incorporated and uses the trade name Dave's Court Reporting Service?

4. D retains your firm to bring lender liability law suits against two of its lenders. After the suits are filed, D's creditors file an involuntary Chapter 7 petition against D. What is the effect of the bankruptcy filing on the lender liability litigation?

5. In *FitzSimmons*, the Chapter 11 trustee was arguing that the earnings from the law practice were property of the estate. Why did he take that position? Who might make such an argument in a Chapter 11 case with no trustee?

6. D, a dentist, files a Chapter 13 petition on January 15th and continues her dental practice. Are the fees that she receives for services rendered after January 15th property of the estate? See section 1306. What if she files a motion to convert and

the case is converted to a Chapter 7 case on April 5th? Will all fees earned from January 15th to April 5th still be property of the estate?

□□□□□□

The Supreme Court considered the question of "property" under the bankruptcy laws in the *Board of Trade of City of Chicago v. Johnson*, 264 U.S. 1, 44 S.Ct. 232, 68 L.Ed. 533 (1924), a case decided under the 1898 Bankruptcy Act. There the "bankrupt"[1] owned a membership on the Chicago Board of Trade. Was this CBT membership property of the estate? The Illinois Supreme Court had earlier held that CBT memberships were not "property" for purposes of Illinois state law. In this case, the Supreme Court held that the CBT membership was "property of the estate" for purposes of bankruptcy law. In declining to limit the definition of property of the estate by state law property concepts, the Court stated: "Congress derives its power to enact a bankruptcy law from the Federal Constitution, and the construction of it is a federal question. Of course, where the bankruptcy law deals with property rights which are regulated by the state law, the federal courts in bankruptcy will follow the state courts; but when the language of Congress indicates a policy requiring a broader construction of the statute than the state decisions would give it, federal courts cannot be concluded by them."

In the *Chicago Board of Trade* case, the Court also was confronted with a question of what interest in the property becomes property of the estate. The rules of the CBT prevented a member from transferring his membership until he had satisfied all of his obligations to other CBT members. The bankrupt owed more than $60,000 to other board members. The Court held that the property of the estate was the membership *subject to* the claims of CBT members, and that the $60,000 owing to other CBT members "must be satisfied before the trustee can realize anything on the transfer of the seat for the general estate."

Notes and Problems

1. Board of Trade of City of Chicago v. Johnson was decided under section 70a(5) of the 1898 Bankruptcy Act. How would Board of Trade of City of Chicago be decided under the Bankruptcy Code?

    A. Would the membership be property of the estate?

---

[1]   While "bankrupt" is not a term used in the 1978 Bankruptcy Code, it was a term used in the 1898 Act.

B. If so, would it be subject to the $60,000 of claims? Cf section 541(c)(1).

2. D, a Chapter 7 debtor, is the holder of liquor license issued by the State of California. Under California state law, the State can refuse to transfer a liquor license until the holder pays state taxes. D owes back California taxes. X has contracted to buy D's liquor license from D's bankruptcy trustee; the State of California is refusing to transfer the liquor license from D to X until it has paid the back taxes.

   a. Is the liquor license property of the estate?

   b. If so, can the bankruptcy trustee sell the license to X without first paying the delinquent state taxes?

3. If a debtor owns property jointly with a nondebtor—in a tenancy in common, joint tenancy, or tenancy by the entirety—the debtor's interest in such property becomes property of the estate. Paragraphs (g), (h), (i), and (j) of section 363 govern the sale of such jointly owned property. If the property is held by the debtor and spouse as tenants by the entirety, then the debtor's interest may be exempt under section 522(b)(2)(B).

3. Exempt Property

Under the Bankruptcy Code, all pre-bankruptcy property in which the debtor has an interest becomes property of the estate, but an individual debtor is permitted to exempt certain property from property of the estate. Section 522 of the Bankruptcy Code deals with exempt property. Basically, it answers two questions

1. What property can be set aside as exempt?
2. What are the legal consequences of setting aside property as exempt?

Paragraph (a) of section 522 contains definitions. Section 522(b), (d), and (m) deal with the question of what property can be set aside as exempt.

a. What Property is Exempt

In bankruptcy, an individual debtor may asset the exemptions to which he is entitled under the laws of the state of domicile and under federal laws other than Title 11, section 522(b)(2). These exemption laws are covered in Unit 1, section B, supra.

In a few states, individual debtors have the choice of instead asserting the exemptions set out in section 522(d). The exemptions in section 522(d) are available only to individual debtors that reside in states that have not enacted "opt out" legislation pursuant to section 522(b)(1). Under section 522(b)(1), a state legislature can enact legislation precluding resident debtors from electing to utilize section 522(d). Most states have enacted such "opt out" legislation.

Bankruptcy Rule 4003 deals with exempt property. It contemplates that an individual debtor will file a list of exemptions within 15 days after filing a bankruptcy petition. The bankruptcy trustee and creditors may challenge the debtor's claim of exemptions.

Notes and Problems

1. Why would a bankruptcy trustee challenge a debtor's claim of exemptions?

2. Why would a debtor in a Chapter 13 case file a list of exemptions?

3. Note the relationship between sections 541 and 522. Section 522(b) begins, "Notwithstanding section 541 of this title, an individual debtor may exempt from property of the estate. . ." If a property interest is not "property of the estate," it is not necessary to determine whether that property interest is "exempt."

   Section 541(c) is not technically an exemption provision but it has the similar effect of permitting a debtor to retain a property interest. More specially, section 541(c) excludes from property of the estate a debtor's beneficial interest in a trust to the extent that interest could not be reached by creditors under nonbankruptcy law. Section 541(c) thus excludes from property of the estate the debtor's beneficial interest in a spendthrift trust.

4. Section 541(c) reaches not only traditional spendthrift trusts but also the debtor's interest in an ERISA pension plan. See *Patterson v. Shumate*, 112 S. Ct. 2242 (1992).

   The Employment Retirement Security Act of 1974 (ERISA) encourages employers to create pension plans by providing tax benefits. To qualify for these tax benefits, the employer pension plan must comply with the requirements of the Internal Revenue Code. Qualified ERISA plans must limit how both the employer and the employee can use the assets. One of these limitations precludes employees from selling their interests or creditors of a participating employee from reaching that employee's interest in the plan as means of obtaining payment on a debt.

   ERISA is directed primarily at employer plans. An individual retirement accounts, IRA, is not required to comply with ERISA and most do not. Most IRA's permit alienation of assignment of funds deposited in the account. In *Patterson v. Shumate*, the Supreme Court in *dicta*, suggested that although a debtor's interest in an IRA could not be excluded under section 541(c)(2) because the plans lack the necessary transfer restrictions, it could be exempted under section 522(d)(10)(E). 112 S. Ct. at 2249.

b. Consequences of Exempt Status

What is the practical significance of property being set aside as exempt?

Generally, an individual debtor is able to retain her exempt property. Exempt property is not distributed to creditors in a Chapter 7 bankruptcy case. After bankruptcy, there are three groups of creditors that will have recourse to exempt property:

- creditors with tax claims excepted from discharge by section 523(a)(1);
- creditors with domestic claims excepted from discharge by section 523(a)(5);
- creditors with liens on exempt property that are neither avoided nor extinguished through redemption. See section 522(c).

As the third group suggests, there are some liens on exempt property that are valid outside of bankruptcy that can be invalidated because of bankruptcy. The general avoidance provisions, discussed infra, are applicable to liens on exempt property. Additionally, section 522(f) empowers the debtor to avoid

- judicial liens on exempt property and
- security interests that are (i) non-possessory, (ii) non-purchase money, *and* (iii) encumber property of a type identified in section 522(f)(2).

The policy behind section 522(f)(2) was explained in the House Report as follows:

> Frequently, creditors lending money to a consumer debtor take a security interest in all of the debtor's belongings and obtain a waiver by the debtor of his exemptions. In most of these cases, the debtor is unaware of the consequences of the forms he signs. The creditor's experience provides him with a substantial advantage. If the debtor encounters financial difficulty, creditors often use threats of repossession of all the debtor's household goods as a means of obtaining payment.
>
> In fact, were the creditor to carry through on his threat and foreclose on the property, he would receive little, for

household goods have little resale value. They are far more valuable to the creditor in the debtor's hands, for they provide a credible basis for the threat, because the replacement costs of the goods are generally high. The creditors rarely repossess, and the debtors, ignorant of the creditor's true intentions, are coerced into payments they simply cannot afford to make.

The exemption provision allows the debtor, after bankruptcy has been filed, and creditor collection techniques have been stayed, to undo the consequences of a contract of adhesion, signed in ignorance, by permitting the invalidation of non-purchase money security interests in household goods. Such security interests have too often been used by over-reaching creditors. The bill eliminates any unfair advantage creditors have.

H.R.Rep. No. 95-595, at 127

Notes and Problems

1. Section 522(f)(2) only applies to security interests that are both "nonpossessory" and "nonpurchase money." What does "nonpossessory" mean? When will a security interest be "possessory"? What does "nonpurchase money" mean?

2. Consider whether D use section 522(f) to avoid the following liens on exempt personal property:

   a. S sells D a television set and retains a security interest in the television set.

   b. D obtains a loan from S to pay her hospital bills and grants S a security interest in her television set.

   c. D borrows money from S to pay for a vacation and grants S a security interest in his car.

   d. D grants S a security interest in the truck that he uses in his work to secure a loan to pay taxes.

3. On January 15, D purchases a stereo system from X paying $100 down and financing the $900 balance of the purchase price with C which takes a security interest in the stereo. On April 15, D refinances the loan with C in a transaction providing $1,400 in total financing. The $1,400 is allocated as follows: $200 cash to D, $899 as balance due on the original loan on the stereo, and $301 for payments to

various third parties. In the refinancing, D executes a new security agreement covering not only the stereo but also ski equipment and a clarinet owned by D at the time of the financing. On November 25, D files a Chapter 7 petition. According to her schedules, her loan balance on the filing date was $1,100. D seeks an order under section 522(f)(2)(A) avoiding the lien on the stereo. What result?

4. Can D use section 522(f) to avoid the following liens on exempt real property:

    a. a second mortgage on D's home;

    b. a judgment lien on D's home?

5. What is the practical significance, if any, of the phrase "to the extent that such lien impairs an exemption to which the debtor would have been entitled" in section 522(f)? Assume that D files a bankruptcy petition and owns a house valued at $100,000 that is encumbered by a $60,000 mortgage held by M and that under relevant state law D is limited to a $10,000 homestead. What are the effects of section 522(f) on a judicial lien of $20,000? A judicial lien of $50,000? *See generally* Margaret Howard, *Multiple Judicial Liens in Bankruptcy: Section 522(f)(1) Simplified*, 67 AM. BANKR. L.J. 151 (1993).

6. Remember that under section 522(b), a state can enact legislation that precludes debtors residing in that state from claiming the exemptions in section 522(d). Can a state similarly "opt out" of section 522(f), i.e., enact legislation that prevents debtors residing in that state from avoiding liens on exempt property under section 522(f). Please reread section 522(b). What if the state amends its exemption statutes to provide?

    a. "Debtors cannot use section 522(f) of the Bankruptcy Code to avoid liens on exempt property."

    b. "A debtor cannot claim exempt status for any property encumbered by a nonpossessory, nonpurchase money security interest." *See generally* C. Robert Morris, *Bankrupt Fantasy: The Site of Missing Words and the Order of Illusory Events*, 45 ARK. L. REV. 265, 294-303 (1992).

B. AUTOMATIC STAY

After the filing of a bankruptcy petition, a debtor needs immediate protection from the collection efforts of creditors. If the petition is a voluntary Chapter 7, the bankruptcy trustee needs time to collect the "property of the estate" and make pro rata distributions to creditors. If the petition is a voluntary Chapter 11 or Chapter 12 the debtor needs time to prepare a plan. And, if the petition is an involuntary Chapter 7 or Chapter 11, the debtor needs time to controvert the petition. Moreover, since creditors will receive payment through the bankruptcy process or the plan of rehabilitation and some claims will be discharged, continued creditor actions would interfere with orderly bankruptcy administration.

Accordingly, the filing of a voluntary petition under Chapter 7, Chapter 11, Chapter 12 or Chapter 13, or the filing of an involuntary petition under Chapter 7 or Chapter 11 automatically "stays," i.e., restrains, creditors from taking further action against the debtor, the property of the debtor, or the property of the estate to collect their claims or enforce their liens, section 362.

There are five stay questions that lawyers (and law students) are asked:

1. When does the automatic stay become effective?
2. What is covered by the automatic stay?
3. When does the automatic stay end?
4. How can a creditor obtain relief from the stay?
5. What are the consequences of violating the stay?

1. Time Stay Arises

The automatic stay is triggered by the filing of a bankruptcy petition. No court action at all is needed for the stay to be created. The filing itself "operates as a stay."

It dates from the time of the filing, not from the time that a creditor receives notice of or learns of the bankruptcy. If D files a voluntary bankruptcy petition on April 5, the stay becomes effective April 5. If D's creditors file an involuntary bankruptcy petition on April 5, the stay becomes effective on April 5. The stay dates from April 5 even if creditors do not learn of the bankruptcy until much later.

UNITED STATES BANKRUPTCY COURT
FOR THE WESTERN DISTRICT OF MICHIGAN
SOUTHERN DISTRICT

In Re:

GIRARDIN SPORTWEAR INC.,   Case No. 93-85931

<u>   Debtors(s)</u>

<u>ORDER AND NOTICE OF STAY</u>

ALL CREDITORS and interested persons are hereby notified that the above noted Debtor(s) has filed a petition for
relief under Chapter 11 of the Bankruptcy Code and is entitled to the protection of the Automatic Stay provisions of
§362.

IT IS ORDERED that, pursuant to §362 of the Bankruptcy
Code, from the time and date of the filing of this case, all
persons, their agents, employees and attorneys are hereby
stayed and restrained from commencing or continuing any
suits, and from levying any attachments, garnishments or
other executions upon earnings or wages, and from
repossessing property (or selling property repossessed) in
the possession or under the control of the Debtor or in
which the Debtor has any interest: and all such persons are
further stayed and restrained from molesting, harassing or
disturbing the Debtor or his employer or other persons on
account of any debt or claim, or with respect to any property which the Debtor has submitted to the exclusive jurisdiction of this Court, unless and until permission and leave
of the Court be first obtained.

This order does not in any way modify the provision of
11 U.S.C. §362. You should consult this statute to determine applicable exceptions.

A copy of this order will be returned to the Debtor
for service on appropriate creditors and interested parties.
The Debtor shall file a proof of service listing all persons
served with this order.

Case filed: Dec. 13 1993

Laurence E. Howard
Bankruptcy Judge

ATTEST: A TRUE COPY

By: *Lupe Wood*
Lupe Wood
Deputy Clerk

Questions

1. What is the purpose of this order? Were creditors stayed before they received this order? Would creditors have been stayed if this order had not been issued?

2. This order is to be served on "appropriate creditors and interested parties." Who pays for the duplication and service costs?

3. Why is Judge Howard's handwriting so nice and neat?

2. Scope Of The Stay

Paragraph (a) of section 362 defines the scope of the automatic stay by listing all of the acts and actions that are stayed by the commencement of a bankruptcy case. It is comprehensive and includes virtually all creditor collection activity.

While paragraph (a) of section 362 indicates what is stayed, paragraph (b) lists actions that are not stayed. For example, section 362(b)(2) provides a limited exception for alimony and child support claims. Such claims can be collected from property that is not "property of the estate."

There is an important limitation on the scope of section 362 that is not dealt with in paragraph (b) of section 362. The automatic stay of section 362(a) only covers the debtor, property of the debtor, and property of the estate. It does not protect third parties. Assume, for example, that D borrows $30,000 from C and G guarantees repayment. If D files for bankruptcy, section 362(a) will stay C from attempting to collect from D. Section 362(a) will not, however, protect G.

The following problems and cases explore the scope of the automatic stay in bankruptcy.

Notes and Problems

1. **Collection Litigation**
    a. Prepetition Debt
        On January 15, D borrows $10,000 from C. On February 22, D defaults. On March 30, C files a collection action. On April 5, D files a bankruptcy petition. What is the effect of the automatic stay on the pending collection action?

    b. Postpetition Debt
        On April 5, D files a bankruptcy petition. On June 1, D negligently injures X. Does the automatic stay prevent X from commencing an action in state

court against D? Does the automatic stay prevent X from enforcing a judgment entered in such a state court action?

2. Lien Enforcement

a. Resale

When D defaulted on her debt, C foreclosed its mortgage on D's building. C's foreclosure sale is scheduled for Thursday afternoon. If D files for bankruptcy on Thursday morning, will the foreclosure sale be stayed?

b. Repossession

S sells D furniture on credit and obtains an Article 9 security interest in the furniture. D defaults. D files a bankruptcy petition. Does the automatic stay bar S from repossessing the furniture?

3. Informal Collection Efforts

After D files for bankruptcy, can his creditors continue to call him demanding payment? Can D's creditors continue to call D's wife demanding that she pay D's debts?

4. Third Parties

a. Guarantors

D borrows $50,000 from C. C obtains a personal guarantee of payment from D's sister, G. D is unable to pay C and comes to your firm for advice. If D files a bankruptcy petition, will C be stayed from collecting the $50,000 from G? See sections 1201 and 1301.

b. Letter of credit

Does the automatic stay bar the beneficiary of an irrevocable letter of credit from collecting from the issuing bank after the customer files a bankruptcy petition? Consider the following illustration. M, a Minnesota food processor, wants to buy peanuts from G, a Georgia peanut producer. M cannot pay cash; G is unwilling to extend credit to M. M and G agree that M will pay for the peanuts by producing a letter of credit from its bank, I Bank, providing that I Bank will pay G when it is presented with bills of lading and other documents establishing that the peanuts have been shipped to M. I Bank and M then agree that I Bank will issue such a letter to G in exchange for M's agreeing to repay all payments I Bank makes on its behalf and M's granting I Bank a security interest in all of its inventory to secure the repayment. I Bank issues the letter of credit to G. G delivers the peanuts. M files a Chapter 11 petition. Does the automatic stay prevent G from drawing on the letter of credit from I Bank? If not, does the automatic stay prevent I Bank from repossessing and selling M's inventory?

In re Olson
United States Bankruptcy Court, N.D. Iowa, 1984
38 B.R. 515

William W. Thinnes, Bankruptcy Judge. The matter before the Court is an Application for Order to Show Cause in re Contempt and Complaint for Damages filed by Ronald D. and E. Sue Olson (Debtors) and against McFarland Clinic P.C. (Defendant). The Court, being fully advised and pursuant to F.R.B.P. 7052, now makes the following Findings of Fact, Conclusions of Law and Orders.

The facts underlying the Application are not in dispute. On June 1, 1982, the Debtors filed a voluntary Chapter 7 Petition in this Court. On Schedule A-3, the Debtors listed the Defendant as a holder of a claim without priority. On June 18, 1982, the Clerk's office sent Notice to All Creditors including the Defendant regarding the Meeting of Creditors and the applicability of 11 U.S.C. §362. On July 27, 1982, the Defendant via its Administrator sent a letter to the Debtors, the relevant portions of which provided: I wish to inform you that the ... McFarland Clinic ... will no longer be able to provide medical care to you and members of your family. This action has become necessary based on your failure to pay for the medical services provided by McFarland Clinic.... Since you have filed bankruptcy, I realize that we cannot legally pursue the collection of this account. However, we are willing to reinstate service if you wish to pay your account voluntarily. Upon receipt of this letter, the Debtors subsequently sought medical services from the Defendant. When the Debtors arrived at the Defendant's premises, they were advised that no medical services would be provided unless the entire balance of the debt owed the Defendant be paid. Being thus unable to obtain care, the Debtors proceeded to another physician and received treatment. It should be noted that at the time of the Debtors' visit, the Debtors offered to pay cash in advance of the medical services to be performed. This offer, however, was rejected by the Defendant. In the Application, the Debtors sought a finding that the Defendant's action violated 11 U.S.C. §362 and 11 U.S.C. §524, and requested an award of actual and punitive damages.

* * *

In enacting §362, Congress' intent was clear:

> The automatic stay is one of the fundamental debtor protections provided by the bankruptcy laws. It gives the debtor a breathing spell from his creditors. It stops all collection efforts, all harassment and all foreclosure actions.

H.R.Rep. No. 595, 95th Cong., 1st Sess 340 (1977), U.S.Code Cong. & Admin.News 1978, 5787, 6296. In particular, the legislative history accompanying §362(a)(6) indicated that the section was purposed at "prevent[ing] creditors from attempting in any way to collect a prepetition debt." Id. at 342, U.S.Code Cong. & Admin.News 1978, at 6296. * * *

Other courts faced with situations similar to the one at bar have found §362(a)(6) violations. For example, * * * the court in In re Lanford, 10 B.R. 132, 134 (Bkrtcy.D.Minn.1981), held that a private college that refused to release a transcript until the student loan account has been brought current violated §362(a)(6). Indeed, the Lanford court observed that "withholding of transcript serves no purpose but the collection of a debt."

Application of the above cases convinces this Court that the purpose behind the Defendant's July 27, 1982, letter to the Debtors was collection of a prepetition debt. While a literal reading of the letter reveals no direct effort at collection, the Defendant is not excused. ***

Further, this Court finds that the Defendant is not committed to refusing services on the basis of nontainted reason. Clearly, the Defendant would not have refused services if the Debtors had paid the prepetition debt. Like Lanford, therefore, the withholding of services by the Defendant "serves no purpose but the collection of a debt." By using the refusal as a lever, Defendant was attempting to collect a prepetition debt.

In sum, this Court finds that the Defendant's letter to the Debtors constitutes an act to collect a claim against the Debtors that arose before the commencement of the case and thus violative of 11 U.S.C. §362(a)(6). By so holding, this Court is not unmindful of the Defendant's assertion that the Bankruptcy Code may not be construed to compel the defendant to provide services to the Debtors. This Court agrees with the Defendant's assertion. Indeed, if the Defendant were to simply refuse service without any mention of the Debtors' bankruptcy filing, §362 would not come into play. However, the Defendant's letter to the Debtors appears motivated by a desire to collect the pre-petition debt under the guise of termination of future services. Because §362(a)(6) prohibits collection attempts "in any way," the Defendant's action violated §362(a)(6).

Turning to the incident during which the Debtors were refused medical services even though they tendered cash in advance of the services, the record is unclear as to the time the incident occurred. Assuming that the incident occurred before the entry of the Order of Discharge on August 17, 1984, it also constituted a violation of §362(a)(6). Conceptually, it was no different than the letter sent to the Debtors. On the other hand, if the incident occurred after the entry of an Order of Discharge, no §362 violation could be found. This is so because §362(c)(2)(C) provides that the stay is terminated when the discharge has been granted. However, a post-discharge action while not violative of §362 may run afoul of 11 U.S.C. §524, to which we now turn.
     * * *

Notes and Problems

1. D owned and operated several retail sporting goods stores in Iowa. D's most important supplier was N. Before D filed for bankruptcy in Iowa, N stopped selling to D because D's account was in arrears. After bankruptcy, D asked N to resume shipments on a C.O.D. basis. Advise N.

2. E is an employee of D. At the time that D filed for bankruptcy, it owed E $2,200 for wages. Under *Olson*, can E refuse to continue working for D unless he is paid the prepetition wages?

3. *See generally* Daniel Keating, *Offensive Uses of the Bankruptcy Stay*, 45 VAND. L. REV. 75 (1992).

United States v. Inslaw

United States Court of Appeals, District of Columbia Circuit, 1991
932 F.2d 1467, cert denied,
___ U.S. ___, 112 S.Ct. 913, 116 L.Ed.2d 813 (1992)

Stephen F. Williams, Circuit Judge:
* * *

[*Inslaw has built itself around one software product, the Prosecutor's Management Information System, known by the acronym "PROMIS". Under a March 16, 1982 contract with the Department of Justice (No. JVUSA-82-C-0074), Inslaw agreed to provide and install the original version of the software (old PROMIS) in certain U.S. Attorneys' offices. Although the parties agree that the original contract required Inslaw only to provide old PROMIS, Inslaw in fact allowed the Department to use a newer version of the software -- enhanced version PROMIS. In November 1982 the Department asked Inslaw, under the terms of the contract, for a copy of "all computer programs and supporting documentation developed for or relating to" the contract. Both sides understood that the Department wanted a copy of the enhanced PROMIS. The request touched off the central, but by no means the only, dispute between the parties -- whether the Department was entitled, under the contract, to receive the PROMIS enhancements without further payments. Following a series of negotiations, the parties agreed to a temporary settlement that would allow the contract to be implemented pending final resolution. Under Modification 12 of the contract, adopted April 11, 1983, Inslaw agreed to deliver a copy of enhanced PROMIS, and the Department agreed to limit and restrict the dissemination of the said PROMIS computer software to certain offices pending resolution of the issues extant between Inslaw and the Government under the terms and conditions of Contract No. JVUSA-82-C-0074. On April 20, 1983, Inslaw sent the Department computer tapes that contained copies of the source and object codes for the version of enhanced PROMIS it* *had been providing * * *." While "object codes" contain unintelligible strings of numbers and letters that actually tell the machine what to do, "source codes" (used to generate object codes) are written in programming languages that can be deciphered by skilled computer programmers.*

From August 1983 until January 1984, Inslaw proceeded under the contract to install enhanced PROMIS on minicomputers in 22 large U.S. Attorneys' offices under the belief that Modification 12 so required. On February 7, 1985, Inslaw filed a petition for reorganization under chapter 11. One month later, Inslaw's contract with the Department expired, by which time Inslaw had received almost all of the original $9.6 million contract price. Between June 24, 1985 and September 2, 1987, the Department installed enhanced PROMIS in 23 additional U.S. Attorneys' offices. A key dispute between the parties is whether this extension of the system beyond the 20 offices slated for the minicomputer version is permitted by Modification 12.]

On June 10, 1986 Inslaw filed a four-count complaint against the government in bankruptcy court, alleging that the Department was willfully violating § 362(a), the automatic stay provision of the Bankruptcy Code. The asserted violation lay primarily in the Department's continuing to use Inslaw's property--enhanced PROMIS--without Inslaw's consent. Inslaw sought declaratory and injunctive relief, as well as compensatory damages, punitive damages, costs and attorney's fees. * * * [The bankruptcy court] found that the government had violated the automatic stay, and issued a declaratory judgment and a permanent injunction against further expansion of the government's use of enhanced PROMIS. It ordered the government to pay nearly $6.8 million in compensatory damages for use of enhanced PROMIS, both the portions installed by Inslaw and those installed by the Department (calculated on the basis of Inslaw's standard perpetual license fees), and almost $1 million in attorney's fees and expenses.

* * *

On appeal, the district court upheld the judgments of the bankruptcy court but reduced the damage award by $655,200. 113 B.R. at 820-21.

* * *

Section 362(a) provides that the filing of a bankruptcy petition operates as a stay, applicable to all entities, of --

> (3) any act to obtain possession of property of the estate or of property from the estate or to exercise control over property of the estate * * *.

11 U.S.C. § 362(a) (1988) (emphasis added). Because we find as a matter of law that none of the acts or omissions alleged by Inslaw would amount to a violation of the automatic stay, we conclude that the bankruptcy court should have granted the Department's motion to dismiss.

* * *

Inslaw's major allegation concerns the Department's use of enhanced PROMIS after the filing of the bankruptcy petition. The bankruptcy court concluded first that the privately-funded enhancements to PROMIS were proprietary trade secrets owned by Inslaw, 83 B.R. at 159, and then that the Department's continued use of these enhancements, and in particular its post-petition installation of enhanced PROMIS in 23 U.S. Attorneys' offices (in addition to the 22 where Inslaw had made installations), were a "willful exercise of control over the property of the estate."

The automatic stay protects "property of the estate". This estate is created by the filing of a petition and comprises property of the debtor "wherever located and by whomever held", including (among other things) "all legal or equitable interests of the debtor in property as of the commencement of the case." 11 U.S.C. § 541(a)(1) (1988). It is undisputed that this encompasses causes of action that belong to the debtor, as well as the debtor's intellectual property, such as interests in patents, trademarks and copyrights. * * * United States v. Whiting Pools, Inc., 462 U.S. 198, 204-05 & n. 9, 103 S.Ct. 2309, 2313 & n. 9, 76 L.Ed.2d 515 (1983). The estate also includes property recoverable under the Code's "turnover" provisions [sections 542 and 543], which allow the trustee to recover property that "was merely out of the possession of the debtor, yet remained 'property of the debtor.'" Whiting Pools, 462 U.S. at 204-09 & n. 11, 103 S.Ct. at 2313-16 & n. 11.

In its brief Inslaw refers rather vaguely to its interest in the enhanced PROMIS software as the "property of the estate" over which the Department supposedly exercised control. But for meaningful analysis, Inslaw's interests must be examined separately. One set of interests consists of (1) the computer tapes containing copies of the source and object codes that Inslaw sent to the Department on April 20, 1983 and (2) the copies of enhanced PROMIS that Inslaw installed on Department hardware between August 1983 and January 1984. As to these, Inslaw held no possessory interest when it filed for bankruptcy on February 7, 1985. Nor can it claim a possessory interest over them through the Code's turnover provisions, as could the debtor-in-possession in Whiting Pools, because, as Inslaw freely admits, the Department held possession of the copies under a claim of ownership (its view of the contract and Modification 12) and claimed the right to use enhanced PROMIS without further payment. It is settled law that the debtor cannot use the turnover provisions to liquidate contract disputes or otherwise demand assets whose title is in dispute. Indeed, Inslaw never sought possession of the copies under the turnover provisions.

The bankruptcy court instead identified the relevant property as Inslaw's intangible trade secret rights in the PROMIS enhancements. It then found that the Department's continuing use of these intangible enhancements was an "exercise of control" over property of the estate.

If the bankruptcy court's idea of the scope of "exercise of control" were correct, the sweep of § 362(a) would be extraordinary--with a concomitant

expansion of the jurisdiction of the bankruptcy court. Whenever a party against whom the bankrupt holds a cause of action (or other intangible property right) acted in accord with his view of the dispute rather than that of the debtor-in-possession or bankruptcy trustee, he would risk a determination by a bankruptcy court that he had "exercised control" over intangible rights (property) of the estate.[1] * * *
    * * *

Inslaw's view of § 362(a) would take it well beyond Congress's purpose. The object of the automatic stay provision is essentially to solve a collective action problem-- to make sure that creditors do not destroy the bankrupt estate in their scramble for relief. Fulfillment of that purpose cannot require that every party who acts in resistance to the debtor's view of its rights violates § 362(a) if found in error by the bankruptcy court. Thus, someone defending a suit brought by the debtor does not risk violation of § 362(a)(3) by filing a motion to dismiss the suit, though his resistance may burden rights asserted by the bankrupt. Nor does the filing of a lis pendens violate the stay (at least where it does not create a lien), even though it alerts prospective buyers to a hazard and may thereby diminish the value of estate property. And the commencement and continuation of a cause of action against the debtor that arises post-petition, and so is not stayed by § 362(a)(1), does not violate § 362(a)(3). Since willful violations of the stay expose the offending party to liability for compensatory damages, costs, attorney's fees, and, in some circumstances, punitive damages, see 11 U.S.C. § 362(h) (1988), it is difficult to believe that Congress intended a violation whenever someone already in possession of property mistakenly refuses to capitulate to a bankrupt's assertion of rights in that property.[2]

The limits of the turnover provisions in the bankruptcy code underscore the improbability that Congress intended § 362(a) to have the sweeping scope that Inslaw would assign it. It is common ground that these cannot be used against property held by another under a claim of legal right. See cases cited at p. 1472 above. As Inslaw's view would turn every act of the possessor that implicitly

---

[1]   Under this view, it does not matter whether the Department has possession of the PROMIS enhancements under a claim of outright title, as they do, or under a more limited lease or license. In both situations, a party in possession of an asset in which the bankrupt has an interest would violate § 362(a) by any act inconsistent with the bankrupt's claims as determined by the bankruptcy court. As a result, a wide range of disputes, such as a bankrupt lessor's claims against a lessee, or a bankrupt co-owner's claims against other holders of concurrent property interests, would slide into bankruptcy court.

[2]   In adding the "exercise control" language to § 362(a)(3) in the 1984 Bankruptcy Amendments, see 98 Stat. at 371, Congress gave no explanation. One court has traced this language to the description of § 362(a)(3) found in the committee reports on the 1978 Bankruptcy Act, which refer to property of the estate as "property over which the estate has control or possession". See In re 48th Street Steakhouse, Inc., 61 B.R. 182, 187 & n. 10 (Bankr.S.D.N.Y.1986), aff'd, 77 B.R. 409 (S.D.N.Y.), aff'd, 835 F.2d 427 (2d Cir.1987); House Report at 341; Senate Report at 50.

asserts his title over disputed property into a violation of § 362(a), it would give the bankruptcy court jurisdiction over all such disputes, creating a kind of universal end-run around the limits on turnover. Our understanding of § 362(a) does not expose bankrupts to any troubling hazard. Here, for example, Inslaw retains whatever intangible property rights it had in enhanced PROMIS at the time of filing. If the Department has violated the contract or Modification 12, Inslaw as debtor-in-possession has all the access to court enjoyed by any victim of a contract breach by the United States government. If Modification 12 was induced by fraud, as the bankruptcy court found, then Inslaw has its contract remedies or perhaps a suit for conversion. Assuming that its privately-funded enhancements to PROMIS qualify as proprietary trade secrets, as the bankruptcy court found, it may be able to sue the government under the Trade Secrets Act or even under the Administrative Procedure Act for improper disclosures of its trade secrets by government officials.

　　　* * *

As the bankruptcy court had no jurisdiction to hear the claims asserted under § 362(a), we reverse the district court and remand the case with directions to vacate all orders concerning the Department's alleged violations of the automatic stay and to dismiss Inslaw's complaint against the Department. So ordered.

Notes and Problems

1. D Inc. is a public corporation with valuable tax attributes such as net operating losses. Under tax law, these tax attributes can be diminished and even extinguished by a change in control. If D Inc. files for bankruptcy, does section 362(a)(3) prevent D Inc.'s shareholders from selling their stock?

2. D is the majority shareholder of X Co. D files for bankruptcy; X Co. does not file for bankruptcy. Does D's bankruptcy filing stay a minority shareholder of X Co. from filing an action in state court for the appointment of a receiver for X Co.?

3. Richard Bearden, Robert Bearden, and J.M. Bearden were partners in Bearden & Sons Fish Farms (the "Bearden Partnership"). The Bearden Partnership entered into and then later breached a licensing agreement with Patton. After the Bearden Partnership filed for bankruptcy, Patton brought a breach of contract action against the Beardens individually. Under relevant state law, (i) partners are liable for partnership debts and (ii) the partnership can compel contributions from its partners for partnership debt. The Bearden Partnership argued that the state court suits against the partners individually violated section 362(a)(3) because Patton's suits against the partners individually would necessarily impair the debtor partnership's right to compel contribution from the partners, thus interfering with the debtor's property. In *Patton v. Bearden*, 8 F.3d 343 (6th Cir. 1993), the court rejected the argument. Do you agree?

4. In the *Robins* bankruptcy, a number of the plaintiffs with Dalkon Shield claims sought to sever their actions against Robins and proceed with their claims against Aetna Casualty and Insurance Company on Robins' products liability insurance policy. In *A.H. Robins Co. v. Piccinin*, 788 F.2d 994 (4th Cir. 1986), the court held that the products liability policy was property of the estate and so actions against Aetna were stayed by section 362(a)(3). Do you agree?

5. *See generally* Note, *The Inequitable Machinations of Section 362(a): Rethinking Bankruptcy's Automatic Stay Over Intangible Property Rights,* 66 S. CAL. L. REV. 659 (1992).

In re F.T.L., Inc.
United States Bankruptcy Court, E.D. Virginia, 1993
152 B.R. 61

MEMORANDUM OPINION

Douglas O. Tice, Jr., Bankruptcy Judge. This adversary proceeding comes before the court on a complaint for injunctive relief filed by debtor and the principals of the debtor. Plaintiffs seek to temporarily enjoin Crestar Bank from foreclosing on the personal residence of Frank Lash, Jr., and Robyn Lash. Crestar Bank is the primary creditor of the debtor, and its lien on the residence arises from the Lashes' personal guarantee of the debtor's obligation to Crestar. A foreclosure sale had been scheduled for January 28, 1993. The court heard evidence on January 21, 1993, and ruled from the bench that unusual circumstances in this case justified an injunction for a period of 90 days. This memorandum opinion supplements the court's bench ruling.

Findings of Fact

Debtor ("FTL") operates a car wash under the trade name Car-Robics Brushless Auto Wash in Newport News, Virginia. On July 31, 1991, debtor filed a voluntary bankruptcy petition under chapter 11. Frank Lash, Jr., and Robyn Lash ("Lashes") are officers and directors of FTL, and together they hold 60 percent of the stock in FTL. Although Frank Lash, Jr., is the president of FTL, his sons Frank Lash, III, and Tom Lash oversee the day to day operations of the business. Frank Lash, Jr., is a pharmacist, and his primary occupation is operating a small pharmacy. However, the Lashes' pharmacy is of inconsequential value, and the Lashes' primary assets are their ownership interest in FTL and their personal residence in which they have substantial equity.

Crestar Bank is the primary secured creditor of FTL, holding secured debt of approximately $785,000.00. Frank Lash, Jr., and Robyn Lash personally guaranteed this debt. In January 1992 Crestar secured a judgment lien against the Lashes and subsequently perfected its lien against the Lashes' personal residence. A foreclosure sale on the residence was scheduled for January 28,

1993. Crestar also issued suggestions in garnishment on the Lashes' personal bank accounts.

Since the commencement of this case FLT has made monthly adequate protection payments to Crestar in the approximate amount of $11,000.00. This amount represents the monthly payments of principal and interest due prepetition. The evidence indicates that FTL is currently operating at a profit and that these adequate protection payments will likely continue throughout the bankruptcy case. All the assets of FTL are fully insured as is the Lashes' residence.

FTL filed its amended plan of reorganization in December 1992. The plan calls for the Lashes to contribute all the equity in their home to the reorganization. The Lashes are prepared to accomplish this through a home equity loan, and they have already obtained a $115,000.00 written loan commitment from First Fidelity Mortgage to be secured by a second deed of trust on their residence. In addition, FTL is conceivably 30-45 days away from a commitment on a SBA loan through NationsBank. However, this loan is conditioned upon the continued ownership and management of FTL by the Lash family and the personal guarantee of the Lashes. Frank Lash, III, and Tom Lash have been able to secure new financing commitments of approximately $41,000.00, and a personal friend of the Lashes, Don Sweeney, has expressed interest in investing up to $30,000.00 in FTL if a plan is eventually confirmed.

Discussion and Conclusions of Law

The plain language of 11 U.S.C. § 362 provides only for the automatic stay of judicial proceedings and enforcement of judgments against the debtor or the property of the estate. This court has previously held that in the absence of compelling unusual circumstances, guarantors of a debtor must file their own bankruptcy petition to receive the benefits of bankruptcy law. Nothing in § 362 suggests Congress intended to strip from creditors of a bankrupt debtor the protection they sought and received when they required a third party to guaranty the debt.[1] Credit Alliance Corp. v. Williams, 851 F.2d at 121. The very purpose of a guarantee is to assure a creditor that in the event the debtor defaults, the creditor will have someone to look to for reimbursement.

While the automatic stay provisions are generally said to be available only to the debtor and not to third party guarantors, the Fourth Circuit has held that in unusual circumstances the bankruptcy court can enjoin proceedings against non-debtor third parties pursuant to 11 U.S.C. § 105(a). A.H. Robins Co. v. Piccinin, 788 F.2d 994, 1002-04 (4th Cir.1986). Where the identity of the debtor and the third party are inexorably interwoven so that the debtor may be said to be the real party against whom the creditor is proceeding a bankruptcy court may

---

[1]   Congress knew how to extend the automatic stay to nonbankrupt parties when it intended to do so. Chapter 13, for example, contains a narrowly drawn provision to stay proceedings against a limited category of individual cosigners of consumer debts. See 11 U.S.C. § 1301(a).

exercise equitable jurisdiction to enjoin proceedings against non-debtor third parties. 11 U.S.C. § 105(a); A.H. Robins Co. v. Piccinin, 788 F.2d at 1004. For example, a situation may exist where proceeding against the third party would actually reduce or diminish property the debtor could otherwise make available to the creditors as a whole. A.H. Robins Co. v. Piccinin, 788 F.2d at 1008. Allowing such action would undermine two basic principles of chapter 11: to provide creditors with a compulsory and collective forum to sort out their relative entitlement to a debtor's assets and to provide the debtor with a realistic opportunity to formulate a plan of reorganization. See A.H. Robins Co. v. Piccinin, 788 F.2d at 998.

However, before the court can grant injunctive relief the court must find:

1. The plaintiff is likely to succeed on the merits;
2. The plaintiff has shown that irreparable injury will result without such relief;
3. Issuing the injunction would not substantially harm other interested parties; and
4. The public interest is best served by preserving the status quo until the merits of the controversy can be fully considered.

I believe this four-part test is satisfied and that this case presents the kind of "unusual circumstances" set forth in Robins that warrant a temporary injunction against Crestar to cease collection activities against the Lashes. A.H. Robins Co. v. Piccinin, 788 F.2d at 999.

First, the evidence establishes that the collection activities against the Lashes arise from FTL debt to Crestar, not direct personal obligations of the Lashes to Crestar. The evidence also establishes that FTL is currently operating at a profit with several promising avenues of new financing on the horizon. With a brief "respite from protracted litigation" the Lash family may be able to successfully reorganize this debtor. A.H. Robins Co. v. Piccinin, 788 F.2d at 998. Accordingly, the court believes the debtor is "likely to succeed on the merits" by proposing a confirmable chapter 11 plan.

Second, the facts establish that proposing a confirmable plan will be virtually impossible without the active involvement of Frank Lash, Jr., in pursuing new financing arrangements. If Frank Lash, Jr., filed his own bankruptcy petition he probably would not be able to contribute the equity in his residence to the debtor's plan of reorganization as proposed, and his ability to secure new financing for the debtor would be foiled. Accordingly, the court must conclude that "irreparable harm will occur" to the debtor's realistic opportunity to reorganize if collection activities against the Lashes are allowed to continue.

Third, the evidence establishes that little or no harm will be caused to Crestar if it is temporarily enjoined from collection activities against the Lashes.[1] What Crestar seeks through foreclosure on the Lashes' residence is effectively being proposed under the plan of reorganization by the Lashes contributing all the equity in their home to the plan; as the primary secured creditor Crestar will be the beneficiary of these funds. The Lashes are not holding back any substantial asset that would otherwise be available to Crestar via the Lashes' guarantor liability. Moreover, since the commencement of this case Crestar has received and will continue to receive monthly adequate protection payments equivalent to the monthly payments of principal and interest due prepetition. Given its predominant secured creditor position it is unlikely that a plan can be confirmed over Crestar's objection. Accordingly, the court must find that issuing a temporary injunction "will not substantially harm" Crestar or any other interested party.

Fourth, the court believes the creditors as a whole are best served by giving this debtor an opportunity to propose a plan of reorganization. By seeking to foreclose on the Lashes' residence Crestar is attempting to opt-out of chapter 11's compulsory and collective forum of sorting out the creditors' relative entitlement to the debtor's assets. The creditors as a whole deserve the opportunity to evaluate and vote on a plan of reorganization in this case. Accordingly, the court concludes that the "public interest is best served by maintaining the status quo" and enjoining Crestar's collection activities against the Lashes for a period of 90 days or until the merits of the debtor's plan can be promptly and fully considered at a confirmation hearing.

Accordingly, the court will enjoin Crestar's collection activities against the Lashes for a period of 90 days.

A separate order has already been entered.

Notes and Problems

1. Could Frank and Robyn Lash stay the Crestar foreclosure by filing personal bankruptcy petitions?

2. Is it likely that the Crestar guarantee is the Lashes' only debt? Are the Lashes other creditors barred from actions and acts to collect their debts?

---

[1]   This injunction is temporary only, and issued to assist the debtor through a crucial point in the reorganization proceedings; the injunction will expire in 90 days or upon confirmation of a plan. The need for permanent injunctive relief in this case is remote because any confirmed plan would likely render unavailable the Lashes' main asset, the equity in their home. Moreover, this court is disinclined to permanently enjoin collection activities against a non-debtor because 11 U.S.C. § 524(e) arguably prevents what would in effect be granting a discharge to a non- debtor. See Peter M. Boyle, Non-Debtor Liability in Chapter 11: Validity of Third-Party Discharge in Bankruptcy, 61 Fordham L. Review 421, 447 (1992). This type of extraordinary relief may be appropriate in rare circumstances like A.H. Robins but should not be liberally granted.

3. *See generally* Howard Buschman & Sean Madden, *The Power and Propriety of Bankruptcy Court Intervention in Actions Between Nondebtors*, 47 Bus. Law. 913 (1992); Barry Zaretsky, *Codebtor Stays in Chapter 11 Bankruptcy*, 72 Corn. L. Rev. 213 (1988).

⌐⌐⌐⌐⌐⌐

The preceding cases and problems have focused on what is stayed—on the scope of paragraph (a) of section 362. Creditors commonly summarize section 362(a) in terms similar to the following: "If something is worth doing, you can't do it because it will be stayed by section 362(a)."

Paragraph (b) of section 362 contains eleven exceptions to the automatic stay. Most of the exceptions are very narrowly drawn; most of the exceptions apply in relatively few bankruptcy cases. The following problems and case deal with some of the more common section 362(b) applications and issues.

Problems

1. When D and W were divorced, the court ordered D to pay $1,000 a month child support. D has missed the last two support payments. D has filed a Chapter 7 petition. Does the automatic stay prevent W from bringing a state court action to collect child support payments? See section 362(b)(2).

2. The United States attorney brings a criminal action against Dr. D, alleging that Dr. D fraudulently obtained $200,000 in Medicare payments. Dr. D then files a Chapter 11 petition. Does the automatic stay affect the pending criminal litigation? See section 362(b)(1)(4). What if the United States attorney is seeking not only a prison term but also restitution? See section 362(b)(5), section 362(a)(6).

3. D owns and operates a chain of convenience stores. The stores have underground tanks for gasoline. In three now-closed locations, the tanks leaked. EPA spends $300,000 on cleanup and brings a cost recovery action against D. D then files for bankruptcy. Does the automatic stay affect the pending EPA cost recovery action?

4. Same facts as Problem 3 except that the EPA has not begun its cleanup. Instead, the EPA obtains a mandatory injunction under CERCLA directing D to cleanup the sites. Should the automatic stay affect enforcement of this mandatory injunction? Do you agree with the Third Circuit's answer to this question in *Penn Terra Ltd. v. Department of Environmental Resources*, 733 F.2d 267 (3d Cir. 1984):

> Penn Terra Limited, P, was the operator of coal surface mines. P's operations caused environmental damage. P entered into a consent order with the Department of Environmental Resources to rectify this damage. P

later filed a Chapter 7 petition. The DER brought an equitable action in state court to enforce the consent order. P contended that this proceeding violated the automatic stay. In ruling for the DER, the Third Circuit stated: "Were we to find that any order which requires the expenditure of money is a 'money judgment,' then the exception to section 362 for government police action, which should be construed broadly, would instead be narrowed into virtual nonexistence. Yet we cannot ignore the fundamental fact that, in contemporary times, almost everything costs something. An injunction which does not compel some expenditure or loss of monies may often be an effective nullity.

It appears that, in defining the scope of the exception to the automatic stay, the Bankruptcy Court in this case placed too much weight on the value of preserving the corpus of the debtor's funds and estate under its own exclusive control. Admittedly, that goal is normally central to the statutory scheme of the Bankruptcy Code. As noted at the beginning of this opinion, however, in some instances this policy is in inexorable conflict with other, no less salutary, governmental goals. We believe that the resolution of this conflict is contained in the statute itself. In enacting the exceptions to section 362, Congress recognized that in some circumstances, bankruptcy policy must yield to higher priorities. Indeed, if the policy of preservation of the estate is to be invariably paramount, then one could not have exceptions to the rule. Since Congress did provide for exceptions, however, we may assume that the goal of preserving the debtor's estate is not always the dominant goal.

We believe that the inquiry is more properly focused on the nature of the injuries which the challenged remedy is intended to redress--including whether plaintiff seeks compensation for past damages or prevention of future harm--in order to reach the ultimate conclusion as to whether these injuries are traditionally rectified by a money judgment and its enforcement. Here, the Commonwealth Court injunction was, neither in form nor substance, the type of remedy traditionally associated with the conventional money judgment. It was not intended to provide compensation for past injuries. It was not reducible to a sum certain. No monies were sought by the Commonwealth as a creditor or obligee. The Commonwealth was not seeking a traditional form of damages in tort or contract, and the mere payment of money, without more, even if it could be estimated, could not satisfy the Commonwealth Court's direction to complete the backfilling, to update erosion plans, to seal mine openings, to spread topsoil, and to implement plans for erosion and sedimentation control. Rather, the Commonwealth Court's injunction was meant to prevent future harm to, and to restore, the environment. Indeed, examining the state order, it is clear that erosion control, backfilling, and reseeding were additionally meant to preserve the soil conditions from further deterioration (as well as to rectify a safety hazard).

5. Both Problems 3 and 4 involved the application of the automatic stay to environmental actions relating to prepetition contamination of property that the debtor is not using postpetition.   Does the automatic stay protect the debtor from environmental actions relating to its postpetition activities?   *Cf.* 28 UCS 959(b) ("a debtor in possession, shall manage and operate the property in his possession . . . according to the requirements of the valid laws of the State in which such property is situated, in the same manner that the owner or possessor thereof would be bound to do if in possession thereof.");   *see generally* Katherine Heidt, *Environmental Obligations in Bankruptcy* (1993); Robert Rasmussen, *Bankruptcy and the Administrative State*, 42 HASTINGS L.J. 1567 (1991); Ellen Sward, *Resolving Conflicts Between Bankruptcy Law and the State Police Power*, 1987 WISC. L. REV. 403; Murray Tabb, *Competing Policies in Bankruptcy: The Governmental Exception to the Automatic Stay*, 21 TULSA L.J. 183 (1985).

6. The application of the bankruptcy discharge to environmental actions is considered later in Unit 9.B.

3. Termination Of The Stay

Remember that the automatic stay begins when the bankruptcy petition is filed and generally bars a creditor from taking any action to collect its debt from the debtor or the debtor's property.

How and when does the automatic stay end? Paragraph (c) of section 362 describes two situations when the automatic stay terminates automatically. Please read section 362(c).

Section 362(c)(1) provides that the automatic stay ends as to particular property when the property ceases to be property of the estate. Assume, for example, that M has a mortgage on D Corp.'s building. D Corp. files a Chapter 11 bankruptcy petition. M is stayed from foreclosing on its mortgage. The bankruptcy trustee then sells D Corp.'s office building to X. M is no longer stayed from foreclosing its lien.

Section 362(c)(2) provides that the automatic stay ends when the bankruptcy case is closed or dismissed or the debtor receives a discharge. The typical Chapter 7 case can be completed in a matter of months. Accordingly, the automatic stay does not often significantly affect creditors in Chapter 7 cases. As the following questions suggest, the automatic stay does often significantly affect creditors in Chapter 11 and Chapter 12 cases.

Notes and Problems

1. According to a study of 1,096 publicly held company Chapter 11 filings from October 1979 to September 1990, the mean time from filing to confirmation was 21 months. *See* Edward Altman, *Evaluating The Chapter 11 Bankruptcy Reorganization Process*, 1993 COLUM. BUS. REV. 1. What does the automatic stay thus mean to the creditors in those cases?

2. Does the automatic stay terminate under section 362(c)(2) when a Chapter 11 plan is confirmed? *See* section 1141(a), (d).

3. In Chapter 13 cases, the plan is generally filed within 15 days and confirmed shortly thereafter. *Cf.* Bankruptcy Rule 3015. Will the automatic stay terminate under section 362(c) when a Chapter 13 plan is confirmed? *Cf.* section 1327, 1328.

4. D files a Chapter 7 petition. M has a mortgage on a building owned by D. The trustee abandons the building to D under section 554. Does the automatic stay terminate under section 362(c) when the building is abandoned to D? Does M have to obtain relief from stay in order to foreclose on the office building?

4. Relief From The Stay

As the preceding questions suggest, creditors in a Chapter 11 case or a Chapter 12 case often would have to wait several years for an automatic stay to terminate automatically. Is there any affirmative action that a creditor can take to obtain earlier relief from the stay?

A creditor can file a motion requesting relief from the automatic stay, Bankruptcy Rule 4001. The bankruptcy court can order the end of the automatic stay or place conditions on continuation of the stay. Paragraphs (d) through (g) of section 362 deal with requests for relief from the automatic stay. Please read these provisions and consider the following questions about stay litigation procedure.

Notes and Problems

1. Is a motion requesting relief from the automatic stay different from a motion to dismiss? D files a bankruptcy petition. D's creditors include A, B, and C. If the court grants C's motion requesting relief from the automatic stay, will A and B be free to proceed against D and D's property?

2. Note the use of the word "shall" in section 362(d). Does that mean that if a creditor establishes one of the grounds for relief from the automatic stay, the bankruptcy court must end the automatic stay as to that creditor?

3. Section 362(d) provides for "terminating" the automatic stay and for "annulling" the automatic stay. How does annulling the automatic stay differ from terminating the automatic stay?

4. What are the time limits, if any, on final resolution of a motion requesting relief from the automatic stay? If a creditor files a motion requesting relief from the automatic stay, is the bankruptcy court required to rule on the motion within 30 days? Within 60 days? Within 90 days? See section 362(e); Bankruptcy Rule 4001(b).

5. Most litigation under section 362(d) involves a holder of a secured claim seeking recourse to or protection of its collateral. The grounds for relief under section 362(d) will be considered in the unit on secured claims infra.

5. Consequences Of Violating The Stay

There are two major consequences of violating the stay. First, the conduct has no legal effect as against the debtor and bankruptcy estate. In appropriate circumstances, however, the court can annul the stay retroactively, so as to let stand and give effect to the conduct *nunc pro tunc*. Second, "[a]n individual injured by any willful violation of a stay provided by this section shall recover actual damages, including costs and attorneys' fees, and, in appropriate circumstances, may recover punitive damages." § 362(h).

IN THE UNITED STATES BANKRUPTCY COURT
FOR THE SOUTHERN DISTRICT OF FLORIDA
WEST PALM BREACH DIVISION

IN RE:

PIPER AIRCRAFT CORPORATION　　　　　Case No.
91-31884-BKC-RAM

       Debtor　　　　　　　　　　　　Chapter 11

_____

PIPER AIRCRAFT CORPORATION
       Plaintiff　　　　　　　　Adv. Pro. No
　-vs-　　　　　　　　　　　　93-1428-BKC-RAM-A

LORI CALABRO, as Executrix
of the Estates of Frank
Calabro and Ruth Calabro
       Defendant

_____

**MOTION FOR STAY PENDING APPEAL AND/OR
FOR REHEARING/RECONSIDERATION OF DEBTOR'S
EMERGENCY MOTION FOR PRELIMINARY INJUNCTION
RESULTING IN ISSUANCE OF INJUNCTION, SUA SPONTE
ADJUDICATION OF CIVIL CONTEMPT AGAINST LORI CALABRO AND
JONATHAN C. SCOTT, IMPOSING FINES AND IMPRISONMENT,
PERMITTING VIOLATION TO BE PURGED BY DISMISSAL OF
STATE COURT ACTION PENDING IN SUPREME COURT OF THE
STATE OF NEW YORK BY 5:00 P.M. ON DECEMBER 21, 1993.**

Movants LORI CALABRO, as Executrix of the Estates of RUTH
CALABRO and FRANK CALABRO and JONATHAN SCOTT, ESQ., hereby
move for an order pursuant to Bankruptcy Rule 8005 for a
stay pending appeal of that portion of this Court's order
dated December 20, 1993 which imposed punishment consisting
of fine and imprisonment and directed the withdrawal by
movants of a post petition lawsuit pending in the Supreme
Court of the State of New York by 5 p.m. tomorrow, December
21, 1993 as a condition of purging the violation. In the
alternative, movants seek reconsideration of this Court's
order dated December 20, 1993 and upon reconsideration, vacatur of those portions of the order determining that Lori
Calabro has a claim under 11 U.S.C. 101(5) and that the
pursuit of that claim postpetition constituted a violation
and willful violation of the automatic stay under 11 U.S.C.
Section 362 and those portions which imposed any sanction.
Movants respectfully contend that the order was improvidently issued. In support thereof, movants state as follows:

1. On July 1, 1991, the debtor commenced this case by filing a voluntary petition for relief under Chapter 11 of the Bankruptcy Code.

2. On July 26, 1991, Ruth and Frank Calabro, the parents of Lori Calabro, were killed when a Piper Aztec airplane used but not owned by them lost engine power upon takeoff, crashed and burst into flames. Both decedents were residents of the State of New York, County of Suffolk.

3. On July 21, 1993, an action was commenced in the Supreme Court of the State of New York, County of Suffolk by LORI CALABRO, Executrix of the Estates of Frank and Ruth Calabro, seeking compensatory and punitive damages against Piper Aircraft Corp. based upon design defect and failure to warn of the known danger of water contamination because of a defect in the fuel system of the aircraft, which defect exists in a fleet of some 1700 presently flying aircraft.

4. On July 27, 1993, debtor forwarded its suggestion of bankruptcy to the Supreme Court of the State of New York, contending that the commencement and continuation of the action would be void under Federal Law as violative of the automatic stay.

5. On August 1, 1993, counsel for Lori Calabro advised E. Glenn Parr, Esq., counsel for Piper Aircraft Corp. that the action was not stayed because it related to a postpetition claim and postpetition lawsuit. Counsel advised Piper that he would proceed with the action within ten days unless Piper indicated the authorities upon which it was relying for the proposition that the action was stayed. Piper did not respond to this letter (See letter attached hereto)

6. On August 27, 1993, Piper Aircraft Corp. was personally served with another copy of the summons and complaint at its office in Vero Beach, Florida.

7. On November 10, 1993, Justice Cohalan of the Supreme Court of the State of New York entered a default judgment against Piper Aircraft for its failure to defend the New York action.

* * *

9. In the emergency application filed this morning, Mr. Singerman sought an order enjoining the state Court proceeding and such other and further relief as the Court may deem just and proper. At the conclusion of the hearing, the Court opined that the prosecution of the postpetition accident and lawsuit was clearly in violation of the automatic stay and the Court indicated that it was imposing a fine of more than $250 million dollars and twenty-five days in prison of both LORI CALABRO and her counsel if the violation was not purged by LORI CALABRO's dismissal of her state court lawsuit by 5 p.m. on December 21, 1993. ***

10. The language of 11 U.S.C. Section 362(a) applies to stay actions which were or could have been brought against the debtor prior to the commencement of the case. It does not apply to post petition claims. Holland America Insurance Company v. Roy et al., 777 F.2d 992 (5th Cir. 1985).

11. To the extent that the debtor asserts that the State Court prosecution is in violation of the automatic stay and is void, it therefore follows that injunctive relief of the nature granted here was neither warranted nor required since the automatic stay is self-executing and any action taken in violation of the stay is void.

12. In light of the fact that movants did not willfully violate the automatic stay, the imposition, extent and amount of the fine imposed is excessive. Further, it is respectfully submitted that the injunction goes far beyond maintaining the status quo pending the determination of this adversary proceeding and will have the effect of rendering the declaratory judgment proceeding moot since movants must either suffer a substantial fine and incarceration or dismiss the State Court lawsuit before a determination has even been rendered in favor of the debtor on its application. This will constitute a violation of due process of law as movants have had no reasonable opportunity to answer the complaint nor to move for the declaration in their favor to which they believe themselves entitled.

13. The order at issue was improvidently entered since there is no basis to find that LORI CALABRO or her counsel willfully violated the automatic stay by prosecuting a postpetition claim for a postpetition accident. Further, the Court's purported determination of the merits is premature and should await an answer being filed to the declaratory judgment action.

14. The sua sponte adjudication of civil contempt should be vacated. It is respectfully submitted that an Article I Court does not have the power to summarily impose a contempt without reasonable notice, hearing or opportunity to be heard, nor may the Court enter such an order except by referral to the United States District Court. Furthermore, the amount of the sanction and the direction for incarceration of both defendant herein and her attorney is not only an abuse of discretion but also constitutes an excessive fine or punishment prohibited by the Eighth Amendment to the United States Constitution.

15. Movants also seek reconsideration on the basis that since the hearing today, movant has learned from the Supreme Court, Suffolk County that on the Court's own motion, and because of scheduling conflicts, it has adjourned this matter to January 11, 1994. This should afford Judge Mark

sufficient opportunity to rule on the automatic stay issue raised in this adversary proceeding. Therefore, it is respectfully requested that the order be modified to strike that portion imposing sanctions and conditions to purge the violation, that the purported determination of the merits and finding of violation of the automatic stay provisions of the United States Bankruptcy Code should be vacated and/or that these provisions should be stayed pending appeal.

16. A stay pending appeal of that provision will not cause any injury to the debtor as the State Court action is stayed until such time as this issue is resolved.

17. A stay or modification is sought on the basis that movant has been unable to contact LORI CALABRO nor is it possible under New York law for counsel to dismiss this proceeding without the consent of the client and of the New York Justice.

18. There are important issues of federalism implicated in this action by the entanglement in an ongoing state Court proceeding.

WHEREFORE, it is respectfully requested the relief set out above and for such other and further relief as is just and proper be granted to movants.

Dated this 20th day of December, 1993.

Johanaton C. Scott
_____

JONATHON C. SCOTT
Attorney for LORI CALABRO
pro hac vice
999 Walt Whitman Road
Melville, New York 11747
516) 4247171

Notes and Problems

1. What, if any, mistakes did the attorney for Lori Calabro make? Did he violate the automatic stay?

2. What, if any, mistakes did the bankruptcy judge make? What is the statutory basis for imposing a fine of more than $250,000,000 and 25 days in jail? *Cf.* section 362(h), Bankruptcy Rule 9020. *See generally* Joan Burleson, *Contempt Proceedings in Bankruptcy Court*, 22 COLO. LAW. 515 (1993).

Unit 9

DISCHARGE

UNIT CONTENTS

"One of the primary purposes of the bankruptcy act is to 'relieve the honest debtor from the weight of oppressive indebtedness, and permit him to start afresh free from the obligations and responsibilities consequent upon business misfortunes.' This purpose of the act has been again and again emphasized by the courts as being a public as well as private interest, in that it gives to the honest but unfortunate debtor who surrenders for distribution the property which he owns at the time of bankruptcy, a new opportunity in life and a clear field for future effort. *** " *Local Loan Co. v. Hunt,* 292 U.S. 234, 244, 54 S.Ct. 695, 699, 78 L.Ed. 1230, 1235 (1934).

This purpose of protecting "honest but unfortunate" debtors is accomplished by means of "discharge."

"Discharge" is not defined in the Bankruptcy Code. A leading practitioner text describes discharge as "the permanent stay," Richard Broude, REORGANIZATIONS UNDER CHAPTER 11 OF THE BANKRUPTCY CODE 14-13 (1986). In general a discharge frees the debtor from any further personal liability on most pre-bankruptcy debts. A law student or lawyer must be able to provide a more specific answer to three discharge questions:

1. Which debtors receive a discharge?
2. Which debts are covered by the discharge?
3. What are the effects of a discharge?

A. WHICH DEBTORS RECEIVE A DISCHARGE?

The answer to the question, which debtors receive a discharge, varies from Chapter to Chapter.

1. Chapter 7

In Chapter 7 cases, the availability of a discharge is controlled by section 727 and Rule 4004. Section 727(a) sets out ten grounds for withholding a discharge. These ten "objections to discharge" are the only grounds for withholding a discharge in a Chapter 7 case. Please read section 727 and Rule 4004 and apply the provisions in the following problems:

Problems

1. What is the policy justification for granting a discharge? See generally Thomas Jackson, *The Fresh Start Policy in Bankruptcy*, 98 HARV. L.REV. 1393 (1985); Frank Kennedy, *Reflections on the Bankruptcy Laws of the United States: The Debtor's Fresh Start*, 76 W.VA. L. REV. 427 (1974). If there is a policy justification for a discharge, why don't all debtors in Chapter 7 cases receive a discharge?

2. D Corp. files a Chapter 7 bankruptcy petition. Can D Corp. receive a discharge? See section 727(a)(1).

3. D files a Chapter 7 bankruptcy petition. At D's section 341 meeting, D told his creditors that he was distressed by a failing relationship and had spent hundreds of dollars each month on drinking and "900" phone calls. Can D receive a Chapter 7 discharge? See section 727(a)(5).

4. The United States attorney filed RICO charges against D. D filed a Chapter 7 petition. Claiming constitutional protection from self-incrimination, D refuses to prepare a Schedule of Assets and Liabilities or a Statement of Financial Affairs and refuses to answer any questions at the section 341 meeting. Can D still receive a discharge?

5. D filed a Chapter 7 petition in February of 1994 and receives a discharge in May. Can her creditors file an involuntary petition under Chapter 7 against D in 1995?

6. Section 727 is not self-executing. The bankruptcy trustee or a creditor must file a complaint to object to the discharge, section 727(c), Bankruptcy Rule 4004. Why would a creditor file a complaint objecting to discharge?

7. According to Professor Joseph Ulrich, "One area in which bankruptcy has been abused is the debtor's conversion of nonexempt property into exempt property on the eve of bankruptcy." See Joseph Ulrich, *Conversions on the Eve of Bankruptcy--There Ought to Be a Law*, 3 FAULKNER & GRAY'S L. REV. 18 (Spring 1991). Can the bankruptcy court withhold a discharge from an individual who sells his nonexempt property and invests the proceeds in exempt property just before filing a Chapter 7 petition? See section 727(a)(2) and *Dofflemeyer* at page 50 *supra*.

2. Chapters 12 And 13

Chapters 12 and 13 and 11, unlike Chapter 7, do not provide for objections to discharge. Remember that those objections are contained in section 727(a), and that none of Chapter 7 (including section 727) applies in Chapters 12 and 13. Thus, if a debtor qualifies for Chapter 12 or 13, files a plan that is confirmed by the bankruptcy judge, and completes payments under the plan, he will receive a discharge.

In re Ciotta
United States Bankruptcy Court, New York, 1980.
4 B.R. 253.

Boris Radoyevich, Bankruptcy Judge.

The above-named debtors filed a Chapter 13 petition, statement and plan with this Court on November 29, 1979. Their plan has been deemed accepted by their one secured creditor, who holds a mortgage on their residence dwelling, in accordance with Section 1325(a)(5)(B) of the Bankruptcy Code. The amended plan also provides for a 12 return over 36 months to general unsecured creditors. A hearing on the confirmation of their plan, as amended, was held on May 5, 1980. Decision was reserved to consider whether a prior discharge in bankruptcy granted to one of these debtors in a proceeding commenced within six years of the filing of the present case should bar confirmation of their proposed Chapter 13 plan.

Section 727(a) of the Bankruptcy Code reinstates the so-called six-year bar against successive discharges formerly contained in Section 14c(5) of the Bankruptcy Act. Section 727(a) provides that:

[t]he Court shall grant the debtor a discharge unless—

(8) the debtor has been granted a discharge under this Section or under Sections 14, 371, or 476 of the Bankruptcy Act, in a case commenced within 6 years before the date of filing of the petition;

(9) the debtor has been granted a discharge under Section 1328 of this title, or under Sections 660 or 661 of the Bankruptcy Act, in a case commenced within six years before the date of the filing of the petition, unless payments under the plan in such case totaled at least—

(A) 100 percent of the allowed unsecured claims in such case; or

(B)(i) 70 percent of such claims; and (ii) the plan was proposed by the debtor in good faith, and was the debtor's best effort;
***

However, Section 103(b) of the Code, provides that the provisions of subchapter II of Chapter 7, of which Section 727 is a part, apply only in cases commenced under Chapter 7. Therefore, the Court is urged to find that the debtor's prior Chapter VII discharge is not a bar to confirmation of the instant Chapter 13 plan.

There is no doubt that the purpose behind new Chapter 13 is to encourage the repayment of debts through future earnings, as an alternative to the liquidation of assets and the payment of a dividend to satisfy and discharge debts. There is no indication in the Code's legislative history, however, that the statute was intended to encourage repeated use of Chapter 13 compositions to escape debt.

It seems absurd to suggest that Congress intended to provide a mechanism for the repeated evasion of honest debt as a means of encouraging financially troubled individuals to use Chapter 13 rather than Chapter 7. It may be that Congress believed the majority of Chapter 13 wage earner plans would provide for the extension of debt only. This was the experience under the Bankruptcy Act, perhaps because of the creditor approval prerequisite contained in Section 652 of the Act. This provision was not continued in the Code. Cf. §1325(a)(5) (secured creditors acceptances required, but only under certain circumstances). The experience of this Court with Code filings, however, is that the greatest majority of Chapter 13 plans are in the nature of compositions. Plans which would provide for the repayment of more than 50 of unsecured debt are few and far between. In a majority of cases, creditors fare only a little better under Chapter 13 than they would in Chapter 7.

Notwithstanding the foregoing, it has long been the rule that the right to a discharge is statutory and should be construed liberally in order to carry into effect the intent of Congress. Accordingly, it has been said that the grounds for opposing discharge should not be extended by construction. This should be the rule in cases under the Bankruptcy Code as well, and particularly in Chapter 13 cases in view of the few exceptions to discharge provided in Section 1328 of the Code. While this Court questions the wisdom of this statutory scheme, it is clear that Congress intended that the so-called six-year bar against successive discharges continued in Section 727 of the Code should not apply to the discharge granted in Chapter 13 cases under Section 1328. This conclusion is supported by the absence of a Chapter 13 provision comparable to Section 602 of the Act, which made Section 14(c) of the Act applicable in Chapter XIII cases to the extent that it was consistent with the provisions of that chapter. Added support is found in Section 1328 of the Code which, by its creation of narrow grounds for objection to discharge, makes it obvious that this was not an oversight on the part of the drafters of the Code.

Accordingly, this Court holds that the six-year bar to successive discharges does not apply in cases commenced under Chapter 13 of the Bankruptcy Code.

Notes and Problems

1. Did the court grant the Ciottas a bankruptcy discharge?

2. If the Ciottas complete their payments under the Chapter 13 plan in December of 1982, when will they next be eligible for a discharge in a case under Chapter 7 of the Bankruptcy Code? In a case under Chapter 13 of the Bankruptcy Code?

3. What happens if the Ciottas cannot complete the payments provided for by the plan? Section 1328(b) permits the court to grant a so-called "hardship discharge." To do so, the court must find that failure to complete the plan was due to circumstances for which the debtors should not justly be held accountable, that creditors have received at least as much as they would have received in a Chapter 7 liquidation, and that modification of the plan is not practicable. A section 1328(b) "hardship discharge" is significantly less comprehensive than a section 1328(a) "regular Chapter 13 discharge."

4. Again, assume that the Ciottas cannot complete the payments provides for by the plan. Can the Ciottas use section 1329 to modify their Chapter 13 plan by reducing their payment obligations, complete the payment obligations under the modified plan, and receive the more comprehensive section 1328(a) discharge?

3. Chapter 11

In Chapter 11, the confirmation of the plan operates as a discharge, section 1141(d). The following hypothetical points out the practical significance of this rule: D Corp. owes X $100,000. D Corp.'s Chapter 11 plan proposes to pay X $70,000 over three years. On confirmation, D Corp.'s only obligation to X is to pay it $70,000 over three years as provided in the plan. The remainder of the debt has been discharged.

The grounds for denying a discharge in a Chapter 11 case are different from the grounds for denying a discharge in a Chapter 7 case. A Chapter 11 debtor will be denied a discharge if *all* of the following requirements are satisfied:

✓ the plan provides for liquidation of all or substantially all of the property of the estate; AND
✓ the debtor does not engage in business after the completion of the plan; AND
✓ the debtor would be denied a discharge if the case were in Chapter 7, section 1141(d)(3).

The following hypotheticals illustrate the application of section 1141(d)(3).

Problems

1. D Corp. files a Chapter 11 petition. Its Chapter 11 plan provides for the sale of all of its assets, distribution of the proceeds from the sale to creditors, and termination of business operations. Will D Corp. receive a Chapter 11 discharge?

2. D Inc.'s Chapter 11 plan provides for the sale of six stores and continued operations of five stores. Will D Inc. receive a discharge?

3. D, an individual who owns and operates several small businesses as sole proprietorships, files a Chapter 11 petition in 1993. D's Chapter 11 plan provides for the continued operation of these businesses. D had earlier filed a Chapter 7 petition and had obtained a discharge in her Chapter 7 case in 1991. Because of her "bankruptcy history," D would be denied a Chapter 7 discharge under section 727(a)(9). Will D receive a discharge in the Chapter 11 case?

4. Do you agree with the following statement about availability of discharge in a Chapter 11 case: "If an individual debtor would be denied a discharge under Section 727(a), the individual will be denied a discharge under Section 1141." Richard Broude, REORGANIZATIONS UNDER CHAPTER 11 OF THE BANKRUPTCY CODE 14-10 (1986).

B. WHICH OBLIGATIONS ARE AFFECTED BY A BANKRUPTCY DISCHARGE

Even when the debtor receives a discharge, she is not necessarily freed from all of her legal obligations. Certain legal obligations are not affected by a discharge. In determining whether a discharge affects an obligation, it is necessary to consider the following three questions:

(1) Is the obligation a "debt" as that term is defined in section 101? [Sections 727(b), 1141(d), 1228 and 1328 discharge the debtor from "debts."]

(2) If so, when did the obligation become a debt? [Subject to limited exceptions, a Chapter 7 discharge reaches only "debts that arose before the date of the order for relief," section 727(b). A Chapter 11 discharge covers debts that "arose before the date of such confirmation," section 1141(d)(1)(A). A Chapter 12 discharge or a Chapter 13 discharge reaches debts "provided for by the plan," sections 1228(a), (c), 1328(a), (c)].

(3) Is section 523 applicable? [Section 523 excepts certain debts from the operation of a discharge. Section 523 applies in all Chapter 7 cases, in all Chapter 12 cases, in Chapter 11 cases involving individual debtors, and in Chapter 13 cases in which the debtor receives a section 1328(b) "hardship discharge," sections 727(b), 1141(d)(2), and 1328(c).]

1. Is The Obligation A Debt?

Ohio v. Kovacs

Supreme Court of the United States, 1985
469 U.S. 274, 105 S.Ct. 705, 83 L.Ed.2d 649

Justice White delivered the opinion of the Court.

Petitioner State of Ohio obtained an injunction ordering respondent William Kovacs to clean up a hazardous waste site. A receiver was subsequently appointed. Still later, Kovacs filed a petition for bankruptcy. The question before us is whether, in the circumstances present here, Kovacs' obligation under the injunction is a "debt" or "liability on a claim" subject to discharge under the Bankruptcy Code.

* * *

Kovacs was the chief executive officer and stockholder of Chem-Dyne Corp., which with other business entities operated an industrial and hazardous waste disposal site in Hamilton, Ohio. In 1976, the State sued Kovacs and the business entities in state court for polluting public waters, maintaining a nuisance, and causing fish kills, all in violation of state environmental laws. In 1979, both in his individual capacity and on behalf of Chem-Dyne, Kovacs signed a stipulation and judgment entry settling the lawsuit. Among other things, the stipulation enjoined the defendants from causing further pollution of the air or public waters, forbade bringing additional industrial wastes onto the site, required the defendants to remove specified wastes from the property, and ordered the payment of $75,000 to compensate the State for injury to wildlife.

Kovacs and the other defendants failed to comply with their obligations under the injunction. The State then obtained the appointment in state court of a receiver, who was directed to take possession of all property and other assets of Kovacs and the corporate defendants and to implement the judgment entry by cleaning up the Chem-Dyne site. The receiver took possession of the site but had not completed his tasks when Kovacs filed a personal bankruptcy petition.

Seeking to develop a basis for requiring part of Kovacs' postbankruptcy income to be applied to the unfinished task of the receivership, the State then filed a motion in state court to discover Kovacs' current income and assets. Kovacs requested that the Bankruptcy Court stay those proceedings, which it did. The State also filed a complaint in the Bankruptcy Court seeking a declaration that Kovacs' obligation under the stipulation and judgment order to clean up the Chem-Dyne site was not dischargeable in bankruptcy because it was not a "debt," a liability on a "claim," within the meaning of the Bankruptcy Code. In addition, the complaint sought an injunction against the bankruptcy trustee to restrain him from pursuing any action to recover assets of Kovacs in the hands of the receiver. The Bankruptcy Court ruled against Ohio, as did the District Court. The Court of Appeals for the sixth circuit affirmed, holding that Ohio essentially sought from Kovacs only a monetary payment and that such a required payment was a liability on a claim that was dischargeable under the bankruptcy statute. We granted certiorari to determine the dischargeability of Kovacs' obligation under the affirmative injunction entered against him.

III

Except for the nine kinds of debts saved from discharge by §523(a), a discharge in bankruptcy discharges the debtor from all debts that arose before bankruptcy. §727(b). It is not claimed here that Kovacs' obligation under the injunction fell within any of the categories of debts excepted from discharge by §523. Rather, the State submits that the obligation to clean up the Chem-Dyne site is not a debt at all within the meaning of the bankruptcy law.

For bankruptcy purposes, a debt is a liability on a claim. §101(11). A claim is defined by §101(4) as follows:

"(4) 'claim' means—
"(A) right to payment, whether or not such right is reduced to judgment, liquidated, unliquidated, fixed, contingent, matured, unmatured, disputed, undisputed, legal, equitable, secured, or unsecured; or
"(B) right to an equitable remedy for breach of performance if such breach gives rise to a right to payment, whether or not such right to an equitable remedy is reduced to judgment, fixed, contingent, matured, unmatured, disputed, undisputed, secured, or unsecured."

The provision at issue here is §101(4)(B). For the purposes of that section, there is little doubt that the State had the right to an equitable remedy under state law and that the right has been reduced to judgment in the form of an injunction ordering the cleanup. The State argues, however, that the injunction it has secured is not a claim against Kovacs for bankruptcy purposes because (1) Kovacs' default was a breach of the statute, not a breach of an ordinary commercial contract which concededly would give rise to a claim; and (2) Kovacs' breach of his obligation under the injunction did not give rise to a right to payment within the meaning of §101(4)(B). We are not persuaded by either submission.

There is no indication in the language of the statute that the right to performance cannot be a claim unless it arises from a contractual arrangement. The State resorted to the courts to enforce its environmental laws against Kovacs and secured a negative order to cease polluting, an affirmative order to clean up the site, and an order to pay a sum of money to recompense the State for damage done to the fish population. Each order was one to remedy an alleged breach of Ohio law; and if Kovacs' obligation to pay $75,000 to the State is a debt dischargeable in bankruptcy, which the State freely concedes, it makes little sense to assert that because the cleanup order was entered to remedy a statutory violation, it cannot likewise constitute a claim for bankruptcy purposes.

Furthermore, it is apparent that Congress desired a broad definition of a "claim" and knew how to limit the application of a provision to contracts when it desired to do so.

The injunction surely obliged Kovacs to clean up the site. But when he failed to do so, rather than prosecute Kovacs under the environmental laws or bring civil or criminal contempt proceedings, the State secured the appointment of a receiver, who was ordered to take possession of all of Kovacs' nonexempt assets as well as the assets of the corporate defendants and to comply with the injunction entered against Kovacs. As wise as this course may have been, it dispossessed Kovacs, removed his authority over the site, and divested him of assets that might have been used by him to clean up the property. Furthermore, when the bankruptcy trustee sought to recover Kovacs' assets from the receiver, the latter sought an injunction against such action. Although Kovacs had been ordered to "cooperate" with the receiver, he was disabled by the receivership from personally taking charge of and carrying out the removal of wastes from the property. What the receiver wanted from Kovacs after bankruptcy was the money to defray cleanup costs. At oral argument in this Court, the State's counsel conceded that after the receiver was appointed, the only performance sought from Kovacs was the payment of money. Had Kovacs furnished the necessary funds, either before or after bankruptcy, there seems little doubt that the receiver and the State would have been satisfied. On the facts before it, and with the receiver in control of the site, we cannot fault the Court of Appeals for concluding that the cleanup order had been converted into an obligation to pay money, an obligation that was dischargeable in bankruptcy.

IV

It is well to emphasize what we have not decided. First, we do not suggest that Kovacs' discharge will shield him from prosecution for having violated the environmental laws of Ohio or for criminal contempt for not performing his obligations under the injunction prior to bankruptcy. Second, had a fine or monetary penalty for violation of state law been imposed on Kovacs prior to bankruptcy, §523(a)(7) forecloses any suggestion that his obligation to pay the fine or penalty would be discharged in bankruptcy. Third, we do not address what the legal consequences would have been had Kovacs taken bankruptcy before a receiver had been appointed and a trustee had been designated with the usual duties of a bankruptcy trustee.[1] Fourth, we do not hold that the injunction

---

[1] The commencement of a case under the Bankruptcy Act creates an estate which, with limited exceptions, consists of all of the debtor's property wherever located. §541. The trustee, who is to be appointed promptly in Chapter 7 cases, is charged with the duty of collecting and reducing the property of the estate and is to be accountable for all of such property. §704. A custodian of the debtor's property appointed before commencement of the case is required to deliver the debtor's property in his custody to the trustee, unless the bankruptcy court concludes that the interest of creditors would be better served by permitting the custodian to continue in possession and control of the

against bringing further toxic wastes on the premises or against any conduct that will contribute to the pollution of the site or the State's waters is dischargeable in bankruptcy; we here address, as did the Court of Appeals, only the affirmative duty to clean up the site and the duty to pay money to that end. Finally, we do not question that anyone in possession of the site—whether it is Kovacs or another in the event the receivership is liquidated and the trustee abandons the property, or a vendee from the receiver or the bankruptcy trustee—must comply with the environmental laws of the State of Ohio. Plainly, that person or firm may not maintain a nuisance, pollute the waters of the State, or refuse to remove the source of such conditions. As the case comes to us, however, Kovacs has been dispossessed and the State seeks to enforce his cleanup obligation by a money judgment.

The judgment of the Court of Appeals is
Affirmed.

Justice O'Connor, concurring.

I join the Court's opinion and agree with its holding that the cleanup order has been reduced to a monetary obligation dischargeable as a "claim" under §727 of the Bankruptcy Code. I write separately to address the petitioner's concern that the Court's action will impede States in enforcing their environmental laws.

To say that Kovacs' obligation in these circumstances is a claim dischargeable in bankruptcy does not wholly excuse the obligation or leave the State without any recourse against Kovacs' assets to enforce the order. Because "Congress has generally left the determination of property rights in the assets of a bankrupt's estate to state law," the classification of Ohio's interest as either a lien on the property itself, a perfected security interest, or merely an unsecured claim depends on Ohio law. That classification—a question not before us—generally determines the priority of the State's claim to the assets of the estate relative to other creditors. Cf. §545 (trustee may avoid statutory liens only in specified circumstances). Thus, a State may protect its interest in the

---

property. §543. After notice and hearing, the trustee may abandon any property of the estate that is burdensome to the estate or that is of inconsequential value to the estate. §554. Such abandonment is to the person having the possessory interest in the property. S.Rep. No. 95-989, p. 92 (1978). Property that is scheduled but not administered is deemed abandoned. §554(c). Had no receiver been appointed prior to Kovacs' bankruptcy, the trustee would have been charged with the duty of collecting Kovacs' nonexempt property and administering it. If the site at issue were Kovacs' property, the trustee would shortly determine whether it was of value to the estate. If the property was worth more than the costs of bringing it into compliance with state law, the trustee would undoubtedly sell it for its net value, and the buyer would clean up the property, in which event whatever obligation Kovacs might have had to clean up the property would have been satisfied. If the property were worth less than the cost of cleanup, the trustee would likely abandon it to its prior owner, who would have to comply with the state environmental law to the extent of his or its ability.

enforcement of its environmental laws by giving cleanup judgments the status of statutory liens or secured claims.

The Court's holding that the cleanup order was a "claim" within the meaning of §101(4) also avoids potentially adverse consequences for a State's enforcement of its order when the debtor is a corporation, rather than an individual. In a Chapter 7 proceeding under the Bankruptcy Code, a corporate debtor transfers its property to a trustee for distribution among the creditors who hold cognizable claims, and then generally dissolves under state law. Because the corporation usually ceases to exist, it has no postbankruptcy earnings that could be utilized by the State to fulfill the cleanup order. The State's only recourse in such a situation may well be its "claim" to the prebankruptcy assets.

For both these reasons, the Court's holding today cannot be viewed as hostile to state enforcement of environmental laws.

Notes and Problems

1. A discharge relieves the debtor from any further personal liability on "debts." Debt is defined in section 101 as "liability on a claim." The definition of "claim" requires a "right to payment." In *Kovacs*, was the State of Ohio asking Kovacs to clean up or to pay up?

2. D owns and operates a chain of convenience stores. The stores have underground gasoline tanks. In three now-closed stores, the tanks leaked, Neither D nor the EPA has cleaned up the sites. The EPA has brought an action seeking a mandatory injunction under CERCLA directing D to cleanup the three closed store sites. D files a Chapter 11 petition. A Chapter 11 discharge, like a Chapter 7 discharge, only affects claims. Does the EPA injunction give rise to a "claim" that D can discharge?

3. *Kovacs* involves the effect of a Chapter 7 discharge on an injunction ordering the debtor to cleanup a contaminated site. Recall that the *Penn Terra* case, discussed on pages 777-78 *supra*, considered the effect of the automatic stay on an injunction to cleanup a contaminated site. Are the two cases consistent?

2. When Did The Obligation Become A "Debt"?

In each chapter of the Bankruptcy Code, the discharge provisions contain time limitations. See sections 727(b), 1141(d)(1)(A), 1228(c), 1328(c). The following problems illustrate some of the issues that arise in applying the time limitations.

Problems

1. D files a Chapter 7 petition on January 5. On February 2, D borrows $20,000 from C. On April 5, D obtains a discharge in her Chapter 7 case. Will the discharge affect D's liability on the February 2 $20,000 loan? See section 727(b).

2. Same facts as Problem 1 except that D files a Chapter 11 petition on January 5. D's Chapter 11 plan is confirmed on April 5. Will the Chapter 11 discharge affect D's liability on the February 2 $20,000 loan? See section 1141.

3. C files a malpractice action against Dr. D. on March 3. seeking damages of $300,000. Dr. D files a Chapter 7 petition on April 5. Dr. D obtains a discharge. The malpractice action is still pending. Cf. section 362. Does C have a "claim"? Will the discharge affect Dr. D's liability if any to C?

4. Same facts as Problem 3 except that C's attorney does not file the malpractice action prior to the bankruptcy filing. Instead, C's attorney sends Dr. D a demand letter on March 3.

5. Same facts as Problem 3 except that C is not aware of Dr. D's malpractice until after Dr. D's Chapter 7 filing. Dr. D treats C on February 2. Dr. D files a Chapter 7 petition on April 5. On April 11, C becomes ill. If C's illness is attributable to Dr. D's prepetition malpractice, does C have a "claim" against Dr. D? A claim " that arose before the date of the order for relief"? What if C's illness attributable to Dr. D's prepetition malpractice did not occur until after the close of Dr. D's bankruptcy case?

3. Is The Debt Excepted From Discharge By Section 523(A)?

Section 523(a) describes twelve kinds of debt that are excepted from discharge.

Recall that generally provisions in Chapter 5 such as section 523 apply in all bankruptcy cases, section 103. Section 523, however, does not apply in all bankruptcy cases. The exceptions to discharge set out in section 523(a) apply only if the debtor is a

- Chapter 7 debtor, or
- Chapter 12 debtor, or
- Chapter 11 debtor who is an individual, or
- Chapter 13 debtor who has received a hardship discharge.

The phrase "exceptions to discharge" is unfortunately similar to the term "objections to discharge." It is very important to understand the differences between section 727(a) objections to discharge and section 523(a) exceptions to discharge. First, section 727 applies only in Chapter 7 cases and some Chapter 11 cases; section 523 applies in all cases under Chapters 7 and 12 and some 11 and 13 cases. Second proof of an objection to discharge benefits all creditors; proof of an exception to discharge benefits only the creditor that establishes the exception.

Assume for example, that Leonard "Bones" McCoy files a Chapter 7 petition. If Christine Chapel establishes a section 727 objection to McCoy's discharge, none of McCoy's creditors will be barred from attempting to collect any unpaid portion of their claims from McCoy. Lt. Commander Montgomery Scott, Lt. Sulu, Ensign Pavel Chekov, Lt. Uhuru and all of McCoy's other creditors will be able to proceed against McCoy personally to recover their claims.

If, on the other hand, Nurse Chapel only establishes a Section 523 exception to McCoy's discharge, all of McCoy's other creditors will be barred from attempting to collect any unpaid portion of their claims from McCoy. Chapel will be able to proceed against McCoy personally after her successful exception to discharge to recover the excepted claim. However, Scotty, Sulu, Chekov, Uhuru, and McCoy's other creditors will be barred by the discharge.

Please review the exceptions to discharge of section 523(a). Note that some of the numbered subparagraphs in section 523(a) focus on the nature of the debt. For example, section 523(a)(1) excepts most tax obligations from the operation of a discharge. Similarly, section 523(a)(8) provides an exception from discharge for educational loan debts. Other exceptions are based on the actions of the debtor. For example, section 523(a)(2)(A) excepts debts resulting from the debtor's misrepresentations. And, section 523(a)(6) provides an exception for debts arising from willful and malicious injury by the debtor.

The following problems illustrate the application of section 523(a).

Problems

1. D files a Chapter 7 bankruptcy petition in March of 1994. She owes 1991 and 1992 state and federal income taxes. Will her Chapter 7 discharge affect her tax liabilities? See section 523(a)(1).

2. D has decided to file a Chapter 11 bankruptcy petition. He wants to buy some new business clothes and is concerned about the effect of bankruptcy on his ability to buy on credit. Accordingly, one day before he files his Chapter 11 bankruptcy petition, he buys three $500 suits at J. Press and charges this purchase to his J. Press account. Advise J. Press. See section 523(a)(2), 523(c).

3. D, a University of Minnesota law student, owes $3,000 to the University for parking tickets. Can she avoid this liability by filing a bankruptcy petition? See section 523(a)(7).

4. S obtained an educational loan from the University of Minnesota. S's mother, D, guaranteed repayment of the loan. The first payment on the loan is due on graduation. S graduates and defaults. Minnesota is now attempting to collect from

D. If D files a Chapter 12 bankruptcy petition and receives a discharge, will the University of Minnesota's claim against D be excepted from the discharge? See section 523(a)(8).

5. D, while intoxicated, drove her car at an excessive rate of speed right into the "dining room" at the Varsity injuring C. C sued D in state court. D then filed a bankruptcy petition. Is C's claim excepted from discharge? See section 523(a)(9), section 523(a)(6).

6. D has filed a Chapter 11 petition. Prior to his Chapter 11 filing, he borrowed $60,000 from your client, C. C required that D provide a financial statement before extending credit. Will C's $60,000 claim be excepted from discharge by section 523(a)(2)(B)? How can you prove

   a. that D's financial statement was "materially false"?

   b. that your client C "reasonably relied" on the financial statement?

   c. that D provided the financial statement "with an intent to deceive"?

Matter of Allison
United States Court of Appeals, Fifth Circuit, 1992
960 F.2d 481

Politz, Chief Judge: Crescentia Roberts, a creditor of bankrupt debtors Dean and Phyllis Allison, appeals the district court's ruling that the Allisons' debt to Roberts is dischargeable in bankruptcy. We conclude that under the provisions of 11 U.S.C. §523(a)(2)(A) the debt of Dean Allison is not dischargeable but that the debt of Phyllis Allison is.

Background
Roberts sold certain immovable property in New Orleans to the Allisons. The contract to sell the two residences called for credit sales, secured by second mortgages covering 80% of the purchase prices. The Allisons defaulted on the notes prior to taking bankruptcy. Citing 11 U.S.C. §523(a)(2)(A), Roberts maintains that their debt to her should not be discharged in bankruptcy because the Allisons obtained her property through false pretenses, false representations, or actual fraud.

[T]he Allisons agreed to limit the first, or primary mortgages on the properties to a maximum of 20% of the purchase price, thus assuring that Roberts would be fully secured for the credit portion. * * *

On the very day that Dean Allison represented that the first mortgages would not exceed 20% of the market value he executed first mortgages for at least four times that amount, effectively negating Roberts' secured position. Roberts did not discover this until after the Allisons defaulted in payment and it became necessary for her to secure a judgment against them in state court for the unpaid balance. Based on these facts the bankruptcy court held that the debt was not dischargeable for Dean Allison but was dischargeable for his wife who was not present at the closing. The matter was appealed to the district court.

The district court * * * reversed the bankruptcy court's ruling as to Dean Allison, holding that the debt was dischargeable as to both Allisons. We now reinstate the disposition of this issue as made by the bankruptcy court.

Analysis

* * * The creditor claiming nondischargeability has the burden of proving, by a preponderance of the evidence, that the debt is exempt from discharge. Grogan v. Garner, --- U.S. ----, 111 S.Ct. 654, 112 L.Ed.2d 755 (1991). * * * Since 1970, however, the issue of nondischargeability has been a matter of federal law governed by the terms of the Bankruptcy Code." Grogan v. Garner, 111 S.Ct. at 657-58 (citations and footnotes omitted). The discharge exception provided by 11 U.S.C. §523 does not discharge a debt

> for money, property, services, or an extension, renewal, or refinancing of credit, to the extent obtained by-- (A) false pretenses, a false representation, or actual fraud, other than a statement respecting the debtor's or an insider's financial condition[.]

Section 523(a)(2)(A) contemplates frauds involving "moral turpitude or intentional wrong; fraud implied in law which may exist without imputation of bad faith or immorality, is insufficient." 3 Collier on Bankruptcy ¶523.08 [4] (15th ed. 1989). The misrepresentations must have been: (1) knowing and fraudulent falsehoods, (2) describing past or current facts, (3) that were relied upon by the other party. Collier, supra. It is undisputed that the Allisons received "property," specifically real estate, from Roberts.

As to the first requirement, the bankruptcy court made the factual determination that Dean Allison effected an intentional and purposeful deception by feigning agreement to the first mortgage limit in order to get Roberts to sign the deeds of conveyance when, in fact, he had already made or was in the process of making arrangements for first mortgage indebtedness far in excess of that limit. Those factual findings are not clearly erroneous and based thereon we must conclude that Dean Allison's statements were knowing and fraudulent within the meaning of section 523(a)(2)(A).

The second requirement is that the misrepresentations be of past or current acts; a promise to perform acts in the future is not considered a qualifying misrepresentation merely because the promise subsequently is breached. In re Bercier, 934 F.2d 689 (5th Cir.1991) (citing Collier); In re Roeder, 61 B.R. 179 (Bankr.W.D.Ky.1986); and In re Boese, 8 B.R. 660 (Bankr.D.S.D.1981). A debtor's misrepresentations of his intentions, however, may constitute a false representation within the meaning of the dischargeability provision if, when the representation is made, the debtor has no intention of performing as promised. The bankruptcy court's finding that Dean Allison misrepresented the current fact of his future intention regarding the mortgages is also supported by the record.

The final criterion is that the creditor relied upon the representation. The nature of this reliance has been the subject of considerable debate. Several courts have held that the reliance must be reasonable. Others consider reasonable reliance to be solely a requisite for exceptions claimed under subparagraph (B) of section 523(a)(2), not of subparagraph (A). [FN4] Indeed, section 523(a)(2)(B), addressing "use of a statement in writing," expressly recites reasonable reliance as an essential element to the discharge exception. [FN5] Section 523(a)(2)(A) contains no such requirement. Further, the legislative history of these subparagraphs recites that "Subparagraph (A) is mutually exclusive from subparagraph (B)." H.R.Rep. No. 595, Cong., 1st Sess. 130-31 (1977), reprinted in 1978 U.S.C.C.A.N. 5787, 6453. Our colleagues in the Eighth Circuit fathomed why Congress intentionally omitted the reasonable reliance language from subparagraph (A):

> Because creditors might induce debtors to falsify financial statements in order to make a debt nondischargeable, Congress explicitly required that nondischargeability under section 523(a)(2)(B) be premised upon a showing of reasonable reliance. H.R.Rep. No. 595, Cong., 1st Sess. 103-31 (1977), reprinted in 1978 U.S.C.C.A.N. 5787. As [In re Fosco, 14 B.R. 918 (Bankr.D.Conn.1981)] explains, "the burden of proving reasonable reliance in section 523(a)(2)(B) to protect the debtor is not only left out of the language of section 523(a)(2)(A), but it cannot be justified by the policy concern expressed in the legislative history regarding false financial statements."

In re Ophaug, 827 F.2d 340, 343 (8th Cir.1987).

Conversely, some courts have required reasonable reliance for subparagraph (A) exceptions on the theory that the statutory policy of giving debtors a fresh start outweighs the rights of creditors who act unreasonably. The recent decision of the United States Supreme Court in Grogan v. Garner sheds new light on the appropriate interpretation of the goals of the Bankruptcy Code. Grogan overruled this court and other federal appellate courts by holding that creditors need only establish fraud by a preponderance of the evidence, not by clear and convincing evidence. In discussing the competing policies central to this issue, the Supreme Court placed the "fresh start" goal into perspective: The statutory provisions governing nondischargeability reflect a congressional decision to exclude from the general policy of discharge certain categories of debts ... [including] fraud. Congress evidently concluded that the creditors' interest in recovering full payment of debts in these categories outweighed the debtors' interest in a complete fresh start. We think in unlikely that Congress, in fashioning the standard of proof that governs the applicability of these provisions, would have favored the interest in giving perpetrators of fraud a fresh start over the interest in protecting victims of fraud. Grogan, 111 S.Ct. at 659. Given this revised pronouncement from the Supreme Court, we find unpersuasive the asserted policy rationale for reading reasonable reliance into subparagraph (A). It is the " 'honest but unfortunate debtor' " to whom the federal bankruptcy laws give refuge. Congressional concern for dishonest or manipulative debtors prompted the reasonable reliance requisite of subparagraph (B). We perceive no justification for interpretative revision of subparagraph (A). In re Ophaug. Both the plain letter and the legislative history of subparagraphs (A) and (B) demonstrate that they espouse separate and independent grounds for the discharge exception. We therefore conclude that reasonable reliance is not, as a matter of law, required under section 523(a)(2)(A). While so concluding we hasten to add that the reasonableness of reliance is strong circumstantial evidence in the factual determination regarding actual reliance, which is an element of subparagraph (A).

In the case at bar, the bankruptcy court concluded that Roberts' reliance was reasonable. We need not make that inquiry; rather, we need only ask whether Roberts, in signing the deeds conveying her property, in fact relied on Dean Allison's representation that the first mortgages would not exceed 20% of the purchase price, thus leaving Roberts adequately secured on the 80% credit portion of the purchase price. After hearing the testimony of those present at the closing of the sales, the bankruptcy court found that Roberts' attorney refused to proceed with the closing without a limitation on the first mortgages as agreed to in the contract to sell, the initial agreement on the transactions. That assurance was forthcoming from Dean Allison. Roberts relied on that assurance in signing the deeds conveying her property on a credit basis. The requisite reliance for section 523(a)(2)(A) purposes exists. We therefore reinstate the ruling of the bankruptcy court that Dean Allison's debt is not dischargeable in bankruptcy.

As to Phyllis Allison we agree with both the bankruptcy court and the district court that the debt is dischargeable. It was stipulated that: she neither met nor spoke with Roberts, her attorney, or daughter; she was not present at the closing; and she was not aware of any agreement to limit the amount of the mortgages placed on the property. "A debtor who has made no false representations may, nevertheless, be bound by the fraud of an agent acting within the scope of the debtor's authority." Collier, supra. The agency theory has been applied to impute the fraudulent acts of one spouse to the other in cases in which the other spouse was involved in a business or scheme. We find no evidence in the record linking Phyllis Allison to false or fraudulent acts or plans. Considering the statutory requirement for fraud involving moral turpitude or intentional wrong, we perceive no basis for applying the agency fraud theory to Phyllis Allison.

We AFFIRM the ruling that the debt as to Phyllis Allison is dischargeable in bankruptcy. We REVERSE the district court and REINSTATE the ruling of the bankruptcy court that the debt of Dean Allison is not dischargeable in bankruptcy.

Notes and Problems

1. What is the statutory basis for the three requirements from Colliers that the court applies?

2. The court in *Allison* concludes that the requirements of section 523(a)(2)(A) are different from the requirements of section 523(a)(2)(B). When does a creditor invoke section 523(a)(2)(A) and when does it rely on (B)?

3. X is a part in the law firm of X, Y, and Z. In the course of representing a savings and loan institution, Y makes fraudulent misrepresentations. X is not involved in the work for the savings and loan client and is unaware of the misrepresentations. Under relevant state partnership law, X is liable for her partner's fraudulent misrepresentations be excepted from discharge? See generally Stephen Resnicoff, *Is It Morally Wrong to Depend Upon the Honesty of Your Partner or Spouse? Bankruptcy Dischargeability of Vicarious Debt*, 42 Case Wes. L. Rev. 147 (1992).

4. See generally, Hon. Nancy Dreher & Matthew Roy, *Bankruptcy Fraud and Dischargeability Under Section 523 of the Bankruptcy Code*, 69 N.D. L.Rev. 57 (1993).

In re Harrell

United States Court of Appeals, Eleventh Circuit, 1985
754 F.2d 902

R. Lanier Anderson, III, Circuit Judge: We consider in this bankruptcy appeal the dischargeability of a debtor's obligation to pay accrued alimony arrearages, and post-majority child support and educational expenses. We conclude that the obligations in question are not dischargeable and accordingly affirm the judgment of the district court.

I. Facts and Decisions Below

The facts as they appear from the bankruptcy court's order and the parties' agreements are essentially as follows. The debtor and his former spouse (defendant herein) entered into a separation agreement in 1971 requiring debtor to pay defendant $100 each month for her support and maintenance during her life or until she remarried, and to pay $100 each month in support of his son until his son became wholly self-supporting, married, or attained the age of 21. The agreement provided that these amounts were to vary with debtor's income. Debtor agreed to pay his son's educational expenses through college and post-graduate school, with debtor's child support payments reduced by one-half during periods he paid education expenses. The separation agreement provided also that debtor would assume the couple's joint debts, and that defendant would acquire the marital residence and responsibility for payments on its mortgage.

Debtor made payments under the agreement, but was substantially in arrears by 1974, at which time the separation agreement was amended. The amended agreement reduced the amounts of alimony and child support to a set amount of $200 monthly for each. The amended agreement required debtor to establish a trust to secure the obligation to pay his son's educational expenses. Defendant agreed to waive the then-existing alimony and child support arrearages. Apparently the parties agree that debtor did not establish the trust required by the 1974 amended agreement. Although the parties dispute the amount of arrearages, the issue they present to this court concerns the dischargeability in bankruptcy of whatever arrearages have accrued.

Debtor filed his Chapter VII [sic] petition October 17, 1980. On December 12, 1980, debtor filed a complaint in bankruptcy court to determine the dischargeability of his domestic debts. Specifically, debtor sought to have declared dischargeable the amounts he owed in alimony and child support arrearages because, he contended, such amounts were not "actually in the nature of alimony, maintenance, or support." Debtor also sought to have declared dischargeable his obligation to make payments on behalf of his son past the age of eighteen because, as expressed in his complaint, "such obligations were not and are not actually in the nature of alimony, maintenance, or support," but were "voluntarily assumed and constitute contractual obligations which are discharged by [debtor's] bankruptcy case."

Debtor's principal contentions on appeal are that: (1) the obligation to pay post-majority child support and educational expenses is dischargeable because the relevant state law does not require a parent to support his child past the age of eighteen; and (2) the alimony arrearages are dischargeable because the parties' separation agreement required debtor to pay more than defendant actually needed for support, and because defendant did not need the arrearages at the time debtor filed his petition in bankruptcy.

II. Dischargeability of Domestic Obligations

A debtor may obtain a general discharge under Chapter VII of the Bankruptcy Code from "all debts that arose before the date of the order for relief." §727(b). The Code makes exceptions for certain obligations, however, among which are alimony and support payments. The language in the Code that provides this treatment states that a discharge under section 727 does not discharge a debtor from any debt:

> (5) to a spouse, former spouse, or child of the debtor, for alimony to, maintenance for, or support of such spouse or child, in connection with a

separation agreement, divorce decree, or property settlement agreement, but not to the extent that—

(A) such debt is assigned to another entity, voluntarily, by operation of law, or otherwise (other than debts assigned pursuant to section 402(a)(26) of the Social Security Act); or

(B) such debt includes a liability designated as alimony, maintenance, or support, unless such liability is actually in the nature of alimony, maintenance, or support;

§523(a)(5). The effect of the statute, then, is that a given domestic obligation is not dischargeable if it is "actually in the nature of" alimony, maintenance, or support.

A. Post-Majority Payments

Debtor contends that his obligation to pay post-majority educational expenses and child support is dischargeable because he was not required under relevant state law to support his son past the age of majority. We do not accept this argument. For several reasons we reject debtor's premise, that an obligation is "actually in the nature of support" only if it could have been imposed under the relevant state law legal duty of support.

First, the language of §523(a)(5) does not refer to a particular state law legal duty of support. If Congress had intended dischargeability to be determined by whether an obligation could be imposed under state law, it might have addressed dischargeability in those terms. Congress chose instead to describe as not dischargeable those obligations in the "nature" of support. We believe that in using this general and abstract word, Congress did not intend bankruptcy courts to be bound by particular state law rules.

This conclusion is directly supported by the legislative history of §523(a)(5). The committee reports that accompanied the new bankruptcy code provide that "what constitutes alimony, maintenance, or support will be determined under the bankruptcy laws, not state law." We take this legislative history as another indication Congress did not intend dischargeability to be determined by reference to a state law legal duty of support.

Most circuit courts of appeal that have considered the question have likewise concluded that state law does not determine whether a domestic obligation is dischargeable in bankruptcy. In *Shaver v. Shaver,* 736 F.2d 1314 (9th Cir.1984), for example, the court considered the effect on dischargeability of a provision under Indiana law that allowed alimony only when a spouse was incapacitated or when the parties agreed in writing to an award of alimony. The court did not follow the state law but looked instead to the substance of the obligation in question to determine if it was one for support. *Id.* at 1316. The court concluded that the parties intended to provide support "and therefore *** the obligation was 'in the nature of alimony, maintenance, or support' under federal law." Having determined that the obligation was in the nature of support under federal law, the court held that it was not dischargeable in bankruptcy.

We are persuaded by the language of §523(a)(5), the legislative history of that section, and the weight of the case law that the absence of a state law duty does not determine that an obligation is dischargeable in bankruptcy. Accordingly, we affirm the district court's decision with respect to the nondischargeability of debtor's obligation to pay post-majority child support and educational expenses.

B. Alimony Arrearages

Debtor argues on appeal that his alimony arrearages are not "actually in the nature of alimony, maintenance, or support" (1) because the payments he did make adequately met his obligation to support defendant as defined under state law; and (2) because, even if federal law applies rather than state law, defendant did not *need* the arrearages as of the time debtor filed his Chapter VII petition, and thus federal law would not classify such amounts as in the nature of support.

We rejected debtor's state law contention in Part II.A. above. Thus, we turn directly to debtor's contention that the bankruptcy court should assess a divorced spouse's needs and arrive at the precise amount that the spouse would require for support. In accepting this proposition, the bankruptcy court followed *Warner v. Warner (In re Warner)*, 5 B.R. 434 (Bankr.D.Utah 1980), which held:

> even if the debt was originally imposed on the basis of the need of the spouse or children, the debt cannot be held nondischargeable unless at the time of filing there exists a present need by the spouse or children that the debt be paid.

The court in *Warner* reasoned that the requirement of present need was "necessary to enforce the general purpose of the bankruptcy laws in providing relief for the debtor." Some bankruptcy courts have followed the holding of *Warner*.

Other courts have rejected the *Warner* approach. The language of the statute itself, the legislative history and considerations of comity, lead us to the conclusion that the district court in this case was correct in rejecting the reasoning and holding of *Warner*.

The language used by Congress in §523(a)(5) requires bankruptcy courts to determine nothing more than whether the support label accurately reflects that the obligation at issue is "actually in the nature of alimony, maintenance, or support." The statutory language suggests a simple inquiry as to whether the obligation can legitimately be characterized as support, that is, whether it is in the *nature* of support. The language does not suggest a precise inquiry into financial circumstances to determine precise levels of need or support; nor does the statutory language contemplate an ongoing assessment of need as circumstances change.

The legislative history is to the same effect. It described the process of determining whether an obligation was in the nature of support as being similar to the determination of whether a payment is actually alimony or in reality a property settlement. The House Report that accompanied the Bankruptcy Code reads, in relevant part:

> This provision will, however, make nondischargeable any debts resulting from an agreement by the debtor to hold the debtor's spouse harmless on joint debts, to the extent that the agreement is in payment of alimony, maintenance, or support of the spouse, as determined under bankruptcy law considerations that are similar to considerations of whether a particular agreement to pay money to a spouse is actually alimony or a property settlement.

Considerations of comity reinforce our interpretation. Debtor's attempt to expand the dischargeability issue into an assessment of the ongoing financial circumstances of the parties to a marital dispute would of necessity embroil federal courts in domestic relations matters which should properly be reserved to the state courts.

We conclude that Congress intended that bankruptcy courts make only a simple inquiry into whether or not the obligation at issue is in the *nature* of support. This inquiry will usually take the form of deciding whether the obligation was in the nature of support as opposed to being in the nature of a property settlement. Thus, there will be no necessity for a precise investigation of the spouse's circumstances to determine the appropriate level of need or support. It will not be relevant that the circumstances of the parties may have changed, *e.g.,* the spouse's need may have been reduced at the time the Chapter VII petition is filed. Thus, limited to its proper role, the bankruptcy court will not duplicate the functions of state domestic relations courts, and its rulings will impinge on state domestic relations issues in the most limited manner possible.

Once the bankruptcy court in this case concluded that the alimony payments were "actually in the nature of alimony," its task was at an end. The obligation was thereby determined to be nondischargeable under §523(a)(5). The district court correctly rejected the bankruptcy court's subsequent excursion to determine the precise level of the wife's need for support.

For the foregoing reasons, the judgment of the district court is in all respects Affirmed.

Notes and Problems

1. Who is the "defendant" referred to in the *Harrell* case? Why did the debtor file a complaint in bankruptcy court to determine dischargeability of his domestic debts? Cf. section 523(c), section 362(b)(2).

2. D and X are divorced. The divorce decree requires D to pay X alimony. D later files a Chapter 7 petition and obtains a discharge. Neither D nor X file a complaint in bankruptcy court to determine dischargeability. After receiving his bankruptcy

discharge, D stops paying alimony. If X brings a state court action against D to enforce the divorce decree, does D have a bankruptcy discharge defense?

3.   *Harrell* was a Chapter 7 case. Could the debtor in *Harrell* have received a discharge from his domestic debts in Chapter 11? In Chapter 12? In Chapter 13?

In re Hudson

United States Bankruptcy Court, Illinois, 1981
9 B.R. 363

Richard L. Merrick, Bankruptcy Judge. [The] cause came on to be heard on the complaint of the Illinois Department of Public Aid (hereinafter "the State") to determine dischargeability of debt.

The debtor received more in public assistance payments from the State than was due to her because she failed to report all income from her employment. The debtor had an affirmative duty to report such income. 1 Ill.Rev.Stat. ch. 23, §11-18 (1979). Debtor Christine Hudson (hereinafter "Hudson") was overpaid $2,443.13 because of her failure to report this income. Judgment was entered against her by a state court for $4,886.26. Subsequently, the debtor filed a petition for relief under Chapter 13 of the Bankruptcy Code. Hudson proposed a plan that provided for 20% repayment to unsecured creditors. There were no objections to confirmation. Hudson's plan was confirmed August 5, 1980.

Conclusions of Law

The State has brought complaints against Hudson to determine dischargeability of debt under sections 523(a)(2) and 523(a)(7) of the Bankruptcy Code. Section 523(a)(2) excepts from discharge any debts for obtaining money, property, or services by false pretenses or false representation.

Provisions in Chapter 5 of the Code apply to Chapter 13 unless superseded by sections within Chapter 13. Section 1328 specifies only three types of debts that are not dischargeable upon successful completion of a Chapter 13 plan: (1) allowed claims not provided by the plan, (2) certain long-term obligations specifically provided for by the plan but which extend beyond the termination of the plan, and (3) claims for alimony and child support. A Chapter 13 discharge is subject to the exceptions in section 523 only if the debtor fails to complete the payments required by the plan. §1328(c)(2).

Nevertheless, the State seeks to have its debts determined to be nondischargeable even though the statute says that such debts are discharged upon successful completion of a Chapter 13 plan. The State contends that under Chapter 13 an unsecured creditor must be treated "at least as fairly" as he would be under a Chapter 7 liquidation. Since an unsecured creditor with a non-dischargeable debt has the possibility (no matter how remote) of collecting a larger part of its debt under Chapter 7 than under Chapter 13, the creditor is not being treated "as fairly" under Chapter 13, according to the State's theory.

The brief of the State asserts repeatedly that it would be illogical to assume that Congress had intended that fraudulent debts might be discharged by partial payment through a Chapter 13 plan. The illogic is to assume that Congress intended anything with respect *** to *** dischargeability. An abnormal number of compromises were involved in shaping a bill which could be passed by both Houses of Congress. The House and Senate Bills did not go through the customary series of subcommittee reports, committee reports, and votes at various levels of the legislative process so that it is more difficult than usual to attribute any given position to any given legislator, much less to assert that there was a consensus among the legislators on a particular matter. ***

Because composition plans under Chapter XIII of the former Bankruptcy Act usually contemplated payment of a significant portion of unsecured debt, and 100 extension plans were more common than composition plans, it may well have been the view of many of the legislators that if a debtor made his best effort and paid off all that he could, the debtor should be forgiven his past mistakes, moral and ethical as well as financial. Whether that was their reasoning or not, the legislators did not require that a Chapter 13 plan be a high payment plan in order to qualify the debtor for relief against the debts due to his creditors generally, which was considerably broader than the relief which would have been received by the debtor under present Chapter 7, or old Chapters I-VII, or XIII. ***

The Court can take judicial notice of the fact that there are many powerful interests within the country that believe that Congress went too far in many areas of the Bankruptcy Code, but particularly with respect to the breadth of discharges under Chapter 13 and the lack of a minimum percentage of payment under Chapter 13 plans. Undoubtedly Congress will be looking at those problem areas during its ensuing sessions, but until it acts all that the Courts can do is to deal with the existing legislation.

Finally, the debts to the State will be discharged only if the plan as confirmed is completed. If the plan is not completed,

> (a) in the event of dismissal, the State may proceed by regular civil process to collect on the debt;
> (b) in the event of a conversion to Chapter 7, the State may present its case of non-dischargeability and if successful, follow normal civil process; or
> (c) in the event of a hardship discharge, the situation respecting fraud debts is the same as under Chapter 7 discharges, (See §§1328(c) and 523(a)) except that the creditor does not have to obtain a determination of non-dischargeability by the Bankruptcy Court before undertaking conventional collection process.

For better or for worse, Congress provided that in a Chapter 13 plan which is completed, under §1328(a), all debts will be discharged except for the alimony and support debts described in §523(a)(5) and long term debts described in §1322(b)(5).

There is no provision in the Bankruptcy Code to contest the dischargeability of a debt under §523 during the time that a Chapter 13 plan is pending after confirmation. At the moment, the State's complaints respecting the discharge of the welfare fraud debts are premature.

The complaints will be dismissed with prejudice toward refiling during such time as the plans are pending and permanently if the plans are completed according to their terms.

Notes and Problems

1. Did Judge Merrick grant Christine Hudson a discharge?

2. Hudson's Chapter 13 plan provides for a 20% repayment to unsecured creditors. If Hudson completes the payments under the plan, will the State of Illinois' claim against Hudson for overpayment of public assistance payments be discharged? See section 1328(a).

3. What if Hudson's Chapter 13 plan provided for 60 repayment of unsecured claims and she lost her job after repaying 55l?

    A. Could Hudson qualify for a discharge under section 1328(b)?

    B. If Hudson received a section 1328(b) discharge, would the State of Illinois' claim against Hudson for overpayment of public assistance payments be discharged? See section 1328(c).

    C. Could Hudson qualify for a discharge under section 1328(a)? Cf. section 1329.[1]

4. According to Judge Merrick, "Section 1328 specifies only three types of debts that are not dischargeable upon successful completion of a Chapter 13 plan: (1) allowed claims not provided for by the plan, (2) certain long term obligations specifically provided for by the plan but which extend beyond the termination of the plan, and (3) claims for alimony and child support." In light of this statement, can a debtor/taxpayer use Chapter 13 to discharge a tax debt? See section 1322(a)(2); cf. section 523(a)(1).

---

[1] In theory, sections 1328(a) and 1328(b) are not strictly alternatives. If modification is possible, a section 1328(b) discharge is not available. See section 1328(b)(3). In practice, who will object if a debtor seeks a section 1328(b) discharge instead of exploring modification possibilities?

5. The *Hudson* case involved the dischargeability of claims that arose before the filing of the Chapter 13 petition. Reconsider the dischargeability of post-petition claims. Assume, for example, that C installed a rebuilt engine in Hudson's car after she filed for Chapter 13 relief.

    a. Can Hudson add C to the list of unsecured creditors receiving 20% under her Chapter 13 plan? Cf. sections 1305, 1322(b)(6).

    b. Is C required to obtain the permission of the Chapter 13 trustee before beginning work on Hudson's car? Cf. section 1305(c).

    c. Should Hudson obtain the permission of the Chapter 13 trustee before incurring the debt to C? Cf. section 1328(c).

    d. If Hudson gets court permission and pays C 20% of the cost of the engine, and Hudson completes the plan and receives a discharge, is C's claim for the other 80% of the cost discharged?

6. Judge Merrick's comment about Congress looking at the level of payments in Chapter 13 plans was somewhat prescient. See section 1325(b).

C. WHAT ARE THE EFFECTS OF A DISCHARGE?

1. On Efforts To Collect From The Debtor

Section 524(a) deals with the effect of a discharge on efforts to collect from the debtor. Please read section 524(a).

In general, section 524(a) protects the debtor from any further personal liability on dischargeable-type claims. Under section 524(a), a discharge not only bars an in personam judgment on such claims but also acts as a permanent injunction against judicial proceedings or even informal collection actions against the debtor with respect to such claims.

Please apply section 524(a) to the following problems.

Problems

1. **Efforts to Collect From the Debtor Personally**

    a. C obtains a $100,000 judgment against D. D files a bankruptcy petition. C receives $11,000 in the bankruptcy distribution. D receives a discharge. What is the effect of that discharge? Can C bring a legal action against D to collect the balance of its prepetition judgment?

b. D files a bankruptcy petition and receives a discharge. You represent C, one of D's prepetition creditors. Can C call D and demand payment of the balance of its prepetition claim?

2. **Efforts to Collect From Third Parties**

a. C lends D $20,000. G guarantees payment. D files for bankruptcy and obtains a discharge. Can D's discharge operate to bar C from collecting on G's guarantee?

b. D negligently injures C in an automobile accident. C sues D. While this litigation is pending, D files for bankruptcy and obtains a discharge. What is the effect of D's discharge on the liability exposure of D's insurer?

3. **Efforts to Collect From Encumbered Property of the Debtor**
According to a text co-authored by five of the leading bankruptcy lawyers in the country, "A lien on the debtor's or the estate's property, if not set aside under one of the avoiding powers," is not affected by a discharge of the underlying obligation that it secures, although any unsecured deficiency would be barred." George Treister, J. Ronald Trost, Leon Forman, Kenneth Klee & Richard Levin, FUNDAMENTALS OF BANKRUPTCY LAW 313 (2d ed. 1988).

a. What is the statutory basis, if any, for this statement?

b. What is the practical significance of this statement? Assume, for example, that F has a mortgage on D's home to secure its $50,000 loan to D. D files a Chapter 7 petition and obtains a discharge. What is the effect of the discharge on F? (See *Johnson v. Home State Bank*, below.)

Johnson v. Home State Bank
United States Supreme Court, 1991
501 U.S. 78, 111 S.Ct. 2150, 15 L.Ed.2d 66

Justice Marshall delivered the opinion of the Court.

The issue in this case is whether a debtor can include a mortgage lien in a Chapter 13 bankruptcy reorganization plan once the personal obligation secured by the mortgaged property has been discharged in a Chapter 7 proceeding. We hold that the mortgage lien in such a circumstance remains a "claim" against the debtor that can be rescheduled under Chapter 13.

I

This case arises from the efforts of respondent Home State Bank (Bank) to foreclose a mortgage on the farm property of petitioner. Petitioner gave the mortgage to secure promissory notes to the Bank totaling approximately $470,000. When petitioner defaulted on these notes, the Bank initiated foreclosure proceedings in state court. During the pendency of these proceedings, petitioner filed for a liquidation under Chapter 7 of the Bankruptcy Code. Pursuant to 11 U.S.C. §727, the Bankruptcy Court discharged petitioner from personal liability on his promissory notes to the Bank. Notwithstanding the discharge, the Bank's right to proceed against petitioner in rem survived the Chapter 7 liquidation. After the Bankruptcy Court lifted the automatic stay protecting petitioner's estate, see 11 U.S.C. §362, the Bank reinitiated the foreclosure proceedings. Ultimately, the state court entered an in rem judgment of approximately $200,000 for the Bank.

Before the foreclosure sale was scheduled to take place, petitioner filed the Chapter 13 petition at issue here. In his Chapter 13 plan, petitioner listed the Bank's mortgage in the farm property as a claim against his estate and proposed to pay the Bank four annual installments and a final "balloon payment" equal in total value to the Bank's in rem judgment. Over the Bank's objection, the Bankruptcy Court confirmed the Chapter 13 plan. The Bank appealed to the District Court, arguing that the Code does not allow a debtor to include in a Chapter 13 plan a mortgage used to secure an obligation for which personal liability has been discharged in Chapter 7 proceedings; the Bank argued in the alternative that the Bankruptcy Court had erred in finding that petitioner had proposed the plan in good faith and that the plan was feasible. The District Court accepted the first of these arguments and disposed of the case on that ground.

The Court of Appeals affirmed. Emphasizing that petitioner's personal liability on the promissory notes secured by the mortgage had been discharged in the Chapter 7 proceedings, the court reasoned that the Bank no longer had a "claim" against petitioner subject to rescheduling under Chapter 13. See id., at 565, 566. Like the District Court, the Court of Appeals disposed of the case without considering the Bank's contentions that Johnson's plan was not in good faith and was not feasible. See id., at 566.

***

II

[W]e must first say more about the nature of the mortgage interest that survives a Chapter 7 liquidation. A mortgage is an interest in real property that secures a creditor's right to repayment. But unless the debtor and creditor have provided otherwise, the creditor ordinarily is not limited to foreclosure on the mortgaged property should the debtor default on his obligation; rather, the creditor may in addition sue to establish the debtor's in personam liability for any deficiency on the debt and may enforce any judgment against the debtor's assets generally. A defaulting debtor can protect himself from personal liability by obtaining a discharge in a Chapter 7 liquidation. See 11 U.S.C. §727. However, such a discharge extinguishes only "the personal liability of the debtor." 11 U.S.C. §524(a)(1). Codifying the rule of Long v. Bullard, 117 U.S. 617, 6 S.Ct. 917, 29 L.Ed. 1004 (1886), the Code provides that a creditor's right to foreclose on the mortgage survives or passes through the bankruptcy. See 11 U.S.C. §522(c)(2).

* * *

The Court of Appeals thus erred in concluding that the discharge of petitioner's personal liability on his promissory notes constituted the complete termination of the Bank's claim against petitioner. Rather, a bankruptcy discharge extinguishes only one mode of enforcing a claim--namely, an action against the debtor in personam--while leaving intact another--namely, an action against the debtor in rem. Indeed, but for the codification of the rule of Long v. Bullard, supra, there can be little question that a "discharge" under Chapter 7 would have the effect of extinguishing the in rem component as well as the in personam component of any claim against the debtor. And because only "claims" are discharged under the Code, the very need to codify Long v. Bullard presupposes that a mortgage interest is otherwise a "claim."

* * *

The Bank resists this analysis. It contends that even if an obligation enforceable only against the debtor's property might normally be treated as a "claim" subject to inclusion in a Chapter 13 plan, such an obligation should not be deemed a claim against the debtor when it is merely the remainder of an obligation for which the debtor's personal liability has been discharged in a Chapter 7 liquidation. Serial filings under Chapter 7 and Chapter 13, respondent maintains, evade the limits that Congress intended to place on these remedies.

We disagree. Congress has expressly prohibited various forms of serial filings. See, e.g., 11 U.S.C. §109(g) (no filings within 180 days of dismissal); §727(a)(8) (no Chapter 7 filing within six years of a Chapter 7 or Chapter 11 filing); §727(a)(9) (limitation on Chapter 7 filing within six years of Chapter 12 or Chapter 13 filing). The absence of a like prohibition on serial filings of Chapter 7 and Chapter 13 petitions, combined with the evident care with which Congress fashioned these express prohibitions, convinces us that Congress did not intend categorically to foreclose the benefit of Chapter 13 reorganization to a debtor who previously has filed for Chapter 7 relief.

The Bank's contention also fails to apprehend the significance of the full range of Code provisions designed to protect Chapter 13 creditors. A bankruptcy court is authorized to confirm a plan only if the court finds, inter alia, that "the plan has been proposed in good faith," §1325(a)(3); that the plan assures unsecured creditors a recovery as adequate as "if the estate of the debtor were liquidated under chapter 7," §1325(a)(4); that secured creditors either have "accepted the plan," obtained the property securing their claims, or "retain[ed] the[ir] lien[s]" where the "the value ... of property to be distributed under the plan ... is not less than the allowed amount of such claim[s]," §1325(a)(5); and that the "the debtor will be able to make all payments under the plan and to comply with the plan," §1325(a)(6). In addition, the bankruptcy court retains its broad equitable power to "issue any order, process, or judgment that is necessary or appropriate to carry out the provisions of [the Code.]" §105(a). Any or all of these provisions may be implicated when a debtor files serially under Chapter 7 and Chapter 13. But given the availability of these provisions, and given Congress' intent that "claim" be construed broadly, we do not believe that Congress intended the bankruptcy courts to use the Code's definition of "claim" to police the Chapter 13 process for abuse.

III

The Bank renews here its claim that the Bankruptcy Court erred in finding petitioner's plan to be in good faith for purposes of §1325(a)(3) and feasible for purposes of §1325(a)(6) of the Code. Because the District Court and Court of Appeals disposed of this case on the ground that the Bank's mortgage interest was not a "claim" subject to inclusion in a Chapter 13 plan, neither court addressed the issues of good faith or feasibility. We also decline to address these issues and instead leave them for consideration on remand.

The judgment of the Court of Appeals is reversed, and the case is remanded for further proceedings consistent with this opinion.

It is so ordered.

Problems

1. Why did Johnson file a Chapter 13 petition instead of another Chapter 7 petition?

2. According to the second paragraph of the opinion, "Petitioner gave the mortgage to secure promissory notes to the Bank totaling approximately $470,000. How did Johnson meet the $100,000/$350,000 eligibility standards of section 109(e)?

3. The second paragraph of the opinion also states that "the state court entered an in rem judgment of approximately $200,000 for the Bank." What was the amount of the Bank's lien? Prior to the Supreme Court's decision in *Dewsnup v. Timm*, 112 S.Ct. 773 (1992), some bankruptcy courts would have "stripped" the Bank's lien to $200,000. Such lien stripping was based on the language of section 506(d) and section 506(a). Section 506(d) begins "To the extent that a lien secures a claim against the debtor that is not an allowed secured claim, such lien is void." Section 506(a) limits allowed secured claims to the value of the collateral. Under lien stripping, since the value of Johnson's property was only $200,000, the Bank's lien would be stripped down to $200,000.

In *Dewsnup*, a 6-2 decision, the Court held that a Chapter 7 debtor may not invoke section 506(d) to strip down an undersecured lien to the value of the collateral. In so holding, the majority relies on (i) an ambiguity in the language of section 506, (ii) the law under the Bankruptcy Act, and (iii) the absence of any indication that Congress intended to change pre-Code law. *Dewnsup* is considered *infra* at pages 903-06.

4.   **Criminal Prosecution**
D buys goods from C and issues a check to C. The check is dishonored for the reason that D's account had insufficient funds. D files a bankruptcy petition and receives a discharge. Will the bankruptcy discharge bar the state's attorney from prosecuting D for violating the state bad check laws?

2. On Agreements To Pay

Under the rules of common law contract, a promise to pay a debt discharged in bankruptcy, i.e., a reaffirmation agreement, is legally enforceable even though there is no consideration or detrimental reliance to support the promise. Section 524(c) and (d) limit the use of these reaffirmation agreements. Please review these provisions and apply them in the following questions and problems:

Questions and Problems

1.   **Reasons for reaffirmation**

Why would a debtor agree to reaffirm a debt?
   a. D files a Chapter 7 petition. Which of the following debts should she reaffirm?
      1. debt owed to family doctor;
      2. debt co-signed by her brother;
      3. debt excepted from discharge;
      4. debt secured by a security interest in her car. Cf. section 722.

   b. Should a debtor who files for Chapter 11, 12, or 13 relief ever reaffirm a debt?

2.   **Procedures for reaffirmation**

   a. Can a reaffirmation agreement be entered into before bankruptcy?

   b. Can a reaffirmation agreement be entered into after the bankruptcy discharge?

   c. Does a reaffirmation agreement have to be filed with the bankruptcy court?

   d. Does the debtor have the right to rescind a reaffirmation agreement? If so, how will he know that he has this right?

    e. What is the role of the bankruptcy judge? Does she have to pass on the fairness of the agreement? See section 524(d)(2); 524(c)(6).

    f. What is the role of the debtor's attorney? Does she have any responsibility? See section 524(c)(3). Any liability?

3. See generally Jeffrey Morris & Joseph Ulrich, *Reaffirmations Under the Consumer Bankruptcy Amendments of 1984: A Loser for All Concerned*, 43 WASH. & LEE L.REV. 111 (1986).

3. On Discriminatory Treatment

Section 525(a) prohibits "governmental units" from discriminating against a debtor in employment, in licensing, or in making similar grants "solely because" she has filed for bankruptcy, failed to pay a discharged debt, or was insolvent before receiving a discharge. Under section 525(b), a private employer is similarly prohibited from discriminating against a debtor on bankruptcy-related grounds.

Notes and Problems

1. Ohio state law provides for suspension of a driver's license for failure to satisfy an accident related judgment within 30 days. The license then remains suspended until the driver/judgment debtor provides proof of financial responsibility. C obtained a judgment against D, arising from an auto accident on January 15. D did not satisfy the judgment. On April 5, D filed a bankruptcy petition. D obtained a discharge. Does D have to meet the Ohio statutory requirement of financial responsibility in order to vacate the suspension of his driver's license?

2. Your client teaches at Biff and Buffie Montessori School. She is considering filing a bankruptcy petition. She is concerned that the school will dismiss her if she does. Advise.

3. See generally Douglas Boshkoff, *Bankruptcy-Based Discrimination*, 66 AM. BANKR.L. J. 387 (1992).

Unit 10

SATISFACTION OF UNSECURED CLAIMS IN BANKRUPTCY

UNIT CONTENTS

The Bankruptcy Code does not define the term "unsecured claim." As you recall, there is a definition of "secured claim" in section 506(a). To the extent that a claim does not come within the definition of "secured claim" in section 506, it is an unsecured or general claim.

In general, a creditor has an unsecured claim if (1) it has not obtained a lien or right of setoff against property of the estate or (2) the value of the property subject to its lien or right of setoff is less than the amount of its claim. Assume, for example, that Watts Landscape, Inc., W, files for Bankruptcy relief. W owes Dick Davenport, D, $1,000 in back wages. D does not have a lien. D's wage claim would be a unsecured claim. W also owes $30,000 to Park National Bank, P. P's debt is secured by W's chain saws that have a value of $22,000. P would have a $22,000 secured claim and $8,000 unsecured claim.

How can D and P collect their unsecured claims after W's bankruptcy filing? Sections 362 and 524 suggest that a creditor with an unsecured claim must look to the bankruptcy distribution for the satisfaction of its unsecured claim. During the bankruptcy case, the automatic stay of section 362 bars a holder of an unsecured claim from taking action against the debtor, property of the debtor, or property of the estate. If the bankruptcy case results in a discharge, section 524 bars the holder of an unsecured claim from legal actions or less formal collection actions to recover the claim from the debtor personally. Accordingly, the holder of an unsecured claim (and its attorney) must look to the bankruptcy case.

In looking to the bankruptcy case, the attorney for the holder of an unsecured claim will be looking for answers to the following questions:

1. What property is available to satisfy unsecured claims?
2. Which unsecured claims are eligible to participate in the distribution?
3. How is the property to be distributed? The answers to these questions vary from Chapter 7, to Chapter 11, to Chapter 12, to Chapter 13.

A. WHAT PROPERTY IS AVAILABLE TO SATISFY UNSECURED CLAIMS?

1. What Property Is Distributed To Holders Of Unsecured Claims In Chapter 7 Cases?

The bankruptcy trustee has a statutory duty to sell the "property of the estate," section 704(1). The net proceeds received from the liquidation of the "property of the estate" are to be distributed to the holders of unsecured or general claims. Such claimants do not, however, receive the net proceeds from the sale of all of the "property of the estate":

- Some "property of the estate" will be turned over to the debtor as exempt property, section 522.
- Some "property of the estate" will be validly transferred after the filing of the bankruptcy petition to third parties, section 549 (considered infra).
- Some "property of the estate" will be subject to liens that are valid in bankruptcy. Encumbered property or the proceeds thereof must be first used to satisfy the holders of secured claims, cf. section 725.
- Some "property of the estate" must be used to satisfy the administrative expenses of the bankruptcy proceeding.

Subject to these four exceptions, holders of unsecured or general claims in Chapter 7 cases receive the net proceeds from the bankruptcy trustee's sale of the "property of the estate."

2. What Property Is Distributed To Holders Of Unsecured Claims In Chapter 12 Cases And Chapter 13 Cases?

In Chapter 12 cases and Chapter 13 cases, the plan controls the payment to holders of unsecured claims. Only the debtor can file the plan.

Section 1222 governs the contents of a Chapter 12 plan; section 1322 governs the contents of a chapter 13 plan. The two sections are markedly similar; in both sections, paragraph (a) governs what the plan *must* provide; paragraph (b) governs what the plan *may* provide.

In Chapter 12 cases and in Chapter 13 cases, creditors do not vote on the plan. Both chapters require the bankruptcy judge to confirm (approve) the plan, and creditors may object to the confirmation. Section 1225 and section 1325 set out the standards for confirmation of a plan. Please read sections 1225 and 1325. Note the similarities. Which of the confirmation standards affect the amount to be paid to holders of unsecured claims?

In re Greer

United States Bankruptcy Court, Central District of California, 1986
60 B.R. 547

Order Confirming Chapter 13 Plan

Samuel L. Bufford, Bankruptcy Judge.

I. Facts

Debtors Phillip and Judy Greer filed this joint Chapter 13 case on February 21, 1986. They filed their Chapter 13 statement and proposed plan on the same date. Mr. Greer is a staff sergeant in the United States Marine Corps, in which he has served for eighteen years. Mrs. Greer is a secretary/office manager at Jacoby and Meyers Law Offices, which is counsel for debtors. They have two teen-age children.

As of the date of filing, the debtors owned their family residence, which had a fair market value of approximately $98,000, and which was encumbered by a first trust deed with an outstanding balance of approximately $88,000 and a second trust deed with an outstanding balance of approximately $3,800. On the date of filing the debtors owed arrearages of $6,000 on the first trust deed and $790 on the second trust deed.

The debtors own two automobiles, on which payments were current at the time of filing. Their 1977 Ford is worth $2,100, and is encumbered by a loan of $2,800, leaving $700 as an unsecured claim. Their 1983 Toyota is worth $8,600, and is fully encumbered. Three other creditors are partially secured on loans for the purchase of home furnishings. Apart from the Chapter 13 Trustee, there are no priority creditors. In addition to the secured debt, at the time of filing the debtors owed unsecured debts totalling more than $18,000 to more than thirty creditors.

The debtors' budget discloses that they receive $3,200 per month in net income. Their monthly expense budget is as follows:

Real estate payments	$1,255
Utilities	241
Food	300
Clothing	100
Laundry and cleaning	75
Auto insurance	146
Transportation	300
Total	$2,417

This budget leaves a surplus of $783, of which the debtors propose to pay $707.43 per month for 36 months to their creditors under their Chapter 13 plan. This will cover the arrearages on the secured debt, plus interest at the rate of 12 per annum. These payments, plus the trustee's fees, take up all but $5.73 per month of the payments. The debtors propose to pay unsecured creditors a total of $206.22 under the plan, which is approximately one percent of the outstanding unsecured debt.

The principal effect of the plan is to cure the arrearages on the home, to discharge one-quarter of the debt on the Ford automobile, and to discharge all of the unsecured debt. The debtors will retain their automobiles, and pay the secured debt on them.

No creditor has objected to the plan. Elsie Davis, the Chapter 13 Trustee, objects to the termination of the plan after 36 months, and argues (1) that the payments should be larger, and (2) that the plan should be extended beyond 36 months to permit a significant payment to the unsecured creditors.

II. Issues Presented

This case presents two related issues: (1) whether a three-year Chapter 13 plan can be confirmed where all of the payments thereunder go to the priority[1] and secured creditors and the trustee's fees, and the general unsecured creditors receive nothing; (2) whether there is "cause" for a Chapter 13 plan to extend more than three years, if the unsecured creditors would otherwise receive nothing thereunder.

Apart from adequate protection and relief from the automatic stay, this is apparently the most litigated issue under the Bankruptcy Code. The vast majority of reported opinions (virtually all of which have been reviewed by the Court), however, involve at least some payments to the general unsecured creditors.[2]

The Court would normally be reluctant to add to the multiplicity of voices on this issue. However, the Court finds two reasons to write yet another opinion on this subject. First, despite the multitude of opinions on this issue, there is no settled law on this subject. Second, one out of every twelve Chapter 13 cases filed in the United States is filed in this district: In 1985 there were 108,059 Chapter 13 cases filed, of which 9,067 were filed in the Central District of California.

The Court holds that such a plan is not disqualified under Chapter 13 solely on the grounds that the general unsecured creditors receive nothing, and that the plan before the Court must be confirmed. The Court further holds that the lack of any payment to the general unsecured creditors in the first three years is not alone cause to extend the plan beyond three years.

---

[1]   Under section 1322(a)(2), unsecured claims entitled to priority under section 507 must be paid in full through a Chapter 13 plan.

[2]   Similarly, the vast majority of Chapter 13 plans proposed for confirmation in this Court involve at least some payment to unsecured creditors. In fact, a substantial portion involve a 100 percent repayment to unsecured creditors.

III. Analysis

The benefit to a debtor of proposing a plan of repayment under Chapter 13, rather than opting for liquidation under Chapter 7, is that it permits the debtor to protect his assets. In a liquidation case, the debtor must surrender his nonexempt assets, as of the date of filing, for liquidation and sale by the trustee. Under Chapter 13, the debtor may retain his property by agreeing to repay his creditors from his disposable income over a period of time.

A. Pre-1984 Law

In the early days of the Bankruptcy Code there were a large number of reported cases on this subject, and several appellate level cases. Cases went both ways at the Bankruptcy Court level. However, the circuit courts took a skeptical view of a requirement of substantial repayment to general unsecured creditors. A number of courts, including the Ninth Circuit, came to the view that, if a minimum payment to unsecured creditors was to be required, it should be mandated by Congress, and not imposed by the courts.

In 1984 Congress adopted the Bankruptcy Amendments and Federal Judgeship Act ("BAFJA"), which, in this Court's opinion, resolved the issues raised in this case.

Among the amendments to the Bankruptcy Code enacted in 1984 in BAFJA was a new subsection of section 1325. The confirmation mandate of section 1325(a) was qualified by a new subsection (b), which provides in substance that, upon objection of the trustee or an unsecured creditor, all of the debtor's projected disposable income for three years must be applied to the plan (alternatively, in the case of an objecting creditor, such creditor may be paid in full). "Disposable income" is defined in section 1325(b)(2) to include all income "not reasonably necessary to be expended *** for the maintenance or support of the debtor or a dependent of the debtor ***"

This statutory provision solves both the problem of excess disposable income and the problem of unreasonably short plans. Under this provision an unsecured creditor cannot be compelled to accept zero payment unless the plan extends at least 36 months, and all of the disposable income is allocated to the plan.

In this case the debtors' budget shows $783 in unallocated income, of which $707.43 is to be paid to the Chapter 13 Trustee for creditors under the plan, which leaves a cushion of approximately $75 per month for contingencies.

Does section 1325(b)(1)(B) authorize a contingency reserve? If a contingency reserve is "reasonably necessary *** for the maintenance or support of the debtor or a dependent of the debtor ***", it is excepted from the section 1325(b)(2) definition of disposable income. The Court considers such a reserve to be reasonably necessary. As the court stated in *In re Otero*, 48 B.R. 704, 708 (Bankr.E.D.Va.1985):

[A] difference of $117.00 a month is not a significant or substantial amount to be extracted from the debtors. It was not intended to take the last son. A cushion of money is necessary in Chapter 13 budgeting to guard against life's unexpectancies. It is not in the public interest to squeeze the last dollar from Chapter 13 debtors to fund a Chapter 13 plan.

Indeed, such a cushion may be required for compliance with section 1325(a)(6), which requires confirmation of a plan if, inter alia, "the debtor will be able to make all payments under the plan *** "

This Court's Chapter 13 relief from stay calendar, which averages more than 100 such motions per week in Los Angeles, indicates that debtors in general have been cutting their budgets too thinly to be able to meet their post-petition obligations, including plan payments. While improvident spending doubtless accounts for a certain portion of post-petition defaults, it appears that most of the relief from stay litigation results from debtors' simple inability to live within their proposed budgets.

The contingency reserve in this case is particularly appropriate, in the view of the Court, because the budget is quite austere. No funds are budgeted for medical or dental expenses, for insurance (except for the automobiles), for recreation or for newspapers and periodicals. The food and clothing budgets are both tight for a family of four adults. While $75 per month for laundry and cleaning may be unusual. Mr. Greer's uniforms and the clothing required for Mrs. Greer's professional employment must be dry cleaned regularly. In fact, the only budgetary item that may be unreasonably generous is an allocation of $150 for heating, which is required in Southern California only for two or three months of the year. In view of the overall leanness of the budget, this item should not hinder confirmation of the plan. Thus the best efforts requirement of section 1325(b) is met by the plan in this case.

However, the Court does not consider it practical to pay $5.73 per month to unsecured creditors. Even if the Chapter 13 Trustee makes a single final distribution to unsecured creditors, only three or four unsecured creditors would qualify for the minimum payment of $15.00 provided by Bankruptcy Rule 3010(b). For this reason, the Court orders that the plan be amended by striking the $206.22 to be distributed to unsecured creditors, and orders that the plan payments be reduced accordingly.

C. Minimum Payment to Unsecured Creditors

The minimum payment to general unsecured creditors under a Chapter 13 plan is governed by section 1325(a)(4). Congress could have required that a Chapter 13 plan provide that unsecured creditors to be paid in full. It could also have provided that unsecured creditors be paid 70, or 30, or some other minimum amount of their claim. However, Congress decided against this approach.

Instead of fixing a minimum percentage payment to unsecured creditors, Congress provided in section 1325(a)(4) that the minimum payment to unsecured creditors should be determined by what they would get under a Chapter 7 liquidation. A Chapter 13 plan may be confirmed if:

> the value, as of the effective date of the plan, of property to be distributed under the plan on account of each unsecured claim is not less than the amount that would be paid on such claim if the estate of the debtor were liquidated under Chapter 7 ***

Thus, if a Chapter 7 case would provide payment to unsecured creditors of 100 of their claims, a Chapter 13 plan must provide 100 also. Similarly, if a Chapter 7 plan would provide 50, the Chapter 13 plan must provide 50. On the other hand, if the unsecured creditors would receive nothing under a Chapter 7 case (which is often true for Chapter 13 cases filed in this Court), section 1325 does not require that they receive more under a Chapter 13 plan.

The Chapter 13 Trustee's argument, that some payment to unsecured creditors should be required, should be addressed to Congress, not to the Court.

Part V of the proposed plan in this case provides a comparison with what the unsecured creditors would receive under Chapter 7. This comparison shows that, after application of the exemptions available to a Chapter 7 debtor,[1] the unsecured creditors would receive nothing in a Chapter 7 case. Although the unsecured creditors are to receive nothing under this Chapter 13 plan, this is not less than the amount that they would receive in a Chapter 7 case.

D. Good Faith

BAFJA relieved the section 1325(a)(3) good faith provision of the "best efforts" excess baggage of certain pre-BAFJA cases.

> Nominal or zero payment to general unsecured creditors may be evidence of bad faith. However, other evidence of bad faith is required to justify the denial of confirmation of a proposed Chapter 13 plan. In this case neither the Chapter 13 Trustee nor any creditor has brought forth any other evidence of bad faith. In consequence, the Court finds that the plan has been proposed in good faith.

E. Cause

A distinction of perhaps more substantial importance between this case and *Goeb* is that *Goeb* involved a five-year plan, while the plan before the Court is a three-year plan. The Chapter 13 Trustee urges that the plan be extended to four or five years to provide a modest payment to unsecured creditors.

---

[1]   The exemptions of Bankruptcy Code §522 normally play no role in a Chapter 13 case, because creditors are paid from the income of the debtor over a period of time, rather than from assets as of the date of filing.

The limits on the length of a Chapter 13 plan are provided by section 1322(c):

Under Chapter XIII of the Bankruptcy Act, plans frequently extended as long as seven to ten years. Congress was concerned that this amounted to involuntary servitude. In consequence, in the Bankruptcy Code Congress limited the duration of a plan to three years, except upon a finding of "cause." "Cause" under section 1322(c) is not defined in the Bankruptcy Code: Congress left it to the courts to determine its dimensions in the light of experience and in the context of particular cases.

Case law has not developed a comprehensive definition of "cause" under section 1322(c), and perhaps none should be expected. Three typical examples of "cause" to extend a plan more than three years have emerged.

First, the payment of 100 of a debtor's unsecured debts provides cause for a plan longer than three years for two reasons: (1) it provides a better credit rating to the debtor; (2) under section 727(a)(9), it does not disqualify the debtor from a Chapter 7 discharge within the ensuing six years.

Second, the payment of 70 of the debtor's unsecured debts also prevents disqualification, under section 727(a)(9), from a Chapter 7 discharge within six years, provided that the plan is proposed in good faith and is the debtor's best effort. In consequence, a 70 payment to unsecured creditors is generally recognized as cause for a Chapter 13 plan to extend beyond three years.

A third category of "cause" may arise after confirmation, if a debtor is unable to make plan payments for a period of time. The debtor may then request a suspension of plan payments and an extension of the plan beyond 36 months to permit full payment of the plan.

A more substantial payment to unsecured creditors, on the other hand, does not qualify as "cause" for a Chapter 13 plan to extend more than three years. Every three-year plan providing less than full repayment to unsecured creditors can be extended to provide more substantial payment to them. If such payment were to qualify as "cause," the Chapter 13 Trustee could routinely object to all such plans, and the three-year Chapter 13 plan would become the exception, rather than the rule. This is surely not a legitimate interpretation of section 1322(c), which contemplates that the three-year plan will be the rule.

This interpretation of section 1322(c) is bolstered by BAFJA's addition of the new section 1325(b) to the Bankruptcy Code. If the proposed plan is less than 36 months, it must be extended to 36 months upon objection of a creditor or the Chapter 13 Trustee. However, in limiting section 1325(b) to 36 months, Congress chose not to require a plan to be extended further to solve low payment problems. If the Chapter 13 Trustee or a creditor contends that a debtor is not proposing sufficient payment to unsecured creditors, such objector should examine carefully the income and expense projections of a debtor to assure that the debtor meets the best efforts requirement of section 1325(b).

Thus low or zero payment to general unsecured creditors is not cause to extend a plan beyond 36 months, and in this case there is no cause for the plan to last more than three years.

IV. Conclusion

The Court concludes that the Chapter 13 plan in this case is proposed in good faith, that it satisfies the "best efforts" requirement, and that there is no cause for it to extend more than 36 months.

The Court does not suggest that Chapter 13 plans that provide zero payment to general unsecured creditors should become the rule, or even that they should be frequent. In the vast majority of cases, the best efforts requirements of section 1325(b) will provide at least some payments to unsecured creditors. In most of the remaining cases the debtor will not be able to repay secured debt arrearages (because the Court requires debtors to repay arrearages on secured debt over 36 months), and confirmation must be denied under section 1325(a)(6). Only the most marginal Chapter 13 case will involve a 36-month plan that provides zero payment to general unsecured creditors.

For the foregoing reasons, the plan is confirmed.

Notes and Problems

1. Section 1225(b) and section 1325(b) require that all "projected disposable income to be received in the three year period" be used to make payments under the plan. Section 1225(b)(2) and section 1325(b)(2) define "disposable income." Note the phrase "reasonably necessary." How should a bankruptcy court determine what living expenses are "reasonably necessary?" What farming expenses are "reasonably necessary?" What business expenses are "reasonably necessary?" How did Judge Bufford deal with this question in *Greer*? See generally Karen Gross, *Preserving a Fresh Start for the Individual: The Case for Narrow Construction of the Consumer Credit Amendments*, 135 U.Pa.L.Rev. 60, 114 (1986).

2. Would Judge Bufford have confirmed the plan in *Greer* if the Greers' debts consisted primarily of debts that would not be discharged in a Chapter 7 case?

3. According to the *Greer* opinion, one out of every twelve Chapter 13 cases filed in the United States is filed in the Central District of California. Does this confirm what you have always believed about Californians?

3. What Property Is Distributed To Holders Of Unsecured Claims In Chapter 11 Cases?

In Chapter 11 cases, like Chapter 12 and 13 cases, the plan controls the payment to holders of unsecured claims. Chapter 11's treatment of holders of unsecured claims is significantly different from Chapter 12 or 13's in that

+ Chapter 11 does *not* require that all of the debtor's "disposable income" be used to make payments under the plan.
+ In Chapter 11, the holders of unsecured claims can file a plan, section 1121(c);
+ In Chapter 11, holders of unsecured claims vote on the proposed plan. If the requisite majorities fail to vote for (accept) a plan, the standards for court approval (confirmation) are more onerous, cf. section 1129(a) and 1129(b).

The formulation, acceptance, and confirmation of Chapter 11 plans are considered later.

B. WHICH HOLDERS OF UNSECURED CLAIMS PARTICIPATE IN THE BANKRUPTCY DISTRIBUTION?

An unsecured claim must go through the allowance process in order to participate in the bankruptcy distribution. Section 502 governs allowance.

The first step in the allowance process is the filing of a proof of claim. In Chapter 11 cases, certain claims listed on the debtor's schedules are deemed filed, section 1111(a). The Bankruptcy Rules and Official Forms prescribe the time for and contents of the filing.

Once a claim is filed or deemed filed it is automatically deemed allowed unless a "party in interest" objects. Grounds for objection to the allowance of a claim are set out in section 502(b), (d), and (e).

The most frequently invoked ground for disallowance of a claim is section 502(b)(1): "The claim is unenforceable *** under any agreement or applicable law for a reason other than because such claim is contingent or unmatured." In other words, a defense that the debtor would have had to the enforceability of the claim outside of bankruptcy is a defense to the allowance of the claim in bankruptcy. Statute of limitations, statute of frauds, and failure of consideration are examples of such defenses.

Read section 502(b)(1) together with section 502(c). Notice: the fact that a claim is speculative or contingent or that its amount is difficult to ascertain is not a basis for disallowance. In these circumstances, the court can either estimate the amount of the claim or delay distribution and closing of the bankruptcy case until the amount of the claim has been determined.

Notes and Problems

1. **Filing Proofs of Claim**

    a. Is there any reason for the holder of an unsecured claim to forego filing a proof of claim? Can a creditor escape the effect of a discharge by not filing a proof of claim?

    b. Section 501(c) authorizes a debtor to file a proof of claim for a creditor who fails to file. What are the reasons, if any, for a debtor using section 501(c) and filing a proof of claim for his creditors?

2. **Objections to Allowance**
    Only a "party in interest" can object to the allowance of a claim. Who is a "party in interest" for purposes of section 502? Who would want to object to the allowance of a claim?

3. **"Unenforceable against the debtor *** under and *** applicable law"**
    D orally agrees to buy goods from C for $700. D breaches. D then files a bankruptcy petition. Is C's claim for damages for breach of contract allowable?

4. **"Unmatured interest"**
    D borrows $20,000 from C. The loan agreement provides for monthly interest payments of $250. D files a bankruptcy petition. Will C have an allowable claim for interest for the months after the filing of the bankruptcy petition and before the distribution in bankruptcy? See section 502(b)(2).

    Interest disallowed under section 502(b)(2) includes not only postpetition interest that is not yet due and payable but also any "original issue discount." Consider the following example of original issue discount: In 1993, D Corp. issues $10,000 face amount debentures, due in 1998, with an interest rate of 8%. The debentures are issued at $7,000 for each $10,000 face amount. Why is D Corp. issuing the debentures for $7,000 each, instead of $10,000? If D Corp. files a bankruptcy petition in 1994, does the holder of a $10,000 debenture have a $10,000 claim? See generally Marc Kirschner, Dan Kusnetz, Laurence Solarsh, & Craig Gatarz, *Prepackaged Bankruptcy Plans: The Deleveraging Tool of the '90's in the Wake of OID and Tax Concerns*, 21 SETON HALL L. REV. 643, 648-51 (1991).

5. **Unliquidated and disputed claims**
    C brings a tort action against D, asserting that she sustained property damages of $500,000 as a result of D's negligence. While this state court tort action is pending, D files a bankruptcy petition which stays the litigation. C files a proof of claim for $500,000. D files an objection to the proof of claim disputing negligence. Section 502(b) empowers the bankruptcy court to decide the merits of the dispute. But cf. 28

U.S.C.A. section 1411. Alternatively, section 502(c) authorizes the bankruptcy court to estimate C's claim. Why would a court use section 502(c)? How does section 502(c) estimation work? Consider the following dicta from the *Baldwin-United* case and the motion from the *Columbia Gas* case.

In re Baldwin-United Corp.

United States Bankruptcy Court, Southern District of Ohio, 1985.
55 B.R. 885.

Randall J. Newsome, Bankruptcy Judge

III. Estimation of the Brokers' Claims

While we have disallowed the Brokers' claims in their entirety pursuant to §§502(e)(1)(A), 502(b)(2), 502(e)(1)(B), 503 and 507, in the interest of setting forth as complete a record as possible we will address the issues raised by the estimation hearings on these claims. For the reasons set out below, were the claims allowable we would estimate their value, pursuant to §502(c), at zero.

Before launching into a discussion of the issues involving the merits of the Brokers' claims, we must first address the Brokers' objections to the estimation process. The Brokers have strenuously and consistently argued that a fair estimation of their claims for contribution and indemnity is impossible, because this Court cannot divine how a judge or jury will decide the SPDA holders' claims against them, and thus cannot possibly determine what debtors' liability to the Brokers might eventually be when the MDL litigation is concluded some years from now. They insist that if this Court estimates their claims at zero or at a nominal amount, "due process will be violated because the risk of erroneous deprivation of claimants' property is far too high."

A bit of history is necessary to establish why these arguments are misguided. Under the Bankruptcy Act of 1898 a claim was required to be both "provable" under §63 and "allowable" under §57 in order to qualify for participation in any distribution from the bankruptcy estate. While certain kinds of contingent and unliquidated claims were provable under §63, they were allowable only if the amount of the claim could be estimated by the Court under §57(d). If the Court determined that a claim was "not capable of liquidation or of reasonable estimation or that such liquidation or estimation would unduly delay administration of the estate," then the claim was disallowed. Although the creditor was precluded from sharing in any distribution from the estate, his claim survived the discharge. Since only provable and allowable debts were subject to discharge, the fresh start afforded to the debtor by the discharge was sometimes more illusory than real. This was particularly true where both liability and the amount of potential recovery on the claim were unknown, since such a claim was often deemed "so incapable of proof as to prohibit allowance." Because disallowed claims were not subject to discharge, a creditor holding such a claim might recover a greater portion of his claim from the debtor than creditors with allowed claims who were limited to a share of the distribution from the debtor's bankruptcy estate.

Disallowance, however, often worked to the severe detriment of a creditor, particularly in corporate bankruptcies. Indeed, disallowance sometimes had the effect of a complete denial of recovery on a claim. Such was the case in *In re Cartridge Television, Inc.*, 535 F.2d 1388 (2d Cir.1976). There, the bankruptcy court determined that the liquidation of claims for securities fraud filed by certain stockholders would unduly delay the administration of the estate under §57(d), and accordingly disallowed the claims. In so doing, the court effectively denied all right of recovery on the claims since the stockholders would have nothing but an assetless shell to look to after the liquidation of the corporation had been accomplished. Nonetheless, the Court of Appeals for the Second Circuit upheld this result.

The inequities to both debtors and creditors inherent in the Act's restrictive approach to claims were swept away with the passage of the Bankruptcy Code of 1978. The concepts of provability and allowability were eliminated in favor of an all-encompassing definition of "claim," which includes any right to payment regardless of how contingent or unmatured it might be. §101(4). As noted in its legislative history, this definition is a "significant departure" from earlier law in that "all legal obligations of the debtor, no matter how remote or contingent, will be able to be dealt with in the bankruptcy case. It permits the broadest possible relief in the bankruptcy court."

To implement this broadened concept of claims and to insure that all claims, however remote, would be subject to discharge in the bankruptcy case, Congress revised the estimation procedures of §57(d) as follows:

> There *shall be estimated* for purpose of allowance under this section—
> (1) any contingent or unliquidated claim, the fixing or liquidation of which as the case may be, would unduly delay the administration of the case;

§502(c)(1) (emphasis added).

By mandating the estimation of *all* contingent claims which cannot be liquidated without undue delay, Congress ameliorated the harsh result of cases such as *Cartridge Television*, and at the same time increased the measure of relief flowing from the debtor's discharge. The combined effect of §101(4) and §502(c) is to bring all claims of whatever nature into the bankruptcy estate, and to give all claimants the same opportunity to share in any distribution from the estate. No longer will some creditors enjoy a windfall or effectively be denied any recovery based upon the provability or allowability of their claims and the financial status of the debtor after bankruptcy. Equally important, Congress has insured that the debtor will receive a complete discharge of his debts and a real fresh start, without the threat of lingering claims "riding through" the bankruptcy.

As an additional measure of protection to creditors, Congress has provided in §502(j), as supplemented by Bankruptcy Rule 3008, that creditors may seek to have any allowed or disallowed claim reconsidered for cause, so long as the case has not been closed. When read together with §502(c), it is apparent that the estimation of a claim conclusively sets the outer limits of a claimant's right to recover either from the debtor or the estate, and that estimated claims are covered by the debtor's discharge, subject only to a §502(j) motion for reconsideration at a later time. The Brokers do not refute Debtors' contention that the liquidation of their claims in MDL 581 would unduly delay the administration of these cases. Indeed, they concede that a final determination of the SPDA holders' claims against them is at least three years away. That estimate may be conservative. Discovery has not yet commenced, and class certification proceedings have not yet begun. Whatever judgment is rendered in the MDL litigation will almost certainly be subject to appeals. Furthermore, it is entirely conceivable that Brokers' third party action will not be tried until after Brokers' liability to the SPDA holders is established. That trial will understandably be a lengthy one, and may very well involve additional appeals. All in all, a time frame of four to five years to liquidate the Brokers' claims against the Debtors might be more realistic.

Notwithstanding this unquestioned delay, and notwithstanding the mandatory language of §502(c), the Brokers insist that this Court is incapable of fairly estimating their claims; that the estimation procedures employed by this Court are unfair; and that their Fifth Amendment due process rights are being infringed. We disagree with each of these contentions.

Initially, it must be emphasized that estimation does not require that a bankruptcy judge be clairvoyant. The court need only arrive at a reasonable estimate of the probable value of the claim: "[i]n so doing, the Court is bound by the legal rules which may govern the ultimate value of the claim."

While the Court concedes that the estimation of the Brokers' claims against the Debtors is not a simple task, we cannot agree that our statutory obligation is impossible to perform.

Section 502(c) makes no mention of the procedure to be followed in estimating claims. The few cases interpreting this provision are in agreement that the bankruptcy court should use "whatever method is best suited to the particular contingencies at issue." *Bittner v. Borne Chemical Co., Inc.*, 691 F.2d 134, 135 (3rd Cir.1982). Because a formal trial on the merits would eviscerate the purpose underlying §502(c), this Court suggested at a September 30, 1985 pretrial conference with the parties that procedures comparable to those used in summary jury trials might govern in the estimation hearing. The parties were given until October 10, 1985 to present alternative suggestions. None was proposed. On October 16, 1985 the Court issued an order establishing procedures for the estimation hearing. While generally consistent with the concept of a summary jury trial, the procedures called for no jury, and allowed live testimony by one witness per party. The order also set a discovery cutoff date, and allotted two days for the hearing.

    * * *

              ⊐⊐⊐⊐⊐⊐

IN THE UNITED STATES BANKRUPTCY COURT
FOR THE DISTRICT OF DELAWARE

In re   :
                                       :   Chapter 11
THE COLUMBIA GAS SYSTEM, INC., and   :   Case No. 91-804
COLUMBIA GAS TRANSMISSION   :
CORPORATION,   :

REVISED MOTION FOR AN ORDER TO ESTABLISH
PROCEDURES TO ESTIMATE CONTINGENT
AND UNLIQUIDATED CLAIMS

       Columbia Gas Transmission Corporation ("TCO"), the debtor and debtor-in-possession, files this Revised Motion for an Order pursuant to Section 502(c) of the Bankruptcy Code to Establish Procedures to Estimate Contingent and Un-liquidated Claims (the "Motion") and respectfully represents:

       1. on July 31, 1991 ("Filing Date"), TCO and its parent, The Columbia Gas System, Inc. ("CG"), filed volun-tary petitions for reorganization under Chapter 11 of Title 11 of the United States Code (the "Bankruptcy Code") with the United States Bankruptcy Court for the District of Delaware. Postpetition, TCO and CG have each continued in the management of their respective businesses and possession of their respective properties as debtors in possession pursuant to Sections 1107 and 1108 of the Bankruptcy Code.

       2. On August 22, 1991, this Court entered an order authorizing TCO to reject pursuant to Section 365 of the Bankruptcy Code, over 4,100 long-term gas purchase and sale contracts between TCO and various natural gas producers. By subsequent orders dated January 6 and 8, 1992, this Court authorized the rejection of additional such contracts.

       3. The Court established Bar Date for the filing of most claims against TCO and CG was March 18, 1992.

       4. Approximately 4,940 timely, non-duplicate claims were filed against TCO by approximately 3,138

different claimants in an aggregate amount of approximately $15.5 billion. Since the Bar Date, TCO has been engaged in analyzing the thousands of proofs of claim submitted.

5. Of that total number of claims, approximately 1,650 were filed by natural gas producers asserting claims purportedly arising from TCO's rejection of long-term gas purchase and sale contracts ("Producer Rejection Claims"). ~ (In many instances, the claims filed also include other types of claims against TCO.) As filed, the Rejection Claims total almost $13.3 billion. However, many of the Producer Rejection Claims set forth amounts that TCO believes are greatly inflated on any reasonable theory of quantification. In addition, many of the claims are so lacking in detail that it is not possible to determine the basis for the quantification of the claim. In all events, as a group, the individual claims were filed based upon radically different theories or measures of claims and upon inconsistent or conflicting assumptions as to common facts or applicable legal principles.

6. TCO has common defenses as to all of the Producer Rejection Claims.

7. TCO has as of this date objected to all Producer Rejection Claims pursuant to Section 502(a) of the Bankruptcy Code. Therefore, TCO submits, the Producer Rejection Claims are contingent or unliquidated within the meaning of Section 502(c) of the Bankruptcy Code.

8. Other claims filed by natural gas producers consist, by dollar amount, primarily of claims for asserted prepetition deficiencies in take-or-pay payments ("Take or Pay Claims") or for the price paid for gas delivered prepetition under particular contracts ("Price Deficiency Claims"). Based upon the information currently available, TCO requests that these estimation procedures apply also to the Take or Pay Claims and Price Deficiency Claims, subject to TCO's right to remove those claims from the process in light of further information about those claims. (Such information on producer contract claims would be collected promptly through an interrogatory propounded to each producer claimant requiring the identification of the type of each gas contract claim being asserted and the dollar amount attributed to each such type of claim.)

9. There are various other types of producer contract claims as well. However, due to the inadequacy of information provided in many of the producers' proofs of claim, TCO is unable to categorize or quantify many of those other producer claims.

10. Therefore, TCO has sought by separate motion of this date authorization pursuant to Bankruptcy Rule 2004 to

obtain additional information from producer claimants as to
claims other than Producer Rejection Claims. (If those
claims become the subject of separate proceedings, TCO will
request that to the extent such other proceedings involve
issues also being addressed as generic issues in these
estimation proceedings, such other proceedings be scheduled
so as to avoid determination of such issues prior to the
determination in the estimation process.) Based upon that
information, TCO will determine whether to object to any or
all of those other claims and, in consultation with the Official Committee of Unsecured Creditors of TCO ("Official
Creditors Committee"), whether other types of claims (beyond
Producer Rejection, Take or Pay and Price Deficiency Claims)
should also be subjected to estimation.

      11. The liquidation of the Producer Rejection
Claims, the Take-or-Pay Claims and the Price Deficiency
Claims through individual or piecemeal liquidation or adjudication clearly would delay unduly the administration of
this case and would impose extraordinary burdens on the resources of this Court and all parties involved.

      12. Section 502(c)(1) of the Bankruptcy Code pro-
vides that "there shall be estimated for purposes of allowance under this section any contingent or unliquidated
claim, the fixing of which, as the case may be, would unduly
delay the administration of the case."

      13. TCO originally moved for an order establishing
estimation procedures on March 27, 1992. That motion was
adjourned to permit communication and negotiation between
TCO and all interested parties concerning the appropriate
and feasible methods for quantifying the Producer Rejection
Claims on a consistent and equitable basis. Since that time,
TCO has been engaged in a continuous dialogue with the
Official Creditors Committee and various unofficial groups
of producer claimants. Those representatives of creditors
have made extensive contributions to the procedures proposed
herein.

      14. By this renewed Motion, TCO requests that the
Court adopt these procedures, which are set forth in Exhibit
A attached hereto, so as to permit the estimation of all
claims based on TCO's rejection of natural gas purchase and
sale contracts and on Take-or-Pay or Price Deficiency
Claims. TCO reserves the right to move to add other categories of producer claims to the process or hereafter to elect
to withdraw Take or Pay or Price Deficiency Claims from the
process.

      15. The Debtor submits that the estimation proce-
dures proposed herein, as detailed in Exhibit A attached
hereto, will achieve the allowance of claims in a manner

which is fair to all claimants with reasonable accuracy and in a reasonable period of time.

16. The Producer Rejection Claims and the Take-or-Pay and Price Deficiency Claims (in the aggregate "Claims") raise various legal and factual issues, many of which are common to all, most or to a significant portion of the individual claims with each category of claims. The procedures outlined in this Motion permit the selection of appropriate procedures for the measurement of Claims and the identification of common factual and legal issues which can be applied to all Claims in fixing their value. Once the common methodologies for measuring damages are determined, and common factual and legal issues identified, analyzed and decided, TCO believes that individual claims may be quickly and efficiently estimated through computations based upon the adopted measure of this type of claim, the application of the various legal and factual criteria and, if necessary, the contract-specific data for each particular claim.

17. The procedures proposed herein are premised upon the appointment by the Bankruptcy Court of a Claims Analyst (the "Analyst") who will be responsible for making proposed determinations regarding the estimation and allowance of all claims included in the process. The Analyst must be mutually acceptable to TCO and the Official Creditors Committee (with input from the unofficial producer committees). TCO contemplates that the Analyst would be a lawyer of stature, with significant commercial experience, such as a senior partner in a law firm, preferably someone located outside of the principal natural gas producing areas. The Analyst will be assisted by staff lawyers and administrative support of his or her choosing.

18. Prior to the hearing on this Motion, TCO and the Official Creditors Committee (with input from the unofficial producer committees) will exchange lists of persons to be appointed Analyst and attempt to agree upon a person to serve as Analyst to be submitted to Court for approval or, if agreement on one person is not reached, a slate of two or more agreed upon proposed candidates for submission to the Court.

19. In advance of the hearing on this Motion, TCO and the Official Creditors Committee will jointly prepare for submission to the Analyst for resolution a proposed outline of generic issues that are expected to arise in the Analyst's determination of the appropriate measure for the quantification of Producer Rejection Claims and a list of the common factual and legal issues that likely would be presented thereunder.

20. The Analyst upon appointment shall first undertake to determine the appropriate manner in which Producer Rejection Claims and other producer claims subject to this process should be estimated, so as to provide consistency and comparability in the quantification of all claims of a particular type. Thereafter, the Analyst shall determine generic issues necessary to the quantification of the Claims.

21. The Analyst will be expected to retain two technical firms with expertise relevant to the evaluation of natural gas deliver abilities and reserves, one firm with Southwest/Midcontinent experience and one firm with Appalachian experience. The Analyst will also be permitted to retain particular fact experts and to delegate to those experts discrete issue determination assignments.

22. The Analyst's recommended determinations as to the appropriate measure of damages and on all generic issues shall be submitted to the Bankruptcy Court for approval when the phases of the process in which those issues are addressed have been completed. TCO and any Parties in Interest may support or oppose these generic recommended determinations before the Court. Generic determinations as to the appropriate measure for the quantification of Claims and as to any generally applicable facts or legal rules will, after approval by this Court, be established as to all parties for purposes of the subsequent proceedings, subject to applicable rights of appeal.

23. After the Analyst has specified the bases upon which the Claims are to be quantified by all claimants and decided the applicable generic issues, each claimant will be required to submit a standardized claim calculation form showing the calculation of its claim in a manner consistent with the Analyst's recommended determinations. This recalculation of claim may be filed under protest pending the ruling of the Bankruptcy Court on the Analyst's recommended determinations and any appeals there from.

24. TCO and other Parties in Interest shall have the right to object to any recalculated claim as contrary to the Analyst's recommended determinations or instructions or as otherwise defective. Claimants may then file responses to objections. In addition, TCO and other Parties in Interest may designate for subsequent resolution specific asserted factors relevant to a particular claim that any party contends require adjustment or modification of the calculation of claims derived pursuant to the generic determinations. Appropriate grounds for designation must be individual to the particular claimant or contract -- such as specific contract defenses, issues of contract

interpretation or facts pertinent to a particular claim --
and not matters already decided as part of the generic
determinations.

    25. The Analyst will consider objections that
claimants failed to recalculate claims in accordance with
the resolution of generic issues and the Analyst's instructions or that contain mathematical errors. If a particular
objection cannot fairly be resolved on the basis of the
written submissions, the Analyst may direct further submissions or a hearing or may defer resolution of the objection
until a later phase of these procedures.

    26. TCO and individual claimants may negotiate
settlements of claims at any time during the estimation
process. However, other Parties in Interest will have an
opportunity to object to any proposed settlements and the
Analyst must approve the settlements to assure fairness and
consistent treatment.

    27. TCO or any other Party in Interest may apply to
the Bankruptcy Court for an order that the recalculated
claims determined pursuant to the Analyst's recommended determinations and instructions (including any corrections
thereto resulting from objections) be temporarily allowed
pursuant to Bankruptcy Rule 3018(a) for the purpose of accepting or rejecting a plan.

    28. Additional proceedings will be held by the
Analyst as necessary to enable the determination of all individual issues preserved during the prior steps.

    29. The Analyst's recommended determinations as to
each claim shall be submitted to the Bankruptcy Court for
approval as the estimation of that claim. Upon approval, the
claim shall be deemed allowed in the amount determined pursuant to Section 502(c) of the Bankruptcy Code.

    30. TCO submits herewith a proposed Order, adopting
a detailed schedule of procedures set forth in Exhibit A, in
order to accomplish the fair and expeditious estimation of
the Claims. The time frames in Exhibit A are intended by TCO
as guidelines in order to achieve the just and speedy estimation of claims. Thereby, TCO contemplates the completion
of the estimation process within a period of about nine
months and the establishment of a basis for the temporary
allowance of claims for voting purposes within four months.

    WHEREFORE, TCO prays that after notice and hear-
ing, as set forth in the accompanying Order, this Court
estimate the aforementioned Claims for purposes of allowance
and for such other and further relief as is just.

Dated: July 1, 1992

Respectfully submitted,

YOUNG, CONAWAY, STARGATT &
TAYLOR

James L. Patton, Jr.

James L. Patton, Jr.

Rodney Square North, 11th Floor,
    P.O. Box 391,
    Willington, Delaware 19899
    (302) 571-6684

CRAVATH, SWAINE & MOORE
    Worldwide Plaza
    825 Elghth Avenue,
    New York, N.Y. 10019
    (212) 474-1000

STROOCK & STROOCK & LAVAN
    Seven Hanovor Square,
    New York, N.Y. 10004-2594
    212-805-5400

Co-Counsel for Debtor and
Debtor-in-Possession

□□□□□□

Notes and Problems

1. Are the procedure for estimation under section 502(c) different from the procedures for allowance of a claim under section 502(b)? How does the Analyst in Columbia Gas differ from a special master? *Cf.* Federal Rule of Civil Procedure 53. Bankruptcy Rule 9031 prohibits the appointment of masters in cases and proceedings under the Bankruptcy Code.

2. Are the consequences of estimation under section 502(c) different from the consequences of allowance under section 502(b). Would the rights of the Brokers in *Baldwin-United* be greater if Judge Newsome estimated their claims at zero under section 502(c) instead of disallowing their claims under section 502(b)? In *Columbia Gas*, would the consequences of the bankruptcy court's estimating the producers' claims at 100 differ from the consequences of the court allowing the producers' claims at 100? See generally Steven McCardell, *Estimation of Contingent and Unliquidated Claims--Binding Effects of Bankruptcy Court Estimation of Claims*, 67th

Annual Meeting of the National Conference of Bankruptcy Judges Educational Materials 4-27 (1993).

3. If the bankruptcy court concludes that C has a 40% chance of prevailing of her $500,000 prepetition tort action against D, should C's claim be estimated at $200,000 for bankruptcy purposes? At 0?

4   Assume that C's $500,000 tort action alleges that D and X were both negligent and jointly and severally liable. When D files for bankruptcy, do both C and X have claims against D? See section 101(5). Should both C and X be allowed to recover from D's bankruptcy estate? See section 502(e)(1)(B); see generally Donald Korobkin, *"Killing the Husband": Disallowing Contingent Claims for Contribution and Indemnity in Bankruptcy*, 11 CARDOZO L. REV. 735 (1990).

5. Consider the consequences of sections 101(5), 502(c), and 502(e)(1)(b) in dealing with environmental liabilities. To illustrate, D was one of hundreds of companies that delivered waste oil to X Oil Co.'s blending and refining facility. Shortly after D files a Chapter 11 petition, the United States Environmental Protection Agency begins investigating the X Oil Co. site for environmental contamination and notifies D and all other customers of X Oil Co. that they are liable for the cleanup costs as "generators" and/or "potentially responsible parties" under section 107 of the Comprehensive Environmental Response Compensation and Liability Act. If you represent the EPA, what, if any, action should you take in D's bankruptcy? If you represent one of the other companies that delivered waste oil to X Oil Co., what, if any, action should you take in D's bankruptcy?

C. HOW IS THE PROPERTY TO BE DISTRIBUTED TO HOLDERS OF UNSECURED CLAIMS?

There are a number of statements in reported cases, books, and articles about equality of distribution to creditors in bankruptcy cases. Such statements must be using the term "equality" in the *Animal Farm* sense. In bankruptcy cases, some creditors are more equal than others. The holders of secured claims are more equal than the holders of unsecured claims. And, some holders of unsecured claims are more equal than other holders of unsecured claims.

1. Priorities

In a bankruptcy case, certain allowed unsecured claims are entitled to priority in distribution over other unsecured claims. Section 507(a) sets out the levels of priorities.

Chapter 7 requires that the various priority classes are paid in the order in which they are listed in section 507, section 726(a)(1). In other words, each first priority claim is to be paid in full before any second priority claim is paid at all. If there are not sufficient funds to pay all claims within a particular class, then generally all claims entitled to that priority are paid pro rata.

Chapter 11, Chapter 12, and Chapter 13, require the plan to provide for payment in full of all priority claims, although the payments of claims within certain priority classes may be stretched over a period of time, sections 1129(a)(9); 1222(a)(2), 1322(a)(2).

In its proof of claim form, a creditor can assert a priority and state the amount and basis therefore. Most of the litigation over whether a claim is entitled to a priority involve assertions of section 507(a)(1) administrative expense status. The next two cases involve such claims.

In re Epstein
United States Bankruptcy Court, District of New Mexico, 1984
39 B.R. 938

Burciaga, Bankruptcy Judge:　This Application for Fees, filed by the Debtors' attorney and opposed by the Trustee, raises for the first time in this District the question of whether fees and expenses incurred by a Chapter 7 Debtor while defending a Complaint for Determination of the Dischargeability of a Debt are payable from the estate as an administrative expense.

The Debtors, Bruce and Penelope Epstein, filed a Chapter 7 petition February 23, 1983. Their schedules listed $311,842.30 of debt and $105,610.00 in property. On May 13, 1983, creditors Richard and Patricia Hataoka filed a dischargeability action, alleging that at least $275,000.00 of the debt was non-dischargeable by virtue of the Epsteins' use of false pretenses, false representations and actual fraud, and further requested punitive damages of $1,000,000.00. The adversary proceeding is currently in the discovery phase.

On February 22, 1984, the Debtors' attorney filed an Amended First Application for Fees, requesting approval of fees totalling $11,284.32. These fees were generated in part through the attorney's representation of the Debtors in a related bankruptcy proceeding in California, for which the Debtors had already paid. The remaining balance of $5,134.32, attributable to the New Mexico bankruptcy, was requested as a priority claim. Of the $5,134.32, the Debtors' attorney represents that $2,344.63 are fees generated by what might be considered core bankruptcy matters, and $2,789.69 was generated by the dischargeability action. The Trustee objected, claiming the fees were excessive and that fees incurred defending the dischargeability action were not properly payable by the estate.

Under the Bankruptcy Act, there was a split of authority as to whether fees and expenses incurred defending dischargeability actions were payable from the estate. Some courts, reasoning from dicta in *Conrad, Rubin & Lesser v. Pender,*

289 U.S. 472 (1933) at 476, to the effect that professional services rendered in the carrying out of the provisions of the Act were compensable from the estate, have ruled that protecting the debtor's fresh start is carrying out the provisions of the Act, and so may be paid from the estate. Other courts have flatly ruled that attorney's fees incurred defending actions relating to discharge are not payable from the estate.

The Act provision, [64a(1)](a), repealed October 1, 1979, allowed priority payment from the estate for:

> "(1) the costs and expenses of administration, including the actual and necessary costs and expenses of preserving the estate subsequent to filing the petition;   *** and one reasonable attorney's fee for the professional services actually rendered, irrespective of the number of attorneys employed, to the bankrupt in voluntary and involuntary cases ***"

This has been interpreted to mean that "attorney's fees are allowed only to compensate for professional services rendered in connection with the preservation of the estate,"

The equivalent Code provision, §503(b) provides that claims will be allowed as an administrative expense, and will therefore under §507(a)(1) have first priority for payment, for:

> "(1)(A) the actual, necessary costs and expenses of preserving the estate. ***
>
> "(3) compensation and reimbursement awarded under Section 330 of this title ***"

Section 330 awards to the debtor's attorney "reasonable compensation for actual, necessary expenses."

The legislative history is essentially silent as to any Congressional intent to effect a change in the law, noting only that Code §503 is derived mainly from Act §64(a)(1), with some case law incorporated, and that "Notions of the economy of the estate in fixing fees are outdated and have no place in bankruptcy code,"

Given this, and the structural similarity of the provisions, it does not appear that Congress intended any further departure from the law under the Act.

Congress was not completely unmindful of the possibility of an overbearing creditor bringing in bad faith a dischargeability action in hopes of forcing a settlement on a debtor unwilling or unable to afford adequate representation. In consumer cases, Section 523(d) mandates granting judgment for costs and attorneys fees, against a creditor that unsuccessfully prosecutes a dischargeability action unless it would be clearly inequitable. This section did not exist under the Act, H.R. No. 95-595, 95th Cong., 1st Sess. 365 (1977), and represents a limited exception to the rule that debtors bear their own expenses while attempting to obtain a discharge. Commercial debtors are not so fortunate, and must rely instead on Bankruptcy Rule 9011 or on the Court's equitable powers for the recovery of attorney fees resulting from a bad-faith complaint.

The goal of all bankruptcy legislation is to achieve a just and equitable distribution of the estate to the creditors and to relieve the honest debtor of his debts, giving him a fresh start. Paying from the estate the attorneys fees of a dishonest debtor, or one whose honesty is legitimately open to question unnecessarily favors the fresh start over the distribution to creditors. Every dollar paid administratively is a dollar less paid to the general creditors. The creditors are already financing the debtor's fresh start through their loss; it hardly seems equitable for them to finance the debtor's attempt to prove he is worthy of discharge. If the debtor has conducted himself in a forthrightly honest fashion, sanctions may be imposed against those impuning his honesty. But where the debtor's honesty is in legitimate question, it is up to the debtor to show that he is as honorable as the Code requires. All should consider in the course of their day-to-day activities that operating in the grey areas might one day prove costly.

Therefore, the Debtors, and not the estate, shall bear the cost of defending the debtors' discharge. An appropriate Order will follow.

Notes and Problems

1. Could Daniel Behles, attorney for the Epsteins, have avoided this litigation (and loss) by obtaining a $12,000 retainer from the Epsteins before filing their Chapter 7 petition? Cf. section 329.

2. In the R.H Macy & Co. bankruptcy, professional fees for August, September, and October of 1992 included:

    (i) Deloitte & Touche, Macy's accountant, $1.88 million fees, $110,473 expenses;

    (ii) fees and expenses of accountants employed by the various creditors' committees, $1.36 million;

    (iii)The Blackstone Group, Inc., Macy's financial adviser, $433,556 fees, $26,192 expenses;

    (iv) fees and expenses of financial advisers employed by the various creditors' committees, $735,847;

    (v) Weil, Gotshal & Manges, Macy's bankruptcy attorneys, $1.46 million in fees and expenses;

(vi) fees and expenses of attorneys employed by the various creditors' committees, approximately $2 million.

In the LTV Corporation bankruptcy, the total legal fees and expenses was $165 million, and an additional $49 million was paid to accountants and financial advisers. Are all of these professional fees a first priority expense of administration under section 503?

3. Section 503's description of administrative expenses includes "actual, necessary costs and expenses of preserving the estate," section 503(b)(1)(A). What are examples of such costs and expenses in a Chapter 7 case? In a Chapter 11 case?

Reading Co. v. Brown
Supreme Court of the United States, 1968
391 U.S. 471, 88 S.Ct. 1759, 20 L.Ed.2d 751

Mr. Justice Harlan delivered the opinion of the Court.

On November 16, 1962, I.J. Knight Realty Corporation filed a petition for an arrangement under Chapter XI of the Bankruptcy Act, §§701-799. The same day, the District Court appointed a receiver, Francis Shunk Brown, a respondent here. The receiver was authorized to conduct the debtor's business, which consisted principally of leasing the debtor's only significant asset, an eight-story industrial structure located in Philadelphia.

On January 1, 1963, the building was totally destroyed by a fire which spread to adjoining premises and destroyed real and personal property of petitioner Reading Company and others. On April 3, 1963, petitioner filed a claim for $559,730.83 in the arrangement, based on the asserted negligence of the receiver. It was styled a claim for "administrative expenses" of the arrangement. Other fire loss claimants filed 146 additional claims of a similar nature. The total of all such claims was in excess of $3,500,000, substantially more than the total assets of the debtor.

On May 14, 1963, Knight Realty was voluntarily adjudicated a bankrupt and respondent receiver was subsequently elected trustee in bankruptcy. The claims of petitioner and others thus became claims for administration expenses in bankruptcy which are given first priority under §64a(1) of the Bankruptcy Act. The trustee moved to expunge the claims on the ground that they were not for expenses of administration. It was agreed that the decision whether petitioner's claim is provable as an expense of administration would establish the status of the other 146 claims. It was further agreed that, for purposes of deciding whether the claim is provable, it would be assumed that the damage to petitioner's property resulted from the negligence of the receiver and a workman he employed. The United States, holding a claim for unpaid prearrangement taxes admittedly superior to the claims of general creditors and inferior to claims for administration expenses, entered the case on the side of the trustee.

Section 64a of the Bankruptcy Act provides in part as follows:

"The debts to have priority, in advance of the payment of dividends to creditors, and to be paid in full out of bankrupt estates, and the order of payment, shall be (1) the costs and expenses of administration, including the actual and necessary costs and expenses of preserving the estate subsequent to filing the petition ***."

It is agreed that this section, applicable by its terms to straight bankruptcies, governs payment of administration expenses of Chapter XI arrangements. Furthermore, it is agreed that for the purpose of applying this section to arrangements, the words "subsequent to filing the petition" refer to the period subsequent to the *arrangement* petition, and the words "preserving the estate" include the larger objective, common to arrangements, of operating the debtor's business with a view to rehabilitating it.

The question in this case is whether the negligence of a receiver administering an estate under a Chapter XI arrangement gives rise to an "actual and necessary" cost of operating the debtor's business. The Act does not define "actual and necessary," nor has any case directly in point been brought to our attention. We must, therefore, look to the general purposes of §64a, Chapter XI, and the Bankruptcy Act as a whole.

The trustee contends that the relevant statutory objectives are (1) to facilitate rehabilitation of insolvent businesses and (2) to preserve a maximum of assets for distribution among the general creditors should the arrangement fail. He therefore argues that first priority as "necessary" expenses should be given only to those expenditures without which the insolvent business could not be carried on. For example, the trustee would allow first priority to contracts entered into by the receiver because suppliers, employees, landlords, and the like would not enter into dealings with a debtor in possession or a receiver of an insolvent business unless priority is allowed. The trustee would exclude all negligence claims, on the theory that first priority for them is not necessary to encourage third parties to deal with an insolvent business, that first priority would reduce the amount available for the general creditors, and that first priority would discourage general creditors from accepting arrangements.

In our view the trustee has overlooked one important, and here decisive, statutory objective: fairness to all persons having claims against an insolvent. Petitioner suffered grave financial injury from what is here agreed to have been the negligence of the receiver and a workman. It is conceded that, in principle, petitioner has a right to recover for that injury from their "employer," the business under arrangement, upon the rule of *respondeat superior*.[1] Respondents

---

[1]   28 U.S.C. §959(b) provides as follows: "A trustee, receiver or manager appointed in

Respondents contend, however, that petitioner is in no different position from anyone else injured by a person with scant assets: its right to recover exists in theory but is not enforceable in practice.

That, however, is not an adequate description of petitioner's position. At the moment when an arrangement is sought, the debtor is insolvent. Its existing creditors hope that by partial or complete postponement of their claims they will, through successful rehabilitation, eventually recover from the debtor either in full or in larger proportion than they would in immediate bankruptcy. Hence the present petitioner did not merely suffer injury at the hands of an insolvent business: it had an insolvent business thrust upon it by operation of law. That business will, in any event, be unable to pay its fire debts in full. But the question is whether the fire claimants should be subordinated to, should share equally with, or should collect ahead of those creditors for whose benefit the continued operation of the business (which unfortunately led to a fire instead of the hoped-for rehabilitation) was allowed.

It is theoretically sounder, as well as linguistically more comfortable, to treat tort claims arising during an arrangement as actual and necessary expenses of the arrangement rather than debts of the bankrupt. In the first place, in considering whether those injured by the operation of the business during an arrangement should share equally with, or recover ahead of, those for whose benefit the business is carried on, the latter seems more natural and just. Existing creditors are, to be sure in a dilemma not of their own making, but there is no obvious reason why they should be allowed to attempt to escape that dilemma at the risk of imposing it on others equally innocent.

More directly in point is the possibility of insurance. An arrangement may provide for suitable coverage and the court below recognized that the cost of insurance against tort claims arising during an arrangement is an administrative expense payable in full under §64a(1) before dividends to general creditors. It is of course obvious that proper insurance premiums must be given priority, else insurance could not be obtained; and if a receiver or debtor in possession is to be encouraged to obtain insurance in adequate amounts, the claims against which insurance is obtained should be potentially payable in full. In the present case, it is argued, the fire was of such incredible magnitude that adequate insurance probably could not have been obtained and in any event would have been foolish; this may be true, as it is also true that allowance of a first priority to the fire claimants here will still only mean recovery by them of a fraction of their

---

any cause pending in any court of the United States, including a debtor in possession, shall manage and operate the property in his possession as such trustee, receiver or manager according to the requirements of the valid laws of the State in which such property is situated, in the same manner that the owner or possessor thereof would be bound to do if in possession thereof." This provision of course establishes only the principle of liability under state tort and agency law, and does not decide from whom or with what priority tort claims may be collected.

damages. In the usual case where damages are within insurable limits, however, the rule of full recovery for torts is demonstrably sounder.

Although there appear to be no cases dealing with tort claims arising during Chapter XI proceedings, decisions in analogous cases suggest that "actual and necessary costs" should include costs ordinarily incident to operation of a business, and not be limited to costs without which rehabilitation would be impossible. For example, state and federal taxes accruing during a receivership have been held to be actual and necessary costs of an arrangement. The United States, recognizing and supporting these holdings, agrees with petitioner that costs that form "an integral and essential element of the continuation of the business" are necessary expenses even though priority is not necessary *to* the continuation of the business. Thus the Government suggests that "an injury to a member of the public—a business invitee—who was injured while on the business premises during an arrangement would present a completely different problem [i.e., could qualify for first priority]" although it is not suggested that priority is needed to encourage invitees to enter the premises.

The United States argues, however, that each tort claim "must be analyzed in its own context." Apart from the fact that it has been assumed throughout this case that all 147 claimants were on an equal footing and it is not very helpful to suggest here for the first time a rule by which lessees, invitees, and neighbors have different rights, we perceive no distinction. No principle of tort law of which we are aware offers guidance for distinguishing, within the class of torts committed by receivers while acting in furtherance of the business, between those "integral" to the business and those that are not.

We hold that damages resulting from the negligence of a receiver acting within the scope of his authority as receiver give rise to "actual and necessary costs" of a Chapter XI arrangement.

The judgment of the Court of Appeals is reversed, and the case remanded for further proceedings consistent with this opinion.

It is so ordered.

Judgment of Court of Appeals reversed and case remanded.

Notes and Problems

1. Thomas Jackson offers the following explanation (criticism?) of the majority opinion in *Reading Co. v. Brown*: "Justice Harlan's view is supported by a slightly different analogy whereby the decision to invoke bankruptcy is itself a triggering event that transfers ownership of the corporation to its creditors. The general creditors are treated as the new equity owners of the corporation during the bankruptcy process. Any debts that the corporation incurs during the bankruptcy proceeding have priority over prepetition unsecured claims because creditor claims take priority over equity claims." Thomas Jackson, *Of Liquidation, Continuation, and Delay: An Analysis of Bankruptcy Policy and Nonbankruptcy Rules*, 60 AM.BANKR.L.J. 399, 425-26 (1986). Do you agree?

2. B Corp. owns and operates a trailer park. On July 5, B Corp. files a Chapter 7 petition. The bankruptcy judge appoints an interim trustee under section 701 to maintain and operate B Corp.'s trailer park pending liquidation. Apply section 507(a) and 503 to the following claims against B Corp.

    a. $2,00 salary claim by W, a B Corp. employee, who did maintenance work during the month of June.

    b. $2,000 salary claim by A, a B Corp. employee, who did maintenance work from July 5 to August 5.

    c. $2,000 claim by T, a tenant who claims he was injured on June 28 by reason of W's negligence in maintaining the trailer park.

    d. $2,000 claim by S, a tenant who claims she was injured on July 28 by reason of A's negligence in maintaining the trailer park.

3. Jartran, Inc. entered into a contract to have advertisements printed in the yellow pages of telephone directories. The contract provided for payment by Jartran, Inc. when the directories were published. After the contract but before the publication of the directories, Jartran, Inc. filed a Chapter 11 petition. The directories with Jartran, Inc.'s advertisements were then published. Should Jartran, Inc.'s obligations to pay for the ads be treated as an administrative expense priority under section 503?

4. Many Chapter 11 cases and Chapter 13 cases are unsuccessful. These cases are either dismissed or converted to Chapter 7 cases. If a Chapter 11 case, Chapter 12 case, or Chapter 13 case is converted to a Chapter 7 case, the administrative expenses in the Chapter 7 case will have priority over the administrative expenses in the prior Chapter 11, 12, or 13 cases. See section 726(b).

5. Consider the scope of section 507(a)(7). Does it cover all tax claims? What about postpetition taxes? Why is the priority of tax claims so low?

2. Subordination

Section 507 provides for priority—payment of certain unsecured claims *before* others. Section 510 provides for subordination—payment of certain claims *after* others. Please read section 510. Note that paragraph (a) of section 510 deals with contractual subordination; paragraph (b) subordinates securities fraud claims; paragraph (c) recognizes the possibility of equitable subordination.

Although the Bankruptcy Code recognizes the possibility of equitable subordination, it does not specify any standards by which the doctrine is to be applied. The legislative history states that section 510(c) is intended to "follow existing case law and leave to the courts development of this principle." 124 Cong.Rec. H32,398 (Sept. 28, 1978). A law review article reviews the case law on equitable subordination and concludes:

> [T]he courts have developed three specific criteria for applying the doctrine of equitable subordination:
>   (i) The claimant must have committed fraud or other inequitable conduct;
>   (ii) The claimant's conduct must have resulted in harm to the other creditors or in an unfair advantage to the claimant; and
>   (iii) The subordination of the claim will not be contrary to the principles of bankruptcy law."

Andrew DeNatale & Prudence Abram, *The Doctrine of Equitable Subordination as Applied to Nonmanagement Creditors*, 40 Bus.Law. 417, 423 (1985).

Notes and Problems

1. D owes C $20,000. D needs additional funds. C is unable or unwilling to extend additional credit to D. X is willing to lend D $30,000 only if C agrees that this $30,000 loan is to be paid before her $20,000 loan. C, knowing that D will be unable to continue its business and pay its debts without the additional $30,000, agrees to subordinate its claim to X's. Two months later, D files a bankruptcy petition. X will receive dividends from the bankruptcy distribution on its claim and the dividends allocable to C's claim. If, for example, the holders of unsecured claims receive only 10 cents on the dollar, X will receive $5,000 and C will receive nothing. See section 510(a).

2. On February 2, C obtains a $200,000 judgment against D Co. based on securities fraud—C bought her stock in reliance on a misleading press release by D Co. On March 3, D Co. files a Chapter 11 bankruptcy petition. The bankruptcy court will subordinate C's claim. See section 510(b).

3. Your client C, is considering extending additional credit to D, a financially troubled computer systems design company. C wants to insure that D uses the new money to pay salaries to key design engineers, not pay trade creditors. C also wants to require D to deposit the loan funds and all cash received from the sale of its inventory in banks that do not have a right to setoff. If D later files for bankruptcy, will C's claim be subordinated under section 510(c)?

Matter of Clark Pipe and Supply Co., Inc.
United States Court of Appeals, Fifth Circuit, 1990
893 F.2d 693

E. Grady Jolly, Circuit Judge: Treating the suggestion for rehearing en banc filed in this case by Associates Commercial Corporation ("Associates"), as a petition for panel rehearing, we hereby grant the petition for rehearing. After re-examining the evidence in this case and the applicable law, we conclude that our prior opinion was in error. We therefore withdraw our prior opinion and substitute the following:

* * *

I

Clark Pipe and Supply Company, Inc., ("Clark") was in the business of buying and selling steel pipe used in the fabrication of offshore drilling platforms. In September 1980, Associates and Clark executed various agreements under which Associates would make revolving loans secured by an assignment of accounts receivable and an inventory mortgage. Under the agreements, Clark was required to deposit all collections from the accounts receivable in a bank account belonging to Associates. The amount that Associates would lend was determined by a formula, i.e., a certain percentage of the amount of eligible accounts receivable plus a certain percentage of the cost of inventory. The agreements provided that Associates could reduce the percentage advance rates at any time at its discretion.

When bad times hit the oil fields in late 1981, Clark's business slumped. In February 1982 Associates began reducing the percentage advance rates so that Clark would have just enough cash to pay its direct operating expenses. Clark used the advances to keep its doors open and to sell inventory, the proceeds of which were used to pay off the past advances from Associates. Associates did not expressly dictate to Clark which bills to pay. Neither did it direct Clark not to pay vendors or threaten Clark with a cut-off of advances if it did pay vendors. But Clark had no funds left over from the advances to pay vendors or other creditors whose services were not essential to keeping its doors open.

* * * When a third unpaid creditor initiated foreclosure proceedings in May, Clark sought protection from creditors by filing for reorganization under Chapter 11 of the Bankruptcy Code.

The case was converted to a Chapter 7 liquidation on August 31, 1982, and a trustee was appointed. In 1983, the trustee brought this adversary proceeding against Clark's lender, Associates. The trustee sought the recovery of alleged preferences and equitable subordination of Associates' claims. Following a one-day trial on August 28, 1986, the bankruptcy court entered judgment on April 10, 1987, and an amended judgment on June 9, 1987. The court required Associates to turn over $370,505 of payments found to be preferential and subordinated Associates' claims. The district court affirmed * * *.

* * *

III

* * * This court has enunciated a three- pronged test to determine whether and to what extent a claim should be equitably subordinated: (1) the claimant must have engaged in some type of inequitable conduct, (2) the misconduct must have resulted in injury to the creditors of the bankrupt or conferred an unfair advantage on the claimant, and (3) equitable subordination of the claim must not be inconsistent with the provisions of the Bankruptcy Code. Missionary Baptist I, 712 F.2d at 212. Three general categories of conduct have been recognized as sufficient to satisfy the first prong of the three-part test: (1) fraud, illegality or breach of fiduciary duties; (2) undercapitalization; and (3) a claimant's use of the debtor as a mere instrumentality or alter ego. Id.

In essence, the bankruptcy court found that once Associates realized Clark's desperate financial condition, Associates asserted total control and used Clark as a mere instrumentality to liquidate Associates' unpaid loans. Moreover, it did so, the trustee argues, to the detriment of the rights of Clark's other creditors.

Associates contends that its control over Clark was far from total. Associates says that it did no more than determine the percentage of advances as expressly permitted in the loan agreement; it never made or dictated decisions as to which creditors were paid. Thus, argues Associates, it never had the "actual, participatory, total control of the debtor" required to make Clark its instrumentality * * * . If it did not use Clark as an instrumentality or engage in any other type of inequitable conduct under Missionary Baptist I, argues Associates, then it cannot be equitably subordinated.

A

We first consider whether Associates asserted such control over the activities of Clark that we should consider that it was using Clark as its mere instrumentality. In our prior opinion, we agreed with the district court and the bankruptcy court that, as a practical matter, Associates asserted total control over Clark's liquidation, and that it used its control in a manner detrimental to the unsecured creditors. Upon reconsideration, we have concluded that we cannot say that the sort of control Associates asserted over Clark's financial affairs rises to the level of unconscionable conduct necessary to justify the application of the doctrine of equitable subordination. We have reached our revised conclusion primarily because we cannot escape the salient fact that, pursuant to its loan agreement with Clark, Associates had the right to reduce funding, just as it did, as Clark's sales slowed. We now conclude that there is no evidence that Associates exceeded its authority under the loan agreement, or that Associates acted inequitably in exercising its rights under that agreement.

We think it is important to note at the outset that the loan and security agreements between Associates and Clark, which are at issue here, were executed in 1980, at the inception of their relationship. There is no evidence that Clark was insolvent at the time the agreements were entered into. Clark was represented by counsel during the negotiations, and there is no evidence that the loan documents were negotiated at anything other than arm's length or that they are atypical of loan documents used in similar asset-based financings.

The loan agreement between Associates and Clark established a line of credit varying from $2.2 million to approximately $2.7 million over the life of the loan. The amount that Associates would lend was determined by a formula: 85% of the amount of eligible accounts receivables plus 60% of the cost of inventory. Under the agreement, Clark was required to deposit all collections from the accounts receivable in a bank account belonging to Associates. Associates would, in turn, re-advance the agreed-upon portion of those funds to Clark on a revolving basis. The agreement provided that Associates could reduce the percentage advance rates at any time in its discretion.

When Clark's business began to decline, along with that of the oil patch generally, Associates advised Clark that it would reduce the advance ratio for the inventory loan by 5% per month beginning in January 1982. After that time, the company stopped buying new inventory and, according to the Trustee's expert witness, Clark's monthly sales revenues amounted to less than one-fifth of the company's outstanding accounts payable. Clark prepared a budget at Associates' request that indicated the disbursements necessary to keep the company operating. The budget did not include payment to vendors for previously shipped goods. Associates' former loan officer, Fred Slice, testified as to what he had in mind:

If he [the comptroller of Clark] had had the availability [of funds to pay a vendor or other trade creditor] that particular day, I would have said, "Are you sure you've got that much availability, Jim," because he shouldn't have that much. The way I had structured it, he wouldn't have any money to pay his suppliers. .... But you know, the possibility that--this is all hypothetical. I had it structured so that there was no--there was barely enough money--there was enough money, if I did it right, enough money to keep the doors open. Clark could continue to operate, sell the inventory, turn it into receivables, collect the cash, transfer that cash to me, and reduce my loans. And, if he had ever had availability for other things, that meant I had done something wrong, and I would have been surprised. To ask me what I would have done is purely hypothetical[;] I don't think it would happen. I think it's so unrealistic, I don't know.

Despite Associates' motive, which was, according to Slice, "to get in the best position I can prior to the bankruptcy, i.e., I want to get the absolute amount of dollars as low as I can by hook or crook," the evidence shows that the amount of its advances continued to be based on the applicable funding formulas. Slice testified that the lender did not appreciably alter its original credit procedures when Clark fell into financial difficulty.

In our original opinion, we failed to focus sufficiently on the loan agreement, which gave Associates the right to conduct its affairs with Clark in the manner in which it did. In addition, we think that in our previous opinion we were overly influenced by the negative and inculpatory tone of Slice's testimony. Given the agreement he was working under, his testimony was hardly more than fanfaronading about the power that the agreement afforded him over the financial affairs of Clark. Although his talk was crass (e.g., "I want to get the absolute dollars as low as I can, by hook or crook"), our careful examination of the record does not reveal any conduct on his part that was inconsistent with the loan agreement, irrespective of what his personal motive may have been.

Through its loan agreement, every lender effectively exercises "control" over its borrower to some degree. A lender in Associates' position will usually possess "control" in the sense that it can foreclose or drastically reduce the debtor's financing. The purpose of equitable subordination is to distinguish between the unilateral remedies that a creditor may properly enforce pursuant to its agreements with the debtor and other inequitable conduct such as fraud, misrepresentation, or the exercise of such total control over the debtor as to have essentially replaced its decision-making capacity with that of the lender. The crucial distinction between what is inequitable and what a lender can reasonably and legitimately do to protect its interests is the distinction between the existence of "control" and the exercise of that "control" to direct the activities of the debtor. As the Supreme Court stated in Comstock v. Group of Institutional Investors, 335 U.S. 211, 229, 68 S.Ct. 1454, 1463, 92 L.Ed. 1911 (1948): "It is not mere existence of an opportunity to do wrong that brings the rule into play; it is the unconscionable use of the opportunity afforded by the domination to advantage itself at the injury of the subsidiary that deprives the wrongdoer of the fruits of his wrong."

In our prior opinion, we drew support from In re American Lumber Co., 5 B.R. 470 (D.Minn.1980), to reach our conclusion that Associates' claims should be equitably subordinated. Upon reconsideration, however, we find that the facts of that case are significantly more egregious than we have here. In that case, the court equitably subordinated the claims of a bank because the bank "controlled" the debtor through its right to a controlling interest in the debtor's stock. The bank forced the debtor to convey security interests in its remaining unencumbered assets to the bank after the borrower defaulted on an existing debt. Immediately thereafter, the bank foreclosed on the borrower's accounts receivable, terminated the borrower's employees, hired its own skeleton crew to conduct a liquidation, and selectively honored the debtor's payables to improve its own position. The bank began receiving and opening all incoming mail at the borrower's office, and it established a bank account into which all amounts received by the borrower were deposited and over which the bank had sole control. The bankruptcy court found that the bank exercised control over all aspects of the debtor's finances and operation including: payments of payables and wages, collection and use of accounts receivable and contract rights, purchase and use of supplies and materials, inventory sales, a lumber yard, the salaries of the principals, the employment of employees, and the receipt of payments for sales and accounts receivable.

Despite its decision to prohibit further advances to the debtor, its declaration that the debtor was in default of its loans, and its decisions to use all available funds of the company to offset the company's obligations to it, the bank in American Lumber made two specific representations to the American Lumbermen's Credit Association that the debtor was not in a bankruptcy situation and that current contracts would be fulfilled. Two days after this second reassurance, the bank gave notice of foreclosure of its security interests in the company's inventory and equipment. Approximately two weeks later the bank sold equipment and inventory of the debtor amounting to roughly $450,000, applying all of the proceeds to the debtor's indebtedness to the bank.

Associates exercised significantly less "control" over the activities of Clark than did the lender in American Lumber. Associates did not own any stock of Clark, much less a controlling block. Nor did Associates interfere with the operations of the borrower to an extent even roughly commensurate with the degree of interference exercised by the bank in American Lumber. Associates made no management decisions for Clark, such as deciding which creditors to prefer with the diminishing amount of funds available. At no time did Associates place any of its employees as either a director or officer of Clark. Associates never influenced the removal from office of any Clark personnel, nor did Associates ever request Clark to take any particular action at a shareholders meeting. Associates did not expressly dictate to Clark which bills to pay, nor did it direct Clark not to pay vendors or threaten a cut-off of advances if it did pay vendors. Clark handled its own daily operations. The same basic procedures with respect to the reporting of collateral, the calculation of availability of funds, and the procedures for the advancement of funds were followed throughout the relationship between Clark and Associates. Unlike the lender in American Lumber, Associates did not mislead creditors to continue supplying Clark. Perhaps the most important fact that distinguishes this case from American Lumber is that Associates did not coerce Clark into executing the security agreements after Clark became insolvent. Instead, the loan and security agreements between Clark and Associates were entered into at arm's length prior to Clark's insolvency, and all of Associates' activities were conducted pursuant to those agreements.

Associates' control over Clark's finances, admittedly powerful and ultimately severe, was based solely on the exercise of powers found in the loan agreement. Associates' close watch over Clark's affairs does not, by itself, however, amount to such control as would justify equitable subordination. In re W.T. Grant, 699 F.2d 599, 610 (2d Cir.1983). "There is nothing inherently wrong with a creditor carefully monitoring his debtor's financial situation or with suggesting what course of action the debtor ought to follow." In re Teltronics Services, Inc., 29 B.R. 139, 172 (Bankr.E.D.N.Y.1983) (citations omitted). Although the terms of the agreement did give Associates potent leverage over Clark, that agreement did not give Associates total control over Clark's activities. At all material times Clark had the power to act autonomously and, if it chose, to disregard the advice of Associates; for example, Clark was free to shut its doors at any time it chose to do so and to file for bankruptcy.

Finally, on reconsideration, we are persuaded that the rationale of In re W.T. Grant Co., 699 F.2d 599 (2d Cir.1983) should control the case before us. In that case, the Second Circuit recognized that a creditor is under no fiduciary obligation to its debtor or to other creditors of the debtor in the collection of its claim. [citations omitted] The permissible parameters of a creditor's efforts to seek collection from a debtor are generally those with respect to voidable preferences and fraudulent conveyances proscribed by the Bankruptcy Act; apart from these there is generally no objection to a creditor's using his bargaining position, including his ability to refuse to make further loans needed by the debtor, to improve the status of his existing claims. 699 F.2d at 609-10. Associates was not a fiduciary of Clark, it did not exert improper control over Clark's financial affairs, and it did not act inequitably in exercising its rights under its loan agreement with Clark.

B

Finally, we should note that in our earlier opinion, we found that, in exercising such control over Clark, Associates engaged in other inequitable conduct that justified equitable subordination. Our re-examination of the record indicates, however, that there is not really any evidence that Associates engaged in such conduct. Our earlier opinion assumed that Associates knew that Clark was selling pipe to which the suppliers had a first lien, but the issue of whether the vendors had a first lien on the pipe was not decided by our court until a significantly later time. In addition, although the trustee made much of the point on appeal, after our re-study of the record, we conclude that it does not support the finding that Associates encouraged Clark to remove decals from pipe in its inventory.

We also note that the record is devoid of any evidence that Associates misled other Clark creditors to their detriment.

When the foregoing factors are considered, there is no basis for finding inequitable conduct upon which equitable subordination can be based. We therefore conclude that the district court erred in affirming the bankruptcy court's decision to subordinate Associates' claims.

* * *

Notes and Problems

1. See generally Benjamin Weintraub & Alan Resnick, *The Application of Improvement of Position and Equitable Subordination Doctrines: Clark Pipe Reconsidered*, 23 UCC L.J. 298 (1990).

2. What is the relevance of a lender's control over a debtor in determining whether to equitably subordinate that lender's claim under section 510?

3. D Corp. is undercapitalized. P, the president and principal shareholder of D Corp., makes a $300,000 unsecured loan to D Corp. D Corp. later files for bankruptcy. Does the trustee have to establish wrongdoing in order to subordinate P's unsecured claim?

3. Classification Of Claims

In a Chapter 7 case, the debtor has no control over how the property of the estate is to be distributed. Section 726 prescribes the scheme of distribution to unsecured creditors in a Chapter 7 case. All allowed, unsecured nonpriority claims are treated alike: a pro rata distribution will be made to the holders of such claims after all priority claims are paid in full, section 726(a)(2). To illustrate, assume that D owes $90,000 to X, $50,000 to Y, and $60,000 to Z for total debts to X, Y, and Z of $200,000. Assume further that X, Y, and Z's claims are allowed, nonpriority, unsecured claims. If there is $100,000 available after satisfying secured claims and priority claims, then X, Y, and Z will each receive 50 of its claim—$45,000 to X, $25,000 to Y, and $30,000 to Z. [Total debts divided by total available funds equals percentage of each claim paid.]

In a Chapter 11 case, a Chapter 12 case, or a Chapter 13 case, a debtor's plan can affect how the property of the estate is to be distributed. The plan can treat some unsecured claims differently than others: it can classify claims and provide for different treatment for each class, sections 1123(a)(1); 1222(b)(1); 1322(b)(1). The next two cases deal with classification of claims.

In re Harris

United States Bankruptcy Court, Eastern District of Michigan, 1986
62 B.R. 391

Arthur J. Spector, Bankruptcy Judge. The debtors filed their joint petition for relief under Chapter 13 on August 19, 1985. In their petition, they list their unsecured debts in two separate categories: one for debts incurred during the operation of their bookstore, The Mustard Seed; the other for unsecured consumer debts. According to their schedules, the business debts are in the amount of $19,697.80, plus a debt of $50,438 to Old Kent Bank-Central representing the unsecured portion of its claim, for a total of $70,135.80; the consumer debts total $1,920.70.

The debtors' proposed Chapter 13 plan continues this distinction between business and consumer unsecured debt. Consumer debts are listed as "Class 3" debts, on which the debtors propose to pay 100 over three years. "Class 5" debts constitute the unsecured business debts. The debtors estimated that there will be no distribution to this class. Moreover, as counsel for the debtors stated on the record, it was their intention not to pay business creditors when they formulated their plan. However, it appears that there may in fact be some distribution to Class 5 creditors due to the failure of some Class 3 creditors to file proofs of claim. Consumer creditors would still receive 100 payment, and business creditors would receive 4.82 on their claims. By way of comparison, if all unsecured creditors are paid without regard to how the debt was incurred, each would receive 7.28 of its claim.

On March 29, 1986, Spring Arbor Distributors, an unsecured business creditor of the debtors, filed an objection to the debtors' plan. The basis of its objection is that the above classification of unsecured creditors unfairly discriminates against the business creditors, and that such treatment is barred by the Bankruptcy Code.

The debtors' authority to classify unsecured claims separately is contained in §1322(b)(1). Under this section the debtors' plan may:

> (1) designate a class or classes of unsecured claims, as provided in §1122 of this title, but may not discriminate unfairly against any class so designated; however, such plan may treat claims for a consumer debt of the debtor if an individual is liable on the consumer debt with the debtor differently than on other unsecured claims.

There is no indication that the unsecured consumer debts being paid 100 under the proposed plan are debts on which third parties are liable as co-obligors; thus, the last clause of §1322 is inapplicable.

Section 1122, to which §1322 refers, does not offer much guidance. It provides that a debtor may designate various classes of creditors, so long as each member of that class holds a claim or interest that is "substantially similar" to the claims or interests of other class members. There is, unfortunately, no statutory definition of what makes claims or interests "substantially similar" to each other.

Fortunately, there have been a considerable number of cases discussing what sorts of classifications of unsecured claims are permissible under §1322. The debtors rely on *In re Cook*, 26 B.R. 187, 7 C.B.C.2d 1079 (D.N.M.1982). There, the debtor sought to pay unsecured debts guaranteed by a co-signor and claims for child support, but nothing to other unsecured creditors. The court adopted the "emergent majority view" that "[a] classification is not *ipso facto* unfairly discriminatory because it provides for a greater percentage of payment to some unsecured creditors than to others." In order to determine whether a particular classification was fair, the court went on to espouse a four-factor test developed by other courts. Those factors are:

(1) Whether the discrimination has a reasonable basis;

(2) Whether the debtor can carry out a plan without such discrimination;

(3) Whether such discrimination is proposed in good faith; and

(4) the treatment of the class discriminated against.

Id. These factors are not rigid rules, but are simply flexible guidelines to assist courts in deciding whether a debtor's plan ought to be confirmed. Each plan should be decided on its own merits. Although to a large extent these guidelines overlap, the reasoning of these opinions is sound and we adopt it.

The standards are consistent with two underlying purposes of the Bankruptcy Code. On the one hand, the remedies provided debtors in the Bankruptcy Code, including Chapter 13, are intended to provide debtors with the opportunity to emerge from bankruptcy with the famous "fresh start". Chapter 13 gives debtors wide latitude to propose a plan which will allow them to pay their debts without undue hardship, yet exit from bankruptcy in sounder financial shape than when they filed for relief. Thus, §1322(b)(1) allows debtors to discriminate among unsecured creditors where it is beneficial to the debtor to do so. However, the objective of providing debtors with a fresh start is counterbalanced by the Congress' intent that the debtor's creditors be treated fairly. More precisely, it is fundamental to the operation of the Code that creditors of an equal status—e.g. priority, administrative and unsecured—be treated equally and equitably. *See* §726(b). Accordingly, while the debtor may classify unsecured creditors differently, they cannot do so in such a fashion that any single class is treated unfairly, that is, inequitably. As the Code presumes that creditors of like position will be treated equally, the debtor has the burden of persuading us that a deviation from that norm is not unfair to creditors.

Applying the four-part test to the facts of this case, we find that the debtor has failed to show that the proposed discrimination is fair. The first factor is whether the discrimination has a reasonable basis. We interpret this to be an inquiry into whether there is any logical or rational foundation for the classification. For example, classifying creditors alphabetically would have no rational basis in the context of a Chapter 13. Here, the debtors have divided their creditors into those who extended credit to them in the operation of their prior business, and those who extended credit for personal consumer purposes. Simply put, the debtors have closed their bookstore and have no further interest in paying the debts incurred therefrom or of maintaining an ongoing debtor-creditor relationship with their business creditors. Conversely, they wish to repay those parties who lent them money or extended them credit for personal needs, and who the debtors will likely encounter post-bankruptcy. The classification thus is rational at least from the debtors' perspective.

The proposed classification makes less sense when evaluated in terms of recourse available to the unsecured creditors. Legally, all of the unsecured creditors in this case, business and consumer, would have the same remedies under state law to pursue collection of their debts. After obtaining a judgment for the balance due, they could attempt to satisfy it through garnishment of wages and deposit accounts or by execution on the debtors' property. In reducing their claims to hard cash, the law cares not whether credit was extended to the debtors for an ill-fated business enterprise or for the debtors' personal needs. Of course, we realize that in practical terms the ability of creditors to pursue their legal remedies may differ; however, it is not the purpose for which the debts were incurred that makes them different. For example, some creditors may hold claims against the debtor for which there may be a co-obligor. Against the debtor, that creditor has the same rights as any unsecured creditor; but the creditor's ability to seek payment from a third-party (often a member of the debtor's family) gives that creditor added leverage against the debtor. Thus, §1322(b)(1) expressly allows debtors to establish a separate class for unsecured consumer debts on which a non-debtor is liable. Additionally, some claimants may possess claims so small that it is impractical for the creditor to pursue its legal remedies. Suppose a creditor holds an unsecured claim for $100.00; even if that creditor could find counsel willing to litigate the matter, it would probably cost more than $100.00 to do so. Because creditors so situated may have *fewer* remedies against the debtor, §1122(b), and by reference §1322, provides that such creditors may be separately classified. As *Colliers* has noted, in enacting an amendment to §1322(b) in 1984.

> Congress has recognized that practical necessity can be a proper reason for separate classification of claims. In doing so, it has apparently rejected the view that unsecured claims may be separately classified only if they would receive differing distributions in chapter 7 and allowed the court to consider the practical justifications for proposed classifications on a case-by-case basis.

Thus some classifications among unsecured creditors may be found to be fair. Suppose, for example, a debtor was compelled to pay a criminal restitution debt or risk imprisonment. There, the debtor would certainly benefit by paying that debt in full and perhaps in advance of other unsecured creditors; but this would likely inure to the benefit of the "lesser" class, because they might receive nothing if the debtor goes to jail. Or, a debtor who wished to continue his or her business might want to pay business creditors *more* as a means of maintaining good relations with essential suppliers, for if those suppliers are not made happy the business might fail, causing both the debtor and the less favored creditors to lose out. Separately classifying these creditors may be reasonable.

In the case at bar, the classification suggested by the debtors was not proposed with any regard to the ability of the various creditors to collect their debts. So far as we can tell, there are no debts on which there is a co-obligor with either of the debtors. Furthermore, the proposed classification has no correlation to the size of the various claims. According to the debtors' schedules, the unsecured business claims range in size from $10.96 to $8,500.00;

the consumer claims range from $154.04 to $988.00. In the instant case, the business creditors would receive no benefit as a result of the proposed classification, either directly or indirectly, nor is there any moral justification for preferring any of the consumer creditors. We also reject the debtors' unsubstantiated assertion that business creditors are more able to take care of themselves than consumer creditors. In short, we find that while the proposed classification may have a rational basis from the debtors' position, it is arbitrary when examined from the creditors' viewpoint. This makes the proposed classification suspect.

The second factor is whether the debtors could consummate a plan without the proposed classification. We find that they could do so. As noted above, assuming the same level of funding and duration of plan as has been proposed, if unsecured creditors are not classified, each would receive 7.28 on its claim. Although plans paying an unusually low percentage may draw closer scrutiny than 100 plans, they may be confirmed if the plan otherwise complies with the standards for confirmation in §1325. Although the debtors might be able to consummate a non-discriminatory plan, it is not necessarily fatal to their plan that they have not done so.

The third factor is whether the discrimination is proposed in good faith. This is where the debtors' plan fails. As we have stated above, the debtors are attempting to wash their hands of their business and the debts they accumulated in its operation. Their stated intent was to pay their business creditors nothing, and it is only because some creditors neglected to timely file proofs of claim that creditors of the business might receive any distribution at all. In attempting to obtain a discharge of these debts without making any payment thereon, the debtors are essentially seeking to file a Chapter 7 petition for their business and a Chapter 13 petition for their personal, preferred creditors. This flies in the face of the policy that similarly situated creditors receive equal treatment under the Bankruptcy Code, and cannot be held to constitute a good faith proposal. The debtors bear the burden of showing that their plan is filed in good faith. Because the debtors have failed to persuade us that their proposed classification satisfies this standard, §1325(a)(3), their plan cannot be confirmed.

Although the above finding makes consideration of the impact of the classification on the adversely affected creditors superfluous, we will discuss it briefly. While the good faith requirement may be regarded as a test of whether the plan is consistent with the spirit underlying Chapter 13 relief, this last factor measures the practical consequences to the affected creditors. Here, the result is obviously unfair. The debtors' consumer creditors will receive full payment; however, their business creditors will receive nothing, or, at best, an inadvertent and insignificant amount. Nonetheless, the debtors' discharge will *not* discriminate between business and consumer debts—each will be discharged. Indeed, because this is a Chapter 13 case, the effect of a Chapter 13 discharge would be more severe than if the debtors filed a Chapter 7 petition, because the business creditors would have no opportunity to seek to have their debts excepted from discharge under §523. On these facts, the harm visited upon the adversely affected class far outweigh any legitimate benefit to be gained by the debtors, thus providing another reason for denying confirmation.

The result we reach here is consistent with the holding in a prior unpublished opinion by this Court, *In re Shands*. There, the debtor filed a petition for relief under Chapter 7. However, because the debtor stated her intention to reaffirm several debts, and her current husband assumed payments on several other obligations, the result was that the only significant creditor not being paid was the debtor's ex-husband, who was owed some $6,000 pursuant to a divorce property settlement. In an answer filed in an adversary proceeding, and in a hearing held to determine whether the case was a substantial abuse of the Bankruptcy Code, §707(b), the debtor admitted that her primary purpose in filing a Chapter 7 petition was to discharge the debt to her ex-husband.

We dismissed the debtor's case as a substantial abuse, pursuant to §707(b). By filing a Chapter 7 petition, then reaffirming or otherwise paying essentially all debts except those to her ex-husband, she was effectively filing a Chapter 7 as to him and a Chapter 13 as to her other creditors. We held such discriminatory treatment to be a substantial abuse of Chapter 7 and dismissed the case. It is equally abusive to attempt to manipulate Chapter 13 to file bankruptcy against only some of a debtor's creditors. When debtors seek to take advantage of the benefits contained in the Bankruptcy Code, one of the conditions placed upon that relief—a "fresh start"—is that they must treat all their creditors fairly.

In the instant case, the debtors' plan fails to treat all similarly situated creditors equally, and thus is not proposed in good faith. Accordingly, confirmation of their plan must be denied. An order consistent with this opinion will be entered contemporaneously herewith.

Problems

1. In *Harris*, Spring Arbor, a creditor of Harris, was able to block the confirmation of Harris' Chapter 13 plan because the plan proposed to pay other creditors more than Spring Arbor. Section 1325(a)(4) requires that the Chapter 13 plan pay Spring Arbor at least as much as it would receive if Harris was in Chapter 7. *Should* a creditor who will be receiving at least as much as it would receive in a Chapter 7 case be able to prevent the debtor from proposing to pay other creditors more in his Chapter 13 plan? Cf. section 1325(b).

2. Why *should* a Chapter 13 debtor ever be permitted to pay certain holders of unsecured claims more than others? Isn't this a preference? Is it inconsistent with the bankruptcy policy of equality of distribution?

3. Most of the early, reported cases under section 1322(b)(1) involve classification of claims on which there is a codebtor. The 1984 amendments to section 1322(b)(1)

added the following language, "such plan may treat claims for a consumer debt of the debtor if an individual is liable on such a consumer debt with the debtor differently than other unsecured claims." Assume that Vern borrows $4,000 from C. Ernest guarantees repayment of this loan. Vern later files a Chapter 13 petition. Vern's Chapter 13 plan places the debt that Ernest guaranteed in a separate class. While Vern's Chapter 13 plan commits all of his "disposable income" to the repayment of his debts, it allocates most of it to the repayment of the debt that Ernest guaranteed. That debt will be paid in full; there will be only a 6 payment on all other unsecured claims. Should the bankruptcy court confirm Vern's plan?

4. Most of the current cases under section 1322(b)(1) involve classification of claims excepted from discharge. Would Judge Spector confirm a plan that proposes to pay Class 3 educational claims 100% and Class 5 other unsecured claims 4.82%?

⊓⊓⊓⊓⊓

    Classification of claims has a different and greater significance in Chapter 11 than in Chapter 13. In Chapter 11, the classification of claims can affect not only what creditors receive under a plan but also whether the plan can successfully pass through the plan approval process contemplated by the Bankruptcy Code.

    Recall that in Chapter 13, creditors do not vote on the plan. In contrast, Chapter 11 creditors vote on a plan, and at least one class of claims must vote to accept the plan. The Chapter 11 plan approval process will be considered later; classification of claims in Chapter 11 is considered below.

In re United States Truck Co., Inc.
United States Court of Appeals, Sixth Circuit, 1986
800 F.2d 581

    Cornelia G. Kennedy, Circuit Judge. The Teamsters National Freight Industry Negotiating Committee (the Teamsters Committee), a creditor of U.S. Truck Company, Inc. (U.S. Truck)—the debtor-in-possession in this Chapter 11 bankruptcy proceeding—appeals the District Court's order confirming U.S. Truck's Fifth Amended Plan of Reorganization. The Teamsters Committee complains that the plan does not satisfy three of the requirements of §1129. The District Court, which presided over the matter after the resignation of Bankruptcy Judge Stanley B. Bernstein, held that the requirements of section 1129 had been satisfied. We agree.

I

    Underlying this appeal is the Teamsters Committee's claim that U.S. Truck is liable to its employees for rejecting a collective bargaining agreement between the local union and U.S. Truck. After filing its petition for relief under Chapter

11 of the Bankruptcy Code on June 11, 1982, U.S. Truck, a trucking company primarily engaged in intrastate shipping of parts and supplies for the automotive industry, sought to reject the collective bargaining agreement. U.S. Truck rejected the agreement with the approval of then-Bankruptcy-Judge Woods, in December 1982. Judge Woods found that rejection of the agreement was "absolutely necessary to save the debtor from collapse." New agreements have been negotiated to the satisfaction of each participating local union. Such agreements have been implemented over the lone dissent of the Teamsters Joint Area Rider Committee. Under the most recently mentioned agreement in the record (due to have expired in March 1985), U.S. Truck was able to record monthly profits in the range of $125,000 to $250,000. These new agreements achieved such results by reducing wages and requiring employees to buy their own trucking equipment, which the employees then leased to the company.

The parties agreed to an estimate of the size of the Teamsters Committee claim against U.S. Truck so that the confirmation plan could be considered. The District Court held a hearing to consider the plan on January 23, 1985. The court considered three objections by the Teamster's Committee to the plan. Consideration of the objections, and the court's treatment of them, requires an understanding of the statutory scheme for approval of a chapter 11 reorganization plan.

II

Section 1129 contains two means by which a reorganization plan can be confirmed. The first way is to meet all eleven of the requirements of subsection (a), including (a)(8) which requires all impaired classes of claims or interests to accept the plan. The other way is to meet the requirements of subsection (b), which, first, incorporates all of the requirements of subsection (a), except for that contained in subsection (a)(8), and, second, imposes two additional requirements. Confirmation under subsection (b) is commonly referred to as a "cram down" because it permits a reorganization plan to go into effect over the objections of one or more impaired classes of creditors. In this case, U.S. Truck sought approval of its plan under this "cram down" provision.

III

The Teamsters Committee's first objection is that the plan does not meet the requirement that at least one class of impaired claims accept the plan, *see* §1129(a)(10), because U.S. Truck impermissibly gerrymandered the classes in order to neutralize the Teamsters Committee's dissenting vote. The reorganization plan contains twelve classes. The plan purports to impair five of these classes—Class VI (the secured claim of Manufacturer's National Bank of Detroit based on a mortgage); Class VII (the secured claim of John Graham, Trustee of Transportation Services, Inc., based on a loan); Class IX (the Teamsters Committee's claim based on rejection of the collective bargaining agreement); Class XI (all secured claims in excess of $200.00 including those arising from the rejection of executory contracts); and Class XII (the equity interest of the stockholder of the debtor). As noted above, section 1129(a)(10), as incorporated into subsection (b)(1), requires at least one of these classes of impaired claims to approve the reorganization plan before it can be confirmed. The parties agree that approval by Class XII would not count because acceptance must be determined without including the acceptance of the plan by any insider. *See* §1129(a)(10). The Code's definition of "insider" clearly includes McKinlay Transport, Inc. *See* §101(28)(B)(iii), (30). Thus, compliance with subsection (a)(10) depends on whether either of the other three classes that approved the plan—Class VI, Class VII, or Class XI—was a properly constructed impaired class. The Teamsters Committee argues that Classes VI and VII were not truly impaired classes and that Class XI should have included Class IX, and hence was an improperly constructed class.[1] Because we find that Class XI was a properly constructed class of impaired claims, we hold that the plan complies with subsection (a)(10).[2]

The issue raised by the Teamsters Committee's challenge is under what circumstances does the Bankruptcy Code permit a debtor to keep a creditor out of a class of impaired claims which are of a similar legal nature and are against the same property as those of the "isolated" creditor. The District Court held that the Code permits such action here because of the following circumstances: (1) the employees represented by the Teamsters Committee have a unique continued interest in the ongoing business of the debtor; (2) the mechanics of the Teamsters Committee's claim differ substantially from those of the Class XI claims; and (3) the Teamsters Committee's claim is likely to become part of the agenda of future collective bargaining sessions between the union and the reorganized company. Thus, according to the court, the interests of the Teamsters Committee are substantially dissimilar from those of the creditors in Class XI. We must decide whether the Code permits separate classification under such circumstances.

Congress has sent mixed signals on the issue that we must decide. Our starting point is §1122.

The statute, by its express language, only addresses the problem of dissimilar claims being included in the same class. It does not address the correlative problem—the one we face here—of similar claims being put in different classes. Some courts have seized upon this omission, and have held that the Code does not require a debtor to put similar claims in the same class.

Further evidence that Congress intentionally failed to impose a requirement that similar claims be classified together is found by examining the "classification" sections of the former Bankruptcy Act. The applicable former

---

[1] Had the debtor included the Teamsters Committee's claim in Class XI, the Committee's vote to reject the plan would have swung the results of the Class XI vote from an acceptance to a rejection. *See* §1126(c) (setting forth the requirement that creditors holding at least two-thirds in amount of allowed claims of a class accept).

[2] For this reason, we need not decide the challenge to the status of Class VI and Class VII.

provisions were sections 597 (from former Chapter X) and 751 (from former Chapter XI).

§597. Classifications of creditors and stockholders

For the purposes of the plan and its acceptance, the judge shall fix the division of creditors and stockholders into classes according to the nature of their respective claims and stock. For the purposes of such classification, the judge shall, if necessary, upon the application of the trustee, the debtor, any creditor, or an indenture trustee, fix a hearing upon notice to the holders of secured claims, the debtor, the trustee, and such other persons as the judge may designate, to determine summarily the value of the security and classify as unsecured the amount in excess of such value.

§751. Classification of creditors

For the purposes of the arrangement and its acceptance, the court may fix the division of creditors into classes and, in the event of controversy, the court shall after hearing upon notice summarily determine such controversy.

Section 597 was interpreted to require all creditors of equal rank with claims against the same property to be placed in the same class. Congress' switch to less restrictive language in section 1122 of the Code seems to warrant a conclusion that Congress no longer intended to impose the now-omitted requirement that similar claims be classified together. However, the legislative history indicates that Congress may not have intended to change the prior rule. The Notes of the Senate Committee on the Judiciary state:

> This section [1122] codifies current case law surrounding the classification of claims and equity securities. It requires classification based on the nature of the claims or interests classified, and permits inclusion of claims or interests in a particular class only if the claim or interest being included is substantially similar to the other claims or interests of the class.

It is difficult to follow Congress' instruction to apply the old case law to the new Code provision. The old case law comes from two different sources. Chapter X of the old Act was designed for thorough financial reorganizations of large corporations. It imposed a very formal and rigid structure to protect the investing public. Chapter XI was designed for small nonpublic businesses, did not permit the adjustment of a secured debt or of equity, and thus contained few investor-protection measures. The idea behind Chapter 11 of the Code was to combine the speed and flexibility of Chapter XI with some of the protection and remedial tools of Chapter X. Thus, Congress has incorporated, for purposes of interpreting section 1122, the case law from two provisions with different language, that were adopted for different purposes, and that have been interpreted to mean different things.

In this case, U.S. Truck is using its classification powers to segregate dissenting (impaired) creditors from assenting (impaired) creditors (by putting the dissenters into a class or classes by themselves) and, thus, it is assured that at least one class of impaired creditors will vote for the plan and make it eligible for cram down consideration by the court. We agree with the Teamsters Committee that there must be some limit on a debtor's power to classify creditors in such a manner. The potential for abuse would be significant otherwise. Unless there is some requirement of keeping similar claims together, nothing would stand in the way of a debtor seeking out a few impaired creditors (or even one such creditor) who will vote for the plan and placing them in their own class.[1]

The District Court noted three important ways in which the interests of the Teamsters Committee differ substantially from those of the other impaired creditors. Because of these differences, the Teamsters Committee has a different stake in the future viability of the reorganized company and has alternative means at its disposal for protecting its claim. The Teamsters Committee's claim is connected with the collective bargaining process. In the words of the Committee's counsel, the union employees have a "virtually unique interest." These differences put the Teamsters Committee's claim in a different posture than the Class XI claims. The Teamsters Committee may choose to reject the plan not because the plan is less than optimal to it as a creditor, but because the Teamsters Committee has a noncreditor interest *e.g.,* rejection will benefit its members in the ongoing employment relationship. Although the Teamsters Committee certainly is not intimately connected with the debtor, to allow the Committee to vote with the other impaired creditors would be to allow it to prevent a court from considering confirmation of a plan that a significant group of creditors with similar interests have accepted. Permitting separate classification of the Teamsters Committee's claim does not automatically result in adoption of the plan. The Teamsters Committee is still protected by the provisions of subsections (a) and (b) [of section 1129], particularly the requirements of subsection (b) that the plan not discriminate unfairly and that it be fair and equitable with respect to the Teamsters Committee's claim.

Notes and Problems

1. In *U.S. Truck,* the Sixth Circuit affirmed the bankruptcy court's decision to confirm the Chapter 11 plan. Confirmation requires compliance with the standards of section 1129. What language in section 1129 calls for the bankruptcy judge to review the classification of claims in the Chapter 11 plan?

---

[1]   We need not speculate in this case whether the purpose of separate classification was to line up the votes in favor of the plan. The debtor admitted that to the District Court.

2. Why is the Teamsters Committee arguing that its collective bargaining claim should have been included in Class XI? Why didn't the debtor include the collective bargaining claim in Class XI?

3. In portions of the opinion that have been omitted, the Sixth Circuit quotes from and relies on Chapter 13 cases on classification of claims. Should the tests for classification of claims in a Chapter 11 plan be different from the tests for classification in a Chapter 13 plan or a Chapter 12 plan? How should the Harris case have been decided if the debtors had filed for relief under Chapter 11 instead of Chapter 13?

4. Most of the recent reported cases dealing with classification of claims in Chapter 11 are "single asset" real estate cases involving facts similar to the following: D is a partnership that owns a building. M has a $4,000,000 mortgage on the building. The value of the building is no more than $1,000,000 so that M has a $3,000,000 unsecured deficiency claim. D's only other unsecured creditors are miscellaneous suppliers who are owed a total of $20,000. D files a Chapter 11 plan that classifies M's deficiency claim separate from all other unsecured claims. *In re SM 104 Limited* on pages 1162-84 *infra* is such a case. We will be better able to deal with a such a case after we have covered about 300 more pages.

Unit 11

EFFECT OF BANKRUPTCY
ON SECURED CLAIMS

UNIT CONTENTS

A. WHAT IS A SECURED CLAIM

Recall that (1) the Bankruptcy Code classifies claims, not creditors; (2) under the Bankruptcy Code, a single credit transaction can give rise to both a secured claim and an unsecured claim; (and) (3) the phrase "secured claim" is defined in section 506(a) of the Bankruptcy Code. Please recall and reread section 506(a) and apply it to the following problems:

Problems

1. **Value of Collateral**

   a. D files a Chapter 7 petition. C has a judgment against D For $100,000, and a judgment lien on real property owned by D. If that property has a value of $60,000, what is the amount of C's secured claim? Of C's unsecured claim?

   b. D files a Chapter 12 petition. D owes M $200,000. M has a second mortgage on D's farm. F holds a first mortgage on the same farm and has a $300,000 claim. If D's farm has a value of $450,000, what is the amount of M's secured claim?

2. **Postpetition Interest**
   In problem 1.B. above, assume that both F's and M's notes and mortgages provide for interest. Will F's secured claim continue to increase postpetition as interest accrues? See section 506(b). Will M's claim increase postpetition as interest accrues? See sections 506(b), 502(b)(2); see generally Craig Averch, Michael Collins, & Stephen Youngman, *The Right of Oversecured Creditors to Default Rates of Interest From a Debtor in Bankruptcy,* 47 Bus. Lawyer 961 (1992); David Carlson, *Postpetition Interest Under the Bankruptcy Code*, 43 U. Miami L. Rev. 578 (1989).

ⵣⵣⵣⵣⵣ

In the above examples, the value of the "creditor's interest in the estate's interest in the property" was hypothesized. In the "real world", the value of the collateral cannot be hypothesized. How does a lawyer establish the value of collateral for purposes of section 506?

Reread the last sentence of section 506: "Such value shall be determined in light of the purpose of the valuation and of the proposed disposition or use of such property and in conjunction with any hearing on such disposition or use or on a plan affecting such creditor's interest."

What does the quoted language mean? How will it be used by a lawyer? By a bankruptcy judge? Is the focus on the value of the encumbered property to the debtor or its value to the holder of the secured claim? Does section 506 look to the value of the collateral as a part of a going concern or its liquidation value? Is it a wholesale or retail standard?

Fortgang & Mayer, Valuation In Bankruptcy
32 UCLA L.Rev. 1061 (1985)

Valuation in Bankruptcy is a Function of Time

For every asset there is a time to use and a time to sell, and depending on its proposed use or sale, an asset may have a "going concern value" or a "liquidation value."

I. Valuing Assets
A. General Principles
1. "Going Concern" and "Liquidation" Values

The value of an asset is not fixed by any one proceeding in a bankruptcy case. Value may vary from proceeding to proceeding, depending upon the context. Congress explicitly recognized the need for different asset valuations in the many different proceedings which value collateral to determine the size of a secured claim. The creditor looking to foreclose on an asset used as collateral may foresee its immediate disposition and, consequently, may attach a "liquidation value" to the asset. The same creditor, seeking to maximize his secured claim under a plan of reorganization, may foresee the same asset's continued use as part of the debtor's business, and consequently may attach a "going concern value" to the asset.

The choice between "liquidation values" and "going concern values" lies at the heart of most disputes over asset valuation in bankruptcy. The terms are so ubiquitous that a prefatory explication of each is essential. The distinction between them often illustrates the function of time in the determination of value.

A "going concern" is a business with some sort of future. Assets of a going concern may be valued based on their present or projected use and their current or future contribution to the production of revenues and profits. Assets of a type normally sold by a going concern may be valued based on their prospective sale, pursuant to the concern's plans or practices, at prices that include the concern's anticipated mark-up or gross margin. Inventory is usually worth more when sold by a continuing business than when sold by a liquidator. A greater percentage of accounts receivable will ordinarily be collected by a going concern than by one in liquidation. Plant and equipment can be valued as integral parts of a revenue-producing enterprise. In short, going concern values assume events going forward. Sometimes values based on this assumption must be discounted for risk and the time value of money.

If an asset is not used as part of a business, or if the business is not viable, the asset is valued at how much it will bring at a sale less the costs of disposition—a "liquidation value." Liquidation values assume no future or a limited future for an asset's relationship to a concern. The liquidation value of an asset will depend on how much time is available for its disposition, who is selling it, and how and where it is sold.

Going concern values generally exceed liquidation values. There are, however, exceptions. If a going concern is not the optimal user or seller of an asset, the asset's liquidation value may exceed its going concern value. A below market lease of prime real estate held by a failing business is one example. A net operating loss (NOL) generated by a failing business is another: It is worth more to a profitable concern than to the business without profits for the NOL to shelter. Surplus assets almost by definition have higher liquidation values than going concern values. If surplus assets do not appreciate enough to generate a fair return on any out-of-pocket expenses of continued possession and the opportunity cost of delayed sale, their going concern value may even be negative. A derelict barge that incurs mooring fees is one example, unproductive land assessed for taxes is another.

Just as a going concern value is not necessarily a high value, so liquidation value is not necessarily a low value. Although the phrase "liquidation value" is often used to mean the value of an asset in a piecemeal forced sale, this may not be a fair liquidation value. An asset may be sold at public auction or private sale, in haste or at leisure. Some of these sales produce higher liquidation values than others. The Uniform Commercial Code, for example, requires disposition in a "commercially reasonable" manner. Even if a foreclosure sale is conducted properly, a court may reject the price realized at the sale as too low to be a true liquidation value. If the asset sold is a publicly traded security or a controlling share of a continuing business, the liquidation values realized at such sales may be indistinguishable from the going concern values of such assets.

Most courts nevertheless cleave to the dichotomy between liquidation and going concern values because the dichotomy expresses a statistical truth: Most asset "liquidations" yield less than the value of the asset if retained by its current owner.

Notes and Problems

1. D has filed for Chapter 7 relief. D owes S $10,000. S has a security interest in D's car. What are the possible methods of establishing the amount of S's secured claim? Is such valuation necessary? What if D had filed for Chapter 13 relief?

2. D has filed for Chapter 11 relief. D owes M $20,000,000. M has a mortgage on a hotel owned by D. what are the possible methods of establishing the amount of M's secured claim? What if D had filed for Chapter 7 relief?

3. H and W file for Chapter 12 relief. They owe the Farmers Home Administration (FmHA) $303,000. The FmHA has a mortgage on their farm. H and W are full-time farmers, and their appraiser testifies that the value of the farm as a working farm is $140,000. The FmHA appraiser testifies that the highest and best use of the property is as a "hobby farm," a country residence for someone who might be interested in keeping a few horses for leisure, and that the farm could be sold to such a person for $250,000. What is the amount of the FmHA secured claim?

4. Issues of the value of collateral can arise at different points in a bankruptcy case -- eligibility for Chapter 13 relief under section 109, relief from stay under section 363(d), adequate protection under section 363 or 364, preference litigation under section 547, and confirmation of plans in Chapter 11, 12, and 13. As you consider these topics, consider again the different possible methods and approaches for valuing collateral.

5. See generally James Queenan, *Standards for Valuation of Security Interests in Chapter 11*, 92 Com. L.J. 18 (1987); Kaaran Thomas, *Valuation of Assets in Bankruptcy Proceedings: Emerging Issues*, 51 Montana L. Rev. 126 (1990).

B. WHAT IS THE SIGNIFICANCE OF SECURED CLAIM STATUS?

Under bankruptcy law, as under non-bankruptcy law, a secured claim is treated more favorably than an unsecured claim.

Under non-bankruptcy law, when the debtor defaults, a secured creditor can seize and sell the property subject to its lien. Additionally, under non-bankruptcy law, a secured creditor has greater rights than unsecured creditors have in both the property subject to its lien and the proceeds from any disposition thereof. Somewhat similar rights exist under the Bankruptcy Code.

First, bankruptcy law does not eliminate the right of a holder of a secured claim to seize and to sell its collateral. However, bankruptcy law makes such seizure and sale subject to the automatic stay: the holder of a secured claim must obtain relief from the automatic stay before seizing its collateral, before selling its collateral. Second, bankruptcy law, in its own way, recognizes that the holder of a secured claim enjoys special rights in the property subject to its lien and in the proceeds from any disposition thereof.

C. RECOVERY OF THE COLLATERAL

If the holder of a secured claim recovers all of the property subject to its lien, it no longer has a secured claim. It might still have a claim; it does not, however, have a secured claim. To illustrate, D owes S $40,000. S has a security interest in D's equipment. D files a bankruptcy petition. S obtains relief from the stay and recovers all of the equipment. S no longer has a secured claim because, in the language of section 506(a), S no longer has a "lien on property in which the estate has an interest." If the value of the collateral that S received was less than the amount that D owed S, S still has a claim, but it is an unsecured claim. If, for example, the value of the equipment is only $17,000, S still has a $23,000 unsecured claim.

How can the holder of a secured claim recover its collateral? Nothing in the Bankruptcy Code bars the voluntary surrender of encumbered property to the creditor that holds a lien on it. Indeed, there are sections in the Bankruptcy Code that provide for releasing encumbered property to the creditor whose claim is secured by it. See sections 725, 1325(a)(5)(C); but cf. section 554. What if the debtor or trustee wants to retain the encumbered property?

1. Postpetition Foreclosure And Section 362(D)

Recall that the automatic stay bars the holder of a secured claim from seizing and selling its collateral, section 362(a). Accordingly, the holder of a secured claim cannot seize and sell its collateral until it obtains relief from the stay. What relief is available? What are the grounds for relief? Section 362(d) and the following cases deal with these questions.

In re Club Tower
United States Bankruptcy Court, N.D. Georgia, 1991
138 B.R. 307

ORDER ON MOTION TO DISMISS OR IN THE ALTERNATIVE
FOR RELIEF FROM AUTOMATIC STAY

Hugh Robinson, Jr., Bankruptcy Judge. On June 14, 1991, Movant, Teacher Retirement System of Texas (TRST) brought the above styled motion and for reasons set forth herein the court will grant the motion by lifting the automatic stay, for cause, per 11 U.S.C. §362(d)(1).

The facts are not in dispute and may be quickly summarized.

On June 6, 1991, Club Tower, L.P. (the "Debtor") commenced this bankruptcy case under Chapter 11 of the Bankruptcy Code.

On April 13, 1988, the Debtor and TRST entered into a Permanent Loan Agreement whereby TRST agreed to loan the Debtor up to $39,000,000.00 in order to provide permanent financing for Club Tower Apartments, a luxury high-rise apartment building owned by the Debtor and located in Fulton County, Georgia (the "Property").

* * *

TRST holds properly perfected first-priority, pre-petition liens and security interests in the Property, Rents and Leases.

Beginning in September 1990, the Debtor defaulted on its obligations to TRST under the Permanent Loan Agreement, as amended, and under the Security Deed.

After workout negotiations, Debtor and TRST entered into an agreement in February 1991, (the "Forbearance Agreement") whereby TRST agreed to forbear from exercising its rights and remedies as a secured creditor until May 31, 1991, provided that the Debtor was successful in raising $1,000,000 in new equity to cover deferred payments of interest on the loan and anticipated future operating deficits on the Property. * * *

As part of the Forbearance Agreement, the Debtor agreed that TRST would be entitled to immediate relief from the automatic stay in the event that the Debtor filed a petition for relief under the Bankruptcy Code.

On May 31, 1991, the Debtor informed TRST that it had been unsuccessful in raising the new equity as required by the Forbearance Agreement and requested an extension of time in which to continue its efforts. TRST consented to an additional extension of the forbearance period, conditioned upon the Debtor's payment of the net operating income generated by the Property during the month of May to TRST by June 6, 1991.

Debtor failed to pay the May net operating income as agreed and on June 6, 1991, filed the instant Chapter 11 bankruptcy proceeding.

Debtor has only one asset, namely, the Club Tower Apartment project.

Debtor has no employees. It has only a few unsecured creditors whose claims are de minimis. The dispute in question is basically one involving the Debtor and its secured lender.

Movant argues that the Debtor acted in bad faith by filing this bankruptcy petition and in the alternative, that the stay should be lifted per 11 U.S.C. §362(d)(1), for cause, because pre-petition, the Debtor had specifically agreed to transfer the Property to Movant if it could not meet the terms of the "Forbearance Agreement" which all agree were not met. This court agrees with Movant on both points.

A. Bad Faith Filing

Section 1112(b) of the Bankruptcy Code provides that the court may dismiss a case under Chapter 11 for "cause". 11 U.S.C. §1112(b). Courts have held that the Debtor's lack of good faith in filing a bankruptcy case constitutes "cause" for dismissing the case.

The courts have not articulated a particular test for determining whether a debtor has filed a petition in bad faith. Instead, they consider a variety of factors which evidence "an intent to abuse the judicial process and purposes of the reorganization provisions" or which demonstrated that the petition was filed "to delay or frustrate the legitimate efforts of secured creditors to enforce their rights." Phoenix Piccadilly, 849 F.2d at 1394 (quoting, Albany Partners, 749 F.2d at 674).

Among the factors considered are:

1. The Debtor has only one asset, the Property;

2. The Debtor has few unsecured creditors whose claims are small in relation to the claims of the secured creditor;

3. The Debtor has few employees;

4. The Property is the subject of a foreclosure action as a result of arrearages on the debt;

5. The Debtor's financial problems involve essentially a dispute between the Debtor and secured creditor which can be resolved in a state court action; and

6. The timing of the Debtor's filing evidences an intent to delay or frustrate the legitimate efforts of the Debtor's secured creditors to enforce their rights.

The Debtor has one asset, Club Tower Apartments. TRST's liens and security interests fully encumber that Property. The Debtor has only a few unsecured creditors whose claims are relatively small. The Debtor has no employees, no cash flow, and no available sources of income to sustain a plan of reorganization or to make adequate protection payments, all income from the Property having been absolutely assigned to TRST.

The court believes that the only objective in filing this case was to delay and frustrate the efforts of TRST to enforce its rights and remedies as a secured creditor. The Debtor and TRST agreed, as part of their negotiations regarding the forbearance period, that a $1,000,000 equity infusion was needed to bring the loan current and to offset future operating deficits on the Property. The Debtor agreed that if it was unsuccessful in raising the needed capital that it would convey title to the Property to TRST, and in fact, tendered a deed to the Property to an escrow agent with instructions to deliver the deed of Trust on June 1, 1991, if the new equity had not been raised. Having been unsuccessful in raising the needed equity and faced with the prospect of honoring its agreement with TRST, the Debtor filed this bankruptcy case.

There is no going concern to preserve, there are no employees to protect, and there appears to be little hope of rehabilitation.

   * * *

A bad faith filing of a bankruptcy petition constitutes "cause" justifying relief from the automatic stay under Section 362(d)(1) of the Bankruptcy Code. The test for determining whether a bankruptcy case was filed in bad faith is the same under Section 362 and Section 1112(b). Accordingly, because the Debtor filed this bankruptcy case in bad faith, TRST is entitled to relief from the automatic stay to exercise its rights and remedies as a secured creditor.

B. Forbearance Agreement and Waiver of Stay Protection

TRST also is entitled to relief from the automatic stay by virtue of the terms of the Second Amendment to Permanent Loan Agreement entered into by the Debtor and TRST as part of their Forbearance Agreement. Paragraph 8 of the Second Amendment to Permanent Loan Agreement provides that in the event that the Debtor files for bankruptcy, TRST "shall thereupon be entitled to relief from any automatic stay imposed by Section 362 of Title 11 of the U.S.Code, as amended, or otherwise, on or against the exercise of the rights and remedies otherwise available to [TRST]."

Pre-petition agreements regarding relief from stay are enforceable in bankruptcy.

* **

[E]nforcing a pre- bankruptcy agreement provision by which a debtor agrees not to oppose the granting to a lender of relief from stay is significantly different from a provision which prohibits a debtor from filing a bankruptcy petition and thus there is no violation of public policy.

First, by agreeing not to contest stay relief, Debtor was not estopped from filing for bankruptcy relief in general and has indeed filed its petition.

Second, Debtor agreed to and did in fact waive a single benefit of the Bankruptcy Code, not all of the rights and benefits provided by the Code as is the case where a borrower agrees to waive its right to file bankruptcy. Moreover, Debtor has already received the benefit of the automatic stay because TRST has been and presently is stayed from enforcing its rights under the Loan Documents. No provision in the Bankruptcy Code guarantees a debtor that the stay will remain in effect throughout the bankruptcy case. To the contrary, Congress specifically provided creditors a means for obtaining relief from stay.

Furthermore, Debtor still retains the benefits of the automatic stay as to other creditors, as well as all the other benefits and protections provided by the Bankruptcy Code including but not limited to the right to conduct an orderly liquidation, discharge debt or pay it back on different terms, assume or reject executory contracts, sell property free and clear of liens, and pursue preferences and fraudulent conveyance claims. Debtor still retains the core rights under the Bankruptcy Code and has the ability to make a "fresh start". Therefore, enforcing Debtor's agreement does not violate the public policy concerns that agreements which prohibit a borrower from filing for bankruptcy violate.

Moreover, enforcing pre-petition settlement agreements furthers the legitimate public policy of encouraging out of court restructurings and settlements. The Bankruptcy Code also recognizes that the filing of a bankruptcy petition might not always be the most efficient means of restructuring the relations of a debtor and its creditors. See 11 U.S.C. §305(a).

Workouts and restructurings should be encouraged among debtors and creditors, particularly where, as here, there is a debt between two parties and a single asset. Under these circumstances, filing for bankruptcy should be a last resort. In order to facilitate this goal, pre-petition agreements should be enforced against a borrower who later files for bankruptcy. To hold otherwise could make lenders more reticent in attempting workouts with borrowers outside of bankruptcy.

Therefore, the court does hereby vacate the automatic stay of 11 U.S.C. §362(d)(1) and will grant the motion of TRST.

IT IS SO ORDERED.

Notes and Problems

1. Under the Bankruptcy Code, "cause" is a basis for dismissing a case under section 1112 and is a basis for granting relief from the automatic stay under section 362(d)(1). Under the *Club Tower* case, bad faith in filing the bankruptcy petition is "cause" for purposes of both section 1112 and section 362(d)(1). Why did TRST move for relief from the stay instead of move to dismiss?

2. Should prepetition agreements between the debtor and a creditor regarding relief from stay be enforceable in bankruptcy? Whom does the automatic stay protect? Would a prepetition agreement regarding relief from stay constitute "cause" for purposes of section 362(d)(1) if

   a. The agreement was a part of the original loan document, rather than the Forbearance Agreement?

   b. The debtor had numerous other significant creditors, instead of "only a few unsecured creditors whose claims are de minimis"?

3. "[A]ll theorists assume that bankruptcy law is a mandatory rule: it is a rule set in place by the government that cannot be altered by those whom it affects. The mandatory nature of bankruptcy, however, in anomalous when viewed in the larger context of general contract law. Most rules governing the consensual relationship among various parties are default rules. In other words, they apply only if the parties do not provide otherwise. Faced with this anomaly, it is time for bankruptcy scholarship to address the question of who should decide when a firm is eligible for corporate reorganization under the auspices of the Bankruptcy Code." Robert Rasmussen, *Debtor's Choice: A Menu Approach to Corporate Bankruptcy*, 71 TEXAS L.REV. 51, 53 (1992).

꠸꠸꠸꠸꠸

Most of the reported section 362(d)(1) cases, and the next two cases in the book, involve the interpretation and application of the statutory phrase "adequate protection of an interest in property."

In re Alyucan Interstate Corp.
United States Bankruptcy Court, Utah, 1981.
12 B.R. 803.

Introduction and Background

Ralph R. Mabey, Bankruptcy Judge. This case raises the question whether an "equity cushion" is necessary to provide adequate protection under Section 362(d)(1). This Court concludes that it is not.

On January 14, 1981, Alyucan Interstate Corporation (debtor), a construction and real estate development firm, filed a petition under Chapter 11 of the Code. On May 4, Bankers Life Insurance Company of Nebraska (Bankers Life), holder of a trust deed on realty owned by debtor, brought this action for relief from the automatic stay under Section 362(d). The complaint alleges that the realty secures a debt in the principal amount of $1,220,000 and that Bankers Life is not adequately protected. On May 20, the preliminary hearing contemplated by Section 362(e) was held. After receiving evidence, the Court fixed the value of the realty on the date of the petition at $1,425,000 and found that there had been no erosion in that value as of the hearing. The debt owing was $1,297,226 as of the petition, and with interest accruing at roughly $8,000 per month, had increased to $1,330,761 as of the hearing. Thus, there was an "equity cushion" of $127,774 or approximately nine percent of the value of the collateral, as of the petition, which had decreased to $94,239, or approximately six and one half percent of the value of the collateral, as of the hearing. As interest accumulates, and if no payments are made, this cushion will dissipate within a year.

The Meaning of Adequate Protection

Section 362(d)(1) mandates relief, in some form, from the stay "for cause, including the lack of adequate protection of an interest in property." The only cause asserted in this proceeding is a lack of adequate protection.

Adequate protection is not defined in the Code. This omission was probably deliberate. Congress was aware of the turbulent rivalry of interests in reorganization. It needed a concept which would mediate polarities. But a carefully calibrated concept, subject to a brittle construction, could not accommodate the "infinite number of variations possible in dealings between debtors and creditors." This problem required, not a formula, but a calculus, open-textured, pliant, and versatile, adaptable to "new ideas" which are "continually being implemented in this field" and to "varying circumstances and changing modes of financing." Adequate protection was requisitioned to meet these needs. Its meaning, therefore, is born afresh out of the "reflective equilibrium" of each decision, understood through analysis of the reorganization context and the language of Section 362(d).

A. The Reorganization Context

Relief from the stay cannot be viewed in isolation from the reorganization process. Bankruptcy in general and Chapter 11 in particular are "procedural devices" for the rehabilitation of financially embarrassed enterprises. The process presupposes dynamic rather than static uses of property and denouement in a plan which accommodates the many, not just the few.

The automatic stay, within this framework, is designed "to prevent a chaotic and uncontrolled scramble for the debtor's assets in a variety of uncoordinated proceedings in different courts." It grants a "breathing spell" for debtors to regroup. It shields creditors from one another by replacing "race" and other preferential systems of debt collection with a more equitable and orderly distribution of assets. It encourages rehabilitation: debtors may seek its asylum while recovery is possible rather than coasting to the point of no return; creditors, realizing that foreclosure is useless, may rechannel energies toward more therapeutic ends.

Although self-help and other unilateral recourse against debtors are forbidden, creditors are not left remediless. They may act through committees with professional assistance, often at the expense of the estate, or by seeking appointment of a trustee or examiner. Conversion to Chapter 7 and dismissal are options. Within certain time constraints, they may file a plan.

In short, the adequate protection vouchsafed creditors in Chapter 11 is interim protection, designed not as a purgative of all creditor ailments, but as a palliative of the worst: re-organization, dismissal, or liquidation will provide the final relief. During this interim, the policies favoring rehabilitation and the benefits derived from the stay should not be lightly discarded. Alternative remedies are available to creditors. Indeed, even relief from the stay need not mean termination of the stay. Section 362(d) provides for relief, *such as* "terminating, annulling, modifying, or conditioning" the stay. Thus, relief may be fashioned to suit the exigencies of the case.

B. The Language of Section 362(d)

Turning from Chapter 11 at large to Section 362(d) in specific, several issues must be addressed. First, what is the "interest in property" being protected? Second, what aspects of the "interest in property" require protection? Third, from what is the "interest in property" being protected? Fourth, what is the method of protection?

(1) What is the "interest in property" being protected? The legislative history mentions only "the interest of a secured creditor or co-owner of property with the debtor" in connection with adequate protection. H.R.Rep. No. 95-595, 95th Cong., 1st Sess. 338 (1977). This classification is important because adequate protection depends upon the interest *and* property involved. Treatment of a secured creditor who faces turnover may be different from treatment of a secured creditor who has not repossessed. Treatment of a senior lienholder may be different from treatment of a junior lienholder. Similarly, protection may

vary if the property is real or personal, tangible or intangible, perdurable or perishable, or if its value is constant, depreciating, or subject to sudden or extreme fluctuations. Also relevant is the proposed use or idleness of the property.

(2) What aspects of the "interest in property" require protection? Adequate protection is concerned with the value of the interest in property. The legislative commentary to Section 361 underscores this point: "Though the creditor might not receive his bargain in kind, the purpose of the section is to insure that the secured creditor receives *in value* essentially what he bargained for." Id. at 339. (Emphasis supplied.) The legislative history reemphasizes this point by noting that adequate protection is "derived from the fifth amendment protection of property interests," id., citing Wright v. Union Central Insurance Co., 311 U.S. 273, 61 S.Ct. 196, 85 L.Ed. 184 (1940) and Louisville Bank v. Redford, 295 U.S. 555, 55 S.Ct. 854, 79 L.Ed. 1593 (1935). In *Wright*, Justice Douglas held that the bank received "the value of the [interest in] property" and that "there is no constitutional claim of a creditor to more than that." Debtors were allowed to redeem the property at its appraised price, despite an obligation which exceeded the value of the collateral by $10,000. Thus, the "interest in property" entitled to protection is not measured by the amount of the debt but by the value of the lien. A mushrooming debt, through accrual of interest or otherwise, may be immaterial, if the amount of the lien is not thereby increased, while vicissitudes in the market, loss of insurance or other factors affecting the value of the lien are relevant to adequate protection. The purpose of adequate protection is to assure the recoverability of this value during the hiatus between petition and plan, or in the event the reorganization is stillborn, between petition and dismissal.[1]

---

[1]   Some cases have interpreted adequate protection more in terms of contractual benefits than economic values. They have focused on language in the legislative history suggesting that secured creditors must receive the "benefit of their bargain." H.R.Rep. No. 95-595, 95th Cong., 1st Sess. 339 (1977). Congress, however, was not referring to the *contractual* bargain between creditors and debtors because the next portion of the House Report acknowledges "there may be situations in bankruptcy where giving a secured creditor an absolute right to his bargain may be impossible or seriously detrimental to the bankruptcy laws. Thus, this section [Section 361] recognizes the availability of alternate means of protecting a secured creditor's interest. Though the creditor might not receive his bargain in kind, the purpose of the section in to insure that the secured creditor receives in value essentially what he bargained for." Id. Whether and to what extent noncontractual or business elements of a bargain may be factored into the adequate protection equation is problematical. Some courts, employing an equity cushion analysis (discussed below), insists that a ratio of debt to collateral is "bargained for" between debtor and creditor and must be considered in determining adequate protection. The stream of inquiry along this path, however, may be difficult to contain. Many business motives, which may or may not be expressed in the documents memorializing a transaction, could then become relevant to adequate protection. As a practical matter, for example, foreclosure may not be an attractive prospect for some lenders who are, after all, in the business of loaning money not managing properties.

(3) From what is the "interest in property" being protected? The short answer is from any impairment in value attributable to the stay. The stay does not cause, but it may forestall a creditor from preventing or mitigating, a decline in value. Some harm to collateral, however, may be unavoidable with or without the stay. Likewise, creditors may acquiesce in some harm to collateral for business or other reasons notwithstanding the stay. In these situations, and others which may arise, any impairment in value may not be attributable to the stay. Hence, not every decline in value must be recompensed, only those which, but for the stay, could be and probably would be prevented or mitigated.

(4) What is the method of protection? The method of affording adequate protection, as noted above, will vary with the interest in property to be protected. In some cases, the debtor[1] need do nothing, either because the value of the interest in property is not declining or because the decline in value is not attributable to the stay. If the stay is responsible for a decline in value, Section 361 states three illustrative methods for providing adequate protection. Some courts, however, have not looked beyond its trilogy of alternatives. Others have insisted on a showing of indubitable equivalence. These approaches miss the mark: they violate the non-prescriptive character of Section 361, and may simply exchange one imponderable for another. Indubitable equivalence is not a method; nor does it have substantive content. Indeed, something "indubitable" is more than "adequate;" "equivalent" is more than "protection;" hence, the illustration may eclipse the concept. At best, it is a semantic substitute for adequate protection and one with dubious, not indubitable, application to the question of relief from the stay.

C. Application to This Proceeding

In this proceeding, the "interest in property" is the lien of Bankers Life on the realty of debtor. It is a trust deed and therefore may be peremptorily foreclosed. It is a first lien with ample collateral to protect Bankers Life. The collateral and therefore the lien are not declining or subject to sudden depreciation in value. Bankers Life is suffering no pain cognizable under

---

Hence, their bargain is primarily for payment with interest and, as a last resort, for liquidation with its burdens of custodial care and costs. Foreclosure may likewise pose regulatory complications. Banks and insurance companies are traditionally limited in the amount of illiquid assets, such as realty, which they can carry at any given time in their portfolio.

[1]   The legislative history notes that the debtor-in-possession or trustee, not the court, must provide adequate protection. Otherwise, the court is forced into an administrative role at odds with the spirit of the Code. Courts, however, have gone beyond this adjudicative function, and in some instances, have actively fashioned protection for creditors. This result may be inevitable given the exigencies and informalities of relief from stay proceedings. Indeed, it grows out of the language of Section 362(d) which mandates relief such as "modifying" or "conditioning" the stay.

Section 362 as a result of the stay, and relief from the stay is therefore, at this juncture, unnecessary.

Moreover, this property is essential to the reorganization of the debtor. Foreclosure and liquidation of the property would run counter to this need and would deprive debtor and other creditors of its going concern value. If liquidation is allowed, it should occur under the aegis of the Court and in the interests of all. Bankers Life is no better qualified to handle this liquidation than the debtor or the trustee. Indeed, Bankers Life may be ill-equipped to undertake this task, both because its interests are parochial and because, for regulatory or other reasons, it may be a reluctant caretaker. In any event, Bankers Life has other remedies under the Code. A trustee has been appointed. It may work with him or with creditor committees to negotiate a sale of the property. It can seek dismissal or conversion to Chapter 7. It can propose a plan of liquidation. In short, the application of adequate protection to the facts of this case avoids the trauma of relief from the stay and maintains the equilibrium of interests in this reorganization.

The Equity Cushion Analysis

In contrast to these principles, there is a trend toward defining adequate protection in terms of an "equity cushion": the difference between outstanding debt and the value of the property against which the creditor desires to act. Where the difference is substantial, a cushion is said to exist, adequately protecting the creditor. As interest accrues, or depreciation advances, and the margin declines, the cushion weakens and the stay may be lifted. Naturally, courts disagree on what is an acceptable margin. The emerging view, however, may be that the stay should be terminated when the cushion will be absorbed through interest, commissions, and other costs of resale. The cushion analysis enjoys practical appeal and ease of application.

This Court rejects a cushion analysis upon four grounds: (1) It is inconsistent with the purpose of adequate protection. (2) It is inconsistent with the illustrations of adequate protection found in Section 361. (3) It is inconsistent with the statutory scheme of Section 362(d). (4) It has no basis in the historical development of relief from stay proceedings.

(1) The cushion analysis, by focusing on the ratio of debt to collateral, obscures the purpose of adequate protection, *viz.*, to guard against impairment of a lien. This blurring of objectives may produce improper results. If Bankers Life had been undersecured at the petition, for example, the absence of cushion would have dictated relief from the stay, even though the stay did not impair its lien and notwithstanding the usual appreciation in the value of realty.

(2) Since the thrust of adequate protection is to assure maintenance of the value of the lien, it is largely compensatory. Sections 361(1) and (2) therefore speak not in terms of preserving equity but in terms of compensating for any "decrease in the value of [an] interest in property." Moreover, the cushion analysis, because it is confined to the relationship between debt and collateral in

a specific property, ignores the recoverability of value, not only from the property at stake but also from other sources. Sections 361(1) and (2), which provide for interim payments and replacement liens, contemplate that value from other assets held by debtors may be appropriated to supply any needed protection. Indeed, the legislative history to Section 361 suggests the use of sureties or guarantors for this purpose. Even if the debtor has no other assets, it is nevertheless conceivable that an enterprise valuation, which approaches value in terms of capitalized earnings, could show an income potential sufficient to meet the adequate protection standard.

(3) Under Section 362(d)(2) a lack of equity, absent a further showing that the property is unnecessary to an effective reorganization, does not warrant relief from the stay. This statutory provision expresses a legislative judgment, first, that it is the *absence* of equity rather than any particular cushion which is the criterion for relief from stay, and second, that the absence of equity is not alone dispositive—the court must still weigh the necessity of the property to an effective reorganization. The cushion analysis is inconsistent with this judgment. It makes surplusage out of Section 362(d)(2) which speaks in terms of equity *and* reorganization. Indeed, this dual requirement emphasizes the role of equity, when present, not as a cushion, but to underwrite, through sale or credit, the rehabilitation of debtors.[1]

Conclusion

Adequate protection is a concept designed to balance the rights of creditors and debtors in the preliminary stages of reorganization. It is, in each case, *ad hoc*. For this reason the cushion analysis, which may be helpful in general, falls short in the particular. It is not fully alert to the legislative directive that "the

---

[1] Sections 362(d)(1) and (d)(2) are separated by the disjunctive "or," which is defined in Section 102(5) to mean "not exclusive." This suggests, as a number of cases have held, that (d)(1) and (d)(2) provide alternate criteria for relief from the stay. This conclusion, however, may be questioned on two grounds. First, the preface to (d)(2) speaks of stays of "an act against property." This suggests that (d)(2) may be the exclusive standard for relief from the stay where property is involved. This suggestion is reinforced by legislative history which earmarks (d)(2) "to solve the problem of real property mortgage foreclosures of property where the bankruptcy petition is filed on the eve of foreclosure." 124 Cong.Rec. H 11,092-11,093 (September 28, 1978). Section 362(e) speaks even more specifically of "the stay of any act against property of the estate." Such particularized draftsmanship may connote a special distinction and purpose. The courts, however, have shown indifference on this score, and have applied (d)(1), which refers to adequate protection of an "interest in property," to relief from stay actions concerning property. Second, the legislative backdrop to "or" is illuminating: "Or" means "not exclusive," which in turn means "if a party 'may do (a) or (b),' then the party may do either or both." Does the court, then, have discretion to apply either (d)(1) or (d)(2) alone or both (d)(1) and (d)(2) together in determining whether relief from the stay is appropriate? And given the legislative history noted above, in the case of a foreclosure on realty, should the court ordinarily defer to (d)(2)?

facts," in each hearing under Section 362(d), "will determine whether relief is appropriate under the circumstances." H.R.Rep. No. 95-595, 95th Cong., 1st Sess. 344 (1977). The facts of each case, thoughtfully weighed, not formularized, define adequate protection.

Notes and Problems

1. Under section 362(d)(1), a holder of a secured claim can obtain relief from the automatic stay by establishing "the lack of adequate protection of an interest in property of such party." What is the meaning of the phrase "interest in property"? From what is this "interest in property" being protected?

2. According to the second paragraph of the edited *Alyucan* opinion, "as interest accumulates and if no payments are made, the cushion will dissipate within a year." Why didn't Bankers' Life wait until the cushion dissipated before seeking relief from the stay? Can Bankers' Life file another stay relief motion after the equity cushion has dissipated?

3. In the *Alyucan* case, interest accumulated postpetition because the value of the collateral was greater than the amount of the debt. Recall that section 506(b) expressly grants postpetition interest to *oversecured* parties. Until the Supreme Court decision in *United Savings Association of Texas v. Timbers of Inwood Forest Assocs.*, 108 S. Ct. 626 (1988), it had been argued that "adequate protection" under section 362(d)(1) provides an "interest-like" entitlement to *undersecured* creditors. The Supreme Court rejected that argument in the *Timbers* case. There a Chapter 11 debtor, an apartment complex limited partnership, owed more than $4.3 million to C, a creditor that had a deed of trust on the apartment complex. The collateral was worth at most $4.25 million and was not depreciating in value. C moved for relief from the stay contending that "adequate protection" under section 362(d) included payment to it of "lost opportunity costs." More specifically, C argued

   (i) part of its "interest in property" is the right to seize and sell its collateral when the debtor defaults;

   (ii) if the debtor had not filed for bankruptcy, C could have sold the apartment complex for $4.25 million;

   (iii) C could have then loaned this $4.25 million to another debtor and received interest on the new $4.25 million loan;

   (iv) accordingly, in order to provide "adequate protection" of C's "interest in the property" as contemplated by section 362(d), the automatic stay should be conditioned on the debtor's making monthly payments to C equal to the amount that C would be receiving in interest payments on a new loan of

$4.25 million. In sum, C's argument was that "adequate protection" means that a debtor is compelled to pay a secured creditor for its "lost opportunity costs."

Looking to both legislative history and statutory language such as section 506(b), the Supreme Court in *Timbers* rejected this argument.

In re BBT
United States Bankruptcy Court, Nevada, 1981
11 B.R. 224

Burt M. Goldwater, Bankruptcy Judge. This is an adversary action to lift the automatic stay in a Chapter 11 reorganization and a counterclaim for accounting and turnover of funds. The background of the parties is as follows:

As of December 30, 1978, BBT had executed four agreements by which 200 general purpose 70-ton boxcars were purchased from a Mexican manufacturer and builder pursuant to a purchase agreement with American Financial Corporation under which: (1) The principal agreement takes the form of a Conditional Sales Agreement between The Provident Bank (Provident), an Ohio banking corporation, as vendor or agent and defendant debtor, a limited partnership, as vendee; (2) BBT as owner appointed Railway Freight Car Services, Inc., as its agent to perform all of the duties of the Conditional Sales Agreement; (3) BBT as owner entered into an agreement with Columbus & Greenville Railway Company (C & G), a short-line railroad in Mississippi, as its manager of the boxcars; and (4) BBT assigned its Agency Agreement and Management Agreement to Provident.

The sales price of the boxcars, $7,500,000, was 80/20 financing. BBT paid a $1,500,000 cash down payment leaving a balance of $6,000,000 payable in quarterly installments over a period of 15 years with interest at 12-1/2, 16-1/2 in the event of default. Debtor paid approximately $1,500,000 in payments on the debt but defaulted on an installment payment of principal and interest on October 30, 1980. The Conditional Sales Agreement also calls for payment to a Maintenance Fund Escrow which payments due quarterly were alleged to be $1,250 short on January 30, 1980, and totally defaulted on October 30, 1980.
* * *

Provident contends there is cause including a lack of adequate protection [§362(d)(1)], and, further, that the property is not necessary to an effective reorganization [§362(d)(2)].

The acquisition of the boxcars in 1978 was at a time when tax laws encouraged investment in rolling stock. The manufacture and acquisition of rolling stock, particularly boxcars, increased rapidly until there were more than adequate numbers to service the nation's railroad freight demands. When the national economy began slowing in 1979, the utilization of boxcars began to drop until today those boxcars which do not have a priority for utilization have little or no use. BBT not only is not in a priority position with C & G, but general purpose boxcars are the last of railroad stock to be put into use. Special boxcars, gondolas, flatcars, and others are usually called up for use before general purpose cars.

The present flat market for general purpose boxcars began in mid-1980 and is expected to continue for at least one year and, according to some experts, eighteen months to two years. It is expected to definitely improve from its low as the business cycle changes.

There are no manufacturers now adding general purpose boxcars to the supply but some manufacturers are gearing up expecting that after the passage of time demand will justify production. Old boxcars are gradually being retired and experience shows there have been low and high demands with changes in the business cycle over the last 35 years.

The BBT boxcars are worth between $20,000 and $25,000 per car at fair market value.[1] A sale of boxcars requires the seller to deliver the cars (per mile charge per unit to place of delivery), paint new logos for the buyer, and pay a commission for the sale. The useful life of a general purpose boxcar is 20 to 40 years. After 20 years a complete overhaul is necessary.

The 200 BBT all-steel 70-ton general purpose boxcars are located at numerous sidings along the C & G lines in Mississippi. They are in good condition. A few minor, easily repairable damages can be seen on examination. They have not been vandalized or rusted. They are standard in grade, desirable in size for American railroad use, and well constructed.

Witnesses on market use and sale value of boxcars testified that there are movements in the market for boxcars from time-to-time but the market for boxcars is a very special area. BBT is engaged in discussions with railroads and others in the market place. Some of these discussions tend to look encouraging but there is nothing definite as to any of the offers or pending negotiations. Various factors affecting market price always must be considered, but, in general, the market price of $20,000 to $25,000 has been a firm plateau since the filing of this case.[2]

---

[1]   Plaintiff's witness David Eckles. Defendant did not use any witness as to market value preferring to rely on $20,000 as a present fair market value. Eckles testified an investor with funds of his own or access to funds at a reasonable rate would be wise at this time to invest his money at $20,000 per boxcar and hold for the future. He further testified that since the middle of 1980 to the present, there has been little fluctuation in the value of railcars.

[2]   In event of depreciation, a method of adequate protection is suggested by §361(1) for periodic cash payments to the extent of a decrease in value. See In re Bermec Corp., 445 F.2d 367 (2d Cir.1971). Collier states: "The most important message of the Code with respect to the treatment of entities with an interest in property of the estate is that their remedies may be suspended even abrogated, their right of recourse to collateral may be terminated as it is consumed in the business, but the *value* of their secured position *as*

The sense of adequate protection is that there be protection for the realization of payment of a claim against the property as of the date of filing the case. As a matter of policy and constitutional law, this protection extends only to a creditor's "allowed secured claim" and the unsecured part of a claim will not be entitled to protection.

An "allowed secured claim" is a determination generally made under §506[1] which provides an allowed claim of a creditor secured by a lien on property has an interest in the estate's interest, and, to the extent that the value is less than the amount of the total allowed claim, the claim is unsecured.

For the purpose of this hearing under Section 362, Provident is adequately secured in that it had, as of the date of filing, a security interest in 200 general purpose boxcars with a market value of $4,000,000 which cars are not depreciating in value and are likely to increase.

During trial BBT produced a letter, backed by reliable bank credit, from Peter S. Bing, its limited partner, which offered Provident $4,150,000 in cash. Provident refused the offer believing it has the right to either (1) vacate the stay or (2) provide its own plan to protect its claim. BBT argues that Provident's success in terminating the stay can only result in Provident's repossession which would required a commercially reasonable U.C.C. sale likely to bring only $4,000,000 or even less after sales costs. However, BBT overlooks Provident's right at such sale to bid its claim, and, if it is the highest bidder, to hold the boxcars until the market justified a sale or other agreement by which it could recoup more than the open court offer.

Provident is entitled to incidental protection from damages, taxes and parking charges. The C & G is not charging for parking the boxcars (usually $7.00 per day per unit). There is sufficient cash held in accounts created by the agreement of the parties to cover insurance premiums (approximately $17,000 per year), repairs, taxes, and other charges.

While BBT has no equity there remains the issue as to whether there may be an effective reorganization. §362(d)(2) is in the conjunctive. Lack of value equity [plaintiff's only burden of proof §362(g)(1)] is conceded here, but that does not alone suffice for lifting the stay. There must also be a failure by defendant to show that the property is necessary to an effective reorganization. §362(d)(2)(B).

The showing here is that these boxcars produced in excess of $1,500,000 between May of 1979 and the end of 1980—a period of 16 months, but the utilization fell from 92 in August of 1979 to 15 in August 1980. Thus there is a record of production when business conditions bring about utilization. An

---

it existed at the commencement of the case is to be protected throughout the case when adequate protection is required." (Emphasis added.) 2 Collier on Bankruptcy 361-6 (15th ed. 1980).

[1] Of course, the value determined in the light of the purpose of vacating the automatic stay may not be the same as the value for another purpose such as confirmation of a plan. §506(a).

effective plan is a plan which is feasible and must be received and weighed in the light of the condition of the economy, the quality of management, the sources of capital necessary to the production of income, and the resiliency of the business to weather the cycles of change.

It is clear than an effective reorganization is a possibility. Every indication is that the future utilization of the boxcars will improve albeit over an extended time. BBT uses professional management and agency teams well known in the railroad area and sophisticated in dealing with general use boxcars, and BBT has shown it has access to a large amount of cash from an outside source.

There cannot be an "allowed secured claim" in excess of the value of the collateral. §506 defines the method of determination of the secured status. It would be anomalous to say that the formula of Section 506 should not be used to determine adequate protection. Naturally, where the property is shrinking in value the secured claimant is not protected without payment or additional security, but, where the value of the collateral is firm, the secured creditor is adequately protected in the sense of the Bankruptcy Code if the collateral is otherwise properly insured, relieved of taxes and properly maintained.

Here the Court finds there is no undue risk of material harm to Provident and there is a possibility of reorganization. In the gap of time between filing and confirmation, plaintiff is entitled only to demand the value continue to be in that amount which was the value of the collateral at the commencement of the case.[1]

It must be remembered that Section 362 is designed as a holding pattern for secured claims under the Code providing there is adequate protection until a plan takes hold. Should the case be dismissed, or confirmation denied, the secured claimant is entitled to the interim adequate protection.[2] If a plan is confirmed the secured claimant is entitled to the rights provided in §1129 and to the election under §1111(b)(2).

To the extent the protection found here proves to be inadequate after the fact, i.e., the value of the collateral falls below the $4,000,000 stipulated to be its

---

[1]   Some courts refer to the "cushion" which may be defined as an excess of value over debt. This is a concept to relieve the necessity of providing further security or payment because there is an area of value which may shrink but yet not fall below the secured claim. In such case where value exceeds debt the interest on the security is also protected. §506(d). In the event the allowed secured claim, at the time of filing is less than the secured claim, interest stops post-petition because there is no collateral security for additional debt. §502(b)(2).

[2]   In the event a Chapter 11 debtor exercises its absolute right to convert the case to Chapter 7 [e 1112(a)], the secured claimant does not have the right to elect under §1111(b)(2), is relegated to the value of its security under §506, and is, if there is recourse, simply an unsecured creditor as to the deficiency. The right of the secured claimant as to the unpaid balance depends upon the existence of a right of recourse. §502(b)(1). Right to recourse is immaterial in the election under §1111(b)(2). A Chapter 11 case converted to Chapter 7 pretty well frees the collateral in most undersecured claims. The trustee may only sell if there is a fair possibility of realizing something for general creditors.

fair market value at the time of filing, Provident would be entitled to request a priority even over administrative expenses. The Court is given power in §361(3) to grant such compensation ahead of priority administrative expense. §503(b)(1). But, when, as here, the secured claimant refused what appears to be the indubitable equivalent ($4,150,000 in cash which was stipulated at the time to be the fair market value) there is a serious question whether the Court should give further protection under Section 361(3), even if the collateral depreciates although a secured claimant has a right to refuse cash out at the time a plan is proposed by the election in Section 1111(b)(2). * * *

 * * *

A debtor cannot arbitrarily and unreasonably stay a secured claimant. The purpose of Chapter 11, as in the entire history of reorganization in bankruptcy, is to relieve the distressed debtor where there is reasonable expectation of continued useful existence of the business. ***

A case must be filed in good faith, else there is cause, independent of lack of adequate protection, to vacate the automatic stay. ***

The petition in this case was filed because of a drastic downturn in the market for utilization of boxcars and it is predicated on the potential that there is an expected upturn in the market. If it is pure speculation, it is not enough. ***

The testimony in this case from both sides is that it will be one to two years for the business cycle to bring about general boxcar utilization.

The issue is now good faith in the light and purpose of the Code that "secured creditors shall not be deprived of the benefit of their bargain." H.R.Rep. No. 95-595, 95th Cong., 1st Sess. 339 (1977).

Provident financed BBT with two general partners having assets of approximately $10,000 and with no "on line" lease or use payments to back up the conditional sale payment schedule. Thus, Provident knew or should have known that BBT was dependent upon the market utilization for general purpose boxcars and would have no recourse to any sources with which to make payments in the event of a slump in utilization. Testimony was that generally lenders require borrowers to show ready source of income by lease or other agreement to amortize a loan.

Provident's bargain is that it is entitled to payment subject to the provisions of the Bankruptcy Code and adequate protection for the collateral until payment.

Essentially, Provident's allegations of cause for lifting the stay is that this case was not filed in good faith because there is no likelihood of an improvement in the market for boxcars within a reasonably foreseeable future and Provident is suffering during the pendency of the stay.

It is true that BBT was able to show only two possibilities in the near future for utilization. In both cases BBT was frank to admit that the opportunities were uncertain and indefinite, and, in one case, dependent upon ICC approval as a condition of its contractual opportunities with one rail line. Provident thus concludes that BBT has no meaningful proposal and only "high hopes".

 * * *

The Court has been shown during the trial of this case that BBT has access to funds outside the limited partnership when BBT's limited partner made a cash offer of $4,150,000. It is as clear as the day follows night that BBT has no present income and has only some cash deposit with Provident and very limited assets of its general partners' corporations. It is eminently clear that BBT cannot be reorganized unless it can provide a plan which will meet its obligation to Provident. It is also patently clear that Provident, at least during the trial will not accept a cash out. Under the circumstances where it appears a debtor has shown a bona fide access to substantial sums of cash that debtor should be given an opportunity to file a plan if during an interim period there is no decrease in the value of the collateral. *** Boxcar deals take time. Hence, BBT should be given an opportunity to present a plan because BBT has shown that it is not totally and wholly without possibility of reorganization and may be able to carry its burden of payments and protection until there is a change in the business cycle which brings about utilization of its property so as to be self-supporting.

This case was filed November 10, 1980. The plan should be filed on or, preferably, before, November 9, 1981, together with a disclosure statement. This is reasonable.

The hearing on the disclosure statement *and* for confirmation of the plan should be consolidated and set for 30 days after filing the plan and statement.

The plaintiff's complaint to vacate the stay should be dismissed.

Notes and Problems

1. In *BBT*, Provident invoked both section 362(d)(1) and section 362(d)(2). What is the relationship between section 362(d)(1) and (d)(2)? According to *In re St. Peter's School*, 16 B.R. 404, 408 (Bkrtcy.S.D.N.Y.1982), "The grounds for relief under subsections (d)(1) and (d)(2) are stated in the alternative. Therefore, a creditor who establishes a basis for relief from the automatic stay under section (d)(2) is not automatically entitled to relief if the debtor is able to prove that notwithstanding such proof the creditor is nevertheless adequately protected under subsection (d)(1)." Do you agree?

2. Please carefully reread section 362(d)(2). How can the court determine whether "the debtor does not have an equity in such property"? Did BBT have an equity in the boxcars? It had made a $1,500,000 down payment and installment payments of another $1,500,000.

    Assume that D owes $500,000 to X and $400,000 to Y and that both X and Y have mortgages in Redacre. If Redacre has a value of $600,000, does D have any equity in Redacre?

3. What is the practical significance of the word "and" at the end of section 362(d)(2)(A)?

4. What is the significance of the word "effective" in section 362(d)(2)(B)? Is the word "reorganization" in section 362(d)(2)(B) important? Will property ever be necessary to an effective reorganization" in a Chapter 7 case? In a Chapter 13 case?

5. Is Judge Goldwater's application and discussion of section 362(d)(2) inconsistent with Justice Scalia's discussion of section 362(d)(2) in *United Savings Association of Texas v. Timbers of Inwood Forest Associates, Ltd.*, 108 S. Ct. 626 (1988): "Once the movant under section 362(d)(2) establishes that he is an undersecured creditor, it is the burden of the debtor to establish that the collateral at issue is 'necessary to an effective reorganization.' *See* section 362(g). What this requires is not merely a showing that if there is conceivably to be an effective reorganization, this property will be needed for it; but that the property is essential for an effective reorganization that is in prospect. This means, as many lower courts, including the en banc court in this case, have properly said, that there must be 'a reasonable possibility of a successful reorganization within a reasonable time.'"

2. Prepetition Foreclosure And Section 542

Section 362 and the preceding cases point up the problems that the holder of a secured claim encounters in attempting to foreclose on encumbered property in the possession of the debtor at the time that a bankruptcy petition is filed. Since postpetition recovery of collateral is so difficult, should secured creditors foreclose prior to bankruptcy, at the first sign of trouble? What are the relevant business considerations? Bankruptcy law considerations? Does a bankruptcy filing affect the rights of a holder of a secured claim who is in possession of its collateral? *See* sections 362, 542, and 543 and the following case.

In re Attinello
United States Bankruptcy Court, Eastern District of Pennsylvania, 1984
38 B.R. 609

Thomas M. Twardowski, Bankruptcy Judge.

At issue in this adversary proceeding is the right to possession of a 1980 Freightliner tractor (hereinafter "tractor"), which is currently in the possession of the plaintiff as a result of the plaintiff's pre-petition repossession of it from the Chapter 13 debtors-defendants. The plaintiff seeks, pursuant to Section 362(d) relief from the automatic stay so that it may pursue its state law remedies with regard to the tractor. The debtors seek turnover of the tractor to them pursuant to Sections 542 and 543 of the Bankruptcy Code. For the reasons hereinafter given, we shall deny the plaintiff relief from the automatic stay and grant the debtors' request for turnover.

I. Facts

The facts essential to our resolution of this matter are as follows. Pursuant to a Transfer and Assumption Agreement (hereinafter "security agreement"), dated January 22, 1982, the debtors became jointly liable to the plaintiff for payment of the $36,639.37 balance due on the aforementioned tractor while the plaintiff retained its perfected security interest in the tractor. The security agreement provided, *inter alia*, for the debtors to make a payment of $890.83 on January 25, 1982, followed by 27 consecutive monthly installment payments of $1,324.02. The monthly installment payments were to be paid on the 25th of each month, beginning with February 25, 1982. The debtors made the required payments through September 25, 1982, but did not make any payments thereafter. Therefore, on January 28, 1983, the plaintiff lawfully repossessed the tractor. At that time and prior thereto, debtor James Attinello had been using the tractor in his employment as a long-haul independent truck driver.

On February 2, 1983, pursuant to the security agreement, the debtors received notification from the plaintiff that the tractor would be sold on February 22, 1983 unless the debtors redeemed the tractor by payment of the $31,157.71 redemption price before the scheduled sale.

The sale was stayed, however, by the debtors' filing of their Chapter 13 bankruptcy petition in our Court on February 15, 1983.

Subsequently, a combined hearing was held on the plaintiff's request for relief from the automatic stay and the debtors' request for turnover of the tractor. The evidence presented at the hearing chiefly concerned the fair market value of the tractor. The plaintiff's valuation witness testified that she believed that the tractor had a fair market value of $28,965.00. The debtors' valuation witness expressed his belief that $38,000.00 was the fair market value.

The evidence adduced at the hearing established a debt of $31,157.71 owing from the debtors to the plaintiff for the tractor. There are no liens against the tractor other than the plaintiff's lien. The tractor is still in the plaintiff's possession.

II. Discussion

In order to resolve this matter, we must first determine the nature of the debtors' interest in the tractor immediately upon their filing of their Chapter 13 bankruptcy petition.

In *United States v. Whiting Pools, Inc.*, 103 S.Ct. 2309 (1983), the Supreme Court held that a Chapter 11 reorganization estate includes property of the debtor that has been repossessed by a secured creditor prior to the filing of the Chapter 11 bankruptcy petition. Such property, therefore, is subject to turnover pursuant to §542 of the Bankruptcy Code. The Court's analysis was based, in part, on the congressional goal of encouraging and facilitating Chapter 11 reorganizations. The Court declined to express its view as to the applicability of its holding in Chapter 7 or Chapter 13 cases.

We see no reason, however, why the holding in *Whiting Pools* should not apply in Chapter 13 cases. The only possible reason for non-applicability, we believe, is if Congress' desire to encourage and facilitate Chapter 13 reorganization and rehabilitation was found to be of a significantly lesser degree than its desire to encourage and facilitate Chapter 11 reorganization and rehabilitation. However, our review of both the Bankruptcy Code and its legislative history convinces us that such is not the case.

Therefore, we find that the repossessed tractor is part of the debtors' Chapter 13 estate and is subject to turnover pursuant to §542.

The plaintiff argues, however, apart from the question of the applicability of *Whiting Pools* in Chapter 13 cases, that *Whiting Pools* is not controlling in the present case because the Internal Revenue Service was the secured creditor in *Whiting Pools* and its repossession of the debtor's personal property was accomplished pursuant to the Internal Revenue Code, whereas, in our case, the plaintiff's repossession was accomplished pursuant to Pennsylvania state law. Therefore, argues the plaintiff, the debtors' interest in the tractor immediately upon the filing of their bankruptcy petition, must be determined according to Pennsylvania law. According to Pennsylvania law, continues the plaintiff, the debtors' interest at that time was merely the right to redemption of the tractor upon full payment of the $31,157.71 redemption price, and not any type of possessory interest. The plaintiff further argues that the case of *Butner v. United States*, 440 U.S. 48, 99 S.Ct. 914, 59 L.Ed.2d 136 (1979), requires that we look to state law and not federal law to determine the debtors' property interest in the tractor.

The plaintiff's interpretation of *Whiting Pools* is incorrect. The analysis and holding in *Whiting Pools* clearly applies to a debtor's interest in repossessed property in general, whether repossessed under state law or federal law, and whether repossessed by the Internal Revenue Service or some other secured creditor. On this matter, the scope of the Court's decision is broad. For example, the Court states:

> "While there are explicit limitations on the reach of §542(a), none requires that the debtor hold a possessory interest in the property at the commencement of the reorganization proceedings."

> "We conclude that the reorganization estate includes property of the debtor that has been seized by a creditor prior to the filing of a petition for reorganization. We see no reason why a different result should obtain when the IRS is the creditor."

We also note that the plaintiff's reliance on *Butner v. United States, supra,* is misplaced. *Butner* held that, in bankruptcy cases, the courts should look to state law to determine a debtor's property interests unless Congress or some other federal interest requires otherwise. In the present context, the *Whiting Pools* decision clearly requires us to be governed by the Bankruptcy Code, particularly §542, and not by state law, in determining the debtors' interest in the tractor.

Having determined that the tractor is part of the debtors' Chapter 13 estate and thus subject to §542 turnover, we must next determine whether the debtors are actually entitled to turnover. To be so entitled, they must show that the plaintiff's secured interest in the tractor is adequately protected. See §363(e) and §361. We find that, under the circumstances of this case, the plaintiff's secured interest is adequately protected by the equity cushion which the debtors have in the tractor. An equity cushion is simply the amount of equity which a debtor has in an item of property, and which is computed by subtracting the amount of all of the encumbrances against an item of property from the fair market value of the property. It is well-established that an equity cushion can provide adequate protection of a secured creditor's interest in property.

In the present case, a witness for each side testified as to the fair market value of the tractor. As indicated *supra*, the plaintiff's witness set the fair market value at $28,965.00, while the debtors' witness arrived at a figure of $38,000.00. For various reasons, we find the appraisal of the debtors' witness to be much more reliable and well-founded. In the first place, the plaintiff's witness is an employee of the plaintiff, whereas the debtors' witness is disinterested in this matter. Secondly, the debtors' witness personally inspected the tractor, whereas the plaintiff's witness did not. Thirdly, the debtors' witness has had considerably more experience in the appraisal of tractors than has the plaintiff's witness. In addition, the debtors' witness has had formal training in the appraisal of tractors, while the plaintiff's witness has not. Finally, both witnesses based their appraisals, in part, upon the Truck Blue Book, which was admitted into evidence as an exhibit in this case. It appears to us that the debtors' witness' use of the Truck Blue Book was more accurate than the use made of it by the plaintiff's witness as it pertains to the value of the particular tractor in question.

For all of the foregoing reasons, based upon the evidence of record, we find the fair market value of the tractor to be $38,000.00. In that, as indicated *supra*, there are no liens against the tractor other than the plaintiff's lien, and the plaintiff's lien was established to be $31,157.71, the debtors have $6,842.29 equity in the tractor. We further find that this represents a sufficient equity cushion to provide adequate protection of the plaintiff's secured interest in the tractor. We are also cognizant of the fact that Mr. Attinello needs the tractor in order to resume his employment as a long-haul independent truck driver and to attempt to fund sufficiently a Chapter 13 Plan for the presumed benefit of all of the creditors of the debtors, including the plaintiff.

Therefore, we conclude that the debtors are entitled to turnover of the tractor from the plaintiff pursuant to §542(a) of the Bankruptcy Code.

Finally, based upon the foregoing, we must deny the plaintiff's request for relief from the automatic stay under both §362(d)(1) and §362(d)(2) of the Bankruptcy Code. As to §362(d)(1), we shall deny relief because we have already concluded that the debtors have provided adequate protection of the plaintiff's interest in the tractor. Also, no other "cause" exists to justify relief from the stay. With regard to §362(d)(2), our finding that the debtors have equity in the tractor precludes relief under this provision.

Therefore, an order will be entered requiring the plaintiff to return possession of the tractor to the debtors forthwith and denying the plaintiff its requested relief from the automatic stay.

Notes and Problems

1. In *Attinello*, Associates Commercial Corp., the plaintiff, had repossessed the tractor prior to the Chapter 13 filing. Why is the plaintiff in possession of its collateral still seeking relief from the stay?

2. Under state law (section 9-506 of the Uniform Commercial Code), the debtor could regain possession of the tractor only by "tendering fulfillment of all obligations secured by the collateral." The *Attinello* opinion concludes that the debtor's interest in the tractor "is to be governed by the Bankruptcy Code, particularly section 542, and not by state law."

    a. What statutory language supports that conclusion?

    b. What statutory language requires a determination of the nature of the debtor's interest in the property held by the creditor?

3. If the plaintiff, Associates Commercial Corp., had sold the tractor before the debtor filed his Chapter 13 petition, could the debtor use section 542 to require the turnover of the proceeds of the sale?

4. Consider the impact of section 542 on Article 9 security interests:

    a. On January 15, your client C, extends credit to D and takes a pledge of 400 shares of Wal-Mart stock. On November 11, D files a Chapter 13 petition. Does section 542 require C to return the Wal-Mart stock to D?

    b. X is indebted to your client C. The loan is secured by a security interest in X's inventory of mobile homes. X is in default. You are concerned that X might file a Chapter 11 petition. Should C repossess the mobile homes?

5. According to the *Attinello* case, a debtor is entitled to turnover under section 542 only if it can show that the secured creditor's interest in the collateral is adequately protected. What is the statutory basis for this rule?

6. *Attinello* is a Chapter 13 case. *Whiting Pools* is a Chapter 11 case. Does section 542 turnover apply in Chapter 7 cases? Assume, for example, that C has a security

interest in D's equipment and repossesses the equipment before D files a Chapter 7 petition. Can the bankruptcy trustee compel C to turnover the equipment to her so that she can sell it?

D. PAYMENTS TO HOLDERS OF SECURED CLAIMS

1. Chapter 7

Chapter 7 contemplates liquidation. The trustee sells the property of the estate and the proceeds from the sale are distributed to creditors. If the trustee sells property that is encumbered by a lien free and clear of the lien, then the lienholder is paid from the net (see section 506(c)) proceeds of the sale.

What if the Chapter 7 debtor wants to retain encumbered property? How much will he have to pay to the holder of a secured claim? Sections 521, 524, 722 and the *Bell* case below answer this question.

In re Bell
United States Court of Appeals, Sixth Circuit, 1983.
700 F.2d 1053.

Krupansky, Circuit Judge. This action joins the legal issue of whether redemption of secured collateral in a Chapter 7 bankruptcy proceeding may be achieved through installment payments.

Debtors, Thomas and Louise Bell (Bells), were parties to a purchase money security agreement with General Motors Acceptance Corporation (GMAC) covering a 1978 Chevrolet Van. The agreement contemplated that the Bells would pay the balance of the purchase price, approximately $6,000 together with financing charges, in equal monthly installments. At the time debtors filed a joint petition in Bankruptcy on March 28, 1980, under Chapter 7 the fair market value of the Van exceeded the outstanding balance on the agreement by approximately $1,000, the debtors had tendered all monthly installments on their obligation to GMAC and had otherwise not defaulted upon any term of the contract.[1] The Van became property of the estate subsequent to which the debtors exempted their equity and the trustee abandoned the estate's interest. GMAC filed a complaint to reclaim the Van and debtors counterclaimed seeking authorization from the bankruptcy court to retain possession of the Van upon continued payment of monthly installments. The Bankruptcy Court permitted installment redemption, and the District Court reversed.

The Bankruptcy Reform Act of 1978 authorizes a Chapter 7 debtor to redeem certain secured property: [722] This provision generally permits a

---

[1] "Default" as predicated upon a provision of the security agreement which authorized GMAC to immediately repossess the Van upon the filing of a bankruptcy petition (bankruptcy clause) is discussed hereafter.

debtor to redeem tangible secured personal property by paying the creditor the approximate fair market value of said property, or the amount of the claim, whichever is less. However, §722 is facially silent as to the mechanics of redemption and, particularly, on whether the redemption may be accomplished through installment payments. The weight of authority has denied installment redemption.

The bankruptcy redemption provision, §722, is a legislative derivative of the redemption provision of 9-506, Uniform Commercial Code. The official comment to 9-506 provides:

> "Tendering fulfillment" obviously means more than a new promise to perform the existing promise; it requires payment in full of all monetary obligations then due and performance in full of all other obligations then matured.

The legislative history of §722 does not reflect a Congressional intent which contemplated anything other than an intent to incorporate the fundamental requirement of "lump sum" redemption as suggested in the underlying UCC provision upon which §722 was predicated.

More importantly, the redemption remedy of §722 must be construed *in pari materia* with the reaffirmation provision, Section 524(c) authorizes a Chapter 7 debtor to seek renegotiation of the terms of the security agreement with the creditor thereby creating an alternative method pursuant to which a debtor may attempt to retain possession of secured collateral. Such an alternative, obviously attractive to the debtor financially unable to redeem the secured collateral through a lump-sum payment, is the equitable complement to §722. Simply, a debtor incapable or unwilling to tender a lump-sum redemption and redeem the secured collateral for its fair market value may reaffirm with the creditor; contrawise, a debtor confronted with a creditor unwilling to execute a renegotiation may retain the secured collateral by redeeming it for its fair market value, which value may be substantially less than the contractual indebtedness. However, §524(c) facially contemplates that the creditor, for whatever reason, may reject any and all tendered reaffirmation offers; §524(c) envisions execution of an "agreement" which, by definition, is a voluntary undertaking. Accordingly, if a debtor is authorized by the bankruptcy court to redeem by installments over the objection of the creditor, such practice would render the voluntary framework of §524(c) an exercise in legislative futility. Phrased differently:

> Of course, if Section 722 payments could be made by installment, no debtor would ever have reason to reaffirm under Section 524(c)(4)(B)(ii), since, by right, he could obtain under Section 722 the same end—continuing possession of his property—under the same terms—payment by installment—for what would often be a significantly

lower price. Thus, installment payments under Section 722 would render useless Congress' carefully laid scheme for voluntary agreement under Section 524—clearly indicating that Congress had no intention to allow such payments under Section 722.

Further, authorization of installment redemption would interpose into Chapter 7 a procedure which Chapter 7 is ill-equipped to implement. A Chapter 7 proceeding, whereby the debtor is discharged through liquidation, may conclude prior to the expiration of the installment payment period. A default by the debtor subsequent to discharge—possibly predicated upon a waste of the collateral, inability to meet the monthly installments or lack of motivation to continue payments on a rapidly depreciating collateral such as a vehicle—would burden the creditor with the expense and effort of reapplying to the bankruptcy court for relief. A bankruptcy court's inability to effectively monitor the installment program and to expeditiously and meaningfully enforce the installment redemption raises serious issues of adequate creditor protection.

A Chapter 7 debtor may assume the anomalous position of being financially unable to redeem the secured collateral by a lump-sum payment and concurrently incapable of persuading a creditor to reaffirm. However, a debtor's inability to exercise the §722 option of redemption, in the absence of *installment* redemption, cannot serve as a basis for the bankruptcy court to abdicate its judicial function of statutory interpretation and resort to legislation by judicial decree. While a bankruptcy court is invested with equity jurisprudence, application of that jurisdiction must comport to and remain compatible with the prevailing legislative intent. A bankruptcy court's imposition of installment redemption clearly contravenes the overall statutory scheme and destroys the delicate balance between §722 and §524(c), and therefore finds no sanction in principles of equity.

Debtors posit that preclusion of installment redemption will precipitate situations wherein a Chapter 7 debtor will possess no viable method of retaining possession of secured collateral. However, a debtor may avoid such an untenuous position by initially filing a petition for bankruptcy under Chapter 13 or converting an existing Chapter 7 proceeding to a Chapter 13 proceeding. Chapter 13 is designed to provide a debtor with a fresh start through rehabilitation, unlike Chapter 7 which provides a fresh start through liquidation. As such, Chapter 13 authorizes redemption by installment over an objection by the creditor (a "cram down"), the very result sought in the action at bar. §1325(a)(5).

In sum, construction of Chapters 7 and 13 *in pari materia* discloses that within the overall statutory scheme a debtor desirous of retaining possession of secured collateral is accorded that election by filing a Chapter 13 petition.

Lastly, the debtors maintain that no default had occurred under the terms of the security agreement and that, upon the trustee's abandonment of the Van under §554, the debtors reacquired the collateral since they held the primary possessory interest. Debtors posit that they enjoyed the same rights after abandonment as before the filing of the bankruptcy petition including the right to continue monthly installments so long as no default, as defined by the security agreement, intervened. Under this theory, the right to continued possession of the secured collateral emanates from the security agreement rather than under a §722 redemption. However, it has been recognized that a return of abandoned property to the party with the primary possessory interest (usually the debtor) merely provides that debtor with time to enforce his right to redeem the property under §722 or to seek a reaffirmation of the agreement under §524(c). The automatic stay of §362(a)(5) continues in effect, and prevents repossession by the creditor until the case is closed, dismissed, or discharge is granted or denied pursuant to §362(c)(2). Analyzing the relationship between §362(a)(5) (debtors protection of the automatic stay) and §554 (abandonment), the Court in *In re Cruseturner* has summarized:

> Accordingly, Section 362(a)(5) grants the debtor time to enforce rights in his property given him under Sections 722 and 524(c).

> The effect of Section 362(a)(5) is to provide the debtor with separate protection of his property. This enables him to exercise his right to redeem either by acquiring refinancing or by otherwise gathering the necessary funds, or to negotiate a reaffirmation. Unless earlier relief is requested by the creditor, the creditor may not repossess property, despite any abandonment by the trustee, until one of the three acts specified in Section 362(c)(2) occurs *** The application of Section 362 to exempt property and abandoned property is co-extensive with the redemption right given in Section 722, for this right extends to exempt property as well as to non-exempt property which may be abandoned by the trustee. Likewise, the stay will cover property which may be the subject of reaffirmation agreements.

In sum, this Court concludes that redemption and reaffirmation constituted the exclusive methods pursuant to which the Bells could retain possession of the secured collateral. The sole method of redemption available to a Chapter 7 debtor under §722 is a lump-sum redemption. Accordingly, the judgment of the district court is Affirmed.

Notes and Problems

1. The *Bell* facts are unusual. In *Bell*, "the fair market value of the Van exceeded the outstanding balance of the agreement by approximately $1,000" and the Bells "had tendered all monthly installments on their obligation to GMAC." Why did GMAC want to repossess the Van? Should GMAC be able to repossess the van even though the Bells were current in their payment obligations?

2. What is the amount of payment required by section 722? What if the fair market value of the Bells' Van was only $2,000?

3. While section 722 does not expressly limit redemption to cash payments, it does contain other limitations as to type of debtor, type of debt, and type of property. Assume, for example, that farmer D owes S $120,000 and that debt is secured by D's farm which has a value of $39,000. If D files for Chapter 7 relief, can he satisfy S's secured claim and extinguish S's mortgage on his farm by paying S $39,000. See sections 722, 506 and the *Dewsnup* decision set out below.

Dewsnup v. Timm
Supreme Court of the United States, 1992
502 U.S. ___, 112 S.Ct. 773, 116 L.Ed.2d 903

Justice Blackmun delivered the opinion of the Court.

We are confronted in this case with an issue concerning §506(d) of the Bankruptcy Code, 11 U.S.C. §506(d). May a debtor "strip down" a creditor's lien on real property to the value of the collateral, as judicially determined, when that value is less than the amount of the claim secured by the lien?

I

On June 1, 1978, respondents loaned $119,000 to petitioner Aletha Dewsnup and her husband, T. LaMar Dewsnup, since deceased. The loan was accompanied by a Deed of Trust granting a lien on two parcels of Utah farmland owned by the Dewsnups.

Petitioner defaulted the following year. * * * [P]etitioner filed a petition seeking liquidation under Chapter 7 of the Code, 11 U.S.C. §701 et seq. Because of the pendency of these bankruptcy proceedings, respondents were not able to proceed to the foreclosure sale. See 11 U.S.C. §362.

In 1987, petitioner filed the present adversary proceeding in the Bankruptcy Court for the District of Utah seeking, pursuant to §506, to "avoid" a portion of respondents' lien. Petitioner represented that the debt of approximately $120,000 then owed to respondents exceeded the fair market value of the land and that, therefore, the Bankruptcy Court should reduce the lien to that value. According to petitioner, this was compelled by the interrelationship of the security-reducing provision of §506(a) and the lien- voiding provision of §506(d). Under §506(a) ("An allowed claim of a creditor secured by a lien on property in which the estate has an interest.... is a secured claim to the extent of the value of such creditor's interest in the estate's interest in such property"), respondents would have an "allowed secured claim" only to the extent of the judicially determined value of their collateral. And under §506(d) ("To the extent that a lien secures a claim against the debtor that is not an allowed secured claim, such lien is void"), the court would be required to void the lien as to the remaining portion of respondents' claim, because the remaining portion was not an "allowed secured claim" within the meaning of §506(a).

    * * *

II

As we read their several submissions, the parties and their amici are not in agreement in their respective approaches to the problem of statutory interpretation that confronts us. Petitioner-debtor takes the position that §506(a) and §506(d) are complementary and to be read together. Because, under §506(a), a claim is secured only to the extent of the judicially determined value of the real property on which the lien is fixed, a debtor can void a lien on the property pursuant to §506(d) to the extent the claim is no longer secured and thus is not "an allowed secured claim." In other words, §506(a) bifurcates classes of claims allowed under §502 into secured claims and unsecured claims; any portion of an allowed claim deemed to be unsecured under §506(a) is not an "allowed secured claim" within the lien- voiding scope of §506(d). Petitioner argues that there is no exception for unsecured property abandoned by the trustee.

Petitioner's amicus argues that the plain language of §506(d) dictates that the proper portion of an undersecured lien on property in a Chapter 7 case is void whether or not the property is abandoned by the trustee. It further argues that the rationale of the Court of Appeals would lead to evisceration of the debtor's right of redemption and the elimination of an undersecured creditor's ability to participate in the distribution of the estate's assets.

Respondents primarily assert that §506(d) is not, as petitioner would have it, "rigidly tied" to §506(a) ***. They argue that §506(a) performs the function of classifying claims by true secured status at the time of distribution of the estate to ensure fairness to unsecured claimants. In contrast, the lien-voiding §506(d) is directed to the time at which foreclosure is to take place, and, where the trustee has abandoned the property, no bankruptcy distributional purpose is served by voiding the lien.

In the alternative, respondents, joined by the United States as amicus curiae, argue more broadly that the words "allowed secured claim" in §506(d) need not be read as an indivisible term of art defined by reference to §506(a), which by its terms is not a definitional provision. Rather, the words should be read term-by-term to refer to any claim that is, first, allowed, and, second, secured. Because there is no question that the claim at issue here has been "allowed" pursuant to §502 of the Code and is secured by a lien with recourse to the underlying collateral, it does not come within the scope of §506(d), which voids only liens corresponding to claims that have not been allowed and secured. This reading of §506(d), according to respondents and the United States, gives the provision the simple and sensible function of voiding a lien whenever a claim secured by the lien itself has not been allowed. It ensures that the Code's determination not to allow the underlying claim against the debtor personally is given full effect by preventing its assertion against the debtor's property.

Respondents point out that pre-Code bankruptcy law preserved liens like respondents' and that there is nothing in the Code's legislative history that reflects any intent to alter that law. Moreover, according to respondents, the "fresh-start" policy cannot justify an impairment of respondents' property rights, for the fresh start does not extend to an in rem claim against property but is limited to a discharge of personal liability.

III

* * *

We conclude that respondents' alternative position, espoused also by the United States, although not without its difficulty, generally is the better of the several approaches. Therefore, we hold that §506(d) does not allow petitioner to "strip down" respondents' lien, because respondents' claim is secured by a lien and has been fully allowed pursuant to §502. Were we writing on a clean slate, we might be inclined to agree with petitioner that the words "allowed secured claim" must take the same meaning in §506(d) as in §506(a).[1] But, given the ambiguity in the text, we are not convinced that Congress intended to depart from the pre-Code rule that liens pass through bankruptcy unaffected.

1. The practical effect of petitioner's argument is to freeze the creditor's secured interest at the judicially determined valuation. By this approach, the creditor would lose the benefit of any increase in the value of the property by the time of the foreclosure sale. The increase would accrue to the benefit of the debtor, a result some of the parties describe as a "windfall."

We think, however, that the creditor's lien stays with the real property until the foreclosure. That is what was bargained for by the mortgagor and the mortgagee. The voidness language sensibly applies only to the security aspect of the lien and then only to the real deficiency in the security. Any increase over the judicially determined valuation during bankruptcy rightly accrues to the benefit of the creditor, not to the benefit of the debtor and not to the benefit of other unsecured creditors whose claims have been allowed and who had nothing to do with the mortgagor-mortgagee bargain.

Such surely would be the result had the lienholder stayed aloof from the bankruptcy proceeding (subject, of course, to the power of other persons or entities to pull him into the proceeding pursuant to §501), and we see no reason why his acquiescence in that proceeding should cause him to experience a forfeiture of the kind the debtor proposes. It is true that his participation in the bankruptcy results in his having the benefit of an allowed unsecured claim as well as his allowed secured claim, but that does not strike us as proper

---

[1] Accordingly, we express no opinion as to whether the words "allowed secured claim" have different meaning in other provisions of the Bankruptcy Code.

recompense for what petitioner proposes by way of the elimination of the remainder of the lien.

2. This result appears to have been clearly established before the passage of the 1978 Act. Under the Bankruptcy Act of 1898, a lien on real property passed through bankruptcy unaffected. This Court recently acknowledged that this was so. See Farrey v. Sanderfoot, 500 U.S. ----, ----, 111 S.Ct. 1825, 1829, 114 L.Ed.2d 337 (1991) ("Ordinarily, liens and other secured interests survive bankruptcy"); Johnson v. Home State Bank, 501 U.S. ----, ----, 111 S.Ct. 2150, 2154, 115 L.Ed.2d 66 (1991) ("Rather, a bankruptcy discharge extinguishes only one mode of enforcing a claim--namely, an action against the debtor in personam--while leaving intact another--namely, an action against the debtor in rem.").

3. Apart from reorganization proceedings, see 11 U.S.C. §§616(1) and (10) (1976 ed.), no provision of the pre-Code statute permitted involuntary reduction of the amount of a creditor's lien for any reason other than payment on the debt.
* * *

Congress must have enacted the Code with a full understanding of this practice.

4. When Congress amends the bankruptcy laws, it does not write "on a clean slate." Furthermore, this Court has been reluctant to accept arguments that would interpret the Code, however vague the particular language under consideration might be, to effect a major change in pre-Code practice that is not the subject of at least some discussion in the legislative history. Of course, where the language is unambiguous, silence in the legislative history cannot be controlling. But, given the ambiguity here, to attribute to Congress the intention to grant a debtor the broad new remedy against allowed claims to the extent that they become "unsecured" for purposes of §506(a) without the new remedy's being mentioned somewhere in the Code itself or in the annals of Congress is not plausible, in our view, and is contrary to basic bankruptcy principles.

The judgment of the Court of Appeals is affirmed.

It is so ordered.

Justice Thomas took no part in the consideration or decision of this case.

Justice Scalia, with whom Justice Souter joins, dissenting.

With exceptions not pertinent here, §506(d) of the Bankruptcy Code provides: "To the extent that a lien secures a claim against the debtor that is not an allowed secured claim, such lien is void...." Read naturally and in accordance with other provisions of the statute, this automatically voids a lien to the extent the claim it secures is not both an "allowed claim" and a "secured claim" under the Code. In holding otherwise, the Court replaces what Congress said with what it thinks Congress ought to have said--and in the process disregards, and hence impairs for future use, well-established principles of statutory construction. I respectfully dissent.
* * *

Notes and Problems

1. *See generally* Margaret Howard, *Stripping Down Liens: Section 506(d) and the Theory of Bankruptcy*, 65 Am. Bankr. L.J. 373 (1991).

2. Does *Dewsnup* affect a Chapter 7 debtor who wants to satisfy a secured claim and extinguish the lien on his family car by making a cash payment equal to the value of the car? See section 722. Does *Dewsnup* affect a Chapter 13 debtor who wants to satisfy a secured claim and extinguish the lien on the family car by making installment payments under a Chapter 13 plan measured by the value of the car? See section 1322(b)(2) which is applied in *In re Klein* below and in *In re Nobleman*, infra.

2. Other Chapters

In a Chapter 11 case, a Chapter 12 case, or a Chapter 13 case, the payments to the holders of secured claims are determined by the provisions of the plan. The plan can completely restructure a secured debt obligation: change the total amount to be paid, change the payment period, change the amount of each payment, change the interest rate, section 1123(b)(1), 1222(b)(2), 1322(b)(2). Consider the following example.

S reluctantly agrees to sell equipment to D on credit. Because of its concerns about D's creditworthiness, S agrees to extend credit for a short period of time at a relatively high rate of interest. The S-D contract provides that (1) S will retain a security interest in the equipment until it is paid in full, and (2) the purchase price of the equipment will be $110,000, and (3) D will pay for the equipment by making six monthly payments of $20,000 each. After making one payment, D defaults and files a bankruptcy petition. In Chapter 11, 12, or 13, D will not necessarily be required to make the remaining payments called for by the contract in order to keep the equipment. Subject to the statutory limitations, D's plan can alter or modify D's payment obligations. The *Klein* case below illustrates such a modification, illustrates the statutory limitations.

In re Klein
United States Bankruptcy Court, New York, 1981
10 B.R. 657

C. Albert Parente, Bankruptcy Judge.

On July 23, 1980, David and Jane Klein (hereinafter "debtors") filed a petition in bankruptcy under Chapter 13 of the Bankruptcy Code. At the confirmation hearing held on November 18, 1980, the Court held a valuation hearing with respect to the partially secured claim held by General Motors Acceptance Corporation (hereinafter "GMAC").

A summary of the pertinent facts elicited at the hearing held on November 18, 1980, follows:

(1) On October 18, 1979, the debtors purchased a 1976 Chevrolet Caprice station wagon for the sum of $3,735.25. The debtors financed said purchase by placing a cash down-payment in the sum of $1,335.25 and executing a consumer credit contract with GMAC in the amount of $3,244.68.

(2) The debtors, in their Chapter 13 petition, listed GMAC's claim as secured in the amount of $1,394.86 and unsecured in the amount of $1,759.69. The debtors fixed the value of the collateral in question at $1,394.86.

(3) Consistent with the debtors' listing of GMAC's claim in the petition, the plan provided for the full payment of GMAC's secured claim plus a discount rate of 12 percent over the term of the plan. The plan further provided for payment of 18 percent of the unsecured portion of GMAC's claim.

(4) On September 4, 1980, GMAC filed a proof of claim in the sum of $3,286.74 and rejected the debtors' plan.

(5) On November 5, 1980, the debtors submitted an amended plan increasing the value of GMAC's secured claim to $1,650.

(6) At the valuation hearing, the expert witness for the debtors, Angelo Merolla, set the wholesale value of the car at $1,100 and the retail value at $1,600. The expert witness for the creditor, Paul Dombrowski, set the wholesale value at $1,850 and the retail value at $2,475.

(7) As of the date of this decision, the debtors' amended plan has not been confirmed.

The above findings of fact give rise to the following issues:

(1) Pursuant to §506(a), what method of valuation should be used to fix a secured claim where the collateral consists of an automobile.

(2) Pursuant to §1325(a)(5)(B)(ii), as of what date should a secured claim be valued.

(3) What is the appropriate discount rate to be paid on GMAC's secured claim in the case at bar.

I.

Section 506 of the Bankruptcy Code provides that a creditor has a secured claim to the extent of the value of the collateral. §506(a).

Where the collateral securing the creditor's claim is valued less than the face amount of the claim, as in the case at bar, the creditor's claim is divided into two parts: an allowed secured claim which is equal to the value of the collateral and an allowed unsecured claim for the deficiency.

Although Section 506(a) sets forth general principles for the courts to follow when called upon to determine the value of a creditor's secured claim, the statutory language does not offer specific guidelines on the question. The statute is extremely flexible and states simply that "(s)uch value shall be determined in light of the purpose of the valuation and of the proposed disposition or use of such property, and in conjunction with any hearing on such disposition or use or on a plan affecting such creditor's interest." §506(a).

The legislative history, while equally as general as the statutory language of Section 506(a), does indicate that the concept of value is to be flexible and grants discretion to the courts to determine value on a case-by-case basis, taking into account the facts and competing interests in each case.

A review of the reported decisions on the issue presented indicates that there are two basic approaches that the courts have followed in determining the value of a secured creditor's claim under Section 506(a):

(1) Where the collateral sought to be valued is an automobile, a majority of the courts have rejected the creditor's claim that the value of the automobile should be set at the retail price unless the creditor was in the business of selling cars in the retail market. The courts found the wholesale price to be the appropriate measure of value.

(2) The second approach followed by the courts entails valuing the collateral by applying the norm which a prudent businessman would employ to dispose of an asset. This approach is derived from Section 9-504(e) of the Uniform Commercial Code, which provides in relevant part that: "(s)ale or other disposition may be as a unit or in parcels and at any time and place and on any terms but every aspect of the disposition including the method, manner, time, place and terms must be *commercially reasonable*." (Emphasis added).

This approach rejects the formulation of a definitive method of valuation to be used in all cases. Rather, the method of valuation is to be determined on a case-by-case basis.

Predicated on the statutory mandate that the value of the collateral should be determined in light of the proposed disposition or use of such property and Congress's intent that the concept of value is to be flexible, the Court finds that the car in question should be valued at an amount which the creditor would receive by its customary or commercially reasonable means of disposition. Such an approach appears to be the alternative most consistent with the statutory language.

At the valuation hearing, Paul Dombrowski, an employee of GMAC, testified as to GMAC's procedure for disposing of abandoned and repossessed cars. Dombrowski stated that said cars are sold on a "bid" market. Although Dombrowski did not elaborate on this method of sale, it is evident that this procedure clearly contemplates a wholesale market value as opposed to a retail or forced-sale (liquidation) market value.

Predicated on the aforementioned discussion, the Court concludes that the car in question should be valued at an amount which could be realized by GMAC in their normal manner of disposing of such vehicles, to wit, on a bid market. Thus, the value of the debtors' car is hereby affixed at $1,650.

II.

The debtors contend that the controlling date for valuation is the date the Chapter 13 petition was filed. In contra-position, GMAC contends that the relevant date is the date of the valuation hearing.

Pursuant to §1325(a)(5)(B)(ii), the value of the collateral establishing the amount of the secured claim is to be determined as of the "effective date of the plan."

Neither the Bankruptcy Code nor the legislative history defines the term "effective date of the plan." The reported decisions indicate that the "effective date of the plan" is one of two dates: either the date the petition is filed, or the date of the confirmation hearing.

The Court rejects the proposition that the date of valuation is the date of the filing of the Chapter 13 petition. This finding posits on the fact that setting the valuation date coordinate with the date the petition is filed does not take into account prospective changes in the value of the property which may occur during the course of administration.

For the purposes of cram down valuation, the Court will determine the value of the collateral as of the date of the valuation hearing, since, as a practical matter, confirmation will almost always follow within a brief time after this hearing.

In comport with the foregoing principles of law, the Court finds that the proper date to value a secured creditor's collateral is the date of the valuation hearing, provided that the plan is confirmed within a reasonable time thereafter.

However, in situations such as the case at bar, where a significant period of time has passed since the date of the valuation hearing, adjustments should be made for any increase or decrease in value which may have occurred during this time.

III.

Under the language of the Chapter 13 "cram down" provisions, the creditor must receive the present value equivalent of the allowed amount of its secured claim. §1325(a)(5)(B)(ii).

To compute the "present value" of a creditor's secured claim requires the Court to determine what the present worth is of a proposed stream of fixed payments over the life of the plan. To accomplish this task, the payments are "discounted" to determine their present value. As a practical matter, the Court is in effect computing an interest rate to be applied to the amount of the creditor's allowed secured claim.

However, such discount rate embodied in Section 1325(a)(5)(B)(ii) should not be confused with a creditor's right to interest on its secured claim under Section 506(b).

For purposes of fixing the value of a creditor's secured claim, Section 506(b) permits the secured claim to include reasonable interest together with any reasonable fees, costs or charges provided for in the security agreement when the value of the collateral exceeds the amount of the allowed secured claim.

The discount rate, on the other hand, does not become part of the secured claim, but is instead incremental adjustments to the secured claim to compensate the creditor for depreciation of the collateral over the term of the plan.

While the Bankruptcy Code is silent as to the value of the discount rate, the legislative history indicates there is a presumption that the discount rate and the interest rate set forth in the contract are equivalent.

Despite the presumption set forth in the legislative history, most of the reported decisions have declined to fix the discount rate at the interest rate stated in the security agreement. The rationale cited in the reported decisions is that the purpose of the discount rate is to protect the secured creditor from any loss caused to it due to the deferred payment of its claim.

Therefore, predicated on the aforementioned principles of law, the Court declines to fix the discount rate at the interest rate set forth in the consumer credit contract, to wit, 19.56 percent. GMAC failed to adduce any evidence to demonstrate that the value of the car in question would depreciate by 19.56 percent over the life of the plan. To fix the discount rate in the case at bar at 19.56 percent would violate the mandate that the determination of the value question in issue must be made to reach a result that is fair and equitable for both the creditor and the debtor.

Absent evidence to the contrary, the Court finds that the method of calculating the discount rate which best comports with legal and equitable considerations found in the Bankruptcy Code, the legislative history and the reported decisions is to take the average of the legal rate of interest in the State of New York (6 percent) and the rate of interest set forth in the consumer credit contract (19.56 percent).

In light of both legal and equitable considerations, the Court fixes the discount rate in the case at bar at 12 percent.

Conclusion

Premised on the aforementioned findings of fact and principles of law, the Court concludes:

(1) the proper method of valuation in the case at bar is the amount which GMAC would realize by its normal means of disposing of such collateral, i.e., commercially reasonable means;

(2) the value of the collateral in question is set at $1,650;

(3) the collateral of GMAC is to be valued as of the date of the valuation hearing; and

(4) GMAC is entitled to a discount rate on its secured claim in the amount set forth in the debtors' amended plan, 12 percent.

Notes and Problems

1. The court valued the Kleins' Chevrolet station wagon at $1,650. On what evidence did the bankruptcy court base this valuation?

2. What is the practical significance of the $1,650 valuation?

    a. Are the Kleins legally obligated to pay GMAC $1,650? If so, when? What about the remaining $1,500 that the Kleins owed GMAC prior to filing a Chapter 13 petition?

    b. What, if any, action can GMAC take if it is not satisfied with the Kleins promising to pay $1,650 and 18 of the balance of its claim? See section 1327(a).

3. The *Klein* decision "fixes the discount rate in the case at bar at 12 per cent."

    a. What is the practical significance of this discount rate?

    b. What is the basis for the 12 rate? Why did the *Klein* decision consider the 6 legal rate of interest? Why didn't the *Klein* decision consider the present prime rate or the present interest rate for car loans?

4. According to *Klein*, the "discount rate embodied in Section 1325(a)(5)(B)(ii) should not be confused with a creditor's right to interest on its secured claim under Section 506(b)."

    a. Which claims accrue interest under section 506(b)?

    b.   Which claims accrue interest under section 1325(a)(5)(B)(ii)?

    c.   Does section 506(b) interest accrue from the time of the filing of the petition?

    d.   Does section 1325(a)(5)(B)(ii) interest accrue from the time of the filing of the petition?

    e.   Does section 506(b) interest accrue after the confirmation of the Chapter 13 plan?

    f.   Does section 1325(a)(5)(B)(ii) interest accrue after the confirmation of the Chapter 13 plan?

5.   Section 1322(b)(2) generally permits a Chapter 13 plan to modify the rights of holders of secured claims. The *Klein* case illustrates the impact of this provision on the holder of a security interest on an automobile. Note the exception in §1322(b)(2) for "a claim secured *only* by *** the debtor's principal residence." Assume, for example, that D obtains financing to buy her house from S Savings & Loan. The mortgage agreement calls for monthly payments of $700. D later files for Chapter 13 relief. D's Chapter 13 plan cannot reduce the monthly payments to S Savings & Loan. See *Nobleman v. American Savings Bank*, infra.

6.   Your client, D, is worrying about losing her home. M has a mortgage on her house. The D-M mortgage agreement calls for payments of $500 a month. D was laid off in March, April and May and missed three monthly payments. D is now working again but is not able to cure the $1,500 default immediately. M has instituted mortgage foreclosure proceedings. Should you advise D to file a petition for relief under Chapter 13? See section 1322(b)(5). What if the mortgage agreement contained an acceleration clause and M has exercised its right of acceleration? See *In re Taddco*, infra.

7.   Chapters 11 and 12, like Chapter 13, empowers a debtor to modify the rights of holders of secured claims in the plan, see sections 1123(b)(1), 1129(b)(2)(A), 1222(b)(2), 1225(a)(5). The treatment of secured claims in Chapter 11 plans is considered in Unites 16 and 17.

Unit 12

LEASES AND EXECUTORY CONTRACTS

UNIT CONTENTS

Section 365 of the Bankruptcy Code deals with leases and executory contracts different from other transactions. Since there is a general understanding of what a lease is and general confusion over what an "executory contract" is, this book first deals with the effect of section 365 on leases and then considers executory contracts.

When D enters into an agreement to lease a building or equipment from L, D is acquiring rights (i.e., the right to keep and use the leased property) and also incurring obligations (i.e., the obligation to make the lease payments). Accordingly, in considering the impact of D's later bankruptcy filing on this lease, it is necessary to consider both what happens to D's obligations and what happens to D's rights.

Under section 365, a bankruptcy trustee can either

(1) reject a lease,

(2) assume a lease, or

(3) assign a lease.

In order to assess the three options in section 365, a lawyer or law student needs to be able to answer these questions:

(1) What are the consequences of a debtor's rejecting a lease? Assuming a lease? Assigning a lease?

(2) What are the procedures and requirements for rejecting a lease? Assuming? Assigning?

(3) What is an "executory contract" and what are the limitations on rejection, assumption and assignment of executory contracts?

A. CONSEQUENCES OF REJECTION, ASSUMPTION, AND ASSIGNMENT

It is clear from section 365 that a trustee can reject, assume, or assign a lease. Section 365 and case law are less clear as to what happens to D's lease obligations and lease rights when a lease is rejected, assumed or assigned.. The following chart provides a general view of the effects of rejection, assumption and assignment, and the problems after the chart involve an application of what is in the chart, in the Code, and in limbo.

	REJECTION	ASSUMPTION	ASSIGNMENT
Property of the estate	No property of the estate	Debtor's rights under contract or lease	Proceeds, if any, from assignment of debtor's rights under contract or lease
Claims	Unsecured claim for (1) pre-petition defaults and (2) breach resulting from rejection; administrative expense priority claim for post-petition obligations, if any	Administrative expense priority claim for all obligations under contract or lease, post-petition or pre-petition	No claim against the estate. Non-debtor party to an assigned contract or lease looks solely to the assignee

Notes and Problems

1. D Corp. leases a building from L. The lease provides for a five-year term and monthly rent of $10,000. A year later, D Co. files a bankruptcy petition and rejects the lease. Does L have an allowable claim? See sections 365(g), 502(g). What is the amount of L's claim? See section 502(a)(6). Can D Co.'s Chapter 11 plan propose to pay L only a part of that amount? See section 1123(b)(1). Can D Co. continue to retain and use the leased building after it rejects the lease? Cf. sections 541(b)(2), 362(b)(10). Would any of your answers be different if the subject matter of the lease was equipment, instead of a building? What if the equipment was a fixture under state law?

2. D leases space in an office building to The Spa , T . The lease provides for a five year term and monthly rent of $10,000, The lease also states that T will be the only exercise facility in the building.. D files for bankruptcy and rejects the lease. Can D evict T and relet the space at a higher rental rate? See section 365(h). Can D raise T's rent? Can D lease other space in the building to another exercise facility? What if the subject matter of the lease was equipment instead of space in a building? Can D get the equipment back from T?

3. D leases a farm from L for $2,000 a month. At the time he files for Chapter 12 relief, D owes L $6,000 in back rent. If D assumes the lease, can his Chapter 12 plan modify the rental terms? See section 1222(b)(2), 1222(a)(2). Can D's Chapter 12 plan decrease or defer the payment of the $6,000 in back rent?

4. D leases machinery from L. D files a Chapter 7 petition and assumes and assigns the lease to X. If X misses a lease payment, will L have an allowable claim. in D's bankruptcy?

B. PROCEDURES AND REQUIREMENTS FOR REJECTION OR ASSUMPTION OR ASSIGNMENT'

Paragraph (a) of section 365 requires court approval of the assumption or rejection of a lease. Paragraph (a), however, does not set out the standards that a court is to apply when ruling on a motion to assume or reject. Courts generally apply a business judgment standard. That is, courts generally defer to the business judgment of the trustee or debtor in possession as to whether a lease should be rejected.

Section 365(d) sets out the time limits within which the bankruptcy trustee or debtor in possession may assume or reject. Section 365(b) contains the requirements for assumption and section 365(f) (2) the requirements for assignment.   Please apply section 365(a), (d), (b), and (f) in the following problems.

Problems

1. D operates a chain of grocery stores. One of its leased stores is in a strip shopping center owned by L. D files a Chapter 11 petition and moves to reject its lease with L. L and L's other tenants testify that they rely on D to attract customers to the shopping center and that if D closes its store in the center, they will have to file for bankruptcy. Should the court approve the rejection of the lease?

2. D leases the apartment his family lives in from L. D files a Chapter 7 petition. The trustee neither assumes nor rejects the lease during the course of D's bankruptcy. During the bankruptcy case and after the close of the bankruptcy case, D continues to pay rent to L. Can L evict D? Cf. section 365(d)(1).

3. D leases a building from L. D files a Chapter 11 petition. D is uncertain as to whether he will need the building in his reorganized building. How long can D delay the decision whether to assume or reject? See section 365(d)(4). Is D required to continue making monthly payments until he decides whether to assume or reject? See section 365(d)(3).

4. D leases machinery from L. D files a Chapter 11 petition. D is uncertain whether she will need the machinery in her "reorganized" business. How long can D delay the decision to assume or reject? What if any action can L take? See section 365(d)(2); cf. section 362(d). Is D required to continue making monthly rental payments until she decides whether to assume or reject?

5. Should Judge Lifland grant Lomas' motion set out below?

□□□□□□

```
UNITED STATES BANKRUPTCY COURT
SOUTHERN DISTRICT OF NEW YORK
- - - - - - - - - - - - - - - - - - - -x
                                        : In Proceedings For A
                                        : Reorganization Under
In re                                   : Chapter 11 Case Nos.
                                        : 89 B 12471 (BRL)
LOMAS FINANCIAL CORPORATION, et al.,    :
                    DEBTORS             : Through
                                        : 89 B 12478 (BRL)
                                        : Inclusive
- - - - - - - - - - - - - - - - - - - -x
```

APPLICATION FOR A SECOND ORDER EXTENDING
DEBTORS' TIME TO ASSUME OR REJECT ALL
<u>NONRESIDENTIAL REAL PROPERTY LEASES</u>

TO THE HONORABLE BURTON R. LIFLAND:

This application of Lomas Financial Corporation ("Lomas"), debtor and debtor in possession, for itself and on behalf of each of the other debtors and debtors in possession herein (collectively, the "Debtors"), respectfully sets forth and represents:

I.

<u>INTRODUCTION</u>

1.   On September 24, 1989 (the "Filing Date"), the Debtors filed petitions for reorganization under chapter 11 of the Bankruptcy Code (the "Code") with the Clerk of this court and were continued in the management and operation of their businesses and properties as debtors in possession pursuant to 1107 and 1108 of the Code. These chapter 11 cases have been consolidated for procedural purposes only and are being jointly administered pursuant to order of this Court. No trustee or examiner has been appointed.

2. By this application, the Debtors herewith seek the entry of an order pursuant to 365(b)(4) of the Code a) further extending the period within which they must assume or reject all nonresidential real property lease agreements under which a Debtor is the lessee (the "Election Period"), through and including June 30, 1990 and (b) providing for automatic extensions of the Election Period of one calendar month each after June 30, 1990, provided that neither the Official Committee of Unsecured Creditors nor any lessor under any nonresidential real property lease agreement under which a Debtor is the lessee (a "Lessor") serves notice to the Debtors of an objection to any such automatic extension at least fourteen days before the expiration of the Election

Period, which objection shall be without prejudice to the Debtors' right to make additional applications to this Court for further extension of the Election Period (the "Order").

II.
BACKGROUND

3. Lomas is a diversified financial services company whose businesses include mortgage banking, funds management, insurance, short-term real estate lending, real estate development, real estate advisory services, information systems services, and commercial leasing. Lomas directly or indirectly owns all of the issued and outstanding common stock of the Debtors and their non-Debtor subsidiaries.

4. The Debtors conduct a substantial portion of their business at four leased locations, three located in Texas and one located in Atlanta, Georgia. The principal corporate headquarters of Lomas are located at 2001 Bryan Tower in Dallas, Texas, where Lomas Financial Corporation leases approximately 140,432 square feet of office and storage space.

5. All of the four leased locations from which the Debtors operate are occupied by the Debtors pursuant to lease agreements which were executed and in force on the Filing Date. The leases under which these locations have been demised to the Debtors are hereinafter referred to collectively as the "Business Leases." Each Business Lease herein is listed and described on a schedule annexed hereto as Exhibit A.

III.
THE ELECTION PERIOD UNDER
§363(d)(4) OF THE CODE

6. The Business Leases are leases of non-residential real property which receive treatment under the Code different from that afforded to other kinds of unexpired leases and executory contracts of the Debtors. Thus, while the Code does not fix a date certain by which unexpired residential and other leases and executory contracts must be assumed or rejected by a debtor in possession, 365(d)(4) of the Code provides that the debtor in possession, at least initially, has sixty (60) days within which to assume or reject an unexpired lease of nonresidential real property under which it is lessee. However, in recognition that the initial sixty (60) day period often imposes upon a debtor an arbitrary and unrealistic deadline, the statute gives the Bankruptcy Court wide latitude to extend such period until a decision to assume or reject can be

made on a rational basis with reference to the facts and circumstances surrounding each particular reorganization case. Accordingly, the statute specifically provides that the Court may extend the Election Period and allow the debtor in possession "such additional time as the Court, for cause shown, within such 60day period, fixes,. . . ." 11 U.S.C. §365(d)(4).

7. *By* order of this Court dated November 27, 1989, (the "First Order Extending the Election Period") the Election Period was extended in these cases to the earlier of (i) March 31, 1990 or (ii) twenty days after the Debtors' presentation of a business plan to the Official Committee of Unsecured Creditors. Given the magnitude and overall complexity of these cases, the Debtors submit that the requisite cause for further extension of the Election Period is amply manifest herein.

IV.

CAUSE EXISTS FOR FURTHER

<u>EXTENSION OF THE ELECTION PERIOD</u>

8. These cases are monumental in their size, scope and complexity. As of the filing of the chapter 11 petitions, the Debtors and their non-filing affiliates had assets and liabilities, on a consolidated basis, in excess of $6 billion. There are thousands of creditors and equity security holders affected by these proceedings.

9. In proceedings as large and complex as these, it would be premature, indeed unreasonable, to require the Debtors to make absolute decisions with respect to the ultimate disposition of their Business Leases in the early months of these cases. Since the entry of the First Order Extending the Election Period, the Debtors have been working diligently toward resolution of numerous pending and weighty matters; these efforts have precluded any searching analysis of the Business Leases. The need to stabilize and maintain existing operations has been the paramount objective in the months since these cases were filed.

10. But perhaps even more significantly, at this early stage of the proceedings, when the Debtors have not yet completed a comprehensive business plan, it would be inimical to the entire chapter 11 reorganization process to compel the Debtors to make elections with respect to their Business Leases. Indeed, the Debtors' creditors would be grossly prejudiced were the Debtors to assume prematurely a particular lease only to have to breach it later (when a business plan is formulated and such lease proves unnecessary), or to reject a particular lease only to later learn that such lease was a valuable asset of these estates which

should have been retained. In either event, creditors of the Debtors would be forced to bear administrative expenses or suffer a diminution of the estates. Such results can be avoided only if the Debtors are given a reasonable opportunity to develop and implement their business plan before they are directed to make Business Lease elections under 365(d)(4).

11. The formulation of a business plan in cases of the magnitude and complexity of those herein requires careful consideration of the many factors which will determine the viability of such a plan. The business plan, when completed, may provide that certain locations are unnecessary for the Debtors' future operations (the "Unnecessary Locations"), while others may be deemed integral to the reorganization process and to the Debtors' restructured businesses. What is more, if a location is identified as an Unnecessary Location the Debtors will require time to evaluate the lease pertaining thereto to determine whether its value is such that the re-marketing of such lease would enable the Debtors to realize maximum value for the benefit of these estates.

12. The Debtors believe that any final election with respect to the Business Leases relating to locations which the Debtors preliminarily determine to retain is necessarily linked to a demonstration of the needs of their restructured businesses. Such demonstration presupposes that once the initial business plan is proposed, the Debtors will be given an opportunity to effect internal changes consonant therewith, to solidify and strengthen their continuing business operations and, if necessary, to continue to develop and refine their business plan. It further presupposes that the Debtors be afforded the requisite time to develop and propose a plan or plans of reorganization predicated upon the business plan.

13. In view of the foregoing, it is only logical that the expiration of the Election Period occur, at the earliest, upon the presentation of a business plan by the Debtors embracing each respective Debtor which is the party to each of the Business Leases. Indeed, the rejection, assumption and/or assignment of leases in the context of a business or a reorganization plan is neither novel nor contrary to the spirit or letter of the Code, as amended. Section 1123(b)(2), which was preserved intact following Congress' enactment of 365(b)(4), expressly authorizes the rejection, assumption and/or assignment of an unexpired lease (not previously rejected) under a plan of reorganization.

14. Extending the Election Period through June 30,
1990 or and providing for additional automatic extensions of
reasonable duration (both subject to the right of the Official Committee of Unsecured Creditors and the Lessors to
apply for entry of an order curtailing such extensions) will
enable the Debtors to assess intelligently the value of each
of the Business Leases in the overall context of these
cases, while avoiding the very real risk of burdening these
estates with the substantial administrative expense claims
which would be occasioned by premature assumption. In addition, the prospect of the premature rejection of a lease
which proves to be a valuable or necessary asset of the estate will be eliminated.

15. Authorization of automatic calendar-month extensions as described at paragraph 2 herein will not prejudice the rights of the Official Committee of Unsecured
Creditors or the Lessors in any way. Under the terms of the
Order, those parties remain free to object to any automatic
extension on fourteen days' notice to the Debtors. Such an
objection would terminate authorization for further automatic extensions and would require the Debtors to apply anew
to this Court for any further extension of the Election Period. Authorization of automatic extensions would, on the
other hand, benefit these estates by eliminating the expense
of repeated applications to this Court should additional
extensions be necessary to allow the Debtors optimal flexibility in advancing a feasible business plan for the benefit
of all parties in interest herein.

16. The Debtors submit that no harm, prejudice or
detriment will befall the Lessors by reason of the Debtors'
request herein. First, the Order is without prejudice to the
right of any Lessor to apply to this Court at any time for
entry of an order shortening the Election Period. Second,
any Lessor may terminate authorization for automatic extensions of the Election Period simply by making an objection
as described at paragraph 15 herein. Third, as required by
365(d)(3) of the Code, the Debtors have paid and intend to
continue to pay all use and occupancy charges due under the
Business Leases until the Debtors have obtained authority
from this Court for the rejection, assumption and/or
assignment of each of the Business Leases. The Lessors will
thus continue to enjoy the full benefit of their original
bargain with the Debtors as embodied in the Business Leases.

17. No previous request for the relief sought
herein has been made to this or any other Court.

WHEREFORE, the Debtors respectfully request the entry of the Order, providing for an extension of the Election Period for each of the Business Leases and for such other and further relief as may be just and proper.

DAVIS POLK & WARDWELL

By _____
A Member of the Firm

1 Chase Manhattan Plaza
New York, NY 10005
(212) 530-4000
Counsel for the Debtors and
    Debtors-In-Possession

Exhibit A

DESCRIPTION OF LEASES

Lessee	Square Footage	Annual Basic Rental Per Sq. Ft.	Monthly Basic Rental	Lease Term	Lessor	Building Description	Comments
(1) Lomas Financial Corp.	140,432	$14.00*	$163,837.33*	May 1, 1989 – April 30, 1999	2001 Tower Limited Partner- ship, A Texas Limited Partnership	2001 Bryan Tower, Dallas, TX 75201 (floors 33, 34, 35, 36, 37, with some storage space on floors 8, 27, 28 and 29)	Headquarters of Lomas Financial Corporation and certain subsidiaries
(2) Lomas Land	10,695	$28.20	$ 25,133.25	N/A	Lomas Mortgage U.S.A.	1600 Viceroy, 7th Floor Dallas, TX 75235	Headquarters of Lomas Realty USA and its subsidiaries
(3) Lomas Land	331**	$14.00	$ 386.17	N/A	Lomas Financial Corp.	2001 Bryan Tower, Suite 3500, Dallas, TX 75201	Lomas Realty USA conference room
(4) Lomas Land	750 Approx.	$16.00	$ 1,000.00	Oct. 20, 1989-Oct. 31, 1990	Hatfield Philips Inc.	Two Concourse Center, Suite 700 Atlanta, GA 30328	Eastern Region office

* Rate applicable from May 1, 1989 through April 30, 1994. From May 1, 1994 through April 30, 1999, the annual rent per square foot will be $17.00 and the monthly basic rental will be $198,945.33. In addition to the monthly basic rental, Lomas Financial Corp. is obligated to pay 13.19595% of the total usage of electricity at 2001 Bryan Tower.

** This space is a portion of the premises described in entry (1).

Matter of U.L. Radio Corp.
United States Bankruptcy Court, S. D. New York, 1982
19 B.R. 537

John J. Galgay, Bankruptcy Judge. Debtor, U.L. Radio Corp., has moved for an order, pursuant to Bankruptcy Code section 365(f), authorizing it to assume its lease ("Lease") with Jemrock Realty Company ("Jemrock"), the landlord, and authorizing U.L. Radio to assign the Lease to Just Heaven Restaurant, Ltd. ("Just Heaven"). U.L. Radio operates the leasehold as a television sales and service store. Just Heaven, the prospective assignee, will operate the premises as a small bistro. Jemrock opposes such an assignment, citing a use clause in the Lease which provides that the lessee shall use the premises only for television service and sale of electrical appliances. Jemrock asserts that the assignment of the Lease to Just Heaven would unlawfully modify the Lease by violating the use clause. Such modification, Jemrock avers, is not permitted under section 365 without the landlord's consent, which consent Jemrock withholds.

After a hearing, the Court ordered the parties to submit proposed findings of fact and conclusions of law (hereinafter "Findings and Conclusions"). The Court has considered all the papers submitted by the parties, the oral arguments and the applicable law and legislative history. The Court grants debtor's motion to assume and assign the Lease to Just Heaven.

I. Background

On September 17, 1979, the debtor entered into the Lease with Jemrock for a store located at 2656 Broadway, New York, New York. The store is located in a building which is also occupied by a grocery store, a Chinese restaurant, a liquor store, and 170 apartments. The term of the Lease is for ten years. * * * Paragraph 43 of the Rider to the Lease provides that the tenant may assign the Lease with the written consent of the Landlord, which consent is not to be unreasonably withheld.

On May 20, 1981, the debtor filed an original petition under Chapter 11 of the Bankruptcy Code and continues to operate its business as debtor in possession. No creditors' committee has been formed. The debtor intends to propose a liquidation plan of reorganization. The debtor is current in the payment of rent and related charges required by the terms of the Lease and is not in default of any of the Lease terms.

In furtherance of its intention to liquidate all of its assets and to propose a plan of reorganization, the debtor, subject to the approval of this Court, entered into an assignment of the Lease to Just Heaven. The proposed assignment provides, inter alia, that Just Heaven will pay to the Debtor as consideration for the assignment as follows: for the period commencing three months after this Court's approval of the assignment to October 31, 1988, the sum of $2000 per month. Such payments will fund a plan paying unsecured creditors 100 percent of their claims. Rockwell International, the largest creditor, recommends the assignment.

The president of Just Heaven has executed a personal guarantee for the payment of rent in favor of the landlord for the first two years of the assignment, together with a statement that her net worth exceeds $50,000.

The Lease provides in paragraph 45 of the rider to the Lease that "any noise emanating from said premises shall be deemed a breach of the terms and conditions of this Lease." Just Heaven has allocated $20,000 for construction, including soundproofing. David Humpal St. James, Vice President and Secretary as well as a director and a shareholder of Just Heaven, is a noted interior designer including the design of commercial restaurants. His design work has involved soundproofing. See Affidavit of David Humpal St. James.

II. Issues

Two issues confront this Court: (1) Have the provisions of section 365, regarding assumption and assignment of leases, been satisfied? (2) Can deviation from a use clause prevent the assignment of a lease, when the assumption and assignment otherwise comport with the requirements of section 365?

III. Assumption and Assignment Under Section 365

Code section 365 governs the assumption and assignment of executory contracts, providing broad authority to a trustee or debtor in possession[148] to assume and assign an unexpired lease. 11 U.S.C. §365(a). The aim of this statutory authority to assume a lease is to "assist in the debtor's rehabilitation or liquidation." House Report at 348, U.S.Code Cong. & Admin.News 1978, p. 6304; Senate Report at 59, U.S.Code Cong. & Admin.News 1978, p. 5845.

Assignment of a lease, which is at issue here, must comply with section 365(f), which states:

> (f)(1) Except as provided in subsection (c) of this section, notwithstanding a provision in an executory contract or unexpired lease of the debtor, or in applicable law, that prohibits, restricts, or conditions the assignment of such contract or lease, the trustee may assign such contract or lease under paragraph (2) of this subsection.
>
> (2) The trustee may assign an executory contract or unexpired lease of the debtor only if-
>
> (A) the trustee assumes such contract or lease in accordance with the provisions of this section; and
>
> (B) adequate assurance of future performance by the assignee of such contract or lease is provided, whether or not there has been a default in such contract or lease.

---

[148] Code section 1107 vests the rights, powers, and duties of a trustee in a debtor in possession.

(3) Notwithstanding a provision in an executory contract or unexpired lease of the debtor, or in applicable law that terminates or modifies, or permits a party other than the debtor to terminate or modify, such contract or lease or a right or obligation under such contract or lease on account of an assignment of such contract or lease, such contract, lease right, or obligation may not be terminated or modified under such provision because of the assumption or assignment of such contract or lease by the trustee.

* * *

A. Requirements of Assumption

The first requirement of assignment under section 365(f)(2) is proper assumption under section 365. The broad authority of a trustee or debtor in possession to assume is limited in Code section 365 by subsections (b), (c), and (d).

Section 365(b)(1) and (2) prescribe conditions to assumption of a lease if a default has occurred. "Subsection (b) requires the (debtor) to cure any default in the ... lease and to provide adequate assurance of future performance ... before he may assume." No default exists under the Lease before this Court; therefore, the subsection (b) requirements for assignment are not applicable.

Section 365(c) prohibits a debtor from assuming a lease if applicable nonbankruptcy law "independent of any language in the contract or Lease itself" excuses the other party from giving performance to or receiving performance from someone other than the debtor. Such "nondelegable" and, therefore, non-assumable contracts and leases include those for unique personal services, as well as those to extend credit, to make loans, and to issue securities. The Lease before this Court does not fall under the prohibition of section 365(c).

Section 365(d) sets time limits on the assumption of unexpired leases. The time requirements of subsection (d) have been met and are not at issue.

B. Adequate Assurance of Future Performance

The second requirement of assignment under section 365(f)(2) is adequate assurance of future performance ("adequate assurance"). Adequate assurance also appears in section 365(b) as a requirement of assumption if an executory contract is in default. The phrase "adequate assurance of future performance" is not found in the Bankruptcy Act.

Adequate assurance is not defined in section 365(f) nor in the legislative history of section 365(f), but "(t)he definition should generally be the same as in section 365(b)." In the legislative history of section 365(b), Congress while discussing assumption under section 365(b) and the bankruptcy clause under section 365(f), provided this explanation of adequate assurance: "If a trustee is to assume a contract or lease, the courts will have to insure that the trustee's performance under the contract or lease gives the other contracting party the full benefit of the bargain."

Beyond equating adequate assurance with the full benefit of the bargain, Congress offers no definition of adequate assurance except in the case of real property leases in shopping centers. The Lease at issue here is not located in a shopping center. Congress described a shopping center as "often a carefully planned enterprise, and though it consists of numerous individual tenants, the center is planned as a single unit, often subject to a master lease or financing agreement." House Report at 348, U.S.Code Cong. & Admin.News 1978, p. 6305. The building in which U.L. Radio is located is primarily a residential apartment building, with a liquor store, a grocery store, a restaurant, and U.L. Radio on the first floor. Thus the specific provisions of adequate assurance in the shopping center case do not apply to the assignment at issue here.

Apart from shopping center leases, Congress "entrusted the courts with the definition of adequate assurance of the performance of contracts and other leases." Adequate assurance of future performance are not words of art, but are to be given practical, pragmatic construction. What constitutes "adequate assurance" is to be determined by factual conditions. The broad authorization of the trustee or debtor to assume or assign unexpired leases, notwithstanding anti-assignment or bankruptcy clauses, prompted the admonition from Congress that the courts must "be sensitive to the rights of the nondebtor party to ... unexpired leases."

The phrase "adequate assurance of future performance" was adopted from Uniform Commercial Code section 2-609. U.C.C. section 2-609 * * * indicates that "adequate assurance" focuses on the financial condition of a contracting party and his ability to meet his financial obligations. Regarding adequate assurance under an assignment pursuant to section 365(f)(2), the Court in In re Lafayette Radio Electronics stated, "(T)he Court's primary focus will be on the ability of (the assignee) to comply with the financial obligations under the agreement."
      * * *

Thus, the primary focus of adequate assurance is the assignee's ability to satisfy financial obligations under the lease. In this case, the president of the assignee has executed a personal guarantee of the payment of rent in favor of the landlord for the first two years of the assignment, together with a statement that her net worth exceeds $50,000. The assignee has budgeted $20,000 for construction, enhancing the chances of success of the assignee's enterprise. The assignee will have operating capital of an additional $30,000. Upon these facts, the Court rules that adequate assurance of future financial performance has been provided by the assignee.

IV. Use Clause
However, adequate assurance of future financial performance is not the complete statutory requirement; adequate assurance of future performance is. The financial capability of an assignee may be sufficient for a finding of adequate assurance under an executory sales contract or a similar commercial

transaction. In a landlord-tenant relationship, more than an assignee's ability to comply with the financial provisions of a lease may be required. More particularly, will compliance with a use clause be required in order to provide adequate assurance?

Congress indicates that adequate assurance will give the landlord the full benefit of his bargain. In its case-by-case determination of those factors, beyond financial assurance, which constitute the landlord's bargain, the Court will generally consider the provisions of the lease to be assigned.

However, it is equally clear that, by requiring provision of adequate assurance under section 365, i.e., "the lessor's receipt of the 'full benefit of his bargain'," Congress did not require the Court to assure "literal fulfillment by the lessee of each and every term of the bargain." Section 365, by its own terms, empowers the court to render unenforceable bankruptcy clauses and anti-assignment clauses which permit modification or termination of a lease for filing in bankruptcy or assignment of the lease. 11 U.S.C. §365(e), (f)(3). Section 365(k) relieves the estate of liability for future breaches of a lease after assignment, notwithstanding lease provisions to the contrary.

The Court in In re Pin Oaks Apartments argued that court authority to abrogate lease provisions extends only to those provisions expressly stated by Congress:

> If Congress intended to give this Court or the trustee the power to abrogate any contractual rights between a debtor and non-debtor contracting party other than anti-assignment and "ipso facto" (i.e. bankruptcy) clauses, it would have expressly done so.

7 B.R. at 367, 6 B.C.D. at 1398.

Such a narrow view of court authority is not supported by the statute or the legislative history. First, such a narrow view would frustrate the express policy of Congress favoring assignment. Under the Pin Oaks reasoning, lessors could employ very specific use clauses to prevent assignment and thus circumvent the Code. Section 365(f), in broad language, empowers the Court to authorize assignment of an unexpired lease and invalidate any lease provision which would terminate or modify the lease because of the assignment of that lease. 11 U.S.C. §365(f)(1), (3). Any lease provision, not merely one entitled "anti-assignment clause", would be subject to the court's scrutiny regarding its anti-assignment effect. The court could render unenforceable any provision whose sole effect is to restrict assignment, "as contrary to the policy of (subsection (f)(3))." House Report at 349; Senate Report at 59.

Further, when Congress intended that all terms and provisions of an agreement remain unaltered, it expressly stated such an intent. Section 1124 sets down stringent requirements to define unimpaired claims, requiring the cure of defaults and the unaltered maintenance of legal, equitable, and contractual rights. * * * Under both sections 1124 and 365, Congress expressly stated the requirements. Under section 365, literal compliance with all lease terms was not required. Even under the tightly drawn definition of adequate assurance in the shopping center case, Congress did not envision literal compliance with all lease provisions; insubstantial disruptions in, inter alia, tenant mix and insubstantial breaches in other leases or agreements were contemplated and allowed.

Thus, provision of adequate assurance of future performance does not require an assignee's literal compliance with each and every term of the lease. The court may permit deviations from strict enforcement of any provision including a use clause.

* * *

Section 365 expresses a clear Congressional policy favoring assumption and assignment. Such a policy will insure that potential valuable assets will not be lost by a debtor who is reorganizing his affairs or liquidating assets for distribution to creditors. This policy parallels case law which disfavors forfeiture. To prevent an assignment of an unexpired lease by demanding strict enforcement of a use clause, and thereby contradict clear Congressional policy, a landlord or lessor must show that actual and substantial detriment would be incurred by him if the deviation in use was permitted.

In this case, the contemplated deviation in use is from an appliance store to a small bistro. The building in which the unexpired leasehold is located already contains a restaurant, a laundry, and a liquor store. The landlord has failed to demonstrate any actual and substantial detriment which he would incur if the proposed deviation in use is permitted. The Court also notes that the contemplated use, along with the planned soundproofing, will have no adverse effect on other tenants in the building. Thus, this Court rules that the use clause may not be enforced so as to block assignment of this lease to Just Heaven. The fact that Jemrock withholds its consent to the proposed assignment will not prevent the assignment. Consent is required only in leases governed by section 365(c). The lease here is not subject to section 365(c).

Finally, the Court briefly addresses the constitutional issue raised by the deviation in the contractual terms of the lease. Can a landlord assert a violation of the Fifth Amendment which prohibits the taking of property without due process of law? The Court in In re Sapolin Paints, Inc., 5 B.R. 412 (Bkrtcy.E.D.N.Y.1980), denied the enforceability of a bankruptcy clause, stating: "Bankruptcy proceedings constantly modify and affect property rights established by state law." The power given Congress by Article I, Section 8, of the Constitution to establish uniform laws relative to bankruptcy gives it broad latitude to effect both contract and property rights.

Congress, in section 365, has stated a general policy favoring assignment. Balanced against this general policy is the requirement that the non-debtor contracting party receive the full benefit of his bargain. Jemrock Realty will receive the full benefit of its bargain under the proposed assignment of the leasehold from U.L. Radio to Just Heaven. No defaults exist under the lease. The lease has properly been assumed and Just Heaven has provided adequate assurance of future performance. The landlord has shown no actual or substantial detriment to him from the proposed assignment. The statutory requirements have been satisfied. The assignment is authorized.

It is so ordered.

Problems

1. The opinion states that the debtor was "not in default on any of the Lease terms." Note the prefatory language in section 365(b) -- "If there has been a default . . ." Since there was no default, why did the court require adequate assurance of future performance?

2. The Lease in *U.L. Radio* provided that the tenant may assign the lease with the written consent of the Landlord. Would the case have been decided differently if

    a. the Lease had prohibited assignments; or

    b. the Lease conditioned assignment on payment of all assignment proceeds to the Landlord.

3. The opinion also notes that the Lease was not in a "shopping center." Special provisions govern the assignment of leases in shopping centers. See section 365(b)(3). Why? Would the case have been decided differently if the building was a shopping center?

4. Note that in the last paragraph, the court finds that "the landlord has shown no actual or substantial detriment to him from the proposed assignment." How could the landlord show such detriment? If the landlord has shown that other tenants were moving out because of a bistro in the building, would Judge Galgay have reached a different decision?

5. See generally Scott Ehrlich, *The Assumption and Rejection of Unexpired Real Property Leases Under the Bankruptcy Code -- A New Look,* 32 BUFFALO L. REV. 1, 35-43 (1983).

C. EXECUTORY CONTRACTS AND LIMITATIONS ON THE REJECTION, ASSUMPTION AND ASSIGNMENT OF EXECUTORY CONTRACTS

1. What Is An Executory Contract?

Section 365 applies to "executory contracts" as well as to leases. The Bankruptcy Code does not define the term "executory contract." The most frequently cited discussion of executory contracts in bankruptcy is in a law review article by Professor Vern Countryman written prior to the enactment of the Bankruptcy Code. In the article, Professor Countryman reviews the pre-Code cases and concludes from those cases that an executory contract for purposes of bankruptcy law is one that is so far unperformed on both sides that the failure of either party to complete its performance would be a material breach, excusing further performance from the other party. Most of the reported cases under the Bankruptcy Code seem to use this "Countryman definition" of executory contracts.

Please apply the "Countryman definition" and section 365 to the following problems.

Problems

1. D contracts to buy 1000 tons of sulfuric acid from T for $25 a ton. D files for bankruptcy before either party performs.
    a. Is the contract an "executory contract" under the Countryman test?
    b. Does D have to "assume" the contract in order to obtain the acid?
    c. What is T's claim if D assumes the contract?
    d. What is T's claim if D rejects the contract?

2. D contracts to buy 2000 tons of sulfuric acid from T for $25 a ton. D files for bankruptcy after T has delivered the acid but before D has paid.
    a. Is the contract an executory contract under the Countryman test?
    b. Does D have to assume the contract in order to retain the acid?
    c. What is T's claim?

3. D contracts to buy 3000 tons of sulfuric acid from T for $25 a ton. D files for bankruptcy after it has paid T but before T has delivered the acid.
    a. Is the contract an executory contract under the Countryman test?
    b. Does D have to assume the contract in order to have a right to the acid?
    c. What is T's claim?

4. In a series of articles Michael Andrew, Morris Shanker, and Jay Westbrook have suggested that the definition of "executory contract" is not important when a debtor wishes to reject the contract -- that the nondebtor party to a rejected executory contract is in the same position as a the nondebtor party to a "non-executory" contract. E.g., Michael Andrew, *Executory Contracts in Bankruptcy: Understanding "Rejection"*, 59 U. COLO. L.REV. 845 (1988); Morris Shanker, Bankruptcy Asset Theory and Its Application to Executory Contracts, 1992 ANNUAL SURVEY OF BANKRUPTCY LAW 97; Jay Westbrook, *A Functional Analysis of Executory Contracts*, 74 MINN. L. REV. 227 (1989). Do you agree?

5. Andrew, Shanker, and Westbrook and the cases following their articles focus on the consequences of "rejection", rather than on the meaning of "executory contract". We first considered the consequences of rejection beginning on page 916 *supra*. What if one of your relatives comes to you with the following problems:

    a. D entered into a contract with your brother-in-law which granted him a ten-year non-exclusive license to utilize a metal processing technology owned by D. A year later, D files for bankruptcy and rejects its contract with your brother-in-law so that it can grant an exclusive license to X. Can your brother-in-law continue to use the technology? See section 365(n)

    b. Your sister owns a hotel in Minneapolis. She operates the hotel as a Days Inn under a franchise agreement with Days Inns of America, Inc (D). D files for bankruptcy, decides to terminate its hotel operations in Minnesota, and rejects the franchise agreement with your sister. Can your sister continue to operate her hotel as a Days Inn?

    c. Your aunt sells her veterinary practice to X and enters into a covenant not to compete with X which provides for four annual payments by X to your aunt. A year later, your aunt files for bankruptcy. Can she reject the covenant not to compete with X and resume her veterinary practice? Is this a section 365 question?

2. What Are The Limitations On Rejection Of An Executory Contract?

Section 365(a)'s requirement of court approval is the only generally applicable limitation on the rejection of executory contracts. Section 365(a) does not indicate what standard the bankruptcy court should apply in determining whether to approve the debtor's rejection of an executory contract. Bankruptcy judges generally apply a business judgment test and give great weight to the business judgment of the debtor. Should the Tampa bankruptcy judge grant Sabal Hotel's motion to reject its franchise contract with Holiday Inn set out below?

IN THE UNITED STATES BANKRUPTCY COURT
FOR THE MIDDLE DISTRICT OF FLORIDA
TAMPA DIVISION

IN RE:)
)   CASE NO. 91-91-35998131
SABAL HOTEL, LTD.,   )
)   CHAPTER 11
        Debtor   )
_____)

MOTION TO REJECT EXECUTORY CONTRACT

SABAL HOTEL, LTD., as Debtor and Debtor-in-Possession, by its undersigned attorneys, moves, pursuant to 11 U.S.C. 365, to reject its executory contract with Holiday Inns Inc. on the following grounds:

1. The Debtor has filed a voluntary Petition under Chapter 11 of the Bankruptcy Code and has been retained in possession of its assets as Debtor-in-Possession. No committee of creditors has been appointed in this case.

2. The Debtor owns and operates a hotel facility located in the Sabal Park industrial-business area in the eastern suburbs of Tampa, Florida. The Debtor's facility is a multi-story hotel comprising of 265 guest rooms and suites as well as various public areas, function rooms, restaurants, and the like. The Debtor's hotel facility is four years old, and can be described a "first rate" hotel facility.

3. On March 6, 1987, Debtor entered into a Holiday Inn License Agreement ("Contract") with Holiday Inns, Inc. The Contract expires on March 5, 2007. The Contract is an "executory contract" for purposes of section 365.

4. The Contract provides for termination by the Debtor on twelve months notice. Because it was the Debtor's business judgment that its Contract costs exceeded its Contract benefits, Debtor sent a termination notice to Holiday Inns, Inc. on or about March 7, 1991.

5. Similarly, it is the business judgment of the Debtor as Debtor-in-Possession that the costs of the Contract to the estate exceed the benefits to the estate from the Contract and that the Contract inhibits rather than enhances the prospects of an effective reorganization.

WHEREFORE, SABAL HOTEL, LTD. prays this Court to enter an order authorizing it to reject its executory contract with Holiday Inns Inc.

JOHNSON, BLAKELY, POPE, BOKOR,
RUPPEL & BURNS, P.A.

By: *Charles M. Tatelbaum*
      Charles M. Tatelbaum
      Michael C. Markham
      201 E. Kennedy Boulevard
      Suite 1700
      Tampa, Florida 33602
      (813) 2252500
      Fla. Bar No. 177540
      Fla. Bar No. 768560
      Attorneys for Debtor

I HEREBY CERTIFY that a true and correct copy of the foregoing has been furnished by regular U.S. mail, postage pre paid, to the Office of the U.S. Trustee, 4921 Memorial Highway, Tampa, Florida 33634 and Holiday Inns Inc., 3796 Lamar Avenue, Memphis, Tennessee 38195, this 21st day of March, 1991.

Charles M. Tatelbaum
Charles M. Tatelbaum

Notes and Problems

1. Is the Holiday Inn License Agreement an "executory contract"?

2. Should the bankruptcy court approve the rejection if Holiday Inn objects? What if the License Agreement provides for liquidated damages of $1,000,000.00 if the License Agreement is rejected in a bankruptcy case?

3. Should the bankruptcy court approve the rejection if the bank that has a mortgage on the hotel objects?

4. If you represented Sabal Hotel, would you have drafted the motion to reject differently?

5. Other provisions in section 365 and elsewhere in the Code restrict the rejection of or the consequences of the rejection of various "special" leases and contracts such as licenses of intellectual property (section 365(n)), aircraft leases (section 1110), and collective bargaining agreements (section 1113).

3. What Are The Limitations On The Assumption Or Assignment Of Executory Contracts?

Obviously, there are some contracts that a debtor can not assign. Assume, for example, that Sharon Stone signs a movie contract and then files for bankruptcy. Ms Stone could not invoke section 365 and assign that contract to David Epstein.

While it is less obvious, there are also executory contracts that can not be assumed by a debtor. Section 365(c)(2) precludes the debtor's assumption of contracts to make loans. For example, C agrees to provide a $100,000 line of credit to D. D files for bankruptcy. D can not assume the financing agreement and require C to lend her the $100,000.

The following case and problems provide even less obvious examples of limitations on assignment and assumption of executory contracts.

In re Pioneer Ford Sales, Inc.
United States Court of Appeals, First Circuit, 1984
729 F.2d 27

Breyer, Circuit Judge. The Ford Motor Company appeals a federal district court decision, allowing a bankrupt Ford dealer (Pioneer Ford Sales, Inc.) to assign its Ford franchise over Ford's objection to a Toyota dealer (Toyota Village, Inc.). The district court decided the case on the basis of a record developed in the bankruptcy court. The bankruptcy court had approved the transfer, which ran from Pioneer to Fleet National Bank (Pioneer's principal secured creditor) and then to Toyota Village. Fleet sought authorization for the assignment because Toyota Village will pay $10,000 for the franchise and buy all parts and accessories in Pioneer's inventory at fair market value (about $75,000); if the franchise is not assigned, Ford will buy only some of the parts for between $45,000 and $55,000. Thus, the assignment will increase the value of the estate. Fleet is the appellee here.

The issue that the case raises is the proper application of §365(c)(1)(A), an exception to a more general provision, §365(f)(1), that allows a trustee in bankruptcy (or a debtor in possession) to assign many of the debtor's executory contracts even if the contract itself says that it forbids assignment.

The words "applicable law" in this section mean "applicable non-bankruptcy law." Evidently, the theory of this section is to prevent the trustee from assigning (over objection) contracts of the sort that contract law ordinarily makes nonassignable, *i.e.* contracts that cannot be assigned when the contract itself is silent about assignment. At the same time, by using the words in (1)(A) 'whether *or not* the contract prohibits assignment,' the section prevents parties from using contractual language to prevent the trustee from assigning contracts that (when the contract is silent) contract law typically makes assignable. *Id.* Thus, we must look to see whether relevant nonbankruptcy law would allow Ford to veto the assignment of its basic franchise contract "whether or not" that basic franchise contract itself specifically "prohibits assignment."

The nonbankruptcy law to which both sides point us is contained in Rhode Island's "Regulation of Business Practices Among Motor Vehicle Manufacturers, Distributors and Dealers" Act, R.I.Gen.Laws §31-5.1-4(C)(7). It states that

> [N]o dealer *** shall have the right to *** assign the franchise *** without the consent of the manufacturer, except that such consent shall not be unreasonably withheld.

The statute by its terms, allows a manufacturer to veto an assignment where the veto is reasonable but not otherwise. The statute's language also indicates that it applies "whether or not" the franchise contract itself restricts assignment. Thus, the basic question that the case presents is whether Ford's veto was reasonable in terms of the Rhode Island law.

Neither the district court nor the bankruptcy court specifically addressed this question. Their failure apparently arose out of their belief that §365(c)(1)(A) refers only to traditional personal service contracts. But in our view they were mistaken. The language of the section does not limit its effect to personal service contracts. It refers *generally* to contracts that are not assignable under nonbankruptcy law. State laws typically make contracts for personal services nonassignable (where the contract itself is silent); but they make other sorts of contracts nonassignable as well. The legislative history of §365(c) says nothing about "personal services." To the contrary, it speaks of letters of credit, personal loans, and leases—instances in which assigning a contract may place the other party at a significant disadvantage. The history thereby suggests that (c)(1)(A) has a broader reach.

The source of the "personal services" limitation apparently is a bankruptcy court case, *In re Taylor Manufacturing, Inc.*, 6 B.R. 370 (Bkrtcy.N.D.Ga.1980), which other bankruptcy courts have followed. The *Taylor* court wrote that (c)(1)(A) should be interpreted narrowly, in part because it believed that (c)(1)(A) conflicted with another section, (f)(1), which states in relevant part:

> Except as provided in subsection (c) ***, notwithstanding a provision *** in applicable law that prohibits *** the assignment of [an executory] contract *** the trustee may assign [it]. ***

As a matter of logic, however, we see no conflict, for (c)(1)(A) refers to state laws that prohibit assignment "whether or not" the contract is silent, while (f)(1) contains no such limitation. Apparently (f)(1) includes state laws that prohibit assignment only when the contract is *not* silent about assignment; that is to say, state laws that enforce contract provisions prohibiting assignment. The section specifically excepts (c)(1)(A)'s state laws that forbid assignment even when the contract *is* silent; they are to be heeded. Regardless, we fail to see why a "conflict" suggests that (c)(1)(A) is limited to "personal services."

Indeed, since it often is difficult to decide whether or not a particular duty can be characterized by the label "personal service," it makes sense to avoid this question and simply look to see whether state law would, or would not, make the duty assignable where the contract is silent. We therefore reject the district court's conclusion in this respect.

Although the district court did not explicitly decide whether Ford's veto was reasonable, it decided a closely related question. Under other provisions of §365 a bankruptcy court cannot authorize assignment of an executory contract if 1) the debtor is in default, unless 2) there is "adequate assurance of future performance." §365(b)(1)(C). Pioneer is in default, but the bankruptcy and district courts found "adequate assurance." For the sake of argument, we shall assume that this finding is equivalent to a finding that Ford's veto of the assignment was unreasonable. On these assumptions, favorable to Fleet, we nonetheless must reverse the district court, for, in our view, any finding of unreasonableness, based on this record, is clearly erroneous.

Our review of the record reveals the following critical facts. First, in accordance with its ordinary business practice and dealer guidelines incorporated into the franchise agreement, Ford would have required Toyota Village, as a dealer, to have a working capital of at least $172,000, of which no more than half could be debt. Toyota Village, however, had a working capital at the end of 1981 of $37,610; and its net worth was $31,747. * * *

Second, at a time when Japanese cars have sold well throughout the United States, Toyota Village has consistently lost money. * * *

* * * In these circumstances, Ford would seem perfectly reasonable in withholding its consent to the transfer. Thus, Rhode Island law would make the franchise unassignable.

One might still argue that under Rhode Island law the only "reasonable" course of action for Ford is to allow the transfer and then simply terminate Toyota Village if it fails to perform adequately. This suggestion, however, overlooks the legal difficulties that Ford would have in proving cause for termination under the Rhode Island "Regulation of Business Practices Among Motor Vehicle Manufacturers, Distributors and Dealers" Act. R.I.Gen.Laws §31-5.1-4(D)(2). The very purpose of the statute—protecting dealer reliance—suggests that it ought to be more difficult for a manufacturer to terminate a dealer who has invested in a franchise than to oppose the grant of a franchise to one who has not. In any event, the law does not suggest a manufacturer is "unreasonable" in objecting to a transfer unless he would have "good cause" to terminate the transferee. And, to equate the two standards would tend to make the "unreasonable" provision superfluous. Thus, we conclude that the Rhode Island law would make the franchise unassignable on the facts here revealed. Therefore, neither the bankruptcy court nor the district court had the power to authorize the transfer.

Notes and Problems

1. The *Pioneer Ford* case deals with a statutory prohibition on assignment. Are there any common-law prohibitions on assignments? In discussing whether a performance is delegable under common law contract principles, Professor Farnsworth notes, "One of the most significant of these circumstances is the extent to which the performance is personal in the sense that the recipient must rely on qualities such as the character, reputation, taste, skill, or discretion of the party who is to render it. For example, an artist who contracts to paint a portrait or a singer who contracts to sing

in an opera cannot delegate performance, even though the delegate's performance might be superior to that of the party delegating it." A. Farnsworth, CONTRACTS 738 (1982). Assume, for example, that Batman contracts to patrol the streets of Gotham. Could he delegate this duty to Billy Batson? If Batman filed a Chapter 13 petition, could he assume this contract and assign it to Billy Batson?

2. *In Pioneer Ford*, there was also a contractual prohibition on assignment. The franchise agreement between Ford and the debtor expressly provided that the franchise was not transferable or assignable. What is the effect of such a contract provision in bankruptcy? Section 365(f)(1).

3. Your client, C, is negotiating a copyright license contract with X. C is concerned about the possibility of X filing for bankruptcy. X's attorney proposes the following contract language: "Either party may terminate this agreement if the other Party is adjudicated a bankrupt, makes an assignment for the benefit of creditors, or otherwise avails itself or becomes subject to any bankruptcy or insolvency statute." Is this helpful?

4. Why did the court in *Pioneer Ford* consider the business record of Toyota Village, the assignee? See section 365(f)(2), 365(k).

5. Judge Breyer held that section 365(c)(1)(A) prevents the Debtor from assigning its Ford franchise to a third party. Does section 365(c)(1)(A) also prevent the Debtor from assuming its franchise agreement with Ford and continuing to operate the Ford dealership itself? Note that section 365(c) begins "The trustee may not assume or assign if * * *."

Unit 13

AVOIDANCE OF TRANSFERS

UNIT CONTENTS

In the absence of bankruptcy, some transfers of a debtor's property can be invalidated under state laws, such as state fraudulent conveyance laws. The Bankruptcy Code incorporates these state laws in section 544(b) so that a transfer of a debtor's property that can be invalidated under state law in the absence of bankruptcy can be invalidated under section 544(b) in the event of bankruptcy.

Chapter 5 of the Bankruptcy Code also contains several other "avoidance" provisions. Accordingly, some payments, sales, exchanges, judicial liens, security interests and other transfers that are valid under state law can be avoided in bankruptcy.

The Bankruptcy Code's avoidance provisions reach both "voluntary" transfers such as a debtor's making a gift to a relative or granting a mortgage to a creditor and "involuntary" transfers such as a creditor's garnishing the debtor's bank account or subjecting the debtor's real property to a judgment lien. Note also that the Bankruptcy Code's avoidance provisions reach both "absolute" transfers such as gifts, payments and sales, and "security transfers" such as mortgages and judgment liens.

In working with these avoidance provisions, law students and lawyers are called on to answer two basic questions : (1) what are the consequences of avoiding a transfer and (2) which transfers can be avoided. Law students are called on to answer these questions both in class and on exams. Lawyers are called upon to answer these questions not only in negotiating and litigating in bankruptcy cases but also in structuring transactions outside of bankruptcy.

To illustrate, assume that your client C buys a business from D for $2,000,000 and pays your firm $100,000 for your legal work on the transaction. If D later files for bankruptcy, you do not want to be in the awkward position of having to call C and tell her that D's bankruptcy trustee has been able to invoke the Bankruptcy Code's avoidance power to recover all of the assets that C purchased from D.

Understanding the Bankruptcy Code avoidance power provisions and the materials on these provisions set out below can be hard. But not as hard as calling C.

A. WHAT ARE THE CONSEQUENCES OF AVOIDING A TRANSFER?

When the bankruptcy trustee avoids an absolute transfer of property, that property then becomes property of the estate. Assume that D owes C $25,000. D repays C $12,000 of that debt. D later files for bankruptcy. At the time of D's bankruptcy filing, the $12,000 paid to C is not property of the estate. If the bankruptcy trustee is able to invoke one of the Bankruptcy Code's avoidance provisions to avoid the $12,000 payment, the $12,000 will then become property of the estate, sections 541(a)(3), 550.

The avoidance of an absolute transfer can also affect the amount of a creditor's claim. In the above hypothetical, C had a $13,000 claim at the time of D's bankruptcy filing. Again, if the bankruptcy trustee is able to recover the $12,000 D paid C from C by avoiding the payment, then C will have a $25,000 claim against D, section 502(h).

The consequences of avoiding a security transfer are similar. Assume, for example, that D borrows $77,000 from C and grants C a mortgage on Blackacre which is worth $120,000. D later files for bankruptcy. Absent the trustee's use of one of the avoidance powers, C has a $77,000 secured claim. Recall that under section 541, Blackacre itself is not property of the estate; rather the estate's interest in Blackacre is only D's limited equity and other rights in Blackacre. If, however, the bankruptcy trustee is able to avoid the grant of the mortgage on Blackacre, then C will have a $77,000 unsecured claim, and Blackacre without any encumbrance will be property of the estate.

In the two examples, the consequences of avoidance were the recovery of the property interest transferred from the party to whom it had been transferred. Under section 550, the consequences of avoidance are not limited to recovery of the property transferred, are not limited to recovery from the party to whom the property had been transferred. Please apply section 550 in the following problems.

Problems

1. **"Or, if the court so orders the value of such property"**

   a. D transfers equipment to C. The equipment is destroyed, and C collects $100,000 from its insurance company. D later files for bankruptcy. What can the bankruptcy trustee recover from C if she is able to avoid the transfer of equipment?

   b. D transfers real property to C. At the time of the transfer, the property was worth $200,000. D later files for bankruptcy. C still owns the real property. Because of declining property values, the property is now worth only $30,000. What can the trustee recover from C if she is able to avoid the transfer?

2. **"Or the entity for whose benefit such transfer was made"**
   C makes a $200,000 loan to D, G guarantees payment. D repays the $200,000 to C. Who benefited from this payment?

3. **"Initial transferee", "immediate transferee"**

   a. Section 550(a)(1) provides for recovery from the initial transferee." Section 550(a)(2) provides for recovery from any "immediate or mediate transferee of such initial transferee." D transfers Blackacre to C. C later transfers Blackacre to X. D files for bankruptcy. If you have read the hypothetical, it should be obvious that C is the "initial transferee" and that X is the "immediate transferee." And, if you will read section 550(b), the reasons that it can be important to identify a transferee as "initial" or "immediate" should also be obvious.

   b. Your client, Bank C loans X $655,000. Subsequently, D, an affiliate of X, remits a $200,000 check to Bank C with instructions directing Bank C to deposit the $200,000 in X's account in Bank C. Bank C complies with this direction. Shortly thereafter, X instructs Bank C to debit $200,000 from its account to pay down the $655,000 loan. If D later files for bankruptcy and the trustee is able to avoid the $200,000 payment, is Bank C an "initial transferee" or an "immediate transferee"? If Bank C is an "immediate transferee", did it "take for value" as required by section 550(b)?

B. WHICH TRANSFERS CAN BE AVOIDED?

1. Fraudulent Transfers And Obligations

Bankruptcy law, like state law, provides for the avoidance of fraudulent conveyances. Indeed, the Bankruptcy Code provisions are very much like the state law fraudulent conveyance laws considered earlier.   Section 548 of the Bankruptcy Code is based on section 67d of the Bankruptcy Act of 1898 which was based on the Uniform Fraudulent Conveyances Act.

Section 548(a)(1) empowers the bankruptcy trustee to avoid transfers made and obligations incurred with actual intent to hinder, delay or defraud. creditors. There is rarely direct evidence of actual intent. Instead, there are certain facts recognized are strong indicia of actual fraudulent intent. Some of these "badges of fraud" are (i) the existence of a family or other close relationship between the transferor and the transferee, (ii) the absence or inadequacy of consideration, and (iii) secrecy of the transfer.

Section 548(a)(2) provides for avoidance of transfers and obligations that are constructively fraudulent. Please read section 548(a)(2) carefully and apply it in the following problems and cases.

Problems

1.   D's creditors are threatening to repossess his boat. D, who is insolvent, gives the boat to his father, F. Within a year, D files for bankruptcy. Can the trustee avoid the gift of the boat as a fraudulent transfer?

2.   Same facts as Problem 1 except that D sells the boat to F for $3,000. Can the bankruptcy trustee avoid the sale of the boat if she can establish that the value of the boat at the time of the sale was $5,000? If so, what are F's rights? See sections 548(c), 550, 502(b)

3.   When D defaulted on his mortgage payments, S foreclosed on D's house. At the foreclosure sale, S bought the house by bidding in its $30,000 debt. In every respect the foreclosure sale and purchase by S complied with the procedures of state law. Within a year of the foreclosure sale, D filed for bankruptcy. Can the bankruptcy trustee avoid the foreclosure sale of the house if the trustee can establish that, measured in terms of comparable properties sold in due course through the ordinary real estate market, the "fair market value" of the D's house at the time of the foreclosure sale was 50,000? Even the Supreme Court is sharply divided. See *BFP v. Resolution Trust Corp.*, 1994 WL 197048 (U.S. May 23, 1994) (5-4) (Scalia wrote for the majority that any price paid at a foreclosure sale is reasonably equivalent value so long as the sale complied with state law.). See generally Frank Kennedy, *Involuntary Fraudulent Transfers*, 9 Cardozo L. Rev. 531 (1987).

In re Young
United States District Court, D. Minnesota, 1993
152 B.R. 939

[Reprinted in Unit 1 at pages 74-78 supra.]

Notes and Problems

1. "The doctrine is firmly declared to be that one must be just before he is generous ***. A donor may make a conveyance with the most upright intentions, and yet, if the transfer hinders, delays, or defrauds his creditors, it may be set aside as fraudulent." *In re Martin*, 124 B.R. 69, 73 (Bankr. N.D. Ill. 1991); see generally 1 G. Glenn, FRAUDULENT CONVEYANCES AND PREFERENCES §§264-72 (rev. ed. 1940)

2. "The parties agreed that the key issue is whether debtors received some sort of property right." Do you agree? What if the Youngs send their child to a private school and paid that school $5,000 tuition within a year of their bankruptcy filing? Is the $5,000 tuition payment a fraudulent conveyance?

3. Were the district court and the bankruptcy court "correct to look to Supreme Court precedent in connection with the Internal Revenue Code for assistance"?

4. In the above problems, insolvency has been assumed. In the *Young* case, the parties stipulated that the debtor was insolvent. How can the trustee's attorney prove insolvency?

□□□□□□

Young and the problems preceding it involved consumer problems. Increasingly, fraudulent conveyance law is being used to challenge commercial and corporate transactions.

Commerce Bank v. Achtenberg
United States District Court, W.D.Missouri, 1993
1993 WL 476510

Sachs, Senior District Judge. Before the court is defendant Commerce Bank of Kansas City's ("Commerce") appeal from the decision of the Bankruptcy Court in favor of David Achtenberg and Steven C. Block ("the Trustees"), the individual acting trustees for the separate bankruptcy estates of George P. Kroh and John A. Kroh, Jr. ("the debtors"). The Bankruptcy Court found that the debtors did not receive reasonably equivalent value in exchange for the personal guarantees the debtors gave to Commerce for loans Commerce made to Kroh

Brothers Development Company ("KBDC"). Accordingly, the Bankruptcy Court voided the guarantees as fraudulent transfers under 11 U.S.C. §548(a)(2).

This court has jurisdiction to hear this appeal pursuant to 11 U.S.C. §158. Commerce contends, and the Trustees concur, that because this appeal only involves the Bankruptcy Court's conclusions of law the court should review those conclusions de novo.

The parties submitted this case to the Bankruptcy Court on a stipulation of the following facts:

1. Plaintiffs are the duly appointed, qualified and acting trustees for the bankruptcy estates of brothers and debtors George and John Kroh.

2. On October 20, 1986, within one year before commencement of debtors' bankruptcy proceedings, Commerce loaned $7 million to KBDC.

3. On October 20, 1986, within one year before commencement of debtors' bankruptcy proceedings, debtors each incurred an obligation to Commerce by guaranteeing KBDC's debt to Commerce in the amount of $7 million.

4. At the time of the $7 million loan and guarantees, debtors were insolvent within the meaning of §101(31).

5. At the time of the $7 million loan and guarantees, debtors were officers and directors of KBDC, and each owned 50% of the issued and outstanding common stock of KBDC.

6. Neither debtor directly received any part of the $7 million loan proceeds.

7. Commerce has not been repaid any of the $7 million loan from either KBDC or debtors, but has filed proofs of claim in all three cases.

8. At the time of the loan and guarantees, KBDC, George and John were all insolvent. Subsequent to the $7 million loan and guarantees, the financial condition of KBDC and its subsidiaries did not improve, but continued to worsen between December 31, 1985, and January 1, 1987.

9. On January 29, 1987, involuntary bankruptcy petitions were filed against debtors. On February 25, 1989, on debtors' applications, the cases were converted from Chapter 7 to voluntary Chapter 11 cases.

10. On April 7, 1989, David Achtenberg, bankruptcy trustee for George, filed an adversary proceeding seeking to avoid George's payment obligation under his personal guarantee to Commerce pursuant to §548. Likewise, on June 9, 1989, Steven Block, bankruptcy trustee for John, filed a similar adversary action.

11. From October 20, 1986, until the date of bankruptcy, George advanced $1,345,500.00 to KBDC and was repaid $171,766.68; John advanced $1,352,018.00 and was repaid $89,966.68.

Based on these facts the Bankruptcy Court made the following legal conclusions:

1. The Trustees met the burden of making a prima facie showing that the debtors did not receive a reasonably equivalent value for their obligation to Commerce by showing that the debtors did not directly receive any of the loan proceeds.

2. The burden then shifted to Commerce to establish that the debtors indirectly received a reasonably equivalent value.

3. The debtors shared an "identity of interest" with KBDC.

4. However, the "identity of interest" finding did not create a presumption of reasonably equivalent value.

5. Commerce did not produce any evidence, let alone fairly concrete evidence, to support a finding of reasonably equivalent value. Accordingly, the debtors did not receive reasonably equivalent value for their obligations to Commerce and the obligations are avoidable as constructive fraudulent transfers.
* * *

A.

A fraudulent transfer is avoidable under §548(a)(2) of the Bankruptcy Code if the Trustee or debtor in possession can establish the following four conditions: first, that there was a transfer of an interest of the debtor in property; second, that the transfer was made within one year before the date of the filing of the petition; third, that the debtor received less than a reasonably equivalent value in exchange for the transfer; and fourth, that the debtor was insolvent on the date the transfer was made. The parties stipulated to the first, second and fourth elements. Thus the only issue before the Bankruptcy Court was whether the debtor received less than a reasonably equivalent value in exchange for the transfer.

Obligations which debtors incur solely for the benefit of third parties are presumptively not supported by a reasonably equivalent value. Rubin v. Manufacturers Hanover Trust Co., 661 F.2d 979, 989 (2d Cir.1981). However, an exception to the rule exists if the debtor and the third party "are so related or situated that they share an 'identity of interests' because what benefits one will, in such case, benefit the other to some degree." In re Ear, Nose and Throat Surgeons, Inc. 49 Bankr. 316 (Bankr.D.Mass.1985) (quoting In re Royal Crown Bottlers, Inc., 23 Bankr. 28, 30 (Bankr.N.D.Ala.1982)). The Rubin court explained the rationale for the exception,

> if the consideration given to the third person has ultimately landed in the debtor's hands, or if the giving of the consideration to the third person otherwise confers an economic benefit upon the debtor, then the debtor's net worth has been preserved.

Rubin at 991. Because the primary consideration is the degree to which the debtor's net worth is preserved, the focus always is on the economic benefit, if any flowing to the debtor as a result of the transfer. However, an identity of interests alone is not enough to validate affiliate guarantees. Rather, the court must analyze all facts and determine the extent to which each guarantor received economic value in exchange for the obligations it guaranteed. * * *

B.

Commerce next argues that the Bankruptcy Court erred in holding that the existence of an identity of interest between the debtors and KBDC, in conjunction with the downstream[1] nature of the transaction, did not create the presumption of reasonably equivalent value. * * *

Commerce is correct that evidence of a downstream guaranty and identity of interest would normally entitle it to a presumption of reasonably equivalent value. However, the court need not decide this issue because KBDC's insolvency at the time of the transaction erased any presumption of reasonably equivalent value. The stipulated evidence is that KBDC was insolvent at the time of the transaction and the loan did not make it more solvent. Thus, the net worth of the guarantor debtors was diminished by the obligation, and the innocent creditors of the debtors were in fact harmed by the transfer. * * * It can hardly be said that the debtor's net worth has been preserved and the interests of the creditors not injured when the debtor guarantees a loan to an insolvent entity. The importance of the "identity of interests" finding and the downstream nature of the transaction loses all meaning in light of KBDC's insolvency at the time of the transaction. Because KBDC was insolvent at the time of the transaction, Commerce bore the burden of producing fairly concrete evidence showing that despite KBDC's insolvency, the debtors still received reasonably equivalent value for their obligation. As the Bankruptcy Court recognized, Commerce failed to produce any such evidence.[2]

* * *

Commerce next argues that the Bankruptcy Court should not have measured reasonably equivalent value against the face value of the guaranty since the obligation was only a contingency. The court rejects this argument. In light of Commerce's failure to provide any evidence establishing reasonably equivalent value, the court need not quantify with specificity the value of the contingent liability. However, it would certainly seem to be worth closer to its face value than zero.[3]

---

[1]   Courts have classified intercorporate guarantees into three categories: first, where a parent corporation or principal guarantees a subsidiary's obligation is termed a downstream guaranty; second, where a subsidiary guarantees the obligation of its sister corporation is termed a cross-stream guaranty; and third, where a subsidiary guarantees the parent's obligations is termed an upstream guaranty. In re Metro Communications, Inc., 95 Bankr. 921, 933 (Bkrtcy.W.D.Pa.1989).

[2]   The court can conceive of situations where there might be evidence that a large loan to a marginally insolvent company might give it a "fighting chance" to escape insolvency. Whether this would be significant in a bankruptcy sense need not be considered; Commerce rests its case without offering any such proof.

[3]   The court does acknowledge that,

> "it is well established, however, that a contingent liability cannot be valued at its potential face amount; rather, 'it is necessary to discount it by the probability that the contingency will occur and the liability become real.'"

Commerce relies almost exclusively on the finding of an identity of interests between the debtors and KBDC and the downstream nature of the transaction to argue that the debtors received reasonably equivalent value. While in some cases this may be adequate to meet a Trustee's prima facie case, in this case the KBDC's insolvent state at the time of the transaction eliminates the significance of these two factual findings. The court finds Commerce's remaining arguments relating to intangible benefits unpersuasive.[1]

Accordingly, the court affirms the decision of the Bankruptcy Court.

Notes and Problems

1. In *Young*, the bankruptcy trustee brought the adversary proceeding to recover $13,450. Why did the bankruptcy trustee bring the adversary proceeding in Commerce Bank? How much will he recover?

2. According to the stipulated facts, Commerce Bank loaned $7,000,000 and has not been repaid any of the $7,000,000. Why is Commerce Bank the defendant in a fraudulent conveyance action? Why isn't the $7,000,0000 loan "reasonably equivalent value" ?

3. The *Commerce Bank* litigation is a part of the Kroh brothers' bankruptcy cases. Why is the insolvency of KBDC important in applying section 548 to the Kroh brothers?

In re Chase & Sanborn Corp., 904 F.2d 588, 594 (11th Cir.1990) (quoting In re Xonics Photochemical, Inc., 841 F.2d 198, 200 (7th Cir.1988)). However, when the evidence establishes, as it does in this case, that the debtors guaranteed a loan to an insolvent entity, the contingency would appear to be "no longer contingent." Xonics Photochemical, 841 F.2d at 201.

[1] Commerce relies on In re Missionary Baptist Foundation, Inc., 24 Bankr. 973 (Bkrtcy.N.D.Tex.1982), to argue that the Bankruptcy Court failed to consider every indirect and intangible benefit that may have accrued to debtors as the result of the debtors' entering into the challenged obligations. Commerce states that the debtors, undeniably received a reasonably equivalent value for their personal guarantees by virtue of the valuable business benefits conferred upon them as a result of Commerce's loan to KBDC. These valuable benefits stem directly from their ownership interest in and interdependence on KBDC. These benefits were certainly no less real and no more intangible than those received by Ministries in the Missionary Baptist case. Appellant's brief at p. 24. Commerce never specifies exactly what these valuable benefits are, nor does the Designated Record On Appeal reveal stipulated facts illustrating these valuable benefits. It would appear that the Bankruptcy Court's finding of an identity of interests would accurately reflect benefits stemming from the debtors' ownership interest and interdependence on KBDC. Moreover, Missionary Baptist appears inconsistent with persuasive precedent within this Circuit. In re Young, 152 Bankr. 939, 949-950 (D.Minn.1993).

4. As the new lawyer for Commerce Bank, you are asked to review the following loan proposal to P Corp. The Bank will loan $4,000,000 to P Corp. and obtain a guarantee from S Inc., one of P Corp.'s three subsidiaries. What are the fraudulent conveyance risks if

   a. Both P Corp. and S Inc. are solvent?

   b. P Corp. is solvent but S Inc. is insolvent?

   c. P Corp. is solvent, S Inc. is insolvent but all of the loan proceeds will be used to acquire new equipment to be used exclusively at S Inc.?

   d. P Corp. is solvent, S Inc. is insolvent and 50% of the loan proceeds will be used to acquire new equipment to be used exclusively at S Inc.?

6. S owns T Co. A wants to buy T Co. from S. for $600,000. A needs to borrow the $600,000. A wants to use the assets of T Co. as collateral for the loan.

   This is an example of a leveraged buyout. It may also be an example of a fraudulent conveyance. As Professor Carlson has explained,

   > An LBO refers to the acquisition of a company ("target company") where a significant portion of the purchase price is borrowed and where the loan is secured by the target company's assets. The structure of an LBO can vary considerably and may include the acquisition of the target company's stock or assets and may also include the merger of the target company and a holding company set up to effectuate the acquisition.
   >
   > A common characteristic of LBO's is that the selling shareholders receive cash for their shares from the proceeds of the LBO loan. Therefore, the target company whose assets have been pledged to secure repayment of this loan do not beneficially receive the loan proceeds. This disparity -- that the target company may appear to suffer a burden without any commensurate benefit -- raises the question of whether the security interests, mortgages and guaranties executed by the target company and its subsidiaries in connection with the LBO may constitute fraudulent conveyances.

   David Carlson, *Leveraged Buyouts in Bankruptcy*, 20 GA. L. REV. 73-75 (1985;.see also Anthony Sabino, *Applying the Law of Fraudulent Conveyances to Bankrupt Leveraged Buyouts: The Bankruptcy Code's Increasing Leverage*, 69 N.D.L.REV. 15 (1993).

ꗠꗠꗠꗠꗠꗠ

Section 548 only applies to transfers made or obligations incurred "within one year before the date of the filing of the petition." State fraudulent conveyance statutes typically have longer time periods. Accordingly, in some instances, a transfer avoidable under state fraudulent conveyance law cannot be avoided under section 548. Consider the following example.

D files a bankruptcy petition in 1987. His bankruptcy trustee learns that D made a transfer in 1985 that would be avoidable by a creditor under state fraudulent conveyance law. The trustee *cannot* use section 548(a)(2) to avoid the 1985 transfer. She may, however, be able to use section 544(b) to avoid the transfer.

Section 544(b) permits the bankruptcy trustee to avoid any prebankruptcy transfer that is "voidable under applicable law by a creditor holding an unsecured claim that is allowable." In essence, section 544(b) permits the trustee to avoid any transaction which the holder of an unsecured claim against the debtor could avoid.

Although the trustee's avoiding powers under section 544(b) depend on the existence of an avoiding power of an actual creditor under state law, the extent of the trustee's avoiding powers under section 544(b) is much greater than those of the actual creditor. Under the rule of *Moore v. Bay*, 284 U.S. 4, 52 S.Ct. 3, 76 L.Ed. 133 (1931), retained in section 544(b), the trustee is not limited in his recovery by the amount of the claim of the actual creditor. A transfer which is voidable by a single, actual creditor, may be avoided entirely by the bankruptcy trustee regardless of the size of the actual creditor's claim.[1]

2. Improvements Of Position Before Bankruptcy

a. Preferences
i. *Elements of a Preference*
Common law does not condemn a preference.[2] Under the common law, a debtor, even an insolvent debtor, can treat some creditors more

---

[1]   The following hypothetical illustrates the significance of the rule of *Moore v. Bay*. Assume that D owes C $1,000. D makes a fraudulent transfer of property with a value of $200,000 to X. Under state fraudulent conveyance law, C can recover only a part of the property fraudulently conveyed to X, an amount sufficient to satisfy her $1,000 claim. Under section 544(b) and *Moore v. Bay*, the bankruptcy trustee can recover all of the property transferred to X.

[2]   Some state statutes void certain transfers because of their preferential character. The trustee may take advantage of such statutes by virtue of his powers under section 544(b): if the state anti-preference provision protects any actual creditor with an allowable claim, it protects the bankruptcy trustee.

favorably than other similar creditors. Although D owes X, Y, and Z $1,000 each, D can pay X in full before paying Y or Z anything.

Bankruptcy law *does* condemn *certain* preferences. A House report that accompanied a draft of the Bankruptcy Code explained the rationale for such a bankruptcy policy as follows:

> "The purpose of the preference section is two-fold. First, by permitting the trustee to avoid pre-bankruptcy transfers that occur within a short period before bankruptcy, creditors are discouraged from racing to the courthouse to dismember the debtor during his slide into bankruptcy. The protection thus afforded the debtor often enables him to work his way out of a difficult financial situation through cooperation with all of his creditors. Second, and more important, the preference provisions facilitate the prime bankruptcy policy of equality of distribution among creditors of the debtor. Any creditor that received a greater payment than others of his class is required to disgorge so that all may share equally." House Report No. 95-595, at 117-18.

Section 547(b) sets out the five elements of a preference; the bankruptcy trustee may void any transfer of property of the debtor if he can establish

1. the transfer was "to or for the benefit of a creditor"; *and*
2. the transfer was made for or on account of an "antecedent debt", i.e., a debt owed prior to the time of the transfer; *and*
3. the debtor was insolvent at the time of the transfer; *and*
4. the transfer was made within 90 days before the date of the filing of the bankruptcy petition, *or*, was made between 90 days and 1 year before the date of the filing of the petition to an "insider"; *and*
5. the transfer has the effect of increasing the amount that the transferee would receive in a Chapter 7 case.

The first three requirements of section 547(b) will usually be easy to apply. To illustrate, a true gift is not a preference—not to or for the benefit of a creditor. A pledge of stock to secure a new loan is not a preferential transfer—not for or on account of antecedent debt.

The third element—insolvency of the debtor at the time of the transfer—requires a showing that debts exceed assets at fair valuation, section 101(26). At first blush, this would seem to present significant problems of proof. Proving insolvency requires establishing the value[1] of the assets and the debts.[2] Proof of insolvency has been made much easier under the Code by section 547(f) which creates a rebuttable presumption[3] of insolvency for the 90 days immediately preceding the filing of the bankruptcy petition.

Section 547(b)(4) establishes the preference period as 90 days or one year for an insider. In determining whether the transfer was made within 90 days of the filing of the petition, look to Federal Rule of Civil Procedure 6(a) which provides that the day on which the transfer occurred is not included.[4] In determining whether the transfer was made to an "insider" so that the relevant time period is 1 year, not merely 90 days, look to Bankruptcy Code section 101(25)'s definition of insider. Remember that the presumption of insolvency is limited to the 90 days immediately preceding the bankruptcy petition. Accordingly, in order to invalidate a transfer that occurred more than 90 days before the filing of the bankruptcy petition the trustee must establish that the transferee was an "insider" and the debtor was insolvent at the time of the transfer.

The fifth element, which essentially tests whether the transfer improved the creditor's position, will be satisfied unless the creditor was fully secured before the transfer or the property of the estate is sufficiently large to permit 100 payment to all general claims. Assume, for example, that D makes a $1,000 payment to C, a creditor with a $10,000 general claim, on January 10. On February 20, D files a bankruptcy petition. The property of the estate is sufficient to pay each general creditor 50% of its claim. A general creditor with a $10,000 claim will thus receive $5,000. C, however, will receive a total of $5,500 from D and D's bankruptcy unless the January 10th transfer is avoided. ($1,000 + 50% X (10,000 - 1,000)). Accordingly,

---

[1]   Courts generally have valued assets at so-called "fair value" or "intrinsic value"—what a willing buyer would pay a willing seller within a reasonable time.

[2]   Note that exempt property is not considered as an asset in determining solvency. The result is that many consumers are insolvent in the bankruptcy sense.

[3]   The Federal Rules of Evidence are incorporated by sections 251 and 252 of Title II of the Bankruptcy Reform Act of 1978. Rule 301 of the Federal Rules of Evidence provides:

> "A presumption imposes on the party against whom it is directed the burden of going forward with the evidence to rebut or meet the presumption, but does not shift to such party the burden of proof in the sense of the risk of nonpersuasion, which remains throughout the trial upon the party on whom it was originally cast."

[4]   If under state law, a transfer is not fully effective against third parties until public notice of the transfer has been given and such public notice is not timely given, then section 547(e) deems the transfer to have occurred at the time public notice was given. The use of section 547 to invalidate transfers not recorded in a timely fashion is considered infra.

the bankruptcy trustee may avoid the January 10th transfer under section 547(b) to "facilitate the prime bankruptcy policy of equality of distribution among creditors."

The problems below are simple applications of the elements of a preference under section 547(b).

Notes and Problems

Antecedent debt

1. On January 10, D buys goods on creditor for $10,000 from C. On May 5, D pays C. On June 6, D files for bankruptcy. Is the May 5 payment, a voidable transfer under section 547(b)?

2. On May 5, D buys goods on credit from C and makes a $20,000 down payment. On June 6, D files for bankruptcy. Is the May 5 payment a voidable transfer under section 547(b)?

Preference period

3. On March 3, D borrows $300,000 from C. D repays $100,000 of the debt on April 5. On December 7, D files for bankruptcy. Is the April 5 payment a voidable transfer under section 547(b)?

4. On March 3, D borrows $40,000 from his law partner, L. On April 5, D repays L $10,000 of the $40,000 debt. On December 7, D files a bankruptcy petition. Is the April 5 payment a voidable transfer under section 547(b)? Do you have enough information to answer this question?

To or for the benefit of a creditor

5. On May 5, D Corp. borrows $50,000 from C; P, the president of D Corp., guarantees payment. On June 6, D Corp. pays C $10,000 of the debt. On December 7, D Corp. is insolvent and files a bankruptcy petition. Is the June 6 payment a voidable transfer under section 547(b)? Is P an insider? Is P a creditor of D Corp.? Was the June 6 payment "to" P? "For the benefit of P"? See pages 966-73 *infra*.

Transfer of an interest of the debtor in property

6. On June 6, D borrows $6,000 from C. On July 7, F. a friend of D, pays C the full amount that D owed C. On August 8, D files a bankruptcy petition. Is the July 7 payment a voidable transfer under section 547(b)?

7. Same facts as 6 except that P gives D a check for $6,000 payable to D to pay the debt. See generally Benjamin Weintraub & Alan Resnick, *The Earmarking Defense to Preference Actions*, 21 UCC L.J. 307 (1991).

The above problems all involved the payment of money. As *In re Zachman Homes, Inc.* illustrates, a bankruptcy trustee can also use section 547(b) to avoid liens on property of the estate.

In re Zachman Homes, Inc.
United States Bankruptcy Court, District of Minnesota, 1984.
40 B.R. 171

Order
Margaret A. Mahoney, Bankruptcy Judge. This matter is before the Court on the motion of the Debtor to reconsider and/or amend an earlier Order of this Court dated April 25, 1984, which found certain transfers to not be preferences under §547(b). Based on the arguments and affidavits of counsel and the writings contained in the file, the Court hereby makes the following:

Findings of Fact
1. Defendants Oredson and Jensen obtained orders for judgment against Debtor Zachman via summary judgment in Hennepin County District Court on November 1, 1983. Judgments in favor of both Oredson and Jensen were docketed in Hennepin County on November 1, 1983. This Debtor filed for Chapter 11 relief on November 2, 1983.

2. The Hennepin County District Court judgment in favor of Jensen was for an amount of $8,700.00, which represented past due rent owed Jensen by Zachman. The judgment in favor of Oredson was for $5,855.00 arising from rent owed to Oredson by Zachman.

3. At the time the State Court judgments were docketed in Hennepin County, the Debtor owned property in Hennepin County in which the Debtor had at least $1,000.00 in equity.

4. Had the State Court judgments not been docketed by Oredson and Jensen, they would have held at best unsecured claims against the estate of the Debtor.

5. This Court entered an Order on April 25, 1984, following a trial pursuant to §547. The April 25 Order determined that no preferential transfer had taken place through the docketing of the State Court judgments.

Discussion
This case presents one narrow issue for consideration by the Court. That issue is the application of §547(b)(5) to the facts arising in this case.[1] That subsection states that any transfer is an avoidable transfer if such transfer "enables" the creditor who received the transfer to receive more than such creditor would receive if:

---

[1]   The parties do not contest the application of subsections (b)(1)-(b)(4) of Section 547. The "transfers" or docketing of the judgments, meet the statutory criteria of (b)(1)-(b)(4).

(A) the case were a case under Chapter 7 of this Title;

(B) the transfer had not been made; and

(C) such creditor received payment of such debt to the extent provided by the provisions of this Title.

Section 547(b)(5) mandates the Court to make a balancing or a comparison between what the creditor would receive had the preferential transfers never been made, the Debtors filed a Chapter 7 liquidation, and the creditors received payments pursuant to the Chapter 7 distribution compared with what the creditors received via the preferential transfer.

Upon docketing in Hennepin County, the judgments obtained by Oredson and Jensen became liens against the real property of the Debtor in Hennepin County. They thus constitute "transfers" for purposes of §547. The transfers, if preferential transfers, were so only to the extent of equity in the real property in the county where the judgments were docketed. Attachment of the judgment liens to the debtor's Hennepin County real property gives these creditors a secured claim at least to the extent of the equity in the property. In this case that means Oredson and Jensen received a transfer, allegedly preferential, to the extent of $1,000.00.[1] As such, the originally entirely unsecured claims of Oredson and Jensen became, in effect, bifurcated claims in that Oredson and Jensen now have secured claims of $500.00 each and unsecured claims for the remainder of the judgment debt exceeding the amount of equity in Hennepin County property owned by the Debtor.

The evidence presented at the earlier trial on this matter indicated that the Debtor had, at the time its petition was filed in bankruptcy, liabilities exceeding its assets in an amount of between $300,000 and $800,000. Such evidence clearly indicates that these creditors, as unsecured creditors, would receive less than 100 percent on the value of their unsecured claims had this matter been originally filed as a Chapter 7 petition and they had received payment pursuant to Chapter 7 distribution.

Against this as yet unknown value received on the claims must be compared another value. That value is what these creditors received through the preferential transfers. Section 547(b)(5) does not clearly indicate what the "enables" language of that subsection requires the Court to compare against this Chapter 7 distribution amount. A review of the legislative history of that section

---

[1]   Whether Oredson's or Jensen's judgment was docketed first is not at all clear in this case. Counsel have treated the two judgments as one for the purposes of the trial. The copies of the judgments in the adversary proceeding file reveal that they were filed in the Hennepin County District Court within the same minute. The docket stamp on Jensen's judgment states it was docketed at 3:10 p.m. on November 1, 1983, while a handwritten addition to the file copy of Oredson's judgment states that it was docketed at 3:00 p.m. on November 1, 1983 in Hennepin County. The judgments were apparently given to the district court clerk at the same instant in time and were docketed serially. As such they would probably be treated as concurrent liens under Minnesota law.

and the reported cases concerning that section convinces me that the proper value to be compared against the Chapter 7 distribution value in this case is the value determined by adding the secured amount of the claim, made secure by the preferential transfer, to the pro-rata amount which would have been paid on the unsecured portion of the creditors' claims had the Debtor filed for Chapter 7 liquidation on the day the petition in chapter 11 was filed. *Palmer Clay Products Co. v. Brown,* 297 U.S. 227, 56 S.Ct. 450, 80 L.Ed. 655 (1936).

Palmer Clay Products, supra, is instructive for present purposes. There, in determining whether a preferential transfer took place under the Bankruptcy Act, the Court stated:

"Whether a creditor has received a preference is to be determined, not by what the situation would have been if the debtor's assets had been liquidated and distributed among his creditors at the time the alleged preferential payment was made, but by the actual effect of the payment as determined when bankruptcy results. The payment on account of say 10 within the four months will necessarily result in such creditor receiving a greater percentage than other creditors, if the distribution in bankruptcy is less than 100%. For where the creditor's claim is $10,000, the payment on account $1000, and the distribution in bankruptcy 50%, the creditor to whom the payment on account is made receives $5500, while another creditor to whom the same amount was owing and no payment on account was made will receive only $5000. A payment which enables the creditor 'to obtain a greater percentage of his debt than any other of such creditors of the same class' is a preference."

Applying the Court's analysis to be present case, the following becomes clear:

1. Payment to unsecured creditors on a Chapter 7 liquidation would be less than 100%.

2. At any level of hypothetical payment of less than 100%, these creditors were preferred to the extent that they received, through the transfers, the hypothetical liquidation payment plus $500. For example, using a 50% payout on Jensen's unsecured claim would entitle him to $4350 (plus the miniscule percentage increase caused by the addition of $1000 to unsecured creditors' pot). With the preference left intact, he would receive $4,100 on his unsecured claim plus $500 on the secured portion for a total payment of $4600. The same holds for Oredson at this level of payout and holds for both at any level of payout of less than 100%.

3. Therefore, the docketing of the state court judgments "enabled" these creditors to receive more than they would have received on a Chapter 7 liquidation had the transfers not taken place.

The (b)(5) language is directed at transfers which diminish the estate available for distribution upon a Chapter 7 liquidation. Any transfer which diminishes or depletes the bankrupt's estate may be seen as a transfer which enables a creditor to receive more than other creditors of equal status and therefore is a preferential transfer. Attachment of a lien to real property is such a transfer as may diminish the bankrupt's estate.

The Court, in determining whether the preferential transfer has occurred, should construct hypothetical situations comparing the distribution to the creditors at various percentage levels of payback on the dollar for unsecured claims under a chapter 7 liquidation to determine whether the preferential transfer has indeed advanced the position of the allegedly preferential transferees. I am convinced the Debtor has made an adequate showing in both its affidavit and the evidence presented at the hearing to show that at any level of distribution to unsecured creditors of less than 100 percent on the dollar, these creditors have advanced their position at least to the extent of the equity in the Hennepin County property. Further, the Debtor has presented satisfactory evidence to the Court that 100 percent payout on the dollar of unsecured claims would be impossible in this case. Therefore, the docketing of the State Court judgments in Hennepin County constitute preferential transfers under §547(b). In that regard, the April 25th Order of this Court was in error and is hereby amended accordingly by this Order.

Conclusion

Therefore, the docketing of the state court judgments on the day before bankruptcy was filed constitute preferential transfers to these creditors. No exception to §547(b) appearing under these facts, the state court judgments are avoidable preferential transfers under §547(b).

Order for Judgment

The April 25, 1984 Order of this Court in the above case is hereby amended in accordance with this Order. The state court judgments obtained by defendants against this debtor are hereby avoided.

Let Judgment be Entered Accordingly.

Notes and Problems

1. In *Zachman*, did the debtor make any payments to Oredson and Jensen? Did the debtor make any transfer to them? What "transfer" did the court avoid?

2. On January 15, D borrows $10,000 from C. On April 5, D grants C a security interest in D's equipment, which is worth $8,000, to secure repayment of the January 15 loan. On June 6, D files a bankruptcy petition. Can the bankruptcy trustee avoid the April 5 security interest under section 547(b)? If so, what would be the practical significance, if any, of the avoidance? Who would benefit? Who would "lose"?

3. On January 15, D borrows $20,000 from C. The loan agreement grants C a security interest in D's equipment which is worth $8,000. C immediately perfects its security interest. On April 5, D files a bankruptcy petition. Can the bankruptcy trustee avoid the January 15 security interest under section 547(b)?

4. On January 15, D borrows $200,000 from C. The loan agreement grants C a security interest in D's equipment which is worth $80,000. C immediately perfects its security interest. D defaults, and C repossesses the equipment on April 5. On June 6, D files a bankruptcy petition. Can the bankruptcy trustee avoid the April 5 repossession under section 547(b)?

5. On January 15, D borrows $200,000 from C. The loan agreement grants C a security interest in D's equipment which is worth $80,000. C immediately perfects its security interest. On April 5, D pays C $80,000. On June 6, D files a bankruptcy petition. Can the bankruptcy trustee avoid the April 5 payment under section 547(b)?

Barash v. Public Finance Corp. (In re Dennis)
United States Court of Appeals, Seventh Circuit, 1981
658 F.2d 504

Jameson, District Judge. This consolidated appeal involves eight bankruptcy cases in which Barry M. Barash, Chapter 7 Trustee for the debtors, sought recovery of alleged preferential transfers. In each case the bankruptcy court found in favor of the defendant creditor. The cases were consolidated on appeal to the district court, which affirmed the decision of the bankruptcy court in all cases.

The sole issue on appeal is whether installment payments voluntarily made by a debtor to an undersecured creditor in the ordinary course of the debtor's financial affairs within the 90 days preceding bankruptcy, but not more than 45 days after their due date, are preferences which may be avoided by the Trustee under Section 547 of the Bankruptcy Code. This is a case of first impression in this circuit; nor do we find that any other circuit court has passed on the question.

I. Factual Background
In each of the eight cases regular installment payments were made to a creditor within 90 days of an order for relief. In each case the value of the creditor's collateral was less than the debt it secured. In all but one case, however, the value of the collateral exceeded the amount of payments made during the 90-day period preceding bankruptcy. All of the payments in question were voluntary, some made through automatic payroll deductions, others by direct payment from the debtor. The bankruptcy court found that none of the

payments were made to cure defaults or eliminate arrearages. All of the accounts in question were considered current.

The orders of the bankruptcy court denying recovery to the Trustee were not accompanied by an opinion; but after notices of appeal were filed, the bankruptcy judge filed identical statements in each case:

> Appellant's [trustee's] statement of the issues he intends to present on the appeal relates only to the grounds for a directed verdict made by appellee [creditor]. The issue on appeal is the Judge's holding, as disclosed by the transcript, that voluntary payments made by a debtor on a secured debt do not constitute a preference.

The district court affirmed the decisions without an opinion.

In resolving the issue presented on this appeal, it is necessary to determine (1) whether the installment payments were preferences under the Bankruptcy Code; and (2) if so, whether the statutory exception removes the transactions from the operation of the preference rules.

II. Elements of a Preference

The Bankruptcy Code prescribes five requirements for a preference, all of which must be met for the Trustee to avoid a transfer. A transfer is preferential if it is (1) to a creditor, (2) on account of a preexisting debt, (3) made while the debtor is insolvent, (4) made on or within 90 days before the date of filing the petition, or made between 90 days and one year before the date of filing the petition if the creditor was an insider who had reasonable cause to believe the debtor was insolvent, and which (5) enables the creditor to receive more than he would receive if the estate were liquidated under Chapter 7. §547(b).

There is no dispute that the first four elements of a preference are established in each case. The installment payments were all made by a debtor to a creditor, on a pre-existing debt, within 90 days of the bankruptcy filing. The debtors are presumed insolvent during the 90-day period, §547(f), and no evidence was presented to rebut the presumption. Appellees argue, however, that they have not improved their position vis-a-vis other creditors, as required by §547(b)(5). The Trustee, on the other hand, contends that the payments received within the 90-day period enabled the creditors to receive a greater proportion of their respective debts than they would if the estate were liquidated under Chapter 7.

As noted above, the debts in all of these cases are undersecured. §506(a) separates undersecured creditors' claims into two parts: a secured component and an unsecured component. A creditor has a secured claim only to the extent of the value of his collateral. Any remaining balance is an unsecured claim. The effect of §506(a) is to classify claims, not creditors, as secured and unsecured. In other words, a single undersecured creditor has both a secured claim and an unsecured claim, each of which is considered in its respective class.

Except for two cases involving valuation of automobiles, it is agreed that the unsecured components of the debts exceed the amounts of the asserted preferences. The Trustee argues that the payments must be charged against the unsecured claims, and therefore the payments enabled the creditors to receive a greater proportion of their unsecured claims than other unsecured claims.

* * *

A principal goal of the preference provisions is the assurance of equal distribution among creditors. Section 547(b)(5) is aimed at achieving that goal.

* * *

For example, if upon liquidation unsecured creditors would be paid 20% of their claims (based on remaining assets and scheduled claims after secured creditors are paid), to defeat a trustee's avoidance rights a creditor would have to show only that the payments received during the 90-day period do not exceed 20% of the creditor's unsecured claim. This sole comparison, however, does not account for what happens thereafter. If the payments made were less than 20%, there would be no preference and the creditor would keep the payments and later also receive a pro-rata share of the balance of his claim. In the final analysis, this would violate the fundamental principle of equal distribution among a class of claims.

Section 547(b)(5) is directed at transfers which *enable* creditors to receive more than they would have received had the estate been liquidated and the disputed transfer not been made. As long as the transfers diminish the bankrupt's estate available for distribution, creditors who are allowed to keep transfers would be enabled to receive more than their share. The creditors in the instant case must account for the payments they received during the 90 days preceding the bankruptcy filing, or they will ultimately receive a larger share of their *unsecured* claims than other unsecured creditors. Of course, they will still receive the full benefit of their collateral as to their secured claims.

IV. Valuation of Collateral

The payments here in dispute are preferential to the extent they are credited to the unsecured components of the debts. Payments on secured claims do not diminish the estate, i.e., they do not enable a creditor to receive more than he would under the liquidation provisions of the Code. Section 506(a) provides that a debt is secured only to the extent of the value of the collateral. Any remaining amount is an unsecured claim. Valuation of collateral is thus crucial to determining the amount of the preferences.

The legislative history of §506(a) indicated that no fixed formula exists for establishing the value of collateral. Congress did not necessarily contemplate the use of forced sale or liquidation value; nor is fair market value always appropriate. "Courts will have to determine value on a case-by-case basis, taking into account the facts of each case and the competing interests in the case." Value should be determined by the purpose of the valuation and the proposed disposition or use of the property.

The present record does not enable us to determine the appropriate value of the cars in these cases. On remand the bankruptcy court should determine the value of the automobiles in light of the competing interests of the parties and the proposed use or disposition of the cars by the secured creditors. The choice of values is not restricted to NADA wholesale or retail, but depends on the facts and circumstances of each case.

V. Conclusion

We hold that regular installment payments on consumer debts, made within 90 days preceding the filing of a bankruptcy petition, may be avoided as preferential transfers to the extent the payments are credited to unsecured claims. The bankruptcy court must determine the value of collateral on a case-by-case basis to ascertain the extent of the preferences, in keeping with the bifurcation of debts into secured and unsecured claims under §506(a).

Reversed and remanded

Notes and Problems

1. In the bankruptcy cases involved in *Barash*, did the debtors grant security interests to creditors? Is a grant of a security interest a "transfer of an interest of the debtor in property"? Why doesn't the bankruptcy trustee attempt to avoid the security interests under section 547(b)?

2. D owes C $20,000. C has a security interest in property owned by D that has a value of $33,000. On January 15, D pays C $4,000. On April 5, D files a bankruptcy petition. Can the bankruptcy trustee avoid the January 15 payment under section 547(b)?

3. D owes C $30,000. *G* has guaranteed repayment of this loan and given C a mortgage on land *G owns* worth $50,000. On January 15, D pays C $30,000. On April 5, D files a bankruptcy petition. Can the bankruptcy trustee avoid the January 15 payment under section 547(b)?

4. In *Barash*, the Seventh Circuit remands to the bankruptcy court for a determination of the value of the two automobiles. What is the relevant date for such valuation: the date that the payment was made, the date that the bankruptcy petition was filed, or the date of the valuation hearing?

5. As a result of the 1984 amendments to the Bankruptcy Code, *Barash* would be decided differently today. The payments to the partly secured creditor would be protected from avoidance by sections 547(c)(2) and 547(c)(7). Paragraph (c) of section 547 is considered below.

ii.   *Indirect Preferences and the Deprizio Problem*

Zachman, Barash and most the above preference problems involve two parties: the debtor transferor and the creditor transferee. The phrase "to or for the benefit of a creditor in section 547(b)(1) contemplates three party transactions in which D makes a transfer to C that is preferential as to S. See also section 550(a)(1) ("or the entity for whose benefit the transfer was made")

Assume, for example, that C makes a loan to D and X guarantees payment of the loan. It is obvious from reading the hypothetical that C is a creditor of D, and it should be obvious from reading section 101's definitions of "creditor" and "claim" that X is also a creditor of D.

If D pays C on January 15, the payment if both a transfer to a creditor (C) and also a transfer for the benefit of another creditor (X). Accordingly, he payment of one creditor can be an "indirect" preference to another creditor if the other elements of section 547(b) can be satisfied.

Finding such an indirect preference can be important to D's bankruptcy trustee where the transferee, C, is insolvent. The transfer is a preference as to X under section 547, and the trustee can recover from X under section 550.

Finding such an indirect preference can also be important where the transfer is not avoidable as to the actual transferee. Assume that D does not file for bankruptcy until six months after she paid C. If C is not an "insider", the payment is not a preference as to C. If X, like virtually all guarantors, is an "insider", the payment would still seem to be a preference as to X. Under these facts, courts have consistently held that D's bankruptcy trustee can recover from X.. Until *Levit v. Ingersoll Rand Fin. Corp., (In re V.N. Deprizio Constr. Co.),* 874 F.2d 1188 (7th Cir. 1989)("*Deprizio*"), courts generally held that the bankruptcy trustee could not recover from C under these facts.

Deprizio held that a payment to a noninsider creditor where there is an insider guarantor could be recovered from that noninsider creditor even though it occurred more than ninety days before the bankruptcy filing. The methodology of *Deprizio* can be outlined as follows:

First, look at section 547(b) and determine if there has been a preference as to anybody;

Second, if there has been a preference as to anybody, look at section 550(b) and determine the possible responsible parties.

In essence, *Deprizio* views sections 547 and 550 as independent provisions to be applied independently. The party responsible under section 550 does not have to be the same party as to whom the transfer was preferential.

After *Deprizio*, law professors spent thousands of hours working on articles explaining, attacking or defending *Deprizio* and practitioners spent even more hours trying to solve possible *Deprizio* problem in transactions involving an insider guarantee and finding possible *Deprizio* problems in very different transactions such as transactions involving a fully secured first mortgage and partly secured second mortgage. and lenders spent even more dollars lobbying Congress. See, e.g., Peter Borowitz, *Waiving Subrogation Rights and Conjuring Up Demons in Response to Deprizio,* 45 Bus.Law. 2151 (1990); Peter Alces, *Rethinking Professor Westbrook's Two Thoughts About Insider Preferences,* 77 MINN.L. REV. 605 (1993).

In re Erin Food Services, Inc.
United States Court of Appeals, First Circuit, 1992
980 F.2d 792

Cyr, Circuit Judge. Appellants, creditors holding partially secured claims ("appellants" or "secured lenders") against property of the estate of the chapter 11 debtor, Erin Food Services, Inc. ("debtor" or "Erin"), challenge a bankruptcy court order setting aside, as voidable preferences, three installment interest payments Erin made to appellants, within one year of the chapter 11 petition, on an antecedent debt guaranteed by an Erin "insider." Appellants argue that (1) Bankruptcy Code §550(a) does not permit direct recovery from the non- insider transferees unless the transfers were made within the conventional ninety-day preference period; (2) even assuming the transfers were directly recoverable from the non-insiders under section 550, the trustee did not establish that the insider-guarantor derived a cognizable "benefit" from the transfers, a prerequisite to their avoidance under Bankruptcy Code §§547(b)(1), (b)(4), and (b)(5); and (3) as transfers in the "ordinary course of business," the installment interests payments are not subject to avoidance under Bankruptcy Code §547(c)(2).

I

BACKGROUND

In 1971, David W. Murray (the "insider") acquired exclusive franchises from Burger King Corporation to own and operate restaurants in parts of New Hampshire and Massachusetts. Murray established Erin to operate the restaurants. By 1987, Erin was operating more than twenty Burger King restaurants on real estate either leased or subleased from Murray, Erin's sole shareholder. Murray retained title to twenty-two parcels of real estate.

In order to fund an expansion, Erin negotiated a long-term refinancing arrangement with the secured lenders in July 1987. As primary obligor, Erin borrowed $45 million, most of which was disbursed by the secured lenders directly to Erin's existing creditors and mortgage lenders. As part of the same refinancing, the secured lenders agreed to provide Erin with a $25 million dollar secured revolving credit account ("RCA"), from which Erin could withdraw funds for future franchise expansion, site acquisition, and working capital. Both loans, totalling $70 million, were secured by an Adjusted Collateral Pool ("ACP"), which included Erin's "cash-flow" assets, such as its equipment and franchise agreements. In addition, the secured lenders obtained Murray's personal non-recourse guaranty on both Erin loan obligations. The guaranty was secured by liens on the twenty-two parcels of real estate owned by Murray.

During the eleven-month period between the loan and the July 5, 1988, installment interest payment, Erin withdrew $3,249,990 from the RCA, including $2,808,290 with which to make the three installment interest payments to the secured lenders as they became due on April 1, July 1, and July 5, 1988. Erin was rendered insolvent. Within a year of the first installment interest payment to the secured lenders, an involuntary chapter 11 petition was filed against Erin and an operating trustee was appointed. At the date of the petition, the real estate securing Murray's personal guaranty had an approximate value of $19.35 million and Erin's total indebtedness to the secured lenders approximated $61.7 million.

The trustee initiated an adversary proceeding against the secured lenders to recover the three installment interest payments as voidable preferences. See Bankruptcy Code §547(b). The bankruptcy court concluded that $2,089,059 was recoverable directly from the secured lenders as voidable preferential transfers. The secured lenders appeal from the district court judgment affirming the bankruptcy court order.

II

DISCUSSION

A. Trilateral Preferences: Transfers to Non-insiders During Extended One-Year Preference Period

The soundness of the avoidance theory adopted by the bankruptcy court ultimately turns on the proper interpretation of Bankruptcy Code §§547(b) and 550(a), governing the avoidability and recovery of preferential transfers. Section 547(b) permits the trustee in bankruptcy to avoid certain prepetition transfers of property of the debtor on account of an antecedent debt as a consequence of which a creditor receives more than it would have received in a chapter 7 liquidation proceeding. Section 547(b)(4), however, distinguishes between (1) preferential transfers to or for the benefit of an "insider," typically a "director," "officer," or other "person in control of the debtor," Bankruptcy Code §101(30), which are avoidable if made within one year of the date of the petition; and (2) transfers to or for the benefit of non-insiders, which are not avoidable unless made within ninety days. Bankruptcy Code §547(b)(4). The one-year preference period is designed to inhibit insiders--entities normally privy to inside financial information long before it becomes available to arm's-length creditors--from influencing the insolvent debtor to deplete its remaining assets for the insider's benefit, to the detriment of non-insider creditors. The secured lenders concede that Murray is an Erin "insider."

The bankruptcy court correctly found that the secured lenders held a secured claim of $53,842,400, a $2,089,059 million unsecured claim, and an equitably subordinated claim in the amount of $5,827,541. On the other hand, Murray, personal guarantor of the Erin debt to the secured lenders, held a contingent unsecured claim against Erin equal to the value of the collateral Murray pledged to secure his non-recourse personal guaranty. The greatly broadened definition of "claim" under Bankruptcy Code §101(4), as any "right to payment, whether or not such right is reduced to judgment, liquidated, unliquidated, ... legal, equitable, secured, or unsecured," 11 U.S.C. §101(4), unquestionably encompasses contingent claims for contribution, reimbursement or indemnification. A "creditor" is an "entity that has a claim against the debtor that arose at the time of or before the order for relief...." Bankruptcy Code §101(9). Thus, both Murray, the insider, and the non-insider secured lenders, independently qualify as Erin "creditors" on the same obligation.

Nevertheless, since Murray alone qualifies as an "insider," only a transfer which conferred cognizable "benefit" on Murray, see Bankruptcy Code §547(b)(1) ("to or for the benefit of a creditor") (emphasis added), would trigger the one-year preference period under Bankruptcy Code §547(b)(4) ("creditor ... was an insider").[1] The insider guaranty by Murray ostensibly provided the last link needed to convert these installment interest payments into trilateral preferences.   There can be no question that an insider-guarantor derives measurable economic benefit from a payment on the guaranteed debt, to the extent the insider's contingent liability on the personal guaranty is reduced. The trustee accordingly contends that the installment interest payments Erin made to the secured lenders conferred a simultaneous "benefit" upon Murray as well as the secured lenders. Finally, the trustee contends that, as "creditor" Murray received benefit from the installment interest payments made by Erin, the one-year preference period applies.

Once the transfer is determined avoidable under section 547(b), the trustee looks to the greatly broadened recovery powers conferred by section 550(a). Thus, a trustee may elect to recover the property (or value) involved in an avoided transfer either from the "entity for whose benefit such transfer was made" (i.e., Murray) or from the "initial transferee of such transfer" (i.e., the secured lenders). Since section 550(a) makes no distinction similar to that found in section 547(b) between the treatment of insiders and non- insiders, the bankruptcy court ordered the secured lenders to remit the installment interest payments to the trustee even though the secured lenders were not "insiders" to

---

[1]   In the typical bilateral preference involving the debtor and one "creditor," there is little difficulty determining the appropriate preference period (ninety days or one year) for application under subsection 547(b)(4). Moreover, were we confronted with a simple bilateral transfer these secured lenders would not have been "preferred," since Erin made all three interest payments more than ninety days before the filing of the involuntary chapter 11 petition.

whom a prepetition transfer would trigger the one-year preference period under section 547(b)(4).

The bankruptcy court relied on the landmark decision in Levit v. Ingersoll Rand Fin. Corp. (In re V.N. Deprizio Constr. Co.), 874 F.2d 1186 (7th Cir.1989) [hereinafter "Deprizio "], which is premised on the presumed "unfair" advantage that non-insider creditors, holding personal guaranties from insider creditors, may have over arm's-length creditors. See id. at 1195 (absent the one-year preference period for outside creditors with "insider" personal guaranties, nervous, "non-guaranteed" creditors might "grab assets themselves ... or precipitate bankruptcy at the smallest sign of trouble, hoping to 'catch' inside preferences before it is too late").

B. The Scope of the Deprizio Rule

The proper interpretation and accommodation of sections 547(b) and 550(a) presents an issue of first impression in the First Circuit. The Deprizio rule represents a radical departure from pre-Bankruptcy Code practice. Under Dean v. Davis, 242 U.S. 438, 443, 37 S.Ct. 130, 131, 61 L.Ed. 419 (1917), and Bankruptcy Act §60, 11 U.S.C. §96, the trustee in bankruptcy could recover a preferential transfer only from an entity in whose hands it represented a "preference" within the terms of the preference avoidance section itself. * * *

We need not revisit the underlying issue addressed in Deprizio. First, the difficulties hampering each attempt (including Deprizio) to unravel the riddle of ill-expressed (or unexpressed) congressional intent are well recorded. Second, a definitive congressional resolution to the riddle may be in the offing. Finally, and more importantly, the particular circumstances before us afford a more conspicuous basis for decision. Therefore, for present purposes, we assume, without deciding, that Deprizio correctly interprets the legislative directives to be applied to the present claim.

Deprizio did not propound a per se rule enabling the recovery of every temporally vulnerable transfer to a non-insider merely because its claim against the debtor is guaranteed by an insider. Even under Deprizio, the trustee is not entitled to recover without first establishing, by a preponderance of the evidence, all five elements of a preference as set forth in section 547(b). In the present case, therefore, the one-year preference period under section 547(b)(4) will not apply unless the trustee can demonstrate that it was Murray, the only "creditor" who was also an "insider," see §547(b)(5) ("that enables such creditor") (emphasis added), who received not only a cognizable "benefit" from the challenged transfers, see 11 U.S.C. §547(b)(1), but a greater benefit than would have been received in the event Erin had been liquidated under chapter 7, see 11 U.S.C. §547(b)(5).

The trustee contends that Murray received at least two types of "benefit" from Erin's interest payments to the secured lenders: (1) whatever unquantifiable benefit Murray realized as a consequence of the resultant one-year delay in the commencement of involuntary chapter 11 proceedings against

Erin, which in turn (i) insulated Murray from more immediate foreclosure proceedings against the collateral pledged to support his non-recourse personal guaranty of Erin's debt to the secured lenders, (ii) preserved his equity in the pledged collateral, and (iii) "bought" valuable operating time in which Erin could try to work its way out of insolvency, and (2) the quantifiable dollar-for-dollar reduction in his contingent liability to the secured lenders on the non-recourse personal guaranty.

1. Delay in Commencement of the Erin Involuntary Chapter 11 Proceedings

* * * [W]e are unpersuaded that whatever unquantifiable "insider" advantage may attend a deferral of bankruptcy proceedings represents a cognizable "benefit" for section 547(b)(1) purposes. No matter the merits of the Deprizio rule, there is no hint in the Code, its legislative history, or in pre-Code law that Congress ever considered, let alone intended, that the term "benefit" might encompass such incorporeal ephemera as "buying time."[1]

* * *

The equation could not be more clear. Unless the creditor for whose "benefit" the transfer was made, realized some quantifiable monetary advantage from the debtor's transfer, there would be no practicable method for determining whether "such creditor ... receive[d] more than such creditor would receive" in the event of a chapter 7 liquidation, 11 U.S.C. §547(b)(5). * * * [W]e believe section 547(b) plainly mandates that the "benefit" inquiry under section 547(b)(1) be confined, as in Deprizio and every other trilateral preference case, see supra notes 10-12 and accompanying text (and cases cited therein), to transfers of the debtor's property which are shown to have resulted in a quantifiable monetary reduction in the insider-creditor's contingent claim against the debtor's chapter 7 estate to the detriment of other creditors of the same class.[2]

---

[1]   An additional flaw in the argument advanced by the trustee, aside from the absence of authority, is that the expansive definition of "benefit," (e.g., "buying time" or the extended opportunity to operate the debtor's business) is at odds with the limited goals of section 547(b), which was never designed to undo every insider transaction which might result in some prepetition diminution of the debtor estate. For example, many transfers to holders of antecedent debts as a consequence of which an insider derives a clear "benefit" would not be subject to avoidance under §547(b) unless the insider was a "creditor" of the debtor estate who was collaterally obligated on the same obligation owed by the debtor. Similarly, if an insider and a non-insider creditor acted with "intent to hinder, delay, or defraud" creditors of the estate, the debtor transfers thus occasioned within one year of bankruptcy would be avoidable as fraudulent conveyances, not as voidable preferences. See Bankruptcy Code §548.

[2]   Even from a policy standpoint, we do not suppose that Congress envisioned that a trustee's burden would be met by evidence of such an elusive "benefit," the recognition of which would have the effect of converting the Deprizio formulation into an absolute rule of law. The preference rules in §547(b) ultimately are concerned with fostering equality of treatment among creditors of the same class. The goal of equality is frustrated when one creditor receives a preferential payment at the expense of other

2. Reduction in Contingent Liability on Non-recourse Personal Guaranty

We return to the question with which we began: whether the interest payments Erin made to the secured lenders reduced the amount of Murray's contingent claim against Erin. * * *

Since the non-insider creditor in a trilateral preference receives direct payment on its antecedent debt, the insider guarantor will realize a corresponding dollar-for-dollar reduction in the amount of his contingent liability on the guarantee, except in cases like the present where the insider has guaranteed less than the full amount of the primary debt, or where the primary debt is fully secured by property of the debtor at the time of the challenged transfer.[1]

Although the secured lenders realized the full "benefit" of the $2.8 million received in interest payments, there was no reduction whatever in Murray's liability on the non-recourse guaranty. The evidence at trial established the value of the collateral securing Murray's non-recourse guaranty at $19.35 million. Since the personal guaranty was "without recourse" at the time the interest payments were made, Murray had no contingent liability to the secured lenders on Erin's $61.7 million debt, beyond the $19.35 million in collateral Murray pledged to secure the guaranty. Unless the net balance on Erin's $61,741,000 debt to the secured lenders fell below $19.35 million as a result of the challenged transfers, or the value of the ACP exceeded $42.39 million at the time of the transfers, no cognizable "benefit" could accrue to Murray. The

---

creditors of the same class. Of course, all creditors benefit if the debtor can defer and ultimately avoid bankruptcy, and Murray, as an inside creditor, would receive no more benefit, qua creditor, from a deferral of Erin's bankruptcy than would other Erin creditors. As a general rule, therefore, insider conduct which "buys time" for the insider will be indistinguishable from actions designed to "buy time" for the debtor and its creditors. Bankruptcy law should not discourage bona fide efforts to save the debtor. Moreover, assuming that Erin's interest payments incidentally prevented immediate foreclosure against the real estate parcels upon which Erin operated its restaurants, and in turn protected Murray's long-term reversionary rights to those properties under his Master Lease with Erin, see supra note 2, the interest payments simultaneously benefitted all Erin creditors by delaying foreclosure on the essential "cash flow" assets (equipment, franchise agreements) in Erin's ACP. We conclude that the delaying effect of an allegedly preferential transfer, standing alone and without proof of any direct reduction in the insider's exposure on the guaranty, does not establish cognizable "benefit" within the meaning of §547(b)(1).

[1] If the non-insider creditor holds collateral of the debtor sufficient to secure the antecedent debt in full at the time of the transfer, payment on the primary debt produces no cognizable "benefit" to the guarantor, whether or not an insider, since the insider has no exposure on the debt at the time of the transfer. Of course the available collateral must be of sufficient value to cover the entire antecedent debt at the time of the transfer. Significantly, the test turns on the value of the collateral in existence at the time of the challenged transfer, and does not take into account future contingencies which might increase or decrease its value.

former proposition cannot be established solely on the basis of a loan payment of $2.08 million, and the trustee did not assert or establish the latter proposition. Accordingly, Murray's exposure on the entire $19.35 million in collateral securing the guaranty remained constant throughout, unaffected by the challenged loan payments to the secured lenders.

As the trustee did not show that the challenged transfers from Erin to the secured lenders resulted in a cognizable "benefit" to Murray, the trustee failed, a fortiori, to establish that the challenged transfers enabled Murray to receive more than he would receive on his claim in a case under chapter 7. See Bankruptcy Code §547(b)(5), 11 U.S.C. §547(b)(5). The bankruptcy court is required to compare the monetary benefit the creditor in fact received from the alleged preferential transfer with the projected amount of any distribution to the same creditor in the event there were an order for relief under chapter 7 and the preferential transfer had never occurred. Even if the defendant- creditor does derive a cognizable "benefit," the transfer is avoidable only if it "'diminish[ed] the fund to which creditors of the same class [as the defendant-creditor] can legally resort for the payment of their debts.'" Kapela, 649 F.2d at 892 (emphasis added) (citation omitted). Transfers to a fully-secured creditor, for example, are not avoidable as preferences, since the secured claim would be satisfied in full in a chapter 7 liquidation. Except in the unusual circumstance where a debtor's estate is adequate to provide payment in full on all unsecured claims, unsecured creditors who receive payment during the applicable preference period will rarely be spared by section 547(b)(5).

Thus, the subsection 547(b)(5) analysis adopted by the bankruptcy court was flawed at the outset as a consequence of its mistaken interpretation of subsection 547(b)(1) ("to or for the benefit of a creditor") (emphasis added). If Erin had not made the three interest payments, Murray would have held a contingent unsecured claim against the debtor estate in the amount of $19.35 million; immediately after the challenged transfers, Murray held a contingent unsecured claim in the same amount.

The district court judgment affirming the decision of the bankruptcy court is reversed, costs to appellants.

iii.   Preferences Excepted From Avoidance

Section 547(b) sets out the elements of a preference. In order to avoid a transfer as a preference, the trustee must allege and establish each of the elements of section 547(b).

Even if the trustee proves his entire case under section 547(b), he may not be able to avoid the transfer. Section 547(c) contains seven exceptions from section 547(b): a creditor/transferee can prevent avoidance of the transfer by proving that the transfer is covered by section 547(c).

Remember the relationship between paragraphs (b) and (c) of section 547(b). Section 547(c) protects transfers that would otherwise be avoidable by the trustee under section 547(b). Section 547(c) applies only in concert with section 547(b). If the trustee fails to establish a preference under section 547(b), it is not necessary to look to section 547(c). It is only after the trustee has proved her entire case under section 547(b) that it becomes necessary to determine whether section 547(c) protects all or part of the transfer from avoidance.

Section 547(c)(1) excepts a transfer which was intended to be a contemporaneous exchange for new value given to the debtor, even though the actual exchange is not contemporaneous. For example, if D purchases goods and mails a check in payment, this is considered to be a contemporaneous transfer and protected by section 547(c)(1) even though the check is not "paid" by D's bank until a week or so after the goods were delivered. Similarly, section 547(c)(1) applies when D borrows $10,000 and agrees to grant a mortgage on Greenacre, but there is a delay of a few days in executing and recording the documents.

The *Tolona Pizza* case below involves section 547(c)(2).

Matter of Tolona Pizza Products Corp.
United States Court of Appeals, Seventh Circuit, 1993
3 F.3d 1029

Posner, Circuit Judge. When, within 90 days before declaring bankruptcy, the debtor makes a payment to an unsecured creditor, the payment is a "preference," and the trustee in bankruptcy can recover it and thus make the creditor take pot luck with the rest of the debtor's unsecured creditors. 11 U.S.C. §547. But there is an exception if the creditor can show that the debt had been incurred in the ordinary course of the business of both the debtor and the creditor, §547(c)(2)(A); that the payment, too, had been made and received in the ordinary course of their businesses, §547(c)(2)(B); and that the payment had been "made according to ordinary business terms." §547(c)(2)(C). The first two requirements are easy to understand: of course to defeat the inference of preferential treatment the debt must have been incurred in the ordinary course of business of both debtor and creditor and the payment on account of the debt must have been in the ordinary course as well. But what does the third requirement--that the payment have been "made according to ordinary business terms"--add? And in particular does it refer to what is "ordinary" between this debtor and this creditor, or what is ordinary in the market or industry in which they operate? The circuits are divided on this question, the bankruptcy judges divided.

Tolona, a maker of pizza, issued eight checks to Rose, its sausage supplier, within 90 days before being thrown into bankruptcy by its creditors. The checks, which totaled a shade under $46,000, cleared and as a result Tolona's debts to Rose were paid in full. Tolona's other major trade creditors stand to receive only 13 cents on the dollar under the plan approved by the bankruptcy court, if the preferential treatment of Rose is allowed to stand. Tolona, as debtor in possession, brought an adversary proceeding against Rose to recover the eight payments as voidable preferences. The bankruptcy judge entered judgment for Tolona. The district judge reversed. He thought that Rose did not, in order to comply with section 547(c)(2)(C), have to prove that the terms on which it had extended credit to Tolona were standard terms in the industry, but that if this was wrong the testimony of Rose's executive vice-president, Stiehl, did prove it. The parties agree that the other requirements of section 547(c)(2) were satisfied.

Rose's invoices recited "net 7 days," meaning that payment was due within seven days. For years preceding the preference period, however, Tolona rarely paid within seven days; nor did Rose's other customers. Most paid within 21 days, and if they paid later than 28 or 30 days Rose would usually withhold future shipments until payment was received. Tolona, however, as an old and valued customer (Rose had been selling to it for fifteen years), was permitted to make payments beyond the 21-day period and even beyond the 28-day or 30-day period. The eight payments at issue were made between 12 and 32 days after Rose had invoiced Tolona, for an average of 22 days; but this actually was an improvement. In the 34 months before the preference period, the average time for which Rose's invoices to Tolona were outstanding was 26 days and the longest time was 46 days. Rose consistently treated Tolona with a degree of leniency that made Tolona (Stiehl conceded on cross- examination) one of a "sort of exceptional group of customers of Rose ... fall [ing] outside the common industry practice and standards."

It may seem odd that paying a debt late would ever be regarded as a preference to the creditor thus paid belatedly. But it is all relative. A debtor who has entered the preference period--who is therefore only 90 days, or fewer, away from plunging into bankruptcy--is typically unable to pay all his outstanding debts in full as they come due. If he pays one and not the others, as happened here, the payment though late is still a preference to that creditor, and is avoidable unless the conditions of section 547(c)(2) are met. One condition is that payment be in the ordinary course of both the debtor's and the creditor's business. A late payment normally will not be. It will therefore be an avoidable preference.

This is not a dryly syllogistic conclusion. The purpose of the preference statute is to prevent the debtor during his slide toward bankruptcy from trying to stave off the evil day by giving preferential treatment to his most importunate creditors, who may sometimes be those who have been waiting longest to be paid. Unless the favoring of particular creditors is outlawed, the mass of creditors of a shaky firm will be nervous, fearing that one or a few of their number are going to walk away with all the firm's assets; and this fear may precipitate debtors into bankruptcy earlier than is socially desirable.

From this standpoint, however, the most important thing is not that the dealings between the debtor and the allegedly favored creditor conform to some industry norm but that they conform to the norm established by the debtor and the creditor in the period before, preferably well before, the preference period. That condition is satisfied here--if anything, Rose treated Tolona more favorably (and hence Tolona treated Rose less preferentially) before the preference period than during it.

But if this is all that the third subsection of 547(c)(2) requires, it might seem to add nothing to the first two subsections, which require that both the debt and the payment be within the ordinary course of business of both the debtor and the creditor. For, provided these conditions are fulfilled, a "late" payment really isn't late if the parties have established a practice that deviates from the strict terms of their written contract. But we hesitate to conclude that the third subsection, requiring conformity to "ordinary business terms," has no function in the statute. We can think of two functions that it might have. One is evidentiary. If the debtor and creditor dealt on terms that the creditor testifies were normal for them but that are wholly unknown in the industry, this casts some doubt on his (self- serving) testimony. Preferences are disfavored, and subsection C makes them more difficult to prove. The second possible function of the subsection is to allay the concerns of creditors that one or more of their number may have worked out a special deal with the debtor, before the preference period, designed to put that creditor ahead of the others in the event of bankruptcy. It may seem odd that allowing late payments from a debtor would be a way for a creditor to make himself more rather than less assured of repayment. But such a creditor does have an advantage during the preference period, because he can receive late payments then and they will still be in the ordinary course of business for him and his debtor.

The functions that we have identified, combined with a natural reluctance to cut out and throw away one-third of an important provision of the Bankruptcy Code, persuade us that the creditor must show that the payment he received was made in accordance with the ordinary business terms in the industry. But this does not mean that the creditor must establish the existence of some single, uniform set of business terms, as Tolona argues. Not only is it difficult to identify the industry whose norm shall govern (is it, here, the sale of sausages to makers of pizza? The sale of sausages to anyone? The sale of anything to makers of pizza?), but there can be great variance in billing practices within an industry. Apparently there is in this industry, whatever exactly "this industry" is; for while it is plain that neither Rose nor its competitors enforce payment within seven days, it is unclear that there is a standard outer limit of forbearance. It seems that 21 days is a goal but that payment as late as 30 days is generally tolerated and that for good customers even longer delays are allowed. The average period between Rose's invoice and Tolona's payment during the preference period was only 22 days, which seems well within the industry norm, whatever exactly it is. The law should not push businessmen to agree upon a single set of billing practices; antitrust objections to one side, the relevant business and financial considerations vary widely among firms on both the buying and the selling side of the market.

We conclude that "ordinary business terms" refers to the range of terms that encompasses the practices in which firms similar in some general way to the creditor in question engage, and that only dealings so idiosyncratic as to fall outside that broad range should be deemed extraordinary and therefore outside the scope of subsection C. Stiehl's testimony brought the case within the scope of "ordinary business terms" as just defined. Rose and its competitors pay little or no attention to the terms stated on their invoices, allow most customers to take up to 30 days to pay, and allow certain favored customers to take even more time. There is no single set of terms on which the members of the industry have coalesced; instead there is a broad range and the district judge plausibly situated the dealings between Rose and Tolona within it. These dealings are conceded to have been within the normal course of dealings between the two firms, a course established long before the preference period, and there is no hint either that the dealings were designed to put Rose ahead of other creditors of Tolona or that other creditors of Tolona would have been surprised to learn that Rose had been so forbearing in its dealings with Tolona.

Tolona might have argued that the district judge gave insufficient deference to the bankruptcy judge's contrary finding. The district judge, and we, are required to accept the bankruptcy judge's findings on questions of fact as long as they are not clearly erroneous. Fed.R.Bankr.P. 8013. But since Tolona did not argue that the district judge had applied an incorrect standard of review, we need not decide whether the district judge overstepped the bounds. Which is not to say that he did. While he did not intone the magic words "clear error," he may well have believed that the record as a whole left no doubt that Tolona's dealings with Rose were within the broad band of accepted practices in the industry. It is true that Stiehl testified that Tolona was one of an exceptional group of Rose's customers with whom Rose's dealings fell outside common industry practice. But the undisputed evidence concerning those dealings and the practices of the industry demonstrates that payment within 30 days is within the outer limits of normal industry practices, and the payments at issue in this case were made on average in a significantly shorter time.

The judgment reversing the bankruptcy judge and dismissing the adversary proceeding is

AFFIRMED.

Notes and Problems

1. As originally enacted, section 547(c)(2) contained an additional requirement that limited its protection to payments made within 45 days after the debt was incurred. In 1984, amendments to the Bankruptcy Code eliminated this requirement.. Until 1991, cases and commentators were divided as to whether payments on long-term

debts could qualify for section 547(c)(2) protection. In *Union Bank v. Wolas*, 112 S.Ct. 527 (1991), a case involving interest payments on a $7,000,0000 revolving line of credit, the Supreme Court held that payments on a long-term debt can qualify for section 547(c)(2) and remanded for a determination of whether the debt was incurred in the ordinary course of business.

2. See generally Charles Tabb, *Rethinking Preferences*, 43 S. CAROLINA L. REV. 981 (1992).

In re Ladera Heights Community Hospital, Inc.
United States Bankruptcy Court, C.D. California, 1993
152 B.R. 964

Lisa Hill Fenning, Bankruptcy Judge.

I. INTRODUCTION
Until the eve of the filing of an involuntary Chapter 7 petition on February 14, 1990, debtor Ladera Heights Community Hospital, Inc. operated the Marina Hills Hospital in Los Angeles. After entry of a consensual order for relief, the case was converted to Chapter 11. A liquidating plan confirmed in early 1992 gave the Successor Official Unsecured Creditors Committee ("Committee") authority to pursue preference litigation against hospital suppliers who had received payments during the 90-day preference period. This adversary proceeding against creditor Bergen Brunswig Drug Company ("Bergen") is one of the more than 30 such proceedings instituted by the Committee.

Both parties moved for summary judgment. All elements of the Committee's prima facie preference action are undisputed. The only issue is whether the pattern of debtor's continuing payments and Bergen's continuing shipments of medical supplies establish either an "ordinary course" or a "subsequent new value" defense under Sections 547(c)(2) and (4) of the Bankruptcy Code. This Court holds that the payments here were not made in the ordinary course, but that Bergen's "new value" constitutes a defense to recovery of all but a small portion of the payments received.

II. FACTUAL BACKGROUND
While the hospital was operating, Bergen shipped drugs and provided pharmaceutical services to the debtor on an "open book account" basis, with invoices payable "net 10 days." At the beginning of the 90-day preference period, Bergen had an unpaid balance of $42,797.17. The debtor was making regular, but late payments, having been substantially in arrears for some period before that. This pattern continued until the bankruptcy filing. Bergen is now an unsecured creditor of the estate holding a claim for $44,541.96, reflecting the unpaid balance on the petition date.

III. DISCUSSION

The Committee's complaint seeks recovery of $76,944.93 in prepetition payments made to Bergen within the 90-day preference period. Bergen acknowledges that the Committee has established by undisputed evidence all material elements of a preferential transfer under Section 547(b). Debtor's payments were made on account of an antecedent debt within 90 days of the petition while the debtor was insolvent. In addition, Bergen's prepetition receipts exceed the amount it would receive under a Chapter 7 liquidation. The estate only has approximately $300,000 available to pay administrative and unsecured claims exceeding $4,500,000, yielding a less than 10% return.

Bergen raises two defenses. First, it asserts that the payments were made in the ordinary course of business and, as such, are protected from recapture by Section 547(c)(2). Examination of the course of payments, however, demonstrates that the payments were not being made within 10 days, as required under the terms of the invoices. As Bergen notes, payment was made on average 15 days after each shipment, but a comparison of the amounts invoiced for each shipment with the amounts paid shows that the payments were on account of invoices at least two or three shipments old, not for the most recent shipment. Bergen has not met its statutory burden of proof on the "ordinary course" defense. See 11 U.S.C. §547(g).

Bergen's second defense is that its continuing shipments constitute "new value" sufficient to preclude recovery by the Committee by application of Section 547(c)(4). Effectively conceding during argument the existence of a partial defense, the Committee nevertheless argues that this defense is available only if the creditor has provided post-preference value that is unsecured and remains unpaid.

A. The Subsequent Advance Rule.

Under Sections 60(a) and (c) of the Bankruptcy Act of 1898 (the "Act"), preference actions seeking recovery of payments made on open accounts were governed by the judicially-created "net result" rule. This rule allowed the creditor to net all transfers made to the debtor during the preference period against all payments by the debtor without regard to their timing. Thus, if a creditor made a shipment early in the preference period, then received several payments on account, the value of that shipment could be offset against the later payments, even though the debtor received no further benefit from having made the payments.

The Ninth Circuit has held that the "net result" rule did not survive enactment of the Bankruptcy Code. It has not, however, directly addressed the question of what standard now applies under the Code's preference provisions contained in Section 547(c)(4). The four circuits that have reached this question uniformly endorse what has become known as the "subsequent advance" rule, most effectively articulated in In re Thomas W. Garland, Inc., 19 B.R. 920 (Bankr.E.D.Mo.1982).

Garland considered whether Section 547(c)(4) constituted a codification of the judicially-created "net result" rule or whether Congress intended a modification instead. Developed to ameliorate the Act's harsh treatment of creditors who had maintained open accounts with debtors, the "net result" rule gave creditors an offset for any shipments they made to the debtor during the preference period.

The court in Garland carefully examined the legislative history and language of Section 547 as well as the net result rule's application under the Act. As Garland notes, the legislative history in the House of Representatives purports to incorporate the net result rule: The fourth exception [547(c)(4)] codifies the net result rule in section 60c of current law. If the creditor and debtor have more than one exchange during the 90-day period, the exchanges are netted out according to the formula in paragraph four. H.R.Rep. No. 95-595, 95th Cong., 1st Sess. 374, reprinted in [1978] U.S.Code Cong. and Admin.News 5787, 6330; S.Rep. No. 95-989, 95th Cong., 2d Sess. 88, reprinted in [1978] U.S.Code Cong. & Admin.News 5874.

The "formula in paragraph four" (i.e., the statutory language of Section 547(c)(4) as enacted), however, contains explicit timing requirements absent from the "net result" rule. It specifies that the new value provided by the creditor must come after the transfer by the debtor, a brand-new requirement. Its inclusion in the statute belies any suggestion that Section 574(c)(4) directly codified that rule. This material difference in the language of Section 547(c)(4) means that only the spirit of the "net result" rule survived the enactment of the Bankruptcy Code.

B. Subsequent Advance Rule Does Not Require New Value to Remain Unpaid.

* * * [T]hree basic principles governing interpretation of Section 547(c)(4) can be derived from Garland: First, §547(c)(4)'s subsequent advance rule makes preferential transfers avoidable until offset by subsequent advances of new value. Second, Congress drafted §547(c)(4) to retain the net result rule's policy of encouraging creditors to continue doing business with troubled debtors by protecting transfers received by creditors from preference actions to the extent goods provided by such creditors replenish the estate during the preference period. Third, §547(c)(4)(B) does not require new value to remain unpaid, but rather acts only as a safeguard against double counting.

Disputing Garland's third principle, the Committee contends that Section 547(c)(4) does require that new value remain unpaid. The Ninth Circuit has not addressed this issue. The three circuits that have directly ruled are split * * *. the plain language of the statute itself. Id. at 890-93. * * *

[T]he plain language of Section 574(c)(4) contains no requirement that new value must remain unpaid. Id. at 890. The legislative history of Section 574(c)(4) is equally devoid of language imposing such a requirement. Most telling, however, is the fact that Congress deleted the restrictive language of former Section 60(c) which limited the new value exception to "the amount of such new credit remaining unpaid at the time of the adjudication in bankruptcy."

* * * The exceptions to the preference laws are designed and intended to encourage creditors to continue doing business with debtors who are struggling to keep making payments. Penalizing creditors in a subsequent bankruptcy case for having continued to do business with such a debtor on a regular open account basis will undoubtedly discourage the very behavior that the preference exceptions purport to seek. Creditors are likely to cut off shipments to the debtor, destroying work-out possibilities and forcing more debtors to file bankruptcy.

C. Offset Credit for New Value Shipments Should Not be Limited to the Immediately Preceding Payment.

Finally, this Court rejects Bergen's assertion that the minority rule promulgated in Leathers v. Prime Leather Finishes Co., 40 B.R. 248 (D.Me.1984), is the appropriate standard for Section 547(c)(4) defenses to preferential transfers. Leathers allows setoff only up to the value of the transfer immediately preceding the infusion of new value.

Under the Leathers approach, new value in excess of the immediately preceding transfer cannot be applied to reduce the existing balance of prior preferential payments. The excess becomes a payment for which the creditor receives no offset credit. In other words, if the creditor ships goods worth $10,000.00, it would receive an offset against a $1,000.00 payment made the week before, but not against a $5,000.00 payment two weeks earlier. *** Such a rule would encourage creditors to limit new shipments strictly to the amount of the prior invoice paid, regardless of the debtor's need for the new value infusion. Such an artificial legal distinction would interfere with the ordinary commercial flow of goods and services to troubled debtors.
    * * *

D. Debtor's Payments are Credited as of Date of Delivery of Check.

For purposes of Section 547(b), "transfers" by check are deemed made on the date that the check is honored by the bank. Barnhill v. Johnson, --- U.S. ----, 112 S.Ct. 1386, 118 L.Ed.2d 39 (1992). But for the purposes of the new value and ordinary course defenses of Section 547(c), the Ninth Circuit adheres to the date of delivery rule, which treats the transfer as occurring upon delivery of the check to the payee, so long as the check is negotiated within a reasonable time thereafter. Thus, in analyzing the stream of payments and shipments between the debtor and Bergen for purposes of Section 547(c) defenses, this Court will deem the transfer date to be the date that Bergen received the check.

E. Application of the Garland Subsequent Advance Rule.

As discussed above, the Garland subsequent advance rule provides that each preferential transfer is avoidable until exceeded by subsequent advances of new value. If the amount of subsequent new value provided by the creditor exceeds a preferential transfer, the defense is complete as to that transfer. Surplus new value, however, cannot be used to offset later preferential transfers.

The chart below applies the subsequent advance rule to the payments made by Ladera to Bergen and Bergen's shipments to Ladera. Bergen has a new value defense that protects all but $9,583.18 of the debtor's transfers to Bergen during the preferential period.

CHECK DATE	CHECK AMOUNT	GOODS SHIPPED	PREFERENCE
11/15/89	$ 12,318.81		$ 12,318.81
		$ 21,416.10	0.00
11/30/89	21,813.79		21,813.79
		9,752.18	12,061.61
12/15/89	11,644.11		23,705.72
		12,190.38	11,515.34
12/29/89	21,416.10		32,931.44
		14,821.70	18,109.74
1/15/90	9,752.12		27,861.86
		17,529.88	10,331.98
		748.80	9,583.18
TOTAL	$76,944.93	$76,459.04	$ 9,583.18

The first column is the date that Bergen received payments from Ladera for previously delivered supplies. The "Goods Shipped" column reflects the value of the supplies delivered by Bergen in between checks. The "Preference" column tallies the net avoidable preference outstanding after any new value is offset against the preceding preferential transfers. If the new value is greater than the preceding transfers, there is a net outstanding preference of of zero, and any difference is not carried forward. In contrast, when the new value is less than the prior transfer, then the difference is carried forward as a preference and added to a future transfer to create a net outstanding preference. The pending balance may then be reduced by the infusion of subsequent value.

For example, the amount of the check Bergen received on November 15th was less than the aggregate value of supplies that were delivered to Ladera after the November 15th check but before the November 30th check. The $21,416.10 in new value supplied by Bergen provides a complete defense to the $12,318.81 preferential transfer. Bergen receives no credit for the $9,097.29 value in excess of the payment received, however, because new value cannot be carried forward to offset later preferential transfers. In contrast, if the "net result" rule under former Section 60 of the Act were applied, this excess value would be credited: the sum of the checks paid would be netted against total shipments, yielding a preference recovery of only $485.89. On the other hand, if the majority rule were applied, Bergen would not be entitled to offset the first two shipments during this period, because it was paid $21,416.10 and $9,752.12 on account of those shipments on December 29th and January 15th respectively. Under the majority rule, the Committee would have recovered an additional $31,168.22.

IV. CONCLUSION

The subsequent advance rule as articulated in Garland is the appropriate standard to be applied under Section 547(c)(4). Both motions for summary judgment are granted in part and denied in part. Bergen's infusion of new value provides a defense to $67,361.75 of the $76,944.93 preferential transfers sought by the Committee, but the Committee is entitled to recover $9,538.18 in preferential transfers from Bergen that were not covered by subsequent advances.

This memorandum opinion constitutes this Court's findings of fact and conclusions of law. An appropriate order and judgment should be submitted forthwith by the Committee.

Notes and Problems

1. Would Bergen have been able to establish a section 547(c)(2) "ordinary course" defense if it had credited each payment to the most recent shipment?

2. Ninety days before D filed for bankruptcy, D owed C $200,000. In that ninety day period, D and C had the following transactions:
    *   D paid C $160,000.
    *   C then extended $70,000 of "ordinary course" credit to D.
    *   D later repaid that $70,000 in the ordinary course.
    If D's $160,000 and $70,000 payments were preferences under section 547(b), what is the effect of section 547(c)?

3.   See generally Lawrence Ponoroff, *Evil Intentions and an Irresolute Endorsement for Scientific Rationalism: Bankruptcy Preferences One More Time*, 1993 Wisc. L.Rev. 1439, 1457 et seq.

ᒡᒡᒡᒡᒡᒡ

Section 547(c)(5) protects security interests in accounts and "inventory" from avoidance by the bankruptcy trustee. It is the longest and most complicated of the preference exceptions. Fifteen lines long. Phrases such as "amount by which the debt secured by such security interest exceeds the value of such security interests for such debts."

A lawyer (and a law student) needs to read section 547(c)(5) carefully and understand the answers to three questions about section 547(c)(5):

1.   Why is section 547(c)(5) necessary?
2.   How does section 547(c)(5) operate?
3.   Why does section 547(c)(5) generally protect the security interest in accounts or "inventory" from the bankruptcy trustee's section 547(c)(5) challenges.

Article 9 of the Uniform Commercial Code and section 547(e)(3) of the Bankruptcy Code make section 547(c)(5) necessary.

Article 9 of the Uniform Commercial Code provides a mechanism for establishing a "floating lien." Such liens are most commonly used in financing accounts or inventory which normally "turn over" in the ordinary course of the debtor's business. Assume, for example, that on January 15, C lends D $100,000 and takes a security interest in D's accounts. Obviously, C wants D to collect its accounts so that it can repay the loan. It is equally obvious that as accounts are collected, the collateral securing C's loan decreases unless C's lien "floats" to cover the proceeds from the collection of the accounts and to cover the new accounts that D generates. Accordingly, the security agreement signed on January 15th will probably contain an after-acquired property clause—will probably grant C a security interest in accounts now owned or later acquired.

Under section 547(e)(3), "For purposes of this section, a transfer is not made until the debtor has acquired rights in the property transferred." Thus, if D generates new accounts on April 15th and files a bankruptcy petition on April 17th, it would seem that the bankruptcy trustee can invalidate C's security interest *in the April 15th accounts* under section 547(b) because there is

1. a transfer of property of the debtor to the creditor (the April 15th accounts);
2. for an antecedent debt (Remember the debt was incurred on January 15th; section 547(e)(3) dates the transfer of the security interest in the April 15th accounts as April 15th.);
3. presumption of insolvency (Remember section 547(f).);
4. a transfer made within 90 days of the bankruptcy petition;
5. the transfer increased the bankruptcy distribution to C (unless C was already fully secured).

Note that the bankruptcy trustee is not using section 547(b) to invalidate C's entire security interest; she is not seeking to avoid the January 15th transfer that created the security interest. Rather, the trustee is contending that in bankruptcy, C's security interest does not reach the April 15th accounts.

That is why section 547(c)(5) is necessary. Absent section 547(c)(5), UCC after-acquired property clauses in accounts and inventory would be largely ineffective in bankruptcy.

Section 547(c)(5) may protect C. Under this provision, D's new accounts result in a preferential transfer to C only to the extent that C improves its collateral position within 90 days of bankruptcy. Section 547(c)(5) uses a two-point test: It compares the secured party's position 90 days before bankruptcy with the secured party's position at the date of the filing of the bankruptcy petition.

There are seven steps involved in applying section 547(c)(5)'s "two-point" test:

1. Determine the amount of the debt on the date of the bankruptcy petition;
2. Determine the value of the collateral on the date of the bankruptcy petition;
3. Subtract # 2 from # 1;
4. Determine the amount of the debt 90 days before the petition;
5. Determine the value of the collateral 90 days before the petition;
6. Subtract # 5 from # 4;
7. Subtract the answer in # 3 from the answer in # 6. This is the amount of the preference.

To illustrate, assume that D's indebtedness remained at $100,000 throughout the 90 day period prior to bankruptcy and that at the date of bankruptcy there was $75,000 of accounts securing the $100,000 of debts. C files a secured claim for $75,000 and an unsecured claim for $25,000. Assume also that 90 days before bankruptcy, the $100,000 debt was secured by accounts with a value of only $60,000. Under these facts, C's collateral position improved by $15,000 within 90 days of bankruptcy. Under these facts, C has realized a $15,000 preference. The bankruptcy trustee can use section 547(b) to reduce C's secured claim to $60,000.

The hypothetical in the preceding paragraph illustrates how section 547(c)(5) operates. It does not, however, illustrate the usual operation of section 547(c)(5). The hypothetical is both unrealistic and atypical in that

- The value of the collateral both 90 days before bankruptcy and on the date of bankruptcy is assumed. In the "real world," such values are difficult to ascertain and almost always disputed.
- The amount of the debt on the date of bankruptcy is exactly the same as the amount of debt 90 days before. No payments, no additional advances, no interest.
- The amount of collateral has increased shortly before a bankruptcy filing. How often will that happen?

Notes and Problems

1. 90 days before bankruptcy, D owes C $100,000. C has a security interest in inventory worth $60,000. 20 days before bankruptcy, D owes C $100,000 and the inventory subject to C's security interest is worth $5,000. On the date of bankruptcy, D still owes C $100,000, and the inventory subject to C's security interest is again $60,000. What result under section 547(c)(5)?

2. 20 days before bankruptcy, D borrows $200,000 from C and grants C a security interest in its inventory of antique coins. On the date of bankruptcy, D still owes C $200,000. Although D has not acquired any additional coins, the value of the inventory increased from $180,000 to $200,000 during the 20-day period. What result under section 547(c)(5)?

3. 90 days before bankruptcy, D owes C $100,000. C has a security interest in accounts worth $40,000. On the date of bankruptcy, D owes C $150,000 and has a security interest in accounts worth $70,000. What result under section 547(c)(5)?

4. 90 days before bankruptcy, D owed C $200,000. C has a security interest in inventory worth $90,000. On the date of bankruptcy, D owes C $140,000 and has a security interest in inventory worth $60,000. What result under section 547(c)(5)?

5. Section 547(c)(5) is a "favorite" of law professors, law review writers, and others of that ilk. See, e.g., Richard Duncan, *Preferential Transfers, the Floating Lien and Section 547(c)(5) of the Bankruptcy Reform Act of 1978*, 36 ARK. L. REV. 1 (1982); Lawrence Ponoroff, *Evil Intentions and Irresolute Endorsement for Scientific Rationalism: Bankruptcy Preferences One More Time*, 1993 WISC. L. REV. 1440; Thomas Ward & Jay Shulman, *In Defense of the Bankruptcy Code's Radical Integration of the Preference Rules Affecting Commercial Financing*, 61 WASH.U.L.Q. 1 (1982). And, it is equally obvious that section 547(c)(5) is not a "favorite" of law students or lawyers. It is a long provision; it is hard to understand; it is hard to apply.

Answers to Problems

1. no avoidance (situation 20 days before bankruptcy not relevant)

2. no avoidance (no transfer)

3. no avoidance ("amount by which the debt secured by such security interest exceeded the value of all security interests for such debt" increased, not "reduced")

4. trustee can reduce amount of secured claim from $60,000 to $30,000)

□□□□□□

How important is section 547(c)(5) in the "real world"? The gist of the exception is that a UCC floating lien on "inventory or receivables or the proceeds of either" is valid in bankruptcy except to the extent that the holder of such a lien has improved its position within 90 days of bankruptcy at the expense of other creditors. How often will such "improvement" occur within 90 days of bankruptcy? How can the holder of a claim partially secured by inventory and/or accounts improve its position within 90 days of bankruptcy? See *In re Ebbler Furniture and Appliances, Inc.*, below.

In re Ebbler Furniture And Appliances, Inc.
United States Court of Appeals, Seventh Circuit, 1986
804 F.2d 87

Flaum, Circuit Judge. The present action is by the trustee in bankruptcy under §§547(b) and (c)(5) (1986), to recover preference payments received by the defendant. Ebbler Furniture and Appliance, Inc. ("Ebbler"), filed a voluntary petition for relief pursuant to the Chapter 7 liquidation provisions of the Bankruptcy Code.

The appellant, Alton Bank & Trust Co. ("the Bank"), was the inventory financier for Ebbler. Although the security agreement is not in the record, it appears that the security agreement granted the Bank a security interest in Ebbler's inventory, and accounts receivable. The record is unclear as to whether the security interest covered proceeds and whether it was properly perfected.

The bankruptcy court made the following factual findings. Purchases made by the debtor within ninety days prior to bankruptcy totaled $170,911.33. The cost of goods sold during the ninety day period equaled $214,065.19. The ending inventory, as of the date of filing bankruptcy, was $67,000.00. The cost of the beginning inventory ninety days prior to the filing of the bankruptcy was calculated by the bankruptcy court in the following manner.

cost of goods sold	($214,065.19)
+ ending inventory	($ 67,000.00)
- purchases	($170,911.33)
beginning inventory	$ 110,000.00

The bankruptcy court also found that there were $19,000 worth of accounts receivable, subject to the Bank's security interest. These receivables were added to beginning inventory. The bankruptcy court then concluded:

12. On the basis on [sic] the foregoing figures, the creditor Bank received a preference as described in §547(c)(5) of approximately $75,000.00, *i.e.,* the difference between what the Bank received on account of the debt it was owed ($204,571.61), less the debtor's beginning inventory ($110,000.00) and its accounts receivable ($19,000).

The bankruptcy court noted that a discrepancy existed in the amount of $15,000 as to the value of the ending inventory. Consequently, the bankruptcy court reduced the preference by $15,000.00, and found a preference of $60,000.00.

Beginning approximately three to four months before filing its petition, Ebbler conducted a going out of business sale. Ebbler ceased doing business on November 30, 1983. At that time Ebbler was indebted to the Bank in the amount of $50,000 and had $67,000 in inventory (valued on a cost basis). The Bank repossessed $50,000 worth of inventory and sold it at cost applying the $50,000 proceeds to the debt.

Finally, and perhaps most important for purposes of this appeal, the bankruptcy court determined that the parties "were relying on the cost basis of the inventory in evaluating the security for the indebtedness."

When a court reviews a bankruptcy court decision on appeal the court must adopt the bankruptcy court's findings of fact unless clearly erroneous. The clearly erroneous rule does not apply to review of the bankruptcy court's conclusions of law.

This case involves a mixed question of fact and law. The definition of value in §547(c)(5) is a legal question, which depends on factual determinations made by the bankruptcy court. The factual determinations are subject to the clearly erroneous standard; but the manner in which these factual conclusions implicate the legal definition of value is subject to a *de novo* review. We note, however, that by deferring to these initial factual determinations, subject to review by the district courts, we are not abdicating our role as the reviewer of the definition of value adopted by the lower courts.

The issue presented is the interpretation of "value" as used in §547(c)(5) of the Bankruptcy Code. Section 547(c)(5) applies to situations where a secured creditor does not have sufficient collateral to cover his outstanding debt. Subparagraph five (5) codifies the "improvement in position test". Section 547(c)(5) prevents a secured creditor from improving its position at the expense of an unsecured creditor during the 90 days prior to filing the bankruptcy petition.

The first step in applying section 547(c)(5) is to determine the amount of the loan outstanding 90 days prior to filing and the "value" of the collateral on that day. The difference between these figures is then computed. Next, the same determinations are made as of the date of filing the petition. A comparison is made, and, if there is a reduction during the 90 day period of the amount by which the initially existing debt exceeded the security, then a preference for section 547(c)(5) purposes exists. The effect of 547(c)(5) is to make the security interest voidable to the extent of the preference. Of course, if the creditor is fully secured 90 days before the filing of the petition, then that creditor will never be subject to a preference attack.

The language of section 547(c)(5), the "value of all security interest for such debt," was purposely left without a precise definition. Thus, the only legislative guidance is "that we are to determine value on case-by-case basis, taking into account the facts of each case and the competing interests in the case."

The method used to value the collateral is crucial in determining whether or not the bank received a preference. The Bank urges that we adopt an "ongoing concern" value standard, which, in this case, would be cost plus a 60 mark-up. We hold that under Section 547(c)(5) value should be defined on a case by case basis, with the factual determinations of the bankruptcy court controlling.

In the present case we affirm the bankruptcy court's use of cost as the method for valuing the collateral for 547(c)(5) purposes. The bankruptcy court found that the parties were using a cost basis for valuing the security. Furthermore, when the Bank removed inventory with a *cost* of approximately $50,000, about a week before the petition was filed, Ebbler was given credit for that amount—$50,000. We do not find the bankruptcy court's factual findings so clearly erroneous as to warrant reversal.

Using these factual findings the bankruptcy court applied cost as the legal definition of "value." We affirm the use of this definition as applied to these facts.

We remand to the bankruptcy court, however, for a determination as to the amount of the preference. The bankruptcy court found, weighing the conflicting evidence, that a preference of $60,000 existed. It is not clear why the bankruptcy court did not consider the $43,000 in cash which the debtor had in hand at the time of filing the bankruptcy petition.

The bankruptcy court held that the Bank had a security interest in the inventory and accounts receivable. The bankruptcy court's opinion is silent as to whether or not this security agreement covered cash proceeds, and whether or not the $43,000 in actuality was cash proceeds of the inventory. It must also be determined if these interests were properly perfected. The only evidence in the record is Mr. Ebbler's testimony that all the proceeds from sales of inventory were deposited into an account at the Bank. The bank statement shows that on the 90th day prior to the bankruptcy the account contained $43,000. Depending on the court's findings on these issues an adjustment downward in the amount of the preference might be appropriate.

For the reasons set forth we affirm the use of cost as a basis for defining value in section 547(c)(5) of the Bankruptcy Code. We remand, however, for a determination as to how the debtor's cash on hand affected the preference amount.

Easterbrook, Circuit Judge, concurring.

This case involves the meaning of "value" under §547(c)(5). I join the court's opinion, which concludes that the statute does not require bankruptcy judges to use one universal definition. The history of condemnation litigation shows that a single definition of "value" is not within judicial grasp. Still, we need not leave bankruptcy judges and litigants adrift. Security interests must be appraised with some frequency in bankruptcy litigation. The greater the uncertainty in the legal rule, the harder it is to settle pending cases. "Anything goes" is not a durable rule. The parties cannot know their entitlements until bankruptcy, district, and appellate courts have spoken. One important function of appellate courts is to provide additional clarity, when that is reasonably possible. It is possible here. The bankruptcy judge did better than to avoid an abuse of discretion. He decided the case correctly.

"Value" is defined for a purpose, which sets limits on the admissible standards of appraisal even though it does not govern all cases. Section 547(c)(5) requires the court to find whether the secured creditor improved its position at the expense of other investors during the 90 days before the filing of the petition in bankruptcy. This calls for two appraisals, one on the day of filing and one 90 days earlier, using the same method each time, to see whether there was an improvement in position. The only standard that might plausibly be used in this case is wholesale cost of goods, because that is the only standard that could have been applied on both dates.

Wholesale cost is also the appropriate standard as a rule because wholesale and retail goods are different things. A furniture store, a supermarket, or the manufacturer of a product (the three situations are identical) uses raw materials purchased at wholesale to produce a new item. In the retailing business the difference between the wholesale price and the retail price is the "value added" of the business. It is the amount contributed by storing, inspecting, displaying, hawking, collecting for, delivering, and handling warranty claims on the goods. This difference covers the employees' wages, rent and utilities of the premises, interest on the cost of goods, bad debts, repairs, the value of entrepreneurial talent, and so on. The increment of price is attributable to this investment of time and other resources. The Bank does not have a security interest in these labors. It has an interest only in its merchandise and cash on hand.[1] The value of its interest depends on what the Bank could do, outside of bankruptcy, to realize on its security. What it could do is seize and sell the inventory. It would get at most the wholesale price—maybe less because the Bank would sell the goods "as is" and would not offer the wholesaler's usual services to its customer. The Bank does not operate its own furniture store, and if it did it would still incur all the costs of retailing the goods, costs that would have to be subtracted from the retail price to determine the "value" of the inventory on the day the Bank seized it.

To give the Bank more than the wholesale value is to induce a spate of asset-grabbing among creditors, which could make all worse off. If the Bank gets the whole increment of value (from wholesale to retail) during the last 90 days, other creditors may respond by watching the debtor closely and propelling it into bankruptcy when it has a lower inventory (and therefore less "markup" for the Bank to seize). The premature filing may reduce the value of the enterprise. There are other defensive measures available to creditors. The principal function of §547(c)(5) is to reduce the need of unsecured creditors to protect themselves against the last-minute moves of secured creditors. It would serve this function less well if goods subject to a security interest were appraised at their retail price.

Too, the Bank's security interest does not reach the "going concern" value of the debtor; it had security in the *goods*, not in the *firm*. To value the inventory in a way that reflects "going concern" value is to give the Bank something for which it did not contract. At all events, this wrinkle does not make a difference. If Ebbler had been sold as a going venture 90 days before the filing of the bankruptcy petition, the buyer of the business would have paid only wholesale

---

[1]   The Bank's interest in the proceeds of sales is not the same as an interest in the whole retail price for unsold inventory. An ongoing financing arrangement provides for operating expenses, too, to come out of proceeds. The security interest on any given day covers only identified proceeds, an asset that is identifiable and significantly smaller than the wholesale or retail value of the entire inventory.

price for Ebbler's inventory. If Ebbler had been at the peak of health, the buyer would have paid no more for inventory. A buyer would not have paid retail, because it would have had to invest the additional time and money necessary to obtain the retail price. So whether Ebbler is valued as a defunct business or as a going business sold to a hypothetical buyer on the critical date, wholesale is the right valuation, because it reflects the price that a willing buyer would pay after arms'-length negotiation. (The "going concern" value of Ebbler is reflected in its name, reputation, customer list, staff, and so on—things in which the Bank did not have a security interest.)

To put this differently, a willing buyer of a flourishing retail or manufacturing business will not pay more than the wholesale price for inventory of goods or parts on hand, because this buyer could purchase the same items on the market from the original sellers. Why pay Ebbler $500 for a sofa when you can get the same item for $200 from its manufacturer? Nothing would depend on whether Ebbler planned to stay in business. The court therefore properly does not allow the outcome of this case to turn on the fact that Ebbler chose a Chapter 7 liquidation rather than a Chapter 11 reorganization. Chapter titles are of little use in valuing assets under §547(c)(5). A "liquidation" may be a sale of the business en bloc as an on-going concern, and a "reorganization" may be a transition from one line of business to another.

The difference between the wholesale and retail prices of the inventory is the compensation that the other factors of production—the employees, landlords, utilities, etc.—obtain for their services. To appraise Ebbler's inventory at "retail" is to award to the Bank the entire value of the work done during the last 90 days by these other creditors of Ebbler. It is to allow the Bank to improve its position at their expense. Because a valuation at "retail" would produce exactly the consequence that §547(c)(5) is designed to avert, the bankruptcy court wisely chose to appraise the goods at wholesale. The court leaves to another day the question whether retail price is ever an appropriate measure of value under §547(c)(5). The observation that the bankruptcy court has leeway, however, does not imply that the court's discretion should be exercised without reference to the function of §547(c)(5) and the limits of the security interest.

Notes and Problems

1. Compare the position of Alton Bank & Trust Company on the date of bankruptcy with its position 90 days before bankruptcy. Did its position improve? If so, what caused the improvement in position? Was the improvement caused by Ebbler purchasing $170,911.33 of new goods?

2. *Ebbler* affirmed the bankruptcy court's use of cost in measuring the value of the inventory. *Ebbler* is a Chapter 7 case. Would the Seventh Circuit affirm the use of "ongoing concern value" in measuring the value of inventory for section 547(c)(5) purposes in a Chapter 11 case?

3. In the typical Chapter 11 case, the debtor will continue to acquire inventory and generate receivables after the bankruptcy filing. Section 547(c)(5) deals with the holder of a secured claim's interest in inventory and other receivables acquired within 90 days BEFORE the filing of a bankruptcy petition. Section 552(a) deals with inventory and receivables acquired AFTER the filing of a bankruptcy petition. Section 552(a) generally provides that a security interest created by a pre-bankruptcy security agreement does not reach collateral acquired after the bankruptcy filing. To illustrate, assume that on January 15, S extends credit to D and obtains a security interest in all of D's inventory, now owned or later acquired. On February 2, D files a Chapter 11 petition. On April 5, D acquires additional inventory. S's claim would NOT be secured by the April 5 inventory, section 552(a).

4. *Ebbler* remands for further findings with respect to the cash proceeds. What is the effect of section 547 on the holder of a secured claim's right to proceeds? Recall that under Article 9, a secured party automatically has a limited security interest in proceeds. Absent an insolvency proceeding, the limitation on the security interest in proceeds is set out in section 9-306(2): "identifiable." In the event of bankruptcy or a state insolvency proceeding, the very different limitations of section 9-306(4) apply.

Consider the possible consequences of the differences between section 9-306(2) and 9-306(4). In some situations, a secured party's interest in proceeds might be greater under section 9-306(4) in bankruptcy than out of bankruptcy under section 9-306(2).

Assume, for example, that S has a security interest in D's inventory. S's security interest would, of course, also reach the proceeds from the sale of inventory. D deposits the cash it receives from the sale of inventory into its general bank account. D files for bankruptcy relief. Assume that prior to bankruptcy, $60,000 of the funds in D's general bank account were "identifiable" as proceeds from the sale of S's inventory for purposes of section 9-306(2). Since D has filed for bankruptcy, the tests of section 9-306(4) apply. Assume that under these tests, S's security interest reaches $80,000 of the funds in D's general bank account. Can the bankruptcy trustee use section 547 to limit S's interest in the bank account to $60,000?

ＤＤＤＤＤＤ

The 1984 amendments added section 547(c)(7) excepting from section 547 avoidance certain "small" preferences. In proposing such an exception in 1973, the Commission on Bankruptcy Laws of the United States argues "Relatively small preferences do not seriously impinge on the goals of equality of treatment. Avoidance of grab-bag effect, and prevention of unwise extension of credit. In addition, the expense of recovery is often disproportionate to the benefit to creditors." Report, Part 1, p. 206.

Please read section 547(c)(7) and apply it in the following problems.

Notes and Problems

1. D, an individual owing primarily consumer debts, owes C $1,000. On January 15, D pays C $1,000. On April 5, D files a bankruptcy petition. Does section 547(c)(7) enable C to retain $600 of the $1,000 payment?

2. D, an individual owing primarily consumer debts, owes C $1,000. On 1/ 15, D pays C $500. On 1/ 22, D pays C the other $500. On April 5, D files a bankruptcy petition. Does section 547(c)(7) enable C to retain the $1,000 in payments?

3. Would the answer to Problem 2 be different if D's debt to C was *not* a consumer debt?

4. According to Professor Countryman, section 547(c)(7) is "unjustifiable. * * * Bankruptcy judges operate within a system that, except for the judges' salaries and expenses, must pay its own costs from the gate receipts. Quite understandably, after a judge has saddled a trustee with some cases in which the trustee received no or little compensation, the judge will try to make it up to him in cases in which assets are available for the fee. Thus, the creditors of consumers get their $600 immunity at the expense of creditors in other cases." Vern Countryman, *The Concept of a Voidable Preference in Bankruptcy*, 38 VAND.L.REV. 713, 815-6 (1985).

b. Setoff, Section 553

Setoff is a nonbankruptcy concept and is discussed in the non-bankruptcy collection materials in Unit 3, *supra*. Setoff is triggered by a fact pattern similar to the following:

+ D owes C $1,000.
+ C owes D $600.
+ If a right of setoff exists, C can reduce its claim against D by the amount of its debt to D. In other words, after the exercise of a right of setoff, D owes C $400.

The determination of whether a right of setoff exists depends upon non-bankruptcy law. The Bankruptcy Code does not create a right of setoff. Rather, section 553 limits the exercise of a state law right of setoff. In bankruptcy it is thus necessary to determine (1) whether there is a state law right of setoff and (2) whether section 553 limits the exercise of that right.

In every state, banks have the right to set off the balance of a customer's checking or savings account against a delinquent loan owed by that customer to the bank. For example, Stephen Weed, W, has a checking account at Kane Citizens Bank, K, with a $1,000 balance. He borrows $6,000 from K to buy a new car. W defaults on the car loan. K has a right of setoff under state law. It can reduce W's checking account from $1,000 to 0 and reduce the amount owed by W on the $6,000 to $5,000.

The use of setoffs is not limited to banks. State law generally recognizes a right of setoff whenever any person is both a creditor and a debtor of another. "Setoff is the cancellation of cross demands between two parties."[1] Zubrow, *Integration of Deposit Account Financing Into Article 9 of the Uniform Commercial Code*, 68 MINN.L.REV. 899, 901, n. 3 (1984). The following hypothetical illustrates a setoff by a creditor other than a bank.

D is the business of supplying ambulance services. Blue Cross has discovered that it has paid $16,000 to D on claims that do not meet the requirements for Blue Cross coverage. D submits a new claim for $20,000 for ambulance services. Blue Cross can set off its $16,000 claim against D's $20,000 claim.

While the use of setoff is not limited to banks, bank setoff is the most common setoff transaction. Accordingly, the following discussion focuses on bank setoffs.

i. *Improvement in Position*

As noted in the discussion of the preference provision, the Bankruptcy Code has a basic policy of discouraging creditors from

---

[1] Some authorities distinguish setoff from recoupment and hold that sections 362(a)(7) and 553 do not apply to recoupment.

> "Recoupment allows a defendant to reduce the amount of a plaintiff's claim by asserting a claim against the plaintiff *which arose out of the same transaction* to arrive at a just and proper liability on the plaintiff's claim. In contrast, setoff involves a claim against the plaintiff which arises out of a transaction which is different from that on which the plaintiff's claim is based. *** I conclude that the defendants here are asserting a right in recoupment which may be asserted independently of section 553."

In re Clowards, Inc., 42 B.R. 627, 628 (Bkrtcy.Idaho 1984). In *Clowards*, the debtor was a masonry subcontractor. Debtor contracted with several builders to do masonry work. Debtor only partially performed under these contracts. Debtor had a claim against the builders for the work it had done; the builders had a claim against the debtor for damages resulting from the debtor's failing to complete the work. Both claims arose out of the same transaction. The court used the label recoupment and refused to use section 553.

improving their positions shortly before bankruptcy. Pre-bankruptcy transfers that result in a creditor's improvement in position are subject to invalidation under section 547(b).

Section 547(b) does *not* apply to setoffs. Note the introductory clause of section 553(b), "Except as otherwise provided in this section and in sections 362 and 363 of this title, this title does not affect any right of a creditor to offset." Accordingly, section 547 "does not affect any right of a creditor to offset." Instead, section 553(b) prevents a creditor from improving its position through a pre-bankruptcy setoff. To understand the exclusion of setoffs from section 547 and the operation of section 553(b), it is necessary to understand how setoffs operate, and how section 506(b) operates.

Bank setoffs generally involve two transfers. The first transfer is the bank customer/bankruptcy debtor's deposit of funds into his bank account. The second transfer is the bank's exercise of its right of setoff against such funds.

As a matter of economic reality, the bank improves its position by exercising a right of setoff. Kane Citizens Bank improved its position by offsetting the $1,000 in Weed's bank account in partial satisfaction of Weed's $6,000 debt.

As a matter of legal theory, the exercise of a right of setoff does not result in an improvement of position. Section 506 equates the right of setoff with a lien: in a bankruptcy case, a creditor's claim will be deemed a secured claim to the extent of any right of setoff under nonbankruptcy law. In other words, Kane Citizens Bank with its right to set off $1,000 is treated the same as a creditor with a lien on $1,000 of property.

The following two hypotheticals illustrate the practical significance of section 506's treatment of the right of setoff:

(1) As of January 15, W owes K $6,000. K has a lien on property of W worth $1,000. On April 5, K forecloses its lien and seizes and sells the collateral for $1,000. On April 10, W files for bankruptcy relief. The bankruptcy trustee will not be able to recover the $1,000 from K under section 547; K did not improve its position within 90 days of bankruptcy.

(2) As of January 15, W owes K $6,000. K has a $1,000 right of setoff (i.e., W has $1,000 in his account in K bank.) On April 5, K exercises its right of setoff, seizing the $1,000 in W's account and reducing W's debt to $5,000. On April 10, W files for bankruptcy relief. The bankruptcy trustee will not be able to recover the $1,000 from K. K did not improve its position within 90 days of bankruptcy.

Without section 506(b)'s inclusion of a right of setoff in its definition of secured claim, every pre-bankruptcy setoff would result in an

improvement in position. With section 506(b), it is necessary to look
to section 553(b) to determine which setoffs result in an impermissible
pre-bankruptcy improvement in position. Section 553(b) is very similar in approach to section 547(c)(5). Please read section 553(b) and
apply it in the following problems:

Notes and Problems

1. 90 days before bankruptcy, D owes C Bank $100,000 and has $20,000 on deposit at
    C Bank. 10 days before bankruptcy, C Bank exercises its right of setoff. At that
    time, D owes C Bank $90,000 and the account has a $50,000 balance. Can the
    trustee recover any part of the $50,000 under section 553(b)? If so, what are C
    Bank's rights? See section 502(h).

2. 90 days before bankruptcy, D owes C Bank $200,000 and has $210,000 on deposit
    at C Bank. 88 days before bankruptcy, D withdraws $170,000 from the account so
    that the account balance is $40,000. Later that same day, a check for $10,100 is
    drawn on D's account is paid by C Bank. 5 days before bankruptcy, C Bank
    exercises its right of setoff. At that time, D owes C Bank $130,000 and the account
    balance is $110,000. Can the bankruptcy trustee recover any part of the $110,000
    setoff under section 553(b)?

3. Note that section 553(b) only applies to pre-petition setoffs. Should the bank in
    Problems 1 and 2 wait until after the bankruptcy petition was filed to exercise its right
    of setoff? See sections 502(h), 506(b), 362(a)(7), 363(c)(2).

4. See generally Philip Lacy, *Setoff and the Principle of Creditor Equality*, 43 S.
    CAROLINA L. REV. 951 (1993).

ii. Other Limitations on Setoff

Improvement in position is not the only bankruptcy limitation on
the exercise of a state law right of setoff in bankruptcy. For example,
section 553(a) requires "mutual debts." This means that the debt
must be between the same parties in the same right or capacity. To
illustrate, a claim against a debt owed to the "bankrupt" as an admin-
istratrix cannot be set off against a claim against the "bankrupt" as
an individual.

Section 553(a) also requires that both the creditor's claim against
the debtor and the debtor's claim against the creditor arose before the
bankruptcy filing. Assume, for example, that farmer D is indebted to
the Farmers' Home Administration, an agency of the United States
Department of Agriculture. D files a Chapter 11 petition in 1993. In
1994, D qualifies for crop subsidies. The FmHA cannot set off D's prepetition debt against the post-petition crop subsidy.

Section 553(a)(3) focuses on the first of the two transfers in a bank setoff—the bank customer/bankruptcy debtor's deposit of funds into the bank account. It invalidates the setoff of funds deposited in a bank within 90 days of the petition for the purpose of increasing the bank's right of setoff. For example, Glen Head Bank makes a $125,000 loan to Oakland Foundry Company. Brede, the president and chief executive officer of Oakland, personally guarantees repayment. Oakland's financial condition deteriorates. In July, Oakland's creditors file an involuntary bankruptcy petition. In the 90 days before the bankruptcy filing, Brede caused Oakland to increase the funds on deposit in Glen Head Bank from less than $10,000 to over $100,000. Shortly before the bankruptcy filing, Glen Head Bank set off $108,783.91 against the $125,000 Oakland owed on the loan. Under these facts—the facts of *Katz v. First National Bank of Glen Head*, 568 F.2d 964 (2d Cir.1977)—the bankruptcy trustee could use section 553(a)(3) to recover from Glen Head Bank.[1]

3. Transfers Not Timely Recorded Or Perfected

A bankruptcy trustee may avoid certain pre-petition transfers that are not timely recorded or perfected. A failure to record or a delay in recording can adversely affect other creditors. If creditor X does not record its lien on D's property, creditor Y might not know that D's property is encumbered. Relying on the mistaken belief that D holds his property free from liens, Y might extend credit, refrain from obtaining a lien, or forebear from instituting collection proceedings.

State law requires recordation or other public notice of many kinds of transfers. Real estate recording statutes require the recording of deeds and real property mortgages. Article 6 of the Uniform Commercial Code requires that creditors be notified in advance of any bulk transfer. Section 2-326 of the Code calls for public notice of sales on consignment. And, Article 9 of the Uniform Commercial Code calls for public notice, i.e., perfection, of security interests.

The Bankruptcy Code does not have its own public notice requirements. It does not simply invalidate all transfers not recorded within 10 days. Rather, the Bankruptcy Code makes use of the notoriety requirements of state law in the following invalidation provisions: sections 544, 547, 548 and 545.

a. Section 544(b)

Section 544(b) empowers the bankruptcy trustee to invalidate any transfer that under non-bankruptcy law is voidable as to any actual

---

[1] Under the *Katz* facts, the Bankruptcy trustee can also recover Glen Head Bank's pre-petition setoff under section 553(b).

creditor of the debtor with an unsecured, allowable[1] claim. In applying section 544(b), it is thus necessary to determine

- whether non-bankruptcy law public notice requirements have been timely satisfied;
- which persons are protected by the non-bankruptcy requirement of public notice; and
- if any actual creditor of the debtor with an unsecured allowable claim comes within the class of persons protected by such state law.[2]

Notes and Problems

1. On January 10, D borrows $10,000 from M and gives M a mortgage on Redacre. On February 2, C lends D $10,000. On March 3, M records its mortgage. The state recording statute provides that a mortgage is not effective against a *purchaser* until it is recorded. On July 7, D files a bankruptcy petition. On the date of the petition, D still owes $10,000 to M and $10,000 to C. Can D's bankruptcy trustee invalidate M's mortgage under section 544(b)?

2. On January 10, D borrows $10,000 from S and gives S a security interest in equipment. On February 2, C lends D $10,000. On March 3, S perfects its security interest. On July 7, D files a bankruptcy petition. On the date of the petition, D still owes $10,000 to S and $10,000 to C. Can D's bankruptcy trustee invalidate S's security interest under section 544(b)? Cf. section 9-301(1)(b).

3. On January 10, D borrows $10,000 from S and gives S a security interest in equipment. On February 2, L obtains an execution lien on the same equipment. On March 2, S perfects its security interest. On July 7, D files a bankruptcy petition. On the date of the petition, D is still indebted to S and L. Can the bankruptcy trustee invalidate S's security interest under section 544(b)?

4. As Problem #3 illustrates, section 544(b) gives the bankruptcy trustee the protection that state law gives to the debtor's actual unsecured creditors. And, as Problems #1 and #2 illustrate, most modern state recording statutes do not protect unsecured creditors. There are, however, a few state recording statutes that protect general creditors that the trustee can invoke under section 544(b). See, e.g., U.C.C. section 2-326 (consignments), U.C.C. section 6-104 (bulk sales).

---

[1] Most creditors' claims are allowable. Section 502, particularly section 502(b), indicates the extent to which claims are disallowed. Section 502 is considered infra.

[2] Remember that under section 544(b), the bankruptcy trustee is not limited by the amount of the actual creditor's claim. A transaction which is voidable (or ineffective) as to a single actual creditor can be completely avoided by the trustee, regardless of the size of that creditor's claim.

b. Section 544(a)

Section 544(b) looks to the rights of *actual* creditors of the debtor; section 544(a) focuses on the rights of *hypothetical* lien creditors and bona fide purchasers of real property. Section 544(a) empowers the bankruptcy trustee to invalidate any transfer that under non-bankruptcy law is voidable as to a creditor who extended credit and obtained a lien on the date of the filing of the bankruptcy petition, or is voidable as to a bona fide purchaser of real property, whether or not such a creditor or purchaser actually exists. In applying section 544(a), it is thus necessary to determine whether

- non-bankruptcy law public notice requirements have been timely satisfied; and
- a creditor who extended credit and obtained a lien on the date that the petition was filed or a bona fide purchaser of real property on the date of the bankruptcy petition comes within the class of persons protected by such state law.

In re Great Plains Western Ranch Co., Inc.
Bankruptcy Court, Central District of California, 1984
38 B.R. 899

[Great Plains Western Corporation (GPW) filed a Chapter 11 petition. GPW promoted tax shelter limited partnerships. Prior to its Chapter 11 filing, GPW formed Wilson County Land Company (WC), a limited partnership, and sold interests in WC to investors. GPW contracted to sell its Triple C Brangus Ranch in Texas to WC. The land sales contract provided that WC would pay $1.5 million in installments over five years to GPW; GPW would transfer a deed to the Triple Brangus Ranch to WC *after* WC made the last payment. Although Texas recording statutes provide for the filing of installment land sales contracts, nothing was filed in the Texas real property records. GPW filed its Chapter 11 petition before WC made all of the installment payments called for by the land sales contract, before GPW transferred the deed to the Triple C Brangus Ranch to WC.

This litigation deals with ownership of the Triple Brangus Ranch. WC claims ownership of the ranch by constructive trust. GPW argues that the Triple C Brangus Ranch is property of the estate.]

John D. Ayer, Bankruptcy Judge.

Introduction

This is a dispute over ownership rights. The debtor holds record title, but the plaintiffs claim ownership by constructive trust. The constructive trust claims rest on an assertion that the record title holder defrauded them out of the purchase price prior to the filing of this Chapter 11 case. For purposes of analysis, I am willing to assume that the record title holder did in fact defraud the plaintiffs. Nonetheless, I hold that the property belongs in the bankruptcy estate.

II
Property of the Estate

Wilson County (the "plaintiffs") rely chiefly on Section 541 of the Bankruptcy Code, defining property of the bankruptcy estate. Property of the estate under Section 541, they argue, includes (with exceptions not here relevant) only property that was property of the debtor. And that is true. As the Supreme Court said, "The Bankruptcy Act simply does not authorize a trustee to distribute other people's property among a bankrupt's creditors." *Pearlman v. Reliance Ins. Co.,* 371 U.S. 132, 135-36, 83 S.Ct. 232, 234-35, 9 L.Ed.2d 190, 193 (1932). For purposes of analysis on this summary judgment motion, they argue, I must assume that this property would not be property of the debtor at state law. And that is true also.

The difficulty with all this is that it is only a partial analysis. For the question is not merely what becomes property of the estate. A bankruptcy proceeding is forum not merely for the adjudication of claims between plaintiff and defendant. Rather, it is a multilateral proceeding for the adjudication of rights among a variety of interests. GPW as DIP has the rights and powers of a bankruptcy trustee. *See* §1107 (1982). As trustee, it takes rights derivative from the rights of a debtor pursuant to Section 541. But as trustee GPW also exercises a broad range of other rights and powers—rights and powers in no way available to the debtor at state law. Among others, the trustee gets certain rights and powers that might have been exercised by third parties at state law, quite apart from any rights of the debtor. One of these is the power of a hypothetical bona fide purchaser of real property, under §544(a)(3) (1982). And it is to this power that I now turn.

III
The Strong-Arm Clause [544(a)(3)]

The strong-arm clause may be read as relying on the principle of ostensible ownership—the principle that, other things being equal, what the creditor sees ought to be what the creditor gets. There seem to be at least two important reasons why the idea of ostensible ownership bulks so large in bankruptcy law. First, it helps to police against fraud on the part of debtors—fraud that may occur with or without the collusion of creditors. Secondly, quite apart from any imputation of fraud, it helps to permit the kind of reliance said to be essential to a dynamic commercial economy.

There are some difficulties here. First, while the strong-arm clause seems to protect against fraud, the Code nowhere requires any showing of actual fraud in order to bring the strong-arm clause into play. Taking the Code as it stands today, it seems to permit me to assume (as I do here assume) that GPW may have defrauded the plaintiffs in this case; still, it appears that I am to permit such a fraud so as to protect against the risk of fraud that might arise if I permitted covert interests.

The point is put even more sharply in the case of reliance. Not only do we require no showing of reliance; quite the contrary, the trustee is expressly excused from showing that there was any competing claimant who might have relied. *Compare* §544(a) *with* §544(b). Evidently, we believe both reliance and fraud to be so likely that we do not wish to put creditors to the expense and inconvenience of proof.

It is no answer to say that the DIP exercising the trustee's power is the same entity as the GPW who committed the supposed fraud. For the DIP, though physically the same as GPW, is conceptually separate for purposes of bankruptcy law. Presumably if the plaintiffs believe that GPW cannot be trusted with that power, they may seek the appointment of a trustee under §1106 (1982) ("for cause including fraud, dishonesty," etc.). But that is another matter. We have already seen how the trustee has at least a dual aspect, deriving rights from the debtor and powers from creditors. Correspondingly, it is fair to say that the DIP also has a dual aspect, as debtor and also as trustee. Similarly, by way of recapitulation, it may be useful to recall that GPW has at least a triple aspect: as debtor, as general partner of other debtors, and as DIP. Like the comic hero of a Gilbert and Sullivan operetta, he is perpetrator in one conception, victim in another, and innocent bystander in a third. This analysis requires some effort at abstraction, but it seems to be what the Code prescribes.

And that is why Section 541 does not end the inquiry in this case. Even conceding that the property rights of the estate are derivative from the property rights of the debtor, still the trustee enjoys additional powers quite independent of his powers under Section 541, and in no way derivative from the debtor's rights at state law. Failure to consider Section 544 together with Section 541 may lead to misleading generalizations and sometimes to unsound results.

IV
The Trustee's Power
Federal Law

The trustee's powers under Section 544(a), like his rights under Section 541, are derivative. Under Section 541, his rights are derivative from the rights of the debtor. Under the predecessors of Section 544(a), his rights were derivative from the rights of creditors. The substance of this provision was carried over into the Bankruptcy Act of 1978. §544(a)(1), (2). With respect to personal property, it makes sense to dovetail the rights of the trustee with the rights of creditors, because the most relevant state priority law is in the Uniform Commercial Code, which builds its priority scheme primarily on the rights of creditors. *See, e.g.*, U.C.C. §9-301(1)(b). But the law of real property is built around the recording acts. And recording acts frequently speak not of the rights of creditors, but rather of the rights of bona fide purchasers. Hence, the 1978 Code added a new provision to the strong-arm clause in Section 544(a)(3). It provides that the trustee shall have the powers of a hypothetical bona fide purchaser of real property. He is limited as a prospective bona fide purchaser would be limited. But he takes free of competing interests of which a bona fide purchaser would take free. The trustee exercises that power without regard to his own actual knowledge. This is particularly important where, as here, there is no independent trustee and the debtor, who by definition has actual knowledge of latent defects in his own title, himself exercises the powers of the trustee. In any event, since we must look to state law to determine the rights of a bona fide purchaser, it is to state law that I now turn.

Texas Law

Texas law provides: "All bargains, sales and other conveyances whatever, of any land, tenements and hereditaments *** shall be void as to all creditors and subsequent purchasers for a valuable consideration without notice, unless they shall be acknowledged or proved and filed with the clerk, to be recorded as required by law."

Thus, in Texas, one who wishes to claim title to real property is bound by adverse claims disclosed by documents recorded with the clerk in the chain of title whether or not she actually saw those documents. Similarly in Texas, one is deemed to know of an unrecorded deed if the party claiming under that deed is in open, visible and unequivocal possession.

Nothing in the chain of title ever showed any interest passing to Wilson County. GPW as DIP/trustee knows nothing of the activities of GPW as transferor/partner, or as an independent entity. Hence GPW as DIP/trustee may exercise the power of a bona fide purchaser under Section 544(a)(3).

Conclusion

The practical result of all this is to bring the property into the estate for the benefit of creditors at the expense of limited partners. At the risk of laboring the point, let me emphasize again that this says nothing at all about the rights of the limited partners *vis a vis* the general partner. On the contingency that creditors are in fact paid off, then the limited partners and the general partners may be left to do battle over the remainder, and it is then that the court may have to face the issue of fraud. But that day is at least a long way away, and in the ordinary bankruptcy case, it is a day that never arrives. There is no point in trying to deal with the issue now.

There are many anomalies here. The strong-arm clause protects reliance, and protects against fraud, without any showing either of reliance or of fraud. The strong-arm clause permits an (assumed) fraud against the plaintiffs in this case to protect against a (hypothetical) fraud by the debtor in which the plaintiffs by definition might have no part. The strong-arm clause permits the alleged wrongdoer to assert the rights of innocent parties against his own supposed victim. All of this is, to say the least, a remarkable result. Nonetheless, as I have tried to show, I think it is consistent alike with the letter and with the spirit of the Bankruptcy Code.   Therefore, I grant GPW's motion for summary judgment.

Notes and Problems

1.   See generally David Carlson, *The Trustee's Strong Arm Power Under the Bankruptcy Code*, 43 S. CAROLINA L. REV. 841 (1993).

2.   The bankruptcy court held that the Triple C Brangus Ranch was property of the estate. What language in section 541 supports that holding?

3.   Would the bankruptcy court have found that the Triple C Brangus Ranch was property of the estate if the land sales contract had been filed as contemplated by the Texas recording statute?

4.   If GPW had *not* filed for Chapter 11 relief, could it use the Texas recording statute to defeat WC's claim to the Triple C Brangus Ranch?

5.   On January 15, D purchased a house. To finance the purchase, D borrows $60,000 from M and grants M a mortgage on the house. On July 13, D files a bankruptcy petition. As of that date, M had not recorded its mortgage. Will the trustee be able to avoid the mortgage under section 544(a)? If so, what are M's rights?

6.   On April 5, D borrows $10,000 from S and grants a security interest in equipment. On November 25, D files a bankruptcy petition. S's security interest is not perfected. Will D's bankruptcy trustee be able to invalidate S's unperfected security interest under section 544(a)?

7.   On January 15, D borrows $10,000 from S to buy equipment and gives S a purchase money security interest in the equipment. On January 18, D files a bankruptcy petition. On January 19, S perfects its security interest. Will D's bankruptcy trustee be able to invalidate S's security interest under section 544(a)? See section 546(b).

8.   On January 10, Dudley Doright, D, borrows $10,000 from Snidely Whiplash, S, and gives S a security interest in equipment. On December 29, S properly files the financing statement. On December 30, D files a bankruptcy petition. Will D's bankruptcy trustee be able to invalidate S's security interest UNDER SECTION 544(a)?

c. Section 547(e)

In the Doright/Snidely Whiplash problem above, Doright's bankruptcy trustee cannot invalidate Snidely's security interest under section 544(a): Section 544(a)(1) gives the bankruptcy trustee the rights and powers of a creditor that obtained a lien on the date of bankruptcy.   The   security   interest   was   perfected   on   the   date   of bankruptcy. A perfected security interest is effective as against a lien creditor. *SHOULD* Doright's bankruptcy trustee be able to invalidate Snidely's lien?

Remember the reasons for invalidating such "secret liens." Creditors of Doright may have been misled by Snidely Whiplash's failure to record or a delay in recording. Unaware of this "secret," unrecorded lien, a creditor might extend credit to Doright that it would not extend if aware of the lien. Unaware of a "secret," unrecorded lien, a creditor might delay in collecting a delinquent debt from Doright that it would try to collect if aware of the lien. Accordingly, the Bankruptcy Code should invalidate transfers that are not timely recorded. And it does. In section 547.

Although it is easy to see the reason for invalidating liens that are not timely perfected, it is difficult to understand why section 547 should be the mechanism for invalidating such liens. The easy way to invalidate such secret liens would be to add a section to the Bankruptcy Code to the effect that any lien required to be recorded by state law must be recorded within 10 (21? 30?) days after it is obtained in order to be valid in bankruptcy. While that is the "easy way," it is not the way of the Bankruptcy Code.

Basically, the Bankruptcy Code's method is to "deem" that, for purposes of applying the requirements of section 547(b), the date of transfer is the date of recordation or perfection, not the actual date of transfer. Thus, a transfer for new consideration that is not timely recorded or perfected will be treated as a transfer for antecedent debt.

The Doright/Snidely Whiplash hypothetical illustrates the practical significance of treating the recordation date as the transfer date. Remember, Doright borrowed $10,000 from Snidley Whiplash on January 10 and gave Snidely a security interest in equipment which Snidely perfected on December 29. Doright filed a bankruptcy petition on December 30. At first, it might seem that section 547 is not applicable—that the January 10 security "transfer" from Doright to Snidely Whiplash was not for an antecedent indebtedness and did not occur within 90 days of the bankruptcy petition. For purposes of section 547, however, the transfer will be deemed made on December 29, not January 10. [Under section 9-301, Snidely Whiplash's security interest would not be effective as against subsequent judicial lien creditors until that date. Accordingly, by reason of section 547(e), the transfer will not be deemed made until that date.] Thus, the "December 29 transfer" would be within 90 days of the bankruptcy petition. Thus, the "December 29 transfer" would be for an antecedent indebtedness, i.e., the $100,000 loaned on January 10. Thus, the trustee would be able to invalidate S's security interest under section 547.

indebtedness, i.e., the $100,000 loaned on January 10. Thus, the trustee would be able to invalidate S's security interest under section 547.

The above hypothetical illustrates that a delay in perfection can result in a security interest actually given for present consideration being deemed made for an antecedent indebtedness and thus a section 547 preference. Section 547(e) does not require immediate perfection; it provides a ten-day "grace period" for perfection in section 547(e)(2). The operation of section 547(c) is illustrated in the following problems.

Problems

1. Section 547(e)(2)(A) deals with the situation in which the transfer *is* perfected within the statutory grace period. For example, on January 15, D borrows $10,000 from C and grants C a mortgage on Greenacre. C records its mortgage on January 19. D files a bankruptcy petition on February 2. What is the time of the transfer for purposes of section 547? Can the trustee avoid the mortgage under section 547(b)?

2. Section 547(e)(2)(B) deals with the situation in which the transfer is *not* perfected within the grace period. Consider the following examples:

    a. On January 15, D borrows $10,000 from C and grants C a mortgage on Greenacre. C records its mortgage on February 12. D files a bankruptcy petition on May 30. What is the time of the transfer for purposes of section 547? Can the trustee avoid the mortgage under section 547(b)?

    b. Does your answer to Problem 2.a. change if the applicable recording statute contains a thirty-day grace period?

3. Section 547(e)(2)(c) deals with *some* transfers not perfected prior to the filing of the bankruptcy petition. Consider the following examples:

    a. On January 15, D borrows $10,000 from C and grants C a security interest in equipment. C does not perfect. On April 5, D files a bankruptcy petition. What is the time of the transfer for purposes of section 547? See section 547(e)(2)(C). Can the trustee avoid the security interest under section 547(b)? Under section 544(a)?

    b. On January 15, S sells D equipment on credit and retains a security interest in the equipment. On January 19, D files a bankruptcy petition. On January 20, S perfects its security interest. Did S violate the automatic stay? See sections 362(a)(4), 362(b)(3), 546(b). What is the time of the transfer for purposes of section 547? See section 547(e)(2)(A). Do you understand why section 547(e)(2)(C) does *not* apply?

c. Does your answer to Problem 3.b. change if S was a lender rather than a seller and its security interest was not "purchase money" ? See sections 544(a), 546(b).

4. Do you understand why section 547(e) is *not* applicable at all in the following problem: On January 15, D borrows $40,000 from C. On January 22, D grants C a security interest in equipment which S perfects. On April 5, D files a bankruptcy petition.

5. Can section 547(c)(1) apply to transfers that are not timely recorded? For example, D borrows $50,000 from C on January 5th. Because a clerk misplaces some of the documents, the mortgage is not recorded until January 29th. D files for bankruptcy on April 20th. Didn't D and C intend "a contemporaneous exchange for new value"? Wasn't it "in fact substantially contemporaneous"?

Answers to Problems

1. January 15 is the date of transfer and so the trustee cannot avoid this transfer for a present debt.

2. February 12 is the date of transfer and so the trustee can avoid this transfer within 90 days of bankruptcy made for a January 15 debt.

3.a. The time of transfer is April 5 and so the trustee can avoid the transfer.

3.b. The time of transfer is January 15 and so the trustee cannot avoid the transfer under section 547. Because of Article 9's ten day grace period for perfection of purchase money security interests, section 546(b) applies and protects the secured party from section 362(a) and section 544(a).

3.c. The time of the transfer is still January 15, and so the trustee still cannot avoid the transfer under section 547. Because Article 9 does not have a grace period for perfection of "non-purchase money" security interests, section 546(b) does not apply. The post-bankruptcy perfection violates section 362. And, the trustee can avoid the security interest under section 544(a).

4. Section 547(e) provides a grace period for perfecting a lien, not a grace period for obtaining a lien.

d. Section 548(d)

Section 548(d) is similar to section 547(e). Section 547(e) fixes the time when a transfer is deemed made for purposes of the preference invalidation provisions of section 547. Section 548(d) fixes the time when a transfer is deemed made for purposes of the fraudulent conveyance invalidation provisions of section 548: when the transfer is so far perfected that no subsequent bona fide purchaser of the property from the debtor can acquire rights in the property superior to those of the transferee.

The purpose of section 548(d) is to prevent a fraudulent conveyance from escaping invalidation by being kept secret. For example, on January 10, 1993, D, an insolvent, gives Greenacre to X. X does not record the deed until November 11, 1994. On December 12, 1994, D files a bankruptcy petition. Remember, section 548 has a one year limitations period. The transfer of Greenacre was actually made more than one year before the bankruptcy petition was filed. The transfer, however, was not effective against a subsequent bona fide purchaser until it was recorded on November 11. Accordingly, under a section 548(d), the transfer is deemed made on November 11, 1994. Without section 548(d), the bankruptcy trustee could not invalidate this gift by an insolvent under section 548.

The transfer from D to X in the preceding paragraph was a "true" fraudulent conveyance: a transfer by an insolvent without "reasonably equivalent value." Section 548(d), however, also may enable the bankruptcy trustee to invalidate some transfers that are not "true" fraudulent conveyances—transfers in which there has been merely a delay in recordation or perfection. Consider the following illustration.

Wallace Cleaver, W, gives Greenacre to his brother Theodore, T, in December of 1993. W is solvent at that time. T, however, does not record the transfer until June of 1994. At that time, W is insolvent. In July of 1994, W files a bankruptcy petition. The bankruptcy trustee will be able to use section 548(a)(2) to invalidate the 1993 gift of Greenacre.

Note that T's delay in recordation is crucial to the bankruptcy trustee's section 548 case. At the time that the gift is actually made, the donor, W, is solvent. There are no legal problems with people who are *solvent* making gifts. This happens every Chanukah and Christmas. Gifts are fraudulent conveyances when made by people who are insolvent.

While the donor, W, was solvent when the gift was actually made, he is insolvent when the gift is deemed made under section 548(d)—at the time the transfer is perfected against bona fide purchasers from the transferor. Section 548(d), like section 547(e), enables the trustee to test all aspects of the transaction as of the time of recordation rather than as of the time of the actual transfer. Since W was insolvent when the transfer is deemed made—at the time of recordation—the transfer was fraudulent as a transfer by an insolvent without reasonably equivalent value.

e. Section 545(2)[1]

Section 545(2) deals with statutory liens that are not timely recorded or otherwise perfected. It empowers the trustee to invalidate a statutory lien on property of the debtor that is not "perfected or enforceable on the date of the bankruptcy petition against a bona fide purchaser that purchases such property on the date of the filing of the petition, whether or not such a purchaser exists."

Section 545(2) is of very limited practical significance for three reasons. First, most statutory liens are enforceable against a bona fide purchaser, i.e., satisfy section 545(2)'s bona fide purchaser test. Second, statutory liens are also subject to section 544(a) which can be used to avoid any statutory lien that is voidable by a hypothetical lien creditor or a bona fide purchaser. Third, section 546(b) permits post-petition recordation of statutory liens in certain circumstances. Please read section 546(b) again. Note that it recognizes any applicable state law "grace periods." If, at the time of the filing of the bankruptcy petition, the statutory lien can still be perfected under state law and that perfection relates back to a pre-bankruptcy petition date, then the bankruptcy trustee will not be able to avoid the statutory lien.

Notes and Problems

1. Your client, C, has supplied material and labor on D's apartment project. D files a Chapter 11 petition before the work on the project is finished and before C is paid. C has not recorded its mechanics' lien (a/k/a construction lien). Under relevant state law, it is not necessary to record a mechanics' lien until after the construction has been completed. Will C's unrecorded mechanics' lien be valid in bankruptcy? Can C record its mechanics' lien? See section 362(a)(4), section 362(b)(3). Should C record its mechanics' lien?

2. Recall that when federal tax liability is assessed, a lien arises on virtually all of the taxpayer's property. This tax lien is not, however, valid against certain third parties—including purchasers from the taxpayer—until public notice of the lien is filed. If the taxpayer files her bankruptcy petition before the IRS files its notice of the tax lien, can the bankruptcy trustee avoid the federal tax lien under section 545? Under section 544(a)?

---

[1] Section 545(1) deals with statutory liens that first become effective on the debtor's insolvency—liens that are more like priorities than like liens. Section 545(3) and section 545(4) invalidate statutory landlord's liens.

C. POST-PETITION TRANSFERS,
SECTIONS 549 AND 542(c)

Sections 544, 545, 547, and 548 deal with the avoidance of transfers that occurred *prior* to the time that the bankruptcy petition was filed. None of these provisions can be used to avoid an unauthorized transfer of property of the estate that occurs *after* the bankruptcy petition is filed. Sections 549 and 542(c) deal with post-petition transfers.

Recall that the filing of a bankruptcy petition creates "an estate." Subject to limited exceptions, property owned by the debtor on that date becomes part of that estate, and property acquired after the date of the bankruptcy petition remains the property of the debtor.

In the typical Chapter 11, Chapter 12, or Chapter 13 case, the debtor retains and uses the property of the estate. But in every Chapter 7 case, the bankruptcy trustee is statutorily required to "collect and reduce to money the property of the estate," section 704.

The date the Chapter 7 petition is filed is not, however, the date that the trustee takes possession of the debtor's property. In a voluntary case, there will invariably be some delay before the trustee takes control of the property even though section 701 provides for the appointment of an interim trustee "promptly after the order for relief." And, in an involuntary case, the debtor will remain in control while the debtor and his creditors litigate whether to grant an order for relief (sometimes called the involuntary gap period). Even if the order for relief is entered, there will usually be a further delay before the trustee obtains control.

During the hiatus between the filing of the Chapter 7 petition and the time the trustee takes control of the property, the debtor will usually have possession and control of the property. Technically, of course, that property belongs to the estate, and the debtor has no right to transfer it to a third party. But, what if she does? For example, assume D files a Chapter 7 petition on January 15. On January 18, D sells her summer home to X, and on January 20 she sells her boat to Y. Obviously, D should not have made those post-petition transfers. Obviously, the trustee can claim any proceeds from the post-bankruptcy transfers as property of the estate, section 541(a)(6). (And, obviously, this claim against D will usually be of limited practical significance.) What is less obvious (and, usually, more important) is whether the bankruptcy trustee can recover the summer house from X and/or the boat from Y? Should the bankruptcy laws protect X and Y?

Section 549 protects X and Y in certain circumstances. Please read section 549. Carefully.

Notice that the general rule of section 549 is that a trustee can avoid a post-bankruptcy transfer, section 549(a)(1). Notice also that this general rule is subject to three exceptions: section 549 protects the transferee if either

- the transfer was authorized by the Bankruptcy Code or the bankruptcy court, section 549(a)(2); or
- the transfer occurred after an *involuntary* petition and was for post-petition consideration, section 549(b); or
- the transfer was a *real* property transfer that was recorded before the bankruptcy was noted in the appropriate real property records, section 549(c).

Please apply section 549 in the following problems.

Problems

1. On January 15, D files a Chapter 7 petition. On January 20, D sells her boat to X for $20,000. X knows of D's Chapter 7 filing. Can the bankruptcy trustee recover the boat from X?

2. Same facts as Problem 1 except that X does not know that D has filed a bankruptcy petition when he buys the boat.

3. On January 15, D's creditors file a Chapter 7 petition against her. On January 20, D sells her boat to X for $30,000. X knows of the bankruptcy petition. Can the bankruptcy trustee recover the boat from X?

4. Same facts as Problem 3 except that X does not know that D's creditors have filed a Chapter 7 bankruptcy petition when she buys the boat.

5. On April 5, D files a Chapter 7 petition. On April 8, D sells Greenacre to Y for $100,000. Can the bankruptcy trustee avoid the transfer? What, if any, additional information is needed to answer the question?

6. Some post-petition transfers of property of the estate are made by persons holding property of the debtor, not the debtor. For example, on January 7, D sends X a $300 check. On January 15, D files a Chapter 7 petition. As of that date, D has $1,000 in her checking account at B Bank. This checking account becomes property of the estate on January 15, section 541. On January 23, B Bank honors a $300 check issued by D to X on January 7 and charges D's account. Can D's bankruptcy trustee recover the $300 from B Bank? *Bank of Marin v. England,* 385 U.S. 99, 87 S.Ct.

274, 17 L.Ed.2d 197 (1966), protected the bank under the Bankruptcy Act of 1898; section 542 protects the bank under the Bankruptcy Code.

Under section 542(c), a third party who in good faith transfers property of the estate after the filing of the petition is protected from the bankruptcy trustee if the third party had "neither notice nor actual knowledge of the commencement of the case." Accordingly, if B Bank has neither actual knowledge nor notice of D's petition, it will not be liable to the bankruptcy trustee. Note that section 542(c) only protects B Bank, the party that transfers the property of the estate; it does not protect X.

7.   All of the above problems have involved Chapter 7 debtors. Provisions in Chapter 5 of the Bankruptcy Code such as section 549 apply to debtors under all chapters of the Bankruptcy Code. Consider the effect of section 549 on the following transactions by D Stores, Inc. (D), that filed for Chapter 11 on April 5:

     a.   On April 7, D advertises "Chapter 11 Celebration Sale." Does section 549 protect the buyers at the sale? See section 363(c)(1)

     b.   On May 1, D pays the prepetition claims of various vendors. Are these payments avoidable under sections 549 and 550?

8.   See generally Darrell Dunham, *Postpetition Transfers in Bankruptcy*, 39 U. Miami L. Rev. 1 (1984).

D. SELLER'S RIGHT OF RECLAMATION

When a seller of goods is not paid, the seller wants the goods returned. Section 2-702 of the Uniform Commercial Code gives an unpaid seller a right to reclaim the goods. Please read section 2-702 below.

Section 2-702. Seller's Remedies on Discovery of Buyer's Insolvency

(1) Where the seller discovers the buyer to be insolvent he may refuse delivery except for cash including payment for all goods theretofore delivered under the contract, and stop delivery under this Article (Section 2-705).

(2) Where the seller discovers that the buyer has received goods on credit while insolvent he may reclaim the goods upon demand made within ten days after the receipt, but if misrepresentation of solvency has been made to the particular seller in writing within three months before delivery the ten day limitation does not apply. Except as provided in

this subsection the seller may not base a right to reclaim goods on the buyer's fraudulent or innocent misrepresentation of solvency or of intent to pay.

(3) The seller's right to reclaim under subsection (2) is subject to the rights of a buyer in ordinary course or other good faith purchaser under this Article (Section 2-403). Successful reclamation of goods excludes all other remedies with respect to them.

What is the impact, if any, of the buyer's bankruptcy on this state law right of reclamation? If S reclaims the goods within 90 days before the bankruptcy petition, hasn't S improved S's position? Has S received a section 547 preference? If, on the other hand, S reclaims the goods after the bankruptcy petition has been filed, hasn't there been a post-petition transfer? Can the trustee avoid this transfer under section 549?

A trustee *cannot* avoid a reclamation under either section 547 or section 549 *if* the seller has completely complied with section 546(c). Please read section 546(c). Compare section 546(c) with section 2-702 of the Uniform Commercial Code. Apply section 546(c) and 2-702 to the following problems.

Notes and Problems

1. **Nature of right of reclamation**

   a. X is one of several companies that delivers sulfuric acid to D. Under 2-702, does X's right to reclaim end when D commingles acid from X with acid received from other suppliers?

   b. Does X's right to reclaim end when D uses the acid? When D sells the acid?

   c. Y Shirt Co. (Y) sells shirts on credit to D Stores, Inc. (D). S has a perfected security in all of D's inventory. Can Y reclaim its shirts?

2. **Effect of bankruptcy on right of reclamation**
   Your client C sold goods on credit to D. D filed for a bankruptcy three days after receiving a large shipment from C. Advise C. Is it necessary to obtain relief from the automatic stay before sending a reclamation letter? Is there any reason to send a reclamation letter if another creditor has a valid security interest in all of D's inventory?

Unit 14

ALLOCATION OF JUDICIAL POWER OVER BANKRUPTCY MATTERS

UNIT CONTENTS

The question of which court has the power to adjudicate the litigation that arises in bankruptcy can be an important one. Many attorneys that represent parties with claims against the "bankrupt" or parties against whom the bankrupt has claims prefer to litigate in some forum other than the bankruptcy court. Some believe that the bankruptcy judge has a pro-debtor bias; others are simply more comfortable or more familiar with state court procedures or state court judges.

In considering the question of which court has the power to adjudicate the litigation that arises in bankruptcy, it is helpful to consider the kinds of matters that can arise in bankruptcy.

Some will involve only bankruptcy law. For example, D files a Chapter 13 petition. At D's confirmation hearing the Trustee argued to the bankruptcy court that the court could not confirm the plan unless the debtor pledged to pay all *actual* disposable income to the trustee during the duration of the plan. The Trustee's objection to the confirmation raised the bankruptcy law issue of whether a Chapter 13 plan must provide for payment of actual or "projected" disposable income.

Other matters will involve both bankruptcy law and non-bankruptcy law. For example, D files a Chapter 7 petition. C files a secured claim that describes its Article 9 security interest. The bankruptcy trustee takes the position that C's security interest is invalid. If this is litigated, it will probably involve both the Bankruptcy Code's invalidation provisions and the Uniform Commercial Code's perfection provisions.

And, still other matters will not involve substantive bankruptcy law. For example, D. Inc., a Chapter 11 debtor, files a breach of contract claim against X.

A. HISTORY

The allocation of judicial power over bankruptcy matters has been and still is one of the most controversial bankruptcy issues. A general familiarity with prior statutory schemes and prior controversies is helpful to understanding the present situation.

1. 1898 Act

Under the Bankruptcy Act of 1898, bankruptcy courts had limited jurisdiction. This jurisdiction was commonly referred to as "summary jurisdiction." (The phrase "summary jurisdiction" is somewhat misleading. First, it incorrectly implies that under the Bankruptcy Act of 1898, bankruptcy courts had a second, non-summary form of jurisdiction. Summary jurisdiction is the only form of jurisdiction that a bankruptcy judge possessed under the Bankruptcy Act of 1898. Bankruptcy courts had only summary jurisdiction; other courts had plenary jurisdiction. Second, it incorrectly implies that in resolving controversies the bankruptcy judge always conducted summary proceedings.)

There was considerable uncertainty over which disputes were within the summary jurisdiction of the bankruptcy court. This uncertainty gave rise to considerable litigation over jurisdictional issues. In 1973, the Commission on the Bankruptcy Laws of the United States recommended to Congress, "A comprehensive grant of jurisdiction to the bankruptcy courts over all controversies arising out of bankruptcy or rehabilitation cases would greatly diminish the basis for litigation of jurisdiction issues, which consumes so much time, money and energy of the bankruptcy system and of those involved in the administration of debtors' affairs." Report of the Commission on Bankruptcy Laws of the United States, Part I, H.R. Doc. 93-137, p. 90.

2. 1978 Code

Apparently for this reason, Congress in 1978 decided to create a bankruptcy court with pervasive jurisdiction. Apparently for political reasons, Congress also decided that this bankruptcy court should *not* be an "Article III court."

As you recall from your Constitutional Law course in law school or civics in high school, Article III of the Constitution vests the judicial power of the United States in the United States Supreme Court and such inferior tribunals as Congress might create. To insure the independence of the judges appointed under Article III (the so-called constitutional courts), Article III provides them with certain protections. These include tenure for life, removal from office only by congressional impeachment, and assurance that their compensation will not be diminished. The constitutional courts created under Article III include the United States Supreme Court, the United States Courts of Appeal, and the United States District Courts.

Congress, in the exercise of its legislative powers enumerated in Article I of the Constitution, may create other inferior federal tribunals—the so-called legislative courts. Judges of these legislative courts need not be granted tenure for life. In addition, they can be removed by mechanisms other than congressional impeachment, and their salaries are subject to congressional reduction. Historically, these Article I legislative courts and their judges have been granted jurisdiction over limited and narrowly defined subject matters, like the Tax Court. In other instances, jurisdiction has been limited to narrowly defined geographical territories, such as the territorial courts, the District of Columbia courts, etc.

In enacting the 1978 Code, Congress gave bankruptcy judges none of the protections required by Article III of the Constitution. While bankruptcy judges were thus Article I judges, Congress nonetheless gave bankruptcy judges far more judicial power and responsibility than granted to other Article I judges. As the House Report stated, "The Bankruptcy court is given in personam jurisdiction as well as in rem jurisdiction to handle everything that arises in the Bankruptcy case." H.R. Rep. 595, 95th Cong., 1st Sess. 445 (1977). Because debtors in bankruptcy cases can be just about any kind of individual or business entity with just about any kind of legal problem, bankruptcy courts had jurisdiction over almost any kind of case or legal issue. In the "numerology" and terminology of constitutional law professors, bankruptcy judges were thus Article I judges exercising Article III powers.

3. *Marathon Pipeline* Decision

The 1978 grant of pervasive jurisdiction to a non-Article III bankruptcy court was quickly and successfully challenged. In June of 1982, the Supreme Court invalidated the entire grant of jurisdiction to the bankruptcy courts in *Northern Pipeline Constr. Co. v. Marathon Pipe Line Co.*, 458 U.S. 50, 102 S.Ct. 2858, 73 L.Ed.2d 598 (1982).

Northern Pipeline, a Chapter 11 debtor, filed a breach of contract lawsuit against Marathon Pipeline in bankruptcy court. There was no question as to whether the bankruptcy court had jurisdiction over this lawsuit under 28 U.S.C.A. section 1471(c). Marathon Pipeline did, however, question whether section 1471(c) conferred Article III judicial power on non-Article III courts in violation of the separation of powers doctrine and filed a motion to dismiss. The bankruptcy judge refused to dismiss; he was reversed by the district judge. On direct appeal, a divided Supreme Court sustained Marathon's challenge.

The Court in *Marathon* was so divided that there was no majority opinion, and therein lies much of the uncertainty about the case. Justice Brennan's opinion was joined by three other justices. Additionally, two justices concurred in the result. The holding of these six is perhaps best summarized in footnote 40 of Justice Brennan's plurality opinion which indicates that (1) the 1978 legislation does grant the bankruptcy court the power to hear Northern Pipeline's breach of contract claim, (2) the bankruptcy court, a non-Article III court, cannot constitutionally be vested with jurisdiction to decide such state law claims, and (3) this grant of authority to the bankruptcy court is not severable from the remaining grant of authority to the bankruptcy court.

4. 1984 Amendments

After *Marathon*, Congress was urged to solve the constitutional dilemma by establishing bankruptcy courts as Article III courts. Congress rejected this solution. Instead, the 1984 amendments make the bankruptcy court a part of the federal district court, confer jurisdiction in bankruptcy on the district court, and allocate judicial power in bankruptcy matters between the federal district judge and the bankruptcy judge. It is easy for any lawyer or law student to criticize the provisions allocating judicial power over bankruptcy matters. It is more difficult (but probably more important) for a lawyer or law student to understand how these provisions operate.

B. PRESENT PROVISIONS

The provisions in Title 28 on allocation of judicial powers in bankruptcy matters deal with three separate issues: (1) jurisdiction of the "district court", (2) authority of the bankruptcy judge and (3) abstention.

1. Jurisdiction Of The "District Court"

Section 1334 of the 1984 legislation, like section 1471 of the 1978 legislation, constitutes an extraordinarily broad grant of jurisdiction.

Section 1334(a) vests original and exclusive jurisdiction in the district court over all "cases" arising under the Bankruptcy Code. "Case" is a term of art as used in title 28, the Bankruptcy Code, and the Bankruptcy Rules. "Case" refers to the entire Chapter 7, 9, 11, 12, or 13 matter—not just some controversy that arises in connection with it. To illustrate, if Sunshine Cab Co. files a Chapter 11 petition, section 1334(a) gives the district court jurisdiction over Sunshine's Chapter 11 case itself.

The term "case" is to be distinguished from the term "proceeding." A specific dispute that arises during the pendency of a "case" is referred to as a "proceeding." Under section 1334(b), district courts are given original but not exclusive jurisdiction over all civil proceedings (i) arising under title 11, (ii) arising in title 11, or (iii) related to cases under title 11.

Section 1334(b)'s three categories of civil proceedings raise the question: Is it necessary to distinguish among proceedings arising under, proceedings arising in, and proceedings related to? Distinguishing among the three categories is important in determining the authority of the bankruptcy judge and in abstention decisions. It is not, however, important in determining jurisdiction issues: it is not necessary to ascertain whether a civil proceeding is arising under, arising in, or related to in determining whether the district court has jurisdiction. So long as a civil proceeding fits in any of the three categories, there is jurisdiction. Accordingly, in Sunshine Cab's Chapter 11, section 1334(b) gives the district court jurisdiction over a complaint filed by Sunshine's trustee alleging that payments to Louie De Palma were preferential (arising under?) or a complaint filed against Sunshine by Elaine Nardo alleging sex discrimination (related to?).

Both the language of section 1334 and the legislative history indicate that the grant of jurisdiction is pervasive, that the district court has jurisdiction over virtually all litigation in which the debtor could be expected to have any interest. And, the reported cases since 1984 have consistently recognized the broad grant of jurisdiction in section 1334. For example, the leading test of what constitutes a proceeding "related to" a bankruptcy case is "whether the outcome of the proceeding could conceivably have any effect on the estate being administered in bankruptcy. Thus the proceeding need not necessarily be against the debtor or against the debtor's property. An action is related to bankruptcy if the outcome could alter the debtor's rights, liabilities, options, or freedom of action (either positively or negatively) and which in any way impacts upon the handling and administration of the bankruptcy case." *Pacor, Inc. v. Higgins*, 743 F.2d 984, 994 (3d Cir. 1984) (dictum).

2. Authority Of The Bankruptcy Judge

Clearly, section 1334 confers jurisdiction over bankruptcy matters to the "district court," an Article III court. Clearly, there are no constitutional problems with a grant of pervasive jurisdiction to an Article III court. It is equally clear that most federal district judges have neither the time nor the inclination to exercise this jurisdiction. Accordingly, the 1984 legislation contemplated that federal district judges would delegate this bankruptcy jurisdiction to bankruptcy judges, see sections 151 and 157.

Please read section 151. Note that it refers to a bankruptcy judge and a bankruptcy court as a "unit" of the district court. Consider the importance of this reference throughout the bankruptcy provisions in Title 28. When the term "district court" appears in section 1334 or in section 157, it could be referring to the United States district judge and/or the bankruptcy judge. After all, the bankruptcy judge is a "unit" of the district court.

Next, please note the title of section 157, "Procedures." As this title suggests, section 157 is not a jurisdictional provision. It does not confer jurisdiction on the bankruptcy judge. Rather, it deals with procedure—the role that the bankruptcy judge, a unit of the district court, is to play in exercising the jurisdiction conferred by section 1334 on the district court.

Paragraph (a) of section 157 permits the district courts to refer all jurisdiction over bankruptcy matters conferred by section 1334 to bankruptcy judges. Every district court in the country has adopted a blanket reference policy.

The extent of bankruptcy judges' power to act in a referred matter turns primarily on whether the matter is a "core" or "noncore" proceeding. In core proceedings, bankruptcy judges may conduct the trial or hearing and enter a final judgment or order, section 157(b). The role of the district court is simply that of an appellate tribunal. As an appellate court, the district court reviews the bankruptcy judge's findings of facts in a core proceeding according to the "clearly erroneous standard."

In noncore proceedings, on the other hand, bankruptcy judges may not enter final orders except with the parties' consent. The bankruptcy judges still hold the trial or hearing but cannot issue the final judgment. In noncore proceedings, dispositive orders are made by the district courts. The bankruptcy judges submit proposed findings of fact and law to the district court for review. The proposed findings in a noncore proceeding are subject to de novo review to the extent that any party has timely and specifically objected to them, section 157(c)(1).

The statute does not define the terms "core" and "noncore." (Indeed, the statute does not even use the term "noncore.") A non-exclusive list of core proceedings is set out in section 157(b)(2). Please review the list. Note that virtually all of the matters considered in the bankruptcy portion of this book are core proceedings. Even though all cases and commentaries agree that almost everything is a core proceeding, there has been considerable case law and law review writing on what is and is not a core proceeding.

A determination that a matter is noncore does not mean that the bankruptcy judge can not hear the matter. A bankruptcy judge can still preside over the trial of a noncore matter and submit proposed findings to the district court. In theory, the district court's review of the bankruptcy judges' proposed findings is *de novo*. In practice, the review is probably more properly described as "de nada".

Similarly, a determination that a matter is a core proceeding does not mean that the district judge lacks power to withdraw the matter from the bankruptcy judge. Section 157(d) authorizes the district judge to withdraw a core or a noncore matter from the bankruptcy judge.

3. Types Of Bankruptcy Hearings

The Bankruptcy Code, title 11, leaves questions of allocation of judicial power in bankruptcy matters to the Judicial Code, title 28. Both title 11 and title 28 leave questions of procedure in bankruptcy matters to the Federal Rules of Bankruptcy Procedure.

The Bankruptcy Rules provide for two different types of hearings: (1) adversary proceedings and (2) contested matters. The pleadings and practice in an adversary proceeding in bankruptcy are much the same as any other civil dispute. Adversary proceedings are commenced by a complaint and are governed by Part VII of the Bankruptcy Rules which are numbered like and incorporate Federal Rules of Civil Procedure. Contested matters are commenced by motion are governed by more streamlined procedures set out in Rule 9014.

Rule 7001 lists adversary proceedings. Adversary proceedings include discharge litigation and avoidance actions. The Bankruptcy Code does not list contested matters. Common contested matters include stay litigation and objections to claims. See Bankruptcy Rules 4001, 3007.

C. MOVING LITIGATION TO AND FROM THE BANKRUPTCY JUDGE

Notwithstanding the good intentions of the Commission on the Bankruptcy Laws of the United States in 1973 and the good intentions of Congress in both 1978 and 1984, tactical efforts to move litigation to and from the bankruptcy judge still consumes much time, money, and energy of the bankruptcy system and of those involved in the administration of debtor's affairs.

1. Withdrawal Of Reference

As noted above, withdrawal of a reference moves litigation from the bankruptcy judge to the federal district judge. Section 157(d) and Federal Rule of Bankruptcy Procedure 5011(a) govern withdrawal. The first sentence of section 157(d) gives the district judge discretion to withdraw an entire bankruptcy case or some specific litigation in a bankruptcy case "for cause shown." The second sentence of section 157(d) sets out the requirements for mandatory withdrawal. Please reread section 157(d).

2. Abstention

Abstention results in the litigation being heard by a state court judge, rather than the bankruptcy judge. There are three separate statutory bases for abstention. Both section 305 of the Bankruptcy Code and section 1334(c)(1) of title 28 provide for permissive or discretionary abstention. Section 1334(c)(2) of title 28 requires mandatory abstention. Please read these sections.

3. Removal

Removal moves a proceeding from state court to the bankruptcy court. If a civil action involving a debtor is pending in state court at the time the debtor files a bankruptcy petition, then any party to that litigation can file an application for removal with the bankruptcy court clerk. *See* 28 U.S.C. section 1452; Federal Rules of Bankruptcy Procedure 9027(a)(1), 9001(1), (3). Section 1452 limits removability to actions within the jurisdictional grant of section 1334. Removal is to the district court for the district where the removed action was pending. Under 28 U.S.C. 1409(a), "in the interest of justice or for the convenience of the party", that court could transfer the action to the district court where the bankruptcy case is pending, and, under the general reference, the action would go to the bankruptcy judge to try.

4. Remand

Remand moves the removed litigation back to the state court. The court may remand a removed action under any equitable ground, 28 U.S.C. section 1452(b).

5. Jury Trial Demand

Because of the uncertainty as to whether a bankruptcy judge can conduct a jury trial, a jury trial demand may be another litigation tactic for moving litigation from the bankruptcy judge.

D. JURY TRIALS IN BANKRUPTCY

A bankruptcy lawyer or law student needs to be able to answer two questions about jury trials in bankruptcy: (1) when is there a right to a jury trial in bankruptcy litigation and (2) can the bankruptcy judge conduct such a jury trial. The Supreme Court has provided a partial and somewhat unclear answer to the first question. To date, the Supreme Court has not directly answered the second question.

1. Right To Jury Trial In Bankruptcy Litigation

The right to a jury trial must arise from either a statute or the Constitution. Section 1411, dealing with personal injury actions, is the only statutory authority for a right to jury trial in bankruptcy cases. Accordingly, the basis for most jury trials in bankruptcy cases is the Constitution.

The Seventh Amendment provides "In Suits at common law, where the value in controversy, shall exceed twenty dollars, the right of trial by jury shall be preserved. . . ." The Supreme Court applied this Seventh Amendment language to bankruptcy litigation in *Granfinanciera S.A. v. Nordberg*, 109 S.Ct. 2782 (1989).

Nordberg was the trustee in the Chase and Sanborn Corporation bankruptcy case. He filed a fraudulent conveyance action in bankruptcy court, seeking to recover $1,7 million from Granfinanciera. In its answer, Granfinanciera requested a trial by jury.

The bankruptcy court, then the district court, then the Eleventh Circuit denied the request. Then, in four opinions and approximately 65 pages, a divided Supreme Court held that *Granfinaciera* had a right to jury trial. Justice Brennan's majority opinion focuses primarily on two legal questions: (1) was there a right to jury trial in fraudulent conveyance actions in England in 1791 and (2) was a fraudulent conveyance action seeking to recover money fundamental legal or equitable in nature.

Both the majority opinion in *Granfinanciera* and the later decision in *Langencamp v. Culp*, 111 S.Ct. 330 (1990) also focus on a question of fact: did the creditor file a proof of claim. In *Granfinanciera* the Court states and in *Langencamp* the Court holds that a creditor that files a proof of claim loses any Seventh Amendment right to a jury trial. The reasoning is that the filing of a proof of claim invokes the bankruptcy court's equitable jurisdiction. By so doing the creditor gives up what would otherwise be its Seventh Amendment right to a jury trial in action at law.

2. Power Of Bankruptcy Judges To Conduct Jury Trials

The power of a bankruptcy judge to conduct a jury trial must be based on both Congressional authorization and Constitutional authorization. In *Granfinanciera*, the Court expressly decided that it was not deciding whether either Congress or the Constitution authorize a bankruptcy judge to conduct a jury trial. 109 S.Ct. 2802.

In re Stansbury Poplar Place, Inc.
United States Court of Appeals, Fourth Circuit, 1993
13 F.3d 122

Williams, Circuit Judge: In October 1990, Stansbury Poplar Place, Inc., Stansbury Timonium, Inc., Stansbury 40 West, Inc., Stansbury Perry Hall, Inc., and International Electronic World Limited Partnership, (the debtors) each filed for relief under Chapter 11 of the United States Bankruptcy Code. In November 1990, the United States Trustee appointed the Official Committee of Unsecured Creditors (the Committee) as the party responsible for all the unsecured creditors in the five Stansbury related estates. In October 1992, the bankruptcy court authorized the Committee to commence actions to recover fraudulent conveyances, preferential transfers, and other claims against several of the officers, directors, insiders and shareholders of the debtors (collectively referred to as Appellants). Appellants answered the complaints and filed demands for jury trials. Appellants then filed motions in the district court to withdraw the order of reference to the bankruptcy court on the ground that the bankruptcy court could not conduct the jury trials to which they were entitled.

This is an interlocutory appeal of the district court's denial of Appellants' motion to withdraw the order of reference to the bankruptcy court. Appellants contend that they have a Seventh Amendment right to a jury trial on the Committee's fraudulent conveyance actions against them, that the bankruptcy court does not have the authority to conduct a jury trial, and, therefore, that the order of reference should be withdrawn immediately.

The Committee, on the other hand, contends that because it requested an equitable accounting as well as actions at law, Appellants are not entitled to a jury trial. It also contends that the bankruptcy court has the authority to conduct a jury trial. However, even if the bankruptcy court could not conduct a jury trial, the Committee believes that court is better able to address the equitable accounting claim and other pre-trial matters, and therefore, the order of reference should not be withdrawn immediately.

We agree that Appellants have a right to a jury trial and that the bankruptcy court does not have the authority to conduct jury trials. This holding, however, does not require that the order of reference be withdrawn immediately. Therefore, we remand for the district court to determine whether to delegate pre-trial matters and the equitable accounting to the bankruptcy court.

I. Background
After appointment by the United States Trustee, the Committee, on behalf of all the unsecured creditors in the five related estates, issued demands upon the debtors to investigate and recover dividend payments and loan repayments made during the three years prior to the filing date, or to provide the Committee with the information necessary to initiate proceedings on its own. According to the Committee, the debtors did not investigate or provide the requested information.

* * * On October 2, 1992, the bankruptcy court authorized the Committee to commence actions against Appellants to recover fraudulent conveyances and preferential transfers and ordered the debtors to make corporate books and records available to the Committee.

* * * On October 9, 1992, the Committee filed five complaints against Appellants in each of the five Stansbury-related bankruptcy cases. The complaints alleged that dividend payments had been paid while the debtors were insolvent in violation of Maryland law, that such payments also breached Appellants' fiduciary duty to creditors, that these dividends were fraudulent conveyances, and that various loan repayments were also fraudulent conveyances and preferential transfers under state and federal law. The last count of each complaint requested an accounting by Appellants of all the money they had received from the debtor corporations for the three years prior to the filing date.

II.

In Granfinanciera, S.A. v. Nordberg, 492 U.S. 33, 36, 64, 109 S.Ct. 2782, 2802, 106 L.Ed.2d 26 (1989), the Supreme Court held that the Seventh Amendment entitled persons who had not submitted claims against a bankruptcy estate to a jury trial when they were sued by the bankruptcy trustee to recover an allegedly fraudulent monetary transfer, notwithstanding the fact that fraudulent conveyance actions are "core proceedings" under the Bankruptcy Code. 28 U.S.C. §157(b)(2)(H) (1988). In reaching this holding, the Court first concluded that fraudulent conveyance actions were actions at law, for which a jury trial is required by the Seventh Amendment. Next, the Court determined that the nature of the relief sought in the action--" 'money payments of ascertained and definite amounts' " with " 'no facts that call for an accounting or other equitable relief,' "--supported the conclusion that the rights involved in a fraudulent conveyance action are legal rather than equitable.

The Committee attempts to distinguish Granfinanciera and offers two arguments why Appellants are not entitled to a jury trial. First, the Committee asserts that because the requested equitable accounting is essential to resolve this action, Appellants are not entitled to a jury trial. Second, the Committee contends that any Appellant who has either filed a claim in one or more of the bankruptcy actions in this case or is listed on Schedule A.1 as a creditor holding a priority claim for wages, salary and commissions, has waived his jury trial right in all the other jointly-administered actions. We reject both of these arguments.

A.

    * * *

While the Committee is correct that the fraudulent conveyance actions in this case are somewhat distinct from the claims for specified amounts presented in Granfinanciera, both are nevertheless legal actions seeking monetary damages. As the Supreme Court held in Granfinanciera, a right to a jury trial attaches to such actions. The Committee's additional requests for equitable accounting do not require that Appellants be denied their constitutional right to a jury trial on the fraudulent conveyance claims.

    * * *

B.

It is clear that by filing a proof of claim against a bankruptcy estate, a creditor "triggers the process of 'allowance and disallowance of claims,' thereby subjecting himself to the bankruptcy court's equitable power." Langenkamp v. Culp, 498 U.S. 42, 44, 111 S.Ct. 330, 331, 112 L.Ed.2d 343 (1990) (quoting Granfinanciera, 492 U.S. at 57-58 & n. 14, 109 S.Ct. at 2798-99 & n. 14). If a subsequent action alleging preferential transfers is filed against the creditor, that action becomes part of the claims-allowance process, "integral to the restructuring of the debtor- creditor relationship through the bankruptcy court's equity jurisdiction," and the creditor is not entitled to a jury trial. If a party does not submit a claim against the bankruptcy estate, the preferential transfer can only be recovered through a legal action and the preference defendant is entitled to a jury trial.

In this case, some Appellants concede that they have filed claims against one or more of the bankruptcy estates. Accordingly, these Appellants do not have a right to a jury trial in the Committee's action against them with regard to that particular bankruptcy estate. The Committee goes further, however, and contends that these Appellants have lost their jury trial right with regard to all the jointly-administered debtor estates. The Committee cites no authority for this contention, and we find no basis for it. We do not believe that the joint administration of these debtor estates, while eliminating duplication and making administration more efficient, should have the substantive effect on a protection as significant as the right to a jury trial as asserted by the Committee.

The Committee also asserts that any Appellants who are listed as creditors holding priority claims for wages, salary and commissions on Schedule A.1 should also be deemed to have filed proofs of claims. According to the Committee, such listings constitute proofs of claim under §1111(a) of the Bankruptcy Code, 11 U.S.C. §1111(a) (1988), and by allowing the listing to stand, without withdrawal, these Appellants have submitted to the bankruptcy court's equity jurisdiction for all purposes. The Committee argues that any Appellants listed on Schedule A.1 are participating in the claims allowance and disallowance process and therefore under Langenkamp and Granfinanciera, they cannot demand a jury trial.

In discussing preferential transfer and fraudulent conveyance actions, the Supreme Court has limited its discussion of the loss of a jury trial right to instances where a creditor has voluntarily filed a proof of claim and chosen to submit himself to the equity jurisdiction of the bankruptcy court. * * * We see no reason to expand the meaning of filing a claim to include a listing as a creditor.

III.

Determining that Appellants are in fact entitled to a jury trial does not end our discussion. We must next address whether the bankruptcy court has the authority to conduct jury trials in core proceedings such as the fraudulent conveyance and preferential transfer actions presented here. This issue of first impression in our Circuit is one on which other circuits are divided, and which the Supreme Court has twice declined to address. * * *
    * * *

[D]ivergence of opinion on whether bankruptcy courts may conduct jury trials is not surprising "given the ambiguous statute and legislative history." Under the Bankruptcy Reform Act of 1978, bankruptcy courts were given an extremely broad grant of jurisdiction, and jury trial rights as they existed prior to the 1978 Act were preserved. 28 U.S.C. §§1471, 1480 (1982). The Supreme Court held, however, in Northern Pipeline Construction Co. v. Marathon Pipe Line Co., 458 U.S. 50, 87, 102 S.Ct. 2858, 2880, 73 L.Ed.2d 598 (1982), that this extremely broad grant of jurisdiction to an Article I court, which included the power to hold jury trials, was unconstitutional.

In response, Congress enacted the Bankruptcy Amendments and Federal Judgeship Act of 1984 (1984 Act), which repealed §1480. The Committee contends that §§157(b)(1) and 151 of the 1984 Act authorized bankruptcy courts to conduct jury trials and that §1411 does not limit the bankruptcy court's power to conduct such trials. While §157(b)(1) grants bankruptcy judges the authority to "hear and determine ... all core proceedings," it contains no express authority to conduct jury trials. 28 U.S.C. §157(b)(1) (1988). Section 151 states only that "[e]ach bankruptcy judge ... may exercise the authority conferred under this chapter...." 28 U.S.C. §151 (1988). Section 1411 merely provides that nothing in the Bankruptcy Code affects rights to jury trials in personal injury and wrongful tort actions. 28 U.S.C. §1411. * * *

The legislative history is similarly unenlightening. * * *
    * * *

Accordingly, we hold that bankruptcy judges are not authorized to conduct jury trials; where the Seventh Amendment provides the right to a jury trial in a core proceeding in bankruptcy, it must take place in the district court.

IV.

In closing, we address the Committee's request that if we hold that Appellants are entitled to a jury trial and that this jury trial must be held in district court, we should direct the district court to consider whether to postpone withdrawal of the order of reference until the parties have conducted discovery and the accounting is accomplished. We think this is an entirely reasonable request. Our holding that bankruptcy judges are not authorized to conduct jury trials does not mean that the bankruptcy court immediately loses jurisdiction of the entire matter or that the district court cannot delegate to the bankruptcy court the responsibility for supervising discovery, conducting pre-trial conferences, and other matters short of the jury selection and trial. The decision whether or not to withdraw the referral immediately "is frequently more a pragmatic question of efficient case administration than a strictly legal decision." * * * This type of pragmatic decision is best left to the district court and we remand for that court to consider the Committee's request.

V.

For the foregoing reasons, we reverse the district court and hold that those Appellants who have not filed a claim against a particular bankruptcy estate are entitled to a jury trial in the Committee's action against them with regard to that estate and the jury trial must be conducted in the district court. We remand for the district court to determine when it will withdraw the order of reference prior to the jury trial.

REVERSED AND REMANDED.

Notes and Problems

1. Your firm represents L, a large, money center bank. One of L's borrowers, D, a popular local athlete who has devoted all of her time and resources to assisting various charities, files for bankruptcy. The bankruptcy trustee brings a preference action against L. L has not yet filed a proof of claim. Should L demand a jury trial? Can D's trustee demand a jury trial?

2. See generally E. Scott Fruehwald, *Jury Trials in Bankruptcy After* Granfinanciera, 24 CUMB.L.REV. 79 (1993-94).

E. APPEALS

Section 158 of title 28 governs jurisdiction of bankruptcy appeals. Under section 158, district courts hear appeals from bankruptcy court final orders and, with leave of court, interlocutory orders. Appeals are taken in the same manner as appeals in civil proceedings generally are taken from the district court to the court of appeals. Appealing a bankruptcy court order does not stay its enforcement. Unless the appellant obtains a stay of the bankruptcy court's order pending appeal, the appeal may become moot. *See generally* Stephen Snyder & Lawrence Ponoroff, Commercial BANKRUPTCY LITIGATION ch.4 (1989).

Unit 15

BUSINESS REORGANIZATION UNDER CHAPTER 11

UNIT CONTENTS

"A corporate reorganization is a combination of a municipal election, an historical pageant, an anti-vice crusade, a graduate school seminar, a judicial proceeding, and a series of horse trades, all rolled into one—thoroughly buttered with learning and frosted with distinguished names. Here the union of law and economics is celebrated by one of the wildest ideological orgies in intellectual history. Men work all night preparing endless documents in answer to other endless documents, which other men read in order to make solemn arguments," T. Arnold, THE FOLKLORE OF CAPITALISM 230 (1937).

Chapter 11 is not limited to corporate reorganization. Many Chapter 11 cases involve partnerships or individuals. Chapter 11 is not even limited to business debtors. Most Chapter 11 cases, however, involve business debtors, and this Unit deals with the reorganization of an operating business.

A. HISTORY: BUSINESS REORGANIZATION UNDER THE BANKRUPTCY ACT OF 1898

The Bankruptcy Act of 1898 contained four separate chapters for the reorganization of businesses. Chapter VIII dealt with railroad reorganizations. Chapter X covered reorganizations of corporations' secured debt, unsecured debt, and equity. Chapter XI was intended to govern arrangements of unsecured debts of individuals, partnerships, and corporations. And Chapter XII, was available only to noncorporate debtors with encumbered real estate.

Leonard Rosen, one of the most prominent practitioners under the Act (and under the Code), charted some of the legal differences between Chapter X and Chapter XI:

	Chapter XI	Chapter X
1. Commencement of proceedings	Voluntary only	Voluntary or involuntary
2. Court approval of petition	Not required	Required
3. Court relief available to	Any "person" (subject to sec. 4 exceptions)	Corporations only
4. Officer conducting proceeding	Usually debtor-in-possession	Disinterested trustee
5. Participation by SEC	By intervention only	Required by statute
6. Judicial officer	Bankruptcy judge	District judge
7. Plan proposed by	Debtor only	Trustee, debtor, creditors, or stockholders
8. Plan may affect	Unsecured debt only	Unsecured debt, secured debt, or stock interests
9. Plan provisions	Must be in "best interests of creditors"	Must be "fair and equitable"

Statement of Leonard M. Rosen, Hearings Before the Subcommittee on Civil and Constitutional Rights of the House Committee on the Judiciary on H.R. 31 and H.R. 32, April 12, 1976, page 2475.

Chapter 11 replaces Chapters VIII, X, XI, and XII. While Chapter 11 has borrowed concepts from all four of these 1898 Act chapters, it also contains new and original concepts.

Notes and Problems

1. For a more detailed discussion of pre-1978 business reorganization laws, see Judge Clark's discussion in *In re Jeppson*, 66 B.R. 269 (Bankr. Utah 1986); see also Peter Coogan, *A Debtor's Choice of a "Chapter" Rehabilitation Proceeding Under the "Bankruptcy Act"*, 1 Vermont L.Rev. 117 (1976).

2. A widely discussed law review article critical of Chapter 11 states, "Chapter 11 significantly changed the law and practice of corporate reorganization, making it easier for managers to invoke bankruptcy protection and strengthening their control of the bankrupt firm. Most notably Chapter 11 does not require that a debtor be insolvent in order to qualify for reorganization and includes a strong presumption favoring retention of management throughout the reorganization process." Michael Bradley & Michael Rosenzweig, *The Untenable Case for Chapter 11*, 101 YALE L.J. 1043, 1044 (1992); see also Edward S. Adams, *Governance in Chapter 11 Reorganizations: Reducing Costs, Improving Results*, 73 BOSTON U. L. REV. 581 (1993); David A. Skeel, *Rethinking the Line Between Corporate Law and Corporate Bankruptcy*, 72 TEX. L. REV. 471 (1994).

B. PEOPLE INVOLVED IN CHAPTER 11 CASES

1. Bankruptcy Judge

A Chapter 11 case involving a business will typically have the following stages:

1. commencing the case, i.e., getting the debtor into bankruptcy;
2. operating the business;
3. preparing a plan of reorganization;
4. seeking creditor acceptance of the plan;
5. obtaining confirmation, i.e., court approval, of the plan;
6. discharge;
7. performing the obligations under the plan.

Each of these seven stages of a Chapter 11 business case is considered below.

A bankruptcy judge is not involved in the first of the seven stages of a Chapter 11 case listed above. She is, however, an important part of each of the other six stages. For example, in operating the business, it is necessary to obtain court approval of sales or leases or even uses of the property that are not in the ordinary course of business.

While the bankruptcy judge is fully involved in the various stages of a bankruptcy case, her involvement is restricted to the performance of essentially judicial functions, i.e., resolution of disputes or issues involving adversary parties and matters appropriate for judicial determination. As John Logan discusses below, one of the significant changes effected by the 1978 bankruptcy legislation was the creation of the United States Trustee to remove the bankruptcy judge from direct involvement in administrative matters.

2. United States Trustee

Statement of John E. Logan, Director, Executive Office for the United States Trustees

before the Economic and Commercial Law Subcommittee on the Judiciary, House of the Representatives, Concerning Oversight of the United States Trustee System, November 1, 1991

Historically and still today, the administration of bankruptcy cases has been primarily committed to the efforts of private individuals, i.e. the debtors, their creditors, stockholders, and the professionals hired to protect their various interests. In a typical chapter 11 case, the debtor remains in possession of his assets, and the bankruptcy laws afford him the opportunity to reorganize his financial affairs. There is no trustee appointed, unless fraud or gross mismanagement is shown.

Until the creation of the United States Trustee Program, this system of rights and responsibilities rested entirely on the efforts of courts and the private parties who had an interest in a particular case. Once the private parties raised issues, the courts could address them and provide any necessary adjudication.

This role placed the judiciary in a difficult position: Extensive oversight and supervision of bankruptcy cases was absolutely necessary to ensure the expeditious and efficient administration of cases. For example, the court needed to appoint committees to represent the interests of creditors, as well as trustees and examiners whenever the courts decided their services were required. In addition, the court determined the size of compensation to be awarded to a trustee or examiner and ruled on litigation involving a trustee or examiner. The courts reviewed monthly financial reports filed by debtors, so as to ensure that assets were not being wasted under chapter 11 if the debtors were unable to reorganize their financial affairs. It was also up to the judiciary to ensure that debtors' assets were properly insured, that debtors' investments and deposits of estate monies were properly collateralized or bonded, and that auctioneers were bonded. The judicial branch also conducted the meetings of creditors under section 341 of the Code and oversaw the general administration of each case.

The active role of courts in such administrative matters took time away from the performance of their adjudicatory responsibilities. The courts' administrative responsibilities necessarily entailed extensive communications with private parties at an administrative rather than adjudicatory level. Just as important, it created the impression of a conflict. To the extent that bankruptcy estate administrators were utilized, those persons were generally viewed as adjuncts of the individual judges. This perception was the impetus for the creation of the Program.

* * *

The creation of the United States Trustee Program reflects the fact that a bankruptcy case is not like a two-party lawsuit, where adversaries actively litigate the issues before the court in furtherance of their own self interests. A chapter 11 case can involve extensive restructuring of business activities and negotiations of a wide variety of claims. Many of these matters do not directly involve particular creditors, even though the matters may eventually have an adverse impact on all creditors. Moreover, it is the unusual case where there is a significant creditor interest.

The court's role as adjudicator and catalyst for moving cases forward remains essential to the administration and supervision of chapter 11 cases, as are the efforts of the private interests involved. The United States Trustee Program adds an important new element: The presence of an independent office having the responsibility to encourage simultaneously greater participation of creditors and other interested parties as well as monitoring and maintaining the efficiency, effectiveness and integrity of how a particular case is moving through the system.

The extent of the Program's participation in a chapter 11 case is often determined by the amount and quality of creditor participation. This approach is premised on both the law's intent, as well as the wise use of resources. The United States Trustee seeks to encourage greater participation in chapter 11 cases through the formation of official committees and by conducting meetings of creditors under section 341 of the Bankruptcy Code. In most cases, creditors committees are appointed from among those creditors with an active interest in serving on a committee. The process seeks to ensure representation of the range of creditor interest present in a case, as well as maintaining communications among creditors and other interested parties.

The Program also conducts extensive reviews of applications to retain professionals and for compensation to ensure that professionals are retained in compliance with the law and are compensated in accordance with the statute's "reasonable and necessary" basis. The Program ensures that professionals satisfy the strict statutory requirements regarding disclosures and the absence of conflicts of interest. The Program's efforts are often resented by professionals in bankruptcy cases because they raise as an issue the very right of a particular professional to be hired and then compensated. The Program's review of employment and compensation matters are essential to its role, as not only does it curtail activity adverse to the law, but it is uniquely an area where private interests often do not come forward.

The nature of the compensation process justifies extensive review, particularly in large cases where it involves enormous amounts of money and paperwork. For example, the interim and final applications for compensation filed by numerous professionals in one recent case, *In re Public Service Co. of New Hampshire*, (D.N.H.), consisted of several thousand detailed pages of billing statements, which sought total compensation in excess of S37 million. Such fee applications threaten to overwhelm the United States Trustee Program, as well as professionals and the courts.

The Program is also active in overseeing the protection of estate assets and monies in chapter 11 cases by establishing procedures to ensure the debtor's fiduciary responsibilities are met. Such procedures typically address such matters as insurance, the payment of taxes during the case, and the filing of monthly operating reports disclosing a debtor's financial status.

One of the Program's goals in chapter 11 cases has been expediting chapter 11 cases through the bankruptcy system. The Program has aggressively moved for the conversion or dismissal of cases, which like in chapter 7 languished in the system for many years where no hope existed to achieve a confirmable chapter 12 plan. Such efforts are particularly important where there is little creditor involvement. Moving these cases through the system has required extensive energy and diligence not only by the Program's attorneys, but also by the Program's bankruptcy analysts who have used their financial expertise in determining which cases should be dismissed or converted to chapter 7 liquidation. The importance of this policy is self evident in light of the fact that approximately 83% of cases filed under chapter 11 never result in a confirmed plan. Of those that do, approximately one-third will still not successfully reorganize.

Most recently, the Program is expanding its efforts in monitoring the chapter 11 area by examining where debtors, having obtained court confirmation of a reorganization plan, fail to comply with the obligations imposed by the plan. These cases similarly remain on the docket, until closed by the court. Such matters may be pursued by creditors and other private parties. The Program's limited experience has taught and the legacy of stagnant cases inherited demonstrate, however, the problems inherent in relying on ad hoc involvement by creditors who, in many cases, have justifiably given up hope of receiving meaningful payment of their claims.

3. Debtor In Possession

In a Chapter 11 case, there will be either a debtor in possession or a trustee. See section 1101. If there is a trustee, there is no debtor in possession. If there is no trustee, then the debtor in possession generally has the rights, powers, and duties of a trustee. See section 1107.

Generally, in Chapter 11 business cases, there is a debtor in possession, not a trustee. Accordingly, the same people that made the business decisions that resulted in a Chapter 11 filing continue to make the decisions while the business is in Chapter 11.

Under the Bankruptcy Act of 1898, the issue of displacement of the debtor's management was determined in large part by the form of chapter proceeding. The appointment of a trustee was mandatory under Chapter X when the debtor's liability exceeds $250,000. In most Chapter XI and Chapter XII cases, however, the debtor remained in control of the business as a debtor in possession unless the court for "cause shown" appointed a receiver.

There is no provision for the appointment of a receiver in Chapter 11 of the Bankruptcy Code. Pre-bankruptcy management will continue to operate the business unless a request is made for the appointment of a trustee and the court, after notice and hearing,[1] grants the request, section 1104. The House Report accompanying a draft of the Bankruptcy Code provides the following justification for this approach:

"The twin goals of the standard for the appointment of a trustee should be protection of the public interest and the interests of creditors, as contemplated in current chapter X, and facilitation of a reorganization that will benefit both the creditors and the debtors, as contemplated in current chapter XI. Balancing the goals is a difficult process, and requires consideration of many factors.

"The public and the creditors will not necessarily be harmed if the debtor is continued in possession in a reorganization case, as has been demonstrated under current chapter XI. In fact, very often the creditors will be benefited by continuation of the debtor in possession, both because the expense of a trustee will not be required, and the debtor, who is familiar with his business, will be better able to operate it during the reorganization case. A trustee frequently has to take time to familiarize himself with the business before the reorganization can get under way. Thus, a debtor continued in possession may lead to a greater likelihood of success in the reorganization. Moreover, the need for reorganization of a public company today often results from simple business

---

[1]   Please read the definition of "notice and hearing" in section 102.

reverses, not from any fraud, dishonesty, or gross mismanagement on the part of the debtor's management. Even if the cause is fraud or dishonesty, very frequently the fraudulent management will have been ousted shortly before the filing of the reorganization case, and the new management, very capable of running the business, should not be ousted by a trustee because of the sins of former management. Nevertheless, there are cases where a trustee is needed, because cases of fraud or gross mismanagement do arise. The policy that has been followed generally in the consolidation of the two reorganization chapters has been flexibility, in place of the absolute rules now contained in chapter X, and determination of the needs of each case on the facts of the case. The current state of reorganization situations suggests that the same need for flexibility and case-by-case determination exists in the development of the standard for the appointment of a trustee.

"The other goal, facilitation of the reorganization to the benefit of the debtor and the creditors, militates against the appointment of a trustee. One of the main reasons that debtors use chapter XI so much more frequently than chapter X is because they know they will not be ousted of possession and operation of the business. In that issue lies much of the controversy surrounding conversion of a case from chapter XI to chapter X. Debtors' lawyers that participated in the development of a standard for the appointment of a trustee were adamant that a standard that led to too frequent appointment would prevent debtors from seeking relief under the reorganization chapter, and would leave the chapter largely unused except in extreme cases. One of the problems that the Bankruptcy Commission recognized in current bankruptcy and reorganization practice is that debtors too often wait too long to seek bankruptcy relief. Too frequent appointment of a trustee would exacerbate that problem, to the detriment of both debtors and their creditors.

"Thus, in consolidating the chapters, the bill adopts the flexible approach of leaving the debtor in possession of the business unless a request is made for the appointment of a trustee. The bill makes no distinction in procedure between cases in which public investors are involved and other cases. Instead, the court will hold a hearing to determine the need for a trustee in any case in which a party in interest, the United States trustee, an indenture trustee, or the S.E.C. requests appointment of a trustee.

"The court may also adopt the less restrictive alternative of ordering the appointment of an examiner to investigate the affairs of the debtor. An examiner might be appropriate instead of a trustee, for example, where current management has recently replaced a former fraudulent management, or where continuance of management is essential to the continued operation of the business during the reorganization, even though there may be some small suspicion of wrongdoing on the part of management."

H.Rep. 95-595, 95th Cong., 1st Sess., pp. 232-34 (1977).

A debtor that remains in possession after a Chapter 11 filing is, not surprisingly, generally referred to as a debtor in possession. The Bankruptcy Code equates the debtor in possession with a trustee, giving him all of the rights and powers of a trustee, section 1107. Case law equates the debtor in possession with a fiduciary, giving him the burden of protecting and conserving the estate's property for the benefit of creditors.

There is considerable language in the case law and the commentary to the effect that the debtor in possession is a new entity, separate and distinct legally from the debtor. It is not clear exactly what this means: most of the cases making such statements involved the ability of the debtor in possession to avoid obligations under collective bargaining agreements. Now, it is not even clear that the statement that the debtor in possession is a separate legal person is even accurate. In *NLRB v. Bildisco*, 465 U.S. 513, 104 S.Ct. 1188, 79 L.Ed.2d 482 (1984), a case involving a rejection of collective bargaining agreement by the debtor in possession, the Court summarily dismissed the notion that the debtor in possession was a separate legal entity from the debtor: "Obviously, if the debtor-in-possession were a wholly 'new entity', it would be unnecessary for the Bankruptcy Code to allow it to reject executory contracts, since it would not be bound by such contracts in the first place. For our purposes, it is sensible to view the debtor-in-possession as the same 'entity' which existed before the bankruptcy petition, but empowered by virtue of the Bankruptcy Code to deal with its contracts and property in a manner it could not have done absent the bankruptcy filing."

Notes and Problems

1. To whom, does a debtor in possession owe a fiduciary duty? Assume, for example, that D Corp, a Chapter 11 can be sold for $5,000,000. If it continues in business, it has some prospect in the next two years of being worth $12,000,000 or more and some prospect of being worth $1,000,000 or less. D Corp. owes $3,000,000 to secured creditors and $4,000,000 to unsecured creditors. The shareholders, of course, want D Corp. to continue business operations; the creditors want D Corp. to sell. What should the management of D Corp., as debtor in possession, do? *See generally* Martin J. Bienenstock, *Conflicts Between Management and the Debtor in Possession's Fiduciary Duties*, 61 U.CINN.L.REV. 543 (1992); Christopher Frost, *Running the Asylum: Governance Problems in Bankruptcy Reorganizations*, 34 ARIZONA L.REV. 89 (1992).

2. Can the law firm that represented the debtor before it filed for Chapter 11 represent the debtor in possession? See section 1107(b). Recall that under section 1107, a debtor in possession has the duties, rights, and powers of a trustee, including the right to hire an attorney. Section 327 which governs the employment of attorneys by trustees is also generally applicable to the employment of attorneys by a debtor in possession. Under section 327, attorneys and other professional persons can not be employed until the bankruptcy court determines that the attorney does not (i) "hold or represent an interest adverse to the estate" and (ii) "are disinterested." Can a King & Spalding lawyer represent D Corp. as debtor in possession if D Corp. owes King & Spalding $100,000 in prepetition fees? What if other King & Spalding lawyers represent the majority shareholder of D Corp.? *See generally* Richard Epling & Claudia Sayre, *Employment of Attorneys by Debtors In Possession: A Proposal for Modification of the Existing Attorney Eligibility Provisions of the Bankruptcy Code and the Existing Conflict of Interest Provisions of the Ethical Rules of Professional Responsibility*, 47 BUSINESS LAWYER 671 (1992).

3. Local rules or United States Trustee guidelines often require business debtors to open new debtor-in-possession bank accounts. For example, in the Northern District of Georgia, the operating guideline provides, "Any bank account over which the debtor has possession or control must be closed immediately upon the filing of the petition. Debtor shall immediately open general, payroll and tax accounts. The checks for each account must bear the words 'debtor in possession' and the bankruptcy case number."

4. Trustee Or Examiner

Section 1104(a) sets out the grounds for the appointment of a trustee. Section 1104(b) sets out the grounds for the appointment of an examiner. While the Bankruptcy Court decides whether there will be a trustee or examiner in a Chapter 11 case, the United States Trustee decides who will be the trustee or examiner, "subject to the court's approval." See section 1104(c). Section 1106 describes the duties of a trustee and of an examiner. Please read sections 1104 and 1106.

IN THE UNITED STATES BANKRUPTCY COURT
FOR THE NORTHERN DISTRICT OF GEORGIA
ATLANTA DIVISION

IN RE:	)
	) CASE NO. 92-62751
National Steel Service Center, Inc.,	) CHAPTER 11
	)
Debtor.	) Judge Cotton

MOTION FOR APPOINTMENT OF A TRUSTEE

USX CORPORATION, WEIRTON STEEL CORPORATION, EMPIRE-DETROIT STEEL CORPORATION (CYCLOPS DIVISION), and BETHLEHEM STEEL CORPORATION (the "Trade Vendors"), parties in interest in the above-captioned bankruptcy case, move the Court pursuant to 1104(a)(2), to appoint a trustee in this case and in support thereof state:

REVIEW OF FACTS

1. National Steel Service Center, Inc. ("NSSC")is a wholly owned subsidiary of Traxxon Holdings, Inc. ("Traxxon"). John Poindexter owns 100% of all outstanding and issued stock of Traxxon Holdings, Inc. Accordingly, NSSC is ultimately owned and controlled by Mr. Poindexter.

2. The Trade Vendors are NSSC's largest present creditors and have filed proofs of claim in this bankruptcy totaling $16,013,993.20. The Trade Vendors are the only secured creditors left in NSSC's bankruptcy case. The Trade Vendors' claim is secured by virtually all of NSSC's real and personal property including

> "[a]ll of Debtor's present and future accounts, contract rights, general intangibles, chattel paper, documents, instruments, inventory, equipment and fixtures constituting personal property..."

It is in the position of the Trade Vendors that "general intangibles" includes NSSC's cause of action that is the subject of the Doveala litigation and NSSC's tax attributes such as its nine to ten million dollars of net operating losses.

3. After discussion initiated by the Trade Vendors
about filing an involuntary bankruptcy petition, NSSC filed
a voluntary petition for relief under Chapter 11 of Title 11
of the United States Code ("Bankruptcy Code") on February
13, 1992.

4.   On February 18, 1992, the United States Trustee
appointed a Creditors' Committee (the "Committee"). All
Trade Vendors are members of the committee, as are the following unsecured trade creditors: Toledo Pickling & Steel
Sales, Inc., Kaiser Aluminum & Chemical Corp., Tomen America, Inc. and Sharon Steel Corp. The Committee is chaired by
a representative of USX Corporation.

5. After discussion initiated by the Trade Vendors
about the appointment of a trustee, NSSC acquiesced to the
position of the Trade Vendors that _all_ its operating
facilities be sold as soon as practicable.

6.   On April 23, 1992, NSSC began a court approved
bidding process which resulted in the acceptance of bids for
the sale of the various operating facilities owned by NSSC:
Atlanta, Tulsa, DOT, Stone Company and Weirton. All sales
except for Weirton have closed. The original bidder for the
Weirton facility withdrew. NSSC negotiated another sale of
Weirton. NSSC will have no remaining business operations
after the Weirton facility sale closes at the end of
September, 1992.

7. NSSC moved for and the Court granted an extension of
its Section 1121 exclusivity.

8.   On September 10, 1992, just prior to the expiration of the extended exclusivity period, NSSC filed its Plan
of Reorganization (the "Plan").

9. The Plan provides _inter alia_ that (i) NSSC's present
owners will retain all equity in NSSC; and (ii) all claims
against Mr. Poindexter and other insiders will be released
for a single payment of $50,000.

10. In addition, the Plan provides that an entity owned
by Mr. Poindexter will obtain use of NSSC's favorable tax
attributes including net operating losses ("NOL"), of between nine to ten million dollars in exchange for a contingent payment over time of no more than seven hundred
thousand dollars.

REVIEW OF LEGAL AUTHORITIES

11. In Chapter 11 cases, there is a strong presumption
that the debtor shall remain in possession. The appointment
of a trustee in a Chapter 11 case is an extraordinary remedy. If the creditors are to prevail in their motion for the
appointment of a trustee, their grounds to this remedy for

the appointment must be shown by clear and convincing evidence.

12. The grounds for the appointment of a trustee are set forth in 1104 which states:

"(a) At any time after the commencement of the case but before confirmation of a plan, on request of a party in interest or the United States Trustee, and after notice and a hearing, the court shall order the appointment of a trustee

(1) for cause, including fraud, dishonesty, incompetence, or gross mismanagement of the affairs of the debtor by current management, either before or after the commencement of the case, for or similar cause, but not including the number of holders of securities of the debtor or the amount of assets or liabilities of the debtor; or

(2) if such appointment is in the interests of creditors, any equity security holders, and other interests of the estate, without regard to the number of holders of securities of the debtor or the amount of assets or liabilities of the debtor."

13. Even if cause is not established within the meaning of 1104(a)(1), the Court <u>shall</u> order the appointment of a trustee under 1104(a)(2) if the interests of creditors and other interest of the estate would be served thereby. <u>See</u> H. Drake & A. Mullins, <u>Bankruptcy Practice 12.06</u>, (2d ed. 1990); R. Ginsberg, <u>Bankruptcy: Text. Statutes. Rules 14.05(b)</u>, (2d ed. 1989).

14. Reported cases are of limited assistance in applying section 1104(a). Whether a trustee should be appointed in a given case is largely a question of fact. "Section 1104(a) decisions must be made on a case by case basis." <u>In re Sharon Steel Corp.</u> 871 F.2d 1217, 1226 (3d Cir. 1989).

15. In determining whether an appointment is in the best interests of the creditors, courts have considered factors such as unresolved intercompany issues, the prospects for the debtor's rehabilitation, and the relative benefits and costs of the appointment of a trustee. E.g., Flatau v. Marathon Oil (In re <u>Craig Oil Co.</u>) 31 8ankr. 402, 409 (Bankr. E.D.N.Y. 1984) <u>aff'd</u> 785 F.2d 1563 (E.D.N.Y. 1986); <u>In re L.S. Good & Co.</u>, 8 B.R. 312 (Bankr. N.D. W. Va. 1980).

16. Courts have appointed trustees to deal with unresolved legal issues in pending Chapter 11 cases and left existing management in place to continue to deal with the day to day business of the debtor. <u>See</u> <u>In re North American</u>

Communications, Inc., 137 B.R. 275 (Bankr. N.D. Ill. 1992);
In re Madison Management Group, Inc.138 Bankr. 175 (Bankr.
W.D. Pa. 1992).

ARGUMENT

17. Because of the differences in the interests of the
owner of NSSC and the estate, and the differences in the
interests of the various members of the Committee, a disinterested trustee can conclude this case more effectively and
efficiently than the Debtor working with the Committee. Over
the last seven and a half months, NSSC, working with the
Committee, has liquidated all of its operating facilities.
While there are still accounts to be collected, litigation
to be resolved, and miscellaneous assets to be sold, the
most significant remaining work is

> (i) determination of whether the estate would
> be better served by liquidation in Chapter 7 than by
> a liquidating Chapter 11 plan;
>
> (ii) assessment of the value of the NSSC's
> $9,000,000 to $10,000,000 net operating losses and
> other tax attributes to Mr. Poindexter and negotia-
> tion with Mr. Poindexter as to payments to the es-
> tate to retain these tax attributes;
>
> (iii) investigation of possible claims against
> Mr. Poindexter and other insiders and a determina-
> tion of whether to litigate such claims or negotiate
> a settlement;
>
> (iv) review of prebankruptcy transfers to all
> holders of claims, including, but not limited to,
> Trade Vendors and all of the other members of the
> Committee;
>
> (v) preparation of a disclosure statement
> that meets the requirements of 1125 and a plan that
> is confirmable.

18. The presence of a trustee will provide the creditors and other parties in interest with an objective party
to resolve these remaining issues. The estate will have a
disinterested and dispassionate party on the other side of
the negotiating table from Mr. Poindexter.
19. Similarly, the estate will have a disinterested and
dispassionate party determining whether to initiate legal
action against Mr. Poindexter, and other insiders, the Trade
Vendors, and other Committee members.
20. And the Court will have an objective and realistic
party to determine whether the benefits to the estate of
continuing to proceed in Chapter 11 justify the time and

resources that will be required. If after her investigation
and negotiation with Mr. Poindexter, the trustee determines
that the estate will be better served by a liquidating
Chapter 11 plan, she can then prepare a disclosure statement
that meets the requirements of Section 1125 and a plan that
meets the requirements of Section 1129.

WHEREFORE, the Trade Vendors respectfully request the
entry of an Order appointing a disinterested person as
trustee pursuant to Section 1104(a)(2) of the Bankruptcy
Code and such other and further relief as this Court deems
just and proper.

Dated: September 25, 1992.

> Respectfully submitted,
> KING & SPALDING
>
> *David G. Epstein*
>
> David G. Epstein
> R. Keith Walton
> 191 Peachtree Street
> Atlanta, Georgia   303031763
> (404) 572-4600
>
> Attorneys for the Trade
> Vendors

Notes and Questions

1. What arguments should National Steel Service Center, Inc., make in its response to the Motion for Appointment of a Trustee?

2. Why did the Vendors seek the appointment of a trustee, rather than the appointment of an examiner? *See generally* Leonard Gumport, *The Bankruptcy Examiner*, 20 CAL. BANKR.J. 71 (1992).

3. As noted in paragraph 6 of the Motion, National Steel had virtually no continuing business operations. What factors should a creditor consider before moving for the appointment of a trustee for an operating business?

4. What factors should a bankruptcy court consider in ruling on a motion for the appointment of a trustee for an operating business:

    a. Number of shareholders?

    b.   Views of the United States Trustee?

    c.   Views of the Creditors' Committee?

    d.   Prepetition financial performance?

    e.   Postpetition financial performance?

5.   What factors should a bankruptcy court consider in ruling on a motion for an examiner?

ᗜᗜᗜᗜᗜᗜ

5. Creditors' And Equity Security Holders' Committees

In re Seaescape Cruises, Ltd.
United States Bankruptcy Court, S.D. Florida, 1991
131 B.R. 241

MEMORANDUM OPINION AND ORDER DENYING DEBTOR'S
OBJECTION TO COMPILATION OF COMMITTEE
OF UNSECURED CREDITORS

Sidney M. Weaver, Chief Judge. THIS CAUSE came on to be heard August 13, 1991 upon the Debtor's Objection To Compilation Of Committee Of Creditors Holding Unsecured Claims, whereby the Debtor seeks to reconstitute the membership of the Committee by removing those members who may assert maritime lien claims. The Court having considered the Debtor's objection and the responses filed by both the Committee and the United States Trustee, having heard the arguments of counsel and examined the evidence presented, and the Court being otherwise fully advised in the premises, denies the relief requested by the Debtor for the following reasons:

Background

The Debtor is in the cruiseline business, specializing in one day cruises. The Debtor filed a voluntary petition for relief under Chapter 11 of the Bankruptcy Code on March 18, 1991. The Committee was appointed by the United States Trustee pursuant to §1102(a) on May 10, 1991. All of the creditors appointed to the Committee were selected from among the Debtor's own lists of unsecured creditors which were included in the Debtor's schedules as filed with the Court. At the time of the formation of the Committee, the United States Trustee was aware that a number of the creditors who were willing to serve on the Committee claimed to hold maritime liens. Notwithstanding this disclosure, the United States Trustee felt that these diverse interests were representative of the types of claims existing in the case and that their appointment to the Committee was not inconsistent with the purpose of Section 1102 of the Bankruptcy Code.

The Committee has participated actively throughout the case, and has recently filed a motion to convert the case to a Chapter 7 proceeding. The motion is presently pending.

Discussion

The Debtor argues that the several members of the Committee who hold maritime liens are secured creditors who do not fairly represent the interests of unsecured creditors; that a conflict of interest exists within the Committee, since the maritime lien claimants would necessarily consider it in their own best interest to resist the Debtor's efforts to reorganize because they will more likely fare better from the liquidation of the Debtor. The Debtor contends that several maritime lien claimants on the Committee have demonstrated their "true colors" by seeking relief from stay to enforce their liens and that the pending the motion to convert the case to a Chapter 7 liquidation is a reflection of the self-serving interests of these particular members. These arguments are unpersuasive.

First, the claims of maritime lien holders are not so readily classified as "secured" claims, especially in the context of a bankruptcy case such as this, where the vessels have not been arrested and where the automatic stay imposed by Section 362 of the Bankruptcy Code precludes the seizure of the vessels or the enforcement of those liens, at least within the jurisdiction of this Court. Virtually every creditor who provided necessary services to the vessels may have a basis for asserting maritime liens. However, whether a maritime lien is enforceable depends on a number of factors, such as the value of the vessel in which the lien arose, the ranking of the maritime lien vis a vis other maritime liens, the law of the jurisdiction in which the vessel is seized, the particular terms of the applicable charter agreement and numerous other variables which must be considered under applicable bankruptcy and maritime law. Whether any of the members of the Committee who claim potential maritime liens are actually "secured" creditors cannot be determined with any degree of certainty at this time.

Further, even if some or all members of the Committee should elect to assert maritime lien claims or other secured claims, they are not required to do so at this stage of the proceeding. The Debtor has sought and obtained an order extending the bar date for filing proofs of claim in this case until October 17, 1991 and also requiring any entity claiming a maritime lien to file a proof of claim by such date. Consequently, creditors need not assert maritime lien claims or make any election at all with regard to their claims until the October 17th bar date. Meanwhile, the Debtor, who listed all of the members as unsecured creditors on the schedules filed in the case,[1] refuses to acknowledge at this stage that any of the members of the Committee hold valid or enforceable maritime

---

[1]   Under 11 U.S.C. §1111(a), these members of the Committee are, accordingly, deemed to have filed unsecured proofs of claim subject to their ability to amend such claims on or before the October 17, 1991 bar date.

liens.[1]   Thus, the Debtor's concerns that members of the Committee assert secured rather than unsecured claims are premature. Furthermore, even if it could now be established that some or all of the members of the Committee are partially secured, such a determination would not justify the removal of any of the members, since section 1102 does not preclude a creditor who holds both secured and unsecured claims from serving on the Committee.

A member of a creditors' committee should not be removed unless there is specific evidence that the member has breached or is likely to breach a fiduciary duty to the class of creditors represented by that member. The fact that the Committee has filed a motion to convert the case to a Chapter 7 case or that some of the members have unsuccessfully sought relief from stay to enforce their maritime liens is not sufficient to demonstrate a conflict of interest among the members of the Committee or any breach of fiduciary duty by the Committee to unsecured creditors. Although Section 1102 of the Bankruptcy Code states no standards regarding who may serve on the creditors' committee, there is nothing in the statute which would prevent service on the creditors' committee of a creditor unsympathetic to the efforts of a debtor to reorganize. A committee's fiduciary obligation extends to members of the unsecured creditor class and not to the debtor.

A creditors' committee is not merely a conduit through which the debtor speaks to and negotiates with creditors generally. An effective committee must necessarily be adversarial if it is to fulfill its role as "watchdog" in a Chapter 11 case. The United States Trustee, with the full appointive power vested in that office pursuant to §1102(a), appointed the members of the Committee in compliance with the statute with full knowledge that the potential members might be holders of maritime liens. The United States Trustee was satisfied then and continues to be satisfied that the Committee is properly constituted. Significantly, no unsecured creditors have come forward to complain that their interests are not being fairly represented. Each member of the Committee, when examined under oath, testified that he or she understood the duties and responsibilities of the members of the Committee and was willing and able to fulfill his or her fiduciary duty to unsecured creditors. Accordingly, the Court is satisfied that no actual conflict of interest exists within the Committee as it is presently constituted and that no member has breached or is likely to breach a fiduciary duty to the class of unsecured creditors. Moreover, the Court is satisfied at this stage of the case that the Committee and its counsel have played an active and productive role in this case and that the Committee has performed its "watchdog" role. Accordingly, it is

ORDERED that the Debtor's objection is overruled and the Debtor's request to remove certain members or to reconstitute the Committee is denied without

---

[1]   See Committee Exhibit "7" in evidence consisting of the Debtor's answer to interrogatories propounded by the Committee on this issue.

prejudice to the Debtor or any interested party in bringing this matter before the Court at some future time should circumstances so warrant.

DONE and ORDERED.

Notes and Problems

1. The opinion notes that "the United States Trustee felt that these diverse interests were representative of the types of claims existing in the case." Why is it important that the members of the committee be representative of the "types of claims existing in the case"? Does a vendor on a creditor's committee represent vendors or all creditors?

2. Which of the following can the United States Trustee appoint to a creditors' committee:

    a. labor union?

    b. Internal Revenue Service?

    c. lawyer who represented the debtor prior to its bankruptcy filing?

3. Note the phrase "willing to serve" in section 1102(b)(1). Should your creditor clients be "willing to serve" on the creditors' committee? What if the debtor is a major customer of your creditor client? See sections 1103(a), 1103(b), 328.

4. Until 1986, the bankruptcy court, not the United States Trustee, appointed the members of the creditors' committee. When Congress amended section 1102 to take the appointment power away from the courts, it did not provide a mechanism for court review of the United States Trustees' appointments. What is the statutory basis for Judge Weaver's review of the United States Trustee's appointments? What standard of review should he apply? Cf. Rule 2020.

5. In *Seaescape Cruises*, the debtor objected to the composition of the creditors' committee. Does the debtor have standing to make such an objection? Does the debtor have an interest in having a strong creditors' committee? Does the debtor have an interest in preventing creditors with secured claims from serving on the committee?

ᘖᘖᘖᘖᘖᘖ

Sections 1103 and 1121(c) set out the duties and powers of the creditors' committees. Please read these provisions. According to Ron Trost of the New York Bar and Professor Lawrence P. King of New York University Law School:

The creditors' committee is to have much greater power and a much more active role in reorganization proceedings than under [the 1898 Act]. In addition to the usual functions of investigation, consultation and negotiations, the creditors' committee will have standing to be heard on all issues that arise during the course of the proceeding. The committee's role in plan formulation and confirmation is greatly expanded. In addition to participating in negotiations with respect to the reorganization plan, the committee may propose its own plan. It is not expected that the committee would often exercise this right, but this reservoir of power should make the debtor more sensitive to the desire of creditors with respect to the actual plan of reorganization.

Trost & King, *Congress and Bankruptcy Reform, Circa 1977*, 33 Bus.Law. 489, 536 (1978).

Notes and Problems

1. What sort of information must the debtor provide to the committee? Can the debtor disclose information only to the committee's professionals? If so, how can the committee's attorney or accountant get guidance from the committee if she is withholding important information from the committee?

2. C supplies goods to D on credit. C is one of D's major suppliers. D makes a large payment to C to reduce its outstanding debt to C. A week later, D files a Chapter 11 petition. Despite requests by the creditors' committee, D has not taken any action to recover the preferential payment from C. Can the creditors' committee file a complaint to recover the preferential payment to C? See sections 547, 1103.

3. Section 1102 contemplates not only a creditors' committee but also an equity holders' committee. Will it be necessary to have an equity holders' committee in every case? How are the interests of the equity holders different from the interests of the debtor?

4. *See generally* Andrew DeNatale, Harold D. Jones, Lori Lapin Jones, Robert Raskin, & Thomas Walper, *Creditors' Committee Manual (1992)*, Letitia Z. Clark, Gregory Kamen, Evelyn Biery & Laura Weiss, *Creditors' Committees: Powers, Rights and Responsibilities* in the 66th Annual Meeting of the National Conference of Bankruptcy Judges Program Materials 9-5 (1992).

C. STAGES OF A CHAPTER 11 CASE

1. Commencing The Case

A Chapter 11 case is commenced by the filing of a petition. The petition may be filed by the debtor or by creditors. Sections 301, 303, and 109 control the commencement of the case. These provisions are considered in Unit 7 of this book.

Notes and Problems

Insolvency

1. Does a debtor have to be insolvent in order to file a Chapter 11 petition?

Authorization

2. If a business is operated as a partnership or a corporation, who signs the petition? Does a partnership debtor have to obtain the approval of all general partners? Cf. section 303(b)(3)(A); Rule 1004. Does a corporate debtor have to call a shareholder meeting and obtain shareholder approval?

Bars to Bankruptcy Filing

3. Your client C is considering extending credit to D. C is concerned about the possibility of D's filing for Chapter 11 relief. Can D make a legally enforceable contract not to file for bankruptcy? According to Professor Rasmussen, D and C should be able to make such a contract but can not under current case law. See Robert Rasmussen, *Debtor's Choice: A Menu Approach to Corporate Bankruptcy,* 71 Texas L.Rev. 51 (1992).

4. Your client C is considering a $400,000 loan to D, an operating corporation. Can C protect itself from the possibility of a later bankruptcy filing by structuring the loan so that (i) D amends its articles of incorporation to provide for the issuance of Class X stock and require the approval of Class X stock in order to file for bankruptcy and (ii) D issues all authorized Class X stock to C?

Joint Administration

5. After cases have been filed, a bankruptcy court can order cases involving two or more separate but related legal entities such as a partnership and its general partner or a parent and subsidiary corporations to be administered jointly. Federal Rules of Bankruptcy Procedure 1015 governs the joint administration of cases. Joint administration may include the use of a single docket, joint listing of filed claims, and combining notices to creditors. Joint administration does not affect substantive rights. The estate of each debtor is kept separate; the creditors of each debtor may look only to the assets of that debtor; and inter-debtor claims survive.

Substantive Consolidation

6. A bankruptcy court can also order the substantive consolidation of two or more separate but related entities, Neither the Bankruptcy Code nor the Federal Rules of Bankruptcy Procedure expressly provide for substantive consolidation. Parties seeking substantive consolidation invoke the general equitable power of a bankruptcy court under section 105. In substantive consolidation, the assets and liabilities of different entities are treated as the assets and liabilities of a single entity and intercompany claims are eliminated. *See generally* Christopher Frost, *Organizational Form, Misappropriation Risk, and the Substantive Consolidation of Corporate Groups*, 44 HASTINGS L.J. 449 (1993); Note, *Substantive Consolidation in Bankruptcy: A Primer*, 43 VAND. L.REV. 207 (1990).

□□□□□□

IN THE UNITED STATES BANKRUPTCY COURT
FOR THE DISTRICT OF DELAWARE

```
-----------------------------------------x
In re                            :   Chapter 11
BUCKHEAD AMERICA CORP., et al.,  :   Case Nos. 91-978
f/k/a                            :      Through 91-986
DAYS INNS OF AMERICA, INC., et al.,  :   Inclusive
                      Debtors    :
-----------------------------------------x
```

APPLICATION OF DEBTORS FOR ORDER
SUBSTANTIVELY CONSOLIDATING THE DEBTOR'S ESTATES
OTHER THAN THE ESTATE OF TOLLMAN-LODGING CORP.

To The Honorable Helen S. Balick
United States Bankruptcy Judge:

NOW COME Buckhead America Corp. ("BAC"), Buckhead Franchising, Inc. ("Franchising"), Buckhead Receivables Holding Corp. ("BRH"), Buckhead Receivables Funding Corp. ("BRF"), Buckhead International, Ltd. ("BIL"), Buckhead Venturer Group, Inc. ("Venturer"), Buckhead Advertising, Inc. ("Advertising") and Buckhead Hotel Management Company, Inc. ("BHMC") eight of the nine debtors herein (collectively, the "Debtors"), pursuant to section 105 of title 11, United States Code (the "Bankruptcy Code"), and hereby file their Application For Order Substantively Consolidating The Debtors' Estates Other than the Estate of Tollman Hundley Lodging Corp. (the "Application").

The Debtors submit, and as described below and in the affidavit of Douglas C. Collins, former Senior Vice President and Chief Financial Officer of the Debtors (the

"Collins Affidavit") annexed hereto as Exhibit "A", that substantive consolidation is necessary and in the best interests of the Debtors, their estates and their creditors, because, among other reasons:

(i) Most, if not all, of the creditors of these estates relied upon the unified assets of all of the Debtors when doing business with each of the individual Debtors;

(ii) Both externally and internally, the Debtors operated as a unified entity and untangling such entities at this late date would create awkward anomalies that serve no purpose and have no grounding in prepetition corporate reality;

(iii) The financial interrelationship between the Debtors is so entangled that any attempt to untangle such relationship would cause undue cost, delay and expense to each estate of the Debtors and would inflict great harm on these estates;

(iv) The Debtors failure to maintain contemporaneous business and record keeping formalities on an entity by entity basis renders it nearly impossible to accurately determine respective assets, property rights and liabilities of the estates;

(v) The cost, expense and delay of attempting to determine and segregate the assets and liabilities of these Debtors will jeopardize any benefit to creditors thereof;

(vi) The nearly identical overlap of both officers and directors of each of the Debtors meant that in practical terms, the Debtors were operated as one unified entity;

(vii) Substantive consolidation will obviate the need for litigating inter-entity claims, which litigation would likely produce de minimis benefit;

(viii) Substantive consolidation will vitiate duplicative claims against the estates;

(ix) Substantive consolidation will reduce significantly administrative expenses by streamlining the claims and distribution processes; and

(x) The benefit to the creditors of these estates dramatically outweighs the minimal prejudice which will result from substantive consolidation of the Debtors.

INTRODUCTION

1. On September 27, 1991 (the "Petition Date"), each of the Debtors filed a voluntary petition for relief under the Bankruptcy Code in the United States Bankruptcy Court for the District of Delaware.

2. Since the filing of their respective petitions, each of the Debtors has remained in possession of its properties and continued to operate its businesses as a debtor in possession pursuant to sections 1107 and 1108 of the Bankruptcy Code.

3. These cases have been consolidated for procedural purposes only and are being jointly administered pursuant to an order of this Court entered on September 30, 1991. No trustee or examiner has been appointed herein.

4. This Court has jurisdiction over this Application pursuant to 28 U.S.C. 157 and 1334 and the "Standing Order of Referral of Cases to Bankruptcy Judges," dated July 23, 1984, by the District Court for the District of Delaware. Venue of this proceeding in this district is proper pursuant to 28 U.S.C. 1408 and 1409. The statutory predicate for the relief sought herein is section 105 of the Bankruptcy Code.

5. The Debtors were engaged primarily in the operation of a franchise system under the "Days Inn" name. The Debtors also managed, and continue to manage, certain Days Inn hotels for investors and certain Days Inn hotels owned by the Debtors. On the Petition Date, Days Inn was the third largest United States hotel brand by number of units and the fifth largest by number of rooms. As of July 1, 1991, there were 1,180 Days Inn hotels and motels operating under various trade names in all 50 states, the District of Columbia, Puerto Rico, Canada, France, Mexico and the Netherlands, of which 23 were managed by the Debtors for investors and 2 were owned and managed by the Debtors.

6. On December 20, 1991, this Court approved the sale of the Days Inn franchise system by the Debtors to Hospitality Franchise System, Inc. ("HFS") and the assumption and assignment of all the Days Inn franchises by the Debtors to HFS (the "Sale"). The sale closed on January 31, 1992.

7. On May 13, 1992, the Debtors, along with Tollman Hundley Lodging Corp. ("THLC"), filed their Joint Plan of Reorganization. On June 12, 1992, the Debtors, along with THLC, filed their Amended Joint Plan of Reorganization and Disclosure Statement relative thereto. On July 2, 1992, the Debtors, along with THLC, filed their Second Amended Joint Plan of Reorganization (the "Plan") and Disclosure Statement (the "Disclosure Statement") relative thereto.

THE MOTION

8. By this Application, the Debtors, eight of the nine debtors in the above-referenced chapter 11 cases, seek an order of this Court substantively consolidating the

Debtors' estates, other than THLC, for all purposes. The facts of these cases and the case law on this issue support substantive consolidation of the Debtors' chapter 11 cases, as more fully set forth in the Collins Affidavit and in the Memorandum of Law in support of the Application, annexed hereto as Exhibit "B".

I. Major Areas in Support of Substantive Consolidation
   A. Corporate
   8. Throughout their history, the Debtors have operated essentially as a single, integrated entity, pursuing shared business paths. Since the acquisition of the Debtors by THLC in 1989, the Debtors have had overlapping boards of directors and officers with only a few distinctions between and among the various Debtors.
   9. Specifically, each of the Debtors, with the exception BRH has the same three directors, Messrs. Tollman, Hundley and Freedman, comprising their respective Boards of Directors. Even with respect to BRH, both Messrs. Tollman and Hundley are members of the board and the third member is an independent outside director.
   10. Through the Sale on January 31, 1992, senior management of each of the Debtors was identical. Each of the Debtors had the following senior and statutory officers:

Officer	Office
Stanley S. Tollman	Co-Chief Executive Officer
Monty D. Hundley	Co-Chief Executive Officer
John D. Snodgrass	President and Chief Operating Officer
Douglas C. Collins	Senior Vice President and Chief Financial Officer
Richard A. Smith	Senior Vice President for Administration
Gregory D. Casserly	Senior Vice President for Franchising
Kevin O. Jeter	Senior Vice President for Marketing
Linda T. Kyles	Treasurer
Robert A. Barnes	Secretary

Sanford Freedman   Assistant Secretary

B.   Financial/Taxes

11. The Debtors employed a consolidated cash management system. Cash being deposited with the Debtors from every source was immediately 'swept' into one depository account in the name of Days Inns of America, Inc. and its subsidiaries. Similarly, all payments to vendors, contract parties and others (other than payments to secured debt holders) were made out of a single disbursement account which is a zero sum account. In other words, most all debts, regardless of which entity incurred the debt, are paid from one account which draws money on an as needed basis from the central depository account.

12. Although the Debtors did keep an intercompany account to track intercompany loans, these loans were never subject to payment and were not used to determine the priority of payment of expenses. Rather, the Debtors ignored such intercompany transactions and looked only to whether the entities as a whole were profitable.

13. The consolidated cash management system furthered the fiction that these entities were one company. All checks had the Days Inns of America, Inc. name on them. Regardless of which entity contracted with the creditor, Days Inns of America, Inc. paid the bill. Because creditors looked to the unified group for payment, it was unnecessary in most instances to differentiate within the group as to which entity possessed the assets and which incurred the liabilities.

14. Historically, the Debtors have prepared consolidated, audited financial statements. Generally, the Debtors, as a closely held corporation, did not disclose their financial statements to third parties. However, on those occasions when the Debtors did choose to reveal financial statements, the financial statements shown were prepared on a consolidated basis. The one exception to this rule was that Franchising prepared its own financial statements to be used in the connection with its state uniform franchise offering.

15. In addition to preparing consolidated financial statements, the Debtors have for more than ten years prepared and filed consolidated federal tax returns.

C. Operations

16. The Debtors have always operated as a unified entity. Internally, all accounting, legal, finance, payroll, human resources, insurance and other administrative services are operated on a consolidated basis. All employees of the

Debtors are either employees of BAC or BHMC. None of the
other entities had employees, yet work was performed for
each entity by employees of both BAC or BHMC.

17. Physically, the Debtors' corporate headquarters
were located at 2751 Buford Highway, Atlanta, Georgia.
Within the building at 2751 Buford Highway, there was no
separation by entity.

18. Other than with respect to BRH and BRF, the
Debtors presented themselves to all creditors as a unified
entity. In dealing with the Debtors, third parties relied on
the good faith and credit of BAC.

II. Major Impacts On Creditors
  A. Asset Ownership

19. The majority of the Debtors assets are owned by
BRF and Franchising. Because the major asset of the Debtors
was the Days Inn franchise system, and because it is difficult to quantify the specific value of a particular franchise agreement licensed by a particular entity, it is not
realistic or reasonable to allocate value between 8RF and
Franchising.

20. Additionally, each of the other entities, other
than BAC which was the parent holding company, was created
as a special purpose subsidiary to service and add value to
the franchise business. In fact, each of the other entities
incurred the substantial majority of liabilities in servicing the Days Inn franchise business. It is inequitable to
penalize creditors who unknowingly had the misfortune to
contract to provide goods or services to an entity with no
assets, while a small minority of creditors who either
inadvertently or purposely are able to take advantage of the
disparate allocation of assets.

  B.   Harm to Creditors

21. It is clear that substantive consolidation will
harm a small minority (both in numbers and amounts owed) of
creditors in that without substantive consolidation a small
minority of creditors would receive a larger distribution
than they would receive if the Debtors are substantively
consolidated. However, there is no question that the benefit
to the Debtors, as well as to the vast majority of creditors, outweighs the limited economic prejudice. Similarly,
the cost and futility of disentangling the Debtors outweighs
the limited economic prejudice.

22. Because of the unified, single entity approach
to business the Debtors have consistently presented to the
world, creditors have always been on constructive notice
that the Debtors are effectively one entity. For a creditor
to argue now that it relied on the asset allocation among

entities prior to engaging in business with the Debtors
stretches the credibility of the creditor.

<u>PROCEDURE</u>
        23. The Debtors have given proper notice of this
Application to all interested parties.
        24. No previous application for the relief sought
herein has been made to this or any other court.

<u>CONCLUSION</u>
        WHEREFORE the Debtors respectfully request entry of
an order substantially in the form annexed hereto as Exhibit
"B" and such other and further relief as is just and proper.

Dated: Wilmington, Delaware
       June <u>15</u>, 1992

                         YOUNG, CONAWAY, STARGATT &
                           TAYLOR
                         Co-Counsel for Debtors and
                           Debtors in Possession

                         By: *David W. O'Connor*
                             James L. Patton, Jr.
                             David W. O'Connor
                         11th Floor
                         Rodney Square North
                         P.O. Box 391
                         Wilmington, Delaware 19899
                         (302) 5716600

                         WILLKIE FARR & GALLAGHER
                         Co-Counsel for Debtors and
                            Debtors In Possession
                         One Citicorp Center
                         153 East 53rd Street
                         New York, New York 10022
                         (212) 9358000

Notes and Problems

1. Paragraph 3 of the *Buckhead* Application states that the cases have been jointly
    administered. Should Judge Balick consider that fact in deciding whether to enter a
    substantive consolidation order?

2. Paragraph 21 acknowledges that "substantive consolidation will harm a small
    minority of creditors." Assume that C has a $1,000,000 judgment against BRH and
    BRF and is the only creditor of BRF which has millions of dollars of assets. Would

substantive consolidation harm C?   Should Judge Balick order substantive consolidation even if C is harmed?

3.   In the *Buckhead America* application, the debtors seek the substantive consolidation of eight entities that filed for bankruptcy.   Can a creditor seek substantive consolidation?   Can a bankruptcy court substantively consolidate a debtor with an entity that has not filed for bankruptcy?

4.   Lawyers are called upon to provide substantive consolidation opinions in connection with structured financings.   Structured financings often involve new entities created for the sole purpose of holding high quality assets that are the primary basis for the bond issuance or other financing.   For example, X creates N, and transfers assets to N.   N then issues and transfers the proceeds to X as the purchase price for the assets.   N, a special purpose entity, has no business activity other than participation in the financing and no creditors with claims against the high quality assets other than the bondholders.   Bondholders and rating agencies are concerned about the possibility of X later filing for bankruptcy and X's bankruptcy court substantively consolidating X and N.   Substantive consolidation would defeat the basic purpose of the structured financing -- that the holders of N's bonds can look to segregated asset pool held by N without concern about the financial condition of X.   Accordingly, legal opinions as to substantive consolidation are regularly required in structured financings.   *See generally Special Report by the Tribar Opinion Committee: Opinions in the Bankruptcy Context: Rating Agency, Structured Financing and Chapter 11 Transactions*, 46 Bus. Law. 718 (1991).

2. Operating The Business Postpetition

Chapter 11 contemplates that the debtor in possession or trustee will continue to operate the business postpetition. during the period between the filing of the bankruptcy petition and the confirmation of the Chapter 11 plan. This period of business operation in Chapter 11 may involve months or even years.

This period of business operation in Chapter 11 will certainly involve sections 361-66 of the Bankruptcy Code. While these statutory administrative powers apply in all forms of bankruptcy cases, they are particularly important in Chapter 11 cases.

For example, most of the property of a debtor that files for Chapter 11 relief will be encumbered. by liens. Section 1108's authorization of continued business operations would be of little practical significance if creditors could repossess or otherwise reach a Chapter 11 debtor's assets. Protection from lien foreclosure and other credit collection efforts is a common motive for Chapter 11 filing. The automatic stay of section 362, considered *supra* in Unit 8, provides that protection.

Similarly, section 362's protection from lien foreclosure would be of limited practical significance in a business Chapter 11 case if the debtor was not able to use and even sell encumbered assets. Section 363(b) and (c)(1), considered earlier, authorizes a Chapter 11 debtor in possession or trustee to use, sell or lease its assets, even its encumbered assets.

And, sections 1108, 362, and 363(b), (c)(1) would be of limited practical significance in a Chapter 11 case if the debtor was not able to fund its business operations postpetition. Cash flow problems is the most common cause for Chapter 11 filing.

a. Postpetition Credit

A company in bankruptcy is not generally viewed as the ideal borrower. Many vendors and most lenders are understandably reluctant to extend credit to such a business. How can a business that was unable to fund its operations outside of bankruptcy now fund its operations in bankruptcy?

See sections 365(c)(2), 502(b)(2), 552, 363(c)(2), 364 and the following problems and materials.

Problems

1. **Prepetition credit commitments**
    D obtains a $100,000 line of credit from C. After borrowing $40,000 from C, D files a Chapter 11 petition. Can D enforce C's remaining $60,000 credit commitment? See section 365(c)(2)

2. **Prepetition payment obligations**
    C makes a $200,000 unsecured loan to D. The loan agreement obligates D to make monthly interest payments of $1,800 and repay the $200,000 in a balloon payment at the end of the loan term. If D files for Chapter 11 does it have to continue making the monthly $1,800 interest payments during the Chapter 11 case? Does interest on this prepetition, unsecured loan even accrue postpetition? See section 502(b)(2). Would your answer be different if C's loan was secured by collateral with a value of more than $200,000? Cf. section 506(b)

3. **Collateral for postpetition loans**
    On January 5, C makes a loan to D that is secured by all of D's inventory. On April 15, D files a Chapter 11 petition. D continues to operate its business postpetition. See section 1108. Will the inventory that D acquires after its bankruptcy filing be subject to C's prepetition security interest? See section 552(a)

4. **Use of cash collateral**

Same facts as above. D continues to sell its inventory in the ordinary course of business. See section 363(c)(1). Does C have a security interest in the proceeds from the sale of the inventory? See section 552(b) Can D use this cash to pay its employees, its utility bills and otherwise fund its continuing business operations? See section 363(a), (c)(2), If not, how can D continue to operate?

5. Consul Restaurant Corp. owned and operated a chain of Mexican restaurants in the Midwest. It filed a Chapter 11 petition and reached an agreement with one its secured creditors, Chrysler Capital Corporation for the use of cash collateral and for adequate protection. That agreement and the Creditors' Committee's objection to the agreement are set out below.

□□□□□□

UNITED STATES BANKRUPTCY COURT
DISTRICT OF MINNESOTA
THIRD DIVISION

In Re:

                            Case No. BKY 3-91-4902
                            Chapter 11 Case

Consul Restaurant Corporation,
        Debtor.

**STIPULATION FOR USE OF CASH COLLATERAL
AND FOR ADEQUATE PROTECTION**

Consul Restaurant Corporation ("Debtor") and Chrysler Capital Corporation ("Chrysler") hereby stipulate and agree as follows:

1. On November 30, 1990, Chrysler loaned to the Debtor the sum of $2,500,000 (the "Obligation") under the terms of a Term Loan and Security Agreement. As of September 9, the dale of filing of Debtor's chapter 11 Petition (the "Filing Date"), the outstanding principal balance owing to Chrysler was $2,425,544.64.

2. The Obligation is secured by a security interest in the Equipment Collateral, Inventory Collateral, Receivables Collateral and Intangibles Collateral located at Debtor's restaurants situated at 18365 West Bluemound Road, Brookfield, Wisconsin, and 9396 U.S. Highway 16, Onalaska, Wisconsin (the "Personal Collateral"). The terms "Equipment Collateral," "Inventory Collateral," "Receivables Collateral" and "Intangibles Collateral" are defined in the Term

Loan and Security Agreement. In addition, the Obligation is secured by a mortgage on the real property of Debtor located at the above two addresses in Brookfield and Onalaska, Wisconsin.

3. Until April 1, 1992, or, until confirmation of a plan of reorganization if earlier, but only if Debtor is not in default under the terms of this Stipulation, the Debtor may use cash collateral which are the revenues of its restaurants located at Brookfield and LaCrosse (Onalaska), Wisconsin, to purchase inventory, pay payroll and payroll expenses and otherwise operate the business of Debtor in the ordinary course.

4. As adequate protection of the security interest of Chrysler in the Personal Collateral:

a. Debtor shall make regular monthly payments of accrued interest at the nondefault rate on the date of the month on which such payments were normally paid prior to the Filing Date for each month commencing with the Filing Date through the last date Debtor is authorized to use cash collateral;

b. Chrysler shall have, and the Debtor hereby grants, a perfected security interest in and a lien on all existing and future property of the Debtor associated with the LaCrosse (Onalaska) and Brookfield, Wisconsin restaurants which is the same type of property in which Chrysler held a security interest on the Filing Date. The newly granted security interest shall have the same priority, dignity and effect as that held by Chrysler on the Filing Date.

5. Debtor shall not grant any postpetition liens on any of the assets subject to Chrysler's lien without Chrysler's prior consent.

6. Except as such rights are modified by this Stipulation, Chrysler's consent to use of cash collateral shall not constitute a waiver of any of its rights under the various agreements with the Debtor, and shall not in any way prejudice its rights to take action, subject to court approval, as may be necessary to enforce or protect its rights under those agreements.

7. Nothing herein prevents Chrysler from filing appropriate instruments so as to notify third parties of the liens granted hereunder, and Chrysler is granted relief from the automatic stay to the extent necessary to file such notices. The Debtor shall execute and deliver to Chrysler any documents necessary to effectuate this Stipulation.

8. Notwithstanding the provisions of this Stipulation, Debtor does not waive the right to seek Court determination as to whether any portion or all of the proceeds received

from the operation of its restaurants constitute cash collateral under 11 U.S.C. 363(a).

9. Chrysler waives its right to collect interest at the default rate under the documents governing the Obligation for any period it receives interest as provided hereunder.

10. If Chrysler is subsequently deemed not to be fully secured under 11 U.S.C. 506(a), all payments received hereunder shall be credited to and reduce Chrysler's secured claim.

11. Any payments made to Chrysler since the commencement of this case and before approval of this Stipulation by the Court shall be credited to the interest payments due hereunder.

CHRYSLER CAPITAL CORPORATION

Dated: December __, 1991

By _Stephen P. Dugan_
Its Division Manager

KING & SPALDING

Dated: December __, 1991

By **David G. Epstein**
David G. Epstein (#249533)

191 Peachtree Street N.E.
Atlanta, Georgia 30303

ATTORNEYS FOR CHRYSLER
CAPITAL CORPORATION

Dated: December _ , 1991

CONSUL RESTAURANT CORPORATION

By **Robert H. Lang**
Its Ex Vice President

RAVICH MEYER KIRKMAN & McGRATH
A PROFESSIONAL ASSOCIATION

Dated December __, 1991

By _Michael L. Meyer_
Michael L. Meyer (#72527)
Michael F. McGrath (#168610)

4545 IDS Center
80 South Eighth Street
Minneapolis, MN 55402
ATTORNEYS FOR CONSUL
RESTAURANT CORPORATION

IN THE UNITED STATES BANKRUPTCY COURT
FOR THE DISTRICT OF MINNESOTA
ST. PAUL DIVISION

```
In re                    )
                         )
CONSUL RESTAURANT        )    BANKRUPTCY NO. 3-91-4902-11
CORPORATION,             )
                         )
          Debtor.        )
-------------------------)
```

OBJECTION OF THE CONSUL RESTAURANT CORPORATION
STATUTORY COMMITTEE OF UNSECURED CREDITORS TO
STIPULATIONS FOR USE OF CASH COLLATERAL

TO THE HONORABLE DENNIS D. O'BRIEN,
UNITED STATES BANKRUPTCY JUDGE

The Consul Restaurant Corporation statutory committee
of unsecured creditors (the "Committee") files this its objection (this "Objection") to (i) the stipulation for use of
cash collateral and for adequate protection between Consul
and Chrysler Capital Corporation (the "Chrysler Stipulation") and (ii) the stipulation for use of cash collateral
and for adequate protection between Consul and The First
National Bank in Sioux Falls (the "Sioux Falls Stipulation")
(the Chrysler Stipulation and the Sioux Falls Stipulation
are collectively referred to as the "Stipulations"), and in
support hereof respectfully shows the Court:

BACKGROUND

1.   On September 9, 1991 (the "Petition Date"), Consul
Restaurant Corporation ("Consul") filed a petition for relief under chapter 11 of title 11 of the United States Code
(the "Bankruptcy Code"). Since the Petition Date, Consul has
been authorized to operate and manage its assets as debtor
in possession pursuant to sections 1107(a) and 1108 of the
Bankruptcy Code.

2.   On September 13, 1991, the United States Trustee
appointed the Committee to serve as a committee of unsecured
creditors in the Consul case pursuant to section 1102(a)(1)
of the Bankruptcy Code. On October 17, 1991, the United
States Trustee filed the second amended appointment of the
Committee. Pursuant to the second amended appointment, the
Committee consists of eleven members.

3.   On November 12, 1991, Consul served on the
Committee by first class mail its notice of continued cash

collateral hearing (the "Notice") and the Stipulations. The
Notice and the Stipulations were received by counsel for the
Committee on November 14, 1991. The hearing on the Stipulations is set for November 25, 1991. The Committee objects to
the approval of the Stipulations on the following grounds:

THE OBJECTION

The Notice fails to comply with Bankruptcy Rule 4001(d)

   4. Bankruptcy Rule 4001(d)(2) of the Bankruptcy Rules
provides that, unless the court fixes a different time, an
objecting party may file its objection regarding the use of
cash collateral within 15 days after the notice of hearing
has been mailed. The Bankruptcy Rules represent minimum due
process requirements. Procedural due process requirements
must be met before the Court can consider a substantive
pleading. The Notice fails to comply with the minimum notice
requirements of Bankruptcy Rule 4001(d). In addition, no
pleading has been filed requesting a reduction of the 15-day
objection period.[1] Therefore, the Court must deny the relief
requested in the Stipulations until compliance with Bankruptcy Rule 4001(d) can be demonstrated.

The Secured Creditors are adequately protected without any
Postpetition payments.

   5. Chrysler Capital Corporation and The First National
Bank in Sioux Falls (collectively, the "Secured Creditors")
are adequately protected. As demonstrated in the memorandum
of authorities filed by the Committee on October 25, 1991 in
support of Consul's motion for use of cash collateral and
for adequate protection, the Secured Creditors are substantially oversecured. More importantly, the collateral of the
Secured Creditors is not deteriorating in value. Indeed,
preserving the going-concern value of Consul through the use
of alleged cash collateral can only enhance the value of the
"hard" collateral held by the Secured Creditors. Thus, the
Secured Creditors are adequately protected for Consul's use
of its operating revenues. No further adequate protection is
necessary.

   6. In addition, as more particularly set forth in the
memorandum filed by the Committee, the postpetition operating revenues of Consul are, at most, only collateral of the

---

[1]   Even if a proper pleading was filed requesting a reduction of
the objection period under Bankruptcy Rule 4001(d), counsel could
not establish "cause" for the reduction. It appears that the
Stipulation with Sioux Fallc was executed October 28, 1991 and the
Stipulation with Chrysler was executed November 8, 1991, yet the
Notice was not filed until November 12, 1991. Consequently, Consul
could have given the required notice if it were so inclined.

Secured Creditors as proceeds of accounts created in favor of Consul as a provider of services to restaurant customers. Because the accounts from which operating revenues are derived arise from the sale of a service, and because those accounts do not come into existence until the service is performed, no accounts arising from postpetition services performed by Consul are collateral securing the claim of the Secured Creditors. 11 U.S.C. §552(a). Consequently, no operating revenues attributable to such postpetition accounts are the Secured Creditors' cash collateral. 11 U.S.C. 552(b). Accordingly, the Committee respectfully asserts that section 552 of the Bankruptcy Code operates to limit the security interest, if any, of the Secured Creditors in operating revenues so that the security interest does not extend to any such revenues generated by the postpetition sale of any restaurant services. Consul should, therefore, be authorized to use all postpetition operating revenues without the necessity of obtaining the consent of any party in interest or providing adequate protection to any party in interest.

As oversecured creditors, the Secured Creditors are not entitled to postpetition interest until confirmation of a chapter 11 plan.

    7. As adequate protection, Consul seeks authority to pay the Secured Creditors' postpetition interest payments. In addition to the postpetition interest payments, the Chrysler Stipulation requires Consul to make principal reductions. Certainly, Section 506(b) of the Bankruptcy Code allows postpetition interest to accrue on an oversecured claim. However, postpetition interest should be paid only if the Secured Creditors are oversecured at the confirmation. Notably, the Secured Creditors are not entitled to interest on interest. Vanston Bondholders Protective Comm. v. Green, 329 U.S. 156 (1946). Consequently, postpetition interest payments can be deferred without compensating the Secured Creditors for interest on interest. Deferring interest payments to the Secured Creditors would allow the Consul estate to benefit from the time value of the sums that would be paid to the Secured Creditors.

    8. Additionally, the value of the collateral held by the Secured Creditors should not be valued for section 506(b) purposes until confirmation. The timing of the payment of accrued interest to an oversecured creditor (after confirmation) is doubtless based on the fact that it is not possible to compute the amount of section 506(c) recovery (and, accordingly, the amount of the net allowed secured claim on which interest is computed) until the termination

of the proceeding. <u>See</u>, <u>In re</u> <u>Timbers of Inwood Forest</u>, 793
F.2d 1380, 1407 (5th Cir. 1986), <u>aff'd</u> 484 U.S. 365 (1988).

<u>RELIEF REQUESTED</u>

    9. The Committee respectfully requests that the Court
(i) deny approval of the Stipulations and (ii) prohibit
Consul from paying postpetition interest to the Secured
Creditors (and postpetition principal reductions as required
under the Chrysler Stipulation) until confirmation.

    WHEREFORE, the Committee requests that the Court grant
the relief requested in this Objection and enter an order
(i) denying approval of the Stipulation; (ii) prohibiting
Consul from paying postpetition interest (and postpetition
principal reductions) to the Secured Creditors until
confirmation; and (iii) for such other relief as may be just
and equitable.

Dated:
November 20, 1991
Dallas, Texas

                        Respectfully submitted,
                        WEIL, GOTSHAL & MANGES

                        By: *Margaret A. Mahoney*
                            Margaret A. Mahoney
                            Texas State Bar No. 12844020
                            Craig H. Averch*
                            Texas State Bar No. 01451020

                        901 Main Street - Ste. 4100
                        Dallas, TX 75202
                        (214) 746-7700
                        ATTORNEYS FOR THE CONSUL RESTAURANT
                        CORPORATION COMMITTEE OF UNSECURED
                        CREDITORS

                        *Admitted <u>Pro</u> <u>Hac</u> <u>Vice</u> 11/8/91

LOCAL ATTORNEYS FOR THE CONSUL RESTAURANT CORPORATION
COMMITTEE OF UNSECURED CREDITORS:

STRINGER & ROHLEDER, LTD.
1200 Norwest Center Tower
55 East Fifth Street
St. Paul, MN 55101
(612) 2277784

Notes and Problems

1. If you represented Chrysler would you consent to the Debtor's use of revenues from its Wisconsin restaurants? What would you try to bargain for?

2. If you represented the Creditors' Committee would you object to the Stipulation?

3. What is the legal reason for the Committee's arguing that the Chrysler Capital Corporation was " substantially oversecured"? See section 363(c)(2)(B); but cf. section 506(b). What is the probable factual basis for this argument?

4. Are the revenues of a restaurant "cash collateral" of a lender with a lien on all of the restaurant's tangible and intangible assets? See U.C.C. section 9-306, section 363(a). Are the room rentals of a hotel the "cash collateral" of a creditor with a lien on all of the hotel's tangible and intangible assets? See generally R. Wilson Freyernuth, *Of Hotel Revenues, Rents and Formalism in the Bankruptcy Courts - Implications for Reforming Commercial Real Estate Finance*, 40 UCLA L. REV. 1461 (1993); Patrick Randolph, *Recognizing Lenders' Rent Interests in Bankruptcy*, 27 REAL PROPERTY, PROBATE & TRUST JOURNAL 281 (1992).

5. What are the probable consequences of a Chapter 11 debtor's using cash collateral in violation of a section 363(c) order? Chrysler provided financing to East County Dodge for the purpose of purchasing vehicles . The loan agreement gave Chrysler a lien on all vehicles and all proceeds therefrom. When East County filed for Chapter 11, the cash collateral order required that East County deposit in a special trust account an amount equal to the wholesale price upon completing the sale of any vehicle. East County instead deposited moneys received from the sale of automobiles in its general operating bank account. Does anything in the Bankruptcy Code or the Uniform Commercial Code give Chrysler a lien on the funds in the general bank account? See sections 363(c), UCC 9-306. Does anything in the Bankruptcy Code give Chrysler any other remedy for violation of the cash collateral order?

□□□□□□

At most, section 363 enables a Chapter 11 debtor to use the cash that its business generates. Generally, a Chapter 11 debtor needs more, needs additional credit and funding. To counter the understandable reluctance of vendors and lenders to extend credit to Chapter 11 debtors, section 364 of the Bankruptcy Code provides incentives. Please read section 364 .

Problems

1. Your client, C, sells dairy products to a group of supermarkets, D. C bills D monthly. D files a Chapter 11 petition. Should C continue to sell dairy products to D on credit? Should C obtain court approval? See paragraphs (a), (b) and (c) of section 364.

2. X has a lien on all of the assets of D stores, including after-acquired inventory, accounts receivable and the proceeds therefrom. The amount owed to X far exceeds the value of X's collateral. D files a Chapter 11 petition. D needs additional financing. What inducements can D offer a new creditor to extend postpetition financing? See sections 552(a), 364(c), (d) and the R.H. Macy & Co. section 364(c) motion set out below.

3. Same facts as 2. The prime source of debtor in possession financing is the creditor that provided the prepetition financing. What inducements can D offer X to extend additional credit? See sections 552(a), 364(c), (d) and *In re Saybrook Manufacturing, Co., Inc.* set out below.

4. D owes C $4,000,000. C has a first mortgage on D's only asset, a building. D files a Chapter 11 petition. D wants to borrow $600,000 to refurbish the building. C is unwilling to extend further credit to D. Can D invoke section 364(d) to grant a new, postpetition lender a first lien on the building? What if an appraiser is willing to testify that the value of the building is $5,000,000? What if the value of the building is no more than $2,000,000 but an appraiser is willing to testify that the planned improvements will increase the value of the building by $900,000?

```
WEIL, GOTSHAL & MANGES        HEARING DATE:
Attorneys for Debtor
  in Possession
767 Fifth Avenue
New York, New York  10153
(212) 310-8000
Lori R. Fife, Esq. {LF 2839}
```

```
UNITED STATES BANKRUPTCY COURT
SOUTHERN DISTRICT OF NEW YORK
-------------------------------x
```

```
     In re                      :
                                   Chapter 11 Case Nos.
R. H. MACY & CO., INC.          :  92B          Through
et al.,                            92B          Inclusive
                                :  (Jointly Administered)

          Debtors.
-------------------------------x
```

MOTION PURSUANT TO SECTIONS 364(c)(1) AND 364(c)(2) OF THE BANKRUPTCY CODE FOR ORDERS (i) AUTHORIZING OBTAINING OF CREDIT AND (ii) AUTHORIZING INTERIM OBTAINING OF CREDIT PENDING A FINAL HEARING

```
TO THE HONORABLE BURTON R. LIFLAND,
UNITED STATES BANKRUPTCY JUDGE:
```

R. H. Macy & Co., Inc. and certain of its direct and indirect subsidiaries (the "Subsidiaries"), as debtors and as debtors in possession (collectively, "Macy's" or the "Debtors"), each move for orders (i) pursuant to sections 364(c)(1) and 364(c)(2) of title 11 of the United States Code (the "Bankruptcy Code"), authorizing Macy's to obtain credit pursuant to the DIP Credit Facility as hereinafter described and (ii) authorizing Macy's to obtain interim credit under the DIP Credit Facility (the "Motion") respectfully represent:

<u>Background</u>

1.   On January 27, 1992 (the "Commencement Date"), each of the Debtors filed with the court a voluntary petition for relief under chapter 11 of the Bankruptcy Code. Pursuant to an order of the court, the Debtors' chapter 11 cases have been consolidated for procedural purposes only and are being jointly administered.

2.   Each of the Debtors continues to operate its business and manage its properties as a debtor in

possession pursuant to sections 1107(a) and 1108 of the
Bankruptcy Code.

Overview of Macy's Operations

3.   The business of Macy's originated in 1858
as R. H. Macy & Co. and was incorporated in New York in
1919. On July 15, 1986, the business and assets of Macy's
were acquired in a leveraged buyout. On May 3, 1988, Macy's
acquired the I. Magnin and Bullock's/Bullocks Wilshire
divisions of Federated Department Stores, Inc., and these
divisions then became wholly owned subsidiaries of Macy's.

4.   As of November 1, 1991, Macy's had assets
of approximately $4.95 billion and liabilities of approxi-
mately $5.32 billion.

5.   Macy's is one of the nation's largest retail department store businesses, having a regular work
force of approximately 69,500 employees. Macy's department
stores are organized into four regional, wholly owned subsidiary store groups strategically located in both major
cities and suburban areas and operated by separate management: (i) Macy's Northeast,Inc. ("Macy's Northeast"),
(ii) Macy's California, Inc. ("Macy's California"),
(iii) Macy's South, Inc. ("Macy's South")/Bullock's Inc.
("Bullocks"), and I. Magnin, Inc. ("Magnin"). Through these
groups, Macy's operates 144 owned or leased retail department stores in 18 states. Macy's also operates 107 specialty stores located mainly in suburban shopping malls
under the names "Aeropostale," "Charter Club," and "Fanta-
sies by Morgan Taylor." All the stores transact business on
cash and credit bases. In addition, to service its retail
organization Macy's operates a warehousing and distributing
system.

6.   Macy's offers a wide assortment of merchandise, principally in the medium-to-higher priced lines.
For the fiscal year ended August 3, 1991, Macy's net retail
sales comprised sales of women's, men's, and children's
ready-to-wear apparel and accessories (79%); furniture, home
furnishings, housewares, and electronics (18%); and other
categories (3%), aggregating $6.675 billion.

7.   The regional department store groups and
the specialty stores are supported by R. H. Macy Corporate
Buying ("Corporate Buying"), which has its principal offices
in New York City and includes foreign buying offices in 18
foreign cities and buying representatives in 4 other foreign
countries. Corporate Buying employs, along with its buying
staff, designers and technical teams to establish
specifications and ensure quality control of Macy's "private
label" merchandise business. In addition to Corporate

Buyer, a specialized corporate staff at Macy's headquarters in New York City provides services in accounting, finance, personnel and labor relations, insurance, real estate, operations, fashion design, store design, engineering and construction, law, and taxation.

8.   As stated above, for the fiscal year ended August 3, 1991, the net retail sales of the four regional store groups totaled approximately $6.675 billion. During this period, Macy's spent approximately $194.6 million for capital projects, including the construction of new stores, renovations of existing stores, and upgrading various support facilities. The improvement program has been directed toward established markets as well as new geographic markets where Macy's management believes it can capture significant market share.

9.   Macy's Northeast currently operates 47 department stores located in Connecticut, Delaware, Maryland, New Jersey, New York, Pennsylvania, and Virginia, and accounts for approximately 45% of Macy's total department store space. Macy's Herald Square, which has been at its present location in midtown Manhattan since 1902, is believed to be the world's largest retail store.

10.   Macy's California operates 25 department stores located in California and Nevada, which account for approximately 17% of Macy's total department store space.

11.   Macy's South operates 26 department stores located in Alabama, Florida, Georgia, Louisiana, South Carolina, and Texas, which account for approximately 17% of Macy's total department store space.

12.   Bullocks consists of 22 department stores located in Arizona, California, and Nevada, which account for approximately 14% of Macy's total department store space.

13.   I. Magnin operates 24 department stores located in Arizona, California, Illinois, Maryland, and Washington, which account for approximately 6% of Macy's total department store space.

Relief Requested

14.   Pursuant to section 364(c) of the Bankruptcy Code and Fed. R. Bankr. Pro. 4001(c), Macy's seeks authorization (i) to enter into the DIP Credit Facility, and (ii) to obtain interim credit under the DIP Credit Facility pending a final hearing to consider the Motion.

15.   Section 364(c) of the Bankruptcy Code provides:

> If the trustee is unable to obtain unse-
> cured credit allowable under section 503(b)(1)
> of this title as an administrative expense, the
> court, after notice and a hearing, may authorize
> the obtaining of credit or the incurring of
> debt --

>> (1)   with priority over any or all
>> administrative expenses of the kind
>> specified in section 503(b) or 507(b) of
>> this title; [or]

>> (2)   secured by a lien on property
>> of the estate that is not otherwise sub-
>> ject to a lien. . . .

11 U.S.C. §364(c). Fed. R. Bankr. Pro. 4001(c) provides, in relevant part:

>> (2) Hearing. The court may commence a
>> final hearing on a motion for authority to ob-
>> tain credit no earlier than 15 days after serv-
>> ice of the motion. If the motion so requests,
>> the court may conduct a hearing before such 15
>> day expires, but the court may authorize the
>> obtaining of credit only to the extent necessary
>> to avoid immediate and irreparable harm to the
>> estate pending a final hearing.

Fed. R. Bankr. Pro. 4001(c). Accordingly, this court is authorized to grant the relief requested.

Macy's Urgent Need for Financing

16.   Macy's urgently needs debtor in possession financing and credit to purchase inventory and continue its businesses and operations. Macy's anticipates that the filing of its chapter 11 case will bring about a cessation of trade credit. Without the availability of bank and trade credit at this critical time, Macy's will not be in a posi-tion to take advantage of the spring and summer seasons and continue to maintain its business. If that were to occur, it would suffer substantial losses.

17.   Without immediate assurance of availabil-ity of credit and a debtor in possession financing facility, Macy's anticipates that its vendors and suppliers will be reluctant to honor Macy's purchase orders. A steady and continual stream of quality merchandise is an essential in-gredient to the maintenance and enhancement of Macy's for the benefit of all parties in interest. Due to the amount

of lead time needed to order merchandise for future selling seasons, any lost inventory may be irreplaceable. This daily loss of inventory may cause a substantial loss of sales with the attendant negative impact on the value of Macy's.

18.   Without a source of postpetition financing, it will be impossible for Macy's to obtain necessary letters of credit required by foreign vendors. Equally important is the sense of confidence that the availability of postpetition financing will instill in Macy's vendors, landlords, customers and employees. The instant case follows in the wake of seriatim filings of chapter 11 cases by major retail organizations over the past two years, beginning with Federated Department Stores, Inc., Allied Stores Corporation and, most recently, Zale Corporation and its subsidiaries. The general decline in consumer confidence in the nation's economy and the substantial debt burden carried by Macy's are the major precipitating causes for the commencement of the cases.

19.   In order to purchase inventory and fund its operation, it is essential that Macy's obtain $600 million in financing under Section 364 of the Bankruptcy Code. Pending a final hearing to consider the Motion, Macy's ongoing business operations and its immediate viability are dependent upon its ability to obtain interim financing in an amount up to $60 million immediately.

The DIP Credit Facility

20.   As a result of extensive, arms-length negotiations conducted by and between Macy's and Chemical Bank, as Agent, and Bankers Trust Company, as Co-Agent (collectively, the "Banks"), the Banks have agreed to make loans and arrange for other financial institutions to make loans to Macy's, as debtors in possession, but only in accordance with and on the terms and conditions to be set forth in the DIP Credit Facility. The major elements of the DIP Credit Facility are set forth in the Term Sheet together with the related Commitment Letter and Fee Letter annexed hereto as Exhibit "A". In summary, it is proposed:

(a)   Borrower and Guarantors. Macy's shall be the borrower and certain of its subsidiaries shall be guarantors of Macy's obligations under the DIP Credit Facility.[1]

---

[1]   The following Macy's subsidiaries are the guarantors under the DIP Credit Facility: (i) Macy Specialty Stores, Inc., Macy Northeast, Inc., Macy's South, Inc., Bullock's, Inc., Macy's California, Inc., and I. Magnin, Inc. and (ii) Macy's other subsidiaries listed on Schedule "A" which is attached to the Term

(b)   <u>Commitment</u>. A total commitment of $600 million for all direct borrowings and letters of credit, with a sublimit of $250 million for letters of credit, with a further sublimit of $20 million for standby letters of credit (the "Commitment").

(c)   <u>Use of Proceeds</u>. The proceeds of all loans are to be used for working capital and inventory purchases by, and for other general purposes of, Macy's and the Guarantors.

(d)   <u>Borrowing Base</u>. The Borrower Base shall be equal to the lower of (i) 50% of the Eligible Book Value of Inventory,[1] and (ii) 40% of the Eligible Retail Value of Inventory.

(e)   <u>Interest</u>. The interest rate shall be equal to Chemical Bank's Alternate Base Rate ("ABR"), plus 1-1/2%; or, at Macy's option, reserve adjusted London Interbank Offered Rate ("LIBOR"), plus 2-1/2% for interest periods of 1, 3, or 6 months. Interest on ABR Loans, 3-month LIBOR Loans, and 6-month LIBOR Loans is to be paid quarterly, in arrears; while interest on each 1-month LIBOR Loan is payable monthly, in arrears. Upon the occurrence and during the continuance of any default in the payment of principal, interest, or other amounts due under the DIP Credit Facility, interest shall, from time of default, be payable on demand at ABR, plus 3-1/2%. All loans are ABR Loans for approximately 45 days after the entry of the Interim Order.

(f)   <u>Term</u>. All borrowings shall be repaid in full at the earlier of (i) February 28, 1994 (the "Maturity Date") and (ii) the substantial consummation (as defined in section 1101(2) of the Bankruptcy Code including the effective date) of a plan of reorganization confirmed pursuant to an order entered by the court in the chapter 11 cases of Macy's, and certain of the Guarantors (the "Consummation Date").

(g)   <u>Closing Date</u>. Closing Date shall occur promptly upon the entry of an order approving the interim financing but no later than ten business days after the Commencement Date.

(h)   <u>Fees and Expenses</u>. Macy's shall pay the following fees and expenses in connection with the DIP Credit Facility:[2]

Sheet, all of which will file petitions under chapter 11 shortly (the "Other Guarantors"). All guarantors referred to in clauses (i) and (ii) above are collectively designated as the "Guarantors."

[1]   Terms not defined in this motion have the meanings ascribed to such terms in the DIP Credit Facility.

(i)   an advisory and structuring fee of
$4,500,000 payable to the Banks
(x) $1,500,000 upon entry of the
Interim Order and (y) the balance
upon entry of the Final Order;[2]

(ii)   a facility fee of $7,500,000, pay-
able in pro rata portions based
upon the amount of the DIP Credit
Facility Macy's is authorized to
utilize;

(iii) an administrative agency fee of
$250,000 per annum payable to
Chemical Bank on the date of the
initial funding under the DIP
Credit Facility and annually on
each anniversary of such date and
a fee to Chemical Bank as administrative agent equal to $1,500,000
payable on the date of the initial
funding under the DIP Credit
Facility;

(iv)   a commitment fee of 1/2 of 1% per
annum on the unused balance of the
Commitment, payable quarterly in
arrears during the term of the
facility;

(v)   a letter of credit fee of 2% per
annum of the outstanding face
amount of each letter of credit,
plus customary fees for issuance,
amendments and processing of the
letters of credit;

(vi)   a fronting fee in the amount to be
agreed upon among Macy's, the
Banks, and the banks issuing the
letters of credit (the "Fronting
Banks"); and

(vii) all reasonable out-of-pocket costs
and expenses of the Banks (including, without limitation, reasonable legal fees and disbursements)
whether or not the transactions

---

[1] The proposal contemplates that the fees referred to above and
set forth in the Fee Letter shall not be refundable under any
circumstances, even if the DIP Credit Facility is not authorized
at the final hearing or is not consummated for any reason.
[2] On January 27, 1992, Macy's paid Chemical $1 million to be
applied against the advisory and structuring fee.

contemplated by the DIP Credit
Facility are consummated.

(i)   Letters of Credit. The DIP Credit Facility sets forth the terms and conditions for the issuance of
letters of credit on behalf of Macy's. All such letters of
credit shall expire no later than 60 days after the Maturity
Date. If the Consummation Date or the Maturity Date occurs
prior to the expiration of any letter of credit, Macy's
shall (i) replace and return each such letter of credit to
the Fronting Bank undrawn and marked "canceled" on or prior
to the Consummation Date or the Maturity Date, as the case
may be, or (ii) in the event of Macy's inability to replace
them, then collateralize such letters of credit by deposit
of cash in a cash collateral account to be maintained in the
name of the Banks in an amount equal to 105% of the undrawn
amount of such letters of credit ("Cash Collateralization").
        (j)   Collateral. The DIP Credit Facility is
unsecured, except to the extent that Macy's may be required
to cash collateralize particular letters of credit under
certain circumstances.[1]
        (k)   Priority. All obligations of Macy's under
the DIP Credit Facility shall constitute the highest administrative expense priority claims under section 364(c)(1) of
the Bankruptcy Code, with priority over any and all
administrative expenses of the kind specified in
sections 503(b) or 507(b) of the Bankruptcy Code. In
accordance with Local Bankruptcy Rule 47, it is noted that
under the DIP Credit Facility, upon the occurrence of an
Event of Default, or an event which with the lapse of time
or giving of notice or both would become an Event of Default, the section 364(c)(1) administrative expense priority
claim to be granted shall be subordinate to (i) the payment
of allowed professional fees and disbursements incurred by
Macy's and the Guarantors, and any statutory creditors'
committee appointed in the chapter 11 cases of Macy's and
the Guarantors in an aggregate amount not to exceed $10
million (the "Cap"), and (ii) the payment of fees pursuant
to 28 U.S.C. e 1930. Notwithstanding the foregoing, so long
as an Event of Default, or an event which with the giving of

---

[1]   Cash collateralization of the letters of credit is required in
the following circumstances: (i) if, prior to the expiration date
of the letters of credit but after the occurrence of the Maturity
Date or the Consummation Date, as the case may be, Macy's is
unable to replace them, or (ii) if, after giving effect to any
mandatory prepayment in full under the DIP Credit Facility, the
sum of outstanding letters of credit, plus unreimbursed draws,
exceeds either the Borrowing Base or the Commitment, but only up
to the amount of such excess.

notice or lapse of time or both would constitute an Event of
Default, shall not have occurred, Macy's and the Guarantors
shall be permitted to pay any and all (i) administrative
expenses incurred in the ordinary course of their business,
and (ii) compensation and reimbursement of expenses authorized by this Court under sections 330 and 331 of the Bankruptcy Code, as the same may be due and payable, without any
reduction of the Cap.

(1)   Remedies. The Banks may, upon the occurrence of certain Events of Default, as more fully set forth
and described in the DIP Credit Facility, take the following
measures:

> (i)   declare outstanding principal and
>   accrued interest thereon to be
>   immediately due and payable;
>
> (ii)   terminate any further commitment
>   to extend credit to Macy's or to
>   issue letters of credit;
>
> (iii)   set off any amounts held as cash
>   collateral or held in any accounts
>   maintained with the Banks;
>
> (iv)   require Cash Collateralization of
>   outstanding letters of credit; and
>
> (v)   take any other action permitted
>   under the DIP Credit Facility or
>   by operation of law;

provided, however, that with respect to items (iii) through
(v) above, the Banks must provide Macy's with two business
days' notice prior to taking the intended action.

21.   Macy's currently is in the process of fi-
nalizing the definitive DIP Credit Agreement with the Banks.
Copies will be served upon all noticed parties and filed
with the Court prior to the hearing. Due to the critical
need for interim financing, Macy's has initiated the process
by using the detailed Term Sheet annexed hereto as Exhibit
"A."

Authorization of the DIP Credit
Facility and the Interim Financing Is In
the Best Interests of Macy's, Its Creditors
and Its Estates

22.   Macy's believes that the terms and conditions of
the DIP Credit Facility are fair and reasonable, and were
negotiated by the parties in good faith and at arm's length.
Indeed, prior to entering into the DIP Credit Facility,
Macy's solicited proposals from other financial institutions

to provide comparable post-Commencement Date financing. The
terms proposed by the Banks, and set forth in the Term
Sheet, represent the financing package which is in the best
interests of Macy's. It is on terms comparable to debtor in
possession, section 364 financings approved in other retail
chapter 11 cases, including <u>Best Products Co., Inc. et al.</u>;
<u>Ames Department Stores, Inc.</u>; <u>Carter Hawley Hale Stores,
Inc.</u>; and others.

     23.   The financing under the DIP Facility will
enable Macy's, among other things, to (i) purchase needed
inventory for the future retail seasons, (ii) maintain continuity of their operations, and (iii) maximize the value of
their businesses and properties. In addition, the funding
under the DIP Credit Facility will install confidence in
vendors, suppliers, and factors and encourage them to extend credit to Macy's that will lead to a successful reorganization as contemplated by chapter 11.

     24.   Accordingly, Macy's urges the court to
approve the DIP Credit Facility. Macy's seeks authorization
to perform all acts and to make, execute and deliver all
such other and further instruments and documents as may be
required for its performance under the DIP Credit Facility,
including, but not limited to, the payment of fees and the
execution of any guarantees by Macy's entities subsequently
becoming debtors in possession.

<u>Emergency Interim Relief</u>

     25.   Pending the final hearing, Macy's requires
immediate interim financing in the amount of up to $60 mil-
lion for, among other things, the purchase of new inventory
and satisfaction of other working capital needs -- all in
order to continue their operations uninterrupted for the
benefit of all parties in interest. Absent interim financing for their continuing business operations, Macy's may
have to curtail continuing operations with concomitant potential harm to the value of its franchise. Such harm is
inimical to the interests of all concerned. The financing
of Macy's businesses is a condition precedent of
rehabilitation and reorganization. Re-establishment of
consumer, vendor and employee confidence is the touchstone
to obtaining the objectives of chapter 11 of the Bankruptcy
Code. Therefore, to enable Macy's to maintain operations
pending a final hearing pursuant to section 364 and Fed. R.
Bankr. Pro. 4001, the interim financing requested must be
authorized.

Good Faith

     26.   Inasmuch as the terms and conditions of
the DIP Credit Facility are fair and reasonable, and were

negotiated by the parties in good faith and at arm's length, the Banks should be accorded the benefits of section 364(e) of the Bankruptcy Code to the extent of any or all of the provisions of the DIP Credit Facility.

Notice

27.   No trustee, examiner, or any statutory committee has been appointed in these chapter 11 cases. In accordance with Fed. R. Bankr. Pro. 4001(c)(1) and (3), notice of this Motion was provided to (i) the United States Trustee for the Southern District of New York, (ii) each of the creditors listed on the lists filed pursuant to Fed. R. Bankr. Pro. 1007(d) in each of the Debtors' chapter 11 cases, (iii) major secured creditors, (iv) attorneys for the Banks, and (v) other parties as directed by the court. Macy's submits that no other or further notice is necessary.

Waiver of Memorandum of Law

28.   Inasmuch as no novel issues of law are presented by this Motion, the Debtors requested that, pursuant to Local Bankruptcy Rule 13(b), the requirement that a motion be accompanied by a memorandum of law be dispensed with and waived.

29.   No previous request for relief sought by this Motion has been made to this or any other court.

WHEREFORE, the Debtors respectfully request (i) entry of an interim order in the form attached hereto as Exhibit B, authorizing the Debtors to obtain credit in accordance with the DIP Credit Facility in an amount up to $60 million, and to pay all fees required in connection therewith; and (ii) after the final hearing, authorize the obtaining of credit pursuant to sections 364(c)(1) and (c)(2) in accordance with the DIP Credit Facility; and (iii) granting such other and further relief as is just.

Dated: New York, New York
          January 27, 1992

                              WEIL, GOTSHAL & MANGES
                              Attorneys for Debtors
                                 in Possession
                              767 Fifth Avenue
                              New York, New York 10153
                                 (212) 310-8000

                              By: _____
                                  Lori R. Fife
                                  LF 2839
                                  (A Member of the Firm)

Notes and Problems

1. Note that Macy filed its bankruptcy petition on January 27, 1992, and filed this motion the same date. The court entered the interim order two days later. Frequently, before commencing its Chapter 11 case, a debtor will reach an agreement with a lender on debtor in possession financing. The definitive loan documents are drafted before the bankruptcy filing. The debtor then files a motion for court authorization of debtor in possession financing at the same time that it files its Chapter 11 petition., Such motions are often heard by the bankruptcy court on an emergency, interim basis, pending a final hearing on the terms of the proposed agreement.

2. According to paragraph 4 of the motion, Macy had liabilities of 5.32 billion and assets of 4.95 billion. Why would Chemical extend credit to Macy?

3. What is the collateral for Chemical's loan? What could Macy use as collateral?

4. What is the purpose of the recitation of "in good faith and at arm's length" in paragraph 25?

Matter of Saybrook Manufacturing Co., Inc.
United States Court of Appeals, Eleventh Circuit, 1992
963 F.2d 1490

Cox, Circuit Judge: Seymour and Jeffrey Shapiro, unsecured creditors, objected to the bankruptcy court's authorization for the Chapter 11 debtors to "cross- collateralize" their pre-petition debt with unencumbered property from the bankruptcy estate. The bankruptcy court overruled the objection and also refused to grant a stay of its order pending appeal. The Shapiros appealed to the district court, which dismissed the case as moot under section 364(e) of the Bankruptcy Code because the Shapiros had failed to obtain a stay. We conclude that this appeal is not moot and that cross-collateralization is not authorized under the Bankruptcy Code. Accordingly, we reverse and remand.

I. Facts and Procedural History

Saybrook Manufacturing Co., Inc., and related companies (the "debtors"), initiated proceedings seeking relief under Chapter 11 of the Bankruptcy Code on December 22, 1988. On December 23, 1988, the debtors filed a motion for the use of cash collateral and for authorization to incur secured debt. The bankruptcy court entered an emergency financing order that same day. At the time the bankruptcy petition was filed, the debtors owed Manufacturers Hanover approximately $34 million. The value of the collateral for this debt, however, was less than $10 million. Pursuant to the order, Manufacturers Hanover agreed to lend the debtors an additional $3 million to facilitate their reorganization. In exchange, Manufacturers Hanover received a security interest in all of the debtors' property--both property owned prior to filing the bankruptcy petition and that which was acquired subsequently. This security interest not only protected the $3 million of post-petition credit but also secured Manufacturers Hanover's $34 million pre-petition debt.

This arrangement enhanced Manufacturers Hanover's position vis-a-vis other unsecured creditors, such as the Shapiros, in the event of liquidation. Because Manufacturers Hanover's pre-petition debt was undersecured by approximately $24 million, it originally would have shared in a pro rata distribution of the debtors' unencumbered assets along with the other unsecured creditors. Under the financing order, however, Manufacturers Hanover's pre-petition debt became fully secured by all of the debtors' assets. If the bankruptcy estate were liquidated, Manufacturers Hanover's entire debt--$34 million pre-petition and $3 million post-petition--would have to be paid in full before any funds could be distributed to the remaining unsecured creditors.

Securing pre-petition debt with pre- and post-petition collateral as part of a post-petition financing arrangement is known as cross- collateralization. The Second Circuit aptly defined cross-collateralization as follows:

> [I]n return for making new loans to a debtor in possession under Chapter XI, a financing institution obtains a security interest on all assets of the debtor, both those existing at the date of the order and those created in the course of the Chapter XI proceeding, not only for the new loans, the propriety of which is not contested, but [also] for existing indebtedness to it.

Otte v. Manufacturers Hanover Commercial Corp. (In re Texlon Corp.), 596 F.2d 1092, 1094 (2d Cir.1979).

Because the Second Circuit was the first appellate court to describe this practice in In re Texlon, it is sometimes referred to as Texlon -type cross-collateralization. Another form of cross-collateralization involves securing post-petition debt with pre-petition collateral. This form of non-Texlon-type cross-collateralization is not at issue in this appeal. The Shapiros challenge only the cross- collateralization of the lenders' pre-petition debt, not the propriety of collateralizing the post-petition debt.

The Shapiros filed a number of objections to the bankruptcy court's order on January 13, 1989. After a hearing, the bankruptcy court overruled the objections. The Shapiros then filed a notice of appeal and a request for the bankruptcy court to stay its financing order pending appeal. The bankruptcy court denied the request for a stay on February 23, 1989.

The Shapiros subsequently moved the district court to stay the bankruptcy court's financing order pending appeal; the court denied the motion on March 7, 1989. On May 20, 1989, the district court dismissed the Shapiros' appeal as moot under 11 U.S.C. §364(e) because the Shapiros had failed to obtain a stay of the financing order pending appeal, rejecting the argument that cross-collateralization is contrary to the Code. The Shapiros then appealed to this court.

II. Issues on Appeal

1. Whether the appeal to the district court and the appeal to this court are moot under section 364(e) of the Bankruptcy Code because the Shapiros failed to obtain a stay of the bankruptcy court's financing order.

2. Whether cross-collateralization is authorized under the Bankruptcy Code.

III. Contentions of the Parties

The lenders argue that this appeal is moot under section 364(e) of the Bankruptcy Code. That section provides that a lien or priority granted under section 364 may not be overturned unless it is stayed pending appeal. Even if this appeal were not moot, the Shapiros are not entitled to relief. Cross-collateralization is a legitimate means for debtors to obtain necessary financing and is not prohibited by the Bankruptcy Code.

The Shapiros contend that their appeal is not moot. Because cross-collateralization is not authorized under bankruptcy law, section 364(e) is inapplicable. Permitting cross-collateralization would undermine the entire structure of the Bankruptcy Code by allowing one unsecured creditor to gain priority over all other unsecured creditors simply by extending additional credit to a debtor.

IV. Standard of Review

Conclusions of law by the bankruptcy and district courts are reviewed de novo.

V. Discussion
A. Mootness

We begin by addressing the lenders' claim that this appeal is moot under section 364(e) of the Bankruptcy Code. Section 364(e) provides that:

> The reversal or modification on appeal of an authorization under this section to obtain credit or incur debt, or of a grant under this section of a priority or a lien, does not affect the validity of any debt so incurred, or any priority or lien so granted, to an entity that extended such credit in good faith, whether or not such entity knew of the pendency of the appeal, unless such authorization and the incurring of such debt, or the granting of such priority or lien, were stayed pending appeal.

11 U.S.C. §364(e). The purpose of this provision is to encourage the extension of credit to debtors in bankruptcy by eliminating the risk that any lien securing the loan will be modified on appeal.

* * *

B. Cross-Collateralization and Section 364

Cross-collateralization is an extremely controversial form of Chapter 11 financing. Nevertheless, the practice has been approved by several bankruptcy courts. * * *

The issue of whether the Bankruptcy Code authorizes cross-collateralization is a question of first impression in this court. Indeed, it is essentially a question of first impression before any court of appeals. Neither the lenders' brief nor our own research has produced a single appellate decision which either authorizes or prohibits the practice.
* * *

The Second Circuit expressed criticism of cross-collateralization in In re Texlon. The court, however, stopped short of prohibiting the practice altogether. At issue was the bankruptcy court's ex parte financing order granting the lender a security interest in the debtor's property to secure both pre-petition and post-petition debt. The court, in an exercise of judicial restraint, concluded that:

> In order to decide this case we are not obliged, however, to say that under no conceivable circumstances could "cross-collateralization" be authorized. Here it suffices to hold that ... a financing scheme so contrary to the spirit of the Bankruptcy Act should not have been granted by an ex parte order, where the bankruptcy court relies solely on representations by a debtor in possession that credit essential to the maintenance of operations is not otherwise obtainable.

In re Texlon, 596 F.2d at 1098. Although In re Texlon was decided under the earlier Bankruptcy Act, the court also considered whether cross-collateralization was authorized under the Bankruptcy Code. "To such limited extent as it is proper to consider the new Bankruptcy Act, which takes effect on October 1, 1979, in considering the validity of an order made in 1974, we see nothing in §364(c) or in other provisions of that section that advances the case in favor of 'cross-collateralization.' " In re Texlon, 596 F.2d at 1098 (citations omitted).

Cross-collateralization is not specifically mentioned in the Bankruptcy Code. We conclude that cross-collateralization is inconsistent with bankruptcy law for two reasons. First, cross-collateralization is not authorized as a method of post- petition financing under section 364. Second, cross-collateralization is beyond the scope of the bankruptcy court's inherent equitable power because it is directly contrary to the fundamental priority scheme of the Bankruptcy Code. Section 364 authorizes Chapter 11 debtors to obtain secured credit and incur secured debt as part of their reorganization. It provides, in relevant part, that:

> (c) If the trustee is unable to obtain unsecured credit allowable under section 503(b)(1) of this title as an administrative expense, the court, after notice and a hearing, may authorize the obtaining of credit or the incurring of debt --

> (1) with priority over any or all administrative expenses of the kind specified in section 503(b) or 507(b) of this title;
> (2) secured by a lien on property of the estate that is not otherwise subject to a lien; or
> (3) secured by a junior lien on property of the estate that is subject to a lien.

(d)(1) The court, after notice and a hearing, may authorize the obtaining of credit or incurring of debt secured by a senior or equal lien on property of the estate that is subject to a lien only if--

> (A) the trustee is unable to obtain such credit otherwise; and
>
> (B) there is adequate protection of the interest of the holder of the lien on the property of the estate on which such senior or equal lien is proposed to be granted.
>
> (2) In any hearing under this subsection, the trustee has the burden of proof on the issue of adequate protection.

11 U.S.C. §364(c) & (d) (emphasis added). By their express terms, sections 364(c) & (d) apply only to future--i.e., post-petition--extensions of credit. They do not authorize the granting of liens to secure pre-petition loans.
  * * *

Given that cross-collateralization is not authorized by section 364, we now turn to the lenders' argument that bankruptcy courts may permit the practice under their general equitable power. Bankruptcy courts are indeed courts of equity, 11 U.S.C. §105(a), and they have the power to adjust claims to avoid injustice or unfairness. Pepper v. Litton, 308 U.S. 295, 60 S.Ct. 238, 84 L.Ed. 281 (1939). This equitable power, however, is not unlimited.

> [T]he bankruptcy court has the ability to deviate from the rules of priority and distribution set forth in the Code in the interest of justice and equity. The Court cannot use this flexibility, however, merely to establish a ranking of priorities within priorities. Furthermore, absent the existence of some type of inequitable conduct on the part of the claimant, which results in injury to the creditors of the bankrupt or an unfair advantage to the claimant, the court cannot subordinate a claim to claims within the same class.

In re FCX, Inc., 60 B.R. 405, 409 (E.D.N.C.1986) (citations omitted).

Section 507 of the Bankruptcy Code fixes the priority order of claims and expenses against the bankruptcy estate. 11 U.S.C. §507. Creditors within a given class are to be treated equally, and bankruptcy courts may not create their own rules of superpriority within a single class. Cross-collateralization, however, does exactly that. As a result of this practice, post-petition lenders' unsecured pre-petition claims are given priority over all other unsecured pre-petition claims. * * *

    * * * We disagree with the district court's conclusion that, while cross-collateralization may violate some policies of bankruptcy law, it is consistent with the general purpose of Chapter 11 to help businesses reorganize and become profitable. Rehabilitation is certainly the primary purpose of Chapter 11. This end, however, does not justify the use of any means. Cross-collateralization is directly inconsistent with the priority scheme of the Bankruptcy Code. Accordingly, the practice may not be approved by the bankruptcy court under its equitable authority.

VI. Conclusion

    Cross-collateralization is not authorized by section 364. Section 364(e), therefore, is not applicable and this appeal is not moot. Because Texlon -type cross-collateralization is not explicitly authorized by the Bankruptcy Code and is contrary to the basic priority structure of the Code, we hold that it is an impermissible means of obtaining post-petition financing. The judgment of the district court is REVERSED and the case is REMANDED for proceedings not inconsistent with this opinion.

    REVERSED and REMANDED.

Notes and Problems

1.   In *Saybrook*, the Eleventh Circuit relied on and quoted from Professor Charles Tabb's article, *A Critical Reappraisal of Cross Collateralization in Bankruptcy*, 60 S. CAL. L. REV. 109 (1986).

2.   What is cross collateralization? N is willing to provide debtor in possession financing to D secured by a lien on all of D's inventory, prepetition and postpetition. Is N seeking crosscollateralization? Will a bankruptcy court in the Eleventh Circuit approve this debtor in possession financing?

3.   D pays its employees on the first and fifteenth of each month. D files a Chapter 11 petition on the fourteenth.. After *Saybrook*, will a bankruptcy court in the Eleventh Circuit permit D postpetition to pay its employees for the work they did prepetition? See *Gulf Air*, infra.

b. Using and Selling Encumbered Property

    Most of the property of a business that files for Chapter 11 relief will be encumbered by liens. To operate its business in Chapter 11, the debtor obviously needs to use and even sell this property. The lienor also has obvious needs. Section 363 balances the needs of the debtor and the lienors.

Under section 363, the trustee (and hence a Chapter 11 debtor in possession) has general authority to use and sell property of the estate, including encumbered property. Section 363 also sets out limits on the use and sale of such property. If a transaction is not within the ordinary course of business, the debtor can act only after notice and a hearing, section 363(b)(1). Regardless of whether a sale is in the ordinary course of business, a party with a lien on the property to be used or sold can insist that its interest be adequately protected, section 363(e), and can bid in its lien at such a sale unless the court orders otherwise, section 363(k).

Encumbered property can be sold free and clear of liens if the sale complies with section 363(f). Section 363(f) is considered below in *Terrace Chalet.*

In re Terrace Chalet Apartments, Ltd.
United States District Court, N.D. Illinois, E.D., 1993
159 B.R. 821

Alesia, District Judge. On June 16, 1993, the Appellants, Franz and Ilse Scherer, appealed to this court to challenge a bankruptcy court's order authorizing the sale of an asset in which the Scherers have a security interest. The Scherers argue the bankruptcy court erred because it did not condition the sale upon compliance with state foreclosure law. In the alternative, they argue the bankruptcy order violates Section 363(f) of the Bankruptcy Code. *** For the reasons set forth in this opinion, the bankruptcy order is remanded for further consideration consistent with this decision.

I. STATEMENT OF FACTS

This appeal is taken from the order entered by the bankruptcy court on April 9, 1993 (the "Order") in the Chapter 11 proceedings of Terrace Chalet Apartments, Ltd. ("Terrace Chalet"). The Order allows for the auction of Terrace Chalet's sole asset, a 180-unit apartment complex known as Camelot Arms.

In October 1984, Terrace Chalet purchased Camelot Arms for $4,250,000 from the Scherers. The Scherers loaned Terrace Chalet $1,050,000 and secured the loan by taking a second mortgage against the property. The Appellee, the Federal National Mortgage Association ("Fannie Mae") holds the first mortgage against the property. After defaulting on both of these mortgages, Terrace Chalet filed for Chapter 11 reorganization on August 13, 1992. As debtor-in-possession, Terrace Chalet is the bankruptcy trustee.

In January of 1993, Fannie Mae moved the bankruptcy court to lift the automatic stay and to allow Fannie Mae to foreclose on its mortgage; Fannie Mae contended its interest in the Camelot Arms was not adequately protected. In February of 1993, the bankruptcy court began to conduct hearings on the issue. At the March 4th hearing, Terrace Chalet and Fannie Mae advised the court they had successfully negotiated a settlement agreement the previous night. The court therefore adjourned the hearings on adequate protection.

According to the proposed agreement, Fannie Mae would attempt to sell its interest in Camelot Arms to a third party for $4,200,000. If Fannie Mae was unable to consummate such a purchase before February 14, 1994, Terrace Chalet would sell the property at a public auction on March 7, 1994 pursuant to Section 363(b) of the Bankruptcy Code.

The proposed settlement agreement further provided that the sale of Camelot Arms at the auction would extinguish the Scherers' security interest. The Scherers filed written objections with the bankruptcy court, and the bankruptcy court heard oral arguments regarding the settlement agreement. The court decided the sale did not violate Section 363(f) and adopted the settlement agreement as a bankruptcy order.

II. DISCUSSION

Whether a Sale Under Section 363 Must Comply With State Foreclosure Law

The Scherers argue that the bankruptcy court erred by failing to condition the trustee's sale of Camelot Arms upon compliance with the procedural requirements of Wisconsin foreclosure law. However, the Bankruptcy Rules--not state law--provide the procedural requirements with which a bankruptcy trustee must comply. The Rules expressly provide that the trustee need only give 20 days notice to sell property pursuant to Section 363(b). FED.R.BANKR.P. 2002(a)(2). The Rules further provide that such a sale may be private or by public auction. FED.R.BANKR.P. 6004(f)(1). Because the United States Supreme Court has established these requirements, it is specious for the Scherers to argue that a trustee must comply with the requirements of Wisconsin foreclosure law. * * *

Whether the Trustee Can Sell the Camelot Arms Pursuant to Section 363(f)(3)

A sale which extinguishes a lien may proceed under Section 363(f)(3) if the proceeds from the sale of the asset exceed "the aggregate value of all liens" on the property. 11 U.S.C. §363(f)(3). The federal courts are sharply divided as to the meaning of the term "value of all liens." Some courts follow the decision of In re Beker Industries Corp., 63 B.R. 474, 477 (Bankr.S.D.N.Y.1986), and hold that "value of all liens" means the actual economic value of the lien. Consequently, these courts hold that Section 363(f)(3) protects only the secured party's equity in the security interest. Thus, if the trustee demonstrates the security interest has no actual value, s/he can sell the secured property free and clear of the security interest.

Other courts, however, hold that "value of all liens" means the face amount of the lien. Under this view, Section 363(f)(3) protects the entire amount of the secured debt. Thus, the trustee cannot sell the property free and clear of the liens unless the sale proceeds will exceed the amount of the secured debt on the property. Under this interpretation, the sale of Camelot Arms may not extinguish the Scherers' security interest unless it produces enough proceeds to fully compensate the Scherers.

    * * *

In discussing Section 363(f), the House and Senate Reports stress that "[t]he trustee may sell free and clear if ... the sale price of the property is greater than the amount secured by the lien." H.R.REP. NO. 95-595, 95th Cong., 1st Sess. 345 (1977); S.REP.NO. 95-989, 95th Cong., 2d Sess. 56 (1978). These reports expressly provide that Congress intended Section 363(f) to protect the amount of secured debt, not the actual economic value of the lien.

    The Bankruptcy Amendments of 1984 further demonstrate that Section 363(f) does not protect merely the actual value of the lien. Previously, Section 363(f)(3) authorized a sale free and clear of liens if the sale proceeds exceeded the value of the "interests" of secured parties in the property. Bankruptcy Amendments and Federal Judgeship Act of 1984, Pub.L. No. 98-353, 98 Stat. 372. In 1984, Congress amended Section 363(f)(3) to authorize a sale if the proceeds exceeded the value of "all liens on the property." Id. When Congress intends to denote the concept of "actual value" in the Bankruptcy Code, it consistently refers to the value of the secured party's interest. E.g., 11 U.S.C. §361 (using the phrase "the interest of an entity in property" to express the concept of actual value); 11 U.S.C. §506(a) (using the phrase "value of such creditor's interest" to denote actual value); 11 U.S.C. §1129(a)(7)(B) (using the phrase "value of such holder's interest" to express actual value). Congress deleted the language of Section 363(f)(3) that courts have consistently interpreted as denoting actual value. This deletion suggests that Congress intended for Section 363(f)(3) to protect other than actual value.

    * * *   The courts that have adopted the interpretation espoused in Beker rely upon the "interplay of [Sections] 506(a) and 363(f)(3)." Beker, 63 B.R. at 476. Section 506(a) defines the amount of a secured creditor's claim as the actual economic value of the security interest. 11 U.S.C. §506(a). The courts reason that because the term "value" in Section 506(a) denotes actual value, this term must mean actual value in Section 363(f). However, to express the concept of actual value, Section 506(a) discusses the "value of such creditor's interest." 11 U.S.C. §506(a) (emphasis added). Section 363(f)(3) discusses the value of the liens. As discussed above, because Congress chose to delete the language in Section 363(f)(3) that was similar to that found in Section 506(a), Congress intended that the "actual value" concept of Section 506(a) would not carry over to Section 363(f)(3).

    * * * Section 363(f) authorizes a sale free and clear of a lien if one of the five exceptions applies. 11 U.S.C. §363(f)(1)-(5). However, if a court interprets Section 363(f)(3) as protecting only actual value, then Section 363(f)(5) becomes superfluous. * * *

Moreover, even if this court would agree with the Beker line of decisions, the holdings of these cases would not apply to the instant case. The instant case involves the sale of the estate's sole asset. The courts that have permitted a sale free of a secured party's interest have expressly cautioned that such authorization may be inappropriate when the contemplated sale involves the estate's only asset. Beker, 63 B.R. at 477 (noting that a court's power to authorize a sale means "little as to its exercise, particularly in the case of a major asset"). Therefore, because Terrace Chalet wishes to sell its only asset, the Beker line of decisions would not disturb this court's conclusion.

* * *

Whether Section 363(f)(4) Authorizes the Sale of Camelot Arms Free and Clear of the Scherers' Interest

A trustee can sell estate property free and clear of a lien if the lien is in bona fide dispute. 11 U.S.C. §363(f)(4). * * * Fannie Mae argues that because it disputes the validity of the Scherers' mortgage, then Terrace Chalet, the trustee, can sell the property free of the mortgage. The case law does not delineate precisely when a dispute between two creditors will constitute a bona fide dispute and consequently allow the trustee to sell the property free and clear of the lien pursuant to Section 363(f)(4).

* * *

It would be nonsensical for a court to allow the trustee to sell property pursuant to 363(f)(4) when the trustee believes the secured party's interest to be valid. However, the bankruptcy court in the instant case authorized the sale pursuant to Section 363(f)(3) and consequently, did not explicitly rule on the applicability of Section 363(f)(4). Therefore, it is appropriate to remand this case so that the bankruptcy court can decide whether (1) the trustee Terrace Chalet can sell the property free of the Scherers' lien because Fannie Mae disputes the validity of the Scherers' interest and if so, (2) whether Fannie Mae's dispute with the Scherers is bona fide.

Whether the Sale Free and Clear of the Scherers' Lien Can Be Authorized under Section 363(f)(5)

Finally, the Appellees urge that the sale will extinguish the Scherers' lien because the Scherers "could be compelled, in a legal or equitable proceeding, to accept a money satisfaction of such interest." 11 U.S.C. §363(f)(5). The federal courts have espoused two interpretations of Section 363(f)(5). Some courts interpret this provision as meaning that the trustee must pay the full amount of the secured party's lien, unless "equitable considerations" will justify lien extinguishment upon realization of less than the full amount of the secured debt. Other courts authorize the sale and consequent lien extinguishment if the creditor could be crammed down pursuant to Section 1129(b)(2). This court adopts the latter interpretation.

First, the clear statutory language suggests a Section 1129(b)(2) cram down. Section 363(f)(5) permits a sale free and clear of a lien if the creditor could be "compelled" to accept a monetary satisfaction of the claim. 11 U.S.C. §363(f)(5).

BANKRUPTCY LAW   Pt. 2

In a cram down, a creditor is compelled to accept monetary satisfaction of her claim and the consequent extinguishment of her lien.

Further, the decisions that require full satisfaction absent a showing of equitable consideration fail to capture the essence of Section 363(f)(5). As discussed supra, Section 363(f)(3) addresses how much a trustee must pay a secured creditor to extinguish the lien. Section 363(f)(5) would repeat Section 363(f)(3) if it were interpreted merely to require a specific amount of money that the trustee could pay in order to sell the property free and clear of a lien. By its express terms, Section 363(f)(5) permits lien extinguishment if the trustee can demonstrate the existence of another legal mechanism by which a lien could be extinguished without full satisfaction of the secured debt. Section 1129(b)(2) cram down is such a provision. Therefore, this court holds that Terrace Chalet can sell Camelot Arms free of the Scherers' lien if it demonstrates it can cram down the Scherers pursuant to Section 1129(b)(2).

As discussed above, a trustee must demonstrate good faith to effectuate a cram down. It is important to emphasize the good faith requirement. In the instant case, Terrace Chalet filed for reorganization. Although reorganizing, it seeks to sell the sole asset of the estate and to accomplish this sale by extinguishing the Scherers' lien. Because the estate will no longer contain any property, it is not clear how Terrace Chalet intends to reorganize or to make a good faith effort to remunerate the Scherers. Because (1) Terrace Chalet's reorganization seems problematic and (2) the proposed sale contemplates the sale of the estate's sole asset (3) at the expense of a secured party's lien, the bankruptcy court must carefully consider whether Terrace Chalet is acting in good faith. The parties in the instant case have not argued the issue, and this court is unprepared to hold that Terrace Chalet cannot demonstrate good faith. Therefore, this case is remanded so the bankruptcy court may determine whether Terrace Chalet can satisfy the requirements of Section 1129(b)(2) and consequently, permit Terrace Chalet to sell Camelot Arms free and clear of the Scherers' lien pursuant to Section 363(f)(5).

III. CONCLUSION

For the reasons set forth above, the bankruptcy court's April 9, 1993 order is vacated and this case is remanded for further consideration consistent with this opinion.

Notes and Problems

1. The Scherers hold a second lien on the apartment complex. Why did the Scherers incur the costs of litigating and appealing the sale of the apartment complex free and clear of liens? How would the Scherers benefit from a judicial determination that the apartment complex could not be sold free and clear of liens?

2.　In interpreting section 363(f)(3), the Court expressed concern about section 363(f)(5) becoming "superfluous." Does the Court's interpretation of section 363(f)(5) render section 363(f)(3) superfluous?

3.　The apartment complex was the debtor's sole asset. As the Court indicates in dicta, courts sometimes treat single asset real estate Chapter 11 cases different from other Chapter 11 cases. This book treats single asset real estate Chapter 11 cases separately in Unit 16.

4.　Why would a debtor use Chapter 11 to sell all of its assets? Are there any limitations on such a use of Chapter 11? See sections 363(b), 1123(b)(4) and the following objection to a sale of substantially all of the assets of LTV Aerospace and Defense Company.

UNITED STATES BANKRUPTCY COURT
SOUTHERN DISTRICT OF NEW YORK

In re CHATEAUGAY CORPORATION, REOMAR INC., THE LTV CORPORATION, et al., *Debtors.*	) In Proceedings For A) Reorganization Under) Chapter 11))) Case Nos. 86 B 11270 (BRL)) Through 86 B 11334 (BRL)) Inclusive 86 B 11402 (BRL)) and 86 B 11464 (BRL))
In re THE LTV CORPORATION, LTV AEROSPACE AND DEFENSE COMPANY, VOUGHT INDUSTRIES, INC. and VOUGHT INTERNATIONAL, INC., *Debtors*	) Case Nos. 86 B 11272 (BRL)) 86 B 11276 (BRL)) 86 B 11329 (BRL)) 86 B 11330 (BRL)))))) RETURN DATE: April 1, 1992) 10:00 a.m.)

OBJECTION OF THE AEROSPACE COMMITTEE TO THE DEBTOR'S APPLICATION FOR AN ORDER AUTHORIZING AND APPROVING TRANSFER OF SUBSTANTIALLY ALL THE ASSETS RELATING TO THE BUSINESS OF LTV AEROSPACE AND DEFENSE COMPANY

The Official Committee of Unsecured Creditors of LTV Aerospace and Defense Company (the "Aerospace Committee"), by and through its attorneys, Wilmer, Cutler & Pickering, submits this objection to the Application of The LTV Corporation ("LTV"), LTV Aerospace and Defense Company ("Aerospace"), Vought Industries, Inc. ("Industries") and Vought International, Inc. ("International") (collectively the "Debtors") for an Order Authorizing and Approving Transfer of Substantially All the Assets Relating to the Business of LTV Aerospace and Defense Company, dated March 3, 1992 (the "Application"), and in support thereof, the Aerospace Committee respectfully represents:

INTRODUCTION

1. The proposed transfer of substantially all of the assets of the missiles and aircraft businesses of Aerospace, Industries and International (collectively the "Transferring Debtors") dictates terms of any plan or plans of

reorganization for those estates. In short, it is a plan outside of a plan: If consummated, it would obviate the protections to which creditors are entitled under the plan confirmation process. Moreover, the Debtors have failed to show that the proposed transfer of assets is in the best interests of the Transferring Debtors or their creditors. In fact, the Transferring Debtors and their creditors would be better served by retention of some or all of the assets included in the proposed transfer. Accordingly, the Debtors' Application should be denied.

BACKGROUND

2. On or about July 17, 1986, LTV and 66 of its subsidiary and affiliated companies -- including Aerospace, Industries and International -- filed separate petitions for relief under Chapter 11 of the Bankruptcy Code, 11 U.S.C. 1101 et seq. The Chapter 11 cases have been consolidated and are jointly administered for procedural purposes only; they have not been substantively consolidated i.e., the assets and liabilities of each of the LTV companies remain separate.

3. Aerospace is a wholly-owned subsidiary of LTV. Through its aircraft and missiles divisions, Aerospace is a leading manufacturer of military and commercial aerospace and defense products. Industries and International are wholly-owned subsidiaries of Aerospace; they own certain assets used in connection with the aircraft and missiles businesses.

4. In the more than five and one-half years during which the Transferring Debtors have been in bankruptcy, their creditors have been foreclosed from filing a plan of reorganization. There is currently no plan of reorganization for any of the Transferring Debtors which this Court has held meets the requirements for confirmation under 1129 of the Bankruptcy Code.

5. The Application seeks Court authority for the transfer, outside of a plan of reorganization, of substantially all the assets of the Transferring Debtors to Vought Corporation ("Vought") pursuant to a Transfer Agreement between the Transferring Debtors and Vought dated as of February 25, 1992 (the "Transfer Agreement").

6. A disclosure statement hearing in respect of the Debtors' Modified Joint Plan of Reorganization, filed February 14, 1992, is currently scheduled for April 30, 1992. However, by letter dated March 24, 1992, the Debtors have requested a postponement of such hearing for at least six weeks. Thus, as the Debtors acknowledge, see Debtors'

Mem. at 14-15, there is no realistic possibility that such plan could be confirmed, if at all, for at least several months.

7. The Transfer Agreement provides that as consideration for the Transferring Debtors' assets, Vought will pay $319 million in cash, will assume certain liabilities, and will issue to the Transferring Debtors 36,000 shares of Vought preferred stock (the "Preferred Stock") which, according to the Debtors, will have a value of $36 million. See App. ¶46; Transf. Agmt. §2.06.

8. Section 5.05 of the Transfer Agreement provides that before chapter 11 plans of reorganization have been "substantially consummated" in the cases of each of the Transferring Debtors, neither the Preferred Stock nor any interest therein may be distributed, directly or indirectly, by plan of reorganization or otherwise, to the Transferring Debtors' creditors or stockholders. See App. ¶48; Transf. Agmt. §5.05(b)(i) & (ii). Section 5.05 of the Transfer Agreement further provides that before chapter 11 plans of reorganization have been "substantially consummated" in the cases of each of LTV, LTV Steel and the Transferring Debtors, (a) neither the stock of Aerospace, Industries or International nor any interest therein may be distributed, directly or indirectly, by plan of reorganization or otherwise, to any creditor of the Transferring Debtors and (b) no new stock in any of the Transferring Debtors may be issued. See App. ¶48; Transf. Agmt. 5.05(b)(iii)&(iv).[1]

9. As reflected in the proposed Order Approving Transfer Agreement and Authorizing Transfer of Substantially All of the Assets Relating to the Business of LTV Aerospace and Defense Company (the "Proposed Order"), the effect of the foregoing provisions of Section 5.05 of the Transfer

---

[1]   Section 1101(2) of the Bankruptcy Code defines the "substantial consummation" of a plan of reorganization as

> (A) transfer of all or substantially all of the property proposed by the plan to be transferred;
> (B) assumption by the debtors or by the successor to the debtor under the plan of the business or of the management of all or substantially all of the property dealt with by the plan; and
> (C) commencement of distribution under the Plan

11 U.S.C. 1101(2). Accordingly, the effect of Section 5.05 is that the plan or plans of reorganization for the Transferring Debtors cannot provide for the creditors to receive any of the Preferred Stock or stock in any of the entities receiving the Preferred Stock pursuant to the Transfer Agreement: Aerospace, Industries and International.

Agreement would be to impose severe restrictions on any plan or plans of reorganization governing any of the Transferring Debtors. <u>First</u>, upon the substantial consummation of any such plan, the Transferring Debtor or Debtors must receive the discharge from liability provided for in 1141(d)(1)(A) of the Bankruptcy Code -- which effectively means that such Transferring Debtor or Debtors must "engage in business after the consummation of the plan." 11 U.S.C. 1141(d)(3). <u>Second</u>, any such plan must provide that no creditor can receive or retain any of the following on account of any claim: (a) the Preferred Stock or any rights therein; (b) any rights to the stock or debt of any subsidiary of the Transferring Debtors; or (c) any rights to any stock or debt of the Transferring Debtors, unless (i) all of the Transferring Debtors have merged with LTV or LTV Steel Company, Inc. ("LTV Steel"), (ii) such reorganized entity owns all of the Preferred Stock, and (iii) the value of the Preferred Stock constitutes less than 5% of such reorganized entity's gross assets and creditors hold less than 20% of such reorganized entity's stock on account of claims arising before consummation of a plan for such reorganized entity. <u>See</u> Proposed Order ¶13. If there is a failure to meet any of these conditions, or if, <u>inter alia</u>, LTV's plan of reorganization does not provide for LTV's retention of all the Aerospace stock, the Preferred Stock, which is valued by the Debtors at $36 million, must be forfeited to a tax-exempt charitable organization. <u>See</u> <u>id.</u>

10. Thus, the Transfer Agreement and the Proposed Order present the creditors of Aerospace, Industries and International with a Hobson's Choice: Either they can adopt a plan or plans meeting the foregoing requirements, and thus forego any interest in $36 million of their estates' value in favor of LTV or a reorganized entity in which the creditors can hold no more than a 20% interest; or they can adopt a plan or plans of reorganization failing to meet the foregoing requirements, and thus forego any interest in $36 million of their estates' value in favor of a tax-exempt charity. Worse still, the Debtors seek to impose this "choice" upon the creditors without having provided them with advance disclosure to that effect, and without having allowed them to cast their votes against it.

11. From the perspective of the creditors of the Transferring Debtors' estates, the consideration for the proposed transfer of assets is <u>not</u> $355 million; it is only $319 million. Pursuant to the terms of the Transfer Agreement and the Proposed Order, the other $36 million in value would be held either in an entity in which the Aerospace creditors are expressly precluded from having an equity interest or,

if LTV can reorganize, an entity in which the creditors are precluded from having any more than a 20% equity interest.[1]

12. At best, then, the Debtors seek this Court's imprimatur on a transaction that would effectively violate the absolute priority rule, see 11 U.S.C. 1129(b)(2)(B)[2] by reserving at least 80% (and most likely more) of $36 million in value of the Transferring Debtors' assets for the benefit of Aerospace's stockholder (i.e., LTV) when there is no assurance (and indeed, it is highly unlikely) that the creditors will be paid in full.

13. Moreover, the Debtors have failed to provide any evidence demonstrating that the proposed transfer of substantially all the assets of the Transferring Debtors at this time and on the terms set forth in the Transfer Agreement is in the best interests of the creditors of the Transferring Debtors. The transaction contemplated by the Transfer Agreement would not yield the highest and best value for the assets.

14. The Aerospace Committee submits that the Transferring Debtors and their creditors would be better served by a retention of some or all of the assets that are covered by the Transfer Agreement.

ARGUMENT

I.   THE RESTRICTIONS ON THE USE AND TRANSFER OF THE PRE-
       FERRED STOCK DICTATE TERMS OF A PLAN OF REORGANIZATION
       AND CANNOT BE APPROVED AS PART OF A 363(b) TRANSFER OF
       ASSETS.

A 363(b) transfer of assets outside the ordinary course of business cannot short-circuit the plan confirmation process by dictating terms for future plans of

---

[1]   Under the Debtors' Modified Joint Plan of Reorganization, the creditors of the Transferring Debtors would receive approximately 11% of the equity of a reorganized LTV.

[2]   Section 1129(b)(2)(B) provides, in pertinent part, that

>   the condition that a plan be fair and equitable with respect
>   to a class [of unsecured claims] . . . require[s that] (i)
>   the plan provide[] that each holder of a claim of such class
>   receive or retain on account of such claim property of a
>   value, as of the effective date of the plan, equal to the
>   allowed amount of such claim; or (ii) the holder of any
>   interest that is junior to the claims of such class . . .
>   not receive or retain under the plan on account of such
>   junior claim or interest any property."

11 U.S.C. 1129(b)(2)(B).

reorganization. The proposed transfer of assets here at issue would do just that. Accordingly, the Debtors' Application should be denied.

In <u>In re Braniff Airways. Inc.</u>, 700 F.2d 935 (5th Cir.
1983), the debtor proposed a sale of assets to Pacific
Southwest Airlines ("PSA") for, among other consideration,
travel scrip for travel on PSA airplanes. The proposed sale
required, however, that the scrip only be used in a future
Braniff reorganization and that it be issued only to former
Braniff employees or shareholders or, in a limited amount,
to unsecured creditors. The Court held that these restrictions were beyond the scope of 363(b). The Court found that
the proposed transaction

> not only changed the composition of Braniff's assets,
> the contemplated result under 363(b), it also had the
> practical effect of dictating some of the terms of any
> future reorganization plan. The reorganization plan
> would have to allocate the scrip according to the
> terms of the PSA agreement or forfeit a valuable as-
> set. The debtor and the Bankruptcy Court should not be
> able to short circuit the requirements of Chapter 11
> for confirmation of a reorganization plan by estab-
> lishing the terms of the plan sub rosa in connection
> with a sale of assets.

<u>Braniff</u>, 700 F.2d at 93940. The <u>Braniff</u> decision has been
followed by this Court, <u>see</u> <u>In re Crowthers McCall Pattern</u>
<u>Inc.</u>, 114 B.R. 877, 883-85 (Bankr. S.D.N.Y. 1990), as well
as numerous other courts.[1]

The restrictions that the Transfer Agreement would impose
on the structure of any plan or plans of reorganization for
the Transferring Debtors mirror those that were before the
court in <u>Braniff</u>. Like the sale agreement in <u>Braniff</u>, the

---

[1]   See. e.g., <u>In re Property Co. of America Joint Venture</u>, 110
B.R. 244, 247 n.6 (Bankr. N.D. Tex. 1990); <u>In re Copy</u> <u>Crafters</u>
<u>Quickprint. Inc.</u>, 92 B.R. 973, 982 (Bankr. N.D.N.Y. 1988) ("Code
363 does not authorize a debtor and the bankruptcy court to short
circuit the requirements of a reorganization plan by establishing
the terms of the plan <u>sub</u> <u>rosa</u> in connection with a proposed
transaction"); <u>In re Fremont Battery</u>, 73 B.R. 277, 279 (Bankr.
N.D. Ohio 1987) ("The bankruptcy court may not circumvent a
chapter 11 reorganization plan by allowing the terms of a plan to
be dictated by the sale of a major asset"); <u>In re Crutcher</u>
<u>Resources Corp.</u>, 72 B.R. 628, 631 (Bankr. N.D. Tex. 1987) ("where
a transaction specifies terms for adopting a reorganization plan,
the Debtor may not bypass 11 U.S.C. 1125, disclosure requirements;
1126, voting requirements; 1129(a)(7) 'best interest of creditors
test;' or 1129(b)(2)tB) absolute priority requirements")).

Transfer Agreement would not only change the composition of the Transferring Debtors' assets; it also would dictate terms of any future reorganization plan or plans. The Transfer Agreement expressly proscribes the Transferring Debtors from consummating a plan of reorganization which gives the creditors any rights to the Preferred Stock, the stock of any subsidiary of the Transferring Debtors or, except in certain circumstances, the stock of any of the Transferring Debtors.[1] The application of <u>Braniff</u> to this case could hardly be plainer.

None of LTV's attempts to distinguish <u>Braniff</u> is persuasive. LTV's contention that the Fifth Circuit subsequently modified <u>Braniff</u> in <u>In re Continental Airlines. Inc.</u>, 780 F.2d 1223 (5th Cir. 1986), <u>see</u> Debtors' Mem. at 23-24, totally misreads that decision. In <u>Continental</u>, the Fifth Circuit confirmed that "363 does not authorize a debtor and the bankruptcy court to short circuit the requirements of a reorganization plan by establishing the terms of a plan <u>sub rosa</u> in connection with a proposed transaction. When a proposed transaction specifies terms for adopting a reorganization plan, the parties and the district court must scale the hurdles erected in Chapter 11." 780 F.2d at 1226 (citations and quotations omitted). The opponents of the proposed transaction in <u>Continental</u> did not contend that it would explicitly dictate terms for a plan of reorganization. Rather, they argued that the transaction could be viewed as part of a "creeping" plan of reorganization.[2] It was in this circumstance that the court in <u>Continental</u> balanced the creditors' concerns over a "creeping" plan of reorganization and the business necessity of the preconfirmation transaction there at issue and held that the objector was required to specify the protections that would be denied if the transaction were effected. Because the Transfer Agreement at issue here does, in contrast to <u>Continental</u>, dictate terms of any plan or plans of reorganization for any of the Transferring Debtors, the <u>Continental</u> balancing test is not applicable here.[3] Moreover, the Aerospace Committee has

---

[1]   In addition, as noted above, the plan or plans must provide for a discharge of the Transferring Debtor or Debtors, meaning that the Transferring Debtors would have to engage in a business after the consummation of their plan or plans of reorganization, even though they would have sold virtually all of their assets.

[2]   The transaction at issue in <u>Continental</u> was a lease of two aircraft. It did not mandate the terms of any future plan or plans of reorganization. In particular, it did not mandate any particular distribution of the estate's assets among various creditors. Accordingly, the district court expressly found that the proposed lease "did not 'dictate the terms of any future plan of reorganization.'" 780 F.2d at 1225.

satisfied the requirements of that balancing test anyway, by specifying certain of the protections that the creditors of the Transferring Debtors would be denied if the Debtors' Application were approved: <u>e.g.</u>, the disclosure requirements, 11 U.S.C. 1125; voting requirements, 11 U.S.C. 1126; the best interest of creditors test, 11 U.S.C. 1129(a)(7); the feasibility requirement, 1129(a)(11); and the absolute priority rule, 11 U.S.C. 1129(b)(2)(B).

LTV errs again in arguing that <u>Braniff</u> is distinguishable because all but a "small portion" of the proceeds of the asset transfer will be available for distribution under an Aerospace plan of reorganization. Debtors' Mem. at 24. The analysis in <u>Braniff</u> did not depend upon the percentage of consideration subject to restriction in future plans of reorganization. Moreover, the Preferred Stock is by any measure a significant portion of the transfer consideration. Assuming, as the Debtors have, that the Preferred Stock would be worth $36 million, it represents more than 10% of the total consideration that would be paid under the Transfer Agreement and over half of the cash distribution LTV proposes to make to the Transferring Debtors' nonpension, unsecured creditors under the Debtor's Modified Joint Plan of Reorganization.

There is no question that the Preferred Stock is a critical element of the consideration that would be received under the Transfer Agreement. And the effect of the Transfer Agreement's imposition of plan restrictions would be to make the Preferred Stock inaccessible to the Transferring Debtors' creditors by requiring that it be given either to LTV, a charity or, if LTV can reorganize, an entity in which the creditors do not have more than a 20% equity interest. Such a "lockup" of estate assets would be contrary to the principles of the absolute priority rule, <u>see</u> 11 U.S.C. 1129(b)(2). The creditors of Aerospace, Industries and International would be forced to renounce their interests in a significant share of their estates' assets when it is virtually certain that they will not be paid in full on their claims. In short, from the creditors' perspective, the consideration to be paid by Vought for the transferred assets would not include the Preferred Stock. The value of the proposed transaction to the creditors of the Transferring Debtors is $319 million rather than $355 million. If the Application were approved, $36 million of the estates' value

---

[1]   Several courts have recognized the continuing vitality of <u>Braniff</u> after <u>Continental</u>. See the cases cited in [earlier] note <u>supra</u>; <u>see also</u> <u>In re Crowthers McCall Pattern, Inc.</u>, 114 B.R. 877, 885 (Bankr. S.D.N.Y. 1990).

would be dissipated without commensurate benefit to the estates' creditors.

The Debtors also erroneously contend that the proposed
transfer of assets would not deprive the Aerospace creditors
of the protections associated with the plan confirmation
process because (1) any other transfer of Aerospace assets
necessarily would be similarly structured, and (2) any plan
of reorganization would provide for the retention of a
"presently undetermined" amount of funds as an operating
reserve. See Debtors' Mem. at 25. The first point ignores
the fundamental tenet of Braniff and it progeny: terms of a
plan of reorganization cannot be dictated outside of the
plan confirmation process. Even assuming that any transfer
of Aerospace assets would necessarily include such "restricted" consideration a premise with which the Aerospace
Committee does not agree[1] -- 363(b) does not provide LTV
with the authority to enter into such a transaction outside
a plan of reorganization. If LTV wishes to enter into the
Transfer Agreement as it is currently structured, it must do
so as part of a plan of reorganization, the confirmation of
which would ensure that creditors have received the full
benefit of the protections accorded to them under the Bankruptcy Code.

The second point is a nonsequitur. In the reorganization
dictated by the terms of the Transfer Agreement and the
Proposed Order, the Transferring Debtors' creditors are
precluded from receiving or retaining any rights whatsoever
in the Preferred Stock. Indeed, they are precluded from receiving stock in Aerospace. In a plan of reorganization that
provided for the retention of working capital, the
Transferring Debtors could as stockholders in the reorganized entity or entities retain an interest in that working
capital. Therefore, the analogy between the Preferred Stock
and working capital is misdrawn.

The Debtors' argument that creditors would retain the
protections accorded to them in the plan confirmation process if the Transfer Agreement were approved is simply
untenable. The Transfer Agreement clearly attempts to dictate terms of a plan of reorganization. And as the Debtors
acknowledge, confirmation of their proposed global plan of
reorganization is not expected, if at all, for a number of
months. See Debtors' Mem. at 14-15. By that time, the

---

[1]   The Debtors provide no support for this contention. The
Aerospace Committee is advised that a transfer of certain of the
Debtors' assets can be effected as a straight sale without adverse
tax consequences. Moreover, the Aerospace Committee submits that
the Transferring Debtors can realize more value by retaining some
or all of their assets rather than disposing of all of them.

Proposed Order, if approved, would have become final, and
the Debtors undoubtedly would argue that the transfer of
assets could not be reviewed as part of the plan confirmation process. They would contend that $36 million in assets
of the Transferring Debtors' estates was beyond the reach of
the Transferring Debtors' creditors -- without having accorded those creditors any of the normal protections of the
plan confirmation process, including the disclosure statement requirements, the voting requirements, the best interests of creditors standard, the feasibility standard, and,
potentially, the cram down requirements.

II.   THE APPLICATION OTHERWISE FAILS TO MEET THE
       CRITERIA FOR A SECTION 363 TRANSFER OF ASSETS.

     Even if the Transfer Agreement did not dictate terms of
any plan or plans of reorganization for the Transferring
Debtors, the proposed transfer nonetheless would fail to
meet the criteria for a 363 transaction.

          A.   The Debtors' Contention that the Transfer "Fits
                Within [the Debtors'] Strategy" of a Global Plan
                of Reorganization Is Misplaced in the Context of
                this Application.

     The Debtors argue that the transfer of assets will "aid
the Debtors' reorganization by refocusing the restructuring
of the Debtors' businesses around those areas [i.e., the
Debtors' steel operations] where the Debtors' [sic] are
likely to be able to compete most effectively after [satis-
faction of pension liabilities and] emergence from chapter
11." Debtors' Mem. at 12-13. But such an argument is misplaced in the context of the Debtors' request for approval
of a 363(b) transfer of assets. It presumes a global reorganization plan embracing LTV and LTV Steel Company, Inc.
("LTV Steel"), as well as the Transferring Debtors and the
creditors of the Transferring Debtors have not had an
opportunity to vote on such a plan.[1] Nor has there been a

---

[1]   The Debtors are careful to say that they believe the proposed
transaction "will aid significantly in the reorganization of the
LTV enterprise as a whole," Debtors' Mem. at 20 not the
reorganization of the Transferring Debtors in particular. The
Transferring Debtors' creditors have never been afforded the
opportunity to pass on a global reorganization, however.
     And of course, in the absence of such a global plan, the
creditors of the Transferring Debtors have absolutely no interest
in a restructuring of the Debtors' operations around the steel
business. They are creditors of Aerospace, Industries and
International not LTV or LTV Steel.

demonstration that such a plan meets the "best interests" test of the Bankruptcy Code. See 11 U.S.C. 1129(a)(7). Moreover, the Debtors have failed to demonstrate to this Court (as they would have to do in connection with the confirmation of a plan of reorganization) that such a plan structure is feasible in accordance with 11 U.S.C. 1129(a)(11). Thus, "the fact that the disposition of Aerospace [may or may not] fit[] within [the Debtors'] strategy" (Debtors' Mem. 14) for that plan structure is simply irrelevant to the Court's assessment of the Application.

The Debtors are asking this Court to commit the creditors to a particular reorganization structure without providing the creditors or this Court with the information necessary to come to an informed opinion on such a plan structure. If the Debtors are going to invoke their as-yet unapproved plan in support of the proposed transfer, the Transferring Debtors' creditors should be afforded the protections of the plan process, including a detailed analysis on the feasibility of such a plan and the opportunity to accept or reject it pursuant to the applicable provisions of the Bankruptcy Code. Absent those protections, the Debtors must demonstrate, independent of any particular reorganization strategy, that the transfer of substantially all of the Transferring Debtors' assets pursuant to the Transfer Agreement would be in the best interests of the Transferring Debtors' creditors. This the Application has failed to do.

        B.   The Debtors Have Failed to Demonstrate that the Transaction Would Be in the Best Interests of the Transferring Debtors' Creditors

Under the controlling precedent in this jurisdiction, a debtor seeking approval pursuant to 363(b) of the Bankruptcy Code for the disposition of substantially all of its assets prior to the confirmation of a plan of reorganization must, at a minimum, demonstrate "some articulated business justification, other than the appeasement of major creditors, for using, selling or leasing property out of the ordinary course of business " In re Lionel Corp., 722 F.2d 1063, 1070 (2d Cir. 1983). This finding must be made from the perspective of what "is best for the estate" from which the assets are proposed to be sold, id. at 1069,[1] and even then, only after a searching, multifactor inquiry. Id. at 1071.

---

[1] See also In re Copy Crafters Quickprint, Inc., 92 Bankr. 973, 983 (Bankr. N.D.N.Y. 1988) (section 363(b) sale of substantially all of debtor's assets can be allowed "if in the best interests of the estate"); Hurley, Chapter 11 Alternative: Section 363 Sale of All of the Debtor's Assets Outside a Plan of Reorganization, 58

One of the factors that <u>Lionel</u> requires a court to consider is "the proportionate value of the asset [to be sold]
to the estate as a whole." <u>Id</u>. In this regard, the Application fails to account for the critical distinction between
this case and <u>Lionel</u>. Here, the Debtors are proposing to
dispose of substantially all the Transferring Debtors' assets. In <u>Lionel</u>, the debtor sought authorization to sell a
stock interest that represented <u>one-third</u> of its consolidated assets.[1]

The <u>Lionel</u> court's directive to consider the proportion
of the debtor's estate to be transferred under 363(b) suggests that a transfer of substantially all of the assets of
a debtor requires a heightened scrutiny of the reasons
proffered by the debtor for the transfer. Thus, in <u>In re Au
Natural Restaurant, Inc.</u>, 63 Bankr. 575 (Bankr. S.D.N.Y.),
Judge Blackshear denied an application for the sale of substantially all of a debtor's assets because, <u>inter</u> <u>alia</u>, the
"debtor's application [was] found to be lacking vis-a-vis
<u>Lionel's</u> proportionality factor, as [the debtor was] at-
tempting to sell all of the assets of the estate . . .
whereas in <u>Lionel</u>, the debtor [was] attempt[ing] to sell
only a portion of its assets." <u>Id</u>. at 580; <u>see</u> <u>also</u> <u>In re
Fremont Battery Company</u>, 73 Bankr. 277, 279 (Bankr. N.D.
Ohio 1987) (proposed sale of substantially all of debtor's
assets denied because, <u>inter</u> <u>alia</u>, "the likelihood of reorganization would dissipate as there would remain no assets
from which a plan could be proposed").

Such heightened scrutiny is needed because the greater
the proportion of assets to be transferred prior to the
confirmation of a plan of reorganization, the greater the
potential infringement on the creditors' and equity security
holders' rights, as conferred by the procedural safeguards
of the confirmation process.[2] Thus, when a sale of

Am. Bankr. L. J. 233, 252 (1984) (section 363(b) sale of
substantially all of debtor's assets can be allowed "[s]o long as
such a sale produces the best possible return for the estate").

[1] The Debtors further fail to take into account the fact that the
Second Circuit <u>denied</u> the debtor's request to enter into the
proposed sale, finding that it was being pursued merely to appease
a single large creditor constituency and that there was no reason
why the sale could not be effected as part of a plan of
reorganization. <u>Lionel</u>, 722 F.2d at 1071-72.

[2] The tension between Chapter 11's safeguards and a 363(b)
transfer of substantially all of a debtor's assets was described
by the Fifth Circuit in <u>Continental</u>, <u>supra</u>, as follows: "The
debtor in a Chapter 11 case cannot use section 363(b) to sidestep
the protection creditors have when it comes time to confirm a plan
of reorganization," for to so allow would render "creditors'
rights under, for example, 11 U.S.C. 1125, 1126, 1129(a)(7) and

substantially all of a debtor's assets is proposed, the "articulated business reason" required by <u>Lionel</u> demands that the Debtors provide, at a minimum, information demonstrating that the current liquidation of the assets will provide the greatest value to the estate.[1] Absent such a showing, the Court cannot find that the proposed sale "is best for the estate." <u>Lionel</u>, 722 F.2d at 1069.

The Debtors, however, provide no evidence -- only the unsupported assertions of counsel -- to support the contention that the Transfer Agreement would maximize the return to the Transferring Debtors' estates. Indeed, it appears that the assertions are merely <u>post</u> <u>hoc</u> rationalizations of LTV's decision to restructure its operations around its steel business. There is no showing that the consideration contemplated by the Transfer Agreement would exceed the value of the Transferring Debtors' business as a going concern or that greater value could not be obtained by dedicating some or all of the future cash to payment of its pensions obligations and other liabilities. The Aerospace Committee submits that the Transferring Debtors and their creditors would be better served by a retention of some or all of the assets that are covered by the Transfer Agreement. Until and unless the Debtors can make a showing to the contrary, the Application should be denied.

1129(b)(2), . . . meaningless." <u>Id</u>. at 1227-28.

[1] As stated by the court in <u>In re Naron & Wagner, Chartered</u>, 88 Bankr. 85 (Bankr. D. Md. 1988), in order for a debtor to sell substantially all of its assets under section 363(b), the debtor is required to provide "appropriate notice [which] should be a functional substitute for the adequate information which would be contained in a disclosure statement concerning the proposed transaction." Id. at 89.

CONCLUSION

For the foregoing reasons, the Aerospace Committee objects to the Debtors' Application for an Order Authorizing and Approving Transfer of Substantially All the Assets Relating to the Business of LTV Aerospace and Defense Company.

Respectfully submitted,

William J. Perlstein

William J. Perlstein (WJP 1073)
Patrick J. Carome (PJC 7218)
Stephen M. Cutler (SMC 3618)
Patrick T. Connors (PTC 1534)
Gregory S. Lane (GSL 0056)
WILMER, CUTLER & PICKERING
2445 M Street, N.W.
Washington, D.C.   200371420
(202) 6636000

Carla E. Craig (CEC 3797)
Steven M. Schwartz (SMS 4216)
Hertzog, Calamari & Gleason
100 Park Avenue
New York, New York   10017
(212) 481g500
*Attorneys for the Aerospace
    Committee*

Dated: March 25, 1992

c. Employees and Unions

A Chapter 11 debtor often can not control the timing of its petition; a debtor which operates as a going concern does not always file for Chapter 11 relief immediately after meeting its payroll. Assume, for example, that D files on Thursday and its employees are due to receive their monthly paychecks the next day. Can D still pay the employees for their prepetition work? Can D continue to operate unless it pay the employees?

In re Gulf Air, Inc.
United States Bankruptcy Court, W.D. Louisiana, 1989
112 B.R. 152

ORDER WITH REASONS AUTHORIZING PAYMENT OF EMPLOYEE-RELATED PRE-PETITION CLAIMS

W. Donald Boe, Jr., Bankruptcy Judge. Gulf Air, Inc. ("Debtor") filed a Chapter 11 petition on December 8, 1989 when it was unable to meet its payroll. This charter air carrier has approximately 550 employees including staff personnel, maintenance personnel, pilots, flight engineers, and flight attendants. These employees are located at various points in the United States including New Iberia, New York City, Los Angeles, Chicago, Boston and Philadelphia. Several days ago, charter escrow funds for completed flights were freed up by Court order, which provides financial wherewithal, though limited, to continue operations.

The Debtor today filed a motion to pay certain pre-petition employee-related expenses. That original motion has for all practical purposes been superseded by an Amended and Supplemental Motion for Authority to Pay Certain Pre-Petition Claims ("the Motion"), which was filed later today, and which is the subject of this Order.

The Motion seeks Court authorization to pay all pre-petition amounts due to salaried employees, hourly employees, and flight crew members, including actual and necessary expenses incurred in the performance of their duties, and flight hours pay, "rig time", and per diem expenses that supplement the base salary owed to flight crew members. The Motion also seeks authorization for payment of pre-petition health and life insurance premiums for employees and their dependents, and workers' compensation premiums. The Motion urges that, without immediate payment, many of the Debtor's skilled employees will abandon their employment, and that immediate payment is essential to reorganization efforts. The Court agrees.

Gulf Air's employees have not received salary or wages for three weeks. The Court finds that, under the particular circumstances of this case, notice and hearing is impractical, because the Court must act immediately to safeguard against loss of going-concern values. See 11 U.S.C. Sec. 102(1).

While pre-petition claims are normally disposed of in a plan of reorganization and in accordance with statutory priorities, there are well-established "necessity of payment" and similar exceptions. These exceptions emerged in 19th Century railroad bankruptcies and have continued to date.

The "necessity of payment" doctrine has been applied in nonrailroad bankruptcies.

* * *

The Court finds and concludes that grant of the Debtor's Motion in its entirety is in the best interest of creditors, the Debtor, and its employees, and is "necessary", in fact, indispensable at this time for any successful reorganization. An air carrier, no less than a rail carrier, is more than the sum of its parts. Despite the capital-intensive nature of the railroad industry, and to a lesser extent, the airline industry, retention of skills, organization, and reputation for performance must be considered valuable assets contributing to going concern value and aiding rehabilitation where that is possible.

ACCORDINGLY, IT IS HEREBY ORDERED that the Motion Requesting Authorization to Pay Pre-Petition Claims of Employees, Principal Life Insurance Company, and Kansas City Fire and Marine Insurance Company be, and it hereby is, GRANTED.

IT IS FINALLY ORDERED that the Clerk of the Court shall serve this Order upon the entire mailing matrix.

Notes and Problems

1. See generally Daniel Keating, *The Fruits of Labor: Worker Priorities in Bankruptcy*, 35 Ariz. L. Rev. 905 (1993); Charles Tabb, *Emergency Preferential Orders in Bankruptcy*, 65 Aм. Bankr.L.J. 75 (1991).

2. Is there any policy basis for treating the prepetition claims of employees different from the prepetition claims of suppliers and other unsecured creditors? Is there any statutory basis for treating the prepetition claims of employees differently?

ꙮꙮꙮꙮꙮꙮ

The Bankruptcy Code now treats collective bargaining contracts different from other executory contracts. Recall that section 365 governs the assumption and rejection of executory contracts. Although section 365 requires court approval of a debtor's decision to reject a contract, courts generally defer to the debtor's business judgment when considering a motion to reject an executory contract. The Supreme Court in *NLRB v. Bildisco & Bildisco,* 465 U.S. 513 (1984), held that a collective bargaining agreement was an executory contract that could be rejected without running afoul of the National Labor Relations Act.

Congress then enacted section 1113 in response to the Supreme Court decision in *Bildisco*. Section 1113 provides strict procedural and substantive standards that a debtor must meet in order to reject an executory contract.

In re Maxwell Newspapers, Inc.
United States Court of Appeals, Second Circuit, 1992
981 F.2d 85

Cardamone, Circuit Judge: This appeal is part of the final acts in a drama--whose denouement is unknown--that will determine whether the Daily News, one of New York City's four venerable newspapers, survives. Nearly 20 years ago the typesetters' union, faced with the reality that technological advances necessary for the continued viability of a modern newspaper had made their skilled craft obsolete, consented to automation. In return, the typesetters obtained a guarantee of lifetime employment.

That July 1974 guarantee was provided for in a collective bargaining agreement and assumed by the Daily News, now a debtor in bankruptcy reorganization. It is at the heart of the litigation before us. As a debtor the newspaper is awash in red ink, having lost over $100 million in the past ten years. It has asked the bankruptcy court to modify the labor contract by eliminating the lifetime guarantees given its 167 typesetters. The typographers' union asks us what such guarantees mean, if they are not honored. All but 15 of these employees, under the debtor's proposal, will lose their jobs over time. To this question there is no convincing answer except perhaps that nothing is forever today.

The circumstances confronting the debtor and the printers are like those facing a Navy ship torpedoed at sea. Drastic damage control instituted at the site seals off that portion of the vessel, with a disproportionate loss of those ill-fated to be in that section. These measures are necessary so that the ship and its remaining crew might survive. The present debtor, like the ship, is in danger of foundering, eliminating not only the typesetters' jobs, but also costing the 1850 other employees their livelihoods as well. Modification of the collective bargaining agreement, like naval damage control, is not something good or pleasing to contemplate, but without it this newspaper will sink.

The New York Typographical Union No. 6 (Local No. 6 or union) and Maxwell Newspapers, Inc., doing business as the Daily News (debtor or Maxwell) cross- appeal from an order of the United States District Court for the Southern District of New York (McKenna, J.), which affirmed in part and reversed in part an order of the Southern District Bankruptcy Court (Brozman, J.). Maxwell is the debtor in a bankruptcy proceeding where a buyer of the newspaper is sought, and Mortimer Zuckerman is the prospective buyer. After filing these appeals on December 10, 1992, the parties moved to consolidate and expedite them so that they could be heard and decided before December 31, 1992 when the issues, if still unresolved, will be rendered moot. On Tuesday, December 15 the motion to consolidate and expedite was granted and the appeals were heard on Thursday, December 17, 1992.

BACKGROUND
A. Overview of Negotiations

This procedurally complex case arises from the effort by the debtor Maxwell to find a buyer for the Daily News with sufficient resources to satisfy not only its creditors and its employees, but also to modernize the Daily News' printing plant so that it can compete in the New York metropolitan market. In September 1992 Mortimer Zuckerman--through his affiliate New DN Company--entered negotiations with the Daily News to buy its assets. These negotiations included a so-called "stand-alone plan of reorganization" that was conditioned on union support. One crucial component of the plan was concessions by Local No. 6 with respect to the July 28, 1974 collective bargaining agreement that guaranteed the printers lifetime employment.

On October 1, 1992 the debtor, in tandem with Zuckerman, proposed to the union that the collective bargaining agreement be modified to eliminate: (1) any obligation of Maxwell to require the purchaser of the assets of the Daily News to employ any member of the union, (2) any obligation of Maxwell to continue to employ any member of the union if Maxwell ceases publication or ceases publication and sells the Daily News pursuant to the bankruptcy proceeding, and (3) any obligation to arbitrate any controversy regarding these matters. Maxwell also provided documentation of the impact of the union's collective bargaining agreement on the financial stability of the Daily News and asserted that it had sought in vain prospective purchasers who would honor the labor agreement.

The union made a counter-proposal on October 14 in which it expressed a willingness to forego the lifetime job guarantees. The union proposed a progressive reduction in the number of shifts worked conditioned upon a cash buyout for each union member, three years' contribution to the pension and welfare funds, and an early retirement enhancement. The parties bargained in terms of shifts rather than jobs. Five shifts per week equals one full-time job; 200 shifts equal 40 full-time jobs. The full-time jobs of the 167 members of Local No. 6 are represented by 835 shifts. The progressive reduction proposed by the union began with an immediate reduction from 835 shifts to 540, then to 425 in 1996, to 300 in 1999, and to 200 in 2002. Translated into jobs that is 108, 85, 60 and finally 40. The initial cut to 540 shifts was designed to induce union members age 62 or older to retire. Although not acceptable to the debtor, Maxwell found this a constructive approach.

The next day, October 15, Maxwell responded with a proposal that hastened the reduction in shifts. The debtor's proposed modification contemplated an immediate cut to 400, a reduction to 300 once a proposed new color printing plant was operational, and then in one year intervals reductions to 250, to 200, and finally to 150. Translated into jobs that is 80, 60, 50, 40 and finally 30. Maxwell's proposal did not provide for any cash buyout or payment to the pension and welfare funds, but it offered an early retirement subsidy that would take the form of adding five years to the age at retirement and five years to the working time at the Daily News (referred to as 5 + 5). On October 19, the union made a counter-proposal that stood firm on the first shift reduction remaining at 540 (or 108 jobs) but accelerated the dates and times of all later reductions down to 200 shifts (40 jobs). It agreed tentatively to Maxwell and Zuckerman's "5 + 5" proposal. It did not address the other changes, awaiting resolution of differences on guaranteed shifts, buyouts, and the publisher's jurisdiction over work assignments.

Negotiations continued on October 21 when the union revised its October 19 offer by dropping the buyout, increasing the "5 + 5" retirement enhancements to 6 years, that is "6 + 6," adding a $10,000 cash payment to retiring employees, and lowering the first shift reduction from 540 to 500 (from 108 to 100 jobs) and the second to 350 (70 jobs). The union also demanded a guarantee that remaining employees would receive at least four shifts per week, but then retreated from this demand in the face of Zuckerman's strong opposition.

Late in the evening of that same day, Zuckerman delivered a final proposal reacting to the union's revised offer. Zuckerman's offer reduced the guaranteed shifts immediately to 400 (80 positions), to 300 (60 jobs) when the new printing plant opened, to 150 (30 jobs) one year later, and to 75 (15 jobs) a year after that. These remaining 15 jobs would be guaranteed for the remainder of the 13 year contract. Zuckerman withdrew his "5 + 5" proposal and did not propose any other continued payments to the pension and welfare fund. He did agree to make one immediate contribution of $1 million, which equals 18 months of continuing coverage.

At oral argument before us it was conceded that the total value of the package offered by Zuckerman to Local No. 6 amounts to approximately $30 million, and that Zuckerman has now reinstated its earlier "5 + 5" offer.

B. Prior Judicial Proceedings

These negotiations between the union, the Daily News, and Zuckerman broke down when the union rejected Zuckerman's final offer to modify the collective bargaining agreement. Zuckerman's final offer came on the eve of an October 22, 1992 hearing in bankruptcy court to consider the debtor's motion to reject Local No. 6's contract and to consider whether the sale to Zuckerman should be approved. The bankruptcy court on October 27, 28 and 29, 1992 issued four orders that are the subject of the cross-appeals before us. It (1) granted Maxwell's motion pursuant to 11 U.S.C. §1113 to reject the union's collective bargaining agreement (rejection order); (2) approved the sale of certain assets that comprise the Daily News as an ongoing business to New DN Company pursuant to 11 U.S.C. §363 (sale order); (3) denied the union's motion under 11 U.S.C. §1104(b) for appointment of an examiner (examiner order); and (4) dismissed as moot the union's adversary proceeding to compel arbitration (adversary dismissal order).

The union appealed these four orders to the district court, which on December 3, 1992 affirmed the sale order, the examiner order, and the adversary dismissal order. It reversed the bankruptcy court's rejection order on the ground that under §1113(c)(2) the union had "good cause" to reject Zuckerman's final offer. The district court held therefore that the Daily News had not satisfied those requirements of the Bankruptcy Code necessary to empower a bankruptcy judge to approve rejection of a collective bargaining agreement. The debtor appeals from this order.

DISCUSSION
I. 11 U.S.C. §1113

* * *

Section 1113 of the Bankruptcy Code "controls the rejection of collective bargaining agreements in Chapter 11 proceedings." The statute put in place "safeguards designed to insure that employers did not use Chapter 11 as medicine to rid themselves of corporate indigestion." Employers may only propose "those necessary modifications in the employees benefits and protections that are necessary to permit" the effective reorganization of the debtor. §1113(b)(1)(A). A debtor may sell the assets of the business unencumbered by a collective bargaining agreement if that agreement has been rejected pursuant to §1113. This statute requires unions to face those changed circumstances that occur when a company becomes insolvent, and it requires all affected parties to compromise in the face of financial hardship. At the same time, §1113 also imposes requirements on the debtor to prevent it from using bankruptcy as a judicial hammer to break the union. Rejection of a collective bargaining agreement is permitted only if the debtor fulfills the requirements of §1113(b)(1), the union fails to reject the debtor's proposal with good cause, and the balance of the equities clearly favors rejection. §1113(c)(1)- (3).

Most importantly, the statute imposes the obligation on the parties to negotiate in good faith. This obligation is properly analyzed under §1113(c)(2), which permits rejection of a labor agreement only when the union has rejected the debtor's proposal without good cause. The district court believed the bankruptcy court's view of "good cause" under §1113(c)(2) was too narrow. The bankruptcy court had held that a union would have good cause to refuse an employer's proposal only in two cases: where its members are "unfairly burdened relative to the other parties," and where the employer's "proposal is not necessary for the debtor's reorganization." This interpretation, as the district court noted, makes the "good cause " requirement of §1113(c)(2) depend entirely upon the satisfaction of the requirements of §1113(b)(1)(A), which are incorporated into the rejection standard at §1113(c)(1). This renders "good cause" surplusage because it would add nothing to the existing substantive requirements of §1113(c)(1) of the statute.

The district court reasoned, in addition, that the statute covers not only the contents of an employer's proposed modification of a labor contract, but also how the offer is made. It ruled because the offer was made on October 21--on the eve of the bankruptcy hearing--and on a take-it-or-leave-it basis, the union had no meaningful opportunity to consider and make a counter- proposal.

II. Section 1113 Applied

We turn to apply §1113 to the instant facts. Here, although the bankruptcy court perhaps took a too narrow view of §1113(c)(2), its findings of fact under that section were not clearly erroneous. Prompted by the bankruptcy judge's view of the statute, the district court ruled that the bankruptcy court's findings of fact also were erroneous. In this conclusion, the district court erred.

What "good cause" means is difficult to answer in the abstract apart from the moorings of a given case. A more constructive and perhaps more answerable inquiry is why this term is in the statute. We think good cause serves as an incentive to the debtor trying to have its labor contract modified to propose in good faith only those changes necessary to its successful reorganization, while protecting it from the union's refusal to accept the changes without a good reason.

To that end, the entire thrust of §1113 is to ensure that well-informed and good faith negotiations occur in the market place, not as part of the judicial process. Reorganization procedures are designed to encourage such a negotiated voluntary modification. Knowing that it cannot turn down an employer's proposal without good cause gives the union an incentive to compromise on modifications of the collective bargaining agreement, so as to prevent its complete rejection. Because the employer has the burden of proving its proposals are necessary, the union is protected from an employer whose proposals may be offered in bad faith.

Thus, for example, a union will not have good cause to reject an employer's proposal that contains only those modifications essential for the debtor's reorganization, that is, the union's refusal to accept it will be held to be without good cause. On the other hand, as we have noted, where the union makes compromise proposals during the negotiating process that meet its needs while preserving the debtor's savings, its rejection of the debtor's proposal would be with good cause.

Whether or not the bankruptcy court may have misstated the good cause rule, its findings clearly were not wrong. For example, it found the debtor measures its workforce by calculating "full time equivalents" (FTEs) derived from dividing payroll expenses by five, which is the number of days in a week worked by a full-time employee. The bankruptcy judge further found that from September 1990 to August 1992, FTEs for debtor's employees declined as follows: for managers 58 percent, guild members 34 percent, drivers 46 percent, pressmen 47 percent, mailers 45 percent, paperhandlers 54 percent, machinists and electricians 21 percent, engravers and stereotypers 27 percent. In stark contrast, the Local 6 typographers workforce declined only 13 percent, and these employees are by far the highest hourly paid employees of the debtor. No other employees or unions suffered so small an FTE cut as Local No. 6.

Moreover, unsecured creditors, the court observed, are estimated to obtain only 13 to 18 cents on the dollar and the value of stockholders' equity is nearly worthless. Yet, the bankruptcy judge declared, the union did not offer an alternative that focused on the needs of its employer's reorganization, but instead adhered to its position that Local 6's excess employees had to be given an incentive to induce them to leave. Neither the debtor or purchaser could fund this demand.

We reverse the district court's ruling not only on the contents of the rejection order but also concerning the manner in which Zuckerman made his final offer to the union. First, Local No. 6 did not complain that it had too little time to respond to the employer's proposal made on October 21. In addition, parties to collective bargaining agreements routinely negotiate for many hours under imperative deadlines. In that negotiating universe, ten hours is ample time to consider and respond to a proposal. Consequently, the bankruptcy court correctly concluded that Local No. 6 rejected the employer's proposal without good cause.

III. Other Issues

Local No. 6 appeals from the three orders of the bankruptcy court affirmed by the district court, that is, the sale order, examiner order, and adversary dismissal order. The union raises several issues, none of which have merit. It contends that the debtor has not shown that a collective bargaining agreement may be rejected to serve the interests of a purchaser of assets. The two lower courts believed that 11 U.S.C. §1113 applied to this transaction because what is to emerge, if the sale is consummated, is the Daily News reorganized as an ongoing business. We agree.

The union also contends that the order approving the sale and finding Zuckerman a good faith purchaser was in error. Section 363 of the Bankruptcy Code provides that a debtor-in-possession may, among other actions, "sell" property of the estate, after notice and a hearing. 11 U.S.C. §363(b)(1) (1988). In the case at hand, the business reasons for the sale were uncontested, only the purchaser's good faith was put in issue. The bankruptcy court held an in camera hearing on this subject. It authorized the creditors' committee to conduct a confidential examination to determine whether allegations of improprieties in the form of bonuses or other payments to the pressmen's and drivers' unions were well founded. The modest wage increase to the pressmen was effected in the normal process of negotiating a new collective bargaining agreement. There were no payments made or promised to be made outside those contained within the four corners of the final collective bargaining agreement, which the creditors' committee examined.

The drivers' union received a first-year bonus based on improvements in returns of newspapers, a matter largely under the drivers' control. The lack of returns results in significant losses annually to the Daily News. In subsequent years, there will be additional bonuses for each percentage of improvement for returns. After consulting labor counsel the committee concluded this kind of payment is proper under a labor contract. Here, too, there were no payments outside the collective bargaining agreement. The creditors' committee therefore supported the sale to Zuckerman because it was assured of the integrity of the sale process. After reading the transcript of this investigation, we are satisfied--as was the bankruptcy court--that the purchaser has acted in good faith in pursuing its offer to buy the Daily News.

The other orders the union appealed from were either well within the bankruptcy court's "broad administrative power", In re Lionel Corp., 722 F.2d 1063, 1069 (2d Cir.1983); accord, In re Chateaugay Corp., 973 F.2d 141, 144 (2d Cir.1992), were fully supported by findings not clearly erroneous, or are now moot.

CONCLUSION

Having ruled in debtor's favor, we hasten to add that our judgment is conditioned on the continuation of offers recently negotiated between the parties, represented to us in open court at the time of the oral argument, which include the offer of 5 + 5. That is, those offers the debtor made to the union that were on the bargaining table as of December 17, 1992 are not now to be withdrawn.

The judgment appealed from is reversed as to the rejection order, conditioned upon terms consistent with this opinion, and otherwise affirmed.

Notes and Problems

1. See generally Carlos Cuevas, *Necessary Modifications and Section 1113 of the Bankruptcy Code: A Search for the Substantive Standard for Modification of a Collective Bargaining Agreement in a Corporate Reorganization*, 64 Am. Bankr.L.J. 133 (1990); Daniel Keating, *The Continuing Puzzle of Collective Bargaining Agreements in Bankruptcy*, 35 Wm. & Mary L. Rev. 503 (1994)

2. The Second Circuit required the Debtor to hold its last offer open as a condition to rejection. What is the statutory basis for this requirement? Do you agree with the following argument by the Debtor's attorneys: "A sophisticated union will adopt the strategy of negotiating with the debtor without actually agreeing to anything. At best, it will convince the bankruptcy court that the rejection is unwarranted because the debtor has failed to establish one or more of the requirements of section 1113. At worst, it will be left with the debtor's last proposal, with no risk that the last proposal will be withdrawn and less favorable terms imposed after rejection. " See Marc Kirschner, Willis Goldsmith, Lawrence Gottesman, Dwena Jenab, & Jay Swardenski, *Tossing the Coin Under Section 1113: Heads or Tails, the Union Wins*, 23 Seton Hall L. Rev. 1516 (1993).

3. Plan Formulation And Filing

a. Who Can File a Chapter 11 Plan?

Unless modified by court order, section 1121(a) of the Bankruptcy Code affords a Chapter 11 debtor the exclusive right to file a plan of reorganization for the first 120 days after the order of relief. If a plan is filed within this period, the Code further provides the Chapter 11 debtor with the exclusive opportunity to solicit acceptances of its plan by impaired classes for 180 days from the order of relief.

Under section 1121(c), however, any other "party in interest" has the right to file a plan if any of the following occurs: (i) a trustee is appointed or (ii) the debtor has not filed a plan of reorganization within the exclusive period or (iii) the debtor has not filed a plan that has been accepted by all classes of impaired claims and interests within 180 days of the order of relief. The 120 and 180 days periods in section 1121 may be either increased or decreased by the bankruptcy court upon a showing of "cause" to justify the adjustment.

The argument most often advanced by debtors seeking an extension of exclusivity is that the case is large and complex. Bankruptcy courts routinely extend exclusivity on this argument.

UNITED STATES BANKRUPTCY COURT
SOUTHERN DISTRICT OF FLORIDA
WEST PALM BEACH DIVISION

CHAPTER 11
CASE NO. 91-31884-BKC-RAM

In re

PIPER AIRCRAFT CORPORATION,

                    Debtor.

_____/

JOINT MOTION OF PIPER AIRCRAFT CORPORATION AND THE OFFICIAL COMMITTEE OF UNSECURED CREDITORS PURSUANT TO SECTIONS 1121(d) and 1125 BANKRUPTCY CODE FOR EXTENSION OF EXCLUSIVE PERIOD FOR THE DEBTOR, THE COMMITTEE AND TELEDYNE INDUSTRIES, INC. TO FILE PLANS OF REORGANIZATION AND OBTAIN ACCEPTANCES

Piper Aircraft Corporation, the above-referenced debtor and debtor-in-possession (the "Debtor") and the Official Committee of Unsecured Creditors (the "Committee"), hereby move jointly for entry of an order of this Court pursuant to sections 1121(d) and 1125 of title 11 of United States Code (the "Bankruptcy Code") and Rules 2002 and 9014 of the Federal Rules of Bankruptcy Procedure, for an extension of the period during which only the Debtor, the Committee and Teledyne Industries, Inc. ("Teledyne" may file plans or further amended plans of reorganization and obtain the acceptances thereof, as more fully set forth herein below. In support of their motion, the Debtor and the Committee, by their undersigned attorneys, respectfully represent as follows:

Background

1. The Debtor commenced this case by filing a voluntary petition for relief under chapter 11 of the Bankruptcy Code on July 1, 1991 (the "Filing Date"). Since the Filing Date, the Debtor has continued in the possession of its property and the management of its business as a debtor-in-possession under sections 1107 and 1108 of the Bankruptcy Code.

2. This Court has jurisdiction over this matter pursuant to sections 157(b)(2)(A), (L) and (O) and 1334 of title 28 of the United States Code. Venue in this district is proper pursuant to section 1409 of title 28 of the United States Code.

3. In accordance with section 1121 of the Bankruptcy Code, the Debtor, the Committee and Teledyne presently maintain the exclusive right to file plans of reorganization in this case through to August 6, 1993, and until October 6, 1993 to solicit the acceptances of any such plans. The Committee and the Debtor respectfully seek a further extension of the exclusive period in which to file plans of reorganization or amended plans and to solicit the acceptances thereof.

4. The Debtor has sought and obtained prior extensions of the exclusive period.

5. By this motion, the Debtor and the Committee jointly seek a ninety (90) day extension through and including November 6, 1993 of the exclusive period for the filing of a plan or amended plans, and a similar extension through and including January 6, 1994 to solicit acceptances thereof, subject to the limitations set forth herein.

6. Since the Filing Date, the Debtor has diligently prosecuted this case and made significant progress in the formulation of a plan of reorganization. Over the past several months, the Debtor has spent a substantial amount of time negotiating with potential purchasers with a view towards obtaining the sale of substantially all of the Debtor's assets or investments from outside sources. Any such transaction has been viewed as constituting the crux of the Debtor's chapter 11 plan in that the proceeds from a sale or investment would, in large part, fund the Debtor's plan.

7. After months of negotiations with numerous parties including, among others, Pilatus Aircraft Limited ("Pilatus"), a Swiss Corporation engaged in the business of manufacturing, selling and developing turboprop trainer and commuter airplanes, the Debtor executed a letter of intent with Pilatus dated April 8, 1993, as subsequently amended, pursuant to which the Debtor agreed to sell to Pilatus, and Pilatus agreed to purchase from the Debtor, substantially all of the Debtor's assets (the "Pilatus Letter"). Pursuant to the Pilatus Letter, the sale of substantially all of the Debtor's assets (the "Assets") to Pilatus is subject to documentation of a definitive "Acquisition Agreement" and the approval of this Court.

8. On June 22, 1993, the Debtor filed with this Court its chapter 11 plan of reorganization (the "Plan"). The Plan provides for the sale of substantially all of the Debtor's assets to Pilatus under terms of an acquisition agreement to be executed, or to another bidder whose bid is determined by the Court to be the highest and best bid received. Subsequently, on or about July 9, 1993, the Debtor filed with

this Court its First Amended Chapter 11 Plan of Reorganization (the "Amended Plan") and its Disclosure Statement in respect thereof (the "Amended Disclosure Statement"). The Amended Plan contains virtually the same provisions as the original Plan, with minor modifications.

9. To date, the Debtor, its attorneys, accountants and principals have been working closely with the Committee, its attorneys and Prudential Securities Incorporated, the Committee's investment bankers, in order to maximize the value of the Debtor's estate for the benefit of creditors. Accordingly, the Debtor and the Committee seek a further extension of the exclusive period herein for numerous reasons. Among other things, the Debtor and the Committee submit that a further extension of the exclusive period will (i) maintain order in this case; (ii) avoid disruption of the Debtor's business; and (iii) enable the Debtor to expeditiously proceed to confirmation herein.

10. As such, the Debtor and the Committee respectfully request a ninety-day extension of the exclusive period for (a) the Committee and Teledyne to file plans of reorganization; and (b) the Debtor to file a further amended Plan. In addition, the Debtor, the Committee and Teledyne seek a ninety-day extension of time within which to solicit acceptances of any such plans or amended plans filed herein under sections 1121(d) and 1125 of the Bankruptcy Code.

11. The Debtor and the Committee believe that an extension of both the exclusive and solicitation periods will enable the Debtor and the Committee to maintain control over this case during this critical period as the Debtor is rapidly approaching confirmation. An extension of the exclusive period will maintain order in this case and will preserve the progress that has been made to date including, inter alia, the Court's approval of bidding procedures, the selection of Pilatus as "stalking horse" and the Plan process as a whole. The termination of the exclusive and solicitation periods could throw this case into turmoil as the Debtor approaches confirmation. The termination of exclusivity would likely impact the Debtor's operations and the value which could be derived from any auction sale of the Assets to be held at confirmation.

12. As such, the Debtor and the Committee submit that a ninety-day extension of the exclusive and solicitation periods will inure to the benefit of, and will not harm or prejudice, any creditors or parties-in-interest since the Debtor is operating at a monthly profit. Moreover, the Committee and the Debtor believe that a further extension of the exclusive period pending their receipt of bids by interested purchasers will enhance the Debtor's prospects

for a successful reorganization by enabling the Debtor to fully analyze all such proposals.

13. In <u>In re UPI</u>, 60 B.R. 265 (Bankr. D.D.C. 1986), the United States Bankruptcy Court for the District of Columbia held that once a debtor files its chapter 11 plan and seeks an extension of the solicitation period under section 1121(d) of the Bankruptcy Code, any such extension constitutes an extension of the exclusive period within which to file a plan as well. <u>See</u> <u>In re UPI International</u>, 60 B.R. at 265. Notwithstanding, the Debtor and the Committee seek an extension of the exclusive period herein for the Debtor, the Committee and Teledyne to file plans or amended plans of reorganization, and to solicit acceptances thereof.

14. The Debtor knows of no authority except for <u>In re Trainer's Inc.</u>, 17 B.R. 246 (Bankr. E.D. Pa. 1982) and <u>In re Barker Estates, Inc.</u>, 14 B.R. 683 (Bankr. W.D.N.Y. 1981), which hold to the contrary of <u>In re UPI</u>. In <u>Trainer's</u> and <u>Barker Estates</u>, the courts held that the exclusivity period ends automatically if any one of the three conditions contained in section 1121(c) of the Bankruptcy Code are met, and that the debtor must meet both the 120 day and 180 day deadlines (or obtain extensions of both deadlines) in order to prevent anyone else from being permitted to file plans. Those courts also held that an extension of one deadline does not automatically extend the other. Though the Debtor in this case respectfully submits that the holding in <u>In re UPI</u> is more persuasive than those in <u>Trainer's</u> and <u>Barker</u>, the Debtor nevertheless seeks an extension of both the exclusive and solicitation periods herein in an abundance of caution.

15. Ms. Amber Donner, the staff attorney from the Office of the United States Trustee with primary responsibility for this case, has no objection to the relief requested. Teledyne has consented to the relief requested. In seeking this relief, the Debtor agrees that any extensions of the exclusive and solicitation periods be without prejudice to the rights of the Debtor, the Committee or Teledyne to file their own plans or amended plans of reorganization during any such extensions, or to seek further extensions, if necessary, of both such periods.

16. In these circumstances, numerous courts have granted extensions of the exclusive period particularly where a case is large or complex. <u>See</u>, <u>e.g.</u>, <u>In re Texaco, Inc.</u>, 76 B.R. 322 (Bankr. S.D.N.Y. 1987); <u>In re United Press International, Inc.</u>, 60 8.R. 265 (Bankr. D.D.C. 1986). The Debtor and the Committee submit that this case is complex. Accordingly, the Debtor and the Committee submit that the

relief requested herein is reasonable and appropriate under the circumstances.

17. Because most of the parties who are likely to attend any such hearing on this Motion are resident in Miami, the Debtor respectfully submits that it would not be opposed to the scheduling of a hearing on this Motion in Miami, Florida at the Court's earliest convenience.

Conclusion

WHEREFORE the Debtor and the Committee respectfully request that this Court enter an order (i) extending the exclusive period for the Debtor, the Committee and Teledyne to file plans or amended plans of reorganization from August 6, 1993 to and including November 6, 1993; (ii) extending the time to solicit acceptances of such plans from October 6, 1993 through to January 6, 1994; and (iii) granting the Debtor and the Committee such other and further relief as this Court deems just and proper.

Dated: Miami, Florida
        August 3, 1993

KLUGER PERETZ KAPLAN & BERLIN   STROOCK & STROOCK & LAVAN
Attorneys for the Official   Attorneys for Piper Aircraft
Committee of Unsecured   Corporation
Creditors   3300 First Union Financial
1970 Miami Center   Center
201 South Biscayne Boulevard   200 South Biscayne Boulevard
Miami, Florida 33131   Miami, Florida 331312385
Telephone: (305) 3799000   Telephone: (305) 3589900

By: *Deborah Talenfeld*   By: *Brent Friedman*
    Howard J. Berlin   Paul Steven Singerman
    Florida Bar No. 276499   Florida Bar No. 378860
                                      Brent A. Friedman
                                      Florida Bar No. 968838

Notes and Problems

1. Note that the Piper bankruptcy petition was filed on July 1, 1991, and this motion seeks an extension of exclusivity through November, 1993. More than two years of exclusivity. Notice also that the motion provides that "In accordance with section 1121 of the Bankruptcy Code, the Debtor, the Committee and Teledyne presently maintain the exclusive right to file a plan." Where does section 1121 provide for such "shared" exclusivity?

2. Under the order requested by the motion, would it be possible for Piper and the Committee to file separate plans?

b. What Can a Plan Provide?

Section 1123 governs the provisions of a Chapter 11 plan. Section 1123 provides that a Chapter 11 plan may alter not only the rights of unsecured creditors but also the rights of secured creditors, and even shareholders. Section 1123 contemplates that the plan will divide claims into classes; section 1122 governs classification of claims.

Compliance with the requirements of sections 1122 and 1123 is not the most difficult part of preparing a Chapter 11 plan. Rather, the hardest questions are how much will creditors be offered by the plan and how will the plan be effectuated.

The plan proponent's answers to these two questions are shaped not only by the various requirements of the Bankruptcy Code but also by the resources and needs of the debtor and the bargaining power and objectives of the creditors. While each Chapter 11 plan is different, Judge John Pearson, a Kansas bankruptcy judge, has suggested that most Chapter 11 plans will fit into one of more of the eight categories listed below:

1. composition and/or extension of payments to creditors;
2. issuance of long-term debt instruments to satisfy creditors;
3. cash-out of creditors;
4. debt-for-equity swap;
5. surrender of assets in satisfaction of debt;
6. spin-off of assets for creditors;
7. creation of a new entity and distribution of assets thereto;
8. liquidation of assets.

See generally John Pearson, DRAFTING REORGANIZATION PLANS ch. 8 (1992)

4. Creditor Acceptance Process

The late Professor MacLachlan described a business reorganization under the bankruptcy laws as a "composition in bankruptcy." James .MacLachlan, BANKRUPTCY 371 (1956). More recently, a prominent New York bankruptcy lawyer, Ron Trost, wrote that "Reorganization plans are essentially contracts between the debtor and its creditors." J. Ronald Trost, *Business Reorganizations Under Chapter 11 of the New Bankruptcy Code*, 34 BUS.LAW. 1309, 1327 (1979). A Chapter 11 plan is similar to a composition, similar to a contract, in that it will be necessary to obtain consent from at least some creditors.

a. Disclosure

While Chapter 11 does not require that all creditors consent to the plan, it contemplates that creditors will receive "adequate information" about the plan and have the opportunity to vote on the plan. According to legislative history, "The premise underlying . . . Chapter 11 . . . is the same as the premise of the securities laws. If adequate disclosure is provided to all creditors and stockholders whose rights are to be affected, then they should be able to make an informed judgment of their own, rather than having the court of the Securities and Exchange Commission inform them in advance whether the proposed plan is a good plan." H.R. 95-595, p. 226. Accordingly, a bankruptcy court does not review a plan before it is submitted to creditors and stockholders for vote. Instead, the bankruptcy court reviews the adequacy of the information about the plan provided to creditors and stockholders.

Section 1125(b) requires the creditors and stockholders be provided with "a written disclosure statement approved after notice and hearing by the court as containing adequate information." "Adequate information" is defined in section 1125(a). Although courts acknowledge that what constitutes "adequate information" varies from case to case, several courts have developed checklists such as the following nineteen points from *In re Jeppson*, 66 B.R. 269 (Bankr. Utah 1986):

- The circumstances that gave rise to the filing of the bankruptcy petition.
- A complete description of the available assets and their value.
- The anticipated future of the debtor.
- The source of the information provided in the disclosure statement.
- A disclaimer.
- The condition and performance of the debtor while in Chapter 11.
- Information on claims against the estate.
- The estimated return that creditors would receive under Chapter 7.
- The accounting and valuation methods used in the disclosure statement.
- Information regarding the future management of the debtor.
- A summary of the plan of reorganization.
- An estimate of all administrative expenses, including attorneys' fees and accountants' fees.
- The collectibility of any accounts receivable.

- Any financial information, valuations or pro forma projections that would be relevant to creditors' determinations of whether to accept or reject the plan.
- Information relevant to the risks being taken by the creditors and interest holders.
- The actual or projected value that can be obtained from voidable transfers.
- The existence, likelihood and possible success of non-bankruptcy litigation.
- Any tax consequence of the plan.
- The relationship of the debtor with affiliates.

Another bankruptcy judge recently prepared a different list -- a list of the causes of delay and expense in Chapter 11. He included disclosure statements on the list, stating: "The process of preparing a disclosure statement and then dealing with the objections and the hearing is an expensive and time consuming process. It is especially troubling in those circumstances in which the creditor objects to the disclosure statement in a strategic effort to improve its treatment under the plan. Regardless, the process can adversely impact the debtor in two ways. First, it can result in substantial fees for attorneys and accountants. Second, it can result in a substantial diversion of the management time from the debtor's business and the reorganization process. . . . The suspicion is that in the average small to medium size chapter 11 case. the time and money spent on his process is largely wasted because creditors are not interested in all of the disclosures that are presently required and thus they do not read the disclosure statement. See Honorable Steven Rhodes, *Eight Statutory Causes of Delay and Expense in Chapter 11 Bankruptcy Cases,* 67 AM BANKR.L.J. 287, 316-17 (1993)

Questions

1. D, a public company, files a Chapter 11 petition shortly after filing its annual 10K with the Securities and Exchange Commission. Can it use its 10K as its disclosure statement?

2. S, a secured creditor of D, files a liquidation plan in D's bankruptcy case. Does S have to file a disclosure statement? If so, how does S obtain the information required by section 1125(a)?

3. D files a plan and disclosure statement in its Chapter 11 case, and the court approves the disclosure statement. The creditors' committee is opposed to the plan and wants to send material to creditors urging them to vote against the plan. Should

the creditors' committee submit any such material to the bankruptcy court for approval?

b. Voting

According to section 1126(a), creditors with claims "allowed under section 502" and shareholders with interests "allowed under section 502" vote on Chapter 11 plans.

The statutory requirement of "allowed under section 502" is often satisfied by the Bankruptcy Code's "double-deeming." In a Chapter 11 case, section 1111 deems filed a claim or interest that is scheduled and is not shown as disputed, contingent or unliquidated. And, under section 502, a claim that is filed is deemed allowed unless objected to by a party in interest.

Section 1126(c) and section 1126(d) deal with the questions of how many creditors and how many shareholders must accept the plan. Please read these provisions. Note that section 1126 focuses on classes of claims and classes of interests. Section 1126 does not require that each member of a class of claims or interests accept a Chapter 11 plan. Under section 1126(c), a class of claims has accepted a plan when a majority in number and two thirds in amount of those actually voting on the plan accept the plan. Under section 1126(d), a class of interests has accepted a plan when two-thirds in amount of those actually voting on the plan accept the plan.

Statutory "deeming" eliminates voting by two classes of claims or interests. First, if a class is to receive nothing under the plan, it is deemed to have rejected the plan, and its vote need not be solicited, section 1126(g). Second, if a class is not "impaired" under the plan, the class is deemed to have accepted the plan and again its vote need not be solicited, section 1126(f).

The concept of "impairment" is unique to Chapter 11. Section 1124 indicates when a class is not "impaired under a plan." A class of claims or a class of interests is impaired under the plan unless one of the three numbered paragraphs of section 1124 is satisfied. Please read section 1124. The *Jones* case below illustrates the application of section 1124.

In re Jones
United States Bankruptcy Court, District of Utah, 1983
32 B.R. 951

Glen E. Clark, Bankruptcy Judge. The issue in this case is whether cure and compensation payments under §1124(2) may be made in deferred cash payments commencing after the effective date of a chapter 11 plan. The ruling is that they may not.

Introduction

Debtors' chapter 11 plan places two allowed secured claims into separate classes, designated B-2 and B-3. The obligation underlying each claim is in default. The plan intends to cure the defaults and leave these two classes unimpaired by complying with Section 1124(2).

Section 1124(2) provides for curing defaults and leaving classes unimpaired under a chapter 11 plan. A class of claims or interests is not impaired even though there has been a default which, under a current or applicable law, triggers the right to demand or receive accelerated payment if, with respect to each holder of a claim or interest of that class, the plan

(A) cures any such default, other than a default of a kind specified in section 365(b)(2) of this title, that occurred before or after the commencement of the case under [title 11];

(B) reinstates the maturity of such claim or interest as such maturity date existed before such default;

(C) compensates the holder of such claim or interest for any damages incurred as a result of any reasonable reliance by such holder on such contractual provision or applicable law; and

(D) does not otherwise alter the legal, equitable, or contractual rights to which such claim or interest entitles the holder of such claim or interest.

Debtors plan to pay the money required to cure and compensate for defaults under subsections (A) and (C) by making monthly cash installment payments commencing thirty days after the effective date of the plan. Class B-2 will receive about $1,436.00 in approximately eighteen and one-half monthly payments of $85.00. Class B-3 will receive approximately $7,000.00 in one $5,500.00 payment on the effective date of the plan and the balance in monthly payments of $50.00. Debtors propose to add 12 percent annual interest to the unpaid cure and compensation amounts.

At the confirmation hearing, the court questioned whether the cure and compensation payments specified by Section 1124(2) may be made over time after the effective date of the plan even if sufficient interest is added to give present value as of the effective date, or whether those payments must be made on or before the effective date. That issue was taken under advisement and is decided by this memorandum opinion.

Discussion

Debtors advance two arguments. First, debtors claim entitlement to make their cure and compensation payments over time after the effective date of their plan because the language of Section 1124(2) fixes no time limits for cure or compensation, unlike Section 1322(b)(5) which requires cure of defaults "within a reasonable time," unlike Section 365(b)(1)(A) which requires cure or adequate assurance of prompt cure of defaults "at the time of assumption" of a contract or lease, and unlike Section 1124(3) which requires payment of cash "on the effective date of the plan."

Second, debtors contend that classes designated to receive installment payments for cure and compensation of defaults do not need the protections given by Section 1129(b) because, in debtors' view, the only Section 1129(b) issues raised by this plan are the interest rate necessary to give present value and the feasibility of the plan. Debtors say these issues can be determined at confirmation just as easily under Section 1124(2) as under Section 1129(b).

In my judgment, debtors' proposal for installment payments after the effective date of their plan, though well-intentioned and arguably not forbidden by the words of Section 1124(2), impairs classes B-2 and B-3.

The bankruptcy code adopts the concept of "private control [of the reorganization process] with a minimum of judicial intrusion." Chapter 11 is "a vehicle to channel negotiation among the parties."

Courts, debtors, and creditors should approach reorganization in ways that discourage litigation and promote negotiation. Chapter 11 supplies useful tools which, in the hands of enlightened debtors and creditors willing to substitute bargaining for brawling, can remedy otherwise irreparable financial disasters. Two provisions of chapter 11 which were designed to limit litigation are Sections 1124 and 1129.

If all classes of claims and interests accept a chapter 11 plan, the plan's proponent need only satisfy the requirements of Section 1129(b) to secure confirmation of the plan. But if any class is impaired under and has not accepted the plan, the plan's proponent must also prove that the plan meets the specifications of Section 1129(b). Section 1129(b) bars confirmation of a plan impairing a class that has not accepted the plan unless "the plan does not discriminate unfairly, and is fair and equitable."

Congress interposed the unfair discrimination and fair and equitable tests as safeguards for dissenting impaired classes. At the same time, however, Congress determined that those protections are not needed and that the burdens and risks of a hearing under Section 1129(b) may be voided for a class not impaired under the plan. Thus, classes left unimpaired by a plan are deemed by Section 1129(f) to have accepted the plan and solicitation of acceptances from holders of claims or interests of those classes is not required.

Debtors, anxious to avoid the perils of a Section 1129(b) hearing, may wish to use Section 1124 to leave unimpaired as many classes as possible. Classes of claims or interests, hoping to have the protection and leverage given by Section 1129(b), may desire to be found impaired under Section 1124.

Debtors may also wish to create unimpaired classes under Section 1124(2) because it enables reversal of contractual or legal acceleration and retention of advantageous contract terms. "Curing of the default and the assumption of the debt in accordance with its terms is an important reorganization technique for dealing with a particular class of claims, especially secured claims."

But creditors who are parties to agreements a debtor wishes to reinstate under Section 1124(2) may argue they are impaired in order to escape a contract with terms favorable to the debtor. Section 1124 and its interpretation therefore occupy a pivotal position.

Barrington Oaks, [15 B.R. 952], offers two approaches to impairment. The first examines the plan in light of the language and purpose of Section 1124 and strictly construes Sections 1124(1) and (2) to find impairment whenever the plan alters rights in any way not expressly permitted by Sections 1124(1) and (2). The second scrutinizes the plan's treatment of the affected classes in light of the protections provided by Section 1129(b) and finds impairment "where necessary to prevent wrongs which are redressable under Section 1129(b)." 15 B.R. at 964. Debtors' plan impairs the two classes designated to receive installment payments of cure and compensation money under either approach.

Impairment Under the First Approach

Classes B-2 and B-3 are impaired under the first approach to impairment of *Barrington Oaks* because the imposition of installment payments to cure and compensate for defaults is an expansion of the permissible alterations intended under Section 1124(2). Debtors' proposal collides, in several particulars, with the intended use and effect of Section 1124. Senate Report 95-989, *supra*, explains Section 1124(2) as follows:

> [A] claim or interest is unimpaired by curing the effect of a default and reinstating the original terms of an obligation when maturity was brought on or accelerated by the default. The intervention of bankruptcy and the defaults represent a temporary crisis which the plan of reorganization is intended to clear away. The holder of a claim or interest who under the plan is restored to his original position, when others receive less or get nothing at all, is fortunate indeed and has no cause to complain.

While it may be argued that Section 1124(2) does not expressly require claim or interest holders to be restored to their original positions by the effective date of the plan, a better interpretation is that "Section 1124(2) requires that the curing of the default occur as of the effective date of the plan because the creditor is impaired until the time the default is cured." Several reasons recommend this interpretation.

Debtors' proposal encourages wasteful litigation over the timing, methods, and effects of cure and compensation under Section 1124(2). The absence of guidelines for the timing of post-effective date payments would multiply litigation. For example, if debtors' proposal for cure and compensation over approximately eighteen months with respect to class B-2 were permissible, what of cure and compensation over twenty-four, thirty-six, or forty-eight months? The court would have no standards by which to decide the issue, causing the proper cure period under Section 1124 to expand and contract without a controlling statutory rationale. Section 1124 is supposed to be a measuring rod for impairment. A measuring rod with inconstant increments, changing between measurements, is useless. Thus, Section 1124 should be strictly construed.

Methods for leaving a class unimpaired under Section 1124 should be exclusive. The non-limiting terms "includes" and "including" do not precede Section 1124's list of options. A class is impaired unless the plan provides one of the three specified alternative treatments. From the outset, parties know that any plan specifying a class as unimpaired must give one of only three treatments. No creativity, with resulting unpredictability, is permitted. Debtors' proposal, if accepted, would broaden the terms "cures" and "compensates" under Sections 1124(2)(A) and (C) and thus create ambiguity and invite disputes.

Section 1124 is meant to be definitive. A class is either impaired or not. There is no middle ground. Section 1124 should establish, as nearly as possible, a bright line test for impairment. "Impairment," explains Norton, "is carefully defined in the Code—an improvement over the Act which failed to furnish any guidelines as to when a claim or interest was materially affected." 3 NORTON BANKRUPTCY LAW AND PRACTICE §62.05 at 8 (1981). The code furnishes "concrete rules *** [and therefore] [t]here should be no difficulty in applying [Section 1124's] standard." Debtors' proposal would cloud the certainty of Section 1124 by requiring the court to inquire into the effects of delay of cure and compensation.

Finally, debtors' proposal encourages litigation over the value of the deferred payments. Section 1124 is designed to be free, for the most part, of disputes over valuation. As explained in *Barrington Oaks, supra* at 962-963, "Value *** is irrelevant under Section 1124; 'any alteration of rights constitutes impairment even if the value of the rights is enhanced.' " Indeed, the purpose of Section 1124 to avoid cramdown would be defeated by requiring valuation of claims to determine impairment. By driving a wedge between the concept of impairment and the vagaries of value, parties may know with greater certainty whether or not they are impaired. This certainty should reduce litigation and aid negotiation toward a plan, the goals which Section 1124 was established to further. The history of the congressional development of Section 1124 illustrates the drafters' "aversion to valuation hearings." Thus, courts should, where possible, construe Section 1124 to eliminate the obscurities of valuation. Debtors' proposal would require the court to value the deferred cash payments. This would necessitate a determination of the appropriate interest rate, a concept which, like value in bankruptcy cases, has proven itself to be "an elusive Pimpernel."

For these reasons Section 1124(2) should be construed to require completion of cure and compensation by the effective date of the plan. While the term "effective date" is subject to interpretation, requiring cure and compensation by the effective date of the plan would minimize litigation over timing, method, and effect of cure and compensation, conform Section 1124(2) to Section 1124(3) which requires payment on the effective date of the plan, and shift litigation over present value to Section 1129(b) where it belongs.

Impairment Under the Second Approach

Debtors' plan impairs classes B-2 and B-3 under the second approach to impairment of *Barrington Oaks*. Because the plan proposes deferred cash payments, both classes need the protection of Section 1129(b). Section 1129(b) was intended to test deferred cash payments. Debtors' plan would permit Section 1124(2)'s use as a cram down device without shielding the affected classes from unfair or inequitable treatment, a use of Section 1124 which was both anticipated and disapproved by the drafters of Section 1124.

Section 1124 was not intended for use as a tool for cram down. An illustration is Section 1124(3)'s requirement of payment in cash.

Conclusions

Classes B-2 and B-3 are impaired under debtors' plan. Cure and compensation required by Section 1124(2) must be completed by the effective date of the plan if impairment is to be avoided. Debtors may treat classes B-2 and B-3 in the same manner proposed in the plan but, if they desire to do so, must amend the plan to specify that classes B-2 and B-3 are impaired and permit them to vote.

Notes and Problems

1. Which of the numbered paragraphs of section 1124 was involved in the *Jones* case?

2. D has filed a Chapter 11 petition. D is insolvent. D's creditors include C. Payment of D's debt to C is guaranteed by G who is also insolvent. D's Chapter 11 plan proposes to substitute Blake Carrington's guarantee for G's. Is C's claim impaired? See section 1124(1).

3. D's Chapter 11 plan creates a separate class, Class 2, for claims of $500 or less. The plan provides that class 2 claims are to be paid in full in cash within 60 days of the confirmation of the Chapter 11 plan. Is Class 2 an impaired class of claims under the Chapter 11 plan? See section 1124(3).

4. One of the ways that a secured creditor will be unimpaired is if its allowed secured claim is paid in full in cash. An understanding of cashing out a secured claim under section 1124(3) requires an understanding of section 1111(b). Section 1111(b) is considered *infra*.

c. Prepackaged Plans

It is possible to obtain acceptance of a Chapter 11 plan from holders of claims (creditors) and from holders of interests (shareholders) before the Chapter 11 petition is filed. Section 1126(b) provides that acceptances solicited prior to the bankruptcy filing may be counted in deciding whether a class of claims or interests has accepted a plan if (i) the acceptances were solicited in compliance with "any applicable nonbankruptcy law, rule or regulation governing the adequacy of disclosure" or (ii) if there was no applicable law, rule or regulation, the acceptances were solicited after disclosure of "adequate information as defined in section 1125(a)(1)."

A Chapter 11 plan that has been negotiated and accepted prior to the filing the bankruptcy petition is now generally referred to as a "prepackaged plan." Prepackaged plans minimize the amount of time that the debtor operates in bankruptcy. The plan has been negotiated and accepted prior to bankruptcy and is filed with the bankruptcy petition. See sections 1126(b), 1121. The most time-consuming tasks of a Chapter 11 case - plan formulation and acceptance - have been completed prior to the bankruptcy filing.

Notes and Problems

1. See generally Marc Kirschner, Dan Kusnetz, Laurence Solarsh & Craig Gatarz, *Prepackaged Bankruptcy Plans: The Deleveraging Tool of the '90's in the Wake of OID and Tax Concerns*, 21 Seton Hall L.J. 643 (1991)

2. Why aren't all Chapter 11 plans prepackaged? What can creditors do to block the negotiation of a prepackaged plan?

d. Selling Claims

Nothing in the Bankruptcy Code addresses the trading of claims. Bankruptcy Rule 3001(e) simply sets forth the procedure required for the transfer of claims.

Increasingly, in Chapter 11 cases of all sizes, the holders of unsecured claims are selling their claims to third parties. Many creditors are eager to sell their claims at a discount rather than wait to collect plan distributions of uncertain amount at an uncertain time.   By selling its claim, a creditor can shift the risk that the debtor's business and its Chapter 11 recovery will decline in Chapter 11 to a party more willing to accept the risk.

The claims buyer may be a "vulture capitalist" who purchases claims at a deep discount from the face amount in the hopes of a larger return when a plan of reorganization is confirmed. Or the claims buyer may be a "corporate raider" who purchases claims in the hopes of gaining control of the bankruptcy case and then control of the debtor. Or, as in *Pleasant Hill Partners* below, the claims buyer may be a prepetition creditor who uses claims trading to block creditor acceptance of a plan.

In re Pleasant Hill Partners
United States Bankruptcy Court, N.D. Georgia, 1994
163 B.R. 388

Margaret H. Murphy, Bankruptcy Judge. This case is before the court on Debtor's Motion to Designate Federal Home Loan Mortgage Corporation Pursuant to 11 U.S.C. §1126(e) (the "Motion to Designate"). * * *

STATEMENT OF FACTS
This is a single-asset real estate case. Debtor's principal asset is an 86-unit apartment complex known as Pleasant Hill Apartments located at 2500 Pleasant Hill Road in Fulton County, Georgia (the "Property"). The Property is secured by a first mortgage in favor of FHLMC executed October 3, 1984 in the original principal amount of $1.2 million. The interest rate is 13.54% with a maturity date of December 1, 1999.
    * * *
On the date the petition was filed, March 2, 1992, the outstanding balance owed to FHLMC was $1,256,006.51. Although the fair market value of the Property has not been established, the parties agree FHLMC is undersecured. The Disclosure Statement sets forth that Debtor obtained an appraisal which showed the fair market value of the Property to be $800,000.

On July 26, 1993, Debtor filed its Second Amended Disclosure Statement and Plan, which was the subject of the hearing scheduled for August 24, 1993. The Disclosure Statement and Plan set forth that Class 1 under the Plan consists of the claim of FHLMC and treats FHLMC's claim as fully secured.

The Plan defines FHLMC's claim to include principal, prepetition interest at the non-default rate, postpetition interest at 7.5% and allowed fees and costs. The monthly payments under the Plan would be interest only. The maturity date remains December 1, 1999. Debtor contemplates sale of the Property or refinancing of the loan on or before the maturity date. Upon the sale or refinancing, FHLMC would receive all the amounts remaining unpaid.

Class 4 under Debtor's plan consists of Debtor's unsecured trade creditors. Debtor shows that it has 18 unsecured creditors whose claims total slightly more than $7,000. The Plan proposes to pay those unsecured creditors 50% of their claims on the effective date of the Plan and 50% sixty days thereafter. The remaining classes in Debtor's Plan are either priority creditors, are unimpaired, or are insiders.

Since the filing of Debtor's petition, FHLMC has purchased 95% in number and 99.6% in amount of the unsecured claims against Debtor. FHLMC contacted the unsecured creditors to offer to purchase their claims for the full amount claimed by the creditor to be owed. FHLMC disclosed that it was a creditor of Debtor with a security interest in the Property. No other disclosures were made: FHLMC did not reveal to the selling creditors that it was buying claims with the intent to block confirmation of Debtor's plan. FHLMC paid the unsecured creditors 100% of their claims. The only unsecured claim which FHLMC has been unable to purchase is a claim for $24; the creditor, without explanation, refused to sell its claim.

FHLMC has announced its intention to cast its Class 1 vote and all the votes for Class 4 against Debtor's plan. As FHLMC has announced its intention to vote its secured claim against Debtor's plan, Debtor may obtain confirmation over FHLMC's rejection only by employing 11 U.S.C. §1129(b), fondly known among bankruptcy practitioners as "cramdown."

In order to effect a cramdown of FHLMC's interests, Debtor must obtain the acceptance of at least one class of non-priority, non-insider, impaired creditors. Pursuant to §1126(c), acceptance by a class requires an affirmative vote by at least two-thirds in dollar amount and more than one-half in number of the allowed claims in a class. FHLMC's purchase of the Class 4 claims, therefore, gives FHLMC control of the acceptance or rejection of Debtor's plan by Class 4, Debtor's only non-priority, non-insider, impaired class. FHLMC has announced that it will cast its votes in Class 4 against the Plan. As a result, if FHLMC is allowed to so vote its Class 4 claims, Debtor will be unable to obtain a consenting class and will be unable to effect a cramdown of FHLMC's interests.

In the Motion to Designate, Debtor asserts the Class 4 votes of FHLMC should be "designated" pursuant to 11 U.S.C. §1125(b) or §1126(e). Pursuant to §1126(c), "designation" of a vote results in that vote not being counted. Debtor, however, requests that, in addition to designating the Class 4 votes of FHLMC, this court should also deem those votes to have been cast in favor of Debtor's plan.

CONCLUSIONS OF LAW

Issues regarding trading claims predate the Bankruptcy Code. During the 1930's, when Congress, the Securities and Exchange Commission and the courts were otherwise addressing trading in securities, trading in claims was also addressed under the Bankruptcy Act. Trading claims was regulated in Chapter X of the Bankruptcy Act with the intent to and for the purpose of protecting the securities-trading public. Trading claims was not regulated, however, in Chapters IX, XI and XII because Congress assumed that trade creditors and bank creditors knew their debtor and needed less protection.

When the Bankruptcy Code was promulgated and Chapter X, XI and XII were combined into the new Chapter 11, no regulation of claims trading was included in the Code or the Bankruptcy Rules. Under the Bankruptcy Code, parties must, therefore, rely primarily upon §§1125(b), 1126(e) and 105, as well as pre-Code law, for the authority of the bankruptcy court to regulate trading claims. As a result of having no clear Congressional mandate regarding trading claims, the case law relating to trading claims is far from well- settled.

SECTION 1125(b)

Debtor contends that FHLMC's purchase of claims constituted an improper solicitation of votes prior to approval of a disclosure statement, in violation of §1125(b), which provides: An acceptance or rejection of a plan may not be solicited after the commencement of the case under this title from a holder of a claim or interest with respect to such claim or interest, unless, at the time of or before such solicitation, there is transmitted to such holder the plan or a summary of the plan, and a written disclosure statement approved, after notice and a hearing, by the court as containing adequate information. Debtor argues that FHLMC's purchase of the unsecured creditors' claims was for the sole purpose of being able to vote those claims and that, therefore, the purchase constitutes the solicitation of a vote against Debtor's plan without proper disclosures.

Debtor cites no case law to support its argument that the purchase of claims may be deemed a §1125 solicitation of votes. Section 1125 "solicitation" is usually construed very narrowly. In the instant case, FHLMC was very careful not to entreat the prospect sellers of unsecured claims to agree to sell in order to assist FHLMC in its plan-blocking maneuver. Apart from simply offering to purchase the claims immediately at full face value, FHLMC used no other stimulus or persuasion to induce the unsecured creditors to sell.

Although not cited by Debtor, however, case law does exist to support a requirement that a purchaser of claims must provide appropriate disclosures to prospective sellers of claims. In the case of In re Revere Copper and Brass, Inc., 58 B.R. 1 (Bankr.S.D.N.Y.1985), Phoenix Capital Corporation sent letters to Debtor's creditors offering to buy their claims for immediate cash equal to 20% of the face value of the claims. Near the time the letters were sent, an article in the Wall Street Journal disclosed that the debtor had announced the outline of its plan of reorganization, which included payment of 65% of the face value of claims to unsecured creditors.

In Revere, Judge Abram concluded that Phoenix Capital's failure to disclose the terms of an announced or filed plan to the prospective sellers of claims permitted the bankruptcy court to withhold approval of the transfers until the selling creditors were provided with such notice, together with 30 days in which to revoke their assignment of claims to Phoenix Capital. One of the evils attendant upon a solicitation of assignment of claims for a cash payment such as is being made by Phoenix is that solicited creditors may be unaware of their rights and options and fall prey to the belief that bankruptcy inevitably will result in their receiving the proverbial 10 cents on the dollar or worse. Similarly, in the case of In re Chateaugay, Case No. 86 B 11270/334, 402 and 464

(Bankr.S.D.N.Y., March 11, 1988), Judge Lifland relied upon a failure of adequate disclosure to withhold approval of an assignment of claims.

Although neither Judge Abram or Judge Lifland cited any case law to support the imposition of a notice requirement upon purchasers of claims, the bankruptcy court's equitable power to impose a notice requirement where none expressly exists in the Code or the Rules may have its genesis in American United Mutual Life Ins. Co. v. City of Avon Park, 311 U.S. 138, 61 S.Ct. 157, 85 L.Ed. 91 (1940).

In the City of Avon Park case, the Supreme Court refused to confirm the city's Chapter IX plan because the city's fiscal agent had solicited votes from bondholders without disclosing that its previous purchases of bonds at 50 percent of their value gave the agent a financial interest in the success of the city's plan. The responsibility of the court entails scrutiny of the circumstances surrounding the acceptances, the special or ulterior motives which may have induced them, the time of acquiring the claims so voting, the amount paid therefor, and the like. Where such investigation discloses the existence of unfair dealing, a breach of fiduciary obligations, profiting from a trust, special benefits for the reorganizers, or the need for protection of investors against an inside few or of one class of investors from the encroachment of another, the court has ample power to adjust the remedy to meet the need. The requirements of full, unequivocal disclosure; the limitation of the vote to the amount paid for the securities; the separate classification of claimants; the complete subordination of some claims, indicate the range and type of the power which a court of bankruptcy may exercise in these proceedings.

In the instant case, Debtor failed to present any indicia of unfair dealing by FHLMC. FHLMC is not seeking to obtain better treatment for itself at the expense of other creditors of the estate. FHLMC paid 100% of the face amount of the claims. FHLMC seeks to gain no competitive advantage over Debtor or any creditor of Debtors. FHLMC sought to purchase all the unsecured claims and achieved that goal except as to a single $24 claim whose holder simply refused to sell. Unlike in the New York cases, the instant case does not involve the purchase and sale of securities. Therefore, no need for more disclosure by FHLMC exists.

SECTION 1126(e)

Debtor also contends FHLMC's votes should be designated because its acquisition of the unsecured claim and its rejection of Debtor's plan is not in good faith. Section 1126(e) provides:

> On request of a party in interest, and after notice and a hearing, the court may designate any entity whose acceptance or rejection of such plan was not in good faith, or was not solicited or procured in good faith or in accordance with the provisions of this title.

The Bankruptcy Code does not define good faith or bad faith. * * *
* * *

In one of the most frequently cited cases involving trading claims, In re Allegheny International, Inc., 118 B.R. 282 (Bankr.W.D.Pa.1990), the court disqualified votes by an investment firm, Japonica Partners, and confirmed the debtor's plan. Japonica was not a prepetition creditor of Debtor but purchased enough claims in two classes to wield a blocking position and to qualify Japonica as a party who could file a competing plan. The two classes in which Japonica purchased claims were "diametrically opposed" in litigation filed by the Creditor's Committee against secured bank lenders. The claims were purchased after approval of the debtor's disclosure statement and balloting had commenced. Japonica presented a competing plan which provided that Japonica would acquire control of the debtor. Neither the debtor's nor Japonica's plan received sufficient affirmative votes for confirmation.

Japonica's purpose was to gain control of the debtor, which the court found to be bad faith. The critical fact which resulted in the court's disqualification of Japonica's votes was that Japonica was a voluntary creditor who purchased claims to give it "unique control over the debtor and the process." Another indicia of Japonica's bad faith was the timing of its purchase and the amounts it paid for the claims. As Japonica approached the attainment of a blocking position, the amount it paid for the claims it purchased increased and then decreased after the critical percentage was reached. Japonica purchased almost exactly the amount required to block the plan.

The court concluded that the facts and circumstances surrounding Japonica's purchase of claims--Japonica's intent to take over the debtor, the timing of the purchases, the amount paid for the claims, Japonica was an "outsider" prior to its purchase of claims, Japonica's use of its veto power to improve its position--established that Japonica's votes were acquired and cast in bad faith and would be disqualified.

In contrast to the holding in Allegheny International is the holding of In re Marin Town Center, 142 B.R. 374 (N.D.Cal.1992). In the Marin Town Center case, as in Allegheny International, an "outsider" purchased an undersecured creditor's claim for the purpose of blocking confirmation in hopes that the creditor could acquire the debtor's main asset. The fair market value of the asset approximately equalled the amount paid for the claim. The court held that merely exercising a blocking position does not constitute bad faith. The creditor must be exercising the blocking position "for the ulterior purpose of securing some advantage to which the creditor would not otherwise have been entitled." Marin Town Center, 142 B.R. 378-79. "Section 1126(e) does not require a creditor to have an interest in seeing the debtor reorganize."
* * *

[G}ood faith does not require a creditor's selfless disinterest. The creditor's conduct in furtherance of its own interest, however, should not result in unfair disadvantage to other creditors or the debtor. The Bankruptcy Code, §1126(c), gives creditors a veto right; therefore, a creditor's taking of a blocking position is not, without more, bad faith.

In the instant case, FHLMC does not seek to gain a competitive advantage over Debtor or any of Debtor's creditors. FHLMC paid 100% to the unsecureds whose claims it bought; Debtor is not offering a better deal. FHLMC attempted to buy all the claims; the only creditor who did not sell holds a claim for approximately $24, and simply did not want to sell. Therefore, all unsecureds have been treated the same by FHLMC. FHLMC has gained no advantage over the unsecureds and has no ulterior motive.

The imprecise definition of "bad faith," however, surrounds the issue of whether FHLMC's determination to vote the purchased claims to block confirmation of Debtor's plan is bad faith. Debtor's position is that the "ill will" existing between Debtor and FHLMC is FHLMC's motive for purchasing the unsecured claims and blocking confirmation--regardless of the treatment of FHLMC's claim in Debtor's plan--and that such a motive constitutes bad faith. Debtor has attempted to show subjective bad faith by FHLMC--i.e., FHLMC has no good business reason for its actions; FHLMC's conduct is motivated by its "ill will" towards Debtor. The only harm Debtor will suffer is foreclosure. FHLMC will gain no unfair advantage over Debtor or any other creditor. In fact, for the purposes of Debtor's suit against FHLMC upon foreclosure, Debtor's damages may no longer be speculative but liquidated.

Debtor directs attention to the proposed treatment of FHLMC's claim in Debtor's plan, which Debtor characterizes as financially much more favorable than liquidation or foreclosure. FHLMC's claim is, however, significantly impaired. FHLMC appears to have concluded that the transaction costs of dealing with this Debtor and its principal exceed the losses it may suffer by foreclosing rather than consenting to a reorganization of Debtor. Even assuming a particular animosity directed by FHLMC towards Debtor, FHLMC's conduct gains it no strategic, competitive or financial advantage and injures no creditor of Debtor's estate. Subjective ill will between Debtor and FHLMC is insufficient to establish a lack of good faith to support disqualification of FHLMC's votes. Further discovery by Debtor on the issue of motive would not be productive or dispositive.

Additionally, Debtor seeks that this court both disqualify FHLMC from voting its Class 4 claims and deem those un-cast votes as acceptances of the plan. Pursuant to §1126(c), (d), and (e), "designation" of a vote means that the vote is not counted. Debtor offers no case law in support of its request to deem the votes as cast in favor of the plan and offers only §105 to sustain such action. No evidence suggests that the transferor creditors would have voted in favor of Debtor's plan. FHLMC's conduct does not appear to justify such a sanction. Accordingly, it is hereby

ORDERED that Debtor's Motion to Designate is DENIED. It is further

ORDERED that, on or before January 21, 1994, Debtor shall file an amended plan and disclosure statement. If no such amended plan and disclosure statement is filed within the time allowed, Debtor will be deemed unable to propose a feasible plan and FHLMC may present an order lifting the automatic stay.

IT IS SO ORDERED.

Notes and Problems

1. See generally Herbert Minkel & Cynthia Baker, *Claims and Control in Chapter 11 Cases: A Call for Neutrality*, 13 CARDOZO L. REV. 35 (1991)

2. In *Pleasant Hills*, FHLMC's goal was to block a plan. Section 1126(c) means that a claims purchaser needs to acquire just over one third in amount of the claims in a class. What if the claims buyer is a corporate raider and its goal as a purchaser is to have a class accept a plan. Assume, for example, that Class 7 has 600 claimants whose claims total $9,000,000. If the claims buyer goal is to have Class 7 accept a plan, can it satisfy section 1126(c) by acquiring just over 2/3 in amount and 1/2 in number of the Class 7 claims? Is the amount that is being paid for the claims relevant?

5. Judicial Confirmation

Chapter 11 contemplates not only a vote on the plan by the debtor's creditors and stockholders but also a review of the plan by the bankruptcy court. A bankruptcy judge has the statutory power to confirm a Chapter 11 plan that has not received the necessary majorities; a bankruptcy judge has the power not to confirm a plan that has been accepted by all holders of claims and interests.

Section 1128 requires the bankruptcy court to hold a hearing on confirmation and give the parties in interest notice of the hearing so that they might raise objections to confirmation. Section 1129 contains the confirmation standards.

a. Plan Accepted By All Classes

Subject to the limited exceptions of section 1129(c) and (d), a plan that has been accepted by every class of claims and interests must be confirmed by the bankruptcy court if the enumerated requirements of paragraph (a) are satisfied. Paragraph (b) of section 1129 does not apply to plans that have been accepted by every class of claims and interests.

In reading paragraph (a) of section 1129, consider the practical problems presented by section 1129(a)(9)(A) which requires that all administrative expenses must be paid in full in cash. Even if every single prepetition creditor consents to a plan, the bankruptcy court can confirm the plan only if there is sufficient cash on hand to pay all of the professionals in full and all other administrative claims.

Consider also the litigation opportunities presented by section 1129 (a)(7) and (11). Under section 1129(a)(7), each individual creditor that does not consent to a plan must receive at least as much under the plan as it would have under a Chapter 7 liquidation. This "best interests of creditors" test would seem to require a determination of the liquidation value of the debtor's assets, an estimation of any additional expenses of administration of the case under Chapter 7, and a valuation of the rights that the dissenting creditor is receiving under the Chapter 11 plan.

Absent opposition to the plan, the bankruptcy court's application of section 1129(a)(7) tends to be perfunctory. A common practice is for the plan proponent merely to proffer the testimony of a representative of the debtor concerning the expected results of a liquidation.

Section 1129(a)(11) requires a showing that the plan will work, that there will not be need for further reorganization or liquidation, that the plan is feasible. Again, absent opposition to the plan, the bankruptcy courts application of the requirement tends to be perfunctory. Possible factors in determining the feasibility of a plan include

- the debtor's prior performance;
- the adequacy of the debtor's capital structure;
- the earning power of the business;
- economic conditions; and
- ability and probable continuity of management.

b. Plan Accepted By One But Not All Classes

Section 1129(a)(8) requires acceptance of the plan by the necessary majority of each class. If, however, all of the other requirements of section 1129(a) have been met except that one or more classes of claims or interests have not accepted the plan, the court may still confirm the plan under section 1129(b).

Confirmation of a plan over the objection of a class of claims of interests is commonly referred to as a "cram down." Section 1129(b) is the "cram down" provision.

A cram down plan under section 1129(b) must satisfy all of the requirements of section 1129(a) except section 1129(a)(8)'s requirement of acceptance by all impaired classes of creditors. In this cram down context, the most strategically important requirement in section 1129(a) is section 1129(a)(10)'s requirement that the plan be accepted by at least one class of claims.

Since a cram down plan proponent needs the affirmative vote of at least one class of creditors whose rights are impaired under the plan, the proponent has an incentive to classify claims in such a way as to create a separate class for a group of creditors that it believes will vote for the plan. Consider *In re SM 104 Limited*, infra and the following example.

Debtor owes 20 trade creditors $600,000 and 3 tort claimants $500,000. The trade creditors are willing to support a plan that reduces their claims and extends the time for payment in order to keep a customer; the tort claimants are unwilling to support such a plan. If such a plan places the trade and tort creditors in the same class, it will satisfy neither section 1129(a)(8) nor section 1129(a)(10). If, on the other hand, the plan can classify the two groups separately, the trade creditors class would vote for the plan, and the plan could be confirmed under the cram down provisions of section 1129(b) notwithstanding the opposition of the tort creditors.

This hypothetical raises questions about the ability of a plan proponent to place unsecured claims in separate classes so that it can satisfy the requirements of section 1129(a)(10) and section 1129(b). Section 112 which governs classification of claims does not answer these questions; the courts in *United States Truck*, supra and *In re SM 104 Ltd.*, infra provide at leas partial answers.

A cram down plan must meet not only the requirements of section 1129(a) (other than section 1129(a)(8)) but also two requirements that are unique to section 1129(b). First, a cram down plan may not "discriminate unfairly" among creditors. Creditors with similar legal rights outside the plan must be treated equally under the plan. Not necessarily identically, but equally.

To illustrate, in the above hypothetical, the debtor's plan could not provide for 80% payments to the trade class but only 10% payments to the tort class. The plan could however provide for cash payment to the trade claimants and payment in notes to the tort claimants so long as the present value of these notes at least equaled the cash.

Second, a cram down plan must be "fair and equitable." This phrase "fair and equitable" was taken from Chapter X of the Bankruptcy Act of 1898. In Chapter X cases, the Supreme Court interpreted the phrase to require "absolute priority", that is classes with legal or contractual priority over other classes must be fully compensated in the order of seniority. For example, unsecured creditors must be paid in full before any distribution is made to shareholders; similarly, any liquidation preference of preferred shareholders must be satisfied before common shareholders receive any value.

Notice that the "fair and equitable" appears in section 1129(b)(1) so is a cram down confirmation requirement but does not appear in section 1129(a) so is not a consensual confirmation requirement.

Notice also that section 1129(b)(2) sets forth minimum requirements for a fair and equitable finding in regard to

- ◆ secured claims in section 1129(b)(2)(A), and
- ◆ unsecured claims in section 1129(b)(2)(B). and
- ◆ interests in section 1129(b)(2)(C).
- ◆

Essentially these provisions are applications of the absolute priority rule.

Consider the application of section 1129(a) and (b) in *Consul Restaurant*:

In re Consul Restaurant Corporation

United States Bankruptcy Court, D. Minnesota, Third Division, 1992
146 B.R. 979

Dennis D. O'Brien, Bankruptcy Judge. This matter is before the Court on contested confirmation hearing of two competing plans. One plan is proposed by the Debtor and the Unsecured Creditor's Committee (Joint Plan); the other by the Debtor's franchisor, Chi- Chi's Incorporated (Chi-Chi's Plan). Appearances are noted in the record. The Court, having heard and received all relevant evidence, and having heard arguments and reviewed briefs submitted by the parties, now being fully advised in the matter, makes this ORDER pursuant to the Federal and Local Rules of Bankruptcy Procedure.

I.

THE JOINT PLAN

Brief History.

Consul Restaurant Corporation is a public corporation that holds a franchise to construct and operate Chi-Chi's Mexican style restaurants within a defined territory in the United States and, until recently, in Canada. The Debtor was organized for that purpose in 1978. At filing of the case, there existed a total of 16,500,000 outstanding common shares of the Debtor.

Beginning in 1983, under former management, the Debtor began an aggressive expansion program of restaurants (stores) within its franchise territory.[1] At its peak development and operation, the Debtor owned and operated as many as 52 stores in the United States and Canada. Financial difficulties ensued, in large part the result of an inadequate management infrastructure to deal with and supervise its growing geographically diverse

---

[1]   The Debtor held a large geographic territory in the United States, including Southern California, Oregon, Washington, Texas, Louisiana and what would later come to be referred to as its core area of key states in the upper midwest. Additionally, it held an exclusive franchise covering much of Canada.

operations, and inadequate capitalization. Management's response strategy to its problems was an attempt to "grow out of them" through more expansion.

By June 1991, it became apparent to the Debtor's board of directors that the strategy would fail and, under new management, the Debtor determined to reverse its course. A petition was filed under 11 U.S.C. Chapter 11 on September 1, 1991, and the Debtor began a program of market and store-by-store analysis with the objective of shrinking its geographic market and divesting itself of unprofitable stores. During pendency of the case, the Debtor sold its Canadian operation and gave up the Canadian franchise. It also shrank the U.S. franchise to its midwest core area and took steps to sell or close unprofitable stores both within and without the core area. The Joint Plan proposes a reorganized operation of 21 stores in its core area, with future expansion under its franchise agreement within the core area of eight more stores over a four year period.

The Plan.

Following is the Joint Plan's classification of claims and interests in the amounts determined by the Court for purposes of considering confirmation issues regarding the Plan:

     Class 1--Priority Non-tax Claims.
        $1,300,000 Administrative.
     Class 2--American Bank Mankato Claim.
        $300,000 fully secured real estate.
     Class 3--Chrysler Capital Claim.
        $2,425,544 fully secured real estate and personal property.
     Class 4--First National Bank Claim.
        $68,000 fully secured personal property.
     Class 5--Ford Motor Credit Claim.
        $9,000 unimpaired.
     Class 5A--GMAC Claim.
        $10,400 unimpaired.
     Class 6--Circle Business Credit Claim.
        6A Secured $1,200,000 personal property.[1]
        6B Unsecured $1,094,000 subordinating debt to Classes 7, 8.[2]

---

[1]   The parties dispute the allowable amount of this claim. The Debtor contends that postpetition adequate protection payments reduced the principal to $960,000. CBC argues that the postpetition payments simply maintained the status quo. The issue is not addressed in this opinion, since resolution of the case is controlled by determination of other issues.

[2]   The Debtor claims that only $400,000 of this amount is senior subordinating debt. However, the entire debt is of the type covered by the contract documents as subordinating debt, and the Debtor, until confirmation, recognized that by separately classifying the entire unsecured amount. If only $400,000 is subordinating debt, then the balance of $694,000 should have been classified with the general unsecured Class 9. No

>Class 7--Senior Debentures.
>>Unsecured $6,233,000 subordinating debt to Class 8.
>Class 8--Subordinated Debentures.
>>Unsecured $3,249,000.
>Class 9--General Unsecured Claims.
>>$6,293,000.
>Class 10--Administrative Convenience Claims.
>>$200,000.
>Class 11--Old Preferred Stock
>Class 12--Old Common Stock
>Class 13--Equity Interests (not including Old Pref. Stock and Old Common Stock).

Classes 2, 3, 4, 8, 9, 10 and 11 voted to accept the Plan, while Classes 6 and 7 voted to reject it. Additionally, Class 6 objected to confirmation on legal grounds of unfair discrimination and failure to meet the fair and equitable standard; and, Class 7 filed a post-hearing brief expressing concern that the Plan might not comply with its absolute priority rights. Chi-Chi's filed similar objections and also objected on grounds of feasibility.

Following is a general presentation of the Joint Plan's proposed payment and treatment of claims and interests on the effective date of the Plan:

>Class 2--American Bank Mankato Claim, fully secured note 5 year term.
>Class 3--Chrysler Capital Claim, fully secured note 12 year amort., balloon 10th year.
>Class 4--First National Bank Claim, fully secured note 5 year term.
>Class 5--Ford Motor Credit Claim, fully secured note per contract.
>Class 5A--GMAC Claim, fully secured note per contract.
>Class 6--Circle Business Credit Claim.
>>6A, secured note, 12 year amort., balloon end of 7th year.
>>6B, $400,000 cash, 321,000 new equity shares, unsecured note to the extent present value of new shares is less than $2.16 per share.
>Class 7--Senior Debentures, $1,469,000 cash, 1,518,000 shares new equity, $997,000 unsecured note.
>Class 8--Subordinated Debentures, 820,000 shares new equity, 263,000 contingent warrants.

---

legitimate purpose has been stated for classification of CBC's unsecured debt separately from Class 9 other than its senior subordinating rights regarding Classes 7 and 8.

> Class 9--General Unsecured Claims, $1,131,000 cash, 1,608,000 shares new equity.
>
> Class 10--Administrative Convenience Claims, $120,000 cash.
>
> Class 11--Old Preferred Stock, 0.
>
> Class 12--Old Common Stock, 0.[1]
>
> Class 13--Equity Interests (not including Old Pref. Stock and Old Common Stock), 0.

Classes 7 and 8 are subordinated by prepetition agreement to CBC's Class 6 unsecured claim. Class 8 is subordinated by prepetition agreement to the Senior Debentures Class 7 claims. Classes 6B, 7, and 8 are of equal priority with the Class 9 General Unsecured Claims.

CBC argues that the payment and distribution scheme of the Joint Plan is unfairly discriminatory against it, and is not fair and equitable, because it does not recognize CBC's subordination rights as to Classes 7 and 8. CBC notes that the proposed cash payment to its subordinated Class 7 on the effective date of the Joint Plan exceeds the entire amount of CBC's subordinating unsecured claim. According to CBC, the Joint Plan not only pays the subordinated class before paying CBC in full pursuant to its subordination rights, but circumstances of the Debtor and the Joint Plan are such that subsequent payment of CBC in full is speculative. Similar concerns are expressed on behalf of Class 7 as its treatment relates to Class 8.[2]

The Debtor argues that nonbankruptcy subordination rights need not be recognized in cramdown under 11 U.S.C. §1129(b), home of the concepts of "unfair discrimination" and "fair and equitable". But even if they need be, the Debtor asserts, the Joint Plan does not violate the subordination rights of either Class 6 with regard to Classes 7 and 8, or Class 7 with regard to Class 8, since both classes are "paid in full" for purposes of cramdown on the effective date of the Joint Plan. The Debtor argues that neither subordination, nor absolute priority fair and equitable concepts, require that a senior class be paid in cash before payments are made to junior classes. All that is required under 11 U.S.C. §1129(b), according to the Debtor, is that senior classes receive property of a present value equal to the allowed amount of their claims. The Debtor argues that the Joint Plan satisfies the requirement through distribution of property to these subordinating classes in combinations of cash, new equity and notes[3] equal to the allowed amounts of their claims.

---

[1]   Classes 11 and 12 would be issued contingent warrants whose value has been assessed by the Debtor at no value for distribution purposes.

[2]   Both CBC and the Senior Debentures argue that the payment to junior classes of stock and/or warrants violates the absolute priority rule if the senior classes have received less than full payment. In order for receipt of shares by Class 7 Senior Debentures to constitute full payment when added to the cash and note the Class is to receive, the newly created equity under the Joint Plan must have value of at least $2.48 per share.

[3]   The Joint Plan provides for the issuance to CBC of an accelerating unsecured note

The positions of the parties on these issues of application of nonbankruptcy subordination rights, unfair discrimination, and fair and equitable standards under 11 U.S.C. §1129(b), as they relate to the payment and distribution scheme of the Joint Plan, are appropriately analyzed in light of feasibility of the Joint Plan and value of the Debtor as a going concern. Accordingly, it is necessary to digress from 11 U.S.C. §1129(b) issues for the moment to consider these important related matters.

Feasibility of The Joint Plan And Value of The Debtor as a Going Concern.

Analysis of feasibility of the Plan and value of the Debtor as a going concern involve many of the same considerations. Feasibility, from an operational standpoint, is considered in light of future projected cash flow probability. Value of the Debtor is determined by using the same cash flow probability over the relevant future, and then reducing it to present value by a discount variable that represents a weighted average cost of capital. The discussion focuses first on feasibility, then on value.

Feasibility. Considerations of feasibility are viewed in the light of a preponderance standard. Accordingly, the Joint Plan would be considered feasible in satisfaction of 11 U.S.C. §1129(a)(11), if it could be said that, more likely than not, confirmation will not be followed by liquidation, or the need for further financial reorganization. The Joint Plan proponents bear the burden of proof regarding feasibility. The burden has not been met.

Accurate prediction of any future course of events is an uncertain endeavor. Accurate prediction of future financial performance of a reorganized business operation often presents significant challenges, particularly where the structure and operations of the reorganized entity bear little relationship to the old one. Prudent prediction of the future financial performance of the Debtor under the proposed reorganization does not support the projected cash flows that drive the Joint Plan.[1]

Prudent prediction of future financial performance in this case is made somewhat easier because the Plan does not propose significant changes in either the structure or operation of the Debtor's core stores; nor does the Joint Plan call for the introduction of any new and untried business endeavor. The Joint Plan is not premised on the infusion of outside capital, but the proposed reorganization is based on a downsized operation in a more limited market with focus on selected profitable stores.

---

for any deficiency that might otherwise result in the payment of its unsecured claim from a finding that the value of the newly created equity under the Joint Plan is less than $2.16 per share. The Senior Debentures are to get a note in the amount of $997,000 in addition to the cash and shares provided it.

[1]   Prudence has been described as the art of accessing memory, analyzing it in light of present circumstances and environment, and applying the analysis to the future for purposes of selecting a course of action that best serves the legitimate interests of the inquirer. See generally: The Art Of Memory, Frances A. Yates, Univ.Ch. Press, 1966.

The projected cash flows in the Joint Plan are based on future performance of core stores that would survive the reorganization. The inquiry to determine validity of the projections begins by comparing them with the historical performance of the same stores. Same store projections reflect substantially higher predicted gross sales and significantly lower predicted key costs of sales than experienced in the past.

Gross sales of same stores project a growth of 2.8% for the 1993 fiscal year over 1992. Gross sales for fiscal year 1992 fell approximately 3.5% from 1991.[1] Gross sales during the summer months of this year failed significantly to meet the cash flow projections, causing the Debtor to postpone or reduce scheduled capital expenditures and reduce its media budget. Gross sales during the weeks immediately preceeding, and during the hearing were mixed, at best, in meeting the projections.

On the cost side, projections are significantly lower or are projected to remain flat during the period. Key costs include: food and beverage; labor; media; and other. The Debtor's general explanation for lower costs in its post-hearing Fact Memorandum is:

> Once the Company emerges from bankruptcy and is not distracted by that process and the other extraordinary matters which have occupied management, such as the divestiture of Canada, it is inevitable that management's renewed focus on the business will result in significantly better operations.

Fact Mem. in Sup. Of Conf. Jt. Plan, p. 11.

Whatever the intended meaning of "significantly better operations" is, it certainly is not inevitable that management could significantly reduce key costs as a percentage of sales. In light of present general economic conditions and intense competition within the industry, the more reasonable conclusion is that operating margins will likely shrink, reflecting greater absorption of costs, thereby increasing key costs as a percentage of sales rather than decreasing them.

In short, explanations furnished to reconcile projected cash flows with substantially underperforming historical individual and collective same store cash flows, are insufficient to overcome the discrepancy. Furthermore, the

---

[1] The Debtor prepared a store-by-store analysis (Joint Exhibit 36), comparing annual sales figures, citing what it refers to as unique factors that caused past poor performance, and offering reasons supporting expected improved future performance. However, the factors cited for the poor performance, such as road construction impeding access to a store and an outbreak of hepatitis at another, while not general common occurrences, are certainly within the scope of occurrences that one might expect to experience in the industry from time to time. Those factors cited in support of expected growth projections for the near term fiscal years, while positive in nature, are only some of myriad factors that can be expected to determine actual store performance.

projections, when viewed in light of present and near future likely economic and industry conditions, do not fare any better. Economic and competitive forces are more likely than not in the near term to keep prices down, shrink operating margins, and require significant capital expenditures, all of which will be necessary to maintain market share, and none of which will have a positive influence on cash flow.

The Debtor has already postponed capital expenditures due to recent shortfalls in actual sales from projected sales. Aside from that, the projections allow for minimal amounts available for store enhancements, with little or no margin for costs exceeding estimates.

The projections assume builder financed construction of new stores under a "build to suit" concept, without initial capital outlay required of the Debtor. Chi-Chi's challenged the availability of the "build to suit" alternative in the current market, and offered testimony that Chi-Chi's itself, with access to more than $25,000,000 in equity, could not attract such an offer from a builder. The Debtor offered no evidence of the availability of "build to suit" construction for its new store construction. Similarly, Chi-Chi's challenged the Debtor's estimated costs of opening new stores, claiming that the actual cost would be substantially higher. Again, the Debtor's projections appear to be thin with no margin for error in cost estimates.

The Joint Plan cash flow projections do not appear realistic under either historical comparison or present conditions analysis. Recent history of operations and present economic and industry conditions indicate a substantial risk of failure of the projections. Aggravating the risk is the weak liquidity position of the Debtor that would result from consummation of the Joint Plan. The Debtor intends to distribute approximately $3,000,000 in cash to various classes of creditors on the effective date of the Plan, which would leave, after payment of administrative expenses and other adjustments, less than $1,000,000 cash going forward. Chi-Chi's offered testimony that, under more conservative but historically consistent cash flow projections, the Debtor would have only $660,000 available going forward, and that the Debtor would run out of cash by August 1993.

In light of the foregoing, the Court finds that the Debtor has not proven by a preponderance that the Joint Plan is feasible.

Value. Six expert witnesses testified relating to the going concern value of Consul. One expert witness (Arthur Cobb), however, did not provide the Court with an independent valuation.[1] These valuations were received:

> (1) Dain Bosworth Incorporated valued Consul at an aggregate
> value in excess of $29 million conservatively, as high as $34

---

[1]   Mr. Cobb's analysis examined and critiqued the valuation report prepared by Dain Bosworth.

million under most liberal assumptions. Larsen, Joint 67,
Joint 53, Joint 54.

(2) R. Steven Tanner valued Consul at a "break-up value" in
excess of $24 million. Tanner, Chi-Chi's EE.

(3) Ernst & Young found that the reorganization value of Consul
exceeded $19 million. Tamosuinas, Chi-Chi's BB.

(4) Don Nicholson adjusted and reduced the Ernst & Young
valuation to approximately $10 million.   Nicholson,
Chi-Chi's KK, Chi-Chi's LL.

(5) Based on Nicholson's projections, Houlihan, Lokey, Howard
& Zukin valued Consul at approximately $12 million.
Daniels, Chi-Chi's OO.

Interestingly, the experts agreed on the better methodology that should be used
in valuing the Debtor, the discounted cash flow method. Similarly, each used
essentially the same formula in the analysis. Yet, a $20,000,000 spread exists in
opinions on the value of the Debtor's business, between $10,000,000 and
$30,000,000.   Each expert's opinion is purportedly based on a conservative
estimate.   The differences are largely accounted for by the use of different
assumptions in determining the variables upon which the formula operates.[1]

At the outset, Mr. Larsen's valuation is rejected for several reasons. Most
important is that the Joint Plan is not based on his valuation. Mr. Larsen
performed the valuation for the Debtor at a time when the Debtor and the
Unsecured Creditor's Committee were not getting along. The Joint Plan is more
the Committee's influence than the Debtor's and is based on the Ernst & Young
valuation.[2]   Seemingly, the Larsen valuation is offered by the Joint Plan
proponents as a frontier position to make the Ernst & Young valuation appear
more conservative and reasonable.

Mr. Larsen's valuation apparently assumes a turned around, financially
healthy Debtor in a robust economy like the late 1980's.   The Debtor is
struggling in an intensely competitive and hostile financial and economic
environment that is nothing like the late 1980's. Furthermore, the Debtor does

---

[1]   The record on this issue verifies that formulas, like trained animals, perform
according to what they are fed.
[2]   If Mr. Larsen's valuation is correct, it would appear that at least $7,000,000 in value
of the Debtor rightfully belongs to prepetition equity security holders, including common
holders. This Plan is not funded by any postpetition capital infusion. Total debts are
approximately $21,000,000 with administrative expenses at approximately $1,000,000.
Yet, the Debtor explained that the common holders were not solicited regarding the Joint
Plan because they were to receive nothing of value and it would be too costly.

not struggle from a position of strength, and would emerge from the protection of the Bankruptcy Court as a relatively weak player in its market. The valuation is simply not credible.

The Ernst & Young valuation presents a more accurate frontier position of the going concern value of the Debtor. That valuation, $19,000,000, assumes the cash flow projections of the Debtor's management. It also draws key cost of capital information from 1980's industry comparables. Despite assertions to the contrary, the valuation is, as a result, a very liberal assessment. A conservative Ernst & Young valuation results from the adjustments made to its assumptions by Mr. Nicholsen in his rework of it with cash flow projections more historically consistent with the same store operations of the Debtor, and with cost of capital assumptions (particularly cost of equity), that are more realistic in the current economic environment.

Having carefully considered all of the substantial, relevant testimony and documentary evidence regarding the issue, the Court finds that the most that can be said with any integral degree of certainty about the going concern value of the Debtor is that the value lies somewhere between $10,000,000 and $19,000,000, probably toward the lower end of the range.

Treatment of CBC And Senior Subordinated Debentures Under 11 U.S.C. §1129(b). Class 6, CBC, objects to confirmation, and the Senior Subordinated Debentures express concern on grounds that their subordination rights are being improperly ignored under the Joint Plan. The Joint Plan proponents disagree.

11 U.S.C. §1129(b)(1) provides: (b)(1) Notwithstanding section 510(a) of this title, if all of the applicable requirements of subsection (a) of this section other than paragraph (8) are met with respect to a plan, the court, on request of the proponent of the plan, shall confirm the plan notwithstanding the requirements of such paragraph if the plan does not discriminate unfairly, and is fair and equitable, with respect to each class of claims or interests that is impaired under, and has not accepted, the plan. (emphasis added). The Joint Plan proponents first argue that subordination rights of classes are not enforceable in cramdown by the plain language of 11 U.S.C. §1129(b)(1). However, it is generally understood that such rights are enforceable under the discrimination and fair and equitable concepts of the statute.

Next, the Joint Plan proponents argue that the subordination rights of these dissenting classes are satisfied because Classes 6 and 7 will receive payment in full on the effective date of the Joint Plan. For Class 7, the Senior Debentures, the question is whether the value of the proposed new shares to be issued the class will have a present value of at least $2.48 per share. For CBC, the question is whether a combination of cash, shares and an accelerating unsecured note with an appropriate interest rate, is fair and equitable when substantial cash payments are proposed for distribution to a subordinated class on the effective date of confirmation.

     * * *

For the present value of the new proposed shares to equal at least $2.48 per share, the present value of the Debtor as a going concern must be at least $19,000,000. For reasons already discussed, that is unlikely. Accordingly, the Joint Plan proponents have not shown that Class 7 would be paid in full on the effective date of the Joint Plan so as to comply with the fair and equitable standards of 11 U.S.C. §1129(b). The scheme appears to violate the absolute priority rule in that a subordinated class would receive property while the subordinating class would be left without full payment.

The Joint Plan would pay CBC's subordinating claim of $1,094,000 by $400,000 in cash on the effective date, 321,000 newly issued shares of equity of the Debtor ($694,000 at $2.16 per share), and an accelerating unsecured note for any deficiency resulting from a finding that the new equity has a present value of less than $2.16 per share. For the proposed new shares to have a present value of $2.16 per share, the going concern value of the Debtor must be approximately $17,700,000. For the reasons already discussed, that is not likely.

The proposed distribution scheme is not fair and equitable to CBC because it would pay out on the effective date of the Joint Plan to CBC's subordinated creditor, Class 7 Senior Debentures, cash exceeding the entire subordinating unsecured debt. CBC would receive 63% of its "payment in full" on the same date in new stock and an unsecured accelerating note.

Under the Bankruptcy Act, such a scheme was not permissible. Under the Bankruptcy Code, the statute specifically allows for the concept of fair and equitable to accommodate payment of senior secured debt through retention of liens and deferred present value payments, with interim distributions of cash to junior classes, secured and unsecured. See: 11 U.S.C. §1129(b)(2). Recognition of such a distribution scheme under the Code is essential to the entire concept of reorganization. The senior secured class is protected by retention of the collateral interest and is compensated for the risk, presumably slight, in going forward by the terms of the note.

The same cannot be said with respect to the distribution scheme here. First, no apparent legitimate purpose is served the reorganization of the Debtor by distributing to the subordinated class available cash that, if distributed to the senior subordinating class, would pay the senior class in full. Such a scheme would materially shift the risk of failure of the Plan from the subordinated to the subordinating class for no apparent reason other than to secure acceptance of the junior class by allowing it to overreach the senior class. Even absent the finding on feasibility, it can hardly be questioned that, should the Joint Plan be confirmed, the Debtor would have significant risk of failure going forward. A class "paid in full" with new equity and unsecured notes has payment without currency when the debtor fails before the note is paid or before the shares can be sold.[1] In the meantime, the junior class would have received irretrievable currency payment at the real cost to the senior class.

---

[1]   Interestingly, none of the experts would record an opinion of what the new shares

The concept of fair and equitable involves more than the application of a mechanical calculation of absolute priority based on distribution of property valued abstractly. When the proposed distribution would substantially shift the risk of failure of the plan from a junior class to a senior dissenting class for no legitimate purpose, the plan is not fair and equitable to the dissenting class.[1] Such is the case here.

Summation on Confirmability of The Joint Plan.

The Joint Plan is not confirmable because the Plan has not been shown to be feasible under 11 U.S.C. §1129(a)(11), and because it has not been shown to be fair and equitable to the dissenting Classes 6 and 7.[2]

II.
CHI-CHI'S PLAN

The Plan.

The Chi-Chi's Plan is essentially a takeover plan. It is one by which the wholly-owned subsidiary of Chi-Chi's, Inc., CCMR, Inc., would purchase the newly issued shares of the reorganized Debtor for $8,700,000 and assume approximately $4,000,000 of the Debtor's secured debt, payment of which is guaranteed by Chi-Chi's. The present common and preferred stock of the Debtor would be cancelled. The $8,700,000 together with certain other assets of the Debtor, including approximately $5,000,000 of cash on hand and the Canadian Notes with a face value of $1,200,000, would be deposited with a Creditors Fund to be distributed in accordance with the priorities of the Bankruptcy Code. In addition, Chi-Chi's filed a motion to assume certain of the Debtor's leases, which

---

would be worth in spendable value, that is, at what price they would trade in the marketplace. The Joint Plan provides for the new shares to be publicly traded like the prepetition equity shares. Those shares traded for 31 cents per share on the last day they were traded.

[1]   Why the Joint Plan proponents chose to distribute cash to Class 7 Senior Debentures and shares and notes to CBC is a mystery. Ultimately, Class 7 rejected the Plan anyway and the proponents are unsuccessful in cramming down the Class. Nevertheless, it seems that there existed from the beginning a better chance to cramdown the subordinated class holding shares where no cash is available for distribution to it because of payment to a senior class, than to cramdown the subordinating class holding the same shares where the cash is not available for distribution to it because of payment to a junior class.

[2]   Chi-Chi's objected to confirmation on the additional grounds that the Debtor could not properly assume the Chi-Chi's franchise under the Joint Plan because of its present net worth deficiency from that required by the agreement, and because of what Chi-Chi's claims is a more rigorous and expanded construction requirement in the agreement for new stores than is provided for under the Joint Plan. These objections are specious and do not merit extended discussion. They are simply overruled, the one in light of 11 U.S.C. §365(b)(2)(A), and the other in light of the good faith prior conduct and dealings of the parties.

payments would also be guaranteed by Chi-Chi's. No objections were filed by any landlord to this motion.

* * * Chi-Chi's anticipated that the claims of Class 6 Circle Business Credit, and the claims of Class 7 Senior Debentures would be paid in full. The claims of the other unsecured creditors, Class 9 would receive approximately 73.7% of their claim, and the claims of Class 8 Subordinated Debentures would receive approximately 9.1% of the estimated amount of their claims. All subordination rights of the classes are recognized and the proposed distribution would be the result of application of the relative priority rights among the subordinating and subordinated classes. One impaired creditor, the Class 6 claim of CBC, voted to accept Chi-Chi's Plan.[1]

The Debtor stipulated at the hearing that the creditors would receive or retain under Chi-Chi's Plan more than they would receive if the Debtor were liquidated under Chapter 7. Also, the Debtor stipulated that Chi-Chi's Plan, which proposes to pay creditors in accordance with the priorities of the Bankruptcy Code, met the absolute priority portion of the fair and equitable cramdown standards of Section 1129(b)(2)(B). Finally, Chi-Chi's Plan was not challenged on any feasibility issue by the Joint Plan proponents.

Objections to the Chi-Chi's Plan.

The Joint Plan proponents object to confirmation of the Chi-Chi's Plan on several grounds.[2] One is that, according to them, the CBC vote was "bought" by more favorable interest rate treatment to CBC than to similarly situated secured creditors. The assertion, however, is not supported by the record in the case.

There is no other similarly situated secured creditor in the case. The creditor coming closest to CBC in size of secured claim is Chrysler Capital and it holds a mortgage on real estate for the full amount. The other secured claims are relatively small and are collateralized with reliable security. The obligation to CBC is collateralized by highly depreciable equipment, whose value in liquidation is speculative. The existing loans were intended to be short term, according to CBC, and the proposed treatment is appropriate and necessary simply to preserve its present position. While the interest on the debt is generous at 500 basis points over the rate provided other secured creditors, that, under circumstances of its six-year term and declining collateral value, is not sufficient evidence that the vote was bought.

---

[1]   The Creditor's Committee has filed a motion to disqualify the CBC vote on the grounds that the vote was "bought." Chi-Chi's has responded to that motion in a separate pleading. The issue will be addressed in this part of the opinion.

[2]   The American Bank Mankato also objected to confirmation of Chi-Chi's Plan. The Bank's objections are specifically related to treatment of its secured claim and are couched in terms of feasibility and fair and equitable considerations. The Bank did not participate in the hearing and, accordingly, offered no testimony or other competent evidence to support its allegations. The objections are specious and are simply overruled without further comment.

* * *

The remaining significant objections by the Joint proponents are that the Chi-Chi's Plan is proposed in bad faith and is not fair and equitable to general unsecured and subordinated creditors. These objections are driven by the premise that the Plan basically is an improperly leveraged hostile takeover attempt that would steal much of the Debtor's value from its junior creditors. The record does not support that assertion.

The Debtor certainly has value. Value in the range assumed by the Joint Plan proponents, however, is more potential future value than real present value. It is apparent that the Chi-Chi's concept and the Debtor's existing stores, are potentially very viable and can be highly competitive in the Debtor's market area. But it is equally apparent that the Debtor's present position is a weak one in a hostile economic and intensely competitive environment.

Former management policies allowed the Debtor to become seriously undercapitalized over a several-year period to the verge of ruin. Apparently, the severe downturn in the economy in 1990 precipitated a crisis for the Debtor. Since then, the new management admirably accomplished the restructuring and downsizing necessary to make a recovery possible. But more than restructuring and downsizing is necessary, especially in the present environment, to make recovery probable. What is needed is a substantial retention or infusion of capital to both provide for necessary capital expenditures, and for maintenance of a healthy liquidity position in anticipation of reasonably expected shortfalls in cash flow over the near term.

The provision for stripping $3,000,000 in cash from the Debtor to pay creditors on the effective date of confirmation, stripped the Joint Plan of feasibility. The provision also betrays the understanding and appreciation by the Joint Plan proponents of the inherent risk of failure of the Plan, and of their unwillingness to accept their own position regarding present value of the reorganized Debtor. Otherwise, presumably, they would have proposed to leave the cash in and convert more debt to new equity, thereby increasing the strength of the Debtor rather than sapping it further.

In order for the Debtor to achieve value in the range that the Joint Plan proponents perceive as present value, substantial risk capital must be committed over the near term that will not positively translate to the near term bottom line net cash flow. The Joint Plan proponents are unwilling to make that commitment. Yet, they value the Debtor as if the commitment has been made, the risk overcome, and the worth realized.

Chi-Chi's is willing to invest the capital and to assume the risk. Because of who Chi-Chi's is, it might have a unique interest in making the investment and, perhaps, Chi-Chi's might stand to benefit more than an ordinary passive investor. But that does not turn the proposal to acquire the Debtor into a bad faith plan; nor is the proposal unfair and inequitable under 11 U.S.C. §1129(b) to creditors who will not receive payment. The proposed price is well within the range of probable present value of the Debtor, and there exists no better offer.

The various objections to confirmation of the Chi-Chi's Plan are insufficient to prevent confirmation.

III.

DISPOSITION

Based on the foregoing, IT IS HEREBY ORDERED: confirmation of the Joint Plan is denied, and the Chi-Chi's Plan is confirmed. All pending motions are granted or denied, consistent with this ORDER.

Notes and Problems

Valuation

1. In considering the Joint Plan, the Court made a finding as to the going concern value of Consul. Why? Will it always be necessary to determine the debtor's going concern value in applying section 1129(b)?

Cram Down of Secured Claims

2. The *Klein* case, supra, involved the cram down of a secured claim. *Klein* is a Chapter 13 case involving a $3,200 debt secured by a station wagon valued at $1,650. In applying section 1325(a)(5)(B)(ii), the court held that the stream of payments proposed by the Kleins' Chapter 13 plan must have a present value of $1,650.

   While the dollars involved in the cram down of a secured claim in a Chapter 11 will obviously be different from the dollars involved in *Klein*, similar statutory language will be involved. Compare section 1325(a)(5)(B)(ii) and section 1129(b)(2)(A)(i)(II). If the *Klein* case had been a Chapter 11 case involving a $3.2 million dollar loan secured by equipment valued at $1.65 million dollars then a cram down of the secured creditor would require a stream of payments with a present value of $1.65 million.

3. Although both section 1129(b)(2)(A)(i)(II) and section 1325(a)(5)(B)(i) use the phrase "allowed amount of such claim", that phrase can have a different meaning in Chapter 11 cases from Chapter 13 cases. In Chapter 11 cases, secured creditors are given two special rights under section 1111(b).

   First, under section 1111(b), loans, whether recourse or not outside of Chapter 11, are recourse in Chapter 11. Assume, for example, that S makes a $3,000,000 loan to D secured by equipment that is nonrecourse. In Chapter 11, S has a $3,000,000 recourse claim against D.

   Second, under section 1111(b), the secured creditor can elect to have its entire claim treated as a secured claim regardless of the value of its collateral. Thus, if S makes the section 1111(b) election, it has a

$3,000,000 secured claim, even if the equipment only has a value of $1,000,000.

Consider the effect of a section 1111(b) election on the application of section 1129(b)(2)(A)(i)(II). In the above hypothetical, could D cram down S by providing for sixty monthly payments of $50,000 each? Section 1111(b) is considered further in *In re SM 104 Ltd.*, 160 B.R. 202 (Bankr. S.D. Fla. 1993), which is included in Unit 16 *infra*.

4. In Consul, the Court did not seem to consider either section 1111(b) or section 1129(b)(2)(A)(i)(II). in holding that the Joint Plan was not "fair and equitable" as to Class 6 and 7. What was the statutory basis for the holding?

5. See generally Jack Friedman, *What Courts Do To Secured Creditors in Chapter 11 Cram Down*, 14 CARDOZO L. REV. 1495 (1993)

Cram Down of Unsecured Claims
6. In Consul, there were no section 1129(b)(2)(B) objections to the Chi-Chi plan. Why? Did the Chi-Chi plan satisfy section 1129(b)(2)(B)(i)? Section 1129(b)(2)(B)(ii)? Section 1129(b)(2)(B)(ii) is considered in *In re SM 104 Ltd.* infra.

6. Effect Of Confirmation

A Chapter 11 case does not end with confirmation. After confirmation, the debtor continues operating its business (providing the plan does not call for liquidation) and makes the payments provided for in the plan.

Even though confirmation requires a finding that the plan is feasible, the debtor may encounter problems in paying or otherwise performing pursuant to the provisions of the plan. Postconfirmation problems raise questions about the effects of confirmation.

Section 1141 is entitled "Effect of Confirmation." Please read section 1141 and determine the effect of confirmation of the Chapter 11 plan in the following problems.

Problems

1. D's Chapter 11 reorganization plan provides for the continuation of business operations and the issuance of notes to holders of unsecured claims. The notes are to be for 40% of the amount owed and are to be payable over five years. The plan is confirmed. What are the rights of X, an unsecured creditor who voted against the plan? Of Y, an unsecured creditor who did not file a proof of claim? What if D is a corporation? Cf. section 727(a)(1)

2. Same facts as #1. What are the rights of D's unsecured creditors if D defaults on its new payment obligations.

3. D's Chapter 11 plan provides for the sale of all of its assets to Newco and the issuance of Newco notes to holders of unsecured claims. The notes are to be 40% of the amount owed and are to be payable over five years. The plan is confirmed. What are the rights of D's unsecured creditors against D? What if D is a corporation? See sections 1141(d)(3) and 727(a)(1)

4. D's Chapter 11 plan that provides for monthly payments to creditors for two years is confirmed. D is able to make the first three payments. Because of an unexpected deep drop in sales, D is not able to make the fourth payment. How can D modify its payment obligations under the confirmed plan? Section 1127(b) prohibits modification after "substantial consummation." See section 1101(c). If D can not modify its confirmed Chapter 11, can D file another Chapter 11 petition, i.e., use "Chapter 22"?

5. See generally David Lander & David Warfield, *A Review and Analysis of Selected Post-Confirmation Activities in Chapter 11 Reorganizations*, 62 Aᴍ. Bᴀɴᴋʀ.L.J. 203 (1988).

Unit 16

SINGLE-ASSET REAL ESTATE CASES

UNIT CONTENTS

A. COMMERCIAL REAL ESTATE

Single-asset real estate cases comprise a substantial portion of Chapter 11 filings. These cases involve a debtor, usually a partnership, that owns a single commercial real estate asset such as an apartment complex, an office or commercial building, or a shopping center or undeveloped land that generates all or substantially all of the debtor's income.

Typically, the real estate asset is fully encumbered by mortgage debt and the deficiency claim of the mortgage holder dwarfs any claims of unsecured trade creditors. The crux of the case is the continuing dispute between the debtor and the mortgagee over control and ownership of the real estate asset. In a sense, the case is not only a single-asset case but also a single creditor case.

The single-asset real estate debtor has few if any employees. Whether reorganized, sold, or foreclosed, the asset will continue to be operated without any loss of going concern value.

The debtor's filing often occurs on the eve of foreclosure. In response to the filing, the mortgagee files (i) a motion to dismiss for lack of good faith, (ii) a motion for relief from stay, and/or (iii) a motion to deny debtor's postpetition use of rents and revenues from the real estate. If the debtor is able to continue in Chapter 11 and file a plan of reorganization, the mortgagee then files an objection to confirmation.

In re Lake Ridge Associates
United States Bankruptcy Court, E.D. Virginia, 1994
163 B.R. 284

Hal J. Bonney, Jr., Bankruptcy Judge. We have a coonskin cap, but can we pioneer?

Can the Court do the extraordinary or are we limited to convention? The intent of the Congress under Chapter 11 of the Bankruptcy Code is to encourage reorganizations to save businesses, but does the proposal by the debtor, Lake Ridge Associates, go beyond this?

Really, the facts in this proceeding are not in dispute. It is the application of the law that provides the rub. NationsBank loaned Lake Ridge Partnership the basic funding to purchase the nearly 1,200 acres of undeveloped, but promising land and is in for about $35 million. Two basic facts have led NationsBank to file a motion to modify the automatic stay (injunction) which prevents a creditor from pursuing its contractual rights of foreclosure without the Bankruptcy Court's authority: 1--NationsBank has not seen the eagle fly its way in 3 years. 2--Admittedly, the debt exceeds the value of the property, i.e., there is no equity for the debtor.

The law says in 11 U.S.C. §362(d):

(d) On request of a party in interest and after notice and a hearing, the court shall grant relief from the stay provided under subsection (a) of this section, such as by terminating, annulling, modifying, or conditioning such stay-- (1) for cause, including the lack of adequate protection of an interest in property of such party in interest; or (2) with respect to a stay of an act against property under subsection (a) of this section, if-- (A) the debtor does not have an equity in such property; and (B) such property is not necessary to an effective reorganization.

First, is there cause to lift the stay? The bank argues, in chief, that (a) there has been no debt service for three years, (2) environmental problems have not been resolved, and (3) a tax payment due under a consensual arrangement was a few days late.

This is not sufficient cause. For such a large debt on such a large piece of dirt in these largely slow times, great caution should be exercised by a court in deciding there is no hope. A lender assumes certain risks and among these is an orderly bankruptcy process that weighs all.

There are apparently no major environmental problems with Lake Ridge. While certain Phase 3 work should have been promptly initiated, this by itself, or coupled with other factors, is not cause to kill a reorganization. The bank is crying wolf. We live in times where the spill of 5 gallons of kerosene outside the house twenty years ago clouds the entire future of the property. Save the environment, yes! But it has some petty features which have unnecessarily impeded the survival of particularly small businesses.

Well, the taxes were paid a few days late. As they say, "big deal." If Chapter 11 entities did not have problems, they would not be here.

NationsBank may not prevail under 11 U.S.C. §362(d)(1).

Under §362(d)(2), the debtor must have no equity in the property and the property not be necessary to an effective reorganization. No one argues that there is equity. There is a hearing on January 31 to set the value of the property for other purposes pursuant to §506.

Is the property necessary for an effective reorganization of Lake Ridge? Indeed, is any reorganization possible?

Some courts hold that no Chapter 11 case may exist where the debtor has but a single asset. This is a narrow, myopic view. There are endless entities possessing but a single asset and application of this rule would deny them the opportunity to reorganize. For instance, the entity that owns the Empire State Building is different from the entity which owns the land under it. If, if, either entity owned nothing else, too bad!

Nevertheless, and on the other hand, a carte blanche highway for a single asset case may not be paved. This court would hold that there can be no place in bankruptcy for a debtor with

　　1. a single asset, particularly raw land;
　　2. no equity in the property;
　　3. there is a plan of liquidation rather than of reorganization; and
　　4. there is no on going business.

Lake Ridge argues, and it is difficult to deny the approach given the history of the patient, that its plan is one of reorganization. Its plan is quite general, too general, but it proposes (1) to have the asset evaluated by the Court, and (2) to have the partners, individually, pay the deficiency as they may be obligated under their personal agreements.

This could possibly pay NationsBank 100% of the indebtedness. Isn't this, then, more than a liquidating plan? Well, it is a strong although a pioneering argument. We say "pioneering" for it is not the prevailing rule of law. A court would have to make "new law" and we are not afraid to do that; however, it would extend the intent of Chapter 11 cases to a point not intended.

On one hand, we have the ominous threat of the bank foreclosing and bidding the property in at a low figure. The bank itself has suggested $9 million. The deficiency would be enormous. Yet this is the right the bank has, the right Lake Ridge gave in the contract. The debtor's plan seeks to alter this contract and could if this were a plan of reorganization. Unhappily, it is an understandable attempt to soften the blow of foreclosure.

Actually, all the debtor proposes in its plan is to bow out as advantageously as possible. This is not permitted.

Modification of the stay to permit NationsBank to pursue its remedies under its secured agreement(s) is proper.

Observations

Not that the Court has a monopoly on wisdom, but that something additional needs to be said leads to these observations. We made some for the bank in the opinion denying its motion to dismiss the case.

We deal with a unique, valuable tract of land, one of the few remaining in the City of Virginia Beach. It was no little thing to gather 1,200 acres into a bundle. It was an ambitious undertaking on both parts, Lake Ridge and NationsBank. In hindsight, too much was paid for it, too much was loaned on it. Both parties engaged in "asset planning," less in the realities of developing the property. The task of developing the property would be, will be, enormous. It was a brave, commendable undertaking by some worthy people, but it was quite a wad to chew.

Could anything have been done to create a plan which might have been workable? Probably. This would have required several millions of dollars up front. Capital. More investors. Those able and willing to wait the term.

As with any case, we would have liked to help, but we are, properly, bound by the law.

In re SM 104 Limited

United States Bankruptcy Court, S.D. Florida, 1993
160 B.R. 202

Robert E. Ginsberg, Bankruptcy Judge. This matter is before the court on the objections of EquiVest Inc., the successor to Realty South Investors, to the confirmation of the plan of the Debtor, SM 104 Limited. For the reasons stated below, the court denies confirmation.

FACTS

The Debtor, SM 104 Limited, is a limited partnership which owns and operates an office complex called Cypress Creek Executive Court in Fort

Lauderdale, Florida. The office complex is situated on land leased from the City of Fort Lauderdale. The Debtor acquired the leasehold in 1984 and, subsequently, built the office complex on it. Construction financing was provided by South Florida Savings Bank.

The Debtor is one of nine limited partnerships set up by William Murphy and Martin Sadkin. Each limited partnership was to own a single piece of commercial real estate. * * *

* * *

On June 18, 1992, * * * the Debtor filed a petition for relief under Chapter 11 of the Bankruptcy Code. On July 28, 1992, Marika Tolz was appointed Chapter 11 Trustee. * * *

On September 18, 1992, the Debtor filed a proposed plan of reorganization. * * * The Debtor's plan divides the claims against the Debtor into 7 classes. Class 1 is EquiVest's disputed nonrecourse secured claim.[1] Class 2 is the claim of Capital Bank, which has a nonrecourse junior mortgage on the Cypress Creek property as a result of a loan it made to SM 108. Capital Bank's claim and mortgage is worthless, because the Cypress Creek property is fully encumbered by EquiVest's senior claim, leaving no equity for Capital Bank's mortgage, and Capital Bank's loan is nonrecourse. See 11 U.S.C. §502(b); §506(a); §1111(b). Class 3 is EquiVest's unsecured deficiency claim.[2] Class 4 is the claim of Fort Lauderdale for rent arrearages and the past-due 1991 property taxes. That claim has been paid in full. Class 5 is the claims of the Debtor's trade creditors, totalling approximately $175,000. Class 6 is the unsecured claims of Murphy. Finally, Class 7 is the interests of the Debtor's equity security holders.

Basically, the Debtor's plan proposes to pay EquiVest's secured claim over 10 years, with interest at 8%, based on a twenty year amortization. The plan also proposes to pay Capital Bank's claim, EquiVest's unsecured deficiency claim, and the general unsecured claims a equal dividend on the effective date, with any balance owed to be paid in equal quarterly installments over the next two years. The plan does not provide for Class 4, which has already been paid in full. Furthermore, the plan waives the Class 6 inside claims. Finally, the plan proposes to wipe out, in effect, the existing equity interests. Under the plan, the equity interests in the reorganized Debtor will go to Murphy in exchange for a one time payment of $200,000 from Murphy to the Debtor on the effective date of the plan. Murphy intends to distribute the new equity interests to the old equity holders.[3]

---

[1] EquiVest's total claim is approximately $5.5 million. The portion of that claim which is secured is disputed by the parties. See Section I below.

[2] Although EquiVest's loan to the Debtor is nonrecourse, EquiVest is treated as a recourse lender under §1111(b). See Section I below. On February 24, 1993, EquiVest filed a notice in which it declared that, provided the Debtor's plan did not materially change, it did not wish to be treated as a fully secured creditor under §1111(b). 11 U.S.C. §1111(b).

[3] In actuality, the plan purports to allow the existing equity security holders to retain

    * * *

On December 7, 1992, EquiVest filed its own plan of reorganization.* * *

    On January 27, 1993, this court approved the Debtor's disclosure statement. The Debtor's plan was submitted to the various parties affected by the plan for a vote.[1]

    * * *

Class 1, EquiVest's secured claim, voted to reject the plan. Class 2, the claim of Capital Bank, originally voted to reject the plan, but, subsequent to the ballot deadline, was permitted to change its ballot to accept the plan. Class 3, EquiVest's unsecured deficiency claim, voted to reject the plan. Class 4, the City of Fort Lauderdale, is unimpaired by the plan, and, therefore, does not vote. See 11 U.S.C. §1126(f). Class 5, the trade creditors' claims, voted to accept the plan. Classes 6 and 7, the claims of insider creditors and interests of existing equity holders, are wiped out by the plan and thus are deemed to reject it. See 11 U.S.C. §1126(g).

    On March 1, 1993, EquiVest filed its objections to the confirmation of the Debtor's plan. The court heard evidence with respect to the Debtor's plan and EquiVest's objections on March 8, 9, and 11, 1993. EquiVest's objections are now before the court for decision.

    * * *

DISCUSSION

I. EquiVest's Claim.

    There is no doubt that EquiVest's claim is undersecured. EquiVest's total claim is approximately $5.5 million. The parties agree that the value of EquiVest's collateral, the Cypress Creek property, does not exceed $2.7 million. Section 506(a) provides that an undersecured claim is to be bifurcated into two claims, secured and unsecured. Under §506(a), EquiVest has a secured claim to the extent of the value of its collateral. 11 U.S.C. §506(a). Thus, EquiVest has a secured claim to the extent of the value of the Cypress Creek property. The remainder of EquiVest's approximately $5.5 million claim is unsecured.[2] Obviously, the key to determining the nature and extent of EquiVest's secured and unsecured claims is to determine the value of the Cypress Creek property.

---

their equity interests. The word "retain" is misused in this context. Unless Murphy pays in $200,000, the old equity holders cannot get anything. Therefore, no "retention," as such, is possible. See Section II B below.

[1]   EquiVest has not asked this court to confirm its amended plan of reorganization in the prayer for relief in any of its pleadings in connection with the confirmation proceeding. Moreover, it is not clear whether EquiVest's plan of reorganization has ever been submitted to the Debtor's creditors for a vote. Therefore, EquiVest's plan is not before the court for confirmation.

[2]   The unsecured deficiency claim of a nonrecourse creditor, such as EquiVest, is afforded special status in a Chapter 11 pursuant to §1111(b). See Section II A below.

In determining the amount of an undersecured creditor's secured claim under §506(a), property is to be valued "in light of the purpose of the valuation and of the proposed disposition or use of such property." 11 U.S.C. §506(a). Where a debtor's plan proposes to retain and use the property, it is appropriate to value the property at its fair market value.

In this case, we have the usual battle of the appraisers. EquiVest's appraiser, John Danner, values the property at $2.7 million. The Debtor's appraiser, Fred Roe, values the property at $2.15 million. The higher value, of course, favors EquiVest by increasing the amount of its allowed secured claim under §506. EquiVest's secured claim must be paid in full under the Code, while its unsecured deficiency claim need only be paid 8.5 cents on the dollar. See 11 U.S.C. §1129(b). The lower value favors the Debtor by reducing the amount it must pay in full and increasing the amount it can settle for 8.5 cents per dollar. Thus, it is no surprise that each appraiser came up with a value more favorable to the interests of its client. It is left to the court to determine which appraisal is to be afforded greater weight.

Real estate appraisers typically use three methods to approximate the fair market value of property. The first method is the "income capitalization approach." This method gives recognition to the view that investors do not buy the bricks and mortar of a building. Rather, they buy the earnings the bricks and mortar will produce in the future. Measuring the fair market value of collateral under the income capitalization approach is a two-step analysis. First, the future net operating income of the property is estimated. Next, that income is divided by a capitalization rate ("capitalized") to obtain the fair market value of the property.[1]

The capitalization rate is computed by determining the annual rate of return a hypothetical investor would be looking for in deciding whether to buy the property. More specifically, the capitalization rate equals the risk-free interest rate available in the marketplace plus some risk premium the hypothetical investor would require to induce her to make the investment. The risk premium is determined by analyzing the risk involved in the business to be valued.

The second method used to determine the value of a business like that of the instant Debtor is the "comparable sales approach." Under that method, the appraiser researches the debtor's marketplace to find several recent sales of similar properties. Since every piece of property is unique, the appraiser then adjusts the actual sales prices of the comparables to account for both positive and negative differences between the comparables and the subject property. This process generates a range of adjusted sales and prices, within which the

---

[1]   Thus, the formula for valuation of a going concern is (1/capitalization rate) * net operating income. The first part of this formula, "1/capitalization rate," is often referred to as the "multiplier." This is because "1/capitalization rate" produces a number that is multiplied times the anticipated net operating income to give value. For example, assuming a capitalization rate of .125, the "multiplier" would be 8. Thus, the value of the property would be equal to its anticipated net operating income times 8.

appraiser places the debtor's property in an attempt to ascertain what the debtor's property would actually sell for in its own market.

The final method is the replacement cost approach. This approach attempts to replicate the precise amount it would cost to reconstruct a piece of property of similar utility or usefulness as the subject property, applying currently used materials and building techniques, and factoring in actual and actuarial depreciation. In effect, this method attempts to determine the actual present value of the debtor's bricks and mortar. This method is most useful in determining value for insurance purposes.

Roe, the Debtor's appraiser, valued the property in July 1992. Danner, EquiVest's appraiser, valued the property in February 1993. Both Roe and Danner analyzed the value of the Cypress Creek property under all three standard methods. Their conclusions as to the value of the Cypress Creek property were not all that far apart. Roe concluded that the Cypress Creek property is worth $2.15 million, while Danner says it is worth $2.7 million. The difference between the valuations reached by the two appraisals stemmed from disagreement about the level of risk involved in running the Cypress Creek property. While Danner concluded that the Cypress Creek property is no riskier than any other similar commercial real estate property in the Fort Lauderdale area, Roe concluded that the property is significantly riskier than other similar properties in the Fort Lauderdale market. The primary basis for Roe's view of the risk associated with the Cypress Creek property is the fact that some 1/3 of the Debtor's space is occupied by a single tenant, Thasc. The Thasc lease is at an above-market rental. Unfortunately for the Debtor, the Thasc lease expires soon, and a new lease will have to be negotiated. In these negotiations, given the glut of office space available in South Florida and the Fort Lauderdale area, the Debtor will be at a significant disadvantage. Thus, in his analysis under the income capitalization approach, Roe chose to employ a much higher capitalization rate than Danner (13.5%, compared to the 10.5% used by Danner).

By the same token, Danner's analysis of comparable sales reached a higher value for the Cypress Creek property than Roe's analysis did. Roe and Danner strongly disagreed about what sales were comparable in terms of geography, the nature of the property and the business, and age.

Both Danner and Roe properly gave little weight to replacement value. Both recognized that the cost of rebuilding the Cypress Creek property is of, at best, limited relevance here. Indeed, if some disaster destroyed the Debtor's building, the appraisers' testimony suggests that, given the excess of available office space in South Florida, it would be fruitless to even rebuild the Cypress Creek property. Instead, a rational investor might well pocket the insurance proceeds and sell the leasehold for some other use. That option is not available to the Debtor; the Debtor's building is in fine condition. Therefore, both appraisers concluded that a rational investor would either hold the buildings to reap the rewards of the Debtor's future earnings or would offer it to the marketplace for sale, and thus emphasized the income capitalization and comparable sales approaches.

Unfortunately, neither appraisal is particularly persuasive. Danner's appraisal contains a number of careless errors that greatly affect the credibility of the appraisal. Furthermore, there is some risk that Danner was not a disinterested witness. He owns an office building within 2 miles of the Debtor's Cypress Creek property. Thus, there is at least some possibility that the shutdown of the Debtor could inure to his benefit. Consequently, the court is hesitant to give Danner's appraisal much weight. On the other hand, Roe appraised the property in July 1992, some eight months before the confirmation hearing. Thus, Roe's appraisal is weakened by its age. Interest rate conditions have changed in the past eight months, affecting the capitalization rate used by Roe in his income capitalization approach. Moreover, the sales comparables used by Roe are outdated, due to changes in interest rate conditions and the Fort Lauderdale area real estate market.

The court does, however, agree with Roe's view that the status of Thasc's lease makes the Cypress Creek property significantly riskier than other similar Fort Lauderdale commercial real estate properties. In addition, because of the admitted errors in Danner's appraisal and his possible conflict of interest, this court is left with little choice but to use Roe's appraisal. Moreover, because of the facts of this case, the court places primary reliance on the income capitalization approach Roe used to value the Debtor.[1]

Roe's appraisal, however, can only be relevant after it is brought up to date. Thus, it must be adjusted to give recognition for the significant reduction in risk-free interest rates over the past eight months. This adjustment is crucial. Under the income capitalization approach, the value of a commercial real estate property is computed by discounting its net cash flows by an appropriate capitalization rate. Where risk-free interest rates decrease, capitalization rates decrease, since capitalization rates are computed by taking the risk-free interest rates and adding a risk premium. Thus, other things being equal, when interest rates decrease, the values of all commercial real estate properties increase.

At the time of the appraisal, the risk-free rate used by Roe was 3.3%. As of the date of the confirmation hearing, that same risk-free rate was approximately 3.15%. See Treasury Bonds, Notes & Bills, Wall St. J., March 15, 1993, at C16 (quoting September, 1993 treasury bill ask yield as of Friday, March 12, 1993). Adjusting Roe's $2.15 million valuation for this significant drop in interest rates, the court values the Cypress Creek property at $2.27 million.[2]

---

[1]   In other contexts, such as in the home real estate market, the comparable sales approach would be the best indicator of the value of property. The reason is that home values do not generate operating income, making the income capitalization approach useless. Moreover, it is generally recognized that identical houses in identical neighborhoods could be sold for identical prices.

[2]   Although this value is computed using the income capitalization approach, it is consistent with the results reached by Roe, as well as Danner, under the comparable sales

Consequently, the value of EquiVest's collateral is $2.27 million. Under §506(a), EquiVest's secured claim is fixed at that amount. EquiVest's unsecured claim is equal to the difference between its total claim of approximately $5.5 million and its secured claim, $3.23 million.

II. EquiVest's Objections to Confirmation of the Debtor's Plan.

EquiVest objects to the confirmation of the Debtor's plan on five grounds. First, EquiVest alleges that the classification of its unsecured deficiency claim separately from other unsecured claims is impermissible under §1122. Next, EquiVest claims that Murphy's purchase of the equity interest in the reorganized debtor violates the absolute priority rule contained in §1129(b)(2)(B)(ii). Third, EquiVest argues that the treatment of its secured claim under the plan is not fair and equitable, in contravention of §1129(b). Furthermore, EquiVest claims that the Debtor's plan is not feasible, in violation of §1129(a)(11). Finally, EquiVest insists that the Debtor's plan was not filed in good faith, as required by §1129(a)(3). [The court's discussion of the last two objections is omitted.]

A. May the Debtor separately classify EquiVest's unsecured deficiency claim created by §1111(b) from the general unsecured claims?

EquiVest's initial objection to the Debtor's plan is that its separate classification of EquiVest's unsecured deficiency claim from the claims of the general unsecured creditors is impermissible. EquiVest's argument in this regard is erroneous.

An attempt to force a Chapter 11 plan on one or more impaired classes of creditors that have rejected the plan is commonly referred to as "cramdown." Section 1129(a)(10) of the Bankruptcy Code provides that before a plan can be crammed down over the objections of a creditor class, at least one impaired class of creditor claims must vote to accept the plan, without regard to any insider votes. 11 U.S.C. §1129(a)(10). Thus, the Debtor, to get its plan confirmed over

---

approach. Under that approach, Roe suggested a value of $2.2 million, while Danner suggested a value of $2.6 million ($3.55 million for the fee, minus $950,000 to adjust for the fact that the Debtor's interest is a leasehold). This is true even when Roe's older comparables are adjusted for the general reduction in interest rates between the confirmation hearing and Roe's appraisal. Moreover, the value is reasonably close to the replacement values suggested by both appraisals. Under that approach, Roe suggested a value of $2.2 million, while Danner suggested a value of $2.61 million ($3.56 million for the fee, minus $950,000 to adjust for the fact that Debtor's interest is a leasehold). The analysis under the replacement cost approach would not have changed significantly between the confirmation hearing and Roe's appraisal, since the inflation rate has been low. The income capitalization value is computed by dividing $302,875 (the stream of net operating income projected by Roe in perpetuity, which Danner agrees was basically accurate) by a 13.35% capitalization rate. That capitalization rate is computed by: (1) determining the implicit risk premium in Roe's choice of 13.5% as the capitalization rate (which is 10.2%, based on a risk-free rate of 3.3% at the time of Roe's appraisal); and (2) adding that risk premium to the current risk-free rate of 3.15%.

EquiVest's objections, must come up with one impaired creditor class that accepts the plan, without regard to any insider votes in that class.

The Debtor has placed EquiVest's §1111(b)--created deficiency claim in a separate class by itself, Class 3. This court has previously held EquiVest's unsecured claim is $3.23 million. The other unsecured creditors' claims are placed by the Debtor's plan in Class 5, and total $175,000. Given the size of EquiVest's §1111(b) unsecured deficiency claim relative to the other unsecured claims and EquiVest's opposition to the plan, it is obvious the reason the Debtor seeks to separately classify EquiVest's §1111(b) deficiency claim from the claims of other unsecured creditors is to satisfy the requirements of §1129(a)(10); i.e., to get one impaired class to accept the plan.[1] EquiVest claims that the Debtor's apparently manipulative motive is improper, and that EquiVest's unsecured deficiency claim should be placed in the same class as the claims of the general unsecured creditors. If the court accepts EquiVest's argument that it should be classified with the other general unsecured creditors in a single class and EquiVest's argument that the Class 5 unsecured creditors were the only impaired class to accept the plan, such a joint classification would be the death knell for the Debtor's plan because the Debtor could no longer satisfy the requirements of §1129(a)(10). EquiVest's deficiency claim would be large enough to overwhelm the claims of the other members of that single class, and, by voting no, EquiVest could prevent the plan from being accepted by two-thirds in amount of the total unsecured claims. See 11 U.S.C. §1126(c).

* * *

Section 1122(a) expressly provides that only substantially similar claims may be placed in the same class. It does not expressly require that all substantially similar claims be placed in the same class, nor does it expressly prohibit substantially similar claims from being classified separately. Nevertheless, many courts, including five circuit courts of appeal, while recognizing that §1122 does not explicitly forbid a plan proponent from placing similar claims in separate classes, have imposed significant limits on the ability of a plan proponent to do so.

* * *

[T]his court believes that the lines of reasoning articulated by the circuit courts and the majority of district and bankruptcy courts have missed the forests for the trees. Section 1122(a) allows joint classification of claims only if the claims are substantially similar in terms of their legal rights. There are, however, significant differences between the legal rights of a general unsecured claim and an unsecured deficiency claim created for the nonrecourse lender by §1111(b). Thus, an unsecured deficiency claim created by §1111(b) is not substantially similar to general unsecured claims, and, under §1122(a), the two types of claims cannot be classified together.

---

[1] The Debtor has suggested no business justification for the separate classification of the EquiVest claim. It is also worth noting that the Debtor's plan offers EquiVest the same 8.5% dividend on its deficiency claim that it offers the general unsecured creditors.

The most obvious difference between a general unsecured claim and an unsecured deficiency claim created by §1111(b) is that the former exists regardless of what chapter of the Bankruptcy Code the case is in, while the latter exists only so long as the case remains in Chapter 11. See 11 U.S.C. §103(f). If the Chapter 11 case is converted to Chapter 7, the nonrecourse lender is confined to its collateral for recovery. It has no deficiency claim against the Chapter 7 estate. See 11 U.S.C. §502(b)(1). This distinction is significant.

One area in which the distinction between the rights of holders of general unsecured claims and the rights of §1111(b) deficiency claimants can be seen clearly is in the application of the "best interests" test of §1129(a)(7). See 11 U.S.C. §1129(a)(7). Section 1129(a)(7) sets out the financial minimum that assenting creditors in an assenting class can impose on dissenting creditors within that class. This minimum was drawn from the best interests test that came to the Bankruptcy Code from the old Chapter XI. See Bankruptcy Act of 1898, §366(2) (repealed 1979); H.R.Rep. No. 595, 95th Cong., 1st Sess. 412-13 (1977), U.S.Code Cong. & Admin.News 1978, p. 5787. Section 1129(a)(7) provides that, with respect to every impaired class, each holder of a claim or interest of such class: (i) has accepted the plan; or (ii) will receive or retain under the plan on account of such claim or interest property of a value, as of the effective date of the plan, that is not less than the amount that such holder would so receive or retain if the debtor were liquidated under chapter 7 of this title on such date ... 11 U.S.C. §1129(a)(7).

Thus, the majority in a class can never force the minority in that class to take less in present value terms than the minority would receive in a Chapter 7 liquidation case involving the debtor.

The application of this standard to a class consisting of both general unsecured claims and §1111(b) deficiency claims can lead to anomalous results. A simple example shows why. Suppose that an unsecured deficiency claim created by §1111(b) is placed in the same class as the general unsecured claims, and that the plan provides for that class to receive a 25% payment of claims on the effective date of the plan. Suppose further that, in a Chapter 7 liquidation, the holders of general unsecured claims would be paid a 35% dividend. The plan would fail the best interests of the creditors test as to the general unsecured creditors, and the plan could not be confirmed unless each general unsecured claim voted for the plan. See 11 U.S.C. §1129(a)(7). This would be true even if a majority in number and two-thirds in amount of the claims in the class that voted on the plan voted to accept. See 11 U.S.C. §1126(c). On the other hand, the plan would propose to give the unsecured deficiency claim created by §1111(b) more than it would receive in a hypothetical Chapter 7 liquidation: in a Chapter 7 case, the unsecured deficiency claim created by §1111(b) would not exist and would not be paid at all.

All that is ever required to satisfy the best interests test as to a §1111(b) nonrecourse deficiency claim is for the claimholder to receive the present value of the collateral. Nevertheless, as long as joint classification is utilized, the holder of a §1111(b) deficiency claim can hold out for a dividend equal to what the general unsecured claims are being paid to satisfy the best interests of the creditors test as to such creditors, even though the undersecured nonrecourse claim is never entitled to any payment in a Chapter 7 case for the amount by which the value of its collateral is less than it is owed. This is because §1123(a)(4) requires a plan to provide for the same treatment of all claims in a class, unless the holder of a claim agrees to less favorable treatment. 11 U.S.C. §1123(a)(4). Thus, in the hypothetical above, if the plan were amended to satisfy the best interests of the creditors test by giving the holders of general unsecured claims a 35% dividend, the holder of the §1111(b) nonrecourse deficiency claim could, as long as the claims are jointly classified, insist on the same 35% dividend, or block confirmation of the plan. It would be hard to believe that the drafters of the Bankruptcy Code intended such an absurd result.

There are other significant disparities between the legal rights of the holder of a general unsecured claim and the holder of a §1111(b) nonrecourse deficiency claim. For example, if the debtor is a partnership, the general partners are liable for the debts of the partnership in the event the case converts to one under Chapter 7. See 11 U.S.C. §723. If the Chapter 11 case shows signs of possible failure, the general unsecured creditors could seek equitable relief to prevent dissipation of the assets of the general partners pending resolution of the Chapter 11 case. It is unlikely that the holder of a §1111(b) nonrecourse deficiency claim could pursue such relief, since the nonrecourse lender is confined to its collateral as a source of payment in Chapter 7. It has no deficiency claim against either the estate or the general partners.

It is clear that the legal rights of creditors holding unsecured deficiency claims created by §1111(b) and general unsecured creditors are, for classification purposes, substantially dissimilar. Therefore, separate classification of unsecured deficiency claims created by §1111(b) and general unsecured claims is not only permissible, but mandatory. See 11 U.S.C. §1122(a).

   * * *

Thus, this court rules that the Debtor's separate classification of EquiVest's Class 3 unsecured deficiency claim and the claims of the Class 5 general unsecured creditors is permissible. Indeed, such separate classification is required by §1122(a). See 11 U.S.C. §1122(a). Since separate classification is required by §1122(a), the Debtor's motive in separately classifying the §1111(b) claim and the general unsecured claims is irrelevant.

B. Does the purchase of the equity interests in the reorganized debtor by its prepetition equity holders for $200,000 violate the absolute priority rule?

EquiVest's second objection to the Debtor's plan is that the Debtor's prepetition equity holders are permitted to purchase full ownership of the reorganized debtor for $200,000. EquiVest claims that such a purchase violates the absolute priority rule, since the Debtor's unsecured creditors are not paid in full but the Debtor's prepetition equity holders wind up owning the reorganized debtor. See 11 U.S.C. §1129(b)(2)(B)(ii). The Debtor argues, however, that the prepetition owners' purchase is permissible under the so- called "new value exception." This court considers the phrase "new value exception" to be an unfortunate misnomer. As long as certain requirements are met, purchase of the equity of the reorganized debtor by the debtor's prepetition equity holders is entirely consistent with the absolute priority rule. In this case, those requirements are met. Thus, the Debtor's prepetition owners' purchase of the equity interests in the reorganized Debtor under the Debtor's plan is perfectly acceptable.

(1) The absolute priority rule and Case v. Los Angeles Lumber.

The absolute priority rule has long been a fundamental tenet of bankruptcy law, tracing back at least to the Supreme Court's ruling in Northern Pacific Ry. Co. v. Boyd, 228 U.S. 482, 33 S.Ct. 554, 57 L.Ed. 931 (1913). Section 77(b) of the Bankruptcy Act of 1898, the statute governing the Boyd case, required that a plan of reorganization be "fair and equitable." In Boyd, the court held that the phrase "fair and equitable" meant that for a reorganization plan to be able to receive judicial approval, each senior class of claims or interests had to be fully satisfied before any junior class of claims or interests could participate in the reorganization. The rule enunciated in Boyd quickly became known as the absolute priority rule.

Subsequently, in Case v. Los Angeles Lumber Products Co., 308 U.S. 106, 121-22, 60 S.Ct. 1, 10, 84 L.Ed. 110 (1939), the Supreme Court appeared to create what has become commonly known as the "new value exception" to the absolute priority rule. In Los Angeles Lumber, the Court considered whether a plan of reorganization that gave prepetition equity holders an equity stake in the reorganized debtor without requiring a fresh contribution of capital and did not pay creditors in full was "fair and equitable" under §77B of the 1898 Act. Such a plan obviously violated the absolute priority rule enunciated in Boyd, and the court so held. However, in Los Angeles Lumber, the Court went on to spell out circumstances under which prepetition equity holders may participate in a plan of reorganization even though not all creditors of the debtor are paid in full under the reorganization plan. The Court stated that participation by prepetition owners without full payment to creditors would not violate the absolute priority rule if: (1) the prepetition owners made a fresh contribution; (2) in money or money's worth; (3) that was reasonably equivalent to the participation accorded those owners; and (4) that was necessary for an feasible reorganization.

Although the court's statement about equity participation in Los Angeles Lumber was dictum, most lower courts have read Los Angeles Lumber as establishing a "new value exception" to the absolute priority rule.

* * *

Although the Bankruptcy Code codified the judicially created absolute priority rule, it did not expressly codify the Los Angeles Lumber dictum.

Incredibly, in the voluminous legislative history of the Code, the "new value exception" is virtually unmentioned. * * *

(2) Current thinking on the purchase by prepetition owners of participation rights in the reorganized debtor.

* * *

Courts take three approaches in considering the vitality of the "new value exception." The most commonly accepted view is that Los Angeles Lumber created a "new value exception" that survived the enactment of the Code. The strongest argument in support of this view relies on Dewsnup, --- U.S. ----, 112 S.Ct. 773, 116 L.Ed.2d 903 in which the Supreme Court stated that the Code did not effect any major change in pre-Code judicially created practice unless there was "at least some discussion" in the legislative history of the Code of Congressional intent to make such a change. Since the Los Angeles Lumber "exception" was clearly part of pre-Code judicially created practice, these courts, relying on Dewsnup, have concluded that because the Code itself is silent and the legislative history of the Code is virtually nonexistent and inconclusive on the issue of the new value exception, it must have survived enactment of the Code.

However, even in the aftermath of Dewsnup, a significant minority of courts have concluded that the Los Angeles Lumber "exception" did not survive enactment of the Code. These courts have reasoned that, in enacting §1129(b)(2)(B)(ii), Congress replaced Los Angeles Lumber 's interpretation of the Act's "fair and equitable" standard with a congressionally enacted definition of that standard. In using the phrase "fair and equitable" in §1129(b)(2)(B)(ii), Congress was aware of the Los Angeles Lumber dictum, yet nevertheless adopted a statutory approach that contains no reference to the "new value exception." * * *

The third approach is to view the phrase "new value exception" as a misnomer, instead holding that the "exception" is not an exception at all, but is merely a corollary to the absolute priority rule. * * *

This third approach, which appears to represent the current trend, starts with the premise that, in a cramdown situation, §1129(b) clearly bars prepetition owners from receiving an interest under the plan " on account of" their prior ownership interests. 11 U.S.C. §1129(b)(2)(B)(ii). However, when prepetition owners infuse into the reorganized debtor necessary new value in the form of money or money's worth, the basis of their equity interest in the reorganized debtor is not their prepetition ownership interest in the debtor, but rather their payment of new value for an interest in the reorganized debtor. Thus, according to this approach, the Los Angeles Lumber court merely enunciated a logical corollary to the absolute priority rule, not some "exception" to the absolute priority rule. Consequently, the corollary was logically included in the Bankruptcy Code as part of Congress's adoption of the absolute priority rule for application in the context of a cramdown of a Chapter 11 plan on dissenting classes of creditors. See id.; 11 U.S.C. §1129(b)(2)(B)(ii).

(3) The new value corollary.

This court finds the view that the "new value exception" is not an exception at all, but merely a corollary to the absolute priority rule, and that, as such, the new value corollary still exists under the Code, to be persuasive. The language of §1129(b)(2)(B)(ii), which codifies the absolute priority rule, supports such a result. See 11 U.S.C. §1129(b)(2)(B)(ii). Section 1129(b)(2)(B)(ii) provides that, in the context of a Chapter 11 cramdown on a dissenting creditor class, "old equity" may not receive any interest "on account of" its prior ownership. The infusion of a reasonable amount of new capital by prepetition owners in exchange for the equity interests of the reorganized debtor does not violate the plain language of §1129(b)(2)(B)(ii) in any way. The equity the old owners receive under a plan is not given to them on account of their prior ownership interests in the debtor. Instead, it is given to them on account of, or in exchange for, the new value contributed. Thus, the purchase by prepetition owners of the debtor of the equity interests of a reorganized debtor for new value is not inconsistent with the absolute priority rule.

Sound policy reasons warrant such a result. Two of the leading commentators on bankruptcy law, Professors Baird and Jackson, have long argued that when a business becomes insolvent, the creditors in effect become the owners of the business. This is because, where a debtor is insolvent, the existing equity is valueless. However, even where a business is insolvent, the going concern value of the business is an asset that can be liquidated to provide at least partial payment for creditors.

In most cases, as in this case, the majority of creditors will not wish to hold the equity in the reorganized debtor and run the business themselves. Instead, they would prefer to sell the equity interests to a buyer who will manage the business of the reorganized debtor and acquire the resources to pay the creditors under the plan. It makes no sense to suggest that the creditor body can sell the equity in the reorganized debtor to anyone except the debtor's prepetition equity holders. Such a blanket rule would, in fact, doom many confirmable Chapter 11 plans, since, as a practical matter, the debtor's prepetition owners may be the only persons who have any interest in buying the equity in the reorganized debtor. Old equity may be interested in purchasing the equity of the reorganized debtor for strictly personal reasons, such as preserving their jobs or continuing a family business. In fact, such personal considerations may cause old equity to purchase the equity of the reorganized debtor at a price that is economically irrational.

Allowing old equity to bid for the new equity also may enhance the return to creditors by setting off a bidding war. It signals the market as to what a party with full information about the debtor and its prospects is willing to pay for the equity in the reorganized debtor. Obviously, creditors are better off if the bid of old equity causes others to investigate an investment in the reorganized debtor and to seek to outbid the debtor's prepetition equity owners. Thus, allowing the debtor's current owners to bid for the equity interests of the reorganized debtor may maximize the return to creditors by producing a true auction for the equity interests.

In fact, it is hard to come up with a logical reason why the debtor's prepetition owners should be barred as a matter of law from purchasing the equity of the reorganized debtor. If the debtor's prepetition owners' offer for the equity interests in the reorganized debtor is reasonable and necessary, contemplates a contribution of real assets, and is the best offer available, the creditors ought to be able to accept it.

This court finds that the "new value exception" is not really an exception to the absolute priority rule. Instead, the court holds that it is a corollary to the absolute priority rule, consistent with the language of §1129(b)(2)(B)(ii) and sound bankruptcy policy. Thus, despite the enactment of the Bankruptcy Code, the new value corollary remains a vital part of bankruptcy law.

(4) When is the purchase by prepetition owners of the equity of a reorganized debtor consistent with the absolute priority rule?

However, before the purchase by prepetition owners of the equity of a reorganized debtor can be accepted as consistent with the absolute priority rule, three requirements must be satisfied. First, the new contribution must be in money or money's worth, meaning that what the creditors are to receive in exchange for the equity in the reorganized debtor must have a present realizable value. It cannot merely be a promise to do something in the future, such as a promise to manage the reorganized debtor or guaranty a loan to the reorganized debtor.

Second, the contribution of new value must be necessary for the implementation of the proposed plan of reorganization. In effect, the plan proponent must show that, without such a contribution of new value for the equity of the reorganized debtor, the reorganization effort may well fail. The necessity requirement is intended to insure that the equity of the reorganized debtor is not given to the prepetition owners in a sham sale for capital in excess of the reorganized debtor's needs. In the case of such a sham sale, the excess, unnecessary capital could be returned to the new owners in the form of a dividend, redemption or the like, resulting in the old owners acquiring the new equity for little or nothing (and on account of their prior ownership) to the detriment of creditors, in violation of the absolute priority rule.

Finally, the purchase price paid by old equity for some or all of the equity in the reorganized debtor must be reasonably equivalent to the value of the new equity; that is, old equity must pay a fair price for the right to participate in the reorganized debtor. Reasonable equivalence is required by §1129(b)(2)(B)(ii). This is because if a plan purports to give the debtor's prepetition owners the equity interests in the reorganized debtor at a bargain price, the prepetition owners will be receiving something "on account of" their prepetition ownership. Thus, the plan would violate the absolute priority rule.

As a matter of auction theory, the ideal method for measuring the fairness of the price paid for the equity in the reorganized debtor is to offer it for sale to a fully informed investing public and to sell the equity to the highest bidder, be it the debtor's prepetition owners or outsiders. This court does not believe such a public auction is necessary. As a practical matter, the prospect of drawing more than a few bidders in such an auction is unrealistic. The market for equity participation for failing business is thin, and the market for failing small businesses is even thinner. Moreover, the market is inefficient; insiders (and possibly a few major creditors) of failing businesses, especially failing small businesses, clearly have superior access to information, giving them a significant upper hand in the bidding process. Finally, a general public marketing of the debtor's equity interests may run afoul of state or federal securities laws, and compliance with such securities laws may be beyond the debtor's financial abilities. Thus, a general public auction of the equity interests in the reorganized debtor need not be held in every case to satisfy the new value corollary.

Rather, at least in all but the largest bankruptcy cases, the disclosure and confirmation procedures provided by Chapter 11 offer an acceptable alternative for marketing the ownership interests of the reorganized debtor. Section 1125 requires a plan proponent to distribute a disclosure statement to all parties that have shown an economic interest in the reorganized debtor; that is, to all creditors and equity holders. The disclosure statement must be approved by the court before it can be used to solicit votes for a plan. See 11 U.S.C. §1125 * * *. In order for the court to approve a disclosure statement, the court must be satisfied that it contains information sufficient for a "hypothetical reasonable investor typical of holders of claims or interests of the relevant class to make an informed judgment about the plan." 11 U.S.C. §1125(a)(1). That level of information should be sufficient to alert claim holders and equity holders whether it is worth pursuing a bid for the equity of the reorganized debtor. Thus, at least in cases the size of the instant case, the disclosure statement is quite adequate to promote an informed bidding process among the parties.

Such a bidding process can take place regardless of whether the debtor's exclusive right to propose a plan has been terminated or has expired. See 11 U.S.C. §1121(b), (c). If the debtor's exclusivity period has ended or been terminated, any creditor can propose a competing plan incorporating an attempt to outbid old equity for the equity in the reorganized debtor. 11 U.S.C. §1121(c). Moreover, even if the debtor's exclusivity period has not ended, any creditor can move to lift exclusivity and then propose its own plan incorporating a competing bid. 11 U.S.C. §1121(d).[1]

---

[1] Several courts have concluded that, if a plan gives prepetition owners of the debtor the exclusive right to purchase the equity interests of the reorganized debtor, the plan violates the absolute priority rule. This is because the plan gives the prepetition owners something "on account of" their prepetition ownership; i.e., the exclusive right to bid.

If the plan process generates competing bids, market theory dictates that the highest bid be accepted. This is because the bidding process itself works to drive the price paid for the equity in the reorganized debtor up towards its fair market value. Thus, as long as the plan process generates competing bids, the court's role ought to be to simply determine which bid is worth more, and accept it.

Of course, the plan process does not guarantee competing bids. Where there is only one bid for the ownership interests in the reorganized debtor, there is no guarantee that the sole bid is at the fair market value of the equity interests in the reorganized debtor. Thus, if only one party bids for the equity interests of the reorganized debtor, the court must determine whether the bid for the equity of the reorganized debtor is reasonably equivalent to the value of the equity interests.

Here, the prepetition owners of the debtor propose to purchase the equity interests of the reorganized debtor for $200,000. Obviously, that infusion of new value is "money or money's worth." Moreover, it is clearly necessary. Without the infusion of new value, the reorganized Debtor could not meet its obligations. Thus, the first two requirements for the purchase by prepetition owners of the equity of a reorganized debtor to be consistent with the absolute priority rule are met in the instant case.

(5) Is the prepetition owners' $200,000 bid for the equity interests of the reorganized Debtor reasonably equivalent to the value of the equity interests?

EquiVest has objected to the prepetition owners' bid to purchase the equity interests of the reorganized Debtor. It has objected even though it made no competing bid for the equity interests in the reorganized Debtor. Nevertheless, to measure whether the plan is fair and equitable with respect to EquiVest, this court must determine whether the prepetition owners' proposed infusion of value is reasonably equivalent to the value of the equity interests of the reorganized Debtor being parcelled out to the old equity owners.

A specific determination of the value of the equity interests of the reorganized Debtor is quite complex; indeed, one scholar has noted that such a valuation would usually be "a guess compounded by an estimate." H.R.Rep. No. 595, 95th Cong., 1st Sess. 222 (1977), U.S.Code Cong. & Admin.News 1978, p. 6181 (quoting Prof. Peter Coogan). Of course, the capitalization of future earnings is accepted to be the appropriate method for determining the value of the equity interests in the reorganized Debtor. Unfortunately, in this proceeding,

See 11 U.S.C. §1129(b)(2)(B)(ii). The auction that the Chapter 11 disclosure and confirmation process creates should minimize the possibility of a prepetition owner being given an exclusive right to bid for the equity of the reorganized debtor. This is because the process allows the debtor's creditors to compete with the prepetition owners for the purchase of the equity interests of the reorganized debtor. Consequently, the process itself prevents old equity from receiving an exclusive right to purchase the ownership interests of the reorganized debtor in all cases.

the income capitalization approach is not useful in valuing the equity interests in the reorganized Debtor.

At first glance, the value of the equity interests in the reorganized Debtor would appear to simply be equal to the market value of the Debtor's lone asset, the Cypress Creek property, net of the liens upon it. Relying principally on the income capitalization approach, this court has determined that the Cypress Creek property is worth $2.27 million. See Section I above. Of course, EquiVest's secured claim and lien, equal to the value of the Cypress Creek property under §506(a), is also $2.27 million. See Section I above. Thus, applying the income capitalization approach, this court would find the equity interests in the reorganized Debtor to be valueless, since the Cypress Creek property is fully encumbered. Thus, any contribution by the prepetition owners of the Debtor, no matter how small, would appear to be reasonably equivalent to its value.

Common sense, however, suggests that the equity interests must be of some value here. If the equity interests in the reorganized Debtor are valueless, why would EquiVest object to the purchase of those interests by the prepetition owners of the Debtor? * * *

In a single asset real estate case, the equity interests in the reorganized debtor might be valuable for a number of reasons. First, the asset could end up being worth more than the court believes it is worth. If this happens, the owners of the equity interests, rather than the holder of an undersecured claim, would be entitled to that residual value, since the secured portion of a creditor's claim is limited to the value which the court determines for the property. In addition, the mere control of the reorganized debtor has some value. Furthermore, those purchasing the equity interests in a reorganized debtor may see things of value that are not generally included in a capitalized earnings valuation of an enterprise. These would include things such as the opportunity to be paid a salary for managing the reorganized debtor and even the prestige of owning an attractive property. All of these things cannot be valued by the capitalization of future earnings approach, since they affect neither projected income nor risk. In single asset real estate cases where the property is fully encumbered, the capitalized earnings value presumably has been entirely allocated to the valuation of the secured claim, as required by §506 and the absolute priority rule. That leaves the question of how to value the highly speculative equity.

* * * This court can only conclude that it must look to the facts and circumstances of each single asset case to determine whether the new value infusion is reasonably equivalent to any quantifiable value being received by the purchaser of the equity. In the instant case, the prepetition owners of the Debtor, meaning essentially Murphy, propose to purchase the equity interests in the reorganized Debtor for $200,000. In light of the facts and circumstances of this case, $200,000 appears to be at least reasonably equivalent to the value of the equity interests in the reorganized Debtor. * * *

Here, economically, old equity appears to be paying something for nothing. However, the prepetition owners' $200,000 bid is, in effect, a bet that the court's valuation of the Cypress Creek property is low, and that there will be some residual value left for the prepetition owners to capture once the EquiVest loan is paid off. It is also a gamble that the Debtor will have future income in excess of that projected by both the Debtor and EquiVest, such that it will be able to service its debt under the plan and have enough left over to pay Murphy and his colleagues nice salaries. Moreover, Murphy clearly has significant personal time and effort invested in running the Debtor. His tone and demeanor while testifying made it clear that he has a great deal of his own ego caught up in saving his SM empire. Murphy seems to believe that he alone can rescue the Debtor and its affiliates from financial disaster. Thus, there are significant noneconomic reasons underlying Murphy's almost desperate desire to retain control of the Debtor. What he is willing to pay for the equity of the reorganized Debtor is not the result of a rational valuation by Murphy; instead, it is determined by how much cash Murphy thinks is necessary to make his proposed plan work. The irrationality of Murphy's bid in economic terms is evidenced by the fact that the reorganized Debtor will be balance sheet insolvent on the effective date of the plan and the fact that Murphy has not produced reasonable projections of the reorganized Debtor's financial future. In buying the equity of the reorganized Debtor, Murphy is playing the lottery, and gambling on a long shot.

Thus, this court finds that the proposed $200,000 contribution by Murphy is at least reasonably equivalent to the value of the equity interests in the reorganized Debtor. Indeed, it probably far exceeds any rational value that the equity interests in the reorganized Debtor could have. Therefore, the prepetition owners' bid for the equity interests of the reorganized Debtor under the Debtor's plan meets the requirements of the new value corollary. Consequently, the prepetition owners may purchase the equity interests of the reorganized Debtor in accordance with the Debtor's plan without violating the absolute priority rule.

C. Is the Debtor's plan fair and equitable to EquiVest's secured claim?

EquiVest's third objection is that the Debtor's plan is not fair and equitable to EquiVest. The court agrees.

Section 1129(b)(1) provides that, for a plan to be crammed down over the objections of an impaired class of creditors or interest holders, the plan must be "fair and equitable" with respect to that class. 11 U.S.C. §1129(b)(1). Section 1129(b)(2)(A) sets forth minimal standards that each plan is required to meet to be considered fair and equitable. Section 1129(b)(2)(A) states, in pertinent part, that a plan must provide, with respect to a class of secured claims:

> (i)(I) that the holders of such claims retain the liens securing such claims, whether the property subject to such liens is retained by the debtor or transferred to another entity, to the extent of the allowed amount of such claims; and (II) that each holder of a claim of such class receive on account of such claim deferred cash payments totaling

at least the allowed amount of such claim, of a value, as of the effective date of the plan, of at least the value of such holder's interest in the estate's interest in such property; (ii) for the sale, subject to section 363(k) of this title, of any property that is subject to the liens securing such claims, free and clear of such liens, with such liens to attach to the proceeds of such sale, and the treatment of such liens on proceeds under clause (i) or (iii) of this subparagraph; or (iii) for the realization of the holders of the indubitable equivalent of such claims.

11 U.S.C. §1129(b)(2)(A).

In this case, the Debtor's plan attempts to meet the requirements of §1129(b)(2)(A) with respect to Class 1, which consists of only EquiVest's secured claim, by making cash payments to EquiVest pursuant to §1129(b)(2)(A)(i). Section 1129(b)(2)(A)(i) has three requirements: the plan must (a) allow EquiVest to maintain its lien on the existing collateral; and (b) provide for cash payments to the EquiVest totaling at least the allowed amount of its secured claim (the "face amount" test); and (c) provide EquiVest with payments of a present value at least equal to the value, as of the effective date of the plan, of EquiVest's interest in the estate's interest in the collateral, i.e. EquiVest's secured claim (the "present value" test). 11 U.S.C. §1129(b)(2)(A)(i). As long as EquiVest's claim is undersecured and EquiVest has not made the §1111(b) election, satisfaction of the present value test with respect to the secured claim will necessarily satisfy the face amount test with respect to EquiVest's secured claim, because payment of EquiVest's secured claim with a present market rate of interest over any period of time requires the Debtor to pay more than the face amount of the secured claim.

Here, the Debtor's plan clearly meets the first requirement §1129(b)(2)(A)(i), since the plan allows EquiVest to maintain its lien. Moreover, EquiVest is undersecured and has not made the §1111(b) election.[1] Thus, as long as the Debtor's plan provides for cash payments to be made to EquiVest at an interest rate sufficient to pay EquiVest the present value of its secured claim, the Debtor's plan meets the requirements of §1129(b)(2)(A)(i) and can be forced on EquiVest.

EquiVest, however, claims that the 8% interest rate the Debtor's plan proposes to pay it is insufficient to provide EquiVest with the present value of its secured claim, and thus that the plan is not fair and equitable to EquiVest.[2] The court agrees.

---

[1] EquiVest did not make the §1111(b)(2) election as of the conclusion of the hearing on the Debtor's disclosure statement. See Fed.R.Bankr.P. 3014. Instead, EquiVest purported to reserve the right to make the election when the Debtor's plan is finalized. Where EquiVest gets that "right" to delay having to make the §1111(b)(2) election is not clear.

[2] EquiVest also claims that the proposed stretchout by the plan of EquiVest's five year loan to the Debtor to ten years (based on a twenty year amortization) makes the plan

(1) Choosing an interest rate: what approach?

Courts differ as to how to calculate the interest rate that provides a secured creditor the present value of its secured claim, as required by §1129(b). EquiVest urges this court to use the "coerced loan" approach, which requires the creditor to be paid "the current market rate of interest used for similar loans in the region" in workout situations. The difficulty with such an approach, of course, is that there usually is no legal market for forced loans. Moreover, even if there were a market for forced loans, that market would be economically inefficient. Vulture capitalists use the urgency of a Chapter 11 debtor's position to extract a premium by charging an interest rate in excess of the actual risks of the loan. The premium approach is inconsistent with the Bankruptcy Code, which requires only that the secured creditor be compensated for the use of its money over the life of the plan, without any premium beyond the rate suggested by the risk of what amounts to a forced loan. Thus, as unrealistic as it sounds at first blush, the existence of the bankruptcy case should be ignored as a factor in computing the interest rate.

Instead, the "time value of money" approach, which appears to be accepted by the majority of courts, should be applied in determining the appropriate interest rate for a cramdown under §1129(b). The time value of money approach takes an appropriate risk- free rate and adds a risk premium, measured in basis points, [1] sufficient to compensate the holder of a secured claim for the inherent risks imposed upon it by the proposed plan. The appropriate risk-free rate is equal to the current interest rate being paid on treasury bonds with a duration similar to the length of the plan. The risk premium reflects the length of the deferment, the quality of the property, and the risk of subsequent default by the debtor.

---

unfair. It is clear that, even if a plan satisfies the technical requirements enunciated in §1129(b)(2) by providing a creditor with an appropriate interest rate, the plan is not necessarily fair and equitable. Section 1129(b)(2) merely states the minimum requirements of a fair and equitable plan. See also 11 U.S.C. §102(3) (defining the term "includes" as not limiting). Rather, this court must consider the plan "in the context of the rights of the creditors under state law and the particular facts and circumstances" of the case. It has been consistently held that the fair and equitable requirement does not prohibit long term payouts. To be fair and equitable, the proposed stretchout must simply be reasonable. In fact, lengthy stretch out periods for real estate have received judicial approval. In this case, the Debtor's proposed twenty year amortization with a ten year balloon is not unreasonable. The fact that the original EquiVest loan to the Debtor was for a term of five years is not dispositive, or even persuasive. As long as the feasibility of a plan can be shown and the creditor is properly compensated and protected for the use of its money via an appropriate interest rate, it is not improper for a plan to stretch out payments, even if the loan was originally intended to be a short term loan.

[1]   A basis point is simply one hundredth of one percent.

(2) Applying the time value of money approach to identify the appropriate interest rate in this case.

Here, the Debtor's plan calls for cash payments of principal and 8% interest over a ten year period based on a twenty year amortization, with a balloon payment of all then-remaining principal in year ten. Thus, the appropriate risk-free rate is the ten year treasury bond rate. As of Monday, August 23, 1993, the start of the week in which this decision was announced, that rate was approximately 5.65%. [1] See Treasury Bonds, Notes & Bills, Wall St. J., August 24, 1993, at C16 (quoting ask yield on August, 2003 treasury bond as of August 23, 1993). Consequently, the base rate to be used in applying the time value of money approach in this case is 5.65%.

Computing the risk premium to be added to the base rate is not quite so simple. Indeed, in this case, computation of the risk premium is made even more difficult by the fact that the Debtor's plan forces EquiVest to make a 100% loan to value. Unfortunately, the Debtor has offered no evidence that an efficient market for loans that are 100% loan to value exists in the real world.

In the absence of an efficient (or, for that matter, any) market for 100% loans, the most appropriate methodology for determining the risk premium on 100% loans is the band of investment technique * * *. The band of investment technique attempts to simulate the financing scheme ordinarily employed by owners of commercial real estate. The band of investment technique divides a 100% loan into two portions: (1) a 75% senior debt portion; and (2) a 25% junior interest portion. Risk premiums are determined for each portion: the senior debt portion earns the risk premium a mortgage-holder would require, and the junior interest earns the substantially higher risk premium an equity investor would require. A weighted risk premium is then computed by multiplying the senior debt risk premium by .75 and the junior interest risk premium by .25.

With respect to the 75% senior debt portion, Robert LaChapelle, EquiVest's interest rate expert, testified that no institutional lenders would make the loan of 100% loan to value that the Debtor's plan requires of EquiVest. However, he

---

[1] Section 1129(b)(2)(A)(i)(II) requires the appropriate interest rate to be measured from the effective date of the plan, which the Debtor's plan provides will be ten days following confirmation of the plan. See 11 U.S.C. §1129(b)(2)(A)(i)(II). "Confirmation" could be construed to mean that the appropriate rate should be measured as of the date on which the court hears evidence on confirmation, or as of the date on which it enters an order confirming the plan. Because information on current risk-free rates is readily available in the marketplace, the court should use the interest rate on the day it rules on the validity of the plan, because that would be the closest date to any hypothetical effective date of the Debtor's plan. The more recent date is more appropriate than the date of the confirmation hearing (in this case, in March 1993), because it is more consistent with the theory underlying this court's approach to identifying the appropriate interest rate. This court's approach gives EquiVest a risk premium for loaning money to the Debtor for ten years instead of purchasing ten year treasury notes, which are riskless. EquiVest could only purchase ten year treasury notes at today's rate, not the rate in effect at the time of the confirmation hearing.

also testified that institutional investors would make a 75% loan to value loan on "acceptable" commercial real estate in the Fort Lauderdale area at a risk premium of 205-230 basis points over the risk-free rate for 10 year loans, depending on the specific risks associated with the borrower in question. * * *

Although the Cypress Creek property is clearly acceptable to serve as collateral for a loan of 75% loan to value, there is greater risk associated with it than with other, similar commercial real estate in the Fort Lauderdale area. Some one-third of the Cypress Creek property is occupied by Thasc, a tenant with an above-market, soon-to-expire lease. In addition, this court * * * is left with serious doubt about Murphy's qualifications to manage the reorganized Debtor. The fact that the plan proposes to allow Murphy to manage the business of the reorganized Debtor is in and of itself another element of risk that must be considered in determining the appropriate rate of interest for the EquiVest claim. Consequently, the court opts for a risk premium at the high end of LaChapelle's scale. The court holds that the risk premium for the senior debt portion of the loan is 230 basis points over the risk-free rate.

Such a holding is, by itself, sufficient to make the court conclude that the Debtor's plan is not fair and equitable to EquiVest's secured claim. The plan proposes to pay EquiVest interest at a rate of 8%, which implies a risk premium of 235 basis points. The risk premium required on the 75% senior debt portion, 230 points, is, by itself, about equal to the risk premium the Debtor's plan proposes. Obviously, the weighted risk premium to be computed using the senior debt risk premium and the substantially higher equity risk premium will also be higher than 8%. Indeed, the risk premium on the equity portion would be in the range of 900 basis points, which would yield a weighted risk premium of 398 basis points.[1]

Thus, it is clear that the Debtor's plan does not propose to pay EquiVest an adequate risk premium, and thus does not propose to pay EquiVest an interest rate sufficient to pay EquiVest the present value of its claim over the life of the plan. Consequently, the court holds that the Debtor's plan is not fair and equitable with respect to EquiVest's secured claim.

D. Is the Debtor's plan feasible?
* * *

---

[1]   [S]uch a computation is inherently an estimate. This court's estimate is based on LaChapelle's testimony that a lender would require a minimum 590 basis point risk premium on a 90% loan to the Debtor. Using this court's adjustment of 230 basis points for the 75% senior debt portion, LaChapelle's testimony implies an adjustment of at least 1668 basis points for the 25% junior interest portion. This implied adjustment is artificially high, since it is weighs heavily the fact that the Debtor is in bankruptcy, a consideration the court has already held is irrelevant for purposes of computing the interest rate required under §1129(b). A premium in the area of 900 basis points on the 25% junior interest portion seems more appropriate.

CONCLUSION

For the reasons stated in this opinion, the court denies confirmation of the Debtor's plan of reorganization. The plan's separate classification of EquiVest's unsecured deficiency claim from the claims of the general unsecured creditors, and the purchase by the old equity owners of the equity interests in the reorganized Debtor for new value are permissible. However, the plan is not fair and equitable to EquiVest, for it does not pay EquiVest an appropriate interest rate. In addition, the Debtor has failed to show by a preponderance of the evidence that the plan is feasible. Finally, the plan violates §1129(a)(5), in that it allows Murphy to be employed as the chief officer of the Debtor.

Notes and Questions

1. *Windsor on the River Associates, Ltd. v. Balcor Real Estate Finance, Inc.*, 7 F.3d 127 (8th Cir. 1993), held that "for purposes of section 1129(a)(10), a claim is not impaired if the alteration of rights in question arises solely from the debtor's exercise of discretion." What would be the effect of that holding in *SM 104*? The claims of the Class 5 trade creditors totaled $175,000. Could the Debtor have paid these claims in full prior to filing for bankruptcy? At the time of the confirmation of its plan? What do you estimate that the Debtor is paying for accountants, appraisers, attorneys, and other professionals in this Chapter 11 case? See generally David Carlson, *The Classification Veto in Single-Asset Cases Under Bankruptcy Code Section 1129(a)(10)*, 44 S.Carolina L.Rev. 565, 610-14 (1993); Benjamin Weintraub & Alan Resnick, *Windsor On the River: The Eighth Circuit Makes It Harder to Find Accepting Impaired Class Needed for Cramdown*, 26 UCC L.J. 359 (1994).

2. Could Equivest have blocked the Debtor by purchasing at least one third of the trade claims and voting the claims against the Debtor's plan? See section 1126(e)

3. Equivest's loan to the debtor was nonrecourse. Why did Equivest have an unsecured claim in this case? If section 1111(b) applies to Equivest's claim, why didn't Equivest make the 1111(b) election? See generally David Carlson, *The Classification Veto in Single-Asset Cases Under Bankruptcy Code Section 1129(a)(10)*, 44 S.Carolina L.Rev. 571, 582-96 (1993). Capital Bank's second mortgage loan was also nonrecourse. Why didn't Capital Bank also have an unsecured claim in this case? See sections 506(a), 1111(b)(1)(A).

4. *In Matter of Greystone III Joint Venture*, 995 F.2d 1274, 1279 (5th Cir. 1991), the court said "thou shalt not classify similar claims differently in order to gerrymander an affirmative vote on a reorganization plan." In *SM 104*, does Judge Ginsberg disagree with or disregard that dictate? See generally Linda Rusch, *Single Asset Cases and Chapter 11: The Classification Quandry*, 1 Am.Bankr.Inst.L. Rev. 43 (1993).

5. You represent C, a creditor with a $14,000,000 claim against D, secured by an apartment building that has a value of $9,000,000. D has filed a plan that proposes inter alia to pay C's $9,000,0000 secured claim in full with interest over six years, to place C's $5,000,000 deficiency claim in a separate class from other unsecured creditors and pay both classes 20% over five years, and to cancel existing equity interests and distribute new equity interests to the present owners who will contribute $300,000. C is willing to pay $300,000 or more in order to obtain control and ownership of the apartment building. Advise C as to what action it can take. See generally Bruce Markell, *Owners, Auctions, and Absolute Priority in Bankruptcy Reorganizations*, 44 STAN.L.REV. 69 (1991); Note, *The Bankruptcy Code and the New Value Doctrine: An Examination into History, Illusions and the Need for Competitive Bidding*, 79 VA.L.REV. 917 (1993).

B. THE DEBTOR'S HOME

A common goal of an individual debtor who files a bankruptcy petition is to save his or her home from foreclosure. Many individual bankruptcy petitions are filed after a lender has accelerated a mortgage and commenced foreclosure proceedings. The bankruptcy filing triggers the automatic stay and that delays the foreclosure.

Can an individual debtor use bankruptcy to accomplish more than a delay of the foreclosure on his or her home? Can the debtor undo the default and reinstate the original mortgage terms? Can the debtor unilaterally alter the original mortgage terms? See section 1322(b) and *In re Taddeo, In re Nobleman v. American Savings Bank,* and *In re Dever* below.

In re Taddeo
United States Court of Appeals, Second Circuit, 1982
685 F.2d 24

.Lumbard, Circuit Judge: Joseph C. and Ellen A. Taddeo live at 6 Ort Court, Sayville, New York. Three years ago they defaulted on their mortgage to Elfriede Di Pierro. Di Pierro accelerated the mortgage, declared its balance due immediately, and initiated foreclosure proceedings. The Taddeos sought refuge under Chapter 13 of the new Bankruptcy Code, staying the foreclosure action under the automatic stay, and proposing to cure the default and reinstate the mortgage under 11 U.S.C. §1322(b)(5). Di Pierro is listed as the Taddeos' only creditor. She rejected the plan to cure the default, and applied for relief from the automatic stay in order to foreclose. Di Pierro contended that once she accelerated her mortgage, the Taddeos had no way to cure the default under the Bankruptcy Code except to pay the full amount as required by state law. Bankruptcy Judge Parente held that the Taddeos could cure the default and reinstate their mortgage, and denied Di Pierro's motion for relief from the stay. We affirm. We do not believe that Congress labored for five years over this controversial question only to remit consumer debtors-intended to be primary beneficiaries of the new Code-to the harsher mercies of state law.

Di Pierro originally owned the house at 6 Ort Court. On June 14, 1979, she sold the house to the Taddeos, taking in return a "purchase money second mortgage" to secure a principal balance of $13,000. The property is subject to a first lien held by West Side Federal Savings & Loan Association, which is not involved in this case.[1] Di Pierro's second mortgage was payable over 15 years at 8.5 percent in equal monthly installments of $128.05.

Upon taking occupancy, the Taddeos notified Di Pierro that they had discovered defects in the property.[2] On advice of counsel, the Taddeos said they would withhold mortgage payments, depositing the money instead with their attorney. The Taddeos and Di Pierro corresponded for several months without reaching an agreement. On October 5, 1979, Di Pierro wrote that she was accelerating the mortgage and declaring the entire balance due immediately. The mortgage contained the acceleration clause specifically approved in N.Y. * * *, which gives the mortgagee the option to accelerate after a default in mortgage payments.

Di Pierro commenced foreclosure proceedings in state court on October 19, 1979. The Taddeos tendered full payment of their arrears by check on October 31, 1979, but Di Pierro refused to accept payment. The state court granted summary judgment to Di Pierro and ordered a referee to determine the amount owed. After a hearing on June 30, 1980, the referee found the Taddeos liable for $14,153.48 in principal and interest, plus interest subsequent to the award.

Before Di Pierro could obtain final judgment of foreclosure and sale, the Taddeos filed a Chapter 13 bankruptcy petition in the Eastern District on July 10, 1980. * * * The petition listed Di Pierro as the only creditor, and stayed Di Pierro's foreclosure action. The Taddeos filed a plan proposing to pay off arrears on the mortgage in installments of $100 per month. The plan further proposed to restore the mortgage and its original payment schedule, * * *. Di Pierro objected to the plan,[3] and petitioned for relief from the automatic stay so that she could proceed with her foreclosure action. Di Pierro contended that her rights as mortgagee could not be affected by the Chapter 13 plan. Bankruptcy Judge Parente, however, held that the Taddeos could pay their arrearages and reinstate their mortgage under this section notwithstanding Di Pierro's acceleration, analogizing §1322(b) to 11 U.S.C. §1124(2), which nullifies acceleration clauses in Chapter 11 corporate reorganizations. Therefore Bankruptcy Judge Parente denied Di Pierro relief from the automatic stay. District Judge Pratt affirmed on similar reasoning.

---

[1]   The record does not indicate the status of the first lien in the Chapter 13 proceeding.

[2]   The nature of the alleged defects does not appear in the record.

[3]   The Taddeos' plan could be confirmed over Di Pierro's protest. 11 U.S.C. §1325(a)(5)(B).

Because Di Pierro is the Taddeos' only creditor, continuance of the stay is justified only if the Taddeos' plan can in fact provide for Di Pierro's mortgage. Otherwise, the stay would serve only to delay foreclosure for delay's sake, and would not be justified. Therefore, although the Taddeos' Chapter 13 plan is not before us for approval, the question of whether under the plan the Taddeos can pay arrearages to Di Pierro and thereby cure the default and reinstate the mortgage is squarely presented for decision.

The relevant parts of §1322(b) read as follows:

> (b) ... the plan may- (2) modify the rights of holders of secured claims other than a claim secured only by a security interest in real property that is the debtor's principal residence, or of holders of unsecured claims; (3) provide for the curing or waiving of any default; (5) notwithstanding paragraph (2) of this subsection, provide for the curing of any default within a reasonable time and maintenance of payments while the case is pending on any unsecured claim or secured claim on which the last payment is due after the date on which the final payment under the plan is due;

When Congress empowered Chapter 13 debtors to "cure defaults," we think Congress intended to allow mortgagors to "de-accelerate" their mortgage and reinstate its original payment schedule. We so hold for two reasons. First, we think that the power to cure must comprehend the power to "de-accelerate." This follows from the concept of "curing a default." A default is an event in the debtor-creditor relationship which triggers certain consequences-here, acceleration. Curing a default commonly means taking care of the triggering event and returning to pre-default conditions. The consequences are thus nullified. This is the concept of "cure" used throughout the Bankruptcy Code. Under §365(b), the trustee may assume executory contracts and unexpired leases only if he cures defaults-but the cure need address only the individual event of default, thereby repealing the contractual consequences. * * *

Policy considerations strongly support this reading of the statute. Conditioning a debtor's right to cure on its having filed a Chapter 13 petition prior to acceleration would prompt unseemly and wasteful races to the courthouse. Worse, these would be races in which mortgagees possess an unwarranted and likely insurmountable advantage: wage earners seldom will possess the sophistication in bankruptcy matters that financial institutions do, and often will not have retained counsel in time for counsel to do much good. In contrast, permitting debtors in the Taddeos' position to de-accelerate by payment of the arrearages will encourage parties to negotiate in good faith rather than having to fear that the mortgagee will tip the balance irrevocably by accelerating or that the debtor may prevent or at least long postpone this by filing a Chapter 13 petition.

Secondly, we believe that the power to "cure any default" granted in §1322(b)(3) and (b)(5) is not limited by the ban against "modifying" home mortgages in §1322(b)(2) because we do not read "curing defaults" under (b) (3) or "curing defaults and maintaining payments" under (b)(5) to be modifications of claims.

It is true that §1322(b)(5)'s preface, "notwithstanding paragraph (2)," seems to treat the power to cure in (b)(5) as a subset of the power to modify set forth in (b)(2), but that superficial reading of the statute must fall in the light of legislative history and legislative purpose. The "notwithstanding" clause was added to §1322(b)(5) to emphasize that defaults in mortgages could be cured notwithstanding §1322(b)(2).

* * * [W]e hold that the concept of "cure" in §1322(b)(5) contains the power to de-accelerate. Therefore the application of that section de-accelerates the mortgage and returns it to its 15-year maturity. Alternatively, we hold that the ban on "modification" in §1322(b)(2) does not limit the Taddeos' exercise of their curative powers under either §1322(b)(3) or (b)(5). Therefore the Taddeos may first cure their default under (b)(3) and then maintain payments under (b)(5).

* * *

Affirmed.

Nobelman v. American Savings Bank
United States Supreme Court, 1993
___ U.S. ___, 113 S.Ct. 2106, 124 L.Ed.2d 228

Justice Thomas delivered the opinion of the Court.

This case focuses on the interplay between two provisions of the Bankruptcy Code. The question is whether §1322(b)(2) prohibits a Chapter 13 debtor from relying on §506(a) to reduce an undersecured homestead mortgage to the fair market value of the mortgaged residence. We conclude that it does and therefore affirm the judgment of the Court of Appeals.

I

In 1984, respondent American Savings Bank loaned petitioners Leonard and Harriet Nobelman $68,250 for the purchase of their principal residence, a condominium in Dallas, Texas. In exchange, petitioners executed an adjustable rate note payable to the bank and secured by a deed of trust on the residence. In 1990, after falling behind in their mortgage payments, petitioners sought relief under Chapter 13 of the Bankruptcy Code. The bank filed a proof of claim with the Bankruptcy Court for $71,335 in principal, interest, and fees owed on the note. Petitioners' modified Chapter 13 plan valued the residence at a mere $23,500--an uncontroverted valuation--and proposed to make payments pursuant to the mortgage contract only up to that amount (plus prepetition arrearages). Relying on §506(a) of the Bankruptcy Code, petitioners proposed to treat the remainder of the bank's claim as unsecured. Under the plan, unsecured creditors would receive nothing.

The bank and the Chapter 13 trustee, also a respondent here, objected to petitioners' plan. They argued that the proposed bifurcation of the bank's claim into a secured claim for $23,500 and an effectively worthless unsecured claim modified the bank's rights as a homestead mortgagee, in violation of 11 U.S.C. §1322(b)(2). The Bankruptcy Court agreed with respondents and denied confirmation of the plan. The District Court affirmed, as did the Court of Appeals. We granted certiorari to resolve a conflict among the Courts of Appeals.

II

Under Chapter 13 of the Bankruptcy Code, individual debtors may obtain adjustment of their indebtedness through a flexible repayment plan approved by a bankruptcy court. Section 1322 sets forth the elements of a confirmable Chapter 13 plan. The plan must provide, inter alia, for the submission of a portion of the debtor's future earnings and income to the control of a trustee and for supervised payments to creditors over a period not exceeding five years. See 11 U.S.C. §§1322(a)(1) and 1322(c). Section 1322(b)(2), the provision at issue here, allows modification of the rights of both secured and unsecured creditors, subject to special protection for creditors whose claims are secured only by a lien on the debtor's home. It provides that the plan may "modify the rights of holders of secured claims, other than a claim secured only by a security interest in real property that is the debtor's principal residence, or of holders of unsecured claims, or leave unaffected the rights of holders of any class of claims." 11 U.S.C. §1322(b)(2).

The parties agree that the "other than" exception in §1322(b)(2) proscribes modification of the rights of a homestead mortgagee. Petitioners maintain, however, that their Chapter 13 plan proposes no such modification. They argue that the protection of §1322(b)(2) applies only to the extent the mortgagee holds a "secured claim" in the debtor's residence and that we must look first to §506(a) to determine the value of the mortgagee's "secured claim." Section 506(a) provides that an allowed claim secured by a lien on the debtor's property "is a secured claim to the extent of the value of [the] property"; to the extent the claim exceeds the value of the property, it "is an unsecured claim." Petitioners contend that the valuation provided for in §506(a) operates automatically to adjust downward the amount of a lender's undersecured home mortgage before any disposition proposed in the debtor's Chapter 13 plan. Under this view, the bank is the holder of a "secured claim" only in the amount of $23,500--the value of the collateral property. Because the plan proposes to make $23,500 worth of payments pursuant to the monthly payment terms of the mortgage contract, petitioners argue, the plan effects no alteration of the bank's rights as the holder of that claim. Section 1322(b)(2), they assert, allows unconditional modification of the bank's leftover "unsecured claim."

This interpretation fails to take adequate account of §1322(b)(2)'s focus on "rights." That provision does not state that a plan may modify "claims" or that the plan may not modify "a claim secured only by" a home mortgage. Rather, it focuses on the modification of the "rights of holders" of such claims. By virtue of its mortgage contract with petitioners, the bank is indisputably the holder of a claim secured by a lien on petitioners' home. Petitioners were correct in looking to §506(a) for a judicial valuation of the collateral to determine the status of the bank's secured claim. It was permissible for petitioners to seek a valuation in proposing their Chapter 13 plan, since §506(a) states that "[s]uch value shall be determined ... in conjunction with any hearing ... on a plan affecting such creditor's interest." But even if we accept petitioners' valuation, the bank is still the "holder" of a "secured claim," because petitioners' home retains $23,500 of value as collateral. The portion of the bank's claim that exceeds $23,500 is an "unsecured claim componen[t]" under §506(a); however, that determination does not necessarily mean that the "rights" the bank enjoys as a mortgagee, which are protected by §1322(b)(2), are limited by the valuation of its secured claim.

The term "rights" is nowhere defined in the Bankruptcy Code. In the absence of a controlling federal rule, we generally assume that Congress has "left the determination of property rights in the assets of a bankrupt's estate to state law," since such "[p]roperty interests are created and defined by state law." Butner v. United States, 440 U.S. 48, 54-55, 99 S.Ct. 914, 918, 59 L.Ed.2d 136 (1979). Moreover, we have specifically recognized that "[t]he justifications for application of state law are not limited to ownership interests," but "apply with equal force to security interests, including the interest of a mortgagee." The bank's "rights," therefore, are reflected in the relevant mortgage instruments, which are enforceable under Texas law. They include the right to repayment of the principal in monthly installments over a fixed term at specified adjustable rates of interest, the right to retain the lien until the debt is paid off, the right to accelerate the loan upon default and to proceed against petitioners' residence by foreclosure and public sale, and the right to bring an action to recover any deficiency remaining after foreclosure. These are the rights that were "bargained for by the mortgagor and the mortgagee," Dewsnup v. Timm, 502 U.S. ----, ----, 112 S.Ct. 773, 778, 116 L.Ed.2d 903 (1992), and are rights protected from modification by §1322(b)(2).

This is not to say, of course, that the contractual rights of a home mortgage lender are unaffected by the mortgagor's Chapter 13 bankruptcy. The lender's power to enforce its rights--and, in particular, its right to foreclose on the property in the event of default--is checked by the Bankruptcy Code's automatic stay provision. In addition, §1322(b)(5) permits the debtor to cure prepetition defaults on a home mortgage by paying off arrearages over the life of the plan "notwithstanding" the exception in §1322(b)(2).[1] These statutory limitations on

---

[1]   Under §1322(b)(5), the plan may, "notwithstanding paragraph (2) of this subsection,

the lender's rights, however, are independent of the debtor's plan or otherwise outside §1322(b)(2)'s prohibition.

Petitioners urge us to apply the so-called "rule of the last antecedent," which has been relied upon by some Courts of Appeals to interpret §1322(b)(2) the way petitioners favor. According to this argument, the operative clause "other than a claim secured only by a security interest in ... the debtor's principal residence" must be read to refer to and modify its immediate antecedent, "secured claims." Thus, §1322(b)(2)'s protection would then apply only to that subset of allowed "secured claims," determined by application of §506(a), that are secured by a lien on the debtor's home--including, with respect to the mortgage involved here, the bank's secured claim for $23,500. We acknowledge that this reading of the clause is quite sensible as a matter of grammar. But it is not compelled. Congress chose to use the phrase "claim secured ... by" in §1322(b)(2)'s exception, rather than repeating the term of art "secured claim." The unqualified word "claim" is broadly defined under the Code to encompass any "right to payment, whether ... secure[d] or unsecured" or any "right to an equitable remedy for breach of performance if such breach gives rise to a right to payment, whether ... secure[d] or unsecured." 11 U.S.C. §101(5). It is also plausible, therefore, to read "a claim secured only by a [homestead lien]" as referring to the lienholder's entire claim, including both the secured and the unsecured components of the claim. Indeed, §506(a) itself uses the phrase "claim ... secured by a lien" to encompass both portions of an undersecured claim.

This latter interpretation is the more reasonable one, since we cannot discern how §1322(b)(2) could be administered under petitioners' interpretation. Petitioners propose to reduce the outstanding mortgage principal to the fair market value of the collateral, and, at the same time, they insist that they can do so without modifying the bank's rights "as to interest rates, payment amounts, and [other] contract terms." That appears to be impossible. The bank's contractual rights are contained in a unitary note that applies at once to the bank's overall claim, including both the secured and unsecured components. Petitioners cannot modify the payment and interest terms for the unsecured component, as they propose to do, without also modifying the terms of the secured component. Thus, to preserve the interest rate and the amount of each monthly payment specified in the note after having reduced the principal to $23,500, the plan would also have to reduce the term of the note dramatically. That would be a significant modification of a contractual right. Furthermore, the bank holds an adjustable rate mortgage, and the principal and interest payments on the loan must be recalculated with each adjustment in the interest rate. There is nothing in the mortgage contract or the Code that suggests any basis for recalculating the amortization schedule--whether by reference to the face value of the remaining principal or by reference to the unamortized value of the

---

provide for the curing of any default within a reasonable time and maintenance of payments while the case is pending on any ... secured claim on which the last payment is due after the date on which the final payment under the plan is due."

collateral. This conundrum alone indicates that §1322(b)(2) cannot operate in combination with §506(a) in the manner theorized by petitioners.

In other words, to give effect to §506(a)'s valuation and bifurcation of secured claims through a Chapter 13 plan in the manner petitioners propose would require a modification of the rights of the holder of the security interest. Section 1322(b)(2) prohibits such a modification where, as here, the lender's claim is secured only by a lien on the debtor's principal residence.

The judgment of the Court of Appeals is therefore
Affirmed.

Justice Stevens, concurring.

At first blush it seems somewhat strange that the Bankruptcy Code should provide less protection to an individual's interest in retaining possession of his or her home than of other assets. The anomaly is, however, explained by the legislative history indicating that favorable treatment of residential mortgagees was intended to encourage the flow of capital into the home lending market. It therefore seems quite clear that the Court's literal reading of the text of the statute is faithful to the intent of Congress. Accordingly, I join its opinion and judgment.

Notes and Problems

1. See generally Jane Kaupmanwinn, *Lien Stripping After* Nobleman, 27 Loy. L.A. L. Rev. 541 (1994); Barry Zaretsky, *Residential Mortgages in Chapter 13*, New York Law Journal, January 20, 1994.

2. In *Nobleman*, the home mortgage lender was partially unsecured. Would the result be different if the home mortgage lender was *completely* unsecured? Assume, for example, that D files for Chapter 13 relief owning a home valued at $94,750 and owing $95,000 to F who has a first lien on the home and $20,000 to S who has a second mortgage on the home. Do section 1322(b) and *Nobleman* prevent D from treating S as an unsecured creditor in her Chapter 13 plan?

3. The majority decision in *Nobleman* cites to *Dewsnup v. Timm*. In *Dewsnup*, at page 903 *supra*, the Court held that a Chapter 7 debtor cannot use section 506(d) to strip an undersecured lien on their farm to the value of the farm. The Noblemans are trying to strip an undersecured lien on their house to the value of their house. Why wasn't *Dewsnup* dispositive of *Nobleman*? Cf. section 103.

4. Could a Chapter 11 plan modify the terms of a home mortgage? If so, why didn't Mr. and Mrs. Nobleman file a Chapter 11 petition? See *In re Dever*.

In re Dever
United States Bankruptcy Court, C.D. California, 1994
164 B.R. 132

Lise Hill Fenning, Bankruptcy Judge.

I. INTRODUCTION
The issue before this Court on cross-motions for summary judgment is whether consumer debtors can use Section 506 of the Bankruptcy Code to "strip down" tax liens on their house in a Chapter 11 case. The Internal Revenue Service (IRS) argues that the holding in Dewsnup v. Timm, 502 U.S. ----, 112 S.Ct. 773, 116 L.Ed.2d 903 (1992), should be extended to Chapter 11 cases to preclude "lien stripping" because Dewsnup held that Chapter 7 debtors cannot use Section 506 for that purpose. The Supreme Court, however, expressly reserved the question as to the applicability of its ruling to cases under the reorganization chapters.

The issue of lien stripping in Chapter 11 is presented here in particularly stark terms, because the debtors converted their Chapter 7 case to Chapter 11 specifically to avoid the Dewsnup result. Thus, the question is whether they can accomplish in a converted Chapter 11 what the Supreme Court has prohibited in the original Chapter 7 case. For the reasons set forth below, this Court concludes that Dewsnup's holding cannot be imported into Chapter 11 cases without eviscerating other key provisions and principles of that reorganization chapter. Being loath to undermine the Chapter 11 statutory framework without compelling cause, this Court holds that Section 506 permits Chapter 11 debtors to strip down liens on real property under a plan.

II. FACTUAL BACKGROUND
Stephen and Susan Dever (the "debtors") filed a Chapter 7 petition to deal with income tax liabilities arising from a disastrous investment in a tax shelter. Their principal objective was to void the statutory liens that the Internal Revenue Service ("IRS") and the California Franchise Tax Board ("CFTB") had placed on all of their property, including their home which they hoped to retain. The Dewsnup decision interfered with that plan. To sidestep the apparent barrier interposed by Dewsnup, debtors converted their case to Chapter 11. Conversion to Chapter 13 was unavailable, since their total debts exceeded the eligibility limits for that chapter.

Debtors have now proposed a plan that revests the house in their names subject to three trust deeds. The trust deeds have been kept current from their earnings as an automobile mechanic and a school teacher. The plan offers to transfer all personal property subject to the tax liens--including furniture and other exempt property--to the IRS on account of the unpaid tax obligations. The debtors propose to pay nothing to the general unsecured creditors of the estate, who would of course receive nothing under a Chapter 7 liquidation either. Only the IRS has objected to the plan, due to the proposed treatment of its claim as unsecured.

Promptly after converting the case to Chapter 11, debtors filed a complaint to determine the secured status and avoid the liens of the IRS and CFTB under 11 U.S.C. §506. The CFTB has since settled with the debtors, consenting to its proposed treatment under the plan. The IRS moved for summary judgment on the ground that Dewsnup barred avoidance of a lien on property to be retained by the debtors in all cases, not just those under Chapter 7. The debtors also moved for summary judgment, countering that Dewsnup should not be extended to Chapter 11 cases.

It is undisputed that the fair market value of the debtors' home is $277,000.00, slightly above the median value for Los Angeles-area homes. The outstanding balance on the first and second trust deeds totals approximately $250,000.00. The only disputed issues of fact concern the validity of the $35,000.00 third trust deed against the property held in the name of debtor's mother, allegedly on account of funds advanced by all of the debtors' parents for the downpayment on the house. Even if that lien were determined to be entirely invalid, however, the $140,000.00-plus junior lien recorded by the IRS would not be fully secured by the remaining $27,000.00 in equity in the property. The IRS lien is either totally unsecured (if the third trust deed is valid), or grossly undersecured (if that deed is invalid). Therefore, partial summary adjudication is appropriate on the question of the avoidability under Section 506 of whatever portion of the IRS lien exceeds the equity value remaining in the property after accounting for the valid senior trust deeds.

III. DISCUSSION

A. Lien-Stripping in Chapter 7 Cases

The question presented here is the proper interpretation and application of Section 506 of the Bankruptcy Code. * * *

* * * In Dewsnup, the debtor sought to invalidate a mortgage lien on her Utah farm. The farm had been deemed abandoned by the Chapter 7 trustee, so the estate no longer had any remaining interest in the property. The Supreme Court held:

> [Section] 506(d) does not allow petitioner to "strip down" respondents' lien, because respondents' claim is secured by a lien and has been fully allowed pursuant to §502. Were we writing on a clean slate, we might be inclined to agree with petitioner that the words "allowed secured claim" must take the same meaning in §506(d) as in §506(a). But, given the ambiguity in the text, we are not convinced that Congress intended to depart from the pre-Code rule that liens pass through bankruptcy unaffected.

Dewsnup, 112 S.Ct. at 778.

This holding appears to have been driven by two factors: (1) as a voluntary lien, the bargained-for result under state law would have been that, if the debtor failed to repay the loan, the lender was entitled to foreclose; and (2) there was no benefit whatever realized for the estate or other creditors from this post-abandonment voiding of the lien. Under the circumstances, the Supreme Court considered unfair an outcome that appeared to place all the risk of a decline in property value on a mortgage lender, and none on the debtor, who would retain the upside potential if the property later appreciates in value. A "windfall," the Court called such a result. Id.

If an undersecured creditor forecloses, one of two things happens: either the creditor is paid in cash the fair market value of the property by a third party purchaser, which in theory should be the equivalent of the collateral value determined by the bankruptcy court; or the creditor buys the property itself by credit-bid if other bids at the sale are not sufficiently attractive to the creditor. The creditor thus has the choice of whether to forego the immediate cash in favor of betting on the property's future appreciation.

What disturbed the Court in Dewsnup was the debtor's attempt to create a third alternative in which the creditor neither received the cash value of the property nor the appreciation potential of ownership. The true effect of lien-stripping in Chapter 7 cases is to allow debtors to redeem their property at a discounted value by installment payments over a protracted period--without giving the creditor any choice whatsoever in the matter.

The issue, therefore, is not really how much of the claim is protected by the lien, but rather who has the right to ownership of the asset when it leaves bankruptcy. Under what conditions does the undersecured creditor have the right to bid for ownership of the property? Framed in this manner, the unfairness of Chapter 7 lien-stripping lies in its failure to require that the creditor receive the cash value of its collateral as the price for being deprived of its opportunity to credit-bid at a foreclosure sale.

B. Lien-Stripping in Reorganization Cases

Dewsnup did not purport to answer the question of avoidability of liens in reorganization cases. It expressly reserved the issue of whether its holding applies under other chapters or, indeed, to any other fact pattern besides the specific situation before it. * * *

In cautioning against an overly broad interpretation of its holding in Dewsnup, however, the Supreme Court apparently failed to consider that Section 103(a) makes the provisions of Chapter 5 of the Code generally applicable to all non-railroad cases under Chapters 7, 11, 12, and 13. In theory, Section 506 should apply uniformly across all of the substantive chapters, unless specifically limited by provisions designed for that chapter * * *.

* * *

Section 1111(b)(2) gives an undersecured, nonrecourse lender some ability to control its destiny in a Chapter 11 case because it allows the creditor to elect to be treated as fully secured, "notwithstanding Section 506(a) of this title," thereby preventing a "cash out" under Section 1129. Ordinarily, a Chapter 11 plan can be confirmed over a dissenting secured creditor if the plan is "fair and equitable" with respect to that class. Section 1129(b)(1). For secured creditors, the plan must either (1) leave the lien in place and pay deferred cash payments equal to the "value of such holder's interest" in the collateral; or (2) provide the "indubitable equivalent of such claims." The plan can also provide for the sale of the collateral, but the secured creditor's treatment must satisfy one of the two foregoing standards.[1] Section 1129(b)(2)(A). In other words, the secured portion of an undersecured creditor's claim is only equal to the value of its collateral, and the creditor can be "cashed out" for the value of the collateral, instead of being paid the full amount of its claim.

* * *

Modifying the rights and interests of secured creditors is at the heart of most reorganizations. Many Chapter 11 cases would be pointless and unreorganizable, if debtors could not reduce secured debt on property that had declined in value. This would particularly apply to single asset real estate cases, where the sole purpose of the case is usually to relieve the burden of a secured debt load that the property can no longer support. At least under current business conditions, very few Chapter 11 plans seek merely to stretch out or reduce payments to unsecured creditors. Most debtors are currently entering Chapter 11 with their assets fully encumbered, which means that their plans must restructure the secured debt in order to make a meaningful difference in their financial well-being.

* * *

In short, liens are affected in Chapter 11 cases in many ways; they do not simply ride through, as the Supreme Court assumed in Dewsnup. Secured creditors are often unhappy about what can happen to their secured lien under a plan. * * *

Chapter 11 limits the nature and extent of such modifications to the interests of secured creditors, most notably in Sections 1129 and 1111. If the Dewsnup premise is correct--that Congress intended that liens continue to attach in full to the property in question, regardless of its value, until paid--then what is the meaning of the "free and clear of claims and interests" language of Section 1141? Or the purpose of Sections 1111(b), and 1129(b)(2)(A)? All of these sections deal with ways to treat secured claims and liens other than leaving the lien intact until full payment.

* * *

---

[1]   The right to credit bid, as set forth in Section 363(k), is another example of the kind of protections that the Code affords to the undersecured creditor. That protection is available whether the property is being sold during the case, or under a plan of reorganization.

IV. CONCLUSION

As set forth above, Chapter 11 expressly contemplates the stripping down of liens to the value of the collateral at the effective date of the plan pursuant to Section 1129, unless the secured creditor invokes its right to make an election under Section 1111(b). To read the Dewsnup prohibition on lien-stripping into Chapter 11 would render these sections meaningless, violating the rule against interpreting statutes so as to render portions superfluous. Therefore, this Court holds that lien-stripping under Section 506(d) is available in Chapter 11.

In this case, the IRS did not exercise its right to make an election under Section 1111(b). Therefore, the debtors have the right under Section 506 and Section 1129 to limit the IRS's secured claim to the fair market value of its interest in the collateral under the terms of their plan. Section 506(d) permits avoidance of the unsecured portion of the lien, leaving the IRS with an allowed unsecured claim for the deficiency.

This Court's conclusion that the Dewsnup rule is unworkable in Chapter 11 strongly suggests that the Supreme Court should reconsider its decision. According to Section 103, Section 506, like all provisions of Chapter 5 of the Bankruptcy Code, should apply uniformly under all substantive chapters. It is anomalous, to say the least, to allow a debtor to achieve opposite results merely by the tactic of converting a case from Chapter 7 to Chapter 11 and doing a liquidating plan. But it is even harder to envision a Chapter 11 without lien-stripping powers. Giving effect to the unique provisions of Chapter 11--specifically Sections 1111(b) and 1129--means that Section 506 must be construed to permit bifurcation of undersecured claims into their secured and unsecured components, and avoidance of the lien to the extent that it exceeds the value of the collateral.

This opinion shall constitute findings of fact and conclusions of law. A separate judgment order shall be entered forthwith.

Notes and Questions

1. Did Judge Fenning confirm the Devers' Chapter 11 plan? Does the plan satisfy the requirements of section 1129(a)(10)? What class of claims impaired by the plan has accepted the plan? Does the plan satisfy the requirements of section 1129(a)(7)? Under the Devers' plan, does the IRS receive "not less than the amount that such holder would receive if the debtor were liquidated under chapter 7"?

2. Will the typical homeowner be able to use Chapter 11 to modify his home mortgage obligation? Recall that California has a very generous homestead statute. Was that relevant to the Dever decision? Recall also the facts in Dever: the Devers' home was valued at $277,000, and the IRS lien was $140,000. Is the Dever decision helpful to the homeowner with a $90,000 home and $120,000 in mortgages? How much would the homeowner have to pay for an attorney, filing fee, and other such costs to confirm a Chapter 11 plan?

3. D, an individual, files a Chapter 11 petition in order to strip down the second
    mortgage on her home. S, the holder of that second mortgage, files a motion to
    convert to the case to Chapter 7. How should the bankruptcy court rule on this
    motion to convert? What if S files a motion for relief from stay under section
    362(d)(2)?

Part 3

WORKOUTS

Unit 17

WORKOUTS

After reading eleven units of the book dealing with bankruptcy, it is important to remember that most debtors pay their debts. And, when a debtor is not able to pay its debts, it generally contacts its creditors to see whether they "can work anything out."

The term "workout" is used to describe a negotiated, nonbankruptcy modification of debts. "Workout" sounds a lot better than "bankruptcy." More positive, more constructive. A private, consensual resolution of financial problems seems more appealing than a public, governmental process. Why then are a million bankruptcy cases filed in some years? The following article by Conrad Duberstein, a bankruptcy judge in New York, explains how workouts work and why workouts do not always work.

Hon. Conrad B. Duberstein, *Out-Of-Court Workouts*
1 Am. Bankr. Inst. L. Rev. 347 (Winter 1993)

* * *

I. Nature of the Out-of-Court Workout

A. Extension or Composition Agreement

The ultimate goal of an out-of-court workout is to effectuate an agreement between the debtor and its creditors. This agreement may either provide an extension of the time period in which the debtor's obligations become due, without altering the amount of the claims of the creditors, or fashion a settlement, sometimes known as a composition agreement, which will reduce the amount to be paid to creditors with provisions for payment either in cash or over a period of time.

Both forms represent a contract between the debtor and the creditors who accept it. The consideration for each creditor's promise is the mutual forbearance of the other consenting creditors. The terms of the agreement bind only those creditors who consent to it. A nonconsenting creditor is not a party to the contract, and its right to obtain a judgment against the debtor is not affected by the agreement. The agreement defines the rights and obligations of the debtor and the assenting creditors. It is an instrument that reflects the terms and conditions, whereby the creditors will permit the debtor to continue in its operations and rehabilitate itself, as expressed in various covenants governing the conduct of the debtor in consideration of the modification of the creditor's rights.

II. The Out-of-Court Workout as an Alternative to Bankruptcy

A. Attractiveness of Workout
* * *

Aside from the possibility that the debtor may consider bankruptcy a stigma, other deterrents to filing a petition for relief under Chapter 11 include the possible appointment of a trustee, who would usurp and interfere with management's control of the company, and the possibility that the creditors and other parties in interest may propose a plan of reorganization. The required appearances in court, the time-consuming element consistent with the bankruptcy reorganization, and the additional expense involved would further contribute to the decision to seek a settlement out of court.
* * *

B. Circumstances Favoring Bankruptcy

Although the out-of-court workout is expeditious, economic, and sensible, the debtor is not provided with the automatic stay protection imposed by section 362 that takes effect upon the filing of a bankruptcy petition. The stay prevents the continuation or commencement of any action or proceeding against the debtor, the enforcement of any judgment against it or its property, any act to obtain possession of its property, or to exercise control over it, and any act to create or enforce a lien against the property. In addition to providing the debtor with a "breathing spell," the automatic stay promotes the efficient administration of the estate. The rights of the parties affected by the stay are not extinguished, but held in abeyance while the debtor endeavors to effect a satisfactory method of providing the creditors with relief or its equivalence, as ultimately determined by the bankruptcy court.

While all entities are not stayed by operation of section 362, its protection remains of paramount importance in considering whether to proceed with an out-of-court workout, or filing a Chapter 11 petition in bankruptcy. Considering the absence of stay protection and its vulnerability to creditors' attacks during the workout, the troubled debtor may be faced with the difficult task of obtaining unanimous creditor approval and participation in the restructuring agreement. Indeed, in the multi-creditor scenario, such a consensus may be difficult, if not impossible to achieve.
    * * *

III. Procedure Preparatory to Structuring the Agreement

A. Meeting of Creditors and Election of Creditors' Committee

Unless circumstances require the debtor to file a petition for reorganization under Chapter 11 immediately, it should first meet with its major creditors, disclose its financial condition, inform them of its intentions for the future, and participate with them in developing a modus operandi. In convening the creditors, consideration should be given to the fact that creditors will undoubtedly elect a creditor's committee designed to be representative of all of the creditors with whom the creditors will negotiate an agreement, and if Chapter 11 proceedings are instituted, will be able to qualify as the creditors' committee in that proceeding. Although section 1102(a) of the Code authorizes the United States Trustee to appoint a creditor's committee in a Chapter 11 case, Bankruptcy Rule 2007(a) also permits the continuation of a committee selected before the petition was filed if it is representative of the different kinds of claims to be represented and was "fairly chosen" as required by section 1102(b)(1). In addition, the requirements relating to the election and formation of a creditors' committee in the out-of-court proceeding, enumerated in Bankruptcy Rule 2007(b), should be followed in order for it to qualify in the Chapter 11 case which may ensue. * * *

B. Functions and Obligations of the Creditors' Committee

The creditors' committee will inquire into the debtor's affairs and the causes of its insolvency or its inability to pay its debts. It will review the balance sheet as well as a profit and loss statement furnished by the debtor, even though unaudited, so as to provide the committee with reasonable information regarding the debtor's condition, past and future operations. The committee should familiarize itself with the cash requirements of the debtor, the status of its relationship with its lender or factor, and its plans with respect to proposed borrowings, particularly when it is intended to secure advances by collateral consisting of accounts receivable, inventory, or fixed assets. The debtor should not be permitted to enter into such agreement without the consent and approval of the committee.

    * * *

VI. Covenants of the Agreement

A. Introduction

    * * *

The agreement will provide for either a cash payment in full settlement, the extension of time for the payment of a part or the whole of the indebtedness, payment out of profits over a limited period of years, or a combination of each. It may provide for the payment to creditors whose claims are in a nominal amount, in a manner different from payment to the remaining creditors, as for example, payment of a substantial portion of the claim or payment in full.

B. Affirmative Covenants of the Creditors

The agreement will also provide for affirmative covenants on the part of the creditors, of which the following are a few examples:

1. As long as the debtor is not in default under the agreement, the creditors will forbear from enforcing their claims and either extend the payment of their claims or accept the composition in full settlement and release their claims in accordance with the terms of the agreement.

2. They will discontinue pending actions and institute no further actions, nor join in the filing of any proceeding under the Code against the debtor.

3. In the event the debtor files a petition for reorganization in the bankruptcy court, and submits a plan of reorganization which embodies the terms of the agreement in principle, the acceptances of the out-of-court settlement shall be deemed acceptances of the reorganization plan in the bankruptcy proceedings.

C. Negative Covenants of the Debtor

These will usually provide that without the prior written approval of the creditors' committee and until the agreement has been completely performed, the debtor shall not be permitted to engage in certain acts that by their very nature, are deemed not to be in the best interests of creditors while the agreement remains unfulfilled. Several examples of those restraints are as follows:

1. Make no purchases of merchandise in excess of an amount fixed by the committee usually based upon the recommendation of the committee's accountants.

2. Incur no obligations other than in the ordinary course of business.

3. Payment of salaries to officers and principals as may be approved by the committee.

4. Sell or otherwise dispose of assets except in the ordinary course of business.

5. Sell no merchandise at prices below cost except upon the consent of the committee based upon its accountant's recommendation.

6. Enter into no factoring contracts or financing arrangements, nor pledge, hypothecate or mortgage any of its assets as security for the payment of any obligations. This restriction may be lifted or modified by the committee in order to enable the debtor to obtain necessary funds to continue in the operation of its business, but in no event, will the debtor be permitted to enter into any of such agreements without the permission of the committee.

7. Pay no dividends nor loan any monies to its officers and principals.

8. Declare or pay any dividends or issue any new stock.

9. Retain accountants except as approved or designated by the committee.

10. Make payments to non-assenting creditors.

11. Incur an operating loss in excess of a fixed dollar amount or, if such loss occurs, fail to supply additional capital or subordinated debt to cure the loss.

12. Fail to prepare and distribute to the members of the committee quarterly unaudited statements and fail to provide and make available to the committee's accountant all information necessary for it to prepare year-end certified statements of its financial condition.

D. Provisions for Collateral and Guarantees

As collateral security for the debtor's performance of the agreement, the settlement may provide for the execution and delivery by the debtor to the representative of the creditors' committee of a security interest in the debtor's assets. This may be evidenced by either a first lien on free property of the debtor, or a secondary or other inferior position on property subject to liens. The debtor will be called upon to avoid encumbering any of its assets which may adversely affect its ability to obtain credit.

The committee will usually endeavor to have the agreement guaranteed by the principals or third parties in order to assure them of payment as provided for by the settlement. The committee will retain the legal controls previously received consisting of the Assignment for Benefit of Creditors, the undated resignations and the stock certificates endorsed in blank to be used in the event of a default so as to enable the committee, if it so desires, to have the Assignment accepted, proceed to liquidation of the debtor's assets, or accept the resignations, of the officers and vote the stock certificates if it decides to sell the corporation as a going concern.

E. Events and Effects of Default

The agreement will set forth events of default including the debtor's failure to comply with any of its provisions, for example, the failure to meet installment payments after the passing of a grace period in which no extension has been granted by the committee, or the breach of any of the negative covenants.

When a default has occurred and it has not been cured, the debtor is not prevented from filing a petition for reorganization under Chapter 11. Public policy will not permit the committee nor any of the creditors to prevent the debtor from seeking such relief.

The debtor may utilize acceptances obtained in the out-of-court settlement in a subsequent Chapter 11 if so authorized by the agreement, which usually will provide for the same as long as the Chapter 11 plan of reorganization is similar to that proposed in the out-of-court settlement.

* * *

Conclusion

The substantial utilization of the out-of-court workout is ample proof of its wide acceptance by sophisticated creditors and attorneys who specialize in the law of insolvency. The benefits derived from the out-of-court workout, particularly those which contribute to the reduction of expense and delay which normally accompany a Chapter 11 proceeding, have prompted its implementation by better serving the interests of debtors and creditors without need to look to bankruptcy court.

Notes and Problems

1. Do Judge Duberstein's suggested covenants of the agreement raise future lender liability concerns? Can a workout agreement be used to eliminate any possible existing lender liability concerns? Should creditors negotiate for a general release of any possible lender liability claims that might exist as a part of a workout agreement? Why couldn't the debtor later argue that any such release was unenforceable because of "duress"?

2. As Judge Duberstein explains, a workout binds only the creditors that agree to it. In a workout, the debtor must rely on its power of persuasion rather than the power of the Bankruptcy Code. The debtor first must persuade creditors to forebear from exercising collection remedies during the negotiation of the workout. Then, after a workout has been negotiated, the debtor must persuade creditors to accept the workout.

    Neither the debtor nor a majority of the consenting creditors has the legal power to control the minority of creditors that choose not to participate in the workout. The fact that 99 out of 100 creditors have agreed to reduce and extend their claims does not prevent that 100th creditor from utilizing the state collection remedies considered in Unit 1 to satisfy its claim in full immediately. And the fear that other creditors will take such action and gain an advantage often prevents creditors from agreeing to a workout.. *See generally,* Susan Block-Lieb, *Fishing in Muddy Waters: Clarifying the Common Pool Analogy as Applied to the Standard for Commencement of a Bankruptcy Case,* 42 Am.U.L.Rev. 337 (1993); Note, *Financial Distress as a*

Noncooperative Game: A Proposal for Overcoming Obstacles to Private Workouts,
102 Yale L.J. 2205 (1993).

3. The existence of Chapter 11 is another impediment to workouts. A debtor can not only obtain Chapter 11 relief in lieu of a workout but can also obtain Chapter 11 relief in addition to a workout. What prevents a debtor from first negotiating a workout with its creditors and then later filing for Chapter 11 relief to obtain further relief? *See* section 109, *In re Club Tower Associates, supra,* and *In re Colonial Ford* below.

In re Colonial Ford, Inc.
United States Bankruptcy Court, D. Utah, 1982
24 B.R. 1014

Ralph R. Mabey, Bankruptcy Judge.

INTRODUCTION AND BACKGROUND

The Bankruptcy Code contains several provisions which promote the private, cooperative, negotiated rebuilding of financially distressed debtors. One of these measures, 11 U.S.C. Section 305(a)(1), is the subject of inquiry in this case. The facts relevant to this inquiry, briefly summarized, are as follows.

In January, 1977, Colonial Ford, Inc., the debtor, ceased operation as an automobile dealership. Since May, 1975, it has been embroiled in litigation with Ford Motor Company, Ford Motor Credit Company, the United States Small Business Administration, and other creditors. This litigation embraces three lawsuits, one of which has journeyed to the Tenth Circuit Court of Appeals and back and resulted in a judgment for $2,897,125 in favor of Ford Credit and against Colonial. Execution on this judgment and liquidation of the former dealership site, which Colonial continues to hold and lease to others, was enjoined by the district court pending resolution of these cases.

In July, 1981, Colonial and its creditors settled their differences. The agreement, in essence, accomplished two objectives. First, with the exception of a single cross- claim, it concluded all three lawsuits. Second, creditors reduced their claims and gave Colonial nine months to sell or refinance the dealership site; if this did not occur, a decree of foreclosure would be entered. Creditors, in other words, were willing to take less in exchange for an end to the litigation and swifter realization on their claims.[1]

---

[1] These reductions, with other concessions, were substantial. Ford Credit, for example, held a judgment for $2,897,125. An injunction barring execution, however, had prevented collection from the fall of 1976 until the settlement in 1981. The settlement reduced the judgment to $1,250,000, provided a moratorium on interest for all but $50,000 of this amount, and postponed foreclosure another nine months. All but three creditors, by default or acquiescence, are dealt with in the settlement. One of these, Ken Rothey, is counsel to and an officer of Colonial. He holds an attorneys lien on the

Colonial was unable to sell or refinance the property and filed a petition under Chapter 11 on March 30, 1982. Ford Credit filed a motion to abstain pursuant to Section 305(a)(1) on June 1. This was heard July 15. The court ruled from the bench August 24. An order was entered September 27. This memorandum decision elaborates the basis for that ruling.[1]

THE POLICY OF ENCOURAGING WORKOUTS

Section 305(a)(1) reflects a policy, embodied in several sections of the Code, which favors "workouts": private, negotiated adjustments of creditor-company relations. Congress designed the Code, in large measure, to encourage workouts in the first instance, with refuge in bankruptcy as a last resort. As noted in the legislative history: "Most business arrangements, that is, extensions or compositions (reduction) of debts, occur out-of-court. The out-of-court procedure, sometimes known as a common law composition, is quick and inexpensive. However, it requires near universal agreement of the business's creditors, and is limited in the relief it can provide for an overextended business. When an out-of-court arrangement is inadequate to rehabilitate a business, the bankruptcy laws provide an alternative. An arrangement or reorganization accomplished under the Bankruptcy Act binds nonconsenting creditors, and permits more substantial restructuring of a debtor's finances than does an out-of-court work-out." H.R.Rep. No. 95-595, 95th Cong., 1st Sess. 220 (1977), U.S.Code Cong. & Admin.News 1978, pp. 5787, 6179-6180. The reasons for blessing the workout are at least threefold.

First, the workout is expeditious. Debtors and creditors, unbridled by bankruptcy, enjoy a flexibility conducive to speed. By contrast, the "bankruptcy machinery [of] today," may be "a very time-consuming and hydraheaded kind of delaying structure" which "frequently works to the detriment of creditors." Hearings on S. 2266 and H.R. 8200 Before the Subcomm. on Improvements in Judicial Machinery of the Senate Comm. on the Judiciary, 95th Cong., 1st Sess. 599 (1977). Indeed, it has been noted, appropos the settlement in this case, that "delay .... is the most costly element in any bankruptcy proceeding and particularly in a business reorganization. The same amount of money received by the senior creditors 4 years from now is worth probably less than half of what would be an amount of money received today. In other words, if [a creditor] can anticipate, after this elaborate procedure, [that he] will receive $1 million, then he would be well-advised and usually is anxious to take $500,000 today because it's worth more to him. He has to consider the investment value and the ravages of inflation. This is worth more than the prospect of getting $1 million 4 years from now." Id. at 490. * * *

---

unsettled cross-claim. The others, LeGrande Belnap and Doris Belnap, shareholders of Colonial, have a claim for wages.

[1]   Ford Credit also sought dismissal of the case for want of "good faith" under 11 U.S.C. Section 1112(b) and relief from the stay under 11 U.S.C. Section 362(d). * * *

Second, workouts are economic. Economy, of course, is improved through expedition, as noted above. But the workout is economic because it avoids the superstructure of reorganization: trustees, committees, and their professional representatives. These and other costs of administration push junior interests "under water," and because they must be paid at confirmation, diminish prospects for a plan. Moreover, bankruptcy may shipwreck relationships necessary to keep a business afloat. Customers are reluctant to deal with the manufacturer who may not survive to honor the warranty of his product or with the lessor who cannot guarantee the habitability of his premises. The cost of overcoming this reluctance, through marketing campaigns and the like, may be high. Sales will be difficult; prices may be low. Suppliers may dwindle. Costs of credit may increase. "[W]hen word of financial difficulty spreads, the debtor's own debtors often decline to pay as they would have in the ordinary course, suddenly reporting that the dresses were the wrong size, were the wrong color, or were not ordered." Coogan, Broude and Glatt, "Comments on Some Reorganization Provisions of the Pending Bankruptcy Bills," 30 Bus.Law. 1149, 1155 (1975). Likewise, "accounts receivable can deteriorate to an unbelievable extent as soon as word gets around that the debtor is headed for the cemetery." Hearings on H.R. 31 and H.R. 32 Before the Subcomm. on Civil and Constitutional Rights of the House Comm. on the Judiciary, 94th Cong., 1st Sess., Ser. 27, pt. 1, at 483 (1975). These circumstances, among others, handcuff a debtor doing business in Chapter 11.

Third, the workout is sensible. Workouts contemplate, indeed depend upon, participation from all parties in interest, good faith, conciliation, and candor. The alternative is litigation and its bedfellows--bluff, pettifoggery, and strife. Moreover, the parties who are "on-site," and prepared by education or experience, are more able than a judge, ill-equipped in resources and training, to rescue a beleagured corporation. "The courtroom," after all, "is not a boardroom. The judge is not a business consultant." In re Curlew Valley Associates, 14 B.R. 506, 511 (Bkrtcy.D.Utah 1981). The problems of insolvency, for the most part, are matters for extra-judicial resolution, calling for "business not legal judgment." Id.

With these advantages in mind, the authors of the Code encouraged workouts in at least two ways.

First, the Code, "[l]ike a 'fleet-in-being' ... may be a force towards mutual accommodation," and as such, sets parameters for negotiations preceding a workout. Hearings on H.R. 31 and H.R. 32 Before the Subcomm. on Civil and Constitutional Rights of the House Comm. on the Judiciary, 94th Cong., 1st Sess., Ser. 27, pt. 1, at 396 (1975). Thus, for example, a creditor may be chary of dictating terms where this might result in the subordination of his claim. A creditor must weigh the possibility that execution on a judgment will be effort wasted if bankruptcy ensues and his preference is avoided, see, e.g., Hearings on H.R. 31 and H.R. 32 Before the Subcomm. on Civil and Constitutional Rights of the House Comm. on the Judiciary, 94th Cong., 1st Sess., Ser. 27, pt. 1, at

394-397 (1975), or that foreclosure will be for naught if the property must be turned over to the trustee, see, e.g., id. at 490-491. A debtor, likewise, may not break faith with creditors by preferring some over others, or by secreting assets, lest they file an involuntary petition.

Second, the Code, in several specific respects, contemplates that workouts will be a prelude to, yet consummated in, bankruptcy. Thus, for example, 11 U.S.C. Section 1102(b)(1), under certain circumstances, allows the continuation, as the official creditors committee, of a prepetition creditors committee. Similarly, 11 U.S.C. Section 1126(b), in some instances, validates prepetition acceptances of a plan. "Congress," according to one authority, "rejecting the opposition of the Securities and Exchange Commission, has provided a flexible reorganization procedure which accommodates prefiling reorganization procedures for both public and private corporations. A plan may be filed with the petition commencing a Chapter 11 case or at any subsequent time. Acceptances obtained before the commencement of the filing may be counted in the voting if there was adequate prepetition disclosure and, if necessary, 'compliance with any applicable nonbankruptcy law .... governing the adequacy of disclosure.' " Trost, "Business Reorganizations Under Chapter 11 of the New Bankruptcy Code," 34 BUS.LAW. 1309, 1325 (1979). Indeed, incentives to use "prepackaged plans" are "written all through the new Act." They lead to a "revolving door" in and out of Chapter 11. Aaron, "The Bankruptcy Reform Act of 1978: The Full-Employment-for-Lawyers Bill: Part V: Business Reorganization," 1982 Utah L.Rev. 1, 38.

SECTION 305(a)(1) AND THE POLICY
OF ENCOURAGING WORKOUTS

Thus, the Code encourages workouts outside, or concluded inside, Chapter 11. Encouragement on both fronts is necessary because dissent from a workout may assume a variety of shapes. Creditors who would otherwise pursue their rights under state law are kept in tow because preferences may be undone following a petition in bankruptcy. Others may be bound, assuming a consensus in number and amount, through confirmation of a plan. What, however, of the maverick who threatens prematurely to disrupt out-of-court negotiations by an involuntary petition, or the party, creditor or debtor, who has "buyer's remorse" and seeks a recapitulation of the settlement in bankruptcy? This form of dissent is the target of Section 305(a)(1) which provides:

> (a) The Court, after notice and a hearing, may dismiss a case under this title, or may suspend all proceedings in a case under this title, at any time if-- (1) The interests of creditors and the debtor would be better served by such dismissal or suspension.
> * * *

APPLICATION OF SECTION 305(a)(1) IN THIS CASE

Colonial questions the applicability of Section 305(a)(1) in voluntary cases, and whether dismissal, under the circumstances of this case, "better serves" the interests of creditors and the debtor.

* * *

Colonial argues that its interests are better served in Chapter 11; otherwise it would not have filed a petition. This argument, however, may be astigmatic for at least two reasons.

First, it ignores the question of who is the debtor for purposes of Section 305(a)(1). If the case is in Chapter 11, for example, the debtor will be a debtor in possession, and hence the trustee or fiduciary for the estate. The interests of the debtor, under these circumstances, are coincidental with the interests of creditors. Indeed, no debtor is an island, self-existent apart from its creditors who supply the capital, goods, and services necessary to his survival. This idea finds expression, not only in the construct of a debtor in possession, but also at common law where insolvent entities became funds managed in trust for the benefit of creditors. From this standpoint, the interests of creditors receive double weight under Section 305(a)(1), once from a partisan and again from a fiducial perspective. In any event, the corporate debtor will be a complex of constituencies, including not only creditors but also a board of directors, management, and shareholders. These parties may be divided on some issues; even when united, their views may change from circumstance to circumstance, or from time to time. To say, with Colonial, that the debtor speaks with one voice on all occasions, and that its interests are circumscribed in the management's act of filing a petition, is oversimple.

Second, it overlooks the benefits which debtors in general may derive from out-of-court workouts and which Colonial in particular obtained in this settlement. The choice to settle out of court rather than to file for reorganization, more often than not, will be enlightened. Management eager for asylum in bankruptcy may pause if faced with displacement by a trustee. Shareholders likewise must reckon with the prospect of a creditor's plan, wresting control of the business and eliminating their interest. Moreover, their equity, already thin or nonexistent, may not survive the burden of administrative debt. Debtors, as well as creditors, are familiar with the old saw that a "good" liquidation out of court is better than a "bad" reorganization in Chapter 11. Since the odds are stacked against obtaining confirmation of a plan, and in light of the probability of conversion to Chapter 7, debtors may be well-advised, where their creditors are cooperative, to forego the dislocations and trauma, the depressed markets, the higher cost of money, and other disadvantages of bankruptcy, and work out an arrangement, even if it contemplates an eventual liquidation.

* * *

These reasons motivated Colonial to make an agreement with its creditors which composed the debt and provided for sale, refinancing, or foreclosure of the property. The alternative of bankruptcy was available then, as now, and entered the calculus of decisionmaking, but was rejected in favor of the settlement. Colonial asserts, however, that reorganization better serves its interests at present. Attempting to divine the interests of Colonial, given this doublemindedness, is problematical. But even if full credit is given to its present protestations, these do not counterbalance the reasons for avoiding bankruptcy. Even assuming that the protestations and the reasons have equal weight, the policy of encouraging out-of-court workouts, embodied in Section 305(a)(1), dictates that the interests of Colonial are "better served" by the settlement than by a petition in Chapter 11.

CONCLUSION

The Code encourages out-of-court workouts. Section 305(a)(1) is one of several instruments useful in achieving this goal. Because an order of dismissal under Section 305(a)(1) is nonreviewable, the statute should be invoked sparingly. Indeed, Section 305(a)(1) permits "suspension" as well as dismissal of a case, suggesting the possibility that efforts toward settlement may proceed on more than one front at the same time. Where, however, the workout is comprehensive, and designed to end, not perpetuate, the creditor- company relations, dismissal under Section 305(a)(1) is appropriate. One "reorganization," under these circumstances, is enough. Section 305(a)(1) precludes an encore, thereby furthering the policies of expedition, economy, and good sense.

Notes and Problems

1. In holding that a voluntary petition could not be dismissed under section 305, Judge Kressel discussed the *Colonial Ford* case in a footnote: "In that case the court concluded that at least in a Chapter 11 case 'the interests of the debtor . . . are coincidental with the interests of the creditor." Most people would find this to be an astounding proposition. I do." *In re G-N Partners*, 48 B.R. 459, 461, n.4 (Bankr. Minn. 1985).

2. D is negotiating for a restructure of its debt to your client C. D offers to agree to forebear from filing for bankruptcy for 12 months in exchange for further concessions. Would a bankruptcy waiver in a workout agreement be enforceable? Should a bankruptcy waiver in a workout agreement be enforceable?

3. What are the effects of a subsequent bankruptcy on the parties to a workout? Assume that D entered into a workout with its three largest creditors, A, B, and C. D agreed to pay them fifty per cent of what she owed them in five monthly installments. After making two of the payments required by the workout agreement, D filed for bankruptcy. What is the effect of the workout agreement on the amount of A, B, and C's claims in D's bankruptcy? Can D recover the payments made pursuant to the workout as preferences or fraudulent conveyances? Can the creditors recover the

professional fees they incurred in negotiating the workout as administrative expenses?

INDEX
(Mainly of Key Terms)

References are to pages

———

0-314-04412-4

90000

9 780314 044129